PRESERVING
OUR HERITAGE

Historic Roosevelt Arch at the north entrance of Yellowstone National Park.

PRESERVING OUR HERITAGE

Perspectives from Antiquity to the Digital Age

Selections and Commentary by
MICHÈLE VALERIE CLOONAN

Neal-Schuman

An imprint of the American Library Association

CHICAGO | 2015

MICHÈLE V. CLOONAN is dean emerita and professor of the School of Library and Information Science at Simmons College and editor in chief of *Preservation, Digital Technology & Culture*. From 2004–2007 she coordinated a Simmons College/Harvard University/UCLA Libraries initiative to train Iraqi librarians. Michèle is a former president of the Association for Library and Information Science Education (ALISE), has held a variety of offices in the American Library Association, has served on the board of the American Printing History Association, has chaired the Northeast Document Conservation Center Board of Directors, and has served on the Preservation Committee of the Council on Library and Information Resources and the Preservation and Conservation Section of the International Federation of Library Associations and Institutions (IFLA). She is on the editorial board of *Libri* and has also served on the editorial boards of *Libraries and Culture* and *Library Quarterly*. Her honors and awards include the 2010 Paul Banks and Carolyn Harris Preservation Award, Association for Library Collections & Technical Services, American Library Association; 2010 Service Award, Association for Library and Information Science Education (ALISE); Robert Vosper/IFLA Fellows Programme award, the Bibliographical Society of America Fellowship; and a fellowship to the Virginia Center of Creative Arts. She has published over 50 articles, chapters, and books, and has been Principal Investigator on numerous grants.

© 2015 by the American Library Association

Printed in the United States of America
19 18 17 16 15   5 4 3 2 1

Extensive effort has gone into ensuring the reliability of the information in this book; however, the publisher makes no warranty, express or implied, with respect to the material contained herein.

ISBN: 978-1-55570-937-2 (paper).

Library of Congress Cataloging-in-Publication Data
Preserving our heritage : perspectives from antiquity to the digital age / Michèle Valerie Cloonan.
   pages   cm.
Includes bibliographical references and index.
ISBN 978-1-55570-937-2 (alkaline paper)
     1. Library materials—Conservation and restoration. 2. Books—Conservation and restoration.
   3. Archival materials—Conservation and restoration. 4. Manuscripts—Conservation and restoration.
   5. Sound recordings—Conservation and restoration. 6. Photographs—Conservation and restoration.
   7. Motion picture film—Preservation. 8. Digital preservation. 9. Museums—Conservation and restoration.
   10. Cultural property—Conservation and restoration. I. Cloonan, Michèle Valerie, 1955– editor of compilation. II. Title.
Z701P7537 2014
025.8'4—dc23
                                            2014000216

Book design by Kim Thornton in the Brandon Grotesque, Meta, and Minion typefaces.

♾ This paper meets the requirements of ANSI/NISO Z39.48-1992 (Permanence of Paper).

To the incomparable Sidney Berger,
helpmate and guiding spirit

CONTENTS

4 COLLECTIONS: DEVELOPMENT AND MANAGEMENT   225

8 PRESERVATION POLICY — 485

9 ETHICS AND VALUES — 533

Selected Conventions, Charters, Declarations, and Professional Association Codes of Ethics

10   MULTICULTURAL PERSPECTIVES   569

11   SUSTAINABILITY   609

ADVISORY BOARD

HOWARD BESSER, Professor, Cinema Studies; Director, Moving Image Archiving and Preservation Program, Tisch School for the Arts, New York University

PAULA DE STEFANO, Barbara Goldsmith Curator for Preservation and Head, Preservation Department, New York University Libraries

ANNE J. GILLILAND, Professor, Department of Information Studies and Moving Image Archive Studies; Director, Center for Information as Evidence, University of California, Los Angeles

KAREN F. GRACY, Associate Professor, School of Library and Information Science, Kent State University

TYRA GRANT, Digital and Electronic Media Preservation Librarian, University of Kansas Libraries

MICHAEL C. HENRY, Watson & Henry Associates, Preservation Architects & Engineers, Bridgeton, New Jersey, and Adjunct Professor of Architecture, University of Pennsylvania

LOIS OLCOTT PRICE, Director of Conservation and Senior Conservator of Library Collections at the Winterthur Museum, and Affiliated Assistant Professor of Art Conservation for the Winterthur/University of Delaware Program in Art Conservation (WUDPAC)

PREFACE

Michèle V. Cloonan

THIS BOOK AIMS TO INTRODUCE STUDENTS AND professionals to readings that will help them in their studies and in their professional practice. For students, the book presents key introductory readings. For professionals, some of the readings will be familiar, though the authors of some pieces have added updates or afterwords. Many other writings will not be familiar, either because they are old or difficult to find, or they were published in different fields. For example, librarians may not be familiar with the historic preservation literature, museum professionals may not read library literature, and so on. I hope that readers will be enriched by the interdisciplinary approach of this volume. Three new pieces appear here in the chapters on "Collections: Development and Management" (Karen F. Gracy, "Preservation in a Time of Transition: Redefining Stewardship of Time-Based Media in the Digital Age"), "Preservation Policy" (Ellen Cunningham-Kruppa's "Exploring Cultural Policy at Humanities Texas"), and "Sustainability" (Rebecca Meyer et al., "Sustainability: A Literature Review"). This anthology should be useful to a variety of audiences.

This book gathers and discusses key readings in preservation and conservation and presents the readings in an accompanying historical timeline. Many current debates about issues such as longevity, reversibility, enduring value, and authenticity have their roots in writings of past centuries. This volume presents the roots and their outgrowths.

Background

Preservation assures the memory of civilizations. Libraries, museums, archives, and other cultural institutions gather, organize, display, and sometimes disseminate their holdings. At the same time, they cannot collect and save everything. And what they do collect and preserve has to do with the mandates of individual institutions. Throughout the histories of institutions, decisions were made about what would not be collected. Thus, what has been preserved is but a small subset of what has been created. Natural and man-made disasters further contribute to the disappearance of objects. Then, too, there are natural and man-made objects that have existed outside the purview of institutions or governments. In those cases preservation has probably been a matter of chance.

Collections cannot be made available if they are not preserved. Yet the systematic practice of preservation management in cultural heritage institutions began only in the twentieth century, though writings about caring for objects date back to antiquity. That is because before the mid-twentieth century, there was a focus on caring for individual items rather than for collections. With the invention of photography in the nineteenth century, it became possible to copy or reformat original materials. It was then subsequently possible to preserve the intellectual content of an object, as well as the object itself. Research into the causes of deterioration led to individual or mass treatments, or to reformatting, or later, with digital media, to migration and other strategies. An interest in preserving collections as a whole led librarians, archivists, and museum curators to make recommendations for improved ambient conditions through environmental monitoring and to advocate for the appropriate design of buildings housing heritage materials. Today, preservation encompasses the care of individual items as well as collections, buildings, and entire communities or habitats. The notion of preservation, then, implies two things: 1) preserving the objects that carry information, and 2) preserving the information itself. The latter of these focuses on the intellectual dimension of an object. Hence, the content of an item can be saved even if the item is lost. Of course, saving the content and losing the original medium is not a full victory because information resides in originals that simply is not inherent in copies. But having a surrogate is better than having nothing. Are photographs of a vase—or even a replica of it—a form of preservation? For written materials the *content* of an item can be saved. For three-dimensional objects, even with the new scanning technology, the "content" is more difficult to preserve.

The onset of digital media means that an increasing amount of information and creative output is born in electronic form and will never be acquired by an institution. Some of the readings, particularly in chapters 4 and 7, address preservation efforts in these areas, including the move to personal archiving and Personal Information Management (PIM), for which there are Personal Information Manager application software systems (PIM or PIM tools). Scholars are already taking measure of users' digital preservation practices.[1] Of course it is easier for someone who creates, for example, a blog, to preserve it than it is for someone to preserve a page that she posts on Facebook—a social utility that may own the content as soon as it is posted. Literature that addresses preservation and social media issues is growing daily.

The evolution of preservation can be charted through its literature. There are many publications in the field which, if students and practitioners had access to them, would help them to understand the context surrounding a host of current issues. Furthermore, the literature comes from a number of disciplines including art, art history, architecture, history, and historic preservation, and, of course, the literature of the library, archives, and museum professions. The sometimes divergent perspectives of the various fields will lead the reader to a broad understanding of the values and ethics of preservation.

Selection of the Readings[2]

The genesis for this book grew out of discussions that Paula De Stefano, Head, Preservation, New York University Libraries, and I had a few years ago about "classic" readings in preservation. We defined classic as those readings that are continuously cited in the literature, referred to repeatedly by professionals, and assigned in preservation courses. In contemplating compiling an anthology, we wanted to know which articles our colleagues thought were the most influential to them. We solicited suggestions from librarians, archivists, and conservators primarily through listservs. We received some fifty suggestions, many of which are included here. Respondents provided lists, or described in detail what each reading had meant to them.

An Advisory Board, whose members represented the fields of librarianship, archives, museum studies, and historic preservation, revised and augmented the original list, and helped me make the final selections.[3] The final selections were further winnowed down either because permissions could not be secured, or the items were too long for inclusion.

I used four selection criteria for the readings. First, I included historical writings that form the basis of contemporary thinking and practices. Classic works can sometimes shed new light on how to approach contemporary problems. Second, I sought readings from a variety of fields that are primarily concerned with the preservation of cultural heritage. These fields include library, information, archival studies, historic preservation, and museum studies and informatics. Sometimes one field is ahead of another in its practices and there is much that can be learned from a new perspective. Third, I looked for readings in new areas of interest, such as sustainability. Finally, I tried to include publications that might not be readily accessible to most readers because they are out of print, were published in un-indexed periodicals, were chapters in books, or were rare and/or difficult to access.

There is necessarily uneven coverage from topic to topic. There has been a tsunami of publications about digital preservation in the past decade, as is reflected by the length of chapter 7, "Frameworks for Digital Preservation." In contrast, while there is a voluminous literature on preservation policies in specific institutions, less has been published about general preservation policymaking in a broader societal context, and I have selected only three pieces for chapter 8. However, policy and public policy issues are considered in some articles in chapters 7, 9, 10, and 11. Other areas are growing rapidly, with new articles

being published frequently. While chapter 11, "Sustainability," has just three contributions, it is a rapidly growing field, with many recent publications.

Terminology

The term *preservation* forms part of the title of this book. However, in various contexts, and at various times, *preservation*, *conservation*, and *restoration*, have been used interchangeably, as the writings in this volume demonstrate. While all three terms are used somewhat differently in librarianship, film archives, art conservation, and historic preservation, they all refer to the care of movable, immovable, natural, man-made, and socially constructed heritage. *Preservation* is an umbrella term that includes conservation and restoration. *Conservation* is the treatment of objects based on scientific principles and professional practices, as well as other activities that assure collections care. The conservation field encompasses art, natural history specimens, archives, and books. In some contexts, *architectural conservation* is used to mean to historic preservation.

Restoration is used in a variety of ways. In film preservation, restoration refers specifically to the process of returning a film to the version that is most faithful to its original release. This process may include restoring lost footage. In art, restoration has a narrower focus than does conservation. Restoration strives to bring objects back as nearly as possible to their original condition, or to a known earlier state. The emphasis is on *presentation* rather than accurate interpretation. Restoration is unethical if it is used solely to make an object appear "new" or "better" than it was before treatment.

Heritage, *cultural heritage*, and *cultural memory* are defined in the introduction to chapter 2. The broad interpretations of these concepts are reflected in the readings.

The book begins with a Timeline that is a reference for the book's readings and which places the readings in context. Thus, the timeline, while providing context and background, is not meant to be a history of the preservation field. Rather it attempts to draw out the many social, political, technological, professional, and economic facets of preservation, and, in so doing, enhance the readings.

The subjects are organized into twelve chapters. chapter 1, "Early Perspectives on Preservation," includes works that span from the Old Testament to the late nineteenth century.

Readers will recognize in these selections some enduring preservation themes.

Chapter 2, "Perspectives on Cultural Heritage," presents a variety of perspectives on the meaning of cultural heritage and how those meanings have shaped our collective pasts. This is followed in chapter 3, "Preservation in Context: Libraries, Archives, Museums, and the Built Environment," with an examination of preservation practices in a variety of institutions and settings.

The relationship between institutional collecting and preservation is the theme of chapter 4, "Collections: Development and Management." A section of the chapter is devoted to time-based media and the distinctions between preservation of paper-based and new media are drawn. Karen F. Gracy has provided an introductory essay to time-based media.

Chapter 5, "Risks to Cultural Heritage: Time, Nature, and People," takes a broad look at risk. While there is a voluminous literature on disaster recovery, risk assessment and management is much less covered.[4] Yet cultural heritage is under constant and inevitable risk; its mitigation is critical to preservation efforts.

Chapter 6, "Conservation," presents a variety of theoretical and practical perspectives on the physical care, treatment, and remediation of collections. Works about the care and treatment of items have been written for centuries, and chapter 1 gives examples of early views on the subject. Chapter 6 represents twentieth and twenty-first century perspectives.

"Frameworks for Digital Preservation" is the subject of chapter 7. Over a thousand publications have appeared on this complex and rapidly changing area, with no diminution in sight. The chapter provides the reader with an overview. It is useful to trace the areas in which great strides have been made and those in which much work remains.

Chapter 8, "Preservation Policy," explores public and cultural policy approaches to preservation. No attempt was made in the chapter to explore legal policy issues. While these are mentioned throughout the book, particularly in chapter 7, this anthology—with its broad coverage of preservation subjects—is not the ideal forum to cover the wide range of legal issues. Readers may want to consult Barbara T. Hoffman's anthology, *Art and Cultural Heritage: Law, Policy, and Practice.*[5]

"Ethics and Values" are covered in chapter 9. The chapter is divided into two sections: a consideration of the topic with readings and a selection of international conventions and declarations, and professional codes of ethics. The subject of moral and ethical conduct has been considered for over 2000 years, and it is no less relevant today. As I write this preface, a new article has just crossed my desk that considers ethical perspectives relating to political-economic issues in the preservation of digital heritage.[6]

Chapter 10, "Multicultural Perspectives," calls into question the assumption that cultural heritage belongs equally to everyone. Who "owns" heritage? How is it to be preserved? By whom and for whom? Some of the authors advocate for collaborative and community-based approaches to preservation while others focus on specific treatment issues. Attitudes in museums, libraries, and archives towards managing diverse cultural materials are changing.

Chapter 11, "Sustainability," the concluding subject of the book, refers to an implied commitment to managing natural and cultural resources into the indefinite future. Parallels are drawn between the stewardship that is implicit in preservation and sustainability.

Finally, the Epilogue identifies several new and potential research foci. The aim is to encourage readers to track these areas in scholarly publications, as well as in the media and on social networking sites.

No volume can do full justice to the broad range of subjects that make up preservation. Certainly, I could have added dozens more excellent pieces to this collection—many items that were on the original list, for instance. It was sometimes painful not to be able to include items that had to be cut. Notes throughout the text refer readers to texts that are not included here.

Infelicities and inconsistencies in bibliographic styling—from one publication to another and even within a single publication––have been retained as they were in the originals.

Audience

The Heritage of Preservation can be a reader for heritage professionals, a textbook for graduate students, or a reference work for professionals and scholars in other fields. Its goal is to bring together a variety of sources, and in so doing represent the depth and scope of this intellectually rich field.

NOTES

1. See, for example, Andrea J. Copeland, "Analysis of Public Library Users' Digital Preservation Practices," *Journal of the American Society for Information Science and Technology* 62.7 (July 2011): 1288–1300.

2. Each article is styled as it originally appeared in print.

3. Though Paula De Stefano was unable to coedit this volume with me, she has served on the Advisory Board, making many useful suggestions for the readings as well as the timeline.

4. One notable example, not excerpted here, is Jonathan Ashley-Smith, *Risk Assessment for Object Conservation* (Oxford: Butterworth-Heinemann, 1999).

5. Barbara T. Hoffman, ed., *Art and Cultural Heritage: Law, Policy and Practice* (Cambridge: Cambridge University Press, 2006; rpt. 2009).

6. Peter Johan Lor and J. J. Britz, "An Ethical Perspective on Political-Economic Issues in the Long-Term Preservation of Digital Heritage," *Journal of the American Society for Information Science and Technology* 63.11 (November 2012): 2153–64.

ACKNOWLEDGMENTS

T TAKES MANY PEOPLE TO BRING A BOOK TO FRUITION, AND I wish to thank those who made this one possible. I wish that there was a word stronger than "thanks" to convey my gratitude to them.

When I came up with the idea of creating a preservation anthology, one of my first supporters was Charles Harmon, formerly Vice President and Director of Neal-Schuman Publishers. He gave me many useful suggestions for this volume and I worked with him until Neal-Schuman was acquired by the American Library Association. Charles, now Executive Editor at Rowman & Littlefield, and Christopher Rhodes and Rachel Chance at ALA, helped to shepherd this volume into print. All three were wonderfully supportive and patient.

Following the early advice of Charles Harmon, I formed an Advisory Board whose names are listed elsewhere. I am grateful to them for their many ideas for items to be included. Unfortunately, I was not able to use all of their suggestions, either because I could not secure the necessary permissions, or because the permissions were prohibitively expensive. No blame should be accrued to them for omissions.

Most of my research was conducted at the Getty Research Institute (GRI). A GRI Library Research Grant in 2007 made it possible for me to begin the Timeline that appears here and to identify some of the texts for this anthology. Subsequent trips to the Getty in 2011 allowed me to finish the research. Special thanks are due to Murtha Baca, Head, Digital Art History Access; Mary Reinsch Sackett, Head of Conservation and Preservation; Marcia Reed, Chief Curator; and Susan M. Allen, formerly of the Getty Research Institute, and currently Director of California Rare Book School (CalRBS). They have been my esteemed colleagues for many years. Their generosity is unparalleled.

Thanks also to Cameron Trowbridge, Manager, Research Services, Dissemination and Research Resources, the Getty Conservation Institute. He and his team were unfailingly helpful to me.

My former and current research assistants have helped me in many ways including bibliographic sleuthing, finding or creating images, translating items, and generally sharing their knowledge: thank you, Patsy Baudoin, Anne Holmer Deschaine, Jonathan Lill, Sarah Spira, Hugh Truslow, and Elizabeth Walters. To Rebecca Meyer I owe a particularly large debt of gratitude. For nearly two years she helped me track down permissions. She also scanned most of the texts for this book.

Linda Chan, Serials Librarian at the Newberry Library in Chicago, has assisted me with more research projects than I can count. She is intrepid at tracking down sources. For this book she helped me locate items relating to Paul N. Banks.

Through ongoing conversations colleagues at Simmons College have helped me shape my ideas. I particularly wish to thank Jeannette Bastian, Ross Harvey, Martha Mahard, and Terry Plum. Former UCLA colleagues Howard Besser and Anne Gilliland continue to be generous supporters of my work.

Rachel Salmond, librarian, consultant, editor, and teacher, has been an intrepid copy editor. She has tracked down many print and digital textual variations in the works. She, too, has been exceedingly generous with her time.

Simmons College granted me a "mini-leave" in 2007, and a sabbatical during spring semester 2011. My special thanks to former president Dan Cheever and current president Helen Drinan, and former Provost Charlena Seymour. I am grateful to them for their generosity.

My final debt of gratitude goes to my husband, Sidney Berger, and my aunt, Marguerite Bouvard. Fine scholars both, they empathize with the agony and the ecstasy of research and writing. I could ask for no better support than they have given me over many years.

The book was longer in the making than I could have anticipated. The process for searching for and securing rights has become increasingly difficult when access should be getting easier. That said, the editor and publisher gratefully acknowledge permission to reproduce previously published material. We made every effort to trace copyrights to their holders for original materials as well as for translations.

PRESERVATION TIMELINE

THIS TIMELINE HAS TWO PURPOSES: TO SERVE AS a reference for the readings and to place them in context. Thus, the timeline provides context and background. For example, in 1823, John Murray laments the poor composition of paper; his letter to *The Gentleman's Magazine* appears in chapter 1. Consulting the timeline, one learns that chlorine bleach had been used in paper since the 1790s—and the harmful effects of it were apparent by the time that Murray's letter was published. Alum-rosin sizing, another prime cause of the deterioration of paper, had been developed at the beginning of the nineteenth century, but was not in widespread use by 1823. Poor-quality wood-pulp paper was not yet being manufactured. John Murray had identified a problem that would only become worse by the middle of the nineteenth century.

Another example dates from 150 years later, in 1976. The publication of Paul Philippot's "Historic Preservation: Philosophy, Criteria, Guidelines" (chapter 3) and of Caroline K. Keck's "The Role of the Conservator" (chapter 6) overlap with a number of preservation-related events in the United States: the Library of Congress holds a major conference on preservation and conservation; the Tax Reform Act of 1976 provides some tax incentives for rehabilitating historic properties; and it is the American Bicentennial with its attendant commemorations and emphases on honoring the past. The publications and the events nurtured the preservation field.

The reader may also use the timeline by selecting a topic, such as Thomas Edison's invention of the phonograph, and then read Mark Roosa's article in chapter 4,

"Sound and Audio Archives," about the preservation of recordings. The timeline and articles are not reflexive, however. There may be events in the timeline that no article in the anthology addresses, and there may be articles for which there are no corresponding events in the timeline. Nor are all of the readings included in the timeline: only pivotal readings such as the *Lieber Code* and the *Salvage of Water-Damaged Materials,* to give but two examples.

In a field as diverse and extensive—and as old—as preservation, no volume, no collection of writings, and no timeline can pretend to approach comprehensiveness. Clearly, many events, inventions, and publications could be added to the timeline. The method here is more suggestive than all-inclusive.

This timeline is not meant to be a history of the preservation field, which has yet to be written. Rather, it attempts to draw out the many social, political, technological, professional, and economic facets of preservation. Its overall aim is to enhance the readings.

ca. 750 BC and ca. 630–580 BC

Old Testament prophets Isaiah and Jeremiah advise on the importance of keeping documents for future use.

ca. 15 BC

Roman architect and engineer Marcus Vitruvius Pollio notes causes of deterioration of domestic buildings in *De Architectura Libri Decem* (Ten Books on Architecture). He advises against having paintings and delicate cornice decoration in dining rooms where smoke from fires and lamps may damage them.

1550

Giorgio Vasari chronicles contemporary artists' techniques, including their art restoration practices, in *Le Vite de' Più Eccellenti Architetti, Pittori, et Scultori Italiani* (Lives of the Most Eminent Italian Architects, Painters and Sculptors).

1560

Queen Elizabeth I of England issues "A proclamation against breakinge or defacing of monumentes of antiquitie, beyng set up in churches or other publique places for memory and not for supersticion."

1627

Gabriel Naudé publishes *Advis pour dresser une bibliothèque* (Advice on Establishing a Library) in Paris, with a chapter addressing preservation concerns.

1631

John Weever decries wanton destruction of Catholic monasteries by Henry VIII in *Ancient funerall monuments within the United Monarchie of Great Britaine, Ireland, and the islands adjacent.*

1774

Chlorine bleach is developed. It was first prepared from hydrochloric acid and manganese by Carl Wilhelm Scheele and was considered a compound until Humphry Davy demonstrated that it cannot be decomposed and that hydrochloric (muriatic) acid consists of hydrogen and another true element, which he named chlorine in 1810. The discovery leads to alternatives to sun bleaching for the removal of stains from paper and fabric.

1783

Chlorine is first used for bleaching fabrics.

1785

French chemist Claude-Louis Berthollet introduces chlorine gas as a commercial bleach.

1789

Berthollet produces the first liquid bleach, *eau de Javel,* a weak solution of sodium hypochlorite.

1791

Thomas Jefferson, in a letter to Ebenezer Hazard of Philadelphia on February 18, laments the loss of documents chronicling early American history. He writes, "The lost cannot be recovered; but let us save what remains: not by vaults and locks which fence them from the public eye and use … but by such a multiplication of copies, as shall place them beyond the reach of accident."

1792

Clement and George Taylor, English papermakers, receive a patent for bleaching linen and cotton in paper manufacture.

1799

Scottish chemist Charles Tennant takes out a patent for bleaching powder (chloride of lime), which is in widespread use in bleaching paper pulp by 1815.

1807

German inventor Moritz Friedrich Illig publishes his method of alum-rosin sizing for paper, which he had developed before 1805. It is later discovered to be a leading cause of paper deterioration.

1823

A letter by John Murray, "On The Bad Composition of Modern Paper," is published in London in *The Gentleman's Magazine*.

1829

John Murray publishes *Practical Remarks on Modern Paper* in which he gives an account of his chemical analysis of pages of a Bible.

1830

Alum-rosin sizing of paper is introduced to the United States.

1835

John Andrews Arnett publishes *Bibliopegia; or, The Art of Bookbinding in all of its branches* in London, in which he describes the use of bleaching to remove stains from paper and improve its color. He refers to the work of French chemist Jean-Antoine Chaptal, who published *Essai sur le blanchiment* in 1801.

1838

French chemist Anselme Payen first identifies cellulose as a substance in plants and determines its chemical composition.

1839

Louis Daguerre develops the daguerreotype, a silver-based system for creating photographs, which he sells to the French government.

Using the daguerreotype process, the first microphotographs are produced.

1840

German paper manufacturers Friedrich Keller and Heinrich Voelter obtain a patent for a wood-grinding machine, which enables the development of techniques for manufacturing wood-pulp paper throughout the 1840s.

1841

After working on his invention at the same time as Daguerre, Henry Fox Talbot takes out a British patent for the calotype process, in which a positive photographic print is made from an in-camera negative.

First ground-wood paper to be made in the West is made in Halifax, Nova Scotia, by Charles Fenerty.

1842

Sir John Herschel publishes his discovery of the first blueprint process based on the photosensitive properties of iron salts in one of his three papers on photographic processes. His discoveries regarding the photosensitive behavior of iron and silver salts underlie the development of most common reprographic processes.

1846

Alfred Bonnardot publishes *Essai sur la restauration des anciennes estampes et des livres rares.* He urges people not to remove early marks of ownership, indications of use, and so on, and includes a bibliography, which was unusual for that period.

ca. 1850

Anselme Payen studies the effects of alum-rosin sizing on paper.

1851

English meteorologist and aeronaut James Glaisher suggests microphotography as a document preservation strategy.

1853

Ann Pamela Cunningham and others found the Mount Vernon Ladies' Association to preserve Mount Vernon, George Washington's home near Alexandria, Virginia.

1858

The second, revised edition of Bonnardot's book is published, with the title *Essai sur l'art de restaurer les estampes et les livres*.

1863

German-American Francis Lieber writes what is generally referred to as the *Lieber Code*, a precursor to the Hague Convention. Section II deals with "Public and private property of the enemy—Protection of persons, and especially of women; of religion, the arts and sciences."

1865

The Commons Preservation Society, the oldest national conservation body in Britain, is founded, with John Stuart Mill among its founders. It continues today as the Open Spaces Society.

1872

The US Congress establishes Yellowstone Park, which is widely held to be the world's first national park. Its purchase heralds the US government's acceptance of responsibility for natural heritage conservation.

1875

Justin Winsor, Superintendent of the Boston Public Library and soon to become President of the American Library Association and Harvard University Librarian, writes the first of frequent pieces on the subject of the deterioration of book paper.

1876

An essay by Librarian of Congress Ainsworth R. Spofford, "Binding and Preservation of Books," is published in the US Bureau of Education report, *Public Libraries in the United States of America: Their History, Condition and Management*.

1877

William Morris and others write a manifesto on the preservation of buildings and help to found the Society for the Protection of Ancient Buildings in Britain.

John Kruesi uses a sketch made by Thomas Edison to build the first phonograph, which records sound onto a metal cylinder wrapped in tinfoil. Within a few years Alexander Graham Bell, Chichester A. Bell, and Charles Sumner Tainter improve Edison's invention, chiefly by developing wax cylinders.

1879

English printer and bibliographer William Blades publishes "The Enemies of Books" in the *Printers' Register*. It was subsequently published as a monograph in 1880 (twice) and frequently thereafter in London, Paris, and New York. It continues to be reprinted and referenced.

1888

The first laboratory designed to conserve cultural heritage collections is opened in Berlin at the Royal Museums. Friedrich Rathgen, the first chemist to be employed by a museum, is hired as its Director.

1889

Eastman Kodak, in Rochester, New York, develops a nitrocellulose-based film, which is used first for snapshots and later for motion pictures.

1890

Jesse Walker Fewkes pioneers a new use for the phonograph–recording—and captures songs of the Passamaquoddy American Indians in Maine.

1894

Prefect Franz Ehrle of the Vatican Library uses silking as a technique for repairing paper documents. (A similar technique may have been used in the United States shortly before that. The French National Archives has claimed that it has used silking since about 1863.)

1895

The National Trust is founded in Great Britain to protect and preserve historic places.

1896

Canadian Reginald A. Fessenden suggests microforms as a compact solution for managing the unwieldy materials that engineers frequently consult.

1897

Ancient Shrines and Temples Preservation Law enacted in Japan.

1898

The International Conference on Preservation and Repair of Old Manuscripts is held at the Abbey of St. Gall, Switzerland, organized by Franz Ehrle of the Vatican Library. He warns of damage to documents caused by corrosive inks and calls for the scientific study of the damage and for the development of effective, durable, and reversible treatments.

Friedrich Rathgen publishes the first manual on the care and treatment of art and archaeological materials, *Die Konservierung von Alterthumsfunden*, in Berlin.

1899

The first of two peace conferences, at which are determined the principles that underpin the 1954 *Hague Convention for the Protection of Cultural Property in the Event of Armed Conflict* and its revisions, is held in the Hague.

1904

American chemist and conservation pioneer William J. Barrow is born. He devotes his life to understanding causes of deterioration in books and documents and publishing his findings. The merits of his work continue to be debated.

1905

The American Library Association appoints its first Committee on Bookbinding.

An English translation of Rathgen's manual is published with the title, *The Preservation of Antiquities: A Handbook for Curators*.

The first German patent for the use of hydrogen peroxide for bleaching.

1906

The US Congress passes the Antiquities Act to protect Native American archaeological sites on federal lands.

Paul Otlet and Robert Goldschmidt, in their Brussels publication *Sur une forme nouvelle du livre: la livre microphotographique*, propose the use of microphotography for making compact copies of books which can be easily distributed to distant readers.

1907

The second of two peace conferences to consider the protection of cultural property is held (see 1899 above).

1909

The Commercial Camera Company of Rochester, New York, introduces the photostat.

1910

Preservation is a topic at the International Congress of Archivists and Librarians in Brussels.

The Society for the Preservation of New England Antiquities (renamed Historic New England in 2004) is founded by William Sumner Appleton and others.

Gertrude Stiles starts teaching courses and workshops on bookbinding and repair at Case Western Reserve University in Ohio; she continues until 1938. She also teaches at the Carnegie Library School, Atlanta (1917–1923) and the University of Wisconsin Library School (1920).

1915

The Vienna Kunsthistorisches Museum uses x-ray and ultraviolet rays for examination and analysis of paintings.

1916

The National Park Service is established in the US.

1919

The British Museum hires Alexander Scott to investigate scientifically the causes of rapid deterioration in its collections as a result of storage underground during the 1914–1918 war.

The Historical Sites, Places of Scenic Beauty, and Natural Monuments Preservation Law is introduced in Japan. It expands on the 1897 law, which covered temples, shrines, and art.

1923

Kalle & Co. of Germany introduces the diazo (blueline) process.

1924

Scottish chemist Harold Plenderleith begins work in the newly created Department of Scientific and Industrial Research at the British Museum.

1925

New York banker George McCarthy obtains a patent for his Checkograph machine for making permanent film copies of bank records.

Harry Lydenburg of the New York Public Library writes about deteriorating book paper.

ca. 1928

Libraries, including the Library of Congress, Harvard University Library, and the New York Public Library, begin microfilming projects that are not aimed specifically at preservation; this paves the way for preservation microfilming.

1928

Eastman Kodak purchases the Checkograph machine and markets it under its Recordak Division.

The Center for Conservation and Technical Studies is established by Edward W. Forbes, director of Harvard University's Fogg Museum, which is the oldest fine arts conservation treatment, research, and training facility in the United States. Rutherford John Gettens and George L. Stout, the Center's first conservator and chemist, respectively, are credited with training the first generation of American conservators.

1929

The National Bureau of Standards Paper Section begins to issue reports on research relevant to library conservation.

1930

The International Conference for the Study of Scientific Methods for the Examination and Preservation of Works of Art, also known as the Rome Conference, is held.

1931

The Athens Charter and the General Conclusions of the Athens Conference on the restoration of historic monuments and buildings introduce important preservation and restoration concepts and principles, including the idea of a common world heritage.

1932

Technical Studies in the Field of the Fine Arts, an international journal, is founded at the Fogg Art Museum; it continues to 1942.

1935

The Library Binding Institute emerges as an outgrowth of the Book Manufacturers' Institute. It establishes a joint committee with the American Library Association, which issues the first of its "Minimum Specifications," which become a de facto standard for library binding.

The Historic Sites Act is enacted by the US Congress. It requires the Secretary of the Interior to conduct surveys of historic places that might be included in the National Park System.

Recordak begins filming and publishing the *New York Times* in microfilm.

The first film archives are founded—the Reichsfilmarchiv in Berlin, Museum of Modern Art in New York City, and the National Film Library in London.

1936

Cinémathèque Française opens in Paris.

Canadian O. J. Schierholtz takes out a US patent for deacidification, titled *Process for the Chemical Stabilization of Paper and Product.*

1937

Randolph G. Adams publishes "Librarians as Enemies of Books" in *Library Quarterly,* an indictment on library practices that damage books, which references William Blades (see 1879).

1938

Eugene Power starts University Microfilms (later University Microfilms International) in Ann Arbor, Michigan.

Harvard University Library launches a microfilming program for its foreign newspapers.

Solon J. Buck, National Archives Director of Research, teaches the first archives course at Columbia University; it covers preservation topics.

1939

The US National Archives decides that federal agencies (rather than archivists) can determine whether records stored in punch cards have historical value and should be preserved. Following this decision, few agencies retain any punch card records.

1939–1945

Widespread damage to European and Asian libraries, archives, and museums throughout the Second World War.

1944

Fremont Rider publishes *The Scholar and the Future of the Research Library,* in which he promotes microfilm as the great space-saver in libraries, maintaining that the rapid growth of academic library collections will make it impossible to store all of them.

1945

The US decides not to bomb Kyoto, the cultural heart of Japan, choosing to attack other Japanese cities instead; "Thus, on May 30, 1945 a top secret memorandum from [General Leslie] Groves to General Lauris Norstad read, in part: 'Will you please inform General [Henry H.] Arnold that this a.m. the secretary of war [Henry Lewis Stimson] and the chief of staff did not approve of the three targets we had selected, particularly Kyoto.'"[1]

American engineer Vannevar Bush publishes "As We May Think" in *The Atlantic Magazine.* He envisions the memex, a machine using the technology of the day (microfilm, screenviewers, cameras), for storing a large library in miniature. His vision later captures the imagination of the creators of the Internet and other technologies for capturing and distributing information.

1946

Pelham Barr publishes an early description of preservation administration, "Book Conservation and University Library Administration" in *College and Research Libraries.*

The International Council of Museums is founded.

1948

Maurice F. Tauber begins teaching, with Bertha M. Frick, a course on technical services that includes preservation—then called conservation—at Columbia University in New York.

The United Nations General Assembly adopts the Universal Declaration of Human Rights on December 10. Article 22 asserts that everyone has "economic, social and cultural rights indispensible for his dignity and the free development of his personality."

1949

The National Trust for Historic Preservation receives its charter from the US Congress.

Suzanne Briet of the French Bibliothèque Nationale writes, and UNESCO publishes, *Bibliothèques en détresse* (Libraries in distress), which serves as an inventory of the damage caused by the Second World War.

1950

The International Institute for Conservation of Museum Objects is founded.

US Federal Records Act expands the definition of a record to include machine-readable materials.

1951

The manufacture of nitrate film discontinued in the US; the film industry switches to cellulose triacetate.

1952

IBM introduces the IBM 701, the first commercial scientific computer.

1954

The Hague Convention (The *Convention on the Protection of Cultural Property in the Event of Armed Conflict*) is signed. It specifies the blue shield as the symbol to mark heritage sites for protection.

1956

Maurice F. Tauber edits the January issue of *Library Trends* on preservation, then called conservation.

The Council on Library Resources is founded through the efforts of Louis B. Wright and a grant from the Ford

Foundation; Verner W. Clapp is named president. Today, as the Council on Library and Information Resources, it continues to fund preservation initiatives.

Ampex introduces the first practical broadcast quality videotape machines at a conference in Chicago.

1957

The Council on Library Resources funds Barrow's research on the physical strength of paper.

1958

The American Group of the International Institute for Conservation of Museum Objects is founded.

1959

Barrow begins a year-long study on manufacturing of durable paper.

International Centre for the Study of the Preservation and Restoration of Cultural Property (ICCROM) is founded in Rome.

1960

The first graduate degree program in art conservation is established at New York University.

The Council on Library Resources funds the ALA Library Technology Program and preservation-related books.

The benefits of Barrow's new chemical wood-pulp paper are promulgated at a conference in Washington, DC.

The Association of Research Libraries appoints a Standing Committee on the Preservation of Research Library Materials.

The American Group of the International Institute for the Conservation of Historic and Artistic Works (IIC-AG) is established.

1961

The Council on Library Resources funds Barrow's laboratory in the new Virginia Historical Society building.

1963

IIC-AG adopts the *Standards of Practice and Professional Relationships for Conservators*, named the Murray Pease Report for the conservator at the Metropolitan Museum of Art, who directed the work of the compiling committee.

The Conservation Analytical Laboratory is established at the Smithsonian in Washington, DC. Today it is the Smithsonian Center for Materials Research and Education (SCMRE).

1964

The International Charter for the Conservation and Restoration of Monuments and Sites (also known as the Charter of Venice, or the Venice Charter) codifies international standards of conservation practice relating to buildings and sites and defines a framework for their permanent maintenance.

1965

The Preservation of Deteriorating Books, a report by Gordon Williams, is adopted by the Association of Research Libraries. The Library of Congress takes responsibility for a national program along the lines of the report.

The first issue of the *National Register of Microform Masters* is published.

The Council of Library Resources gives a grant to the Library of Congress to begin testing the distribution of cataloging records in machine-readable format, which becomes known as machine-readable cataloging (MARC), to other libraries.

Alkyl ketene dimers are first used in sizing hand-made conservation papers at Hayle Mill, Maidstone, England.

The National Endowment for the Arts and the National Endowment for the Humanities are established in the United States, both of which fund conservation and preservation projects.

1966

Richard D. Smith publishes a preliminary report on his experiments on deacidification of whole books in *Library Quarterly*.

Salvage of damaged items following the Florence flood of November 4 raises the level of awareness of conservation treatments and options and attracts international attention.

The National Historic Preservation Act is signed into law. According to Robert Stipe, "it catapulted the movement forward and gave us the unified national system that has been in effect ever since."[2]

The Association for Recorded Sound Collections (ARSC) is founded in the United States.

1967

Library of Congress centralizes preservation activities and funding, creating the position of the Assistant Director for Preservation and renaming the Office of Collections Maintenance and Preservation the Preservation Office; Frazer G. Poole is appointed to the position.

1969

The Conference on Deterioration and Preservation of Library Materials is held August 4–6 at the University of Chicago; its proceedings are edited by Richard Daniel Smith and Howard Winger.

The New York Library Association establishes an ad hoc committee on preservation.

The American Association of Museums produces *America's Museums: The Belmont Report: A Report to the Federal Council on the Arts and the Humanities*, which publicizes the need for the conservation of museum collections.

1970s

Personal computers (PCs) take off with the development of microprocessors.

1970

The Preservation Research Office at the Library of Congress is established with help from Verner W. Clapp and a grant from the Council on Library Resources.

The Bookbinding Committee of the ALA Resources and Technical Services Division expands its functions and becomes the Preservation of Library Materials Committee.

1971

OCLC (Ohio College Library Center) introduces an online catalog, which is today the most comprehensive database of library materials in the world.

Project Gutenberg is founded by Michael Hart, a student at the University of Illinois, to make electronic texts readily and widely available to anyone with access to the Internet. The first e-text published is the US Declaration of Independence.

IBM makes the 8-inch floppy disk commercially available.

1972

The American Institute for Conservation of Historic and Artistic Works is organized from the IIC-AG; the name change occurs in 1973.

The Convention Concerning the Protection of the World Cultural and Natural Heritage (the World Heritage Convention) is adopted by the General Conference of UNESCO at its 17th session on November 16.

1973

The New England Document Conservation Center, the first regional center in the United States, is founded and begins to provide telephone and on-site disaster assistance, and consultation on climate, building maintenance, security, fire prevention, and storage and handling. It continues today as the Northeast Document Conservation Center.

The Library of Congress establishes its Preservation Research and Testing Office.

National Historic Preservation Week is celebrated in the US for the first time.

The National Conservation Advisory Council is established. It continues today as Heritage Preservation, the National Institute for Conservation.

1975

Ellen McCrady produces the first issue of *Abbey Newsletter*, an important early preservation and conservation resource, which she publishes until 2003.

"Procedures for Salvage of Water-Damaged Library Materials," written by Peter Waters, then a restoration officer at the Library of Congress, is published.

1976

The Library of Congress hosts a planning conference for a national preservation program, December 16–17.

The Institute of Museum Services is established. It funds conservation projects in the United States.

Roots: The Saga of an American Family is published. A documentary based on the book airs on ABC the following year, which stimulates widespread interest in genealogical research.

The Tax Reform Act is passed in the United States, providing some tax incentives for rehabilitating historic properties and eliminating tax benefits for their demolition.

Events celebrating the US Bicentennial showcase American history.

1977

The television show *Antiques Roadshow* premieres in the UK.

The Conservation Center for Art and Historic Artifacts is established by Marilyn Kemp Weidner in Philadelphia.

Apple Computers releases the 5¼-inch floppy disk.

1979

The Book and Paper Group of the American Institute for Conservation of Historic and Artistic Works is founded.

The ALA Committee on Preservation of Library Materials becomes the Preservation of Library Materials Section.

The Australian National Committee of the International Council on Monuments and Sites (Australia ICOMOS Inc.) adopts the *Charter for the Conservation of Places of Cultural Significance* (Burra Charter). Further versions are issued in 1981, 1988, 1999, and 2004.

1980

The New England Document Conservation Center becomes the Northeast Document Conservation Center after it expands activities to New York and New Jersey.

Don Etherington creates a conservation department in the Harry Ransom Humanities Research Center at The University of Texas at Austin.

1981

3½-inch floppy disks and drives are introduced by Sony.

The Economic Recovery Tax Act offers further tax benefits for rehabilitating historic sites in the United States.

1982

Compact disk-digital audio (CD-DA) is introduced to the market jointly by Philips and Sony.

The National Information Systems Task Force of the Society of American Archivists develops the first two formally recognized archival description standards in the United States—*Data Elements Used in Archives, Manuscripts and Records Repository Information Systems* and the MARC *Format for Archives and Manuscripts Materials*.

The J. Paul Getty Trust commits to supporting four major activities, one of which is conservation.

1983

The Research Libraries Group embarks upon several decade-long projects to preserve members' "Great Collections" on microfilm and includes preservation microform information in online records for the first time.

1984

The New York State Conservation and Preservation Program, the first statewide program, is established with enabling legislation.

1985

The Office of Preservation is established at the National Endowment for the Humanities.

Digital audio tape (DAT) is introduced by Sony.

The Getty Conservation Institute begins operation in Marina del Rey, California.

1986

The Council on Library Resources establishes the Commission on Preservation and Access.

Microfilming Institute is held at the Library of Congress on March 6–7.

Tagged Image File Format (TIFF) is developed by Aldus Corporation.

1987

Cons DistList online forum begins.

The Twenty-Fifth International Archival Round Table conference is held at Gardone Riviera, Italy, and produces its proceedings, titled *Policies for the Preservation of the Archival Heritage.*

Public Broadcasting Service broadcasts the Council on Library Resources film *Slow Fires: On the Preservation of the Human Record.*

1988

The Berne Convention Implementation Act, officially titled *An Act to Amend Title 17, United States Code, to Implement the Berne Convention for the Protection of Literary and Artistic Works, as Revised at Paris on July 24, 1971, and for Other Purposes*, is signed into law. The United States agrees to the terms of the Berne Convention, promoting international standards in copyright protection and eliminating the need for copyright notice for copyright protection.

Z39.50 becomes the international standard defining a protocol for computer-to-computer information retrieval.

The US Congress passes the first National Film Preservation Act, which directs the Librarian of Congress to establish the National Film Preservation Board.

Patricia Battin, President of the Commission on Preservation and Access, appears before the US Congress on March 17 to propose a model for a national cooperative microfilming program.

1989

The Society of American Archivists Conservation Section changes its name to Preservation Section.

1990

The Native American Graves Protection and Repatriation Act is passed by the US Congress.

The National Trust for Historic Preservation adopts the Charleston Principles, eight guidelines for community conservation, at its meeting in Charleston, SC.

Martin Scorsese and others establish the Film Foundation to raise money for film preservation.

Kodak announces Photo CD, a system for "digitizing and saving" photographs.

The Film and Television Archives Advisory Committee becomes the Association of Moving Image Archivists.

Tim Berners-Lee writes a program called "WorldWide-Web."

1991

The Association of Moving Image Archivists becomes a professional association.

Philips introduces the Compact Disc Interactive (CD-i) player for music and video.

The Joint Photographic Expert Group introduces JPEG image compression, which is adopted as a standard by the International Telecommunications Union and the International Organization for Standardization in the following year.

Yale University's Project Open Book begins a multiphase study on the conversion of library materials from microfilm to digital format.

1992

The UNESCO Memory of the World Programme is launched; analogous to the World Heritage Convention, it addresses the poor state of documentary heritage throughout the world.

The Commission on Preservation and Access publishes *A Hybrid Systems Approach to Preservation of Printed Materials*, by Don Willis.

The Second National Film Preservation Act is passed, reauthorizing the National Film Preservation Board.

1993

The Librarian of Congress publishes a report, *Film Preservation 1993: A Study of the Current State of American Film Preservation.*

The Pitt Project begins, a three-year research effort funded by the National Historical Publications and Records Commission and centered at the University of Pittsburgh School of Information and Library Studies.

1994

The ALA Preservation of Library Materials Section merges with the Reproduction of Library Materials Section to become the Preservation and Reformatting Section of the Association for Library Collections & Technical Services.

The Conference on Authenticity in Relation to the World Heritage Convention held in Nara, Japan, drafts the *Nara Document on Authenticity.*

Tim Berners-Lee establishes the World Wide Web Consortium.

Cornell University's Digital to Microfilm Conversion Project begins evaluating the use of high-resolution imaging in the production of computer output microfilm (COM).

1995

The Library of Congress proceeds with the National Digital Library Program after a five-year pilot.

JSTOR, a nonprofit organization, is started to create online storage space for long runs of scholarly journals.

eBay, a web-based consumer marketplace that includes antiques, is founded.

The Kodak DC40 and the Apple QuickTake 100 are the first digital cameras marketed to consumers.

HTML 2.0, the first formal HTML standard, is published.

Dublin Core Metadata Initiative begins.

1996

The Institute of Museum and Library Services is formed, combining the Institute of Museum Services and the Library Program Office of the Department of Education. It supports conservation and preservation.

The George Eastman House in Rochester, New York, establishes a moving image archiving education program.

The Northeast Document Conservation Center holds its first School for Scanning seminar on digitization.

The International Committee of the Blue Shield is set up to protect cultural heritage threatened by wars and natural disasters globally.

The Commission on Preservation and Access and the Research Libraries Group publish *Preserving Digital Information: Report of the Task Force on Archiving of Digital Information*, written by John Garrett and Donald Waters.

Australia's Preserving Access to Digital Information Initiative (PADI) receives government funding and the National Library of Australia assumes responsibility for PADI the following year.

Brewster Kahle launches the Internet Archive, a nonprofit organization, in San Francisco; it aims to provide permanent access to digital materials.

The National Library of Australia's PANDORA (Preserving and Accessing Networked Documentary Resources of Australia) Project is launched.

1997

The Regional Alliance for Preservation commences as a pilot project of the Commission on Preservation and Access. It continues today as a national network of organizations with expertise in preservation and conservation.

The National Film Preservation Foundation is established by the US Congress.

RLG DigiNews is published as a forum for managers of digital initiatives; it continues publication until 2007.

DVD discs and players become commercially available in the US.

The US Department of Defense shifts from paper to electronic records.

Boston's public broadcasting station WGBH introduces the American version of the television program *Antiques Roadshow*.

1998

The Copyright Term Extension Act, also known as the Sonny Bono Extension Act and the Mickey Mouse Protection Act, is passed by the US House of Representatives, extending the period of time that works remain under copyright.

Public Broadcasting Service broadcasts the Council on Library and Information Resources film *Into the Future: On the Preservation of Knowledge in the Electronic Age*, a follow-up to *Slow Fires*.

The National Archives and Records Administration Electronic Records Archives project begins.

Encoded Archival Description Version 1.0 is introduced.

Google Search engine is launched.

1999

A draft recommendation for the Open Archival Information System reference model is issued.

Project CAMiLEON begins at the Universities of Michigan and Leeds to study long-term digital preservation strategies. The British project continues to 2002 and the US component to 2003.

The Arts and Humanities Data Service in the UK begins research into the management of digital information, a major outcome of which was *Preservation Management of Digital Materials: A Handbook*, by Neil Beagrie and Maggie Jones (2001).

2000

The Library of Congress establishes MINERVA, a Web archiving project, to collect and preserve websites.

The Library of Congress receives funding to establish the National Digital Information Infrastructure and Preservation Program (NDIIPP) as a permanent program.

The Research Libraries Group publishes *Moving Theory into Practice: Digital Imaging for Libraries and Archives* by Anne R. Kenney and Oya Y. Rieger.

XHTML 1.0 is accepted as a web standard.

MIT Libraries and Hewlett-Packard develop DSpace, an open-source digital repository system.

2001

UNESCO adopts the Universal Declaration on Cultural Diversity.

Bamiyan Buddhas are destroyed in Afghanistan on March 11.

METS 1.1 schema is introduced as an XML standard for encoding metadata in digital libraries.

The Internet Archive unveils the Wayback Machine to provide access to its World Wide Web archive.

The National Library of Australia, with funding from the Council on Library and Information Resources, begins the Safekeeping project within PADI.

The Digital Preservation Coalition is established in the UK.

The New York Historical Society is one of the earliest institutions to actively preserve artifacts from the September 11 disaster in New York.

2002

OCLC launches Digital Archive.

Research Libraries Group and OCLC publish *Trusted Digital Repositories: Attributes and Responsibilities* and *Preservation Metadata and the OAIS Information Model: A Metadata Framework to Support the Preservation of Digital Objects*.

The Consultative Committee for Space Data Systems releases the first *Reference Model for an Open Archival Information System (OAIS)*.

The National Archives in the United Kingdom develops PRONOM, a database of file formats and technical information about digital preservation.

The PDF/A initiative begins with the goal of creating an international standard to define the use of the Portable Document Format (PDF) for preservation of digital documents.

The National Initiative for Networked Cultural Heritage publishes *The NINCH Guide to Good Practice in the Digital Representation and Management of Cultural Heritage Materials.*

UCLA launches the Moving Image Archive Studies program.

2003

UNESCO adopts the Convention for the Safeguarding of the Intangible Cultural Heritage.

UNESCO releases *Guidelines for the Preservation of Digital Heritage.*

OCLC and Research Libraries Group form the Preservation Metadata: Implementation Strategies (PREMIS) Working Group.

The Council on Library and Information Resources publishes *A Survey of Digital Cultural Heritage Initiatives and Their Sustainability Concerns,* by Diane M. Zorich.

New York University establishes the Moving Image Archiving and Preservation program.

2004

The most recent version of the Burra Charter is issued.

Google begins working with university libraries to digitize books for the Google Books project.

The Digital Curation Centre, based in Edinburgh, is founded in the United Kingdom.

2005

YouTube, a video-sharing website, is created.

Hurricane Katrina, one of the deadliest hurricanes in American history, strikes, with most of the damage occurring in New Orleans. Several foundations provide funds to assist libraries and other cultural heritage institutions affected by Katrina.

The National Digital Newspaper Program distributes $1.9 million in grants to six institutions to create a web-accessible archive.

The PREMIS Working Group publishes *PREMIS Data Dictionary for Preservation Metadata.*

2006

dPlan: The Online Disaster-Planning Tool for Cultural and Civic Institutions, funded by Institute of Museum and Library Services, is released by the Northeast Document Conservation Center.

The Art Materials Information and Education Network is launched.

2007

Eastman Kodak ceases production of Kodachrome, a film stock noted for its color stability.

2008

A lawsuit entitled The Authors Guild, Inc., et al., v. Google Inc., Case No. 05 CV 8136.(S.D.N.Y.) is heard. The District Court for the Southern District of New York preliminarily approves the Original Settlement (Google Book Settlement) in November. (See 2013 update.)

HathiTrust Digital Library is started by a group of American universities in order to establish a repository for archiving and sharing digitized collections.

Cloud computing emerges as a system for managing and storing digital information.

2009

The District Court for the Southern District of New York preliminarily approves an Amended Settlement Agreement in the Google Book lawsuit, November. (See 2013 update.)

The Salzburg Declaration on the Conservation and Preservation of Cultural Heritage, October 31, is prepared at the Salzburg Global Seminar session on Connecting to the World's Collections: Making the Case for the Conservation and Preservation of our Cultural Heritage.

2010

The Council on Library and Information Resources publishes *Digital Forensics and Born-Digital Content in Cultural Heritage Collections* by Matthew G. Kirschenbaum, Richard Ovenden, and Gabriela Redwine in December, following a symposium, Digital Forensics and Cultural Heritage, held at the University of Maryland in May to solicit comment and feedback on a draft of the report.

2011

The three remaining producers of 35mm professional quality motion picture film cameras, ARRI, Panavision, and Aaton, cease production of their analog models to focus on digital cameras, leading to industry prediction that the end of analog filmmaking is approaching.

The District Court for the Southern District of New York on March 22 denies the parties' request for final settlement approval in the Google Book law suit. (See 2013 update.)

2013

In November, Judge Denny Chin, US Circuit Court, dismisses the *Authors Guild, Inc., et al., v. Google Inc.*, lawsuit and affirms that the Google Books program meets all legal requirements for "fair use." The Authors Guild announces that it will appeal the ruling.

Further Reading

Bewer, Francesca G. *A Laboratory for Art: Harvard's Fogg Museum and the Emergence of Conservation in America, 1900–1950.* Cambridge, MA: Harvard Art Museum; New Haven, CT: Yale University Press, 2010.

Clavir, Miriam. *Preserving What Is Valued: Museums, Conservation, and First Nations.* Vancouver: University of British Columbia Press, 2002.

Collings, Thomas, and Derek Milner. "A New Chronology of Papermaking Technology." *The Paper Conservator* 14 (1990): 58–62.

Cunha, George Martin, and Dorothy Grant Cunha. *Library and Archives Conservation: 1980s and Beyond.* Metuchen, NJ: Scarecrow Press, 1983. 2 vols.

Darling, Pamela W., and Sherelyn Ogden. "From Problems Perceived to Programs in Practice: the Preservation of Library Resources in the U.S.A., 1956-1980." *Library Resources & Technical Services* 25 (1981): 9–29.

Gracy, Karen, and Michele Valerie Cloonan. "The Preservation of Moving Images." *Advances in Librarianship* 27 (2004): 49–95.

Higginbotham, Barbra Buckner. *Our Past Preserved: A History of American Library Preservation, 1876–1910.* Boston, Mass.: G. K. Hall, 1990.

Hunter, Dard. *Papermaking: The History and Technique of an Ancient Craft.* New York: Dover, 1974.

Ogden, Sherelyn. "The Impact of the Florence Flood on Library Conservation in the United States of America: A Study of the Literature Published 1956–1976." *Restaurator* 3 (1979): 1–36.

Swartzburg, Susan G. "Preserving the Cultural Patrimony." In *A la recherche de la mémoire, le patrimoine culturel : actes du colloque* édité *par Huguette Rouit et Jean-Marcel* (IFLA Publication 62), 81–86. München: K.G. Saur, 1992.

NOTES

1. Cary, Otis. *Mr. Stimson's "Pet City": The Sparing of Kyoto,* 1945. (Kyoto: Amherst House Doshisha University, 1987), 14.

2. Stipe, Robert E., ed. *A Richer Heritage: Historic Preservation in the Twenty-first Century.* (Chapel Hill, NC: University of North Carolina Press, 2003), vii.

chapter 1

EARLY PERSPECTIVES ON PRESERVATION

THE NEED FOR THE PRESERVATION OF DOCUMENTS has been recognized for nearly 3,000 years, although conservation and preservation have emerged as formal fields only in the twentieth century. This recognition is manifest in many texts that talk of preserving history, documents, ideas, and the oral and written record, though only rarely do these early writers propose strategies for achieving the longevity of cultural heritage.

This chapter introduces a host of early sources relating to preservation, which are presented chronologically. (No doubt many other sources exist.) Together, the sources included here weave an uneven but persistent narrative of the reasons we preserve our heritage. These include religious, political, cultural, educational, historic, philosophical, scholarly, aesthetic, fiscal, and personal motivations.

In **Jeremiah 32:14** (ca. 630–580 BC) we see that to ensure the return of the people of Israel to the Land of Israel, and thus to the restoration of their promised status, a key document—the deed of purchase—needed to be preserved. Storage in earthenware jars was a contemporary preservation strategy. In fact, systems were then in place throughout the Middle East for the creation and keeping of records.

Similarly, in **Isaiah 30:8–11** (ca. 740–700 BC) the prophet is commanded to write God's prophecy down on a tablet so that it may serve as "a witness forever" that God warned against an alliance with Egypt. "That Isaiah is commanded to write this prophecy specifically suggests that he often delivered prophecies as speeches without writing them down."[1]

Ernst Posner, writing about archives in the ancient world, observed that

> Where business considerations had an influence on the mind of the record creator, he could be expected to provide for the long-term preservation of his documents. In an oblique sense, such consideration would prompt the temple priests to build and keep collections of omen tablets, [the prediction of events] just as the priests of the Apollo temple at Delphi later maintained their oracle archives. Businessmen would naturally see to it that their records were kept for future use, and they did so quite effectively. The records of the Egibi banking family in Babylon, to give but one example, document the activities of six generations of that family from 690 to 480 BC.[2]

Vitruvius (ca. 75–15 BC) takes a preventive approach to preservation in his *On Architecture*. For example, he observes that smoke from fire and soot from lamps can cause damage to paintings and thus it is better not to place paintings in dining rooms. Similarly, he notes that continuous dampness in a building can cause injury to plaster and stucco. One of his pragmatic suggestions is that in constructing a house, builders should determine its style by the climate in which it is built. Today such thinking is central to sustainable architecture. Unfortunately, architects throughout the ages have failed to follow his sound preservation advice.

Martial (ca. 40 AD and 104 AD), a poet and social commentator whose works are known for their sharp wit (as well as for their obscenities), wrote over a dozen books of epigrams. Included here is Epigram 2 of Book 10, "To the Reader on Issuing a Second Version of this Book." ("This book" refers to Book 10 of his Epigrams.) Of interest to us are his reflections on the art of writing and the preservation of recorded texts. Martial suggests that words are more enduring than physical monuments because they are preserved in multiple copies of books.

A passage from the **Koran**, Surah 85 (ca. 632), "The Constellations," verses 17–22, reminds us that the Koran is preserved on a tablet, presumably for

Clay tablet; legal document of the Egibi banking family concerning a sale of land. Dated 2nd Nisan, 10th year of Darius; i.e., 512 BC. Image courtesy of the British Museum.

the ages. The tablet is a metaphor for the permanence of the Koran; once recorded it is unchangeable and imperishable.

The idea that multiple copies of works will help to assure their longevity, as Martial asserted, was taken up by **Thomas Jefferson** nearly 1,700 years later in a letter to Ebenezer Hazard on February 18, 1791. Jefferson was concerned that if the history of "the infancy of our country" was not kept in "the public eye," it would not be preserved. The idea that multiplicity will place items "beyond the reach of accident" is current in the digital-information world. For example, LOCKSS, "Lots of Copies Keeps Stuff Safe," based at Stanford University, is an international community initiative that provides libraries with digital-preservation tools and support for preserving e-content. It uses open-source software, a contemporary approach to keeping material in "the public eye." The home page of the site prominently displays a quotation from the same Jefferson letter that is reproduced in this volume (www. lockss.org).

Martial's epigram was quoted by **John Weever** (active 1630s) in his 1631 book *Ancient Funeral Monuments within the vnited monarchie of Great Britaine, Ireland, and the islands adiacent, with the dissolued monasteries therein contained*; he also quoted classical authors Horace (*Lyric poesie*) and Ovid (*Metamorphoses*, Book 15), who were similarly contemplating the preservation of their work. Relevant to Weever's interest in preserving heritage, Martial, Ovid, and Horace each expressed the belief that books were the most permanent of all "monuments." Martial, Horace, and Ovid composed their works long before the invention of printing, when every book produced was as unique as the monuments that Weever sought to preserve. Yet even if the various copies of manuscript books had textual variations, at least some portions of the texts had a chance of survival. And it is certainly easier to copy a text than to make a copy of a piece of sculpture. Additionally, books were portable and hideable, further aids to their survival.

The overarching theme of *Ancient Funeral Monuments,* however, is another age-old preservation dilemma: how to protect works from war and other social, political, or religious conflicts. His aim was to preserve the monuments and sepulchers of the dead which, he maintained, were not preserved as well in the "British Isles" as they were in other countries.

This was in part because of King Henry VIII's destructive actions against monasteries. In response to the looting of churches and other Catholic religious sites in England that came as a result of the dissolution of the monasteries, Queen Elizabeth I sought to end such destructive practices. Her proclamation against breaking or defacing "Monuments of Antiquity"[3] —quoted in Weever—was possibly more symbolic than successful. To declare such a sentiment is one thing; to enforce the law is another. Weever implies that the declaration was not particularly enforced. Nonetheless, the Queen's *Declaration* does stand as an early example of governmental protection over sacred or otherwise charitable or cultural sites. Later, in the nineteenth century, local, national, and international laws would be enacted to protect cultural heritage, also with varying levels of success (see chapter 9). All the laws in the world will not stop fanatics, enemies, or repressive regimes from defacing or destroying historical objects or records.

Writing at about the same time as Weever, **Gabriel Naudé** (1600–1653) viewed the very act of gathering collections and forming libraries as aspects of preservation. During his career he became the librarian of some of the greatest collectors of his time, including Cardinal Francesco Barberini. Luckily for us, he wrote down his views of librarianship in the remarkable work *Advice on Establishing a Library* (1627). Later, as librarian to Cardinal Jules Mazarin, Naudé traveled throughout Europe to enhance the Cardinal's great library in Paris. Mazarin eventually acquired some 40,000 items and allowed his library to be used by the public. Sadly, Mazarin's library was sold by the French government, and Naudé closed out his career as librarian to Queen Christina, of Sweden.

Gabriel Naudé's important book stands as a testament to all that he learned as a librarian as well as to his natural brilliance. In chapter 5, he discussed the process of building collections. He acquired entire libraries with verve, tenacity, and wisdom. He recognized the research value of items that others did not. Today we would describe such items as ephemera. Some of the principles in this chapter address the integration of preservation into collection development—a theme that is picked up again in chapter 4 of the present volume, "Collections: Development and Management."

For example, Naudé stresses the importance of conserving whatever is acquired. Paraphrasing Ovid, himself an avid collector, he writes: "that which is gained by being protected is not less valuable than that which is gained by being searched for." Yet at the same time, Naudé cautions against lavishing too much attention on fancy bindings:

> The fourth principle is to cut the excess expenditure many waste on the binding and ornamentation of their volumes, in order to use this money instead to purchase books that are missing, so as not to be liable to Seneca's criticism, who took pleasure in making fun of those 'to whom the covers and titles of their books give the most pleasure.'

Gabriel Naudé's work deserves to be better known.

John Murray (1786?–1851), a scientific writer,[4] identified some of the causes of deterioration in paper in "On the Bad Composition of Paper," a letter to the editor published in 1823 in *The Gentleman's Magazine.* He later expanded his observations and published *Practical Remarks on Modern Paper* in

1829.[5] Although it would be nearly a hundred years before all of the causes of deterioration in machine-made papers would be determined, Murray's work was important in two ways. First, he identified problems with manufacturing that existed even before the development of wood-pulp paper. Second, he voiced his concerns in a popular publication, *The Gentleman's Magazine,* where it was read by a number of people throughout the English-speaking world. Thus Murray turned preservation into a public concern.

Francis Lieber (1800–1872) was a German-American jurist. In 1863 he prepared "Instructions for the Government of Armies of the United States in the Field," more commonly referred to as "The Lieber Code." It was revised by the Army's board of officers and approved by President Abraham Lincoln. The Code sets out rules of engagement for war. Of particular significance for readers of this volume is that the Code also sets out rules for the "public and private property of the enemy," with specific instructions about the protection of works of art, libraries, and hospitals. These ideas would be further developed in the 1954 Hague Convention, which includes a section on "The Protection of Cultural Property in the Event of Armed Conflict." Thus, in the Lieber Code, Weever's concerns about the wanton destruction of monuments were addressed within the context of war. Although codes and conventions are not always followed—as many of the armed conflicts of the twentieth and early twenty-first century have demonstrated—they carry moral weight as well as legal authority. (See also chapters 5, "Risks to Cultural Heritage: Time, Nature, and People," and 9, "Ethics and Values.")

William Morris (1834–1896), a founding member of the Society for the Protection of Ancient Buildings (SPAB) in 1877, advocated for a minimalist approach to the repair of historic buildings. Inspired by the architectural writings of John Ruskin,[6] he decried poor restoration practices in the manifesto that he and others wrote for SPAB. Morris set an ideal, but not one that can always be met. Sometimes intervention is necessary in order to save a historic structure. In his 2009 work, *Time Honored: A Global View of Architectural Conservation,* John H. Stubbs (see chapter 3, "Preservation in Contexts") describes degrees of intervention for architectural conservation ranging from laissez-faire (least intervention) to re-creation *in situ* or at a different site with new materials (replication or facsimile).[7]

Three poets, **Hakīm Abu'l-Qāsim Ferdowsī Tūsī** (940–1020), **William Shakespeare** (1564–1616), and **Percy Bysshe Shelley** (1792–1822), address variations of the themes we have considered here, and their poems round out this chapter. Like the classical poets before him, Ferdowsi hopes that his work will remain in the world because it carries the wisdom of the ancients. His lines "from this famous book of the ancients" is probably a reference to the work of which this poem is a part, the *Shahnama,* his national epic about the Persian empire before the Islamic conquest.

In Shakespeare's Sonnet 18, "Shall I compare thee to a summer's day?," the poet intones with confidence that "So long lives this, and this gives life to thee"; his words will be immortalized as long as there are people to read his sonnet. Archivist and computer scientist Jeff Rothenberg, in the documentary *Into the Future: On the Preservation of Knowledge in the Electronic Age,* about digital preservation,[8] quotes the last lines from the sonnet. Shakespeare could be confident that his work would survive, so reasons Rothenberg, because of the fixity of the printed word. However, for authors who compose their work online, Rothenberg raises the concern that there is much less chance that such creations will survive. (See his article in chapter 7, "Frameworks for Digital Preservation.")

For the Romantic poet Shelley, "Ozymandias" provides a metaphoric read into the almost complete decay of a statue (of Egyptian King Ramses II, here referred to by his Greek name) and the entire civilization it stood in front of. Although once a mighty king, he is no more immune from oblivion than anyone else. Even his entire physical world has turned to dust ("Round the decay of that colossal wreck, boundless and bare, the lone and level sands stretch far away.") Shelley's poem seems to anticipate the many nineteenth century writings about ruins that would follow.

With these writings, then, we can trace the roots of preservation concerns that today's practitioners continue to express and grapple with.

NOTES

1. *The Jewish Study Bible.* Jewish Publication Society, Tanakh trs. Edited by Adele Berlin and Marc Zvi Brettler. (Oxford and New York: Oxford University Press, 2004): 843.

2. Ernst Posner, *Archives in the Ancient World.* (Cambridge, MA: Harvard University Press, 1972): 66.

3. Queen Elizabeth I, *A Proclamation against breakinge or defacing of monumentes of antiquitie, beyng set up in churches or other publique places for memory and not for supersticion.* (Imprinted at London in Powles Churchyarde: By Rycharde Iugge and Iohn Cawood, Printers to the Quenes Maiestie, [1560]). The proclamation is included on pages 52–54 of Weever's book, which was published in London, by Thomas Harper, in 1631. This copy (DA28.W37 1631) was consulted at the Getty Research Institute, on March 3, 2011.

4. There is little information to be found about John Murray. Perhaps the best source is a reprint of Murray's *Practical Remarks on Modern Paper* with an introductory essay by Leonard B. Schlosser (North Hills, PA: Bird & Bull Press, 1981).

5. John Murray, *Practical Remarks on Modern Paper with an introductory account of its former substitutes; also observations on writing inks, the restoration of illegible manuscripts, and the preservation of important deeds from the destructive effects of damp.* (Edinburgh: William Blackwood; London: T. Cadell, 1829).

6. Ruskin's influence on Morris is described throughout Fiona MacCarthy's *William Morris: A Life for Our Time.* (New York: Alfred Knopf, 1995).

7. John H. Stubbs, *Time Honored: A Global View of Architectural Conservation*, 2009, pp. 23–24, "Nomenclature and Common Understandings," and p. 127, the graph "Architectural Conservation: Degrees of Intervention."

8. Terry Sanders, director. *Into the Future: On the Preservation of Knowledge in The Electronic Age* (Washington, DC: Commission on Preservation and Access, Council on Library and Information Resources, 1998).

Selection 1.1

THE JEWISH STUDY BIBLE

The translations of these two passages are from The Jewish Study Bible. *Jewish Publication Society, Tanakh translation. Edited by Adele Berlin and Marc Zvi Brettler (Oxford and New York: Oxford University Press, 2004).*

Jeremiah 32:14
Thus said the Lord of Hosts, the God of Israel: "Take these documents, this deed of purchase, the sealed text and the open one, and put them into an earthen jar, so that they may last a long time."

Isaiah 30:8
Now, go, write it down on a tablet, and inscribe it in a record, that it may be with them for future days, a witness forever.

MARCUS VITRUVIUS POLLIO

Excerpts from *De Architectura*

Edited by F. Krohn (Leipzig: Teubner, 1912).
New translation for this volume by Coleman Connelly.

De Architectura 6.1.1–2

These [private residences] will be properly designed if one has first taken into account which of the world's regions and climes they are being built in. It is clear that one should build one type of building in Egypt and another in Spain, and build differently near the Black Sea than at Rome, and so forth according to the qualities of other lands and regions. For in one part of the world the earth is close to the sun's course, whereas in another it is far removed from it, and in a third it is situated in the middle. Therefore, just as the world is arranged such that the circle of the zodiac and the sun's course naturally bestow different properties on any given area of the earth, in the same way is it clear that one should fit the design of a building to the type of region and its variety of climate.

In the north, buildings should clearly be well-roofed and as closed as possible, not open but rather oriented toward the direction of warmth. By contrast, in southern regions where the force of the sun creates oppressive heat, buildings should be designed to be more open and oriented toward the north. Thus what nature spoils craft shall amend. Likewise in the other regions one should modify one's designs to fit the climate of that part of the world.

De Architectura 7.4.1–5

I have already given the reasons why in dry places one should use stucco. Now I will explain how in damp places one may achieve smoothed surfaces that can last without cracking. First, in rooms that are of level footing, apply plaster using burnt tile instead of sand-mortar at a height of roughly three feet above the base of the floor and lay it down such that those parts of the stuccoing will not be cracked by dampness. If a wall should suffer from permanent dampness, retreat a ways back from it and construct a second thin wall standing as far apart from as the situation will allow, and conduct a channel between the two walls that is on a gradient with the room and has vents at the opening. Likewise, when the wall has been built up to its full height, one should leave air-holes. For if the dampness cannot exit through vents both at the base and at the top, it will unfailingly spread out over the new structure. Once all this has been carried out, plaster the wall using burnt tile, straighten it, and then smooth it using stucco.

If however the location will not allow for such construction, create channels and have the vents lead out to the opening. Then on one side place tiles of two feet each, while building on the other side a foundation of pillars made from eight-inch bricks,[1] upon which the corners of two tiles can rest. Have the pillars stand apart from the wall such that resulting space is no more than a palm's breadth. Next, set up studded tiles above from the base to the top and fasten them to the wall. Carefully coat their inward-facing sides with pitch so that they will resist water. Likewise make sure that they have air-holes on the base and the top above the vault.

Then whitewash them in turn with slaked lime so that they will not resist the tile-plastering, since because of their dryness from being fired in the kiln they cannot take and hold onto the plaster unless one puts lime underneath to glue the two substances together and force them to cohere. Once the plastering has been put on, lay down burnt tile instead of sand-mortar and complete all the other steps described above in the section on the reasons for using stucco.

The smoothed surfaces for their part ought to have decorations adapted as befits them, such that they possess worthy qualities suited to the location and not foreign to the distinctions between types.[2] In winter dining rooms, subtle decoration with artistic depictions, grand paintings, or cornice work in the vaulting is not practical, because they are marred by the smoke from the fire and the constant soot from the torches. In these rooms, panels decorated with black varnish should be installed below the dadoes and polished, with wedges dyed in ochre or vermillion placed between them. The vaulting should then be smoothed out, after first being polished clean. Regarding floors, if one cares to consider the style of Greek winter dining rooms, this cost-effective and practical method will prove quite satisfactory.

First, below the level of the dining room one digs to a depth of roughly two feet and after packing down the soil spreads out a layer of lime and gravel or of burnt tile, sloped such that it has vents in the drainage channel. Then, having heaped in charcoal and stamped it down, one spreads out a mortar mixed from sand, lime, and ash, a half-foot thick. Once rubbed down with a whetstone to the measures of a rule and level, the surface gives off the appearance of a black floor. Thus during the Greeks' banquets, whatever anyone spills from a cup or spirts out dries up as soon it falls, and the servants who stand in waiting do not catch cold from that type of floor, even if they go about barefoot.

TRANSLATION NOTES

1. Reading laterculis between besalibus and pilae.

2. Translation of this sentence can only be approximate since, to follow Krohn, there is a lacuna between *autem* and *politionibus*.

M. VALERII MARTIAL

Epigrammaton

Edited by W.M. Lindsay (Oxford: Clarendon University Press, 1902).
New translation for this volume by Coleman Connelly.

Liber 10.2

My first hurried efforts on this tenth book have forced me to recall it after the work had already slipped from my hands. You will read some familiar poems, but they have been polished by a more recent file; the greater part are new. Reader, be kind to both since, reader, you are my mainstay. For when Rome gave you to me, she said "We have nothing greater to give you. Through this man you will escape the sluggish flows of thankless Lethe and in your better part will survive. A fig-tree splits Messalla's marble and a rash mule-driver laughs at Crispus' defaced horses. But writings no theft can harm and the passing centuries profit them. These monuments alone cannot die."

THE KORAN

Excerpt from Surah 85, "The Constellations"

From The Koran Interpreted. *Translated by A.J. Arberry (New York: Simon & Schuster, 1955).*

Hast thou received the story of the hosts,
    Pharoah and Thamood?
Nay, but the unbelievers still cry lies,
And God is behind them, encompassing.
Nay, but it is a glorious Koran
    In a guarded tablet.

HAKĪM ABUL-QĀSIM FERDOWSĪ TŪSĪ

Excerpt from "When the Sword of Sixty Comes Nigh His Head," from *Shahnameh*

Translated by Basil Bunting, in World Poetry: An Anthology of Verse from Antiquity to Our Time, *edited by Katharine Washburn and John S. Major (New York: W.W. Norton, 1998, p. 469).*

[Final stanza]
I ask the just Creator
so much refuge from Time
that a tale of mine may remain in the world
from this famous book of the ancients
and they who speak of such matters weighing their words
think of that only when they think of me.

WILLIAM SHAKESPEARE

Sonnet 18: "Shall I Compare Thee to a Summer's Day?"

Shall I compare thee to a summer's day?
Thou art more lovely and more temperate.
Rough winds do shake the darling buds of May,
And summer's lease hath all too short a date.
Sometime too hot the eye of heaven shines,
And often is his gold complexion dimmed;
And every fair from fair sometime declines,
By chance, or nature's changing course, untrimmed;
But thy eternal summer shall not fade,
Nor lose possession of that fair thou ow'st,
Nor shall Death brag thou wand'rest in his shade,
When in eternal lines to Time thou grow'st:
    So long as men can breathe, or eyes can see,
    So long lives this, and this gives life to thee.

GABRIEL NAUDÉ

Advis Pour Dresser Une Bibliothèque (Chapter 5)

New translation for this volume by Laurence Bouvard (Paris: François Targa, 1627).

The Means by Which a Collection Can Be Created

And so, Monsieur. After having shown in these first three discussions the method that should be followed in order to learn how to establish a library, how many books it is suggested it should be provided with and what qualities to look for in their selection, what follows now is an investigation of the means by which one can obtain the books themselves, and what must be done to improve and increase the collections. In this regard, I will honestly say that the foremost principle pertaining to this point is to carefully preserve those books that are acquired and that one acquires on a regular basis without allowing them to be lost or damaged in any way. "It is far more easily bearable," says Seneca, "never to acquire than to lose, and thus it can be seen that those who have never had any fortune are happier than those who have lost it."

> In addition to this is the idea that there is no point in greatly increasing a collection if the books that have been so carefully and diligently acquired are then lost or damaged through lack of care. Keeping this in mind, Ovid and other wise men were right to say that to preserve is no less a virtue than to acquire: "That which is gained by being protected is not less valuable than that which is gained by being searched for."

The second principle is not to overlook anything that could be considered at all important or have some use, whether in your view or that of others; such as writs, placards, theses, fragments, essays, and other similar items that one should be careful to collect together and assemble according to their different types and subjects, as this is the best way to consider them and take them into account: "Since that which is of no benefit on its own, is useful when taken

together." Otherwise what often happens is that by neglecting these little books that do not appear to be anything more than trifles and items of small importance, one ends up losing a number of wonderful little collections that are sometimes the most interesting parts of a library.

The third point can be gleaned from the methods which were used by Richard de Bury, Bishop of Durham and Lord Treasurer and then Lord Chancellor of England, which involved publicly declaring and otherwise making known to everyone the regard he had for books and the great desire he had to establish a library. If such a project is well and widely known, and if the person who champions this idea has the ability and the authority to do his friends favors, these friends will undoubtedly be led to present him with the most interesting books that come into their possession, invite him into their own library and that of their own friends, in short, do everything they possibly can to aid and support such a plan. This has been well documented by the above-mentioned Richard de Bury in the very words that I transcribe here, all the more willingly because his book is extremely rare and counts among those that are being lost through our negligence: "When I began to be successful," he says, "I came to the notice of the King's Majesty and was received into his household, giving me a greater opportunity to explore wherever I wanted and to hunt through, as it were, some wonderful public and private libraries, both secular and religious." And a little afterward, "I received free access through his Royal favor to search out the most hidden books. The knowledge of my love of books soon spread very quickly, and it was even reported that I was languishing from desire for them, especially the most ancient books, and that my favor was more easily obtained by quartos than by money. For this reason, supported by the authority of the above-named Prince, I could greatly hinder and benefit, advance and impede, both the strong and the weak; and instead of presents and rewards, in place of gifts and jewels, there flowed to me filthy quartos and timeworn Codices, valuable both in my sight and in my affections. Then the most illustrious monasteries threw open their safes, chests were unfastened, and cabinets undone, etc."

To this he also adds the many voyages he made as an ambassador and the great number of erudite and diligent people whose hard work and industriousness served him in his research.

What also leads me to believe that these methods were effective is that I knew a man who was so interested in medals, paintings, statues, brooches, and other such items and ornaments that he collected more than twelve thousand pounds worth by this means alone without ever having paid out more than four. And in all honesty, my motto is that any well-bred and naturally virtuous person should always support the laudable intentions of his friends, as long as they do not hinder his own. So that those who have books, medals, or paintings that they have received more or less by chance and that they take no pleasure from, will have no trouble in accommodating those of his friends whom he knows desire and are interested in these items. I would willingly liken this third principle to the ploy which magistrates and people with power of office may make use of; but I do not want to explain this more overtly than by the simple narration of the strategy which the Venetians used to obtain Pinelli's best manuscripts the moment he had passed away. Having been informed that his library was going to be transported from Padua to Naples, they immediately sent one of their magistrates who seized one hundred bales of books, among which were fourteen that held the manuscripts, two of which containing more than three hundred commentaries covering all of Italy's affairs. They gave as their reason the fact that although Signor Pinelli had been given permission to copy the archives and registers of their affairs, as a result of his position, his purpose, his noteworthy and virtuous life, and above all the loyalty that he had always exhibited towards the republic; nonetheless, it was neither relevant nor advisable for them that these documents should be divulged, disclosed and revealed after his death. His

heirs and executors, being powerful and within their rights, filed suit in response, so that only two hundred of these commentaries were retained by the Venetians, and put into a special chamber with this inscription: "Herein collected the Pinelli library by order of the Imperial Senate."

The fourth principle is to cut the excess expenditure many waste on the binding and ornamentation of their volumes, in order to use this money instead to purchase books that are missing, so as not to be liable to Seneca's criticism, who took pleasure in making fun of those "to whom the covers and titles of their books give the most pleasure;" and to do so especially given that a binding is nothing but an incidental mode of appearance without which, or at least without one so beautiful and opulent, books would be no less useful, convenient, and sought-after, as it is only ever ignorant people who attach importance to a book due to its cover; (since it is not the same with books as it is with people, who are only recognized and respected through their apparel); as it is more useful and necessary to have, for example, a large number of books with ordinary bindings than to have a tiny room or cabinet full of volumes that have been cleaned, gilded, ordered, and adorned with every kind of ornate, luxurious, and superfluous decoration.

The fifth principle concerns the procurement of the volumes, and can be divided into four or five articles according to the different ways in which this can be done. However, of these I will willingly put first and foremost the quickest, easiest, and most worthwhile method of all the others, which entails the acquisition of another complete library in its entirety. I call it quick because in less than a day you can obtain a large number of scholarly and unusual books that otherwise might only be rarely available, once or twice in a lifetime. I call it easy, because you are spared the time and trouble that goes into acquiring them separately. And finally, I call it worthwhile, because if the libraries which are acquired are noteworthy and unusual, they will increase the reputation and authority of those that are enriched by them.

From this we can see why Possevino makes much of the library of Cardinal de Joyeuse, because it incorporated three others, one of which had belonged to

Mr. Pithou; and that all the most famous libraries have grown in this way, such as for example, that of St. Mark's in Venice which received as a gift Cardinal Bessarion's own library; that of Lescurial, which was given the enormous library collected by Hurtado de Mendoza; the Ambrosiana in Milan, which received ninety bales in one go from the shipwreck carrying the ruin of Pinelli's; that of the Leyden, which was bequeathed more than two hundred manuscripts in Oriental languages in Scaliger's will; and finally, that of Ascagno Colonna which was bequeathed Cardinal Sirlette's outstanding collection. This leads me to conclude, Monsieur, that your own will certainly be one of the most famous and renowned of all the greatest libraries, arising as it does from that of your own most eminent father, which is already celebrated and well-known from the account that has been made of it for posterity by Lacroix, Fauchet, Marcillius, Turnebus, Passerat, Lambinus, and virtually all the gentlemen of this rank, who are not unaware of the pleasure and education they have obtained from it.

It seems to me that the next best method for establishing a library that is closest to what has been previously described, is to rummage through and frequently revisit all the secondhand bookstores and the old sources and shops, looking for both bound books and those that have remained unbound for such a long time that many people of a lesser education and understanding of this type of research would deem them nothing but a nuisance: "Let not wrappers be wanting for tuna, nor for olives."

Yet one often finds among them some excellent books, and if bargained for carefully, it is possible to buy more for ten crowns than could have been purchased for forty or fifty, if they are bought piecemeal from several different places; provided, nevertheless, that one has the time and patience to gather them, and taking into consideration that one cannot say of a library what certain flattering poets have said about our city: "It was great from the moment of its birth," it being impossible to be able to quickly come to the end of something in a situation that Solomon deemed infinite—"There will be no end to the creation of books;" and that this accomplishment took Monsieur de Thou twenty years, Pinelli fifty, and many others

their entire lives; it must not be believed, even so, that they arrived at ultimate perfection, as no matter how much one desires it, one can never actually complete a library.

However, as it remains necessary for the growth and development of such a collection to carefully provide it with all the latest books of such worth and esteem that they have been printed throughout Europe, and since Pinelli and the others maintained a correspondence with an endless number of foreign friends and stallholders for this very reason; it is recommended to do exactly that, or at least to choose and select two or three wealthy, expert and experienced merchants, who due to their various knowledge and travels could provide a variety of new discoveries, as well as carry out diligent research and investigation for those that have been ordered from catalogues.

All this is not necessary in the case of older books, where the best way to collect the most at the lowest prices is to search extensively through all bookstores where time and happenstance have a way of scattering and spreading them.

I do not wish to imply, however, by everything I have discussed up to this point, that it will not sometimes be necessary to exceed budgetary limits in order to buy, at extraordinary expense, certain books that are so rare that this is the only way to wrest them from the hands of those who know their value. However, the best attitude to have to this difficult circumstance is to consider that libraries are only built up and valued for the service and use they give, and that consequently it is not necessary to take into consideration all those books and manuscripts which are only valued for their age, their pictures, illustrations, bindings and other insignificant factors, such as the Froissard that certain booksellers wanted to sell for three hundred crowns, not so long ago; Boccaccio's *On the Fates of Famous Men* which was valued at one hundred; Guinart's Missal and Bible; books of hours, which are often said to be priceless because of their illustrations and engravings; Livy and other historical illuminated manuscripts; books from China and Japan which are printed on parchment, colored paper, or very thin cotton, with big margins; and many other similar items, in order to use the large sums of money they would have cost on books that would be more useful for a library, in place of all those mentioned or similar such volumes, which would never be as valuable to those passionate collectors such as Ptolemy Philadelphus who paid fifteen talents for Euripides' works; Tarquin who purchased three Sibylline books at a price that would have bought all nine of them; Aristotle who paid seventy-two thousand sesterces for the works of Speusippus; Plato who acquired those of Philolaus for a thousand denarii; Bessarion, who spent thirty thousand crowns on Greek books; Hurtado de Mendoza who obtained an entire shipload from the Levant; Pico della Mirandola, who spent seven thousand crowns on Hebrew, Chaldean, and other manuscripts; and finally, that king of France who pawned his gold and silver plate to obtain a copy of a book that was in the medical library of this city, as is fully witnessed by the historical accounts and records of its faculty.

I would like to add that it would also help to know from the relatives and heirs of a variety of gentlemen whether they have left behind any manuscripts which these family members may wish to part with, as it often happens that most of these gentlemen are never able to have even half of their works printed, either because they die too soon; or because of cost; worry about criticism or judgment, and the fear of not having any response to it; the boldness of their arguments, the reluctance to be public, and other similar reasons which have deprived us of many books by Postel, Bodin, Marcillius, Passerat, Maldonatus, etc. Such manuscripts are often found in certain private libraries or in booksellers' shops. In a similar way, it is important to find out what papers the most learned university professors will be giving in their public lectures and private tutorials from one year to the next, in order to be sure to make copies and in this way easily obtain a great number of writings as good and as valuable as many manuscripts which have been purchased at great cost due to their age and antiquity, such as The Treatise on the Druids by Monsieur Marsille, The History and Treatise of the French Magistrates by Monsieur Grangier, Monsieur Belurgey's geography, and various writings by Messieurs Dautruy, Isambert, Seguin, du Val, D'artis and, in a word, of the most famous professors in all of France.

Finally, people who have as much regard for books as Signor Vincent Pinelli, could visit, as he did, the stores of those who often buy old papers or parchments, in order to ascertain whether something has fallen into their hands by chance which would be worthy of being collected for a library. And indeed, we should be inspired in this search by the example of Poggio who discovered Quintilian on a butcher's counter while he was at the Council of Constance, as well as by that of Papire Masson who found Agobardus at a bookbinder who was going to use it to cover his books, and that of Asconius whose manuscript was unearthed in a similar manner. However, given that this method is as unusual as the enthusiasm of those who employ it, I would rather leave it to the discretion of those who wish to use it, rather than recommend it as a general and necessary rule.

JOHN WEEVER

Excerpts from *Ancient Funeral Monuments, of Great Britain, Ireland, and the Islands Adiacent*

(London: Thomas Harper, 1631).

WEEVER FIRST PROVIDES an accounting of the deeds carried out under Henry VIII "to pull down and cast out of all Churches, Roodes, graven Images, Shrines with their reliques, to which the ignorant people came flocking in adoration" (50). This supposedly continued until the "second yeare of the raigne of Queene Elizabeth, of famous memory, who, to restraine such a savage cruelty, caused this Proclamation (following) to bee published throughout all her dominions; which after the imprinting thereof, shee signed (each one severally) with her own hand-writing, as this was, which I had of my friend, Master Humphrey Dyson" (51–52).

Weever defines monuments as

a thing erected, made, or written, for a memorial of some remarkable action, fit to bee transferred to future posterities. And thus generally taken, all religious Foundations, all sumptuous and magnificent structures, Cities, Townes, Towers, Castles, Pillars, Pyramids, Crosses, Obeliskes, Amphitheaters, Statues, and the like, as well as Tombes and Sepulchres, are called Monuments. Now above all remembrances (By which men have endevoured, even in despight of death to give unto their Fames eternitie) for worthiness and continuance, books, or writings, have ever had the preheminence (Chapter 1, I B).

On pages 52–54 is Elizabeth's A Proclamation against breaking or defacing of Monuments of Antiquitie, being set up in Churches, or other publike places, for memory, and not for superstition.

She acknowledges that, "by the meanes of sundrie people, partly ignorant, partly malicious, or covetous; there hath been of late yeares spoiled and broken certaine ancient Monuments some of metal, some of stone, which were erected up as well in Churches, as in other publike places within this Realme, onely to shew a memory to the posterity of the persons there buried, or that had been benefactors to the building or dotations of the same Churches or publique places, and not to nourish any kinde of superstition. ..." (52).

For structures already damaged, the Queen "chargeth and commandeth" that these sites be visited by all Archbishops, Bishops, and other "Ordinaries, or Ecclesiastical persons, which have authoritie to visit the Churches or Chappels" (53). They must assess and repair the sites. If not repaired, such people could be Excommunicated or face "her Maiesties Councell in the Starre-chamber at Westminster" (53).

She further states that she wants to redress "such contempts done from the beginning of her Maiesties raigne" (53), that is, the first year of it.

No mention is made of books and manuscripts.

At the end of the document: "Yeuen at Windsor the xix of September the second year of her Maiesties raigne. God save the Queene. Imprinted at London in Pauls Churchyard by Richard Iugge and Iohn Cawood, Printers to the Queenes Maiestie. Cum privilegio Regiae Maiestatis" (54).

Weever notes that a second proclamation was issued in the fourteenth year of Elizabeth's reign, and writes: "these Proclamations tooke small effect, for much what about this time, there sprung up a contagious broode of Scismatickes..." (54). Nonetheless, an important precedent was set by Queen Elizabeth I.

THOMAS JEFFERSON

Letter to Ebenezer Hazard, February 18, 1791

See http://memory.loc.gov/master/mss/mtj1/013/1000/1030.jpg.

Sir,

I return you the two volumes of records, with thanks for the opportunity of looking into them. They are curious monuments of the infancy of our country. I learn with great satisfaction that you are about committing to the press the valuable historical and State papers you have been so long collecting. Time and accident are committing daily havoc on the originals deposited in our public offices. The late war has done the work of centuries in this business. The lost cannot be recovered, but let us save what remains; not by vaults and locks which fence them from the public eye and use, in consigning them to the waste of time, but by such a multiplication of copies, as shall place them beyond the reach of accident. This being the tendency of your undertaking, be assured there is no one who wishes it more success than Sir,

your most obedient & most humble servt.

Thomas Jefferson

PERCY BYSSHE SHELLEY

"Ozymandias"

From Francis Turner Palgrave, ed. The Golden Treasury. *(London and Glasgow: Collins Clear-Type Press, n.d., p. 238).*

I met a Traveller from an antique land,
Who said, "Two vast and trunkless legs of stone
Stand in the desert. Near them, on the sand,
Half sunk, a shattered visage lies, whose frown,
And wrinkled lip, and sneer of cold command,
Tell that its sculptor well those passions read,
Which yet survive, stamped on these lifeless things,
The hand that mocked them, and the heart that fed;
And on the pedestal these words appear:
'My name is Ozymandias, King of Kings.
Look on my works, ye Mighty, and despair!'
Nothing beside remains. Round the decay
Of that colossal wreck, boundless and bare,
The lone and level sands stretch far away."

JOHN MURRAY

"On the Bad Composition of Paper"

Gentleman's Magazine 93 (1823): 21–22.

I APPRECIATE THE honour you have done me, in the insertion of my remarks on the "Mermaid" by way of reply to your anonymous Correspondent.

Allow me to call the attention of your readers to the present state of that wretched compound called *Paper*. Every printer will corroborate my testimony;* and I am only astonished that the interesting question has been so long neglected and forgotten. It is a duty, however, of the most imperative description — our beautiful Religion, our Literature, our Science, all are threatened.

Every person in the habit of writing letters on "Bath wove Post," must have been sensible of what I complain. Specimens there are, that being folded up, crack at the edges, and fall asunder; others, that being heated at the fire, disintegrate and tumble to pieces.

I have seen letters of a recent date already become a *carte blanche*. One letter, which I forwarded by post, fell to pieces by the way, and I have noticed more than once a description of writing-paper, that being bent, snapped like a bit of watch-spring. I have in my possession a large copy of the Bible printed at Oxford, 1816 (never used), and issued by the British and Foreign Bible Society, *crumbling literally into dust*. I transmitted specimens of this volume to the Lord Bishop of Gloucester, and to Mr. Wilberforce. No doubt it must be difficult to legislate on such a subject, but something must be done and that early. I have watched for some years the progress of the evil, and have no hesitation in saying, that if the same ratio of progression is maintained, a century more will not witness the volumes printed within the last twenty years. *M.S. Records* are in the same fatal condition.

Our typography does credit to this "our dear, native land," and the paper is *apparently* good. The *ink*, however, betrays the fatal secret; there is the canker worms the ink of our most brilliant specimens of modern typography, and those of Ballantine, Bulmer,

&c. has already become *brown*. I now see clearly, that "*Black* letter" books are so called by a just and proper emphasis; for those of modern times are "*brown* letter" volumes.

The causes of destruction are two-fold: the *material*, and the mode of bleaching the rags.

The use of *cotton* rags was very happily superseded by those of *linen*, yet I fear some manufacturers are not very scrupulous in the selection.

The application of quicklime to the rags, once prevalent in France, but very properly subsequently interdicted, was a serious evil, for it actually decomposed the material. Are you entirely guiltless? Such a process must needs disorganize the fibre.

The Chinese dip their paper in alum water; it is thereby rendered brittle. Alum is clearly indicated, even to the taste, in the copy of the sacred volume already referred to.

I take it however, that the chief causes of destruction consist in the employment of sulphate of lime, &e. in the pulp, and bleaching the rags previously, or the paper subsequently, with oxymuriatic gas (*chlorine*).

The tissue of paper will be more or less firm and permanent according to the substance from which the pulp is obtained. I am disposed to think that nettles (*urtica urens*) would be an excellent substitute for linen rags, if linen cannot be obtained in sufficient quantity. In the North of Italy they manufacture a beautiful cloth from the parenchematous fibre of the nettle.

Various have been the substitutes for, and materials of, paper. The *medulla* of the "cyperus papyrus," (not the *epidermis* of that plant, as has been erroneously supposed); the bark of tress, as of the "paper mulberry," white cotton, silk, &c. have afforded materials for the pulp. The "paper reeds" are adverted to in holy writ; and it has often occurred to me, that the Wasp ("Vespa Vulgaria,") first gave the important hint of our present paper tissue to man.

I have specimens of paper made from *Amianthus* (incombustible paper), leather, (not parchment, &.c) wood, straw, silk, &c.

Having examined the paper, taken from the copy of the Bible, 1816, and already mentioned as in a state of ruin, by chemical re-agents, I presume leave to sub-join the results.

To the tongue it presents a highly astringent and aluminous taste.

On a heated metallic disc the lead evolves a volatile acid, evincing white vapours with ammonia.

The paper is brittle as tinder, and of a yellowish tint. The ink is brown.

Litmus paper was reddened in a solution of the leaves in distilled water.

Hydriodate of potassa became greenish yellow, from free sulphuric acid, or rather from the excess of that acid, obtaining in the supersulphate of alumina (alum).

Osallate of ammonia gave the usual indications of lime.

Nitrate of silver exhibited the presence of muriatic acid, no doubt resulting from the chlorine employed in whitening the rags or paper.

Nitrate of baryta proved the presence of sulphuric acid, or of a sulphate.

The interference from these tests follows:

Free muriatic acid (from the chlorine).

Sulphate of lime.

This analysis has been submitted to the University of Oxford, through the medium of a friend.

Yours, &c.,

J. Murray

* We insert this letter of our ingenious Correspondent with much pleasure, as we can from sad experience confirm the truth of his assertions; and we are not without a hope of his hints producing some beneficial results. It is notorious that the great mass of printing papers are now made of cotton rags; and that to produce a better colour, the pulp undergoes a chemical process, which materially injures its durability.–Edit.

FRANCIS LIEBER

Excerpts from General Orders No. 100:
The Lieber Code: *Instructions for the Government of Armies of the United States in the Field, April 24, 1863*

Avalon.law.yale.edu/19th_century/lieber.asp#sec2.

Art. 34.

As a general rule, the property belonging to churches, to hospitals, or other establishments of an exclusively charitable character, to establishments of education, or foundations for the promotion of knowledge, whether public schools, universities, academies of learning or observatories, museums of the fine arts, or of a scientific character such property is not to be considered public property in the sense of paragraph 31; but it may be taxed or used when the public service may require it.

Art. 35.

Classical works of art, libraries, scientific collections, or precious instruments, such as astronomical telescopes, as well as hospitals, must be secured against all avoidable injury, even when they are contained in fortified places whilst besieged or bombarded.

Art. 36.

If such works of art, libraries, collections, or instruments belonging to a hostile nation or government, can be removed without injury, the ruler of the conquering state or nation may order them to be seized and removed for the benefit of the said nation. The ultimate ownership is to be settled by the ensuing treaty of peace.

In no case shall they be sold or given away, if captured by the armies of the United States, nor shall they ever be privately appropriated, or wantonly destroyed or injured.

WILLIAM MORRIS, ET AL.

"The Manifesto" of The Society for the Protection of Ancient Buildings

www.spab.org.uk/what-is-spab-/the-manifesto.

A SOCIETY COMING before the public with such a name as that above written must needs explain how, and why, it proposes to protect those ancient buildings which, to most people doubtless, seem to have so many and such excellent protectors. This, then, is the explanation we offer.

No doubt within the last fifty years a new interest, almost like another sense, has arisen in these ancient monuments of art; and they have become the subject of one of the most interesting of studies, and of an enthusiasm, religious, historical, artistic, which is one of the undoubted gains of our time; yet we think that if the present treatment of them be continued, our descendants will find them useless for study and chilling to enthusiasm. We think that those last fifty years of knowledge and attention have done more for their destruction than all the foregoing centuries of revolution, violence and contempt.

For Architecture, long decaying, died out, as a popular art at least, just as the knowledge of mediaeval art was born. So that the civilised world of the nineteenth century has no style of its own amidst its wide knowledge of the styles of other centuries. From this lack and this gain arose in men's minds the strange idea of the Restoration of ancient buildings; and a strange and most fatal idea, which by its very name implies that it is possible to strip from a building this, that, and the other part of its history—of its life that is—and then to stay the hand at some arbitrary point, and leave it still historical, living, and even as it once was.

In early times this kind of forgery was impossible, because knowledge failed the builders, or perhaps because instinct held them back. If repairs were needed, if ambition or piety pricked on to change, that change was of necessity wrought in the unmistakable fashion of the time; a church of the eleventh century might be added to or altered in the twelfth, thirteenth, fourteenth, fifteenth, sixteenth, or even the seventeenth or eighteenth centuries; but every change, whatever history it destroyed, left history in the gap, and was alive with the spirit of the deeds done midst its fashioning. The result of all this was often a building in which the many changes, though harsh and visible enough, were, by their very contrast, interesting and instructive and could by no possibility mislead. But those who make the changes wrought in our day under the name of Restoration, while professing to bring back a building to the best time of its history, have no guide but each his own individual whim to point out to them what is admirable and what contemptible; while the very nature of their task compels them to destroy something and to supply the gap by imagining what the earlier builders should or might have done. Moreover, in the course of this double process of destruction and addition, the whole surface of the building is necessarily tampered with;

so that the appearance of antiquity is taken away from such old parts of the fabric as are left, and there is no laying to rest in the spectator the suspicion of what may have been lost; and in short, a feeble and lifeless forgery is the final result of all the wasted labour. It is sad to say, that in this manner most of the bigger Minsters, and a vast number of more humble buildings, both in England and on the Continent, have been dealt with by men of talent often, and worthy of better employment, but deaf to the claims of poetry and history in the highest sense of the words.

For what is left we plead before our architects themselves, before the official guardians of buildings, and before the public generally, and we pray them to remember how much is gone of the religion, thought and manners of time past, never by almost universal consent, to be Restored; and to consider whether it be possible to Restore those buildings, the living spirit of which, it cannot be too often repeated, was an inseparable part of that religion and thought, and those past manners. For our part we assure them fearlessly, that of all the Restorations yet undertaken, the worst have meant the reckless stripping a building of some of its most interesting material features; whilst the best have their exact analogy in the Restoration of an old picture, where the partly-perished work of the ancient craftsmaster has been made neat and smooth by the tricky hand of some unoriginal and thoughtless hack of today. If, for the rest, it be asked us to specify what kind of amount of art, style, or other interest in a building makes it worth protecting, we answer, anything which can be looked on as artistic, picturesque, historical, antique, or substantial: any work, in short, over which educated, artistic people would think it worth while to argue at all.

It is for all these buildings, therefore, of all times and styles, that we plead, and call upon those who have to deal with them, to put Protection in the place of Restoration, to stave off decay by daily care, to prop a perilous wall or mend a leaky roof by such means as are obviously meant for support or covering, and show no pretence of other art, and otherwise to resist all tampering with either the fabric or ornament of the building as it stands; if it has become inconvenient for its present use, to raise another building rather than alter or enlarge the old one; in fine to treat our ancient buildings as monuments of a bygone art, created by bygone manners, that modern art cannot meddle with without destroying.

Thus, and thus only, shall we escape the reproach of our learning being turned into a snare to us; thus, and thus only can we protect our ancient buildings, and hand them down instructive and venerable to those that come after us.

chapter 2

PERSPECTIVES ON CULTURAL HERITAGE

WHAT IS CULTURAL HERITAGE, AND HOW is it linked to preservation?[1] To put it simply, the term *culture* refers to socially constructed behavior and attitudes that are manifest in arts, beliefs, customs, and institutions. Or as anthropologist Lourdes Arizpe describes it, *culture* "provides the building blocks of identity and ethnic allegiance; moulds attitudes to work, saving and consumption; underlies political behavior; and … builds the values that can drive collective action for a sustainable future in a new global context."[2] *Heritage* is perpetuation of culture—its historical scope and reach. *Cultural heritage*, then, refers to "monuments, habitats, artifacts, ideas, beliefs, and oral and written communication"[3] that have survived and/or have been documented. Cultural heritage can refer to the tangible (buildings, works of art, documents) and the intangible (customs, beliefs, languages). The domain of preservation is assuring the longevity of cultural heritage. (However, whether or not to preserve particular artifacts is sometimes called into question, as is discussed in chapter 9, "Ethics and Values.") By understanding the many dimensions of cultural heritage, we may become effective stewards of it.

But if defining cultural heritage were that straightforward, why has so much been written on the topic and across such diverse disciplines as history, art history, philosophy, geography, anthropology, archaeology, sociology, heritage studies, architecture, museum studies, conservation, archives, library science, and other fields? This chapter includes perspectives on cultural heritage from several disciplines that should aid our understanding of the preservation of it.

At least one scholar has observed that cultural heritage may be "all things to all people."[4] David C. Harvey takes a more systematic approach to defining it when he reasons that heritage has always been "produced by people according to their contemporary concerns and experiences."[5] By viewing heritage as a historical or social process, it is possible to consider cultural heritage in the context of particular societies at particular times.

A closely related, but narrower, concept is *cultural memory*. According to Robert DeHart, it is

> used to describe the interpretations of the past shared by a group of individuals. The need to address contemporary concerns, such as preserving group identity or sustaining support for a political ideal, influences the creation and content of cultural memory. Thus cultural memory represents a reconstructed past that serves the present needs of a group.... A group's cultural memory is reinforced and transmitted to other individuals in forms such as commemorations, rituals, monuments, oral traditions, museum exhibits, books, and films.[6]

DeHart writes that the concept was born in part as an element of the reaction to the devastation caused by the First World War. However two early twentieth-century scholars, Aby Warburg and Maurice Halbwachs, were already exploring the idea that individuals construct a past within a social context. **Jan Assmann**, author of the first piece in this chapter, observes that, "according to Nietzsche, while in the world of animals genetic programs guarantee the survival of the species, humans must find a means by which to maintain their nature consistently through generations. The solution to this problem is offered by cultural memory, a collective concept for all knowledge that directs behavior and experience in the interactive framework of a society and one that obtains through generations in repeated societal practice and initiation."

The French historian Pierre Nora further developed the social context for memory in *Lieux de mémoire* (*Realms or Places of Memory*), a multi-volume work. With contributions by a number of French historians and edited by Nora, it examines historic and cultural sites as representations of collective memories. In volume 3 of the English edition of the work, Nora explains how *lieu de mémoire* came to be coined as a phrase in France, as evidenced by its inclusion in the 1993 edition of *Le Grand Robert de la langue française*.[7] Nora's work was the beginning of a wave (even a tsunami) of cultural-national memory studies which continues to the present. But as Nora contends, his work "makes sense only for the present moment. By the time the French have settled on another way of living together, by the time they have settled on the contours of what will no longer even be called 'identity,' the need to exhume these landmarks and explore these *lieux* will have disappeared. The era of commemoration will be over for good."[8]

Or will it? The readings in this chapter offer a variety of perspectives about cultural heritage, and, in some cases, cultural memory. The Preamble of the **Burra Charter**, the Australia International Council on Monuments and Sites (ICOMOS) Charter for Places of Cultural Significance, provides a rationale for conservation:

> Places of cultural significance enrich people's lives, often providing a deep and inspirational sense of connection to community and landscape, to the past and to lived experiences. They are historical records, that are important as tangible expressions of Australian identity and experience. Places of cultural significance reflect the diversity of our communities, telling us about who we are and the past that has formed us and the Australian landscape. They are irreplaceable and precious.
>
> These places of cultural significance must be conserved for present and future generations.[9]

Places of cultural significance are described in the Charter as synonymous with heritage significance and cultural heritage value.[10] The *Burra Charter* takes the long view that these cultural and natural places will hold significance for Australians for the indeterminate future, and that strategies must be developed to *ensure* their longevity.

The *Burra Charter* has its critics. Laurajane Smith, in her *Uses of Heritage*, expresses the opinion that

> ...the text is dialogically closed, thus reducing the ability of community perceptions of heritage and its conservation to fully engage in dialogue with the underlying philosophy of the Charter. Utilizing language which does not invite dialogue, the text becomes authoritative and reduces difference, or dialogue, between 'author' of the text and other voices completely. This is at odds with the desire of the 1999 version of the Charter to involve a range of stakeholders in the management and conservation process.[11]

Smith is concerned with the *discourse* of preservation. The risk is that works such as the *Burra Charter* legitimize a certain view of what heritage *is*.

Peter Burman considers value in "What Is Cultural Heritage?" He considers *Burra* and other charters in his overview. He points out that what we value as cultural heritage is part of a continuing philosophical and ethical debate. Value may include context, association, economics, aesthetics, and traditions. In the twentieth century, a series of international documents demonstrate shifts that have taken place in our values. These are the *Conclusions of the Athens Conference* and the *Athens Charter*, the *Venice Charter,* the *Burra Charter,* and the *Nara Document on Authenticity.* These publications demonstrate that we have moved from a western-centric and monumental perspective of cultural heritage to a more nuanced and multicultural approach to the value of cultural heritage. There are many issues in preserving cultural heritage. Burman thinks we must justify the preservation of cultural heritage on the grounds that "(a) its survival is essential for the spiritual and emotional well-being of human beings and (b) it contributes handsomely to our economic well-being." There is a dialogue, according to Burman, and it will continue to evolve.

Over the past twenty-five years, David Lowenthal has become the preeminent writer about cultural heritage in society. In particular, *The Past is a Foreign Country* and *The Heritage Crusade and the Spoils of History*[12] are frequently cited by scholars in a variety of disciplines. In these works, Lowenthal shows us the myriad ways in which the past is either celebrated or reviled, and how our reading of the past shapes the present. One of his most recent pieces, "Stewarding the Future," is reproduced in chapter 11. In it, Lowenthal focuses on sustainability and its implied commitment to manage natural and cultural resources into the indefinite future. He advances several reasons for his futurist stance: ethical, conscientious, familial, and pragmatic, all of which he considers in some detail. As in all of his works, Lowenthal draws on philosophers and historians as well as popular culture and advertising. At the same time, he notes that "the contemplated future gets ever more attenuated." He suggests that perhaps a renewal of "the stewardly commitment" is needed to mitigate the many potential political, social, and environment risks that we now face.

Throughout history, various cultures have been represented in several ways, but usually in isolation from the circumstances of their creation. **Susan M. Pearce** has written prolifically about museums, and about how they can make objects more historically coherent and exhibitions more culturally sensitive than they would be without some curatorial mitigation and explanations. In "The Making of Cultural Heritage," she explores the genesis of cultural heritage with three goals in mind: to define what cultural heritage is; to examine the factors that bear on its creation; and to arrive at some sense of how and where, in the real world, we might look to see new heritage created before our very eyes.

Pearce views heritage, from a legal perspective, as that which can be passed on from generation to generation, and to which descendents of the original owners have rights. However, "law itself, like the heritage it defines, draws its authority from the traditions of the ancestors." *Cultural* is more or less the physical manifestation of heritage. "This physicality is why cultural heritage requires such a large superstructure of operation and maintenance, why it can be directly politically contested, why it can be owned, and why no group can afford to preserve all of its heritage in the style that it might wish."

Laurajane Smith approaches heritage studies as an area of policy analysis *and* as a cultural process, as we have seen above. Other passages from her *Uses of Heritage* are included in this chapter. Her work delves into the meaning of heritage as it relates to social institutions. She also addresses the politics of heritage, tackling such issues as the interplay between class and heritage; multiculturalism and heritage representation; community heritage and heritage tourism; and heritage public policy. Her work extends the perspectives of the other authors in this chapter by challenging the assumptions that we make about heritage. For Smith, heritage and, presumably the preservation of it, is social action, "not something that is frozen in material form."[13]

Pierre Bourdieu's analysis of the field of cultural development and the economy of cultural power relations provides us with still another lens from which to examine the longevity of cultural heritage. *Distinction: A Social Critique of the Judgement of Taste* is a critical study of cultural practices of different French social classes. A sociologist, Bourdieu surveyed and interviewed people to determine their cultural habits and predilections. Among his findings he concluded that

> scientific observation shows that cultural needs are the product of upbringing and education: surveys establish that all cultural practices (museum visits, concert-going, reading, etc.), and preferences in literature, painting or music, are closely linked to educational level (measured by qualifications or length of schooling) and secondarily to social origin. ...[A]nd the influence of social origin is strongest—other things being equal—in 'extracurricular' and avant-garde culture.[14]

Bourdieu posits that specific judgments matter less than one's aesthetic outlook in general. And, he believes, upper-class prestige is an instrument of domination in status and power. Systems of domination are manifest in all areas of cultural practice and symbolic exchange. "Taste classifies, and it classifies the classifier."[15] The denial of lowbrow culture on the part of the upper classes implies the superiority of highbrow culture. In this scenario the implications for preservation are clear: it is the taste-makers who will determine what gets preserved.

Cultural heritage will continue to exist as long as societies leave behind traces of themselves. But what gets preserved, how it gets preserved, why and by whom, will continue to defy definitive answers. The answers will be as diverse as the perspectives presented in this chapter. Cultural heritage will yield different truths to each person trying to define it.

NOTES

1. The terms *cultural heritage* and *heritage* are often used interchangeably; their use in this chapter reflects that practice.

2. Lourdes Arizpe, ed. *The Cultural Dimensions of Global Change: An Anthropological Approach*, Culture and Development Series (Paris, France: UNESCO Publishing, 1996), p. 11. In the context of this chapter, *sustainable* refers to cultural heritage generally. Chapter 11 focuses specifically on sustainability and stewardship.

3. Michèle Valerie Cloonan, "Conservation and Preservation of Library and Archival Materials," *Encyclopedia of Library and Information Sciences*, 3rd ed. (2010): 1250.

4. Peter J. Larkham, "Heritage as Planned and Conserved," in D. T. Herbert, ed. *Heritage, Tourism and Society* (London): Mansell, 1995, p. 85, and cited in David C. Harvey, "Heritage Pasts and Heritage Presents: Temporality, Meaning, and the Scope of Heritage Studies," *International Journal of Heritage Studies* 7.4 (December 2001): 2.

5. Harvey, p. 2.

6. Robert DeHart, "Cultural Memory," *Encyclopedia of Library and Information Sciences,* 3rd ed. (2010): 1363.

7. Pierre Nora, ed., *Realms of Memory*, vol. III: "Symbols" (New York: Columbia University Press, 1998), pp. 608–09.

8. Nora, p. 637.

9. Australia ICOMOS, *The Burra Charter*, 1999, "Preamble," (N.p.: Australia ICOMOS, Inc., 2000), p. 1.

10. *Burra Charter*, p. 2.

11. Laurajane Smith, *Uses of Heritage* (London and New York: Routledge, 2006), p. 103.

12. David Lowenthal, *The Past is a Foreign Country* (Cambridge, UK: Cambridge University Pr., 1985); in an e-mail, Lowenthal notified the author that he was preparing a new edition of *The Past,* (e-mail, 8/23/11). David Lowenthal, *The Heritage Crusade and the Spoils of History* (Cambridge, UK: Cambridge University Pr., 1998).

13. Smith, p. 83.

14. Pierre Bourdieu, *Distinction: A Social Critique of the Judgement of Taste.* Trs. by Richard Nice. (Cambridge, MA: Harvard University Pr., 1984), p. 1.

15. Bourdieu, p. 6.

Selection 2.1

JAN ASSMANN

"Collective Memory and Cultural Identity"

New German Critique *65 (Spring-Summer 1995): 125–33.*

Problem and Program

In the third decade of this century, the sociologist Maurice Halbwachs and the art historian Aby Warburg independently developed[1] two theories of a "collective" or "social memory." Their otherwise fundamentally different approaches meet in a decisive dismissal of numerous turn-of-the-century attempts to conceive collective memory in biological terms as an inheritable or "racial memory,"[2] a tendency which would still obtain, for instance, in C.G. Jung's theory of archetypes.[3] Instead, both Warburg and Halbwachs shift the discourse concerning collective knowledge out of a biological framework into a cultural one.

The specific character that a person derives from belonging to a distinct society and culture is not seen to maintain itself for generations as a result of phylogenetic evolution, but rather as a result of socialization and customs. The "survival of the type" in the sense of a cultural pseudo-species[4] is a function of the cultural memory. According to Nietzsche, while in the world of animals genetic programs guarantee the survival of the species, humans must find a means by which to maintain their nature consistently through generations. The solution to this problem is offered by cultural memory, a collective concept for all knowledge that directs behavior and experience in the interactive framework of a society and one that obtains through generations in repeated societal practice and initiation.

We[5] define the concept of cultural memory through a double delimitation that distinguishes it:

1. from what we call "communicative" or "everyday memory," which in the narrower sense of our usage lacks "cultural" characteristics

2. from science, which does not have the characteristics of memory as it relates to a collective self-image. For the sake of brevity, we will leave aside this second delimitation which Halbwachs developed as the distinction between memory and history and limit ourselves to the first: the distinction between communicative and cultural memory.

Communicative Memory

For us the concept of "communicative memory" includes those varieties of collective memory that are based exclusively on everyday communications.

These varieties, which M. Halbwachs gathered and analyzed under the concept of collective memory, constitute the field of oral history.[6] Everyday communication is characterized by a high degree of nonspecialization, reciprocity of roles, thematic instability, and disorganization.[7] Typically, it takes place between partners who can change roles. Whoever relates a joke, a memory, a bit of gossip, or an experience becomes the listener in the next moment. There are occasions which more or less predetermine such communications, for example train rides, waiting rooms, or the common table; and there are rules—"laws of the market"[8]—that regulate this exchange. There is a "household"[9] within the confines of which this communication takes place. Yet beyond this reigns a high degree of formlessness, willfulness, and disorganization. Through this manner of communication, each individual composes a memory which, Halbwachs has shown, is (a) socially mediated and (b) relates to a group. Every individual memory constitutes itself in communication with others. These "others," however, are not just any set of people, rather they are groups who conceive their unity and peculiarity through a common image of their past. Halbwachs thinks of families, neighborhood and professional groups, political parties, associations, etc., up to and including nations. Every individual belongs to numerous such groups and therefore entertains numerous collective self-images and memories.

Through the practice of oral history, we have gained a more precise insight into the peculiar qualities of this everyday form of collective memory, which, with L. Niethammer, we will call communicative memory. Its most important characteristic is its limited temporal horizon. As all oral history studies suggest, this horizon does not extend more than eight to (at the very most) one hundred years into the past, which equals three or four generations or the Latin *saeculum*.[10] This horizon shifts in direct relation to the passing of time. The communicative memory offers no fixed point which would bind it to the ever expanding past in the passing of time. Such fixity can only be achieved through a cultural formation and therefore lies outside of informal everyday memory.

Transition

Once we remove ourselves from the area of everyday communication and enter into the area of objectivized culture, almost everything changes. The transition is so fundamental that one must ask whether the metaphor of memory remains in any way applicable. Halbwachs, as is well known, stopped at this juncture, without taking it into account systematically.[11] He probably thought that once living communication crystallized in the forms of objectivized culture—whether in texts, images, rites, buildings, monuments, cities, or even landscapes[12]—the group relationship and the contemporary reference are lost and therefore the character of this knowledge as a mémoire collective disappears as well. "Mémoire" is transformed into "histoire."[13]

Our thesis contradicts this assumption. For in the context of objectivized culture and of organized or ceremonial communication, a close connection to groups and their identity exists which is similar to that found in the case of everyday memory. We can refer to the structure of knowledge in this case as the "concretion of identity." With this we mean that a group bases its consciousness of unity and specificity upon this knowledge and derives formative and normative impulses from it, which allows the group to reproduce its identity. In this sense, objectivized culture has the structure of memory. Only in historicism, as Nietzsche perceptively and clairvoyantly remarked in "On the Advantage and Disadvantage of History for Life,"[14] does this structure begin to dissolve.[15]

The Cultural Memory

Just as the communicative memory is characterized by its proximity to the everyday, cultural memory is characterized by its distance from the everyday. Distance from the everyday (transcendence) marks its temporal horizon. Cultural memory has its fixed point; its horizon does not change with the passing of time. These fixed points are fateful events of the past, whose memory is maintained through cultural formation (texts, rites, monuments) and institutional communication (recitation, practice, observance). We call these "figures of memory." The entire Jewish calendar is based on figures of memory.[16] In the flow of everyday communications such festivals, rites, epics, poems, images, etc., form "islands of time," islands of a completely different temporality suspended from time. In cultural memory, such islands of time expand into memory spaces of "retrospective contemplativeness" [*retrospective Besonnenheit*]. This expression stems from Aby Warburg. He ascribed a type of "mnemonic energy" to the objectivation of culture, pointing not only to works of high art, but also to posters, postage stamps, costumes, customs, etc. In cultural formation, a collective experience crystallizes, whose meaning, when touched upon, may suddenly become accessible again across millennia. In his large-scale project Mnemosyne, Warburg wanted to reconstruct this pictorial memory of Western civilization. That of course is not our problem; our inquiry is more general. But we are indebted to Warburg for emphatically directing attention to the power of cultural objectivation in the stabilizing of cultural memory in certain situations for thousands of years.

Yet just as Halbwachs in his treatment of the mnemonic functions of objectivized culture, Warburg does not develop the sociological aspects of his pictorial memory. Halbwachs thematizes the nexus between memory and group, Warburg the one between memory and the language of cultural forms. Our theory of cultural memory attempts to relate all three poles—memory (the contemporized past), culture, and the group (society)—to each other. We want to stress the following characteristics of cultural memory:

1) "*The concretion of identity*" or the relation to the group. Cultural memory preserves the store of knowledge from which a group derives an awareness of its unity and peculiarity. The objective manifestations of cultural memory are defined through a kind of identificatory determination in a positive ("We are this") or in a negative ("That's our opposite") sense.[17]

Through such a concretion of identity evolves what Nietzsche has called the "constitution of horizons." The supply of knowledge in the cultural memory is characterized by sharp distinctions made between those who belong and those who do not, i.e., between what appertains to oneself and what is foreign. Access to and transmission of this knowledge are not controlled by what Bleumenberg calls "theoretical curiosity," but rather by a "need for identity" as described by Hans Mol.[18]

Connected with this is

2) its *capacity to reconstruct*. No memory can preserve the past. What remains is only that "which society in each era can reconstruct within its contemporary frame of reference."[19] Cultural memory works by constructing, that is, it always relates its knowledge to an actual and contemporary situation. True, it is fixed in immovable figures of memory and stores of knowledge, but every contemporary context relates to these differently, sometimes by appropriation, sometimes by criticism, sometimes by preservation or by transformation. Cultural memory exists in two modes: first in the mode of potentiality of the archive whose accumulated texts, images, and rules of conduct act as a total horizon, and second in the mode of actuality, whereby each contemporary context puts the objectivized meaning into its own perspective, giving it its own relevance.

3) *Formation*. The objectivation or crystallization of communicated meaning and collectively shared knowledge is a prerequisite of its transmission in the *culturally institutionalized heritage of a society*.[20] "Stable" formation is not dependent on a single medium such as writing. Pictorial images and rituals can also function in the same way. One can speak of linguistic, pictorial, or ritual formation and thus arrives at the trinity of the Greek mysteries: legomenon, dromenon, and deiknymenon. As far as language is concerned, formation between the communicative memory and the cultural memory is *not* identical with the distinction between oral and written language.

4) *Organization*. With this we mean a) the institutional buttressing of communication, e.g., through formulization of the communicative situation in ceremony and b) the specialization of the bearers of cultural memory. The distribution and structure of participation in the communicative memory are diffuse. No specialists exist in this regard. Cultural memory, by contrast, always depends on a specialized practice,

a kind of "cultivation."[21] In special cases of written cultures with canonized texts, such cultivation can expand enormously and become extremely differentiated.[22]

5) *Obligation.* The relation to a normative self-image of the group engenders a clear *system of values* and *differentiations in importance* which structure the cultural supply of knowledge and the symbols. There are important and unimportant, central and peripheral, local and interlocal symbols, depending on how they function in the production, representation, and reproduction of this self-image. Historicism is positioned firmly against this perspectival evaluation of a heritage, which is centered on cultural identity:

The particle α"ν and the entelechy of Aristotle, the sacred grottos of Apollo and of the idol Besas, the song of Sappho and the sermon of the sacred Thekla, the metric of Pindar and the altar of Pompeii, the fragments of the Dipylon vases and the baths of Caracalla, the deeds of the divine Augustus, the conic sections of Apollonius and the astrology of Petosiris: everything is a part of philology because it all belongs to the subject that you want to understand, and you cannot leave anything out.[23]

As is well known, there has been no lack of countermovements against relativism of such a value-free science (M. Weber). In the name of "life," Nietzsche opposed the dissolution of horizons and perspectives of historical knowledge through the historical sciences. W. Jaeger and other neo-humanists opposed it in the name of education. To add a relatively recent voice of protest to this list, we quote Alexander Rüstow's monumental work, *Ortsbestimmung der Gegenwart*, a plea for the "humanistic standpoint":

—If you leave it (that standpoint, J. Cz.), then the history of the Botocudo, the Zulucafer, or any other people is just as interesting, just as important, just as directly linked to God, and we find ourselves in the midst of an aimless relativism.[24]

The binding character of the knowledge preserved in cultural memory has two aspects: the *formative* one in its educative, civilizing, and humanizing functions and the *normative* one in its function of providing rules of conduct.

6) *Reflexivity.* Cultural memory is reflexive in three ways:

a) It is practice-reflexive in that it interprets common practice in terms through proverbs, maxims, "ethno-theories," to use Bourdieu's term, rituals (for instance, sacrificial rites that interpret the practice of hunting), and so on.

b) It is self-reflexive in that it draws on itself to explain, distinguish, reinterpret, criticize, censure, control, surpass, and receive hypoleptically.[25]

c) It is reflexive of its own image insofar as it reflects the self-image of the group through a preoccupation with its own social system.[26]

The concept of cultural memory comprises that body of reusable texts, images, and rituals specific to each society in each epoch, whose "cultivation" serves to stabilize and convey that society's self-image. Upon such collective knowledge, for the most part (but not exclusively) of the past, each group bases its awareness of unity and particularity.

The content of such knowledge varies from culture to culture as well as from epoch to epoch. The manner of its organization, its media, and its institutions, are also highly variable. The binding and reflexive character of a heritage can display varying intensities and appear in various aggregations. One society bases its self-image on a canon of sacred scripture, the next on a basic set of ritual activities, and the third on a fixed and hieratic language of forms in a canon of architectural and artistic types. The basic attitude toward history, the past, and thus the function of remembering itself introduces another variable. One group remembers the past in fear of deviating from its model, the next for fear of repeating the past: "Those who cannot remember their past are condemned to relive it."[27] The basic openness of these variables lends the question of the relation between culture and memory a cultural-topological interest. Through its cultural heritage a society becomes visible to itself and to others. Which past becomes evident in that heritage and which values emerge in its identificatory appropriation tells us much about the constitution and tendencies of a society.

NOTES

1. Warburg however quotes Durkheim in his Kreuzlinger Lecture of 1923 in which the concept of "social memory" appears in his work for the first time. Cf. Roland Kany, *Mnemosyne als Programm: Geschichte, Erinnerung und die Andacht zum Unbedeutenden im Werk von Usener, Warburg und Benjamin* (Tübingen: Niemeyer, 1987). H. Ritter has informed me that according to unpublished notes, Fritz Saxl had referred Warburg to the work of Maurice Halbwachs.

2. Ernest H. Gombrich, *Aby Warburg: An Intellectual Biography* (London: The Warburg Institute, 1970), 323ff.

3. Warburg's most important source for his own theory of memory was Richard Semon. See Richard Semon, *Die Mneme als erhaltendes Prinzip im Wechsel des organischen Geschehens* (Leipzig: Engelmann, 1920).

4. Erik Erikson, "Ontogeny of Ritualization," PUB. INFO London (1965):21; Irenaus Eibl-Eibesfeldt, *Krieg und Frieden aus der Sicht der Verhaltensforschung* (Munich: Piper, 1984).

5. The use of the plural refers to the coauthorship of Aleida Assmann in the formulation of these ideas. See Aleida and Jan Assmann, *Schrift und Gedächtnis: Beiträge zur Archäologie der literarischen Kommunikation* (Munich: Fink, 1987).

6. Maurice Halbwachs, *Das Gedächtnis und seine sozialen Bedingungen* (Frankfurt/Main: Suhrkamp, 1985); and Maurice Halbwachs, *La mémoire collective, ed. J. Alexandre* (Paris: PU de France, 1950).

7. Of course, everyday communication is found in non-reciprocal role constellations such as medical anamnesis, confession, interrogation, examination, instruction, etc. But such "habits of speech" (Seibert) already demonstrate a higher degree of cultural formation and constitute a stage of transition between everyday and cultural communication.

8. Pierre Bourdieu, *Esquisse d'une théorie de la pratique. Précède de trois études d'ethnologie kabyle* (Geneve: Droz, 1972).

9. In his work, the sociologist Thomas Luckmann speaks of the "communicative household" of a society.

10. According to T. Hölscher, that corresponds exactly to the timespan treated by Herodotus. Tacitus expressly noted in Annals III 75 the death of the last witnesses of the republic in the year AD 22; cf. Cancik-Lindemeier in A. and J. Assmann. As to the meaning of saeculum as the maximal life span of those who remember a generation, see Gladigow, "Aetas, aevum and saeclorum ordo. Zur Struktur zeitlicher Deutungssysteme," *Apocalypticism in the Mediterranean World and the Near East*, ed. D. Hellholm (Tübingen: Mohr, 1983).

11. Halbwachs dealt with the phenomena beyond this border. Maurice Halbwachs, *La topographie légendaire des Evangiles en Terre Sainte; étude de mémoire collective* (Paris: PU de France, 1941). There, he presents Palestine as a commemorative landscape that transforms through the centuries. In Palestine, change in the image of the past follows theological positions that are made concrete in the construction of monuments.

12. The classical example for a primarily topographically organized cultural memory is that of the Australian Aborigines with their attachment to certain sacred rites. Cf. Cancik in A. and J. Assmann, and Halbwachs, *La topographie légendaire* for other examples of sacred or commemorative landscapes.

13. Friedrich Ovebeck, *Christentum und Kultur* (Basel, 1963) 20ff. and similarly Halbwachs, *La topographie légendaire* 261ff. treat such a transformation under the rubric of falsification and in the conceptual framework of primeval history and theology.

14. Friedrich Nietzsche, *Werke*, vol. 3, ed. K. Schlechta (Munich: Hanser, 1964).

15. Cf. Aleida Assmann, "Die Ünfähigkeit zu vergessen: der Historismus und die Krise des kulturellen Gedächtnisses," A. and J. Assmann.

16. Halbwachs designated it as the object of religion to maintain the remembrance of a time long past through the ages and without allowing it to be cor-

rupted by intervening memories. Halbwachs, *Das Gedächtnis* 261. The sharpness of this formulation, however, only applies to the Jewish religion, which Halbwachs as an assimilated Jew did not treat and hardly even mentions. For the problem of Jewish remembrance see Yosef Yerushalmi, *Zachor, Jewish History and Jewish Memory* (Seattle: U of Washington P, 1982), and Willy Schottroff, *Gedenken im alten Orient und im Alten Testament* (Neukirchen: Neukirchner Verlag des Erziehungsvereins, 1964).

17. The inevitable egoism of cultural memory that derives from the "need for identity" (Hans Mol) takes on dangerous forms, if the representations of alterity, in their relation to the representations of identity (self-images), become images of an enemy. Cf. Hans Mol, *Identity and the Sacred* (Oxford: Blackwell, 1976); Gladigow; and Eibl-Eibesfeldt.

18. Mol.

19. Halbwachs, *Das Gedächtnis*.

20. For the problem of the stability of cultural meanings see Eric Havelock, *Preface to Plato* (Cambridge: Belknap, Harvard UP, 1963), where he speaks of "preserved communication" as well as A. and J. Assmann, 265–84. For the technology of conservation and its intellectual implications see J. Goody, *La logique de l'écriture: aux origines des societés humaines* (Paris: A. Colin, 1986).

21. In this connection, Niklas Luhmann refers to "cultivated semantics." Niklas Luhmann, *Gesellschaftsstruktur und Semantik* (Frankfurt/Main: Suhrkamp, 1980).

22. We distinguish in this between three dimensions: the cultivation of text, i.e., the observation of word by word transmission; the cultivation of meaning, i.e., the culture of explication, exegesis, hermeneutics, and commentary; and mediation, i.e., the retranslation of text into life through the institutions of education, upbringing, and initiation.

23. Wilamowitz, quoted in Werner Jaeger, *Humanistische Reden und Vorträge* (Berlin: De Gruyter, 1960), 1–2.

24. Alexander Rüstow, *Ortsbestimmung der Gegenwart; eine universalgeschichtliche Kulturkritik* (Zurich: E. Rentsch, 1952), 12.

25. About this concept cf. *Identität*, ed. Odo Marquardand and Karlheinz Stierle (Munich: Fink, 1979) 358: "About νπ\ληγιζ: relate to that which the previous speaker has said; compare J. Ritter, *Metaphysik und Politik — Studien zu Aristoteles und Hegel* (Frankfurt\Main 1969), esp. p. 64, p. 66."

26. Niklas Luhmann, *Soziologische Aufklärung* (Köln: Westdeutscher Verlag, 1975).

27. George Santayana. Aleida Assmann is the source of this citation.

PIERRE BOURDIEU

Excerpts from Chapter 1 of *Distinction: A Social Critique of the Judgement of Taste*

Translated by Richard Nice (Cambridge: Harvard University Press, 1984), 11–12.

SOCIOLOGY IS RARELY more akin to social psychoanalysis than when it confronts an object like taste, one of the most vital stakes in the struggles fought in the field of the dominant class and the field of cultural production. This is not only because the judgement of taste is the supreme manifestation of the discernment which, by reconciling reason and sensibility, the pedant who understands without feeling and the *mondain* who enjoys without understanding, defines the accomplished individual. Nor is it solely because every rule of propriety designates in advance the project of defining this indefinable essence as a clear manifestation of philistinism—whether it be the academic propriety ... from the most scholastic commentators on the classics to the avant-garde semiologist, [who insist] on a formalist reading of the work of art; or … upperclass propriety which … cannot conceive of referring taste to anything other than itself.

… It is not sufficient to … relate taste, the uncreated source of all 'creation', to the social conditions of which it is the product, knowing … that the very same people who strive to repress the clear relation between taste and education, between culture as the state of that which is cultivated and culture as the process of cultivating, will be amazed that anyone should expend so much effort… . [The sociologist] must also question that relationship, … and unravel the paradox whereby … educational capital is just as strong in areas which the educational system does not teach… . Hidden behind the statistical relationships between educational capital or social origin and … applying it, there are relationships between groups maintaining different … relations to culture, depending on the conditions in which they acquired their cultural capital … .

PETER BURMAN

"What Is Cultural Heritage?"

In Rational Decision-making in the Preservation of Cultural Property, *edited by Norbert S. Baer and Folke Snickars (Berlin: Dahlem University Press, 2001), 11–22.*

ONE OF THE commonly accepted foundation documents of cultural heritage, especially as regards buildings with their settings and their historic contents, is the *Manifesto* drafted by William Morris (with the assistance of George Wardle and Philip Webb) on the founding of the Society for the Protection of Ancient Buildings in 1877.[1] As though anticipating that one of the first questions needing to be answered would be, "What, then, *is* of value, in this particular context," he declared:

> If, for the rest, it be asked us to specify what kind of amount of art, style, or other interest in a building makes it worth protecting, we answer, anything which can be looked on as artistic, picturesque, historical, antique, or substantial: any work, in short, over which educated, artistic people would think it worth while to argue at all.

Take out the expression "a building" and substitute "cultural heritage" and we have an answer that is still relevant in the late 20th century, and that can be analyzed in our terms. The qualities that Morris specifies are:

- artistic
- picturesque
- historical
- antique
- substantial
- any work that educated, artistic people would think it worthwhile to argue about at all.

If we take the last quality first, we may understand this as saying something about the inclusive nature of heritage; in other words, it is easier to put things into a definition of heritage than to take them out. Among those things that we might wish to include is the concept of fashion, which is a very potent force in questions of heritage. We have only to look at the evidence of landscapes, buildings, and artifacts destroyed in the 1960s and 1970s to find ourselves asking: How could it be that our predecessors failed to realize that they had something very special there? How on earth could they neglect or destroy it and still sleep easily in their beds and even, in some cases, still consider themselves good preservationists?

Another concept that we might wish to insert is context. To give an example, I would suggest that a very ordinary object (e.g., a letter, bill, pair of shoes, dress, bus, etc.) can seem especially significant if we encounter it in a particular context. I remember feeling this strongly when I visited the New England house which Walter Gropius had built for himself, his wife, and daughter after he became Professor of Architecture at Harvard University. The house itself, together with its garden and relationship to the wider landscape, is certainly beautiful and of cultural value. However, what gave the place special resonance to me were not only the pictures, furniture, and textiles that had been made, in many cases, for them by equally artistic and cultivated friends, but also the wardrobe full of Mrs. Gropius's dresses, his typewriter, their cutlery and china, and all the artifacts relating to the intimacy and tenderness of daily domestic life. This is not, I believe, a question of sentiment or of association but of cultural value. Because of daily service to one of this century's great architectural geniuses and his family, even the humble early-morning tea tray becomes an object of cultural value through context. Seen in this way, cultural heritage is something generous and inclusive; it has something to say about the *wholeness* of culture.

Again, Morris's first six qualities seem very apposite in themselves, but what do they mean now compared to the sense in which he meant these terms, and what do they mean when seen through the dimension of time? Moreover, did he leave anything else out besides fashion and context? If we briefly review some of the main 20th-century formulations for identifying cultural value to see what we might wish to add, we find the following:

1. The *Conclusions of the Athens Conference* (*Athens Charter* 1931) refer chiefly to "monuments and works of art," without defining them further, and it may be that the fathers of the Athens Conference would have found it difficult to accept Mrs. Gropius's dresses as part of cultural heritage. Presumably, though, they would have been able to accept the court dress of Sir Christopher Wren or the drinking vessel of Praxitiles as being of cultural value. In other words, is it true that the further we go back in time, the more likely it is that we shall find "ancientness" of

context, or association with clearly recognizable "creative geniuses" of the past, to be acceptable criteria?

2. The *Athens Charter,* which arose from the conference in 1933 (Le Corbusier 1941), refers to a wider spectrum in the expression "lay-outs and building structures," which seems to respect town planning and urban form as well as individual structures (such as a constructionally significant bridge) as being part of cultural heritage.[2] The Charter also evokes them as "precious witnesses of the past which will be respected, first for their historical or sentimental value, and second, because certain of them convey a plastic virtue in which the utmost intensity of human genius has been incorporated." Then, in a phrase that seems to prefigure the 1970s concept of world heritage or universal value, the preamble declares that such artifacts "form a part of the human heritage, and whoever owns them or is entrusted with their protection has the responsibility and the obligation to do whatever he legitimately can to hand this noble heritage down intact to the centuries to come."

3. The *Venice Charter* (1964) builds on the foundations and thinking patterns of the two Athens documents and is also influenced by Ruskin (1849, 1854), Morris, and the Italian *Carta del Restauro* (1926). The *Venice Charter* has been more influential for two reasons: (a) it became the basis for the work of the *International Council on Monuments and Sites* (ICOMOS) and its national committees, which are spread throughout the world, and (b) it was adopted by many governments as a basis for their perceptions of heritage and for drafting the increasing amount of legislation that sought to protect cultural heritage. A specific example is provided by the former Soviet Union and various satellite countries of Central and Eastern Europe. From the mid to late 1960s onwards, many of these governments began to adopt a more generous attitude toward cultural heritage, formulating policies and practices that were sometimes even exemplary (e.g., in former Czechoslovakia) and taking part in international discussions about cultural heritage. Presumably, what was found to be helpful and even inspiring in the *Venice Charter* was the declaration that "monuments" (now understood to be almost anything from a palace or cathedral to a battlefield or sailing ship) were "living witnesses of their age-old

traditions"—"traditions" being politically acceptable or at least neutral to most political regimes. Further, Article 1 declared that "the concept of an historic monument embraces not only the single architectural work but also the urban or rural setting in which is found the evidence of a particular civilization, a significant development or a historic event," and this applied "not only to great works of art but also to more modest works of the past which have acquired cultural significance with the passing of time."

This brings us back, of course, to the core question of what cultural significance, cultural value, or cultural heritage actually are. Is it still possible only to say that cultural heritage constitutes "any work ... over which educated, artistic people would think it worth while to argue at all"? If we accept this definition, is it necessary for people to be "educated" and "artistic"—terms that are arguably elitist and restrictive—or should people simply possess some sort of balanced, experienced, and well-informed view of their (and therefore our) heritage that is conscious of the limitations of time, place, knowledge, and fashion?

Let us imagine a historic room of, perhaps, the 18th or 19th century and see which elements it might contain that could be said to possess cultural or heritage values:

1. The space itself; its volume, planning, and internal disposition; its relationship to its function as a dining room, library, etc.;
2. Plasterwork, either plain or decorative, but in either case authentic to the period of that room or to a significant change in the ordering and decoration of that room;
3. Painted decoration, perhaps even wall paintings or wall coverings of paper, textiles, leather, or metals;
4. Floors and floor coverings;
5. Furniture, probably made principally of wood but perhaps also incorporating different woods, gesso, metals, painted decoration, upholstery, etc.;
6. Paintings, perhaps in frames which themselves are of cultural value;
7. Impedimenta of use and daily living which might include technical systems for heating and ventilation or the summoning of servants, framed photographs, fire-dogs, screens, cutlery, glass and china, books, etc.

This all looks fair and easy enough to identify cultural value in all or most of these manifestations of human culture. But let us go on from that imaginary list to compare two rooms: one designed by the 18th-century Scottish architect Robert Adam (a figure well known and respected in many countries), and the other designed by no one in particular but representing a remarkable accretion of living culture. The latter room could be either of high status (e.g., a castle, country house, or palace) or of lower status (e.g., one of those remarkably well-preserved farmhouses or town houses seen in museums of buildings in Central and Eastern Europe or the United States, or the astonishingly complete prefab of 1947, which is shown in the Avoncroft Museum of Buildings near Worcester, England, and which represents the high watermark of enlightened planning and housing provision in the period immediately following World War II when resources of all kinds were scarce). Who is to say that one of these rooms has "greater" cultural value than the other? If that assertion should be made, then what criteria have been used in confidence? Let us imagine a third case in which everything in the room is relatively commonplace (this is not the case with Walter Gropius's house, referred to earlier) but belonged to or was used by a recognized writer, composer, poet, politician, soldier, architect, priest, administrator, etc. Does that context again change the nature of our perception of the term "cultural value" or "cultural heritage"? If so, then how? Or are those values, as I would argue, being increasingly accepted for their inclusiveness and not their exclusiveness?

Let us move forward in time to the Australian ICOMOS Charter for the Conservation of Places of Cultural Significance, the well-known *Burra Charter* (1981, 1988), which is particularly helpful in its definitions. "Cultural significance means aesthetic, historic, scientific or social value for past, present or future generations" (*Burra Charter* 1981, 1988). Could anything be more inclusive than that?

Later on, in the "Guidelines to the Burra Charter: Cultural Significance," these concepts are more fully defined. Cultural significance is defined as "a concept which helps in estimating the value of places." Place has already been defined as a "site, area, building or other work, group of buildings or other works together with associated contents and surrounds." In other words, Capability Brown's first great designed landscape, Croome Park, is such a place, encompassing the mansion, church (the shell designed by Brown, but the interior by Robert Adam), temples, bridges, lodges, gates, sculptures, furniture within the buildings (one room of the mansion is in the Metropolitan Museum of Art in New York, where we experience it out of context as perhaps a modified form of cultural heritage), modeling of contours, trees, greenswards, water (whether still or moving around the landscape), axes, ways of distinguishing one feature from another, literary and philosophical references, agricultural, economic, and social aspects, ways of managing the totality, and so on.

If all this is *not* cultural heritage, then what do we dare exclude? The "Guidelines to the Burra Charter: Cultural Significance," also include the following:

1. Aesthetic value "includes aspects of sensory perception for which criteria can and should be stated. Such criteria may include consideration of the form, scale, colour, texture and material of the fabric; the smells and sounds associated with the place and its use."

2. Historic value "encompasses the history of aesthetics, science and society," and a place "may have historic value because it has influenced, or has been influenced by, an historic figure, event, phase or activity. It may also have historic value as the site of an important event. For any given place the significance will be greater where evidence of the association or event survives *in situ,* or where the settings are substantially intact, than where it has been changed or evidence does not survive. However, some events or associations may be so important that the place retains significance regardless of subsequent treatment."

3. Scientific or research value of a place "will depend upon the importance of the data involved on its rarity, quality or representativeness, and on the degree to which the place may contribute further substantial information."

4. Social value "embraces the qualities for which a place has become a focus of spiritual, political, national or other cultural sentiment to a majority or minority group."

Finally, but essentially, the guidelines recognize that these four categories represent only one possible approach to understanding the concept of cultural significance and that "more precise categories may be developed as understanding of a particular place develops." So, to take one example, investigation of the ruined abbey at Glastonbury in Somerset or the ruins of St. Mary's Abbey in York would lead us in due course into an understanding of a particular kind of community which was focused on spiritual activities such as prayer and liturgy in the church, but which required a whole spectrum of supporting activities ranging from manuscript illumination to beekeeping, herb-growing, caring for the sick, animal husbandry, agriculture, financial management, etc.

It would be possible to adduce numerous other formulations that attempt to provide a satisfactory definition of cultural value. However, such refinements serve to show that in a particular context *anything* may be considered cultural heritage, from a whole mixed landscape such as the English "Lake District" to the German *Ruhrgebiet,* the Rhine valley, the French *Carmargue,* and a cup and saucer. Essentially, cultural heritage depends on many factors, and the great virtue of the Burra Charter is that it encourages us to do our research so that we define those factors—and understand them—more precisely.

There is a rapidly growing literature on values, and it would be helpful to review this literature more thoroughly. However, reference must at least be made to William D. Lipe's (1984) essay, "Value and Meaning in Cultural Resources." Lipe identifies four "value contexts" that depend upon four types of value: economic, aesthetic, associational/symbolic, and informational. In addition, a major contribution to the necessary dialog between different cultures and traditions was provided by the 1994 Nara Conference held in Nara, Japan, which specifically considered authenticity in relation to the World Heritage Convention. The meetings that preceded and followed the Nara Conference were triggered by Japan's decision to sign the World Heritage Convention. As Herb Stovel explains (see Foreword in Larsen 1995), "the Japanese feared that their practice of periodically dismantling significant wooden structures would possibly be seen as inauthentic if judged from within a Western framework. In fact, their fears were legitimate; levels of understanding of Japanese heritage and its conservation outside Japan are relatively low." The result of the Nara Conference and the signed protocol known as the *Nara Document on Authenticity* (1994) is that, according to Knut Einar Larsen (1995), "international preservation doctrine has moved from a eurocentric approach to a post-modem position characterized by recognition of cultural relativism." The *Nara Document* is far from being a prose poem (as the *Venice Charter* arguably is) or a practical guide to good conservation practice in the field of cultural heritage (as the *Burra Charter* undoubtedly is), and the debate about values and authenticity must continue if only because our perceptions change through time, and because fashion and context will always have a part to play. Reference could also be made to the value systems defined either in writing or through tradition by particular professionals, e.g., archaeologists, architects, archivists, conservators, and craftsmen. These professions may also vary from culture to culture.

This is not to deny the value of attempts to define cultural heritage. However, beyond a certain point, it may be more fruitful to consider and develop specific examples. For instance, taking landscape as a concept, how many varieties can we identify? Here is a beginning:

1. ecological;
2. wilderness;
3. cultural, i.e., consciously formed by humans, such as agricultural, designed (in the sense that a landscape park, a garden, or an urban park is designed), or industrial landscapes;
4. a combination of all or some of the above.

For example (and would that his example had been more widely emulated since), the late 18th-century Prince Franz[3] of Anhalt-Dessau, Germany, sought to turn his entire small principality into a landscape park in which the contented peasantry toiling in the fields, the royal and noble families in their palaces and parks, the smiling hedgerows, fruit trees, lakes, rivers, and buildings all played their part. In the late 20th century, when much of this Arcadian landscape had been altered by brown coal mining and other industrial activities, it was realized with great imagination and good sense that the *whole* of this landscape could be regarded as having cultural value. It is now being studied, conserved, managed, and presented as an *Industrielles Gartenreich*. It has also been realized that by celebrating it as a whole, instead of going back to some idealized moment in its past, there could be greater motivation and a wider spectrum of funding available for its reclamation, regeneration, and interpretation, as well as the renewal of activities of various kinds, including tourism.

Similarly, in regard to building culture, we can identify:

1. Archaeological evidence of early settlement and living patterns, such as the remarkably well-preserved prehistoric village of Skara Brae,[4] on the mainland of Orkney.
2. Vernacular building culture, varying widely from country to country, region to region, or even area to area, and always depending upon the underlying geology and topography for its distinctive building materials and character.
3. Designed architecture, ranging from castles and country houses in the countryside to grand town houses, row houses, and shop houses in urban areas; or from cathedrals, mosques, and temples of world-class craftsmanship and design to humbler yet well-crafted chapels and shrines of many traditions.
4. Combinations of many of these, such as may be seen in York, where the Minster, city churches, city walls and gates, town houses, mansions, shops, etc., all add up to a totality, i.e., the historic city, which is of greater value than its individual parts.
5. Combinations of buildings with their collections: (a) York Minster and its stained glass; (b) the Borthwick Institute with its historic

and living archives of the Archbishop of York, for many centuries one of the most important citizens of the kingdom; (c) the neighboring Castle Howard with its collections of paintings, furniture, antique sculpture, its 18th-century lead sculpture in the designed landscape, and archives and books of a great noble land-owning and politically influential family; (d) the City Art Gallery with its rich holdings of paintings and ceramics; (e) Fairfax House with its collection of furniture; (f) the York city churches with their stained glass, furnishings and works of art, etc.

Thus it is clear that an inclusive view of cultural heritage allows even minor artifacts to have cultural value. A non-European example is provided by the restaurant and resthouse *At the Sign of the Kiwi,* located outside Christchurch, New Zealand, and designed by the Arts & Crafts architect Hurst Seager in 1911. The owner of the locale has taken steps to recover the furniture, cutlery, and china that were part of the original *Gesamtkunstwerk,* in recognition of the fact that these items possess cultural value as parts of a whole. The owner's motivation to pursue this restoration arises from the fact that her predecessors did not recognize this cultural value and proceeded to sell, give, or throw these items away. Thus it is important to recognize that opinions as to what constitutes cultural heritage can change significantly. In particular, there is now a recognition of *completeness* that has arisen during the most recent era. It is a moot point whether this change in opinion is influenced by the astonishing rise in financial value of such items of heritage, or vice versa.

In assigning cultural value, we should include such items as engines and tools. In England, there are few more romantic and inspiring experiences than traversing Coniston Water in the Lake District—under the very eye of Ruskin's *Brantwood* house—in the 1860s steam gondola that the National Trust has rescued from the lake floor and restored as a working piece of industrial machinery. Additional examples can readily be provided: Many different kinds of machinery have recently been restored and returned to use. Waterwheels and water mills are turning again, and for their original purposes. Canal systems have been dredged, bridges and tunnels repaired, and the waterways brought back into use for commerce and recreation. Historic railway engines and their accompanying rolling stock have likewise been restored in many different countries and brought back into use. In York, home of the National Railway Museum, several magnificent, restored engines are occasionally put back on the rails and have a good day's outing once again pulling trains. A distinction may be made here, however, between artifacts or aspects of cultural heritage that are restored primarily for interpretative purposes and those that are brought back into use primarily or partly to serve their original purpose.

With regard to architecture, we can also include specialist structures that were not necessarily regarded as part of cultural heritage until relatively recently, and that in some countries and cultures still need to have their case made for them. Such structures include:

1. buildings for industrial production processes such as mills, factories, power stations, gas-works, turbines, lime-kilns, etc.;
2. more specifically rural equivalents such as wind- and water mills, farmsteads, horse-engine houses, and barns as well as buildings and machinery associated with the production of olive oil, wine, beer, cider, etc.;
3. buildings for mercantile activities such as warehouses, go-downs, offices, and administrative buildings;
4. structures (i.e., not necessarily buildings) associated with transportation, such as harbors, wharves, quays, trams and tramways, railroads and trains, canals and their towpaths and tunnels, roads and embankments, petrol stations, the specific contribution that motorways have made to 20th-century culture, airfields, and airports;
5. technical infrastructure such as aqueducts, viaducts, bridges, drains; water-pumping stations as well as sewage disposal and treatment systems;

6. housing associated with all of the above, such as mill or factory villages (Saltaire, Bradford, and Ackroyden, Halifax, are among notable Yorkshire examples); colliery villages; estate villages, associated with the economy of a country house or castle of a landed estate; also the houses in which owners or managers lived, in symbolic relationship to the "works" and to the workers' housing;

7. natural sites used for industrial exploitation such as open-cast mines, mine shafts, and pit-head structures, or that were used in the processing of oil, coal, salt, etc.

So far, all that has been said may be held to contribute toward defining cultural heritage. There are other questions to be considered as well. One might ask whose heritage are we considering, and what is the purpose of defining, and consequently protecting, cultural heritage, and for whom. It is also warranted to ask whether there is such a thing as universal cultural value, and what is the significance of boundaries, for example, in cultural, racial, religious, or political terms.

There is still a wall in Nicosia dividing Turkish and Greek Cyprus. The removal of the physical wall in Berlin did not remove the psychological barrier. There is much sad evidence that, in the late 20th century, boundaries of all kinds are maintained as often as they are broken down, and that destruction of heritage for political, cultural, racial, or religious reasons is still distressingly common.

Perhaps the overriding justification for being concerned about cultural heritage is that every aspect of it has some significance for *someone*. For this person, that particular aspect of cultural heritage contributes to his or her feelings of acceptance and wholeness as a human being.

A perfectly framed heritage policy would recognize the delicate, sensitive, and specific nature of particular forms of heritage for particular people. Bruce Chatwin's travel book, *The Songlines* (1987), for example, made many people—especially people of white European origin—aware of the significance for Australian aborigines of places associated with the naming of specific animals, the continuity of meaning, and the continuity of cross-country routes that had a special, sacred significance. Such an understanding may make us more aware of the fact that cultural heritage may exist in many layers and may be revealed by different kinds of evidence.

Similarly, many if not all the world's major religious traditions have an understanding of the concept of pilgrimage: a journey to a specific place, along a specific route, where specific goals are sought, and where specific rituals or devotions are to be performed. Examples are not difficult to find. In England, there are annual pilgrimages to the Shrine of Our Lady at Walsingham and to the Shrine of St. Alban in the great Abbey Church of St. Albans. There is an endless stream of pilgrims on foot, bicycle, and motorized transport to the Shrine of St. James at Santiago de Compostela in northern Spain. In India, the purifying function of the waters of the river Ganges plays a significant role in the lives of devout Hindus. In addition, a constant stream of Buddhist monks, nuns, and lay people pay their respects to the Dalai Lama at Dharamsala in northern India. This last case is especially interesting, in that a conscious attempt is being made to keep Tibetan Buddhist culture alive in a generous host country, and this culture embraces the bedrock of ritual and language as well as music, dance, poetry, costume, etc.

The purpose of defining, and then seeking to protect, cultural heritage is so that none of this delicacy of meaning or significance is heedlessly swept away. However, apart from destruction, there are many other ways—ranging from careless to malevolent—in which cultural heritage is at risk. It is a commonplace of heritage policy, not only in the West, that the worst threat to cultural heritage is simply neglect, lack of maintenance, absence of repairs, inability to take responsible action, etc. To counteract this tendency, the United Kingdom and other countries have invented such mechanisms as (a) the regular quinquennial inspection of the 17,500 Anglican churches and also the secular properties of the National Trust, and (ii) the *Monumentenwacht*, a regionally organized initiative in the Netherlands and Flanders (Belgium), which allows building owners to receive regular "check-ups" on their buildings—

whether sacred or secular, large or small—for a modest fee. These check-ups enable owners to monitor maintenance and repair requirements, thus helping to prevent the development of major, potentially cost-intensive problems. There are also a variety of incentives and penalties for neglect or disrepair, such as compulsory repair notices or compulsory purchases by public authorities. Such compulsory purchases are difficult to enforce, however, and public authorities are wary of potential political backlash in response to large expenditures. Thus more positive policies—such as regular inspection and maintenance, education, and the promotion of awareness—tend to be preferred.

The category of threats includes a large gamut of actions such as destructive or inappropriate re-use, or the use of destructive or inappropriate materials for repairs. This is not to deny that re-use can be extremely positive, benign, and socially beneficial. Such positive examples include the conversion of churches in the city of York into senior citizens' day-care centers, archaeological resource centers, restaurants, Christian resource centers, arts centers, etc. The point here is that re-use activities must be well-considered, well-designed, and well-executed, in order to avoid spoiling the cultural significance of various buildings.

Sharper attention must be focused on the threat posed by deliberate defacing or destruction of cultural heritage, especially in times and places of racial, religious, or political conflict. For example, during the Communist era, the Soviet Union and its satellite countries destroyed countless mosques, temples, churches, and cathedrals, or deliberately used these buildings for utilitarian, propagandistic, or often shocking secular purposes. The furnishings and decorations of these buildings were often smashed to pieces or exposed to the elements. Worse still, in recent conflicts not far from the heart of Europe, cultural heritage has been attacked or destroyed in a deliberate attempt to inflict pain upon the enemy. Such attacks inflict pain because, at a fundamental level, cultural heritage is closely connected to human value systems and provides all individuals with a sense of validity as human beings.

Cultural heritage is also of vital importance as we seek to redress the overexploitation of materials and nonrenewable resources. The maintenance of cultural heritage seeks to maximize the utility of what we already possess and to use human ingenuity in adapting, rather than replacing, existing buildings or structures. What is the relationship between cultural heritage and sustainability? What policies can help make cultural heritage more sustainable? One might argue that cultural heritage policy-makers have been slow to recognize the importance of the *Brundtland Report,* the report of the World Commission on Environment and Development (WCED 1987). However, a considerable amount of published material on the topic of sustainability has recently become available to committed heritage specialists (cf. English Heritage 1999a, b; Jarmon 1999; National Trust.)[5] In addition, the National Trust—whose holdings include precious works of fine art, furniture, and decorations from castles and country houses, industrial archaeology, wild upland landscapes, and extensive stretches of coastline—has begun encouraging its members, staff, and committees to "think sustainably." The Trust has also engaged in a number of experiments in sustainability. For example, it has encouraged diversification among its farm tenants as a way of focusing attention on cultural heritage in a different manner: rather than merely driving or walking through landscapes, public visitors are encouraged to take "bed and breakfast" in the historic houses of working farms. In this way, visitors can contribute to the survival of the landscape and its precious balance between nature and human society. In certain cases, such as the 18th-century designed landscape of Prior Park, Bath, visitors are required to come via public transportation or on foot.

In short, rational decision-making with regard to cultural heritage requires us not only to understand, define, and identify cultural heritage but to justify its preservation on the grounds that (a) its survival is essential to the spiritual and emotional well-being of human beings and (b) it contributes handsomely to our economic well-being. Threats to cultural heritage are as pressing today as ever, a fact that is disconcerting in light of today's higher levels of education and awareness. However, this may be partly due to the increasing recognition of the propaganda value of cultural heritage, i.e., the destruction of cultural heritage, by inflicting pain and damage upon a society or state, provides yet another weapon to be deployed in contemporary conflicts. In contrast to these concerns is the more positive consideration that, in countries that are at peace with themselves and their neighbors, cultural heritage has never been more popular, and citizens enjoy an ever-increasing range of cultural opportunities. Nevertheless, enormous numbers of visitors, as well as the effects of "wear and tear" and environmental pollution, bring their own problems. Ensuring that cultural heritage will be preserved for the enjoyment of our successors has therefore become one of our most urgent preoccupations. As a result, those responsible for cultural heritage must explore and adopt policies of sustainability before it is too late.

REFERENCES

Athens Charter. 1931. Conclusions of the Athens Conference, October 21-30, 1931. In: *La conservation des monuments d'art et d'histoire*, pp. 448–453. Intl. Office of Museums. http://www.icomos.org/docs/athens_charter.html.

Burra Charter. 1981, 1988. The Australian ICOMOS Charter for the Conservation of Places of Cultural Significance. Adapted 1979, with revisions in 1981 and 1988. http://www.icomos.org/docs/burra_charter.html.

Chatwin, B. 1987. *The Songlines.* New York: Viking.

Clarke, D., and P. Maguire. 1989. *Skara Brae: Northern Europe's Best Preserved Prehistoric Village. The Official Historic Scotland Guidebook.* Edinburgh: Historic Buildings and Monuments Scotland.

English Heritage. 1999a. *The Heritage Dividend: Measuring the Results of English Heritage Regeneration* 1994-1999. August, 1999.

English Heritage. 1999b. *Sustaining the Historic Environment: New Perspectives on the Future.* March, 1999.

Jarmon, R. 1999. *Green is the color.* Paper presented at RIBA seminar in London, in March, 1999.

Jokilehto, J. 1999. *A History of Conservation.* Oxford: Butterworth-Heinemann.

Klein, N., ed. 1984. *The Collected Letters of William Morris.* Princeton, NJ: Princeton Univ. Press.

Larsen, K.E. 1995. *Nara Conference on Authenticity in Relation to the World Heritage Convention.* Paris: UNESCO, ICCROM and ICOMOS and the Japanese Agency for Cultural Affairs.

Le Corbusier, C.-Ed. 1941. *La Charte d'Athenes.* Paris.

Lipe, W.D. 1984. *Value and meaning in cultural resources. In: Approaches to the Archaeological Heritage: A Comparative Study of World Cultural Resource Management Systems,* ed. H. Cleere. Cambridge: Cambridge Univ. Press.

Nara Document on Authenticity. 1994. Convention Concerning the Protection of the World Cultural and Natural Heritage. Report of the Experts Meeting, Nov., 1994. http://www.unesco.org/who/archive/nara94lhtml.

Ruskin, J. 1849. *The Seven Lamps of Architecture.* London: Smith, Elder and Co.

Ruskin, J. 1854. Lectures on architecture and painting, delivered at Edinburgh in November, 1853.

Venice Charter. 1964. Intl. Charter for the Conservation and Restoration of Monuments and Sites. http://www.icomos.org/docs/venice_charter.html.

Waterfield, G. 1999. *Prince Franz's Garden Kingdom. Country Life* April 29, pp. 68–73.

WCED (World Commission on Environment and Development). 1987. *Our Common Future.* Oxford: Oxford Univ. Press.

NOTES

1. The *Manifesto* is reproduced in every annual Report of the Society for the Protection of Ancient Buildings from 1878 until the present day. It can also be found printed in, for example, Klein (1984, pp. 359–360).

2. For a more detailed explanation of both Athens documents, see Jokilehto (1999, pp. 284–285).

3. Prince Leopold III Friedrich Franz of Anhalt-Dessau, 1740–1817. His enlightened patronage was

celebrated in an exhibition entitled *For the Friends of Nature and Art: The Garden Kingdom of Prince Franz von Anhalt-Dessau in the Age of Enlightenment* at Osterley Park, Middlesex, in the summer of 1999, and in an article by Waterfield (1999).

4. In the official Historic Scotland guidebook to *Skara Brae,* Clarke and Maguire (1989, p. 1) state that "the village of Skara Brae was inhabited before the Egyptian pyramids were built and flourished many centuries before construction began at Stonehenge.

It is some 5000 years old. But it is not its age alone that makes it so remarkable and so important. It is the degree to which it has been preserved. The structures of this semi-subterranean village survive in impressive condition. And so, amazingly, does the furniture in the village houses. Nowhere else in northern Europe are we able to see such rich evidence of how our remote ancestors actually lived."

5. The National Trust. Environment and Conservation website. http://www.nationaltrust.org.uk.

AUSTRALIA INTERNATIONAL COUNCIL ON MONUMENTS AND SITES (ICOMOS INC.)

The Burra Charter: The Australia ICOMOS Charter for Places of Cultural Significance 1999 with Associated Guidelines and Code on the Ethics of Co-existence

Preamble

Considering the International Charter for the Conservation and Restoration of Monuments and Sites (Venice 1964), and the Resolutions of the 5th General Assembly of the International Council on Monuments and Sites (ICOMOS) (Moscow 1978), the Burra Charter was adopted by Australia ICOMOS (the Australian National Committee of ICOMOS) on 19 August 1979 at Burra, South Australia. Revisions were adopted on 23 February 1981, 23 April 1988 and 26 November 1999.

The Burra Charter provides guidance for the conservation and management of places of cultural significance (cultural heritage places), and is based on the knowledge and experience of Australia ICOMOS members.

Conservation is an integral part of the management of places of cultural significance and is an ongoing responsibility.

Who Is the Charter For?

The Charter sets a standard of practice for those who provide advice, make decisions about, or undertake works to places of cultural significance, including owners, managers and custodians.

Using the Charter

The Charter should be read as a whole. Many articles are interdependent. Articles in the Conservation Principles section are often further developed in the Conservation Processes and Conservation Practice sections. Headings have been included for ease of reading but do not form part of the Charter.

The Charter is self-contained, but aspects of its use and application are further explained in the following Australia ICOMOS documents:

- Guidelines to the Burra Charter:
  Cultural Significance;
- Guidelines to the Burra Charter:
  Conservation Policy;
- Guidelines to the Burra Charter: Procedures
  for Undertaking Studies and Reports;
- Code on the Ethics of Coexistence
  in Conserving Significant Places.

What Places Does the Charter Apply To?

The Charter can be applied to all types of places of cultural significance including natural, indigenous and historic places with cultural values.

The standards of other organisations may also be relevant. These include the Australian Natural Heritage Charter and the Draft Guidelines for the Protection, Management and Use of Aboriginal and Torres Strait Islander Cultural Heritage Places.

Why Conserve?

Places of cultural significance enrich people's lives, often providing a deep and inspirational sense of connection to community and landscape, to the past and to lived experiences. They are historical records that are important as tangible expressions of Australian identity and experience. Places of cultural significance reflect the diversity of our communities, telling us about who we are and the past that has formed us and the Australian landscape. They are irreplaceable and precious.

These places of cultural significance must be conserved for present and future generations.

The Burra Charter advocates a cautious approach to change: do as much as necessary to care for the place and to make it useable, but otherwise change it as little as possible so that its cultural significance is retained.

Articles

ARTICLE 1. DEFINITIONS

For the purposes of this Charter:

1.1 *Place* means site, area, land, landscape, building or other work, group of buildings or other works, and may include components, contents, spaces and views.

1.2 *Cultural significance* means aesthetic, historic, scientific, social or spiritual value for past, present or future generations. Cultural significance is embodied in the *place* itself, its *fabric, setting, use, associations, meanings*, records, *related places* and *related objects*. Places may have a range of values for different individuals or groups.

1.3 *Fabric* means all the physical material of the *place* including components, fixtures, contents, and objects.

1.4 *Conservation* means all the processes of looking after a *place* so as to retain its *cultural significance*.

1.5 *Maintenance* means the continuous protective care of the *fabric* and *setting* of a *place,* and is to be distinguished from repair. Repair involves restoration or reconstruction.

1.6 *Preservation* means maintaining the *fabric* of a *place* in its existing state and retarding deterioration.

1.7 *Restoration* means returning the existing *fabric* of a *place* to a known earlier state by removing accretions or by reassembling existing components without the introduction of new material.

1.8 *Reconstruction* means returning a *place* to a known earlier state and is distinguished from *restoration* by the introduction of new material into the *fabric*.

1.9 *Adaptation* means modifying a *place* to suit the existing use or a proposed use.

1.10 *Use* means the functions of a place, as well as the activities and practices that may occur at the place.

1.11 *Compatible* use means a use which respects the *cultural significance* of a *place*. Such a use involves no, or minimal, impact on cultural significance.

1.12 *Setting* means the area around a *place,* which may include the visual catchment.

1.13 *Related place* means a place that contributes to the *cultural significance* of another place.

1.14 *Related object* means an object that contributes to the *cultural significance* of a *place* but is not at the place.

1.15 *Associations* mean the special connections that exist between people and a *place*. Associations may include social or spiritual values and cultural responsibilities for a place.

1.16 *Meanings* denote what a *place* signifies, indicates, evokes or expresses to people. Meanings generally relate to intangible aspects such as symbolic qualities and memories.

1.17 *Interpretation* means all the ways of presenting the *cultural significance* of a *place*.

Conservation Principles

ARTICLE 2. CONSERVATION AND MANAGEMENT

2.1 *Places* of *cultural significance* should be conserved.

2.2 The aim of *conservation* is to retain the *cultural significance* of a *place*.

2.3 *Conservation* is an integral part of good management of *places* of *cultural significance*.

2.4 *Places* of *cultural significance* should be safeguarded and not put at risk or left in a vulnerable state.

ARTICLE 3. CAUTIOUS APPROACH

3.1 *Conservation* is based on a respect for the existing *fabric, use, associations* and *meanings*. It requires a cautious approach of changing as much as necessary but as little as possible.

3.2 Changes to a *place* should not distort the physical or other evidence it provides, nor be based on conjecture.

ARTICLE 4. KNOWLEDGE, SKILLS AND TECHNIQUES

4.1 *Conservation* should make use of all the knowledge, skills and disciplines which can contribute to the study and care of the *place*.

4.2 Traditional techniques and materials are preferred for the *conservation* of significant *fabric*. In some circumstances modern techniques and materials which offer substantial conservation benefits may be appropriate.

ARTICLE 5. VALUES

5.1 *Conservation* of a *place* should identify and take into consideration all aspects of cultural and natural significance without unwarranted emphasis on any one value at the expense of others.

5.2 Relative degrees of *cultural significance* may lead to different *conservation* actions at a place.

ARTICLE 6. BURRA CHARTER PROCESS

6.1 The *cultural significance* of a *place* and other issues affecting its future are best understood by a sequence of collecting and analysing information before making decisions. Understanding cultural significance comes first, then development of policy and finally management of the place in accordance with the policy.

6.2 The policy for managing a place must be *based* on an understanding of its *cultural significance*.

6.3 Policy development should also include consideration of other factors affecting the future of a *place* such as the owner's needs, resources, external constraints and its physical condition.

ARTICLE 7. USE

7.1 Where the *use* of a place is of *cultural significance* it should be retained.

7.2 A *place* should have a *compatible* use.

ARTICLE 8. SETTING

Conservation requires the retention of an appropriate visual *setting* and other relationships that contribute to the *cultural significance* of the *place*.

New construction, demolition, intrusions or other changes which would adversely affect the setting or relationships are not appropriate.

ARTICLE 9. LOCATION

9.1 The physical location of a *place* is part of its *cultural significance*. A building, work or other component of a place should remain in its historical location. Relocation is generally unacceptable unless this is the sole practical means of ensuring its survival.

9.2 Some buildings, works or other components of *places* were designed to be readily removable or already have a history of relocation. Provided such buildings, works or other components do not have significant links with their present location, removal may be appropriate.

9.3 If any building, work or other component is moved, it should be moved to an appropriate location and given an appropriate use. Such action should not be to the detriment of any *place* of *cultural significance*.

ARTICLE 10. CONTENTS

Contents, fixtures and objects which contribute to the *cultural significance* of a *place* should be retained at that place. Their removal is unacceptable unless it is: the sole means of ensuring their security and *preservation;* on a temporary basis for treatment or exhibition; for cultural reasons; for health and safety; or to protect the place. Such contents, fixtures and objects should be returned where circumstances permit and it is culturally appropriate.

ARTICLE 11. RELATED PLACES AND OBJECTS

The contribution which *related places* and *related objects* make to the *cultural significance* of the *place* should be retained.

ARTICLE 12. PARTICIPATION

Conservation, interpretation and management of a *place* should provide for the participation of people for whom the place has special *associations* and *meanings,* or who have social, spiritual or other cultural responsibilities for the place.

ARTICLE 13. CO-EXISTENCE OF CULTURAL VALUES

Co-existence of cultural values should be recognised, respected and encouraged, especially in cases where they conflict.

Conservation Processes

ARTICLE 14. CONSERVATION PROCESSES

Conservation may, according to circumstance, include the processes of: retention or reintroduction of a *use;* retention of *associations* and *meanings; maintenance, preservation, restoration, reconstruction, adaptation* and *interpretation;* and will commonly include a combination of more than one of these.

ARTICLE 15. CHANGE

15.1 Change may be necessary to retain *cultural significance*, but is undesirable where it reduces cultural significance. The amount of change to a *place* should be guided by the *cultural significance* of the place and its appropriate *interpretation*.

15.2 Changes which reduce *cultural significance* should be reversible, and be reversed when circumstances permit.

15.3 Demolition of significant *fabric* of a *place* is generally not acceptable. However, in some cases minor demolition may be appropriate as part of *conservation*. Removed significant fabric should be reinstated when circumstances permit.

15.4 The contributions of all aspects of *cultural significance* of a *place* should be respected. If a place includes *fabric, uses, associations* or *meanings* of different periods, or different aspects of cultural significance, emphasising or interpreting one period or aspect at the expense of another can only be justified when what is left out, removed or diminished is of slight cultural significance and that which is emphasised or interpreted is of much greater cultural significance.

ARTICLE 16. MAINTENANCE

Maintenance is fundamental to *conservation* and should be undertaken where *fabric* is of *cultural significance* and its maintenance is necessary to retain that *cultural significance*.

ARTICLE 17. PRESERVATION

Preservation is appropriate where the existing *fabric* or its condition constitutes evidence of *cultural significance*, or where insufficient evidence is available to allow other *conservation* processes to be carried out.

ARTICLE 18. RESTORATION AND RECONSTRUCTION

Restoration and *reconstruction* should be culturally significant aspects of the *place*.

ARTICLE 19. RESTORATION

Restoration is appropriate only if there is sufficient evidence of an earlier state of the *fabric*.

ARTICLE 20. RECONSTRUCTION

20.1 *Reconstruction* is appropriate only where a *place* is incomplete through damage or alteration, and only where there is sufficient evidence to reproduce an earlier state of the *fabric*. In rare cases, reconstruction may also be appropriate as part of a use or practice that retains the *cultural significance* of the place.

20.2 *Reconstruction* should be identifiable on close inspection or through additional *interpretation*.

ARTICLE 21. ADAPTATION

21.1 *Adaptation* is acceptable only where the adaptation has minimal impact on the *cultural significance* of the place.

21.2 *Adaptation* should involve minimal change to significant fabric, achieved only after considering alternatives.

ARTICLE 22. NEW WORK

22.1 New work such as additions to the *place* may be acceptable where it does not distort or obscure the *cultural significance* of the place, or detract from its *interpretation* and appreciation.

22.2 New work should be readily identifiable as such.

ARTICLE 23. CONSERVING USE

Continuing, modifying or reinstating a significant *use* may be appropriate and preferred forms of *conservation*.

ARTICLE 24. RETAINING ASSOCIATIONS AND MEANINGS

24.1 Significant *associations* between people and a *place* should be respected, retained and not obscured. Opportunities for the *interpretation,* commemoration and celebration of these associations should be investigated and implemented.

24.2 Significant *meanings,* including spiritual values, of a *place* should be respected. Opportunities for the continuation or revival of these meanings should be investigated and implemented.

ARTICLE 25. INTERPRETATION

The *cultural significance* of many places is not readily apparent, and should be explained by *interpretation*. Interpretation should enhance understanding and enjoyment, and be culturally appropriate.

Conservation Practice

ARTICLE 26. APPLYING THE BURRA CHARTER PROCESS

26.1 Work on a *place* should be preceded by studies to understand the place which should include analysis of physical, documentary, oral and other evidence, drawing on appropriate knowledge, skills and disciplines.

26.2 Written statements of *cultural significance* and policy for the *place* should be prepared, justified and accompanied by supporting evidence. The statements of significance and policy should be incorporated into a management plan for the place.

26.3 Groups and individuals with *associations* with a place as well as those involved in its management should be provided with opportunities to contribute to and participate in understanding the *cultural significance* of the place. Where appropriate they should also have opportunities to participate in its *conservation* and management.

ARTICLE 27. MANAGING CHANGE

27.1 The impact of proposed changes on the *cultural significance* of a *place* should be analysed with reference to the statement of significance and the policy for managing the place. It may be necessary to modify proposed changes following analysis to better retain cultural significance.

27.2 Existing *fabric, use, associations* and *meanings* should be adequately recorded before any changes are made to the *place*.

ARTICLE 28. DISTURBANCE OF FABRIC

28.1 Disturbance of significant *fabric* for study, or to obtain evidence, should be minimised. Study of a *place* by any disturbance of the fabric, including archaeological excavation, should only be undertaken to provide data essential for decisions on the *conservation* of the place, or to obtain important evidence about to be lost or made inaccessible.

28.2 Investigation of a *place* which requires disturbance of the *fabric,* apart from that necessary to make decisions, may be appropriate provided that it is consistent with the policy for the place. Such investigation should be based on important research questions which have potential to substantially add to knowledge, which cannot be answered in other ways and which minimises disturbance of significant fabric.

ARTICLE 29. RESPONSIBILITY FOR DECISIONS

The organisations and individuals responsible for management decisions should be named and specific responsibility taken for each such decision.

ARTICLE 30. DIRECTION, SUPERVISION AND IMPLEMENTATION

Competent direction and supervision should be maintained at all stages, and any changes should be implemented by people with appropriate knowledge and skills.

ARTICLE 31. DOCUMENTING EVIDENCE AND DECISIONS

A log of new evidence and additional decisions should be kept.

ARTICLE 32. RECORDS

32.1 The records associated with the *conservation* of a *place* should be placed in a permanent archive and made publicly available, subject to requirements of security and privacy, and where this is culturally appropriate.

32.2 Records about the history of a *place* should be protected and made publicly available, subject to requirements of security and privacy, and where this is culturally appropriate.

ARTICLE 33. REMOVED FABRIC

Significant *fabric* which has been removed from a *place* including contents, fixtures and objects, should be catalogued, and protected in accordance with its *cultural significance.*

Where possible and culturally appropriate, removed significant fabric including contents, fixtures and objects, should be kept at the place.

ARTICLE 34. RESOURCES

Adequate resources should be provided for conservation.

Words in italics are defined in Article 1.

SUSAN M. PEARCE

"The Making of Cultural Heritage"

In Values and Heritage Conservation: Research Report, *edited by Erica Avrami, Randall Mason, and Marta de la Torre. (Los Angeles: The Getty Conservation Institute, 2000), pp. 59–64.*

THIS PAPER IS meant to contribute to the ongoing debate surrounding the genesis of cultural heritage and perhaps to stimulate responses. In it, I hope to do three things: to reprise (briefly) what cultural heritage is; to analyze the factors that bear upon its creation; and to arrive at some sense of how and where, in the real world, we might look to see new heritage being created before our very eyes.

Genesis of Cultural Heritage

The term *heritage*, a borrowing from legal terminology, may be described as embracing that which can be passed from one generation to the next and following generations, and to which descendants of the original owner(s) have rights deemed worthy of respect. This legal genesis is one of the reasons that landscapes, buildings, and objects loom large in the management of heritage at a practical level, because these are entities that the law recognizes as property and. Consequently, as being capable of transmission across generations (for discussion, see Carman 1996). The term also presupposes an intrinsic relationship between those who went before and those who come after, with concomitant notions of responsibility and "holding in trust." Equally—and I write now as someone brought up in the English system—law only exists as a mixed bundle of customs and judgments that run back to the beginning of legal memory in 1086; consequently, law itself, like the heritage it defines, draws its authority from the traditions of the ancestors.

The idea of "cultural" heritage is an extension of the basic concept of heritage. Here, inheritance is extended to encompass ideological elements that, like physical transmissions, enable the inheritors to enter into their rightful state and be their true selves. The separation of ideology—ideas and feelings—from property (in the legal sense of material goods and real estate) is, however an unreal dichotomy, a wrongful slicing up of the seamless garment of culture. No social idea can exist without its physical manifestation—whether it be land, objects, food, body use, or performance space; correspondingly, no physical manifestation lacks its ideological information. This physicality is why cultural heritage requires such a large superstructure of operation and maintenance, why it can be directly politically contested, why it can be owned, and why no group can afford to preserve all its heritage in the style that it might wish.

This analysis leads to the next significant point. Cultural heritage is cognitively constructed, as an external expression of identity, operating in a range of ways and levels. It is a social fact, and like all social facts, it is both passive and active. Its passivity rests in its role as an arena of selection: most elements (of whatever kind) do not make it into the heritage zone. Its activeness lies in its influence: once particular elements are established as heritage, they exercise power; they have a life of their own that affects people's minds and that consequently affects their choices. Heritage becomes a representation of beliefs about self and community which nest in with other related belief systems to create a holistic structure that ramifies through all the areas—politics, economics, use of resources—where social life touches us as individuals.

Heritage is the cultural authority of the past, as well as a selective construction of individual and corporate identity. Heritage (in the sense being discussed here) is also part and of that complex of beliefs and actions that it is convenient to call European modernism. It relates to attitudes that emerged and developed in Europe, chiefly northwestern Europe, between about 1500 and 1750, and that engage particular notions of the nature of history, the force of scientific reason, the rights of the individual, and the rule of law, all of which have been shadowed in the foregoing paragraphs. And heritage shares with modernism its dark side: the selection and cultivation of heritage, by definition, draws on distinctions between "ours" and "theirs," "us" and "them," and brings all the nationalistic and fascist horrors that can flow from its misuse. Like most modernistic notions, ideas of heritage have spread over the world, but we must remember that they are not native to most cultures and are not by any means necessarily the only or the best way of constructing a relationship of identity on the cusp between past and present.

Factors in the Construction of Cultural Heritage

Given this broad context within which cultural heritage operates as construct and practice, it is helpful to seek out ways in which we can analyze, and so begin to understand, how the selective process that results in heritage works—that is, to distinguish the elements involved and the force field created by their modes of interaction (Table 1). The notion of scale is significant here. Each human being lives within a range of nesting scales, all of which arc a field for cultural practice. Plainly, the precise definition of these is difficult, but as a working guide—given relative validity by its standard use and in the pragmatic experience of most of us—we can make some suggestions.

As individuals, we all have patterns of thought and action that draw on and help to sustain cultural practice, in the sense that even a person marooned alone on a desert island can be said to be cultured. On the next scale, humans live in family groups, which are carriers and creators of culture; the exact composition of family groups is, of course, a key cultural element. The same considerations apply to the local community and to the self-perceived "ethnic" group, both made up of families and their composing individuals. In the contemporary world, all ethnic groups exist as parts of sovereign states, and the

states together make up the world community, which, along with all the other wavelengths of scale, has a certain collective culture expressed through transnational organizations.

The relationship among the different scale levels is both intimate and complex and embodies the ideological tensions that in part arise from and in part are expressed by conflicting cultural traditions, and which create a force field across the system. These may be broken down into a number of interlocking agencies. Utilitarian pressures of population and space; clashes of ideology and religion with, among many other discords, the potential for ethical clashes over perceived "bad" cultures (e.g., those that carry out female circumcision); the media and its "sound bite" agendas; professionalism and its resistance to change: specific economic pressures (e.g., globally on woodland): all these spring to mind, and others could be distinguished, like conflicts between elite and popular culture, or pressures associated with the speed of communication. All these cultural traditions, of course, have arisen among ourselves, in relation to interactions among the different scales, and with the natural environment as the battlefield.

Across the force field of interscale tension plays a range of generic elements that are implicit in the human condition, and through which, therefore, culture and heritage are habitually constructed. These can be defined in various ways, but key areas do emerge. "History" is plainly important—the term being used here to mean the appropriation of the record as a legitimizing technique. Similarly significant is the way in which Nature is produced as Culture, particularly in the areas of land and food. The symbolic action of material culture is implicit in the ways in which the natural environment is used to create things, which then embody and order social relationships and our expression of ourselves. Notions of "good ordering" or "right relationships" are crucial and are embodied in explicit religions and in political and ideological codes and practices. The operation of all these things gives rise to direct political/economic competitive pressures. Finally, the explicit actions a culture takes to reproduce itself (over and above the reproductive drive implicit in all cultural

TABLE 1.

Activities, interactions, and emergent tensions relating to the construction of heritage at various scales of social organization.

Activity / Scale	Tensions	History	Nature (i.e., view and use of land and its raw materials)	Material culture	Beliefs (religious/political/ ideological, etc.)	Direct political/ economic pressure	Mode of self-conscious cultural reproduction
Individual	Conflict between Us and Other (racial, cultural, religious)	Desire to preserve memories; selective autobiography	Competition to secure appropriate share	Individual tastes; clothes; possessions; souvenirs; psychology of shopping	Personal beliefs	Individual compromises	Chosen attitudes of conformity and rebellion
Family	Human fallibility (greed, voyeurism, callousness, nostalgia, etc.)	Desire to preserve family memories, create family histories	Production and consumption practices seen as "appropriate"	Choice of domestic interiors; clothes; heirlooms; shopping practices	Nature of family tradition	Aspirations to improve status, often seen in technological terms	Mother's knee; father's stories; "learning from Nelly"
Local community	Perceived "economic" pressures of raw material, labor, debt, etc.	Selection of origin stories, local accounts	Chosen construction of nature as land allocation; building; food	Creation of culture through pick a mix fashion	Mix of local family traditions, which constantly change	Efforts to channel local resentments, resistance to pressure to change	Accredited seniors: religious, "big men" employers, local institutions
Ethnic group	Clash between elite and popular culture; speed of global communication, including electronics, travel, tourists	Creation of origin stories; "ancestors" management of discourses	Creation of narratives about "well-ordered landscape," "good food," "proper work"	Manipulated use of material symbol; creation of relics	Construction of cultural identity as a holistic worldview	Perceived fragility of "traditional ways of life"; threats to craft production	Choice of those vested with cultural reproduction role, associated institutions
Nation/ sovereign state	Media agendas; political and military force; pressures of population and space	Harnessing of major resources to production of selected elite historical narratives	Construction of narratives about, e.g., "the rice paddy landscape," "French cuisine"	Creation of icons; effects of mass production; raw material pressures; "high culture" and art	Chosen attitudes of inclusion and exclusion, and their "real" effect	Creation of stance favoring production over consumption; tax generation; internal suppressions	State education system; agencies of cultural stewardship; roles of these in hierarchy
World	Professionalisms and others	Competition between grand narratives involving concepts like neocolonial, Western, Oriental	Choice of various narratives to be disputed/reconciled—e.g., Unesco list of world heritage sites	Creation of world-class icon—e.g., Mona Lisa	Construction of major competing system—e.g., Christianity/ Islam/Judaism; capitalism/ communism	Permitted actions of transnational companies; warfare; terrorism	International agencies; travel and communication; international media; pressure groups; think tanks

action) need consideration. These embrace notions of "education" and "stewardship." These elements are appropriated simultaneously by the community at each scale in ways that each finds satisfactory, and each appropriation is a site of conflict with community groups in the surrounding scales. The result is a matrix of cultural production and clash.

An effort to express this has been set out in Table 1. Plainly this is the merest sketch or skeleton of the complexities of cultural dynamic and can never express the fine grain of actual cultural experience. It may, however, help provide a framework that can give some insights into how choices about what constitutes heritage come to be made. Two examples must suffice, and I have chosen the Watts Towers, Los Angeles (Goldstone and Goldstone 1997), and the Tower of London. These have in common their physical presence in the landscape, their important cultural heritage and tourist status, and their definition as towers, but little else.

The Tower of London (a heavily visited site) emerged as significant on the scale of national sovereign state, and at this level its constructed significance runs across the generic categories. It is "old," and the state has harnessed major resources to produce a selected elite of historical narratives that dwell on its ancient image of stability spiced with ancient tyranny to make it a bit sexy (but safe sex), on its centrality to the image of London, and on an association with the English resistance to Continental threat. It is, therefore, a major narrative about Englishness. It embraces symbolic material culture icons of potency interwoven with national life in the shape of the crown jewels, the regimental relics of the Royal Scots, and the legendary ravens turned into material culture by their tamed status and their clipped wings. The Tower is part of the ideology that embraces all these elements, but today it is part of the production of consumption, since its only "real" role is as a state revenue-generating tourist site, and hence it has been incorporated into the national agencies of stewardship.

At the ethnic level, the Tower is exclusive: Scots and Welsh see it as a symbol of oppression. At the local community level, it has little impact. At the family and individual levels, it has an important role as part of family trips to London, which are embalmed in

souvenirs, photographs, and memories, all of which feed into personal beliefs, chosen attitudes, and so on. It still features strongly as a narrative of Englishness that is beamed into our living rooms in, for example, the BBC costume dramas featuring stories about Henry III and Elizabeth I. The world at large also sees these dramas, but what it makes of the Tower of London images—if anything—is hard to say.

The Watts Towers have emerged into heritage by an entirely different route. Here the focus is upon a single individual. Simon Rodia was born in 1879, into a poor Italian family that lived near Nola, in southern Italy. Rodia emigrated to America about 1894, and in 1921 he moved to 1765 East l07th Street in the city of Watts, then a small town near Los Angeles. In the side garden of the house, over a period of some years, he constructed seventeen sculptures, including three tall spires and several smaller ones, a ship, walls, and a gazebo. All were constructed with scrap steel, wire or wire mesh, and Rodia's own cement mixture. Bits of salvaged ceramic, bottles, tiles, and shells form a mosaic that decorates the surfaces of the structures.

Nola has a famous yearly festival of Saint Paul, its ancient bishop, in which the citizens carry a ship and wooden towers on their shoulders, and it is clear that the design of Rodia's construction embodies personal and family memories and that in building the towers he was making an individual statement about being Italian and Nolan and about his personal attitudes. Here, family, personal, and ethnic/immigrant elements are fused together.

The local community—mostly not of Italian descent but equally poor and dispossessed—took little interest in his work, a circumstance furthered by Rodia's difficult personal disposition. But by 1959 the towers had become unsafe, and suddenly, when demolition was imminent, they began to attract the attention of the Los Angeles artistic and intellectual elite, and they became headline news across the United States. This situation can be seen to have come about because the belief system had now begun to embody notions about "folk art as icon" and about the significance of the bricolage approach to art and life signified by the "found" nature of Rodia's structures and decoration. Once this change in the belief system had happened, the towers could be constructed

TABLE 2.
Potential sites for the invention of heritage

	Theme	Sites	Parameters
When cultures collide	How multicultural, or creole, culture is created from a hybrid mix, or clash of traditions.	• Newly or recently discovered tribal communities in, e.g., Brazil and New Guinea and how they interact with outside culture. • Relationships between minority and dominant culture, e.g., the Indian Gujarati community in contemporary Britain. • Eclectic fashion, e.g., Pacific Rim cuisine.	• Nature of small-scale groups as cultural entities, role of economic pressures and of ideas of "preservation not fossilization." • Identification of "heritage" sites, monuments, material culture, and practices as they emerge. • Role of international media.
Parents and children	How culture is transformed across the generations, how it is not, how it is changed, and why.	Selected communities and the relationships among grandparents/parents/children.	• How individual passions create significance. • How "ancestor" narratives work. • How families construct memories and autobiographies.
Catalytic significance of world-class icons	How the life and (sudden or mysterious) death of icon figures create "instant" heritage as material culture, places, customs; how this bears on the notion of popular culture.	Selected individuals and culture that focuses upon them (i.e., John Lennon, President Kennedy, Elvis, Marilyn Monroe, Malcolm X, President Mandela, and Princess Diana).	• The nature of "relic" and "icon." • The manipulation of symbols. • The psychology of grief and self-identification; "recreational mourning."
Workplaces	How we are, or were, at work until very recently (is anybody preserving a seventies/early eighties typing pool office?).	Selected modes of working in offices, farms, workshops, etc.	• Relationship between community and workplace (mine, steel mill, textile factory, etc.) and what happens to work traditions when workplaces close. • Industrial community narratives of origin and identity.
Consuming passions	How shopping constructs its sites.	Shopping malls, mail-order operations, car boot (garage) sales.	• Feminist ideology and its bearing on consumption. • National and international companies in operation. • Obstinate nature of personal choice. • What are "quality goods" and "rubbish"?

into a local, national, and international iconic narrative of self-creation and life as art—with universal resonance. Consequently, they have been designated a city, state, and national landmark.

In the case of these contrasting heritage sites, analysis drawn from the information in Table 1 has been directed toward illuminating what has happened. This tool may provide a framework for improved understanding of the sites within which contemporary cultural production is now taking place. It could help researchers break up the cultural process into useful segments and define research projects that can hone in on particular issues of specific scale, animated by particular versions of the generic cultural production and worked upon by specifically identified pressures, within a specific time and place. A project being investigated could thus be placed within an investigative context aimed at a better understanding of the dynamic. This would illuminate the specific cultural community issues, encourage the development of overarching critical or theoretical perspectives, and provide material (at both levels) for engagement in the actual political process through which change can he brought about on the ground, however difficult this may be.

Cultural Heritage in the Making

We can, without great difficulty, single out some factors in the contemporary world that have global significance and that bear on issues relating to the construction of cultural heritage. One key factor is the breakup of the grand explanatory narrative, keystone of the modernist mindset, and of its direct political expression, the great empire. The result is an increasing cultural mix within which people everywhere wish to define themselves self-consciously, in terms of what they see as their own cultural style. This produces very complex societies with many tapering and intersecting layers, where the notion of scale is a particularly important mode of understanding what happens. In these complex societies, interactions of many possible kinds among the entities will evoke ideas of brokerage and negotiation as significant players in the cultural game. From this condition arise notions of

cultural fission and fusion which give us a perspective on hybrid or creole forms and on notions of pastiche and appropriation—now perceived as creative and significant in their own right. This state of affairs is the postmodern context, where today's "lifestyle" is being transmuted into tomorrow's "cultural heritage," and it prompts the identification of a number of interesting themes that are potential sites for the invention of new heritage. These are presented below in Table 2. The "sites" and "parameters" should be taken only as suggestions drawn from a large range of possibilities.

These are the merest suggestions from an enormous possible range. They are, however, interesting areas in which, a few years or decades on, legitimated heritage sites will have emerged.

Final Suggestions

The forward path to an improved understanding of the nature and construction of heritage clearly lies in the articulation of properly constructed and managed research projects geared to illuminate this aspect of ourselves. Such projects will inform the debate by enhancing theoretical perspectives (an urgent task) and by broadening the scope of the field in ways that bring it closer to the issues that concern real individuals and communities.

Deciding upon research topics that will develop the theoretical base while illuminating particular areas or issues is a difficult art—and one that the cultural heritage studies grid roughed out here in Table 1 is intended to facilitate through the focusing on salient topics and tensions. The next step must be the implementation of research.

REFERENCES

Carman, J. 1996. *Valuing Ancient Things: Archaeology and Law*. London and New York: Leicester University Press.

Goldstone, B., and A.P. Goldstone. 1997. *The Los Angeles Watts Towers*. Los Angeles: The Getty Conservation Institute and the J. Paul Getty Museum.

LAURAJANE SMITH

Uses of Heritage

(London and New York: Routledge, 2006), chapter 2, pp. 45–53.

Heritage as Experience

Before the conceptual heritage suitcase is repacked, however, I want to unpack it a little bit more and outline a particular experience that led me, someone trained in archaeology, to reconsider my adherence to the dominant and framing concept that heritage *is* a material object or site. In 1999, while undertaking research work (reported in Chapter 5; see also Figure 2.1) in northern Queensland, Australia, senior Indigenous women from the Waanyi community approached two colleagues and myself to be involved in a project they were developing. The Waanyi Women's History Project aimed to get Waanyi women's concerns about their heritage, and the sites that they had cultural custodianship over, onto the local land management agendas. The women considered that, as women, their concerns had not been given adequate attention or legitimacy by governmental land management agencies. Many of their cultural heritage sites fell within the boundaries of Boodjamulla National Park, which was at this time moving to joint management between the Waanyi community and the Queensland Parks and Wildlife Service. It had become vital to the women for them to secure a strong voice in these negotiations. As has been detailed elsewhere (Smith et al. 2003a, 2003b), our invitation to participate as heritage archaeologists was, in part, a move to grant authority to the project: if experts were involved, then government agencies would more likely pay attention. However, it was the Waanyi women who determined the nature, specific aims and outcomes of the project. Two field seasons were undertaken during 2000, ostensibly, at least as the archaeologists involved in the project understood, to record women's heritage sites. However, as the project unfolded we spent much of our time recording oral histories and these, rather than the site recordings, became a central feature of the project.

What was interesting for us was that for the Waanyi women these oral histories were perceived to be as much their heritage as the sites we had intended to record. More significantly, however, it became obvious that it was important for the women to recite and record these histories, not at home over a table, but in their cultural territory or 'country'[1] and, where relevant, at the appropriate cultural site. Passing on the oral histories and traditions was, for the women, an act of heritage management, as this heritage was being recorded and preserved as recordings. However, in also passing on histories and traditions to the younger Waanyi women who were present, the project became itself an act of heritage. Heritage was not the site itself, but the act of passing on knowledge in the culturally correct or appropriate contexts and times. The sites and the 'country' we were in were more than *aide-mémoire*, but rather, following Samuel (1994), were 'theatres of memory'. That is, while the sites, and indeed the whole Boodjamulla landscape or country, did play a mnemonic role, they also provided background, setting, gravitas and, most importantly, a sense of occasion for those both passing on and receiving cultural meaning, knowledge and memories. While the sites were intrinsically important to the women, it was the *use* of these sites that made them heritage, not the mere fact of their existence.

In addition to oral history recordings, a significant amount of time was spent fishing during the project. At first, this was difficult for archaeologists trained in a certain work ethic to accept. However, for the women, simply being in their cultural landscape, being 'in country', was to experience a sense of heritage. For many of the women involved, the project offered a rare chance to visit their country or cultural territory. Almost all of the women lived some distance from Boodjamulla, and had to be flown to the park by light aircraft due to the hazards and time involved in driving long distances in far northern Queensland. In addition, although many of the elderly women taking part in the project were related, or had known each other since they were girls, many had not seen each other for lengthy periods due to the difficulties and costs involved in travelling in the region. Just being in country and having the time to enjoy 'just being there' was significant. It allowed women to not only affirm a sense of their historical and cultural identities but also to network, meet and renew old friendships and pass on news about mutual friends and relatives. This socializing was also knitting together a sense of community, sometimes frayed by geographical separation, in a place that symbolized certain cultural values and meanings and at a time that was politically important to them.

What emerged from this project was a sense that heritage had to be experienced for it to be heritage and that, moreover, it *was* the experience (Smith et al. 2003a: 75). What also becomes apparent is a sense of the importance of memory, remembering and of performance. While women were affirming a sense of their gendered cultural identity at Boodjamulla, it was both culturally and politically important to reinforce its value by locating it in a particular place of performance. The Waanyi women undertook a range of heritage acts or actions that in themselves conveyed and carried meaning, but took on particular force because of the context in which they occurred. These acts, or performances, not only concerned keeping cultural heritage and knowledge alive by passing on their meanings and values to younger women, but also involved asserting a sense of their identify as Waanyi women both for themselves and the audience in the Queensland Parks and Wildlife Service.

Heritage also involved acts or performances of remembering, not just performances of remembering in terms of recounting oral histories, but also in embodying that remembering. Taking time to fish was, in part, a needed break during the project from oral history recording, but it also allowed time to reflect and to experience and re-embody those memories and acts of remembering in the Cultural landscape of Boodjamulla. New memories were also being cre-

ated, which was especially significant for the younger women who were gaining new collective memories passed on from the elder women, but everyone was also gaining new memories through the process of being at Boodjamulla, whilst also negotiating new meanings about what it meant to 'be' at Boodjamulla. In this sense, then, heritage as experience meant that heritage was not static or 'frozen in time', as the conservation ethic tends to demand, but rather was a process that while it passed on established values and meanings was also creating new meanings and values. Ultimately, this project also illustrates the degree to which different conceptualizations of heritage stand outside of the dominant discourse. Although we had little conceptual role to play in the development of the project, it was the presence of archaeological 'experts' that facilitated an awareness of this project within government agencies—that helped make at least one of the audiences pay attention. Our expertise was used as a commodity to broker the legitimacy of the project, precisely because the project stood outside of the dominant, and to a certain extent androcentric, concepts and values embedded in the AHD [Authorized Heritage Discourse].

This example identifies a range of concepts such as 'identity', 'power', 'memory', 'place' and 'performance', amongst others, which need elaboration and consideration. The following sections explore a reworking of the idea of heritage around these themes.

Heritage as Identity

The association between heritage and identity is well established in the heritage literature—material culture as heritage is assumed to provide a physical representation and reality to the ephemeral and slippery concept of 'identity'. Like history, it fosters the feelings of belonging and continuity (Lowenthal 1985: 214), while its physicality gives these feelings an added sense of material reality. As Graham et al. (2000: 41) state: 'heritage provides meaning to human existence by conveying the ideas of timeless values and unbroken lineages that underpin identity'. How the links between identity and heritage are developed and maintained, however, is an area that has not had much scrutiny in the heritage literature. The sorts of 'identity work' that people actually do at heritage sites, and how these links are constructed and maintained, are often assumed and unproblematized in the literature (Urry 1996; Bagnall 2003; McLean 2006).

Certainly, the representational and symbolic value of heritage in constructing and giving material reality to 'identity' is well recognized, although analysis of the way heritage is thus used is often articulated in terms of national identity. A great deal of critical attention has been paid to the ways in which the ideologies of nationalism and national identities have been consciously and unconsciously articulated and legitimized in terms of heritage (Diaz-Andreu and Champion 1996; Meskell 2002, 2003; Crouch and Parker 2003; Carrier 2005). This focus is a consequence of the way the AHD both constructs the idea of heritage and the official practices of heritage, both of which stress the significance of material culture in playing a vital representational role in defining national identity. Indeed, as identified in Chapter 1, the AHD was itself both constituted by, and is a constitutive discourse of, the ideology of nationalism. In identifying 'national heritage', the 'nation' is symbolically and imaginatively constituted as a real entity (Brett 1996: 156). In heritage literature and practice the monumental, the grand, rare, or aesthetically impressive is most often identified as being quintessentially representative of national identity. However, Billig (1995) draws our attention to the banal and the vernacular, arguing that it is often the commonplace symbols and everyday activities and habits that work to continually 'flag' or remind people of their national identity. While his argument draws on a range of practices and habits, he also shows that it is the banality and frequency of various symbols, the flag on the government building being the most obvious, that work to unconsciously remind and identify. To some degree the pervasiveness of the nationalizing discourse of heritage has itself become banal in the sense that Billig uses the term. The everyday ubiquities, and thus banalities, of nationalizing heritage through increasing leisure and heritage tourism activities, even at its most monumental, has perhaps facilitated and helped drive the heritage industry critique.

The process that Billig (1995) identifies may also work on a sub-national level in helping members of particular social, ethnic, cultural or geographically regional or local groups to define their sense of identity. Specific communities also use the same symbolic elements to define and constitute who they are—and who they are not—and to adhere to particular sets of group values and habits. Brett (1996: 8-9) uses Bourdieu's idea of 'habitus'—the ideational environment that reflects durable dispositions and values that defines individual and group conduct, taste and expectations and helps to ensure regularity in new situations—to develop this link between identity and heritage. As modernization erodes customs and expectations, Brett argues, individuals and communities are forced to re-articulate and recover a sense of the past and to affirm or renegotiate a sense of habitus. It is important at this point, however, to draw a distinction between authorized or received and subversive expressions of identity. The heritage industry critique has stressed the degree to which heritage often propagates received notions of identity, both at a national and class level. Bourdieu's idea of cultural capital is an influential one in the heritage literature, and one that facilitates a sense that received identity dominates the heritage process. Heritage is identified as part of the cultural capital that may be invested in to help identify a person's membership to a particular social group or class, but may also require a particular attainment of cultural literacy to ensure that the meanings and 'messages' believed to be contained within or represented by various heritage forms may be read and understood. However, heritage may also be actively used to reject or contest received notions of identity, and the dominance of the cultural capital thesis tends to obscure the possibility of subversive uses of heritage (Graham 2002: 1004).

As much of the globalization literature proclaims, however erroneously, the end of the nation state, critical attention has begun to focus more assiduously on expressions of sub-national, and particularly 'local', constructions of identity and the role of heritage (Inglehart and Baker 2000; Berking 2003). Greater critical analysis of how specific class identities are articulated and communicated through heritage has emerged from this (Bruno 1999; Dicks 2000;

DeBlasio 2001; Linkon and Russo 2002; Macdonald 1997; Kirshenblatt-Gimblett 1998), how ethnic and cultural identities are defined in multicultural contexts (Hayden 1997; Knecht and Niedermüller 2002; Littler and Naidoo 2004, 2005), how gender and sexuality is identified (Butler 1993; Holcomb 1998; Dubrow 2003) and how regional and local communities, amongst others, articulate a sense of identity (Derry and Malloy 2003; Jones 2005). What emerges from this literature is a much greater sense of conscious agency in the expression of identity than is found in the literature that has focused on the nationalizing uses of heritage. This may in part be an expression of the way in which the AHD focuses and frames research in this area, or a real element associated with these types of identity formations (see chapters in Part III). However, the articulations of identities, which often stand in opposition to nationalizing and other received identities, and to the AHD itself, must require an active sense of construction and expression.

The issue of agency and heritage audiences will be discussed in more detail below; however, it is useful to consider here the active way in which heritage is used in 'identity politics'. As Crouch and Parker (2003: 405) show, heritage is used as a legitimizing discourse in constructing and maintaining a range of 'identities'. Heritage can give temporal and material authority to the construction of identities, especially if the heritage in question has been recognized as 'legitimate' through state-sanctioned heritage management and conservation practices, and/or through the research attentions of experts such as archaeologists, historians, historical architects and so on. The interplay between authorized and subversive identities is quite revealing about the work that the AHD does in helping to de-legitimize and legitimize certain forms of identity. In earlier work, drawing on a critical reading of the Foucaldian thesis of 'governmentality', I documented how certain archaeological conceptualizations of 'heritage' became embedded within heritage or 'cultural resource' legislation and the state-sanctioned heritage management process in both the United States and Australia (Smith 2004). I argued that in governing or regulating the political and cultural legitimacy of Indigenous cultural iden-

tity, policy makers and state bureaucracies used specific archaeological knowledge about the nature and meaning of Indigenous heritage. In this way, those things that archaeologists objectified as 'material culture', and those things that Indigenous people were identified as treating subjectively as 'heritage', became resources of power in struggles over the legitimacy of certain claims to sovereignty, land and other economic and social resources that Indigenous people made in wider political negotiations with the state. They became resources of power because claims to cultural identity often framed the political legitimacy with which policy makers viewed wider claims to sovereignty and economic and social justice. Although this work focused on quite specific and explicit conflicts over identity claims, and was concerned with the power/knowledge consequences of archaeological expertise and the specific use this is put to in state agencies, it offers some insights for the current project of understanding how heritage is used in much more diffused ways.

There are three points I want to draw on from this previous work. The first is that expert knowledge and experts are not simply another interest or stakeholder group in the use of heritage. Expert values and knowledge, such as those embedded in archaeology, history and architecture amongst others, often set the agendas or provide the epistemological frameworks that define debates about the meaning and nature of the past and its heritage. One of the ways this is actively done is through the whole process of cultural heritage management, wherein wider social debates about the meaning of the past, and its utility for the present, are relegated to bite-sized and manageable chunks by reducing them to specific debates over the meaning, 'ownership' and/or management of specific sites, places or artefacts. A second, and related, point is that experts often have a vested interest in maintaining the privileged position of their knowledge claims within both state apparatuses and wider social debates about the meaning of the past. The position of privilege ensures that they are not treated as just another stakeholder but as stewards for, and arbitrators of, debates over the past. In turn, this helps to facilitate access to sites, artefacts, places and other resources that are part of the database of these disciplines. The ability to possess, control and give meaning to the past and/or heritage sites is a re-occurring and reinforcing statement of disciplinary authority and identity.

The third point relates to the governmentality thesis itself and the idea of a heritage 'mentality'. The governmentality thesis argues that expert knowledge in the social sciences can [be] and has been mobilized by bureaucracies to govern the 'conduct of conduct' of populations (Foucault 1991). Intellectual knowledge becomes incorporated into the act of governing populations and social problems by 'rendering the world thinkable, taming its intractable reality by subjecting it to the disciplined analyses of thought' (Rose and Miller 1992: 182; see also Dean and Hindess 1998; Dean 1999). Subsequently, particular social problems become 'amenable to interventions by administrators, politicians, authorities and experts' (Rose 1993: 289). This process is based on liberal modernity and its emphasis on rationality and the universality of knowledge. In this process, expert knowledge about the meaning and nature of the past, and the heritage objects that represent that authorized and universalized past became useful in defining populations. These may be Indigenous populations as I have already documented (2004), or they may be national or a range of sub-national populations. The application of 'rational' expert knowledge renders any social problems or debates over the legitimacy of certain identities it may govern as 'non-political'.

Specifically, identity debates are reduced to debates over 'ownership' issues—'who owns the past', a recursive theme in the heritage literature, is a discursive devise that hides the more politically significant and charged issue of 'control'. Who controls the past, or who controls the meaning and value of heritage, is a much more unambiguous question for examining the identity politics of heritage, and as such it is often made more tractable and open to regulation by reducing it to technical issues of owning and possessing. What the governmentality thesis does here, however, is highlight the degree to which we can conceptualize heritage as a 'mentality', or in Graham's (2002) terms 'a knowledge', for regulating and governing identity claims and making sense of the present.

The AHD constructs not only a particular definition of heritage, but also an authorized mentality, which is deployed to understand and deal with certain social problems centred on claims to identity. Heritage is, in a sense, a gaze or way of seeing. Urry (1990) identifies the institutionalization of the 'tourist's gaze' and the way this gaze constructs reality and normalizes a range of touristic experiences. As Hollinshead (1999: 10-11) points out, the idea of the gaze has an intellectual debt to Foucault, and refers to the ways different professions learn to see and how this may be used to govern others. For Hollinshead, as for Wright, Hewison and others, authorized heritage becomes a form of social control (1997: 186). However, what happens when, as Coleman and Crang (2002b) point out, those gazed upon gaze back?

As I identified in terms of Indigenous identity politics those gazed upon, or subjected to the governance of certain 'mentalities', are not passive, and can and do use heritage in subversive and oppositional ways. Although the Foucaldian idea of governmentality only theorizes the process in which bodies of expertise and knowledge deploy power, it is often those very resources of power that are then utilized to contest received knowledge and, in this case, identity. Heritage thus becomes not only a tool of governance, but also a tool of opposition and subversion. Heritage can therefore be understood as an important political and cultural tool in defining and legitimizing the identity, experiences and social/cultural standing of a range of sub-national groups as well as those of the authorizing discourse. However, it may also be an important resource in challenging received identity and cultural/social values. This latter use of heritage is often undervalued, but is as important and significant as is its use in constructing and validating identity. How this is undervalued is evident in the often strident criticism of the phrase 'identity politics'. This criticism becomes particularly disparaging when minority groups overtly and self-consciously engage in identity politics. However, this criticism is simply revealing of the extent to which the identity politics played out as authorized heritage is so naturalized and taken for granted. It is also indicative of the political power of the politics of recognition. As Nancy Fraser (2000) argues, recognition or misrecognition of identity and cultural values is politically powerful and harmful. In the so-called 'culture wars' in North America and other post-colonial countries, the ability to validate identity is as important as the ability to challenge and overthrow misidentification. This ability is no less significant for other subaltern groups whose self-perception may be at odds with, or sits entirely outside of, received ideas of their heritage and identity.

In summary, the theoretical task then is to construct a sense of the links between heritage and identity that recognizes the various nuanced ways identity is constructed, reconstructed, and contested. As I am suggesting here, the links between heritage and identity can be expressed in any number of ways: actively or passively within the AHD (Chapters 4 and 5), or in active and self-conscious opposition to the AHD (see Chapter 8), or in ways that are less self-conscious and are constructed without reference to or outside of the AHD (see Chapters 6 and 7). In complicating the issue further, no community, group or individual aligns themselves to a single identity. Individuals have layered identities and may belong to any number of 'communities,' further any community may within itself have layers or a range of sub-community identities (Corsane 2005: 9). It is also suggested that these identities need not necessarily be constituted or symbolized by the monumental, and that even the grand narratives of identity such as those of nation and class may be built upon the commonplace or banal. Further, it is argued that these constructions are by their nature political, in that they often involve the deployment of resources of power and prestige.

Heritage, it is argued above, has power as a legitimizing or de-legitimizing discourse. However, there is another dimension to the political power of heritage. This power rests within the naturalization of heritage as material object. Material heritage objects are symbolic not only of identities but also of certain values. Heritage may be embodied as objects of desire and prestige in and of themselves, not because of any inherent value, but in so far as the symbolic ability to control desired, fetishized, and prized objects reinforces not only the identity, but the power of the identity of the nation, group or individual in possession (Weiner 1992; Lahn 1996). The materiality of heritage is itself a brutally physical statement, at least within the confines of the AHD, of the power, universality, objectivity, and cultural attainment of the possessors of that heritage. The physicality of heritage also works to mask the ways in which the heritage gaze constructs, regulates and authorizes a range of identities and values by filtering that gaze onto the inanimate material heritage. In this gaze, the proper subject of which *is* the material, a material objective reality is constructed and subjectivities that exist outside or in opposition to that are rendered invisible or marginal, or simply less 'real.'

NOTE

1. 'Country' refers to the land or landscape that Aboriginal people associate themselves with, and it is the area of land from which is drawn a sense of place; that is, identity, sense of belonging and community, For further discussion of this, see Rose and Clarke (1997) and Head (2000).

REFERENCES

Bagnall, G. (2003) 'Performance and performativity at heritage sites', *Museum and Society*, 1(2): 87–103.

Berking, H. (2003) '"Ethnicity is everywhere": On globalisation and the transformation of cultural identity', *Current Sociology*, 51(3–4): 248–264.

Billig, M. (1995) *Banal Nationalism*, London: Sage.

Brett, D. (1996) *The Construction of Heritage*. Cork: Cork University Press.

Bruno, R. (1999) *Steelworker Alley: How Class Works in Youngstown*, Ithaca, NY: Cornell University Press.

Butler, J. (1993) *Bodies that Matter: On the Discursive Limits of 'Sex'*, New York: Routledge.

Carrier, P. (2005) *Holocaust Monuments and National Memory Cultures in France and Germany Since 1989*, New York: Berghahn Books.

Coleman, S. and Crang, M. (2002b) 'Grounded tourists, travelling theory', in S. Coleman and M. Crang (eds) *Tourism: Between Place and Performance*, New York: Berghahn Books.

Corsane, G. (2005) 'Issues in heritage, museums and galleries: A brief introduction', in G. Corsane (ed.) *Heritage, Museums and Galleries: An Introductory Reader*, London: Routledge.

Crouch, D. and Parker, G. (2003) '"Digging-up" utopia? Space, practice and heritage," *Geoforum*, 34: 395–408.

Dean, M. (1999) *Governmentality: Power and Rule in Modern Society*, London: Sage.

Dean, M. and Hindess, B. (eds) (1998) *Governing Australia*, Cambridge: Cambridge University Press.

DeBlasio, D. (2001) 'The immigrant and the trolley park in Youngstown, Ohio, 1899–1956', *Rethinking History*, 5(1): 75–91.

Derry, L. and Malloy, M. (eds) (2003) *Archaeologists and Local Communities: Partners in Exploring the Past.* Washington, DC: Society for American Archaeology.

Diaz-Andreu, M. and Champion, T. (eds) (1996) *Nationalism and Archaeology in Europe*, London: UCL Press.

Dicks, B. (2000) *Heritage, Place and Community*, Cardiff: University of Wales Press.

Dubrow, G. (2003) 'Restoring women's history through historic preservation: Recent developments in scholarship and public historical practice', Baltimore, MD: Johns Hopkins University Press.

Foucault, M. (1991) 'Governmentality', in G. Burchell, C. Gordon and P. Miller (eds) *The Foucault Effect*, London: Wheatsheaf Harvester.

Fraser, N. (2000) 'Rethinking recognition', *New Left Review* at http://www.newleftreview.net/ NLR23707.shtml (accessed 12 November 2003).

Graham, B. (2002) 'Heritage as knowledge: Capital or culture?' *Urban Studies* 39(5–6): 1003–1017.

Graham, B., Ashworth, G. and Tunbridge, J. (2000) *A Geography of Heritage: Power, Culture and Economy*, London: Arnold.

Hayden, D. (1997) *The Power of Place*, Cambridge, MA: MIT Press.

Head, L. (2000) *Second Nature: The History and Implications of Australia as Aboriginal Landscape*, New York: Syracuse University Press.

Holcomb, B. (1998) 'Gender and heritage interpretation', in D. Uzzell and R. Ballantyne (eds) *Contemporary Issues in Heritage and Environmental Interpretation*, London: Stationery Office.

Hollinshead, K. (1997) 'Heritage tourism under post-modernity: Truth and the past', in C. Ryan (ed.) *The Tourist Experience: A New Introduction*, London: Cassell.

——— (1999) 'Surveillance of the world of tourism: Foucault and the eye-of-power', *Tourism Management*, 20: 7–23.

Inglehart, R. and Baker, W. (2000) 'Modernization, cultural change, and persistence of traditional values', *American Sociological Review*, 65: 19–51.

Jones, S. (2005) 'Making place, resisting displacement: Conflicting national and local identities in Scotland', in J. Littler and R. Naidoo (eds) *The Politics of Heritage: The Legacies of 'Race'*, London: Routledge.

Kirshenblatt-Gimblett, B. (1998) *Destination Culture: Tourism, Museums and Heritage*, Berkeley, CA: University of California Press.

Knecht, M. and Niedermüller, P. (2002) 'The politics of cultural heritage: An urban approach', *Ethnologia Europea*, 32(2) 89–104.

Lahn, J. (1996) 'Dressing up the dead: Archaeology, the Kow Swamp remains and some related problems with heritage management', in L. Smith and A. Clarke (eds) *Issues in Archaeological Management*, St Lucia: Tempus Publications, University of Queensland.

Linkon, S.L. and Russo, J. (2002) *Steeltown USA: Work and Memory in Youngstown*, Lawrence, KS: University Press of Kansas.

Littler, J. and Naidoo, R. (2004) 'White past, multicultural present: Heritage and national stories', in H. Brocklehurst and R. Phillips (eds) *History, Nationhood and the Question of Britain*, Basingstoke: Palgrave Macmillan.

—— (eds) (2005) *The Politics of Heritage: The Legacies of 'Race'*, London: Routledge.

Lowenthal, D. (1985) *The Past is a Foreign Country*, Cambridge: Cambridge University Press.

Macdonald, S. (1997) 'A people's story? Heritage, identity and authenticity', in C. Rojek and J. Urry (eds) *Touring Cultures: Transformations of Travel and Theory*, London: Routledge.

McLean, F. (2006) 'Introduction: Heritage and identity', *International Journal of Heritage Studies*, 12(1): 3–7.

Meskell, L. (2002) 'The intersections of identity and politics in archaeology', *Annual Review of Anthropology*, 31: 279–301.

—— (2003) 'Pharaonic legacies: Postcolonialism, heritage and hyperreality', in S. Kane (ed.) *The Politics of Archaeology and Identity in a Global Context*, Boston, MA: Archaeological Institute of America.

Rose, D.B. and Clarke, A. (eds) (1997) *Tracking Knowledge in North Australian Landscapes*, Darwin: North Australia Research Unit.

Rose, N. (1993) 'Government, authority and expertise in advanced liberalism', *Economy and Society*, 22(3): 283–299.

Rose, N. and Miller, P. (1992) 'Political power beyond the State: Problematics of government', *British Journal of Sociology*, 43: 173–205.

Samuel, R. (1994) *Theatres of Memory. Volume 1: Past and Present in Contemporary Culture*, London: Verso.

Smith, L. (2004) *Archaeological Theory and the Politics of Cultural Heritage*, London: Routledge.

Smith, L., Morgan, A. and van der Meer, A. (2003a) 'Community-driven research in cultural heritage management: The Waanyi Women's History Project', *International Journal of Heritage Studies*, 9(2): 65–80.

—— (2003b) 'The Waanyi Women's Project: A community partnership project, Queensland, Australia', in L. Derry and M. Malloy (eds) *Archaeologists and Local Communities: Partners in Exploring the Past*, Washington, DC: Society for American Archaeology.

Urry, J. (1990) *The Tourist Gaze*, London: Sage.

—— (1996) 'How societies remember the past', in S. Macdonald and G. Fyfe (eds) *Theorising Museums*, Oxford: Blackwell.

Weiner, A.L. (1992) *Inalienable Possessions: The Paradox of Keeping-While-Giving*, Berkeley, CA: University of California Press.

chapter 3

PRESERVATION IN CONTEXT

LIBRARIES, ARCHIVES, MUSEUMS, AND THE BUILT ENVIRONMENT

ULTURAL HERITAGE RESIDES IN MANY types of settings; this chapter provides an overview of its care in libraries, archives, museums, and the built environment—which is commonly referred to as "historic preservation." While preservation is essential to any collecting institution, the way it has been practiced varies not only from place to place but from profession to profession. The literature in each field reflects overlapping yet distinct professional practices and philosophies. First, we will consider writings with a broad approach to cultural heritage or that compare one kind of institution to another. The text then presents literature about libraries, archives, and museums, followed by a look at historic preservation. Although these institutions may themselves be housed in historic buildings—many of which are in need of preservation—historic preservation as a field includes practices and concerns which are distinct from library, archive, or museum preservation issues and practices.

David Carr describes the many roles that museums and libraries play in a civil society in his "In the Contexts of the Possible: Libraries and Museums as Incendiary Cultural Institutions." Libraries and museums facilitate learning, creativity, and entertainment, but they also rescue, conserve, and sustain "the treasures of culture and identity" across generations. Preservation assures that the human record will be available to the future. In many ways, Carr is a contemporary stand-in for John Cotton Dana, whose piece "Why This Series is Begun: The Old Museum and the New," is also contained in this chapter.

In "To Represent Us Truly: The Job and Context of Preserving the Cultural Record," **Stanley Chodorow** addresses the issue of defining *culture* as the prelude to his discussion of what it means to preserve the cultural record. To him it "has become a weapon of mass distinction of the social sort" and "definition of the word must sail above social and political value judgments and find a meaning that is broader than one that only denotes the arts or the particular mores of a people." In other words, the cultural record is the total of everything that we have created and we must be deliberate about what we can preserve. This deliberateness is particularly important since not everything can be preserved.

A 1993 article by **Michèle V. Cloonan**, "The Preservation of Knowledge," considers the shift in focus in conservation and preservation from treating individual objects to developing strategies for preserving digital collections. Yet all categories of materials—ephemeral as well as permanent—must be preserved. In the twenty years since this piece was published, the preservation field has evolved to traverse the increasingly complex landscape for information creation and dissemination. New partnerships and structures must continue to inform the field.

Archivists should select the information that will create for the future "a representative record of human experience in our time," observed **F. Gerald Ham** in his 1974 SAA presidential address, "The Archival Edge." But at the time those words were written, there was little evidence to support any claims of representational selection for preservation by archivists. Instead, according to Ham, the custodial model of archives prevailed. Ham advocated a more activist approach to preservation. For example, archivists could conduct oral histories, and sponsor other activities to actively preserve the archival record, particularly of contemporary social and political movements. Collaborations with various stakeholder groups would assure a more deliberative approach to preservation. Ham himself was an activist archivist,

and some of his suggestions have gained currency since this piece was published.

Today there is a tendency to draw comparisons between libraries and museums. Both institutions collect cultural heritage materials and make them available to the public through exhibitions and other educational programming, or through lending. Both have as primary goals to preserve the human record. But G. Thomas Tanselle, in his "Libraries, Museums and Reading," puts a different spin on the comparisons by calling into question the ways in which we contrast the activities of each type of institution.[1] For example, the notion that libraries are for scholarly pursuits and museums are for entertainment, or that museums contain objects while libraries house information. Museums are centers of study just as libraries are and libraries contain objects whose physical properties make them worthy objects of study. The role of artifacts to the study of the past is critical and Tanselle entreats us to approach books as museum objects so that "we most fully and productively read them" (p. 5).

Tanselle believes that there is a fundamental difference between how librarians and museum curators approach preservation: librarians may reformat objects, comfortable in preserving the "content" and not necessarily focused on the physical objects—except in special collections. Museum curators are more likely to understand the full significance of the objects that are under their care. Tanselle insists that "all books should be regarded as rare books" (p. 13) and takes issue with **Paul Banks** who in his own article, "A Library Is Not a Museum," takes the view that not all books have aesthetic or artifactual value. Tanselle has been the foremost champion of the book as artifact and it is incumbent upon preservationists to understand the crux of his arguments in order to be thoughtful stewards of collections.

The authors whose works appear in this opening section offer general insights into preservation which are picked up in more detail in the readings in the rest of the chapter. Ham and Chodorow emphasize the importance of collaboration and interdisciplinarity in the cultural heritage fields. Cloonan discusses how the changing nature of information has influenced approaches to preservation. Carr's piece examines libraries and museums as social institutions. These pieces provide a backdrop to the institution-specific pieces that follow.

Libraries and Archives

Historically, the roles of the library were to collect, organize, and preserve collections and to make them available to users. Preservation was implicit rather than explicit: in early libraries, collecting and organizing materials *were* acts of preservation (See Naudé, in chapter 1). As university libraries were established in the Middle Ages, and public libraries were started in the nineteenth century, the number and types of library users expanded. Libraries ran out of space for their collections, and items were often placed in inappropriate storage areas such as basements and attics. By the late nineteenth century, articles were regularly written in the American and British library press about damage to collections caused by wear and tear, pollution, and poor storage facilities. In an 1876 report issued by the US Bureau of Education, preservation was used as the term to describe the actions that could be taken to assure the longevity of materials—such actions as binding, proper shelving, and the overall care of collections.[2] According to Barbra Buckner Higginbotham, "Melvil Dewey appears to have been the first administrator to use the term *preservation* as an actual heading in a library annual report. In 1891, as director of the New York State Library, he introduced a section entitled 'Preservation,' with the subsections 'Binding,' 'Shelving,' and 'Building.'"[3]

Conservation facilities, research laboratories, and formal conservation and preservation graduate programs are modern developments which evolved in the twentieth century. Today, preservation practices are rooted in the collecting as well as the service aspects of the profession as is reflected in the American Library Association policy on preservation which

- is based on its goal of ensuring that every person has access to information at the time needed and in a useable format. ALA affirms that the preservation of library resources protects the public's right to the free flow of information as embodied in the First Amendment to the Constitution and the Library Bill of Rights.
- The Association supports the preservation of information published in all media and formats. The Association affirms that the preservation of information resources is central to libraries and librarianship.
- Librarians must be committed to preserving their collections through appropriate and non-damaging storage, remedial treatment of damaged and fragile items, preservation of materials in their original format when possible, replacement or reformatting of deteriorated materials, appropriate security measures, and life-cycle management of digital publications to assure their usefulness for future generations. Preservation issues should be addressed while planning for new construction or the renovation of existing buildings.
- Librarians who create, maintain, and share bibliographic records and other metadata associated with physical and digital objects in their collections enhance security, access, and preservation and facilitate collaborative efforts to protect the Nation's cultural heritage.
- Librarians must educate the public about the choices and the financial commitments necessary to preserve our society's cultural and social records (ALA, Preamble, document revised, 2001; www.ala.org/ala/mgrps/divs/alcts/resources/preserv/01alapres policy.cfm; accessed 3/8/12).

From an American library perspective, preservation is tied to the access of information and a user's constitutional right to that access.[4] Before the digital information explosion, preservation consisted of the actions taken to maintain items after they were created. As Jan Merrill-Oldham points out, today librarians "must cultivate a stronger and more focused message regarding the role of preservation programs in a modern information environment. We are well equipped to do so. Over the course of the past thirty years, we have learned and confirmed much about the physical nature and aging characteristics of library materials, what strategies are most effective for extending their useful lives, and how to apply these in cost-effective ways" (Merrill-Oldham, p. 91).

The library readings in this chapter include a historical overview (**Darling** and **Ogden**) and descriptions of preservation programs (**Harvey** and **Merrill-Oldham**). Writings about collection development and management appear in chapter 4.

To archivists, preservation grows out of the creation of records. Thus preservation activities might take place as soon as an item is created. This is described in the Society of American Archivists *Core Values of Archivists*:

> **Preservation:** Archivists preserve a wide variety of primary sources for the benefit of future generations. Preserving materials is a means to this end *not an end in itself* [emphasis added]. Within prescribed law and best practice standards, archivists may determine that the original documents themselves must be preserved, while at other times copying the information they contain to alternate media may be sufficient. Archivists thus preserve materials for the benefit of the future more than for the concerns of the past (Approved by SAA council, May 2011; www2.archivists.org/statements/saa-core-values -statement-and-code-of-ethics#core_values; accessed 3/8/12).

The aim of archival preservation, then, is not so much immediate access; it focuses more on preserving and managing the cultural record in its many formats—and contexts. Archivists preserve primary sources created by organizations, communities, and individuals by taking custody of them. Library collections may include decontextualized or stand-alone information, while museums contain discrete objects. For all of these different types of collections, the preservation strategies must vary.

The preservation of records and archives is similar to and distinct from the preservation of library materials and museum objects. Libraries, with the exception of special collections, generally collect items that exist in multiple copies, while archives collect unique records. Modern archives administration began during the French Revolution with the establishment of the Archives Nationales in 1789—which was created to maintain documents and records without alteration. The significance of this development was that "for the first time an independent national system of archives administration was set up, for whose preservation and maintenance the state was responsible and to which there was public access."[5]

Preserving archives differs from preserving other kinds of information objects in another way: although records may exist singly (a letter, a memo) they are also part of a group that was created or received by an individual, family, or organization. To assure the integrity of records, one must maintain the order in which they were created. If a record is removed from its *fonds*, it may lose its context and therefore it may lose its meaning. Further, the principle of provenance dictates that "records of the same provenance should not be mixed with those of a different provenance, and the archivist should maintain the original order in which the records were created and kept" (Gilliland). Preservation must adhere to the principle of provenance while also respecting models such as the records continuum and life-cycle approaches. An individual record never truly "stands alone" as does a book or a painting.

Archival collections are organic and organized according to principles of description, which include "the process of creating a finding aid or other access tools that allow individuals to browse a surrogate of the collection to facilitate access and that improve security by creating a record of the collection and by minimizing the amount of handling of the original materials."[6] Librarians view preservation as the care of collections of discrete objects, with the exception of serials. Although there are strategies for preserving whole collections—such as building maintenance, security procedures, and environmental controls—

there is also an emphasis on caring for the individual items within the collection through library binding, conservation, and reformatting.

An archive is primarily a collection of collections of records rather than a collection of discrete items. Preservation strategies include the same ones used to stabilize library collections, such as environmental controls. Archivists use a number of strategies to care for individual collections, including re-housing items into acid-free containers and copying deteriorating items. However, these actions must always be carried out in such a way as to respect provenance and order when possible and practicable.

The archives readings consider how archives are linked to memory and culture (**Foote**); retention, preservation, and permanence (**Bearman** and **O'Toole**); archival administration and preservation (throughout); and archives in a digital environment (**Cox** and **Gilliland**).

Museums

For the most part, museums contain collections of unique items. Museums interpret their collections to the public through exhibitions. The uniqueness of objects as well as how they can be best presented in exhibitions drive preservation decision making. For example, the types of decisions that are made in conserving a unique vase or painting are different from decisions that might be made about a circulating book. Museums must also make objects exhibition-presentable, and the objects must be able to withstand the physical rigors of being exhibited. While archives and libraries have exhibits, these exhibits are not generally organized on the same scale as museum exhibitions. There is less emphasis in library and archives preservation programs on display and education.

The American Alliance of Museums (until recently, the American Association of Museums) *Code of Ethics for Museums* makes the role of preservation clear:

Museums make their unique contribution to the public by collecting, preserving and interpreting the things of this world. Historically, they have owned and used natural objects, living and nonliving, and all manner of human artifacts to advance knowledge and nourish the human spirit. Today, the range of their special interests reflects the scope of human vision. Their missions include collecting and preserving, as well as exhibiting and educating with materials not only owned but also borrowed and fabricated for these ends (Adopted by the Board of Directors, 1993;http://www.aam.org/museum resources/ethics/coe.cfm; accessed 3/8/12).

In museums, preservation responsibilities tend to be more distributed than they are in a library or archive where almost all preservation-related activities take place in a single department. For example, preservation responsibilities may reside with collections managers, registrars, exhibition designers, conservators, curators, photographers, building operators, and other museum personnel whose role it is to safeguard collections.

With digital collections, preservation concerns are the same no matter the institutional setting: the rapid obsolescence of information technology means that digital objects will survive only if strategies are developed to maintain them. Digitization of information and objects, combined with the ever-increasing capacity of digital information storage and the rise of social networking, are causing the traditional models of libraries, archives, and museums to expand. People want to access library, archival, and museum collections from anywhere at any time. Some scholars even question whether digital strategies are really forms of preservation. Digital practices increase access, but whether they add to the longevity of materials is being questioned.

The lack of fixity of digital objects means that the paradigm of benign neglect is no longer acceptable for library materials, archival records, or museum objects.[7] Digital preservation is discussed at length in chapter 4, "Collections: Development and Management," and chapter 7 "Frameworks for Digital Preservation".

Readings from the museum literature cover conservation functions and the longevity of art (**Alexander** and **Alexander**); preservation and the role of museums (**Goode, Cuno, Dana**); and the transformation of the museum and its implications for preservation (**Cuno**).

Historic Preservation and Architectural Conservation[8,9]

William Murtagh provides a detailed description of the language of preservation.[10] Three terms are basic to the field: "preservation," "restoration," and "reconstruction." Preservation is "the act or process of applying measures to sustain the existing form, integrity and material of a building or structure, and the existing form and vegetative cover of a site." Restoration is "the act or process of accurately recovering the form and details of a property and its setting as it appeared at a particular period of time by means of the removal of later work or by the replacement of missing earlier work." Reconstruction is defined as the "act or process of reproducing by new construction the exact form and detail of a vanished building, structure, or object, or a part thereof, as it appeared at a specific period of time."[11]

Murtagh further describes how preservation also has a generic meaning, "the historic preservation movement."[12] The movement has included professionals and amateurs, from the earliest historic preservation to the present. This makes historic preservation distinct from archival or library preservation, and more allied with the environmental conservation movement. For example, in both movements there may be issues relating to property values or business interests; however, while conservation of the environment may be viewed as a societal good, proponents of historic preservation may also have personal or aesthetic reasons for wanting to preserve a structure or structures. In library, archival, and museum preservation, there are no widespread movements; for the most part it is the professionals who have advocated for their fields. This is not to say that librarians, archivists, and museum curators do not engage with their publics about the importance of preservation, but activities tend to be driven by the professionals

rather than by citizens. There is no equivalent figure in archives and libraries to Ann Pamela Cunningham, the nineteenth-century American who rallied support and funding to preserve Mount Vernon, and any of the other people who have served as advocates for the historic preservation cause more recently.

Historic preservation in the United States, referred to as "conservation of historic buildings" in the UK, has benefited from the establishment of organizations, agencies, and legislation to address issues of property stewardship. Passage of the Antiquities Act of 1906, creation of the National Park Service (NPS), a federal agency, in 1916, and the Historic Sites Act of 1935, as well as the founding of the National Trust for Historic Preservation in 1949, assured that some sites and monuments would be preserved. However, far more wide-reaching was the National Historic Preservation Act of 1966, which included a system for evaluating sites. The National Register of Historic Places, also part of the legislation, assured identification and documentation of sites, buildings, districts, and structures of significance. The law shepherded the Department of the Interior and the Department of Housing and Urban Development towards responsible planning. Further, the law enabled local jurisdictions to secure financial assistance from the government. Finally, some tax incentives were created for rehabilitating buildings. Historic preservation efforts consist of networks of citizens, businesses, attorneys, politicians, the government, scholars, and professionals. Architects, archaeologists, historians, engineers, and other professionals make up the network of local and national preservation initiatives.

Although the brief overview above focuses on historic preservation in the United States, a wider variety of perspectives on historic preservation is included in the readings. Four pieces consider the theory and philosophy of preservation and restoration (**Brandi, Fitch, Jokilehto,** and **Philippot**).

Taken together, the readings in this chapter provide examples of overlapping and distinct issues that preservation professionals in a variety of settings face. In the end, however, the aim is the same: to assure that future generations will be able to benefit from the cultural heritage of the past.

NOTES

1. See G. Thomas Tanselle, "Libraries, Museums, and Reading," in *Literature and Artifacts* (Charlottesville, VA: The Bibliographic Society of the University of Virginia, 1998): 3–23. Because of the length of this article, it was not possible to use this essay in the present volume.

2. *Public Libraries in the United States of America: Their History, Condition, and Management: Special Report* (Washington, D.C.: U.S. Bureau of Education, 1876), 673–78.

3. Barbra Buckner Higginbotham, *Our Past Preserved: A History of American Library Preservation, 1876–1910* (Boston, MA: G. K. Hall, 1990), 9.

4. "Each House shall keep a Journal of its Proceedings, and from time to time publish the same, excepting such Parts as may in their Judgment require Secrecy; and the Yeas and Nays of the Members of either House on any question shall, at the Desire of one fifth of those Present, be entered on the Journal" (U.S. Constitution, art. 1, sect. 5). Thus, explicit in our Constitution is that a representative democracy keep records of the work of its elected officials. Implicit is that such records must be preserved.

5. *Encyclopedia Britannica*, 15th ed., "Libraries," v. 22 (2005): 956.

6. Richard Pearce-Moses, *A Glossary of Archival and Records Terminology*. Chicago: Society of American Archivists, 2005; see http://www.archivists.org/glossary/index.asp; accessed February 12, 2012.

7. Ross Harvey discusses the preservation paradigm shift from paper-based materials to digital objects in his *Preserving Digital Materials*, 2nd ed. (Berlin and Boston: De Gruyter Saur, 2012), pp. 8–13.

8. According to John H. Stubbs, in his *Time Honored: A Global View of Architectural Conservation* (New York: John Wiley, 2009), "historic preservation" is the term generally used in the United States, and "architectural conservation" is preferred in the United Kingdom. He discusses terminology at length in chapter 2, "What is Architectural Conservation?" pp. 21–31.

9. Michael C. Henry further explained that in North America, historic preservation refers to the *built* environment while architectural conservation refers to the building materials level. (E-mail to Michèle V. Cloonan, August 22, 2011, in response to her inquiry about the terms.)

10. William J. Murtagh, *Keeping Time: The History and Theory of Preservation In America*, 3rd ed. (New York: John Wiley, 2006), p. 5. No excerpt from this work is included in this volume.

11. Murtagh, p. 5.

12. Murtagh, p. 4.

PAUL N. BANKS

"A Library Is Not a Museum"

In Training in Conservation: A Symposium on the Occasion of the Dedication of the Stephen Chan House, *Institute of Fine Arts, New York University, edited by Norbert S. Baer (New York: Institute of Fine Arts, 1989), pp. 57–65.*

"A LIBRARY IS Not a Museum" is a nicely provocative title offered—on a "negative-option" basis, like book clubs—by Norbert Baer. I wonder if some of the rest of you who are speaking today were so lucky? In any case, I feel honored to have been included in such distinguished company, to talk about a new aspect—training in library and archives conservation—of a larger endeavor—conservation training in general, which has recently reached its majority as an academic discipline. This seems an appropriate moment to step back to take a look.

There are at least as many different kinds of libraries as there are museums, and it should be understood that I am talking today about the research library: the type of library (to use one possible definition) that attempts to build collections in depth on one or many subjects, for present and future scholarly use. By this definition, materials are collected for long-term (if not precisely predictable) goals, and the need for preserving the materials is clearly entailed.

The first great library that seems to have served other than a primarily liturgical or archival purpose—in other words, probably the first research library—was the original or "mother" Alexandrian, and it was, after all, part of the *mouseion*, the precursor of the museum.

Ian Willison of the British Library (still physically if no longer administratively part of the British *Museum*!) states:

" ... it seems clear that success of the [Alexandrian] library was due to the four techniques ... that have since become fundamental for research library administration: catholic acquisition; rationalization of the format, and even the content of books; systematic author and subject cataloging ... ; and a continuing conservation program, largely in the form of recopying."

But we are certainly at the beginning of a revolution—and I don't believe that revolution is too strong a word—in the ways of handling current, useful information that is starting to influence profoundly the ways that all four of the basic functions of research librarianship are carried out. Not only are business and governmental records handled digitally, but laboratory research, work in progress, current scholarship, and the like, will be handled in digital form, with the attendant problems of large masses of information often at best only partially digested. The questions of what of this type of material is worth capturing for posterity, who is to have responsibility for deciding, and in general, how can it all be managed, are formidable, and fortunately beyond the scope of this paper. (Parenthetically, despite my comments on the "information revolution," I am not among those who believe in the imminent demise of the book; for one thing, publishing statistics belie such predictions. But the amount of information handled digitally will almost certainly continue to grow at an ever-accelerating rate.)

The result of this impending revolution in the way at least current information is handled is that the research library is increasingly becoming on the one hand an automated information center, and on the other a repository of retrospective knowledge. The library as information center tends to deal with current information in the sciences, technology, medicine and law, while the retrospective collections consist largely of books, journals, manuscripts, and the like, predominantly in the humanistic disciplines, that are deteriorating at a seemingly accelerating rate.

Needless to say, this schema of the bifurcation in research librarianship, with its echoes of C.P. Snow's two cultures, is oversimplified, but it is real and profound as exemplified by the identity crisis that library schools are undergoing as they add "information science" to their names and their curricula.

The advance into automation—including the beginnings of full-text data bases in addition to operational and bibliographical ones—is clearly essential to the continuing viability of research libraries. However, the costs are large, and the initial primary beneficiaries tend to be such areas as the health and "hard" sciences and law, which have what one might call a higher standard of living than the humanistic disciplines. (Automation certainly has important potential benefits for the humanistic disciplines also, and its benefits will continue to grow.)

While it may not be possible to document instances of conscious decisions to favor automation over preservation of retrospective collections, or the sciences over the humanities, the pressures to automate, and consequent competition for resources, seem inexorable.

This issue of competition for resources is in part a reflection of a more basic difference between research libraries and museums: While I believe that it is generally felt that museums must continue to acquire, libraries, which are generally dependencies of other organizations, must ordinarily continue to collect in areas that are of interest to their parent organizations and those interests are often very broad. A university library, for example, has no choice but to collect current materials in the fields in which the university has programs. Thus, because of acquisition commitments, research libraries usually have little flexibility in the way that their funds are spent.

Meanwhile the retrospective collections, that in large measure define the research library, present conservation problems that seem overwhelming because of their size and complexity.

The collections of the members of the Association of Research Libraries, which includes nearly all of the major research libraries in the U.S. and Canada, contain upwards of 300,000,000 volumes and 200,000,000 microforms. Statistics for manuscripts are even more slippery than those for books, but for what it is worth, the Library of Congress alone reports 34,627,783 pieces of manuscripts, as well as nearly 4 million maps, nearly 9 million photographs, and so on. The National Archives is estimated to have some three billion pieces.

By comparison, *The New York Times* announced recently that the Smithsonian, the world's largest museum complex, has something like 20,000,000 items, not counting "snails and bugs," to use the *Times*'s phrase, and they add items at the rate of about a million a year.

When these figures on collection size are multiplied by the results of some recent surveys suggesting that 25% or more of the paper in the non-rare books in these collections is so brittle that the books may not withstand more than one or two more uses before pages begin to break out (if they are not already doing so), we begin to get a sense of the dimensions of what has been called, with a resolutely stiff upper lip, "the preservation challenge." The dimensions of the problems are so enormous that they almost earn the misnomer "enormity" that is so often applied to them. It may be worth underlining, considering the title of my paper, that normally books cannot be isolated from users in the way that most museum objects can; they must have enough physical ruggedness to withstand repeated use that is moreover under little or no surveillance.

These figures deal primarily with non-rare books in general collections. A comparably alarming figure concerning the needs of special collections materials has been given by Peter Waters: 11,500 person-years are needed to treat the deteriorating items in the rare book collections of the Library of Congress.

One of the greatest complicating factors in library preservation is the diversity of the collections, which include materials ranging from those solely of interest for their overt information to those of great artifactual value. While museums certainly have objects of varying value, I think that once an object has found its way into the museum, it is assumed to have some artifactual or esthetic value. Lest you boggle at this assertion from an outsider, I would ask whether museums regularly discard parts of their collections outright, and make copies of others on a large scale, discarding the original objects after making the copies. Both of these operations—weeding and preservation microfilming of "brittle books"—are normal operating procedures in the research library world.

A further complication is that a large percentage of retrospective materials—perhaps a majority—do not fall neatly into either the artifactual category or the category in which the physical embodiment of the information is irrelevant. When does an author or event become important enough that the associated books assume artifactual value? Or old enough? When does the always diminishing number of, say, ordinary eighteenth-century trade bookbindings make them eligible as an endangered species?

Most of what I have said thus far tends to support the thesis implied in my title. But to the extent that research libraries contain materials of artifactual value—and it can be safely assumed that all do contain such materials—they take on aspects of a museum.

This museum aspect of libraries is certainly no new thing. Most research libraries have special collections departments (once called rare book rooms), and there are a few unabashedly rare book libraries, such as the Pierpont Morgan or the Houghton at Harvard. Special collections departments have many traits in common with museums—their key personnel may be called curators rather than librarians; they may have the primary responsibility within the library for exhibitions; use is more closely controlled than in general collections, and so on. Their collections get a higher level of care than general ones, or at least books are not apt to be threatened with heavy buckram library bindings. However, unlike museums they usually do not have conservators as yet.

As more current information is handled electronically, as existing collections, especially in the humanities, become older, and as the value of cultural property in general increases, the retrospective parts of research collections are becoming more museum-like. Many of the now rare books in Harvard's or Columbia's or Yale's libraries were, after all, the current reference books of the 17th or 18th centuries when they were acquired.

Another aspect, then, of the "preservation challenge" is the question of how to deal with those general collections, especially in the humanistic disciplines, that contain books of unrecognized, potential, or partial artifactual value. At present, large research libraries often can only deal with general collections of books as if they were current and expendable.

To summarize, then, some salient characteristics of the library "preservation challenge": The amount of material to be preserved is enormous; the materials have a whole spectrum of artifactual values, ranging from none to almost total; books must have enough strength to be extensively and often carelessly handled by users; and flexibility in allocation of resources is severely limited by the necessity to acquire extensively in an ever-expanding universe of information.

It is increasingly understood that the preservation of artifactual materials requires highly skilled and educated treatment conservators, and that specialized administrators are needed to manage broad conservation programs. What is less understood is that the needed preservation effort is so large that all categories of materials require mass preservation strategies that are outside the scope both of existing conservation education and libraries' organization charts. The urgency of what one might call conservation engineering is in buying time until greater resources—fiscal, human, and technological—are available for the application of "conventional" solutions or until better solutions are available. Time must be bought both for deteriorating non-artifactual materials, because there is little hope for filming them or otherwise converting their overt information to another format in time with present methods, and for artifactual materials, as Peter Waters' astronomical figure for treatment of the rare materials just in the Library of Congress tells us.

The type of position that is needed would seem logically to be called the *collections conservator*, whose charge and training would be in broad systems methods, in technical and engineering approaches to collections care, including housing, storage, environment, and in mass treatment. I might expand a little on what I mean by an engineering approach or by the collections conservator as quasi-engineer.

Part of this idea of an "engineering approach" deals with perfectly conventional aspects of engineering, especially building design, climate control, exhibition cases, and the like. I'm not trying to suggest that the collections conservator should be trained to actually design such systems; that is certainly the province of mechanical engineers. But it is crucial that there are people who first of all take the part of the collections and the institution, and who are able to set convincing and realistic specifications for architects, mechanical engineers, and those who operate buildings and systems once they are built. This entails enough knowledge of engineering to be able to communicate.

The other engineering approach that I have in mind is the need for systems methods for a multiplicity of library and archives conservation problems. This relates to the developmental research that Robert Feller was talking about this morning. Sometimes the issues are almost ludicrously prosaic: designing storage containers that can be manufactured inexpensively in large quantities and that really enhance the preservation of different kinds of objects.

One of the most urgent needs in library conservation is the development of systems of methods and materials that can be used for routine mending or binding of books that actually do help to preserve them, as many current ones do not, and that are as respecting as possible of potential artifactual values.

The need for conservators as quasi-engineers seems to me to be quite clear. What is considerably less clear, however, is how to fulfill that need. There are several issues: the aptitudes that attract people to conservation are not always accompanied with aptitude for the broader and more quantitative types of conservation; the need for any kind of full-time conservation specialist is only beginning to be recognized in libraries, and where there is only one conservation person that person is usually trained in librarianship rather than conservation; and the prevailing image of the conservator is of someone who treats individual rare books. The most important question, perhaps, is what means libraries and archives could devise to support such specialists.

The program for library and archives conservators offered jointly by the School of Library Service, Columbia University and the Conservation Center, Institute of Fine Arts, New York University stresses the importance of mass approaches including such fundamental aspects as building planning and climate control, and to give some rudimentary understanding of these subjects within the always frustrating limitations of the time available. However, the program is modeled largely on the pre-existing museum conservation programs, and the students who are attracted to it seem to lean toward treatment conservation rather than collections conservation.

A large task that remains is to sell the library and archives world on the need for collections conservators or conservation engineers, and at the same time to learn how best to train them.

You may be aware that similar ideas have been offered in the museum context. (Parenthetically, while it appears to me that the substance of Nathan Stolow's plea for the sort of "quasi-engineer" for museums is very much to the point, I think that his proposed terminology, "exhibition conservator" for the person involved with overall collections care, and "collections conservator" for the person who treats individual objects, is unfortunate.) Despite my catalogue of differences between libraries and museums, many aspects of broad collections care are virtually identical in the two types of institutions, and just as the new library and archives conservation training program is a cooperative undertaking between a library school and a museum conservation program, perhaps there are further opportunities that could be to our mutual advantage.

I might also mention the preservation administrator program at the School of Library Service. This might be said schematically to consist of a one-year master's degree in library science and a one-year advanced certificate concentrated in preservation courses. It occurs to me that the idea of specialized training for preservation administrators may be of interest in the museum field as well.

DAVID W. CARR

"In the Contexts of the Possible: Libraries and Museums as Incendiary Cultural Institutions"

RBM: A Journal of Rare Books, Manuscripts, and Cultural Heritage *1.2 (September 2000): 117–34.*

GREAT CULTURAL INSTITUTIONS—incendiary cultural institutions—feed flames that illuminate the human capacity to imagine the possible. When we consider our institutions as dramatic stages or provocative forums—places where human beings present themselves to each other, act to change their cognitive lives, perform the passions of their searches, frame their hopeful inquiries, tentatively assert their aspirations—we begin to understand that we preside over a place where something essential and revolutionary goes on. But what situations for learning could live up to the metaphor of flame and fire? What would such an institution be? How might an incendiary cultural institution think of itself?

Whenever we speak about libraries and museums, and whenever we consider the power of institutions to address and respect the integrity of human intellect and human becoming, the incendiary minds and watchful eyes of Thomas Jefferson and James Madison are in the room. So are the minds and eyes of our communities and cultures, those who live and grow strong in our civil societies, our families and schools, all contemplating the challenges of their lives and hoping to be addressed and assisted in the course of their own individual human becoming.

When people come together as learners, they have an opportunity to understand that cultural institutions—libraries, museums, historical societies, botanical gardens, archives, zoos, parks—are grounded in the idea that a culture requires places, forums, working laboratories for cognitive change, where voices can be heard expressing hopes and aspirations in the contexts of the possible. When we capture and express such possibilities, we come to own a view of the future. In such places, the truly open sources of our society, there is also equality in those possibilities of ownership, ensuring that knowledge is not privi-

leged to any but those who can learn from the records and objects at hand and from other people in mutual engagement with a common world.

In this coming together we find several challenges: *overcoming the isolations of experience*, our separations and insularities, the anxieties and distances among us; creating *the language of observation*, exploration and common exchange; *building accord on what we want to have happen*, deciding what we want our institutions to do and be; and *finding the courage* to consider the mutual unknown. This is exactly why cultural institutions exist: to manage our cognitive challenges by creating good processes and educative structures, to recognize and celebrate good questions when they appear, and to engage with the personal narratives of human beings as they learn.

And yet, the "personal" has become increasingly elusive, as our connections and transactions become both increasingly virtual and increasingly transient. As we negotiate our way to the learning structures we need, we may feel that something of our own is missing or possibly lost in the tensions that define our lives—tensions between our families and our work, feeling safe and feeling fearful, continuity and change. These are all tensions of knowledge, discrepancies between what we know and what we do not yet know, the hopes of having enough information to manage a complex life with extraordinary unknowns in it.

To these tensions, we might add the observation that the values that define our lives, inform our educational systems, and are transmitted to our children may not be coming from us but, instead, from somewhere outside us. Where, then, do they begin, and how do they reach us and shape our environments? These are times when the unresolvable tacit questions we are asked to live with may be: What does it mean to be a human being? What are the values of a person and of personal acts? What does it mean to be a human being among other human beings?

We who are advocates for cultural institutions as sources of structure, continuity, and transformation may be sensitive to less identifiable, even subtler, erosions in public altruism. In our own lives we may notice fewer opportunities for reflection and self-renewal, more difficult connections to others, an inability to find a common voice. In our work we may experience less cooperation and outreach, less mutual respect, less self-respect. These erosions are especially important, of course, because they affect the grounding impulses for teaching, learning, self-exploration, and confident engagement with one's life. To lose them, even a bit of them, is disheartening; and so we must seize what we have.

In "Utterance," by the poet W. S. Merwin,

"Sitting over words / very late,"
hears
a kind of whispered sighing
not far
like a night wind in pines or like the sea in the dark
the echo of everything that has ever
been spoken...[1]

Against the "the echo of everything that has ever been spoken," the tensions and senses of loss, we take the life we have, create communities of all kinds, and build harbors in them: the institutions and collective settings where commonalities and stories and the mutual transmissions of cultural gifts are exchanged. These are the institutions and settings doing the formative cultural mediation that is the practical work of civil society, the ways a community has of causing or encouraging favorable things to happen.[2,3]

In the case of libraries and museums, the favorable thing we want to have happen is the development of learners, alone and in groups and families, whose lives are engaged with each other, embracing each other over their mutual reflections. For us, it is also the confirmation of observers, readers, and thinkers, nourishing and encouraging them to experience and synthesize new information. That critical work is the setting of minds on fire in such a way that they

inch their edges forward toward new knowledge and each other. Jean Bethke Elshtain writes, "Civil society isn't so much about problem solving as about citizen and neighbor creating."[4] And I will add learner creating, memory creating, and future creating. As Senators Dan Coats and Rick Santorum write, "When civil society is strong, it infuses a community with its warmth, trains its people to be good citizens, and transmits values between generations."[5] To me, this is what our cultural institutions must be about, what we who work in them must be for.

Certainly, it is what we at our best do better than anyone else. We find the energy of people who arrive in the library, the garden, the museum, or the zoo to renew and reinvent themselves and so to renew and reinvent their awareness of the culture they inhabit and own. Our cultural institutions recognize that every mindful person is a community's treasure. To serve in such institutions is to exist in an alliance of trust and common weal with a community. The preposition is important: it is the institution that is not just *for*, but *with* its community in trust that thrives most fully.[6]

———

How are cultural institutions part of common human motives, beyond the fundamental idea of keeping things and preserving them against the threat of loss and forgetfulness? Having a museum and a library in a community is always about the community having an informed present and future. These institutions are devoted to the unknown and to the evidences of possible knowledge constructed on the foundations of the known.

Museums and libraries share common themes.

- They share a horizon, attending to the cognitive, educative, and developmental possibilities of people over the life span, apart from the interests and expectations of schools. They do not give credits or certificates. They do not graduate anyone. There are no bells, no recess. But museums and libraries are for learning as it perhaps ought to happen best, in what we might call an open configuration of structures and structures-within-structures evoking the natural continuities of cognitive experience.

- They have similar logic and patterns of organization. Although we may be challenged as independent observers, we can expect to find our ways in museums and libraries by paying reasonable attention and with minimal intervention and instruction. In my experience, every public cultural setting is constructed for direct, independent entry by users who typically are given articulate, logical, public organization systems and coherent narratives for passage or process. Each institution employs professionals and others whose specific task is to consult, direct, facilitate learning, and assist the user in designing an individual experience of the collection. Apart from the more or less logical systems created for access (such as catalogs and maps), the physical structures of museum and library buildings generally reflect a logical likeness or design and a continuity of discipline, topic, or material. Museums and libraries are designed structures with a logic that is, at its best, visible and coherent. They are settings that evoke a path that we can experience as our own path.

- In what they offer and how they offer it, museums and libraries are laboratory-like environments. In content and power, they are potentially volatile and surprising, and they require acute attention to detail. Borrowing from John Dewey, one might say that museums and libraries are places for events that have not happened yet. By their nature, our cultural institutions are designed for cognitive experiments, for proximities and juxtapositions of images and ideas that cannot occur in any other institutions. And in libraries or museums, every user's step is a form of question, from generic to specific. Because library and museum use is active

and experimental, not passive, we might further say that such experiences are empirical, revealing logical connections and decisions that require direct cognitive impressions of artifacts and tools. Holding these artifacts and tools for us, they are places where our handmade lives, our crafted truths, are shaped.

- Both institutions, even those with limited collections and services, are engaged in organizing provocative and complex realms of knowledge that exist in parallel to corresponding experiential worlds outside. Both institutions must forge illuminating links to the world beyond their walls. They are culturally charged in the connections they make to situations and settings beyond the institutions themselves. In fact, they depend on the world outside, each a treasury that is renewed by the progress of its exterior cultures. As institutions, they are complex in their potential interactions with their communities and each other. It also is clear that libraries and museums never become simpler; their content never becomes less complex.

- In a museum or library, nothing moves forward without a question, pursuit, or objective, a mix of risk and hope. Even casual use of a cultural institution typically takes on an aim or plan within the limits of time, interest, or skill. It follows from the need to find something, even if invisible or inexplicable. Purposeful use in both institutions might be described in searching language: "I am looking for," "I want to see," "I am trying to find," and so on. Museums and libraries need to cultivate and follow the multiple forms of a searching sensibility.

- Museums and libraries integrate past and present, embodied in the user. A thoughtful person in the museum or library brings a history of knowing, reflecting, and understanding to bear upon the moment of use and the design of the search at hand. In the learner's intellectual processes, everything discovered is compared to past experiences and previous knowledge. (Of course, he or she also carries a history of confusion, questioning, and mystery.) Not only does the user encounter the new and the historic, he or she also encounters the past that is carried within, as well as an emerging new idea. The here and now blends its dimensions with the once and past. No other institutions require their users to travel in so many private dimensions of time and space at once.

- Wherever inquiry takes place, literacy guides the discoveries of the user. Language helps the user to find information and to understand and process it. The critical intellectual factors of explanation, articulation, and synthesis are experiences of language. Without words and a level of fluency, we cannot articulate in public or private what has happened in the presence of a work, an idea, an object, or a text. Words enable us to capture and then hold and contain what we witness.

- Museums and libraries let us work and think for as long as we live. Among institutions of learning, only libraries and museums allow multiple generations to reflect side by side. This means that the interests of an individual across the life span can be explored and renewed over time, transmitted to others, and will never be exhausted from youth to old age. It also means that young and old can gather to tell the stories stimulated by words and things. In museums and libraries, age, knowledge, family, and educational or economic status are not barriers to use. Perhaps it is time to suggest that formative cultural institutions construct the lifelong learner far more directly than any classroom does.

- Inside cultural institutions, we are free within limits to do as we care to do and free with no limits to think as we care to think. Unlike the school, where the learner

typically must submit to the values and interpretations of an instructor, in the cultural institution the user is largely in control of the situation for experience. Moreover, the institution succeeds only when it has responded to the needs of the individual user. The responsive institution makes direct, authentic, and unrestricted experiences possible for the user and then helps the user to illuminate those experiences and see them in further, deeper, richer, more extensive contexts.

- Museums and libraries succeed through the useful tensions combining intellectual work and intellectual play, the known and the unknown, the conventional and (sometimes right next to it) the revolutionary. When we enter a cultural institution, we find an environment that challenges and tempts us, even as we find more to know than we can possibly master. For the mindful learner, a single possibility can create a powerful tension between the desirable and the actual, the clear and the shrouded. These are the tensions of learning.

- The structure and process of the museum and the library are the same for every learner: One must begin where one is, assessing the parts of knowledge to be grasped and mastered over time. The learning is connective and integrative, evolving slowly and not arriving as if for an examination. Here, learners fabricate and build their own minds; they do not wait to receive the mind of a professor or other teacher. Here, learners combine pieces for themselves. Nothing about this is easy.

- Ultimately, both museums and libraries are institutions that give information to their users—through vision, words, comparisons, suggestions, or the powerful presence of a reorganizing concept, an insightful connection. Libraries connect information to the processes of individual cognitive, personal, imaginative, economic energy. Museums connect information to the experiences of awe and surprise that follow from seeing the thing itself that has been brought before us.

Increasingly, we are challenged to understand how these common themes take different forms in museums and libraries, how they might be woven together more explicitly in the cultural institution, and how our historic community genius can invigorate the patterns of thought and aspiration that unify their missions. We are challenged to understand what these two institutions might become, together. We are challenged to encounter the idea that cultural institutions have a common agenda and that libraries and museums both hold and construct a powerful vision of inquiry and knowledge in culture.

————

If we agree on some of these common qualities among cultural institutions, we also might consider several fundamental ideas that seem to sustain such institutions in our lives. Why do human beings need these institutions, these collections, this information? What unknowns, wants, and urgencies do these institutions mirror in our hearts and minds? This is an individual perspective on reasons for having museums and libraries; reasons for rescuing, conserving, and sustaining the treasures of culture and identity; and reasons for sharing their conjoint value and power with fellow citizens.

Human beings collect, organize, and keep evidence of their lives and cultures for multiple reasons: the pleasures of ownership; personal identification; the cultivation of knowledge and the advancement of scholarship; the possibility of change through reflection. We are certain, because we see the events of our own lives and the lives of our ancestors as worthy, that we are obligated to contain and illuminate the artifacts and ideas of persons now gone. Objects of art, memory, identity, or wisdom bear in common the touch of human, caring hands. Their presence in a contemporary world suggests that among their qualities, simple endurance may be worth our attention and reflection. And so *we keep these institutions in*

order to understand and ensure the enduring qualities of a handmade life.

Reasons for keeping and understanding objects and texts and for explaining their lasting strength are more than private. They are sources of insight and recognition for the individual and for other learners in groups. But if we assume that such insight and thought go *with* the user, *beyond* the institution, we also must assume that cultural treasures are alike in that *they are about the future more than they are about the past.* If our record is to be of use, it must be given to the future. The formal institutions we have built to hold evidence of our civilization are too often regarded as precious reliquaries or display cases. Instead, they should be seen as formative and interactive, creating whatever is to happen next in the cognitive life of the user. Having a museum or library in a community is about the community having both a present and a future because these institutions are devoted to exploring the evidence of the possibilities at hand.

Across time and geography, our public cultural institutions are grounded in concepts and intentions that we rarely articulate. What are the deepest cultural purposes of cultural institutions? Why do we strive to contain, keep, and narrate the documents and artifacts of human knowledge and activity? What do we construct when we construct a cultural institution? What do we assemble for ourselves when we build a library or a museum?

- We build collections because we strive *to keep and preserve* evidence of human continuity and to sustain remembrance. We strive not to forget how we have become who and what we are in order to be mindful of where we began. Cultural institutions hold artifacts and their legacies when our memories as humans cannot. This makes possible the transmission of meanings among distant generations.
- We construct and systematize collections because we strive *to contain and organize* authoritative materials for reference and verification. By looking at the original

artifact—the edited manuscript, the sculpted bone, the tortured score—we are nearly able to look at (and into) the moment of its inspiration. By retaining the records of masterful ideas and objects, we keep the possibility of drawing new insights from them. Museums and libraries allow us the opportunity, generation after generation, to respond separately to the questions, "Is it true? And what, exactly, is its truth?"

- As inquirers, we strive to *discover and study* materials for new knowledge and new syntheses of evidence. Driven by questions, we use our cultural institutions as places where we can first follow threads and then weave garments. If every school were to close tomorrow, intellectual growth might continue in cultural institutions, where we would likely find and teach each other. These settings are always poised to rescue human cognitive processes when schools fail to sustain and nurture them and even when the Internet undoes the tendency to have an original, private, unshared thought.

- In museums and libraries, we strive *to delight and inform* ourselves with observations and reflections on human accomplishment. Human beings have always reserved their greatest delights for moments of learning. Parent and child are bonded as much by the learning transmitted between them as they are by blood. What we find delightful, we wish to have held forever before us, Faust-like. The museum or library does this, while generously allowing us to retain our souls.

- We strive to integrate and verify our experiences in the larger culture. Our cultural institutions are mirrors for the people and societies that construct them, naturally. But in each personal discovery or observation a learner also finds a mirror of lived experience: "I remember an object like this in San Francisco." "The quality of light in this work appears sometimes in Copenhagen." "The evolution of tools fascinates me and leads me

on." "My grandparents were once in this part of the world." We enter and leave with what we know, but our knowing is different when we depart the institution because we have clarified, augmented, or revised what knowledge we had. Or what we know is in the process of becoming different knowledge because we are present, working to understand things. Because what we know configures who we are, we also might say that the crafting of truth in cultural institutions is a process of becoming, renewing, or confirming ourselves.

- We strive to *settle fears* of loss. We seem at times to be particularly haunted by loss and the fear of loss. Change, the arrival of strangers, the frequency of feeling discontinuous with the past, the terror of beginning again all advance the sense of eroding integrity in our lives. As the greatest of cultural educators, the cultural institution can make explicit links between the past and future, drawing us toward an understanding of great, immutable themes. In doing so, it can help us gain cognitive control over an otherwise unimaginable transition and to place ourselves clearly within our own times, integrated and not excluded. A museum or library collection allows us to revisit and reconsider the differences between what was and what is and to see ourselves in continuity with those who preceded us and those who will follow us.

If museums and libraries are to recognize their common future and reorganize themselves to address it, generalizations such as those offered in this text will require exploration and reflection based on a strong grounding in empirical observations and educational theory. The individual learner; the family as a learning organism; the process of sensemaking in the presence of an unknown; the continuities and connections among learners who speak to each other and make their stories, fears, and learnings known—we need to understand these invisible things even more than we need to understand the histories of texts and objects. Museums and libraries have one research agenda that overshadows all others: we need to know more about how individual learners renew themselves by exploring their literacies and possibilities, and we can learn this best by talking directly to people.

The final concept unifying museum and library is the idea that all cultural institutions must act on the tenet that *every mindful person is a community's treasure*. As our culture changes, the culture of every institution needs to find new forms of professional thought grounded in a new cognitive environment. The truly educative institution will experiment with new ideas of professional service to the exploring user. In a world that becomes increasingly virtual, cultural institutions must be challenged to redesign themselves to become face-to-face forums where the questions and controversies of a living culture can find their form and be debated. It is through such forums that human beings will experience the realities of democratic cultural literacy and may come to embody the tensions of being both responsible citizens and mindful people. There is no country on earth without the need for such forums.

––––––

How does the incendiary institution think of itself? It must understand its own energy and how that energy attracts and engages its users. How does it lead people in, involve them with their own choices and with other human beings, help them to understand the structures at hand, and teach them how to move among those structures with eyes open? The incendiary institution never compromises its respect for the open-eyed user.

Such users will increase in number when the institution addresses them and the problems that learning presents to a contemporary life. As people experience the inexorable growth of both the tasks and the information at hand, there also will be a common increase in ambiguity and irresolution. How do we know what we need next? How do we confirm the accuracy or truth of our observations? What does learning in one

frame of our lives (as parent or companion) mean to the learning we carry out in other frames of our lives (as colleague, designer of new experiences, educator of other adults)?

It is a commonplace that receiving and deciding about immense amounts of information increasingly requires our time and attention if we are to be appropriately responsive to our world. And yet, our lives then become less our own because as messages and information increase, the more we must think on the horizons of others, contend with the structures and assumptions of others, and negotiate meaning and think critically in worlds designed or deeply influenced by others.

And so the living challenge to any person is double-edged: to live strongly on one's own horizon and yet also to adapt our horizons among others in order to find contexts of what we want, what we see, and what we hope for. No one can meet the challenges of such a life without being a passionately critical thinker, an author of one's own experience, and a cautious master of one's own intellect. In a culture where "knowledge" arrives unbidden instantly, it is problematic to confirm its authority, value, and relevance; and so we need to question. The design of real, not surrogate, experiences becomes important as we become increasingly remote from living a self-constructed life; and so we need ways to determine what is authentic. And when information is unlimited in both speed and density, it is not good for reflection; and so we need to slow it down and leaven it with our own salient ideas and values.

As I tell my students, our task is to slow down the information revolution. This is also every learner's task.

Reflection is essential for understanding the configuration of the world-the mass of influences that create human experience-and its concomitant tensions, balances, processes, and assumptions. It will always be essential for any person who strives to move forward toward wholeness against fragmentation, toward integrity against compromise, and toward fearlessness in the presence of things unknown. As ever, learning and reflection will depend on engaging ceaselessly with the processes that configure a cognitive experience: planning, questioning, remembering, pursuing, discovering, evaluating, constructing, and connecting.

When we face our primary task as adults—*to arrive at a working sense of identity and integrity*—we have no choice other than to do it as learners led by our own thoughts and not solely by the thoughts and horizons of others. In cultural institutions, people must always undertake this courageous task against the odds. The mass, the authority, and sometimes the intractability of our institutions require great strength of mind if we are to overcome both brilliance and awe in order to see the small traces of an inspired hand. But even in our mindfulness (and here is one of the tensions that will not go away), we also must be permeable to the living experiences and words of others. We must feel safe enough in our own lives to encounter new questions that expand our grasp, even though they may at first make us fearful of change.

Learning will take place as it has always taken place in the contexts of the possible:

1. A human being will create a question in a situation of complexity.
2. His or her question will stimulate a felt need to pursue information in multiple formats, wherever that may lead.
3. The information will create more questions, lead to more or less useful information.
4. The problem, its contexts, what it means to the learner, and an array of possible questions will all become clear.
5. The first step toward changes in thought, attention, or behavior also will become clear.

These are all incendiary moments. They cannot occur without structures and processes or a logical system of informing paths.

These elements must be present in the situation if learning is to take place:

- *assistance*, freely given by a mentor, a model, a source of information or referral, a person who speaks the language of the learner; and *access* to this person, meaning

opportunities to create questions and develop a relationship;

- *tools*, a broad array of adaptive and generative, convivial tools (the term is Ivan Illich's); tools that suggest syntheses, ideas for recombination and exploration; tools that lead a learner on, stimulating new responses to experience; tools that assist the user to transfer skills and observations to another place and time;

- *autonomy*, meaning independence from authority, freedom from any evaluation other than meeting the learner's own satisfaction, freedom to accept or reject a mentor;

- *control* and *authorship* of an inquiry, for example, frequent opportunities to revise the themes and patterns of an inquiry or to abandon it altogether;

- a *forum* or a *conversation* in an open environment where learners can participate in mutual conversations with other learners.

People come to museums and libraries and look to them as places to hold things still, as the world has fewer and fewer places of stillness in it. That is a critical thing to do. And yet, at the same moment that it offers stillness in a turning world, the great cultural institution also must understand itself to be *challenging*, a *creator* of learners and thinkers, a setting where mindfulness cannot possibly be abjured. For any learner, of any age, the great library or the great museum must be an advocate for new thinking, based on the astonishing, moving evidence in treasured texts and objects. Only the place that has a heart of fire (and not of ice) is the one where learning can happen best.

Sustenance for the mind of the future will come from excellent information near at hand, as it always has; but it also will come from collaboration among human beings in an alliance for knowledge, identity, and mere connection to another person, as it always has. Every day of service in a cultural institution provides an opportunity to reinvent the idea of a helping mind, reconfigure a repertoire of ideas and tools, and construct connections to whatever might happen next. We may slowly come to understand that every life bears its own unfinished issues and is unfinished in a different way. In a world often characterized by loss and fear, certain acts of human rescue and survival can occur only in the places where a culture continuously transforms itself through human associations, forged in the presence of the unknown. In this way, the constructive cultural institution contributes to the integrity of its culture.

Our questions, like telescopes or microscopes, are instruments that concentrate our attention and allow us to focus on those parts of the unknown that engage us most. Without such mechanisms, we cannot understand the dimensions hidden from our vision. Whenever we come together to engage in such conversations, we have made a place that is, of course, full of questions itself; and these questions do not become fewer as an evening wears on. And so we must arrive at last at what may be the best question of all, here left for others to consider through the arts of practice and the human gifts of reciprocity and mutual engagement: What happens when caring minds meet? It is with this question that the incendiary cultural institution must regard itself.

NOTES

1. W. S. Merwin, "Utterance," in *A Book of Luminous Things*, ed. Czeslaw Milosz (New York: Harcourt Brace, 1996).

2. E. J. Dionne Jr., "Introduction," in *Community Works: The Revival of Civil Society in America*, ed. E.J. Dionne Jr. (Washington, D.C.: Brookings Institution Pr., 1998), 3.

3. Former Senator Bill Bradley defines civil society in this way: "Civil society is the place where Americans make their home, sustain their marriages, raise their families, hang out with their friends, meet their neighbors, educate their children, worship their god. It is in the churches, schools, fraternities, community centers, labor unions, synagogues, sports leagues, PTAs, libraries and barbershops. It is where opinions are expressed and refined, where views are exchanged and agreements made, where a sense of common purpose and consensus are forged. It lies apart from the realms of the market and the government, and possesses a different ethic. The market is governed by the logic of economic self-interest, while government is the domain of laws with all their coercive authority. Civil society, on the other hand, is the sphere of our most basic humanity—the personal, everyday realm that is governed by values such as responsibility, trust, fraternity, solidarity, and love. In a democratic civil society such as ours, we also put a special premium on social equality—the conviction that men and women should be measured by the quality of their character and not the color of their skin, the shape of their eyes, the size of their bank account, the religion of their family, or the happenstance of their gender." ("America's Challenge: Revitalizing Our National Community," in *Community Works*, ed. E.J. Dionne Jr. [Washington, D.C.: Brookings Institution Pr., 1998], 108–9.)

4. Jean Bethke Elshtain, "Not a Cure-All: Civil Society Creates Citizens, It Does Not Solve Problems," in *Community Works*, ed. E.J. Dionne Jr. (Washington, D.C.: Brookings Institution Pr., 1998), 27.

5. Dan Coats and Rick Santorum, "Civil Society and the Humble Role of Government," in *Community Works*, ed. E.J. Dionne Jr. (Washington, D.C.: Brookings Institution Pr., 1998), 102.

6. The author is grateful to the Children's Museum of Indianapolis for this awareness of prepositions and much more.

STANLEY CHODOROW

"To Represent Us Truly: The Job and Context of Preserving the Cultural Record"

"Libraries & the Cultural Record" 41.3 (Summer 2006): 372–80.

THE PRESERVATION OF government records has been a natural activity of governments since the establishment of the first government. The earliest libraries were really archives of government documents, including the records of rituals that kings performed to assure the favor of the gods. Those documents made up the collections of the first libraries in Mesopotamia, dating to about 1500 BC, and of the classics on which Chinese civilization has rested for more than three thousand years. Historians rely on the government records preserved in those libraries and classical works—truly they are anthologies—to reconstruct the ancient cultures that produced them. For them, government records are cultural records. They still are, but when we moderns talk about the cultural record, we have in mind a much broader range of cultural productions than those produced by government, even a government that had religious as well as secular functions.

The word "culture" now calls forth notions of social class and function. We speak of political cultures, of the arts, of social practices, and of *mentalités,* to borrow a useful French term. We speak of high-, middle-, and low-brow culture. To a significant extent "culture" has become a weapon of mass distinctions of the social sort, and in the United States the reaction of some people to the word is a product of our egalitarianism and populism. The word bears the burden of what its user thinks of academics, of aesthetes, of modern artists and composers, of all those big-city folk who don't think life exists beyond the city limits—or, conversely, of blue-collar workers, rural folks, and Lawrence Welk and his musical descendants.

The William and Margaret Kilgarlin Center for Preservation of the Cultural Record must establish a meaning for the term *culture* in order to organize and carry out its work. Its definition of the word must sail above social and political value judgments and find a meaning that is broader than one that only denotes the arts or the peculiar mores of a people. How broad should the center's conception be? It is hard to find its boundaries and hard to define it.

To begin with, the cultural record is the sum of the things we put away and drop on the floor as we, the whole society, go through life. It is the detritus of our ways of life and our ways of thinking, of our knowledge and beliefs, and of our superstitions and nightmares. None of these descriptive words outline the shape of something we can grasp, because the cultural record, which contains our cultural heritage, seems to incorporate the whole, unabbreviated body of evidence of everything we produce.

Or, rather, it incorporates everything that has survived and that will survive by conscious and unconscious decision or by accident. In fact, for historians the cultural record appears always to have an accidental character. Our cultural record will be just what got saved because someone put it in a safe place or in a place that turned out to be safe because that place did not burn up or rot or get eaten by moths or get dissolved in floods. Yet as ordinary people not defined by our professions, we cannot accept that our understanding of our culture rests on such accidental processes. Scientists take reassurance from randomness because they can apply statistical techniques to random events that have great predictive authority. But in our everyday lives, in our ordinary activities, we want to know that our understanding of ourselves as individuals and as a society is not produced by accident or by statistics. None of us believes that what we and our compatriots think is an accident. When we turn our attention to ourselves and our culture in order to analyze ourselves, in order to find out how we deal with unusual events, or to confirm our good ideas or to change our bad ones, we want to be sure that the records we study are true to ourselves. They must represent us truly.

Our need for the cultural record does not arise only from our need to understand who we are. Often, we call on the record to solve practical problems. Here's an example from my field of medieval studies.

In 1938 and 1939 Edith Pretty, a widow who owned Sutton Hoo, an estate in East Anglia in England, decided to instigate excavations on some mounds on her property. She enlisted the curator of the local museum, who called in a local amateur archaeologist named Basil Brown, who very quickly found that the mounds were a seventh-century burial ground for important people. In Mound 1 Brown found a ship burial, and in the collapsed central chamber of this ship tomb he found the richest trove of Anglo-Saxon burial goods ever uncovered.

Nineteen thirty-nine was not a good time to open up a delicate excavation in the eastern part of England, and so the trench was covered and camouflaged. But as the grave goods were being put away in an unused tunnel of the London subway, the government undertook to find out who owned them. The county coroner of East Anglia held an inquest to determine whether Mrs. Pretty or the Crown owned the Sutton Hoo treasure. Under the ancient law of treasure trove, the answer to this question depended on whether the goods had been buried to be dug up later or buried to go with a deceased person to the underworld. If the former, then the buriers, said the law, presumptively were trying to avoid taxes and the trove belonged to the Crown; if the latter, then the owner of the property on which the treasure was found owned it. The question turned on the Anglo-Saxon cultural heritage, and the lawyers involved in the hearing found the record of that heritage principally in the fragments of early Anglo-Saxon poetry that still exist. They spent a good part of the hearing reciting these poems to one another, the poor coroner, and a no-doubt small, bemused audience. This record, contained in bits and pieces of writing that for myriad reasons were passed on from genera-

tion to generation until librarians took them in hand as invaluable artifacts of the nation's cultural record and put the fragments into their vaults, showed that the burial was an interment and that Mrs. Pretty owned it. The cultural record of England gave her a million-pound windfall—in 1939, when a million was emphatically a million. She then gave the trove to the British Museum, the largest gift the institution had ever, to that point, received from a living donor.

One of the striking characteristics of this charming story is the way it reveals that our cultural heritage often survives only in a handful of broken jewelry and scraps of poetry. It is the work of historians, principally, to put these fragments in some order and to make sense of them. How do the pieces fit together? What meaning should we read into the assemblage? There may be competing reconstructions and interpretations. Our cultural heritage is contested ground, but, as the case of Sutton Hoo shows, sometimes we cannot leave it unsettled. Ownership, wealth, and the national patrimony may be at stake.

Another example, which stems from the work I do as a scholar, shows how tiny or incidental the evidence on which we construct our knowledge of our heritage might be. Contrary to what most Americans believe, the idea of inalienable rights did not originate with the philosophers of the seventeen the century—Hobbes, Locke, Pufendorf, and the like—but with the lawyers and law professors of the late twelfth and early thirteenth centuries. Interpreting the legal texts they had received from their tradition, law teachers led their students into discussions that explored the possible meanings of the old language. At the end of the twelfth century an ancient text that incidentally distinguished between those who had plenty and those who did not was the occasion for professors to ask their students whether a starving man who stole food from a rich person committed theft. Then, in the manner of law professors of all times and places, the professors and students spun out analyses of the hypothetical situation to reveal the legal principles at work. The consensus of the faculty and students of the time was that such a taking was not theft because the starving man, assuming he was truly needy, had a right to the necessities of life.[1]

The *word* the lawyers seized on to represent this right was *ius,* which appeared in many ancient texts but with no settled meaning. It could mean "right," "law," or "faculty" (i.e., the ability to do something), and it was often ambiguous in context. Gradually, however, one of its main meanings came to be *right* in our sense of the term, a property that inhered in a person, real or fictive, by definition. By the end of the thirteenth century a person, by virtue of being a person, was said to have a right not only to the necessities of life but also to his or her property and to what we would call due process. As the lawyers said, even though God knew that Adam had violated his command he asked him whether he had done so and waited for a reply. The first trial, based on Adam's right to due process, took place in Eden.[2]

How early did ordinary people who were engaged in ordinary legal business—as opposed to professors and students—consolidate their ideas about rights? (Before one can speak of a class of professional lawyers who had specialized education one can recognize that there were people who represented their institutions in court and read law books. They constituted the vast majority of those who appeared in courts.) The academic treatises and commentaries represent the exploratory and playful processes of the classroom, which are not a sound foundation for judging common opinion. Yet if one looks at the law books kept in church and monastery libraries–and most such institutions had law books because they were often engaged in litigation–one can see the common or popular jurisprudence in formation. In a law book copied between 1170 and 1180, preserved in the city archive of Cologne, a contemporary reader wrote an interlinear explanation over the word "nations." The original sentence defines the natural law *(ius naturale)* as the law common to all nations. The user of the book wrote above the phrase "to all nations" the phrase "to all persons."[3] Voila! More than ten years before the extant commentaries of the law schools we have evidence that people had begun to attribute rights and capacities to persons. We can see,

therefore, that the sophistication of the law professors and their students was an outgrowth of the legal culture—or, more broadly, of the cultural heritage of the late twelfth century. Some medievalists talk of the rise of individualism in that period, long before the Renaissance was supposed to have invented the idea. The textual comment entered into Cologne's manuscript is a cultural record that provides evidence for that claim.

But many would say that these examples only reveal the problems of reconstructing our ancient selves—the deepest roots of our cultural being and of the ideas that govern our political life. It is reasonable to view these reconstructions of our culture as resulting from the accidents through which the record was preserved. The counterargument—that people preserve what is most telling about themselves—contains some truth, perhaps, but skeptics consider that defense to be wishful thinking. Responding to the uncertainty about our old cultural records, we have become determined to do better than our ancestors. The Kilgarlin Center is a response to that determination.

The center will not look backward (except to make sure the bad practices of the past are not gaining on us) but forward. It will study the condition of the cultural record we are producing now and will produce in the future. Thus the problems it will try to solve are the reverse of what those who dig deep into the soil of our culture face. Modern historians and all those others who must do research in the records of recent times—political scientists tracking voting behavior, economists plotting trends in the markets, intelligence officers trying to piece together a coherent picture or an enemy's or an ally's intentions and capabilities—do not have all they need. However, the problem for them is that they cannot with certainty distinguish the pure metal from the dross. They face such a mass of material that it is nearly as difficult for them to find the gems in the apparently endless stream of data as it is for medievalists to understand and weigh the significance of the fragments with which they must work. Understanding the task of the Kilgarlin Center requires understanding the irony in its work. The irony is that we can only save our cultural record by throwing out the majority of it.

Let's start by imagining the process by which a collection of usable materials is created. I'm not talking now of those collections put together by individual collectors. Those special collections are products of human passion. I'm talking about the collection that is extracted from the high-pressure outflow of modern science and scholarship, of government operations, and of modern artistic and literary production. Many readers of this journal could tell you how the outpouring of scholarship has grown since the early seventeenth century. The first catalog, issued in 1602, of the Bodleian Library of the University of Oxford listed two thousand volumes; the second, produced in 1620, contained sixteen thousand. And the production of scholarship has continued to grow exponentially, especially after Sir Edmund Halley's—he of the comet and the man who funded the publication of Newton's *Principia*—article in the late seventeenth century. In 1991 the Association of Research Libraries (ARL) reported that of the 118,500 journals then published, 70,000 had come into existence since 1970. The growth of the number of journals has been over 11 percent per annum since 1970. Beginning in 1991, ARL has published an annual list of electronic journals, newsletters, and academic discussion lists that are a kind of living journal through which scholars collaborate on research; they are often called e-conferences.[4] The first edition of the catalog contained about 400 items, mostly discussion lists. The second edition cataloged 769 such discussion lists and e-journals. The third, published in 1993, contained 240 journals and 1,152 e-conferences. A year later, the fourth edition listed 443 journals and 1,785 discussion boards and recorded the first Web-based journals. To jump ahead, the seventh edition in 1997 listed 3,400 journals and newsletters and 3,800 e-conferences. The growth of publications has, among other effects, such as overwhelming library budgets, forced scholars to narrow their fields of research. One can only keep up with a sliver of what was once considered one's discipline.

The production of government records and of works of art has followed the same pattern. When records were kept and documents prepared with quills, they were produced at a stately pace and accumulated slowly. Steel-nib pens increased the pace somewhat; one did not have to sharpen them regularly. The typewriter sped up the production line significantly, but its greatest contribution to the accumulating of documents was the carbon copy, which also increased the likelihood that the record would survive. The computer has so vastly increased the production of records and documents that we *feel* the speed and overwhelming flow of information rather than *count* it. It is beyond counting.

In the other products of human creativity—the arts in all their forms—the older technologies are being replaced, with similar effect. When I was dean of arts and humanities at the University of California at San Diego I had to deal with the composers and visual artists and to learn something of the world they inhabit. One thing that struck me was that contemporary music compositions tend to be much shorter than those of the early twentieth century and before. My colleagues explained that the recording media—first tapes and records and then electronic media—make it unnecessary to include the repeats that we humans needed when the only way we could hear music was in the concert hall or coffee house or on the street corner. Moreover, compositions generated by computers can be produced at a much greater rate than those handwritten on a five-line staff. The electronic media have increased not only the speed of production but also its variety. Composers are inventing new musical forms and new ways to represent those forms.

Meanwhile, one of my colleagues in visual arts, the painter Harold Cohen, was creating a computer program to draw pictures using artificial intelligence. His machine could produce dozens of works each day, from which he selected a few for coloring, which he did himself. To that point, the machine sped up art production, but the completion of the process had to wait on Harold's hand-coloring. The technology is now way beyond what Harold was doing, and artists are producing and disseminating work at a much higher rate than ever before. They also are producing works that contain a prodigious amount of data.

Yet certainly the most significant change in our cultural record is not scholarship, government records, and music and visual art but audio and video recordings. We cannot hope to understand the culture of the twentieth century, much less of the twenty-first, if we do not study movies, radio programs, and the spate of TV programs. We need to preserve these materials, and we need to ensure access to them—a legal as well as technical matter—if we are to know anything about what we believe, what we think, and how we view things. The information contained in these media is now and will increasingly be the basis for our understanding of our culture.

Our cultural record is composed of all of this stuff–the scholarship that gathers, sorts, and analyzes what we know or think we know, the government records, the artistic works, the movies and broadcast programs, and now the millions of Web sites. He or she who would study that record or search in it for the answer to questions that might determine who owns something or how we should understand the complex tradition of our ideas—and therefore how we should understand our ideas, period—must find the telling and true indicators in that overwhelming ocean of data.

When I think of the task of the modernists or of the judges, members of commissions, bureaucrats, and ordinary citizens who want or need to know about our cultural ideas, attitudes, or tendencies, it calls to mind discussions I had when I was at the University of Pennsylvania with physicists involved in gargantuan experiments. These great enterprises, such as the Hubble Telescope, produce so much data at such a pace that scientists had to develop a whole new approach to coping with them. They defined a new unit of information, the LOC, that amount of data contained in the Library of Congress (some experiments were expected to produce a LOC a day), and they developed a technique for extracting the significant data that they called data mining, an automated process. Unfortunately, we cannot use such automated techniques in the selection of materials that we ourselves produce. We need new techniques and approaches, but we cannot design a computer program to make the selections for us.

The Kilgarlin Center can and should become a leading institution for the creation and teaching of these new techniques and approaches. The tasks are formidable and will not be completed soon or by one center. We need to define principles of selection, techniques for the preservation of fragile media, and new ways to catalog materials that our existing cataloging processes and techniques never contemplated. How do you describe a movie so that students and scholars fifty years from now will know, from the catalog, whether they want to spend two hours viewing it? What about radio programs, television programs, Web sites? Web sites present the greatest challenge of the future. They change continually; they are bodies of information that have come alive; they die and disappear. How do we preserve them? Which version or edition should be preserved? How do we catalog them so that users of our collections will understand the history of the site as well as its content? How much of all these technical requirements can be automated? How much must remain in the hands of sentient beings?

The mention of sentient beings brings me to my final point. The last time the library community reviewed the qualities and education of those who would be librarians or archivists was in a 1921 study funded by the Carnegie Corporation. Melvil Dewey was the instigator of the undertaking; Charles Williamson carried it out. Before the Carnegie study, librarians were trained in the major public libraries. Their entering qualifications were not consistent from program to program or perhaps even from person to person. Literacy was the only common denominator. Williamson's study led to the founding of university-based library schools and to the definition of their curricula. It also determined that library schools should be graduate schools—that is, their students should arrive with a college education. It is time for a national reassessment. The schools of library science have become, as here at UT Austin, schools of information. The curricula of the schools have dispersed, like a crowd going home after a ball game. And there is a widespread feeling among university and other research librarians that something is missing in the graduates of these schools. From my standpoint as an observer, what is missing is not that the schools are failing to teach information science as it now exists but that the students do not have the other education—in the humanities, sciences, or social sciences—that they need to perform the tasks that must now be performed. Whatever systems or techniques we develop to manage or at least cope with the ocean of cultural records now washing over us, the people who operate those systems and use those techniques must be learned. They must know what the various disciplines consider important so that they can plug in the descriptors and the operants most likely to select, catalog, and preserve those exemplars of the data that contain the significant information about the subject so that when we search the cultural record we find something true and telling.

NOTES

This article is based on remarks delivered on 22 October 2004 to celebrate the opening of the William and Margaret Kilgarlin Center for Preservation of the Cultural Record at The University of Texas at Austin. I began those remarks by congratulating Justice William Kilgarlin and the university on the founding of this important center.

1. See Brian Tierney, *Medieval Poor Law: A Sketch of Canonical Theory and Its Application in England* (Berkeley: University of California Press, 1959) and *The Idea of Natural Rights: Studies on Natural Rights, Natural Law, and Church Law, 1150–1625* (Grand Rapids, Mich.: William B. Eerdmanns, 2001).

2. See Kenneth Pennington, *The Prince and the Law, 1200–1600: Sovereignty and Rights in the Western Legal Tradition* (Berkeley: University of California Press, 1993).

3. The manuscript is Cologne, Library of the Archiepiscopal Diocesan and Cathedral, Cod. 127. It contains a copy of *Gratian's Decretum*, the fundamental textbook of canon law in the Middle Ages. Kenneth Pennington pointed this manuscript out to me in an e-mail.

4. In the early 1990s these online discussions were carried out through listservs, which distribute contributions by email; since about 1995 they have been increasingly carried out on the Web.

MICHÈLE VALERIE CLOONAN

"The Preservation of Knowledge"

Introduction

Library Trends *41.4 (Spring 1993): 594–605.*

Midway life's journey I was made aware
That I had strayed into a dark forest,
And the right path appeared not anywhere
—*Dante Alighieri,* The Inferno, *Part 1, Canto 1*

THOSE MIDWAY THROUGH careers in preservation now find themselves in a forest that, if not dark, is dusky. As information is stored increasingly in electronic formats, as the very concept of the form and substance of the book is changing, it is time to re-examine the principles of preservation under which we were trained and under which we are still guided in decision making. These principles need to be compared to recent technological advances in the formation and storing of texts so that points of convergence or divergence can be evaluated. Only then can we either follow a new path or continue down the current one.

One can argue that preservation dates back to the origin of written records. In ancient times, one form of preservation consisted primarily of protecting items from all kinds of human and natural enemies by placing them in earthenware vessels and other types of containers. Once libraries were established, the three broad areas of librarianship were acquisitions, the organization of texts (for access), and guardianship, which implies preservation of the collection (the circulation of library collections is a relatively recent development in library history). Yet, although preservation has always been one of the primary aspects of librarianship, it has only become a recognized specialty within the library profession in recent times. In other words, storage, safekeeping, and repair of library collections have always been integral parts of librarianship, but these activities were not formally designated as preservation.

As the preservation of library materials became a specialization within librarianship, certain principles evolved which grew out of the guardianship mandate of librarianship, the discipline of bibliography, and the art conservation field.[1] The guardianship aspect of librarianship is the assumption that, generally speaking, once libraries acquire books, they are kept permanently. The second assumption is that the books will be stored in buildings that are structurally sound and secure; these buildings are usually owned, rented, or leased by the library or the organization to which the library belongs. Therefore, the books are usually "owned" by the library. This is an important concept to keep in mind, for in today's electronic environment, the ownership of texts by libraries can no longer be assumed or expected (the general historical concern for suitable library structures has been well described by Swartzburg and Bussey [1991] and the late nineteenth- and early twentieth-century debates have been documented by Higginbotham [1990]).

Regardless of how one defines bibliography, it goes back centuries. For the purposes of this discussion, it is adequate simply to state that the existence of rare book departments in libraries demonstrates that the value of particular books has been recognized for a long time. These books have been valued for such attributes as their artifactual, historical, or associational significance. Therefore, there is a long tradition of appreciating books as artifacts where the underlying assumption is that each book requires special care and handling.

The influence of art conservation dates from the twentieth century. It lies in the artifactual one-by-one approach to treating items, and in the principle that, whenever possible, treatments should be reversible.[2] This influence can be seen in the curriculum of the book conservation program which was offered at Columbia University from 1981 to 1992. The curriculum was partially based on the art conservation programs at the University of Delaware, New York University, and Cooperstown (now Buffalo State College). Everyone who took those courses at Columbia was exposed to the artifactual approach.

From these sources the following broad preservation principles have evolved:

- When materials are treated, the treatments should, when possible, be reversible.[3]
- Whenever possible or appropriate, the originals should be preserved. Only materials that are untreatable should be reformatted.
- Library materials should be preserved for as long as possible.

These principles have come increasingly into conflict with the enormity of the library preservation problem—i.e., millions of deteriorating books. The sheer size of the problem, as well as the high cost, has diverted us from the artifactual approach toward such measures as preservation microfilming and mass deacidification. These approaches have meant that many more texts could be preserved. However, the effects of deacidification are not necessarily reversible, and, in the case of microfilming programs, some institutions discard the books once they have been filmed. So, two of the three principles have already diminished in importance. The third is open to interpretation: should the objects be preserved for as long as possible, or should we preserve only the texts?

The Preservation Problem

The use of mass deacidification and microfilming assumes that the items to be treated are paper based to begin with. The forest in which we now find ourselves is replete with new media such as audio- and videotapes or computer and optical disks, all of which are constantly changing form. In some instances—for example, e-mail—the electronic format is the first and only format unless the information is printed out. The trend is a shift from information in permanent formats to information conveyed in formats *so* transitory that it can disappear at the touch of a command key.

Kurzweil (1992a, 1992b, 1992c) presents a world in which the "book" is a personal computer, telephone, television, and cybernetic research assistant all in one. Though he says that the electronic book "falls short in some of the fundamental characteristics of paper and ink in the areas of flicker, contrast, resolution, and color …, computer technology is anything but static, and already some of these limitations are being overcome" (Kurzweil, 1992b, p. 141).

More immediate than the Kurzweil "powerbooks" are the electronic formats already available in libraries—e.g., digital media such as CD-ROMs. These media have become an integral part of library collections and yet they are deteriorating at a rate that is much quicker than originally thought (De Whitt, 1987a; "Special Report: ALA Back to Basics," 1990; Stielow, 1991; Zachary, 1991). However, Lesk (1992) reminds us that perhaps of more import than deterioration is the fact that from now on data will have to be frequently "refreshed" (reformatted) because of technological obsolescence—e.g., the equipment used to convey information will be obsolete or cease to be manufactured as vendors go bankrupt or as data are moved to more sophisticated storage media. "On the good side, the intervention of machinery between the actual object and the reader means that the users are unlikely to become emotionally attached to the particular physical media, and thus reformatting of advanced technology should not produce the objections that accompany reformatting of books" (Lesk, 1992, p. 3).

In an ideal world, where time, manpower, and money exist in equal shares, such regular reformatting could be expected. In the meantime, a lot of valuable information is disappearing, particularly in government archives. Sniffen (1991) has described information such as census data, which has been lost because it is stored only on old computer tape from discarded systems (p. 46). Anderson (1985) describes administrative records from the 1980s "created in machine-readable form and … stored on media which at best had only a few years of reliable life and at worst were subject to regular overwritings in the interests of economy of data storage" (p. 79).

How do our preservation principles hold up to these situations? We can evaluate the principles in the context of the life cycle of information which consists of three stages: creation, life (or use), and disposal (reformatting, replacement, or disposal with no form of replacement). Preservation administrators are concerned with all of these stages.

The Life Cycle of Information

The deterioration of an item begins during creation. For books, deterioration is caused by many things, among which are poor methods of manufacture such as adding alum-rosin sizing to paper pulp, the use of sulphuric acids to accelerate the leather tanning process, and so on. In recent years, the preservation community has lobbied paper manufacturers to produce permanent/durable papers and the publishing industry to use such papers and to designate that use with an infinity sign on the verso of title pages. Nevertheless, even though some manufacturers can guarantee 250 years of life for their papers, all organic materials will disintegrate eventually, so there is ultimately a limit to what can be done.[4]

The useful life of library materials can be extended not only through proper methods of manufacture but also by improving conditions of storage and use. Controlling the environment of buildings, proper shelving, and careful handling of materials will make them last longer. Preservation administrators have made great strides in extending the use of library materials and in educating manufacturers, librarians, and users.

Finally, disposal may take place when individual items deteriorate beyond the possibility or practicality of repair. Replacement with a like item such as a reprint or by reformatting are all solutions (this stage usually requires collaborative decision making with other librarians as well as with the vendors who can provide the necessary services).

How does the life cycle differ with new media? At the media creation point, the preservation community has less knowledge and expertise about the development and manufacture of new formats than it does about more familiar formats such as paper. Also, physical durability of new media is not the ultimate problem but rather obsolescence (Lesk, 1992, p. 2). Therefore, preservation administrators will have to plan for an ongoing process of media conversion beginning at the point of acquisition (Cloonan, 1991; Lesk, 1992).

The life of media is another consideration. Storage conditions can be controlled for some new media, but not all electronic information is replicable and, therefore, it is not necessarily in a physical form which can be stored or saved. Librarians will need to decide what will be stored, how and when it will be stored, and by whom—the library, the creator, the end-user, or the publisher (the issue of how information could be stored and transmitted is examined by Fiddes and Winterbottom, 1991).

Reformatting will also be an integral part of this stage. Four areas of concern in media conversion are: (1) fragility (the inherent strength or inherent weakness of each medium), (2) rapidity of obsolescence of the operating apparatus of each medium, (3) the ease of altering documents (the ability to manipulate, change, or reformat data easily), and (4) proprietary rights and preservation (who owns the information, and who will take responsibility for its preservation—an area potentially far more complex than copyright issues) (Cloonan, 1991, p. 3). Disposal of media is a third concern. Content or format—which will we preserve? To a certain extent, these decisions will be market driven. No matter how much people resist, they will eventually give up their LP collections in favor of the predominant CDs, which they will then collect only as long as CDs are manufactured. So, ultimately, we have no control over formats and will have to focus on the content. Yet we must also realize that, in changing formats, something of the original is lost. The CD version of the Beethoven piano sonatas performed by Artur Schnabel may sound cleaner and crisper than the original LPs, but some of the original atmosphere is gone.

Given these new scenarios, let us examine the principles of longevity and the importance of the artifact.

There is no doubt, given the current technological environment of the late twentieth century, that the notions of both are changing radically. New technologies last a shorter and shorter time than do the older ones—papyrus, paper, vellum, vinyl records, etc. So much for the artifact; under these circumstances, preservation administrators will have to be more concerned with the longevity of the information.

However, even as some new materials are being created only in electronic formats, what about the hundreds of millions of books currently housed in libraries? Most books will not disappear within our lifetimes. Preservation managers will need to continue to use established methods for the maintenance of these materials.

Yet the emergence of electronic information will result in a fundamentally different way of approaching the preservation field which has been object based (books, broadsides, maps, etc.) and time oriented (e.g., permanent/durable paper should last for at least 250 years). Thus the notion of saving object X for Y years may become obsolete. We will need to secure the longevity of information so that the information itself does not disappear. And it must be done in concert with librarians, publishers, manufacturers, and anyone else involved in the handling of the information. Malinconico (1992) makes an articulate plea for library educators to teach students how to cooperate with the whole community of individuals who are involved with the dissemination of information—computer and telecommunications specialists, vendors, community service agencies, and educational organizations—so that there is an understanding of the problems from all perspectives (pp. 233–34).

Lesk (1992, p. 16) also calls for cooperation but cites as his reason the technical aspects of the digital world. But such cooperation is already an integral part of the preservation field: deacidification, standards for microfilming, and other developments required collaboration among preservation managers, conservators, scientists, and corporations. The only difference in the digital world is that we may need to look more toward industry in our collaborative efforts.

Current Initiatives or Paths out of the Forest

There are a number of interesting initiatives currently underway that suggest more than one path to be taken. Some projects are sponsored by the Commission on Preservation and Access and the British Library. A description of these will give the reader some idea of the directions in which librarians, researchers, and corporations are headed.

The Commission on Preservation and Access, since its formation in 1986 as the Committee on Preservation and Access of the Council on Library Resources (Byrne & Van Deventer, 1992, 313), has been charged with creating a structure to set the conditions for a national preservation program. In 1988, it became an independent nonprofit organization. Since then, it has sponsored research, organized task forces and symposia, and published numerous technical reports.

It has succeeded in accomplishing so much because it is an independent organization funded by universities, foundations, and granting organizations. It is an example of a network, a way of organizing activities that, according to Naisbitt (1982, pp. 192-94), is largely replacing the old hierarchies. In the case of preservation, it has, in a sense, replaced such hierarchies as the National Preservation Office at the Library of Congress. The National Preservation Office was dependent on staffing and support from the Library of Congress which, in recent years, has had fewer resources. Without the burden of a large hierarchy, the commission has had the freedom to pursue a number of initiatives. Patricia Battin, president of the commission, has often said in public speeches that the commission will last only as long as it takes to fulfill its mandate. No matter how long the commission lasts, its method of organizing a variety of activities through networks may well turn out to be a model that will be followed for some time to come.

Perhaps the most striking example of the commission's networking has been through the work of Hans Rütimann (1992), international project consultant to the commission. Through Rütimann's extensive travels, he has reported on a variety of preservation initiatives, including the Archivo General de Indias in Seville, Spain, which is seeking to make accessible the contents of 45 million documents and 7,000 maps and blueprints which chronicle Spain's 400 years of influence in the Americas. The project comprises three parts: (1) the creation of an image database, (2) a bibliographic database, and (3) implementation of an archive management system. The technical work is being carried out by IBM Spain at its Scientific Center north of Madrid, and the cataloging and scanning are being done at the archive (Rütimann & Lynn, 1992, p. 1). Rütimann (1992) has also reported on the possibilities for cooperation with preservation initiatives in China.

The Technology Assessment Advisory Committee of the commission has conducted and authored several pieces of research (Brown, 1991; Lynn et al., 1990; Waters, 1991). One of the members of the committee, M. Stuart Lynn, vice president of information technologies at Cornell University, is also involved in a collaborative effort between Cornell and Xerox (with the support of the commission) to test a prototype system for recording the text of deteriorating books as digital images. High-quality and archivally sound paper facsimiles can be produced from the digital images on demand. The project is described in detail by Kenney and Personius (1991).

At Yale, a study is being conducted (under contract to the commission) to determine the means, costs, and benefits of converting library materials on microfilm to digital images. The idea for this study was based in part on Lesk's 1990 report to the commission which affirmed the current use of microfilm as a preservation medium but suggested that, in the future, digital imaging technologies would be realistic only after the costs become lower (Lesk, 1990).

Meanwhile, the British Library Research and Development Department is sponsoring its own research into the electronic storage and transmission of texts. One of these projects was to examine the feasibility of acquiring data for storage in an electronic archive directly from the printer after it was typeset into electronic form. The text could be acquired in ASCII code, which is compact. In this manner, the British Library could maintain an accessible record of the intellectual content of published works. The user would have access to the information online. In order to determine the feasibility of such a plan, two researchers undertook a survey of printers to ascertain current technology and practices in Britain. The study concluded that it should be possible to convert much of the text held into an electronic form (Fiddes & Winterbottom, 1991, pp. 1-2).

The purpose of the projects described here is to capture the information, store it centrally, and then make it available to users on demand. The emphasis is on the information itself rather than on the artifact, and, in the case of both the Yale and British Library projects, they will be carried out at some future date.

There is still another path to be taken, one in which the new formats are treated as objects, much as we have treated books, archives, maps, and so on. Some of the preservation literature describes storage, handling, and use of various formats; this literature is becoming more voluminous every day. To cite a recent example, St-Laurent (1991) has written *The Care and Handling of Recorded Sound Materials* which discusses the physical characteristics of these formats, how they deteriorate, and how best to minimize their deterioration. As libraries acquire more of these new formats, they will depend increasingly on such literature.

Out of the Forest to Where?

After spending considerable time in preservation, where will we find ourselves? Which principles will be practiced? Will books be treated much as museum objects are today, as rare items because so few are being manufactured? Will reversibility become a dead issue because we will no longer expect books to last for hundreds of years? Will our very concept of permanence change in the next generation as consumer goods become disposable at an even faster rate than today's average paperback book? The answer to most of these questions is likely to be "yes." Concepts will change as the work environment changes and as the materials change. But the commitment to preserving information for future generations will certainly remain.

The Law of the Situation

Naisbitt (1982, pp. 85–86) directly and Kurzweil (1992c, p. 63), indirectly refer to the Law of the Situation, which asks "what business are you really in?" The law was formulated in 1904 by Mary Parker Follett (1942), the first management consultant in the United States (pp. 58–59). The question is usually asked when the business environment changes and a company or industry must reconceptualize its mission, though Follett saw it as being applicable to all organizations. Naisbitt uses the railroads as an example of an industry that did not understand the Law of the Situation. Instead of seeing themselves in the transportation business, they saw themselves only as railroads and almost became obsolete.

Kurzweil uses the blacksmith at the turn of the century as a metaphor for the position that libraries and other public institutions are in today. The blacksmith, who saw himself as a facilitator of transportation, traded in his forge for a gas pump. Kurzweil (1992c) contends that if libraries see their mission broadly as gathering information and making it universally available (not confined by library buildings or adversely influenced by current perceptions of librarianship), then they will become even more important in time (p. 63).

Applying the Law of the Situation to the field of preservation, we must consider the primary underpinnings of what we do. Are we ultimately concerned with the preservation of individual items or with the preservation of knowledge? If the former, then the field will merely respond to changes brought about by each new technology. If the latter, then we must help to shape the sources that will create and distribute information. Both items and knowledge must be preserved. We must continue to save as much information as possible, regardless of the format or the means by which it is stored and disseminated.

NOTES

1. For the past decade, librarians have used the term *preservation* to denote the aggregate care of collections, and *conservation* to refer to the treatment of individual items. In art, the term *conservation* denotes both.

2. The principles of longevity and reversibility are part of the *Code of Ethics and Standards of Practice* which deal specifically with conservation treatment issues. Written by The American Institute for Conservation of Historic & Artistic Works (AIC) and currently under revision, the code applies to books, paintings, objects, and so on (American Institute for Conservation of Historic & Artistic Works). AIC principles have influenced not only book conservators but preservation administrators as well.

3. Actually, many conservators have argued that no treatment is truly reversible. So, reversibility means that, inasmuch as possible, conservators will use the least intrusive treatments available. For example, thirty years ago, lamination was a common method of strengthening documents. Today conservators are more likely to encapsulate an item.

4. For a cogent discussion of recent scientific findings about the behavior of different types of paper, see Sparks (1991).

5. Knowledge of these projects is based, in part, on this author's discussion with Terry Cannon at the Research and Development Department of the British Library on July 29, 1992.

REFERENCES

Alighieri, D. (1975). *The portable Dante: The Divine Comedy, La Vita Nuova, excerpts from the Rhymes, and the Latin prose works.* Harmondsworth, Middlesex, England: Penguin Books.

The American Institute for Conservation of Historic & Artistic Works. (1985). *Code of ethics and standards of practice,* amended ed. Washington, DC: AIC (currently under revision).

Anderson, M. (1985). The preservation of machine-readable data for secondary analysis. *Archives, 17*(74), 79–93.

Brown, R. C. W. (1991). Mixed microform and digital. *Inform,* 5(9), 10–13.

Byrne, S., & Van Deventer, B. (1992). Preserving the nation's intellectual heritage: A synthesis. *College & Research Libraries News* 53(5), 313–315.

Cloonan, M. (1991). *Introduction to the program: Text, lies, & videotape: A discussion of reformatting technologies.* Unpublished oral presentation in San Marino, California, at The Huntington Library.

De Whitt, B. L. (1987a). Long-term preservation of data on computer magnetic media: Part I. *Conservation Administration News,* 29 (April), 7, 19, 28.

De Whitt, B. L. (1987b). Long-term preservation of data on computer magnetic media: Part 11. *Conservation Administration News,* 30 (July), 4, 24.

Document preservation by electronic imaging, vol. I: Synopsis. (1989). Bethesda, MD: Communications Engineering Branch, Lister Hill National Center for Biomedical Communications, National Library of Medicine.

Fiddes, R.G., & Winterbottom, D. R. (1991). *The feasibility of electronic accession of archive material at the printers.* [London, England]: British Library Research and Development Department (British Library R & D Report 6061).

Follett, M. P. (1942). *The giving of orders.* In H. C. Metcalf & L. Urwick (Eds.), *Dynamic administration: The collected papers of Mary Parker Follett* (pp. 58–59). New York: Harper & Bros.

Higginbotham, B. B. (1990). *Our past preserved: A history of American library preservation, 1876–1910.* Boston, MA: G. K. Hall.

Kenney, A. R., & Personius, L. K. (1991). *Update on digital techniques.* Insert in The Commission on Preservation and Access, Newsletter, 40 (November–December), [1–61 (this insert has separate pagination from the newsletter).

Kurzweil, R. (1992a). "The futurecast: The future of libraries. Part 1: The technology of the book." *Library Journal,* 117(1), 80, 82.

Kurzweil, R. (1992b). "The futurecast: The future of libraries. Part 2: The end of books." *Library Journal,* 117(3), 140–141.

Kurzweil, R. (1992c). "The futurecast: The future of libraries. Part 3: The virtual library." *Library Journal,* 117(5), 63–64.

Lesk, M. (1990). *Image formats for preservation and access: A report of the Technology Assessment Advisory Committee to the Commission on Preservation and Access.* Washington, DC: Commission on Preservation and Access.

Lesk, M. (1992). *Preservation of new technology.* Washington, DC: Commission on Preservation and Access.

Lynch, C. A., & Brownrigg, E. B. (1986). Conservation, preservation, and digitization. *College & Research Libraries,* 47(4), 379–382.

Lynn, M. S., & The Technology Assessment Advisory Committee to the Commission on Preservation and Access. (1990). *Preservation and access technology, the relationship between digital and other media conversion processes: A structured glossary of technical terms.* Washington, DC: The Commission on Preservation and Access.

Malinconico, S. M. (1992). What librarians need to know to survive in an age of technology. *Journal of Education for Library and Information Science,* 33(3), 226–240.

Naisbitt, J. (1982). *Megatrends: Ten new directions transforming our lives.* New York: Warner Books.

Naisbitt, J., & Aburdene, P. (1990). *Megatrends 2000: Ten new directions for the 1990's.* New York: William Morrow and Co.

Research issues in electronic records: Report of the working meeting. (1991). St. Paul, MN: The Minnesota Historical Society, for the National Historical Publications and Records Commission, Washington, D.C.

Rutimann, H. (1992). Preservation and access in China: Possibilities for cooperation: Report of a visit to the People's Republic of China (September 19–October 12, 1991). Washington, DC: The Commission on Preservation and Access.

Rutimann, H., & Lynn, M. S. (1992). Computerization project of the Archivo General de Indias, Seville, Spain: A report to the Commission on Preservation and Access. Washington, DC: The Commission on Preservation and Access.

Sniffen, M. J. (1991). "Lost in tapes: History fades as computer efforts focus on future." *The Courier-Journal* (Louisville, KY), (January 2) Al, A8 (report in The Abbey Newsletter, 15[3], 46–47).

Sparks, P. G. (1991). Some thoughts on paper as an information storage medium. The Commission on Preservation and Access: Newsletter, 40 (November/December), 3–4.

Special report: ALA back to basics. (1990). Wilson Library Bulletin, 65(1), 34–38, 43–51.

St-Laurent, G. (1991). The care and handling of recorded sound materials. Washington, DC: The Commission on Preservation and Access.

Stielow, F. J. (1991). Biting the WORM: Theory and tales of electronic media preservation. *CAN: Conservation Administration News*, (47), 10.

Swartzburg, S. G., & Bussey, H., with Garretson, F. (1991). Libraries and archives: Design and reno-vation with a preservation perspective. Metuchen, NJ: Scarecrow Press.

Waters, D. J. (1991). From microfilm to digital imagery: On the feasibility of a project to study the means, costs and benefits of converting large quantities of preserved library materials from microfilm to digital images: A report of the Yale University Library to the Committee on Preserva-tion and Access. Washington, DC: The Commis-sion on Preservation and Access.

Zachary, G. P. (1991). Compact disks for data aren't forever, it turns out. *The Wall Street Journal*, (Wednesday, October 16), B1, B4.

F. GERALD HAM

"The Archival Edge"

The American Archivist 38.1 (January 1975): 5–13.

This presidential address was delivered in Toronto, Ontario, Canada, on Thursday evening, October 3, 1974, at the thirty-eighth annual meeting of the Society of American Archivists. Mr. Ham, a Fellow of the Soci-ety since 1969, elected to the SAA Council in 1966, and Secretary of the Society (1968-71), is the State Archivist and head of the Division of Archives and Manuscripts, State Historical Society of Wisconsin.

OUR MOST IMPORTANT and intellectually demand-ing task as archivists is to make an informed selec-tion of information that will provide the future with a representative record of human experience in our time. But why must we do it so badly? Is there any other field of information gathering that has such a broad mandate with a selection process so random, so fragmented, so uncoordinated, and even so often accidental? Some archivists will admit the process is a bit out of kilter. They say a simple formula of more cooperation, less competition, increased governmen-tal largess, and bigger and better records surveys—a logistical device we often mistake for an acquisitions strategy—should be sufficient to produce a national mosaic that will bequeath to the future an eminently useable past.

A handful of critics, however, have suggested that something is fundamentally wrong: our methods are inadequate to achieve our objective, and our passiv-ity and perceptions produce a biased and distorted archival record. In 1970, Howard Zinn told an SAA audience that the archival record in the United States is biased towards the rich and powerful elements in our society—government, business, and the mili-tary—while the poor and the impotent remain in archival obscurity. To correct this, the chief spokes-man for history's new Left urged archivists "to com-pile a whole new world of documentary material about the lives, desires and needs of ordinary peo-ple."[1] How this task was to be done he shrewdly left to the archivists. In 1971 Sam Bass Warner, a noted historian of urban life, urged us to make our archives more useful. Like Zinn, Warner subscribed to Carl

Becker's notion that history should help people to understand the world they live in. To do this Warner asked archivists "so far as it is humanly possible" to "abandon the pursuit of the classic subjects of American history" and turn instead to the collection of data that would yield a "historical explanation of the major issues of our own time."[2] Warner had specific notions of how this should be done which were dismissed as the half-baked product of an archivally uninformed mind.

Even earlier there were rumblings in Columbus, Ohio, where a young and untamed archivist suggested that his colleagues' concern with quantity and competition inhibited discussion of advantages of quality and cooperation; that many, if not most, archival institutions operated "as introspective units justifying their existence solely on their own accomplishments rather than in terms of their role in the overall historical collection process"; and if this "egocentric attitude" was not abandoned competing archival programs would become so proliferated that the possibility of inter-institutional cooperation would be jeopardized.[3]

But the most sweeping indictment in what was emerging as a radical critique of the way archivists go about documenting history and culture came from the Cornell University historian and archivist, Gould P. Colman. Colman, in the *American Archivist* "Forum," charged that lack of concern about acquisition guidelines had produced possibly "the most serious problem facing archivists ... the politicalization of our profession," politicalization in the sense of "skewing the study of culture by the studied preservation of unrepresentative indicators of that culture." For example governments, particularly the one in Washington, preserved documents out of all proportion to government's impact on culture while other important institutions, such as the family, are poorly documented. Shouldn't archivists, Colman asked, have a responsibility to redress this balance? Documentation was biased further by our propensity to collect what is most easily accessible and by limiting oral history resources primarily to those relatively well-documented aspects of culture which could pay the expensive oral history piper.[4]

The empirical evidence—from published accession notes, from NUCMC, from recently issued guides, from anywhere an archivist keeps a record of what he collects—validates these charges. But the evidence reveals more than a biased record; it reveals incredible gaps in the documentation of even traditional concerns. Take the case of a midwestern state known both for its production and consumption of fermented beverages. Neither brewing nor the brewing industry is mentioned in any of the state's archival finding aids. It is possible that 1000 years from now some researcher will conclude that in a city known as Milwaukee the brewers [sic] art was unknown. The evidence also showed that many archivists waste time and space preserving random bits and pieces, as well as large accessions, of the most dubious value.

But the real cause for concern is that there doesn't seem to be any concern. With a few notable exceptions, there is no realization that our present data gathering methods are inadequate or that our fundamental problem is the lack of imaginative acquisition guidelines or comprehensive collecting strategies at all levels of archival activity. You search archival literature in vain to find something more helpful than a "how we did it here" article on a particular collecting program or an essentially "nuts and bolts" piece on the mechanics of collecting. Equally barren are the annual reports of the SAA committees dealing with identification and acquisition of archives. Further, an examination of the works on historical methodology and social science research indicate that our clients do not think the matter deserves much attention either.[5] For the archivist, the area of acquisition strategies remains a vacuum.

These criticisms, even if correct, are irrelevant for some archivists. To them the archival endeavor is primarily a custodial one. And the so-called dean of Canadian bookmen, Bernard Amtmann, would agree with them. In the May issue of the *Canadian Archivist* he stated, "archivists are by definition custodians of the material in their possession and their professional training and qualifications do not exactly encompass the ... historical evaluation of material." This evaluation, he said, "must surely be the responsibility of the historian."[6] Whether it was arrogance or ignorance, Bernard Amtmann was only echoing archivists. In 1969 as reported in the *New York Times* the archivist of New York City was asked what he saved. "Aside from the mayors' papers," he answered, "we try to keep only things which will protect the city against a suit or help it to document a suit against somebody else." He went on to suggest that "some of the historical societies" might be interested in examining the records he was destroying. "You never can tell," he said, "when you're going to come across something valuable."[7] And, in an uninformed way, he was only practicing what Hilary Jenkinson and others have preached.

Small wonder the custodial image is still widely held by our allies in the research community. Indeed, the persistence of the custodial tradition has not only been a major factor in the archivist's failure to deal with acquisition policy on a coherent and comprehensive basis, but has resulted in an obsession—with the "nuts and bolts" or craft aspects of our work.

Reinforcing the custodial tradition is a parallel tradition, that of the researcher as data gatherer. We all know that many of the great manuscript collections—those of Belknap, Draper, and H. H. Bancroft come easily to mind—were brought together in this fashion. The American Historical Association through its committees on source material perpetuated this tradition and even today there are archival programs where the history faculty are the collectors while the archivists are the "keepers of the past."[8]

This tradition, of course, leaves the archivist too closely tied to the vogue of the academic marketplace. For example, only after historians rediscovered the importance of the city in American history did a few so-called urban archives come into existence. Similar efforts, often initiated by the action of concerned historians, were developed to meet the needs for documentation on the black community; on ethnic groups and immigrants; on social welfare; on architecture; on popular culture; the history of science; and so forth. These responses to changing patterns in the pursuit of history, and to the increase of other studies once considered outside the proper use of archives, are a temporary corrective. There is a dilemma here. Most researchers are caught in their own concerns and do

not worry about all the history that needs to be written; yet in terms of documentary preservation this is precisely what the archivist must do. Small wonder, then, that archival holdings too often reflected narrow research interests rather than the broad spectrum of human experience. If we cannot transcend these obstacles, then the archivist will remain at best nothing more than a weathervane moved by the changing winds of historiography.

Turning from those traditions which have prevented the archivist from developing a larger acquisition design, let's consider five interrelated developments that are forcing him into a more active and perhaps more creative role.

The first is structural change in society. The process of institutionalizing and nationalizing decision-making, for example, has had a profound impact on documentation, making the archives of associations, pressure groups, protest organizations, and institutions of all sorts relatively more important than the papers of individuals and families. Accession data in the *American Archivist* reflects this change. Thirty years ago personal and family archives accounted for 38 percent of all reported accessions; but they account for only 14 percent today. In this same period, records of labor, of social and political protest, and of social welfare increased from less than 1 percent to nearly one-fourth of all accessions. Unlike family papers these archives usually do not fall unsolicited into the hands of a waiting archivist, and their percentage rise on the accession charts is partly the result of the sensitivity and hard work of many archivists. Further, as the government has become the primary instrument of social and economic policy the records of its dealings, especially with non-elite population groups, have become more important. But archival holdings do not reflect this change. One reason is the disorganization of state, county, and municipal records; another is the narrow appraisal criteria used by many public record archivists. The result has been the destruction of vast quantities of important social and economic data.

Closely related to institutionalized decision-making and increased governmental activity, is a second and more prosaic factor: bulk. With records increasing at an exponential rate, it is Utopian to believe that society could ever afford the resources for us to preserve everything of possible value; for it to do so would be irresponsible. We must realize that when we preserve one body of data it probably means that something else won't be preserved. But I do not think we have adequate methodological tools to make these critical choices. In fact, we might be better off if we forget what we have been taught. It is irresponsible and unrealistic to argue for the integrity of a file of gubernatorial papers that fills up 1500 document cases of which 80 percent is either duplicate or of marginal worth.

If the volume of documentation has greatly increased, the quality of the information has greatly decreased. Arthur Schlesinger, commenting in the *Atlantic Monthly* on this third problem—missing data—wrote: "In the last three quarters of a century, the rise of the typewriter [and to this we should add modern quick copy machines of all sorts] has vastly increased the flow of paper, while the rise of the telephone has vastly reduced its importance … . If a contemporary statesman has something of significance to communicate, if speed and secrecy are of the essence, he will confide his message, not to a letter, but to the telephone."[9] An examination of files similar to the gubernatorial papers above is proof that there is much more bulk of much less usefulness.

If the archivist is going to fill in the gaps he will have to become, as Warner suggests, "a historical reporter for his own time." He can use any of several techniques: he can create oral history, he can generate a photographic record, and he can collect survey data. As a reporter he can produce oral history, not as a painstakingly edited source for written texts about the Presidents and their men, but rather as documentation of the day to day decisions of lower echelon leaders and of the activities and attitudes of ordinary men and women. He can use photography to supplement the written record and make it more meaningful. But today, though most archival institutions collect photographs, virtually none has an active field program. And he could, if he has the courage and energy, do as one archivist suggests and create his own mail questionnaires and use other survey techniques to establish a base line of social and economic data.

A fourth factor in the making of the active archivist is that of vulnerable records or what we might call "instant archives." It is documentation that has little chance of aging into vintage archives, that is destroyed nearly as fast as it is created, and which must be quickly gathered before it is lost or scattered. At my own institution, for instance, the collections which deal with the major 1960's movements on the left—civil rights, student activism, and the anti-Vietnam War protest—probably would not exist today if we had not initiated contacts before many of the organizations quietly dissolved.

Technology is a fifth development. We are all aware that electronic impulses easily and rapidly disappear from magnetic tape, that photographic images often fade beyond recognition, that files with quick copy documents are literally self-destructing, and that the program documentation to important EDP data sets often disappears long before the archivist is aware the set was ever created. Because of its short life-cycle, we must collect this material on a current basis or not at all.

Taken together, these five factors—institutionalization, bulk, missing data, vulnerable records, and technology—have expanded the universe of potential archival data, have given a contemporaneous character to archival acquisition, and have permanently altered the job of the archivist, forcing him to make choices that he never had to make before. I see three developments on the archival landscape which, in part, are responses to these conditions—the specialized archives, the state archival networks, and an emerging model for urban documentation. The specialized archives, particularly those built around a subject area—the Archives of Social Welfare at the University of Minnesota is an example—have great appeal. They offer the possibility of well-defined parameters, and exhaustive documentation. They also allow the development of real staff expertise and may be easier to fund. The apotheosis of this type of program was the recent Eugene McCarthy Historical Project, described by its director as the most systematic attempt ever undertaken "to collect and organize all retrievable material of a political campaign for the presidential nomination." The records are voluminous and the project was expensive and the institutional competition for this prize was keen.[10]

But these archives, especially those centered around the life and times of an individual, do not come to grips with acquisition problems. They sidestep them. They contribute to the problem without adding to the solution. But they can contribute to the solution by plugging into larger conceptual frameworks, they can build the kind of inter-institutional linkages and coordination they now lack.

The need to link specialization with coordination was stressed by Sam Bass Warner. Speaking of the urban scene he argued that there is insufficient variation among American cities to justify the repetition everywhere of the same sort of collection. He urged historians and archivists to get together and divide up the archival turf. "San Francisco," he suggested, "might establish a business archive, Detroit, a labor archive, Los Angeles, a housing archive, … and so forth."[11] These specialized archives, in turn, would be *linked* with existing local, state, and federal programs. This was Warner's half-baked product that was dismissed out of hand.

But the concept of linkage is a key to the new state archival networks such as those in Ohio, Minnesota, Texas, and Wisconsin. The best of these have a coordinated acquisition program which seeks to be representative in subject coverage, inclusive in informational formats, and statewide in competence.[12] In these regards the Ohio network is one of the most advanced, conceptually if not operationally. The eight centers, most of which are part of a university, function as an integrated archives-library program for their assigned geographic area. Overall collection administration is provided by the Ohio Historical Society which supplies field service assistance in both the public and private sector and assumes responsibility for collections of statewide scope. Furthermore, interconnection assures that the activities of the centers are coordinative rather than competitive.[13] The network concept and structure offer not only a means to document society more systematically, but also to utilize better the limited resources of participating archival units.

In a similar fashion the Houston Metropolitan Archives Center hopes to do for one urban area what the networks have done for their states. Not only is the center the most ambitious urban archives program ever launched, it is also the most handsomely funded—a quarter of a million dollar grant from the National Endowment for the Humanities. The project is backed by a consortium of the three major urban universities and the Houston Public Library. In affiliation with the new statewide Regional Historical Research Depositories system, it serves as the public records depository for Houston and Harris County. Manuscript records, printed and non-text material, and oral history are part of its collecting program; and it will provide a fully automated bibliographic control system for all resources regardless of their location in Houston. And two historians—not archivists—using traditional archives-library components, created this comprehensive model for documenting urban life.[14] These approaches can be a beginning. But we must do much more.

First. We must change old habits and attitudes. The view, held by many in our profession that, in collecting, cooperation is synonymous with abdication, must become an anachronism. Given our limited resources, the competition which produces fragmentation and the idiosyncratic proprietary view of archives must yield to integrated cooperative programs which have easily available information on the location of their resources.

Second. We must commit a far greater proportion of our intellectual resources to developing guidelines and strategies for a nationwide system of archival data collecting. And let me say that I am talking about concepts and flexible programs, not rigid structures or uniform procedures. Let me suggest some beginnings. Our subject area committees must give as much attention to appraisal and acquisition criteria and methods as they do to the preparation of technical manuals and directories. Conceptualization must precede collection and, while this methodology is equally applicable to all subject areas, church archives provide a finely drawn example of how this process can be applied. Why couldn't archivists determine the documentation needed to study contemporary religious life, thought, and change and then advise denominations and congregations on how their records selection can contribute to this objective?

We must also develop empirical studies on data selection. For example, why don't college and university archivists compare the documentation produced by institutions of higher learning with the records universities usually preserve, to discover biases and distortions in the selection process and to provide an informed analysis on how archivists should document education and its institutions?

We need more seminars similar to the recent Midwest Archives Conference seminar on state networks to deal with collecting plans and strategies. One on labor documentation would be especially timely. The goal of that seminar might be a consortium of labor archives. Such a cooperative effort would conserve and amplify rather than waste limited resources. Researchers would be better served if the consortium determined weaknesses in labor documentation and then did something about it. And the individual labor archival institutions *might* even find some workable way to decide who should knock on whose door.

We need to develop methodologies to cope with the important but vast time-series now produced by public and private agencies. Series such as case files of all sorts are so massive that wholesale preservation even on microfilm is impossible. The sample techniques of the various social sciences may offer a solution to the construction of a "representative" sample and suggest the limits and advantages of using one approach rather than another. Similarly, the conceptualization that went into the development of first economic and later social indicators may be transferrable to archival documentation. And the models built by anthropology, economics, sociology, and psychology may give clues to the direction of future research as well as a vision of what constitutes social relevance. The uneasy partnership of the archivist and the historian must be strengthened and expanded to include other students of society.

If our literature is an index to our profession's development, then we need a new body of writings because our old catechisms are either inadequate or irrelevant when they deal with contemporary archives and the theory and practice related to their acquisition. And without needed conceptual and empirical studies, archivists must continue to make their critical choices in intellectual solitary confinement.

Third. We need to reallocate our limited resources for collecting. The critics also present a strong case that far too much effort and money go to document the well documented. In addition, we need archival revenue sharing that will enable the states and localities to meet their archival responsibilities better. The passage of the National Historical Publications and Records Act would be a modest beginning by encouraging statewide planning and providing funds to implement these programs.

Finally, the archivist must realize that he can no longer abdicate his role in this demanding intellectual process of documenting culture. By his training and by his continuing intellectual growth, he must become the research community's Renaissance man. He must know that the scope, quality, and direction of research in an open-ended future depends upon the soundness of his judgment and the keenness of his perceptions about scholarly inquiry. But if he is passive, uninformed, with a limited view of what constitutes the archival record, the collections that he acquires will never hold up a mirror for mankind. And if we are not holding up that mirror, if we are not helping people understand the world they live in, and if this is not what archives is all about, then I do not know what it is we are doing that is all that important.

As archivists we must be in a more exposed position than we have been in the past, one that is more vulnerable. We might well heed the advice of one of Kurt Vonnegut's minor characters, Ed Finnerty, "a chronically malcontent boozer" and the real hero of the novel *Player Piano.* When someone suggested he should see a psychiatrist, Ed replied: "He'd pull me back into the center, and I want to stay as close to the edge as I can without going over. Out on the edge you see all kinds of things you can't see from the center... Big, undreamed-of things—the people on the edge see them first."[15]

NOTES

1. Howard Zinn, "The Archivist and Radical Reform," unpublished manuscript, pp.12–13, 18.

2. Sam Bass Warner, "The Shame of the Cities: Public Records of the Metropolis," unpublished manuscript, 1971, pp. *2, 3.*

3. David R. Larson, "The Ohio Network of American History Research Centers," *Ohio History* (Winter 1970): 62.

4. "The Forum: Communications From Members," *American Archivist* 35 (July/October 1972): 483–85.

5. Examples of the historian's superficial approach to acquisition problems are the "Report of Ad Hoc Committee on Manuscripts Set Up by the American Historical Assoc. in December 1948," *American Archivist* 14 (July 1951): 233; and more recently, Walter Rundell, Jr., *In Pursuit of American History: Research and Training in the United States* (Norman: University of Oklahoma Press, 1970), pp. 104–07.

6. An abbreviated version of this article by Amtmann, "Historical Manuscripts at Auction," was widely circulated in the United States in the July 22, 1974, issue of the *Antiquarian Bookman,* pp. 356–57.

7. *New York Times,* November 23, 1969.

8. See William F. Birdsall, "The American Archivist's Search for Professional Identity, 1909–1936" (Ph.D. dissertation, University of Wisconsin-Madison, 1973), particularly ch. 5.

9. Arthur Schlesinger, Jr., "On the Writing of Contemporary History," *Atlantic Monthly* (March 1967), p. 71.

10. Werner Peters, "The McCarthy History Project," *American Archivist* 33 (April 1970): 155.

11. Warner, "Shame of the Cities," p. 4.

12. Richard A. Erney and F. Gerald Ham, "Wisconsin's Area Research Centers," *American Libraries* 3 (February 1972): 135–40; James E. Fogerty, "Minnesota Regional Research Centers," *Minnesota History* (Spring 1974): 30–32; Marilyn von Kohl, "New Program Focuses Attention on Local Records," *Texas Libraries* (Summer 1972): 90–93.

13. The Ohio Network of American History Research Centers: Charter; Agreement Number One, Administration of Local Ohio Government Records; Agreement Number Two, Ohio Newspapers; and Agreement Number Three, Ohio Manuscripts. Xerox copies.

14. Proposal, "Houston Metropolitan Archives Center," National Endowment for the Humanities, Division of Research Grants.

15. Tim Hildenbrand, "Two or Three Things I know About Kurt Vonnegut's Imagination," in The *Vonnegut Statement,* Jerome Klinkowitz and John Somer (eds.) (New York: Delacorte, 1973), p. 121.

PAMELA W. DARLING AND SHERELYN OGDEN

Excerpt from "From Problems Perceived to Programs in Practice: The Preservation of Library Resources in the U.S.A., 1956–1980"

Library Resources & Technical Services 25.1 (January/March 1981): 9–29; excerpts.

Twenty-five years ago preservation was largely a neglected area. This historical review focuses on major events, activities, and publications that have contributed to the emergence of preservation as a vital specialty within librarianship.

IN 1946 PELHAM Barr wrote, "Silence, rarely broken, seems to surround the subject of book conservation ... Conservation, as responsible custody, is the only library function which should be continuously at work twenty-four hours a day ... concerned with every piece of material in the library from the moment the selector becomes aware of its existence to the day it is discarded. The reason this sounds so exaggerated is that it is a forgotten platitude ... There was a time when library administration was simpler, when these platitudes were living, activating principles. But, with the increasing complexity of universities and their libraries, the custodial function of the library—the 'care and custody of the collection'—has deteriorated through neglect. ... It became harder and harder to develop a program and procedures for book conservation, and therefore it was more and more neglected."[1]

Barr's experience as a founding member and first executive director of the Library Binding Institute brought him into close contact with the results of this neglect, and his analysis of the causes and outline of administrative remedies are astute and still remarkably valid. But he was ahead of his time, and the silence about conservation deepened in following decade.

What then of the quarter-century to be reviewed in this paper? How has conservation, or preservation, fared? (The reader will here note that the terms *con-servation* and *preservation* are used interchangeably. Despite numerous efforts to define and distinguish between them, no working consensus has yet emerged within the library profession, and rather than attempt to impose our own versions—the authors don't altogether agree either!—we shall flow fuzzily with the crowd on this point.) Since Barr's time, the silence about conservation has ended. These twenty-five years just past have been increasingly noisy. Indeed at the risk of irritating proper historians, we shall here suggest that the modern field of library preservation was born in 1956, for two events occurred in that year that can be considered the beginning of our profession's serious and sustained attention to preservation.

First Steps

The first of these events was the publication in January 1956 of a *Library Trends* issue entitled "Conservation of Library Materials."[2] Edited by the late Maurice F. Tauber, the issue included articles on the conservation of old and rare books, stack problems, lamination, binding, discarding, and personnel for preservation functions. Tauber's introduction to the issue was titled "Conservation Comes of Age," a premature assertion as we can now see, but the infant was definitely alive and growing.

Tauber had reported that committees of the Association of Research Libraries (ARL) and the Council of National Library Associations had considered plans for the protection and preservation of library materials in 1954 and 1955, apparently motivated chiefly by wartime and cold war fears of military attack and the threat of nuclear devastation. The seeds of several "national plans" can be found 'in these deliberations. Although these seeds have germinated (if not flourished) in the years since, in 1956 many critical ingredients were still missing. As Tauber's introduction concluded: "The reader may not find in these pages as many guideposts for a conservation theory as he might like ... the major usefulness of the papers, however, is in pointing up the many areas which are still in need of basic investigations."[3]

Who was to carry out these investigations? A potent new force, for preservation as for most other areas of librarianship, emerged through the other major event of 1956, the establishment of the Council on Library Resources (CLR). Funded by the Ford Foundation and guided through its first fifteen years by the extraordinary Verner W. Clapp, CLR from the start recognized preservation as an urgent problem and set in motion the "basic investigations" necessary for its solution. A full history of the Council's role in preservation is well beyond the scope of this review, but the Council's significance as a guiding hand will appear throughout the account that follows.

Repeatedly associated with the names of Clapp and the Council during these early years is that of William J. Barrow. A document restorer at the Virginia State Library, Barrow became fascinated by the problems of aging paper. In the late 1930s he developed the cellulose acetate and tissue method of lamination that bears his name, and, in the mid-1940s, the first of his deacidification processes. His work became known to the larger library community through the 1956 *Library Trends* issue.[4] Perhaps sensing that the time was now ripe, the Virginia state librarian, Randolph W. Church, approached CLR with a proposal that Barrow be supported in an extensive study of the "paper problem." Clapp agreed, and on June 1, 1957, Barrow began his first study on the physical strength of the paper used for nonfiction book publishing between 1900 and 1949. The shocking results, suggesting that only 3 percent of the volumes studied had paper which could be expected to last more than fifty years, led to a second study on the stabilization of modern book papers. A report of these two studies appeared in 1959,[5] and in March of that year, again with CLR support, Barrow began a year-long investigation of the feasibility of manufacturing durable paper.

That same year, CLR provided support to the American Library Association (ALA) for the establishment of the Library Technology Project (LTP), brainchild of Clapp and CLR vice-president Ruggles. LTP came into being with Frazer G. Poole as director, and although LTP's activities have by no means been confined to preservation, its role and Poole's were nonetheless significant, as we shall see.

Following publication of the report for Barrow's second Council-funded project on the manufacture of stable paper,[6] a one-day conference was held on September 16, 1960, "to explore the potential benefits for the users of books offered by the new chemical wood pulp paper recently developed under the auspices of the Virginia State Library by W. J. Barrow .... "[7] Cosponsored by the Virginia State Library and ALA, the meeting in Washington's Cosmos Club brought together a group of librarians, publishers, paper manufacturers, and CLR staff for a general review of the situation and of the effects Barrow's findings might be expected to have on future publishing. The final recommendation was that ALA establish a committee to "continue some discussion of this problem, looking toward mutually agreeable solutions."[8]

Two other events of 1960 moved forward the cause of preservation—one directly, and the other indirectly but, in the long run, as significantly. In June 1960, after a discussion of Barrow's findings at a meeting of the Association of Research Libraries, a standing Committee on Preservation of Research Library Materials was appointed.[9] Since the formation of the committee led in the next twelve years to the articulation of a broad-scale cooperative approach to the nation's preservation problems, this action was evidence of the trend Tauber had earlier identified—"that a problem of national significance is receiving earnest attention from library leaders."[10]

The other event, virtually unnoticed within the library world, was the formal recognition of the profession of art conservation in the United States by the establishment of the American Group of the International Institute for Conservation of Historic and Artistic Works, and by the admission of the first class to the country's first graduate training program for art conservators at the Institute of Fine Arts of New York University. The development of professional education programs in this area, with its obvious parallels and areas of overlap with library preservation, is now strongly influencing the pattern of professional development for the latter. And it is worth noting that the first graduate of NYU's program, art-on-paper conservator Mary Todd Glaser, became senior conservator of the New England Document Conservation Center, the first cooperative regional center with a special focus on library materials. But we are getting ahead of our story.

In 1961 the search for answers to technical problems was accelerated when CLR funded the W. J. Barrow Research Laboratory, a permanent facility located in the new Virginia Historical Society building. Here Barrow and a small staff of scientists pursued investigations on permanence and durability of the book.[11]

Early National Planning

In 1962 the first published report from the ARL preservation committee sought to establish, through a CLR-funded sampling study, a framework for national planning by assessing the "magnitude of the paper-deterioration problem."[12] The findings—that nonserial titles listed in the National Union Catalog in 1961 contained just under three billion pages, of which nearly 60 percent were probably printed on paper that was rapidly deteriorating—were perhaps more stunning than stimulating to specific action. But by the end of the year CU had provided new funds for a major project to determine potential solutions to the paper-deterioration problem.

This study was conducted by Gordon Williams, director of the Center for Research Libraries. His report, *The Preservation of Deteriorating Books: An Examination of the Problem with Recommendations for a Solution*,[13] was unanimously adopted by ARL in January 1965 and has been called "the most significant single document on the subject."[14] Williams concluded that the best way to deal with the problem of the deterioration of library materials would be

to establish a centralized federal agency to preserve a physical copy of every significant written record and make copies available to all libraries. Microfilming of materials as an adjunct to physical preservation, to preserve the text and reduce wear on the original, was also an important element of the proposal, and Williams commended the Library of Congress' work toward a central listing of microform masters. The first issue of *National Register of Microform Masters* appeared in September 1965 and has since become an essential tool in all preservation microfilming activities.[15]

At its June 1965 meeting, ARL recommended that the Library of Congress take responsibility for implementing a program based on the Williams report, and LC accepted the challenge.[16] At a meeting on December 6, 1965, among senior staff at the Library of Congress and the ARL Preservation Committee, the Librarian of Congress "stated that the Library of Congress will assume responsibility for a program for the preservation of deteriorating books in accordance with the principles set forth in the Report ... by Gordon R. Williams."[17]

Basic Investigations

Meanwhile, the Library Technology Project had been at work on a variety of projects related to preservation—studying adhesives and pressure-sensitive tapes; developing the Se-Lin system for safe, durable call number labels; undertaking an extended project with the Barrow Laboratory for the development of performance standards for library binding; sponsoring Hawken's work on reprographic techniques, including his landmark *Copying Methods Manual*;[18] supporting Barrow's work on permanent/durable catalog cards. In 1965 a special CLR grant supported an LTP project intended to produce a series of manuals on conservation practices. In fact, LTP engaged in a whole range of projects relating to the physical quality of library materials and methods.[19]

In a related development, the first report on Richard D. Smith's experiments in search of a deacidification treatment for whole books appeared in 1966.[20] Thus during this period the Library Technology Project and the Barrow Research Laboratory, supported by the Council and often working together, and Smith (soon to be supported by CLR), were carrying out "basic investigations" and developing technical tools for building library preservation programs, while the deliberations and projects of ARL and LC, also Council-supported, were setting up the policy framework for those programs. Much had occurred in the ten years since the *Library Trends* issue on conservation.

Local Developments— The Newberry Example

To what extent was all this activity affecting operations on the local level? Librarians have been caring for materials, in some fashion, since libraries began, but the intensity and effectiveness of the care has varied considerably. Although binding and mending sections and stack maintenance units have been common for generations, and the microfilming of deteriorating materials to preserve their intellectual content began in the early 1930s,[21] programs encompassing the full range of preservation activities as we now define them are of very recent origin. For most libraries in the fifties and sixties, a wide range of problems was arrayed under the rubric of *preservation* or *conservation.* Many the technical solutions to these problems were still experimental and problematic at best. Further, the organizational complexities implicit in any attempt to assign responsibility for programs addressing all these problems to a single administrative unit prevented the development of a unified program.

One institution particularly suited to the task of developing a program through the happy coincidence of place and personality quietly moved ahead during the first decade of our review. The Newberry Library, private and scholarly, is free of heavy patron pressures from faculty and student body, Congress, or a taxpaying citizenry, and has a specialized collection interest in the history of the book. One Newberry board president, Everett D. Graff, brought a special concern for preservation to his duties, and by 1961 air conditioning was installed in the dignified old Chi-

cago building to retard deterioration of its contents. The next year, Lawrence W. Towner was appointed librarian and began working to extend Graff's concern to the total care of the collections. In 1964 Towner appointed Paul N. Banks as the Newberry's first "conservator," giving him broad responsibilities for reshaping the in-house bindery operations and developing a library-wide conservation program.[22] With scientific research and the resulting technical tools, broad national policies backed up by a steady flow of funds through CLR, and the development of local procedures for adaptation elsewhere, the stage seemed set. Surely development of preservation as a discipline within librarianship would be rapid from then on.

The Florence Interlude

Nature has a way of interfering in the affairs of humankind, however, and on the night of November 4, 1966, the waters of the Arno swirled through Florence, Italy, leaving a trail of mud and destruction throughout homes, businesses, churches, museums, and libraries. Conservation activities in the rest of the world virtually came to a halt as binders, restorers, and conservators joined a massive international salvage effort. Much has been written about Florence, the salvage operation, and its effects on the conservation field which we shall not repeat here.[23] It is appropriate for this review, however, to observe that although the Florence "event" temporarily interrupted developments in the United States, both the focusing of public attention on the subject of conservation and the techniques and professional relationships established through the salvage effort stimulated and influenced subsequent activities here to an extraordinary degree.

This is not to say that nothing else happened while the mud was being cleaned up in Florence. In May of 1967 the American Group of the International Institute for Conservation of Historic and Artistic Works adopted the first code of ethics for art conservators, a companion document to its 1963 standards of practice, the latter of which is often referred to as the "Murray Pease Report" after the chairman of the committee that prepared it.[24] In June the Library of Congress appointed Frazer G. Poole as LC's first preservation officer, and he began a long series of reorganizations and expansions of LC's preservation activities. In the fall of that year, LTP published the first edition of Carolyn Horton's now classic *Cleaning and Preserving Bindings and Related Materials,*[25] the New York Library Association held a symposium on preservation during its annual conference, and the first edition of the Cunha work, *Conservation of Library Materials,* appeared.[26]

The Pilot Preservation Project (which became known as the Brittle Rooks Project) was conducted at the Library of Congress during this period. This study concluded that establishment of a national preservation collection was administratively feasible in terms of identification of material, that compilation of a register of best copies would present few difficulties, and that problems still to be resolved included development of a more efficient and economical method of deacidification, determination of optimal storage conditions, and choice of a secure site.[27]

By 1969, almost everybody was back from Florence and the pace began to increase. A second edition of Horton's manual, revised and expanded and in great demand, appeared from LTP. The New York Library Association established an ad hoc committee on preservation. Binder-restorer Laura Young was commissioned to do a preservation survey for the library of the New York Botanical Garden, and in August a conference was held at the University of Chicago.

The Chicago Conference and Subsequent Developments

The Thirty-fourth Annual Conference of the Graduate Library School, a three-day event entitled "Deterioration and Preservation of Library Materials," included formal papers and discussions covering the scholarly needs for preservation, the nature of library materials, and the physical requirements for insuring their survival, organizational considerations, and personnel needs. The conference organizers "hoped that the wide representation here of various parties concerned with the problems of preservation may contribute to a wider communication of knowledge and cross-fertilization of ideas so important in scientific advance."[28] They succeeded in their aims, for the conference served to summarize what was then the state of the art and to stimulate renewed activity, while the proceedings remain one of the most frequently cited documents of the field.

In the next year, Poole's labors at the Library of Congress began to bear fruit, as CLR provided funds to establish a laboratory, and Peter Waters—a major organizer of salvage operations at the Biblioteca Nazionale Centrale di Firenze and prominent English binder-restorer—was brought in as consultant to guide the laboratory development. Also under Poole's leadership, the Bookbinding Committee of ALA's Resources and Technical Services Division expanded its functions and changed its name to the Committee on Preservation of Library Materials. At the Newberry Library, Banks' operation was expanded through the establishment of a conservation laboratory. The New York Public Library, actively concerned about preservation since at least the days of Lydenberg, moved closer toward a formal program with the publication of Henderson's *Memorandum on Conservation of the Collections,*[29] an amplification of the paper he and Robert Krupp had prepared for the Chicago conference.

Attention was also focusing again on the need for a national program. The LC Pilot Preservation Project had pointed up the wide range of technical and organizational questions surrounding the "national collection" idea, and the ARL Preservation Committee pressed forward the effort to answer those questions. With a grant, this time from the U.S. Office of Education (the first significant federal fund for library preservation), the ARL committee, under the chairmanship of Warren J. Haas, launched a new effort that culminated in the publication of *Preparation of Detailed Specifications for a National System the Preservation of Library Materials.* Originally the project was aimed at establishing the operational details necessary for implementation of the Williams proposals of 1964, but as work progressed the purpose was modified. Noting that "the objective ... of suggesting specific steps that seem necessary to help move the research library community towards the preservation goals it has set for itself remained unchanged,"[30] the Haas report takes the Williams report as its starting point but moves considerably beyond it in making recommendations for future action.

While the Haas report was still in preparation, important steps we being taken. Waters was appointed restoration officer of the Library of Congress. Yale University Library began a Preservation Office, under Susan Swartzburg, who was succeeded by Gay Walker; the New York Public Library established its Conservation Division under John P. Baker; the Boston Athenaeum sponsored a major conference on' library and archives conservation;[31] Jean Gunner was appointed conservator/bookbinder at the Hunt Botanical Institute Library; and Paul Banks began teaching conservation of library materials for the University of Illinois.

Information was becoming much more available. The second edition of *Conservation of Library Materials* appeared; Clapp produced his remarkable "Story of Permanent/Durable Book Paper, 1115-1970";[32] LTP brought out the second volume in its conservation series, Middleton's *Restoration of Leather Bindings;*[33] LC published the first edition of Peter Waters' pamphlet on salvaging water-damaged materials;[34] the Library Binding Institute published Tauber's *Library Binding Manual;*[35] and a major treatment of deterioration, by Carl J. Wessel, appeared in the new *Encyclopedia of Library and Information Science.*[36]

As techniques for physical treatment expanded and improved, the professional structure grew. The American Group of the International Institute for Conservation of Historic and Artistic Works reorganized as the American Institute for Conservation of Historic and Artistic Works (AIC). This small but vigorous group, including conservators of library materials, grew dramatically in the following years, stimulating the development of improved techniques, educational programs, and an increasingly scientific approach to vexing technical problems.

[...]

Collective Action

The ARL/OMS project is one among many examples of collective action supporting the efforts of individual institutions. These collective activities may be grouped under three major headings: program support from professional organizations and associations, cooperative efforts within a regional or network framework, and progress towards a "national program."

Within the American Library Association, preservation grew rapidly in the years following the transformation of the Bookbinding Committee into the division-level Committee on Preservation of Library Materials. While continuing its interest in binding, the committee was also actively concerned with the availability of permanent/durable paper and sponsored a series of tours, programs, and exhibits during ALA conferences on a variety of preservation topics. As interest within the profession grew, committee meetings were crowded with observers hoping to pick up useful information and by 1976 there was sufficient support for the establishment of a Preservation Discussion Group to provide a structured channel for the exchange of news, views, and developments. The following year the committee set up a subcommittee on library/binders relations to work on specifications and other areas of mutual concern, and an ad hoc group undertook the creation and periodic updating of the *Preservation Education Flyer.* In 1979, the RTSD Board approved the recommendation of the preservation committee that it be reorganized and given full section status within the division. The new section numbered approximately fifteen hundred members in the first year, with its first elected officers taking over in the summer of 1980. Such formal recognition of the importance of preservation by the nation's largest library association did much to encourage preservation developments and stimulate leadership in the field.

During the same period, the role of library conservation within the American Institute for Conservation grew in significance. Perhaps the most important factor in this process was the activity of Paul Banks, whose service as treasurer, vice-president, and then president, in 1978-80, kept the particular preservation problems of libraries clearly in focus within this organization of art and object conservators. By 1980, many librarians were members of AIC, and when specialty groups emerged the book-and-paper group was among the largest and most active.

In 1973, the National Conservation Advisory Council was established to "identify and offer recommendations for the solution of preservation problems" and to "serve as a forum for cooperation and planning among institutions and programs concerned with the conservation of cultural property."[64] Its Study Committee on Libraries and Archives, chaired by Banks, published an excellent summary of "national needs" in 1978,[65] a policy document expected to influence funding and program initiatives in the future.

The Society of American Archivists and the American Association for State and Local History were also increasingly active in preservation, conducting workshops and producing publications to support the work of their constituencies. In 1980, the National Endowment for the Humanities awarded a major grant to the former for the development of manuals and an extensive series of workshops. Communication between librarians and other groups was limited, but as the sheer numbers of preservation-conscious professionals in various fields increased, the opportunity for cooperative development also grew.

The need for institutional cooperation in coping with the massive problems of preservation has long been recognized, but the development of actual mechanisms has been slow and painful. One major cooperative approach, borrowed from the art conservation field, is the of the regional center, which can provide consultation and conservation treatment services and perform some educational and training functions for many institutions that could not afford to support such programs individually.

In 1973, the Council on Library Resources provided start-up funds for the New England Document Conservation Center, the first regional center established primarily to meet the conservation needs of libraries.[66] Governed by the New England Library Board, which continues to provide limited operating support, the nonprofit center offers a wide range of conservation services to libraries, historical societies, archives, and town record offices on a fee-for-

service basis. In its early years the center was directed by George M. Cunha, former conservator of the Boston Athenaeum. At his retirement in 1977, the center was reorganized to allow for the appointment of a full-time administrator, Ann Russell, and a full-time senior conservator, Mary Todd Glaser. In 1980, the professional staff also included a book conservator, an assistant conservator with a specialty in photographs, and a records specialist who directed the preservation microfilming service. The center had experienced serious financial difficulties, and in its early years had trouble finding enough people with appropriate training to provide the full range of services; but by 1980 both staff and budget were well balanced and the center had received an NEH grant to expand its field service program.

The New England Document Conservation Center has provided a valuable test of the regional center approach, but as 1980 ended, although it was still the only full-service center devoted primarily to library materials, a significant portion of its income derived from the conservation of art on paper for museums and other nonlibrary customers. The continued scarcity of trained book conservators, together with the inability or unwillingness of libraries to allocate substantial funds for what is a very expensive process, probably accounts for this imbalance.

Another approach to the provision of conservation services on a regional basis took shape in New York. In 1979, with initial funding from the H. W. Wilson Foundation, the New York Botanical Garden Library established a Book Preservation Center to provide advisory services and training in proper care and minor repair of library materials to institutions throughout the metropolitan New York area. This center does not offer treatment services, but assists many small and medium-sized libraries to evaluate their preservation needs and improve their maintenance and repair programs.[67]

Other joint efforts have focused on programs not requiring the immediate establishment and staffing of a center. The Research Libraries Group (RLG) in its first incarnation as a consortium of Harvard, Yale, Columbia, and the New York Public Library had an active preservation committee. This committee established standards for the care of "master copies"—

titles that one member agreed to preserve and make available for all other members; developed shipping containers for the safe transport of interlibrary loan volumes among members; recommended pricing policies, and operated a pilot project of coordinated preservation microfilming; and prepared a number of reports and recommendations regarding the bibliographic control and joint storage of microform masters. When RLG was restructured and expanded in 1978, preservation activities temporarily ceased; future efforts will probably focus on exploiting RLG's emerging bibliographic system to coordinate preservation decisions.

The California Library Authority for Systems and Services (CLASS) made preservation an important priority in 1977, sponsoring a colloquium on conservation followed by extensive consultations that resulted in a major planning document for the state.[68] Case Western Reserve, with support from an LSCA grant in 1977, conducted a survey of conservation needs in Ohio, producing a report that recommended establishment of a regional center to serve a six-state area. In 1979, funds from the National Historic Publications and Records Commission enabled the Western Council of State Libraries to conduct a Western States Materials Conservation Project to "form a cadre of conservation advocates," identify needs, develop an action plan, and take preliminary implementation steps. The project concluded with a feasibility colloquium, from which came a Western Conservation Congress; which is to follow through on establishing a conservation information clearinghouse as a first step toward a complete range of services.[69]

Planning studies, reports, and recommendations play an important role in advancing the thinking of a profession on particular topics and create an environment in which desired change can be accomplished. The process, however, is often a slow and cumbersome one, the more so in relation to the number of people and institutions involved. Nowhere is this more apparent than in the attempts to develop a "national preservation program" for libraries in the United States. We have already mentioned the early ARL studies by Gordon in 1964 and by Warren J. Haas

in 1972, and the Library of Congress' Pilot Preservation Project in the late 1960s. In 1976 the Library of Congress made another effort, calling a "Planning Conference for a National Preservation Program." The two-day meeting, supported by CLR, brought together librarians, conservators, publishers, and representatives of funding agencies to review the existing state of affairs and respond to a set of proposals developed by Poole.[70] The conference endorsed the major elements in the proposals, and an ad hoc advisory committee was appointed to work with LC on development. Norman Shaffer, who had directed the Brittle Books Project, was appointed National Preservation Program Officer, and the advisory committee met twice, focusing its attention initially on the need for bibliographic control of master microforms as the foundation for a coordinated preservation filming program. However, in 1977 Poole retired, LC was passing through a series of major reorganizations, and Congress began a series of budget slashings that endangered LC's ability to keep up with existing program responsibilities. It became evident that LC would have to dedicate its preservation resources to coping with the needs of its own collections, and once again prospects for a "national program" dimmed.

From this vantage point it may be appropriate to make several observations. The seemingly sensible recommendation that a national program be administered by a federal agency may have been a strategic error, in effect passing the buck to a government grappling with inflation and an increasing number of worthy programs seeking funding and creating the illusion for many that the responsibility no longer lay within the profession. In addition, the scope of preservation needs is so vast, the masses of materials affected so overwhelming, and the state of procedural development still so primitive that a national program would probably have been impossible even if staffing and funding problems had not intervened. A great deal more experimentation and development of program elements on a small scale will be necessary before large-scale programs can be implemented. Finally, effective coordination of large-scale programs will not be possible until a fast, accurate, comprehensive bibliographic system exists to support decision making and eliminate costly duplication of effort. We must not conclude, however, that national planning efforts have been wasted. The fundamental theories are still valid, and the very absence of a national program has stimulated local and regional efforts that will form the foundation for a national system.

In this review we have concentrated on the major events and activities that have contributed to the emergence of preservation as a vital specialty within librarianship in the United States, an emphasis that has meant ignoring significant developments in Canada and elsewhere, giving short shrift to the activities of archivists, conservators, and others in related fields, and omitting mention of many U.S. libraries and librarians who have participated in the remarkable growth of preservation activities. For the adequacy of the record these omissions are unfortunate, but for the long life of our collections it bodes well: preservation is no longer the province of the few, and as the rapid multiplying of activities exceeds our ability to recount them all, it enhances our collective capacity to preserve the materials entrusted to our care.

REFERENCES

1. Pelham Barr, "Book Conservation and University Library Administration," *College & Research Libraries* 7: 214, 219 (July 1946).

2. Maurice F. Tauber, ed., "Conservation of Library Materials," *Library Trends* 4: 215–334 (Jan. 1956).

3. Maurice F. Tauber, "Conservation Comes of Age," *Library Trends* 4: 221 (Jan. 1956).

4. Ray O. Hummel and W. J. Barrow, "Lamination and Other Methods of Preservation," *Library Trends* 4: 259–68 (Jan. 1956).

5. Randolph W. Church, ed., *Deterioration of Book Stock: Causes and Remedies: Two Studies on the Permanence of Book Paper Conducted by W. J. Barrow* (Richmond: Virginia State Library, 1959).

6. Randolph W. Church, ed., *The Manufacture and Testing of Durable Book Papers, Based on the Investigations of W. J. Barrow* (Richmond: Virginia State Library, 1960).

7. Permanent/Durable Book Paper: Summary of a Conference Held in Washington, D.C., September 16, 1960 (Richmond: Virginia State Library, 1960), p. 15.

8. Ibid., p. 28.

9. Association of Research Libraries, Minutes of the Fifty-fifth Meeting of the Association Research Libraries, June 18, 1960 (Washington, D.C.: Association of Research Libraries, 1960), p. 1–7.

10. Tauber, "Conservation Comes of Age," p. 218.

11. *Permanence/Durability of the Book*, 7v. (Richmond: W.J. Barrow Research Laboratory, 1963–74).

12. Edwin E. Williams, "Magnitude of the Paper-Deterioration Problem as Measured by a National Union Catalog Sample," *College & Research Libraries* 23: 499, 543 (Nov. 1962).

13. Gordon R. Williams, *The Preservation of Deteriorating Books: An Examination of the Problem with Recommendations for a Solution* (Washington, D.C.: Association of Research Libraries, 1964). Reprinted in revised form in *Library Journal* 91: 51–56, 189–94 (Jan. 1 and Jan. 15, 1966).

14. Edwin E. Williams, "Deterioration of Library Collections Today," *Library Quarterly* 40:7 (Jan. 1970).

15. *National Register of Microform Masters* (Washington, D.C.: Cataloging Distribution Service, Library of Congress, 1965–).

16. Paul E. Edlund, "The Continuing Quest: Care of LC's Collections," *Library Journal* 90: 3401 (Sept. 1, 1965).

17. Douglas W. Bryant, "Notes on a Conference Held at the Library of Congress ..." in *Minutes of the Sixty-seventh Meeting of the Association of Research Libraries, January 23, 1966* (Washington, D.C.: Association of Research Libraries, 1966), p. 39.

18. William R. Hawken, *Copying Methods Manual* (Chicago: Library Technology Program, American Library Assn., 1966).

19. Verner W. Clapp, "LTP—the Rattle in an Infant's Fist," *American Libraries* 3: 795–802 (July-Aug. 1972).

20. Richard D. Smith, "Paper Deacidification: A Preliminary Report," *Library Quarterly* 36: 273–92 (Oct. 1966).

21. James W. Henderson and Robert G. Krupp, "The Librarian as Conservator," *Library Quarterly* 40: 178–79 (Jan. 1970).

22. Sherelyn Ogden, "The Newberry Library," *Guild of Book Workers Journal* 14, no. 1, 11–14 (Fall 1975).

23. See, for example, Carolyn Horton, "Saving the Libraries of Florence," *Wilson Library Bulletin* 41: 1034-43 (June 1967), and Sherelyn Ogden, "The Impact of the Florence Flood on Library Conservation in the United States of America: A Study of the Literature Published 1956–1976," *Restaurator* 3: 1–36 (1979).

24. American Institute for Conservation of Historic and Artistic Works, "Code of Ethics and Standards of Practice." For the latest approved version see the current *AIC Directory* (Washington, D.C.: American Institute for Conservation, 1980).

25. Carolyn Horton, *Cleaning and Preserving Bindings and Related Materials,* 1st ed., LTP Publication 16 (Chicago: Library Technology Program, American Library Assn., 1967). A second edition, revised, was issued by the same publisher in 1969.

26. George M. Cunha and Dorothy G. Cunha, *Conservation of Library Materials: A Manual and Bibliography on the Care, Repair and Restoration of Library Materials,* 1st ed. (Metuchen, N.J.: Scarecrow, 1967). A second edition was issued by the same publisher in 1971 in two volumes.

27. Norman J. Shaffer, "Library of Congress Pilot Preservation Project," *College & Research Libraries* 30: 5–11 (Jan. 1969).

28. Howard W. Winger, ed., "Deterioration and Preservation of Library Materials," *Library Quarterly* 40:2 (Jan. 1970). Note that these proceedings constituted the entire January 1970 issue, and were also published as a separate volume edited by Winger and Richard D. Smith. with the same title (Chicago: University of Chicago Pr., 1970).

29. James W. Henderson, *Memorandum on Conservation of the Collections* (New York: New York Public Library, 1970).

30. Warren J. Haas, *Preparation of Detailed Specifications for a National System for the Preservation of Library Materials* (Washington, D.C.: Association of Research Libraries, 1972), p. 2.

31. George M. Cunha and Norman P. Tucker, eds., *Library and Archives Conservation: The Boston Athenaeum's 1971 Seminar on the Application of Chemical and Physical Methods to the Conservation of Library and Archival Materials* (Boston: Library of the Boston Athenaeum, 1972).

32. Verner W. Clapp, "Story of Permanent/Durable Book Paper, 1115–1970," *Scholarly Publishing* 2: 107–24, 229–45, 353–67 (Jan., Apr., July 1971).

33. Bernard C. Middleton, *The Restoration of Leather Bindings*, LTP Publication 18 (Chicago: Library Technology Program, American Library Assn., 1972).

34. Peter Waters, *Emergency Procedures for Salvaging Flood or Water-Damaged Materials* (Washington, D.C.: Library of Congress, 1972). A revised edition was issued by the same publisher in 1975, under the title "Procedures for Salvage of Water-Damaged Materials," one of the LC Publications on Conservation of Library Materials.

35. Maurice F. Tauber, ed., *Library Binding Manual: A Handbook of Useful Procedures for the Maintenance of Library Volumes* (Boston: Library Binding Institute, 1972).

36. Carl J. Wessel, "Deterioration of Library Materials," in *Encyclopedia of Library and Information Science* (New York: Marcel Dekker, 1972) 7: 69–120.

[Notes 37–64 are in the text that was cut from this volume.]

65. Study Committee on Libraries and Archives, *National Needs in Libraries and Archives Conservation* (Washington, D.C: National Conservation Advisory Council, 1978).

66. Walter T. Brahm, "Regional Approach to Conservation: The New England Document Conservation Center," *American Archivist* 40: 421–27 (Oct. 1977).

67. Judith Reed, "A Nucleus of Guidance, a Center for Preservation," *Library Scene* 9: 12–13 (Sept. 1980).

68. J. Michael Bruer, *Toward a California Document Conservation Program* (San Jose: California Library Authority for Systems and Services, 1978).

69. Howard P. Lowell, "Conservation Planning in the West," *Library Scene* 9: 28–29 (Sept. 1980).

70. Frazer G. Poole, "A National Preservation Program: A Working Paper" (Washington, D.C.: Library of Congress, 1976).

ROSS HARVEY

"Developing a Library Preservation Program"

Chapter 10 in his Preservation in Australian and New Zealand Libraries, *2nd ed.*
Riverina, Australia: Centre for Information Studies, 1993, pp. 259–80.

Minor editorial emendations have been made by the author.

Introduction

The introduction to this book notes four premises on which the book is based:

1   that preservation is a management responsibility, at the highest level;
2   that all collections need a preservation plan;
3   that the preservation plan must be adequately funded as part of the ongoing budget;
4   that preservation must be the concern of all library staff at every level and a part of all library routines: it is not only a technical specialist matter which takes place in a separate laboratory.

Preservation must not be limited to large research libraries or archives, but must be a high priority for every librarian. That this has not been the case in the past is firmly stated by one of the many librarians, Scottish in this instance, writing in recent years on preservation:

Many currently in senior management positions know little of even the bare essentials for an environment conducive to document preservation. Worse, many lower-grade staff actually inflict gratuitous damage on existing bookstocks by mishandling, clumsy or excessive photocopying, injudicious rebinding and improper storage conditions.[1]

The key question which this chapter addresses is *how* preservation can be integrated into all aspects of

library management and into every library procedure. Other related questions are raised and the answers indicated in preceding chapters: those of *why* preservation should be integrated into library management, and of what techniques are at our command.

Preservation is a library management problem and must be considered in relation to other library management decisions. Consider a few examples. We know that books are best housed at temperatures lower than those at which humans thrive: if we choose to lower the temperatures of the stack areas, what is the effect on the humans who work in that area? What is the additional cost of maintaining the temperature at the lower level? Is there a cost saving? If the reading room temperature is lowered, will the library have to supply hot rum toddies to users who complain of the cold? If a flimsily bound thick monograph which is likely to be heavily used is received in the library, and is rebound as two thinner volumes to offer protection when being photocopied, what are the implications for other library procedures? Will it cause any problems in the cataloguing process? Will its separation into two volumes cause security problems? If one half of the work is lost or stolen, will the other half be completely useless?

The importance of having a policy statement for the library which clearly notes preservation as an essential part of that library's activities is noted in several places later in this chapter. Some examples here are not out of place. The National Library of Australia's preservation policy contains the words: 'The Library takes appropriate preservation measures to ensure the longevity of its collections, consistent with the aim of maintaining a distributed national collection. The National Library of New Zealand notes that its mission is to enrich the social, cultural and economic well-being of New Zealand by:ensuring equitable access to information and recorded knowledge [and] collecting, preserving and making available the documentary heritage of New Zealand.

Further, one of its objectives is stated as: 'Passing on to future generations the accumulated heritage of New Zealand. Preserving and conserving of New Zealand's recorded heritage, its documentary heritage. Providing access to the documentary heritage in such a way as to safeguard access for future generations.'[2] The State Library of New South Wales' mission statement is succinct and ambitious: 'We are creating for the community a thriving dynamic organisation, leading the NSW library system so that it becomes one of the world's best in collecting, conserving and communicating information.'[3] A description of the contents of a preservation policy is given by Chapman, and a selection of preservation policy statements can be found in *Preservation Guidelines in ARL Libraries.*[4] That of the Columbia University Libraries begins with the unequivocal statement: 'The Columbia University Libraries is committed to the preservation of its collection.'[5]

Two further points, both already made in preceding chapters, are worth reiterating here. The first is that the aim of preservation is to make library materials usable; it is about helping items in library collections to last as long as they are wanted. In this definition preservation becomes the concern of all staff working in libraries and of all users of libraries, not only of the special materials librarian or conservator. The second point is that in the past library preservation has been reactive. It is essential that it become proactive, that is, that a large part of the resources available to preservation be applied to preventive preservation measures.

Integrating Preservation and Management: Some General Concerns

One of the basic texts about library technical services stateis unequivocally that 'there is no set pattern for the organization of a library preservation pro-gram.'[6] How the preservation program is organized and where it is placed in the overall library structure depends on a number of factors, organizational structure being only one. The establishment of preservation sections as separate units within the organization is of relatively recent origin, dating back to the 1970s, when preservation came to be considered as part of more general library concerns (most notably in North American libraries) and more specifically as part of the collection development function. More and more preservation departments are being established, as indicated by the example of member libraries of the Association of Research Libraries, where the number rose from 27 in 1985 to 73 in 1989.[7]

Although there may be no set pattern for organizing the preservation program, some key ingredients necessary for the successful operation of such programs can be identified, and the steps essential in planning such a program can be isolated. Two essential ingredients are commitment on the part of the library's administration and staff, and the status of the preservation unit and its staff within the library. Although the initial impetus for the preservation program may not have come from the top, the continued support and commitment of the library's administration are necessary for the maintenance and well-being of preservation as a central activity. Commitment on the part of library staff at all levels is also essential. This is noted in Chapter 5.

The status of the preservation unit and its staff, and more particularly the status of the head of the preservation unit, within the library's hierarchy is another critical factor. The manager of the preservation program needs to be accorded a status high enough within the organization for that person to be privy to major administrative decisions, to be able to influence those decisions, and to implement those which are relevant. High status is also required to be effective in coordinating, liaising, advocating, planning, and educating.

Carolyn Clark Morrow has examined seven case studies of successful preservation programs in libraries in the United States, and has established their common features which, it could reasonably be concluded, have contributed to their success. They are:

a redefining of the activities which constitute preservation (for example, including care and handling activities in addition to the more traditional repair activities);

hand in hand with the redefinition, a reorganisation of administration to better coordinate preservation activities;

employment of a professional (either a conservator or a librarian with preservation knowledge and experience) to develop and organise the program;

knowledgeable library staff, and the establishment of formal liaison between the preservation staff and the rest of the library staff;

an in-house treatment facility, for example, a workshop tailored to the need of the individual library.[8]

Funding of the preservation effort at adequate levels is required for success. It is instructive to note that Association of Research Libraries members are 'increasingly' spending '10 per cent of their materials budget on preservation', and some are spending higher amounts, ranging up to 50 per cent.[9] By comparison, university libraries in the U.S. Midwest (in Indiana, Illinois and Ohio) spent on average 2.68 per cent of the total library expenditure on preservation.[10] Much of the preservation literature originating from the United States notes that funding can be obtained from charitable foundations and similar philanthropic organizations. Australia and New Zealand do not have bodies of similar wealth and generosity and such sources have not made significant contributions to funding for preservation activities. One exception is the donation in 1990 of $250,000 by the Vincent Fairfax Family Foundation to the State Library of New South Wales to establish the Vincent Fairfax Family Conservation Laboratories.[11]

Steps in Implementing a Preservation Program

Writers on preservation planning are in general agreement about the steps which are needed to implement a successful library program. Robert Patterson notes

that these are: first, to examine the environment in the library and the condition of the collection, and make recommendations; second, to prepare a disaster plan; third, to examine current practices (for example, binding, handling, processing, repair techniques) and recommend changes and ascertain additional requirements to meet current standards; fourth, to ascertain what professional conservation advice and expertise is available to the library; fifth, to develop a collection development approach for the library; sixth, to identify sources of funding; seventh, to establish an in-house clearinghouse for preservation information for staff; and, finally, to explore the feasibility of participating in regional or national cooperative conservation efforts.[12]

An experienced preservation administrator, Sally Buchanan, notes the general administrative concerns which are applicable to a preservation program; her list is similar to that of Patterson, above. She notes that the first step is to assess needs. Next, priorities need to be established; here Buchanan suggests one useful way in which activities might be grouped for administrative purposes: maintenance of collections (both circulating and non-circulating collections), stabilization (of the environment, and through handling and housing), security (including disaster planning), and preservation of deteriorating volumes. The activities then need to be organized and funding sought (but note that some activities, for example disaster response planning, require relatively little financial support). The staffing requirements need to be addressed. Education of both staff and users is an essential step to ensure that both groups recognize the preservation program, which will make extra demands on them, as being worthwhile. Finally, evaluation of the program—of progress, and also regular monitoring—needs to be carried out.[13]

The need to establish priorities is an essential part of planning and implementing a preservation program. Here the concept of 'phased preservation' can assist. First developed at the Library of Congress in 1973 as 'phased conservation', this concept has proved to be of assistance in selecting materials for treatment, helping to avoid the selection of items which visibly need attention but which may not warrant a high priority if other factors such as use, value and rate of deterioration are also taken into account. If the phased preservation concept is adopted, it needs to be integrated into the library's administrative structure.[14]

Responsibility for Developing and Implementing the Program

Once the steps to be carried out have been decided on, then the question arises of who does the planning and who implements the program? There are three possibilities. Specialists can be appointed, on a full-time or consultancy basis, to establish the program; a staff member can be charged with gaining experience in preservation and overseeing the preservation program (and hiring expertise on a consultancy basis where necessary); or a committee approach can be used. Specialist staff may be easier to locate on a consultancy basis than on a full-time permanent basis, especially in Australia and New Zealand. The current shortage of trained conservation staff with sufficient library experience may mean that the best route to follow is to turn a professionally qualified librarian into a preservation librarian, that is, to assist that person to gain what preservation expertise he or she can. It can be said that ideally the preservation program should be under the control of a single administrator. This was certainly acknowledged to be an important factor in the success of the preservation program of the National Museums of Canada libraries. A full-time preservation officer 'focussed' the efforts to achieve preservation objectives and also 'conferred a much higher profile on the preservation programme'.[15] However, the committee approach has met with considerable success in some libraries and is applicable to libraries of all sizes except the very smallest.

The preservation committee approach has been described in the library literature and is not therefore explained in any detail here.[16] It can be applied either in part or in full. That is, preservation programs can be planned, implemented, and operated under the direction of a committee, or the committee approach can be applied only to some of the implementation stages. This latter approach is the basis in the United States of the 'assisted self-study' Preservation Planning Program of the Association of Research Libraries. It is intended for libraries with sufficient staff to assign about twenty-four people to the task, each spending on average five or six hours per week over four to six months. The self-study results in a detailed examination of the preservation needs of the library, essential for the further development of a preservation program. In outline, the Preservation Planning Program is made up of the following steps: preliminary matters (getting the plan organized); an assessment of environmental conditions; an assessment of the physical condition of the collections; an assessment of organizational issues; disaster control; identifying preservation resources in the library; and final reporting.[17]

A local example of the use of a committee approach is the University of Otago, Dunedin, New Zealand, described below in the section concerned with Model 3 libraries. The University of Texas at Austin General Libraries has used the committee approach to determine the initial needs of a preservation program.[18] The immediate result of this approach was that a report was produced which provided data about the nature and extent of preservation needs and made recommendations about implementing a preservation program. There were also less tangible results which may be of more lasting benefit to the institution. A number of staff members developed preservation expertise, and the general preservation awareness of the staff was heightened, as between 10 and 20 per cent of the total number of staff were involved in one way or another. The committee approach allows for a wide representation of interests, which can be increased if required by rotating the membership periodically. In the words of Mark E. Cain, author of the article describing The University of Texas at Austin experience,

> Libraries need not delay initiating a preservation program until they can afford fulltime staff for that purpose. Much groundwork can be laid by employees already onboard who have only a few hours each week to devote to the task in a committee framework.[19]

Another result of this approach is that it can indicate areas where improvements can be made in preservation without major expenditure and without new staff positions being established.

What Is in a Preservation Program?

The precise contents of an integrated preservation program will vary from library to library, but it is possible to indicate in general terms what its major components will be.[20] These are all described in detail in preceding chapters. There will be an understanding of the factors which affect the library's physical environment and an application of these factors to control that environment; a disaster prevention plan and recovery procedures; an emphasis on security; 'positive control' of binding; regular use of professional conservation expertise and facilities, perhaps in an in-house conservation laboratory, in the largest libraries, but more likely using the services of conservators and facilities available on a contract basis; an in-house facility for preventive conservation and simple repair techniques to be carried out; an emphasis on treatment of the collections as a whole, and not on single item treatment; a strong and ongoing staff training and education component; active participation in cooperative conservation efforts on a regional level and also on a national level if appropriate; and a concentration on finding alternative sources of funding for large-scale preservation activities such as major microfilming or reformatting projects.

[...]

Conclusion

In what direction is the field of library preservation heading? Fascinating as it is to conjecture, prophecy is at best an imprecise art. Many have written on this topic, and some general directions can be perceived. It is of interest to note some of these as a conclusion to this book.[48]

The application of new technologies to preservation will become more widespread, but only after the problems associated with them—of archival standards of permanence, and compatibility between systems—have been more effectively addressed. There will be an increasing use of the older technology of microfilming, until—say by the year 2000—digitizing equals it in popularity. However, despite the increasing use and availability of these technologies, the originals will still be retained wherever possible.

Mass deacidification processes will be more widely available and more widely used, but mass paper strengthening methods will not be wholly successful. More permanent paper will be manufactured and used in book production, to the benefit of libraries.

All major libraries will have a disaster preparedness plan. There will be increased emphasis on education for preservation in library schools. Preservation administrators will be more likely to be librarians with preservation training than conservators, as a detailed knowledge of libraries and their administration will be more important to effective preservation programs than will mastery of manual skills. Contracting out of preservation services will probably increase.

For Australia and New Zealand, the situation is less clear, and what follows may perhaps be categorized more as wishful thinking than as potential reality. Some of the indications are already apparent, for example, the place of preservation at the Australian Libraries Summit in 1988, although little action has resulted as yet. The major trends will be these: the importance of preservation in libraries will slowly increase; the library profession will become better organized and some large-scale projects will eventuate; and more administrators of large libraries in Australia and New Zealand will divert resources into preservation activities.

Let us end this book as we began it, by quoting John Feather.

International conferences, Unesco reports and European Commission plans can sometimes seem a little remote from the work of the ordinary librarian or archivist, struggling to keep a decaying collection in a condition in which it can be used, often in an inadequate building and almost always with insufficient funds. The perception is understandable, but it is false. A profession, which is, by definition, self-regulating, creates for itself the climate in which it conducts its activities. Within the broad scope of providing the service demanded by its clients, it largely determines its own agenda. In the last 20 years, and more markedly so during the 1980s, the library profession in many countries has apparently reached the conclusion, through its various representative bodies, that preservation is an area of significant and serious professional concern ... A consensus is emerging which will carry us through the new decade and into a new century. There is a broad general agreement that preservation is important, not least because our central professional activity—to transfer information from source to user—will be frustrated if we lose the media which contain the information. Therefore we need to be able to determine whether to preserve information in its original format, or whether to reformat it and preserve the surrogate. We need to have the technologies which will permit the reformatting to take place, and then to preserve the surrogates themselves. We need to be able to repair, restore and preserve those damaged originals which we prefer not to sacrifice. In short, ten years of revitalized concern for the physical media of information have forced us to rethink the way in which we manage our information resources.[49]

NOTES

1. Antonia Bunch, 'Conservation and the Library Community', *Library Review* 35 (1986): 58.

2. National Library of New Zealand, *Report...for the Year Ended 30 June 1990* (Wellington: Government Printer, 1990), p. 3.

3. State Library of New South Wales, *Mission Statement* (1989).

4. Patricia Chapman, *Guidelines on Preservation and Conservation Policies in the Archives and Libraries Heritage* (Paris: Unesco, 1990); *SPEC Kit* 137 (1987).

5. *SPEC Kit* 137 (1987): 17.

6. A. Dean Larsen, 'Preservation and Materials Processing', in *Library Technical Services: Operations and Management*, ed. Irene P. Godden (Orlando, Fla: Academic Press, 1984), p. 195.

7. Jutta Reed-Scott, 'Preservation Organization and Staffing', *SPEC Flyer* 160 (January 1990).

8. Carolyn Clark Morrow, *The Preservation Challenge: A Guide to Conserving Library Materials* (White Plains, N.Y.: Knowledge Industry Publications, 1983), pp. 115–117.

9. Reed-Scott.

10. Robert S. Lamb, 'Library Preservation Survey', *Conservation Administration News* 45 (April 1991): 4–5.

11. *InCite* 11, 9 (25 June 1990): 12.

12. Robert H. Patterson, 'Conservation: What We Should Do Until the Conservator and the Twenty-First Century Arrive', in *Conserving and Preserving Library Materials*, ed. Kathryn Luther Henderson, William T. Henderson (Urbana-Champaign, Ill.: Graduate School of Library and Information Science, University of Illinois, 1983), p. 14.

13. Sally A. Buchanan, 'Administering the Library Conservation Program', *Law Library Journal* 77.3 (1984–1985): 569–574.

14. Peter Waters, 'Phased Preservation: A Philosophical Concept and Practical Approach to Preservation', *Special Libraries* 81, 1 (1990): 35–43.

15. Antony Pacey, 'Library Preservation: The Approach of the National Museums of Canada', *Canadian Library Journal* 47, 1 (1990): 27–33.

16. Some examples are Robert H. Patterson, 'Organizing For Conservation', *Library Journal* (15 May 1979): 1116–1119; Robert H. Patterson, 'Conservation: What We Should Do Until the Conservator and the Twenty-First Century Arrive', in *Conserving and Preserving Library Materials*, p. 14.

17. Pamela W. Darling and Duane E. Webster, *Preservation Planning Program: An Assisted Self-Study Manual for Libraries*. Expanded 1987 ed. (Washington, D.C.: Association of Research Libraries, Office of Management Studies, 1987).

18. Mark E. Cain, 'Analyzing Preservation Practices and Environmental Conditions: A Committee's

Systems Approach", *Collection Management* 4, 3 (1982): 19–28.

19. Cain, p. 27.

20. George Martin Cunha and Dorothy Grant Cunha, *Library and Archives Conservation: 1980s and Beyond* (Metuchen, N.J.: Scarecrow Press, 1983), Vol. 1, p. 119; Chapman.

[...]

48. Gleaned from Peter Waters, "The Florence Flood of 1966 Revisited," in *Preserving the Word: The Library Association Conference Proceedings,* Harrogate 1986, ed. R. Palmer (London: Library Association 1987).

49. John Feather, *Preservation and the Management of Library Collections* (London: Library Association, 1991), pp. 105–106.

JAN MERRILL-OLDHAM

"Taking Care: An Informed Approach to Library Preservation"

Essays from the symposium held at the Library of Congress, October 30-31, 2000. Washington, DC: Library of Congress, 2002, pp. 90–105.

THE BURGEONING OF information resources in electronic form, created and distributed worldwide, has had a profound methodological, organizational, and financial impact on the research enterprise. Today, the users of any large academic library expect organized access to vast numbers of electronic journals, books, works of art, and databases, as well as the equipment required for viewing, printing, downloading, and manipulating them. The cost of licensing and purchasing electronic publications of enduring value, and of the hardware, software, and technical expertise required to deliver them, is steep. And even as communications technologies are transformed by leaps and bounds, the flow of paper, film, magnetic tape and discs into traditional library collections continues unceasingly.

The dawn of a new and volatile information environment—an environment that will surely change in ways that cannot yet be predicted—raises questions about the ability of institutions to embrace and manage an ever-broadening range of services and stewardship responsibilities. As a growing body of information is distributed over networks, concerns are inevitably raised regarding the bibliographic, reference, and instructional attention being deflected from collections of books, paper, and other materials amassed over the course of centuries. It is not clear how we will fund the costly systems that will be required to provide sustained access to electronic resources and simultaneously find the means to do the same for traditional collections. There is nothing new about complexity and competition for dollars in libraries, but the stakes are being raised.

In order to be effective advocates for the care and long-term preservation of library collections, we must cultivate a stronger and more focused message regarding the role of preservation programs in a modern information environment. We are well equipped to do so. Over the course of the past thirty years, we have learned and confirmed much about the physical nature and aging characteristics of library materials, what strategies are most effective for extending their useful lives, and how to apply these in cost-effective ways. Following is a review of the preservation tools with which we must continue to work effectively: environmental control, emergency preparedness and response, collections care and handling, conservation, commercial binding, and reformatting. What strategies have been successful and are well worth championing in a new information age that also carries with it most of the technologies of the past?

We have been hearing for decades that controlling environmental conditions is the single most important action that a library can take to ensure a long life for collections of all types. The aging of books, papers, photographs, film, magnetic tape, and discs is inextricably linked to the conditions under which they are stored. In general, an environment that promotes the longevity of organic materials is characterized by cold, dry air that is free from gaseous and particulate pollutants. Light is filtered to screen out ultraviolet radiation and is controlled for intensity and duration. Furnishings and surface finishes are composed of materials that are free from harmful gas emissions.

In recent years, many of the world's oldest and largest libraries have upgraded environmental systems in existing buildings and have constructed new libraries and storage facilities designed to promote the preservation of their collections. The development and maintenance of hospitable environmental conditions is a truly strategic act, affecting materials collectively rather than selectively. Also strategic are such building routines as rigorous testing, maintenance, and replacement of pumps, motors, and fans; changing of air filters; integrated pest management; regular cleaning of floors and other surfaces; and skilled vacuuming of collections.

Alongside requests for expanded technical capabilities and increased collections purchasing power, funds for environmental management must appear predictably and persistently in every annual budget proposal. We cannot allow the need for ongoing maintenance and physical improvements to slip off the radar screen as pressure to offer distance learning and other important new services mounts. Paper- and plastics-based collections will not disappear as electronic sources become more prominent, nor will our responsibility to provide safe housing for them.

If a high-quality off-site storage facility is part of the library's strategy for managing ever-expanding holdings, take full advantage of the options that cool, orderly, secure storage presents for establishing truly rational preservation priorities. Never before have we had so good an opportunity to invest typically lean preservation resources in those holdings that are at greatest risk of being lost if they are not conserved or copied promptly. Storage at fifty degrees Fahrenheit and 35 percent relative humidity slows down the aging process enough to truly legitimize long-

range preservation planning. The power of integrated library systems can also be brought to bear on the highly systematic development and implementation of preservation priorities. If the incidence of damage and embrittlement can be recorded, for example, either as material, are transferred to storage or are circulated from it, it will be possible to address preservation problems in a meaningful sequence, however slowly.

Like environmental control, emergency preparedness and response support and legitimize all other preservation activity. Although many institutions have put disaster preparedness plans into place, few go far enough in their efforts to prepare for incidents that could result in major loss. We must be more organized in our efforts to train an adequate number of staff to respond to collections emergencies large and small in a deliberate and informed way. Responsibilities should be built into job descriptions rather than left to personal preference and chance. Staff with diverse skills and experience must be involved in emergency readiness to ensure that a range of talents can be mobilized when they are needed. Too much homogeneity strips the library of its ability to manage an emergency skillfully when a conference calls away too many members of disaster team.

Well-stocked emergency supply closets that include such tools as water vacuums, dehumidifiers, fans, and extension cords are a high priority. Experience has shown that access to the tools needed in a library emergency must be restricted. Flashlights, plastic sheeting, and other supplies are mysteriously attractive and can dwindle if they are not kept under lock and key, hampering the first hours of a cleanup effort. Emergency power-generating capacity should be reviewed throughout the library system and improved when necessary, even if it takes time and a concerted effort to analyze systemwide needs, set priorities, and move adequate funding into place.

Be certain that the emergency support systems needed at 2:00 A.M. on a Saturday morning can really be mobilized and that every important vendor is called periodically to ensure that companies are still in business and telephone numbers are still working. Be sure that there are multiple options available for securing freezer space for wet library materials, and plan to use a disaster recovery vendor for freezing rather than a firm whose main job it is to store and distribute the public food supply.

Finally, staff must have time to read the library emergency preparedness and response literature, to assign roles and responsibilities, to create documentation specific to the local situation, and to organize and participate in emergency training programs and exercises. While no degree of preparation suffices in certain situations, many collections emergencies involving water can result in minimal loss if they are managed by a trained response team.

Cultivating an environment for library collections care and handling that promotes longevity requires observation, analysis, planning, and a commitment of resources. Guidelines for storing and using library collections have appeared repeatedly in the literature, and although such prescriptions may be shopworn, they remain important blueprints for action. The job of communicating good care and handling practices to library staff and users is difficult to manage convincingly. Signs, exhibits, news articles, and Web sites can trivialize the issues or be effective consciousness-raising tools, depending on how ideas are expressed. Seek tough criticism when creating educational products for staff and users. Remember that messages gradually become invisible in a familiar landscape and must be refreshed. Goals for an education program are various because of the many material types that a research library collects and preserves, but the overarching one is to get as many users as possible to buy into the principle of the public good. Library resources must be cared for and protected by the entire user community on behalf of the community.

The way that collections are treated in public areas suggests their ultimate fate. We can choose to let books and journals pile up on floors around copy machines, or we can provide book trucks for materials awaiting return to the stacks. We can opt for the convenience of book drops, or take the extra care required for human intervention. The politics of closing book drops is dicey, but the argument against them can be made in compelling ways. Over-the-counter returns

coupled with good staff training can have significant long-term benefits.

We must communicate regularly with vendors and manufacturers to ensure that fast-disappearing right-angle book copiers are carried forward into the digital age, and we must continue to encourage people to copy pages one at a time, at least when to do otherwise would be to ruin a volume. Microfilm readers, videocassette recorders, and other readers and playback equipment should be kept as clean as possible to avoid the transfer of dirt from machine to medium. Budgets may not support an optimal level of care, but it is important to allocate reasonable resources to machine maintenance to help minimize the damage that media can sustain during reading and playback. We must reconsider once again the ways in which the stacks are managed, and whether they might be kept cleaner. Cyclical vacuuming is an effective way to reduce abrasive dirt and grit and the damaging moisture that can be trapped around books and papers by blankets of dust. While a full collections vacuuming cycle may not be completed for years, it ensures that there is continual improvement in the condition of the stacks and that there is a mechanism in place for dealing with trouble spots.

Regarding processing, it is important to foster an environment in which all materials are handled consistently, according to an established protocol, from the time they enter the acquisitions workflow. Materials check-in, temporary storage, cataloging, and end-processing are among the junctures at which handling decisions can affect permanently the condition of a library collection. Procedures that promote longevity are often as straightforward as ensuring that books do not lean on shelves and that compact discs are rehoused in jewel cases. Regarding processing supplies, care must be exercised in making selections. Acidic pamphlet binders, for example, can still be purchased through standard library supply catalogs and obviously should be avoided.

End-processing is a point at which the library's security program can get a big boost. Although bookplates are an elegant vehicle for acknowledging ownership, edge stamping is a more aggressive way to mark an object as library property and therein to make it a less desirable object of theft. Edge stamps are easily seen signs of ownership and are hard to eradicate. They lower the value of an object, often significantly, thus providing some protection against resale.

Regarding the decades-long debate over whether to mark items in special collections, the guidelines that have been developed by the Rare Books and Manuscripts Section of the American Library Association's Association of College and Research Libraries provide a structure within which a variety of approaches can be considered. In general, libraries must navigate conflicting needs and goals, caught between the desire to preserve value and aesthetic characteristics and the need to prevent accidental and intentional loss. For general collections, electronic library security systems, while not foolproof, are effective deterrents to theft, particularly when security devices are inserted in all circulating materials.

Despite our best efforts, damage to library materials is unavoidable and likely to be widespread, and thus conservation must be a priority. A great deal of attention was devoted during the 1980s and 1990s to the development of methods and work flows for carrying out high-quality book repair for circulating collections. Likewise, the conservation of materials in special collections has evolved considerably in recent decades, with conservation treatments tending to be less invasive and more likely to retain evidence of original intention whenever possible. Methods and mending materials are chosen for their chemical, mechanical, and structural advantages: and in the case of general collections, work is done in batches to increase productivity. Custom-fitted boxes are constructed to protect library materials from light, dust, and handling and to substitute for treatment when the workload is overwhelming.

Significant space is required to manage an effective collections conservation program for research library materials. The larger the collection, the more tending—and therefore the more square footage—its care will require. Ideally, every item that circulates and is returned to the library in damaged condition will be repaired before it is sent back to the shelf. Programs must be balanced so that the more important bindings are saved through conservation and other materials are commercially rebound. There is an inevitable gap, however, between the amount of repair and rebinding required for a circulating collection and the work to which a library can afford to commit. Setting priorities is no easy task, even if a library chooses to concentrate almost exclusively on the treatment of materials that are heavily used.

Certain classes of damaged materials must be earmarked for rapid turnaround, and in such cases, the repair team must deliver services that demand skill and speed. When a damaged reference book leaves the shelf one day and is repaired and put back in use the next, the conservation program can be judged a success. For all but the most pressing needs, however, repair problems in most institutions often go unaddressed, and the condition of collections tends to worsen significantly as the collections age. We have not yet made the case successfully to funders that library holdings require significant upkeep. As a result, resources for collections maintenance are lean. If salaries for skilled conservation staff and a suitable work space are beyond reach, commercial binding is an option. Although instructions for carrying out basic treatment procedures are documented in several important publications, it nonetheless makes little sense to proceed with an in-house treatment program if the program cannot be staffed adequately. It is easy for the preservation unit to become a black hole into which damaged materials pour and from which little emerges.

This is not to paint a gloomy picture of the state and practice of conservation in libraries. Today we understand the nature and behavior of the kinds of materials that we collect even better than we did only a decade ago, and research in conservation science is ongoing. More staff members in research libraries are dedicated to collections treatment than ever before, and more practitioners recognize the need to expand and strengthen these efforts. More conservation positions are migrating to the permanent ranks, and more are recognized as part of the professional workforce.

For general collections, goals are generally similar across institutions. In special collections, however, to treat the letters and poems of Emily Dickinson, the page proofs of James Joyce's *Ulysses,* or the globes of

Gerardus Mercator requires consummate skill. We know that objects ultimately deteriorate, but uninformed conservation treatment can do far more damage to library materials than time and wear. We must ensure that the conservators of rare books, manuscripts, photographs, and other unique and important objects have at their command years of training, ample technology, established channels of communication with knowledgeable curators, the time to research unknown objects, and generous opportunities for continuing education.

In the absence of access to trained conservators, in-house treatment of special collections begins and ends with proper housing. If resources allow, conservation treatments are contracted out. Neither a sizable professional staff, however, nor a generous budget for contract work eases the difficulty of setting conservation priorities. The gap between need and capacity is simply overwhelming.

One viable approach to setting conservation priorities for special collections is to focus on minor treatment, with the goal of maximizing the number of items restored to good condition. Another is to treat damaged materials that scholars are slated to use in the coming year. Planned classroom use can be an important criterion upon which to base treatment priorities, as can exhibition requirements. Although the conservation of materials for the purpose of display is sometimes viewed as a deterrent to accomplishing more systematic goals, scholarly exhibits naturally highlight significant works and can be as good a strategy as any for establishing goals. Yet another approach is to focus on major treatment of a few great treasures each year—objects of indisputable and enduring importance.

Institutions can sometimes pursue multiple treatment strategies, but every choice requires careful consideration, and every treatment will be undertaken at the expense of another. Special collections conservation is a compelling enterprise, however, and its potential for attracting new funds should not be overlooked.

Few institutions can keep up with the need to repair books in circulating collections in particular, and the importance of commercial binding services for modern general collections is widely recognized.

Managing a binding program is not as straightforward as it may appear to those who have never been involved in the decision making and preparation process. The way a volume is bound dictates to a great extent whether it will open well, will be able to withstand repeated photocopying, and will retain most of its original features after binding. Bindery preparation staff must also be able to assess book structure, the condition of paper, and the way that these features influence the development of a binding specification. Staff members should have the opportunity not only to develop basic skills but also to master the more sophisticated aspects of binding that result in a better outcome.

Often discussed are methods for dealing with paperback volumes when the budget is not adequate to fund comprehensive binding. It may be better to commercially bind paperbacks selectively based on patterns of use than to employ in-house binding techniques that work in the short term but cause damage and failure in the long term. If budgets will not stretch to accommodate needs, journals must take first priority and monographs that have truly become unusable, second. The efficacy of early intervention, and the difficulty and cost of delayed binding, argue for a prompt response to binding needs.

Among the most daunting of challenges for research libraries is the mandate to retain a large part of their collections "permanently," a challenge that can be met through reformatting. Although the job of managing materials while they are being processed is a logistical puzzle, it pales beside the difficulty of monitoring and managing ongoing preservation needs once materials are absorbed into the collections. Looking across rows of deteriorating nineteenth-century books, or boxes of important nineteenth-century papers that have become brittle, it is hard to imagine how we will grapple with physical problems that are too massive to solve exhaustively. Certain modern materials decay so rapidly that we have not formulated a response to their physical problems, let alone resolved them.

By way of example, many of the papers that record the work of great thinkers can no longer be manipulated without damaging them each time they are handled. Some collections are huge, and most are made up of items that have considerably more value in the aggregate than as discrete objects. Preservation surrogates allow us to depend less on failing paper. They ensure that intellectual access persists and, in the case of microfilm, serve as a platform for making new microform, paper, or electronic copies on demand. Microfilm can be exploited as a source for new versions, and at the same time it promises hundreds of years of reliable access to the master copy. There have never been large budgets for copying deteriorated materials, and with every passing year preservation resources must stretch further. Nonetheless, libraries continue to identify and copy aging collections of significance, and a segment of our holdings could potentially survive for a very long time.

Fundamental to the microfilming process are both strict adherence to national standards and unrelenting quality control. These goals apply whether film has been treated in-house or by a commercial service. Image capture must be of consistently high quality if it is to serve as a permanent record of the original work or as a platform for making digital copies. Unless paper is so brittle that it fractures with gentle handling, we can retain original copies of reformatted materials for consultation until they are no longer able to serve a useful purpose.

When making film, the printing negative is all-important. In addition to protecting the master negative from damage, it is the source from which the use copy is produced. That copy can be created on film, paper, or as an electronic resource. Regarding bibliographic control, there is no point in expending resources to reproduce a text if readers cannot discover it easily. There are untold numbers of aging pamphlets in the stacks of some of our oldest libraries, for example, that will become known to scholars for the first time as we clean up or create cataloging records during reformatting projects. Our international system for preserving and distributing fragile and rarely held titles depends upon identifying and describing materials accurately and noting missing issues and other anomalies.

Modern materials such as videotapes, many types of sound recordings, nitrate negatives, and CD-ROMs (compact discs with read-only memory) have begun to present us with an overwhelming array of physical and management challenges. Sound and video recordings, for example, have an unpredictable shelf life, are costly to copy, and, unlike a microfilmed book, will need to be copied repeatedly over the years if they are to survive. Currently, the average cost to remaster one hour of video play time is approximately two hundred dollars plus materials.

Copyright permissions present vexing issues in preservation, for we must be able to migrate short-lived forms of information long before they are in the public domain. To preserve some materials will require that we secure permissions that we currently do not have. Furthermore, preservation reformatting promises to be expensive, and we are unlikely to be able to do very much of it. It is hard to imagine that we will find the means to support conversion and maintenance of any significant percentage of our nonprint resources if current costs and the legal environment remain unchanged. And it will be many decades before we begin to realize the impact of the resulting losses on our intellectual life.

The electronic environment promises to provide new and sometimes better ways to preserve information, provided that we are able to devise strategies that guarantee the persistence of electronic flies into the indefinite future. Digital copying, if executed expertly, eliminates the gradual degradation of text, images, and sound that characterizes analog reproductions. New frontiers are opening before us that only a short time ago seemed remote and improbable. Consider, by way of example, the revisiting of history through early photographs. The daguerreotypes held in fourteen repositories at Harvard are a useful case in point. These images are among the earliest ever captured by photographic means and are of great value to scholars and researchers in many fields. Until recently, they could be accessed only by the Harvard community and visitors to the collections in Harvard's libraries and museums. Because of their delicacy, fragility, and uniqueness, the daguerreotypes could be consulted only a few at a time and could not be borrowed for research purposes, however compelling. Repeated handling threatened glass and seals and generally increased the exposure of the unique, silver-coated copper plates to risk.

Comprehensive photographing and subsequent digitizing of every known daguerreotype in Harvard's libraries and museums have addressed the problem of access and created unprecedented opportunities for study and research. Copying and online display are creating new audiences for Harvard's photographs, making images widely available for examination, comparison, and use in new ways.

Electronic reproductions are no substitute for the real thing when it comes to experiencing history first-hand, but they fulfill most purposes admirably and open up brand new avenues for exploration. The conversion of traditional library resources to more convenient, and sometimes more functional, electronic files is an attractive option for everything from movies and news broadcasts to newspapers and science treatises. It is practical, however, only in cases where materials merit the cost of creating, maintaining, and migrating digital files to ever newer forms, and where adequate funds are available to do so.

The delivery of searchable texts over networks is rapidly becoming a mainstream approach to publishing, much to the satisfaction of those readers who are fortunate enough to have access to fast networks and unlimited printing. The convenience and power of electronic texts and images prompt us to wonder what place paper, film, discs, and other physical instances of information resources will have in tomorrow's publishing world, what will replace them, and to what extent we will backtrack to capture existing resources in new forms. In the preservation arena, to make, store, and deliver microfilm costs a small fraction of what it costs to scan and process an electronic text. It seems likely that we will proceed on multiple tracks, taking advantage of existing copying techniques for some classes of material and pursuing more expensive, more flexible forms of access for others. The beauty of film is that it addresses preservation problems relatively inexpensively and can serve as source material for creating digital access should that prove desirable at any time.

Over the coming decades, digital table of contents projects will rescue unindexed serial runs from neglect. Existing finding aids will be converted from paper to machine-readable form, and new and important indexes and finding aids will be created. Large numbers of visual resources will be made available electronically and used as never before. Historic scores, essays, and logbooks will blend with modern demographic and economic data to create altogether new relationships. And as texts and indexes are recycled for new uses, some will at the same time also be preserved.

We have difficult choices before us regarding what information to gather and what to save for the long term, as has been the case since we first began to collect, organize, and store information, and these choices will be greatly complicated by the fact that modern documents need never be finished—no version need be finalized. Despite logistical, financial, and legal issues, however, we will build digital collections that are critical for teaching and research, and we will use them in harmony with information resources in many other forms. We will preserve materials at great risk of being lost forever and imbue them with new power. We will rescue films and databases, ephemera, and great works.

In contemplating these possibilities, libraries, library users, and society at large must come to grips with major financial needs and how they might better be met. We must do more to raise awareness regarding the fragile nature of library resources, ancient and modern, and to stimulate public interest in their survival. We must build on our successes to make a stronger case to federal and state governments, to major funding sources, and to the community at large for ongoing support. The forging of connections between the past and the present, and between our accomplishments and our aspirations, is, after all, a large part of what it means to be human.

DAVID BEARMAN

"Retention and Preservation"

Chapter 2 in his Archival Methods. Archives and Museum Informatics Technical Reports, *no. 9.*
N.p.: Archives & Museum Informatics, 1989.

The Problem

When archivists determine that records possess evidential or informational value sufficient to warrant their archival retention, they designate them as "permanent" or of "enduring value" and accession them. They tell themselves, their institutions and their donors, that they intend to keep such records forever. Nevertheless, they must recognize that recorded memory is a material manifestation of the past, and as a material manifestation it will need to be stored and it will undergo material decay. Indeed, these two physical requirements, storage and conservation, are closely related.

The media on which mankind has been recording its history since the advent of literacy have become increasingly fragile and susceptible to decay with each succeeding technological development. The shift from stone to clay tablets, from clay to papyrus, from cloth paper to wood pulp paper, from paper to photographic media and now to magnetic recordings has produced ever shorter format lifetimes. Along the way, we have introduced media and recording techniques which are not "eye-readable". To listen to a wax cylinder or analyze a data tape we also need the hardware or software which was designed to use them. The generations between such technological changes are shorter now than ever before—thousands of years elapsed between stone and clay, hundreds between clay and papyrus and cloth paper, wood pulp paper is less than three hundred years old, photography and sound recording only one hundred-fifty, magnetic tapes only fifty, and optical storage media are less than ten years old.

Against such rapid change stands a concept of permanence, dwarfing any of the scales which apply to the realm of recorded memory or the preservation of its material manifestation.[1] Recorded history is measured in tens of thousands of years. The immediate ancestors of modern man have populated the earth for about one million years. Man has been evolving recognizably for the past ten million years. Mammals emerged a little over one hundred million years ago. Permanent is a very long time indeed! In this context, it is odd and somewhat frightening that traditional conservation efforts still refine methods to extend media by factors as little as two or three times.[2] Usually the costs of these approaches are such that one cannot extend them to more than a fraction of the archival record, even then without any particularly sound reason for believing that the ravages of time will thereby be suspended.[3] If the intent of such intervention is to save the cultural record even for one thousand years, that is, for a noticeable period in the scale of recorded history, these interventions will have to take on heroic and untested proportions.[4]

The importance of preservation of the record is such that both the Society of American Archivists and American Association of Museums reports on the future of these professions identify it as central to the purposes of the administration of cultural repositories, and major preservation programs have been launched in the past several years by the National Endowment for the Humanities and other national organizations to secure the preservation of important cultural documentation.[5] The breadth of the cultural commitment to preservation, and the scale of its potential technical and financial requirements, are illustrated in the 1984 report of a panel convened at the request of the U.S. Senate Subcommittee on Science, Technology and Space to recommend policies for the archiving of weather and earth satellite data in the event that the satellites were sold to a private corporation. The panel found that "it is in the public interest to maintain an archive of land remote sensing satellite data for historical, scientific and technical purposes. The data in question are a national resource worthy of preservation ... and while the cost of archiving these data is not insignificant, it is extremely small relative to the investment in the space segments of the satellite remote-sensing systems ... ." At the same time, the challenge of preservation is underscored in the body of the report where the Earth Resources Observation Data Center proudly asserts that "with proper environmental conditions and handling procedures the data and black and white film) are expected to be good for 20 years—color film for ten years."[6]

A recent study by the National Association of Government Archives and Records Administrators (NAGARA) estimated that the costs of preserving the one million cubic feet of records (2.5 billion items) currently held by state and local government archives at almost half a billion dollars over the next decade ($135 million from non-state sources to match an additional state expenditure of $350 million in addition to the $17 million that would be spent based on 1986 spending levels).[7] This expenditure would go toward the passive maintenance of materials, improved storage conditions, and the transfer of information on media that are seriously deteriorated to more stable media, not toward active conservation treatment. The report does not attempt to estimate the length of time by which such an investment in preservation would extend the life of the records. In any case, the costs of conserving the relatively small volume of records already held by state government archives exceeds the current social expenditure for the maintenance of these archival records by a factor of ten. To fund the preservation of existing records, suspending all new acquisitions or public services, would require more than a tripling of current budgets. Such findings led NAGARA to call for increases in expenditures sufficient to offset the expense of the estimated conservation effort; they lead me to ask whether there isn't something fundamentally wrong with our goals.

The recent emphasis within libraries, archives and museums on collections management has fostered a revision of the traditional focus of conservation pro-grams on the repair and restoration of individual items. Increased emphasis is being placed on collection wide storage and handling practices which slow deterioration or stabilize the current situation. While commendably more realistic, both information oriented "preservation" and collections management fail ultimately to prevent decay, and both represent financial drains of unprecedented magnitude. Archivists must adopt a considerably more radical stance.

Archival Methods

If we are really going to store and preserve records forever, of course, preservation measures would need to be taken forever and space for records storage would have to be maintained forever. The costs of doing anything forever are infinite, by definition. Because the very concept of permanent retention is preposterous and flies in the face of the laws of physics and economy, archivists have permitted themselves to ignore the consequences of acts of preservation that fall short of permanent retention. They have overlooked the obvious fact that conservation of the original records of contemporary society, comprised as they are of materials that nearly defy preservation, is impractical in the extreme.

The problem is, of course, of our own making in that archivists have declared that certain records are to be retained "permanently". The life of 19th and 20th century records on paper is estimated at less than fifty years.[8] With exacting storage conditions and treatment to deacidify the paper and stabilize the inks used to record information, this can be extended to several hundred years. Extending the life of such materials to one thousand years, would require regular intervention such as on-going deacidification and heroic measures of storage, such as retention in cryogenic vaults.[9] On the other hand, copying onto microform combined with reasonable storage measures and low use may be able to assure an information life approaching one thousand years at acceptable cost.

Even with the best care, the magnetic records of the twentieth century, including sound tape, videotape and data tapes, will lose their signal after less than twenty-five years without recopying. The signal recorded on optical recording media may well last two or more times as long, but this is more likely to impede future access than to improve it.[10] The problem with preservation of electronic media is that the media can easily be preserved longer than the capability of reading the signals recorded on them. Magnetic and optical media for recording of sound, image and data are all subject to market forces and technological change which are occurring at a rate that requires us to continuously recopy media to newer physical and logical formats in order to preserve access. Archival guidance concerning sound recordings in various formats recommends that older types of recordings be transferred to reel-to-reel tape in order to avoid having to maintain a museum of outdated sound playback equipment,[11] but this assumes that archivists have the playback equipment now and that reel-to-reel tape won't soon suffer the same obsolescence. In a recent study for the United Nations, this author concluded that such recopying of records will almost certainly have to take place within offices with each migration they make to new systems, media or software.[12] The recommendation is based on the presumption, which is urged as a matter of policy, that there will be a continuing requirement to migrate the information, certainly not less often than once a decade.

A strategy which can instantly reduce the dimensions of the problem to manageable size and free archival energies for other tasks is to simply declare the problem away. Rather than setting our sights on posterity, we need to replace the concept of "permanent retention" with the more realistic concept of "retention for period of continuing value" and adopt policies based on the premise that no preservation measures should be taken to extend the "format life" of the materials. Format life is the length of time which, given reasonable care, the information contained in the records will remain usable in its original format. Materials should be reformatted when format life has expired, if the information in them has continuing value. These redefinitions are not simply a sleight of hand means for instantly reducing the size of the threatened volume of "permanent" materials in custody, or a bureaucratic ploy to provide a more convenient definition of reality (both of which they are to some extent); they are offered as a way of redefining archival purposes.[13]

In their definition of archival, the authors of the official glossary of the Society of American Archivists defined archives as records kept for their "continuing value."[14] But archivists have not taken the concept of continuing value seriously as a policy framework. If they decided to keep materials for their "continuing value" only, archivists would need to reassess this continuing value on a regular basis, freeing archives to deaccession materials found to no longer deserve retention. I suggest this is the only responsible management strategy. But my proposal is not equivalent to Leonard Rapport's 1981 proposal to deaccession existing collections.[15] While I am sympathetic to Rapport's proposal, and it would save us some resources for storage of records over the longer run, it does not contribute significantly to the resolution of our preservation problems because it employs the same appraisal methods that have already been demonstrated to be inadequate. Further, it intimates that the need for reappraisal arises from previously impaired decision making, rather than that it should be a regularized function that is a desirable consequence of recognizing changing constituency needs and cultural values. What is proposed here is that we rethink the entire framework of accessioning materials and make all decisions about their continued preservation based on realistic assumptions about the length of time that they will be retained.

Minimal preservation measures, called "holdings maintenance," do little to extend the life of the medium, they simply make it possible for the medium to be usable for its full physical life. Yet even extending such minimal measures to all their holdings is clearly beyond the capabilities of most archives. After several years experience, it is clear that the substantial investment that the U.S. National Archives has made in "holdings maintenance," toward its 20 year plan to preserve the records of the Federal government, will prove inadequate.[16] In 1988 NARA was able to provide "holdings maintenance attention" for 121,700 cubic feet of records at a time when the holdings of the archives were increasing by over 100,000 cubic feet annually.

Even if we were able to extend holdings maintenance treatment to all our holdings, the aggregate cost of storing records in specially constructed facilities, and environmentally controlled, space approaches $25 per square foot per year. The costs of storing the 1 million cubic feet that the state archives wish to preserve at a cost of $500 million will be an additional $250 million per decade. The costs of storing the 100,000 cubic feet accessioned annually by the National Archives, is $2.5 million, a sum greater than the average annual increase to the NARA budget over the past few years. Clearly, even holdings maintenance is unaffordable if permanent retention remains our goal.

Once we shake the commitment to retain materials permanently, we are free to determine which materials in our custody ought to be retained as cultural artifacts, as well as information sources, and which might require preservation only as information sources, without concern for their physicality. The National Archives itself estimates that only .4% of its holdings possess intrinsic value. Thus 99.6% of its holdings should be subject to media transformation, and an equal percentage of new intake should be transformed upon accessioning.[17]

Recognizing these realities, some pragmatists within the archival community have begun to express the view that since we cannot prevent the eventual disappearance of most of this record, only halt the relative speed of its displacement and decay, we should focus less attention of the conservation of the physical medium, and more on the preservation of its information content. Advocates of this position promote the concept of "preservation microfilming", in which originals are relegated to the ravages of time, but microfilm copies are retained, presumably forever.[18] However, the basic text for American archivists on conservation, Mary Lynn Ritzenthaler's SAA Manual, mentions microfilming only once, and only as an alternative to photocopying materials that might be damaged by the kind of handling required to photocopy them.[19]

Traditionally, conservators have found preservation microfilming alarming because it violates the "rule of reversibility," which states that we should not take actions (finding and destroying originals) that cannot be reversed, and because it is arguably not the "appropriate treatment" in that it takes an action that is not necessary in order to forestall future conservation requirements. I would suggest that both doctrines lead to bad management and should be reconsidered. Preservation microfilming is a contradiction in terms only if we accept the dogmatic definition of preservation offered by the National Conservation Advisory Committee that "preservation is action taken to retard or prevent deterioration or damage in cultural properties by control of their environment and/or treatment of their structure in order to maintain them as nearly as possible in an unchanging state".[20]

We must begin by accepting the information life of specific recording formats as a fact of physics. While we can influence the production of new media and formats and encourage current information recorders to use formats with longer lives, the "format life" of any given format is the outside boundary beyond which we cannot rationally plan to retain the information without transforming the medium. If the expectation is to keep the information beyond that time, then plans to reformat it should be made when it is acquired, and executed as soon as it is cost-effective to do so, usually immediately. If the expectation is to retain a record for less than its format life, a probable retention period should be estimated and the benefits of reformatting should be calculated. Media should be reformatted if they meet economic tests to do so. Retaining records in the formats in which they were created, even employing the most minimal preservation measures, simply to achieve format life is almost never the most economical solution.

If we were to accept the NAGARA premise that 2.5 billion documents in state archives should be preserved at a cost of $500 million, the job could be done more cheaply, last longer, cost less to maintain, and have greater potential impact on more possible uses, if we microfilmed the entirety and made it available on interconnected Computer-Aided-Retrieval systems nationwide. By William Saffady's calculation, at 580,000 pages per cubic foot, microfilm storage of the contents of all the state archives would require 4310 cubic feet![21] According to the latest price lists from the Mid-Atlantic Preservation Service (MAPS), the costs of copying documents is now $0.15 per page or $375 million for 2.5 billion documents. The state archives are, thus, looking to preserve their existing holdings largely in the form of paper at a cost greater than the cost of microfilming the entire lot, and have convinced themselves to retain holdings in future decades at costs thousands of times greater than the cost of storing preservation microfilm.[22]

In facing the requirement for preservation of information content, archivists will find several new challenges. One of these challenges will be to consider the nature of the use to which records will be put, and make decisions about appropriate media transformation based on those findings. Microform is not the only media transformation we should consider. For example, records now of value only for genealogical research might well become important sources for social history research if converted to machine-readable databases.[23]

Another emerging challenge is that even when we decide to retain records that require machine reading for their format life, whether computer data, images or sound recordings, we will have to cope with the rapid transformation of our modes of producing, recording and storing information. The changing requirements of "playback" threaten even the most immediate aims of the archival profession. The challenge we face in managing the technological change of even as short a time as one hundred years, far exceeds that which confronts, and largely confounds, businessmen and government planners in our age.[24] The challenge is to manage a revolution in the nature of information acquisition, storage and transmission more radical than any since the invention of writing. With ongoing maintenance of current electronic information systems and software costing 15% of the acquisition costs of equipment per year, and equipment and software becoming obsolete after 5-7 years, the costs of retaining operating information systems for obsolete data can easily run between 25% and 50% of the cost of the system annually, as long as it is even possible to maintain. Therefore, as a practical matter, no electronic information can, or should, be retained in its original systems environment after that system is migrated to new equipment and software. When the

National Research Council studied the question of preserving electronic information five years ago, it recommended that this data should be preserved in Computer-Output-Microfilm because all other media were inherently too unstable and would require such massive investments over time.[25] The suggestion provoked an outcry from data archivists who correctly recognized that the greater benefit of manipulability possessed by electronic records would be sacrificed to the demands of preservation.[26] The dilemma presents a classic case of trading the preservation of the data for the loss of the ability to use it conveniently (and the loss of its evidential context). If the technologies of computer-input-microfilm could be improved to an extent that it was possible to recover the electronic databases in a reasonable amount of time for manipulation as test sets and destruction when the researcher was through with them, it would warrant further consideration As it is now, the preservation of electronic information systems leaves archivists in the proverbial position between a rock and a hard place.

In addition to the obvious challenges of coping with the new physical formats of information in the electronic age, two more fundamental challenges confront us. First, we will have to confront what may be a culturally intrinsic threat posed by communication across time: we might not, for the very reasons which make our archive so important to us, so defining of our culture and our modes of thought, be able to communicate to persons in the future, or they to understand us. Secondly, we will need to confront the preservation of the evidential context of information creation, a context we have long claimed is essential to understanding the meaning of records, and which is now threatened by changes in our modes of communication.

Because evidential data has meaning only in the context of its use, and because that context is not self-evident for machine-readable data in the way that it is for paper records, which leave behind their "original order" and the evidence of how they were exploited in their active setting, archivists will need to concern themselves in the electronic era with the preservation of system functionality. Indeed, archivists will need to migrate both archival data and functionality along with current records, and make provisions to continue to do so for as long as the data is to be retained. This part of the problem of preservation will be with us even if we decide not to keep anything longer than its natural period of use.

Conclusions: An assessment of the demands of preserving records permanently forces us to discard the notion of permanent retention in favor of a more responsible management formula based on "continuing value".

When we accept continuing value as the basis for retention, we are forced to address whether to retain records in their original formats. In place of the presumption that records should be kept in such formats, we should substitute a serious assessment of format life of different recording media and take actions, such as microfilming and media migration, required to maintain the information content of records in a usable form, for the period and purposes, for which it is required.

In keeping the information content of records, we must become more sensitive than we have been to the preservation of evidential context, and to the preservation of the functionality associated with the use of records. In addition we will need to consider (and here we can wait until we address other issues associated with use) erosion of accessibility to records caused by changes in cultural frameworks and modes of expression over time.

NOTES

1. After completion of this article, I received the Winter 1989 issue of the *American Archivist* with a fine article by James O'Toole, "On the Idea of Permanence," which affirms some of the ideas expresses here, but appears not to draw the ultimate conclusions for administration of an archives that I draw. I regret not having the opportunity to consider O'Toole's views and incorporate reference to them in this piece.

2. New York Document Conservation Advisory Council, *Our Memory at Risk: Preserving New York's Unique Research Resources* (Albany, NY: New York State Document Conservation Advisory Council, March 1986).

3. For example, so-called Perma-Life Paper, which has a pH of 8.5, has a durability of 1200 folds and a half-life of 200 years, an obvious improvement over papers with lifetimes of less than 50 years, but at the cost of having to copy the originals onto new paper, for which no simple and inexpensive methods have yet been devised. It is possible to extend the life of paper by deacidification, but the intervention is too expensive on scales approaching those which confront archives. For further discussions, see *The Laboratory: Current Developments in Instrumentation & Technique,* 1964, pp. 98–101, on Permalife.

4. Perhaps the most elaborate efforts to maintain records are those of the Church of Latter Day Saints Genealogical Society, and they illustrate why such efforts are not being undertaken elsewhere on an effective scale. See *Records Protection in an Uncertain World* (Salt Lake City, UT: LDS Church Genealogical Society, n.d.). Millions of rolls of microfilm are being made and stored in subterranean vaults constructed 700 feet deep in granite mountains where the temperature is 57 degrees Fahrenheit year round and humidity is 40–50%. The initial construction included space for 885,400 rolls of 35mm microfilm.

5. National Conservation Advisory Council, *Conservation of Cultural Property in the United States* (Washington, DC: National Conservation Advisory Council, 1976); *Proposal for a National Institute for the Conservation of Cultural Property* (Washington, DC: National Conservation Advisory Council, 1982) for further discussion for the growing importance of preservation.

6. National Commission on Libraries and Information Science Panel on the Information Policy Implications of Archiving Satellite Data, *To Preserve the Sense of Earth from Space* (Washington DC: NCLIS, 1984).

7. Howard Lowell, *Preservation Needs in State Archives* (Albany, NY: NAGARA, February 1986).

8. Mary Lynn Ritzenthaler, *Archives & Manuscripts: Conservation. A Manual on Physical Care and Management,* SAA Basic Manual Series (Chicago: Society of American Archivists, 1983).

9. At normal room temperatures. This life can be doubled for each ten degrees the storage temperature is reduced.

10. Margaret Hedstrom, "Optical Disks: Are Archivists Repeating Mistakes of the Past?" *Archival Informatics Newsletter* 2 (Fall 1988): 52–3.

11. Ritzenthaler, *Archives & Manuscripts: Conservation,* p. 46.

12. David Bearman, "Electronic Records Guidelines: A Manual for Policy Development and Implementation" (Report prepared for the United Nations Administrative Coordinating Committee, Administrative Committee for the Coordination of information Systems, Technical Panel on Electronic Records Management, [1989]).

13. In a delightfully provocative talk to the SAA meeting in 1979, newly elected President Maynard Brichford noted that "let them rot" might be the appropriate attitude to take towards records requiring active conservation. He went on to state that "we are keepers for a purpose and that purpose is not 'keeping' but using." I only wish he had pursued the issue and supported his arguments at the same time. See "Seven Sinful Thoughts," *American Archivist* 43 (Winter 1980): 13–16 for the text of Brichford's address.

14. Evans, Frank B., Donald F. Harrison and Edwin A. Thompson, "A Basic Glossary for Archivists, Manuscript Curators and Records Managers," *American Archivist* 37 (July 1974): 415–34.

15. Rapport, Leonard, "No Grandfather Clause: Reappraising Accessioned Records," *American Archivist* 44 (Spring 1981): 143–50.

16. National Archives and Records Administration, Annual Report for the year ending September 30, 1988 (Washington DC: NARA, 1989).

17. Alan Calmes, *National Archives and Records Service 20 Year Preservation Plan* (Washington, DC: NARS, November 1984). National Archives and Records Service, "Intrinsic Value in Archival Material," *Staff Information Paper* 21 (Washington, DC: NARS, 1982).

18. Microform was adopted as the preservation technique of preference by the national newspaper project because it reduces the space requirements for storage by 98%, assists in retrieval speed, and allows for low cost distribution. In spite of this, the National Archives microfilms a mere 20 million images a year in its Federal Records Centers, and does very little microfilming of archival records, none for the simple reason of saving long term storage costs. See National Archives and Records Administration, *Annual Report for the Year Ending September 30, 1988* (Washington, DC: NARA, 1989).

19. Ritzenthaler, *Archives & Manuscripts: Conservation,* p. 59.

20. National Conservation Advisory Committee, *Conservation of Cultural Properties in the United States* (Washington, DC: NCAC, 1976), 313.

21. William Saffady, *Optical Disks vs. Micrographics as Document Storage and Retrieval Technologies* (Westport, CT, Meckler, 1988) estimates the cost of labor and equipment for microfilming and a CAR implementation at $166,000 per million documents, or $415 million for the 2.5 billion documents in state archives. In this implementation, copies would be easily distributable, inter-archive loans could be launched remotely, and digitized images could be linked over networks at little added cost or using existing fax machines.

22. The *MAPS Newsletter* includes a price list for microfilming services in each issue. The prices quoted are from the spring 1989 issue.

23. Frederic Miller, "Use, Appraisal, and Research: A Case Study of Social History," *American Archivist* 49 (Fall 1986): 371–92.

24. Clifford A. Lynch, "Optical Storage Media, Standards & Technology Life-Cycle Management," *ARMA Quarterly* (January 1986): 44–54.

25. National Research Council, Committee on Preservation of Historical Records, *Preservation of Historical Records* (Washington, DC: National Academy Press, 1986). In support of the Council's recommendation see John C. Mallinson, "Preserving Machine-Readable Archival Records for the Millennia," *Archivaria* 22 (1986): 147–152.

26. Sue Gavrel, "Preserving Machine-Readable Archival Records: A Reply to John Mallinson," *Archivaria* 22 (1986): 153–5.

RICHARD J. COX

"Digital Curation and the Citizen Archivist"

Paper given at Digital Curation: Practice, Promises & Prospects, April 1–3, 2009.
Chapel Hill, NC: School of Information and Library Science, pp. 102–09.

1. Introduction

Much has transpired with personal information technologies in the past two decades, suggesting that personal archiving, from websites and blogs to digital photograph albums and scrapbooks, is already a prominent feature of our society, as well as a prominent preservation issue.

The present interest in personal archiving represents a major new opportunity for archivists to re-imagine and better communicate their mission in society by aiding individuals who have already developed some interest in the archival enterprise. We need archivists to develop innovative publications, Web sites, and other training materials to assist the public. Archivists now have the opportunity to connect with a growing portion of the public looking for advice about preserving personal and family documents. Archivists may need to alter their mission and priorities, but the possible results may be unprecedented in terms of gaining public support and understanding.

My question in this paper is whether the new interest in digital curation and in developing a multi-faceted curriculum for educating the next generation of archivists has some value for working with the public. This paper is conceptual. It is difficult to pin down the present digital curation effort because it is in development. However, given the purpose of this project, it is possible to make some proposals for why we need to develop some spin-offs to be used for equipping citizen archivists to work with their own personal and family archives, increasingly created or stored as digital objects.

2. Archival Appraisal and Individual Collecting

Collecting is a basic human instinct and books and articles pour forth regularly about the history and meaning of collecting. Personal collecting can seem quirky or frivolous, but it always reveals some deeper inner meaning to life's purpose. Traditional and official archival repositories have long operated on the basis of collecting personal and family papers, juxtaposing their public, institutional role against that of individual, private collecting. The nature of this contrast has been exploded by the advent of the digital era, complicating institutional collecting and empowering individual archiving, both possibly at the expense of the work of future historians and other researchers (or maybe not, instead just redirecting researchers to the World Wide Web as an archival repository, as the number of practical manuals on the topic grows, such as Brown).[1]

One of the continuing promises of our present digital age is the idea that individuals will be able to save every scrap of information about their lives and families and call them forth effortlessly and seamlessly whenever needed. No one will deny that this is an intriguing prospect, or that it is an engaging topic to reflect on. Designers and researchers exploring the MyLifeBits software, designed by Gordon Bell, certainly reveal why digital personal archives can be so captivating. Reviewing the advances in cheap storage, desktop search tools, and metadata development, these software advocates describe a database supporting the range of personal documents each of us is likely to produce in our lifetime (Gemmell, Bell, and Leuder).[2] What we hear is the mantra, save everything. Then when we examine the uses of FaceBook and MySpace, we hear another refrain, display most everything publicly (with some personal control and restrictions).

3. Personal and Family Archives

Whether we consider the use of personal information technology or traditional technologies involving ink, paper, and leather bound notebooks, there is little question that the interest in personal and family archiving is growing. We are witnessing an upsurge in diary writing, journaling, and calligraphy—perhaps part of a reaction to the bits and bytes of the digital world (see Serfaty).[3] Self-help publications appear regularly to assist individuals in taking up these pastimes. Attics, basements, and garages, even in the heralded era of cyberspace, often still contain boxes and bags of old family papers. As time passes, however, the kinds of documents we discover in these spaces seem more and more foreign to us.

It is important for records professionals to remember the emotions that might be associated with even the most mundane looking document. And this is certainly the case when we consider personal and family papers, especially in their traditional forms. Sometimes it is easy for archivists to lament the times that they have been forced to watch and listen as someone carefully pulls out documents one at a time and tells a story about each one. Yet, this very human response to interacting with the archival documentation giving them meaning and placement in our age ought to tell archivists something about the value of their work.

While one can read transcripts of such documents on the World Wide Web or their digital counterparts by contemporary writers, the experience between this kind of reading and possessing a physical document is not quite the same. In the past, while there has always been tension between private and public (institutional) collectors, it has been the institutional collectors—archives, libraries, museums, and historic sites—that have won out. In the future, there may be less certainty about this, especially as so many personal papers are digitally born and pose challenges to the public archives. The good news is, however, many private citizens care as passionately about the documents as do the institutional repositories.

People may be increasingly reluctant to turn over their original documents to archives, libraries, and other institutions because of sentimental and emotional meanings not being afforded by the new and emerging digital documents. Before the computer, of course, people worried about the increasing number of technologies encouraging oral rather than written transmission, and their impact on written records. However, there may be less to learn looking backwards because of the remarkable advances in affordable information technologies. Whatever perspective archivists might assume about shaping the documentary heritage through planned appraisal approaches, private individuals will continue to save their own personal and family archives and, different than what has occurred in the past, we might see these documents not hidden away but visibly posted on the Web. Archivists must explain and advise about the basic tasks necessary to maintain archival documentation, requiring new depths of technical and other knowledge, such as intellectual property and personal privacy.

4. Archiving and Expertise

The world is changing, at least in how it views expertise. It may seem ironic, but the many preservation challenges posed by digital technologies also suggest more empowerment to individuals to administer their own personal papers. Individuals who are not archives and records management professionals may be interested in developing their own expertise to administer their part of the larger documentary heritage (even though solving the challenges cannot occur without some expertise or more resources, public policies, and laws and regulations). We can learn a lesson from the historical development of writing: computers will become so essential that they will become available to all and in ways that are seamless and painless, just as formal scripts were supplanted by the less formal cursives for everyday recording and communicating (see Fischer series on language, writing, and reading, 1999-2003).[4]

It is worth noting that for all the claims made about digital writing and the World Wide Web that the prospects for preservation seem all the more dim.

Those working within the digital curation movement reflect this as their reason for working on technical models and methods. Martin Halbert writes, "CMOs [cultural memory organizations] hold virtually innumerable archives of idiosyncratic material that are rapidly being digitized in local initiatives. This digital content has important long-term value for both research and cultural identity purposes. But CMO professionals frequently lack effective, scalable DP infrastructures. This lack of access to effective means for long term preservation of digital content is aggravated by a lack of consensus on DP issues and professional roles and responsibilities" (Halbert).[5] This perspective also helps us to understand that the reason people cling to old family papers or try to administer their own records may have little to do with some noble societal cause, but everything to do with personal interests, curiosity, and self-identity—or recognition of the fear of the loss of digital stuff that they read and hear about. Archivists should want to nurture such interests, not diminish them, because they support the mission to preserve our documentary heritage.

Is it no wonder then that even as every home acquires a personal computer the shelves in the home are also being filled with leather-bound, acid-free journals for diaries and commonplace books? The only differences between these earlier revolutions and the present computer era is the amount of time involved; centuries have shrunk to decades, decades to years, years to months (it is often the compression of time in new technical developments that is identified as the main attributes of the present information age). One can practically use and cherish an old fountain pen or camera for decades, but every few years we need to replace our computers (even after they have been upgraded numerous times) (Gleick).[6]

5. The Changing World of Personal Recordkeeping

We have new challenges involving personal recordkeeping. The theft of laptops, identity theft, ownership and responsibility for personal medical records, shifting and confusing notions of personal privacy, and digital documents replacing paper forms and posing new maintenance challenges have all transformed the notion of personal and family papers. How well we do with these personal papers is critical to our identity. We are surrounded by documents marking the activities of our lives, the history of our families, and the unrelenting passage of time. Bills to be paid pile up on our desks at home. Papers from our workplaces can usually be found nearby, or, if we are efficient and organized, in our briefcases, packed and ready to be consulted and worked on. We save certain documents, an interesting letter from a family member or an annotated greeting card from a friend, as mementos of important events in our lives. We assiduously maintain our financial records, carefully organized by accounts and functions, and usually reflecting our sense of how we will tackle the unpleasant annual chore of filing our income tax statements. Photographs, diplomas, and certificates of awards are framed and decorate parts of our houses and offices. Sometimes we use the most routine documents, such as checks, to recreate a life (Mallon).[7]

These witnesses have been with us for a very long time. The impulse to record extends back tens of thousands of years and is seen in the cave paintings, decorated objects, and other material culture remains left us by early humans. Writing systems are, of course, much more recent innovations, but they tell us remarkable things about ancient societies, including what they ate, how they traded with each other, who the rulers were, evil acts perpetrated on people, stories of miracles and great beneficences, natural disasters, wars, what people wore, and how they built residences and public buildings. Although we view our own age as the time when great quantities of information are created, maintained, used, and abused, such recording is endemic to human nature—and that all eras are eligible to be termed "information" ages (Hobart and Schiffman).[8]

Even if one could argue that the impulse to document our activities is not part of our human nature, it is hard to argue that the sources driving writing and recording were not connected to the most basic of human functions. The most mundane of all recordkeeping, tracking financial transactions, is probably the oldest records system known to us. The most common financial record is our check book. Although many banks have ceased sending cancelled checks back to the customer, there are billions of these checks floating about.

Letter writing has been around since the ancient world, and it shows little signs of disappearing. Most Americans take for granted the daily arrival of mail at their doorsteps, even as their increasing use of electronic mail has affected how, when, and why they choose to write a letter, affix a stamp, and drop it into a corner mailbox. Somehow, however, the letter continues to hang in there. People certainly use short-cuts in our faster-paced world, such as writing long messages in pre-fabricated greeting cards or postcards or mass-producing on word processors what appears to be personalized letters, but the function and allure of the letter remains intact. The major change in letter writing has come in the form of electronic mail, and electronic mail is one of the primary features of our modern networked society, where one can communicate nearly instantly with others where it used to take days or weeks before. The use of digital letter writing poses problems regarding the maintenance of a personal archive.

Most of us, at least those of us at a socio-economic level where we own substantial property, also are cognizant of the need to maintain property records as a form of protection and a manifestation of the responsibility that comes with property. Like financial records, property records extend back to antiquity. As commerce and government developed, the need for documenting the ownership of land and houses emerged, and the nature of marking physical features on the landscape soon proved unreliable as the ownership of property became more complicated (although the earliest records, predating scientific systems of surveying and mapping, often documented immense amounts of these features and that of oral tradition as well) (see Clanchy as an example).[9] All those old metal document boxes we find in antique stores and flea markets are testimony to the fact that people have been maintaining property and other vital records in safe places for a very long time; examples of the predecessors of such document boxes date back to ancient society, and the storage devices

and the function they represent provide an easy to comprehend link between what organizations and governments do with their records and why we manage our personal papers.

The intensely practical merits of financial and property records and personal correspondence ought not to overshadow the equally intensive personal needs to create and maintain records. One historian's study of Abigail Adams, the wife of John Adams, describes her letter writing as having a "therapeutic function." "Abigail had the rare capacity to express her grief, anger, and fear in words on paper. In doing so, she also helped to raise her own spirits. By transferring her emotions to paper and then mailing the letter, she banished her unhappy temper." Abigail's letter writing was a means for her to "unconsciously transform the raw experience of her daily observations into a strongly formulated system of values. Writing to the folks at home about the strange scenes encountered in her travels confirmed their reality in her own mind as well" (Gelles, 26, 102).[10] Whether one is using quill, ink, and paper or tapping away on a computer keyboard, the therapeutic aspects of personal recordkeeping have not lessened.

6. Human Impulses and Personal Archiving

We have a great need to consult regularly many of our personal archives. We re-examine property records when we are contemplating selling them or refinancing them. We inventory when we are working on a will or updating one. We check financial records when we believe we have been over-charged for a purchase. We pour over old family papers when we need a photograph of an ancestor or a remembrance of a past event to be used in the production of a greeting card, wedding invitation, or renewal of wedding vows. These human impulses to record events and then to save records are reflected in legal matters, societal customs and traditions reflected both in the actual forms of the records and other sources such as etiquette manuals, and in our display of older records—framed and strategically situated—in our houses, workplaces, and our wallets and computers.

New technologies have changed the process but not necessarily the aim of how we interact with our personal and family archives. Digital photography has a more tenuous relationship to reality than that of earlier photographic forms. Now a photograph is information and does not become an image until called up and tinkered with, exaggerating all of the earlier debates about just what a photograph's image is—art or reality, for example. Critics, historians, and other scholars long ago abandoned thinking of any photographic image as just a frozen moment in time and space, adopting far more complicated concepts of what the image is, but a digital photograph seems more complex by many orders of magnitude, mainly because it is so much more malleable (Mitchell).[11]

Iconography is the study of images and their symbolic role in our lives, institutions, and society. And, as such, it also speaks to the use of documents in displays in our homes and offices meant to interpret our life. Often displayed with the care of a museum exhibit, these spaces tell us much about how and why people want to preserve at least a portion of their private archives. The public display of documents is a means by which we connect with the past. The mere retention and management of our personal archives suggests this purpose as well, but such administration is often done behind the scenes, with records neatly stored in boxes and folders, on disks, and on personal computers. The public display employs a much more selective process of interpretation, whereby we assemble key documents—sometimes selected as much for their aesthetic value as for their evidence—to portray a certain image or to assume a particular identity.

We can understand more of this role of personal archives if we understood why we carry certain records with us. The photographs, receipts, credit cards, licenses, and membership cards we transport with us every day in our wallets, purses, and briefcases speak loudly about us as citizens of the world. Some of these cards, such as a driver's license, we carry with us because we are required to by government agencies. We keep these documents with us because they provide some identity for us, especially as we relate to others. And, with the aid of laptop computers, PDA's, and cell phones, we can now carry far more personal information, some of it quite symbolic of who we are and much of it as carefully arranged and catalogued as an exhibition at a museum (or at least as good as the hallway outside the kitchen).

Recordkeeping we associate with government responsibilities as public data managers, such as vital family records—like death, birth, marriage, and baptismal documents—and a large array of licenses (from hunting to driving, passports and professional certification) have seemed to be with us nearly forever. Many people associate such vital records with government responsibilities, and, indeed, such recordkeeping did become an essential and ubiquitous aspect of government bureaucracies as social, health, and legal services expanded. Some associate such government recordkeeping as being synonymous with bureaucracy, the filling out of endless forms that every citizen experiences every time they visit a government office. Nevertheless, our effort to complete such records or to provide the information essential for completion leaves traces everywhere of us, adding to the accumulation of personal records we generate on our own volition.

Vital recordkeeping was not always a government responsibility. Non-governmental organizations, most notably churches, recorded births, deaths, marriages, and baptisms as part of their sacramental responsibilities—and it is reasonable to assume that if government had not become the official agent for this that such private groups would have continued to perform this function. Many of us have copies of these documents in our family scrapbooks or framed and hanging on the wall, especially since many of these documentary forms are in beautiful calligraphic hands and are associated with landmarks in our lives and those of our families. The rapid growth of interest in genealogy through the past century shows no signs of abating and, along with other hobbies such as scrapbooking and diary writing, suggests a continuing interest in personal archives. (For example, we can see this in the study of scrapbooks, such as Tucker, Ott, and Buckler[12]). If government was not recording so many of our activities, even with all the reasons of privacy invasions and misuse of personal data that should concern us, would we simply ramp up our own self-recording? The relationship between governmental and organizational recordkeeping and the individual impulse to develop personal archives is a complex, but quite real and useful, one.

The level of commitment we might want to invest in such personal documentation, even to the point of forging our own documentary past, can also be seen in other document forms, such as diaries. The writing of diaries has been a human activity for centuries, and nearly everyone can think of a famous one that has been published. And, perhaps, the best window into the process can be seen in the words of diarists themselves, such as in the those of Rev. Francis Kilvert, a nineteenth century English curate, quoted by Bret Lott in his book on writing: "Why do I keep this voluminous journal? I can hardly tell. Partly because life appears to me such a curious and wonderful thing that it almost seems a pity that even such a humble and uneventful life as mine should pass altogether away without some record such as this" (quoted in Lott, 79).[13] The process of diary writing may be the quintessential act of personal recordkeeping, where the daily—or some regular occurrence—of scribbling in a bound book can become an obsession of trying to record every activity, or, at least, an interpretation of every activity.

Whatever diaries might be, they have become popular again. It seems that nearly everyone at least starts compiling a diary, although most do not sustain the process (committing to a diary over an extensive period of time has about the same success rate as dieting and New Year's resolutions). There is a contemporary revolution in diary writing. Diaries are portrayed as the place to write down those salacious thoughts about illicit or immoral activities, a kind of protest against authority (but, also, I would argue, really intended to be read as well). Now, of course, every bookstore chain devotes an entire section to "archival" quality notebooks, beautiful and sleek fountain pens, and books about how to compile a diary (along with family histories, photograph albums, and scrapbooks). There is a public invitation to creating personal archives everywhere one looks, and it is sometimes hard to ascertain whether the vendors are driving and creating a market or whether a market

has emerged all on its own. The popularity of diary writing can be seen in the growing presence, since 1995, of online diaries on the Web, with their writers searching for an audience, a connection with others.

Blogging eliminates the middle agent, removing the question of whether the diary is intended for personal use or for public consumption by going instantly to a public (one much larger than when occurs when diaries are placed in archives or even when they are published). Blogging suggests that personal archives are becoming more public, as people also put scrapbooks with family photographs and scanned images of memorabilia online for their family and friends. As one thinks about their personal recordkeeping, it is not difficult to imagine a clear or precise role for the diary. It is the backbone of a personal archive, providing the basic outline of a life and its activities, a frame of interpretation for other records.

As photography became cheaper, more portable, and more adaptable for a wider range of activities, individuals and families took to photography as a means of documenting all facets of their lives. Photographs of travels and tourism became a normal personal pastime for the use of the camera. Family events, such as picnics, baptisms, and reunions, were all documented less formally than before. Informal images, people reading or talking over dinner, proliferated and filled scrapbooks and document boxes. A fuller sense of the personal archive became possible because of the advent of photography, and it is safe to say that newer technical developments, such as Polaroid instant photography and portable digital cameras, added to the possibilities of a richer documentary foundation (although posing new preservation problems).

Another essential part of any personal archives is the array of certificates one gathers over the years. We accumulate diplomas, award citations, and certificates indicating the completion of a special course or program through the years, with the largest clumps coming in our earliest and latter years. Our parents dutifully keep those certificates we receive in grade, middle, and high school, and we generally start holding onto them when we enter our college years. Most of these documents are intended to be framed and displayed, much like what we do with photographs. These documents are markers of personal progress, expertise, and authority, and they are most often displayed in public spaces such as our offices.

Such records exude symbolic value and provide a connection between modern records and their ancient antecedents. Documents such as modern diplomas have little, if any, legal value as they are issued merely for decorative purposes, mimicking older parchments and more ancient forms of records. They speak eloquently to the symbolic role of archives, a role whereby the documents take on more of a cultural rather evidential purpose. They provide a source of identity, prestige, and status, especially as they are usually displayed before us, usually hung in a place where they will be best seen. These documents manifest much of the overall symbolic value of our personal archives, including those parts of the archives that we carry around with us.

Certificates and diplomas often wind up in scrapbooks, another essential aspect of our personal archives, and now a modern multi-billion dollar a year industry with millions of people creating scrapbooks in one recent year, some using software enabling digital scrapbooks to be created as well. Scrapbooks are what many people think of if you ask them about their family archives, and, in many ways, they are another form of symbolic personal archives, with their arrangements creating order and meaning. Assembling a scrapbook is the amateur's approach to the classification and ordering of information done by librarians and archivists, portraying what their families have been up to through the decades. Individuals select documents and enhance their value as they sort through boxes and file cabinets jammed with records, ephemera, and artifacts and shape to their own and family's history by arranging the materials in volumes with narratives and interpretations. Menus, postcards, ticket stubs, letters, receipts, and other items serve as mementos of favorite or benchmark events, allowing individuals to construct a narrative of their past, as deliberately as others write diaries.

7. Traces of Ourselves

Personal archives can be viewed as crucial aspects for knowing about ourselves, our families, and our times, as important as licenses and memberships enabling us to function on a daily basis. There is some security in being surrounded by evidence of our lives and families. And there ought to be a feeling of insecurity when we lack such knowledge, equivalent to being illiterate. When we lack the right records, and hence the necessary information, we weaken our ability to read and cope with the world. Some of our fascination with old manuscripts, photographs, and other original documents derives from romanticized aspects of creating and interacting with such materials, but there are other utilitarian aspects motivating our personal recordkeeping.

The next time you are walking on a busy street or traveling through an airport, observe what people are carrying. Nearly everyone is laden with a briefcase, a large purse, or a backpack of some variety. Some of these devices indicate a businessman or -woman or a student, but they have become so ubiquitous that it is difficult to assign such identities so easily. What kinds of things are in these various contraptions? Some are filled with their business documents and readings, especially since so many carry laptops so that they can fire up and work anywhere (in the year 2003, laptops began outselling personal computers).[14] But they also carry many parts of personal archives. Photographs, credit cards, membership identifications, drivers' licenses, and other items either include or represent the trail of documentary evidence that follows us everywhere we go, work, and play. With the laptops and digital cameras, most of us seem able to take nearly our entire personal archives with us wherever we travel, provided we have taken the time to scan in the older papers and photographs. It represents just one reason why digital curation might become as much a public concern. While efforts such as the PARADIGM project at the Universities of Oxford and Manchester are working on digital personal archives, recognizing that "there is a marked lack of research and development dedicated to the preservation of this kind of content," since "to date, digital preservation projects have tended to be sponsored by corporate bodies or state archives." Even so, this project has as its "principal audience … organizations, of any flavor, which care for the personal archives of politicians, scientists, writers, journalists, academics or of other individuals" (PARADIGM).[15] My point is that we need to focus as well on the digital curation needs of average citizens, even if very little of their personal archives might ever reside in a repository.

Much of our personal space is occupied by older devices, from furniture to built-in shelving and filing cabinets, reflecting very traditional document systems. We reside in a world where we are bombarded by advertisements suggesting that most of this is obsolete or that it should be only of interest to us if we are engaged by the use of antiques and more comfortable with obsolete technologies (and I write this on a laptop on a hundred year old desk where sits a fountain pen and an old letter sorter). The maintenance of personal archives will be contested in this environment, raising many of the same issues archivists and records managers face in striving to administer both paper and digital systems in our transitional era from analog to digital formats. How we engage such challenges and incongruities with our personal and family records ought to make us better in how we explain, engage with, and resolve such situations in other organizations supporting the archival programs we normally think of when we imagine the archival mission.

8. Digital Challenges

It is difficult to know just what the impact of the Internet (and other digital documentary forms) has been on the sense of the personal archive. As I have discussed in this paper, the Internet has provided a new space for displaying personal archives, such as blogs and personal photograph galleries, but there has been enough debate about the preservation of digital records that no one should view the newly emerging digital personal archives with unbridled confidence. Electronic mail has proved to be a particularly testy

challenge, as it generates great gobs of documents testing maintenance and control systems, posing new security problems, and, like the telephone before it, has probably lessened the reliance on the traditional letter. A child writing from college is now likely to ask for money by dispatching quickly an email, perhaps with digital images attached, a scan of a professor's positive comments on an essay, and other documents. Saving these kinds of records suggests both greater problems and more imagination. No longer can we casually jam stuff into a box in the closet, planning to look at and assess the records at a later time. Now we must more consciously plan out what our personal archives will look like and the functions it will serve, understanding that it will consist of paper records, printed ephemera, photographs, memorabilia, and digital materials.

It is likely that the increasing use of digital formats will enhance interest in the preservation of personal archives and that this will strengthen the public's awareness of the importance of archives, records, and information management. For example, as digital photography has captured the public's interest, now constituting a billion dollar a year industry, with its ease of making and reproducing images, other problems have emerged. These images are easily manipulated, but just as easily lost. If archivists can step forward and provide advice about such problems, a new public comprehension of the archival mission may be gained.

Personal records and artifacts immerse us into the world in a way that gives us meaning beyond the superficial material stuff we acquire. All we have to do is to determine how best to care for the archival goods, recognizing that the personal sensibilities associated with family archives may be far more important than all the scholarship and theorizing being devoted to studying such documents. All we may need to do is to read the testimony of a writer like Ivan Doig rediscovering his mother and his childhood after he receives a packet of his mother's letters years after her death, suddenly "sensing the carrying power of ink as a way to go on" (Doig, 4).[17] We have to acquire a sense of the digital version of this "carrying power."

9. We Are All Archivists

Most people have little sense of what an archivist does, or even know that such a profession exists. It is difficult for the public to understand archival work because of the shifting notions of archives in scholarly and popular usage. A lot of scholarship about the nature of the "archive" has twisted and expanded the concept beyond any sense of the traditional meaning of the term as a repository where scholars and other researchers use historical records to try to decipher the past.

Fortunately, there are places to turn for assistance. Enough people struggle with administering their own personal papers that a number of self-help books have appeared offering advice and promising solutions. Even the vendors of the latest glitzy software products have gone after the market for managing personal records.

Maintaining one's own personal or family papers is a crucial activity for preparing a family history, and while there are similarities between archiving and writing there are also differences. Americans have been blessed with an abundance of historical agencies providing many programs offering advice and instruction on family history work. And these organizations have been doing this for a long time.

Archivists can gain valuable assistance by understanding the nature of personal recordkeeping. For the archivist, some of these personal archives may ultimately be offered to their repositories, and it behooves the archivist to provide advice about the care of such documentary sources to ensure that they arrive in good order. Some professionals have awakened to this role, as reflected in the recent book by Don Williams and Louisa Jaggar on *Saving Stuff*, offering basic advice on the care of personal artifacts and documents.[18] Of course, the vast majority of personal records will not be offered to archives, as they are of much greater value to the individuals and families they relate to. But for the archivist, the key importance may be tapping into the concept of personal archives as a way of explaining the importance of administering records. Too often we assume that others do not share any sense of this important work,

when, in fact, many are quite engaged in trying to preserve their own family and personal papers.

The archival profession needs to concentrate on developing new mechanisms for educating the public about how to care for their personal and family archives. Perhaps, this has already started to happen, as we note that one of the expanding sections of the major chain bookstores is the self-help section. In this section there is a growing number of books about organizing personal papers, what to keep, how to avoid cluttering up one's life, preserving family archives, and so forth. Any of these self-help guides provides as good a reason as any why there is a need for people to follow the advice being offered. However, professional archivists can do better than most of the advice currently being offered in such publications, but, in order to do so, archivists need to shift some of their attention from mostly serving the needs of academic and experienced researchers to working with amateurs committed to preserving their personal and family archives.

Archivists need to be careful in how they might criticize the role, old or new, of individual preservers of documentary materials. A historical perspective clearly indicates that the source of many holdings in now established archival repositories is that of the work of individual collectors or the efforts of some family member to preserve the family archival legacy. While archivists often see or portray themselves as the documenters or collectors of our society, if the truth be told many of their holdings were already somewhat formed by individual collectors who built aggregations of documents or who worked to preserve their own family archives; their disposition in an established archival repository with a more public mission was simply the last stage of a process. What I am getting at is that we may be seeing a very different role for family archivists because of the digital platform on which they work. Whether this new archival desire emanates from simply a utilitarian interest in maintaining personal and family papers or whether it reflects a new kind of competition with archival repositories, it is too early to tell.

The transformation of archival perspectives has usually occurred because of rapidly growing volumes of documents and increasingly complex hybrid doc-umentary technologies. Over the past two decades especially, new networked digital technologies have pushed archivists, at least some, to rethink the custo-dial model and to consider new kinds of distributed or post-custodial strategies. This seems to be where we now are with personal and family archives, and the prospects for continuing archival work are both daunting and exciting. Continuing archival work is challenging because the digital recordkeeping and information technologies continue to perplex archi-vists, especially those working in smaller institutions with limited resources, in their abilities to apply tra-ditional notions of record reliability and trustwor-thiness to the new environments; the result has been almost an avoidance of dealing with these documen-tary forms, an approach bound to cause problems with the future prospects of the archival profession. Dire predictions of the demise of the archival com-munity have not come true, although it is also the case as much because there are still vast reservoirs of paper records to be analyzed and administered. It is unlikely that sanguine predictions will continue if archivists working through society simply do not deal with digital formats; this avoidance will result in other disciplines or new disciplines stepping in to fill the void.

The exciting aspect of rethinking how archivists will work in preserving personal and family archives is that it may re-open a much greater possibility for reaching the public with a clearer sense of the archival mission, an objective archivists and their professional associations have struggled to do for several decades with very mixed results. It is, however, clearly the case that the public itself is actually sowing the ground for archivists to seed. As individuals and families continu-ally invest in new technologies that are portable and use them to store ever-growing amounts of records and information, they will encounter increasing chal-lenges for maintaining these sources. Even as people grow more aware of the potential loss of these mate-rials because of technical glitches and design weak-nesses, they may be loath to give up on them because of their convenience and ease of use (similar to peo-ple being hesitant to stop using credit cards and retail

discount cards even as they become more aware of the increased threats to personal privacy).

In addition to archivists adopting a broader cam-paign to assist the public, they must redirect part of their attention and resources from acquisition of archival materials and to assisting onsite researchers to developing workshops, self-help publications, and other tools for the purpose of equipping more and more citizens to care for their own archives. There is an emerging scholarly discipline, personal informa-tion management that archivists need to begin both to dig into and to influence (and there is probably a natural connection to the other emerging area, digi-tal curation).

Partnerships with other disciplines to develop solutions for personal archives management and a greater dedication to research about the reasons why personal and family archives are formed and main-tained are good commitments for the archival com-munity to make. Archivists, either on their own or in collaboration with others, need to write and publish guides about the management of personal and family archives directed at the lay audience. Maybe we are becoming poised to do this as we begin to see new attempts to provide such publications. The Council of State Archivists, for example, published in late 2007 a guide on saving family records in disasters [Car-michael[19]]. Advisory publications such as this are a by-product of what might be a new role for profes-sional archivists. In this role archivists will function more as advisors rather than acquirers, educators giv-ing their knowledge away rather than protecting the secrets of a guild, and advocates rather than reactors in seeking to preserve the portion of the documen-tary universe that possesses archival value. Some of this should seem familiar because it relates to some notions promulgated by those working with elec-tronic records a decade or more ago, although some of these views have been greeted with criticism or silence.

I am not arguing that established, institutional archives will not acquire and preserve personal and family archives in the future. What I am suggesting is that the vast and rapidly growing digital documen-tary universe of such archives requires that archivists first try to advise the creators and amateur caretakers of these materials and only intercede when valuable or unique personal and family archives are endangered. This will require new and more intense archival appraisal approaches, ones that have not been devised yet, as well as new standards for the maintenance and use of personal and family digital archives. These are interesting and engaging problems that should be the increasing focus of what educators teach, what doctoral students conduct research about, and what working archivists experiment with and develop into reliable systems.

10. Whither Digital Curation?

The digital age is such that we read of new terms, concepts, jobs, and even disciplines on a regular, sometimes frightening basis. Digital curation is, of course, just another new entry in our new cyberuniverse, and the question of whether it has staying power or not depends on how relevant and practical it proves to be in supporting archivists and their allies to develop new training programs both for records professionals and for private citizens interested in preserving digital documentation.

The efforts in the digital curation project to catalog required knowledge and to define and explain this knowledge with specificity in order to build a logical curriculum are quite important. Terms like "systems engineering and development," "harvesting," "ingest," "digital objects or packages," and so forth, all seem perfectly at home in a graduate-level curriculum. However, there also needs to be some thought given as to how to condense or spin-off elements of this curriculum, minus the technical or professional jargon, in order to create guides, training programs, and other forms of advice for public use and consumption.

My hope is that we can build on the digital curation initiative in order to develop the means by which to help private citizens to care for their materials. However, even thinking in this way might be far too limited. Nicholas Carr, in his latest book, predicts the rise of private computer systems companies pro-

viding centralized data processing services and storages. Carr also hints that these services will not just be directed at large companies with their immense computing needs, but that individuals might also be in line to use such services. Already, Carr suggests, "our PC's are turning into terminals that draw most of their power and usefulness not from what's inside them but from the network they're hooked up to—and, in particular, from the other computers that are hooked up to that network" (Carr, 27).[20] Some archivists might think that this means they should contemplate developing such a service role, but I believe that would involve resources far beyond the archival profession. However, it might mean that archivists should target these emerging computer services and data companies to educate them about the archival issues. The digital curation definitions and curriculum might provide one means to do this.

Acknowledgments

This is a shortened version of a book by the author, *Personal Archives and A New Archival Calling: Readings, Reflections and Ruminations*, recently published by Litwin Books, LLC, 2008.

11. REFERENCES

1. Brown, A. 2006. *Archiving websites: A practical guide for information management professionals.* Facet.

2. Gemmell, J.; Bell, G.; and Leuder, R. 2006. *MyLifeBits: A personal database for everything.* Communications of the ACM, vol. 49.

3. Sefaty, V. 2004. *The mirror and the veil: An overview of American online diaries and blogs.* Rodopi.

4. Fischer, S.R. 1999, 2001, 2003. *A history of language. A history of writing. A history of reading.* Reaktion.

5. Halbert, M. 2008. *Comparison of strategies and policies for building distributed digital preservation infrastructure: Initial findings from the MetaArchive Cooperative.* 4th International Digital conference, Edinburgh, Scotland.

[...]

7. Gleick, J. 1999. *Faster: The acceleration of just about everything*. Vintage.

8. Mallon, T. 1993. "Memories held in check: Pursuing a lifetime of my father's expenditures." *Harper's Magazine*, vol 287, 75–81.

9. Hobart, M.B. and Schiffman, Z.S. 1998. *Information ages: Literacy, numeracy, and the computer revolution*. Johns Hopkins.

10. Clanchy, M.T. 1993. *From memory to written record: England 1066–1367*. Blackwell.

11. Gelles, E.B. 2002. *Abigail Adams: A writing life*. Routledge.

12. Mitchell, W.J.T. 1992. *The reconfigured eye: Visual truth in the post-photographic era*. MIT.

13. Tucker, S.; Ott, K; and Buckler, P.B., eds. 2006. *The scrapbook in American Life*. Temple University.

14. Lott, B. 2005. *Before we get started: A practical memoir of the writer's life*. Ballantine Books.

15. Thornton, C. 2003. Laptop era dawns. *P.C. World* 21 (October 2003), 22–26.

16. PARADIGM, http://www.paradigm.ac.uk/workbook/introduction/index.html.

17. Doig, I. 1993. *Heart Earth*. Harcourt.

18. Williams, D. and Jaggar, L. 2005. *Saving Stuff: How to care for and preserve your collectibles, heirlooms, and other prized possessions*.

19. Carmichael, D.W. 2007. *Rescuing family records: A disaster planning guide*. Council of State Archivists.

20. Carr, N. 2008. *The big switch: Rewiring the world from Edison to Google*. W.W. Norton.

KENNETH E. FOOTE

"To Remember and Forget: Archives, Memory, and Culture"

American Archivist 53.3 (Summer 1990): 378–92.

The Memory Metaphor

Archivists have long been interested in the theoretical dimensions of their work as well as its institutional and social goals. With a view toward improving archival documentation strategies, some writers have drawn attention to the question of why societies maintain archives.[1] In addressing this broader question, archives are sometimes said to be society's collective memory. From this perspective, archives transcend the immediate tasks of documentation, education, enrichment, and research to help sustain cultural traditions and values. Although the view of archives as collective memory is sometimes employed metaphorically, it is a claim that can be placed on firmer theoretical foundations. Previous writings in anthropology, sociology, linguistics, and semiotics argue that material objects, artifacts, and documents—including those contained in archival collections—play a special role in human communication.[2]

Unlike verbal and nonverbal action, which is ephemeral and disappears as it occurs, the physical durability of objects, artifacts, and documents allows them to be passed from person to person and from place to place over long periods of time. Their durability defines them as communicational resources that can be used to transmit information beyond the bounds of interpersonal contact. The first of the two key points of this article is, then, that archives can be seen as a valuable means of extending the temporal and spatial range of human communication.

The coevolution of writing systems and early civilizations provides an example of the relationship between the use of documents and communicational range. Although many factors were involved in the rise of early civilizations, the beginning of complex social organization seemed to require a means of notating the spoken word.[3] Writing allowed information to be transferred from place to place and from year to year, even if the information pertained at first only to commonplace business transactions and government decrees. In this way, documents and archives facilitated transfers of information that were difficult to accomplish through means such as oral and ritual tradition.

Yet, the fact that documents and artifacts can extend the temporal and spatial range of human communication does not mean they are the only resource available for meeting this need. Oral and ritual tradition can serve a similar function and, indeed, *memory* may even be said to reside in the institutional mission of organizations such as archives, museums, universities, some government agencies, and the like. In this light, the idea of *collective memory* assumes a double meaning. First, as discussed in sociology and psychology, collective memory refers to beliefs and ideas held in common by many individuals that together produce a sense of social solidarity and community.[4] In the second sense—of interest here—the term implies that many individuals and organizations act *collectively* to maintain records of the past, even if these records are shaped by the demands of contemporary life. From this perspective, the activities of, say, archives and museums are interwoven. Each particular institution may sustain a *representation* of the past quite specific to its institutional mandate, but these representations can be interrelated.[5]

The value of this point is that it guards against assuming that collective memory is invested in any single type of human institution, such as the archives. Any view of the past conserved by the archival record can be placed, profitably, in the context of the representations maintained by other institutions. The task of assessing this archival contribution is made no easier by the variability in the way different societies come to sustain important information. In one society, oral and ritual traditions may predominate, while in another society they may be allied with archival records, written documentation, and even elements of material culture such as monuments and memorials.[6]

This second key point—about the collective, interdependent nature of institutional memory—implies that the cultural role of the archives is hard to isolate from the contributions of other institutions and traditions. Setting archives in such a broad context, however, gives us a better understanding of how social pressures influence and shape the archival record. No matter how tempting it is to discount these forces, understanding the force of their influence is a natural outgrowth of viewing archives in relation to, rather than as set apart from, the goals of other cultural institutions.

The two key points of this discussion can be set in bolder relief with examples, the first of which arises from recent attempts to isolate high-level radioactive wastes from living ecosystems. Warning future generations about the location of waste sites is a serious public policy issue and raises the possibility of archives being used to help communicate across spans of time greater than any single civilization has ever endured. The second example emphasizes some of the forces that shape a society's view of its past. It derives from study of landscape history and the selective way in which tragedies and acts of violence have been marked with monuments and memorials in order to outline an almost mythological representation of the national past.

Sustaining Warnings for Ten Millennia

Since the dawn of the Atomic Age during World War II, the United States has produced large quantities of high-level nuclear waste. These radioactive byproducts of weapons production and commercial power generation require up to ten thousand years to decay into less dangerous isotopes. No solution has yet been found to the problem of this material's safe disposal. Current plans call for its solidification and burial deep in stable geologic formations. However, quite apart from uncertainty about natural processes that might breach the storage chambers, human violation of the waste dumps is an important concern. No matter how securely the waste is stored, it is virtually impossible to prevent people from disturbing the waste—

intentionally or unintentionally—during the next ten millennia. If some of the buried waste becomes of value to future generations, it may even be "mined."

Recognition of the dangers of possible human penetration of waste deposits led to the formation of a Human Interference Task Force by the U.S. Department of Energy in 1980.[7] The task force included specialists in semiotics and communication and was charged with proposing long-term warning systems for disposal sites.[8] It recognized from the start that disturbance of the sites by future generations could never be completely prevented. Indeed, the task force was unwilling to assume responsibility for safeguarding the waste from deliberate violation. However, it did accept the obligation to reduce the likelihood of inadvertent, ill-informed penetration of the storage areas.[9] Long-term communication regarding the location of waste deposits was seen as crucial to this goal.

The key to understanding the interplay of archives and communication in this instance lies in the task force's pursuit of long-lasting means of communication employing a variety of transmission techniques. Durable physical markers at the storage sites were seen as a long-lasting, but insufficient, technique. It would be impossible to hope that such markers could retain their meaning for three hundred generations, or that they would even remain physically intact. After all, some of the most durable building materials known are, by virtue of their durability, prime quarry for scavengers. The task force therefore proposed that other techniques be employed to supplement the warning conveyed by physical markers.

Written documents maintained in on-site vaults and off-site document collections would be the most important of these supplements. At the site of the waste deposit, written warnings could be placed in an above-ground document vault to explain the nature and danger of the radioactive materials. In this way, detailed information about the design and layout of the storage area would be available for careful study. Future generations would be encouraged to periodically translate the documents from their original languages into languages that may emerge over the next ten thousand years, thereby enhancing the effectiveness of the on-site written documents. The task force

saw periodic translation of the materials as a means of creating a sort of temporal "relay system" of information transmission.

In addition to this relay system of translation, the task force proposed distributing information about the disposal sites and their location to off-site library and archival collections. Printed records produced on acid-free paper were judged the most durable for distribution, but microfilm, magnetic tape, and electronic storage media were viewed as possible alternatives if periodically copied and replaced.[10] Entrusting the care and updating of these new records to established libraries and archives would serve to extend their longevity. History has shown that collections gathered by libraries and archives have been maintained with care for long periods—in some cases for many centuries—without serious disruption.[11] Worldwide distribution of warning messages in this manner would mean that the potential loss of a record from any one place would be offset by the conservation of copies in other collections.

The task force also recommended that information about nuclear waste sites be added to maps and included in the national land survey system. Maps were seen as an effective means of communicating with future generations because they are used extensively, are produced in great number, and are constantly revised under the supervision of established national, state, and local government agencies. To encourage mapping of the waste sites long into the future, each site would have established vertical and horizontal reference points within the national geodetic survey system. These reference points would provide surveyors and cartographers with the incentive to retain information about the location of the storage areas. Furthermore, it was recommended that the locations of waste storage sites be included in recently created *geographical information systems*. These are large computer databases developed by government agencies and private corporations to store plat and tax maps and plans of public utility systems. Geographical information systems are among the largest databases ever created in the world of computer technology. The high cost of their creation provides some assurance that investment in their maintenance will continue long into the future. The task force concluded that this plan of distribution would extend the longevity of warnings by again entrusting their care to a variety of established and long-lived organizations.[12]

Beyond the use of records stored in onsite vaults and off-site document collections, the task force considered the possibility of employing oral tradition to communicate with future generations.[13] Disagreement exists among historians, anthropologists, and folklorists about the effectiveness of oral traditions in accurately transmitting information over long periods of time.[14] Instances can be found in which factual information has accurately been maintained orally for hundreds of years, but in many other cases oral tradition has fallen far short of sustaining factual accuracy. Of all the means of conveying information, oral tradition was judged the most difficult to assess in terms of potential long-term effectiveness. Legend-like tales and stories might well arise, or be created, to convey the dangers of the waste deposits. But the task force held little confidence that such stories would transfer enough information to guarantee safety, unless one or more of the other long-term communicational techniques succeeded, too.

Finally, as part of its recommendations, the task force suggested creation of a universal biohazard symbol as a two-fold aid to communicational durability. First, the symbol would depict the deadliness of the waste in a form that could be marked on a wide variety of monuments and written documents. Second, use of a single legible symbol would permit its meaning to be assimilated more readily and accurately into oral and social traditions.

Taken together, these efforts reflect the varied resources societies have at their disposal for extending the temporal range of communication. Given the need to communicate through ten millennia, the Human Interference Task Force recommended that both durable markers and documentary records be employed as the cornerstones of long-term warning systems. The task force did, however, find value in other communicational resources, such as legend-like stories. The task force also argued that synergistic relationships can be expected to emerge from the interplay of communicational resources. For example, the longevity of markers and written records could be improved significantly if their safekeeping could be made an ongoing concern of existing human institutions, such as libraries, archives, and government mapping agencies. The conclusions imply that even though documents and markers may be the preeminent means of sustaining memory in human communication, they are not the only way, and they benefit from interaction with other communicational resources.

The Effacement of Memory

If archives can play a part in extending the range of communication, they can just as readily be implicated in any attempt to thwart communication by diminishing its temporal and spatial range.[15] In George Orwell's novel *1984*, the Ministry of Truth ("Minitrue" in the language of Newspeak) revised records to reflect current dogma. By translating documents from Oldspeak into Newspeak, Minitrue workers could manipulate the past to support "goodthink." In real life, people do sometimes choose to keep secrets, to lie, and to distort information to control others. Bureaucracies and corporations may seek to control the flow of damaging information by destroying incriminating records and employing oaths of secrecy.[16]

Despite the prevalence these days of paper shredders in high government offices, professional archivists would not condone effacement of records in their care. Nonetheless, as was earlier made clear, archives are subject to the same social pressures that shape the collective memory of other institutions. Perhaps archivists are more successful in resisting these pressures, but effacement does sometimes occur with respect to representations of the past maintained by other institutions and by society at large. Insight into how such forces aid *forgetting* can be gained by turning to the history of places that have been stigmatized by violence and tragedy.

These are cases stemming from landscape history, an active area of research in contemporary geography. To draw a parallel with archival theory, this research has stressed, among other themes, the interrelationship between cultural landscape and collective memory. Such studies are based on observations of the close connection between the places a society values and that society's view—or "myths"—of its past.[17] Like archives, cultural landscapes can be said to maintain a representation of the past. In some early civilizations and primitive societies, this representation was legible in the layout of cities and villages that were designed according to sacred cosmological principles.[18] In modern secular societies, the organizational principles that guide the shaping of cities and landscapes are considerably more complex and elusive. Yet, as the historian Catherine Albanese has noted, Americans are not without a sort of "civil religion," despite claims to the contrary.[19] This civil religion has attained a sort of cosmographical representation in the American landscape, in the national parks, battlefields, museums, monuments, and memorials that are maintained at public expense and are the object of pilgrimage by tourists.[20]

One of the most interesting aspects of this landscape cosmography is the selectivity with which sites are commemorated to recall great victories, watershed events, historical turning points, and the women and men who made sacrifices for the cause of nationhood. Not infrequently, however, darker events—tragedies and massacres—are marked as well. The value of turning to episodes of violence and tragedy lies in the fact that the memory of such events is so prone to be held in tension. A society's need to remember is balanced against its desire to forget, to leave the memory behind and put the event out of mind. Few events produce such strong ambivalent feelings as acts of violence, and as societies grapple with these feelings in public debate, the struggle comes to imprint itself on landscape. If a tragedy seems to illustrate a lesson of human ethics or social conduct worth remembering, or if it demands that warnings be forwarded to future generations, tension may resolve in favor of a permanent monument or memorial.[21] If the violence fails to exemplify an enduring value, there is greater likelihood of the site, artifacts, and documentary record being effaced, either actively or passively. As the geographer David Lowenthal has written, "Features recalled with pride are apt to be safeguarded against erosion and vandalism; those that reflect shame may be ignored or expunged from the landscape."[22]

This point about effacement can be illustrated with striking, but contrasting, examples from Salem, Massachusetts, and Berlin, Germany. Today in Salem, no one knows exactly where the town's "witches" were executed.[23] Soon after the witchcraft episode of 1692, witnesses retracted their testimony and the trials were discredited. Through the years, the exact location of the site of the executions was forgotten. Tourists visiting Salem today can stop at the Witch Museum (the building and site are unrelated to the events of the seventeenth century), and visit a house where it is believed accusations were leveled against some of the victims. The sense of shame engendered by the trials, combined with Salem's subsequent growth as a prosperous seaport, led to the passive effacement of the execution site. All records of the site, both oral and written, were lost. Still, with the tercentenary of the trials approaching in 1992, the executions remain part of Salem's public life. Proposals to raise a memorial, and thereby publicly accept the event as a valid part of Salem's past, are countered by the desire of many to leave the episode unmarked and unremarked.

In Berlin, buildings closely associated with Nazi power have been destroyed. The Berlin Wall was originally begun close to the heart of the former Nazi government district as an intentional means of breaking apart this stigmatized area. The site of the Gestapo headquarters remains vacant more than forty years after the building's destruction. In Berlin, this conscious effacement of buildings was based on renouncement of this vicious genocidal episode, as well as on the belief that effacement would waylay attempts to create pro-Nazi monuments. The destruction of Spandau Prison, following the death of Rudolph Hess, was predicated on the latter motive. Some Germans go so far as to call for the razing of all remaining Nazi buildings, such as the libraries and galleries that still stand in Berlin and elsewhere.[24]

In Germany, of course, this active effacement of buildings has been matched by the demand that sites of Nazi atrocities be memorialized for eternity. Without question, the Holocaust has inspired some of the most forceful memorials of modern times. The pressure to sustain these sacred places is growing ever stronger as members of the last generation of Holocaust survivors seek, in their remaining years, to leave enduring testimony to the evil of the Holocaust.

These cases bring to mind other events of violence and tragedy where calls for monuments divide opinion and provoke heated public debate. Generally, this debate is resolved in favor of one of four outcomes for landscape: sanctification, designation, rectification, or effacement. As was the case above with respect to concentration camps, sanctification entails construction of a memorial—perhaps a building, monument, or park—and ritual dedication of a site to the memory of an event, martyr, great individual, or group of victims. Designation revolves around the marking of an exceptional event without the religious overtones borne of sanctification. Rectification occurs, generally, after accidental tragedy, when a place or building is "put right" and reused. As was noted above for Salem and Berlin, effacement occurs both actively and passively after particularly shameful events and involves obliteration of the evidence of violence.

The most striking aspect of all four outcomes is the length of time required for transformation to occur. Even in cases where tragedy sites become transfigured into shrines of national, state, or civic identity, their sanctification frequently involves a lengthy struggle. In the first place, as many historians have noted, historical conceptions of a national past are almost entirely retrospective and take time to evolve.[25]

The American Revolutionary and Civil Wars had to be won, for instance, before people became interested in identifying key events of the struggle. Second, as has been noted above, tragedies carry intense equivocal meaning and people may hesitate to sanctify sites of tragedy without first reinterpreting their meaning. The initial horror of a tragedy usually must pass before its significance can be assessed and its site sanctified. As a consequence, years or decades may pass before sites achieve the status of national shrines. Until then, the sites may lie abandoned and virtually ignored.

Nowadays, the Boston Massacre of 1770 is viewed as the first act of violence of the Revolutionary War era, but more than one hundred years passed before it was permanently marked. Even after this was accomplished, people argued against the marker on the grounds that the massacre was little more than a street fight, an undignified provocation of British troops unfit for commemoration as part of America's "glorious" struggle for independence.[26] Similarly, many years passed before Texans sanctified the Goliad and Alamo battlefields, both sites of needless massacres. In fact, the Alamo was almost lost to urban development before it was rehabilitated and enshrined to mark an almost mythical view of Texas's origin as a republic and state. The same delay occurred in the cases of Chicago's civic tragedies: the Fort Dearborn Massacre of 1812, and the Chicago Fire of 1871. Initially these were viewed as at least inauspicious, and perhaps even shameful, events. Only later did they become reinterpreted —and marked—as episodes demonstrating Chicago's civic spirit as a hardworking, enduring, and enterprising city.

In contrast to these landscape "stigmata" of national, regional, and local identity, places go unmarked and even unnoticed when defaced by other types of violence. Accidents, for example, seem to have little effect on landscape, unless they claim many victims of a single group and induce a feeling of community loss. Society seems to find little redeeming value in accidental tragedy. Once the immediate causes have been deduced and rectified, the site of an accident is usually forgotten. As a result, the sites of many accidental tragedies have remained unmarked or have been reused.

Among these are the sites of many of the worst accidental tragedies in American history, such as the Iroquois Theater fire (1903) and the Our Lady of Angels School fire (1958), both in Chicago, and the Cocoanut Grove fire (1942) in Boston. By isolating, cleansing, and returning such sites to everyday use, people absolve them of guilt in a manner common to other ritual processes.[27]

In the case of accidental tragedy, the passage of time is a useful means of absolution. But when a tragedy is not accidental, rectification resulting from the healing action of time is not always acceptable, and this is where social pressure is most outwardly evident. People may be so outraged and shamed by the appearance of violence in their community, perhaps caused by someone they knew and trusted as a neighbor, that they demand active, not passive, effacement. In the case of many mass murders, for instance, people have not hesitated to destroy the site of the massacre—or even the murderer's home—as soon as possible after the violence.[28] Apart from assassinations of prominent individuals, which tend to inspire memorials, the general trend is for murder sites to be rectified gradually, as are places of accidental tragedy.[29] But slow decay is unacceptable in instances of particularly heinous crimes. In some cases, the sense of shame and stigma is so great that a place, once effaced, will remain isolated and unused indefinitely, never to be reincorporated into the activities of daily life.[30] Perhaps the "silence" of these sites actually does "speak" to the senselessness of the violence as eloquently as any monument would.[31] In the end, all these cases show how social pressures shape landscape into an acceptable representation of the past. The disposition of the tragedy sites comes to mirror society's view of its own motives and aspirations.

Implications for Archival Appraisal and Retention

The issue of sustaining or effacing memories of tragedy has a direct bearing on debate concerning the collection and appraisal of archival materials. In 1970, historian Howard Zinn faulted archivists for neglecting to collect records documenting significant social minorities outside the mainstream of American life.[32] In a sense, Zinn was maintaining that archives err in favor of preserving records of dominant social groups at the expense of the less powerful. As the discussion of tragedy shows, the issue of selectivity is even more involved. The American landscape, too, is notably silent in regard to these less powerful groups. Few monuments mark the course of American racial and ethnic intolerance. But even with respect to the activities of dominant groups, powerful forces may intervene to influence the record of the past, regardless of whether it is represented in the landscape or in an archival collection.

The Dallas County Historical Foundation had difficulty raising funds to open an exhibit entitled "The Sixth Floor" in the former Texas School Book Depository from where Lee Harvey Oswald shot President

John Kennedy. The foundation's fund-raising efforts were hampered by a division of public opinion concerning the exhibit. Some people felt that an exhibit was needed, whereas others believed it would only serve to glorify the assassin, since Dallas had already built a cenotaph honoring President Kennedy.[33] The Historical Museum of South Florida was severely criticized for collecting the motorcycle of a black man whose alleged murder by Miami police in 1980 sparked a major riot. Some museum sponsors withdrew their support in the wake of rumors that the motorcycle was to be put on display.

Archivists have never come to terms with the concept of the cultural effacement of memory. They have long recognized the necessity of selective retention, but have done so to avoid squandering limited archival resources on redundant or relatively unimportant records. Similarly, they have accepted the necessity of restricting access to certain records, at least temporarily, in order to balance national security, personal privacy, or competitive business considerations against the value of public availability. But the possibility that a positive purpose might be served by conspiring to efface the collective memory of a particular event is alien to prevailing archival values, at least in contemporary Western civilization. The point here is not to realign those values, but to help understand the conflicts inherent in any society's attempts to remember and deal with its past. A critical role for archives may well be to serve as a countervailing force to effacement as a "source of last resort."

For archivists, the idea of archives as memory is more than a metaphor. The documents and artifacts they collect are important resources for extending the spatial and temporal range of human communication. This view implies that attitudes toward the past, as well as visions of the future, can sometimes condition collecting policies. In regard to the long-term storage of nuclear waste, it may be imperative that archives be employed to protect future generations from danger. Conversely, the history of tragedies exposes the power of social pressure to shape society's view of the past as represented in cultural landscapes and, by extension, archival collections. At the same time, the examples discussed in this article suggest how much remains to be learned about the dynamics of collective memory. Theorists must eventually come to terms with how archives, as communicational resources, are to be related to other means of memory conservation, and why some events are so well documented and stir so much interest while others leave such a small mark on the historical record, to the point where archives become a memory of last resort. Pursued in these directions, research can yield insight into the relationship of societies to their archives so that the concept of memory is not overlooked—or forgotten—in archival theory.

NOTES

1. Frank Burke, "The Future Course of Archival Theory in the United States," *American Archivist* 44 (1981): 40–46; Lester Cappon, "What, Then, Is There to Theorize About?" *American Archivist* 45 (1982): 19–25; F. Gerald Ham, "The Archival Edge," *American Archivist* 38 (1975): 5–13; Andrea Hinding, "Toward Documentation: New Collecting Strategies in the 1980s," in *Options for the Eighties: Proceedings of the Second Annual Conference on American College and Research Libraries,* eds. V. Massman and M. Kathman (Greenwich, Conn.: JAI Press, 1982); Michael Lutzker, "Max Weber and the Analysis of Modern Bureaucratic Organization: Notes Toward a Theory of Appraisal," *American Archivist* 45 (1982): 119–30; Society of American Archivists, Task Force on Goals and Priorities, *Planning for the Archival Profession* (Chicago: Society of American Archivists, 1986).

2. Kenneth E. Foote, "Object as Memory: The Material Foundations of Human Semiosis," *Semiotica* 69 (1988): 243–68, and "Space, Territory, and Landscape: The Borderlands of Geography and Semiotics," *Recherche Semiotique/Semiotic Inquiry* 5 (1985): 158–75. The case made in those two articles is based on a number of sources: Victor Yngve, *Linguistics as a Science* (Bloomington: Indiana University Press, 1986); Ferrucio Rossi-Landi, *Linguistics and Economics* (The Hague: Mouton, 1977) and *Language as Work and Trade: A Semiotic Homology for Linguistics and Economics* (S. Hadley, Mass.: Bergin and Garvey, 1983); Mary Douglas and Baron Isherwood, *The World of Goods: Towards an Anthropology of Consumption* (New York: Norton, 1979); Jean Baudrillard, *Le systeme des objets* (Paris: Gallimard, 1968); and Pierre Bourdieu, "Le marche des biens symboliques," *L'Annee sociologique* 22 (1973): 49–126.

3. Jack Goody, *The Interface Between the Written and the Oral* (Cambridge: Cambridge University Press, 1987), 1–56, and *The Logic of Writing and the Organization of Society* (Cambridge: Cambridge University Press, 1986); Roy Harris, *The Origin of Writing* (London: Duckworth, 1986), 76–157; Geoffrey Sampson, *Writing Systems* (London: Hutchinson, 1985), 46–61.

4. Maurice Halbwachs, *The Collective Memory,* trans. F. J. and V. Y. Ditter (New York: Harper & Row, 1980) and Edward S. Casey, *Remembering: A Phenomenological Study* (Bloomington: Indiana University Press, 1987).

5. Mary Douglas, *How Institutions Think* (Syracuse: Syracuse University Press, 1986), 69–90.

6. Jan Vansina, *Oral Tradition as History* (Madison: University of Wisconsin Press, 1985). The literature of oral history is of interest also in this regard, including David Stricklin and Rebecca Sharpless, eds., *The Past Meets the Present: Essays on Oral History* (Lanham, Md.: University Press of America, 1988) and William W. Moss, "Oral History: An Appreciation," *American Archivist* 40 (1970): 429–39.

7. The following discussion summarizes an argument found in Kenneth E. Foote, "Object as Memory: The Material Foundations of Human Semiosis," *Semiotica* 69 (1988): 253–59.

8. Thomas A. Sebeok, *Communication Measures to Bridge Ten Millennia* (Columbus, Ohio: Battelle Memorial Institute, Office of Nuclear Waste Isolation, 1984) and Percy H. Tannenbaum, *Communication Across 300 Generations: Deterring Human Interference with Waste Deposit Sites* (Columbus, Ohio: Battelle Memorial Institute, Office of Nuclear Waste Isolation, 1984).

9. Battelle Memorial Institute, Office of Nuclear Waste Isolation, Human Interference Task Force, *Reducing the Likelihood of Future Human Activities That Could Affect Geologic High-Level Waste*

Repositories (Columbus, Ohio: Battelle Memorial Institute, 1984); U.S. Department of Energy, *Statement of Position of the U.S. Department of Energy in the Matter of Proposed U.S. Nuclear Regulatory Commission Rulemaking on the Storage and Disposal of Nuclear Waste (Waste Confidence Rulemaking)* (Washington, D.C.: Department of Energy, 1980); U.S. Environmental Protection Agency, "Environmental Standards for the Management and Disposal of Spent Nuclear Fuel, High-Level and Transuranic Waste," *Federal Register* 47, 29 December 1982, 53196; U.S. Nuclear Regulatory Commission, "Disposal of High-Level Radioactive Wastes in Geologic Repositories, Technical Criteria," *Federal Register* 48, 21 June 1983, 28194.

10. Battelle Memorial Institute, "Reducing the Likelihood," 67.

11. Ibid., 72.

12. Abraham Weitzberg, *Building on Existing Institutions to Perpetuate Knowledge of Waste Repositories* (Columbus, Ohio: Battelle Memorial Institute, Office of Nuclear Waste Isolation, 1982).

13. Sebeok, Communication Measures.

14. Battelle Memorial Institute, "Reducing the Likelihood," 74, and W.L. Montell, *The Saga of Coe Ridge: A Study in Oral History* (Knoxville: University of Tennessee Press, 1970).

15. Further discussion of the following issues can be found in Kenneth E. Foote, "Object as Memory: The Material Foundations of Human Semiosis," *Semiotica* 69 (1988): 259–63 and in "Stigmata of National Identity: Exploring the Cosmography of America's Civil Religion" in *Person, Place, Thing: Essays in Honor of Philip Wagner,* ed. S.T. Wong and M.E.E. Hurst, (in press).

16. Sissela Bok, *Secrets: On the Ethics of Concealment and Revelation* (New York: Vintage, 1984) and *Lying: Moral Choice in Public Life* (New York: Pantheon, 1978).

17. Foremost among these works are those of David Lowenthal, including "Past Time, Present Place: Landscape and Memory," *The Geographical Review* 65 (1975): 1–36, and *The Past is a Foreign Country* (New York: Cambridge University Press, 1985), 185–259. Other related works are: John B. Jackson,

The Necessity for Ruins (Amherst: University of Massachusetts Press, 1980); John Gold and Jacquelin Burgess, eds., *Valued Environments* (London: George Allen & Unwin, 1982); and Yi-Fu Tuan, *Landscapes of Fear* (Minneapolis: University of Minnesota Press, 1979).

18. Paul Wheatley, *The Pivot of the Four Quarters: A Preliminary Enquiry into the Origins and Character of the Ancient Chinese City* (Chicago: Aldine Publishing, 1971), 225–476.

19. Catherine L. Albanese, *Sons of the Fathers: The Civil Religion of the American Revolution* (Philadelphia: Temple University Press, 1976).

20. An informal but provocative account of cosmographical representations and "pilgrimage" routes to be found in the capital cities of Europe is provided by Donald Home, *The Great Museum: The Re-Presentation of History* (London: Pluto Press, 1984).

21. In this context it is useful to recall that the etymological root of the word *monument* is the Latin verb *monere*—"to remind, to warn." Monuments may arise from other impulses, but their power to remind and to warn often overshadows secondary considerations. Further insight into this issue is offered by Kurt Forster, "Monument/Memory and the Mortality of Architecture," *Oppositions* 25 (1982): 1–19; Alois Riegl, "Der moderne Denkmalskultus, sein Wesen und seine Entstehung," in *Gesammelte Aufsätze* (Augsburg: Dr. Benno Filser, 1929); and John Ruskin, *The Seven Lamps of Architecture* (London: J.M. Dent, 1907), 182.

22. David Lowenthal, "Past Time, Present Place: Landscape and Memory," *The Geographical Review* 65 (1975): 31.

23. Sidney Perley, *Where the Salem "Witches" Were Hanged* (Salem, Mass.: Essex Institute, 1921). For an account of the witchcraft episode, see Paul Boyer and Stephen Nissenbaum, *Salem Possessed: The Social Origins of Witchcraft* (Cambridge: Harvard University Press, 1974).

24. The fate of these sites of Nazi terror is an active topic of debate in Germany and is discussed in Reinhard Riirup, ed., *Topographie des Terrors: Gestapo, SS und Reichssicherheitshauptamt auf dem "Prinz-Albrecht-Gelande"* (Berlin: Verlag Willmuth

Arenhovel, 1987); Gottfried Korff and Reinhard Riirup, eds., *Berlin, Berlin: Die Ausstellung zur Geschichte der Stadt* (Berlin: Nicolai, 1987), 543–60; and Benedikt Erenz, "Der Ort, der Stort," *Die Zeit,* 9 September 1988. Debate about the disposition of this "landscape of terror" is closely related to attempts by Germans to come to terms with the Nazi legacy, a topic discussed by Lucy S. Dawidowicz, *The Holocaust and the Historians* (Cambridge, Mass.: Harvard University Press, 1981) and Richard J. Evans, *In Hitler's Shadow: West German Historians and the Attempt to Escape from the Nazi Past* (London: I.B. Tauris and Co. Ltd., 1989). This debate is likely to increase in intensity in the wake of East and West German unification; many sites are likely to be reappraised in light of this development.

25. Some of the most useful sources in this large literature are Eric Hobsbawm and Terence Ranger, eds., *The Invention of Tradition* (Cambridge: Cambridge University Press, 1983); George Allan, *The Importances of the Past: A Meditation on the Authority of Tradition* (Albany: State University of New York Press, 1986); Bernard Lewis, *History: Remembered, Recovered, Invented* (Princeton, N.J.: Princeton University Press, 1975); Richard Johnson, Gregor McLennan, Bill Schwarz, and David Sutton, eds., *Making Histories: Studies in History-Writing and Politics* (London: Hutchinson, 1982); Michael Kammen, *Selvages and Biases: The Fabric of History in American Culture* (Ithaca, N.Y.: Cornell University Press, 1987); John Lukacs, *Historical Consciousness, or, The Remembered Past* (New York: Harper and Row, 1968); Patricia N. Limerick, *The Legacy of Conquest: The Unbroken Past of the American West* (New York: Norton, 1987); and Paul Thompson, *The Voice of the Past: Oral History,* 2nd Edition (New York: Oxford University Press, 1988).

26. Franklin J. Moses, "Mob or Martyrs? Crispus Attucks and the Boston Massacre," *The Bostonian* 1 (1895): 640–50.

27. Victor Turner, *The Ritual Process: Structure and Anti-Structure* (Chicago: Aldine, 1969) and Arnold Van Gennep, *The Rites of Passage* (Chicago: University of Chicago Press, 1960).

28. Perhaps the best known of these demolitions followed the 1984 mass murder in a fast-food restaurant in San Ysidro, California. The restaurant was razed and the land donated to the City of San Diego. There are, however, many less well-known cases. During the course of the investigation of a serial murder in a suburb of Chicago in 1978–79, the killer's house and garage were leveled by public officials. In the case of a series of murders discovered in 1957 in Plainfield, Wisconsin, the killer's house was destroyed by arson. Many sites of mass murder are rectified, but about half are effaced.

29. For example, see the Martin Luther King, Jr., Memorial shown in the cover illustration for this issue. The memorial is on the balcony of the Lorraine Motel in Memphis, Tennessee, where King was assassinated; it was created by the motel's owner, Walter Bailey. It took nearly twenty years for supporters of a memorial to gain public funding that would convert the motel into a civil rights educational center. Similar tensions have been aroused by attempts to memorialize victims of American violence of the 1960s at Kent State University, Jackson State University, and the John F. Kennedy assassination site in Dallas, and with respect to the Vietnam Veterans Memorial in Washington, D.C.

30. Shame and stigma may have a powerful effect on the shaping of landscape and the archival record. Future research in this area is supported by a suggestive literature on shame and stigma and their bearing on interpersonal relationships, including Erving Goffman, *Stigma: Notes on the Management of Spoiled Identity* (Englewood Cliffs, N.J.: Prentice-Hall, 1963); Agnes Heller, *The Power of Shame: A Rational Perspective* (London: Routledge & Kegan Paul, 1985); and Edward Jones et al., *Social Stigma: The Psychology of Marked Relationships* (New York: W.H. Freeman, 1984).

31. Bernard P. Dauenhauer, *Silence: The Phenomenon and Its Ontological Significance* (Bloomington: Indiana University Press, 1980) and Peter Ehrenhaus, "Silence and Symbolic Expression," *Communications Monographs* 55 (1988): 41–57.

32. Hinding, "Toward Documentation."

33. Candace Floyd, "Too Close for Comfort," *History News,* September 1985, 9–14.

ANNE J. GILLILAND

Enduring Paradigm, New Opportunities: The Value of the Archival Perspective in the Digital Environment

An extended version of this paper was published in February 2000 by the Council on Library and Information Resources, Washington, DC, as report no. 89. The author excerpted and updated her report in August 2011 for this volume.

Abstract

As the digital information environment has expanded and diversified, so too has the community of professionals responsible for designing, managing, disseminating, and preserving digital information resources. This community, really a metacommunity, includes, but is not limited to, librarians, archivists, preservationists, museum professionals, information system designers, technical information specialists, and sometimes information creators themselves. Each of these parties has a unique perspective developed from its societal role and manifested in specialized paradigms and practices. Unparalleled opportunities to enhance the processes of knowledge creation, dissemination, and use in the digital environment have come coupled with critical and often seemingly intractable issues relating to the heterogeneity, scale, validation, information life cycle, intellectual accessibility, and preservation of digital resources. The paradigms of any of the information professions come up short when compared with the scope of the issues continuously emerging in the digital environment. An overarching dynamic paradigm—that adopts, adapts, develops, and sheds principles and practices of the constituent information communities as necessary—needs to be created. This paper discusses some of the ways in which the archival perspective can make a major contribution to a new paradigm for the design, management, preservation, and use of digital resources through its evidence-based approach to the management of recorded knowledge.

Introduction: Enduring Paradigm, New Opportunities[1]

There is no doubt that in recent years a real shift has been occurring within which new or re-discovered recordkeeping theories are emerging as fresh discourse, and equally that there are members of the recordkeeping profession(s) now looking to see how the archival perspective can inform the conceptual models of other information professionals.[2]

Today's concept of whom and what the information professions comprise has expanded and diversified in direct relation to the expanded concept of what kinds of information resources and services make up or should make up the digital information environment. This broadened vision encompasses everyone who manages information content as well as those who design, document, and exploit information context and structure. This includes librarians, archivists, curators, preservationists, technical information specialists, and information systems and museum professionals. The important roles played by the creators of digital information are also being recognized.

The drive to develop transparent, networked, multimedia, multi-repository resources has brought these professional communities and information creators into a new metacommunity. The members of this metacommunity are converging around issues of metadata standards and interoperability, electronic record-keeping systems design, interface design, intellectual property, preservation of digital content, and professional education. Each community brings a unique perspective developed out of its societal role and is manifested in specialized paradigms and practices. As a result, convergence requires that each community learn the others' vocabularies and the principles and practices to which they relate and determine what needs to be accommodated and where new practices need to be devised or new principles articulated.

The rapid development and widespread implementation of networked digital information technology have presented this metacommunity with critical and often seemingly intractable issues relating to the heterogeneity, scale, validation, and information life cycle of digital resources. The paradigms of any one of the information professions do not provide adequate guidance for addressing the scope and size of the issues continuously emerging in the digital information environment. This metacommunity needs to develop a dynamic paradigm that draws on those of its constituent communities. However, the metacommunity must also understand and accommodate the distinctiveness of the societal roles and missions of the different information professions as the boundaries among their practices and collections begin to blur.

The archival community is one of the smallest and, arguably, the least well understood of the professional communities working in the digital information environment and in knowledge management in general. It comprises practicing archivists, manuscript curators, archival academics, and policy makers who work to define and promote the social utility of records and to identify, preserve, and provide access to documentary heritage, regardless of format. Archival holdings are noncurrent organizational records of enduring value that are preserved by the archives of the creating organization. Manuscript collections, however, are also often collocated with archival holdings. Manuscript collections are unpublished materials that are created or gathered by an organization or individual but are transferred from the original custodian to an archives, historical society, or library.

The archival perspective brings an evidence-based approach to the management of recorded knowledge. It is fundamentally concerned with the organizational and personal processes and contexts through which records and knowledge are created and with the ways in which records individually and collectively reflect those processes. This perspective distinguishes the archival community from other communities of information professionals that manage decontextualized information and tend to be focused more on users, systems, or institutions.

In his 1958 address to the annual meeting of the Society of American Archivists, preeminent American archival theorist Theodore R. Schellenberg demonstrated with remarkable prescience his understanding of the exponential at work in twentieth-century information production resulting from the acceleration of record-keeping, information, and communication technologies. He predicted that archival practices, with their focus on the nature of materials, would be shaped by the dominant characteristics of those materials: their organic character, diverse form and content, and sheer volume. Schellenberg[3] also predicted that these practices would be the archival profession's most important contribution to information management in general.

Exhortations for archivists to move beyond customary custodial roles and become advocates for information that must be preserved because of its enduring legal, fiscal, administrative, research, or other societal value[4] reflect a growing awareness among archivists that along with their concern for the nature of archival materials, there is a critical need to promote the materials' long-term requirements and enduring value to society. Maintaining massive quantities of digital materials of continuing value, especially the evidential qualities of those materials, over time is essential but complex. The challenge of identifying and maintaining such materials has led archivists to work with information creators to design systems capable of keeping records that will endure with their evidential integrity intact and with the preservation community to provide testbeds and evaluation for new preservation technologies and processes.

The Archival Perspective

There are several essential and intellectually-related principles that support the archival perspective, including:

- the sanctity of evidence;
- *respect des fonds*, provenance, and original order;
- the life cycle of records;

- the organic nature of records; and
- hierarchy in records and their descriptions.

These principles reflect the concerns of a profession that is interested in information as evidence and in the ways in which the context, form, and interrelationships among materials help users to identify, trust, interpret, and make relevant decisions about those materials. The following discussion will focus specifically on archival notions of evidence and how it should be preserved across its life.

The Sanctity of Evidence

History in the true sense depends on the unvarnished evidence, considering not only what happened, but why it happened, what succeeded, what went wrong.[5]

The perfect Archive is *ex hypothesi* an evidence which cannot lie to us: we may through laziness or other imperfection of our own misinterpret its statements or implications, but itself it makes no attempt to convince us of fact or error, to persuade or dissuade: it just tells us. That is, it does so *always provided that it has come to us in exactly the state in which its original creators left it.* Here then, is the supreme and most difficult task of the Archivist— to hand on the documents as nearly as possible in the state in which he received them, without adding or taking away, physically or morally, anything: to preserve unviolated, without the possibility of a suspicion of violation, every element in them, every quality they possessed when they came to him, while at the same time permitting and facilitating handling and use.[6]

Many of the information professions interact closely with other disciplines and derive much of their outlook from those relationships. For example, the practices and perspectives of information scientists have been strongly influenced by science and computer science. Archivists are closely aligned with professions such as law, history, journalism, anthropol-

ogy, and archaeology. Evidence in the archival sense can be defined as the passive ability of documents and objects and their associated contexts to provide insight into the processes, activities, and events that led to their creation for legal, historical, archaeological, and other purposes. The concern for evidence permeates all archival activities and demands complex approaches to the management of information; it also sets high benchmarks for information systems and services, particularly with respect to archival description and preservation. Recently, the paramount importance of identifying and maintaining the evidential value of archival materials has been reemphasized, partly as a result of the challenges posed by electronic records, but partly also to differentiate the information and preservation practices of the archival community from those of the library community.

The integrity of the evidential value of materials is ensured by demonstrating an unbroken chain of custody, precisely documenting the aggregation of archival materials as received from their creator and integrated with the rest of the archives' holdings of the same provenance, and tracking all preservation activities associated with the materials. Jenkinson described this process as the physical and moral defense of the record.[7] Schellenberg expanded archival notions about evidence when he discussed the values that archivists should use to help them decide which materials to retain.[8] The primary values of archival records are related to the legal, fiscal, and administrative purposes of the records creators; the secondary values are related to subsequent researchers. Schellenberg maintained that the secondary values of public records can be ascertained most easily if they are considered in relation to "(1) the evidence they contain of the organization and functioning of the Government body that produced them, and (2) the information they contain on persons, corporate bodies, things [e.g., places, buildings, physical objects], problems, conditions, and the like, with which the Government body dealt."[9] His argument acknowledges both the strict legal requirements of records that must be satisfied by archival processes and the wider concept of historical and cultural evidence that is contained in the materials and can be interpreted by secondary users.

The archival concern for the description and preservation of evidence involves a rich understanding of the implicit and explicit values of materials at creation and over time. It also involves an acute awareness of how such values can be diminished or lost when the integrity of materials is compromised. Evidential value in the widest sense is reflected to some extent in any information artifact, but only a subset of all information is subject to legal or regulatory requirements concerning creation and maintenance. Publications, for example, can be analyzed for evidence of the motivations and processes associated with their creation by studying their physical and intellectual form, examining different editions of the same work, and learning about the history of the publishing house or printer that produced them. Primary sources (unpublished or unsynthesized materials) particularly lend themselves to such kinds of analysis and interpretation, and such materials are increasingly being incorporated into digital information resources.

Maintaining the evidential value of information is important not only to creators of materials that are subject to legal or regulatory requirements but also to many researchers. In particular, reformatting, description, and preservation need to be considered. Reformatting has been discussed extensively in the professional literature in relation to the digitization of library and archival collections. Information professionals involved in digitally reformatting their collections must understand when a user may need to work with the original information object to appreciate some intrinsic characteristic, such as the weight of the paper, when a digital copy will do, and whether a copy needs to be high- or low resolution, color, or black-and-white. Information professionals must also decide how much of a collection needs to be digitized and what kind of metadata will enable a user to place information objects in context.

Archival practice places a premium on both collective and contextual description. The key is to explain the physical aspects and intellectual structure of the collection that may not be apparent and to provide enough contextual information for the user to understand the historical circumstances and organizational processes of the object's creation. Description should also demonstrate that the physical and the intellectual form of the materials have not been altered in any undocumented way.

Counterintuitively, perhaps, it is during the preservation of digital materials that evidential value is often most at risk of being compromised. Digital preservation techniques have moved beyond a concern for the longevity of digital media to a concern for the preservation of the information stored in those media during recurrent migration to new software and hardware. In the process, many of the intrinsic characteristics of information objects can disappear; data structures can be modified and the presentation of an object on a computer screen can be altered.

The Life Cycle of Records

If we can become overarching information generalists with an archival emphasis, we will be able to bring to bear what should be a deep and thorough knowledge of the documentary life-cycle theory … it may be our most important asset in relation to (I do not say in competition with) our colleagues, the librarians and other information specialists, who in time are likely to become not so much separate professions as special skills within a larger and more encompassing occupational group, which, in fact, may cease to be a "profession" as we understand the term.[10]

The U.S. National Archives and Records Administration (NARA) developed the concept of the records life cycle to model how the functions of, use of, and responsibility for, records change as records age and move from the control of their creator to the physical custody of the archives. In the first phase of this model, administrators create and use records (in archival terms, primary use). Records creators must develop logical systems for classifying or registering records and implement procedures to ensure the integrity of the records. Records managers and archivists also ensure that active records are scheduled for systematic elimination or permanent retention. As records age, they gradually become less heavily referenced and finally become inactive. During the second phase, the archives is a neutral third party responsible for ensuring the long-term integrity of the records. When the records enter the archives, they are physically and intellectually integrated with other archival materials of the same provenance, thus establishing the archival bond.[11] Their physical integrity is ensured through preservation management; their intellectual integrity, through archival description. Archival records are then available for secondary use.

Changes in methods of record creation and in perceptions of their continuing value have recently led archivists to consider if and how to apply the life-cycle model in a digital environment. The principles underlying the life cycle have been refined through projects such as Preservation of the Integrity of Electronic Records, conducted from 1994 to 1996 by archival researchers at the University of British Columbia (known as the UBC Project). An alternate model—the records continuum—has been proposed.[12] This model now undergirds the conceptualization of the role and activities of the record-keeping professions in Australia and is gaining in acceptance in the United States and Europe.

The UBC Project sought to develop a generic model to identify and define by-products of electronic information systems and methods for protecting the integrity of the by-products, which constitute evidence of action.[13] Using a deductive method drawing on the principles of diplomatics and archival science, the project identified the procedures necessary to ensure control over reliable records creation during the first phase of the records' life cycle and to maintain the integrity of archival records during the second phase. The project reiterated the need in the digital environment for completed records to be placed under the jurisdiction of the archives. These findings subsequently became the basis for the InterPARES 1, 2 and 3 Projects that have been examining the creation and preservation of permanent authentic records in electronic systems.[14]

The records continuum model takes a different approach. Records managers and archivists are involved with records from the time that a record-keeping system is designed. Physical transfer to the archives is not required; archivists establish requirements for appropriate maintenance of the records and monitor compliance by records creators. The intellectual interrelationships of active and archival records are established by integrating metadata from active records into the archival authority's information system.[15] This postcustodial model expands the role of the archivist to include active participation in the production and use of records.

The benefits of modeling the life, uses, and shifting values of information materials extend to information management in general by

- providing for the management of information resources from birth to death and identifying the points at which responsibilities for managing those resources change or certain actions must occur;
- integrating the communities responsible for creating, disposing of, and preserving information resources with those focusing on the organization and use of information;
- recognizing the motivations of different parties to ensure the integrity of information materials and points in the life cycle at which those motivations become less compelling, thus putting the materials at risk; clearly elucidating the process of creating and consuming knowledge and using it to create new knowledge;
- making it possible to meet different user needs; and
- enabling prediction of levels of use and management of information storage requirements.

Utility of the Archival Perspective in the Digital Environment

Information is not a natural category whose history we can extrapolate. Instead, information is an element of certain professional ideologies ... and cannot be understood except through the practices within which it is constructed by members of those professions in their work.[16]

The principles and practices discussed in the preceding section demonstrate how the archival community constructs information as evidence and why this construction needs to be understood and addressed in the digital environment. These principles and practices, independent of the archival construction of information, can also contribute to the management of digital information. Implementing the archival paradigm in the digital environment encompasses the following:

- working with information creators to identify requirements for the long-term management of information;
- identifying the roles and responsibilities of those who create, manage, provide access to, and preserve information;
- ensuring the creation and preservation of reliable and authentic materials;
- understanding that information can be dynamic in terms of form, accumulation, value attribution, and primary and secondary use;
- recognizing and exploiting the organic nature of the creation and development of recorded knowledge;
- identifying evidence in materials and addressing the evidential needs of materials and their users through archival appraisal, description, and preservation activities; and
- using collective and hierarchical description to manage high volumes of nonbibliographic materials, often in multiple media.

The archival community is making significant contributions to research and development in the digital information environment by encouraging the protection of integrity, the use of metadata and the application of approaches and techniques of knowledge management, risk management, and knowledge preservation.

Integrity of Information

Integrity implies a degree of openness and auditability as well as accessibility of information and records for public inspection, at least within the context of specific review processes. Integrity in an information distribution system facilitates and insures the ability to construct and maintain a history of intellectual dialog and to refer to that history over long periods of time.[17]

Ensuring the integrity of information over time is a prominent concern in the digital environment because physical and intellectual integrity can easily be consciously or unconsciously compromised and variant versions can easily be created and distributed. This concern has two aspects—checking and certifying data integrity (associated with technical processes such as integrity checking, certification, digital watermarking, steganography, and user and authentication protocols) and identifying the intellectual qualities of information that make it authentic (associated with legal, cultural, and philosophical concepts such as trustworthiness and completeness).

Functional requirements are particularly well articulated in highly regulated communities such as the pharmaceutical and bioengineering industries. Less well explored is how to identify and preserve the intellectual integrity of information. The intellectual mechanisms by which we come to trust traditional forms of published information include a consideration of provenance, citation practices, peer review, editorial practices, and an assessment of the intellectual form of the information. In the digital environment, information may not conform to predictable forms or may not have been through traditional publication processes. A more complex understanding of information characteristics and management procedures is required for the intellectual integrity of information to be understood. Attempts are often made to implement digital versions of procedures traditionally used in record-keeping and archival administration. Such attempts include establishing trusted servers or repositories that can serve as a witness or notary public, distributing information to multiple servers, thus making it harder to damage or eliminate all copies, developing certified digital archives as trusted third-party repositories, and identifying canonical versions of information resources.[18]

Risk Management

> If archivists are to take their rightful place as regulators of an organization's documentary requirements, they will have to reach beyond their own professional literature and understand the requirements for recordkeeping imposed by other professions and society in general. Furthermore, they will have to study methods of increasing the acceptance of their message and the impact and power of warrant.[19]

Evaluation practices of library and information retrieval systems have traditionally been based on four factors—effectiveness, benefits, cost-effectiveness, and cost benefits.[20] Research on electronic archival records has postulated another form of evaluation, risk management, borrowed from professions such as auditing, quality control, insurance, and law. Although this concept has not been applied directly to other information environments, it has implications for assessing risk in terms of ensuring the reliability and authenticity, appropriate elimination, and preservation of digital information.

Archivists seeking to develop blueprints for the management of electronic records have undertaken several important projects in recent years. Their research has shown that electronic records are likely to endure with their evidential value intact beyond their active life only if functional requirements for record-keeping systems and policies and procedures for record-keeping are addressed during the design and implementation of the systems. Addressing these increases the likelihood that appropriate software and hardware standards will be used, making the records easier to preserve. Records will also be created in such a way that they can be identified, audited, rendered immutable on completion, physically or intellectually removed, and brought under archival control.

Missing from this approach is the motivation for organizations to invest the resources required to implement expensive archival requirements in their active record-keeping systems. In a digital asset management approach such as might be found in the knowledge management community, the motivation to preserve usable digital information comes from the organization itself and is intimately tied to enterprise management. Recent Australian metadata projects apply two other strategies.[21] The first is demonstrating that well-designed record-keeping systems and metadata will enhance organizational decision-making. The second is risk management—persuading the organization that the resources invested in electronic record-keeping will reduce the organizational risk incurred by not complying with archival and record-keeping requirements. Organizations such as public bodies and regulated industries are generally aware of the penalties for noncompliance. Noncompliance by a public body could result in a costly lawsuit; noncompliance by a regulated industry could result in not getting regulatory approval to market a new product. The cost of noncompliance with record-keeping requirements may be significantly higher than that of compliance. In other environments the risk analysis may be less straightforward because the risks may be less evident or the costs of noncompliance less tangible.

The risk management approach developed by the Recordkeeping Functional Requirements Project at the University of Pittsburgh between 1993 and 1996 greatly influenced subsequent electronic record-keeping research and development projects, including the Australian metadata projects. The Pittsburgh project was an inductive project based on case studies, expert advice, precedents, and professional standards.[22] There were four main products of the research:

- functional requirements—a list of conditions that must be met to ensure that evidence of business activities is produced when needed;
- a methodology for devising a warrant for record-keeping derived from external authorities such as statutes, regulations, standards, and professional guidelines;
- unambiguous production rules formally defining the conditions necessary to produce

evidence so that software can be developed and the conditions tested; and

- a metadata set for uniquely identifying and explaining terms for future access and for using and tracking records.

The contribution of the Pittsburgh project, beyond the development of the functional requirements and metadata set, was the development of the concept of warrant and a methodology for creating a warrant relevant to the individual circumstances of an organization. Warrant relates to the requirements imposed on an organization by external authorities for creating and keeping reliable records. If organizations understand warrant as it applies to how they manage their electronic record-keeping systems, they can assess the degree of risk they might incur by not managing their systems appropriately.[23]

Knowledge Preservation

The digital world transforms traditional preservation concepts from protecting the physical integrity of the object to specifying the creation and maintenance of the object whose intellectual integrity is its primary characteristic.[24]

Preservation is perhaps the single biggest challenge facing everyone who creates, maintains, or relies on digital information. Awareness of the immense scope of the potential preservation crisis has brought many groups together to experiment with new preservation strategies and technologies. Preserving knowledge is more complex than preserving only media or content. It is about preserving the intellectual integrity of information objects, including capturing information about the various contexts within which information is created, organized, and used, their organic relationships with other information objects, and characteristics that give them meaning and evidential value. Preservation of knowledge also requires appreciating the continuing relationships between digital and non-digital information.

Concern for retaining the evidential value of records has placed the archival community at the vanguard of research and development in digital preservation and authentication. Moreover, because archives focus on records, archivists have an awareness of the societal, institutional, and individual construction of memory and an understanding of the implications of how that memory is represented and transmitted over time. This awareness becomes increasingly important as more of the world's collections are reformatted and represented online. It is also important for retaining evidence in time and over time, especially through digital preservation processes.

Archives today are engaged with both the creation of information and its ultimate disposition (either destruction or permanent retention). Since the 1960s, the archival community has worked increasingly closely with the creators of records and record-keeping systems to develop means to identify and preserve digital records that have no paper counterpart. The problem of what to do about records that are born digital has forced archivists to reexamine and reinvent their principles and practices in light of a digital challenge that emerged before the advent of digital libraries. This engagement at various points in the life cycle of materials also helps to establish a bridge to information and knowledge production processes and communities—from electronic publishing to digital asset management—that have traditionally fallen outside the domain of bibliographic information.

The archival mission of preserving evidence over time has resulted in demanding criteria for measuring the efficacy of the range of strategies proposed for digital preservation, including migration, emulation, bundling, and persistent object preservation (later referred to as persistent archives technology). Projects using archival testbeds have been undertaken in several countries with the aim of understanding the extent to which different strategies work with a range of materials and what limitations need to be addressed procedurally, through the development of new technological approaches.

THE CEDARS PROJECT

The Cedars Project was a United Kingdom collaboration of librarians, archivists, publishers, authors, and institutions (libraries, records offices, and universities). Working with digitized and born-digital materials, Cedars used a two-track approach to evaluate different preservation strategies through demonstration projects at U.K. test sites, formulate recommendations and guidelines, and develop practical, robust, and scaleable models for establishing distributed digital archives.[25] Cedars also examined other issues related to the management of digital information, including rights management and metadata.

THE DIGITAL REPOSITORY PROJECT

The Digital Repository Project of the National Archives of the Netherlands aims to create a Trusted Digital Repository for the Dutch central government and some of the Netherlands regional archival institutions that will ensure the authenticity, accessibility, and longevity of archival records created by Dutch government agencies.[26] The project brought together two important concepts—the emulation technique devised by Jeff Rothenberg and the reference model for an open archival information system (OAIS) developed by the U.S. National Aeronautics and Space Administration and adopted as an ISO standard in 2003.[27] The emulation technique involved creating emulators for future computers to enable them to run the software on which archived material was created and maintained, thus recreating the functionality, look, and feel of the material.[28] The OAIS reference model is a high-level record-keeping model developed to assist in the archiving of high-volume information. It delineates the processes involved in the ingestion, storage, administrative and logistical maintenance, intellectual metadata management, and access and delivery of electronic records.[29]

The Digital Repository Project is most concerned with determining the functionality of the repository, scope of the metadata, standards to be applied, and differentiation of the intellectual, physical, and technical form of the records. As with the Cedars Project, a two-track approach has been taken. One track built a repository to preserve simple records in a stand-alone environment implemented by the National Archives.

The other track developed a testbed and experimental framework for examining the application of preservation strategies such as migration, emulation, and XML to electronic records acquired by applying the OAIS reference model.[30]

PERSISTENT OBJECT PRESERVATION

Persistent object preservation is a highly generic technological approach that was developed jointly by the U.S. National Archives and Records Administration and the San Diego Supercomputer Center. This project addressed the National Archives' need to find efficient and fast methods for acquiring and preserving, in context, millions of files that can be applied to many types of records and that comply with archival principles. The approach focuses on storing infrastructure independent proxies (IIPs) for the original information objects that make up a collection and identifying their metadata attributes and behaviors that can be used to recreate the collection. Persistent object preservation also exploits inherent hierarchical structures within records, predictable record forms, and dependencies between them. It is designed to be consistent, comprehensive, and independent of infrastructure.[31]

Like the Digital Repository Project, persistent object preservation was built around the OAIS reference model. It supports archival processes from accessioning through preservation and use, and it recognizes the importance of collection-based management. It went on to become the basis for the Persistent Archives Testbed, which sought to develop, in collaboration with several state and university collaborators, the Archivist's workbench, a community model for electronic records management, with archival and technological functions including appraisal, accessioning, arrangement, description, preservation and access performed within in a distributed network using data-grid technology.[32]

Achieving the Full Potential of Cross-Community Developments in the Digital Environment

The long-term preservation of information in digital form requires not only technical solutions and new organizational strategies, but also the building of a new culture that values and supports the survival of bits over time. This requires that a diverse community of experts—computer scientists, archivists, social scientists, artists, lawyers, and politicians—collaborate to ensure the preservation of a new kind of cultural heritage, the digital document.[33]

Much of this paper has focused on explicating the archival perspective and demonstrating how it can contribute to the management of digital information. It has also pointed out some of the opportunities resulting from the extension of archival principles to the management of electronic records. A similar explication of the perspectives and functional requirements for digital information and information systems of other information communities, such as museum professionals, preservationists, and systems designers, is now needed. This will enable everyone engaged in the digital environment to see points of commonality and divergence and develop technological, procedural, policy, and educational approaches accordingly.

Several other activities would assist in this endeavor. First, more opportunities are needed for cross-community dialog on issues relating to the development of digital information infrastructure. Such dialog has increased in recent years, as shown by the development of the Dublin Core, the ongoing debate over intellectual property in the digital environment, and the collaborative projects mentioned above. Workshops and conferences hosted by the Council on Library and Information Resources, the Institute of Museum and Library Services, National Science Foundation, and Northeast Document Conservation Center, among others, have brought the different communities together to discuss key issues such as digital preservation and access and the education of boundary-spanning professionals. More could be done, however, to bring together rank-and-file members of the professional communities.

Second, identifying substantive documentation on the various projects under way can be difficult, despite the presence of substantial project Web sites. A clearinghouse of project-related papers, especially final reports, would help, as would additional interdisciplinary publishing outlets.

Third, and perhaps most important, professional education and continuing education mechanisms need to be reevaluated. A new kind of professional is needed, one whose primary domain is the information metacommunity and who can function effectively in the dynamic interdisciplinary information environment. This might involve

- changing the core curricula in library and information science programs to include additional professional perspectives,
- developing more intensive education in archival science and museum administration under a more interdisciplinary rubric, such as information studies, and
- developing new interdisciplinary or inter-professional programs.

Similarly, a pressing need exists to develop effective mechanisms for keeping practicing professionals abreast of techniques and issues in the digital environment. The information professions lack a coherent continuing education infrastructure to systematically address this need.

The archival community has come a long way in the past 200 years. Challenged by increasingly rapid changes in record-keeping and reproduction technologies as well as by changes in bureaucratic structures and collaborative processes, the archival paradigm has evolved into a sophisticated and confident articulation of an evidence-based approach to information management. The archival community has made the following important contributions individually and collaboratively:

- articulating functional requirements for information systems and records creation processes to ensure the reliability and authenticity of records and the preservation of their evidential value;
- providing testbeds for implementing and evaluating preservation techniques and technologies;
- exploiting the roles of context and hierarchy in information retrieval; and
- developing interoperable metadata.

Such contributions demonstrate the relevance and utility of the archival perspective in the digital environment and argue for consideration of its principles and practices in the development of a new paradigm for the emerging metacommunity of information professionals.

NOTES

1. An extended version of this paper was published in February 2000 by the Council on Library and Information Resources, Washington, D.C., as its Publication no. 89. The author has selected excerpts from that publication and updated them for this volume in August 2011.

2. Frank Upward and Sue McKemmish, "Somewhere Beyond Custody," *Archives and Manuscripts* 22 (1994): 136.

3. Theodore R. Schellenberg, "The Future of the Archival Profession," *American Archivist* 22 (1959).

4. Bruce W. Dearstyne, *The Archival Enterprise: Modern Archival Principles, Practices, and Management Techniques* (Chicago, Il.: American Library Association, 1993).

5. Frank G. Burke, *Research and the Manuscript Tradition* (Lanham, Md.: Scarecrow Press, 1997), 20.

6. Hilary Jenkinson, "Reflections of an Archivist," *Contemporary Review* 165 (1944).

7. Hilary Jenkinson, *A Manual of Archive Administration*, New and rev. ed. (London: Percy Lund, Humphries, 1937).

8. Theodore R. Schellenberg, *The Appraisal of Modern Public Records* (Bulletin of the National Archives 8) (Washington, D.C.: National Archives and Records Service, 1956), accessed February 29, 2012, http://www.archives.gov/research/alic/reference/archives-resources/appraisal-of-records.html.

9. Schellenberg, *The Appraisal of Modern Public Records.*

10. Hugh Taylor, "Information Ecology and the Archives of the 1980s," *Archivaria* 18 (1984): 32.

11. Luciana Duranti, "Archives as a Place," *Archives and Manuscripts* 24 (1996).

12. Frank Upward, "Structuring the Records Continuum Part One: Postcustodial Principles and Properties," *Archives and Manuscripts* 24 (1996), and "Structuring the Records Continuum Part Two: Structuration Theory and Recordkeeping," *Archives and Manuscripts* 25 (1997).

13. Luciana Duranti and Heather MacNeil, "The Protection of the Integrity of Electronic Records: An Overview of the UBC-MAS Research Project," *Archivaria* 42 (1996).

14. InterPARES Project, International Project on Permanent Authentic Records in Electronic Systems: Project Overview, accessed February 29, 2012, http://www.interpares.org.

15. Upward and McKemmish, "Somewhere Beyond Custody."

16. Philip Agre, "Institutional Circuitry: Thinking About the Forms and Uses of Information," *Information Technology and Libraries* 14 (1995): 225.

17. Clifford A. Lynch, "The Integrity of Digital Information: Mechanics and Definitional Issues," *Journal of the American Society for Information Science* 45 (1994): 738.

18. Commission on Preservation and Access and Research Libraries Group, *Preserving Digital Information: Report of the Task Force on Archiving of Digital Information* (1996), accessed February 29, 2012, http://www.clir.org/pubs/reports/pub63 watersgarrett.pdf; Lynch, "The Integrity of Digital Information."

19. Wendy Duff, "Harnessing the Power of Warrant," *American Archivist* 61 (1998): 105.

20. F. Wilfrid Lancaster, *Information Retrieval Systems: Characteristics, Testing, and Evaluation*, 2nd ed. (New York: Wiley, 1979).

21. Records Continuum Research Group, Monash University, "Recordkeeping Metadata Project" (1999), accessed February 29, 2012, http://www.infotech.monash.edu.au/research/groups/rcrg/projects/spirt/about.html.

22. Richard J. Cox, "Re-Discovering the Archival Mission: The Recordkeeping Functional Require-

ments Project at the University of Pittsburgh, A Progress Report," *Archives and Museum Informatics* 8 (1994).

23. Duff, "Harnessing the Power of Warrant."

24. Paul Conway, *Preservation in the Digital World* (Washington, D.C.: Commission on Preservation and Access, 1996), accessed February 29, 2012, http://www.clir.org/pubs/reports/conway2/index.html.

25. Cedars Project, CURL Exemplars in Digital Archives (1999), accessed February 29, 2012, http://www.webarchive.org.uk/ukwa/target/99695/.

26. Jacqueline Slats, "The National Archives as a Trusted Digital Repository for Record Creators and Archival Institutions in the Netherlands" (paper presented at the 16th Congress of the International Council on Archives, Kuala Lumpur, Malaysia, July 21–27 2008).

27. Consultative Committee for Space Data Systems/ International Organization for Standardization, *Space Data and Information Transfer System: Open Archival Information System: Reference Model* (Geneva: International Organization for Standardization, 1999).

28. Jeff Rothenberg, "Ensuring the Longevity of Digital Documents," *Scientific American* 272 (January 1995), and Rothenberg, *Avoiding Technological Quicksand: Finding a Viable Technical Foundation for Digital Preservation* (Washington, D.C.: Council on Library and Information Resources, 1999), accessed February 29, 2012, http://www.clir.org/pubs/reports/rothenberg/contents.html.

29. Don Sawyer and Lou Reich, *Archiving Referencing Model, White Book,* Issue 5 (Consultative Com-

mittee for Space Data Systems, 1999), accessed February 29, 2012, http://nssdc.gsfc.nasa.gov/nost/isoas/ref_model.html.

30. Hans Hofman, "National Archives of the Netherlands' Digital Repository" (paper presented at the DLM-Forum, Brussels, October 18–19, 1999).

31. Kenneth Thibodeau, "Persistent Object Preservation: Advanced Computing Infrastructure for Records Preservation" (paper presented at the DLM-Forum, Brussels, October 18–19, 1999); Moore, Reagan, Chaitan Baru, Arcot Rajasekar, Bertram Ludaescher, Richard Marciano, Michael Wan, Wayne Schroeder, and Amarnath Gupta, "Collection-based Persistent Digital Archives: Part 1," *D-Lib Magazine* 6.3 (2000), accessed February 29, 2012, http://www.dlib.org/dlib/march00/moore/03moore-pt1.html and "Collection-based Persistent Digital Archives: Part 2," *D-Lib Magazine* 6.4 (2000), accessed February 29, 2012, http://www.dlib.org/dlib/april00/04moore/03moore-pt2.html.

32. Richard Marciano, "Archivist's Workbench: A Framework for Testing Preservation Infrastructure", (paper presented at an InterPARES symposium, UCLA, May 15, 2004, accessed February 29, 2012, http://www.interpares.org/display_file.cfm?doc=ip2_dissemination_cs_marciano_us-interpares_symposium_2004.pdf).

33. Peter Lyman and Howard Besser, "Defining the Problem of Our Vanishing Memory: Background, Current Status, Models for Resolution," in *Time and Bits: Managing Digital Continuity*, ed. Margaret MacLean and Ben H. Davis (Los Angeles: Getty Research Institute for the History of Art and the Humanities, 1998).

JAMES M. O'TOOLE

"On the Idea of Permanence"

American Archivist *52.1 (Winter 1989): 10–25.*

In time, the Rockies may crumble,
Gibraltar may tumble;
They're only made of clay....
                                    —Ira Gershwin

LIKE THE PRACTITIONERS of most other professions, archivists possess a vocabulary of their own, a set of words and phrases that hold special meaning for them and that help them structure and define what they do. Most of this vocabulary is perfectly recognizable to those outside the profession, but the peculiar meaning and significance of its elements are different for those within the field. *Arrangement* and *description,* for example, are words that both archivists and nonarchivists use, perhaps every day, but when an archivist uses them, they are intended to denote very specific activities and concepts that are generally absent when a layman uses them. Professional vocabulary may degenerate into jargon, a term with a distinctly negative connotation, but regardless of that danger a particular set of terms and meanings is both inevitable and necessary for the development of any profession.[1]

Because the professional vocabulary of archivists is acquired and employed fairly readily, archivists generally do not reflect on the words they use or on how those words define and control the way they think and what they actually do. Just as no one can communicate at all by pausing to analyze every word that is uttered, so archivists cannot carry their glossaries with them at every moment and indeed have no need to. Too much reflection is paralyzing, but too little reflection risks obscuring distinctions that are rightly made, as well as blocking the consideration of new ideas and techniques that may be improvements over the accepted way of doing things. Periodically, therefore, it is useful to "pause in the day's occupations" to examine professional vocabulary, to understand how the words archivists use have changed over time and therefore how archival ideas have themselves developed. Such an exercise is more than just historical, tracing what ideas and words have meant at different times; it is also of benefit in present professional practice because it may open up new perspectives and possibilities.

One word in the archival lexicon used repeatedly without reflection is the word *permanent.* Archivists speak almost instinctively of their collections as being the permanent records of an individual or entity. The materials in archives are separated from the great mass of all the records ever created and are marked for special attention and treatment because they possess what is frequently identified as permanent value. Whether by accident or design—and the distinction is at the heart of the modem idea of appraisal—certain materials are selected by archives for preservation into the indefinite future. They are in that sense permanent. The word *permanent* does not appear in the standard glossary definition of *archives,* though the reverse is true: the entry for *permanent records* says simply, "*See* archives." The term has been employed in less formal sources and most archivists do indeed use it as a way of distinguishing archival records from those of lesser value.[2] Ironically, though archivists have not formally defined permanent records, the records managers have. The glossary of that profession specifies permanent records as those that are kept "indefinitely," often for legal reasons, and provided with "continuous preservation because of reference, historical or administrative significance."[3] By judging some records to be permanent, archivists make a substantial commitment to them, a commitment of time and resources, a commitment that is intended to last well beyond the tenure or lifetime of any individual professional. From that judgment and that commitment, a whole range of specific activities seems logically to flow.

But what do archivists really mean when they talk about their holdings as permanent records? As Leonard Rapport has noted, permanent is "a convenient term for which no simple substitute comes to mind."[4] The timelessness of such a term is difficult to grasp, but the idea of permanence offers nonetheless all the comforts of any absolute. The word's meaning is so self-evident, why should it trouble us? To say that archival records are permanent seems to fix their nature beyond doubt and to establish beyond challenge the full extent of the archivist's responsibility to them. Permanence is like pregnancy: there is apparently no middle ground. In fact, however, *permanent* has always been a more complicated, even relative, term than it appears, and an examination of its shifting meaning and use over time may illuminate its current and future usefulness as a category in archival thinking.

Permanence in Oral and Written Cultures

Recording information and preserving it for long periods of time are very old problems, and human culture has found different ways of accomplishing these tasks. Before the invention of writing, a relatively late development for the species, all information had to be stored mentally and transmitted orally, and oral cultures evolved particular means of doing so efficiently and effectively.[5] By emphasizing certain characteristics that enhanced the memory—the use of formulaic language and rhythm; the embodiment in ritual of key stories, values, and pieces of information; the association of physical objects with certain events; the reliance on social and interpersonal communication of things to be remembered—all oral cultures, even those that survived into the twentieth century, achieved a degree of permanence in what they knew, preserved, and handed on to the indefinite future.[6] Some degree of timelessness was achievable in such cultures: a kind of permanence was possible.

The advent of literacy, however, changed these mnemonic necessities and offered a more objective means of recording information and of preserving it intact for the indeterminate future. Specific texts, particular ways of expressing ideas, and not just the general thrust of a story or argument, could themselves be fixed and given permanence. *Accuracy* took on a new, more precise meaning based on continuity of text.[7] Since knowledge could now be written down and stored outside the brain, it would not be lost through forgetfulness, and it could be called back to life whenever necessary or desired. It could be more securely transmitted from one place to another or from one time to another. Permanence could be more reliably achieved through the preservation of writing. The ancient adage stated this advantage succinctly: *verba volent, littera scripta manet*—words are fleeting, written letters remain. It was by remaining that writing could emerge as triumphant, even "pre-emptive," over oral means of preserving information.[8] Thus, the very act of writing something down would invest it with a permanence it would not otherwise have had. To be sure, not all writing was intended to be kept literally forever; indeed, early in literate cultures a distinction was drawn between writings created for posterity and those with only a limited effect or usefulness. St. Paul's letters to the Christian churches of the Mediterranean world, for example, were "near-oral" means of communication not necessarily intended to be enduring; in the Middle Ages, drafts of documents, meant to be transitional and impermanent, began to appear, writings produced on materials (such as wood blocks covered with wax) that were cheaper than those used for formal records.[9] Still, in comparison to purely oral systems, writing seemed a better, more reliable guarantee of permanence.

The distinction between the kind of permanence offered by oral cultures and that which was available to cultures with writing was most readily apparent at the times of transition from one system to the other. The history of writing is long and complex, but at least since the perfection of an alphabetic system by the Greeks (about 700 B.C.E.) writing has come to different cultures at different times, and the change has not always been smooth. Socrates, for example, was skeptical of writing, fearing that "it will implant forgetfulness" in the human mind, offering "no true wisdom, ... but only its semblance." What is more, writing broke down the human links that were at the heart of the information storage and transfer process in the oral world. "Written words … seem to talk to you as though they were intelligent," the philosopher said, "but if you ask them anything about what they say, from a desire to be instructed, they go on telling you the same thing forever."[10] Writing could not be cross-examined as a speaker could, and Socrates found this a distinct disadvantage in the process of advancing understanding. Similarly, in ancient Jewish culture, both oral and written means of long-term storage of information coexisted for centuries, but social dislocation as well as religious and political turmoil led at different times to the encoding of certain basic tenets in written form. One such occasion was the emotionally powerful return to Zion (ca. 450 B.C.E.), which resulted in the codification of the Torah books known to Christians today as the Old Testament; another came after the destruction of the Jerusalem temple in 70 C.E. during the rise of Christianity, leading to the writing down of the teachings of the Talmud and the Mishnah, which had previously been available only in oral form.[11]

The key element in any such transition was not, as the historian M.T. Clanchy has pointed out with reference to Norman England, the mere fact of literacy itself (i.e., who can read and write and who cannot). Rather, the critical shift came with the reliance on written records rather than on individual recollection as the basis for society, by literates and nonliterates alike. Thus, the authors of the Christian gospels, which had been transmitted orally for a generation or two before being written down, were deliberate in choosing language that emphasized the legal validity of the writing as an acceptable replacement for the actual eyewitness testimony of the members of the apostolic generation, whose stories they told.[12] By writing the gospel narratives down, the authors hoped that they had thereby "guaranteed longevity, if not perpetuity."[13] Similarly, in medieval England transfers of land and other property, as well as other forms of agreements and contracts, came to be expressed in documents, and both the legal system and the language itself had to change as a result. Whereas in Edward I's time a nobleman could prove his title to a piece of land by displaying the rusty sword with which he had seized

it years before, a generation later a charter was the only acceptable proof. At the same time, the word *deed* came to denote not only the act itself, but also the document that embodied and recorded the act and thus preserved the memory of it for future generations.[14] The results of this shift were both practical and symbolic, and it was the symbolic significance that underlined the greater degree of permanence that was available through writing. "A document could indeed make time stand still," Clanchy says of England (though the same could apply to other cultures in the process of accepting literacy); "it could pass on a record of an event to remote posterity."[15]

PERMANENCE IN AMERICAN ARCHIVES

The seemingly inherent ability of written records to freeze time in this way, to make more reliably permanent what would remain fragile and evanescent if retained orally, meant that once records were preserved in archives they would attain a degree of permanence they might not otherwise have had. Because some records survived in archives while others did not, those that were preserved would naturally be valued more highly and therefore retained indefinitely. In eighteenth- and nineteenth-century America, as elsewhere and earlier, formal archival agencies readily accepted the responsibility to do just that. The subsequent discovery that archival records could be used for broad research as well as for administrative purposes reinforced this long-term view of the archives and their functions. As writing spread to all areas of American society and written records multiplied, not everything written down could be permanent, but everything gathered into an archives would be.

Most early American archival repositories, especially those founded with a specific commitment to research, stated this desire to ensure or enhance the permanence of their holdings. Though earlier preservation efforts had had similar motivations, the historical societies founded at the beginning of the nineteenth century took as their primary goal "the responsibility to safeguard their collections," and this responsibility was echoed by their many successors and imitators.[16] The American Antiquarian Society, established in 1812, proclaimed that "its immediate and peculiar design" was "to discover the antiquities of our own continent, and, by providing a fixed and permanent place of deposit, to preserve such relicks of American antiquity as are portable." The Society optimistically observed that "all things … are in their nature durable, if preserved from casualty and the ravages of time." Accordingly, "a depository like this may not only retard the ravages of time, but preserve from other causes of destruction many precious relicks of antiquity, … which once lost could never be restored."[17] Even the location of the repository was a deliberate choice in the desire to preserve records indefinitely. Given "the destruction so often experienced in large towns and cities by fire, as well as the ravages of an enemy … in times of war," the Society decided that, "for a place of deposit for articles intended to be preserved for ages," an inland, out-of-the-way place (like Worcester, Massachusetts) was preferable.[18]

By offering a "fixed and permanent place of deposit" for "articles intended to last for [the] ages," other historical and archival collections likewise had permanence in mind as a rationale for their activities. One historical society in Ohio in the 1840s announced its intention "to preserve the manuscripts of the present day to the remotest ages of posterity," adding almost theologically, "or at least … as near forever as the power and sagacity of man will effect." To accomplish this it proposed to store its manuscript and archival holdings in "airtight metallic cases, regularly numbered and indexed, so that it may be known what is contained in each case without opening it."[19]

Preserving records in archival repositories was thus intended to ensure their permanence, but the promoters of such efforts recognized the potential dangers inherent in such an effort. Unusual circumstances could put carefully preserved records at risk. In 1814, for example, a committee of the New York Historical Society prepared to move that organization's collection out of the city in the event of a British attack; many smaller organizations, uncertain that they would be able to maintain the interest of a sufficient membership, provided for the relocation of their collections in the event of the organization's demise.[20] Fire was the most obvious hazard, and

the destruction of some of the holdings of the Massachusetts Historical Society in 1825 and of most of the holdings of the Vermont Historical Society in 1857 provided sobering examples of how records that had been preserved and were intended to be permanent could be lost. "By all manner of means," a colleague wrote Lyman C. Draper after one such disaster, "have a *fire-proof building*. Don't now look at size and splendor—but safety."[21]

Concern for the safety of archival materials led those responsible for them to consider other means of preserving them "as near forever as the power and sagacity of man will effect," and understandably they turned to whatever technology, the fruit of that sagacity, was available to them. The society that had proposed air-tight containers with detailed descriptions on the outside apparently hoped to safeguard its holdings from the possible deleterious effects of the environment and from the wear and tear of handling—both of these concerns entirely recognizable to modern conservators. Even more common among these archives was the aim of preserving their collections by publishing them. "Repositories of every kind, however desirable, are exposed to … accidents, from the hand of time, from the power of the elements, and from the ravages of unprincipled men, as to render them unsafe," the Massachusetts Historical Society declared in 1806. "There is no sure way of preserving historical records and materials, but by *multiplying the copies*. The art of printing affords a mode of preservation more effectual than Corinthian brass or Egyptian marble."[22]

Permanence of Information

Among the many early archives and historical organizations that sought to preserve their materials by publishing and diffusing them, there developed a surprisingly modern distinction between the permanence of the archival documents themselves and the permanence of the information they contained. Initially, historical collections were valued principally for their information, information that testified to the "pastness of the past" and thereby certified "the reality of progress." Only later did repositories come to value their collections as things worthy in their own right and, later still, as sources for specialized study by professional scholars.[23] Preserving the documents was certainly worthwhile, but it was not ultimately as important as preserving the information. By relying on printing as a preservation technology, one repository hoped to "secure our treasures by means of the press from the corrosions of time and the power of accident," while another sought to "preserve and perpetuate by publication."[24] The same principle could be applied to public records as to the holdings of private historical organizations. "Let us save what remains," Thomas Jefferson wrote in 1792, endorsing Ebenezer Hazard's first compilation of *American State Papers,* "not by vaults and locks, which fence them from the public eye and use in consigning them to the waste of time, but by such a multiplication of copies as shall place them beyond the reach of accident."[25] There were enough examples of the permanent preservation of the information contained in records through printing before the loss of the originals to highlight the importance and the usefulness of achieving permanence through publication. The most famous of these was the original journal of Massachusetts's Puritan governor John Winthrop, a portion of which had been destroyed by fire in 1825 after the publication of a documentary edition.[26]

As technology advanced, archivists gained access to other means by which they could hope to safeguard their collections and preserve them "as near forever" as they desired. The development of practical microfilm technology, for example, seemed to offer a better means of reproducing documents than letterpress publication—better because it preserved actual images of the items themselves, not just the information they contained, thereby in some sense preserving both. This use of microfilm for storing records of permanent value had been suggested as early as 1853, and by the early 1870s it was actually being employed. In 1871 a French insurance company was regularly producing a microfilm copy of all its policies; three years later an enterprising Irishman received a patent to record property deeds in this way, using what seems to have been a lineal ancestor of the modern-day rotary camera.[27]

Permanence of Original Documents

In the twentieth century still newer technological developments focused on archival records and eventually worked a near revolution in the way archivists looked at and cared for the permanent records they held. Concern for the information in records was still strong, but concern for better treatment of the originals themselves increased, in part because it now seemed possible to do something about them. At least since the mid-nineteenth century, archivists had worried about the physical deterioration of their collections, even those that were already published or microfilmed, and about how to preserve them permanently; now the advance of preservation theory and practice offered the possibility that the long-desired goal could in fact be achieved. Preservation technicians learned more about the physical properties of documentary materials and the forces that caused them to deteriorate, and they began experimenting with methods for retarding, stopping, and reversing that deterioration.[28] In the process, the technical distinction between extending the so-called usable lifetime of documents (a more modest and realistic goal) and preserving them literally forever was often blurred. The "ravages of time" that had for so long troubled those in charge of archives could at last be controlled: real, physical permanence seemed within reach.

There may well have been a significant psychological predisposition in favor of preserving and repairing the original documents, of not being satisfied with printed or micrographic substitutes that preserved the original information, but in a different form. "Copies are never totally satisfactory," said the pioneer preservation researcher William J. Barrow in explaining the motivation for his work at the Virginia State Library, "for the originals possess unique and desirable characteristics lost in copying."[29] Though he did not specify what those "unique and desirable characteristics" were, he probably did not have to. The desire to preserve unusual original papers was often what had attracted many archivists to their profession in the first place. In its earliest manifestations, the collection of manuscripts was closely associated with the collection of other interesting curiosities, including museum objects and specimens in the physical and natural sciences.[30] These efforts were reinforced by a broader cultural disposition that preferred to see even historic items in their pristine condition. Deterioration "symbolizes failure," the philosopher of history David Lowenthal has observed, serving perhaps as a reminder of our own transience and mortality. Accordingly, "however venerated a relic, its decay is seldom admired"; indeed, "decay is more dreadful when it seems our fault."[31] With the advent and apparent perfection of preservation technology, archivists seemed capable of mastering decay; not to do so would only increase the "fault" of those whose responsibility it was to keep the permanent records of society.

As a result of the work of Barrow and others throughout the middle of the twentieth century, an active concern for the details and techniques of conservation developed and flourished among archivists. They learned more about the physical characteristics of their holdings, and they were increasingly disposed to act on the basis of that knowledge. Advancing far beyond early methods of "silking" or backing documents with synthetic crepeline, Barrow had perfected a method for deacidifying archival materials by about 1940, later maintaining that such a procedure extended their life expectancy "by a factor of from 8 to 10."[32] Archivists reported happily that they were using these procedures to good effect, along with the eventually controversial process of lamination (also developed by Barrow): Leon deVallinger, state archivist of Delaware, endorsed Barrow's method, reporting that his state archives had treated 5,000 documents in its conservation laboratory's first year of operation.[33] A kind of technological imperative took hold in archival thinking. Archivists could actively preserve their holdings; they could approach more nearly the long-desired goal of physical permanence. In the process, they did not doubt either the wisdom or the efficacy of doing so. They could do it, and they naturally assumed that they should.

Concern for conservation was suddenly everywhere in the archival profession. The very first article published in the new journal, the *American Archivist,* in 1938, dealt with the subject of "manuscript repair," and it was followed in subsequent issues by a string of related papers, many of them describing preservation and restoration laboratory techniques in great detail.[34] The Historical Records Survey of the Depression-era Works Progress Administration was actively concerned with preservation problems as it went about its business of surveying the documentary holdings of the various states.[35] Barrow appeared regularly on the programs of archival meetings, describing his own research and not unnaturally promoting his own methods and procedures. He and other preservation specialists found interested audiences among their archival colleagues. A session at the Society of American Archivists' second annual meeting in Springfield, Illinois, in 1938 dealt with "Fumigating, Cleaning, and Repairing Archival Material," and the large audience greeted the formal presentations with "an animated discussion."[36]

Throughout the 1940s and 1950s the number of program sessions and journal articles on preservation activities, most focusing on specific techniques and positive steps that archivists could take, continued to grow.[37] At the same time, though the concern for microfilm techniques and applications remained strong, consideration of preserving archival records through publication virtually disappeared from professional discussion.[38] With so much attention focused on the care and treatment of documents in their original form, archivists were—perhaps unconsciously, perhaps deliberately—restricting their notion of permanence. Increasingly, *permanence* became a technical term, a term that was defined by conservators and accepted by archivists in a limited, specific sense. More and more, *permanence* meant the physical permanence of archival collections, a goal which, thanks to the forward march of archival science, seemed attainable. "Today, for the first time," one technical report said expansively in 1964, "the possibility of preserving mankind's most significant records—in their original form and almost indefinitely—is at hand."[39]

Conservation Consciousness

Other aspects of professional culture reinforced this growing conservation consciousness. In April 1950, Arthur Kimberly of the National Archives announced the results of a study on archival record containers, approving the use of pressboard boxes (not specifically identified as being acid-neutral) covered with foil to retard fire damage. Two years later, the Hollinger Corporation advertised such a box for sale, again without any reference to its acid content, but highlighting the box's "unique metal edge construction, ... no paste or glue to attract vermin."[40] Hollinger introduced in 1961 an archival file folder, "tested and approved by leading authorities," that was "100% Rope Manila Paper; PH Neutral Guaranteed," and in 1963 the Milltex Paper Company produced archival quality paper "for document, map and picture folders and for other uses where permanence is essential."[41] The Council on Library Resources funded a project to develop a "safer" archival box at about this same time. The result was the birth of what quickly became an archival staple and cynosure: the acid-free box, first advertised in the *American Archivist* in July 1966.[42] That journal had added a regular section of "Technical Notes" in April 1963, the first of which centered on some newly available microfilm equipment and, more significantly, on a test of various ballpoint pens to determine their suitability for use in making "permanent" records. In the following year, the journal took the next logical step. Deciding to practice what it preached with regard to physical permanence, the principal periodical for the archival profession in the United States changed the paper on which it was printed to one defined as durable (i.e., able to withstand wear and tear) and permanent (i.e., sufficiently stable chemically to withstand internal deterioration).[43]

As concern for the physical permanence of their collections grew, archivists and conservators naturally began to study the deterioration and preservation of records more intensively. The results were both a greater understanding of the nature of the problem and a greater realization that active, ongoing programs were needed to address it. A number of national studies were commissioned, and the dimensions of the preservation challenge began to emerge. The Association of Research Libraries (ARL) surveyed the condition of deteriorating library and archival materials and, with an activism that was typical of the

Great Society era in which it appeared (1964), proposed a central national agency to address the problem. Ten years later ARL was working on "detailed specifications for a national system for preservation of library materials," which resulted in the formation of a National Conservation Advisory Council. On the regional level, too, archivists and librarians were banding together to advance the preservation cause in the interests of ensuring the permanence of their holdings. The New England (later Northeast) Document Conservation Center (NEDCC) was organized in 1973 to provide preservation and restoration services for that part of the country; several studies later explored the idea of setting up similar organizations elsewhere, especially in the West. The founding director of the NEDCC, George M. Cunha, became a sort of traveling missionary for the conservation gospel, and his works quickly became standard reading and reference points for archivists concerned about preserving their collections. In 1976 the Library of Congress sponsored a conference to outline the scope of a "national preservation program"; by the early 1980s the Society of American Archivists (SAA) had embarked, with money from the National Endowment for the Humanities, on a basic conservation program that sought, through workshops and publications, to spread awareness of physical conservation issues even more widely through the archival profession.[44]

So much thinking and worrying about the physical permanence of records resulted in archivists' and conservators' beginning to appreciate just how massive the problem was. This recognition was only aggravated as the number of archives holding valuable records grew throughout the 1970s, with more and more bulky collections expanding at an alarming rate. The spread of new technologies, especially those that were computer-based (tapes and disks, for example), further complicated the problem by adding new media for storing information, media that had their own particular problems and required their own special treatments. The 5,000 manuscript documents treated by the Delaware State Archives in the late 1930s, impressive in its own day, were now seen as only the very small tip of a very large iceberg.

A kind of preservation apocalypticism set in, as archivists came to understand graphically not only what was needed to make their collections truly permanent, but also just how impossible it would be to do so with the time and resources that would ever conceivably be available. "The magnitude of the deterioration problem in American manuscript and printed records appears to be far greater than realized," William Barrow had said calmly enough in the 1960s, but in the following decades a steadily gloomier tone became the standard in any consideration of preservation and permanence. Cunha spoke of the "dire straits" the archival profession was in and estimated that as much as 80 percent of all materials in archives and library special collections was in need of some kind of treatment. Daniel Boorstin, the Librarian of Congress, described the problem, which was of "cataclysmic proportions," as being "all the more serious because it [i.e., the slow deterioration of materials] is so undramatic."[45] Drama was not lacking from other quarters, however, as one report showed a conservator blowing on a handful of paper that scattered through the air like so much confetti. A film produced in 1987 and broadcast widely on public television showed a deputy librarian of Congress performing the same trick and, while a funeral bell tolled a steady peal of doom on the soundtrack, the narrator spoke sonorously of "these precious volumes [that] are burning away with insidious slow fires, … falling apart within their covers and within the very fortress meant to preserve them."[46] A study prepared for the National Association of Government Archives and Records Administrators (NAGARA) concluded that no state even approached "the goal of providing adequate preservation" and estimated that a colossal $500 million would be needed to remedy the situation and to provide satisfactorily for the "permanently valuable government records [the state archives] need to preserve and make accessible."[47] Having become convinced of how important it was to preserve their physical holdings permanently, archivists began to realize how impossible it would be to do precisely that.

Retreat from the Absolute

Virtually everywhere in the profession there was a subtle but steady retreat from the idea of physical permanence as archivists had come to understand it. The National Archives had recognized as early as 1950 that "a selective, rather than a comprehensive, rehabilitation of records" was the only realistic choice, especially in large collections, though this distinction was often lost in the conservation euphoria of the following decades.[48] More to the point, archivists began to grow uncomfortable with the apparently limitless commitment that adherence to a notion of absolute permanence implied, and they began to view questions of appraisal and preservation in much more relative terms. Maynard Brichford, author of what became a standard manual on appraisal, felt constrained in 1977 to put the word *permanent* in quotation marks while describing how the value and usefulness of records changed over time, thereby intimating that what was permanent about archives might not in fact endure. "The documented past is represented by a static body of surviving records," he wrote, "but the human perception of the past is dynamic." Archivists erred, therefore, if they imputed too great a degree of immutability to their collections.[49] Shortly thereafter, Brichford applied this belief specifically to the subject of preservation in archives, proposing a blunt "let it rot" philosophy. "Documents that need the conservator's attention, if they are to be preserved for posterity, may not be worth the cost of conservation," he argued before an SAA annual meeting. While acknowledging such an attitude as potentially "sinful," he added pointedly: "We have wasted a lot of money placing acid-laden documents in acid-neutral folders and boxes."[50]

A significant aspect of the retreat from the absolute of permanence was a renewed emphasis on the idea of the intrinsic value of records. T. R. Schellenberg had hinted at this idea in his discussion of the form and uniqueness of certain records, and the notion had been current in archival and preservation circles for some time. The archival glossary of 1974 included *intrinsic value,* prescribing its use to designate the worth of documents "dependent upon some unique factor," a not particularly helpful designation in singling out materials in collections the entirety of which claimed to be unique.[51] Concern over the possibility of throwing money into a bottomless conservation pit in the hope of achieving permanence led to a renewed consideration of intrinsic value. The National Archives formed a committee on the subject in 1979, which sought to outline the criteria for assessing the "qualities and characteristics that make the records in their original physical format the only archivally acceptable form for preservation." All records had such characteristics, of course, but some had them "to such a significant degree" that the originals had to be maintained and, if necessary, restored.[52] The report itemized nine standards by which to judge intrinsic value, including aesthetic value, exhibit potential, and cases where the physical form of the record might itself be a legitimate object of study. Far more tricky was the issue of "general and substantial public interest because of direct association with famous or historically significant" persons or events, a category that presumably covered items like the Declaration of Independence.[53] As with Justice Potter Stewart's supposed remark about pornography—"I can't define it, but I know it when I see it"— archivists were left with some guidelines for judging intrinsic value but with something less than a precise formula for evaluating it.

The decision to subject any particular records to preservation treatment remained an involved process, one in which priorities and desires had to be balanced against available resources and potential benefits. For the first time, archivists began to examine and rethink the technological imperative that had previously governed much of their approach to preservation work. The National Archives, for example, determined that only 0.5 percent of its holdings—a far cry from Cunha's 80 percent—should ever receive preservation laboratory treatment, with the remainder receiving no treatment, "maintenance" through proper housing in a good environment, or copying.[54]

At the same time, the focusing of renewed attention on the subject of appraisal led archivists to rethink the triple meaning of the idea of "preserving"

records: collecting and acquiring the original documents; intervening to conserve or restore their physical condition; and preserving the information in an alternative format. The implications for the idea of permanence were to reemphasize the relative at the expense of the absolute. Leonard Rapport presented the case for reappraising and destroying records that already were in archives, in what was a serious blow to the notion of archives as truly permanent records. Arguing that there should be "no grandfather clause" for records, Rapport raised the possibility that permanence was a quality that was subject to change or even outright revocation: records that were permanent today might not be so permanent tomorrow.[55] Though his argument was controversial and, in fact, few archives have as yet followed his advice on a large scale, Rapport's point of view helped underline a growing archival attitude in which permanence seemed an unrealistic and unattainable ideal.

Other examples of this reconsideration of the idea of permanence emerged in professional discussion. In the middle 1980s, the SAA task force on goals and priorities (GAP) in its monumental and comprehensive report, *Planning for the Archival Profession,* nowhere referred to archives as permanent records, preferring instead to speak of "records of enduring value."[56] This distinction, relying on the participial form, was more than semantic or purely stylistic: the implication was that once the enduring value stopped enduring, the permanence of the records was at an end. At about the same time, even a preservation group recognized the problem and spoke of the idea of "acceptable permanence," treating information in its original form or copying it into some other form so that it could survive and be useful to a certain degree.[57] If the GAP report implied that permanence could exist for a time and then come to an end, this group seemed to argue that a limited amount of permanence might be enough. In either case, the absolute had been dethroned, and archivists were left with the vague sense that permanence simply meant nothing any more. Whether consciously or not, the word permanent seemed to be disappearing from the archival lexicon, even as it was lingering in the archival mind.

Archives without Permanence

Thus, the idea of permanence as it is understood by archivists has changed considerably over time, passing from an unattainable desire to an absolute value within the realm of achievement to an extremely relative notion of little clarity. Today, the idea may be in the process of evolving out of usage altogether. This should not come as a surprise; the twentieth century is not a congenial climate for absolutes of any kind. At the same time, an information-rich society such as the modern one is inclined to accord any particular datum or document a lesser value than would an information-poor society. If this is the case, however, what are the implications for archival theory and practice? How should archivists think and what should they do in a professional world without the security of the traditional idea of permanence? As might be expected, there are more questions than answers.

First, do conservation decisions become simpler or more complex? The restriction of the idea of permanence to mean primarily physical permanence instilled in archivists a set of instinctive habits, the value of which seemed impossible to doubt. Would any archivist, given the choice, actually prefer to store records in acidic folders rather than acid-free ones? Is not Brichford's sinful thought precisely that, and even foolhardy as well? From one perspective the benefits of acid-free storage appear so self-evident as to defy challenge. From another, such an activity is at best an exercise in fighting a rear-guard battle that will only delay the inevitable for a brief time. Not even the most enthusiastic conservator can say with any certainty what the measurable benefits of acid-free storage are. At worst, therefore, archivists may indeed have simply wasted their money. At the same time, preservation activities become a slippery slope, leading inexorably to ever more elaborate and expensive procedures. In the way conservators have "sold" conservation consciousness and in the way archivists have been disposed to "buy" it, archivists have been lulled into a false sense of security about the permanence of their collections. As a result, they have lost sight of the larger purposes of their work—

preserving over time information that is of benefit and use to society—and have restricted the available options for approaching that goal.

Refocusing their attention on the permanence of the information in records rather than on the documents themselves will restore a broader view and will reemphasize the possibilities and the usefulness of preserving information in formats other than the original. For larger archives, this will inevitably mean a better use of scanty resources: the National Archives found, for example, that physical conservation of one large group of heavily-used records was more expensive by factors of two or three to one than transferring the information they contained to other media.[58] For smaller repositories, unable to provide or acquire sophisticated alternative technologies, the implications will be less dramatic but no less real: acid-free folders (which actually touch the documents) might still be a necessity, for example, but the money spent on acid-free boxes (which touch only the folders) might well be applied to other purposes. In repositories of whatever size, the intrinsic value of records might be assessed more rigorously, perhaps with the assistance of subject specialists, before materials are submitted to the conservation laboratory. A harsher, more demanding standard of what archivists wish to preserve—and why—might restrict even further the amount and nature of material that is submitted for conservation treatment.

Second, do appraisal and accessioning decisions become simpler or more complex in a world without physical permanence? Abandoning the implicit guarantee of permanence that archival preservation has come to entail, will certain repositories not have freer reign to define and redefine the scope and purpose of their collections, as well as greater flexibility in managing them? Will an active documentation strategy approach to assembling archival materials make constant redefinition of what is permanent and what is not more likely? Despite their reluctance to do so heretofore, will repositories not be in a better position to follow Rapport's advice and to cross the line between permanent and valuable on the one hand and impermanent and valueless on the other? Though no one would argue for archival collections that respond only to research fads (real or perceived), the result may be archives that are more regularly forced to reexamine their basic purposes and to respond more directly to the needs of their users and of society at large. At the same time, however, the ongoing reappraisal of collections will surely complicate the acquisition of material. Will records creators—whether private individuals seeking repositories for their papers (as traditionally defined) or officers of the parent organizations that archives serve—be reluctant to entrust their recorded memory to archivists without the assurance that it will be safeguarded as long as possible? The abandonment of permanence as an archival ideal may open new options in the management of historical records, but it may also lead the creators of those records to look elsewhere for assistance in preserving them.

Third, what impact will new technologies have on the notion of permanence? By almost any standard, virtually all of the newer means of recording information, though more flexible, are less permanent than older ones. The contrast is most visible at the extremes: magnetic impulses on computer disks are certainly more unstable than baked clay tablets. The continued development of the technological means for recording information will therefore increase the options available to archivists for preserving information and for transferring it from one medium to another. Like physical conservation, however, such transfers are not without cost, and archivists will be forced to evaluate their options repeatedly, resisting the natural human temptation to rely on similar solutions to different problems. Choice is a fine thing and seems to possess inherent value. The availability of choice, however, does not make the choosing any easier.

Finally, does the decline of archival permanence shed any light on the fundamental motivations that cause creators to create records and archivists to keep them? Why do individuals or administrators not simply throw their records away once their immediate usefulness is passed? Why do they give them to archivists, and why do archivists lavish such attention on them? What are the intrinsic values of certain records, whether for individuals—diaries, love letters, records

of significant life-events; for corporate bodies—the company's charter, the denomination's organizational minutes, the school's first enrollment register; or for whole societies—the Declaration of Independence? What is the basis for the human disposition to keep these records, to keep them in as near pristine condition as possible for as long as possible? Is it merely revulsion at even the smallest reminders of our own mortality, as Lowenthal maintains, or is there a larger, even quasi-religious meaning? What are the connections between records and relics? How do both attempt to ensure the continued presence of past events, persons, and things, and what ongoing meaning do they therefore have? To argue that permanence is devoid of meaning may be possible, but do certain basic human impulses thereby go unfulfilled?

Such larger questions are surely beyond the scope of the archivist's daily professional practice. They do, however, constitute appropriate subjects for future research and reflection. Questions about the meaning of archival vocabulary are always relevant because they lead to greater clarity in thinking about what archivists do and why they do it. In maintaining a healthy balance between theory and practice, the tension is helpful for any living and growing profession.

NOTES

1. On the importance of precision in professional vocabulary, see Frank B. Evans, et al., "A Basic Glossary for Archivists, Manuscript Curators, and Records Managers," *American Archivist* 37 (1974): 415–16. On the general characteristics of professions, see Richard J. Cox, "Professionalism and Archivists in the United States," ibid., 49 (1986): 23–233.

2. Evans, "Basic Glossary," *American Archivist* 37 (1974): 417. No less an authority than Ernst Posner defined archives as "records considered worthy of permanent preservation" in *Collier's Encyclopedia*, 6th ed., s.v. "Archives."

3. Association of Records Managers and Administrators, *Glossary of Records Management Terms* (Prairie Village, Kansas: ARMA, 1985).

4. Leonard Rapport, "No Grandfather Clause: Reappraising Accessioned Records," *American Archivist* 44 (1981): 148.

5. For a general theory of the oral transmission of information, see Frederick J. Stielow, *The Management of Oral History Sound Archives* (New York: Greenwood Press, 1986), 11–33.

6. The literature on oral cultures is fascinating and extensive. For the best guide through the issues it raises, see Walter J. Ong, *Orality and Literacy: The Technologizing of the Word* (London: Methuen, 1982), esp. 31–57. On the use of formula and rhythm, see Eric A. Havelock, *The Literate Revolution in Greece and Its Aftermath* (Princeton: Princeton University Press, 1982), esp. 226, and Ananda E. Wood, *Knowledge Before Printing and After: The Indian Tradition in a Changing Kerala* (Delhi: Oxford University Press, 1985), 7–9. For ritual, see Jacob Neusner, *The Oral Torah: The Sacred Books of Judaism, An Introduction* (San Francisco: Harper and Row, 1986), 26–27, and Robert Goldenburg, "Talmud," in *Back to the Sources: Reading the Classic Jewish Texts*, ed. Barry W. Holtz (New York: Summit, 1984), 131, and Werner H. Kelber, *The Oral and Written Gospel: The Hermeneutics of Speaking and Writing in the Synoptic Tradition, Mark, Paul, and Q* (Philadelphia: Fortress Press, 1983), 168–177. For the use of objects as *aides-memoires,* see M. T. Clanchy, *From Memory to Written Record: England, 1066–1307.* (Cambridge, Mass.: Harvard University Press, 1979), 21–24. For the social context of records, see Kelber, *Oral and Written Gospel,* 23–24 and 92–93, and Albert B. Lord, *The Singer of Tales* (Cambridge, Mass.: Harvard University Press, 1960).

7. Edward P. Dirringer, *The Book Before Printing: Ancient, Medieval, and Oriental* (New York: Dover, 1982), 15; Lord, *Singer of Tales,* 138.

8. Ong, *Orality and Literacy,* 11-12 ("pre-emptive," p. 12); Havelock, *Literate Revolution in Greece,* 87.

9. Kelber, *Oral and Written Gospel,* 168–169; M. T. Clanchy, *From Memory to Written Record,* 116–125; see also Ernst Posner, *Archives in the Ancient World* (Cambridge, Mass.: Harvard University Press, 1972), 4–5.

10. Plato, Phaedrus, 274C-275D. In this connection it is worthwhile to note that Socrates himself left no written account of his thinking, this task being performed for him by his next-generation, fully literate successor, Plato.

11. Neusner, *Oral Torah,* 26, 222.

12. Kelber, *Oral and Written Gospel,* 92-93; Birger Gerhardsson, *Memory and Manuscript: Oral Tradition and Written Transmission in Rabbinic Judaism and Early Christianity* (Uppsala: Gleerup, 1961), 221–222.

13. Kelber, *Oral and Written Gospel,* 105.

14. Clanchy, *From Memory to Written Record,* 2, 21–22, 36–37, 204.

15. Ibid., 20.

16. Leslie W. Dunlap, *American Historical Societies, 1790-1860* (Madison: Privately printed, 1944), 79.

17. *Archaeologia Americana: Transactions and Collections of the American Antiquarian Society* (Worcester, 1820), 1:18, 29, 30–31. The repeated association of documents with "relicks" is noteworthy.

18. Ibid., 31. This argument may simply have been an attempt to make a virtue of necessity, since the society's founders and benefactors were all located in Worcester already.

19. Quoted in Dunlap, *American Historical Societies,* 142. The organization in question is the Logan Historical Society of Cincinnati.

20. Ibid., 79.

21. Quoted ibid., 79–80.

22. *Collections of the Massachusetts Historical Society* (Boston, 1806), 1:3.

23. Henry D. Shapiro, "Putting the Past Under Glass: Preservation and the Idea of History in the Mid-Nineteenth Century," *Prospects: An Annual of American Cultural Studies* 10 (1985): 243–278, describes the evolving viewpoint of collecting organizations; the quotations are at 258.

24. Walter Muir Whitehill, *Independent Historical Societies* (Boston: Boston Athenaeum, 1962), 40; Dunlap, *American Historical Societies,* 177.

25. Quoted in Whitehill, *Independent Historical Societies,* 4.

26. *Winthrop's Journal: "History of New England,"* 1630-1649, ed. James Kendall Hosmer (New York: Barnes and Noble, 1908), 1:17–18.

27. Frederic Luther, *Microfilm: A History, 1839–1900* (Annapolis: National Microfilm Association, 1959), 24–25, 84, 94–95.

28. For some of the early history of preservation work and research, see James L. Gear, "The Repair of Documents—American Beginnings," *American Archivist* 26 (1963): 469–475.

29. William J. Barrow, "Deacidification and Lamination of Deteriorated Documents, 1938–1963," *American Archivist* 28 (1965): 285.

30. Shapiro, "Putting the Past Under Glass," 244–245.

31. David Lowenthal, *The Past is a Foreign Country* (Cambridge: Cambridge University Press, 1985), 147, 175, 143.

32. William J. Barrow, *The Barrow Method of Restoring Deteriorated Documents* (Richmond: Virginia State Library, 1965), 7. On silking and other methods of document repair and reinforcement, see Gear, "Repair of Documents," 470–475.

33. Leon deVallinger, "Lamination of Manuscripts at the Delaware State Archives, 1938–64," *American Archivist* 28 (1965): 290–293.

34. L. H. Smith, "Manuscript Repair in European Archives: I. Great Britain," *American Archivist* 1 (1938): 1–22. See also Smith's "Manuscript Repair in European Archives: II. The Continent (France, Belgium, the Netherlands)," ibid., 51–77.

35. William F. McDonald, *Federal Relief Administration and the Arts: The Origins and Administrative History of the Arts Projects of the Works Progress Administration* (Columbus, 1969), 751–828.

36. *American Archivist* 1(1938): 233; ibid., 2 (1939): 23.

37. See, for example, Adelaide E. Minogue, "Some Observations on the Flattening of Folded Records," *American Archivist* 8 (1945): 115–121, and Minogue, "Treatment of Fire and Water Damaged Records," ibid., 9 (1946): 17–25; James D. Breckenridge, "Have you Looked at Your Pictures Lately?" ibid., 17(1954): 25–36; Harry F. Lewis, "The Deterioration of Book Paper in Library Use," ibid., 22 (1959): 309–322.

38. The National Historical Publications Commission, revitalized in the early 1950s, did begin to promote documentary publishing during this period, but its main goals were scholarly use and wider dissemination of materials rather than preservation. See Mary A. Giunta, "The NHPRC: Its Influence on Documentary Editing," *American Archivist* 49(1986): 134–141, and Lester J. Cappon, "A Rationale for Historical Editing Past and Present," *William and Mary Quarterly,* 3rd ser., 23 (1966): 56–75.

39. " 'P' for Permanent," *The Laboratory: Current Developments in Instrumentation and Technique* (1964): 101.

40. Arthur Kimberly, "New Developments in Record Containers," *American Archivist* 13 (1950): 233–236; Hollinger advertisement, ibid., 15 (1952): 46.

41. Hollinger advertisement, *American Archivist* 24 (1961): 131; Milltex advertisement, ibid., 26(1963): 468.

42. Gladys T. Piez, "Archival Containers—A Search for Safer Materials," *American Archivist* 27 (1964): 433-438; Pohlig Brothers advertisement, ibid., 29 (1966): 393.

43. "Technical Notes," *American Archivist* 26 (1963): 263–266; announcement, ibid., 27 (1964): 562.

44. Many of these developments are described in Carolyn Clark Morrow, "National Preservation Planning and Regional Conservation Efforts," *Conserving and Preserving Library Materials,* ed. Kathryn Luther Henderson and William T. Henderson (Urbana-Champaign: University of Illinois, 1983), 37–53. See also Ann Russell, "The Northeast Document Conservation Center: A Case Study of Cooperative Conservation," *American Archivist* 45(1982): 45–52; ARL, *The Preservation of Deteriorating Books: An Examination of the Problem with Recommendations for a Solution* (Washington, D.C.: Library of Congress, 1980). Cunha's work is summarized in his *Conservation of Library Materials: A Manual and Bibliography on the Care, Repair and Restoration of Library Materials,* 2 vol. (Metuchen, New Jersey: Scarecrow Press, 1971), and its updated version, *Library and Archives Conservation: 1980s and Beyond,* 2 vol. (Metuchen, New Jersey: Scarecrow Press, 1983).

45. Barrow, *Barrow Method for Restoring Deteriorated Documents,* 3; Cunha, *Conservation of Library Materials,* 1: 233, 140; *A National Preservation Program* (Washington: Library of Congress, 1980), 11–12, 13. Boorstin painted a picture of documentary deterioration as a kind of "silent killer" of civilization which had to be checked.

46. *Slow Fires: On the Preservation of the Human Record* (Council on Library Resources, 1987). When the author showed this film to an introductory archives class recently, the students giggled through this melodramatic introduction to the problem.

47. National Materials Advisory Board, *Preservation of Historical Records* (Washington, D.C.: National Academy Press, 1986), 40; NAGARA, *Preservation Needs in State Archives* (Albany: NAGARA, 1986), 13, 2–3, 5.

48. "The Rehabilitation of Paper Records," *National Archives Staff Information Paper No. 16* (December 1950), 5.

49. Maynard J. Brichford, *Archives and Manuscripts: Appraisal and Accessioning* (Chicago: SAA, 1977), 5.

50. Maynard J. Brichford, "Seven Sinful Thoughts," *American Archivist* 43 (1980): 14. That Brichford felt compelled to label this notion "sinful" is an indication of how much archivists had come to accept the responsibility of at least attempting to ensure the physical permanence of their collections.

51. Evans, "Basic Glossary," *American Archivist* 37 (1974): 424. See also T. R. Schellenberg, *Modern Archives: Principles and Techniques* (Chicago: University of Chicago Press, 1956), 150–151, and Schellenberg's chapter on "Record Attributes" in *The Management of Archives* (New York: Columbia University Press, 1965), 119–143.

52. The committee's report, originally contained in *NARS Staff Information Paper No. 21* (September 1980), is reproduced in its entirety in the *Report of the Committee on the Records of Government* (Washington, D.C.: Government Printing Office, 1985), 117–125; the quotations are at 118.

53. Ibid., 120–121.

54. National Archives and Records Service, *Twenty Year Records Preservation Plan* (Washington, D.C.: NARS, 1984), no pagination.

55. Rapport, "No Grandfather Clause," 143–150.

56. *Planning for the Archival Profession* (Chicago: SAA, 1986), 8 and elsewhere.

57. Materials Advisory Board, *Preservation of Historical Records,* 6.

58. NARS, *A Study of the Alternatives for the Preservation and Reference Handling of the Pension, Bounty-Land, and Compiled Military Service Records in the National Archives* (Washington, D.C.: NARS, 1984), esp. Table 6.2.

EDWARD PORTER ALEXANDER
AND MARY ALEXANDER

"To Conserve"

Chapter 9 in Museums in Motion: An Introduction to the History and Functions of Museum*s. 2nd ed. (Lanham, MD: Rowman Altamira, 2008), pp. 217–34.*

Anything, absolutely anything—from a flint arrowhead to a spacecraft, from a dugout canoe to the Queen Mary—may end up in a museum, and the museum must know how to care for it.
—*Philip R. Ward, 1991[1]*

There's a silent thief stealing away with millions of dollars of artwork each year. The thief's name? Poor conservation.

—*David Hugh Smith, 1982[2]*

Collections have suddenly become something of a burden to museums. Most museum directors now feel like directors of geriatric hospitals whose budgets are devastated by patients whose survival for another day depends on expensive, high technology support systems. Conservators in museums are like a host of relatives who guard the wall plug of the life support systems.
—*Miriam Clavir, 2002[3]*

NOT UNTIL THE 20th century did museums clearly realize that one of their chief functions as well as an all-important duty was to pass on their collections in pristine condition to succeeding generations. Science had advanced far enough to point out that, just as all human beings must die, so all objects must deteriorate. At the same time, scientists learned to slow the degradation of museum materials, and a new profession of scientifically knowledgeable "conservators" began to replace the artists and craftsmen commonly known as "restorers." Conservators know how to preserve materials, that is, to prevent, stop, or retard

deterioration, and also how to restore objects that had undergone decay or alteration. In France today, the preferred term for these professionals is *conservator-restorer*, acknowledging the duality of the role in caring for collections.[4]

A 2005 *Heritage Preservation Heritage Health Index* outlines the status of U.S. museums' collection care practices this way:

Eighty percent have no paid staff responsible for collections care.

Seventy percent have not assessed collections condition or needs.

Eighty percent do not have adequate environmental controls in place.

Sixty-five percent of collections suffer from improper storage conditions.

Eighty percent do not have a plan to protect collections in case of emergency.

A Public Trust at Risk: The Heritage Health Index Report on the State of America's Collections published by Heritage Preservation with funding from the Institute of Museum and Library Services (IMLS) is based on a project involving more than three thousand museum professionals from institutions large and small across the United States. The survey sample includes collecting museums, historical societies, collecting libraries, and archives.[5]

And, on a more local level, consider this exchange from the Small Museum Association summer workshop in Hagerstown, Maryland, in 1998. The first speaker was a staff member of a local historical society. The society had been given a collection of assorted buttons from a local collector, including political campaign buttons. The staff had no experience caring for a collection like this, so the speaker went to the Internet for advice and found the websites of button collectors who described how to clean and care for buttons. She went on to describe in detail what products she used and how she went about cleaning each button. After her talk, she moved to the back of the room. Next on the program was a professional conservator, who walked up to the podium, hesitated, shuffled her papers, and seemed uncomfortable. Eventually, she took a deep breath and said, "Please disregard everything the first speaker just said." The audience gasped. It was a pretty dramatic moment because the Internet advice from hobbyist collectors was absolutely contrary to what a professional conservator would have done.

This chapter outlines desirable museum principles and practices to care for objects, concluding with more generalized discussions of professional conservation concerns. Where there are references to conservators, it should be understood that this position does not exist in most museums and therefore these activities are carried out by a wide variety of staff from the director to volunteers. Nonetheless, all museums and museum professionals should strive to meet the basic standards described here. The goal is to protect the objects, a mainstay of museums' missions. The footnotes provide more in-depth reading.

The Nature of Museum Objects

The conservator is interested in the materials of which museum objects are made—not primarily their aesthetic form, but their molecular/atomic composition and structure. These objects range from the everyday, used detritus of life to those made from the finest materials to adorn their owner or for public display. The conservator wants to know about their condition—how much they have deteriorated and how they can be stabilized for a long future. In doing this work, he or she is dealing with four chief classes of substances: organic materials, metals and their alloys, siliceous and equivalent materials, and easel and mural paintings. Harold J. Plenderleith, former keeper of the British Museum research laboratory, authored *The Conservation of Antiquities and Works of Art: Treatment, Repair, Restoration* (1962), the classic reference for scientific museum conservation. In the revised second edition (1971), A. E. A. Werner, then the keeper of the laboratory, collaborated with Mr. Plenderleith. These volumes remain valuable basic reference tools.[6]

Organic materials include hides, leather, parchment, paper, bone, ivory, textiles, and wood. They are of animal or vegetable origin, carbon based, and with cellular structure. They are susceptible to deterioration by light, variations in humidity and temperature, dryness or brittleness, and excessive humidity (dampness) that produces molds, mildew, and other biological reactions.

Gold, silver, lead, tin, copper (and its alloys), iron, and steel are the chief metals. They are inorganic, much more stable than organic materials, and little affected by light, temperature variations, or biological reaction. They differ in their resistance to deterioration from variations in humidity and from impurities in the air or the ground. Gold is the only metal that remains virtually intact under all conditions. The others suffer from corrosion that may produce a pleasing patina or heavy incrustation that ultimately transforms the metal into the mineral ore from which it was extracted. Silver exposed to air tarnishes and, if underground for a long period, may take on a patina. Copper and iron are easily oxidized in air and especially in the ground. Copper and bronze show brown, blue, or green patinas, and iron can be completely transformed into rust.

Siliceous and equivalent materials consist of natural stone, bricks, pottery and other ceramics, and glass. Natural stone varies in its resistance to deterioration. Granite and basalt are relatively impervious, but limestone and sandstone are vulnerable to industrial sulfur fumes, automobile emissions, temperature and humidity variations, saline efflorescences, and cryptomatic vegetation (molds and mosses). Bricks and pottery, both of clay, are similar to natural stone in their resistance. If baked at higher temperatures, they are equivalent to stone of average resistance; if baked at low heat or air-dried, they correspond to soft natural stone. Ceramics fired at high temperatures have great resistance to deterioration, but water with salt in solution can produce efflorescences in them. High humidity can dull the transparency of normally stable glass and lead to crizzling with a multitude of small cracks.

Easel and mural paintings are complex chemical compounds that contain in their various layers both organic and inorganic materials. The outer layer of varnish is completely organic; the paint layers and ground or coating are usually a combination of organic and inorganic; the support, if wood or canvas, is organic, or if metal or a wall substance, inorganic. Adhesives used between the layers are organic. Varnish, which normally lasts only twenty to fifty years before losing its elasticity, also turns yellow. Mediums or vehicles of oil or distemper in the paint layers become brittle and subject to dampness, while the ground or foundation is susceptible to high humidity. Soft wood and canvas supports of easel paintings attract insects and are distorted by dampness; saline efflorescences and mold attack murals. Decay also weakens the adhesives between layers and results in unsticking and blisters.

These categories of objects may, of course, be combined in ways that make their care more complicated. These descriptions neglect the collections of botanical gardens and zoos that have their own special concerns regarding the professional standards of care for living collections. Botanical garden herbariums carefully preserve dried plants and seeds, allowing gardens to exchange species. Today these simple practices are complemented with international seed banks protecting species' DNA, sometimes in cooperation with botanical gardens or even international governmental initiatives. Norway's effort to freeze DNA samples on the island of Svalbard reflects heightened international concerns. The zoos' Species Survival Plans (SSPs) are a cooperative approach to maintaining biodiversity, a special form of conservation. The SSPs form an international matrix for "matchmaking" to ensure the maximum biodiversity within zoos. The fundamental elements include good animal care in terms of nutrition, social systems, mating systems,

reproductive and parental influences, environmental factors, medical health, and reproductive biology and genetics. With the vanishing of wild animals of so many types, zoo populations form the future for many species. In the basic sense, they are the ultimate conservators.[7]

Basic Conservation Practices

The environment has a powerful influence on objects, which tend to establish equilibrium with their surroundings. Whenever the environment changes, the objects are likely to suffer. Thus, when archaeologists open a tomb, objects apparently in perfect condition may shrink or warp and sometimes even turn to dust. The changes in the relative humidity and temperature of the atmosphere cause such deterioration.

Museums therefore need to provide a stable environment with constant relative humidity and temperature for the varied objects in their collections. The two qualities are closely related; in fact, relative humidity is defined as the ratio of the amount of water vapor present in the air to the greatest amount possible at the same temperature. As those familiar with central heating so well know, increasing the temperature of a building in winter reduces the humidity markedly and may result in too dry an atmosphere, while lowering the temperature may raise the humidity so much that it reaches the dew point and water condenses on walls and objects. A temperature of sixty to seventy-five degrees Fahrenheit or about twenty degrees centigrade is comfortable for museum visitors year round. At that temperature the relative humidity should not fall below 50 percent or organic materials such as paper, parchment, and leather will become brittle; canvas will go slack; and textiles and the adhesives used in making furniture will dry out and deteriorate. Similarly, if the relative humidity exceeds 65 percent, mold and mildew will grow on glue, leather, and paper; wood will swell and canvases tighten; and oxidation of metals will increase. The ideal relative humidity for most museum objects at temperatures of about seventy degrees Fahrenheit is 50 to 65 percent. But, keep in mind that it's the very variation of a stable environment that can be most damaging.

Air-conditioning systems can provide the constant relative humidity and temperature desirable for the museum environment and mitigate atmospheric pollution. Obviously, every museum should strive to obtain such climate control for its entire buildings, but especially for its exhibition and storage spaces. Contaminated air may blacken lead pigments, tarnish metals, or bleach out or stain materials. And, Nathan Stolow warns that merely crowded galleries can produce high levels of carbon dioxide and ammonia that are damaging to paintings.[8] Though it may be difficult to raise money for such a purpose (the saying goes that nobody every gave a museum a ton of coal in memory of his mother), air-conditioning in the long run is more important for the museum than the acquisition of million-dollar objects. In instances where controlling the conditions of large spaces becomes impossible, museums can create "microclimates" for objects. These can be individual areas within a room or actual cases that allow for closer control of the conditions for the objects. They can be as simple as covering the glass of an exhibit case with fabric that the visitor removes to see the object and replaces afterward, or as complicated as individual controls for the case's internal atmosphere.

Another important part of the museum environment is lighting. Strong light or ultraviolet rays damage watercolors, paintings, paper, textiles, and other materials, usually by fading or embrittlement. Although enjoying a return to favor in art museums out of aesthetic considerations, natural light is especially destructive because of ultraviolet radiation and should be controlled by blinds, curtains, or special glass. Incandescent bulbs give off heat, which must be lessened in museum cases. The ultraviolet emissions of fluorescent tubes can be reduced to safe levels by plastic sleeves. Too much light intensity from spotlights or too high a general illumination should also be avoided.

The *Heritage Health Index Report* suggests that museums begin their conservation efforts with the most basic environmental conditions for their objects. Even with the most limited resources museums can establish conditions so that they "do no harm" to artifacts. A critical element to maintain this most basic standard is that storage areas, while out of the public view, are central to the ongoing conservation/preservation needs of collections. Clean, dry, temperature-controlled spaces are fundamental to caring for objects. Although complex, expensive conservation practices may be out of the reach of many museums, careful storage practices are not.[9]

Negligence results in exposure of objects to excessive light, heat, or humidity, infestations of pests, or actual accidents that result in physical destruction of the object. Stolow recounts an arresting incident that happened in a Canadian art gallery. "A cleaner was operating an electric floor polisher when he moved too far ahead, unplugging the machine. Forgetting to 'turn off' the polisher he then walked over to plug in the cord. Since the electric polisher was still 'on,' it proceeded to dance along the floor on its own before he could rush to stop it. As it careened over the floor and swerved to the wall the metal handle scraped and scuffed a number of paintings before it could be turned off."[10]

Common sense precautions include:

Ensuring the relative humidity and temperature in storage and display areas are kept stable and at appropriate levels for items;

Ensuring the light levels are at an appropriate level for objects on display;

Keeping storage areas unlit when access is not required;

Checking that materials used in storage and display—wood, fabrics, paints, adhesives, plastics, and rubber—are not harmful to items;

Keeping storage areas clean, tidy, and uncluttered;

Providing sufficient space in storage containers to avoid crushing or abrasion of items;

Not storing items on top of or inside one another;

Raising stored items/storage containers off the floor in case of flooding;

Cleaning items only following expert advice;

Storing items in secure areas;

Checking collections on a regular basis against pest infestation;

Avoiding handling whatever possible, and then only using cotton gloves;

Not smoking, eating, or drinking in the vicinity of collections;

> Ensuring all staff (and volunteers) understand the principles and practice of preventive conservation.[11]

These descriptions of the care of objects reflect current museum practice and tradition, but it is important to understand that as the very nature of museums is expanding, so too are the demands on conservation. For example, interactive exhibitions change the nature of the gallery space that impacts on the environment and security of the objects regardless of their origin. One example will reveal the demands of changing museum practices. What should a technology museum do with an automobile? Should their resources be put into keeping the car in "running order," or into maintaining it as a static artifact? If the former path is chosen, as time goes by mechanical elements of the car will need to be replaced, and some would argue that compromises its integrity as an object, while meeting its needs as an operating machine. One compromise seems to be establishing "archival" machines that are not kept in running order, but rather maintained as a record of the car as artifact of a time period, complete with original engine parts, upholstery, and even paint finishes.[12]

Exhibition Concerns

Special exhibitions are increasingly used by museums to attract visitors, promote scholarly research, and increase public enlightenment. They usually involve borrowing materials from several museums, and the curator ought to have a leading role in deciding when objects in his or her care should be lent. The curator may approve highly of the purposes of a temporary or traveling exhibit and also know that the museum may wish to borrow materials from other museums from time to time. The curator, however, should carefully consider the dangers to which such exhibits expose objects. Can they stand the jolting and jarring of travel and the changes in humidity and temperature they are sure to encounter? Can they be properly packed for transport? Will the borrower provide careful handling, dependable environmental con-

trol, and protection against fire, vandalism, and theft? These practical questions will help the curator decide whether the proposed exhibit is important enough to justify the risks to the objects in his or her care.[13]

In order to respond rationally to requests for loans, the wise curator may well decide, with advice from conservators, to classify objects as to their ability to travel safely. Some objects will be too delicate and fragile to stand any shipping. Others may be allowed to travel only occasionally to exhibits of exceptional importance with strictly specified conditions of packing, handling, and protection during transit and on exhibition. In another category will be placed objects sound, stable, and structurally strong enough to be included in traveling exhibitions. Once the decision has been made to lend objects, arrangements must be made for their packing, transport, exhibition, repacking, and return travel. The whole transaction must be covered by written agreements and by insurance. A new role, that of exhibition conservator, who joins a team that may include security, registrar, designer, and architect, assumes the following duties: evaluation of conditions, establishment of environmental controls for each object, assessment of safety (in transport, especially), monitoring storage and gallery conditions, and coordination with designers and architects to ensure safety and special conditions for each object on view.[14] Once again, many museums will assign such a role to a staff member, regardless of his or her title and normal responsibilities.

The packing can be as elaborate as the situation requires. If the distances involved are short, the objects may be taken by car or van with abundant padding and careful separation but without special cases. Caroline Keck's *Safeguarding Your Collection in Travel* shows the small museum how to instruct a carpenter to build a solid, watertight, shock-absorbing case in which objects can be "floated" with inner cushioning provided by some of the new plastic foam materials. A reliable commercial packing firm may be used, though its work should be carefully supervised. A larger museum will have its own trained packing staff. In instances of important international exhibitions of extremely rare objects, as Nathan Stolow points out, conservators know how to build ideal containers with preconditioned packing materials or silica gel panels that will maintain about the same humidity and temperature that the objects enjoy in their "home" museum. Trained packers should do the packing, unpacking, and repacking of loans, because at these points the most damage to objects is likely. Packing material should be stored in the same atmospheric conditions as the exhibition spaces. Those who did the unpacking should do the repacking, and the same materials should be used.[15]

Transport should be carefully planned. If a carefully checked and reliable moving company is used, the lending and receiving museum staffs should supervise the loading and unloading. The transportation should be direct, without layovers or transshipments. For extremely rare objects, a museum staff member should accompany the shipment, going and coming. Upon arrival, the objects still within their packing cases should be allowed to "rest" reaching equilibrium in their new setting. Ideally that atmosphere is the same whether in a storage area or gallery. Even the conditions of the packing materials, if they are to be reused, should be kept in near-constant conditions. The installation of borrowed materials is the responsibility of the curator of the borrowing museum; he should see that they have the same protection as those of his own museum. All of the arrangements should be clearly written down and agreed to by both parties. The lending museum will photograph the objects before they leave and describe any weaknesses or defects, and the borrowing museum will do likewise before returning them. In addition to physical security, overall protection, including insurance, should be provided with written agreements between lender and borrower.[16]

Conservation Tasks

At the start of the 20th century, international purchases of artworks flourished. The traffic flowed from Europe west to the United States. Art dealers in European capitals sought artworks and offered them to American industrialists intent on adding luster to their surroundings and prestige. Dealers promoted restoration practices to attract buyers and make a sale. Restorers worked to make the object more attractive; their interests lay in sales and not in the integrity of the work. From these beginnings emerged in the mid-20th century professional conservation practices overseen by museums with responsibilities for protecting cultural artifacts for the public good rather than profit. As the 21st century begins, the role of conservation has become even more complex with museums recognizing that objects document the past and that their modification or restoration should be rare and guided by the "intent" of the maker, or in some cases their owner.[17]

The conservator that we know today has developed since the mid-20th century. Previously, the restorer took an empirical approach to conservation. He knew certain practical treatments to use on deteriorating art and historical objects and with skilled hands applied them; he would frequently describe himself as an artist. Charles Wilson Peale, for example, made himself sick using arsenic to preserve his specimens.[18] The conservator uses knowledge of science (especially chemistry and physics) to examine objects/artifacts, to determine appropriate treatment to maintain them in stable condition, or to restore them to a previous condition. Within the museum, he or she is responsible for establishing and maintaining environmental conditions to protect the object, whether in storage, on display, or in transit.

The conservator has two classes of duties. As adviser on preventive conservation, he or she helps the curator work out operating procedures and practices, and as a skillful scientist and craftsman diagnoses and treats deteriorated or altered objects. The first role may be the most important as the conservator can establish institutional practices that protect objects, and thereby avoid the necessity for restoration. Today, this is called preventative conservation. Some of the more practical elements of a conservator's advice have been described. A second role begins with inspection of a museum's holdings in cooperation with the curator and assignment of priorities for objects that need treatment; which often becomes a continuing responsibility with periodic inspections of which written records are kept.

In this treatment work, the conservator observes several guiding principles. One of these is to examine the objects to be worked on, using the latest scientific methods, in order to understand as thoroughly as possible the nature and prognosis of the deterioration and any alterations. A second principle requires the conservator to make as few changes as possible and to keep any changes reversible in the future. For example, fifty years ago a restorer might have decided that a polychrome wood sculpture was so worm eaten that he would replace a considerable portion with new wood, shaped and painted as nearly like the original as he could make it. A more conservative kind of restoration—say, fumigation of the statue to stop worm damage and minimum repainting with soluble paint—would have preserved it for the better treatment that could be given now. The treatment options change with scientific research. A detailed account of everything discovered about the object, good or bad, and every step taken in repairing or restoring it should become part of the museum record of the object. If further work is needed in the future, judgments can be made based on the record.

Another of the conservator's rules is not to use conjecture in restoration or reconstruction of objects. If he or she cannot find out by research what their actual appearance was, restoration should not proceed. This area is a very dangerous one, for conservators sometimes know so much about objects and their normal appearance in a historical period that they are tempted to go ahead intuitively, even when they lack authentic evidence. Another pitfall here is to use today's taste in restoring an object. For example, the H.F. du Pont Winterthur Museum acquired an early-19th-century wooden sculpted man's bust with several bad cracks; it had been cleaned down to the wood. In restoring it, the question arose whether to paint it a stone color or to use a natural finish that would show off the wood grain. Modern taste would have dictated the latter course, but research into the early-19th-century practice and faint traces of paint led to painting it stone color. Conservation must be guided by careful research beyond science into the fundamental cultural context of the object, Miriam Clavir argues that: "Conservation is more than a set

of physical preservation techniques, it is also an interpretive activity which involves a complex of artistic, scientific and historical ideas which influence the approach to treatment whether they are acknowledged or not."[19]

Two roles have expanded for conservators. The first is involved with protecting the museum's environment from insects and other pests that can harm the objects. "Integrated pest management" (IPM) seeks to protect the collection, and even the museum environment, by using natural approaches and compounds that will get rid of the pests, but not harm the environment, either inside or outside the museum. Some large museums actually have integrated pest managers on staff who keep up with the latest "natural" solutions to protecting collections areas. Nathan Stolow argues: "Traveling exhibitions and exchanges are increasing in frequency, involving movement of possible infected objects between tropical and more temperate countries ... measures for control of insect and fungus deterioration is of global concern; ethnographic, natural history and archival materials are especially vulnerable."[20]

Secondly, conservators also are often involved in the creation of institutional emergency plans with detailed instructions on how to protect the collections in time of fire, flood, or other disaster. Conservators not only assist in creating the plans, but also in carrying out special "triage" activities as a museum staff responds to disasters. Often conservators assemble disaster "carts" that hold items for use in protecting or stabilizing collections in case of emergencies. In the 1980s there was a national emphasis on creating operative disaster plans for museums across the country. The Getty Institute's *Building an Emergency Plan* identifies thirty recent disasters affecting cultural heritage institutions around the world ranging from fires, floods, earthquakes, hurricanes, and volcanic eruptions to wars and terrorist bombings from 1981 to 1997.[21] The recent experiences of New Orleans' museums during Hurricane Katrina are extreme cases, while broken water pipes and invading squirrels are much more common.

At the close of the 20th century, object conservation has stepped out of the office and lab spaces of museums and entered the galleries. In 1996 the Walters Art Gallery in Baltimore, Maryland, dedicated major gallery space to revealing to visitors the tasks performed by the museum's conservators. The objects on view reflected the care and attention of the conservator to the object and its context. Some of the exhibition cases included scientific instruments and explained their use by conservators. The purpose of the exhibition was to alert visitors to the role of conservation, the importance of the decisions made by the conservator, and on another level the investment of the museum as a public institution in caring for objects for public benefit. As the 21st century opened, when the original Star Spangled Banner required conservation, the National Museum of American History placed the work-in-progress on view as an exhibition. Visitors could watch the conservators as they worked and from surrounding label texts understand the decision-making process for restoring and conserving the object to protect it for future generations. Another brilliant example is the Lunder Conservation Center at the Smithsonian American Art Museum that opened in 2006. On the museum's top floor, visitors can watch conservators at work through glass walls. Conservation practices have become a permanent exhibition. No longer is conservation seen as a supporting function carried out in labs and offices out of public view.[22]

As an example of a comprehensive approach to conservation policies, in the Netherlands there is a project underway to address the needs of that nation's collections. It may hold important lessons (or guidance) to future museum conservation practices. There are some nine hundred museums in the Netherlands, and about twenty are funded and operated by the central government. In 1989 the government sought to measure the needs of the collections in all the nation's museums. The Delta Plan for Preservation of the Cultural Heritage began by identifying the "backlogs for registration and conservation," thereby quantifying the need and following on by creating a strategy to improve museum collections protections. The first steps involved simply identifying the number of collections, creating a national typology, and from there establishing priorities for conservation

needs. "The Plan has results in ... a far more professional approach with regard to collection management and conservation. Norms, guidelines, and standards of quality with regard to collections have been developed." The Delta Plan ended in 1999 and the Cultural Heritage Authorities (Erfgoed Inspectie), who are responsible for the inspections of all national museums to ensure proper preservation of collections, warned in their evaluation of the plan (2000) that it is crucial that the government not forget about museums after this investment. Such massive support has really helped by increasing awareness of collection preservation/conservation needs, providing air-conditioning in storage facilities, and improving conditions. This important attention should not lapse because of diminished financial support.[23]

Challenges

TECHNICAL AND CULTURAL ASPECTS OF CONSERVATION

As science has allowed for greater understanding of the physical nature of objects, the cultural interpretation of the artifact may be misunderstood. As museum donors and audiences expand, the important of understanding both the cultural and physical aspects of objects becomes more complex, and perhaps more important. Canadian conservator Miriam Clavir summarizes the issues this way: "[T]he conservation professional bases much of his or her decisions on scientific examination, knowledge of materials, and scientific reasoning, he/she also recognizes the importance of cultural knowledge. For example, the artist's intent and the object's social history are important foundations for making decisions regarding the object. Conservation work often adds to the information regarding both these phenomena. However, the conservator is expected to unearth this new information on the basis of expert observations of the physical object rather than on the basis of the traditional curatorial specializations of art and history. It is important to recognize that cultural information informs both the conservation decision-making process and conservation objectives."[24] These complexities especially impact the training process for museum conservators.

CARING FOR NEW MATERIALS

These changes in the very nature of museum collections affect museum storage and display techniques along with the training required for the museum conservation staff. Canadian conservator R. J. Barclay describes the challenges this way, suggesting that the very nature of museums is undergoing important changes when it comes to collections. "Conservators are anything but conservative. Even so, the greatest challenge is yet to come: the twentieth century can be characterized by the widespread use of synthetic materials in the creation of artefacts and works of art coupled with an abandonment, or at least a subjugation, of traditional techniques. These two facts together will oblige the discipline of museum conservation to face wider and more diverse demands in the next century—provided, of course, that the artefacts of our material culture continue to occupy centre stage in our museums."[25]

NEW MUSEUM MODELS AND CONSERVATION

What should be the role for conservation as museums change their emphases from collecting and scholarship to public service? Adding conservation practices to exhibition cases is one way that museums engage the public with their preservation functions. American anthropologist Carolyn Rose opines: "While the last decade has been challenging for museum conservation, even more challenges lie ahead. What really constitutes a museum today? Certainly it is not what we thought of at the beginning of the century, or even 30 years ago. As museums struggle with evolving and often mandated roles as businesses rather than institutions of higher education or research, and as entertainment centers rather than collections repositories, many traditional conservation approaches are outdated. To be effective, conservation strategies must consider the museum's changing objectives."[26]

CONSERVATION AND HISTORIC PRESERVATION

What of the impact of the changing nature of the museum "envelope" from a stand-alone building to a site, or perhaps even a town? American anthropologist Carolyn Rose writes: "[P]roblems...arise when whole groups of objects or entire historic city centers fall into disuse. One no longer wonders only how to conserve paintings, art, and archaeological objects in the great traditional museums, but also how to prevent the destruction of those monuments, urban contexts, craft items and ethnographic objects in danger of being either destroyed or dispersed by the tide of modernization...one must negotiate a very narrow path with destruction on one side and mummification on the other."[27]

PROTECTION AND PUBLIC ACCESS

Alessandra Malucco Vaccaro argues: "Striking a balance between the demands of conservation and the rights of the public is one of the most difficult challenges, but it is also the most urgent to undertake in order to secure the future of the past."[28] The caves at Lascaux in southwestern France are a perfect example of these conflicting demands. Four teenagers discovered the fifteen-thousand-year-old paintings 250 meters below ground in late 1940. With the end of World War II, the entry was expanded and visitors began to arrive at the rate of more than one thousand a day. After little more than twenty years of such visitation, the paintings began to show damage from the elevated levels of carbon dioxide. In the spring of 1963 the caves were permanently closed to the public and the atmosphere returned to its earlier levels. In 1980 the Dordogne Tourism Department created a replica of the cave, duplicating both its contours and ancient images. This replica opened to public viewing in 1983. Thus, today the public is excluded from viewing these ancient images to ensure their very existence.

NOTES

1. Philip R. Ward, "Conservation: Keeping the Past Alive," *Museum International* 43, no. 1 (1991): 7.

2. David Hugh Smith quoted in *Museums for a New Century*, Washington, DC, American Association of Museums, 1984, p. 40.

3. Miriam Clavir, *Preserving What Is Valued: Museums, Conservation, and First Nations*, Vancouver, Canada: University of British Columbia Press, 2002, p. 28.

4. H.J. Plenderleith and A. E. A. Werner, *The Conservation of Antiquities and Works of Art: Treatment, Repair, Restoration*, London: Oxford University Press, 1971; Patrick Boylan, "The Conservator-Restorer," *Museum International* 39, no. 4, 1987; Nicholas Stanley Price, M. Kirby Talley Jr., and Alessandra Malucco Vacarro, eds., *Historical and Philosophical Issues in the Conservation of Cultural Heritage*, Los Angeles: Getty Conservation Institute, 1996; Marcia Lord, "Editorial" and Gael de Guichen, "Preventive Conservation: A Mere Fad or Far-reaching Change?" and Eleonore Kissel, "The Restorer: Key Player in Preventive Conservation," *Museum International* 51, no. 1 (1999); Giorgio Torraca, "The Scientist in Conservation," *Getty Conservation Institute Newsletter* 14, no. 3 (1999); Graeme Gardiner, "Prevention Rather Than Cure: Preservation versus Conservation," *Museum International* 46, no. 3 (1994): 54–56; R. J. Barclay, "The Conservator: Versatility and Flexibility," *Museum International* 45, no. 4 (1993); "Conservation and Preservation Issue," *Museum News* 68, no. 1 (January–February 1989); Calvin Tomkins, "A Picasso Face-lift," *New Yorker*, May 24, 2004; Gregory J. Landrey et al., *The Winterthur Guide to Caring for Your Collections*, Winterthur, DE: Henry Francis Du Pont Winterthur Museum, 2000.

5. *A Public Trust at Risk: The Heritage Health Index Report on the State of America's Collections*, Washington, DC: Heritage Preservation, 2005. The full report can be accessed at www.heritagehealth index.org.

6. Plenderleith and Werner, *The Conservation of Antiquities and Works of Art;* The Getty Conservation Institute offers up-to-date information on conservation approaches on their website www.getty.edu/conservation.

7. Melissa Fay Greene, "Breeding Zoo Stock," *Museum News* 68, no. 1 (January–February 1989): 58–59; Nigel Rothfels, *Savages and Beasts: The Birth of the Modern Zoo*, Baltimore, MD: Johns Hopkins University Press, 2002, p. 199.

8. Nathan Stolow, *Conservation and Exhibitions: Packing, Transport, Storage and Environmental*

Consideration, London: Butterworth, 1987, p. 173; Karen Motylewski, "A Matter of Control," *Museum News* 69, no. 2 (March–April 1990).

9. *A Public Trust at Risk;* The following websites are very helpful in answering basic conservation inquiries: the Canadian Conservation Institute, www.cci-icc.gc.ca; the Getty Institute, www.getty .edu/conservation/institute; and the American Institute of Conservators, www.aic.stanford.edu.

10. Stolow, *Conservation and Exhibitions*, p. 214.

11. Timothy Ambrose and Crispin Paine, *Museum Basics*, London: Routledge with the International Council of Museums, 1993, p. 163; *Caring for Collections*, Washington, DC: American Association of Museums, 1984.

12. Peter Mann in *Care of Collections*, ed. Simon Knell, Routledge, Leicester University, 1994, pp. 36–37; Suzanne Keene, *Fragments of the World, Use of Museum Collections*, Oxford, UK: Butterworth, Heinemann, 2005, p. 164.

13. Rebecca A. Buck and Jean Allman Gilmore, *The New Museum Registration Methods*, Washington, DC: American Association of Museums, 1998.

14. Stolow, *Conservation and Exhibitions*, p. 2.

15. Caroline K. Keck, *Safeguarding Your Collection in Travel*, Nashville, TN: American Association for State and Local History, 1970; Stolow, *Conservation and Exhibitions*.

16. Marie Malaro, *A Legal Primer on Managing Museum Collections*, Washington, DC: Smithsonian Institution, 1985, pp. 156–183, 276–290.

17. Clavir, *Preserving What Is Valued*; Meryle Secrest, *Duveen: A Life in Art*, New York: Knopf, 2005, pp. 219, 252, 376–377; Jonathan Ashley-Smith, "The Ethics of Conservation," in *Care of Collections*, Simon Knell, ed.

18. Edward P. Alexander, "Charles Willson Peale," in *Museum Masters: Their Museums and Their Influence*, Nashville, TN: American Association of State and Local History, 1983, p. 60.

19. Clavir, *Preserving What Is Valued*, p. 41; Sherman E. Lee, *Past, Present, East and West*, New York: George Braziller, 1983, p. 37; James Cuno, ed., *Whose Muse? Art Museums and Public Trust*, Princeton University Press and Harvard University Press, 2004, pp. 32–35; Tony Bennett, "Out

of Which Past?" *The Birth of the Museum: History, Theory and Politics*, New York: Routledge, 1995.

20. Stolow, *Conservation and Exhibitions*, p. 23; David Pinniger, *Pest Management in Museums, Archives and Historical Houses,* London: Archetype Publications, 2001; David Pinniger and Peter Winsor, *Integrated Pest Management: Practical, Safe and Cost-effective Advice on the Prevention and Control of Pests in Museums*, London: Museums and Galleries Commission, 1998; Lynda Zycherman. ed., *A Guide to Museum Pest Control*, Washington, DC: Association of Systematics Collections, 1988; Mary-Lou Florian, *Heritage Eaters*, London: James and James, 1997.

21. *Building an Emergency Plan: A Guide for Museums and Other Cultural Institutions,* Los Angeles, CA: Getty Conservation Institute, 1999; K. Sharon Bennett, ed., *SEMC Disaster Response Handbook,* Charleston, SC: South East Museums Conference, 1999; *Field Guide to Emergency Response,* Washington, DC: Heritage Preservation, 2006; "Recovering from Disaster," *History News* 61, no. 2 (Spring 2006), this is a special issue with a comprehensive resource list, including Internet aid.

22. Joyce Hill Stoner, "Conservation Center Stage," *Museum News* 76, no. 3 (May–June 1997).

23. M. Kirby Talley Jr., "The Delta Plan: A Nationwide Rescue Operation," *Museum International* 51, no. 1 (1999): 11–15; Clara von Waldthausen, restorer of photographs, personal correspondence.

24. Clavir, *Preserving What Is Valued*, p. 42; Karen Zukowski, "The Importance of Context," in *Conservation in Context: Finding the Balance for the Historic House Museum Conference Proceedings,* National Trust of Historic Preservation and Andrew W. Mellon Foundation, 1994.

25. R. J. Barclay, "The Conservator: Versatility and Flexibility," *Museum International* 45, no. 4 (1993).

26. Carolyn L. Rose, "Conservation of Museum Collections," *GCI Newsletter* 14, no. 3 (1999): 17.

27. Malucco Vaccaro, "Introduction, Section III," in *Historical and Philosophical Issues*, p. 205.

28. Malucco Vaccaro, "The Emergence of Modern Conservation Theory," in *Historical and Philosophical Issues*, p. 206.

JAMES CUNO

Excerpt from "The Object of Art Museums"

In Whose Muse? Art Museums and the Public Trust, *ed. by James Cuno.*
Princeton: Princeton University Press and Harvard University Art Museum, 2003, pp. 52–53.

I WANT TO focus on the object because while museums do many things—like provide their visitors relative safety, a sense of place, distractions from everything else that is going on in their lives, a place to meet their friends and make new ones, to buy, eat, and drink things, hear concerts and lectures, and to feel empowered as they recognize that museums are here for them and work on their behalf without regard to their age, race, ethnic origin, religion, or sexual identity—nothing museums do is more important than adding to our nation's cultural legacy and providing visitors access to it, if only, as in the National Gallery during the Blitz, one object at a time.

Acquiring, preserving, and providing access to works of art is the basis for an art museum's contract with the public and the foundation of the trust that authorizes that contract. I do not mean simply physical access to the object, although that's very important: I also mean access to knowledge about and a deeper appreciation of the object. The museum is not just a treasure house, it is also a center of a very special kind of research and education. Its mode of research and teaching does not duplicate that which is conducted in schools, colleges, and universities, where the study consists of text- or image-based activities. In the art museum, research and teaching are object-based: prompted by the object, engaged with the object, and offered up by the particular way objects are experienced in space as physical things made of matter of a certain size and scale, worked in a certain way, and presented under certain circumstances, whether they be those of the gallery or the study room.

For these reasons, I want to reflect on the experience of engaging with works of art, especially in their most fundamental sense—as objects, manufactured things making claims on our close and sustained attention. This is not always easy with museums, especially in this age of extraordinary attendance. We have all had the experience of crowds in special exhibitions, where we've had to sneak quick glances over people's shoulders at the objects put temporarily on view. But it is difficult to engage with art in our permanent collection galleries too, because of the combination of things that were never intended to be seen together or in the way we them.

The French poet Paul Valéry reminds us of this in his 1925 essay "The Problem of Museums":

I make my way into a room of sculpture where a cold confusion reigns. A dazzling bust appears between the legs of a bronze athlete. Between repose and vehemence, between silliness, smiles, constrictions, and the most precarious states of equilibrium, the total impression is something quite intolerable. I am lost in a turmoil of frozen beings, each of which demands, all in vain, the abolition of the others—not to speak of the chaos of sizes without a common scale of measurement, the inexplicable mixture of dwarfs and giants, nor even of the foreshortening of evolution presented to us by such an assemblage of the complete and the unfinished, the mutilated and the restored... the eye, within the angle of its sweep, and at an instantaneous glance, is compelled to take in a portrait and a seascape, a study of food, and a triumph, along with views of people in the most varying states and sizes; and it must also accept mutually incompatible color harmonies and styles of painting, all in the same look.

Valéry is staggered and repelled by the accumulation of different things on view in a museum, and so might we be. The finer the works of art are, "the more exceptional as landmarks of human endeavor, the more distinct they necessarily be. They are rarities whose creators wanted each one unique."

JOHN COTTON DANA

"Why This Series Is Begun: The Old Museum and the New"

In The New Museum, *Woodstock, VT: The Elm Tree Press, 1917, pp. 9–21.*

THERE ARE ABOUT eighty live museums in the United States. Of these, indeed, it is doubtful if the term "live" can be properly applied to more than fifty. Of the total of six hundred institutions in the country which assume the name museum, only the number above noted combine the essentials of museum existence,—a home, collections properly so called, an income and, most important of all these essentials, such activities as may fairly be supposed to produce beneficial effects on their respective communities.

The above data are gathered from the three reports on museums which Mr. Paul M. Rea, director of the Museum of Charleston, S. C., has published in recent years through the U. S. Bureau of Education.

Mr. Rea says quite plainly that these few live museums are doing all the work in the museum field which is worthy of serious consideration. If, then, we assume that a good museum is a proper and helpful institution to any community which may establish and maintain the same; and if we note that there are in this country several thousand towns and cities without museums, good or poor, alive or dead; and if we note that other figures in Mr. Rea's reports show that the number of active museums is increasing quite rapidly, we arrive inevitably at these conclusions: (1) that the museum idea is abroad; (2) that in many communities the wish to establish a museum of some kind is in the minds of at least a few of the more public-spirited citizens; and that, consequently, (3) there is now a wide-spread, if not an intense and popular, demand for suggestions on museum founding and on the elements of museum management.

The literature of this subject is quite meagre. Of all that has been written on it, by far the greater part consists of histories of museums, of descriptions of their contents or perfunctory museum reports, of elaborate and technical discussions of individual objects and of methods of installing costly special objects or special groups. Notable exceptions to this statement are

G. Brown Goode's Report on the U.S. National Museum for 1892-3, and other writings by him, and the ten annual volumes of the Proceedings of the American Association of Museums. From these and from a few other sources, which are noted in the appended list of books, journals and proceedings, have been drawn much of the information and many of the suggestions on which we have for eight years based our activities here in Newark.

Our Search for Information

From the very beginnings, eight years ago, of our still modest enterprise, we have felt the need of sources of information on such topics as these:

How to organize a museum association.

How to stimulate interest in a local museum.

How to construct a museum which shall interest and help its community.

How to record acquisitions.

How to install the simpler and commoner classes of museum objects.

How to store safely and compactly objects which are not in use.

How to prepare and display modest temporary exhibits.

How to secure such printing of labels, lists, etc., as befits a museum.

How to get expert museum advice and competent museum workers.

How to discover the latest and best things that have been published on museum work of each and every kind.

These and many other queries we have met and answered as best we could. Our problems have not been large ones, in the sense that they involved large expenditures; they have been large, in the sense that they were broad and fundamental, that is, of the kind that every museum must meet in beginning its career.

We have felt so keenly the lack of printed information which gave clear, precise and definite answers to our many queries, that we decided several years ago that, if fortune favored us by keeping our museum alive and growing, we would, in due course, set down in print our own experiences, the results of our inquiries, studies, observations and experiments. And it is precisely because we are young, inquisitive and, we hope, unprejudiced, and have felt so keenly our own ignorance and our own shortcomings, that we are willing to run the risks that go with the offering of advice and suggestion, especially by the young and inexperienced. Often it is those who are just beginning to learn who can give most help to others who are but one step behind them in the learning process.

Our Opposition to Museum Conventions

Another aspect of our museum attitude has helped so to embolden us as to make us willing to put down for others that which we are in the very process of learning for ourselves, and that is our frankly confessed opposition to most of the accepted museum conventions. This opposition is addressed not so much to conventions of management as to conventions of purpose.

We decided, quite early in our history, that the art-gallery type of museum would be, for our city, not at all worth the money it would cost to establish and maintain. Special local conditions were in part responsible for this conclusion. Newark is only nine miles from New York, and any Newarker who wishes can, at the cost of fifty cents and three hours time, make a long visit either to the world's best museum of science or to its best museum of art. This cost in money and time will be, in a few years, even less than it is today. To set up in Newark a poor imitation of either of these great institutions; poor at least in its contents, and in its home a mere ostentatious product of a foolish desire to add the façade of a marble palace to the city's insignia of culture,—to do these things

seemed to us foolish and wasteful and unproductive of good results.

The Kind of Museum Newark Seems to Need

Obviously the thing needed by Newark in the museum field, was something which should supplement locally the great storehouses of wonderful, beautiful, and educational objects in the collections of the city next door, the richest city in the world, and a city of which Newark each year becomes more essentially a component part. This supplement, so we felt, and still feel, should be adapted with special care to the needs of the people of Newark; through careful study it should be made something the people of Newark would use and, using, would find pleasure and profit therein. It should not be constructed, in its home, or in its collections, or in its activities, after any preconceived pattern. What Newark men and women and children would welcome, and would use to add to the interests of their lives and to the improvement and general efficiency of their business and work-a-day lives,—this we thought should be slowly and carefully discovered by study, observation and trial,—and so the museum would grow. To build first an expensive home, a palace, a temple or any grandiose and permanent structure on the conventi[on]al lines of so-called museum architecture was, so we seemed clearly to see, to do a foolish, wasteful, antiquated thing; a thing possible only to those who knew little of modem community life, still less of American educational practice, and least of all of modern museum ideas. Vast sums, it is true, are invested in some of our large cities, and relative large sums in some of our smaller cities, on buildings and collections of museums of the conventional art-gallery type: and sums also very large are spent on the maintenance of the same. But a very brief study of these museums and of the use made of them in adding to the pleasure, to the broadening and enlightening, and to the definite education of their respective communities, convinced us that they are among the least effective products of community enterprise that American development has brought forth. We came to a like conclusion concerning conventional scientific and historical and industrial collections. They have shown themselves to be collections, and little more; gratifying to a few, awesome to a few, tiresome to many, and helpful to almost none.

The Coming of the New Museum Idea

The same open-minded study,—did we not believe it was open-minded we would never presume to offer to our colleagues any suggestions whatever,—which seemed to us to demonstrate the general futility of conventional museums of whatever character, brought to our attention a movement, within the museum field, which precisely fell in with the notions we had already acquired concerning museum work. This movement or activity within certain museums, suggested long ago by Mr. Goode, and hinted at broadly by a few students long before his day, has scarcely yet embodied itself in a museum. It is too new, on the one hand, and the old "art-gallery" and "collections" ideas of museums are still too powerful, on the other hand, to permit it to express itself fully in an active, complete and well-rounded institution. There are seeming exceptions to this statement here and there, which will be alluded to later.

This new movement, with which we have tried to identify ourselves and in which we have tried to do our part, is difficult of description. It is not directed to the erection of Greek or Renaissance façades in parks or corners remote from a city's center. It is not concerned with the construction, behind those façades, of a few grand courts and galleries. Its galleries or work and study rooms to be are not invested with that ancient and ghastly fetish, a top light—something which one may properly hope to escape when he enters a modern building. It is not friendly to that "museum" atmosphere which is depressing and numbing to the sensitive visitor in direct ratio to the self-conscious grandeur and refinement of its architectural container. Nor does this new museum method aim at the acquisition of rare and priceless objects with which to fill rows of cold and costly cases; all peculiarly well-fitted, if they do nothing else, to aggravate the foolish pride of the thoughtless citizen;

nor at the acquisition of so many objects within any-one field as to make a museum distinctly a museum of a certain kind.

The Value of Mere Collections

Parenthetically it should be said, lest some misunderstand our attitude toward the preservation of rare and beautiful objects, toward the creation of art galleries, toward the making of science collections and collections in any field whatever, that all these things are manifestly useful, and have their proper place. We merely hold to the theory that in most cases their immediate utility is vastly over-rated; that their cost is out of proportion to their value; that their managers usually too greatly exalt their acquisitions and forget the entertainment and instructions of those for whom they were professedly acquired; and that their presence, and the dominance of the conventions which go with them, make very difficult the introduction of homelier, more attractive and more useful objects and methods into the museum world.

Most of us prefer to copy. It is one of the limitations of wealth that it can not be original in its exercise of one of its prime functions, the practice of conspicuous wastefulness. The rich like to collect what other rich have collected. They add the lust of possession to the practice of patronage of art or science. They think of "grand" public homes of the public's treasures only in terms convention has fixed. Hence, remote palaces full of things whose accepted merits in beauty, rarity, age and cost are excelled only by the paucity of their visitors.

But, as it is well for the public to become possessors of the rich and rare, and as the rich will supply them only under certain architectural and administrative conditions, it is obvious that it would be quite as foolish as it would be unwise to oppose the growth of the conventional museum.

Our attitude of criticism which is, we fully realize, quite negligible as such, is born merely of the belief that a better type of museum, a museum properly so-called, indeed, is possible, is in fact inevitable, and that some of the energy and money which now goes to the old kind of museum store-house may well be diverted to the new kind of museum work-shop. And that belief is expressed in this pamphlet as a partial explanation of the character of the constructive suggestions we make later.

The General Theory of the New Movement

The general theory of the new movement we are trying to describe seems to be this:

Each community can use to good advantage a certain quantity of material in formal and informal training through the eye. This training, this visual instruction, every member of every community is gaining in some measure every working moment, of his life. In each community there is a tendency toward rather special and somewhat limited interests in the visual field, by reason of the special industrial, commercial and educational activities of that community. We believe that it will pay any community to add to its educational apparatus a group of persons which shall form: the staff of a local institution of visual instruction and to put in the hands of these persons modest sums with which they shall acquire, label, describe, arrange for show and prepare for lending, such objects as careful study and experiment shall suggest; in the expectation that staff and objects combined will do for the community these things at least, and, one may hope, in time many others—

1. Entertain, and be ready to try to interest and instruct, such as may have the wish and the time to visit casually the institution's headquarters.

2. Entertain and more definitely and generally instruct, in classes and conducted groups, by labels, leaflets, handbooks, talks and illustrated lectures, such adults as may be induced to come to see special exhibits, also at the institute headquarters.

3. Entertain, interest and still more definitely instruct children who may be sent to the institute's headquarters from schools on stated occasions, and for certain specific observations; the objects observed, and the talks and the reading expounding the objects, being closely related to school work and to the age and stage of mental development of each group that comes.

4. Prepare for schools single objects and groups of objects with such labels, leaflets, lantern slides and instructors as the proper use of each may demand, and lend these to schools as the school authorities may designate; all being fitted, of course, to make easier the work of teaching and to make broader and more effective the work of the pupils.

5. Place in schools, as opportunity and fit occasions and the felt need of teachers, supervisors and the management may indicate, single objects and large and small collections of objects, fully labeled and accompanied by pictures, leaflets and pamphlets; all being such as may entertain and instruct both teachers and pupils, and particularly such as may be found to give constant and almost daily assistance in adding interest and value to studies and in broadening the experiences of pupils and in awakening new interests in them. These to be changed as use and circumstance suggest.

6. Place in convenient and easily accessible rooms, like store rooms on business streets, and in special rooms with separate entrances in school buildings, single objects and small, well-rounded collections in art, science, industry, ethnology and other fields, such as experience shows will attract a large number of visitors. Manage these branch institutes, when possible, as veritable independent teaching centers, with leaflets and cards descriptive of the museum's work and its acquisitions for distribution, and with skilled attendants who can describe and instruct as opportunity offers.

7. Discover collectors and specialists and experts in the community and secure their cooperation in adding to the museum's collections; in helping identify, describe and prepare labels and leaflets; in arousing the interest of young people in the museum's work and in finding such boys and girls as may wish to make collections of objects of any kind for themselves or for the museum.

This development of the collecting habit among the young, with its accompanying education of powers of observation, its training in handwork, its tendency to arouse interests theretofore· unsuspected even by those who possess them, its continuous suggestions toward good taste and refinement which lie in the, process of installing even the most modest of collections, and its leadings toward sound civic interest through doing for one's community a helpful thing,—

this work of securing the cooperation of boys and girls, making them useful while they are gaining their own pleasure and carrying on their own education, is one of the coming museum's most promising fields.

8. Lend to individuals, groups and societies, for any proper use and for any reasonable length of time, any of the museum's objects, whenever it is clear that things thus lent will be of more service to the community than when they are resting, relatively unseen and unused, in the museum's headquarters.

9. Prepare and display, at the headquarters, at branches and in schools, carefully selected objects which are products of the community's activities in field, factory and workshop. These will be local industry exhibits. They may be so small as to show in a very easily transported case a few of the major steps in the manufacture of a simple object. They may include merely a group of completed objects, interesting for their beauty or complexity, or for the high technical skill of the craftsman who made them. Or they may be so extensive as to fill every available inch of space the museum controls and to illustrate many aspects of one field of industry; and so general as to give a bird's-eye view of all the industries of the whole community. These may be planned to attract and interest the business man, or to draw to them the women, or to arouse in young people a healthful curiosity in the activities of their community and the results of the daily labor of men and women,—their fathers, mothers, brothers and sisters, in the field, the store and the factory.

10. Keep the museum and its activities continually before the community in the daily press, and publish and distribute as many leaflets, posters, broadsides and cards descriptive of the museum's acquisitions as conditions seem to warrant. At the proper time publish leaflets and booklets, based on the museum's material, proper to be used as reading lessons in the schools.

11. Connect the work the museum may do, its objects and all the activities of its staff, with all the resources of the public library. In doing this, many books and journals will be displayed near objects on view, references to books and journals will be made on labels and in leaflets of all kinds, and the library will be asked to show placards and notes and to dis-tribute things the museum may publish descriptive of its purposes and activities.

———

The activities thus very briefly described form a small part only of the work that, as we conceive it, the coming museum will do. Though they are suggestions only, they seem to demonstrate their reasonableness merely by the statement of them. They are ample, in our opinion, to show to the open-minded that the new museums are to be museums properly so-called,—homes and work-shops of the Muses. They are not to be storage warehouses, or community attics, or temples of dead gods, or copies of palaces of an extinct nobility, or costly reproductions of ancient temples, or grand and elaborate structures which are of service only as evidences of conspicuous waste by the rich and as ocular demonstrations of the unwise expenditure of public funds.

The New Museum
An Institute of Visual Instruction

The coming museum, being entitled to the ancient name by virtue of its activities, will ultimately be called The Museum; though it will be for a time quite properly conceived of by many as an Institute of Visual Instruction. Museums of the old kind we contend, are truly not museums at all. They are "collections" of variable extent and cost and of slight definite utility. They will become each year a little less considered, less esteemed and less used; or they will, as is the case with some of them already, transform themselves slowly into living organisms, with an abundance of teachers, with ample workshops, classrooms and spaces for handling the outgoing and incoming of objects which they lend. In the new museums, as in the old ones which are informed with the new spirit, the experts will use their expertness partly on objects, as now; but they will sweeten much of it generously with the simple syrup of sympathy and use it for the pleasure and profit of the common man.

We have purposely presented emphatically the difference between the museum of today and the museum we are trying to develop, and shall try in this series to foreshadow, in the hope that, in so far as our emphasis is disturbing, in so far will the differences we mention be more clearly seen.

Many Old Museums Are New in Part

These differences, it should again be said, are not of our creation. We found the new movement active in many institutions old and young. Indeed, there are few museums to-day, few at least of the very small number which Mr. Rea tells us are alive, in which the management does not claim that it is doing the new work and developing into the new kind.

That is, to say over once more what we have already said, of the activities above prophesied for the new museum, there are few, if any, which are not being somewhere carried on or being promised for the future.

We have simply conceived of a museum as a living thing, definitely living as is the school; and upon this conception we have grafted such activities of present day museums as one may properly call alive, and have added such others as the thought of a museum as an active to "institute of visual instruction" inevitably brings to mind.

Of the things named above, or suggested elsewhere in this volume, we are doing very, very few. Our limitations, psychological and social, are many; our financial limitations are very definite and narrow. We have placed here, in this the first number of our Museum Series, this statement of what we believe a museum should try to be, only because we felt that unless we made our position in this fundamental quite clear, the experiences we shall set forth and the suggestions we shall make would not be accepted as we intend them and the spirit in which we present them would not clearly be understood.

This Is Not a Museum Manual

Once more; what we are putting down for publication is by no means entirely the product of either our own experience or our own invention. We have stud-

ied museum literature; we have visited museums; we have gathered where we could, and we shall try to give due credit always.

———

Again it should be said that we plan to put into these publications such of a learner's acquisitions as we hope may be useful to other learners. We are not compiling complete museum manuals. We had hoped that workers in old, rich and experienced museums, far better equipped for the purpose than we are, would undertake what we are doing; but they do not. We dare hope that, by setting forth plainly the lessons we have learned and the principles we have been forced to accept, we can help the beginner. We can hope to do little more.

Our Experience in Museum Work

As to some of the elements of museum management in general and of our fitness to speak of them, perhaps this should be said; for 15 years, seven of them before our museum was organized, we did in the library many of the things that are done in modern museums. We had several unused rooms. In these, in ten years, there were held about 5,382 meetings, large and small, of 662 different civic and educational organizations, with a total attendance of 167,335. Perhaps no library in the world, and certainly no museum, ever enjoyed so ample an experience as was ours in the management of a center for the voluntary expression by the community of its civic and self-educational impulses. We cared for all these meetings. We helped to make the library a welcome place for them. And from them we learned much in the line of public service.

In the same years we prepared or supervised and directed the installation and the public visitation of 74 exhibitions. These ranged from paintings of the best type to book-plates, guns and school handiwork. They were visited by 300,000 persons. The installation of every one of them was carefully studied and as carefully carried out as funds permitted; and on the printing of posters, announcements, and catalogs, no time was spared to make it as good as our judgment could dictate and as our local printer could produce.

The management of these many meetings and exhibitions was in the hands of the library staff, and that same library staff,—not the same throughout in personnel, but the same in intent and skill,—has managed all the museum's affairs since its foundation.

Our experience, then, and our learnings, in those elements of museum work which we plan to include in this series, have not come solely from the management for a few years of a very small museum.

Hence, in part, the boldness which permits us to put into print some of the things we have found helpful.

G. BROWN GOODE

"The Relationships and Responsibilities of Museums"

Science N.S. 2.34 (August 23, 1895): 197–209.

Part of a paper on "The Principles of Museum Administration," read before the Museums Association, at Newcastle-on-Tyne, July 23, 1895.

IN AN ARTICLE on 'The use and abuse of Museums,' written nearly fifteen years ago by Professor William Stanley Jevons, attention was directed to the circumstance that there was not, at that time, in the English language a treatise analyzing the purposes and kinds of museums, and discussing the general principles of their management and economy. It is somewhat surprising that the need then made so evident has not since been supplied and that there is not at the present day such a treatise in the English or any other language. Many important papers have in the interval been printed in regard to particular classes of museums and special branches of museum work. Notable among these have been those written by Sir William H. Flower, Professor W. A. Herdman, Dr. J. S. Billings, Dr. H. H. Higgins, Dr. Albert Günther and General Pitt Rivers, and there had previously been printed the well known essay of Dr. J. E. Gray, Edward Forbes' suggestive paper on 'Educational Uses of Museums,' in 1853, and the still earlier one by Edward Edwards on 'The Maintenance and Management of Public Galleries and Museums,' printed in 1840.

No one has as yet attempted, however, even in a preliminary way, to formulate a general theory of administration applicable to museum work in all its branches, except Professor Jevons, who, in the paper already referred to, presented in an exceedingly impressive manner certain ideas which should underlie such a theory.

It is still true, as it was when Professor Jevons wrote, in 1881, that there is not in existence 'a treatise analyzing the purposes and kinds of museums and discussing the general principles of their management and economy.' With this fact in mind I have ventured to begin the preparation of such a treatise and to attempt to bring together in one systematic sequence the principles which I believe to underlie the practice of the wisest and most experienced of modern museum administrators.

My ideas are presented, it may be, in a somewhat dogmatic manner, often in the form of aphorisms, and to the experienced museum worker many of them will, perhaps, sound like truisms.

I have had two objects in view:

It has been my desire, in the first place, to begin the codification of the accepted principles of museum administration, hoping that the outline which is here presented may serve as the foundation for a complete statement of those principles, such as can only be prepared through the cooperation of many minds. With this in view, it is hoped that the paper may be the cause of much critical discussion.

My other purpose has been to set forth the aims and ambitions of modern museum practice, in such a manner that they shall be intelligible to the persons who are responsible for the establishment of museums and also to the directors of other public institutions founded for similar purposes, in order to evoke more fully their sympathy and cooperation.

Museums of art and history, as well as those of science, are discussed in this paper, since the same general principles appear to be applicable to all.

The theses proposed are two hundred and fifteen in number and are arranged under the following heads or chapters:

I. The Museum and its Relationship; II. The Responsibilities and Requirements of Museums; III. The Five Cardinal Necessities in Museum Administration; IV. The Classification of Museums; V. The Uses of Specimens and Collections; VI. The Preservation and Preparation of Museum Materials; VII. The Art of Installation; VIII. Records, Catalogues and Specimen Labels; IX. Exhibition Labels and Their Function; X. Guides and Lecturers; Hand Books and Reference-books; XI. The Future of Museum Work.

[The introductory portion, consisting of the first three chapters, and the last chapter are here printed. The remainder of the paper is more technical and is intended especially for the consideration of persons engaged directly in museum work.]

The Museum and Its Relationships

A. THE MUSEUM DEFINED.

1. A museum is an institution for the preservation of those objects which best illustrate the phenomena of nature and the works of man, and the utilization of these for the increase of knowledge and for the culture and enlightenment of the people.

B. THE RELATION OF THE MUSEUM TO OTHER INSTITUTIONS OF LEARNING.

1. The Museum in its effort for the increase and diffusion of knowledge aids and is aided by (a) the university and college, (b) the learned society and (c) the public library.

2. The special function of the museum is to preserve and utilize objects of nature and works of art and industry; that of the library to guard the written records of human thought and activity; that of the learned society to discuss facts and theories; that of the school to educate the individual, while all meet together on common ground in the custodianship of learning and in extending the boundaries of existing knowledge.

3. The care and utilization of material objects being the peculiar duty of the museum, it should not enter the field of other institutions of learning, except to such a degree as may be found absolutely necessary in connection with its own work.

[For example, its library should contain only such books as are necessary for use within its own walls. Its publications should be solely those which are (directly or indirectly) the outgrowth of its own activities. Its teaching work should be such as cannot be performed by other institutions.

On the other hand, schools may advantageously limit their cabinets with reference to the needs of their lecture rooms and laboratories. The library and the learned society should not enter the field of the museum, except in localities where museum agencies are not provided.]

C. THE RELATION OF THE MUSEUM TO THE EXPOSITION.

1. The Museum differs from the Exposition both in its aims and in the method of its activity.

2. The Exposition, or Exhibition, and the Fair are primarily for the promotion of industry and commerce; the Museum for the advancement of learning.

3. The principal object of the former is to make known the names of the exhibitors for their own professional or financial advantage; in the latter the name of the exhibitor is incidental, the thing chiefly in mind being the lesson taught by the exhibit.

4. Into the work of the former enters the element of competition, coupled with a system of awards by diplomas or medals; in that of the latter the element of competition does not appear.

5. The educational results of expositions, though undeniably important, are chiefly incidental, and not at all proportionate to the prodigal expenditure of energy and money which are inseparable from any great exposition.

D. MUSEUM FEATURES ADOPTED IN EXPOSITIONS.

1. Museum methods have been in part adopted by many expositions, in some instances to attract visitors, in others because it has been desired to utilize the occasion to give museum lessons to multitudes to whom museums are not accessible.

2. Those expositions which have been most successful from an educational standpoint have been the ones which have most fully availed themselves of museum methods, notably the London Exhibition of 1851 and the Paris Exposition of 1889.

3. Special or limited exhibitions have a relatively greater educational value, owing to the fact that it is possible in these to apply more fully the methods of the museum. Examples of this principle were afforded by the four expositions held in London from 1883 to 1886—Fisheries, Health, Inventions and Colonial.

4. The annual exhibitions of the academies of art are allied to the exposition rather than to the museum.

5. Many so-called 'museums' are really 'permanent exhibitions,' and many a great collection of pictures can only be suitably described by the name 'picture gallery.'

E. TEMPORARY MUSEUMS.

1. There are many exhibitions which are administered in accordance with museum principles and which are really temporary museums. To this class belong the best of the loan exhibitions, and also special exhibits made by public institutions, like the 'Luther Memorial Exhibition' of 1874, the material for which was derived chiefly from the Library of the British Museum, and similar exhibitions subsequently held under the same auspices.

F. MUSEUM METHODS IN OTHER INSTITUTIONS— 'MUSEUM EXTENSION.'

1. The zoölogical park, the botanical garden and the aquarium are essentially museums, and the principles of museum administration are entirely applicable to them.

2. An herbarium in its usual form corresponds to the study series in a museum, and is capable of expansion to the full scope of the general museum.

3. Certain churches and ecclesiastical edifices and classical antiquities in place, when they have been pronounced 'public monuments,' are subject to the principles of museum administration.

4. Many cities, like Rome, Naples, Milan and Florence, by reason of the number of buildings, architectural features, sculpture and other objects in the streets and squares, together with the historical houses duly labeled by tablets, have become practically great museums, and these various objects are administered much in the manner of museums. Indeed, the number of 'Public Monuments' in Italy is so great that the whole country may properly be described as a museum of art and history. A government commission for the preservation of the monuments of history and art regulates the contents of every church, monastery and public edifice, the architectural features of private buildings, and even private collections, to the extent of requiring that nothing shall be removed from the country without governmental sanction. Each Italian town is thus made a museum, and in Rome the site of the Forum and the adjacent ancient structures has been set aside as an outdoor museum under the name of the *Passegiata Archeologica*.

Similar government control of public monuments and works of art exists in Greece and Egypt, and in a lesser degree in the Ottoman Empire, and for half a century there has been a Commission of Historic Monuments in France, which has not only succeeded in protecting the national antiquities, but has published an exceedingly important series of descriptive monographs concerning them.

The Responsibilities and Requirements of Museums

A. THE RELATION OF THE MUSEUM TO THE COMMUNITY.

1. The museum meets a need which is felt by every intelligent community and furnishes that which cannot be supplied by any other agency. The museum does not exist except among enlightened peoples, and

attains its highest development only in great centres of civilization.

2. The museum is more closely in touch with the masses than the university and learned society, and quite as much so as the public library, while, even more than the last, it is a recent outgrowth of modern tendencies of thought. Therefore,

3. THE PUBLIC MUSEUM IS A NECESSITY IN EVERY HIGHLY CIVILIZED COMMUNITY.

B. THE MUTUAL RESPONSIBILITIES OF THE COMMUNITY AND THE MUSEUM.

1. The museums in the midst of a community perform certain functions which are essential to its welfare, and hence arise mutual responsibilities between the community and the museum administrator.

2. The museum administrator must conduct his work with the highest possible degree of efficiency, in order to retain the confidence of the community.

3. The community should provide adequate means for the support of the museum.

4. A failure on the part of the one must inevitably lead to a corresponding failure on the part of the other.

C. THE SPECIFIC RESPONSIBILITIES OF THE MUSEUM.

1. The museum should be held responsible for special services, chiefly as follows:

   a. *For the advancement of learning.*—To aid learned men in the work of extending the boundaries of knowledge, by affording them the use of material for investigation, laboratories and appliances.

   To stimulate original research in connection with its own collections, and to promote the publication of the results.

   b. *For record.*—To preserve for future comparative and critical study the material upon which past studies have been made, or which may serve to confirm, correct or modify the results of such studies. Such materials serve to perpetuate the names and identifications used by investigators in their publications and, thus authenticated, to serve as a basis for future investigation in connection with new material. Specimens which thus vouch for the work of investigators are called *Types*. Besides types museums retain for purposes of record many specimens which, though not having served for investigation, are landmarks for past stages in the history of man and nature.

   c. *As an adjunct to the class room and the lecture room.*—To aid the teacher either of elementary, secondary, technological or higher knowledge in expounding to his pupils the principles of art, nature and history, and to be used by advanced or professional students in practical laboratory or studio work.

   To furnish to the advanced or professional student materials and opportunity for laboratory or studio training.

   d. *To impart special information.*—To aid the occasional inquirer, be he a laboring man, school boy, journalist, public speaker or savant, to obtain, without cost, exact information upon any subject related to the specialties of the institution; serving thus as a 'bureau of information.'

   e. *For the culture of the public.*—To serve the great general public, through the display of attractive exhibition series, well-planned, complete and thoroughly labeled; and thus to stimulate and broaden the minds of those who are not engaged in scholarly research, and draw them to the public library and the lecture room. In this respect the effect of the museum is somewhat analogous to that of travel in distant lands.

2. A museum to be useful and reputable must be constantly engaged in ag[g]ressive work, either in education or investigation, or in both.

3. A museum which is not ag[g]ressive in policy and constantly improving cannot retain in its service a competent staff and will surely fall into a decay.

4. A FINISHED MUSEUM IS A DEAD MUSEUM, AND A DEAD MUSEUM IS A USELESS MUSEUM.

5. Many so-called 'museums' are little more than storehouses filled with the materials of which museums are made.

D. THE RESPONSIBILITY OF MUSEUMS TO EACH OTHER.

1. There can be no occasion for envious rivalry between museums, even when they are in the same city. Every good museum strengthens its neighbors and the success of the one tends to the popularity and public support of the others.

2. A system of coöperation between museums, by means of which much duplication of work and much expenditure of work may be avoided, is seemingly possible.

3. The first and most important field for mutual understanding is in regard to specialization of plan. If museums in the same town, province or nation would divide the field of work so that each should be recognized as having the first rights in one or more specialities, rivalry would be converted into friendly association and the interests of science and education better served.

4. An important outcome of such a system of coöperation might be the transfer of entire groups of specimens from one museum to another. This would greatly facilitate the work of specialization referred to, and at the same time relieve each museum of the responsibility of maintaining collections which are not germane to its real purpose. Such transfers have occasionally been made in the past, and there are few museums which might not benefit individually, in a large degree, by a sweeping application of this principle. If its effect upon the effectiveness and interest of any local or national group of museums is taken into account, no one can doubt that the result would be exceedingly beneficial.

5. Another field for coöperation is in joint expenditure of effort and money upon labels and catalogues and in the economical purchase of and in supplies and material.

6. Still another would lie in the coöperative employment of expert curators and preparators, it being thus practicable to pay larger salaries and secure better men.

The Five Cardinal Necessities in Museum Administration

THE ESSENTIALS OF SUCCESS IN MUSEUM WORK.

A museum cannot be established and creditably maintained without adequate provision in five directions:

1. A stable organization and adequate means of support.

2. A definite plan, wisely framed in accordance with the opportunities of the institution and the needs of the community for whose benefit it is to be maintained.

3. Material to work upon—good collections or facilities for creating them.

4. Men to do the work—a staff of competent curators.

5. Appliances to work with—a suitable building, with proper accessories, installation material, tools and mechanical assistants.

A. Stability of Organization.

1. The only absolute assurance of permanence for a museum lies either in governmental protection, in a connection with some endowed institution of learning, or in special organization with ample endowments.

2. The cabinets of unendowed societies, or those gathered and supported by the efforts of individuals, must in time inevitably be dispersed or destroyed.

B. Definiteness of Plan.

1. No two museums can be or ought to be exactly alike. Each should be devoted to one or more special subjects, and should select those subjects not only in reference to opportunity and the needs of the community, but also with regard to the specialties of other museums in the same region, with a view to coöperation.

2. It is the duty of every museum to be preeminent in at least one specialty, be this specialty never so limited.

3. The specialties or departments of any museum may be few or many, but it is important that its plan should be positively defined and limited, since lack

of purpose in museum work leads in a most conspicuous way to waste of effort and to failure, partial or complete.

4. It will undoubtedly be found desirable for certain museums, founded for local uses, to specialize mainly in the direction of popular education. If these cannot also provide for a certain amount of scholarly endeavor in connection with their other activities, it is of the utmost importance that they should be associated (by a system of administrative cooperation) with some institution which is a centre of original work.

5. The general character of a museum should be clearly determined at its very inception. Specialization and division of labor are essential for institutions as well as for individuals. It is only a great national museum which can hope to include all departments and which can with safety encourage growth in every direction.

6. Small museums, it is needless to say, cannot attempt specialization in the same degree as large ones, but the principles just enunciated should be constantly kept in view, even by the least of them.

C. Collections.

1. The sources of collections are the following: (a) By gift; (b) by purchase; (c) by exchange; (d) by collection and exploration; (e) by construction; (f) through deposit or temporary loan.

a. *By gift.*—Acquisition by gift is a most important source, but very uncertain. If a museum has a plan to which it intends to adhere, a large proportion of the gifts offered to it will be unavailable; while, on the other hand, only a small proportion of the desiderata will ever be thus obtained. A museum may properly, by the offer of a large and complete collection illustrating a subject outside of its plan, be induced to expand its scope. In the case of a large benefaction of this kind, necessitating extensive changes in installation, there must always be careful consideration of the result. It should be borne in mind, however, that the random, thoughtless acceptance of proffered gifts, which in the course of a few years produces results by no means insignificant in the consumption of space and money for their care, may modify the plan of a museum in a most radical manner. It requires quite as much judgment and mental effort on the part of a museum officer to keep out unsuitable objects as to bring in those which are desirable.

b. *By purchase.*—Acquisition by purchase is often the only means of obtaining desirable objects, particularly so in the case of art museums, least so in natural history museums. Money is especially necessary for the filling of gaps in series obtained by gift or otherwise.

c. *By exchange.*—Acquisition by exchange is especially advantageous, since it enables a museum to dispose of unavailable duplicate material. When exchanges are made with well-conducted museums there is the additional advantage that the materials thus obtained have been studied and identified by expert authorities. Little is gained by conducting exchanges in a commercial spirit and in insisting on too exact valuations and balancing of equivalents, especially when the parties to the exchange are public institutions. Large museums in dealing with small ones may often advantageously give largely and receive comparatively little in return, since they not only become disembarrassed of useless duplicates not desired by institutions of equal rank, but are also building up sister institutions which may in time afford them much more substantial aid. Exchanges with private collectors may well be carried on in the same spirit, since the collector is thus encouraged to gather more material, in the midst of which unexpected treasures may come to light, and is also aided to build up a private collection which in time will probably fall into the hands of some public museum.

d. *By collecting and exploration.*—For all museums save those of art this is usually the most profitable and satisfactory, since by gathering fresh material in unexplored fields, new facts are discovered, science is enriched, and the reputation of the institution improved. Furthermore, material is obtained in such large quantities that there always remains much in the way of duplicate specimens valuable for exchange. A museum which carries its activities into unexplored fields secures for itself material which is unique and unobtainable by others, and thus makes itself a centre of interest for the entire world.

The smallest museum may enrich its collections by modest explorations under its own walls; it can do much by simply encouraging the people in the adjacent region to save what they accidentally encounter in the course of their daily pursuits. Explorations of this kind are preeminently the function of local and provincial museums.

e. *By construction.*—Any museum may do much to improve its exhibition series by the construction of models and the making of drawings and maps and by taking copies of important objects in its own collections, to secure material to be used in exchange. Even small museums may do this, for extensive workshops are not necessary and a specialist, himself devoid of mechanical skill, may accomplish marvelous things with the aid of a patient mechanic.

f. *Through deposit and temporary loan.*—Possessors of private collections will often lend them for purposes of exhibition or study, if assured that they will be properly cared for. Such loan collections often become permanent gifts. Single specimens, or small groups of objects, are still more frequently offered on deposit, and such deposits, when within the province of the museum, should be encouraged. [...]

2. Collections which are encumbered by conditions as to manner of disposition and installation are usually sources of serious embarrassment. It is especially undesirable to accept either as a gift or as a loan any unimportant collection with the pledge that it shall be kept intact and installed as a unit. The acceptance of any collection, no matter how important, encumbered by conditions, is a serious matter, since no one can foresee how much these conditions may interfere with the future development of the museum.

3. Gifts, deposits and coöperation of all kinds may be greatly encouraged by liberal acknowledgment upon labels and in public reports. This is but simple justice to the generosity of the benefactor. It is also a legitimate way to gratify a natural and praiseworthy sentiment; for a collection to the accumulation of which a man has devoted a lifetime becomes so connected with his own personality that it is but natural that he should wish his name to be permanently associated with it. If acknowledgment of this kind is made upon the individual label of each specimen, this will usually fully satisfy the desire of the donor that the individuality of his gift should be preserved—an arrangement much more satisfactory than a plan requiring that the objects shall be kept together and treated as a unit of installation.

Gifts and deposits are also encouraged by the fact that the buildings are fire-proof, the cases so built as to afford perfect protection, and the scheme of installation dignified and attractive. Collections of great value may well be afforded accommodations of a specially sumptuous character and such protection, in the case of priceless objects, as is afforded by special electric attachments.

4. Since the plan and character of a museum is largely determined for all time by the nature of the collections which fall first into its possession, at the time of its organization, the authorities in charge of such an institution at the time of organization should be exceedingly careful in accepting materials which are to serve as a nucleus for its future growth. [...]

D. *Museum Officers.*

1. A museum without intelligent, progressive and well-trained curators is as ineffective as a school without teachers, a library without librarians, or a learned society without a working membership of learned men.

2. Museum administration has become one of the learned professions, and success in this field can only be attained as the result of years of study and expe-

rience in a well-organized museum. Intelligence, a liberal education, administrative ability, enthusiasm, and that special endowment which may be called 'the museum sense ' are prerequisite qualifications.

Each member of the museum staff should become an authority in some special field of research, and should have time for ·investigation and opportunity to publish its results.

3. A museum which employs untrained curators must expect to pay the cost of their education in delays, experimental failures and waste of materials.

4. No investment is more profitable to a museum than that in its salary fund, for only when this is liberal may the services of a permanent staff of men of established reputation be secured.

Around the nucleus of such a staff will naturally grow up a corps of volunteer assistants, whose work properly assisted and directed will be of infinite value.

5. Collaborators, as well as curators, may be placed upon the staff of a large museum, the sole duty of the former being to carry 'on investigations, to publish, and, if need be, to lecture.

6. Volunteers may be advantageously employed either as curators and custodians, or collaborators. Such cooperation is especially desirable and practicable when a museum is situated in the same town with a college or university, or, in a national capital where there are scientific bureaus connected with the government. Professors in a university or scientific experts in the government service often find it a great benefit to have free access to the facilities afforded by a museum, and are usually able to render useful service in return. Younger men in the same establishments may be employed as volunteer aids, either in the museum or in the field.

7. No man is fitted to be a museum officer who is disposed to repel students or inquirers, or to place obstacles in the way of access to the material under his charge.

8. A museum officer or employee should, for obvious reasons, never be the possessor of a private collection.

9. The museum which carries on explorations in the field as a part of its regular work has great advantage over other institutions in holding men of ability upon its staff and in securing the most satisfactory results from their activities. No work is more exhaustive to body and mind than the care of collections, and nowhere are enthusiasm and abundant vitality more essential. Every museum must constantly obtain new material through exploration, and it is better that this exploration should be done by the men who are to study the collections and arrange them in the museum than that this work should be placed in the hands of others.

10. In a large museum staff it is almost essential that certain persons should give their attention chiefly to administrative and financial matters, thus leaving their associates free from occupation of this description. The business affairs of a museum cannot be conducted with too great promptness and precision. It is desirable, however, that the administrative officers of a museum should be men who comprehend the meaning of museum work and are in sympathy with its highest aims; and that its business affairs and scientific work should be controlled by the same executive head.

E. Museum Buildings.

1. The museum building should be absolutely fireproof and substantially constructed; the architecture simple, dignified and appropriate—a structure worthy of the treasures to be placed within.

2. Above all things the interior should be well lighted and ventilated, dry and protected from dust. The halls should be well proportioned, the decoration simple and restful to the eye. No decorative features should be permitted which might draw attention from the collections or reduce the floor or wall space.

3. While the museum building should be planned with reference to the character of the collections it is to contain, the fact that unexpected development of rapid growth in some one direction may necessitate the rearrangement and reassignment of halls to different departments should always be kept in mind.

4. Since no two museums can be alike, there can be no general uniformity in their buildings. It is manifestly undesirable then that a board of trustees should erect a building for a museum before its character is decided upon or its staff appointed; or that the

opinion of the architect of a museum building should be allowed to outweigh the judgment of the experts who are responsible for its utilization after completion. Museum architecture affords no exception to the principle that an edifice should be perfectly adapted to the purpose for which it is designed. No architectural effect which lessens the usefulness of the building can be pleasing to an intelligent public.

F. Accessories to Museum Work.

1. A well-equipped museum requires as accessories to its work:

a. A reference library for the use of staff, students and visitors.

b. Laboratories for the classification of material, for the storage of the study-series, and for the use of students and investigators.

c. Workshops, for preparation, mounting and repair of specimens, and the making and adjustment of mounts and cases, and storage rooms for material not yet available. A printing press is a most essential feature.

d. An assembly hall, for public lectures, society meetings and special exhibitions.

e. A bulletin, or other official publication, to preserve the history of its activities, to maintain its standing among similar institutions, to serve as a means of communication with correspondents, and to exchange, for specimens and books for the library.

2. In addition to local accessories, the opportunity for exploration and field work are equally essential, not only because of considerations connected with the efficiency of the staff, but for the general welfare of the institution. Other things being equal, exploration can be carried on more effectively by the museum than by any other institution of learning, and there is no other field of research which it can pursue to better advantage.

The Future of Museum Work

A. THE GROWTH OF THE MUSEUM IDEA.

1. There can be no doubt that the importance of the museum as an agency for the increase and diffusion of knowledge will be recognized so long as interest in science and education continues to exist. The prediction of Professor Jevons in 1881, that the increase in the number of museums of some sort or other must be almost coextensive with the progress of real popular education, is already being realized. Numerous local museums have been organized within the past fifteen years in the midst of new communities. Special museums of new kinds are developing in the old centres, and every university, college and school is organizing or extending its cabinet. The success of the Museums Association in Great Britain is another evidence of the growing popularity of the museum idea, and similar organizations must of necessity soon be formed in every civilized country.

2. With this increase of interest there has been a corresponding improvement in museum administration. More men of ability and originality are engaging in this work, and the results of this are manifest in all its branches.

The museum recluse, a type which had many representatives in past years, among them not a few eminent specialists, is becoming much less common, and this change is not to be regretted. The general use of specimens in classroom instruction and, still more, the general introduction of laboratory work in the higher institutions, has brought an army of teachers into direct relations with museum administration, and much support and improvement has resulted.

3. Museum administration has become a profession, and the feeling is growing more and more general that it is one in which talents of a high order can be utilized. It is essential to the future development of the museum that the best men should be secured for this kind of work, and to this end it is important that a lofty professional standard should be established.

B. PUBLIC APPRECIATION OF THE MATERIAL VALUE OF COLLECTIONS.

1. The museum of nature or art is one of the most valuable material possessions of a nation or a city. It is, as has well been said, 'the people's vested fund.' It brings not only world-wide reputation, but many visitors and consequent commercial advantage. What Alpine scenery is to Switzerland, museums are to many neighboring nations. Some one declares that the Venus of Melos has attracted more wealth to Paris than the Queen of Sheba brought to King Solomon, and that but for the possession of their collections (which are intrinsically so much treasure) Rome and Florence would be impoverished towns.

This is thoroughly understood by the rulers of modern Italy. We are told that the first act of Garibaldi after he had entered Naples in 1860 was to proclaim the city of Pompeii the property of the nation, and to increase the appropriation for excavations so that these might be carried on with greater activity. He appreciated the fact that a nation which owns a gold mine ought to work it, and that Pompeii could be made for Naples and for Italy a source of wealth more productive than the gold mines of Sacramento. If capital is an accumulation of labor, as economists say, works of art which are the result of the highest type of labor must be capital of the most productive character. A country which has rich museums attracts to itself the money of travelers, even though it may have no other source of wealth. If, besides, the populace is made to understand the interest which is possessed by their treasures of art they are inspired with the desire to produce others of the same kind, and so, since labor increases capital, there is infinite possibility for the growth of national prosperity. It is evident then that too much money cannot be devoted to the formation of museums, to their maintenance, and to the education of the people by this means.

Suggestive in this same connection is this remark of Sir William Flower to the effect that the largest museum yet erected, with all its internal fittings, has not cost so much as a single fully equipped line of battleships, which in a few years may be either at the bottom of the sea or so obsolete in construction as to be worth no more than the material of which it is made.

This principle was well stated more than half a century ago by Edward Edwards in his treatise on the 'Administrative Economy of the Fine Arts in England,' as follows:

"In addition to the broad principle that public funds can never be better employed than in the establishment of institutions tending at once to refine the feelings and to improve the industry of the whole population, there is the subordinate but yet important ground of inducing and enabling private persons greatly to benefit the public by contributing towards the same end."

"No country," he continues, "has more cause to be proud of that munificent spirit of liberality which leads private individuals to present or bequeath to the community valuable' collections which it has been the labor of their lives to form; but to give due effect to this liberality and to make that effect permanent, it is necessary that the state step in and contribute its sanction and its assistance; and in many cases the very munificence of spirit which has formed an immense collection, and given birth to the wish to make it national, has, by its own excess, made that wish powerless without the active aid of, the legislature. The· actual cost, and still more the inherent value—of the collections of Sloane, Elgin and Angerstein, made them in reality gifts to the nation, although they could never have been acquired (without gross injustice to the descendants of the large minded collectors) had not Parliament made certain pecuniary advances on account of them. Whilst but for the foundation of the British Museum and of the National Gallery, the collections of Cracherode and Holwell Carr, of Beaumont, of Sir Joseph Banks and of King George III., would have continued in the hands of individuals."

C. PUBLIC APPRECIATION OF THE HIGHER FUNCTIONS OF MUSEUMS.

1. Museums, libraries, reading rooms and parks have been referred to by some wise person as 'passionless reformers,' and no better term can be employed to describe one of the most important of their uses.

The appreciation of the utility of museums to the great public lies at the foundation of what is known as 'the modern museum idea.' No one has written more eloquently of the moral influence of museums than Mr. Ruskin, and whatever may be thought of the manner in which he has carried his ideas into practice in his workingmen's museum, near Sheffield, his influence has undoubtedly done much to stimulate the development of 'the people's museum.' The same spirit inspired Sir Henry Cole when he said to the people of Birmingham in 1874:

"If you wish your schools of science and art to be effective, your health, your air and your food to be wholesome, your life to be long and your manufactures to improve, your trade to increase and your people to be civilized, you must have museums of science and art to illustrate the principles of life, wealth, nature, science, art and beauty."

I myself never shall forget the words of the late Sir Philip Cunliffe Owen, of South Kensington, who said to me some years ago:

"We educate our working people in the public schools, give them a love for refined and beautiful objects, and stimulate in them a desire for information. They leave school; go into the pursuits of town life, and have no means provided for the gratification of the tastes which they have been forced to acquire, and are condemned to a monotonous, depressing life in the midst of smoky chimneys and dingy walls. It is as much the duty of the government to provide them with museums and libraries for higher education as it is to establish schools for their primary instruction."

The development of the modern museum idea is indeed due to Great Britain in much greater degree than to any other nation, and the movement dates from the period of the great Exhibition of 1851, which marked an epoch in the intellectual progress of English speaking peoples.

2. The future of the museum, as of all similar public institutions, is inseparably associated with the continuance of modern civilization, by means of which those sources of enjoyment which were formerly accessible to the rich only, are now, more and more, placed in the possession and ownership of all the people (an adaptation of what Jevons has called 'the principle of the multiplication of utility') with the result that objects which were formerly accessible only to the wealthy, and seen by a very small number of people each year, are now held in common ownership and enjoyed by hundreds of thousands.

In this connection the maintenance of museums should be especially favored, because, as has been shown, these, more than any other public agency, are invitations to the wealthy owners of private treasures, in the form of collections, to give them in perpetuity to the public.

3. If it be possible to sum up in a single sentence the principles which have been discussed in the present paper, that sentence should be phrased in these words:

THE DEGREE OF CIVILIZATION TO WHICH ANY NATION, CITY OR PROVINCE HAS ATTAINED IS WELL INDICATED BY THE CHARACTER OF ITS PUBLIC MUSEUMS AND THE LIBERALITY WITH WHICH THEY ARE SUPPORTED.

Selection 3.18

CESARE BRANDI

Excerpts from "The Concept of Restoration," in *Theory of Restoration*

"The Concept of Restoration," in the Theory of Restoration, *first published as* Teoria de restauro, *Rome: Edizioni di Storia e Letteratura, 1963. New translation for this volume by Laurence Bouvard.*

RESTORATION IS GENERALLY taken to mean any operation intending to return a product of human activity back to its use. In this general idea of restoration, which is the same as what should more precisely be called a preconceptual scheme[1], can already be found a priori the concept of operating on an object of human activity; any other type of operation either in the biological or physical arena is not included, not even in this common idea of restoration. Therefore, in advancing from a preconceptual scheme to the concept itself, it is inevitable that the conceptualization will occur with regard to the variety of products of human activity to which this particular operation that is called restoration is applied. There will therefore be a restoration meant for industrially manufactured items and a restoration meant for works of art; but if the former is synonymous with repair or a return to the initial state, the latter differs from it, and not just in the many different operations with which it is carried out. In relation to industrial products, meaning those on the greatest scale going from the tiniest craft item, the goal of restoration will clearly be to restore the object's functionality, and thus, the nature of the restoring operation will be exclusively focused on realizing this aim.

[...]

As a product of human activity, a work of art makes a double case: the aesthetic case that corresponds to the fundamental concept of art where a work is a work of art; the competing historic case which sees it as a human object created in a certain time and place and found in a certain time and place. It is clear that it is not necessary to add the case for usefulness, which is the only advancement other human objects have, because this very usefulness, if it is present, as it is in architecture, cannot be taken into consideration on its own in a work of art, but rather must be taken on the basis of the work's physical consistency and on the two fundamental cases with which the work of art is constructed in order to have an impact on conscious perception.

Having re-established a connection between restoration and the recognition of a work of art as such, it is now possible to give it a definition: Restoration constitutes the methodological moment in which the work of art is recognized, in its physical consistency and in its dual aesthetic and historic polarity, with a view to transmitting it to the future.

[...]

The coexistence of the two purposes represents the dialectic of restoration, as exactly that methodological moment in which a work of art is recognized as such.

NOTE

1. For more on the "preconceptual scheme" see Cesare Brandi, *Celso o della* Poesia, Einaudi, Torino 1957, pp. 37ff.

JAMES MARSTON FITCH

"The Philosophy of Restoration: From Williamsburg to the Present"

Chapter 14 in his Selected Writings in Architecture, Preservation, and the Built Environment, *New York: W.W. Norton, 2006, pp. 172–81.*

This talk was given on May 15, 1992, at a symposium in Washington D.C., titled "Evolution of the Restoration Process: New Directions Symposium," sponsored by The American Architectural Foundation and the Washington Chapter of the Association for Preservation Technology. Also published in The Octogon, *American Architectural Foundation, 1993.*

I WAS CANDIDLY intimidated initially by the size of my assignment and the small time slot I was given to fill it until I got the most recent version of the agenda, when I learned I was assigned the task not only of opening this promising conference but also of closing it. So that gives me the opportunity to read the paper that I originally wrote for this occasion and then, at the end, to talk to you at a little greater length about matters which might crop up in the conference itself. I have another caveat, which is that in this prepared paper there are certain references to the profession of architecture which some of you may find derogatory. I look around the table and I see that practically every speaker here including myself is a member of the AIA. And this suggests that the preservationists have either captured the profession of architecture, or what's much more likely and much more dangerous, is that the profession of architecture has captured us. Historically there's been a certain ambivalence between the ambitions of the architectural profession, i.e., the creative artists, and the curatorial responsibilities of its preservationists, i.e., the caretakers. And this dichotomy exists right up to the present time. Indeed it may always exist, since it's really a dichotomy between two temperaments. It's one that this conference should face and do what it can to resolve, because many of our problems spring from these two attitudes toward the historic patrimony.

The Colonial Williamsburg Restoration, which began in the late 1920s, is a benchmark against which to measure subsequent developments in our field. But Historic Preservation, as an institutional affair, actually first appears with Miss Pamela Cunningham and the ladies of the Mount Vernon Ladies Association in 1859. Williamsburg was indeed our first fully professional restoration project, in which architects, landscape architects, archaeologists, and historians had collaborated on a programmatic basis. Developments in the subsequent sixty years have been mixed; enormous, on both conceptual and quantitative terms, it was these developments that led ultimately to the creation and the publication of the Secretary of the Interior's Standards, which attempted to establish another set of criteria for the field. These developments have been so immense that, in my own case, I have been compelled to add a modifying clause to the term historic preservation, as being the curatorial management of the built world, because it seems to me that nothing less can define conceptually the true scope of our work.

Our assignment has long ago passed beyond the preservation of isolated works of architecture, from historic buildings, houses, and gardens of upper class gentry to the conservation of whole districts and indeed whole towns, and from wholly urban sites to suburban and even rural ones. We have come to understand the equal cultural importance of all styles of buildings, folkloristic and vernacular as well as monumental and high style, and by the same token to broaden our definitions historically as extending from pre-Columbian dwelling sites to significant skyscrapers as recent as New York City's Lever Building and Seagram Building. In other words, willy-nilly, and without those of us in the historic preservation field necessarily willing it, our jurisdiction has broadened to awesome dimensions. Our stewardship of the whole built world is really the only adequate description of our responsibility. Parallel with this development, of course, there's been another development: the appearance of a movement for the preservation and conservation of the natural environment. For an audience like this, it's probably not necessary to stress this too much. Because the analogy between our efforts, those who preserve the manmade and those of the conservation movements to preserve the God-made world of nature are very close. Obviously here too the field has broadened immensely from local efforts to conserve Walden Pond or the California redwoods to international campaigns to conserve the ecological systems of tropical Brazil, or rescue northern Quebec from the giant hydro-Quebec project that threatens to flood the entire northern half of that province and drown entire native cultures. Such fields of action by historic preservationists and conservationists of nature are so far only parallel and symbiotic. They just more or less happen to run in the same general direction, they're tangent to each other. But of course they are rapidly being fused in the even larger global issues such as the carbon dioxide mantle which contributes to the dreaded greenhouse effect; and the hole in our ozone layer, which protects all life on earth from solar radiation.

So these are two larger macroscale developments of which, whether we like it or not, we're not only partners, but actually very important partners. And this establishes, it seems to me, the scale of our actions between the very microdiscussions that we're having here today (and when I say micro, I don't mean unimportant, I mean just what I say, micro), and the macrodiscussions, which our lame duck President is currently trying to evade at the Rio Conference, on the worldwide problems which confront us. They're not mutually exclusive; in fact, they're just different ends to the same environmental scale. These are huge problems, and our own contribution may constitute only a small part of the solution, but it constitutes a very important part.

I'd like to suggest that the preservation of the historic built world is critical to man's psychic and emotional well-being. Its preservation and adaptive reuse is also an urgent aspect of the conservation of energy. The clear understanding of these broader implications can only illuminate and enrich our everyday practice and put a much firmer basis under our arguments in defense of our field. As regards the first issue, the growing interest of modern man in his past, in antiques and antiquities, in old cities and gardens, in antiquities of every sort, seems to me an expression of his growing sense of alienation in his radically changing personal environment. In that connection, I'd like to modify the statements of surface, a superficial interest in the field. I think we ought to remind ourselves that the initial founders of this field were all civilians, they were all consumers. The little old ladies with blue hair and tennis shoes who met with Pamela Cunningham in 1859 were actually the founders of our movement, and these have been precisely the core of our movement ever since. They're the core of our movement today. You all know from what we draw our strength, it's from exactly this section of the population, of the so-called *amateur*, using the term in its original meaning: someone who does the work for the love of it and not the pay.

And I think it's critically important that professionals like us keep this constantly in mind, and keep constantly in close alliance with those sections of the population who long before we did recognized the importance of protecting the environment that we share. As regards these issues, of the way in which our habitat affects our psychic and emotional well being, we have only so far drawn upon generalities. I think all of us would agree on this, but there's a surprisingly small amount of factual data that we can cite to prove it. Man has developed across the millennia an environment which offered a dynamic equilibrium between status quo and change. Archaeology shows us that there's always been change in human society, but the rate of that change has been too slow to be perceptible to the individual. Environmental changes were seldom large or rapid enough to be stressful to the ancient societies which caused them. For example, the deforestation and desiccation of the Italian peninsula by the wood-burning brick and tile industries of Imperial Rome led to a radically drier and more hostile micro-environment. But the rate of change and hence the environmental degradation and habitat destruction was too gradual to be perceptible. It began to accelerate with the Industrial Revolution in the eighteenth century. It has been accelerating ever since until today it affects the personal environment of every creature on earth.

Ironically enough, the very instruments with which this brave new world was built—the steam engine, the electric motor, and the internal combustion engine—are now seen as the cause of the world's most profound environmental crisis. Waste gases from burning fossil fuels are causing the greenhouse effect, waste gases from compressors are destroying the ozone. The direct connection between human distress and environmental degradation, whether the smog in Mexico City or the nuclear meltdown in Chernobyl, is too well-established to need any amplification here. But so far as I am aware, there has been little effort to quantify the moral and psychic nourishment and support offered by the historic habitat to the people who inhabit it. I'm not trying to romanticize or gloss over the drawbacks of life in the slums of fifteenth-century Rome and Florence or the lives of blacks and Latinos in the Harlem of James Baldwin or Alvin Ailey. Both habitats were the locus of uniquely brilliant cultures which would not survive dispersion or transplantation to another venue. Such historic habitats should be restored with acceptable levels of amenities and new structures inserted. But they should be restored for their original population and not for a new population which has historically no right to be there in the first place. That, of course, is the great danger of most historic preservation on the urban scale today: it gentrifies neighborhoods. It exiles the original population (usually to other slums elsewhere), the people who historically probably built those buildings to begin with, and most certainly are entitled to benefit from the process of restoration itself. As far as I'm aware, psychologists have paid little attention to this special aspect of psychic disorientation as a result of physical displacement. I've read one such account which described the demoralized collapse of the U.S. Army in North Korea during the winter of 1952 as attributed to the sheer bitter foreignness of the environment in which the troops were

expected to function. Obviously there were other factors involved too, but they weren't the normal ones of lack of food, ammunition, clothing, and so forth. The psychologist came to the conclusion that the fundamental cause of this collapse of morale was that these men were expected to operate in an environment so new, so hostile, so strange, that they could no longer function. Obviously very few people have studied this kind of situation, and it may be very difficult to quantify, but many living Americans have felt this pain of lost habitat, whether of our own or our neighbors. This is a loss which Jane Jacobs described thirty years ago in her great book, *Death and Life of American Cities*. Certainly it was this sense of loss which has driven these anonymous citizens into the movement which we call historic preservation today. And their instinct has proven to be profoundly correct and often much earlier than the professionals themselves. If you are familiar with the struggle that went on in Savannah some thirty years ago to save that historic fabric, you must know that it was done in the face of every professional organization in the city, state, and nation. And it was done by something like twenty-two laymen and laywomen, who mobilized themselves into a kind of vigilante; there wasn't a single professional in the whole group. Yet it was the group that saved central Savannah from destruction by the planners, organized the restoration of dozens of historic houses and persuaded citizens to buy them and move back to them. It was they who saved Savannah and gave it its biggest industry: tourism. There is another way in which we can quantify the value of the built world that we're trying to save, and that is in terms of energy, the huge amount of deposited energy which this built world represents. The term, "embodied energy," is now used to describe all activity, human and mechanical, required to process any artifact, from a brick to a building. Thanks to computer technology, embodied energy can now be precisely calculated for any artifact, not only for man and machine hours expended on the site in the construction of the building, but also to trace all energy costs back through its transportation factors, to steel furnaces, brick kilns, salt mills, iron and coal mines, and so forth. In other words, you can trace the energy impact all the way back to its original raw materials. This enables us to express costs in BTUs rather than in dollars and cents: i.e., in absolute terms rather than in shifting values of dollars and cents. This enables us to express the value of a given building as being so many billion BTUs of energy. Before anyone proposes to dismantle it, to dislocate it, or throw it out, these values need to be considered very carefully. The results of this kind of computation are often astonishing though ignored usually within this profession. A study by the late Richard Stein, a New York architect, compared two high-rise structures of comparable size and shape and different only in their construction. One was a high energy-intensive steel frame system. The other was a low energy concrete system. The dollar cost of the two systems was found to be roughly equal. But the steel system ran 32 percent higher than the concrete system in terms of the energy consumed. If we brought this approach to bear in our own built world, we would have a totally new picture of what it was worth. Beyond all the photographic images that we see, or the images that we like or dislike, the basic fact is that all artifacts are worth something. I don't know if any comparable effort has been made in the field of historic preservation. In fact, this suggests that there might be a very useful doctoral dissertation by some American preservation student on precisely this subject. Obviously this would put us, on a stronger basis in dealing with the so-called practical world, to deal with it in terms that they are compelled to understand. It would support the realization that the old building, which the so-called realists propose to demolish, is a reservoir of energy. To demolish it will require additional energy. The new building proposed to be built in its place will require still more energy and all this activity of demolition, cleaning, and new construction will be carried on with motors, whether they're electric, gasoline, or diesel, will also consume more fossil fuels, further adding to our problems with the environment. The arguments for a careful curatorial attention to our built world are overwhelming, whether we regard the moral and physical well-being of the inhabitants or the simple cash value of the habitat itself. I begin this with a caveat: there are few architects who have not been

guilty of two errors in the handling of the historic fabric of our country: They saw their task as being exclusively that of constructing a new built world, and this misconception leads to a frightening neglect of, if not a contempt for, the already-built world around them. The planners were especially guilty of this conceptual posture, forgetting both the past and the present in their sponsorship of the notorious urban renewal program of the 50s and 60s, which came so near to destroying the heart of many American cities. The preservationists, whatever their shortcomings, were never guilty of this error, being by definition site-specific and time-specific. When Williamsburg was opened sixty years ago, it was all too easy to accuse preservationists of being parochial. Their favorite slander was, of course, "little old ladies with blue hair and tennis shoes" whose sole preoccupation was the protection of George Washington's last sleeping place. But time has proved this estimate of them quite wrong. In those American cities whose centers have been saved from the evisceration of urban sprawl and returned to some measure of viability, preservation has proved to be the central energizing force. In Portland, Maine; in Boston's North End; in Philadelphia's Society Hill; in the redemption of the historic centers of Charleston and Savannah and New Orleans; conversion of the little river in San Antonio from an open sewer into one of the beauty spots of the Southwest; in San Francisco, where the preservationist's spirit has put a limit on the height and number of high rise buildings in the center city and caused the demolition of the elevated highway which had cut the city off from its own harbor. Even in those Midwestern cities where urban attrition was most ferocious, in St. Louis, Cincinnati, and Kansas City, the preservation ethic is now helping to knit together the damaged fabric. And far from having preserved only those historic buildings which survived this flood of demolition, district preservation has also generated impressive amounts of new buildings. The only analogy I can think of is what happens in severe burn cases, when the transplantation of some healthy skin tissue from other parts of the body grafted onto the center of the burned tissue accelerates enormously the recovery of the whole damaged section. This phenomenon we've seen in every state in the country in which the preservation movement played a decisive role. This is most brilliantly demonstrated in the city of Boston, where it has affected—in fact, completely changed—-the ethics of the city planners, reversing their policies of thirty years ago, unraveling the outrageous network of highways by burying them and placing new parks where the highways were. The Boston planners have played an admirable role in this change of position. But I maintain that it's the preservationists who first saw the necessity for it and had the perspective to demand it, even though at the time, the realists said, "Oh, it may be a good idea, but it'll never happen." Just yesterday, Amtrak announced that it is proposing to take over the old Beaux Arts New York City Post Office Building, which of course looks across Eighth Avenue to where the great Pennsylvania Station once stood. And Amtrak says the reason for doing this is because New York City needs a port of entry such as it had in the Pennsylvania Station. A bunch of hard-headed railroad men finally speaking the language of preservation. Despite the ridicule that we've endured and the many defeats, the fact is that the preservation ethos has won, and won irrevocably. It will not be reversed. There may be temporary setbacks, I'm sure there will be. But the fact is that the majority of the American people understands that our whole habitat, man-made and God-made alike, is at risk. Unless steps are taken to preserve it, we'll all go down together.

I'm not, of course, suggesting that this battle of saving the built American world can be won without the full participation of planners and architects. They'll be the essential members of any team which will be able to rescue us from environmental disaster. But, in my opinion, they have to purge themselves of recent error. The planners must understand that they cannot handle the future until their feet are firmly planted in the actually existing present. And the architects must understand that they cannot meet the important demands of history with the historicizing eclecticism of the postmodernists. If these two professions can reorient their conceptual grasp of what the problem really is, then they'll be viable partners in the process of historic preservation. As for preservation-

ists themselves, God forbid that you think me smug, but I think the very agenda of today's session is proof enough that the preservationists have the curatorial task as well in hand as a squirrel with his acorn... .

Closing Remarks

One of the greatest problems of architects, planners, historians, preservationists, and our whole society is the unforgivable sloppy, slovenly, cynical fashion in which work is done. I don't want to sound like a Quaker minister, but the thing that distinguishes all the work that we've heard today was that it was principled. All the decisions were with principle, and without apology. They were not unrealistic. On the contrary, the reason that they were so thrilling was that they dealt with the most concrete and specific problems. There wasn't any suggestion of compromise. All of these people indicate that we live in a really very dangerous world, and as far as preservationists are concerned, we're surrounded by man-eating tigers who see in the present administration the chance to undo all the legislation of the last twenty to twenty-five years. So it's not that we think that we're home safe. There was no kind of false optimism in today's discussions. I think that this is a central lesson that we can learn from today. I don't think we can be accused of being self-deluding. I mean, I think we're just describing a simple fact when we say that. I think that this attitude clearly has been centered in the preservation field, not in our allied professions of architecture and planning, and has actually radiated these contiguous fields of activity. And in so far as we see planners behaving in a different manner from how they behaved in the 50s and 60s when they embraced urban renewal, in so far as they've changed their tune, I think it's due to the fact that they too have been alienated by this attitude toward the real built world.

Most of us are products of schools in which such factors as immaculate workmanship or pride in craft were never discussed. I doubt if there's anybody in this room who went through school or participated in a curriculum in which any of these aspects of work were discussed, unless you were lucky enough to have gone to one of the few preservation programs that have been established in recent years. So it seems to me that this is a principal lesson to learn from. I've heard for example that the preservationists are to blame for the postmodernists. Now in some kind of insane fashion, of course, this may be true, because it's the preservationists who have made the past respectable. We're guilty of that; there's no question about that. But no preservationist has ever advocated imitations or facsimiles, none that I have ever met. On the contrary, preservationists have always fought for preservation of the prototype, the original, first of its kind. Prototype in Greece meant the first blow. That's what prototype meant. And the battle to preserve, protect, and extend the influence of the prototype is not a bit of romantic nonsense; it's the most sensible and practical issue that we face today.

The moral we can draw from the lectures today: even the lectures that seemed in a way most dull, like those dealing with fire protection, every one of these lectures was focused on this very specific question. Really, ultimately, on the conservation of energy. Today, I think, we couldn't possibly have a more moral task than this or a more noble task. The organizers of this program are to be congratulated, and I think the [American Architectural] Foundation and the Association for Preservation Technology must be uniquely pro-preservation agencies to organize such a celebration. I've had now about sixty years' experience in the architectural field, largely from the vantage point of the architect. It was my increasing disillusion with the vantage point of the architects that led me by degrees to look at the world from the vantage point of this conference. I am really convinced that this is uniquely the way that we have to look at the world, if indeed the real world is to be saved. I think you're on the right track. So, good luck to all of you.

Selection 3.20

JUKKA JOKILEHTO

"Preservation Theory Unfolding"

Future Anterior 3.1 (Summer 2006): 1–9.

Present Debate

While examining the history of modern preservation practices, one notices how these have evolved from individual initiatives to national legislation, subsequently becoming the basis for international doctrine. The role of international organizations, and particularly of the United Nations Educational, Scientific and Cultural Organization (UNESCO) has however become increasingly decisive. It has been sustained by the activities of the International Centre for the Study of the Preservation and Restoration of Cultural Property (ICCROM) and the International Council on Monuments and Sites (ICOMOS), and guided by international conventions and recommendations. In terms of theory, the *International Charter for the Conservation and Restoration of Monuments and Sites* (the Venice Charter) in 1964, started a compendium of international doctrine, which gradually expanded the thinking process. Alternatively, as a legal instrument, the UNESCO 1972 *Convention Concerning the Protection of the World Cultural and Natural Heritage* (the World Heritage Convention) has become crucial. By March 2005, it had been ratified by 181 states—nearly all the countries of the world. More recently, UNESCO has adopted the *Convention for the Safeguarding of the Intangible Cultural Heritage* (2003), emerging from the earlier *Proclamation of Masterpieces of the Oral and Intangible Heritage of Humanity* (1997). We should also remember that the UNESCO *Universal Declaration on Cultural Diversity* (2001) was groundbreaking in recognizing the value of all cultures. Through this process, new notions of heritage, such as "cultural landscape" and "intangible heritage," are rapidly having an impact on national and local policies.

The current debate has raised a number of issues that are significant for the formulation of principles and philosophy for safeguarding heritage resources as well as reviving a new interest in preservation-conservation-restoration theory. At the same time, we should take note that the meanings that we associate even with familiar words can vary from language to language and from country to country. For example, the North American expression "historic preservation" would generally correspond to "conservation of historic buildings" in the United Kingdom and "restoration of monuments" in Latin countries. International documents often use the terms "conservation" or "restoration," depending on the emphasis of treatment. For example, the Venice Charter emphasizes that "conservation of monuments" should imply maintenance and appropriate use, while restoration is considered a highly specialized operation, aiming "to preserve and reveal the aesthetic and historic value," respecting original material and authenticity.

The principles emerging from the debate have sometimes been accused of "Euro-centricity," intending that they would be mainly applicable to historic monuments that correspond to those in the Mediterranean region. The 1994 Nara Conference on Authenticity was an attempt to rebalance the debate and take into account the cultural situations outside the Western world. During the conference, there was a hard debate between those who emphasized the importance of "monuments" and those who stressed the qualities of "vernacular built heritage." In fact, the question was raised whether the whole concept of "authenticity" actually existed outside Europe![1] Special attention was drawn to cultural diversity and the "authenticity of values." Furthermore, in the French language, a fundamental difference was seen between the concepts of *"monument"* and *"monument historique,"* which are defined by Alois Riegl as "memorial" and "historic building."[2]

Notwithstanding all of these differences in meanings and approaches, the conference was able to draft

the Nara Document on Authenticity, which was only finalized after additional efforts by the two rapporteurs, Raymond Lemaire and Herb Stovel. We should remember that Lemaire had been rapporteur of the drafting group that produced the Venice Charter in 1964. In the new document, he stressed material authenticity and the spirit of this Charter. Stovel, on the other hand, represented a younger generation, and gave importance to cultural diversity and the continuity of traditions. Both of these issues were integrated into the Nara Document, which emphasizes the fundamental importance of cultural diversity and "the respect for other cultures and all aspects of their belief systems."[3] The document notes that the judgments of values attributed to heritage may differ from culture to culture,[4] but it also insists that the importance of "credibility and truthfulness of related information sources be verified in each case."[5] The concept of authenticity thus emerges as a notion related to the credibility and truthfulness of sources of information, which may include a great number of parameters depending on the character and values of the heritage concerned. At the same time, the truthfulness, i.e., "authenticity" and "genuineness," of the sources of information must be verified.

Restoration Theory

A line must be drawn between principles or ethics of preservation, on the one hand, and the relevant theory, on the other. International doctrinal documents, such as the Venice Charter or the Nara Document on Authenticity, offer principles, which are often referred to in debates. The *US Secretary of the Interior's Standards of Preservation* and the Australian *Burra Charter* have comparable sets of principles. However, the theory of restoration or preservation means something different, and should be understood as the description of the methodology of approach to the critical survey and assessment of a heritage, and the step-by-step decisions for its treatment and maintenance.

A fundamental reference for the theory of restoration was published by Cesare Brandi in 1963. In his work, Brandi distinguished between the common understanding of "restoration" as "any intervention that permits a product of human activity to recover its function,"[6] and the restoration of works of art, which he defines as "... the methodological moment in which the work of art is recognized, in its physical being, and in its dual aesthetic and historical nature, in view of its transmission to the future."[7] Brandi's name is well known outside Italy, but little other than his theory of restoration has been translated. His other works, however, *are* essential for understanding his thought and his definition of the work of art. Paul Philippot, the former director of ICCROM, has translated a fundamental book by Brandi, *Le Due Vie* ("the two paths"), into French. Without going into more depth here, we still want to emphasize that Brandi's concept of art is in the human mind, and therefore, a work of art cannot be conceptualized in the same way as other types of existing physical reality.[8]

In his lectures at ICCROM in the 1970s, Philippot often emphasized restoration as a fundamentally cultural problem. Restoration and preservation of cultural heritage should thus be understood as a form of culture—another aspect of modernity of our time. It is based on values generated by us, values that can be quite different from those in the traditional society. Today, we are experiencing the phenomenon of globalization, but we are concurrently aware of the conflicts between modern societies and communities that have retained their traditional beliefs and ways of life. These differences can be seen in various realms, such as religion and family life. In such situations, the question can be raised whether the international principles of preservation and the theory of restoration can be applicable and, if not, what is the alternative.

Taking in to account the notion of cultural diversity as declared by UNESCO, we should respect the values and the specificities of culture and heritage in different contexts. Following Brandi's definition, restoration is a process in which the first phase consists of the "recognition" of the heritage and understanding what it signifies. It is only then that an intervention can be contemplated. Recognition is a fundamental part of the process, because this is the basis

that will guide one's critical judgment of the necessary analysis and treatments that should follow. It is not by accident that Brandi's theory has been called in Italian "*restauro critico*" or restoration based on critical judgment.

"Restoration" ("conservation," "preservation") can thus be defined as a cultural approach to our inherited environment and understood as a methodology based on critical judgment of the qualities and the identification of the significance and associated values of a heritage resource. The principles indicated in restoration charters can be kept in mind as a general guidance. However, the process must necessarily be based on a critical judgment. Therefore, restoration cannot be a template distinguished from miles away. It must take into account the specificity of each heritage as a resource reflecting the cultural and historical context where it was created and with which it associates. David Lowenthal has spoken about the past as "a foreign country."[9] One should approach any heritage with the same critical mind, in such a way that the methodology is not dependent on the "nationality" or the age of the heritage.

Since the 1994 Nara Conference on Authenticity, there has been ongoing debate about the applicability of restoration principles in different cultures. It is obvious that no principles should be applied without a critical recognition and assessment of the character and significance of a particular heritage. Such a notion has been recognized by Seung-Jin Chung of Korea, who has claimed that East Asian societies are determined in relation to the spiritual and naturalistic sensibilities of their culture and that such ideas are more appropriate than the approaches ("mainly aesthetically oriented"!) developed in Western countries.[10] Following from the previous and also referring to the Nara Document, one can obviously conclude that each heritage needs to be based on the knowledge and understanding of its qualities and attributed values. The differences and similarities of our cultures can be discussed at length. In this discussion, we can also refer to the on-going international debate and research on new types of heritage. Each culture has its own spirituality, relationship with nature and environment, and aesthetic appreciation.

Heritage Values

The World Heritage Convention has been remarkably successful in encouraging the various states to identify suitable properties that meet the requirements of outstanding universal value. By 2005, there were 812 sites in total on the World Heritage list, including 628 cultural, 160 natural, and twenty-four mixed (both cultural and natural values). With the growing number of sites on the list, the evaluation for inscription has become an increasingly demanding operation. As long as a site is well known, such as the Taj Mahal or Yellowstone Park, there is enough reference material to assess it. However, evaluation becomes much more demanding when a state proposes a cultural landscape, a vernacular settlement, or an archaeological site of which the significance has only recently been recognized and not yet described in general or art histories. It is also true that the so-called Western values tend to be overwhelmingly present in international reference literature. Therefore, it is not always easy to find unbiased assessment of lesser known sites, particularly in regions that have been less studied. One of the future challenges for the World Heritage Convention is certainly to promote new research in to the history and heritage of the different peoples and cultures of the world.

The UNESCO World Heritage Global Strategy meeting of 1998 in Amsterdam stated that:

> The outstanding universal value characterizing cultural and natural heritage should be interpreted as an outstanding response to issues of universal nature common to or addressed by all human cultures. In relation to natural heritage, such issues are seen in bio-geographical diversity; in relation to culture in human creativity and resulting cultural diversity.[11]

Taking further this line of thought, ICOMOS has studied the representation of the World Heritage list in relation to three frameworks: 1) typological framework of heritage categories, 2) chronological regional framework, and 3) thematic framework. Of these, the thematic framework is the key for the identification of the universal value of a particular site, and it lists the following main themes: expressions of society, creative responses and continuity, spiritual responses, utilizing natural resources, movement of peoples, and developing technologies.

This is an open framework which can be edited and provided detailed subcategories if necessary. Once a potential heritage resource has been identified, the relevant themes should be determined. Subsequently, for the World Heritage purposes, it will be necessary to make a comparative study of the relative significance of the site seen in its chronological and cultural-regional contexts. Such studies are increasingly important not only to inscribe something on the UNESCO List, but also to define appropriate strategies for the national territory.

Heritage Diversity

The definition of what is intended by "heritage" has been greatly broadened in the late twentieth century. In addition to the previous categories of historic buildings and historic towns, there is increasing interest in identifying industrial heritage, modern architecture and town planning schemes, and cultural landscapes. While certain regions of the world have preserved a rich heritage of historic structures built in stone and brick, others may have buildings mainly in wood, mud or straw. Here, the question is sometimes less about the preservation of the historicity of materials, and more about the continuity of traditional use of materials and techniques. Therefore, rather than speaking about the authenticity of ancient elements, the emphasis may be in the continuity of genuine traditions and how such continuity can, if at all possible, be guaranteed in the future.

The ICOMOS Charter on the Built Vernacular Heritage (adopted in 1999) states:

> [Vernacular building] is a continuing process including necessary changes and continuous adaptation as a response to social and environmental constraints. The survival of this tradition is threatened world-wide by the forces of economic, cul-

tural and architectural homogenization. How these forces can be met is a fundamental problem that must be addressed by communities and also by governments, planners, architects, conservationists and by a multidisciplinary group of specialists.[12]

This consideration places the definition of heritage values in a much broader context, including culture itself, such as the intangible heritage, the subject of the 2003 UNESCO Convention. It can be stated that all heritage has an intangible aspect. A work of the imagination by humankind of any era and culture is based on ideas and concepts that have guided material expressions. In a traditional living settlement or cultural landscape, however, we are dealing with values and ways of life that may change over time. In traditional societies, it was common for older generations to instruct the young in order to guarantee continuity. In our increasingly globalizing world, such indoctrination is rare. Nevertheless, even modern preservation policies should pay due attention to increasing awareness and training. In traditional rural settlements, the challenge is to maintain the integrity of the place, particularly in terms of materials and techniques, which in themselves represent traditional continuity. On the other hand, there are plenty of examples in countries with wood construction, including North America and Northern Europe as well as East Asia, where modern design has been well integrated within traditional context. The question is about finding a critical balance.

In Japan and Korea, there has long been legislation encouraging the identification of skilled persons or groups of persons who agree to pass their knowledge and know-how of traditional building crafts to younger generations. Even the Council of Europe has long made efforts to promote training of craftspersons. Additionally, the question is about building a market for traditional crafts and making such solutions accepted by [a] modern way of life. Therefore, it is fundamental to improve public awareness of the value and role of traditional crafts and materials as well as to provide constructive examples of suitable solutions.

The Way Forward

We have discussed various issues related to preservation theory and its implementation in the future. In looking forward, the first challenge in this process is raising awareness of the existence of such a theory—defined as a methodology and based on critical judgment—and introducing this into relevant education programs. ICCROM has long been working on developing the application of preservation methodology into training programs. ICOMOS instead has contributed through systems of communication involving professionals. The most recent initiative, in 2005, has been the establishment of an International Committee for Preservation Theory. We have stressed the notion of cultural diversity and the need to take into account the specificity and values of heritage. We should not forget, however, that it is also necessary to identify common parameters and definitions that can be shared by all. This is particularly important for the credibility of international collaboration and the implementation of such initiatives as the World Heritage List. In this context, for example, the concept of authenticity has been defined in reference to truthfulness of the sources of information, which already states a common reference applicable to other cultures. A shared critical methodology is fundamental, but it should also offer the possibility to take into account the specificities of heritage resources in different cultures and times.

Another challenge is the continuation of surveying of our heritage, both cultural and natural, and the recognition of its significance as a vital component of the culturally and environmentally sustainable development of the world. Furthermore, past responsibility for heritage management was often assumed by a form of public authority. Since the 1980s, however, due to increasing privatization and the expansion of the notion of heritage, problems cannot be faced by a single authority alone. On the contrary, it is the responsibility of the society as a whole. While the role of specialists and experts in the preservation process remains vital, the informed participation of the other stakeholders is imperative. Since the nineteenth century, non-governmental organizations (NGOs) have been fundamental promoters of this process, not only in the Western world and other industrialized countries, but also increasingly in the so-called developing world. The participation of a large number of interest groups and stakeholders can only become meaningful if there are common objectives based on shared values.

Going beyond the mere principles, the scope of preservation theory is to define heritage and the methodology for its preservation and restoration. However, it can only be reached through an appropriate system of negotiation, arbitration and conflict solving, sustained by a fitting legal and administrative framework. Communication is an important tool for preservationists. In fact, preservation is communication, an understanding of and dialogue with the existing built environment, and it means information flows between all stakeholders.

ENDNOTES

1. Knut Einar Larsen, ed. *Nara Conference on Authenticity, Nara, Japan, 1–6 November 1994: Proceedings.* (Trondheim: Tapir Publishers, 1995), 329.

2. Ibid., 101.

3. *Nara Document on Authenticity* (1994), par. 6.

4. Ibid., par. 11.

5. Ibid., par. 12.

6. Cesare Brandi, *Theory of Restoration*, trans. C. Rockwell. (Rome: Instituto Centrale del Restauro, 2005), 47.

7. Ibid., 48.

8. Ibid., 27.

9. David Lowenthal, *The Past is a Foreign Country* (Cambridge: University Press, 1985).

10. Seung-Jin Chung, "East Asian Values in Historic Conservation," *Journal of Architectural Conservation,* vol. 11., no. 1. (March 2005), 55–70.

11. B. Von Droste et al. eds., *Linking Nature and Culture, Report of the Global Strategy Natural and Cultural Heritage Expert Meeting,* Amsterdam, UNESCO (March 1998), 221.

12. H. Cleere, S. Denyer and M. Petzet, in an ICOMOS study compiled by J. Jokilehto, *The World Heritage List: Filling the Gaps—an Action Plan for the Future* (Munich, 2005). The study is also available in PDF format on ICOMOS website: www.icomos.org.

PAUL PHILIPPOT

Excerpts from "Historic Preservation: Philosophy, Criteria, Guidelines"

Preservation and Conservation: Principles and Practices: Proceedings of the North American International Conference, Williamsburg, Virginia, and Philadelphia, Pennsylvania, September 10–16, 1972. *Ed. by Sharon Timmons, Washington, D.C.: The Preservation Press and the Smithsonian Press, 1976, 367–82.*

THE ORIGINS OF historic preservation are linked with those of the modern historical consciousness, which matured toward the end of the 18th century.[1] The word *preservation*—in the broadest sense, being equivalent in some cultures to *conservation* or restoration—can be considered, from this point of view, as expressing the modern way of maintaining living contact with cultural works of the past. This way of maintaining contact evolved after the outburst of the Industrial Revolution and the development of a historical conscience brought an end to the traditional link with the past, which may be said to have lasted, in various forms, from the origin of civilization to the end of the 18th century.

Indeed, since this rupture, the past has been considered by Western man as a completed development, which he now looks at from a distance, much as one looks at a panorama. On one hand, this new historical distance has produced the conditions necessary for a more objective, scientific approach to the past in the form of historical knowledge. But purely scientific knowledge cannot in itself insure the continuity that was guaranteed by tradition. To bridge the gap that the historical conscience opened between the past and the present, a new kind of contact developed, based on the feeling that the past has indeed been lost, but continues to live through nostalgia. This romantic nostalgia of the past, which replaced the traditional continuity between the past and the present, combines historicism and nationalism and has led, since the end of the 18th century, not only to various revivals of past styles of art and architecture but also to an unfortunate confusion of preservation and reconstruction.

A scientific archaeological approach to the past and nationalistic revival are closely interwoven in Eugène Viollet-le-Duc's theory[2] and in all 19th-century restoration work in Europe, where these ideas have not yet died out completely. Modern nationalism also seems to foster revivals and reconstructions in most young countries that have recently become independent.

In the meantime, however, the scientific approach to the past has surpassed national borders and now considers products of all cultures as part of one cultural patrimony of mankind. Living contact with this patrimony can no longer be achieved in revivals—nor, consequently, in reconstructions based on the symbolic value given to a style of the past by romantic nationalism. It can be achieved only through a new approach that will acknowledge simultaneously the uniqueness of every creation of the past and the distance from which it is appreciated in the present.

John Ruskin was the first to express a full awareness of the consequences of this break in the continuity of tradition introduced by the development of the modern historical consciousness:

Neither by the public, nor by those who have the care of public monuments, is the true meaning of the word restoration [meaning the reconstruction, whether total or partial, suggested by revivalism] understood. It means the most total destruction which a building can suffer: a destruction out of which no remnants can be gathered: a destruction accompanied with false description of the thing destroyed. Do not let us deceive ourselves in this important matter; it is impossible, as impossible as to raise the dead, to restore [meaning reconstruct] anything that has ever been great or beautiful in architecture. That which I have above insisted upon as the life of the whole, that spirit which is given only by the hand and eye of the workman, can never be recalled. Another spirit may be given by another time, and it is then a new building; but the spirit of the dead workman cannot be summoned up, and commanded to direct other hands, and other thoughts.[3]

Modern developments of aesthetics and principles of historical criticism and philology can only confirm the truth expressed by Ruskin.[4] Each work of art, each piece of decoration, each historic document is unique and cannot be repeated without faking. It is like a dead language: One can know and understand Latin or Sanskrit, but one cannot speak these languages anymore because such speech could not be genuine expression. The genuine voice of the past is exactly what must be safeguarded by preservation/conservation. The survival of traditional crafts should not mislead one here. What survives of the craftsman's tradition in the new industrial world is its practical skill, and while this skill can certainly be of great use in conservation, it is no longer a genuine expression either of the past or of the present. To ignore this would mean to close one's eyes to the fact that the modern historical consciousness has irreversibly broken the traditional continuity and, therefore, would lead to a faked expression. If the conservation of an object or building requires an intervention or substitution, the intervention should be recognized as a modern, critical action. How to integrate the modern intervention without faking the original object is an essential question of conservation, and the way in which the modem intervention is handled makes the difference between the restorer or conservator and the traditional craftsman.

What to Preserve and Inventory: Criteria

Every object (or complex of objects) that is recognized to be of artistic or historical significance is entitled to be safeguarded as an item of cultural value and as a legacy of the past to the present and the future. The recognition of such significance, however, does not depend upon the fulfillment of preestablished criteria, but rather upon the progress of the development of the historical consciousness and the culture of the people involved. This progress is expressed by the work of historians and the sensitiveness of cultivated people.[5] As a matter of fact, the range of interest

in this connection has been continuously expanding since the beginning of the 19th century, progressively including all cultures of the world and all kinds of folklore and reaching up to the threshold of the present, which in turn will deserve protection whenever its objects qualify as items with artistic or social value. The universality of this modern viewpoint, as compared to the classicistic or nationalistic one, does not prevent some fluctuation of values from one nation to the other. In fact, this fluctuation is quite justified inasmuch as the significance of the past is indeed relative to the peoples who recognize it as their past. Any other view of universal values would be a purely abstract one.

Since the first step toward conservation is to establish an inventory of what should be conserved, criteria that recognize the creative quality, documentary significance and impact of the object on human consciousness must be established. Such criteria will, of course, never crystallize in fixed rules but will reflect the development of each country's culture.

Methodology

THE APPROACH TO THE OBJECT

The first operation in any conservation process is to assess accurately the substance of the object to be safeguarded. This may seem obvious but, alas, is not, and ignoring this operation by considering it to be obvious may result in irreparable mistakes. The problem's main aspects may be summarized in three questions: (1) What is to be considered the whole of the object, to which all operations must be referred? (2) What is the context of the object? and (3) What has been the history of the object?

The whole of the object. The importance of the whole must be stressed because positivistic habits of classification have accustomed us to divide various arts according to technique and to split the whole of a monument into various pieces scattered throughout various sections of museums and galleries. What was once a Gothic altarpiece may be dismantled into isolated sculptures, easel paintings and decorative carvings, the result being that the experience of the altarpiece as a whole has to be rediscovered. This rediscovery includes, for example, defining the artistic relationships that existed among sculptures, reliefs and paintings.

The same situation applies to architecture, which today is often reduced to that part of the building that can be expressed in architectural drawings, thereby arbitrarily separating structure and decoration. One especially vivid example of this kind of separation concerns the plasterwork within a structure and its color. The result of this separation is that today original plasterwork is becoming so rare that it is difficult to know its genuine character in various periods and styles.

Germans have a convenient word to stress this importance of the whole of the monument. By *Gesamtkunstwerk*, they mean the unity resulting from the cooperation of the various arts and crafts that combine to make a monument and cannot be divided from it.

It is obvious that what is a whole must be treated consistently as a whole, and this implies that close cooperation among various specialists in preservation—architects, conservators, artisans—under one consistent policy is necessary. On the other hand, each fragment will have to be treated as such, keeping in mind the whole to which it once belonged.

Context. Context refers to an object's immediate surroundings, inasmuch as these determine the approach and, thus, the correct interpretation of the object; that is, the frame of a picture, traditional surroundings of a monument that are essential to its scale and significance and social circumstances in which the object is or was used, this consideration being especially important for liturgic or ethnographic objects.

In some cases, the context may be an object, as is the case, for instance, of minor architecture in historic centers, when no individual building is a work of art but the whole becomes a monument in itself (e.g., the Campo dei Fiori in Rome). An object should never be deprived of its context, if the object is to avoid becoming isolated and "museumized," that is, segregated from life.

The recognition of the value of the whole and the object's context leads logically to the principle that every object should, whenever possible, be conserved in situ if one wants to save the full value of the whole

and of the parts. This applies to wall paintings, altarpieces and sculptured decoration. It also applies to architecture and to its architectural or natural surroundings. Exceptions to this principle must be made, however (e.g., in situations where a fresco or building can be preserved only by disassembling and moving it, even though the movement will produce unavoidable and irreparable damage). The open-air museum is an emergency solution and is almost a contradiction in itself, since vernacular architecture is existentially linked to its surroundings, even more so than major monuments that can impose themselves on their surroundings. Hence, there is the almost inherent tendency of the open-air museum to evolve into a Disneyland: No longer is it a preservation of history in the present, but rather a projection of fantasy into objects of the past, which is a special variety of faking.

The object's history. A monument of the past, be it architecture, sculpture, painting or any combination of these forms of art, has come to man through time and history. During this period, it usually undergoes changes of various kinds—additions, reductions or modifications in shape, use or sense due to man's interventions and material alterations due to physical and chemical processes.[6] Furthermore, the way the object is perceived is continuously evolving as the result of the historic development of a culture, especially aesthetic sensitiveness. Each new experience in art changes one's view of the history of all art in the way that one's vision of colors is no longer the same after experiencing Impressionism.

All this history must be taken into consideration when establishing what is the whole to be safeguarded. Indeed, history and time cannot be undone; they are irreversible. However, those additions that are recognized to be of no historical or artistic significance and that distort or obliterate the object can rightly be removed. But removal always requires a justified decision, thus showing the inescapable freedom and cultural responsibility of the restorer in making history.

It is an illusion to believe that an object can be brought back to its original state by stripping it of all later additions. The original state is a mythical, unhistorical idea, apt to sacrifice works of art to an abstract concept and present them in a state that never existed.

Tendencies, much supported by archaeologists, to strip medieval churches of their baroque or even 19th-century decoration in order to discover naked walls without their original plaster or furnishing and to undo old restorations of classical sculpture have led to a great deal of destruction without ever succeeding in reestablishing the appearance of the work at a real historic moment.[7]

The patina resulting from material alterations of an object has been the subject of much controversy, especially in the field of easel paintings.[8] This, however, should be considered as only a particular case of a more general problem. Physical and/or chemical alterations of original materials are unavoidable and usually irreversible. They may, however, up to a point, be anticipated by the artist or accepted as an additional aesthetic value, like the traditional acceptance of the patina of bronzes, sometimes called "noble" patina. The point when such alterations are felt to be distortions of the object's value and not enhancements of its aesthetic quality cannot be defined objectively and is, therefore, a matter of critical interpretation and cultural responsibility. It should be clear, in any case, that simple removal of the patina on a bronze or a painting will not recover the object's original appearance, but only uncover the present state of the original material. Furthermore, what is the original appearance? At what moment can it be fixed? Obviously, the original state is an abstract idea and not a historical reality. Bear in mind also that any attempt at removing a patina, which is, of course, a modification of the original material, will necessarily result in a further alteration of the material. It should be admitted, therefore, that the patina is a part of the object's original substance as transmitted to man through history and that any attempt to eliminate it will damage the original substance and introduce a historical contradiction, inasmuch as removal will show an old object in fresh, or new-looking, material. For example, the drastic cleaning of pictures or bronzes is in no way an objective approach to the object, and it would be easy to show that the decision in recent times to so treat an object being "restored" has been greatly determined by a definite aesthetic approach, influenced by the new sensitivity to materials developed by Expressionism and the Bauhaus.

The cleaning of facades, inaugurated in Paris as a matter of political prestige, brings to the fore the complicated nature of this problem. Assuming that cleaning will not harm the original material, it remains that the appearance of each building will look "correct" only when all the surrounding buildings are equally clean, but the patina, or dirt, forms again so quickly on the freshly cleaned facades that such a general unity is never reached. What results is that cleaned buildings look like white ghosts in their darkened context. Even regular maintenance is hardly a solution as long as the causes of pollution are not eliminated.

THE FRAGMENTED OBJECT; LACUNAE AND THEIR INTEGRATION; ARCHAEOLOGY AND MUSEUM OBJECTS

The problem of lacunae (i.e., missing parts of objects) and the object in fragments may best be approached from the viewpoint used in dealing with museum objects and archaeological remains which, being free from the requirements of practical functions, allow for the strictest interpretation of basic principles. The lacuna, be it in a picture, sculpture or monument of architecture, appears to be an interruption of the continuity of the object's artistic form and its rhythm. Since the object's completeness is no longer a necessity (and often, the fragmented object has acquired a value in its fragmented state, as is the case for a ruin or a torso), the only aim of restoration should be to reduce or eliminate the disturbance caused by lacunae in such a way that the intervention can be unmistakably identified as such (i.e., as a critical interpretation).

Philology has shown the way to achieve that aim in a long tradition of the editing of old manuscripts. In the editing, the missing word or words are never added by the editor unless they can be safely reconstructed, and this interpretation is then clearly indicated as a reconstruction by the use of special printing devices and footnotes. Missing words are never written on the original manuscript. Since in the case of a work of art the editing has to be done on the object itself, the same principles require that special practical devices be applied to a painting, sculpture or monument of architecture, while the basic philosophy is fundamentally the same as that applied in philology. Therefore, in each case, it is necessary to make a distinction between lacunae that may and lacunae that should not be reintegrated.

Reintegration will be justified only when lacunae are relatively small and so situated that there can be no doubt about what was lost and when the new work is sufficiently limited so as to avoid the reconstruction's appearing to quantitatively overwhelm the original parts and making the whole seem to be a fake or a copy. The reintegration (used in preference to the terms "retouching" and "in painting") should then aim to reestablish the continuity under normal conditions, while being easily identified on closer inspection. There are various technical solutions to this problem, and the restorer will have to use his artistic feeling, as well as his knowledge of materials, to find the best answer, one essential point being the consistency of the reintegration system. Hatchings in paintings and changes of material or of surface treatment (akin to but different from the original) in sculpture and architecture have given satisfactory results.

When lacunae cannot be reintegrated because this process would be too hypothetical or because there would be more lacunae reintegrated than there would be remains of the original, restoration should consist of treating lacunae in such a way that their disturbance is reduced to a minimum. As Cesare Brandi has shown in a penetrating study where he refers to the structures of perception according to Gestalt psychology,[9] the treatment should consist of preventing lacunae from becoming so patterned over the work that the original image recedes into the background. Lacunae should, on the contrary, be made to appear as the background before which the work is perceived. The disturbance due to lacunae will then be reduced to a minimum. Here again, the technical devices may be many, but consistency in approach is essential. As a rule, the object's technical construction, especially that of a painting, will suggest solutions, such as lacunae being treated as the receding surface of the ground or the support or arriccio in wall paintings, with a conveniently adjusted texture and color if necessary.

A special problem arises in the archaeological field. A ruin is normally considered the object to be preserved, not as a fragment of the object, since ruins themselves are cultural objects with their own specific emotional values and appeals to the imagination, which would be completely destroyed by an attempt to restore the ruin to its original state.

There is one case, however, where such an intervention may be contemplated. When all fragments of a part or the whole of a building have been preserved and can be reassembled with the certainty that in so doing the original shape is restored, then one may be justified in performing an *anastylosis* (i.e., the reconstruction of the object from its scattered fragments), with modern additions being strictly limited to what is required for static safety and justified as reintegration. Obviously, anastylosis can be contemplated only when the building is of dry masonry (i.e., joints allow for an exact restitution of the original shape) and pieces have not suffered deformation by erosion.

When joints are made with mortar, as in brick structures, disassembling and reassembling even a complete building will result in faking, as the old mason's peculiar rhythm in laying the bricks is replaced by a mechanical dryness and hardness of line due to the modern way of working.

As is stated in the Venice Charter of 1964, anastylosis is the only justified form of archaeological reconstruction, because it is the only one that can reestablish the genuine object. Any other kind of reconstruction that the archaeologist may be able to achieve on the basis of fragments, iconographic documents or descriptions can refer only to a knowledge of the lost object. Such a knowledge cannot be identified with the real object without faking it should, therefore, be materialized in drawings or models, but never in actual reconstruction of the object.

The Object Still in Use and Its Context

Once the guidelines for safeguarding an object's value have been defined in the "pure" situation of archaeological and museum objects, one may consider what special adjustments may be necessary for objects that have retained a practical social function; this refers in particular to architecture and to ethnographic objects in traditional societies.

As regards architecture, it is obvious that lacunae may have to be supplied to a much larger extent than may be justified on aesthetic grounds for archaeological remains. However, the two basic requirements for reintegration and easy identification of the intervention are still valid in this instance, their validity extending up to the point where the intervention would become hypothetical or so extended that only a modern creation would avoid faking. When an entirely contemporary intervention is called for, original parts of the structure (or group of structures) will constitute the basic elements of the design problem, the aim being to achieve a harmony within the larger unity of a contemporary environment.

Such creative integration requires a study of the old building, its context and perhaps the whole historic center where it is located in order to establish the peculiar rhythm of the old complex and to adjust the scheme of the modern creation to the basic modules and materials that already exist. Since control of social and economic factors will also be essential in achieving a harmonious development, a new, dynamic and multisided systematic study of historic complexes in the larger, town-planning frame of reference will have to be developed in order to bridge the gap between the classical conservation approach to the structure and the need to maintain a living, human environment.[10] One point ought to be stressed in this regard: A detailed evaluation, through a thorough study of the structure or complex of buildings, must always precede any study of adaption to new functions. Otherwise, restoration will unavoidably give way to exercises in modern architecture made at the expense of old buildings.

Ethnographic objects, although when taken individually do not differ from other museum objects, present a number of special problems when they are considered in their contemporary contexts. For instance, an object may lose all its sense once separated from its original function. Hence the question: What is to be preserved? Should interest be limited to the object and not to its social environment? It is clear that conservation activity cannot be separated from information gained in the collection of materials and documentation in the field. This is all the more true when the material of the object may make conservation almost impossible: Shall the symbolic wedding cake be conserved or the ceremony carefully documented? The tendency of modern art to overemphasize the event (or happening) and to despise the resulting object might lead to similar considerations.

The deeper problem of the conservation of the ethnographic patrimony of traditional cultures is that of a "museumization" of a culture through an anthropological approach. But is this situation not in a way parallel to that of functioning buildings in a historic center? Here again, a creative integration is needed. This, however, is threatened by two terrible forces: the tourist coming from the industrialized world who, in the same manner as King Midas who changed into gold everything he touched, (1) changes tradition into an empty show and (2) fosters the illusion that traditional crafts can remain genuine when kept unchanged in a changing society, which in fact results only in encouraging new varieties of cultural kitsch.

Fighting the Causes

Any long-term conservation policy must be concerned more with fighting causes of deterioration than with repairing its effects. It should be realized, therefore, as Max Dvorak has,[11] that the main causes of the deterioration of cultural property are human ones, which may be identified and classified as follows:

1. Neglect due to ignorance or lack of cultural interest.
2. Purposeful disrepair or destruction for ideological reasons.
3. Destruction due to priorities being given to economic considerations and traffic.
4. Fake reconstruction due to various factors:

   a. The romantic confusion of a revival versus a genuine historical experience.
   b. The illusion that the survival of traditional craftsmanship can express traditional values in a world where values have changed.

    c. The confusion of archaeological
       knowledge and the actual monument
       or structure.

    d. The exploitation of monuments or
       structures of the past for symbolic-
       ideological purposes.

No philosophy of restoration based on safeguarding the authentic witness of the past will ever be successfully carried out unless these adverse forces are fought and defeated.

NOTES

1. On the history of restoration, see Carlo Ceschi, *Teoria e Storia del Restauro* (Rome: Mario Bulzoni, 1970).

2. Eugene Viollet-le-Duc, *Dictionnaire raisonné d'Architecture* (Paris: F. de Nobele, 1967), s. v. "Restauration."

3. John Ruskin, *The Seven Lamps of Architecture* (London: George Allen and Unwin, Ltd., 1925), chap. VI, aphorism 31, pp. 353–54.

4. See Cesare Brandi, *Teoria del Restauro* (Rome: Edizioni di Storia e Letteratura, 1963).

5. See Giulio Carlo Argan, "La Storia dell'Ane," *Storia dell'Arte* nos. 1–2 (1969): 5–36. See also Roland Günter, "Glanz und Elend der Inventarisa-tion," *Deutsche Kunst und Denkmalpflege* 28, nos. 1–2 (1970): 109–17.

6. Brandi, *Teoria del Restauro*, pp. 99–103.

7. On the unjustified removal of baroque decoration in medieval churches, see Benedikt Nicolson, "Restoration of Monuments in Tuscany," *Burlington Magazine* 113, no. 813 (December 1970): 789–92; on the equally unjustified removal of Renaissance, baroque and classicistic restoration of antique sculptures, see Jürgen Paul, "Antikenergänznng und Ent-Restaurierung," *Kunst-Chronik* no. 4 (April 1972): 85–112.

8. See Paul Philippot, "Le notion de patine et le nettoyage des peinture," *Bulletin de l'Institut Royal du Patrimoine Artistique* I, no. 9 (1966): 138–43.

9. Cesare Brandi, "II trattamento delle lacune e la Gestalt-psychologie," in *Studies in Western Art: Acts of the XX International Congress of History of Art,* ed. Millard Meiss et al. (Princeton, N.J.: Princeton University Press, 1963), vol. 4, *Problems of the 19th and 20th Centuries,* pp. 146–51.

10. Compare, in this regard, Ingrid Brock, Paolo Giuliani and Cristian Moisescu, *Il Centro antico di Capua: Metodi di analisi per la pianificazione architettonico-urbanistica* (Padua, Italy: Marsilio Editori, 1972) and D. Stephen Pepper, "Conservation and Its Social Context," *Paragone* 22, no. 257 (July 1971) 77–85.

11. Max Dvorak, *Katechismus der Denkmalpflege* (Vienna: Julius Bard, 1918).

chapter 4

COLLECTIONS

DEVELOPMENT AND MANAGEMENT

THIS CHAPTER EXPLORES THE DEVELOPMENT AND management of library, archival, and museum collections. Preservation is a key component of managing collections, but to care for them wisely, we must consider a number of issues that surround analog and digital holdings. Before considering these issues, we must first understand what is meant by the term *collections*.

Susan Pearce views museums as a part of modern European cultural expression serving an educational function, and sees museum objects as "the lumps of the physical world to which cultural value is ascribed."[1] *Lumps* is her term for the individual things, objects, specimens, and goods that make up institutional collections. Collections are the expression of *material culture*, which in the words of anthropologist James Deetz, whom she quotes, "is that segment of man's physical environment which is purposely shaped by him according to a culturally dictated plan."[2] Although *lumps* can also refer to the broader physical world, this chapter focuses only on the discrete items that find their way into the collections of cultural heritage institutions.

Museums, libraries, archives, or historical societies are sometimes created to document the work or records of a particular group. In "We Are What We Collect, We Collect What We Are: Archives and the Construction of Identity," an article not reprinted here, Elisabeth Kaplan considers "the role of archives and archivists against a backdrop of contemporary debate on identity, illustrated by research on the establishment and early years of the oldest extant ethnic historical society in the United States—the American Jewish Historical Society—and the construction of American/Jewish Identities… . Archivists appraise, collect, and preserve the props with which notions of identity are built."[3] The example that Kaplan uses is more than a representation of, or showcase for, material culture; it is an active forum for identity, diversity, and difference. However, Kaplan warns us that "the reification of ethnic identity does not foster tolerance or acceptance; it constructs communities and then draws hard, arbitrary lines between them, creating differences and making them fixed, constricting the freedom of the individual to define or understand him or herself in multiple ways."[4]

Collections define and shape cultural heritage institutions. Almost every function in a library, archive, or museum relates in one way or another to the collections: selection, organization, appraisal, security, legal issues, (including copyright), preservation, exhibition, education, outreach, and the dissemination of information. There is a rich and voluminous literature about developing and managing collections in libraries. While archives and museums devote as many resources to collecting activities and policies as libraries do, their professional literature is not as extensive on the subject as is the library literature.

An important aspect of managing collections is preserving them. Nearly every author in this chapter addresses the practical concerns of collection development and management with respect to preservation. Preservation decision-making usually begins before items are acquired. Selectors, curators, and bibliographers may make decisions about potential purchases and gifts based on the condition of items. Or, if there is no option but to acquire something in poor condition, preservation plans might be made at the outset to treat an item, place it in a protective enclosure, or take some other measure. For digital media, provisions must be made early in the life cycle of an item to create metadata, and to reformat or migrate the media over time. (Copyright or rights restrictions may further impact acquisition decisions

and/or preservation strategies. An institution may not want to acquire items that it will not have the rights to preserve.)

Decisions regarding the preservation of collections are not confined to the collecting institution itself. Sometimes a donor will put restrictions on an item that will affect its preservation. Or there may be external stakeholders who have a say in whether, or how, something is preserved. For example, such situations may exist in institutions that house indigenous collections, such as aboriginal, First Nations, or Native American materials. If there are no professional staff who understand these perspectives or rights, it is incumbent upon the museum, library, or archive to develop meaningful relationships with these communities. **Miriam Clavir** addresses these relationships thoroughly in *Preserving What Is Valued*,[5] an excerpt of which is included in chapter 10, "Multicultural Perspectives."

Decision making is critical to the preservation of collections, and several authors in this chapter focus on it. **Paula De Stefano** provides an excellent overview of the history of collection building and the pros and cons of four selection-for-preservation methodologies that librarians have used. The "clean-sweep" approach, practiced in the 1980s, targeted all publications in selected subject areas that were published in the period in which most books were printed on acidic paper. The Research Libraries Group (RLG) refined this method by focusing on the "great collections" identified through the *RLG Conspectus*. A third approach was the condition-and-use model, which sought to focus on items that were actually used—as these were the most vulnerable to damage.[6]

The fourth approach was developed by **Ross W. Atkinson**, and it is described in his "Selection for Preservation: A Materialistic Approach,"[7] which is included here. (Additional perspectives on this work are provided in Margaret S. Child's, "Further Thoughts on 'Selection for Preservation: A Materialistic Approach.'"[8] Atkinson begins with the proposition that "[b]ecause decisions to preserve library materials affect the quality and composition of library collections, such decisions clearly must be made in consultation with collection development staff."[9] By now the collection development/preservation relationship is well established and, in fact, preservation is a collaborative effort across institutional functions and departments. But Atkinson was really advocating for a conceptual framework for decision making. He proposed a typology of preservation consisting of three classes: class 1 materials of "high capital value," special collections and unique items; class 2, "high-use items" in current demand for courses and research; and class 3, "low-use materials" with future research value. The class level determined the strategy for treatment: class 1 items warranted conservation treatment; class 2, replacement or preservation reproduction; and class 3, microfilming. Atkinson's piece was written before the development of digitization, although he predicted that there would be new technologies to replace microfilm. However, he could not have anticipated that the "new technology" most in use today, digitization, makes no sense for class 3 materials, as is demonstrated by De Stefano.

Atkinson's framework needs to be modified for today's digital culture. Class 1 items are the ones most frequently digitized, though it is as much for access to wider audiences as for preservation, e.g., to reduce wear and tear on originals. And, as De Stefano points out, now that digital conversion has largely replaced microfilming, it is not likely that costly digitization would be used on class 3, or low-use, materials.[10]

Digitization provides excellent access to analog collections and offers new opportunities for researchers to gain access to information not previously accessible. At the same time, digitization increases the cost of preservation because the original and the digital surrogate must be preserved. Also, the long-term costs of digitization must be considered, checking on the accessibility of the digital items, migrating to newer platforms, emulation, acquiring new hardware and software, and so forth. These issues are addressed in chapter 7, "Frameworks for Digital Preservation."

Selecting Research Collections for Digitization, by **Dan Hazen, Jeffrey Horrell, and Jan Merrill-Oldham**,[11] is a useful transition to the next section of the chapter, on time-based media, for some of the issues that the authors touch on, such as copyright, play defining roles in digitizing analog materials and

in preserving digital media. Other similar concerns include the current and potential use of digital items, and the projection of costs in relation to the benefits of reformatting and preserving items. The authors conclude that "disciplined efforts to address the themes and questions outlined in this essay will help ensure that new digitizing projects fulfill the expectations of libraries, students, and scholars."[12]

Collections: Time-based Media

According to *Wikipedia*, the term "time-based media" was coined by the British artist David Hall in 1972 to refer to moving image and sound work that was created by visual artists.[13] Time-based media include analog film, audio, video, and digital works which are dependent on technology to be heard or viewed, and include duration as a dimension. The articles in this chapter reflect a variety of perspectives on collecting and preserving media collections. **Karen Gracy**, known for her research in this area, has provided an overview of the field.

Howard Besser ("Digital Preservation of Moving Image Material?")[14] reflects not only on how digital imaging and broadband networks have changed the moving image and distribution process, but how preservationists must change their practices because of the paradigm shift from preserving completed works to now also preserving partial works, or even disembodied content. Along with these shifts, user needs and expectations have changed as well.

Gregory Lukow considers the thorny issues surrounding the preservation of "orphan films."[15] This term is used variously to refer to moving images that have been abandoned by their owners or copyright holders; films that have suffered neglect; films of unknown provenance; and so on. While Lukow offers no definition, he dates the use of the term to the early 1990s and the writing of the National Film Preservation Act of 1992. He further spells out all the issues associated with collecting, and preserving this category of moving images.

Mark Roosa's "Sound and Audio Preservation"[16] gives an overview of the history of sound media and a description of the various formats. He considers collecting and preservation issues, as well as the role of audio archives in the use of these media. The literature about sound recordings is dominated by technical pieces; this piece is a counterbalance to that tendency. However, some technical information is critical for curators, librarians, and archivists to have knowledge of current trends in the preservation of sound recordings. Recent research by Carl Haber, at the Lawrence Berkeley National Laboratory in Berkeley, California, applies digital imaging to recorded sound. Haber and his collaborators have developed IRENE (Image, Reconstruct, Erase Noise, Etc.).[17] This technology makes it possible for researchers to gain access to historical recordings that might otherwise have been lost. As Carl Haber has written, "these efforts demonstrate the relevance of quantitative science to other fields of humanistic research and culture."[18]

Dietrich Schüller describes audiovisual media as follows:

They are partly artistic creations in their own right, like film and music productions, and partly documents of political, historical and cultural events and phenomena. Most justifiably, audiovisual documents have been called the media of modernity: no adequate understanding of the past 100 years would ever be possible without them.[19]

Schüller advocates for the identification of hidden audiovisual collections around the world to ensure their survival. He believes that there is only about a twenty-year window to complete this work if many of these media collections are to survive. Much will also depend on the political will of some countries to do this work.[20] His advocacy for the preservation of time-based media rounds out the chapter.

NOTES

1. Susan M. Pearce, *Museum Objects and Collections: A Cultural Study* (Washington, D.C.: Smithsonian Press, 1992), p. 5.

2. Pearce, p. 5.

3. Elisabeth Kaplan, "We Are What We Collect, We Collect What We Are: Archives and the Construction of Identity," *The American Archivist* 63.1 (Spring/Summer 2000): 126.

4. Kaplan, p. 151.

5. Miriam Clavir, *Preserving What Is Valued: Museums, Conservation, and First Nations* (Vancouver, BC: University of British Columbia Press, 2002), chapter 3.

6. Paula De Stefano, "Selection for Digital Conversion in Academic Libraries," *College & Research Libraries* 62.1 (January 2001): 63–64.

7. Ross W. Atkinson, "Selection for Preservation: A Materialistic Approach," *Library Resources & Technical Services* 30.4 (October/December 1986): 341–53.

8. Margaret S. Child, "Further Thoughts on 'Selection for Preservation: A Materialistic Approach,'" *Library Resources & Technical Services* 30.4 (October/December 1986): 354–62.

9. Atkinson, p. 341.

10. De Stefano, p. 64. The editor of this volume described criteria for selecting items for preservation—including condition-and-use in Michele Valerie Cloonan, "Developing a Brittle Book Program at the Newberry Library," 10.4 *Library Scene* (December 1981): 22–25.

11. Dan Hazen, et al., *Selecting Research Collections for Digitization* (Washington, D.C.: Council on Library and Information Resources, August 1998).

12. Hazen, p. 12.

13. "Time-Based Media," *Wikipedia,* http://en.wikipedia .org/wiki/Time-Based_Art_Festival, accessed May 12, 2012.

14. Howard Besser, "Digital Preservation of Moving Image Material?" *The Moving Image* 1 (Fall 2001): 39–55.

15. Gregory Lukow, "The Politics of Orphanage: The Rise and Impact of the 'Orphan Film' Metaphor on Contemporary Preservation Practice," a paper delivered at the *Orphans of the Storm* annual conference, University of South Carolina, September

23, 1999 (www.sc.edu/filmsymposium/archive/ orphans2001/lukow.html), accesed May 12, 2012.

16. Mark Roosa, "Sound and Audio Archives," *Encyclopedia of Library and Information Sciences*, 3rd ed. (New York: Taylor & Francis, 2010): 4913–20.

17. Carl Haber, "Imaging Historical Voices," *International Preservation News* 46 (December 2008): 23–28.

18. Haber, p. 27.

19. Dietrich Schüller, "Socio-cultural Challenges of Audio and Video Preservation," *International Preservation News* 46 (December 2008): 5.

20. Schüller, p. 7.

ROSS W. ATKINSON

"Selection for Preservation: A Materialistic Approach"

Library Resources & Technical Services 30.4 (October/December 1986): 341–53.

Ein wirklich historisches Denken muss die eigene Geschichtlichkeit mitdenken.
—Hans-Georg Gadamer[1]

BECAUSE DECISIONS TO preserve library materials affect the quality and composition of library collections, such decisions clearly must be made in consultation with collection development staff. To date, however, very little effort has been made to describe the processes and criteria of preservation selection from the perspective of collection development. This is partially because preservation has in most libraries only recently acquired the status of a fully legitimate library operation deserving coordination with other library functions, but also because some of the values that underlie selection for preservation are alien to those that inform current collection development, as I will try to show in this paper.

The fundamental preservation problem facing collection development is, as Gordon Williams put it ten years ago, that, while "everyone ... will agree that not everything needs to be preserved forever," there is "far less agreement ... on exactly which books [and other materials] need not be preserved."[2] Dan Hazen, therefore, whose 1982 article remains far and away the best treatment of preservation selection, sees it as the primary responsibility of collection development in the preservation process to make item-by-item preservation selection decisions on the basis of criteria similar (but not identical) to the criteria used for the selection of current materials.[3]

The extent to which the function posited by Hazen is valid will be considered in the course of this paper. One must, in any event, agree with Hazen that the most productive approach to the topic of the interface between collection development and preservation is from the standpoint of selection decision making. Therefore, I will first define the location of collection development in the preservation decision process. While many detailed descriptions of preservation programs are now available, it will be useful for any future study of these programs, or for the creation of a program where none has previously existed, to attempt to reduce the activity of decision making for preservation to a minimal model, which might then be adapted to different organizational situations. Second, once the location of collection development in the decision-making process has been determined, I can then turn around, so to speak, and examine the activity of preservation from this perspective. In order to clarify from the standpoint of collection development the basic functions of preservation and their relationship to each other and to determine where the particular mode of microfilming fits into the whole scheme, I will make some suggestions for a rudimentary typology of preservation. Finally, using the characteristics of preservation that emerge from this typology, I can begin to speculate on the obstructions to large-scale cooperative preservation efforts and offer some suggestions for the qualities that a cooperative plan must contain to overcome such impediments.

Throughout this paper, the term *microfilming* will be used to refer to the best method of inexpensive and efficient reformatting generally available. If another method of reformatting becomes broadly available that is more inexpensive or efficient or will result in a more durable or accessible product, that new method should certainly be adopted, and what I have to say in this paper with respect to microfilming will be valid for such a new method as well.

The Decision Cycle

It is a basic purpose of all human communication to make a text available in some material form long enough for that text to have some meaning assigned to it by someone other than the author. If that meaning is judged for whatever reason to be of some special significance, the length of time the text is available can be extended to afford the opportunity for further evaluation. The decision to reproduce a spoken text in written form, the decision to publish a written text, the decision to include a publication in a library collection—all of these extend the text's availability. By the time a document reaches a point at which a library must decide to preserve it through microfilming or any other means, the text of that document has been subject to a series of decisions, beginning with the expression of the text in phonic or graphic form, all of which have resulted in the material extension of the text's accessibility. The extreme discomfort of preservation selection derives in no small part from the realization that a negative decision (i.e., a decision not to preserve) represents a reversal—and in many cases a permanent reversal—of a series of positive "preservation" decisions made throughout the history of the text. Not to preserve is therefore always to silence a voice, which, in the opinion of a number of

people in the past (authors, editors, publishers, librarians), has had something to say significant enough to warrant extended consideration.

The decisions made at any stage in the history of a text to extend its availability are clearly of two general types: (a) should the text be made further available, and, if so, (b) by what material means? These decisions are, needless to say, distinguishable but not separable. The minimal decision cycle in the library's preservation operation continues to conform to this pattern, as depicted in figure 1.

Figure 1. The Decision Cycle

	Pre-i.d.	Identification	mode
technical		what needs preservation?	which modes are possible?
	a	1	3
critical		what should be preserved?	which mode should be used?
	b	2	4

The two fundamental decisions that must be made in all cases of preservation—identification for preservation and determination of the mode of preservation—are, moreover, invariably two-dimensional, involving both technical and critical considerations. In each instance, the critical decisions can be made only subsequent to and on the basis of the technical decisions; it is, in fact, the essential purpose of the technical decisions in this process to define the options available for the critical decisions.

The first decision that must be made in this cycle of decision making is this: Which items in the collection are physically in need of preservation? Which will not last the decade? or the year? or another circulation? Which will fall apart in marking before they can even be put on the shelf? This is a technical decision based on a knowledge and experience of such matters as printing, binding, and paper chemistry. Only after that set of materials in need of preservation has been identified on the basis of technical criteria (step 1) can the subset of materials that should in fact be preserved be isolated (step 2).

It should be noted that, especially in larger collections, the first technical decision may need to be preceded by a preidentification phase, which would consist of a critical decision (step b) as to which segments of the collection should be surveyed in order to identify items in need of preservation. This preidentification critical decision may, moreover, also be preceded by a preidentification technical decision (step a) concerning, for example, which segments of the collection are most likely to contain the highest proportion of disintegrating materials.

Once decisions concerning identification have been made, the proper mode of preservation must be considered. The technical questions to be answered at this point (step 3) are these: Of the modes of preservation available, which are possible for the materials identified and what are the projected costs for each mode? The standard options have been outlined in a number of publications, perhaps most clearly in Gay Walker's chapter of Carolyn Morrow's *Preservation Challenge*.[4] With respect to microfilm, there are also a number of other formal considerations, which have been delineated by Pamela Darling, concerning the suitability of microfilm for certain types of materials.[5] Once the technical experts have determined the options, it is the responsibility of the critical decision makers to determine from among the modes available the one that will as nearly as possible balance cost with projected use.

It should also be noted that technical decisions in the cycle not only provide the options for the following critical decisions but also can affect earlier critical decisions. If, for example, the technical determination is made in step 3 that the only practical method of preservation is restoration, then the decision made in step 2 to preserve that item may be cancelled if the value of the item does not justify the cost of such treatment.

This very simplified decision cycle for preservation applies, I would expect, in virtually all cases for printed materials. In smaller libraries the critical and technical decisions may be made by the same person, while in larger libraries preservation experts will be entrusted with the technical decisions, and different collection development staff will usually be assigned responsibility for many of the critical decisions.

It is also possible, and in some cases highly desirable, for the critical decisions to be macrodecisions.[6] It may be that in a given project aimed at a discrete collection segment, a single decision can be made in step 2 that all items identified to be in need of preservation within that segment should in fact be preserved. Or in step 4, the single decision could be made, for example, that all materials determined in the previous (technical) step to be conducive to microfilming should indeed be microfilmed.

Toward a Typology of Preservation

The fundamental question, from the standpoint of collection development, remains why certain items should survive while others should not, i.e., how to respond to the need for a system of "planned deterioration" for printed materials.[7] Until we can answer that question in a consistent and generally acceptable fashion, we have very little chance of establishing standards for preservation selection in individual libraries, let alone of handing over to the twenty-first century a true research collection, i.e., one that consists, to use Mosher's word, of a "community" of documentation[8] rather than a random assortment.

Let me suggest, therefore, a rudimentary typology of preservation based upon three different and, to my mind, equally legitimate answers to the question of why certain categories of library materials deserve preservation (see figure 2). This typology can be summarized as follows.

Class 1 Preservation

We must begin by admitting that certain library materials need to be preserved in order to protect their capital value. Special or unique items, e.g., rare books (and manuscripts), must be preserved if the library is not to forfeit a considerable investment tied up in a relatively small number of documents. The purpose of what I will call class 1 preservation, therefore, is to preserve materials or groups of materials that have a high economic value. Emphasis on the economic value is not to deny, of course, that such materials have research value. Certainly they do, but the decision to preserve these materials must be made on the basis of their economic rather than their research value; for there are, after all, many other materials with potential research value moldering throughout the library, and to define special collections as having greater research value, and therefore as being more worthy of preservation, than main stacks collections would be highly problematic—especially, as I will explain shortly, at this particular time in the history of valuation.

Figure 2. Typology of Preservation

	Class 1	Class 2	Class 3
object	high capital value	high use value	low use/ future research
primary mode	restoration	replace/ repair	microform
decision locus	local	local	regional/ national
decision type	macro	micro	macro

Because the artifactual worth forms much of the basis of the capital value of many of the objects of class 1 preservation, its primary mode is clearly restoration. I am assuming that the microfilming of special collection materials is probably exceptional and would usually be done only to produce working copies of the originals or to save materials so totally decrepit that their content is jeopardized.

Class 1 preservation cannot, however, be limited to the type of documentation found in special collections. There is another type of material that does fit (albeit with some squeezing) into class 1 and which is often conducive to microfilming—especially if mass deacidification is not an option. Level-five collections (as defined by the Conspectus)[9] can also be of significant capital value, if for no other reason than for the amount of labor that has been invested in their development. In such collections the special value or uniqueness often lies in the combination or compre-

hensiveness of the materials rather than in any single item by itself. The capital (and research) value of such a collection, in other words, exceeds the combined value of its individual parts. Individual pieces of such collections must be preserved, therefore, if the capital value of the whole is to be protected.

Critical decision making in class 1 preservation is usually of the macro variety and, at least in the case of special collections, should require very little input from collection development staff. All materials of significant capital value in special collections must be preserved, and the order of their preservation will normally be determined by the technical estimate of their degree of deterioration in combination with the amount of their capital value. In the case of level-five collections, however, collection development will have an important role in what we defined above as the preidentification stage of critical decision making. Once the parameters of the level-five collection have been defined by a bibliographer, however, the macrodecision will usually be made to preserve all of the items within the collection segment in need of preservation. It should also be the responsibility of the bibliographer to identify for preservation any stray materials, such as any classified outside of the relevant collection segment, which the bibliographer would define as being part of or intimately related to the collection.

Finally, class 1 preservation is always a local decision-making operation; it is mandated by local constituencies and is intended to serve (for the most part) local needs. Since the materials are to a great extent unique (either individually or in combination with each other), and since the primary criterion for class 1 preservation is economic rather than bibliographical, cooperation among institutions is not usually an option.

Class 2 Preservation

At the opposite end of the bibliographic spectrum from the materials targeted in class 1 preservation are those to be identified for class 2 preservation. Class 2 preservation consists of higher use items that are currently in demonstrable demand for curriculum and research purposes. A major source of information about such material is circulation, and the need for preservation of such materials often derives from overuse. It is in class 2 decisions that the classical studies of use patterns, such as those by Trueswell or Fussler and Simon, are most applicable.[10] Christinger Tomer has devised a statistical method for identifying candidates for this kind of preservation, based on date of publication (as an indicator of physical condition) and date of last circulation (as a measure of frequency of use).[11] From a less quantitative perspective, the criteria developed by Hazen, which include the note that "some priority should be attached to the materials people actually use," would appear to be aimed, in my opinion, largely at this type of preservation.[12]

The objective of class 2 preservation, then, is to preserve materials currently being used, or very likely to be used as projected on the basis of what is currently being used. It is in class 2 preservation, moreover, that bibliographers have the most important role to play in the preservation process, for the knowledge amassed by bibliographers as to the current needs and activities of users and the current trends in the subject are precisely the criteria that must be applied to class 2 preservation selection decisions. Class 2 preservation is, in fact, really only an extension of or supplement to the core building and maintenance done by most selectors in most libraries. It is, in a manner of speaking, simply current selection by other means. Because it also clearly involves item-by-item selection (microdecisions), it would seem to correspond to Hazen's view of preservation selection.

Because of the high use of Class 2 materials, the primary mode of preservation tends to be replacement. If copies or reprints are not available, then bound photocopies within the limits permitted by copyright are probably the most preferable mode. Microfilm can, of course, be used for class 2 preservation, and I expect it is used occasionally for some core serials. For the most part, however, use of microfilm for class 2 preservation occurs, in my opinion, only when the appropriateness of the item for class 2 is in some doubt—when, in other words, the utility of the item has been projected more on the basis of proba-

bility than observation. The parameters of a core (or even of a canon) are always fuzzy, so that there is a tendency for class 2, which aims at high-use items, to blend into what we will shortly define as class 3, the class directed at low-use items and which does indeed take microfilm as its primary mode of preservation.

Like class 1, true class 2 preservation is activated exclusively by local values. Decisions to preserve are based directly on the demonstrated needs of current local clientele. Unlike class 1 items, however, most class 2 materials are being preserved simultaneously at many different institutions. Such duplication of preservation is, moreover, thoroughly justified by high use. Cooperation is once again, therefore, usually not an option, because such material must be available in-house.

Class 3 Preservation

The most problematic category of preservation is the third class, which has as its function to maintain for posterity lower-use research materials. Because it consists of less-frequently used materials, class 3 preservation has microfilm (or its equivalent) as its main mode of preservation.

Although there is clearly a great deal of class 3 preservation being done at local institutions throughout the country, local needs are not the main motivation for class 3. Indeed, the clientele for whom this material is being preserved has not yet, for the most part, arrived on the scene. Because of the absence of direct local motivations—which are to a great extent satisfied by class 2 and to a lesser degree by class 1 preservation and because of the magnitude of the problem, class 3 preservation is the exclusive source of cooperative preservation projects. To complete this equation, therefore, if the three classes defined here provide something approaching a sufficient typology of preservation, then a primary use of microfilm as a mode of preservation is for projects that usually require and deserve coordination among libraries. For a library to engage in a large-scale preservation microfilming effort without such coordination would be, in my opinion, a very questionable undertaking.

While selection criteria for classes 1 and 2 are, as we have seen, relatively easy to define, the criteria for class 3 present significant difficulties. Why preserve this material, anyway? Just what is it that posterity is not going to be able to do if it lacks access to this documentation? Will whatever posterity could do with access to this material tomorrow be of sufficient value to justify the considerable expenditure of resources today necessary to prepare that access?

The purpose of large-scale, coordinated preservation is not merely to help the future understand the past, but also to provide the future with the ability to understand itself—to supply a ground of knowledge upon which the future can build and against which the future can contrast and thus identify and define itself. Orwell was quite right: who controls the past controls the future. In this sense, it is certainly we who control the future, because the future will only be able to understand and define itself in relation to what we give it. This responsibility requires that we devise effective and reliable methods to supply the future with the best possible collection—as defined, of course, by our own values at this time.

The most appropriate publications for preservation must always be selected on the basis of the values in place—or, if you prefer, the "dominant ideology"— at the time of the decision. There is absolutely no escaping this requirement—not in the past and not now. We have no alternative but to make our selection decisions for class 3 preservation on the basis of the late-twentieth-century values, which inform all of our decisions. The only problem is that late-twentieth-century values are thoroughly permeated by a highly developed and all-encompassing network of ethical and epistemological relativism.

We are all products of an age, a nation, and a profession that has become increasingly unwilling to accept or to apply absolutes. The vital role of libraries in the opposition to political censorship is indicative of this position. The Library Bill of Rights is a noble document, and it expresses eloquently the ethical relativism and humanistic tolerance that characterize our era and profession—but as a determinant of values for any discriminating activity such as preservation selection, it leaves us completely helpless.

Closely related to this ethical position is the epistemological relativism that so clearly pervades contemporary thought. Kuhn's analysis of scientific revolutions,[13] Patrick Wilson's theory of research quality as consensus,[14] the historicity of phenomenology and the textuality of poststructuralism, the rejection of positivism even by Western Marxism, the increasing acceptance of the centrality of interpretation in the social sciences[15]—all of these (and many other) current and extremely influential concepts and trends render highly unlikely the possibility of developing a broadly acceptable and stable scale of values, which would be restrictive enough to permit the final rejection of certain library materials.

American research libraries in the late twentieth century have embraced and promoted such relativistic trends. There is no doubt in my mind that this is a major reason research collections have been increasingly driven by an ideal of inclusiveness. The Library of Congress is considered the greatest library in the country; it is not just a coincidence that it is also the largest. Quantity is quality in the research library, and this perspective has evolved, I would maintain, primarily because of our inability to define or measure bibliographical quality in any other terms.

Another obvious manifestation of this syndrome is our attitude toward weeding—which, from a critical point of view, is simply preservation done in reverse. While much has been written on the methods and values of weeding, research libraries, as Curley and Broderick realistically note, "will rarely weed, aware that what seems superfluous today may contain the essence of our times for the researcher of tomorrow."[16] The reason for such a reluctance to weed is that we lack at this time the epistemological apparatus to distinguish a level of quality or veracity that would clearly permit a decision to reject or retain. In the absence of an absolute measure, any statement has potential value, and any statement is thus worthy of retention. One wonders whether there has ever been an age so monumentally ill equipped to devise a system of planned deterioration. This, from the standpoint of collection development, is the ultimate problem of class 3 preservation.

Toward a Coordinated Program for Class 3 Preservation

There are many and varied preservation programs in operation throughout the country today. Some of these are cooperative and as such are aimed at class 3 materials. But there remains, partially for reasons I have just described, a clear lack of a general strategy linking these programs. Indeed, it is becoming increasingly likely that the major threat to the systematic preservation of library materials will turn out to be not an excess of acidity in paper but rather a shortage of coordination among libraries. How is such coordination to be achieved?

A successful coordinated program for class 3 preservation must satisfy certain general requirements:

First, it must provide scholars of the future with access to some kind of representative collection of documentation.

Second, it must be economically feasible and practicable; a library must be able to afford to take on a regionally or nationally coordinated class 3 responsibility in addition to accommodating its local responsibilities for class 1 and 2 preservation.

Third, it must be politically acceptable, i.e., it must not strain faculty-library relations at the institutional level, nor must it place undue pressure on relations among research libraries.

Fourth, it must be structured in such a way that it will permit, but not depend for its success on, indefinite expansion, so that more and more materials can be preserved as time and resources become available.

Fifth, it must be in operation relatively soon.

To these requirements we might add the excellent summary recommendation of Margaret Child that we "should not agonize too much over the fine points of definition of scope, but should begin to deal with the most easily grasped portion of the problem in an organized way as soon as possible."[17]

One view of the problem of valuation in preservation selection is represented in figure 3.

Let the vertical axis represent the scale of values in effect and the horizontal axis some division of the collection, such as by subject. Because we are operating under severe time constraints, it is clear that we should want to proceed in the diagram horizontally, i.e., we want to preserve all of the most valuable materials on all subjects first, then the second most valuable, and so on. In the cases of class 1 and class 2 preservation, these values (capital value and current use value respectively) are relatively definable, so that a horizontal process is feasible in local institutions. When we attempt to implement a program at a regional or national level for class 3 preservation, however, we find it impossible, because, as I have tried to explain above, we have not succeeded in defining a uniform scale of values. It has therefore frequently been the practice in cooperative preservation projects to proceed vertically, i.e., to select a subject (perhaps with formal limitations such as format or imprint) and to try to preserve everything (within those limitations) on that subject found in the collections of the participating institutions down to some vague point (the dotted line) below which items are no longer of sufficient value to be preserved. Clearly, the risk of such a procedure is that, whatever scale of values is being used, materials of less value (according to that scale) in one subject are being preserved, while materials of greater value (according to the same scale) in another subject are being permitted to disintegrate.

Figure 3. Cooperative Preservation Planning

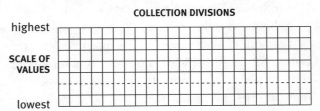

There is, in my opinion, only one practical method for a large-scale cooperative preservation program that has any chance of success and that is to begin to build the program not around subjects but rather exclusively around subject collections in place. We must agree, in other words, to decline the qualification of a document for class 3 preservation solely by virtue of its current inclusion in a designated collection of record. Systematic class 3 preservation of this type would thus result in a stringing together of different subject collections in different libraries into a single cooperative collection. Although each subject collection at each institution is obviously built in response to local needs, each collection will also, if it is a research collection (Conspectus level-4) built by competent bibliographers, represent the scholarship on the subject in a relatively balanced and unbiased manner. Each bibliographer is, after all, subject to and struggling with the same ethical and epistemological relativism described above. Any research-level subject collection is by necessity representative of a variety of trends and biases, and therefore should be acceptable as the minimally adequate subject segment of a cooperatively preserved collection. Material in such a designated subject collection would be preserved by the holding institution, and material on the subject not in that collection would be left (for the time being) at risk. This would provide us with an initial, practicable, and (procedurally and critically) achievable method of "planned deterioration" for printed materials.

The first step in such a plan should be to identify in a general fashion the strengths of collections by subject throughout the region or country. This is, of course, precisely the purpose of the Conspectus, so this should present few difficulties. We need to identify strong research collections through this method, but not special collections aimed at inclusiveness. (These special level-five collections will, in any case, probably survive through class 1 preservation.)

The second step would be for preservation specialists to determine a ratio of deterioration among subjects and then to annotate the Conspectus accordingly. It does not matter that collections at different institutions are deteriorating at different rates. Such a ratio of deterioration by subject would presumably hold for all institutions, even though the rates of deterioration may vary. (Use a code like a = probable large percentage of materials on this subject are deteriorating; b = moderate percentage; c = small percentage.) Using also the latest shelflist data, it should then be possible to gain some idea of the extent of the problem in each general subject area.

Finally, this information should be used to assign as equitably and systematically as possible respon-

sibility for preservation of particular subject collections among cooperating institutions. For each subject area, a strong (level-4) collection should be identified, which will serve as the collection of record. It would then be the responsibility of that institution to monitor this collection and to microfilm all deteriorating materials before they are lost. All cooperating institutions should accept the past work of the different bibliographers who have built the particular subject collections of record as informed and the resulting collections as sufficiently representative to satisfy many of the needs of future scholarship.

A shared bibliographic database with the capacity to identify items that have been preserved, such as RLIN and, in the near future, OCLC, is clearly essential for such a cooperative class 3 program, since it will permit the library of record to avoid preserving items it holds that are already preserved elsewhere. In many cases such preservation elsewhere will have been the result of class 2 decisions, especially those, mentioned above, involving items microfilmed because they fall on the fuzzy border between classes 2 and 3.

Let me emphasize that such a method would require the preservation of all materials in the designated subject collection of record identified as being in need of preservation. Never mind the current bibliographer's current evaluation of those materials. Such an evaluation, in fact, should not be solicited. Never mind the opinion of faculty or other experts as to which items are eternally significant and which are worthless. A certain amount of the collection may be trash, but it is our duty to pass that on in a representative collection, because a certain quantity of the reality the collection is to represent consists of what currently looks like trash. Let posterity decide it is trash. The only way to recognize quality material is, in any case, to have some trash with which to contrast it.[18]

Such a method of dividing responsibility among a large number of institutions could be implemented fairly quickly and would not place significant financial strain on any single institution—especially if the information on collection sizes, strengths, and the ratios of deterioration by subject are figured into the planning and if a shared database is available. Serious political problems with current users should not arise, because the identification of especially relevant documents (in the judgment of users) should always be accommodated as part of class 2 preservation. Clearly what would stand most in the way of such a plan and what has impaired our ability to establish such programs in the past is our reluctance to abandon in such circumstances the principles of current collection building. We must recognize that we cannot preserve cooperatively using the same values and procedures that we use to build a current local collection. We cannot approach a coordinated class 3 preservation project as if it were simply an expanded version of class 2 local preservation. Even if there were time for bibliographers to evaluate every item on every subject in a variety of libraries in the same way that bibliographers make current selection decisions—which there obviously isn't—we nevertheless demonstrably lack the criteria to make those judgments in a coordinated fashion at this time.

Coordinated class 3 preservation decisions must therefore be administrative decisions relating to material and which, in the absence of known users and trends, are best regulated by a material system of values. Let us return to figure 3. To initiate a cooperative class 3 preservation project, let the horizontal axis represent not subjects, but rather subject collections in place (i.e., a different subject collection in each library). Let the value system in the vertical column then be the rate of material decomposition, so that the most rapidly disintegrating items will then receive the highest value. In this way we can achieve a kind of horizontal parity by having all institutions (each responsible for a different subject) proceed vertically in a coordinated fashion according to a relatively measurable set of values. The dotted line in this case will separate materials disintegrating (above the line) from those not disintegrating (below it).

Once such a designated collection has been brought to a condition of stability, i.e., once all items in the collection in need of preservation have been preserved and a mechanism is in place to ensure that all items in future need of preservation will be preserved, a second phase of the program, which can be expanded indefinitely, can be undertaken to identify and preserve subject materials not contained in the designated collections of record. If we never attain such an advanced phase, however (and I am somewhat doubtful that we ever would), we can still be certain that such a program would safeguard a minimally adequate representative research collection for the future.

In conclusion, let us return to the original question: why undertake class 3 preservation? Perhaps in the effort to answer how to go about it, we have also managed to formulate a rationale. For the past four thousand years, civilization has found classes 1 and 2, for the most part, adequate. Now it is necessary to introduce a new kind of preservation, what I have been calling class 3. It is necessary not because we have more library materials than ever before, nor because their rate of disintegration is faster than ever before, nor even because there now are better and more accurate methods of preservation. The reason for undertaking large-scale coordinated class 3 preservation is that the values by which we live and work demand it. That very system of values that makes it so difficult to decide what to preserve provides us at the same time with the moral and epistemological imperative to secure for the future a balanced and representative collection, one that will provide posterity—in the same way that we provide current use—the opportunity for evaluation and for the acceptance and rejection of ideas embodied in library materials. We are, in a sense, obligated to confront and solve the complexities of cooperative class 3 preservation as much for ourselves as for the readers of the future who will rely on our judgment. The sooner we get on with it, therefore, the better for them—and the better for us.

REFERENCES AND NOTES

1. Hans-Georg Gadamer, *Wahrheit und Methode: Grundzüge einer philosophischen Hermeneutik*, 2d ed. (Tübingen: Mohr, 1965), p. 283.

2. Gordon R. Williams, "Objectives of a National Preservation Program," in *A National Preservation Program: Proceedings of the Planning Conference* (Washington, D.C.: Library of Congress, 1980), p. 29.

3. Dan C. Hazen, "Collection Development, Collection Management, and Preservation," *Library Resources & Technical Services* 26: 2–10 (Jan./Mar. 1982).

4. Gay Walker, "Preserving the Intellectual Content of Deteriorated Library Materials," in *The Preservation Challenge: A Guide to Conserving Library Materials* by Carolyn Clark Morrow (White Plains, N.Y.: Knowledge Industry, 1983), pp. 101–106.

5. Pamela W. Darling, "Microforms in Libraries: Preservation and Storage," *Microform Review* 5: 94–95 (Apr. 1976).

6. Hazen, "Collection," p. 6–7. See also Hendrik Edelman, "Selection Methodology in Academic Libraries," *Library Resources & Technical Services* 23: 3 (Winter 1979).

7. Margaret Child, "Deciding What to Save," *The Abbey Newsletter* 6, no. 4: suppl. 2 (Aug. 1982).

8. Paul Mosher, keynote address delivered at the Collection Management and Development Institute, Trinity University, San Antonio, Texas, 15 May 1985.

9. The Conspectus, as most collection development librarians are aware, is a tool, developed originally by the Research Libraries Group and now in use in many North American research libraries, to rate subject collections on a scale of 0 (out of scope) to 5 (comprehensive). See Nancy E. Gwinn and Paul H. Mosher, "Coordinating Collection Development: The RLG Conspectus," *College & Research Libraries* 44: 128–40 (Mar. 1983).

10. See, for example, Richard L. Trueswell, "Some Behavioral Patterns of Library Users: The 80/20 Rule," *Wilson Library Bulletin* 43: 458–61 (Jan. 1969); Herman H. Fussler and Julian L. Simon, *Patterns in the Use of Books in Large Research Libraries* (Chicago: Univ. of Chicago Pr., 1969).

11. Christinger Tomer, "Identification, Evaluation, and Selection of Books for Preservation," *Collection Management* 3: 34–54 (Spring 1979).

12. Hazen, "Collection," p. 8.

13. Thomas S. Kuhn, *The Structure of Scientific Revolutions*, 2d. ed. rev., (Chicago: Univ. of Chicago Pr., 1970). See also Gerald Doppelt, "Kuhn's Epistemological Relativism: An Interpretation and Defense," in *Relativism: Cognitive and Moral*, ed. Jack W. Meiland and Michael Krausz (Notre Dame, Ind.: Univ. of Notre Dame Pr., 1982), pp. 113–46.

14. Patrick Wilson, *Second-Hand Knowledge: An Inquiry into Cognitive Authority*. Contributions in Librarianship and Information Science, 44. (Westport, Conn.: Greenwood, 1983), pp. 81–121.

15. Daniel Bell, "The Turn to Interpretation: An Introduction," *Partisan Review* 51:217 (1984).

16. Arthur Curley and Dorothy Broderick. *Building Library Collections*, 6th ed, (Metuchen, N.J.L Scarecrow, 1985), pp. 308–09.

17. Child, "Deciding," p. 2.

18. See Daniel Boorstin's remark in *A National Preservation Program*, p. 72: "But a larger epistemological concern—and one reason why I think this subject [i.e., preservation selection] is of cosmic importance—is that we are always tending to second guess the future, to think we know what's trash and what isn't."

PAULA DE STEFANO

"Selection for Digital Conversion in Academic Libraries"

College & Research Libraries *62.1 (January 2001): 58–69.*

SELECTION DECISIONS IN academic libraries have never been clear-cut or straightforward. One has only to examine the literature to confirm that. However, a rudimentary principle that library professionals historically have agreed on is this: Like other processes in the library, selection should be aligned closely with the mission and goals of the parent institution. This simple, but important, tenet of academic librarianship is supremely meaningful in light of the resources that digital conversion activities consume, such as staff and funding. More strongly stated, it is incumbent upon the academic library community to develop a carefully reasoned approach to the selection of library materials for digital conversion that is fiscally responsible to both itself and its parent institution. To select and select well is critical to the success of the digital library. As Clifford Lynch has pointed out:

> Libraries face both opportunity and potentially unmanageable budgetary demands from all quarters. The questions now facing libraries arise less from the availability of technology than out of the development of strategies for collection development and management and supporting resource allocation choices.[1]

Despite the urgency to develop a coherent and sustainable approach to the selection process, the academic library community has yet to produce one. Perhaps the biggest reason for this hesitation has been the newness of digital technology itself. Much experimentation has taken place in the formative years of this technology in libraries, and more research and development is needed to explore the capabilities of digital technology, specifically, for what it has to offer the research community. Those efforts should be deliberate, well planned, and designed for the greater good of this community on a global scale. At the same time, however, it now is clear that a critical mass of a newly reformatted body of knowledge must be created to assist in this new electronic approach to research.

This article examines the process involved in developing an implementable rationale for the selection of library materials for digital conversion by reviewing analogous conditions in collection-building history. In the hope that the past may inform the future (if not in practice, at least in principle), what follows is a reexamination of past collection building, including the advent of the printing press and the ensuing drive to develop print collections; an overview of the selection process as it evolved in modern research libraries; and the selection criteria developed to cope with brittle books and preservation microfilming. Then, turning to contemporary efforts, a small sampling of project managers of recent digital projects provides information about some of the contemporary selection methods used in today's projects.

Developing Print Collections

The act of selecting and acquiring books to build and develop printed book collections has evolved over the centuries since the time of the manuscript book. During the secular period of the manuscript book and the early rise of the university in the twelfth century in Europe, the demand for books began to move beyond the monasteries. The drive to produce manuscript books was fueled by the need for books in education and research. Universities employed professional craftsmen to copy texts by hand "expeditiously and cheaply" for their courses.[2] Following Johannes Gutenberg's invention of the printing press and William Caxton's perfection of movable type and the inking process, both in the mid-fifteenth century, the race was on to duplicate and convert scholarly works from manuscript books to printed books. In the words of Lucien Febvre, the book

> rendered vital service to research by immediately transmitting results from one researcher to another.... By doing so, it gave their ideas a new lease on life and endowed them with unparalleled strength and vigour [sic]. They came to have a new kind of coherence and, by the same token, an incomparable power for both transformation and propagation. Fresh concepts crossed whole regions of the globe in the very shortest time, wherever language did not deny them access.[3]

This produced a remarkable transition in both library history and the book trade, and in many ways is comparable to the transformation facing libraries today. Febvre goes on to say that the magnitude of reproducing texts in print was quite staggering at the time: "[S]oon the potential of the new process became obvious, as did its role as a force for change as it began to make texts accessible on such a scale as to give them an impact which the manuscript book had never achieved."[4]

With respect to the selection of texts for printing, Febvre reminds us that the process of setting up a printing shop—acquiring equipment and supplies—required a significant investment. Therefore,

> 15th-century publishers only financed the kind of book they felt sure would sell enough copies to show a profit in a reasonable time. We should not therefore be surprised to find that the immediate effect of printing was merely to further increase the circulation of those works which had already enjoyed success in manuscript, and often to consign other less popular texts to oblivion. By multiplying books by the hundred and then thousand, the press achieved both an increased volume and at the same time more rigorous selection.[5]

Most of the earliest books were religious because clerics generated most of the demand. But as the demand for books broadened, "selection soon became imperative as the decision had to be made as to which of the many thousands of medieval manuscripts were worth printing."[6] Febvre aptly mines the depths of this issue, but for the purposes of this article, what his research distills very clearly is that the selection of manuscripts for printing was based on the profitable demands of an elite society for education and knowledge. Later, this would expand to include a broader audience with a thirst for learning.

What is most strikingly similar in this limited comparison between the early days of printing and the current status of electronic technology is the need to develop a body of knowledge. Today, this endeavor supports an effort to realize the potential of electronic technology similar to what Febvre recognized when he said the printing effort sought "to make texts accessible on such a scale as to give them an impact the manuscript book had never achieved." We now seek to realize the potential of electronic technology "to make texts accessible on such a scale as to give them an impact" that, indeed, surpasses what the printed book has achieved. If today's libraries are to take any direction from the past, they would not go wrong to follow the example of their medieval counterparts and focus resources and attention on the education of the communities they serve. For academic libraries, this is the research community, with faculty and students of the university being the primary beneficiaries. Strictly followed, this entails allocating internal funds for the digital conversion of collections exclusively to support the needs of the immediate user community. It is this mandate of the academic library that precludes a focus on K–12 education, leaving those needs for digital materials to places such as the Library of Congress, the New York Public Library, and other public libraries.[7]

The exclusive application of resources for specific mission-related uses and needs may be construed as something too obvious to point out. However, much of what has been scanned by libraries and archives to date are low-use special collection materials, simply because they are "signature" collections. Although these efforts produce educational information sites, rarely do they actually produce a digital collection deep enough to satisfy the broader research needs of the local constituency. In effect, many of these sites are more suitable to the needs of the K–12 audience, rather than higher education. Given the costs of conversion, selection decisions must remain organic to the mission of the parent institution, or the library stands to lose its credibility within the university and its scholarly structure.

Overview of Past Collection-building Practices

Though in no way new, the question of how libraries should proceed in building a body of knowledge is quite daunting in the electronic environment. In a very broad assessment of what digital technology portends, Carla Hesse saw the current environment as an opportunity to achieve the "most cherished ideal of modern democratic polities and the libraries they have created: universal access to all forms of human knowledge."[8] For academic libraries and their selecting policies, the idea of collecting "all forms of human knowledge" is an old one. In the nineteenth century, early book selection in academic libraries began to adhere to the ideal of comprehensiveness and completeness.[9] However, in the twentieth century, the idea of completeness was

> given up as its practical impossibility came to be realized. The cause was the enormous proliferation of knowledge and the resulting vast increase in publication.[10]

Now, with the technology and the demand in place to convert library materials into digital form, we find ourselves in a situation comparable to our earlier counterparts. As in the traditional print environment, the stultifying problem of overabundance amplifies the need for selectivity and increases the need for professionals to do the selecting: "the more there is to select out there, the more subject expertise is needed to select quality and specifically in order to satisfy needs and demand."[11]

In the early days of collection building in American academic libraries, most collections were built by

faculty.[12] J. Periam Danton emphasized the vagaries that resulted in this practice:

> The majority of titles in the book stock of the typical American university library are there as the result of scores of thousands of individual, uncoordinated, usually isolated decisions, independently made by hundreds of faculty.[13]

Danton was not the earliest or only critic of the system that permitted faculty the exclusive responsibility for selecting library materials. Corroborating this view, Raven Fonfa cited the period 1876–1939 as a period of widely shared discontent and criticism among librarians and others, noting that data collected for the Waples and Lasswell study, published in 1936 and entitled *National Libraries and Foreign Scholarship,* stated that collections developed by faculty in academic institutions were both unbalanced and lacking, whereas collections developed by librarians in public institutions "showed significantly more balanced holdings."[14] Danton also cited the Waples and Lasswell study, which found that Harvard and the universities of Chicago, California, and Michigan had significantly lower percentages of 500 English, French, and German works in the areas of social sciences, "judged by specialists in those fields to be of primary scholarly importance," whereas the New York Public Library, "where book selection is … entirely the responsibility of a corps of subject specialist librarians, held 92 percent."[15] In the years after 1939, as librarianship became more professional, librarians began to win support for collection development in academic libraries, and the theories and practices that inform materials selection evolved simultaneously.

Undoubtedly, at its most basic level, the "selection of materials has almost always been based on clientele."[16] In the academic environment, the university, as the parent institution, dictates the development of collections for the research and teaching needs of the faculty and students. Ross Atkinson, clarifies this condition by saying,

> [w]hile the individual library can make the micro-decisions concerning the particular items

to which access should be provided, the broader policy decisions that define the parameters within which the library's collection building effort must operate, are largely based upon stipulations made in advance by the supported (and in support of) [the] user community.[17]

As stated above, the huge expense of digital conversion of library and archive materials requires a fiscal responsibility to the academic library's parent institution. In fact, this responsibility to the university is heightened further by potential misjudgments and technical vagaries that could grossly waste precious resources and would, in the end, represent a glaring disservice to the library's clientele. With this in mind, there is an amplified need for an implementable plan that adheres to the basic tenet that collection development—what John Rutledge and Luke Swindler defined as the "macro-decision"—should coincide with the directives of the parent institution.[18] In addition, libraries' collecting decisions should be consistent and cognizant of holistic responsibilities. Hendrik Edelman broadly defined collection development as the first level in the development of a policy or plan that considers

> the goals of the library as far as the collections are concerned, taking them into account and correlating them with the environmental aspects such as audience demand, need, and expectation, the information world, fiscal plans, and the history of the collections.[19]

In the digital environment, conformity to this established principle is certainly possible and looms as a fiscal imperative. However, David Fielding and Carl Lagoze raised a good point in the context of digital libraries when they asked, "is it really necessary to select materials in specific groupings or 'collections' to begin with, or just proceed on [a] use basis, or curriculum needs basis?"[20] In other words, does the "distributed digital library" or "virtual library" obliterate the need to follow traditional collection development principles as they have been applied broadly to the macro-collection-building function? Indeed, digital technology affirms the capability to forego the need for one institution to build and develop isolated "collections," especially when such an endeavor can otherwise be accomplished on a multi-institutional, collaborative basis with individual institutions contributing on what Rutledge and Swindler call a micro-decision level. As long as an institution's selection efforts coincide with the goals of the parent institution, cooperatively built virtual collections can satisfy the needs of the immediate user community as well as the pressing need to be fiscally responsible.

Proceeding from the idea that traditional (macro-level) collection building could be jettisoned, the need to formulate a strategy to build digital collections still persists. It is possible that the clue to a coherent selection strategy is embedded elsewhere in traditional collection development practices. Moving on to Edelman's second level of collecting practice, he defined the title-by-title selection process as implementation of the library's overall collection development policy.[21] Rutledge and Swindler called this the micro-decision and set out the six "most relevant" factors that a selector must consider in title-by-title selection: "(1) subject, (2) intellectual content, (3) potential use, (4) relation to collection, (5) bibliographic considerations, and (6) language."[22] These categories could be adopted easily in a micro-level decision-making process for electronic collection development; however, they are too broad and too inclusive to be selective enough. Even more than in the print world, the caution to "remember that selection implies selectivity" is profoundly relevant.[23] Here, at this micro-level of collection building for the digital library, is where the real crux of the problem exists. Following the established traditions of the omnivorous library ("which sees nothing as out of scope") is no longer appropriate, nor is the "just-in-case" model of selecting.[24] Both are far too inclusive to be compatible with the implied fiscal responsibility of digital technology.[25]

Selection Methodologies for Preservation

A third avenue to explore as a path toward a digital conversion strategy lies in the methodologies that evolved to support the decision making for the preservation of brittle books using microfilm technology. This, too, is a reformatting decision and, perhaps, explains why there is a persistent practice in the library community of linking preservation and digitization particularly with regard to selection activities. The choices involved in microfilming brittle books are recognizably similar to the choices libraries must make in deciding what to reformat digitally, but that intersection is brief and extends only backward, not forward. Whether driven by the demands of researchers or the demands posed by poor condition, the similarity between microfilm and digital technologies lies only in the initial desire to duplicate what already exists. Beyond that, the two technologies diverge significantly in purpose. Nevertheless, a brief tour of the selection decisions established for preservation microfilming is a useful exercise and possibly may distill a vision of purpose in developing digital collections, even if only in the obverse. What follows is a brief description of the decision processes applied to microfilming.

An early and popular selection methodology for brittle books was developed in the 1980s and adopted by the Research Libraries Group (RLG) for use in cooperative preservation microfilming projects. The "clean-sweep" approach utilized date parameters applied to subject areas of a collection. The date parameters attempted to approximate those years in which paper manufacture produced highly acidic paper, 1870 and 1910.[26] The distinctive feature of this approach was its comprehensiveness: It sought to include *all* materials within a subject area between the chosen date parameters on the grounds that what had been collected in the past would have potential use in the future. Initially, this method had great attraction primarily because "little time is expended on decision making... . And it is argued that there might someday be a use even for materials whose importance is not evident at present."[27] Thus, the merit of this approach lies squarely in its lack of selectivity. The efficiency of such a prospective approach works well when applied to microfilm technology, due to microfilm's low storage costs. But the inherent weakness of the clean-sweep approach "is that materials which may never

be needed by scholars take up time and money and thus displace more important materials that aren't in the chosen group."[28] High labor costs associated with pre- and post-microfilming activities hardly justified the benefits of its built-in decision-making efficiencies, and the clean-sweep method of selection fell out of favor. In the electronic world, the vagaries of this approach are equally intolerable given the high cost of digital conversion. Therefore, this paradigm is clearly one to avoid.

In an effort to improve upon the clean-sweep approach, the RLG later fostered the concept of great collections based on the RLG Conspectus rating of a collection as a measure of its worth for preservation.[29] This selection method also was subject driven and focused attention on those comprehensive research collections, built over time, that were in danger of disappearing due to embrittlement. The great-collections approach retained many of the characteristics endemic to the clean-sweep approach but also introduced the element of physical condition. Date parameters were still observed, but if an item was not brittle, the great collections approach excluded it from microfilming. Comprehensive in its approach, this method also was not very selective. Again, microfilm technology lends itself well to the massive attempt to reformat brittle books, but evaluated from the perspective of digital technology, the problem of what to do with low-use materials resurfaces. In the digital environment, it makes little sense to enhance access to low-use materials because it is difficult to justify their costly conversion.

A more practical approach to selection for preservation was provided by Ross Atkinson, in "Selection for Preservation: A Materialistic Approach," in which he discussed three classes of library materials and their appropriate corresponding preservation treatment.[30] Class 1 includes special collection and unique materials, such as rare books and manuscripts; class 2 "consists of high-use items that are currently in demonstrable demand for curriculum and research purposes"; and class 3 are low-use, or less frequently used, research materials.[31] The preservation treatments that Atkinson advises for these groupings of materials are conservation treatment for class 1; replacement and/or preservation photo-copying for class 2; and microfilm reformatting for class 3. This is an acceptable formula, generally, for organizing preservation treatments, and it works well for low-use materials when microfilm is your reformatting tool of choice. Unfortunately, like the previous two methods described above, this approach is not appropriate either. A strict translation of Atkinson's paradigm would substitute digital conversion as the reformatting agent for class 3 materials instead of microfilm—a fruitless and costly undertaking for low-use materials.

Before leaving Atkinson's model, it cannot be overlooked that many, if not most, digital projects to date have focused largely on Atkinson's class 1 special collections and unique materials. These efforts have attracted funding and attention and have provided fertile ground for testing this new technology. Whether they do now or ever will suit the research objectives of academic libraries is debatable. Research requires in-depth collection building. Converting that depth to electronic technology in a specific subject area for scholarly use would be extremely expensive and inefficient because it would lead to the conversion of materials that are used by only a small segment of researchers. In addition, building electronic collections on this basis requires the bibliographer, as in print collections, to speculate and project which materials will be needed by the researcher, an activity that has been deemed both subjective and difficult, often leading to overbuying.

Still pursuing the analogy of selection methodologies for preservation microfilming, additional strategies include the condition-and-use model and the editorial model. Selection based on condition and use for preservation microfilming was an approach first suggested by Christinger Tomer in 1979 (and again in 1985) and then later by Barclay W. Ogden in 1987.[32] Proponents of this method argue that scarce resources should be allocated for preservation based on poor condition and the amount of use an item receives, the theory being that the combination of use and poor condition places an item in a higher-risk category than those items that remain untouched on the library shelf. Tomer logically explained that

the documents at most serious risk are those whose interest to readers exceeds in longevity their physical capacity to support the consequent handling.[33]

As part of this process, identification of items in need of preservation occurs at the point of use. Condition plays the largest role in the decision and, thereby, makes access to materials currently in demand its initial priority. Of course, bibliographic review of these materials is essential because everything used in a library is not necessarily worth preserving. The condition-and-use selection decision proceeds on a title-by-title basis and assumes that the heart of the preservation mission should first consider the end user for whom the material is saved.

The condition-and-use selection method brings us closer to a translatable decision-making paradigm for digital conversion primarily because of its focus on use; however, the element of condition is misplaced. In the digital environment, it is important to distinguish between the factors that motivate a preservation decision and those that seek to enhance access. The two decisions may "overlap where materials are both endangered and in demand," but in the context of collection building (i.e., creating a body of knowledge in a new medium for research purposes), selection decisions for digital conversion need not consider physical condition of the original.[34] Digital technology is ideal when used to enhance access but assists in preservation only when creating surrogate copies of materials that are likely to benefit by reduced handling. It cannot be used to actually preserve an item.[35]

The editorial model of selecting materials for retrospective collection development has been employed commonly by commercial microfilmers as a method of distributing collected works and genres. It was not widely used as a method for selecting materials for preservation microfilming. Only a few preservation-microfilming projects explored the use of editorial boards of scholars and national bibliographies to identify important titles and core materials. Most notable among them are the American Theological Society Serials Project and the American Philological Association's effort to preserve classics materials.[36] It is not entirely clear why the editorial method was not used more widely to make preservation decisions. Perhaps the general distaste among scholars for microfilm is responsible, compounded by a fractious relationship between faculty and the library in the wake of large microfilming grants. Digital technology seems to be bridging that chasm as libraries look to their respective faculties to assist them in selection decisions for digital conversion. Currently, several conversion projects are using this method to develop digital collections in specific subject areas: the Perseus Project and the National Agriculture Library's CORE Project.[37]

For the most part, it seems that selection models for preservation microfilming are inapplicable to digital technology. The clean-sweep approach is wholly unsuited to guide the selection decision for digital conversion because it is far too inclusive and would involve the reformatting of items that may never be needed or used. Likewise, the great-collections approach is equally inappropriate for the same reason. Although Tomer's condition-and-use approach is more appealing, strictly applied, it is only appropriate in digital conversions where protection of the original is an issue. It appears that even though the choices involved in digital conversion are reminiscent of the choices required for preservation microfilming, they are not translatable. True, both approaches involve a reformatting decision, but their trajectories diverge from there because their intents conflict in purpose. At the most basic level, one thwarts or decreases access whereas the other enhances or increases it.

Tangentially, it is too tempting to resist the observation that digital technology may serve to rescue much of what exists on microfilm—a format that researchers tend to avoid. Just as Febvre recognized that printing in the fifteenth century "resurrected long-forgotten writings in which the fifteenth century seem[ed] to have new interest," it is possible that when libraries begin to offer on-demand digital conversion of microfilmed materials, much of the scholarship "hidden" on microfilm will be "resurrected" in the same way.[38] Conversely, Febvre's notion that printing was responsible for "consigning ... less popular books to oblivion" has a rather unattractive, yet valid, modern-day correlation to the reformatting of brittle books to microfilm.

Conclusion

Salient points taken from the collection-building and selection decision-making models offered above settle most harmoniously around the overriding directive of research libraries to align their collection development practices with their parent institutions and the utility of doing so. The idea of use, especially high use, is fundamental to collection development and is the common thread in all selection decisions. Coupled with the extraordinary access capabilities permitted by digital technology, use holds significant promise as a guiding factor in selecting materials for digital conversion. It represents an opportunity to extend more resources and offer highly improved services to the academic library's local user community—undergraduates, graduates, faculty, and scholars alike. Whether digitizing core collections, following a curriculum-based approach, or creating partnerships with faculty, collection-building efforts based on use are more likely to garner the support of the parent institution.

A use-based directive never succeeded in preservation reformatting, but it has been widely accepted and, indeed, very successful in replacement and physical treatment decisions in collections conservation activities—where funding tends to be most scarce and decision making most practical. Here, Atkinson's proposal for class 2 materials is quite relevant. In its application to digital conversion, it offers three advantages: first, it could dovetail nicely with the work of faculty and students and thus support the teaching process and curriculum. Second, high-use items suffer from the wear and tear of heavy handling, which digital reformatting would alleviate, or at least reduce. And third, because high-use materials are the most likely to be duplicated across academic collections, it might foster opportunities for interinstitutional collaboration. In fact, because use is often similar across institutions, especially at the core collection and curriculum levels, the latter could lead to the development of a digitized core collection and, in so doing, force the issue of cooperation to exploit the efficiencies and economies of sharing, carefully tailored to avoid duplicate efforts and expenditures.

In Atkinson's parsing of library materials into three classes, he says,

> the objective of class 2 [high-use] preservation … is to preserve materials currently being used, or very likely to be used as projected on the basis of what is currently being used. It is in class 2 preservation, moreover, that bibliographers have the most important role to play in the preservation process, for the knowledge amassed by bibliographers as the current needs and activities of the users and the current trends in the subject are precisely the criteria that must be applied to class 2 preservation selection decisions. Class 2 preservation is, in fact, really only an extension of or supplement to the core building and maintenance done by most selectors in most libraries.[39]

This statement is just as pertinent when read in the context of today's environment and applied to selection efforts for digital conversion, using the same argument in favor of converting materials in support of an institution's core curriculum. Demonstrable use motivated current efforts such as the National Science Foundation's Digital Library Initiative Phase II (1998–2002), which seeks to "explore the linking of digital library research efforts and testbeds for undergraduate education" in science, mathematics, engineering, and technology.[40] Similarly, one of the findings of the studies conducted as part of the Columbia On-line Book Project was that faculty had a high regard for the usefulness of offering students Internet access to reading assignments.[41]

Except for a few examples such as these, however, it seems that a use-based approach still is no more popular as a selection criterion for digital conversion than it was a selection criterion for preservation microfilming.[42] Having reviewed an array of possible selection criteria and approaches deployed in the past

to develop book collections and preserve brittle books in academic libraries vis-à-vis digital conversion, it is surprising to discover what is actually driving the endeavor to create digital collections in academic libraries today. An informal survey of twenty-five current digital projects in academic libraries showed that the most popular approach to selecting collections for digital conversion is a subject-and-date-parameter approach applied, by and large, to special collections, with little regard for use, faculty recommendations, scholarly input, editorial boards, or curriculum.[43] When queried about their goals, project managers most often responded that improved and/ or enhanced access was the primary goal of converting collections to an electronically accessible format. It is hard to imagine that a broad-based local user community benefits by the improved access to special collections. It is only a matter of time until the question emerges as to how long the parent institution will be satisfied with supporting the costly conversion of their library's materials to improve access for narrowly defined audiences that may not even be their primary local constituents. Harking back once more to the mid-fifteenth century, the building of printed book collections in libraries was driven initially by the education and research needs of the academic community. Simplistic as it sounds, half a millennium later, the education and research needs of the academy are still the academic library's primary responsibility; thus, it must be prepared to account for a digital conversion selection methodology that supports and complements that relationship.

NOTES

1. Clifford Lynch, "The Role of Digitization in Building Electronic Collections: Economic and Programmatic Choices," in *Selecting Library and Archive Collections for Digital Reformatting*, proceedings from an RLG Symposium held Nov. 5–6, 1995, Washington, D.C. (Mountain View, Calif.: Research Libraries Group, 1996), 2.

2. Lucien Febvre and Henri-Jean Martin, *The Coming of the Book*, trans. David Gerard, eds. Geoffrey

Nowell-Smith and David Wooton (New York: Verso, 1997), p. 19; first published as *L'Apparition du livre* (Paris: Éditions Albin Michel, 1958).

3. Ibid, 11.

4. Ibid, 248–49. Febvre says, "Some 30,000–35,000 different editions printed between 1450 and 1500 have survived, representing 10,000–15,000 different texts, and if we were to take into account those which have not survived the figures would perhaps be much larger. Assuming an average print run to be no greater than 500, then about 20 million books were printed *before 1500,* an impressive total even by 20th-century standards." However, he further qualifies this estimate in a footnote saying, "Of course we mean only to indicate some idea of scale. According to Vladimir Loublinsky, production would be somewhere between 12 and 20 million copies."

5. Ibid., 249.

6. Ibid., 260.

7. An exception to this would be when grant and/or donor funds are available to the academic institution to scan and make available on the Internet educational materials that would benefit an outside constituency or, perhaps, in those cases where the institution of higher education is publicly funded and mandated to provide K–12 access to their collections. The idea expressed here—that the academic library's commitment to higher education (to the exclusion of K–12) as part of their mission—is most appropriate to research libraries and is based on a historic and economic perspective that acknowledges the traditional purposes of the academic library. This, however, is an emphasis that could undergo radical changes in the future. See the Library of Congress's "American Memory Collections" for an excellent example of selection for a broader constituency that includes K–12 and others.

8. Carla Hesse, "Humanities Scholarship in the Digital Age," in *What's Happened to the Humanities*, ed. Alvin Kernan (Princeton, N.J.: Princeton Univ. Pr., 1997), 110–11.

9. J. Periam Danton, *Book Selection and Collections: A Comparison of German and American University Libraries* (New York: Columbia Univ. Pr., 1963), 34.

10. Ibid.

11. William S. Monroe, "The Role of Selection in Collection Development: Past, Present and Future," in *Collection Management for the 21st Century* (Westport, Conn.: Greenwood Pr., 1997), 114.

12. Danton, 71. See also Raven Fonfa's, "From Faculty to Librarian Materials Selection: An Element in the Professionalization of Librarianship," in *Leadership and Academic Librarians,* eds. Terrence F. Mech and Gerard B. McCabe (Westport, Conn.: Greenwood Pr., 1998), 22–36.

13. Danton, *Book Selection and Collections*, 74.

14. Fonfa, "From Faculty to Library Materials Selection," 29.

15. Danton, *Book Selection and Collections*, 75.

16. Robert N. Broadus, "The History of Collection Development," in *Collection Management: A New Treatise*, eds. Charles B. Osburn and Ross Atkinson (Greenwich, Conn.: Jai Pr., 1991), 9.

17. Ross Atkinson, "The Conditions of Collection Development," in *Collection Management: A New Treatise*, eds. Charles B. Osburn and Ross Atkinson (Greenwich, Conn.: Jai Pr., 1991), 36.

18. John Rutledge and Luke Swindler, "The Selection Decision: Defining Criteria and Establishing Priorities," *College & Research Libraries* 48, no. 2 (Mar. 1987): 125, 128.

19. Hendrik Edelman, "Selection Methodology in Academic Libraries," *Library Resources & Technical Services* 23.1 (Winter 1979): 34.

20. David Fielding and Carl Lagoze, "Defining Collections in Distributed Digital Libraries," in *D-Lib Magazine* (Nov. 1998). Available online at: www.dlib.org/dlib/november98/lagoze/11lagoze.html.

21. Edelman, "Selection Methodology in Academic Libraries," 34.

22. Rutledge and Swindler, "The Selection Decision," 128.

23. Monroe, "The Role of Selection in Collection Development," 107.

24. Ibid., 106. See also Broadus, "The History of Collection Development," 3–28, for a deeper treatment on the subject of size of collections and for an excellent bibliography on the history of collection development.

25. Interestingly, John Price-Wilkins takes the opposing view and argues in favor of just-in-case collections, and has applied the just-in-time selection model to the decision to create and store derivatives (i.e., images derived from larger TIFF images) in "Just-in-time Conversion, Just-in-case Collections," 5 Aug. 1999. Available online at: http://www.dlib.org/dlib/ may97/michigan/ 05pricewilkin.html.

26. For an excellent overview of selection methods for preservation, see Margaret S. Child, "Selection for Preservation," in *Advances in Preservation and Access,* vol. 1, ed. Barbara Buckner Higginbotham (Westport, Conn.: Meckler, 1992).

27. Roger S. Bagnall and Carolyn L. Harris, "Involving Scholars in Preservation Decisions: The Case of the Classicists," *Journal of Academic Librarianship* 13, no. 3 (July 1987): 141.

28. Ibid., 141.

29. Child, "Selection for Preservation," 149–151.

30. Ross Atkinson, "Selection for Preservation: A Materialistic Approach," *Library Resources & Technical Services* 30 (Oct./Dec. 1986): 344–48.

31. Ibid., 346.

32. See Christinger Tomer, "Identification, Evaluation, and Selection of Books for Preservation," *Collection Management* 3, no. 1 (Spring 1979) and "Selecting Library Materials for Preservation," *Library and Archives Security* 7, no. 1 (Spring 1985). See also Barclay W. Ogden, "Preservation Selection and Treatment Options," in *Preservation: A Research Library Priority: Minutes of the 111th Meeting of the Association of Research Libraries* (Washington, D.C.: ARL, 1987), 38–42. Margaret Child's summary of the condition and use methodology is excellent in "Selection for Preservation," 153–55.

33. Tomer, "Selecting Library Materials for Preservation," 2.

34. Janet Gertz, "Selection Guidelines for Preservation," in *Guidelines for Digital Imaging: Papers Given at the Joint National Preservation Office and Research Libraries Group Conference in Warwick 28th–30th Sept. 1998.* Available online at: http://www.rlg.org/preserv/joint/gertz.html. See also her more recent article, "Selection for Preservation in the Digital Age: An Overview," *Library Resources and Technical Services* 44, no. 2 (Apr. 2000): 97–104.

35. Paula De Stefano, "Digitization for Preservation and Access," in *Preservation: Issues and Planning* (Chicago: ALA, 2000): 307–22. See also Stephen Chapman, Paul Conway, and Anne Kenney, "Digital Imaging and Preservation Microfilm: The Future of the Hybrid Approach for the Preservation of Brittle Books." Available online at: http://www.clir.org/cpa/archives/hybridintro .html#full.

36. The American Theological Society's serials microfilming project lasted more than twenty years in which "selection seems to have been mainly by consensus among the theological librarians who constituted the Board," see Child, "Selection for Preservation," 148. For the American Philological Association's microfiche project, see Bagnall and Harris, "Involving Scholars in Preservation Decisions: The Case of the Classicists," 140–46, and "Who Will Save the Books? The Case of the Classicists," *New Library Scene* 6 (Apr. 1987): 17.

37. See Mary Summerfield, "Online Books: What Roles Will They Fill for Users of the Academic Library?" 23 Apr. 1999. Available online at: http://www.columbia.edu/cu/libraries/digital/texts/paper. See also the "Perseus Project: An Evolving Digital Library," ed. Gregory Crane, Tufts University. Available online at http://www.perseus.tufts.edu, July 16, 1999; R. Entlich et al., "Making a Digital Library: The Contents of the CORE Project, " *ACM Transactions on Information Systems* 15, no. 2 (Apr. 1997): 103–23.

38. Febvre and Martin, *The Coming of the Book,* 260.

39. Atkinson, "Selection for Preservation," 346.

40. "Digital Libraries Initiative—Phase 2," sponsored by the National Science Foundation, Defense Advanced Research Projects Agency, National Library of Medicine, Library of Congress, National Aeronautics & Space Administration, National Endowment for the Humanities, in partnership with the National Archives and Records Administration and the Smithsonian Institution. Final draft version: Feb. 18, 1998; announcement number NSF 98-63 (NEW).

41. Summerfield, "Online Books."

42. Paula De Stefano, "Use-based Selection for Preservation Microfilming," *College & Research Libraries* 56 (Sept. 1995): 409–18.

43. This author queried twenty-five project managers at academic libraries through an informal e-mail survey. Many thanks to those individuals who responded to my questionnaire. Sources used to identify digital projects were: the National Endowment of the Humanities "Top Humanities Web sites" (http://edsitement.neh.gov, 6/24/99); IFLA's IFLANET Web site document, "Digital Libraries: Resources and Projects" (http://www.ifla.org/II/ diglib.htm, 7/16/99); Rutgers "Digital Library Resource Page," 7/16/99; and the University of California, at Berkeley's, SunSITE Hosted Projects (http://sunsite.berkeley.edu/R+D, 7/3/99).

Selection 4.3

DAN HAZEN, JEFFREY HORRELL, AND JAN MERRILL-OLDHAM

Selecting Research Collections for Digitization

Washington, D.C.: Council on Library and Information Resources, August 1998; Report 74; excerpts.

Summary

Selection for digitization is a complicated process having much in common with selection for purchase, microfilming, and withdrawal, and with other strategic decision-making that is integral to the work of libraries. The conversion of textual, visual, and numeric information to electronic form from preparation and conversion to presentation and archiving encompasses a range of procedures and technologies with widely varying implications and costs. The judgments we must make in defining digital projects involve the following factors: the intellectual and physical nature of the source materials; the number and location of current and potential users; the current and potential nature of use; the format and nature of the proposed digital product and how it will be described, delivered, and archived; how the proposed product relates to other digitization efforts; and projections of costs in relation to benefits.

Copyright assessments play a defining role in digitization projects and must be addressed early in the selection process. If a proposed digitizing project involves materials that are not in the public domain, permissions must be secured and appropriate fees paid. If permissions are not forthcoming, the materials cannot be reproduced and the focus of the project must change. We will be able to convert to electronic form only a small percentage of existing scholarly materials, and to do even that will require substantial investments. Therefore, the intellectual value of the original sources, together with the types and levels of use, must shape priorities for conversion. Ideally, the electronic version of a source will permit new kinds of use and more sophisticated types of analysis. Decisions to digitize must also take into account the physical size, nature, and condition of source materials as they affect the characteristics of the desired product. Decisions must be based on the current state of technology, but they must also anticipate how changes in technology could enhance or make obsolete an investment in digitization. One must also assess how the product will be described for users, delivered to them, and managed over time.

Digitization, like other reformatting endeavors, takes place within a context larger than a single institution, discipline, or country. Selection decisions should be informed by both duplicative and complementary efforts. This may prove challenging, because it is difficult to determine whether an item has been already digitized and by what means. Cost-benefit analysis for digital conversion may also be hard to conduct reliably, because the costs of creating electronic resources vary considerably. File size, associated storage needs, and processing requirements account for part of the differences, though labor requirements are even more important. Functions such as preparation of materials for scanning, indexing, bibliographic description, post-scan processing, and long-term file management often fail to be factored into cost equations. Incomplete cost analyses can impute benefits that are difficult to represent on a project balance sheet. Though digitizing projects must calculate the likely costs and benefits, our ability to predict either of them is as yet rudimentary. Thus, the decision to digitize must begin with an inquiry into copyright and an assessment of the nature and importance of the original source materials, but it must then proceed to analyze the nature and quality of the digitizing process itself, how well relevant information is captured from the original, and then how the digital data are organized, indexed, delivered to users, and maintained over time.

Introduction

Electronic resources are immensely appealing to nearly everyone concerned with education and scholarship. The potential benefits of information in digital form—unfettered access, flexibility, enhanced capabilities for analysis and manipulation—are profound. The widely held notion that existing collections of books, manuscripts, photographs, and other materials should (and will) be digitized wholesale is not surprising. In reality, of course, the creation and

maintenance of electronic resources require funding, skill, and ongoing commitment. Those that are intended for permanent use, moreover, will almost certainly require repeated intervention to ensure that they remain viable as technologies evolve. In creating digital products, libraries are called upon to balance the competing worlds of boundless promise and limited resources. Because hard choices are unavoidable, the decision-making process must be well organized and its results fully consonant with the institution's goals and values.

Selection for digitization is a complicated process having much in common with selection for purchase, microfilming, and withdrawal and with other strategic decision-making that is integral to the work of librarians and curators. Conversion of textual, visual, and numeric information to electronic form, however, involves additional layers of complexity. The digitization process, from preparation and conversion to presentation and archiving, encompasses a range of procedures and technologies with widely varying implications and costs. Digital reformatting of library collections is still in its infancy, at once limiting what can be accomplished now and forcing decision-makers to anticipate future improvements. Scanned images optimized for viewing on today's computer monitors, for example, will display poorly on tomorrow's high-resolution screens and will require reprocessing. The same may ultimately be true of bitmap texts, which, if they are not made word-searchable once conversion is affordable, may be underutilized by researchers who have come to rely on key-word search capability. Considerations such as these make selection for digitizing more challenging than selection for purchase.

The judgments we must make in defining digital projects require consideration of many factors, including: assessment of the intellectual and physical nature of the source materials; the number and location of current and potential users; the current and potential nature of use; the format and nature of the proposed digital product and how it will be described, delivered, and archived; how the proposed product relates to other digitization efforts; and projections of costs in relation to benefits.

Copyright: The Place to Begin

There are many interdependent and interacting factors to be weighed in selecting materials to digitize. The specific choices that result from the selection process will reflect subjective judgments, any of which may change over time. Nuanced assessments, ambiguity, and shades of gray are all to be expected.

Questions concerning copyright, however, are far more clear-cut. Simply stated, if a proposed digitizing project involves materials in the public domain, the work can proceed. If the source materials are protected by copyright but rights are held by the institution or appropriate permissions can be secured, the work can move ahead. If permissions are not forthcoming for copyrighted sources, however, the materials cannot be reproduced and the focus of the project must change. Copyright assessments thus play a defining role with regard to digitizing projects. Since the impact of copyright is so decisive, we have given it pride of place in this discussion.

Copyright issues in the digital environment are still very much in flux and have provoked ongoing international discussion. While the broad thrust of digital technology is toward enhanced access, diminished costs, and more versatile capabilities, it is far less clear that copyright law will likewise encourage wider use. The legal strictures applicable to a particular project will vary depending on the country in which the project is based, the country in which the source materials were produced, and prevailing international agreements. Different kinds of materials, moreover, usually pose different types of rights-management issues. The performance rights associated with musical scores, for example, or exhibition rights for films, differ from rights for nonperformance materials such as electronic journals or documentary photographs. To complicate matters, all these rights are susceptible to change over time.

Digital projects must be undertaken with a full understanding of ownership rights, difficult as they often are to ascertain, and with full recognition that permissions are essential to convert materials that are not in the public domain. Rights that must be negotiated with the copyright holder often entail fees.

The institution hosting a project may also have policies and procedures that inform intellectual property negotiations. The general counsel or legal office of most institutions can provide guidance. The Internet site IFLA: Copyright and Intellectual Property Resources is a good resource for maintaining current awareness. It includes articles, reports and white papers, discussions, and information about organizations related to copyright issues, intellectual property in general, and electronic distribution of intellectual property.

The Intellectual Nature of the Source Materials

The following sections of this paper separately discuss the complement of considerations that bear on decisions to digitize. The elements are presented in a sequence that moves from relatively abstract assessments of intellectual value to nuts-and-bolts issues concerning whether available resources and technology can provide a product that meets expectations. In practice, the pieces interact in ways that are often complex.

Decisions about what to digitize must first and foremost address the intellectual value of the original sources. We are likely to be able to convert only a small percentage of existing scholarly materials to electronic form, and doing even this will require substantial investments. We therefore need to determine what it is truly worthwhile to convert.

QUESTIONS TO ASK

Does the intellectual quality of the source material warrant the level of access made possible by digitizing?

Materials with marginal scholarly value are best left in their original form or made accessible in a less costly manner. Scholarly value, of course, is a subjective assessment and even the most marginal materials can support some kinds of research. Most users, nonetheless, would opt for electronic access to original monographs rather than to derivative works, or to the papers of a prominent scholar over the administrative records of a university department. Bibliographers regularly make purchase decisions that reflect their evaluation of the intellectual quality of single items or collections of materials. Similar judgments apply in choosing what to digitize.

Will digitization enhance the intellectual value of the material?

Scholarship can be facilitated when texts are made fully searchable by rekeying (retyping) them or by employing OCR software. Comparisons between successive drafts of a text and the final published work, for example, or with later editions and translations, are vastly simplified when the words and phrases are searchable. A concordance or thesaurus is likewise most easily mined when it is in searchable form. Electronic texts can be moved readily from one environment to another (from the World Wide Web onto the hard drive of a personal computer, and then into a word processing program, for example), shared with other users, and manipulated and reconfigured for multiple purposes. Digitized prints, drawings, and other visual resources can be viewed in groups at low resolution or inspected individually for very fine detail. Digital charts and tables, appropriately coded, can be loaded directly into statistical software packages for additional analysis. Census results, for instance, are most easily used when the data have been formatted and imported into the Statistical Package for the Social Sciences.

Will electronic access to a body of information add significantly to its potential to enlighten, or are the original books, manuscripts, photographs, or paintings sufficient to the task?

A collection of thousands of portrait images, however promising a resource, might be nearly unapproachable because of its size and the condition and dimensions of individual items. Well-indexed and in digitized form, however, the collection could be searched with relative ease for images of a particular person or for some indexed characteristic (the country from which the portrait originates, for example). Likewise, the digitization of large-format architectural draw-

ings could enable comparisons of small- and large-scale drawings, different views of the same architectural feature, or sequential phases of construction.

To what extent will the combination or aggregation of original sources increase their value?

Digitizing related scholarly monographs, like building a coherent collection of paper copies, can strengthen the context within which each title is approached. Ephemera leaflets from a political campaign, for example, are often most useful when studied in the aggregate, as are posters, broadsides, and popular literature. Harvard has digitized daguerreotypes from thirteen repositories to facilitate the combinations and comparisons that are otherwise precluded by the fragility, value, and dispersion of the original images.

Current and Potential Users

Some scholarly resources are heavily used; others are consulted infrequently. With only limited funds available for reformatting, types and levels of use can help to shape priorities.

QUESTIONS TO ASK

Are scholars now consulting the proposed source materials? Are the materials being used as much as they might be?

These are complicated questions. Intensive use does not automatically make a collection a good candidate for digitizing. If the primary audience is local, for example, and if competition for a particular resource is not a problem, access may already be sufficient. Ephemera produced by a community political organization may be of great interest to local scholars and of limited value to a worldwide audience. On the other hand, if use is heavy and widespread, digitizing may at once guarantee convenient and reliable access, and make it possible for some institutions to discard their original copies. The JSTOR project, through which a large array of core scholarly journals is being made accessible in digital form, is a prime example of an initiative focusing on high-use materials.

Is current access to the proposed materials so difficult that digitization will create a new audience?

Low use may signal that a collection has marginal intellectual value, but there are many other reasons for valuable materials to have generated little interest. A collection may be held in a remote location, for example, or be owned by an institution with highly restrictive access policies. Bibliographic records may be poor, as is often the case with pamphlets. The value of digitizing such materials may go beyond the simple fact that the resulting files can be widely distributed. Broader access, as it creates a new community of users, can also facilitate more active scholarship.

Does the physical condition of the original materials limit their use?

Some resources are too fragile to be consulted. Aging newspapers or palm-leaf manuscripts that break at the slightest flex simply cannot be browsed. In such cases, a digital copy might be provided to improve access, and a microfilm or other photographic surrogate made to ensure long-term survival. (Film can be made from a digital file or vice versa.)

Sources may also be at risk because of high user demand or extraordinary monetary value. A nation's founding documents, glass-plate negatives of vanished architectural sites, or rare maps may benefit from the creation of digital copies that satisfy the purposes of most users. These files do not necessarily need to meet archival standards. They are created to protect the originals from handling.

Are related materials so widely dispersed that they cannot be studied in context?

Cooperative efforts to digitize disparate pieces of a greater whole can create or restore a more usable collection. Papyrus fragments, a prominent individual's far-flung correspondence, scattered photographs of a particular subject or by a specific photographer, and broken serial runs are among the many materials whose coherence, accessibility, and scholarly utility can be enhanced through digitization.

Will the proposed digital files be of manageable size and format?

Digital resources need to match users' technical capabilities and equipment. Most require Internet access and standard web browsers, or a CD-ROM drive. Images delivered to the Internet in formats other than JPEG or GIF require additional software for viewing or printing. Even when electronic resources are optimized for on-screen delivery, some network connections, particularly those via modem, are still far too slow to support browsing of digital collections at satisfactory speeds. And scholars in some locations may lack training opportunities or the ongoing technical support needed to take advantage of the electronic environment. These limitations, however, are not necessarily reasons to rule out digitizing. The worldwide trend is toward greater capabilities. Moreover, the more important the resources available electronically, the greater the incentive to acquire the network, viewing, and printing technology necessary to use those resources. Digitization may, in and of itself, stimulate improved access.

Will digitization address the needs of local students and scholars?

Immediate demand can inject a measure of practical reality into decisions to create electronic resources. An art historian might seek to scan art images and make them available to students as electronic reserves, as an alternative to slide-based classroom presentations and reviews. A historian may choose to teach from digitized images of manuscripts that would otherwise be unavailable to a large class. Because ready access to shared electronic files can transform the classroom, proposals to digitize in support of immediate teaching needs may garner faculty support.

Actual and Anticipated Nature of Use

A person reading a book, looking at a photograph, or consulting a manuscript encounters few barriers to use. One might have to handle an object carefully, or use a magnifying glass to read fine print, but in general the work is immediately approachable. The same resource, when digitized, should be equally accessible and approachable. Ideally, the electronic version will also permit new kinds of use and more sophisticated types of analysis.

QUESTIONS TO ASK

How do scholars use the existing source materials? What approach to digitization will facilitate their work?

Different digitizing techniques result in electronic files with different characteristics. These in turn can correspond well or poorly with scholarly needs. If the goal is to provide an image-based finding aid that helps users identify original materials of interest, for example, mounting slow-loading high-resolution images would be counterproductive. If, on the other hand, the intention is to reduce or eliminate handling of original materials, an image that fails to convey all critical information embodied in the original will fail to serve its intended purpose.

The simplest approach to digitizing involves use of a scanner or digital camera to create electronic pictures (bitmap images) of original materials. Decisions concerning the number of dots recorded by the scanner (resolution), how many shades of gray or colors will be recorded (bit depth), and other factors related to scanning equipment and settings will determine how well the digital product replicates the original. High-quality bitmap images can usually capture all the significant detail in texts or graphics. Scanning rare and unique texts or visual resources can make them accessible to users who would otherwise never see them. In such a case, merely reproducing the original in electronic form represents an extraordinary enhancement.

For textual materials, post-scan processing can support expanded capabilities. Scanned text can be processed with Optical Character Recognition software to produce searchable indexes. OCR software is now only occasionally employed in digitizing projects because it cannot yet interpret accurately all fonts and alphabets, and because it adds significantly to per page costs. Text can also be rekeyed to create ASCII files, very straightforward digital text files that permit searching by keywords or phrases. In some cases

this enhancement is the primary justification for digitization. Directories, dictionaries, and indexes are all significantly easier to use when specific words can be searched within a well-designed digital file.

ASCII texts accommodate key-word searching (e.g., searching for all instances of the word "temperance") and some kinds of analysis, but they do not readily replicate the structure and format of an original document. Without special coding, researchers cannot directly consult the seventh paragraph of the third chapter of a particular text. Nor can they search for all occurrences of ?welcome? used as a verb rather than a noun. These capabilities become possible in marked-up texts, which are coded to highlight elements of structure, format, and syntax. The Standard Generalized Markup Language (SGML) is the emerging model. One SGML application, the Encoded Archival Description (EAD), is being used to create electronic versions of archival finding aids.

These and other approaches to digitizing carry very different costs, benefits, and resource requirements. While electronic versions can be more versatile than original materials, in some cases they hinder research. A scholar studying bookbindings or papermaking, for example, is poorly served by a reproduction of any kind. So too is the scholar whose immediate access to a large and important collection of literary works is sacrificed in order to serve a worldwide constituency, perhaps because bound volumes have been disbound for scanning.

Will digitization increase the utility of the source materials? Will it enable new kinds of teaching or research? Do scholars agree that the proposed product will be useful?

Digitization can enhance original materials in many ways. Image quality can be improved by eliminating extraneous stains and marks. Thumbnail images of visual resources (photographs, drawings, paintings) can be browsed to discover patterns, trends, and relationships among individual items, and specific images can then be scrutinized at higher resolution. Likewise, patrons can review scanned images to identify needed materials before requesting that they be retrieved from storage.

Electronic transcriptions of texts, in ASCII format or marked-up files, can be linked to bitmap images of original documents. Readers can then decide for themselves whether "authoritative" transcriptions are in fact accurate. Comparisons of different versions of a text are likewise simplified. Related texts and images can be assembled together within a single, unified corpus. Examples such as the Dante Project mounted by Dartmouth College, which reproduces and links related texts and commentaries concerning the Divine Comedy, and Tufts University's Perseus Project, an interactive, multimedia database on Archaic and Classical Greece, suggest the potential of electronic texts.

Almost all electronic products will provide basic links that allow users to navigate them (to locate a particular map within a printed text, for example). The degree to which a digitization project exploits electronic links will depend upon its intended use. For digital resources created as pedagogical tools, predetermined connections are part of the package. Products intended for research tend to be less aggressive in ordaining relationships among sources, since their creators assume that researchers will build their own structures of meaning.

Are there other scholars, librarians, and archivists who can collaborate to create a useful product?

Colleagues and potential users can clarify ideas, help select meaningful materials for conversion, improve project design, and stimulate early interest. "User demand" reflects both the intrinsic utility of specific source materials as well as a social context of participation and promotion.

The Format and Nature of the Digital Product

Decisions to digitize must take into account the physical size, nature, and condition of source materials as they affect the characteristics of the desired product. They must likewise address whether available means of conversion can satisfy expectations for the result. Projects must also, from the very first, consider how users will be guided through the electronic version.

QUESTIONS TO ASK

What critical features of the source material must be captured in the digital product? Are very high resolution copies, accurate rendition of colors, a seamless combination of images and text, or other qualities considered essential?

The cost and nature of digitizing hardware and software continue to evolve, and preferred solutions are likely to shift as well. It may sometimes make sense to defer certain digitizing projects so that technology can catch up to needs. The success of a project to digitize oversized maps at Columbia University, for example, depended partly on the ability of users to see detail and read place names. As a result, the maps were scanned at relatively high resolution, thereby creating challenges for digital image delivery and presentation. File sizes were very large and initially outran the capacity of the library's computers and network. Greater bandwidth and more powerful machines have enhanced functionality.

If the original sources are to be retained, can they withstand the digitization process?

Automatic sheet feeders are fast and efficient, but they may destroy brittle paper. Digital cameras can minimize the manipulation of source materials, but subjecting certain media—watercolors, for example—to prolonged lighting is problematic.

What type of hardware should be used for conversion?

Color slides, for instance, cannot be fully represented by scanners that create only black-and-white images. Even a color scanner with limited capacity to reproduce tonalities will be inadequate when high-quality images are important. Digitizing equipment can be expensive, and the costs may be difficult to justify when use is sporadic. Some projects may thus be done most economically if they are contracted out. Agreements with external vendors, in addition to specifying technical conditions, performance expectations, and handling guidelines, must fully define ownership and distribution rights for all digital products.

Will a digitized sample meet users' needs?
If so, how should the sample be constructed?

Many collections are too large to convert in their entirety. In the case of an artist's drawings, one might select materials from each of the artist's major periods, or representatives of the various media in which he or she worked, or particular subjects, such as cityscapes or portraits. Subsets of large collections can be defined in many ways and for many purposes. Collaboration with scholars and other experts is essential.

Will the information resources upon which the project is based continue to grow?

Ongoing commitments and extended arrangements for copyrights may be required when collections are still expanding, as is the case with current journals and annual reports, or the papers of a living individual. Consultations with scholars and other experts can be particularly useful, since the long-term value of current materials is often difficult to discern.

How will users navigate within and among digital collections?

Printed sources orient readers by means of tables of contents, chapters and sections, pagination, indexing, and formatting cues. Manuscript materials often rely on finding aids linked to the organization of file folders. Photographs may be mounted in albums. At a minimum, electronic products need to provide the same kind of functionality. The process may require several steps. For a multi-volume work that has been scanned page by page, for instance, each page is a separate computer file that must be individually labeled and stored. The files for critical pages of the work, for example, the title page, table of contents, and the first page of every new chapter, must then be linked to electronic navigational tools so that they can be easily located.

Describing, Delivering, and Retaining the Digital Product

While libraries can point with pride to their collective achievements in organizing and describing an enormous number and variety of collections and material types, some perplexing issues have not yet been resolved. There is still no consensus on how to handle ephemera that cannot realistically be cataloged by the piece and that are too insubstantial to shelve like most books and journals. Providing access to mixed media (a book accompanied by a floppy disk or CD-ROM, for example) is likewise problematic. But these issues, complicated as they are, pale next to the challenges of making digital products available to users. Decisions as to what resources should be digitized must be informed by an understanding of how the product will be described for users, delivered to them, and managed over time.

QUESTIONS TO ASK

How will users know that the digital file exists?
Bibliographic records, finding aids, and indexes can all be adapted to include references to electronic resources. Nonetheless, our ability to determine what has been digitized remains well behind what we know about materials that have been microfilmed or photocopied.

One of the principal challenges is to determine what information is essential in describing an electronic product. The Dublin Core (see http://purl.oclc .org/metadata/dublin_core/) and other special initiatives for structuring and standardizing descriptive data propose to combine information about the technical characteristics of digital files (how they were created), their location, and a summary of their contents. The resulting records are known as metadata. Their function is to provide users with a standardized means for intellectual access to digitized materials. Despite these and other initiatives, projects to catalog digital files are only in the developmental stage. No system has yet been widely adopted for tracking the digitizing activities of libraries, archives, and museums, although new approaches continue to emerge.

How can the digital product best be delivered to users?

Alternative modes of digital storage and delivery must be considered from the outset of a project. CD-ROMs, for instance, are distributed and used differently from information made accessible over the Internet. The differences are reflected in hardware requirements, software, and ease of use. CD-ROMs are sometimes bundled with software for searching and analysis that is superior to that generally provided for Internet files. On the other hand, access to CD-ROMs is limited to individual workstations or small networks, while Internet files can be made available to a very broad audience. And Internet resources, by nature, can be updated or augmented without requiring users to replace objects that have become obsolete.

Internet products, however, generate questions of their own. How immediate must access be?

Files can be mounted on a server so that they are instantaneously available on-line. They can be stored on disks in a jukebox and loaded on demand (near-line access), or kept off-site (off-line) and retrieved and delivered on demand. Near-line and off-line access can save on server space and requirements, though there are countervailing staff costs associated with retrieving and mounting the files. Expected demand, file sizes, fee structures, and available staffing and equipment must all be considered.

Who will be authorized to use the digital resource, and under what circumstances?

Copyright holders may limit distribution rights, institutions may be unable or unwilling to provide the infrastructure needed to support universal access, and cost-recovery enterprises cannot by definition make their products available without restriction. Digitizing projects must thus consider access policies and control, pricing mechanisms, and billing procedures. Access issues impinge upon selection decisions in a number of ways. A university may mount high-resolution images of unique holdings for scholarly use (a medieval manuscript, an important collection of drawings), but would not allow unauthorized publication of those images. Moreover, electronic resources cost money that must be secured through subsidies or fees. When neither internal budgets nor external subventions provide adequate financial support, digitization will require a paying audience.

Access, when it is not universal, must be managed. Current alternatives include passwords, direct user fees, and limitations according to organizational affiliation. Different capabilities for viewing, downloading, and printing may be offered at different prices or to different sets of users. There are many options, each reflecting a different pathway toward a self-sustaining endeavor.

How will the integrity of the digitized data be ensured?

The malleability of electronic products makes them particularly useful for many kinds of scholarship. Digitized files must be embedded with detailed information concerning the methods used to create them. The same information should be included in external bibliographic or descriptive records. Users who are consulting or copying the sources must also be able to confirm that the files they see or receive match the originals. Means to authenticate and protect digital products, long available in financial and industrial applications, are only beginning to take hold.

Particularly for digital products created to meet local demand, is the existing technology infrastructure adequate?

Robust computer systems and an appropriate number of work stations are perhaps more easily provided than such ancillary features as network printing capabilities in the library and in offices, classrooms, and residences.

What are the long-term intentions for the digital file?

In the case of electronic document delivery systems such as ARIEL (a product of the Research Libraries Group, Inc.), the goal in most cases is to provide very rapid access to specific articles or chapters. While images must be legible, they need not be perfect replicas; and copyright constraints, indexing complexities, and storage economies make it simpler to rescan on demand than to organize and retain random files. In other cases, the file may be kept for a longer, but still limited, period and then discarded, a reserve reading list or copyrighted images of artworks scanned to support classroom teaching, for example.

Is the long-term preservation of deteriorated materials a project goal?

Preserving documentary resources in electronic format presumes that, to the greatest extent possible, all the information contained in the original material has been captured completely and accurately. This requires careful attention to significant detail, whether the smallest text character on a page or all the shades and tones of blue and green in a seascape. Targets for resolution, grayscale, and rendition of color either exist or are being developed to ensure the needed detail and fidelity.

Digital preservation also requires a supporting organization and infrastructure dedicated to storing the electronic files and to migrating them to new formats and/or media as technologies change. Unless these capacities are all in place, digital files cannot be regarded as permanent. Creating an enduring digital preservation master file is a multidimensional task with long-term implications. Hybrid projects, in which digital files are complemented by copies on microfilm, alkaline paper, or some other stable medium, provide the insurance that exclusively electronic projects do not.

Digital processes meet preservation objectives without pretending to permanence. In the case of Spain's Archivo de Indias, for instance, low-resolution grayscale images were prepared so that fragile original documents, some more than five hundred years old, could be spared the rigors of repeated consultation. The digital files, while they fall well short of capturing all the information in the originals, nonetheless fulfill a vital preservation function.

Relationships to Other Digital Efforts

Digitization, like other reformatting endeavors, takes place within a context larger than a single institution, discipline, or country. Selection decisions should be informed by both duplicative and complementary efforts.

QUESTIONS TO ASK

Have the materials proposed for digitization already been converted to electronic form?

As we have seen, it can be difficult to determine whether a specific item has been digitized and by what means. If an electronic copy does exist, is it accurate, satisfactorily functional, and accessible? Does it take advantage of the capabilities of current technologies? If the existing product does not serve the intended purposes of the proposed project, a new version may be warranted.

Can cooperative digitization efforts bring together a cohesive body of material that would otherwise remain disassociated?

Standardized descriptors and a common approach to indexing and storage can allow dispersed materials to be combined in an amalgamated digital resource. The process involves institutional alliances as well as technological conventions. Different levels of participation and different expectations for returns may affect the result. If one institution provides the majority of materials for a digital project, for example, with many others completing the whole, the lead institution may claim special consideration or returns, requiring extra negotiation.

Successful projects to combine digital resources through a common system for organization and delivery suggest a new kind of model for collection building. Even in preservation microfilming, cooperative efforts to preserve a single title typically involve assembling dispersed materials at a central location for filming, or bringing together film prepared at various locations for splicing and duplication. The workflow of digital collection development can remain radically decentralized provided a robust infrastructure for collaboration is in place. The Research Libraries Group project, Studies in Scarlet: Marriage, Women, and the Law, 1815–1914, is a case in point (see http://www.rlg.org/scarlet/sis.html). Six U.S. libraries and one in Great Britain have scanned trial accounts, case law, statutes, treatises, and other materials related to the theme expressed in the project title. RLG established file-naming conventions and other guidelines, designed the interface, and will store the images—

one of several models being explored for the creation of virtual collections. The conceptual kinship with traditional collection development is clear.

Costs and Benefits

Cost-benefit analysis assesses the relationship between functionality, demand, and expense. Limited resources and competing demands on organizational time and energy mean that the analysis must be rigorous and complete. The costs of creating electronic resources vary considerably. File size (and the associated storage needs) and processing requirements account for part of the differences, though labor requirements are even more important. Bitmap images in black and white are relatively inexpensive to produce and store. Grayscale images, currently capable of capturing up to 254 shades of gray plus black and white, are more costly; color images are the most costly of all. In each case, images with higher resolution result in larger digital files.

Accurate ASCII files of searchable text, even though occupying far less computer memory than any image file, are more expensive to produce than bitmaps of the same material. The main reason is that OCR software is not yet fully reliable. Materials converted by machine must be painstakingly proofread, or the source documents must be rekeyed in combination with careful attention to the detection and correction of errors. Costs rise even more for marked-up text, which entails yet another level of analysis and intervention. Creating other kinds of special databases or enhanced capabilities, for image files or for text, likewise raises the costs.

Costs vary even within specific approaches to digitization. All other things being equal, for example, it is less expensive to scan from single sheets than from bound volumes. Small sheets are less expensive to scan than oversized ones. Items in good condition are less costly to process than those that are deteriorated and thus require special handling.

Available cost figures for digitizing projects are often misleading. Cost projections seek to pin down a rapidly moving target. Although the prices of computer storage and processing power, for example, continue to fall, most projections simply extrapolate from available information about current price structures. Analyses often fail to account for certain categories of effort that, were they included, would alter cost calculations significantly. Labor expenses, for instance, often reflect only a pro-rated price per page that overlooks the real cost of a full-time employee. Crucial pieces of the workflow are sometimes written off as one-time research and development expenses. Functions such as preparation of materials for scanning, indexing, bibliographic description, post-scan processing, and long-term file management may not be factored into cost equations. Incomplete cost analyses can impute benefits that are difficult to represent on a project balance sheet. It may be true, for example, that ready access to backfiles of digitized journals will ultimately reduce or eliminate construction costs for new stack space. Unfortunately, money not spent on capital projects is unlikely to be reflected in support for other library initiatives. Though digitizing projects must calculate the likely costs and benefits, our ability to predict either of them is as yet rudimentary.

QUESTIONS TO ASK

Who will benefit from the proposed digital product?
It is important to consider whether the product will support better teaching or research and enable students to learn more, or in different ways if, for example, texts or images are more fully revealed. Digitization may allow librarians to manage collections and provide services more effectively, or to provide traditional services such as copying or interlibrary loan at lower cost or at less risk to collections.

Is the intellectual value of the proposed product commensurate with the expense?
The limited resources available for digitization might have greater impact if they were directed at another project, or directed toward an entirely different approach to providing access through exhaustive indexing perhaps, or microfilming, or some other type of reformatting that would prove in the end more useful to scholars.

Could an acceptable product be created at lower cost?

When materials are scanned to support short-term course work, for example, careful (and expensive) post-scan processing to eliminate extraneous marks and speckles or to deskew misaligned images may be a waste of time. Likewise, an adequate substitute for full-text scanning of little-used journals might be provided by linking scanned tables of contents and indexes to bibliographic records and relying on traditional forms of document delivery.

How will the proposed project address the long-term costs associated with digital files?

The accumulated body of digital products may enable savings elsewhere in the institution—for example, by reducing staff costs for reshelving bound journals, or by lowering the costs of storage, circulation, and preservation, and these savings could offset some or all of the expense of digitizing. But such savings as may be realized are difficult to predict. It is essential to realize that the costs of digitization are just beginning at the time of initial capture. The programmatic capacity to distribute and maintain electronic resources, and to migrate them to new forms as original digital platforms fail and formats and software are superseded, is fundamental to long-term efforts. In addition, there are staff costs associated with training and user support. Finally, rising user expectations may require that existing digital files be reprocessed in new ways. When OCR software is perfected, for example, unsearchable bitmap images of texts could be thought unsatisfactory. Projects that do not plan for change may become obsolete, and therefore irrelevant.

Can external funding be secured to support the proposed project?

Some foundations are particularly interested in electronic products, and specialized scholarly initiatives may attract their support.

Conclusion

Research libraries are eagerly embracing the digital world. They are acquiring access to great quantities of electronic materials produced outside their walls and are making digital versions of their own holdings. These projects, as they become more common, are bringing both the broad issues and the nuances of the digitizing process into sharper relief.

Projects based on careful review, analysis, and planning can yield electronic resources that are functional and faithful to the original sources, and that support new kinds of scholarship. A detailed plan of work, regular assessment of progress, closely documented adjustments and corrections, and the retention of other project-related data can strengthen the knowledge base for future efforts. Each success, as well as each failure, will bring us closer to fulfilling the promises of the electronic environment.

The process of deciding what to digitize anticipates all the major stages of project implementation. Digital resources depend on the nature and importance of the original source materials, but also on the nature and quality of the digitizing process itself—on how well relevant information is captured from the original, and then on how the digital data are organized, indexed, delivered to users, and maintained over time. Disciplined efforts to address the themes and questions outlined in this essay will help ensure that new digitizing projects fulfill the expectations of libraries, students, and scholars.

KAREN F. GRACY

"Preservation in a Time of Transition: Redefining Stewardship of Time-Based Media in the Digital Age"

Written for this volume.

THE TECHNICAL PRESERVATION challenges resulting from the transition to digital formats in media preservation often dominate professional discourse.[1] This preoccupation with technological change and its impact on archival work, while understandable, often overshadows other equally important shifts in the field. To reflect deeply on the stewardship of audiovisual materials in the twenty-first century requires one to also contemplate how radical disruptions in modes of media production, distribution, and consumption have begun to irrevocably transform the preservation landscape. These changes in media infrastructure and economics, preservation politics, and social uses of audiovisual materials have greatly influenced archival work by readjusting preservation priorities and creating new frameworks to guide policy and practice.

No Turning Back? The Tipping Point for the Digital Transition

In the various media industries, production companies, distribution networks, and manufacturers of player devices have for the most part completed their transition to digital formats. Digital media communication tools and formats have largely replaced analog technologies in the motion picture, television, and recording industries. In the domestic and commercial spheres, media consumers now create, use, and share material digitally in their daily lives.

Media archivists have differed in their response to the digital transition, with some areas switching to digital archiving workflows more quickly than others. The audio archival community, faced with the quick fade of most analog formats, largely abandoned analog carriers *en masse* as target formats for reformatting projects by the end of the 1990s. As Schüller indicates, the assumption was that "audio preservation has to concentrate on the safeguarding of the content, not of the original carriers."[2] The digital transition has occurred more slowly for moving image archivists, with the reaction being slower but still deliberate.[3] Archivists' concerns about the quality of highly compressed proprietary digital video formats made large-scale reformatting to digital somewhat controversial, particularly for higher resolution material such as 35 mm. and 70 mm. motion picture film.

The true tipping point for those working with analog motion picture film was the rapid decline of business prospects for key players in the motion picture industry in the first decade of the twenty-first century. Motion picture camera manufacturers have ceased production of new film cameras in order to focus on the digital production market.[4] Reduced demand for motion picture stock led film manufacturers such as Kodak and Fuji to dramatically reduce production. In the case of Kodak, the free fall in the market for motion picture film partially contributed to their decision to declare Chapter 11 bankruptcy in 2012.[5] Fuji has ceased production entirely.[6]

Most theater chains in the United States will have made the switch to digital projection by the end of 2015, which means that projection equipment, spare parts, and the technicians trained to maintain projectors will disappear relatively quickly.[7] Archivists who wish to continue showing film as a projected medium will face limited options for sustaining that mode of exhibition going forward.

The demand for laboratory services has also decreased, as fewer and fewer production companies shoot on film and demand for distribution prints has dried up in the wake of conversion of most commercial movie theaters to digital distribution. Many labs, such as restoration specialist Haghefilm in the Netherlands, have already declared bankruptcy or are narrowly avoiding it at this time.

These recent developments indicate the rapid acceleration of the digital transition, and will have a significant impact on archival work. While many film archivists still have grave reservations about transferring analog motion pictures to digital formats because of their concerns for costs of long-term storage and quality of transfers, the archival market is probably too small to sustain more than a handful of specialist laboratories for those who would prefer to continue making preservation copies on film.

Media preservation professionals have long relied upon access to new film stock and knowledgeable laboratory technicians in order to create preservation-quality transfers. Given the rapid decline of the infrastructure needed to support most analog formats, the archival community understands that the facilities and resources available to them to complete their preservation work are rapidly disappearing and they must adjust their expectations and workflows accordingly. While film archivists have historically defined preservation as film-to-film transfer, the pressure to rethink those standards is intense and may soon invoke policy changes not just for institutions, but also funding agencies that support preservation work.

Materiality of Time-based Media in a Digital World

In the wake of this digital transition, media archives have reconsidered their aspirations and made many adjustments to their policies and practices. As the nature of engagement with time-based media evolves, goals for preservation and access will change in turn. The die appears to have been cast: convert to digital media formats or risk failure in carrying out the critical missions of preservation and access.

Yet, not all archivists have completely acquiesced to this imperative. Running counter to this inevitability are those who see media archives at a crossroads for redefining their relevance. While the perceived inevitability of the digital takeover may seem to have closed the door on the study of analog material as historical objects, the materiality of these objects continues to pique interest in media histories and preservation research.

Cultural historians, format enthusiasts, and artists often revive interest in media cast-offs. In the recent collected volume *Residual Media*, scholars such as Jonathan Sterne, Kate Egan, and John Davis explore how continued fascination with older media formats by enthusiasts creates niche markets and may even provide a window into society's view of itself.[8]

Conservation scientists also remain interested in artifactual information embedded in analog media; they often investigate the techno-histories of media formats in the process of considering how best to represent significant properties of analog formats in digital forms. Carl Haber's work on how to create digital images of wax cylinder grooves has been informed by his research into the science of recording sound waves in the late nineteenth century.[9] Mark Roosa notes that many sound archives originated as medium-centered institutions, focusing on the particular conservation needs of a certain format and the associated social and historical contexts associated with a particular format.[10] Although the sound-archiving community has embraced a digital future, it is likely that those medium-centered archives will still cling to an identity at least partially shaped by their format-specific origins.

While many of those archivists working with older sound and moving image systems continue to find evidential value in analog source material, proponents for the digital changeover often see little value in archives clinging to obsolete formats. The suggestion that media archives might risk irrelevance by becoming "museums of dead media" has thus spurred the transition to digital formats for many institutions. Yet, many scholar-archivists in the field maintain that only by restoring historical and cultural context to analog objects will media archives find renewed purpose. Paolo Cherchi Usai argues that with the decline of analog motion pictures as a communication method and subsequent scarcity of prints in the wake of their replacement with digital copies, films finally have the opportunity to be taken seriously as cultural artifacts.[11] Similarly, David Francis contends, "Art museums display the original artifact, and the public has been educated to believe that a copy, however good, is no substitute. It was hard to make a similar case for films, until now, but with the possibility that film stock will no longer be manufactured and that existing viewing prints will be as much unique artifacts as the negatives from which they were produced, the case has become much stronger."[12]

Exhibition is one area of moving image archival work that will be heavily impacted by the digital transition, particularly exhibition in theatrical venues. As the available facilities and equipment to screen analog films dwindles and as moving images are consumed almost exclusively via digital devices, archivists working with motion picture material in cultural heritage institutions find themselves debating whether they should be maintaining projectable analog film collections, for how long, and for what purposes. Those archives that wish to continue to support analog motion picture projection will need to develop and sustain resources through cooperative efforts such as those by the Projection and Technical Presentation Committee of the Association of Moving Image Archivists, which has devoted considerable time to the consideration of standards and infrastructure required to keep analog projection a reality for those archives that choose to continue to support this access method.

Imminent Impacts of the Digital Transition on Preservation Policies and Practices

While this brief introduction cannot serve as a comprehensive review of all potential changes for preservation workflows and policies, the author suggests that the digital transition will affect all aspects of media archives. In particular, the field must consider the following impacts:

- As day-to-day archival work of acquisition, storage, preservation, and access becomes more and more focused on the management of digital materials and conversion of analog materials to digital formats, archivists will finally coalesce to create commonly accepted guidelines and best practices for digital workflows. In particular, archivists need frameworks for measuring and conducting quality control over transfer processes and products.

- While digital workflows continue to evolve, other processes such as cataloging and metadata creation will reflect new description and access requirements. More metadata, particularly technical and provenance information, will be needed at the time of acquisition, and many types of cataloging actions may be automated, or semiautomated, such as basic record creation at time of ingest into systems or creation of digital versions of analog materials.

- The increasing separation between content and carrier may spur development of interest and expertise in the study of certain analog moving image and sound materials as physical objects, particularly in cases where either formats or the materials themselves are acknowledged to have artifactual or historical value.

- As Gregory Lukow and others have noted, the copyright status of many media objects still restricts the options of archivists to reproduce material for preservation and access purposes. In the next decade, archivists will be advocating for revisions to copyright law to permit them to take action for purposes of preservation and increasing action for material in the purgatory of uncertain copyright status.[13]

- Finally, archives will continue to acquire and provide access to material in new ways. Roosa predicts that many institutions will become aggregators of materials from many different institutions and commercial sources. Scholars, artists, students, and other consumers of archival media objects will no doubt welcome the expansion of access to a wider variety of material.[14]

It is hoped that this brief introduction to the following sources on time-based media preservation will provide additional evidence of the current state of the field. The forces advocating the digital transition have irrevocably altered the nature of media stewardship, affecting both daily work practices and archival missions. By contemplating these shifts and their potential impact, the field may better understand how the next generation of media archives and preservation professionals will adapt and endure.

NOTES

1. Howard Besser, "Digital Preservation of Moving Image Material?" *The Moving Image*, 1.2 (Fall 2001): 39–55.

2. Dietrich Schüller, "Socio-technical and Sociocultural Challenges of Audio and Video Preservation," *International Preservation News*, no. 46 (December 2008): 6.

3. Nicola Mazzanti, "Goodbye, Dawson City, Goodbye: Digital Cinema Technologies from the Archive's Perspective: Part 2," *AMIA Tech Review* 3 (2011), accessed January 13, 2013, http://www.amiaconference.com/techrev/V11-01/mazzanti.htm.

4. Debra Kaufman, "Film Fading to Black," *Creative Cow Magazine* (2011), accessed January 13, 2013, http://magazine.creativecow.net/article/film-fading-to-black.

5. Michael J. de la Merced, "Eastman Kodak Files for Bankruptcy," *New York Times*, January 19, 2012, accessed January 11, 2013, http://dealbook.nytimes.com/2012/01/19/eastman-kodak-files-for-bankruptcy.

6. Joe Marine, "Fuji Ceasing Motion Picture Film Production, Kodak is on Life Support. Is Celluloid Done For?" October 1, 2012, accessed January 13, 2013, http://nofilmschool.com/2012/10/fuji-ceasing-film-production-kodak-on-life-support-is-celluloid-done-for/.

7. Gendy Alimurung, "Movie Studios are Forcing Hollywood to Abandon 35mm Film. But the Consequences of Going Digital Are Vast, and Troubling," *LA Weekly*, April 12, 2012, accessed January 11, 2013, http://www.laweekly.com/2012-04-12/film-tv/35-mm-film-digital-Hollywood/full.

8. *Residual Media*, ed. Charles R. Acland (Minneapolis, MN: University of Minnesota Press, 2007).

9. Carl Haber, "Imaging Historical Voices," *International Preservation News*, no. 46 (December 2008): 23–28.

10. Mark Roosa, "Sound and Audio Archives," in *Encyclopedia of Library and Information Sciences*, 3rd ed. (Taylor & Francis, 2010), 4914.

11. Paolo Cherchi Usai, "The Conservation of Moving Images," *Studies in Conservation* 55 (2010): 250–257.

12. David Francis, "The Way Ahead," *Journal of Film Preservation*, no. 82 (2010): 11.

13. Gregory Lukow, "The Politics of Orphanage: The Rise and Impact of the 'Orphan Film' Metaphor on Contemporary Preservation Practice," accessed January 11, 2013, http://www.sc.edu/film symposium/archive/orphans2001/lukow.html.

14. Roosa, 4919.

HOWARD BESSER

"Digital Preservation of Moving Image Material?"

The Moving Image *1.2 (Fall 2001): 39–55.*

DIGITAL IMAGING AND broadband networks are changing the moving image production and distribution process. In response to these changes, preservationists not only need to rethink some of their daily practices, but also need to engage in some fundamental paradigm shifts in how they view the preservation process. This article describes some of the technologically induced changes in moving image production and distribution, how those changes are altering viewer habits and expectations, and how those in turn affect how we will need to deliver and store moving image materials. Various approaches to preserving digital materials are explained. Finally, the author points to two paradigm shifts that will be likely for moving image preservation: from preserving completed works as a whole to asset management, and from preserving an artifact to preserving disembodied content.

The advent of digital technology is leading to widespread changes in moving image production. These changes are reverberating through all aspects of moving images—from distribution channels to user expectations. Though the time lines and extent of many of these changes are overly inflated, these changes are still likely to force a dramatic shift in the film preservation paradigm. Key shifts will cluster around two areas. The first is a movement from saving finished works as a whole to an asset management approach that deals both with component parts of works and with ancillary materials that relate to the work. The second involves learning how to shift from a mode focused on preserving an original negative or print as a physical artifact to one instead focused on saving a digital work that has no tangible embodiment.

Electronic works are encoded and usually stored on a physical storage device such as digital or analog tape. The most obvious impediment to electronic longevity is what this author has termed "the viewing problem" (Besser, "Digital Longevity," 2000). While the default for physical artifacts is to persist (or to deteriorate in slow increments), the default for electronic objects is to become inaccessible unless someone takes an immediate proactive role to save them. Thus, we can discover and study three-thousand-year-old cave paintings and pottery (even though the pottery may be in shards that we need to piece together). But we are unable to decipher any of the contents of an electronic file on an eight-inch floppy disk from only twenty years ago.

The Problem of Digital Changes and User Expectations

Digital technology and high-speed networks are leading to sweeping changes throughout society, and moving image production and distribution are in no way immune to either the technological changes or the social expectations that these changes have induced.

Thus far, the most far-reaching changes in production have been felt in the arena of special effects. For years most special effects have been done digitally. In the past the completed digital effects were transferred back onto film and intercut with the rest of a production, but as general moving image production itself becomes increasingly digital, this intermediary transfer to film will become far less common.

Small-budget independent productions are increasingly being shot and edited in digital form. According to director Mike Figgis, "there is clearly a technical revolution taking place. You can edit a film on a laptop, and there is the Internet, the streaming and downloading capabilities. These are the technical elements of the revolution." He believes that this is leading to massive changes in the industry: "Like anything, once you open up a system to those outside the tight corps who control it, you get a massive increase in product. You also get a lot more talent exposed to the possibilities of creating something new. I'm really looking forward to that kind of chaos and the results…. But the real revolution will come when we challenge what I call our biblical way of making films—the way we edit, shoot and score our films, which is very stagnant. I hope that young filmmakers will continue to say, 'I don't want to do it like that.' Hopefully, with the new technologies, nothing will stop them" (Silverman 2000).

It is only a matter of time before high-budget productions are entirely shot and edited in digital form. The most talked-about foray into this field is Star Wars Episode II, scheduled for release in summer 2002. According to George Lucas, "The tests have convinced me that the familiar look and feel of motion picture film are fully present in this digital 24P system, and that the picture quality between the two is indistinguishable on the large screen" (Laguna 2000). According to Jim Morris, president of Lucas Digital, "The image quality of the new Sony camera and the Panavision lenses exceeded our expectations, and really validate the 24P system as a great new tool for moviemaking. All of our hopes about doing digital capture for the big screen have started to be realized" (Laguna 2000). Though most productions don't have the budget of Lucasfilm, it is only a matter of time before further demand for this technology drops the prices enough that digital production becomes commonplace for the studios.

Digital distribution coupled with digital theater projection is not nearly as imminent. The first such distribution was June 6, 2000, when Cisco Systems and Qwest Communications transmitted Fox's animated adventure movie *Titan A.E.* from Los Angeles to Atlanta. There have been other experiments since, and a number of competing digital projection standards have emerged; one of these standards claims to have equipped more than two dozen theaters worldwide (Digital Light 2001). Some analysts contend that

this number will jump to five hundred by the time of the release of *Star Wars: Episode II* (Laguna 2000),[1] but the process is far from mainstream. Competing standards (NIST 2001) and the large cost of installing digital projection equipment will slow the growth of this type of projection. It is also unclear whether the recent bankruptcy of major theater chains (Loews, United Artists) will slow or accelerate this type of distribution. When we eventually reach the point where digital distribution of commercial releases is widespread, economics will dictate that many of those works will never be converted to film or video. But this is unlikely to happen this decade.

Technological changes have altered users' expectations in a variety of ways. One can make the claim that the time-shifting features of the VCR helped instill a user mindset of viewing a video any time of day or night, and that this in turn created a market for video-on-demand and for cinema multiplexes that staggered starting times so that a particular new release might be seen every half hour.

The World Wide Web is leading to further expectations of immediacy, as well as increased desires to see both massive amounts of related materials and to view material in fragmented ways. Web surfing involves a user bouncing from one tangentially related fragment of information to another. Web surfers seldom read an entire lengthy document online, but skim part of a document, jump to something related to it and briefly read that, then jump to still another related fragment.

Recent enhanced DVDs appeal to the Web-surfer mentality. Adding additional material about the making of the film, interviews with cast and crew, stills from the set, outtakes, and other ancillary materials all appeal to the Web-surfer expectation of having a vast array of related primary-source material available. Over time we may very well see a demand for users to just view particular clips (Besser 1994) within a completed movie. And on the horizon is a whole new set of products that involve repurposed clips that we can only begin to imagine.[2] We do know that today's primary multimedia delivery vehicles (both DVDs and the Web) are enhancing user expectations of extensive interactivity.

From Saving Completed Works to Managing Assets

The digital impact mentioned here is likely to promote widespread changes within the moving image archival community. The increasing amount of material originating in digital form (some of which may never be transferred to film or video), the release of moving image products that contain a variety of ancillary material, the increased focus on fragments that need to be easily found and that sometimes may be repurposed and reused in multiple digital products—all these elements imply significant changes in practices for moving image archives.

Technological developments have led to a large number of users no longer being satisfied with merely viewing end products. The high demand for additional content implies that some organization needs to supply the ancillary material that helps contextualize the finished product. Interviews, scripts, correspondence, sketches of sets, special effects, outtakes, and even moving images of initial casting calls are all valuable assets that surround a completed work. In the past, only a limited amount of this type of material was saved, and often it was saved outside the moving image archive (in records management units, print archives, or special collection libraries). In the future, as new digital products and services emerge, there will be increasing pressure to minimize the dispersal of these assets. And moving image archivists who do not move quickly to widen their areas of responsibility may soon find themselves marginalized and subordinated to digital asset managers.

Archivists need to shift from a paradigm centered around saving a completed work to a new paradigm of saving a wide body of material that contextualizes a work. They also need to proactively seek out material (particularly moving image material) that today may be thrown away routinely, but in the future may prove historically and/or commercially valuable. And they need to fulfill their traditional role of making sure that this material will persist over time.

Archivist involvement in the stages before the final cut implies new skill sets. Ingesting outtakes means developing new skills for organizing and managing this type of material. And doing a good job of managing special effects data implies understanding how to keep software files accessible over time.

Preserving special effects files may prove to be critically important. Several decades from now, a person looking back on a film like *The Matrix* will be far less interested in the film as a whole and much more interested in the special effects and how they were done. Access to the special effects data files is likely to be valuable in understanding the historical development of moving image material, and the final cut on film reveals little of the groundbreaking processes involved.

As we have seen with both the Web and DVDs, there is increasing demand to view material in fragments. This type of fragmented use is a perfect complement to a postmodern era, where mass cultural elements are repeatedly recontextualized. Promotional units within a studio, advertisers, production companies, and end users all periodically request to see and/or use a particular clip. This implies an increasing need for access at lower levels of granularity than a completed work. Moving image archivists need to prepare themselves for requests at this lower level of granularity, and would do well to follow some of the literature on methods for finding clips that do not rely upon human labor to catalog and index all the subparts of a work (Besser, "Bibliography," 2000; Turner 1999; Goodrum 1998).

Archivists shifting to articulate an asset management approach can have strategic advantages. Some of the greatest influx of money for preservation in the past twenty years emerged when studios realized that there was an after-market for older films. Today we are living in an age where content repurposing is a driving economic force, and there is high expectation that any given media asset will be used in a variety of secondary multimedia products (from a clip on the Web to incorporation within a video game, to a variety of DVDs and CD-ROMs, even to including clips of one film within a subsequent film [like *The Limey*]). Savvy administrators recognize that today's capital investment in adequately preserving and indexing media assets can pay off in long-term repeated use and reuse.

Still, the shift from managing completed works as a whole to managing a range of assets will be a profound one. And much of this shift requires background and knowledge about how to make digital files persist over time.

Problems with Preserving Anything Digital

Information encoded and stored in digital form is fragile, but in very different ways from film stock. And though digital storage shares some characteristics with video storage, it is different from that as well. There are several special problems with preserving works in digital form, but I will begin with the simplest aspect: the physical storage medium. Film is a rather durable storage medium; barring a few exceptions (such as nitrate and Eastmancolor), film stored under proper conditions is stable and relatively long-lasting. Video storage, on the other hand, is unstable. Compared to film, videotapes have a relatively short shelf life. The physical strata used to store videos decays relatively quickly, and video preservationists recognize that they need to periodically refresh the contents of a videotape by copying it onto another physical stratum before the original deteriorates.

Digital storage, like video storage, requires periodic refreshing because the physical storage stratum decays.[3] Digital storage offers the illusion that preservation is not a problem because, unlike analog storage formats (such as film and video), a digital copy is ostensibly an exact replica of what was copied (whereas each copy of a film or video loses quality from that of the previous copy).

But though digital refreshing is itself near lossless, works stored in digital form raise other preservation problems that are enormous. Chief among these is the problem of rapidly changing file formats—files encoded in AVI or MPEG-1 or the various flavors of MPEG-2 can be periodically refreshed onto new physical strata, but it is highly unlikely that those formats will be viewable a decade from now. To understand this problem, we need only to turn to recent experience with much simpler word processing documents.

Word processing files (which are primarily ASCII text, and thus much simpler formats than moving or even still images) are generally readable for half a dozen years after they are created. But even these word processing formats become inaccessible after a dozen years. Fifteen years ago WordStar had (by far) the largest market penetration of any word processing program. But few people today can read any of the many millions of WordStar files, even when those have been transferred onto contemporary computer hard disks. Even today's popular word processing applications (such as Microsoft Word) typically cannot view files created any further back than two previous versions of the same application (and sometimes these still lose important formatting). Image and multimedia formats, lacking an underlying basis of ASCII text, pose much greater obsolescence problems, as each format chooses to code image, sound, or control (synching) representation in a different way.

Elsewhere I have outlined other digital longevity problems such as "the translation problem." "the custodial problem," "the scrambling problem," and "the inter-relational problem" (Besser, "Digital longevity," 2000).1 have also specifically applied these problems to electronic art (Besser forthcoming). All of these are relevant to digital preservation of moving image material. Particularly notable are the custodial problem and the translation problem.

The custodial problem focuses upon who should be in charge of making something persist over time. Though we have developed traditions of which organizations (and who within a given organization) should take responsibility for preserving and maintaining various types of analog material (film, video, stills, correspondence, manuscripts, printed matter), no such traditions exist yet for digital material. As a result of this, much current material originating in digital form falls through the cracks and is unlikely to be accessible to future generations.

For example, print archivists and special collections librarians who aggressively pursue print-based collection development in their particular specialty areas claim that it should be the responsibility of their organizations' computing staff to pursue collection development of material originating in digital form.[4]

Yet the computing staff claim that it should be the subject-matter specialists' responsibility to pursue collection development of digital materials. Meanwhile, much of this fragile material is not collected at all. Motion picture animation studio archives that have had established procedures for saving sketches and cells typically have no procedure in place for saving the digital files that are now replacing those sketches and cells.

Many moving image archivists feel they have neither the resources nor the technical knowledge to take charge of digital files of moving image materials. They have no money for file servers and no idea of how to develop a long-term digital migration strategy. So either digital moving image files end up not being collected at all, or they become the responsibility of a department that has not been trained in archival and preservation practices (such as an information technology department or a digital asset management department).

Though at the present time resource allocation and technological skills may force the handling of digital material into another department, this is a dangerous long-term strategy. Archivists have well-developed training and skills for handling moving image materials, and these skills are seldom found in staff from other departments. As costs for handling digital materials diminish and as strategies for long-term maintenance of digital files become better known, reasons for handling digital material separately will start to fade, and administrators will begin to realize that digital files of moving images have much more in common with film and video than with word processing files and databases. At some point, the idea of handling digital moving image files in a separate department will sound as old-fashioned as establishing separate departments for 16mm., 35mm., and CinemaScope film formats.

A number of experiments are underway to explore strategies for maintaining digital content over time. We still need to develop guidelines and best practices so that organizations and individuals who want to make the effort to try to make digital information persist will know how to do so. A key function of archives is ensuring the authenticity of a work. Print archives

do this by amassing "evidence" and by maintaining a "chain of custody" (Council 2000). Film archives follow a variation of this through strategies like identifying the release negative. But when works are subject to repeated acts of "refreshing," as most approaches to digital longevity propose (see the next section of this essay, "General Approaches to Digital Preservation"), these traditional ways of ensuring authenticity break down. Files repeatedly copied to new strata face the likelihood that changes will be introduced into these files, and we know little about how to control mutability across repeated refreshments. This set of problems constitutes the custodial problem.

Another important issue is how a work translated into new delivery devices changes meaning (the translation problem). While a lay person may occasionally confuse the two, people in the cultural community are aware that a photograph or poster of an oil painting is definitely different from the painting itself, and that a video of a motion picture film is not the same as the film. We clearly understand that a reproduction of a work (particularly in another format) may convey certain characteristics of that work, but is dramatically different from that work. The faithfulness of photographic reproduction processes has raised questions about differences between originals and reproductions (Benjamin 1978; Besser 1997; Besser 1987), particularly of photographs. But those of us in the cultural community still recognize that a digitized photograph displayed on a screen is quite different from the paper-based photograph it was digitized from, and that a motion picture film converted and shown on a video screen is quite different from the original film.

Today, most electronic moving image works (both video and digital) are displayed on cathode-ray-tube (CRT) screens. With the advent of liquid-crystal and other flat-panel display units, a decade from now CRT screens may be as rare as black-and-white monitors are today. And fifty years from now, it is unlikely that one would even be able to find a working CRT screen. For some electronic works (certainly for artistic ones that concern themselves with the "look" of a CRT screen), attempting to display that work on a flat-panel screen would result in something that the creator would regard as a poor reproduction of his or her work (perhaps akin to a photograph of an oil painting). For one of his pieces that opened in the new Tate Modern Museum, video artist Gary Hill told the museum that they can replace fading CRT screens with other similar-sized CRT screens, but he was adamant that replacing any of them with flat-panel screens would significantly alter the meaning of his work (Laurenson 2000).

Computer-based moving image works are often designed for particular screen dimensions. As screen resolutions get higher, these older works end up looking smaller and smaller on contemporary screens. (For example, a work created to fill a 640 x 480 screen would take up about one-third of a contemporary 1024 x 768 screen.) This raises issues of how best to display older digital works on newer digital screens. Though there are certainly parallels between this problem and those experienced by film archives wanting to display older films with proper lenses, in appropriate aspect ratios, and original frame rates, digital works convey the illusion that one merely needs to play them and they will be displayed appropriately. With traditional media, the separation between the work (stored on film or video) and the display device is clear; with digital media the public often does not understand the separation between the stored work and the display device (particularly since the stored work may be repeatedly copied from device to device or even streamed).

General Approaches to Digital Preservation

The following is a brief history of the approaches to preservation of simpler types of digital materials. In the mid-1990s the library community began to worry about the fragility of works stored in digital form. The Commission on Preservation and Access and the Research Libraries Group formed a task force to explore how significant this problem really was. The task force report sounded an alarm: "Rapid changes in the means of recording information, in the formats for storage, and in the technologies for use threaten

to render the life of information in the digital age as, to borrow a phrase from Hobbes, 'nasty, brutish and short'" (Task Force 1996). As the problem of digital longevity had repercussions within the arts community as well, the Getty Conservation Institute and Getty Information Institute collaborated with leading technologists to put together a conference and book trying to broadly outline and bring attention to the problem (Maclean and Davis 1998). Both of these seminal works identified the depth of the digital longevity problem but only pointed out very general approaches that might possibly lead to solutions. Others have pointed to the problem, again with little beyond generalities in terms of offering solutions (Besser, "Digital Longevity," 2000; Rothenberg 1999; Lyman and Besser 1998: Sanders 1997). Only one conference proceeding (Hummelen and Sille 1999) and one article (Besser forthcoming) have been directed specifically toward multimedia artistic content, and none have been specifically addressed toward moving image material. But these seminal works have identified key concepts that we need to understand before considering digital preservation of moving image material.

The concept of *refreshing* (first outlined for records by Mallinson (1986) and identified for a wide body of digital works by the Task Force on Archiving of Digital Information (1996)) involves periodically moving a file from one physical storage medium to another to avoid the physical decay or the obsolescence of that medium.[5] Because physical storage media (even CD-ROMs) decay, and because technological changes make older storage devices (such as eight-inch floppy disk drives) inaccessible to new computers, some ongoing form of refreshing is likely to be necessary for many years to come (Besser, "Digital Longevity," 2000). Besides raising the issue of assuring authenticity, this suggested approach ignores the even more substantial problem of constantly changing file formats.

Two key approaches have been proposed to deal with the problem of changing file formats: migration and emulation (Task Force 1996). These are seen as alternatives to one another, but both approaches are supposed to be used in conjunction with refreshing.

Migration is an approach that involves periodically moving files from one file encoding format to another that is usable in a more modern computing environment. (An example would be converting a WordStar file to WordPerfect, then to Word 3.0, then to Word 5.0, then to Word 97. etc.) Migration seeks to limit the problem of files encoded in a wide variety of file formats that have existed over time by gradually bringing all former formats into a limited number of contemporary formats.

Emulation seeks to solve a similar problem, but its approach is to focus on the applications software rather than on the files containing information. Emulation backers want to build software that mimics every type of application that has ever been written for every type of file format, and make them run on whatever the current computing environment is. (So, with the proper emulators, applications like WordStar or Word 3.0 could effectively run on today's machines.) Emulation is most closely associated with the writings of Rand scientist Jeff Rothenberg (Rothenberg 1995, 1999, 2000).

Moving Away From Artifact-based Approaches

The conventional paradigm that has shaped all types of conservation efforts for centuries is focused on preserving the artifact. Though moving image archivists are much more aware of the limitations of this paradigm (having dealt with reformatting of nitrate and Eastmancolor) than conservationists in charge of other formats, the field still focuses on saving original artifacts like negatives and release prints.

But in a digital world, the concept of saving an original artifact carries little meaning. First of all, it is unlikely that there is a single original; there will be at least several copies that are absolutely identical (back-up copies, copies stored off-site, etc.). Second, unlike film or video where copies lack some of the pristine qualities of originals, a digital copy is indistinguishable from the digital work that was copied. Finally, as we have seen earlier, any digital work will have to be copied and refreshed on a periodic basis.

A digital archivist needs to move away from an artifact-based approach and instead adopt an approach that focuses on stewardship of disembodied digital information. This requires some knowledge about strategies for making digital content persist (such as refreshing, migration, and emulation). It also requires honing skills to determine the definitive version of the work to be saved.

In a digital environment, the concept of a master is likely to be more useful than the concept of an original. Unlike the word "original," "master" does not necessarily convey physical embodiment. But it does convey the idea that this is the definitive version of a work, though not in such strong terms that it prevents the possibility of multiple variant forms.

The moving image material of the future will resist any attempts to try to put it back onto a linear medium like film or video. We are already seeing multimedia creations complete with moving images, still images, and audio files. We have DVDs with various levels of navigation and degrees of interactivity. And we even have works that are designed to periodically change their attributes (somewhat analogous to various cuts of a single film). This type of material just can't be effectively put back onto a linear medium. And the plethora of media types and file formats pose serious problems for maintaining such a work over time (Besser forthcoming).

Once digital archivists have shifted their conceptual framework to focus on preserving disembodied masters, the question remains of how to do that best. Moving image archivists can learn from other fields, such as conservators of electronic art, who have begun meeting regularly to share approaches and best practices, as well as to develop some generally agreed-upon standards (Hummelen and Sille 1999; Besser forthcoming). Promising developments may come from the May 12, 2000, meeting of moving image archivists in the Los Angeles area entitled "Issues of Preservation and Media Production: New Paradigms for the Digital Age" (Davis 2000).

Embracing the key approaches of refreshing and either migration or emulation will go a long way toward ensuring digital longevity. But the file format problem can best be approached by standardizing on a limited number of file formats among the large number of formats currently used for moving images, sound, still images, synching, and special effects.

Because formats for storing works are so rapidly changing and outdated, custodians of these works may need to involve themselves in standardization processes (Besser, "Digital Longevity," 2000; Lyman and Besser 1998). Encoding files and records in widely adopted standard formats acts as a hedge against rapidly changing software—the more people who are using a standard for encoding, the more likely that new formats will recognize that encoding standard. A wide variety of standards may be useful for moving image materials.

High-order multimedia encoding standards (like SMIL and MPEG-4) may make moving image material less fragile and subject to changes in application software such as Director, Acrobat, and Flash. And capturing and encoding postproduction information such as Edit Decision Lists (EDL) can be critical for future viewing of today's moving image materials. The moving image archivist community needs to involve itself in the standardization process for these high-level encoding standards and make sure that they incorporate the features future users will need. And these same archivists need to press the production community to use more standardized formats and to hand over more material than simply final polished productions. Groups like the Los Angeles-area moving image archivists and AMIA may be effective places for this effort to begin.

Conclusion

Digital encoding is not just another new format for moving image archivists to handle. And though many traditional archivist skills can be applied to the new digital material (which is why this material should be handled by archivists rather than technologists), digital works force a new paradigm of preserving disembodied content and making sure that that content will be viewable far into the future. This is more than a hardware problem of saving a projector for a particular film gauge; it is a software problem involving file formats and applications software. In addition to

moving away from an artifact-based paradigm, digital archivists will need to learn about refreshing, migration, and emulation and will need to get involved with multimedia standards developments.

At the same time, moving image archivists need to be aware of changes in the production process and changes in viewer expectations. The World Wide Web and enhanced DVDs have created a world where all kinds of ancillary materials have become important parts of an enhanced production, and where viewers want to see small fragments of a work almost as much as they want to see a work in its entirety. Moving image archivists need to respond by moving from a focus on completed works to a focus on managing a large set of assets related to a particular work (which itself may have numerous versions). Again, this community has a breadth of knowledge in this area, but for many it will be a large conceptual leap to see themselves as asset managers.

By combining their vast set of skills in handling analog objects as well as moving to new paradigms provoked by the digital age, moving image archivists can continue to play a critical role in preserving our cultural heritage and ensuring that today's works will last well beyond the use of the team that produces them.

NOTES

This article would not have been possible without the encouragement of Ben Davis, who organized the May 2000 meeting of moving image archivists to discuss preservation in the digital age, as well as the Getty's Time and Bits conference. Jan-Christopher Horak provided encouragement and enthusiasm for this topic, and James Turner provided insightful comments. Under a small grant from UCLA's Committee on Research, Snowden Becker contributed research assistance. Karen Gracy also provided help on fact checking and contextualization.

1. Michael Schwartz (sales coordinator for Sony Pictures High Definition Center in Culver City) has indicated that the studios may partially finance the retooling of movie theaters to digital projection.

2. Such as make-your-own videos from existing clips—a kind of video clip art.

3. This is true even with optical digital storage devices like CD-ROMs. These were originally rated with life expectancies of 150 years, but recent experience has shown that many CD-ROMs have become unreadable a decade after they were recorded. As early as 1990 real-life use had revealed a variety of dangers: chemical damage from the ink used to print the label information leaking through to the information layer, separation of the bonded physical layers, and crazing of the metal information-bearing layer, causing the laser beam to deflect so it could not read the information.

4. "Collecting at the Margins: Social Protest and Counterculture Materials," American Library Association Midwinter 1999 Conference, Philadelphia, Collection Development Librarians of Academic Libraries Discussion, January 30, 1999.

5. Refreshing is not viable for analog storage, as each successive copy is inferior to the previous copy. Typically, fourth-generation video copies have lost so much information that they are unviewable.

REFERENCES

Benjamin, Walter. "The Work of Art in the Age of Mechanical Reproduction." In *Illuminations*. New York: Schocken, 1978.

Besser, Howard. *Longevity of Electronic Art*. Proceedings of the International Conference on Hypermedia and Informatics in Museums, September 2001 Forthcoming.

——. "Digital Longevity." In *Handbook for Digital Projects: A Management Tool for Preservation and Access*, ed. Maxine Sitts, 155–66. Andover, Mass.: Northeast Document Conservation Center, 2000.

——. "Bibliography of Moving Image Indexing," 2000, http://www.gseis.ucla.edu/~howard/Classes/287-mov-index-bib.html.

——. "The Changing Role of Photographic Collections with the Advent of Digitization." In *The Wired Museum*, ed. Katherine Jones-Garmil, 115-27. Washington, D.C.: American Association of Museums, 1997.

——. "Fast Forward: The Future of Moving Image Collections." In *Video Collection Management and Development. A Multi-type Library Perspective*, ed. Gary Handman, 411–26. Westport, Conn.: Greenwood, 1994.

——. "Digital Images for Museums." *Museum Studies Journal* 3, no. 1 (fall/winter 1987): 74–81.

Council on Library and Information Resources. *Authenticity in a Digital Environment*. Washington, D.C : Council on Library and Information Resources, May 2000.

Davis, Ben. "Digital Storytelling." *Razorfish Reports* no. 24 (June 16, 2000), http://reports.razorfish.com/frame.html?rr024_film.

Digital Light Processing. "Where is DLP Cinema?" 2001, http://www.dlp.com/dlp/cinema/where.asp.

Goodrum, Abby. "Representing Moving Images: Implications for Developers of Digital Video Collections." Proceedings of the American Society for Information Science, 1998.

Hummelen, Ijsbrand, and Dionne Sille, eds. *Modern Art: Who Cares? An Interdisciplinary Research Project and International Symposium on the Conservation of Modern and Contemporary Art*. Amsterdam: Foundation for the Conservation of Modern Art and Netherlands Institute for Cultural Heritage, 1999.

Laguna Research Partners. Notes from INFOCOMM 2000 (Industry Brief), June 22, 2000, http://www.lrponline.net/infocomm2000_1.PDF.

Laurenson, Pip. "Between Cinema and a Hard Place: The Conservation and Documentation of a Video Installation by Gary Hill." Presented at Preservation of Electronic Media session, twenty-eighth annual meeting of American Institute for Conservation of Historic and Artistic Works. Philadelphia, June 9, 2000.

Lyman, Peter, and Howard Besser. "Defining the Problem of Our Vanishing Memory: Background, Current Status, Models for Resolution." In *Time and Bits: Managing Digital Continuity*, ed. Margaret Maclean and Ben H. Davis, 11–20. Los Angeles: Getty Information Institute and Getty Conservation Institute, 1998.

MacLean, Margaret, and Ben H. Davis, eds. *Time and Bits: Managing Digital Continuity*. Los Angeles: Getty Information Institute and Getty Conservation Institute, 1998.

Mallinson, John C. "Preserving Machine-Readable Archival Records for the Millennia," *Archivaria* 22 (summer 1986): 147–52.

National Institute for Standards and Technology. Digital Cinema 2001 Conference, Gaithersburg, Md., January 11–12, 2001, http://digitalcinema.nist.gov.

Rothenberg, Jeff. *An Experiment in Using Emulation to Preserve Digital Publications*. NEDLIB Report series, no. 1. Den Haag: Koninklijke Bibliotheek, 2000, http://www.kb.nl/coop/nedlib/results/emulationpreservationreport.pdf.

———. *Avoiding Technological Quicksand: Finding a Viable Technical Foundation for Digital Preservation*. Washington, D.C.; Council on Library

and Information Resources, January 1999, http://www.clir.org/pubs/abstract/pub77.html.

———. "Ensuring the Longevity of Digital Documents." *Scientific American* 272, no. I (1995): 42-47.

Sanders, Terry. *Into the Future: Preservation of Information in the Electronic Age*. Santa Monica, Calif.: American Film Foundation, 1997. 16mm film, 60 min.

Silverman, Jason. "Digital Cinema Plays with Form." *Wired News* (April 12, 2000), http://www.wired.com/news/culture/0,1284,35098,00.html.

Task Force on Archiving of Digital Information. "Preserving Digital Information." Commission on Preservation and Access and Research Libraries Group, 1996, http://www.rlg.org/ArchTF/tfdadi.indcx.htm.

Turner, James M. "Metadata for Moving Image Documents." Proceedings of the Twentieth National Online Meeting, New York, May 18–20, ed. Martha E. Williams, 477–86. Medford, N.J.: *Information Today*, 1999.

Selection 4.6

GREGORY LUKOW

"The Politics of Orphanage: The Rise and Impact of the 'Orphan Film' Metaphor on Contemporary Preservation Practice"

A paper delivered at the conference, "Orphans of the Storm I," University of South Carolina, September 23, 1999 (www.sc.edu/filmsymposium/archive/orphans2001/lukow.html); (accessed February 14, 2014).

I SHOULD START by saying that I am not here to define the term "orphan film preservation." That implies pinning it down. I don't want to pin it down. Rather, I want to expound on it as a matter of public policy interest and concern. I want to offer more of a historical meditation, perhaps even a historical critique, of the rise of this metaphor, a metaphor which has taken on an active role as a rhetorical devise within the archival field today. My goal is to examine what orphan film preservation means. It certainly is not

intended to limit the thinking about orphan films as simply a matter of "films produced before 1923 and in the public domain."

Beginning in the early 1990s, the concept of the "orphan film" emerged as the dominant metaphor within the moving image archival community for use in positioning film preservation as a legitimate enterprise on the national public policy cultural agenda. As such, the undeniably wholesome and heartfelt evocation of "Save the Orphan Film" effectively replaced the early-1980s credo of "Nitrate Won't Wait" as an unofficial, field-wide motto. In both instances, these themes were designed to serve as a totemic plea to both the general public and to potential funders alike.

By the end of the 1980s, the rhythmic rallying cry of "Nitrate Won't Wait" had disappeared from everyday preservation discourse, having lost its credibility as a legitimate appeal for specific historical reasons. Namely, gradual recognition was brought about by new scientific research that, indeed, nitrate film *can* "wait," and that all film materials, whether nitrate or acetate—or even now the first rumors of issues with polyester—are potentially equally at risk in the absence of proper storage.

The contemporary turn to and embrace of the "orphan film" metaphor arose within its own specific historical circumstances and under unique public policy pressures. It is important to remember that the use of the term "orphan film" was non-existent within the archival field prior to the early 1990s. This situation changed when the term was brought into the linguistic foreground as a result of the passage by the U.S. Congress of the National Film Preservation Act of 1992.

In a number of ways, this 1992 Act was fashioned in direct contrast to its predecessor, the National Film Preservation Act of 1988. The earlier 1988 Act was the first piece of U.S. federal legislation ever to contain the words "film preservation" in its title. In reality, however, the 1988 Act had almost nothing to do with actual film preservation. But this was ironic only on the surface, until one understood that the roots of the legislation lay in the artists' rights controversies of the late 1980s, controversies then centered in the now near-forgotten debates over computer colorization and film labeling.

The 1992 Film Preservation Act, by contrast, did, finally, have something to do with actual film preservation. The 1992 Act was designed to implement a fieldwide study and national planning initiative on film preservation, an initiative whose recommendations were intended from the outset to pave the way for the establishment of a new mechanism for increased preservation funding support—including, most importantly, federal appropriations. This

mechanism was later realized with the passage of the National Film Preservation Act of 1996 and through it, shortly thereafter, the establishment of the federally-chartered National Film Preservation Foundation.

But to secure Congressional support and federal matching dollars for this new foundation, U.S. law-makers needed reassurances regarding a crucial public policy dilemma that had never been confronted head-on within the moving image archival community: that is, the *prima-facie* concern of utilizing public funds for the preservation of moving image materials whose rights of intellectual property and commercial exploitation were still maintained by private sector corporations, regardless of whether or not the materials *themselves* were held by or the physical property of public or non-profit cultural institutions.

In other words, what was needed prior to securing Congressional support for any national preservation foundation was the drawing of a clear boundary between the types of moving image materials that public sector archives might legitimately expect to be eligible for and deserving of federal support, and, on the other hand, the types of materials whose preservation should necessarily be carried out by corporate or other private-sector rights holders.

At base level, then, the "orphan film" metaphor eliminated a political problem. Its political utility came in the way it serves to identify and describe types of moving image material that qualify for federally recognized, chartered or otherwise supported preservation funding. Within the context of the publication of the seminal report *Film Preservation 1993: A Study of the Current State of American Film Preservation* (published by the Library of Congress in 1993), the concept of the "orphan film" was first proposed and strategically reified as the new public policy metaphor. In its follow-up report, *Redefining Film Preservation: A National Plan* (published in 1994), this new metaphor enabled the Library of Congress to navigate past this public policy contradiction and proceed with its recommendations for new forms of federal preservation funding.

As an historical aside, it should be noted that this was not the first attempt by the federal government to address the dilemma of how best to spend—or not spend—federal dollars in support of film preservation. An earlier attempt was set forth during the early years of the Reagan administration by that administration's first appointed chair of the National Endowment for the Arts, Frank Hodsoll. To the surprise of many in the traditional arts and cultural communities, the Arts Endowment under Hodsoll embraced film preservation with perhaps more passion than any other activity on the Endowment's agenda. But consistent with Reagan-era economic philosophy and its ideological critique of public funding for the arts, the Endowment was also motivated to articulate for the first time the federal government's qualms about appropriating public monies to preserve movies owned by Hollywood studios.

The Endowment's solution was articulated in its oft-stated goal to "avoid duplication of effort," another familiar motto from an earlier era in the archival field that now has been surpassed by the more sharply drawn distinctions embedded in the "orphan film" metaphor. But at that time, in the early 1980s, the NEA's policies ultimately led to the establishment in 1983 of the National Center for Film and Video Preservation at the American Film Institute. The NCFVP at AFI was an agency initially intended to serve as an instrument of national coordination that would assist in this effort to "avoid duplication of effort," most specifically through one of its key programs, the National Moving Image Database (or NAMID for short). Indeed, the NAMID database was an NEA-mandated brainchild, and insofar as it was designed as an earlier model for sorting out public and private holdings and "avoiding duplication of preservation effort," it can be seen as a conceptual precursor to the role that the "orphan film" metaphor has come to play in contemporary archival practice. The fact that NAMID, over time, failed to involve private sector collections in any meaningful way within its holding databases (it did gather a lot of public sector information) can be seen today as in no small way responsible for the need for and rise of the "orphan film" metaphor.

———————

To return from this historical aside to our consideration of the metaphor itself, as a by-product of its

political utility, the "orphan film" concept has also emerged as an extraordinarily valuable device for promoting many types of moving image collections and materials that previously did not receive sufficient public attention. These holdings include the nation's output of documentaries, newsreels, avant-garde and independent film, home movies, amateur and local productions, educational and industrial shorts, etc. The orphan film metaphor has been largely responsible for putting these moving images on the map of our cultural heritage.

Yet despite the undeniably positive and productive "save the children" connotations of the "orphan film" appeal, the question remains as to whether or not there are attendant costs to the public archives—or, indeed, more generally, to the public interest—that emerge in the wake of this new metaphor. Is it a double edged sword? This paper argues that the metaphor carries with it several such restrictions on the public interest—clear challenges now more securely in place within the archival field that are the flip side of the opportunities borne out in its appeal to save the "orphans."

First, it is important to acknowledge that the definition of an orphan film is ineluctably bound up within the discourses and legal distinctions of U.S. copyright law and the various and complex revisions to these laws that have occurred in the past decade. Those revisions were brought about first by NAFTA, then by the GATT treaty, and more recently the 20-year term extension signed into law in October 1998. (Indeed, as an ironic footnote, we can note the utter and absolute lack of impact that the "orphan film" metaphor had within the recent debate on copyright term extension.)

But the definition of the "orphan" is not always or necessarily a simple matter of declaring a specific film title to be unpublished, or never copyrighted, or not renewed, or in some other way having entered the public domain. All too often, such determinations are elusive at best. With such difficulties in mind, I would suggest that both the legality and the politics of "orphanage" need to be defined so that the key criteria is *not* that a public archive can determine, in all cases, films or footage that are guaranteed to be in the public domain with no rights holder legally on the books. Rather, the initial key criteria should be that there is no private-sector entity actively responsible for such materials. For example, what if—purely in terms of historical chronology— a given set of films were clearly still within their term of copyright, but the corporate rights holder no longer exists, or was dissolved without a clear disposition of assets, or the materials have otherwise fallen through the proverbial cracks? Such situations do not describe rare occurrences, but rather the classic cases of thousands of films abandoned or held against debt in laboratories across the country. Or, conversely, what if there is a clearly identified corporate rights holder, but one which over time has changed its business activities, or demonstrated no involvement with its film holdings, or otherwise disavowed any interest in taking responsibility for their preservation? Ultimately, as such examples demonstrate, the flip side of the need to identify and prioritize preservation "responsibilities" is the need to untie the "orphan" concept from strict (and restrictive) considerations of copyright.

Perhaps more pointedly for the moving image preservation community as a whole, the ultimate and most powerful impact of the "politics of orphanage" has been to reinforce in a new way the historic "division of labor" between the public and private sector archives. On the one hand, this division of labor provides the challenge and opportunity for vital new public/private partnerships of the kind embodied in recent years by the Sony Pictures Film and Video Preservation Committee. On the other hand, where private rights holders are less motivated to engage in such collaborative partnerships with the archives, this "division" keeps public sector archives at arm's length from dealing with materials they previously might have more proactively sought to preserve—materials for which a compelling case can often be made that they should remain and be conserved within cultural institutions.

The division of labor fostered by the orphan film metaphor should not be limited to the simple sorting out of *who*—the public sector or the private sector— will preserve *what* materials, under the assumption that it does not matter "who" does the preserving as long as the materials themselves are preserved. No, there is another relevant "division," that between raw "preservation" and preservation within cultural institutions, whether archives, libraries, museums, or historical societies. This is the distinction between, on the one hand, "asset protection" (to use the current parlance) within the context of commercial re-purposing and exploitation, and, on the other hand, cultural preservation and access in the context of national, regional or local institutions with public interest mandates.

Ultimately, while the term "orphan film" evokes the emotional appeal of saving the individual film, television or video "child," a variation on this metaphor, which might more properly and resonantly capture the dual nature of the problem for the field, is that of the "Orphan Library" or orphan collection. Orphan library I use not in the sense of a building, but in terms of all of the materials that are still out there and at risk as a result of what we might reasonably refer to as "orphan producers." It is perhaps only by viewing the politics of "orphanage" in these larger and more expansive terms that one can begin to address both the scale and contradictions within the continuing problem of "orphanage," while also anticipating the new cultural canons that will be established through their adoption or forever lost through their abandonment.

MARK S. ROOSA

"Sound and Audio Archives"

Encyclopedia of Library and Information Sciences, *3rd ed.*
(New York: Taylor & Francis, 2010), pp. 4913–20.

Introduction

To a large extent, the rise of sound archiving directly parallels the development of recorded sound technology itself. Indeed, some of the earliest efforts to archive sounds came in the wake of the invention of the Edison phonograph in 1877, a device which recorded sound onto a wax cylinder. For an illustrated overview of sound record technology, http://history.sandiego.edu.[1] Archival safe keeping of sound recordings during this early period was tied to the commercial distribution of recordings of popular and classical music. As molded wax (and later plastic) cylinder production was limited, these artifacts from the early period of sound recording history have become increasingly rare and valuable. "In the 1890s it became possible to duplicate cylinders and discs on a large scale and, after the turn of the century, the commercial production of recordings really got under way."[1] Cylinders were collected chiefly by private individuals, museums, and historic societies. Federal institutions in the United States, such as the Smithsonian Institution and the Library of Congress, which housed centers for the study of folk culture, amassed large numbers of cylinder recordings. Many of these cylinders, made by anthropologists, musicologists, ethnomusicologists, and folklorists, recorded for the first time the words, sounds, music, and cultural expressions of Native Americans, Eskimos, and African Americans.

Recognizing a need to archive and preserve the growing number of cylinders in institutional hands, the Library of Congress launched the Federal Cylinder Project.

It began in June 1979, with three main goals:[1] to preserve wax cylinder recordings in federal collections by transferring them onto modern Mylar tape,[2] to document and catalog the recordings, and to disseminate the results of the project to the public, particularly to those culture groups from which the recordings were originally recorded [from a review by Richard Keeling which appeared in the Journal of American Folklore (101, 1988), 82].

In recent years, institutions and individual collectors have paid increasing attention to the preservation of cylinders as important artifacts. Several important projects aimed at providing increased public access to sounds recorded on these antique information carriers have been undertaken, including one notable initiative by the library at the University of California, Santa Barbara. The project, made possible through support from the Institute for Museum and Library Services, has produced a digital collection of nearly 8000 cylinder recordings held by the library's department of special collections. The digitized recordings can be freely downloaded or streamed from the library's Web site.[3]

Recording Culture

Elsewhere in the world, ethnographic and anthropological museums holding collections of cylinders have taken steps to identify and preserve collections of early recordings, including, for example, the Berlin Phonogramm-Archiv— one of the most significant collections of ethnographic recordings in Europe— which contains some of the earliest recordings of the indigenous peoples of Africa, North America, Asia, Australia, Oceania, and Europe. Today the Phonogramm-Archiv, which is part of the musicological section of the Ethnographical Museum, State Museum at Berlin, Prussian Cultural Heritage Foundation, holds, "more than 145,000 recordings of music representing the heritage of many cultures all over the world."[4]

Sound archives have also developed, "within research and educational institutions which took up sound recordings as yet another source of information in their specialized fields (e.g., music, ethnomusicology, and dialectology, political or social history)."[5] For example,

> In 1890 the anthropologist Jesse Walker Fewkes pioneered the use of the phonograph when he recorded songs of the Passamaquoddy Indians. In Europe, the Hungarian Bela Vikar (1859–1945) is regarded as a pioneer for his work in recording traditional folk music and dialects. With the opening in 1899 of the Phonogrammarchive (Phonographic Archive) of the Academy of Science in Vienna, the first scientific sound archive in the world was established, having as its aim the systematic collection of this new type of source material by the production, acquisition and preservation of sound recordings for all areas of scholarship.[6]

The organization of sound archives in cultural institutions has developed along two chief lines. The *medium-centered* archive is one that collects recordings of like type, such as long playing (LP) phonograph records. The assumption here is that, "the needs of the medium take priority over any other consideration."[7] For certain formats such as early cylinders, the medium-centered approach can help in the long-term preservation of an endangered or artifactually important format. By contrast, the *content-centered* approach involves collecting recordings on the basis of how they relate to a particular topic or discipline. For example, an archive containing all known commercial recordings of works by Beethoven regardless of format would be an example of a content-centered approach.

Some examples of sound archives organized by content include:

- Linguistic
- Folklore
- Oral history
- Ethnographic
- Dialectic
- Music
- Ethnomusicology
- Bioacoustic (e.g., ornithology, etc.)
- Spoken word

Sound archives have also developed around national library and archives collection development mandates. For example, the British Library and the U.S. Library of Congress are both copyright depository libraries which are required by law to collect, describe and preserve copies of all copyrighted materials in their respective countries. For these institutions, the business of sound archiving is integrated into the larger mandate of serving the public good by maintaining a collection of all items protected under copyright. Today, along with the Library of Congress in the United States, the British Library Sound Archive is one of the world's leading repositories of sound recordings in all genres and formats.

> The sound archive holds over a million discs, 185,000 tapes, and many other sound and video recordings. The collections come from all over the world and cover the entire range of recorded sound from music, drama and literature, to oral history and wildlife sounds. They range from cylinders made in the late nineteenth century to the latest CD, DVD and mini disc recordings. We keep copies of commercial recordings issued in the United Kingdom, together with selected commercial recordings from overseas, radio broadcasts and many privately made recordings.[8]

Pekka Gronow notes, "The idea of a national collection of commercial recordings was first introduced in France, where the Phonotheque Nationale was founded in the 1930s."[9] In the United Kingdom, the British Institute of Recorded Sound collects not only commercial recordings but also wildlife sounds, documentary recordings, folk music, and broadcasts. In Sweden, the Arkivet for Ljud och Bild is the central archive for commercial recordings, radio and television broadcasts, and films. In Denmark, the Nationaldiskoteket is part of the National Museum. In the United States, the Motion Picture, Broadcasting and Recorded Sound Division of the Library of Congress, established in 1978,[9] serves as a national repository for sound recordings.

Large, broad-based national sound archives collections help assure that a representative cross-section of the total output of recorded culture produced in a particular country or region is collected, described, preserved, and made available. For those with particular research needs, however, large broadly focused collections may be of limited value. Instead, smaller topic-specific sound archives may be more useful to those perusing specific topics such as folk music, the spoken word, or jazz.

Music for the Masses

With the introduction of the mass-produced Edison disc, manufactured by means of a stamping process, the availability of sound recordings skyrocketed. The Edison phonograph with its hand crank and ornate funnel-shaped horn rapidly became a fixture in households across America and around the world. Discs were aggressively marketed by the Edison Company. Competitors began to enter the scene and with this we see the rise of the so-called "format wars" which persist today. The competitive climate that defined the early years of commercial sound recording is described in great detail in Gelat's, *The Fabulous Phonograph: From Edison to Stereo* (see the Bibliography entry by Besek, J.M.). Subsequent improvements in the disc manufacturing process enabled more grooves per inch to be added to a disc thus extending its playback time. Extended play enabled more varied repertory to be recorded. This significant improvement enabled extended popular and classical works to be recorded for the first time in their entirety usually on a series of discs. When packaged together these multidisc sets were referred to as record "albums." The push to increase disc program time led to the development of the LP record. Gronow notes [that] "In the 1950s, the introduction of the microgroove (long playing and single) record and the general improvement in the standard of liv-

ing increased the demand for records, and for thirty years world sales increased."[2] The open reel tape format—the chief format for recording sound in a studio setting—was only moderately successful in the consumer market. More popular as a distribution medium was the Compact Cassette introduced by Philips in the 1960s for which many varied types of players were produced, including notably units fitted in automobiles.

A major change in the way in which sound was recorded came in 1979 with the introduction of pulse code modulation (PCM) recording technology. Pulse code modulation, the first digital music recording system for commercial use, was quickly adopted by recording studios because it was much better suited to studio recording, editing, and production than its analog counterpart. The digital compact disc (CD), and the CD player, was introduced in 1982. The CD remained the prevailing format collected by most popular and classical music sound archives throughout the 1980s and 1990s. With the rise of the Internet as the primary means of distributing digital data (including text, moving images, and sound), the downloading of sound (currently in MP3 format) to computers and to portable devices (such at the Apple I Pod) is now a preferred means of accessing sound. This mode of delivery continues to gain in popularity each year as retail sales of CDs drop at a corresponding rate.

The Rise of Music Archives

While initial efforts to archive sound began in step with the commercial development of the earliest sound recordings, the formal shaping of archives for the purposes of supporting research and to assure preservation of the cultural record is a more recent phenomenon. National libraries and archives, university libraries and archives, and private libraries and archives have each contributed uniquely to the development of a network of repositories for commercial and noncommercial sound recordings. Archives, such as the American Folklife Center at the Library of Congress (http://www.loc.gov/folklife/index. html), the Smithsonian Center for Folklife and Cultural

Heritage (http://www.folklife.si.edu/index.html), and specialty archives such as the Rutgers Institute of Jazz Studies Archive (http://newarkwww.rutgers.edu/IJS/), state-based folk life centers, university-hosted centers, such as the Archives of Traditional Music at Indiana University (http://www.indiana.edu/_libarchm) each play an important role in shaping a community responsible for collecting, preserving, and providing sustained access to recorded sound.

In Europe and in the United States, institutions holding substantial collections of sound recordings have aligned themselves with one another through participation in the work of professional associations such as the International Association of Sound Archives (IASA) and in the United States the Association for Recorded Sound Collections (ARSC). Within this latter organization resides the Association of Audio Archives, a group composed of leading institutional sound archives, including those located at the New York Public Library, Yale University, Stanford University, and the Library of Congress.

Serving User Needs

The users of sound archives vary widely and extend beyond the realm of traditional scholarship. Writing on the role of sound archives in the field of Ethnomusicology, for example, Anthony Seeger notes, [that] "Scholars are not the only people who use archives. They are also used by musicians, students, members of the public interested in a certain part of the world or learning a language, members of the society recorded, and refugees." Seeger continues, "Field collections serve all these users better than commercial recordings because they usually provide more material and are closer to the original live performances than most commercial releases."[10]

Both private and corporate sound archives have contributed significantly to development of a network of sound repositories who serve a diverse range of needs. Symphony orchestras, for example, frequently possess archives which document live performances, rehearsals, and radio or television broadcasts. Jones and Trebble note that archives of sound recordings in broadcasting organizations (including the archives

of the British Broadcasting Corporation, one of the world's leading broadcast archives) were not developed until the middle of the 1930s when recording techniques, such as instantaneous recording onto lacquer discs, began to be used in radio production.[11]

Collecting Policies

Collection development policies which set forth the type of material to be acquired by an archive are essential for effective collection management and for providing patrons with the materials they require. These written guidelines should be explicit and updated periodically. Jones and Trebble suggest the following questions be asked of items or collections being considered for acquisition:

- Is the recording likely to be of use in future broadcasts?
- Does the recording possess significance in sound, over and above the information and/or style of the script?
- Does the archive possess similar material and if so, does the new recording increase the value of the existing collection by providing additional examples, improved performances, or better technical quality?
- Is the recording technically suitable for preservation?
- Are there copyright, contractual, or other restrictions on the use of the recording?
- Should the recording be selected as a whole or in part?[12]

Techniques of Sound Archiving

Effective technical processing of sound recordings is essential to providing sustained access to content. This involves making certain that procedures and policies are in place for the acquisition of materials. Written collection development guidelines which define the types of materials collected by an archive and preferred formats (e.g., 78s, LPs, CDs, etc.) are of fundamental importance. Such guidelines should also articulate retention and deaccession policies and procedures and provide archives staff with direction regarding how and when to copy recordings. Copying may be required when an item is deteriorated to the extent that information is at risk of being lost. Copying may also be carried out as a means of converting sound from an obsolete or noncompliant format to one that is supported by the archive. In addition, archives staff may copy for distribution provided they are in compliance with copyright law. In each case, procedures and guidelines are critical for the consistent and correct transfer of sound from one carrier to the next.

Correct documentation tailored to the level and type of access an archives wishes to provide is also of critical importance. This begins with compilation of a complete inventory of holdings. Once items are accounted for, cataloging and description can focus upon individual items or collections depending on the level of user access required. Cataloging or metadata records can be either minimal or full. This depends on a number of factors, including the relative importance or value of particular items to a collection. Indexing provides users a means for identifying specific performers, topics, and works within an archive's cataloged collections. A variety of cataloging standards have been used over the years to describe sound recordings. Two standards currently in common use are Machine-Readable Cataloging (MARC) and International Standard Bibliographic Description for Non-Book Material (ISBD NBM).

Preservation and Access

Of equal importance in the responsible stewardship of sound is managing use of collections in ways that provide users with the resources they need while assuring good preservation. Effective preservation begins with development and use of written collection access policies which set forth the terms under which collections may be used, security guidelines, and care and handling policies. Such policies may also articulate the ways in which patrons may access recordings (onsite or remotely), how to use equipment, procedures for obtaining copies, etc. Depend-

ing on an archive's clientele and scope of activities, policies may also be needed to address such things as providing permissions for using sound recordings in publications, loan of materials for exhibitions, use of recordings for educational purposes, and broadcast.

Supporting Materials

A collection of sound recordings is of limited value without a catalog that enables a user to locate recordings of specific interest. Catalogs are usually organized by subject, author, genre, format, location, etc. Of special importance is supporting reference materials, such as bibliographies, discographies, and books or electronic resources pertinent to the types of recorded materials collected. Manufacturer catalogs, for example, can be invaluable reference sources for archives that collect commercially issued sound recordings.

Professional Associations

The development and general availability of best practices for archiving sound recordings has been made possible in large part due to the growth of the profession of sound archivists. Today's sound archivist in search of information, best practices, and like-minded colleagues has a number of professional organizations to choose from. These associations and organizations serve as both convening bodies for professionals and clearing houses for information about sound archiving. In the United States, the ARSC, a nonprofit organization founded in 1966, is the largest professional association for sound archivists. As its Web site states, ARSC is, "dedicated to the preservation and study of sound recordings in all genres of music and speech, in all formats, and from all periods." Association for Recorded Sound Collections is unique in bringing together private individuals and institutional professionals. Archivists, librarians, and curators representing many of the world's leading audiovisual repositories participate in ARSC alongside record collectors, record dealers, researchers, historians, discographers, musicians, engineers, producers, reviewers, and broadcasters. The peer-reviewed ARSC Journal, first published in 1968, represents a wealth of landmark articles, papers, and reviews. The ARSC Newsletter delivers timely announcements, short articles, and a calendar of coming events. Topics explored in ARSC publications, at ARSC conferences, and on the ARSC List e-mail forum include, "preservation of sound recordings, access to recordings, audio conservation and restoration, biography, cataloging, discography, history and technology, archival practices, training and education, bibliography, copyright and intellectual property issues."[13] The work of ARSC and its members has made a tremendously positive impact on the management of sound archives in the United States. Several of its publications, such as the landmark study by Pickett and Lemcoe, Preservation and Storage of Sound Recordings (1959, reprinted in 1991) are in wide use in both private and public sound archives throughout the world.

At the international level, IASA serves as the chief organization for sound archivists.

The International Association of Sound and Audiovisual Archives (IASA) was established in 1969 in Amsterdam to function as a medium for international cooperation between archives that preserve recorded sound and audiovisual documents. IASA has members from more than 60 countries representing a broad palette of audiovisual archives and personal interests which are distinguished by their focus on particular subjects and areas, e.g., archives for all sorts of musical recordings, historic, literary, folkloric and ethnological sound documents, theater productions and oral history interviews, bio-acoustics, environmental and medical sounds, linguistic and dialect recordings, as well as recordings for forensic purposes.[14]

IASA, which maintains operational relations with UNESCO, holds a conference each year in a different location. Committees responsible for various issues convene at these conferences. IASA publishes its Information Bulletin and Journal on a regular basis, as well as special publications on various topics. At the conference there are ample opportunities for sound archives professionals to gather, network, hear papers, present papers, visit exhibitions, and tour the libraries and archives of the host country.

Assessing the State of Collections

During the twentieth century, collections of sound recordings especially those in academic settings have grown to support campus learning, teaching, and research. The relative state of these collections was not well understood until 2004 when the Council on Library and Information Resources (CLIR) undertook a survey of academic library repositories to better understand their preservation needs. Staff from more than 80 institutions responded to the CLIR survey which found that, "recorded sound collections on campuses are rich and diverse ... and [that] campuses report increased demand for the use of audio in teaching and research. But with few exceptions, barriers to such use are high and institutional readiness for improving the condition and accessibility of audio holdings is low, especially for rare and unique materials."[15] Respondents tended to identify lack of funding as the greatest barrier to access. Other commonly cited barriers included:

> 1) the absence of appropriate standards and tools for cost-effective inventory and bibliographic control; 2) the lack of effective and cost-efficient means of treating and reformatting analog materials; 3) the absence of clear mandates about how to provide access to valuable collections the rights to which are ambiguous or unknown; and 4) the lack of staff who are sufficiently trained and conversant in the genres, formats, and rights issues unique to recorded sound collections.[15]

Preservation

Implicit in an archive's mission to provide sustained access to sound recordings is a deep-seated obligation to responsibly preserve its recordings so they are available for research, study, and enjoyment. To achieve this, an archive initially conducts a preservation needs assessment of its collections. Data derived from this work help an archive understand its preservation challenges and forge a strategy to address areas of concern.[16] Ideally this risk assessment and management process produces series-coordinated measures to reduce risks to collections through preventive measures while providing remedial treatment for content in imminent danger of loss.

Preventive measures include making certain that the collection storage environment is conducive to long-term preservation of the media being stored. This begins with assuring the temperature and humidity levels are stable and within acceptable parameters for the materials being archived. It also requires that all materials (storage containers, record sleeves, tape storage boxes, etc.) which come in contact with the recordings are constructed of permanent and durable materials that will not interact adversely with the recordings they are designed to protect.

A frequent cause of damage to collections is through mishandling by staff and patrons. Investing in an educational program to address care and handling issues is money well spent, as it reduces unnecessary damage. Various manuals, bibliographies, and guides covering the care, handling, and storage of discs,[17] tapes,[18] and CDs[19] are available.

Due to the relatively unstable physical nature of many of the recorded sound formats that have been introduced over the years, and due to the increasing obsolesce of the hardware needed to play back some of these older formats, copying (or preservation reformatting) of endangered content is often the only viable remedial preservation option available. Several useful guides are available to assist archives personnel in this exacting work.[20] Preservation reformatting requires the skills of a trained individual (preferable a sound engineer), the correct equipment properly calibrated, and the investment of time and money. Selected guidelines and best practices for the effective and accurate extraction of sound from older formats and its transfer (usually to digital systems) are described in *Capturing Analog Sound for Digital Preservation, Report of a Roundtable Discussion of Best Practices for Transferring Analog Discs and Tapes* (CLIR, March, 2006).[21] Another useful guide is Sound Directions: Best Practices for Audio Preservation by Mike Casey and Bruce Gordon (2007). Research and development into the art and science of extracting sound from antique or obsolete formats is ongoing. One recent effort, led by Dr. Carl Haber in the Lawrence Berkeley Labs in California, involves the use of techniques borrowed from high-energy particle physics to extract sound from grooved media using a noncontact method. This approach potentially eliminates the need for a traditional analog playback machine in the reformatting process.[22]

Following established guidelines and best practices for copying is a good starting point for extending the life expectancy of endangered recorded sounds. Following existing technical standards is also useful, including those developed by the Audio Engineering Society (AES).[23] Unfortunately, as the 2006 CLIR study mentioned above notes, due to the idiosyncrasies of individual application of these guidelines and standards and the variables associated with equipment used and personal preferences for attaining the "best sound" no firm technical standards for doing audio transfer have been universally adopted such as those which exist for more well-established preservation techniques such as preservation-microfilming.

Funding and Support

Because of the exacting and costly nature of much of the work associated with the preservation of sound recordings and the shortage—relative to the print world—of experts trained to do this work, institutions must often seek external sources of funding to accomplish their preservation objectives. Several federal agencies in the United States offer financial assistance for sound preservation.

The National Endowment for the Humanities (NEH), "an independent grant-making agency of the United States government dedicated to supporting research, education, preservation, and public programs in the humanities"[24] is one such agency. The National Endowment for the Humanities offers, through its various program components, preservation support for humanities collections and resources and preservation education and training for individuals, organizations, and institutions.

The Institute for Museum and Library Services (IMLS) strives to, "provide leadership and funding for the nation's museums and libraries, resources these institutions need to fulfill their mission of becoming centers of learning for life crucial to achieving personal fulfillment, a productive workforce and an engaged citizenry."[25]

Both funding agencies offer, through their Web sites and program officers, a wealth of information and guidance to organizations seeking funding.

Copyright

Copying recordings for preservation and access purposes is a core activity in most sound archives. U.S. copyright law provides a framework for legal copying. The Digital Millennium Copyright Act, enacted in 1998, amended portions of the copyright law to address the preservation practices of libraries and archives, but it was not a comprehensive revision. For example, direction concerning pre-1972 sound recordings not presently covered by federal copyright law was omitted from the revision. This prompted the Council on Library and Information Resources and the Library of Congress to publish a study in 2005 on this issue.[26] Concerned further with the exceptions and limitations applicable to libraries and archives under section 108 of the Copyright Act, the U.S. Copyright Office and the National Digital Information and Preservation Infrastructure and Preservation Program of the Library of Congress formed The Section 108 Study Group, "to conduct a reexamination of the exceptions and limitations applicable to libraries and archives under the Copyright Act, specifically in light of digital technologies."[27] Their report, published in March 2008, contains specific recommendations for amending copyright law to reflect the preservation and access needs of cultural repositories, including sound archives.

Challenges of the Digital Era: Meeting User Needs and Expectations

Since the late 1990s, the distribution of music has shifted from being format-based to being streamed or otherwise distributed digitally. Today's consumers increasingly expect their favorite music and sounds to be available through their choice of digital distribution channels. This shift in user expectations is impacting sound archives. As the format era draws to a close, sound archives interested in collecting contemporary music, for example, are being challenged to refocus efforts to address a media-less environment. Increasingly, the distribution of contemporary music will be on-demand, which is to say made available to users on a "pay-as-you-go" basis, downloaded from an Internet resource. Evidence of this trend can be seen today in the degree to which commercial music distribution services (e.g., Apple iTunes, etc.) have proliferated. How long a commercial release remains available will depend directly on demand: if an item does not sell well, it will likely not remain available for long. Fundamental changes in the ways in which commercial recordings are distributed will challenge sound archives to develop new methods of harvesting content, including perhaps, employing mechanisms for the automatic retrieval of digital content from creators, publishers, and aggregators.

Within the past decade, a growing number of libraries on academic campuses around the world have developed institutional digital repositories to preserve and provide sustained access to owned and leased scholarly material. Increasingly, these repositories are acquiring more and more sound content, much of it locally produced. This movement toward intuitions functioning as aggregators and stewards of distinctive, locally produced works represents perhaps a polar opposite to the prevailing practices of the twentieth century in which large regional or national sound archives served as the primary repositories of our recorded sound culture. The emergence of distributed models for archiving sound reflects the changing ways in which content is being created, aggregated, and used and also its value to the communities it serves.

Reflective of the proliferation of smaller institutions taking part in the archiving of sound, an increasing number of digital audio projects aimed at acquiring, describing, preserving, and distributing "born-digital" and digitally converted audio have appeared within the past 5–7 years. Several of these are noted at http://palimpsest.stanford.edu/bytopic/audio/ a Web site devoted to preservation and conservation. A particularly useful resource, developed by the University of Washington Libraries, "Digital Projects and Developing Technologies in Music and Media" (http://www.lib.washington.edu/music/projects.html) provides an overview of select digital audio projects, readings on digital audio technologies, information on music metadata (documentation), audio encoding and markup language, and other tools for the production and management of digital audio and video.

Along with the emergence of new models for archiving sound, several national efforts have also been mounted to create digital sound and moving image repositories and service centers. One such initiative is the National Audio Visual Conservation Center operated under the auspices of the Library of Congress. "Located at the foothills of the Blue Ridge Mountains in Culpepper, Virginia, the Library's newly completed Packard Campus of the National Audio-Visual Conservation Center provides underground storage for this entire collection on 90 miles of shelving, together with extensive modern facilities for the acquisition, cataloging and preservation of all audio-visual formats." In addition to being a national repository for sound and moving image formats where digital conversion takes place, the Culpepper facility is also designed to acquire, preserve, and make available "born-digital" sound and moving image content.

Conclusion

Moving forward, and facilitated to a large extent by tools which enable one to create a sizable archive of sound recordings on one's laptop computer, one can easily imagine a time in the not-too-distant future when the infrastructure for sharing personal archives, globally mining institutional holdings, and rapidly accessing historical recordings from the collections of the great sound repositories of the twentieth century will be upon us. While there are significant cultural, institutional, and legal barriers to realizing this future, the technology needed to make possible this future is readily available today. With the strategic use of this technology directed toward providing seamless access to content, coupled with the continued

good stewardship of those who are entrusted to care for recorded sounds wherever they reside, we may well reach that future sooner than expected.

REFERENCES

1. http://history.sandiego.edu/gen/recording/notes.html (accessed November 2008).

2. Gronov, P. Commercial recordings. In *Sound Archives, a Guide to Their Establishment and Development*; Lance, D., Ed.; IASA: Vienna, Austria, 1983; 77.

3. UCSB, http://cylinders.library.ucsb.edu (accessed November 2008).

4. UNESCO, http://www.unesco.org (accessed November 2008).

5. Schuursma, R. Approaches to the national organization of sound archives. In *Sound Archives, a Guide to Their Establishment and Development*; Lance, D., Ed.; IASA: Vienna, Austria, 1983; 1–9.

6. Schüller, D. Ethnomusicology. In *Sound Archives, a Guide to Their Establishment and Development*; Lance, D., Ed.; IASA: Vienna, Austria, 1983; 122.

7. Schuursma, R. Approaches to the national organization of sound archives. In *Sound Archives, a Guide to Their Establishment and Development*; Lance, D., Ed.; IASA: Vienna, Austria, 1983; 22.

8. British Library Sound Archive, http://www.bl.uk/collections/sound-archive/nsaabout.html (accessed November 2008).

9. Grenow, P. Commercial recordings. In *Sound Archives, a Guide to Their Establishment and Development*; Lance, D., Ed.; IASA: Vienna, Austria, 1983; 76.

10. Seeger, A. The role of sound archives. In *Sound Archives, a Guide to Their Establishment and Development*; Lance, D., Ed.; IASA: Vienna, Austria, 1983; 264.

11. Jones; Trebble, Broadcasting. In *Sound Archives, a Guide to Their Establishment and Development*; IASA: Vienna, Austria, 1983; 76.

12. Jones; Trebble, Broadcasting. In *Sound Archives, a Guide to Their Establishment and Development*; IASA: Vienna, Austria, 1983; 70–71.

13. ARSC, http://www.arsc-audio.org (accessed November 2008).

14. IASA, http://www.iasa-web.org/pages/00 homepage.htm (accessed November 2008).

15. Smith, A.; David, R.A.; Karen, A. *Survey of the State of Audio Collections in Academic Libraries. Optimizing Collections and Services for Scholarly Use*; Council on Library and Information Resources: Washington, DC, 2004; 10.

16. A particularly useful preservation needs assessment tool is FACET, http://www.dlib.indiana .edu/projects/sounddirections/facet/index.shtml (accessed November 2008).

17. http://www.loc.gov/preserv/care/record.html (accessed November 2008).

18. http://www.clir.org/pubs/abstract/pub54.html (accessed November 2008).

19. http://www.clir.org/pubs/abstract/pub121abst .html (accessed November 2008).

20. Dale, R. Audio Preservation: *A Selective Annotated Bibliography and Brief Summary of Current Practices*; The Association: Chicago, IL, 1998.

21. Council on Library and Information Resources, National Recording Preservation Board (U.S.), and Library of Congress, *Capturing Analog Sound for Digital Preservation, Report of a Roundtable Discussion of Best Practices for Transferring Analog Discs and Tapes. Optimizing Collections and Services for Scholarly Use*; Council on Library and Information Resources and Library of Congress: Washington, DC, 2006.

22. http://irene.lbl.gov/ (accessed November 2008).

23. http://www.aes.org/publications/standards/list .cfm for a list of AES standards (accessed November 2008).

24. NEH, http://www.neh.gov/whoweare/index.html (accessed November 2008).

25. IMLS, http://www.imls.gov/about/about.shtm (accessed November 2008).

26. Besek, J.M. *Copyright Issues Relevant to Digital Preservation and Dissemination of Pre-1972 Commercial Sound Recordings by Libraries and Archives*; Commissioned by the National Recording Preservation Board, Library of Congress; Council on Library and Information Resources and Library of Congress: Washington, DC, December 2005.

27. *The Section 108 Study Group Report. An Independent Report sponsored by the United States Copyright Office and the National Digital Information Infrastructure and Preservation Program of the Library of Congress*; United States Corporate Office: Washington, DC, March 2008, http:// www.section108.gov/docs/Sec108ExecSum.pdf (accessed November 2008).

BIBLIOGRAPHY

Besek, J.M. *Copyright Issues Relevant to Digital Preservation and Dissemination of Pre-1972 Commercial Sound Recordings by Libraries and Archives. Optimizing Collections and Services for Scholarly Use*; Council on Library and Information Resources: Washington, DC, 2005.

Boston, G. Archiving the Audio-Visual Heritage: Third Joint Technical Symposium: May 3–5, 1990, Canadian Museum of Civilization, Ottawa, Canada; [S.l.]: Technical Coordinating Committee, 1992.

Council on Library and Information Resources, National Recording Preservation Board (U.S.), and Library of Congress. *Capturing Analog Sound for Digital Preservation, Report of a Roundtable Discussion of Best Practices for Transferring Analog Discs and Tapes. Optimizing Collections and Services for Scholarly Use*. Council on Library and Information Resources and Library of Congress: Washington, DC, 2006.

Gelatt, R. *The Fabulous Phonograph; From Edison to Stereo;* Appleton Century: New York, 1966.

Lance, D. *Sound Archives: A Guide to Their Establishment and Development*; International Association of Sound Archives: Vienna, Austria, 1983.

Pickett, A.G.; Lemcoe, M.M. *Preservation and Storage of Sound Recordings;* Library of Congress: Washington, DC, 1959.

Smith, A.; David, R.A.; Karen, A. *Survey of the State of Audio Collections in Academic Libraries. Optimizing Collections and Services for Scholarly Use;*

Council on Library and Information Resources: Washington, DC, 2004.

Stielow, F.J. *The Management of Oral History Sound Archives*; Greenwood Press: Westport, CT, 1986.

Welch, W.L.; Leah, B.S.B; Oliver, R. *From Tinfoil to Stereo: The Acoustic Years of the Recording Industry, 1877–1929*; University Press of Florida: Gainesville, FL, 1994.

DIETRICH SCHÜLLER

"Socio-technical and Socio-cultural Challenges of Audio and Video Preservation"

International Preservation News *46 (December 2008): 5–8.*

Slightly updated version of the paper prepared for the 3rd Memory of the World Conference, Canberra, February 2008.

AUDIO AND VIDEO documents are the most significant primary sources of linguistic and cultural diversity. With all respect to the role of language and written texts in human communication, the limits of these traditional tools to communicate and describe cultural phenomena are obvious and undisputed. It must be noted that scientific interest was the driving force for the invention of audiovisual recording technology: the study of language and the human voice paved the way for the invention of sound recording while the interest to analyse fast movements, which could not be explored by the naked eye, triggered the invention of cinematography. Several disciplines like linguistics, ethnomusicology and parts of anthropology did not really flourish until the advent of audiovisual documents which—more or less perfectly and more or less objectively—permit the creation of adequate primary sources of or about the phenomena of interests themselves: language, music and dance, rituals, artefacts, etc. Consequently, it was the academic world that installed the first sound archives, 1899 in Vienna, 1900 in Paris and Berlin, 1908 in St. Petersburg.

Commercial exploitation, though not at the cradle of the new recording technologies, started even before 1900: the products of the phonographic and film industries soon quantitatively surpassed the aca-

demic activities. It is noteworthy, however, that systematic collection and archives for the products of the entertainment industry emerged only by and by in the 1920s and 1930s, as libraries and archives started to include audiovisual materials in their collections. In those years, independent units in the sound archives were created (*e.g.* the *Discoteca di Stato* in Italy or the French *Phonothèque nationale*), while film archives were founded in the Netherlands, the UK, the Soviet Union, France, and Germany. As Radio broadcasters also developed from 1922 onwards, radio sound archives came into existence.

The consolidation of audiovisual archiving only happened after World War II, heavily supported by the international spread of magnetic tape recording technology for audio, which had been in existence in Germany already since the mid-1930s. From 1956 onwards magnetic video recording became available and gradually replaced film recording in television stations. Outside broadcasters, magnetic tape recording, specifically the availability of battery-operated portable equipment, enormously furthered the production of research materials, as it became possible to record language, music and rituals everywhere in the world in good quality. This also created the corpora that constitute the primary source materials of our present-day academic knowledge of the linguistic and cultural diversity of mankind. While the creation of film documents for research was not very widespread because of the considerable costs involved in the production and development of film, moving image documentation for scholarly and cultural purposes mushroomed, since in the 1980s truly portable video-recorders became available which permitted the creation of video documents in a fashion similar to what had already existed over the past decades for audio.

These three creative sectors in audiovisual production—the record and film industry, the radio and televisions broadcasters, and the academic and cultural bodies—have accumulated a remarkable legacy of primary source materials, which form the most significant sources of cultural and linguistic diversity of mankind. They are partly artistic creations in their own right, like films and music productions, and partly documents of political, historical and cultural events and phenomena. Most justifiably, audiovisual documents have been called the media of modernity: no adequate understanding of the past 100 years would ever be possible without them.

Concentrating now on audio and video recordings, the worldwide holdings are estimated to be 100 million hours for each of the two categories. While photographic materials and films can be preserved as originals, provided stringent storage and handling conditions are met, this is not possible for audio and video recordings in the long term. Historical cylinders become brittle and mouldy, unique instantaneous disks deteriorate beyond retrievability, life expectancy of magnetic tape can be assumed to be only in the order of decades, and recordable optical disks must be considered to be at great risks, unless produced under tight quality control, which practically can hardly be met in practice.

Carrier instability, however, is only part of the problem. As machine-readable documents, all audio and video recordings depend on the availability of format-specific replay equipment, some of considerable sophistication. Thanks to the technical development over the past 20 years, we have experienced ever shorter commercial life cycles of dedicated audio and video formats. Whenever a format had been superseded by the next, industry swiftly ceased production of new equipment, spare parts, and professional service support.

Around 1990, this foreseeable development led to a shift of paradigm amongst sound archivists: it was realised that the classic aim to preserve the document placed in the archives' care would ultimately be in vain, because even if carefully kept carriers survived over longer periods, the unavailability of replay equipment would make these stocks soon irretrievable, and thus useless. Audio preservation has to concentrate on the safeguarding of the content, not of the original carriers, by copying contents losslessly from one digital preservation platform to the next. Analogue contents have to be digitised first.

This new paradigm met with some scepticism from traditionally-minded archivists; however, German radio broadcasters took the lead to develop digital mass storage systems, which soon became state of the art in audio archiving. The incentive for their installation was not so much preservation, but automated access to huge archival holdings, which was considered to become a strong weapon in the fight of these previously monopolistic institutions against upcoming competition from private broadcasters. Video archiving is following that path, with some time delay however, as storage quantities for video are significantly higher. Outside the radio world, national archives and libraries, but also some research archives followed.

Feeding analogue and single digital carriers into digital repositories is a demanding and time-consuming process. Principles have been standardised by the International Association of Sound and Audiovisual Archives (IASA), which had also issued practical guidelines for the production and preservation of digital audio objects. The transfer of originals is in need of modern replay equipment, of test equipment and expertise for their proper maintenance. The time needed for one transfer operator must be estimated to be at least triple the duration of audio, and even significantly more in the case of video documents. Bigger radio and national archives are solving that problem by simultaneously transferring three or four audio tapes at one time, making use of special quality control software to replace the aural control of the operator. This works with fairly homogeneous source material as typically available in radio archives. Holdings of research materials, because of their diverse technical nature, hardly lend themselves to this kind of "factory transfer".

Yet there is more to it than solving the transfer of originals. Digital preservation is equally demanding, as it requires an ongoing investment to keeping digital data actively alive. Appropriate professional storage technology and management software is expensive and needs subsequent renewal at least at the pace of migration intervals, which are generally in the order of five years. It must be clearly stated that the use of recordable optical disks as sole digital target media constitutes a great risk, although it is unfortunately widespread, specifically amongst small and less wealthy institutions. Professional digital preservation currently costs 5 USD/GB/year, however with a clear tendency to come significantly down in the short term. According to latest developments, costs in the order of 1 USD/GB/year, a mid-term vision only a year ago, may be within realistic reach pretty soon.

It can be assumed that the challenges as outlined above will be met by the radio and television archives as well as the national collections of fairly wealthy countries within the next 20 years. Because of the impending unavailability of replay equipment, this is the time frame generally considered to be available for safeguarding what we have accumulated so far. Several postcommunist and developing countries, however, will face considerable problems in safeguarding their holdings, even in a selective manner. The most significant problem is lack of funds. While it is fairly popular to finance digitisation projects in the course of international development cooperation, the lack of commitment to finance long-term preservation of the digital files makes many such projects a dead-end road.

The great majority of small and hidden collections in all parts of the world, which preserve a considerable part of the world resources of cultural and linguistic diversity, have a different, generally much greater problem. The first is awareness. While generally "digitisation" is recognised to be an action to be carried out, there is little knowledge about prerequisites needed and standards to adhere to. Most typically, inadequate replay equipment is regarded to be sufficient, and there is no realistic perspective about standards and costs to preserve the digitised documents. The other notorious problem is lack of money, which mainly—apart from, of course, unfavourable general economic situations—means lack of awareness on the part of parent organisations, governing financing bodies, and/or of the public at large.

From the technical prerequisites, the required expertise, and the necessary financial resources it becomes clear that autonomous audio and video preservation requires critical mass amounting to several thousands of carriers within each format. As many important collections are held by relatively small institutions, many even still at the private homes of the researchers that had recorded them, the only viable solutions for these holdings are cooperative projects, which can be arranged in different forms: the transfer of original contents to digital files should be seen separately from digital preservation. And even the transfer of originals could be subdivided according to the various formats. Often very specific formats, like cylinders, are outsourced, while e.g. magnetic tapes are transferred inhouse. A typical cooperative model at universities could be the recording and annotation of new audio and video materials by the institutes concerned, accompanied by the transfer of analogue and historical digital single carriers in specialised audiovisual units, while the computer centres of the universities take responsibility for the long-term preservation of digital files.

On the way to improve the situation of audiovisual collections within the academic world, which often amount to considerable sizes, different obstacles can typically be spotted in the Western and the former Eastern Bloc world.

Typical of the Western World and its socioeconomic situation is the fact that success of research institutions is measured by the degree of advancement in their respective disciplines, generally expressed in the number and size of publications, and not by preserving resources for future generations. Hence, unless they have a specific mission as an archive, institutes have the tendency to emphasise research at the expense of archiving, specifically when it comes to financial constraints. Sad experiences can be told especially of the fate of audiovisual collections at American universities, which are notoriously endangered by their parent organisations whenever financial re-allocations have to be made. Even internationally highly respected archives have come under severe threat, which has often triggered international rescue rallies; once, however, a renowned collection was frozen, and another even dissolved.

The most efficient counteraction to such inherent threats is to enhance the use by making catalogues of the holdings available on the Internet. This has been started successfully by collections within libraries and is now gradually followed by dedicated audiovisual research collections, which generally provide more detailed descriptive metadata on their holdings than libraries. Another factor serving to enhance attractiveness of archival materials is a recent shift of research priorities in anthropology and ethnomusicology. While previous schools have overemphasised the importance of relying on self-generated materials, there is a clear tendency to re-discover the potential of already existing sources, provided, however, the limitations of those materials are critically examined and understood.

A stereotype found in post-communist countries is the notorious mistrust in contracts and in the honesty of partners. Typically, researchers were working in relatively small units, all more or less orderly shelving their respective field tapes. Often research units with similar aims work under the same umbrella organisation, without ever having shared audiovisual field equipment or archiving infrastructure. Although these resources have been gathered with institutional, and governmental, support they are considered to be private possessions. With analogue field recordings, predominantly open reel tape and compact cassettes, this has so far worked but sub-optimally, because recording equipment was generally amateur standard, and tapes have suffered from bad storage condition and from being used for transcriptions, as working copies were rare. Against this background, specifically the older generation has developed a notorious mistrust in sharing resources such as archives, because of the firm belief that this would lead to an expropriation of their recordings by their scholarly competitors. There is also a remarkable mistrust in the reliability of contracts granted by official institutions.

This typical and strong attitude would of course be an obstacle to any attempts of solving the problems of safeguarding small audiovisual collections through cooperative projects. A recent study, however, seems to indicate clearly that almost two decades after the political changes in post-communist countries this notorious mistrust is being eroded. In a survey of 107 European field workers, predominantly ethnomusicologists, 80% expressed their readiness to safeguard their field collections in the course of cooperative projects. The percentage of Western vs Eastern respondents was almost the same.

In summarising, it can be stated that the greater part of audio and video collections, held by the broadcast and national archives of wealthy countries, will be safeguarded and made available in the long term. Whether also in developing countries these kinds of institutions will be able to solve their problems within the time frame of the next 20 years, remains open. Much will depend on the political will of these countries to safeguard their audiovisual cultural heritage and to allocate the necessary funds. There is some reason to hope that the development in this field in the West over the past 20 years can be optimistically extrapolated to other parts of the world. This concerns, however, only the greater part of the accumulated collection.

In terms of importance, a major part of the entire audiovisual heritage is held in small and scattered, often hidden research and cultural collections all over the world. Without them, our view of the cultural and linguistic diversity of mankind would be incomplete. Their loss would mean a substantial deprivation of cultural, linguistic, and ethnic minorities in terms of their heritage, their history and their identity. The veritable challenge of a worldwide strategy of audiovisual preservation is to spot these collections and to organise their physical survival.

REFERENCES

Boston, George (Ed.). *Safeguarding the Documentary Heritage: A Guide to Standards, Recommended Practices and Reference Literature Related to the Preservation of Documents of All Kinds.* Paris:

UNESCO, 1998. Web version: <http://www .unesco.org/webworld/mdm/administ/en/ guide/guidetoc.htm> Extended CD-ROM version, Paris, UNESCO, 2000 (available from a.abid@uneso.org)

Bradley, Kevin. "Risks Associated with the Use of Recordable CDs and DVDs as Reliable Storage Media" in *Archival Collections—Strategies and Alternatives*. Paris: UNESCO, 2006. Web version: <http://www.unesco.org/webworld/risk>

Bradley, Kevin. *Towards an Open Source Repository and Preservation System. Recommendations on the Implementation of an Open Source Digital Archival and Preservation System and on Related Software Development*. Paris: UNESCO, 2007. <http://www .unesco.org/webworld/en/mow-open-source>

IASA Task Force on Selection, Majella Breen et al. *Selection criteria of analogue and digital audio contents for transfer to data formats for preservation purposes*. International Association of Sound and Audiovisual Archives (IASA), 2004. Web version: <http://www.iasa-web.org/downloads/ publications/taskforce.pdf >

IASA Technical Committee. *The Safeguarding of the Audio Heritage: Ethics, Principles and Preservation Strategy*, edited by Dietrich Schüller. (IASA Technical Committee—Standards, Recommended Practices and Strategies, IASA TC-03), Version 3, 2005. Web version: <http://www.iasa-web.org/ downloads/publications/TC03_English.pdf> Also available in French, German, Italian, Russian, Spanish, and Swedish.

IASA Technical Committee. *Guidelines on the Production and Preservation of Digital Audio Objects*, edited by Kevin Bradley. (IASA Technical Committee—Standards, Recommended Practices and Strategies, IASA TC-04), 2004. Spanish translation: *Lineamientos para la producción y preservación de objetos de audio digitales. Radio Educación*, Mexico, 2006. Italian Translation: *Linee guida per la produzione e la preservazione di oggetti audio digitali*. Roma: Discoteca di Stato, 2007. Second English edition in print.

Memory of the World, Sub-Committee on Technology. *Preserving our Documentary Heritage*. Paris: UNESCO, 2005. http://portal.unesco.org/ci/en/ ev.php-URL_ID=19440&URL_DO=DO_TOP IC&URL_SECTION=201.html Also available in French, Spanish and Arabic.

Plathe, Axel, and Dietrich Schüller, Coordinators. *Safeguarding Documentary Heritage: Virtual Exhibition*. Web version: <http://www.unesco.org/web world/virtual_exhibit/safeguarding/expo00.html>

Schüller, Dietrich. "Preservation of Audio and Video Materials in Tropical Countries". *IASA Journal 7* (1996): 35-45 Reprint in: *International Preservation News* 21/2000, 4–9.

Schüller, Dietrich. *Audiovisual research collections and their preservation*. http://www.knaw.nl/ecpa/ TAPE/docs/audiovisual_research_collections.pdf (published 2.4.2008)

Schüller, Dietrich. *Audio and video carriers. Recording principles, storage and handling, maintenance of equipment, format and equipment obsolescence*. http://www.knaw.nl/ecpa/TAPE/docs/audio_and _video_carriers.pdf (published 21.2.2008)

chapter 5

RISKS TO CULTURAL HERITAGE

TIME, NATURE, AND PEOPLE

ULTURAL HERITAGE IS UNDER CONSTANT AND
inevitable risk, and its causes are easy to catalog: the natural aging process of objects, neglect, extinction (of intangible heritage), the internal and external physical environment, natural disasters, and human depredations, such as
war, theft, vandalism, and other willful destruction. The
last category ranges from local incidents of protest to state-
sponsored campaigns against heritage buildings and/or
entire collections and cultures. (The destruction of images is referred to as iconoclasm, and of books, biblioclasm or libricide.) The literature in all of these areas is
voluminous. This chapter provides readings that address one fundamental question:
how do we understand, prepare for, protect, and manage risk to collections? With a
clear understanding of the dimensions of risk management, the reader may consult
these myriad sources for further information.

Readings that deal with aspects of risk appear in other chapters. For example, in
chapter 1, "Early Sources on Preservation," most of the authors address risk, though
they may use the words *jeopardy, peril, hazard, menace,* or *threat.* Vitruvius seeks
to minimize risks to objects through careful building design. Gabriel Naudé suggests that properly creating a library assures the survival of ephemeral items that
might otherwise be lost or destroyed. Thomas Jefferson believes that multiple copies of records will assure their survival. William Morris urges us to cast a critical

eye on certain restoration practices to minimize further damage to historic buildings. Francis Lieber seeks to establish a code for the handling of cultural objects in times of war to assure their survival. Chapter 9, "Ethics and Values," includes *The Hague Convention for the Protection of Cultural Property in the Event of Armed Conflict*, which further develops the "Lieber Code." Chapter 10, "Multicultural Perspectives," includes an essay by Sven Haakanson, Jr., who considers the many issues surrounding the preservation of Native American objects, including potential risks. Throughout chapter 7, "Frameworks for Digital Preservation," the authors discuss aspects of risk management in creating, using, and retaining digital collections.

Considerations of risk, then, are threaded throughout this book. Risk management is an integral part of preserving individual objects, structures, and collections. In this chapter, the focus is on risk itself. But what is risk? It is the *possibility* or *probability* of damage or loss. It is the chance that an unwanted event may occur. According to the entry on "Risk" in the *Stanford Encyclopedia of Philosophy*, "since the 1970s, studies of risk have grown into a major interdisciplinary field of research in which there may be several philosophical sub-disciplines."[1] These are: epistemology, philosophy of science, philosophy of technology, ethics, and economic analysis. (To these disciplines should be added conservation, preservation, and other related heritage-based fields.)

The article gives five meanings of risk that are used across their selected disciplines:

1. risk = an *unwanted event* which may or may not occur. 2. risk = the *cause* of an unwanted event which may or may not occur. 3. risk = the *probability* of an unwanted event which may or may not occur. 4. risk = the statistical *expectation value* of an unwanted event which may or may not occur. 5. risk = the fact that a decision is made under conditions of *known probabilities* ("decision under risk" as opposed to "decision under uncertainty.")[2]

All five of these definitions are applicable to preservation, though number 5 is probably most usefully applied to the aspects of the field that focus on science (conservation) or engineering (buildings; environmental systems.)

How, then, can we apply risk management in practice? This chapter contains distinct aspects of risks to cultural heritage. **Rebecca Knuth** (author of two books on cultural destruction)[3] draws parallels between the destruction of books, libraries, and archives, and acts of genocide and ethnocide. She identifies three types of destruction: vandalism, biblioclasm, and libricide—which is the ideological and systemic destruction of books and libraries. For example, the destruction of vital records might be a form of genocide. If the intent is to erase all records of a group of people, such an act would qualify as libricide. In contrast, the vandalism of records could be the random act of one person. While books have often been destroyed for ideological purposes, the destruction of records may make possible the erasure of historical events. How can risk management be applied to such irrational forces as Knuth describes in "Understanding Modern Biblioclasm?" As Knuth observes, "Our attention to the circumstances in which the violence occurs is imperative if we seek to revise our responses to social outcasts, acknowledge and respond to protests of marginalized groups before they progress to violence, and strengthen the humanistic foundations upon which international peace and the modern democratic state depend."

More pragmatically, to respond to hazards, such heritage may need to be documented with surrogates such as photos or moving images, some items may need to be hidden, security may need to be strengthened, and so on. Depending on the nature and extent of the threats, none of these actions may be enough. András J. Reidlmayer's work in Bosnia exemplifies strategies to document heritage that has fallen victim to systematic attempts at its destruction. After the Balkan Wars of the early 1990s, Reidlmayer traveled to Bosnia to survey architectural heritage sites as well as archives and libraries that had been damaged by nationalistic extremists. He photographed the sites that he could locate, collected eyewitness statements, and photographed the sites again, but from the vantage of those whom he interviewed. To capture manuscripts that were destroyed, Reidlmayer organized an international project to find and gather microfilm copies of those that had been filmed or photocopied. His efforts have led to the risk management *ex post facto* of surviving heritage as well as to copies of records that were destroyed.[4]

Knuth's suggestion that we "strength[en] the humanist foundations upon which international peace and the modern democratic state depend" moves well beyond risk management. It depends upon governments in all countries where heritage is under threat to work with one another—an unlikely possibility. Yet at the same time, international treaties, codes, or any document with legal standing, can hold force. For example, the 1999 protocol of the *Hague Convention for the Protection of Cultural Property in the Event of Armed Conflict* provides for "exceptional protection" of significant sites, monuments, and institutions. Extradition for some crimes against cultural heritage is possible—even if unlikely, and legal precedents have yet to be set. Still, the international courts play an important role in preserving the world's heritage, as do international bodies such as UNESCO, and other institutions such as universities, foundations, non-governmental organizations (NGOs), non-profit organizations (NPOs), and professional associations. Seen in this light, international initiatives to preserve heritage may be considered to be a global approach to risk management.

Sociologists **Dennis Mileti** and **Lori Peek** (formerly L. A. Peek-Gottschlich) focus on the societal aspects of disasters. The authors, together, singly, and with other colleagues, have written about risk analysis, ongoing public education for disaster preparedness, how disasters disproportionly effect women, children, and minorities, and the advantages and disadvantages to technological strategies for disaster mitigation, among many other topics. Some of these themes are addressed in "How Do Societies Manage Risk?" Mileti and Peek consider ways in which risk is distributed unevenly in society as a result of social, political, and economic forces. In choosing to address some risk factors, we may ignore others, thus shifting losses to future generations. The authors refer to this as dichotomizing risk. Similarly, decisions might be made to take actions that mitigate for one group of people but not for another. (Possible examples: building high-cost housing in an area of town that is less prone to flooding than a low-cost housing area; shipping waste to other countries, and so on.) The ramifications of decisions that favor one group of people over another may have catastrophic effects, as was seen in New Orleans in 2005 after Hurricane Katrina, an event that took place after this article was written but that illustrates its points well: the people who lived in the poorest neighborhoods were hardest hit. And earlier decisions surrounding the building of the levees proved catastrophic as well because they were not built solidly enough to withstand a hurricane of Katrina's magnitude.

Actions that redistribute risks, costs, and losses can occur in the preservation of cultural heritage, too. Emergency management is the strategic process that is used to protect the assets of an organization from hazard risks. There are four processes: mitigation, preparedness, response, and recovery. In any of these phases, decisions that are made will effect what is preserved. Emergency management must be strategic not tactical.

Mileti and Peek further suggest that we might be overreliant on technology to protect collections from the forces of nature. "Societies that highly value technology put less emphasis on alternate mitigations to natural hazards, since approaches such as land-use restrictions contradict other basic values like individualism and the sanctity of private property."

To address these issues, the authors suggest six sustainable development objectives for the management of natural-hazards risk: maintain and enhance environmental quality; maintain and enhance people's quality of life; foster local resiliency and responsibility; recognize that vibrant local economies are essential; ensure inter- and intra-generational equity; and adopt local consensus building. In other words, use long-term holistic approaches to ensure societal resiliency to natural disasters.

In "Inside Installations, Preservation of Installation Art," **Pip Laurenson** presents a new approach to risk management. Rather than address individual items, or collections as a whole, as do most conservators, Laurenson provides a strategy for the assessment of "ensembles" such as rooms constructed for exhibition with a variety of objects. Laurenson, and colleagues, used case studies from different types of installations to develop their own cases that "high-lighted the different risks and vulnerabilities of artists' installations." By the end of the project the team had established a framework for assessing the value of different elements of artists' installations.

The last piece in this chapter is an excerpt from **Peter Waters's** "Procedures for Salvage of Water-Damaged Materials," first published in 1975. The advice that he gives still has currency. Waters authored this now-classic manual based, in part, on his extensive salvage experience in the aftermath of the flooding of the Arno River that occurred in Florence, Italy, on November 4, 1966. Often referred to simply as the Florence Flood, it was perhaps the most damaging of the many devastating floods in the city's history. Extensive damage occurred to collections in nearby libraries and museums. The Biblioteca Nazionale Centrale Firenze (BNCF) was particularly hard hit. Flood waters carried mud and heating oil that had been released from tanks that had broken throughout the city due to the incredible pressure of the Arno's waters. Tens of thousands of valuable books and manuscripts, shelved in the basement of the BCNF, and below the level of the water, were submerged by the flood waters.

Over many years, Waters led the preservation efforts at the BCNF, which consisted of many phases. In 1966, there were few resources available for large-scale disaster recovery of cultural objects. First, materials had to be removed from the library to be dried. The drying was done in tobacco kilns. Once back in the library, the materials had to be organized, and treatment options had to be determined. The magnitude of the damage was such that flood-damaged items still await treatment, nearly 50 years later. Waters trained and managed volunteers, conservators, and other staff at the BCNF, and binders and conservators from other countries who went to Florence.

Today there are hundreds of organizations around the world that conduct disaster-recovery training and offer general information about recovery. Many corporations now exist to aid in recovery efforts. So it is difficult to measure the long-term impact of Waters's work. Perhaps his most significant contribution was to systemize the various components of emergency management, which we now refer to as mitigation, preparedness, response, and recovery. The important lessons he imparted through his manual, lectures, workshops, and international consulting have made possible the recovery of millions of items throughout the world.

The four pieces in this chapter address the inevitability of risk. The authors present us with a number of complex social, political, legal, economic, and logistical challenges that should be addressed in risk management. A failure to understand these complex forces will make us less capable of responding to unwanted events.

NOTES

1. *Stanford Encyclopedia of Philosophy*, "Risk," first published March 13, 2007; substantive rev., August 11, 2011. http://plato.stanford.edu/entries/risk.

2. *Stanford*, "Risk." In all definitions, italics are in the original.

3. *Libricide: The Regime-Sponsored Destruction of Books and Libraries in the Twentieth Century* (Westport, CT: Praeger, 2003), and *Burning Books and Leveling Libraries: Extremist Violence and Cultural Desctruction* (Westport, CT: Praeger, 2006).

4. For a description of some of these activities, see András J. Reidlmayer, "Crimes of War, Crimes of Peace: Destruction of Libraries During and After the Balkan Wars of the 1990s." *Library Trends* 56.1 (Summer 2007): 107–132.

REBECCA KNUTH

"Understanding Modern Biblioclasm"

Chapter 1 in her Burning Books and Leveling Libraries: Extremist Violence and Cultural Destruction. *Westport, CT: Praeger, 2006, pp. 1–16.*

"Each decision we make, each action we take, is born out of an intention."
—*Sharon Salzberg, "The Power of Intention"*

IN 1795, AT the height of the French Revolution, moderate revolutionary Francois-Antoine Boissy d'Anglas pronounced, "France is bathed in blood, both at the hand of the enemy and of its executioners ... [It is] devastated by anarchy, suffocated by acts of vandalism, prey to the ravages of greed and a victim of the excesses of ignorance and savagery" (Poulet 1995, 196). His observation describes much more than the event of his times, unparalleled though it was in modern history. In many modern social conflicts, deepseated strife has led both sides to commit extreme acts of violence, and just as often, the bloodletting has been accompanied by the destruction of books. D'Anglas's sentiment in expressing the reaches of the tragedy resonates with Western civilization's collective memories of sixth-century Vandals sacking Rome, Saracens burning the Alexandrian Library, Vikings attacking the Christian monasteries that had sustained learning through the Dark Ages, and the burning of heretics and their texts during the Spanish Inquisition. We carry a distinct sense of loss at these events, despite their historical distance, and we share the view that the destruction of culture is senseless and perilous to society.

More recent events have also been formative to our condemnation of cultural destruction, especially those involving the destruction of books and libraries. The Nazis' book fires of 1933 (among the regime's other atrocities) exposed the vulnerability of the very foundations of modern civilizations. The Nazi regime shook the world with the reality of how effective unchecked vandalism and unbounded racial pride could be in reversing our progress toward a moder-

nity based on pluralism and tolerance. Though Germany's book fires were by far the most well-known incidents of cultural destruction from the last century, the phenomenon recurred in many forms across the globe, and by century's end a litany of pejorative terms had been cemented into our vocabulary. "Vandals!" "Fanatics!" "Fascists!" we have cried repeatedly in horror and denunciation. But by our judgments we have admitted an inability or reluctance to probe the behavior for a cause.

Condemnations imply that the destruction has no meaning other than to signify the presence of irrational forces. They effectively dismiss the destroyers of books as barbaric, ignorant, evil—as outside the bounds of morality, reason, even understanding. If instead we acknowledge the perpetrators as human beings with concerns and a goal—albeit misguided—of effecting social change, a number of questions emerge that usher us into the subject with clearer meaning and purpose. What is it about texts and libraries that puts them in the line of fire during social conflict? What compels a group to enact its alienation through violence aimed at print materials and the institutions and buildings that house them? What do various incidents of book destruction have in common, and what makes them unique? And, is there an identifiable pattern to such acts?

Modern conflicts involving books have ranged from sporadic local incidents of protest and isolated programs of censorship to systemic crusades aimed at totalitarian implementation of a new orthodoxy. Hindu nationalists destroyed the Bhandarkar Oriental Research Institute in Pune, India, because it provided documentation for historical works that challenged their myths. The National Socialist Party in Germany dismantled Berlin's Institute for Sexual Knowledge to purge the nation of "un-German" elements: homosexuality, cosmopolitanism, independent inquiry, and humanism in general. Afghanistan's Taliban regime purified the nation's print collections in the name of the Koran, and Pol Pot's Communist regime purged Cambodia of its texts and intellectual community for the cause of socialist transformation. Cultural destruction has become an almost familiar gesture of defiance that signals the immediate threat of censorship and cultural homogenization. The destruction of books and libraries is at once a public assertion of choice and a radical repudiation of intellectual freedom, individualism, pluralism, and tolerance. In the name of the common man, an ethnic group, or a belief system, modern radicals have sought to reestablish pre-Enlightenment prerogatives of absolutism, threatening to bring 300 years of history full circle.

This book argues that modern biblioclasm occurs when books and libraries are perceived by a social group as undermining ideological goals, threatening the orthodoxy of revered doctrine, or representing a despised establishment. Although it seems a precursor to more extensive violence (as so famously put forth by Heinrich Heine: "When they burn books, they will also, in the end, burn human beings"), biblioclasm is actually a signal that social discord has progressed to a critical point and that the foundations of modern civilization are at risk. Our attention to the circumstances in which the violence occurs is imperative if we seek to revise our response to social outcasts, acknowledge and respond to protests of marginalized groups before they progress to violence, and strengthen the humanist foundations upon which international peace and the modern democratic state depend.

Book and library destruction shares many elements with iconoclasm, the destruction of images that a perpetrator associates with corrupt establishments ("Iconoclasm" 1989, 609). I have chosen to use the term *biblioclasm* in this book because of its linguistic relation to iconoclasm and because, by association, it suggests that there is a moral judgment, on the part of the perpetrator, concerning what the target represents. In the *Oxford English Dictionary*, *biblioclasm* is defined as "the breaking of books" and cited

as first appearing in print in 1864 in a text on religious theory. Twenty years later, a passionate scholar used the term to denounce the Catholic priests who had burned Maya and Aztec manuscripts after the Spanish conquest: "May these bishops expiate their crimes in the purgatory of biblioclasts!" ("Biblioclasm" 1989, 169). In this book the term is used not to levy judgment, but to denote purposeful action that is rooted in moral repugnance or judgment.

The history of biblioclasm is entwined with the history of vandalism and political violence in general. In ancient times, libraries were routinely destroyed in wars over territory. Texts were lost in combat, and, because the leveling of cities was a prominent feature of conquest, through fire, exposure to the elements, and burial in the rubble. Neglect destroyed many of the texts that had survived the initial violence. As scrolls gained in commercial value, the looting of libraries eventually (especially during the Roman Empire) became a prerogative of victors, who sold the enemy's patrimony for personal profit or co-opted its symbols and institutions for the glory and use of their own empire. As generals carried off entire libraries as trophies of war, deposed elites came to associate the loss of written works with both political and spiritual subjugation. From very early on, the wholesale annihilation of texts had much to do with the perception that they carried heretical beliefs. Although seizing the enemy's texts enforced a victor's dominance and lent some legitimacy to the central power structure of the expanding empire, many texts were intentionally destroyed because they were seen as repositories of antithetical religious beliefs and identity. The powerful association between texts, group identity, and preservation of a society's belief system is evidenced in apocryphal stories recounting the destruction of many cultures' texts by paranoid or fanatical rulers who sought to extinguish opposing beliefs and cultures. The Chinese cite Emperor Ch'in Shih-huang as the embodiment of political tyranny for his decimation of books and scholars, and Iraqis remain traumatized by the thirteenth-century destruction of Baghdad's books by the Moguls. The destruction of the Library of Alexandria by Omar the Caliph (though largely apocryphal) haunts Western civilization to this day. By the same token, resistance to cultural extinction has, throughout history, triggered heroic efforts to preserve books. Over centuries of persecution and diaspora, the cultural survival of the Jewish people was related in large part to their tenacious guarding of sacred works. The past provides a powerful incentive for groups concerned with preventing cultural decline and extinction: preserving texts is a necessary condition for cultural autonomy and survival.

When the Vandals plundered Rome in 455 A.D., they carried away all of the city's portable treasure. Although contemporary historians disagree as to whether the Vandals were quite as savage as portrayed in the historical record (Jones 1999, 890), the Roman people were united in the devastation they felt at the ignorance of their attackers and, with time, came to see all Germanic tribes as a singular danger to civilization itself. During the Dark Ages that followed the fall of Rome, the original losses were compounded by Viking raids on monasteries in Ireland and northern Europe. Here, recorded knowledge survived only tenuously as handwritten manuscripts were looted, burned, or ripped apart for their decorative elements. Viking depredations served as an intermediate step in etching the trauma of cultural violence into the collective consciousness of Western civilization. The Vandals, characterized by historical sources as the "great destroyers of Roman art, civilization and literature," ultimately became a term for any people demonstrating "a general barbaric ignorance" (Cohen 1973, 34). The *Oxford English Dictionary* cites the first written use of the general term vandal as occurring in 1663, in reference to a "willful or ignorant destroyer of anything beautiful, venerable or worthy of preservation" ("Vandal" 1989, 425).

The term *vandal* accrued further nuance during the French Revolution (1789-1799), when the people revolted and destroyed monuments, paintings, books, and documents in public ceremonies that celebrated their freedom from despotism. Abbé Grégoire, an influential deputy in the Constituent Assembly and a member of the National Convention (the ruling bodies during the revolution), cemented the association of cultural destruction with barbarism and

ignorance when he used the term *vandalisme* (vandalism) to condemn the revolutionaries' actions. In his *Mémoires*, Grégoire wrote "I invented the word to abolish the act" (Poulet 1995, 195). Attacks on symbols of the monarchy and the Ancien Régime were especially rampant during the Reign of Terror, a radical and bloody period, 1793-1794. In calling for an end to the destruction, Grégoire recalled the invasion of Rome and judged his contemporaries as indistinguishable from the Vandals, whom he viewed as the epitome of tyranny and ignorance (Baczko 1989). In a series of reports to the convention, Grégoire listed examples of damage, singling out books in particular, and advocated preservation efforts to curtail a "destructive fury" that, at its fiercest, called for burning the Bibliothèque Nationale and all libraries (Baczko 1989, 860). His followers would eventually publicly decry the ethos of revolutionary terrorists, "riff-raff disguised as patriots" who "debased all public life" by acting out their hatred of culture (Baczko 1989, 862). They legislated protection for books and records, redefining them as the common property of the nation.

Grégoire's response to biblioclasm was based on a strand of Enlightenment thinking that recognized the importance of intellectual freedom and books as crucial pillars of reason and cultural progress—and their destruction, consequently, as regression of tragic proportions. He used the Enlightenment's recognition of human agency to construct a view of books as an integral part of a group's heritage, a source of intellectual stimulation, and the foundation of civilized living—much more than mere fetishes of the elite. In France and the rest of Europe, the term *vandalism* soon became commonplace, as did *vandalistes* (vandals)—those who commit violent acts against the symbols of the establishment or those who profit from such violence. In later centuries, many educated and respectable people adopted Grégoire's premises along with the term, and the upper classes tended to reject vandalism as hysterical violence committed by the lowest sort of people (Gamboni 1997, 15, 22). This is a departure from the spirit of his ideas, though, polarizing the classes yet again. In the nineteenth and early twentieth centuries, with mass literacy fostered by public education, the importance of preserving books became a relatively stable and widespread sentiment, a collective attitude or value-based "unit of thought-feeling" embraced by society as a whole (Leighton 1959, 415). A case can now be made that when biblioclasm occurs, it is because books (as well as art) stand at "the center of interest of all civilized people ... [they are] a guarantee for the modern spirit and thus, at the same time, its Achilles heel, the point at which the cultivated may most easily be touched" (as quoted in Gamboni, 1997, 105-106).

In the mid-twentieth century, as sociology came into its own as a discipline, the term *vandalism* acquired still another nuance, beyond its association with cultural destruction: it came to signify the seemingly random destruction of public property that had become prevalent in industrialized urban settings. Sociologists used the term in this narrowed sense and developed the view that vandalism, like all forms of violence, was a rational expression of frustration. Summarily rejecting the common interpretation of modern vandalism as merely random and ignorant, sociologists argued that acts such as disfiguring telephone booths, breaking windows, and scribbling graffiti are complicated, purposeful behaviors that send an important message to society of underlying social malaise and unfulfilled needs (Lumsden 1983, 4). To interpret the message, we must consider not only the target itself, but also the society in which this target is embedded (Sperandio 1984, 106). By destroying a telephone booth, a person may be reacting not only to a malfunctioning phone or a negative call, but to a system in which the perpetrator cannot find work, for example, or meaningful identity. Interpreting the message can be difficult because it is being conveyed through action and symbol. Modern vandals often attack public property because it is the accessible, material aspect of a society that they perceive as having marginalized them. By understanding the motivation of vandals, the sociologist argues, society can better respond to the needs of these alienated members. It has been an ongoing battle to avoid simplistic conflation of vandalism with deviance, but sociologists have generated a knowledge base about the subject and advanced theories and models that

have beneficially affected social policy. I believe their work may profitably be applied to book destruction because, as Grégoire so presciently established, biblioclasm can be seen as a form of vandalism.

Of particular interest in this application are explanations of vandalism that acknowledge the presence of diverse emotional influences at the individual perpetrator's level. Acts of vandalism can express feelings of fear, hate, and frustration. Some perpetrators find satisfaction in the physical act of destruction and the state of mind that emerges from seizing the opportunity for destruction. A major affective motivation of vandalism has been identified by Vernon L. Allen (1984, 80), who determined that the act of destruction can be intrinsically enjoyable in itself—"an aesthetic experience" that links creation and destruction. Smashing a window can be experienced as an imaginative and original act. Scrawling graffiti on public surfaces superimposes a personal statement on an otherwise static environment. With his colleague David Greenberger, Allen (1980b) has also identified cognitive impulses behind violent acts: the increase in an individual's perception of personal control or efficacy that destruction can effect. If vandalism is, as Allen and Greenberger (1980b, 85) claim, influenced by self-identity and subjective states, including alienation and frustration, a lowered level of "perceived control" (efficacy or competence) will, under certain conditions, stimulate attempts to change the environment through acts of destruction.

A third motivation—social identity—provides "theoretical unification of aesthetic factors and perceived control" and suggests "a link between internal psychological processes and units in the social environment such as role, group, and social structure" (Allen and Greenberger 1980a, 194). Destruction, which is cathartic and empowering (affective and cognitive motivations), can also feel noble to the perpetrator when he or she perceives it as serving a higher purpose (social identity). In the case of the Nazis, who exuberantly participated in book-burning ceremonies, the ideas of National Socialism appealed to those who were humiliated by the World War I defeat, alienated by values of the Weimar Republic, and victimized by economic depression. Participants in the book fires were persuaded by propagandists and orators of a fundamental connection between creation and destruction: out of the ashes of the un-German element would rise the new reich. It was exhilarating for participants to repudiate all that had held them back, to unleash their power in a public spectacle. In standing with their comrades and pledging allegiance to National Socialism, they were united in a transformative and affirmative act, their social identity fused by an intensely satisfying emotional experience.

The usefulness of Allen and Greenberger's tripartite approach to vandalism is apparent when we look at the most commonly cited typology of vandalism, which directly categorizes incidents according to the perpetrator's motivation. Stanley Cohen's (1973) seminal work on vandalism in the 1970s distinguished six categories of vandalism, while acknowledging that a mixture of motivations is common. These are Cohen's terms and his definitions, which are based on motivation; for comparative purposes, Allen and Greenberger's motives have been placed in italics and parentheses after each definition.

> *PLAY:* Heedless damage that results from play
>   or self-entertainment (*Affective*)
> *MALICIOUS:* Destruction motivated by hatred
>   or pleasure in destroying but is relatively
>   non-specific in target (*Affective and Cognitive*)
> *VINDICTIVE:* Damage carried out as a form
>   of revenge (*Affective and Cognitive*)
> *ACQUISITIVE:* Destructive actions aimed at
>   acquiring money or property (*Cognitive*)
> *TACTICAL:* Damage that results from a considered, planned initiative to reach a goal
>   beyond money (*Social*)
> *IDEOLOGICAL:* Damage calculated to support
>   a specific social or political cause, similar to
>   tactical (*Social*)

As we juxtapose Cohen's categories of vandalism against Allen and Greenberger's schemata of motivations, we see that as one progresses down the list, the emotional aspect is overshadowed by more deliberate elements. *Play* and *malicious* forms of vandalism display a strong affective component. *Malicious* vandalism, which is non-specific in target, expresses both affective (impotence, hatred, hostility, and rage) and cognitive motivations (the desire for control and efficacy); it resonates in emotive quality with the *vindictive* category, in which damage is carried out as a form of revenge. Although often perceived as senseless, malicious vandalism is akin to the vindictive category in that both are responding to a perceived violation or irritant (which may or may not be evident to an observer). The grievance that triggers a destructive response may be real or imagined, and the eventual target only indirectly or symbolically related to the original cause of hostility. In incidents of *acquisitive* vandalism, cognitive motivations are prominent, and the motive is laced with opportunism, although the perpetrators justify their actions as a response to deprivation and lack.

The social aspect of motivation identifies other, ostensibly higher roads that may be taken in pursuit of psychological satisfaction: *tactical* vandalism, the pursuit of a goal beyond money, and *ideological* vandalism, similar behavior committed in the name of a cause. Individuals aggrieved by debilitating or alienating social circumstances may embrace extreme ideas and identities and, in their thrall, engage in acts of violence that they believe will achieve desirable goals beyond benefit only to themselves. Cohen (1973) suggests that most ideological vandalism is tactically motivated, committed in the interest of drawing attention to a certain cause. In both tactical and *ideological* acts of vandalism, the choice of target is deliberate, and an attempt is made to anticipate the possible consequences of the action before it is carried out. Together, Allen and Greenberger's focus on internal states leading to destruction and Cohen's typology of vandalism according to motivation effectively dismantle explanations that attribute pleasure in destruction to a simple frustration aggression reflex.

Sociologists in the 1980s built on Cohen's idea that motivations might overlap and continued the process of investigating their relative influence. Some viewed perception of power as a key construct and perceived control over one's circumstances as both an "antecedent and consequence of destruction" (Allen and Greenberger 1980b, 85). Social psychologist David Canter (1984, 346-347) surveyed research on the vandals' locus of control and concluded that the vandal might be both motivated from within and challenged from without to respond to a threatening physical and sociopolitical environment. In other words, both internal and external circumstances were catalysts to action. Reuben Baron and Jeffrey Fisher's (1984, 65) examination of the influence of external factors on internal states led them to describe the contemporary vandal as driven by a sense of injustice. They posited that people's perceived control over influences in their personal lives exerts a proportional influence on their ability to cope with inequity; a low sense of control leaves an individual little with which to combat frustration and can lead to vandalism. Claude Lèvy-Leboyer (1984) has argued that vandals' perception of injustice may be a reaction to a social or political system that rejects them. For marginalized people who feel thwarted by mainstream society and unable to control their circumstances, defacing or destroying public property can increase feelings of power and control. Allen and Greenberger's (1980b) studies show that destroying something, and the feeling of control this engenders, lessens the individual's sense of helplessness. This work confirmed the observations of earlier researchers that vandalism often attracts those with little attachment to others, who lack any sense of control over the future, and who live in milieus in which there is a stress on toughness and tests of masculinity (Baron and Fisher 1984).

Identification with a group assuages feelings of powerlessness and fosters a "herd mentality" that vastly expands the scope of the vandalism that results. When there is a progression from individual and anonymous acts to group and public acts of vandalism, it is usually because the perpetrators' sense of control and perception that their actions are legitimate have been strengthened by identification with like-minded others and a system of values. And although individual destructive impulses are often reactive and spontaneous, group consensus may channel such impulses into broader protests against larger and more symbolic targets: motivations shift

from affective and cognitive to social as the perpetrators find company and identity. In this process the destruction takes on a more decidedly tactical and ideological orientation. Taking action, with the security of a group, comes to be seen as a way of changing entire systems, and is no longer merely an outlet for personal frustration and a question of the affective domain. Physical objects and structures (institutions, businesses) lend themselves to being viewed in a symbolic way, which gives special meaning to acts of destruction targeting them. The target of destruction is selected on an instrumental basis, based on its appropriateness in terms of reaching the goal of change.

Group dynamics strongly influence the development of consensual values and the translation of the values into action. During social conflict, values that are not altogether discontinuous with more accepted ones may become radicalized. In the 1980s, recourse to violence seemed a logical step for Dutch anti-apartheid protestors whose movement began as one dedicated to peace and nonviolence. As apartheid remained in place and frustration mounted, their thinking became more rigid and doctrinaire: destroying Amsterdam's South African Institute became a "reasonable" and honorable act of protest. The Buddhists in Sri Lanka embraced ethnic nationalism and racial supremacy to such a degree that their nonviolent creed became a fundamentalist platform that rationalized the murder of Hindu Tamils and the destruction of their beloved Jaffna Library. In both cases, group identity drove the translation of values into action.

Regardless of their motivation, vandals show little remorse for their destructive acts. Indeed, vandals driven primarily by affective and cognitive influences rarely are able to reflect on their actions. Either they are nihilistic and random, hedonistic, or they view themselves as chronic victims entitled to a period of dominance—however brief. Perpetrators who are socially motivated and who commit ideological or tactical vandalism generally give their actions a political context or religious justification. Insulated by the knowledge that they derive no direct benefit from destruction, they evade any awareness of wrongdoing and even see their actions as laudatory. Their beliefs about themselves and their actions, reinforced by their group, run counter to the general public's view, which associates vandalism with hostility rather than political purposefulness and routinely condemns all vandals for violating the social contract. Vandals are dismissed as brutal, immature, and degenerate and or diagnosed as sick or evil—labels that have become psychiatric metaphors for deviance. Vandals construct their social identity in opposition to dominant mores. Criticism of their actions merely reinforces their distance from the mainstream and may, in fact, encourage extreme reactions against systems that they, in turn, see as socially deviant.

By interpreting rule-breaking activities as meaningful action, sociologists have suggested that a rule-breaker is trying to engage society in a conversation or transaction (Cohen 1971, 14), or that the rule-breaker is attempting to respond to something about which dialogue is not welcome. Of course, the sociologist is inferring the perpetrator's motive from his or her action and circumstance, and this inference can differ markedly from the perpetrator's own belief about the reason for his or her actions. The "vocabularies of motive" that vandals use to justify or normalize their actions was a prominent feature of Stanley Cohen's *Images of Deviance*, which came out in 1971, just prior to his typology (Nard 1973, 19). Perhaps the most cited sociologist of vandalism, Cohen (1984, 55) suggested that judgments about vandalism almost always involve struggles between perpetrators and their audience over respective interpretations of a particular act.

This is particularly true when biblioclasm is committed by extremists who are labeled by society as terrorists. Terrorism is the systematic use or threat of violence to communicate a political message. Its perpetrators often employ symbolic targets. A defining characteristic of terrorism is that "its users expect rewards that are out of proportion to both the resources they possess and the risks they assume" (Crenshaw 2001, 15604). Here are two examples of messages gone astray. In the early part of the twentieth century, the British feminist movement split and one faction turned militant, targeting public prop-

erty to draw attention to its cause. In 1914, Suffragettes firebombed a public library in an act designed to arouse a complacent public to put pressure on the government to grant women the vote. Arson seemed one of the few options left to their beleaguered movement, and the horrors of female disenfranchisement to them far outweighed the costs of property loss. But an outraged public branded them terrorists and summarily rejected their message. Another example of biblioclasm as terrorism, possibly coincidental, is the loss of historic documents and texts in the 1993 bombing of Florence's renowned Uffizi Gallery. The phrase "cultural terrorism" was employed for the first time after this disaster, expressing public dismay at the damage to the gallery, its contents, and the historic documents that were housed in a nearby archive. Whether or not the archive was the intended target, the perpetrators were clearly attacking "symbolic places, tokens of the very culture and identity of the state and the nation" and thus its authority and legitimacy (Gamboni 1997, 105). When the cause is construed as a moral one, the exercise of force against an opponent is, to the perpetrator, a legitimate and even exalted activity. Like other extremists, terrorists find it easy to slip into totalistic thinking, and they acknowledge no limitations to their actions. The violence of terrorism is provocative, and it is typically committed by small numbers of people who otherwise lack the capacity to challenge those in power. Labeling vandals as terrorists is, however, an attempt to silence them. Terrorists demand attention, yet their actions set up a reaction that closes the public mind and guarantees that the intended message will not be heard.

If the destruction of books is an attempt to communicate, then the targeting of an entire library—its physical structure, furnishings, and books—must have a meaning that is unique and distinct from the destruction of books alone. Destroying a library may bring the usual affective pleasure from destructiveness as well as cognitive rewards—a heightened release from powerlessness that comes with targeting an institution associated with the establishment and given status by the elite. When a library's contents offend a group's beliefs or ideology, destroying the entire structure can be a way of weakening the group to whom the collection belongs (the tactical element). By attacking libraries that are public institutions, vandals may be facing off against the state, a specific social group, or authority in general. In such cases, there is often a strong iconoclastic force at play. The iconic status accorded texts by those in power is offensive to groups who feel undervalued and misunderstood by global and local social systems that do not recognize the superiority of their moral framework. During conditions of civil unrest, rebellion, and war, various motivations for biblioclasm operate simultaneously as violence is fed by the polarization and dehumanization that accompany militant mindsets. In these circumstances, the full range of biblioclasm can occur. The enemy and its possessions are considered to be outside the bounds of moral obligation, and under the cover of general chaos, brutalized troops and civilians turn to destroying books for reasons of cathartic play, malice, or vindictiveness. Sometimes economic or practical advantage is the goal of the destruction. Books may be torn apart and used for practical purposes in a mixture of disdain and pragmatism, or they may be stolen to be resold or kept as trophies (acquisitive). Books are easy targets because of their symbolic nature and relative vulnerability. They are fragile and easily destroyed by fire, pulping, and exposure to the elements. A library may be damaged in the generalized shelling and door-to-door fighting that is a prelude to the taking of a city. The collateral damage that is usually written off by the military as an unfortunate byproduct of direct combat is associated, nevertheless, with tactical and ideological goals. The destruction of the enemies' texts eliminates antithetical beliefs and documentation that support claims to contested lands and identities. The loss of libraries signals to the population that they are vulnerable to the enemy and a superior army. Invading troops may set fire to a library to reinforce their victory over the deposed government, or to exact revenge for civil resistance, or as a preliminary step to colonizing occupied territory—all of which comprise tactical and/or ideological motives.

Cohen's (1973, 53) observation that urban vandalism is the ideal form of rule-breaking "both in

expressive (expressing certain values) and *instrumental* terms (solving certain structural problems)" can be extrapolated to wartime vandalism against libraries. Armed conflict sets an open stage for biblioclasm by setting up conditions in which affective, cognitive, and social motivations find the outlet of action. These same conditions can make it hard to discern primary forces behind an incident of biblioclasm. In a paper on the Russian Revolution, historian Richard Stites (1981, 6-7) recounted the story of an insurgent army of Ukrainian peasants entering the city of Ekaterinoslav in 1918 and firing point-blank into the "tallest and most beautiful buildings." They set fire to the prisons, libraries, and archives. Stites posed several questions:

"Was this playfulness—the warrior ebullience and military macho which takes joy from ejaculating shells into a passive target...a mere act of drunkenness...deep hatred of the city...[or] a crude example of military tactics? Was it class war and political vengeance against the bourgeoisie?" His final question approaches an answer: "Or was it all of these things?"

Full-scale war is the most frequent host to biblioclastic events, but it is not the only arena. Civil conflicts can intensify to the point of mimicking war in their destructive potential. Because vandalism and biblioclasm are inextricably entwined with conflict in its many forms, throughout this book we will return to the perspective of sociology to ask about each case: What conflicts existed and gave rise to extremism and violence? What motivated the perpetrators, and what did they hope to achieve? How can we interpret their acts? What does this case tell us about the nature of biblioclasm and social conditions that open the door to cultural destruction? These questions, plus those posed earlier about what it is about books and libraries that causes them to be targeted, will surface repeatedly throughout this book.

Often (though not always) the impulse behind biblioclasm is religious or quasireligious dedication to an ideology. Religious texts (and sometime political texts, like Mao's Red Book) play a symbolic role as the material representations of a community of belief. It is common for members of a group that defines itself by its beliefs to showcase and celebrate their hallowed texts and dedicate themselves to preserving the volumes. These texts contain the basic articles of faith and, in the eyes of followers, the "truth." The influence of sacred texts is so powerful that devout followers tend to fear the texts of other religious groups as Trojan horses, vessels of alternate perspectives with the potential to undermine their belief system. For much of history, in the interest of spreading their faith and achieving homogeneous societies, competing religious groups have destroyed the books of their rivals, and sometimes the rivals themselves. Orthodoxy has been enforced by government and by mob alike. The familiar tale of the destruction of the Alexandrian Library (ca. 640 A.D.) had Caliph Omar rationalizing it thus: "If these writings of the Greeks agree with the book of God [the Koran], they are useless and need not be preserved: if they disagree, they are pernicious and ought to be destroyed" (Gibbon 1994, 284-285). Though Omar's forces may not have been solely responsible for the library's loss (evidence now points to several hundred years of purging by competing groups—pagans, Christians, and Muslims alike), all versions attribute the destruction of the famous library to religious conflict (Thiem 1979). Like their predecessors, twentieth-century fundamentalists and zealots practiced little restraint in ordering the obliteration of libraries, and they were highly effective in mobilizing their followers to destroy the texts of those with beliefs differing from their own.

Throughout history, books have been destroyed by extremists because they offended the religion, morals, or politics of the day (Farrer 1977, 4). Religious motives, however, have often exacted the highest price. The Greeks and Romans burned books, but it was the Christians who burned the books and their authors, and the fifteenth, sixteenth, and seventeenth centuries were particularly dangerous times for heretics and their texts. Biblioclasm was standard policy for powerful Western religious-based governments throughout this time. In both France and England, the official hangman was also charged with burning offensive books in public ceremonies. In sixteenth-century France, book-burning served as a popular form of "street theater": "In one instance a Catholic

mob hanged a Protestant printer and burned his 'seditious' volumes as part of the same public ceremony" (O'Toole 1993, 254). In sixteenth-century England, the fury of biblioclasts was terrible during conflicts over religion. Tens, possibly hundreds, of thousands of texts were lost in attempts by Henry VII and, later, by Protestant reformers, to purge England's monasteries of manuscripts, religious images, and icons of the Roman Catholic Church. But, by the eighteenth century, the decoupling of church and state had caused a decrease in imposed orthodoxy and put government-sponsored book burning out of fashion in Europe (Gillett 1964). In many parts of the world, however, biblioclasm for religious reasons remains a prevalent feature of ethnic conflict, especially when secular governments are overtaken by groups with messianic religious missions. In Bosnia, for example, the destruction of Muslim books and libraries by the Serbs in the 1990s, while an expedient function of rampant nationalism, was linked also to religious extremism.

During the twentieth century, book destruction increasingly became the prerogative of groups whose ideals served as the basis for attacks on rival ethnic and political groups. During times of social and political discord, mainstream values radicalized into immoderate principles that rationalized intemperate, often violent actions. Deteriorating conditions within a country led groups to polarize over possession of resources or opposing beliefs. In the scramble for power, books and libraries sometimes fell victim to communal demonstrations, as in India, where right-wing Hindu groups regularly attacked Muslims and their institutions, or in Kashmir, where the Muslims purged the region of Hindu Pandits and their books. The group that managed to assert control in situations of ethnic polarization, where the central government was weak, was often the one that most effectively mobilized followers behind a compelling program, based on charismatic ideas, that promised to solve immediate social and economic problems. The solution to socioeconomic issues under these circumstances inevitably involves taking back from an enemy that which is due to their own people. Leaders took advantage of chaotic conditions to seize and expand their power. With assumption of absolute power came the ability to transform beliefs into dogma, legislate orthodoxy, and put into effect systemic library destruction.

In a previous book, I have made a case that the ideologically driven, systemic destruction of books and libraries emerged, in the twentieth century, as patterned behavior (Knuth 2003). And I introduced the term *libricide* for this kind of campaign. Its etymology and dynamics implicitly link it to genocide and ethnocide. Libricide is an organized form of biblioclasm that stems from an extremist regime's pursuit, at all costs, of millennial ambitions and territorial claims that are held as the solution to social chaos (Knuth 2003). Ideals alone determine for extremists what institutions and groups must be swept out of the way. If the regime is racist, it will destroy the books of groups deemed inferior; if nationalistic, the books of competing nations and cultures; if religious, all texts that contradict sacred doctrines and teachings. Libricide often occurs during struggles over territory, when ideas imposed within a nation's borders are used to justify the colonization of neighboring states. Ideologues in possession of absolute power follow the template of history; their decisions mirror in fanaticism those of Ch'in Shih-huang or Omar the Caliph. Contemporary extremist regimes have repeatedly elevated nationalism into an ideology, channeling nationalistic sentiments into reinforcing the primary belief system. As modern secular societies have used texts to bolster national identity and built national libraries and archives that stand as monuments to the nation's strength, libraries have become increasingly attractive targets.

And with increasing frequency, extremist regimes have attacked libraries during war precisely because they understand the role of these institutions in sustaining cultural vitality, national identity and pride, and the will to resist outside aggression.

Extreme forms of nationalism (often laced with racism, militarism, and imperialism) have also joined forces with modern technology to give new impetus to historic patterns of library destruction during war. All types of governments have used the doctrine of total war to justify extreme acts of violence—including strategic urban bombing in World War II, which resulted in horrific losses of life and property. The extreme tactics of total warfare are adopted by both those who initiate aggression and those who merely respond to incursions. War is, by nature, a situation of extremities in which ordinary norms and civic order break down, inviting physical violence and cultural vandalism and opening the door to the rationalized ethnic and political cleansing favored by extremists. For twentieth-century totalitarian regimes, war was a way to achieve righteous ideological mandates and impose orthodoxy on a chaotic world. As biblioclasts, they were soldiers fighting for a "better" world. Their opponents summoned a like intensity to withstand such offensives because they realized that they were fighting for cultural survival. Imposition of the enemy's ideology would mean the end of life as they knew it. Such was the virulence and countervirulence that ideological duels were often fought to the point of national collapse and unconditional surrender. Attackers and defenders alike were vested in extremism and cultural destruction.

Outside of war and revolution, book and library destruction has occurred when the social and political environment is conflict-ridden, and when social groups become polarized, reactive, and prone to extreme gestures. Biblioclasm is a public protest that releases tension and often takes tactical form. Books, of course, are part record, part artifact, and part symbol of forces or ideas that are taken by extremists to be dangerous or oppressive; when they are destroyed, they are symbolically standing in for something that cannot be so readily touched (O'Toole 1993, 238, 254). Books can serve as surrogate targets for a competing religious and ethnic group, caste, or political and ideological enemy; a public building like a library may stand for "the State, Law and Order, Repression, Money or a particular social class" (Sperandio 1984, 106). The protest may be sponsored by a regime but staged to look spontaneous (like the book fires of the Nazis and Maoists), or it may be carried out by a maverick group in service to a particular cause.

Twentieth-century biblioclasts were extremists of a new breed. They were moderns, sophisticated about using the enemy's own symbols against them and garnering maximum attention. Many mastered the technique of using ideas to tap into popular discontent, muster support, and rationalize their seizure of power. Theirs was a deliberate choice to operate outside of and against prevailing norms. The essence of extremism is dissatisfaction with the status quo and a desire for its replacement with "better" circumstances albeit through the imposition of a homogeneous worldview. This brings in its wake a compulsion to challenge prevailing values and reject the pluralism associated with cosmopolitan, secular, and modern attitudes. Like vandalism and others forms of violence, book destruction enacts a struggle for power. At stake is the form society should take: Is a healthy society a homogeneous autocracy, where orthodoxy prevails and decisions are made by the few in the collective interest of all? Or is it a liberal democracy, where, in the end, individual human rights, pluralism, and intellectual freedom truly matter?

REFERENCES

Allen, V.L. 1984. "Toward an Understanding of the Hedonic Component of Vandalism." In *Vandalism: Behaviour and Motivations*, ed. Claude Lèvy-Leboyer. Amsterdam: Elsevier Science, 77–89.

Allen, V.L., and David B. Greenberger. 1980a. "Aesthetic Theory, Perceived Control, and Social Identity: Toward an Understanding of Vandalism." In *Violence and Crime in the Schools*, eds. Keith Kather and Robert J. Rubel. Lexington, Mass: Lexington Books, 193–207.

Allen, V.L., and David B. Greenberger, 1980b. "Destruction and Perceived Control." In *Advances in Environmental Psychology*, Vol. 2, eds. Andrew Baum and Jerome E Singer. Hillsdale, N.J.: Lawrence Erlbaum, 85–109.

Baczko, Bronislaw. 1989. "Vandalism." In *A Critical Dictionary of the French Revolution*, eds. Françoise Furet and Mona Ozouf, trans. Arthur Goldhammer. Cambridge, Mass: Belknap Press, 860–868.

Baron, Reuben M., and Jeffrey D. Fisher. 1984. "The Equity-Control Model of Vandalism: A Refinement." In *Vandalism Behaviour and Motivations*, ed. Claude Lèvy-Leboyer. Amsterdam, Elsevier Science, 63–75.

"Biblioclasm." 1989. In *Oxford English Dictionary*, Second Edition, Vol. 2, prepared by J.A. Simpson and E.S.C. Weiner. Oxford: Clarendon Press, 169.

Canter, David. 1984. "Vandalism: Overview and Prospect." In *Vandalism Behaviour and Motivations*, ed. Claude Lèvy-Leboyer. Amsterdam, Elsevier Science, 63–75.

Cohen, Stanley. 1971. "Introduction." In *Images of Deviance*, ed. Stanley Cohen. Harmondsworth, England: Penguin, 9–24.

Cohen, Stanley. 1973. "Property Destruction: Motives and Meanings." In *Vandalism*, ed. Colin Ward. London: Architectural Press, 23–53.

Cohen, Stanley. 1984. "Sociological Approach to Vandalism." In *Vandalism Behaviour and Motivations*, ed. Claude Lèvy-Leboyer. Amsterdam, Elsevier Science, 51–61.

Crenshaw, M. 2001. "Terrorism." In *International Encyclopedia of the Social and Behavioral Sciences*, Vol. 23, eds. Neil J. Smelser and Paul B. Baltes. Amsterdam: Elsevier, Science, 15604–15606.

Farrer, James Anson, 1977. *Books Condemned to be Burnt*. Reissue of 1892 Edition (London: Elliot Stock). Norwood, Penn.: Norwood Editions.

Gamboni, Dario. 1997. *The Destruction of Art: Iconoclasm and Vandalism since the French Revolution*. New Haven, Conn.: Yale University Press.

Gibbon, Edward. 1994. *The History of the Decline and Fall of the Roman Empire*. Vols. 5 and 6. Ed. David Womersley. London: Allen Lane.

Gillett, Charles Ripley. 1964. *Burned Books: Neglected Chapters in British History and Literature*. Port Washington, N.Y.: Kennikat Press.

"Iconoclasm." 1989. In *Oxford English Dictionary*, Second Edition, Vol. 7, prepared by J.A. Simpson and E.S.C. Weiner. Oxford: Clarendon Press, 609.

Jones, Tom B. 1999. "Vandals." In *Encyclopedia Americana International Edition*. Danbury, Conn.: Grolier, 890.

Knuth, Rebecca. 2003. *Libricide: The Regime-Sponsored Destruction of Books and Libraries in the Twentieth Century.* Westport, Conn.: Praeger.

Leighton, Alexander H. 1959. *My Name is Legion: Foundations for a Theory of Man in Relation to Culture.* New York: Basic Books.

Lèvy-Leboyer, Claude. 1984. "Vandalism and the Social Sciences." In *Vandalism: Behavior and Motivations,* ed. Claude Lèvy-Leboyer. Amsterdam: Elsevier Science, 1–11.

Lumsden, Malvern. 1983. "Sources of Violence in the International System." In *International Violence,* eds. Tunde Adeniran and Yanah Alexander. Westport, Conn.: Praeger, 3–19.

O'Toole, James. 1993. "The Symbolic Significance of Archives." *American Archivist* 56 (2): 234–255.

Poulet, Dominique. 1995. "Revolutionary 'Vandalism' and the Birth of the Museum: The Effects of a Representation of Modern Cultural Terror." In *Art in Museums,* ed. Susan Pearce. London: Athlone, 192–213.

Salzberg, Sharon. 2004. "The Power of Intention." *O Magazine* (January 2004): 83–84.

Sperandio, J.C.L. 1984. "Vandalism as a Fact of Life in Society." In *Vandalism: Behavior and Motivations,* ed. Claude Lèvy-Leboyer. Amsterdam: Elsevier Science, 105–107.

Stites, Richard. 1981. "Iconoclasm in the Russian Revolution: Destroying and Preserving the Past." Kennan Institute for Advanced Russian Studies, Occasional Paper Number 147. Conference on the Origins of Soviet Culture. May 18–19, 1981. Washington, D.C.: The Wilson Center.

Thiem, Jon. 1979. "The Great Library of Alexandria Burnt: Towards the History of a Symbol." *Journal of the History of Ideas* 40 (4): 507–526.

"Vandal." 1989. In *Oxford English Dictionary,* Second Edition, Vol. 19, prepared by J.A. Simpson and E.S.C. Weiner. Oxford: Clarendon Press, 425.

Ward, Colin, 1973. "Introduction." In *Vandalism,* ed. Colin Ward. London: Architectural Press, 13–22.

PIP LAURENSON

"Inside Installations. Preservation and Presentation of Installation Art. Part 1: Risk Assessment"

May 2007 (web document: www.inside-installation.org/OCMT/mydocs/RiskAssessment.pdf).

Introduction

Traditionally, risk assessment has been used in conservation to examine risks to entire collections and to establish priorities, often with regard to preventative conservation measures.[1] Recently this approach has been expanded to consider the risks associated with 'ensembles'; for example rooms in historic houses.[2] This work indicated interesting parallels to artists' installations, in that in both cases the value of the individual components is, in part, determined by its relationship to the whole ensemble.

The Benefits of Risk Assessment

The risk assessment approach provides the following benefits as a method of developing a conservation plan for a complex artwork:

- It provides a more or less rational ranking of risks based on their expected magnitude which allows for setting priorities in treating or reducing them.
- It facilitates the involvement of key stakeholders in shared decision making; politically this can help create 'buy-in' for conservation efforts across an organization.
- It requires that participants think more holistically about what it is that is important to preserve for the whole installation. For example it encourages decision makers to consider both the tangible and intangible aspects of an installation rather than simply considering the material elements.

- It pools expertise in considering where the greatest risks lie of not being able to display the work in the future.
- It encourages strategic thinking.

Although clearly the main goal of any risk assessment is to come up with a plan which will benefit the long term care of a work of art or collection, the process in itself has a number of added benefits. In particular it provides a space for structured thinking about the assumptions of the different stakeholders and their notions of value and risk.

Methodology

Following two meetings in Amsterdam and building on the work carried out by the Dutch case study researchers for Jeffrey Shaw's work 'Revolution', Agnes Brokerhof adapted currently used methodologies to be applied to installation artworks. A group of 13 case study researchers were recruited to work together to learn more about risk assessment and test the methodology on their case studies.

This group of case study researchers 'met' via conference calls every week during the months of October and November 2006. During each conference call the group was introduced to a consecutive homework assignment in preparation for a two day workshop at Tate Modern, London. During this workshop each participant carried out the actual qualitative, semi-qualitative or quantitative assessment of the risks to their installation.

The stages of the methodology are as follows:

1. Establishing the anatomy of the installation
2. Developing a 'Statement of Significance'
3. Determining the relative value to the whole of the elements identified
4. Developing scenarios and identifying the risks
5. Exploring the possibility of recovering lost value
6. Carrying out a qualitative or (semi)-quantitative assessment of risks.

Results

Given that risk is expressed in terms of expected loss of value in the future, risk assessment proved to be a valuable tool for creating a dialogue within the museum about what is important to preserve for any given installation. Where traditional preservation is very much oriented towards the material aspects of an artwork or collection, the preservation of installations focuses much more on the intangible. This exercise allowed participants to reflect on their perception of the 'object' and on their working practice and also to gain insight into their decision making processes. 'It rationalises your intuitive everyday way of working' was the comment of one participant.

The Value of a Statement of Significance

Understanding the significance of a work of art is vital to designing an appropriate preservation strategy. 'A statement of significance should be a reasoned, clear summary of the values, meaning and importance of an object or collection'[3]. One very practical way for a conservator and curator to jointly develop a statement of significance, is to relate it directly to the process of interviewing artists about the preservation and presentation of their work. This builds on the value of artist's interviews as a key element in the development of good practice for the care and management of installation art.

Recoverability

Traditional preservation has a strong emphasis on 'authenticity' and 'originality' of material.

Hence, in risk assessment the possibility of restoration of lost value is usually considered separately from the actual assessment. For works of art which include technology-based components or elements that are mass produced, replacement of parts and recoverability of lost functionality are often considered as part of standard maintenance. Therefore for these works it was considered important that the possibility to recover lost value was brought into the risk assessment. This uncovered a shift in thinking for conservators and meant that the specific value associated with 'original' components proved more complex than that assumed in traditional risk assessment.

Time

All museums, including contemporary art museums, plan for their collections to last 'a very long time'. Within a contemporary art context, the survival of a work of art is not always synonymous with the survival of a specific unique material object or set of objects. In some installations elements can be substituted without significant loss to the work and in others, the fact that the work has no permanent material remains is central to its nature. In the case of traditional objects the two main models of deterioration are: gradual accumulative damage or catastrophes. Eventually the small, but high probability, accumulative effect of minor losses will lead to the same magnitude of loss as the low probability catastrophe. Hence probability and consequence have a similar weight on the final magnitude of risk. Does this model work as well for all contemporary works, in particular technology-based works of art?

Technology based works of art have different modes of failure—in some cases we can predict at what point (after how many hours of usage) a piece of technology will fail. As its function is usually very important to the installation, this failure brings about sudden high loss. This loss can, in many cases, be mitigated by repair and the value recovered. Obsolescence is another very particular type of failure. How then can we best factor in to our risk assessments both the way in which these elements fail and their recoverability?

Shifting Roles

Because the risk assessment methodology highlighted the different risks and vulnerabilities of artists' installations it provided a point of focus for the participants to reflect on their changing role as conservators. This linked to the second point of focus for the B1 activity (see below).

Areas of future research and development for the risk assessment methodology are

- The development of a framework for assessing the value of different elements of an artist's installation and a method of determining their 'relative value'.
- A method for incorporating recoverability in the final assessment and evaluation risk
- The development of reference scenarios specific to the risks associated with installation art
- The generation of applicable data on the rates of loss and 'mean-time-to-failure' of materials and components used in installations.

We would like to thank Agnes Brokerhof of ICN for all her hard work and commitment to this project and for Bart Ankersmit for his patience and expert guidance during the London meeting.

NOTES

1. Examples include the work of Rob Waller—Waller, R.R. (2003) Cultural property risk analysis model: development and application to preventive conservation at the Canadian Museum of nature. Acta Universitatis Gothoburgensis, Goteborg, Sweden and Jonathan Ashley Smith—Ashley-Smith, J. (1999) *Risk assessment for object conservation*, Butterworth-Heinemann, Oxford, 358 pp. and Stefan Michalski—Michalski, S. (1990) 'An overall framework for preventive conservation and remedial conservation'; in *Preprints of the 9th Triennial Meeting of the International Council of Museums Committee for Conservation*, Dresden, ICOM, pp. 589–591.

2. Brokerhof, A.W., Luger, T., Ankersmit, H., Bergevoet, F., Schillemans, R., Schoutens, P., Muller, T., Kiers, J., Muething, G., and Waller, R. (2005) 'Risk Assessment of Museum Amstelkring: Application to an historic building and its collections and the consequences for preservation management'; in *Preprints of the 14th ICOM-CC Triennial Meeting*, The Hague, pp. 590–596.

3. Australian Heritage Collection Council 2001 'A guide to assessing the significance of cultural heritage objects and collections.'

DENNIS S. MILETI
AND LORI PEEK

"How Do Societies Manage Risk?"

In Rational Decision-making in the Preservation of Cultural Property, ed. by Norbert S. Baer and Folke Snickars. Berlin: Dahlem University Press, 2001, pp. 35–45.

MANY OF THE currently accepted methods for coping with natural hazards and disasters have been based on the idea that societies can use technology to control nature to make themselves totally safe. What is more, most strategies for managing hazards have followed a traditional planning model: study the problem, implement one solution, and move on to the next problem. This approach casts hazards as static and mitigation as an upward, positive, linear trend. Events over the past quarter-century, however, have shown that natural disasters are not linear problems that can be solved in isolation. Rather, they are symptoms of the complex interaction of broader and more basic problems. Losses from hazards—and the fact that no contemporary developed or lesser-developed society seems able to reduce them—result from shortsighted and narrow conceptions of the human relationship to the natural environment.

We propose that societies have traditionally used two fundamental approaches in dealing with and managing the risk of losses from the occurrence of future natural disasters, such as earthquakes, floods, and hurricanes. First, societies dichotomize risk, that is, societies make choices—both directly and indirectly—to address some of the risks imposed by certain hazards while ignoring others. A second approach is to take no action, or to take actions to mitigate risk for one group in a society while shifting losses onto others and future generations. This occurs when actions taken to deal with today's risks postpone losses into the future and shift risks onto future generations. Also, actions taken today may protect select groups of people while shifting risks and losses onto the less powerful and affluent segments of a society's population. These approaches are rarely used in isolation by any given society, and it is more prevalent for a combination of approaches to be used that emphasizes one over the other. Each approach draws on mitigation actions that can include land-use planning and management; building codes and standards; insurance; prediction, forecast, and warning; engineered solutions such as control and protection works; and emergency response, recovery, and reconstruction. We make the point, in reference to each of these approaches, that what has been recently learned in the area of natural hazards risk management is transferable to managing risk in the preservation of cultural property, and examples are provided. We also illustrate how societies select approaches to manage risks that match their fundamental cultural values, rather than selecting approaches that would most effectively deal with impending disasters. These fundamental cultural values are what impact the approach, or approaches, that societies choose to implement when dealing with risk. We conclude by providing a sustainable development paradigm that values a holistic and long-term approach for managing risks from the natural hazards arena, and will provoke what we think are significant questions about risk management decision-making for the preservation of cultural property.

Societies Dichotomize Risk and Risk Assessment

An underlying inconsistency exists between how professionals estimate risk from natural hazards and how people and societies perceive and deal with those same risks. Engineers, scientists, statisticians, and some others view risk probabilistically and often presume that people and societies will act rationally to mitigate losses and costs in proportion to the risks faced; however, this is not always nor even often the case (Mileti et al. 1992). In general, human beings, as individuals and groups—even groups as large as entire societies—dichotomize future risks into those that will be acted on and those that will be ignored. Because human risk perception does not follow from objective estimates and definitions of risk, and human and societal action to mitigate risk can often be inconsistent with estimated scientific probabilities (Tweeddale 1996), professional risk estimators are often frustrated in their attempts to motivate people and societies into what would constitute appropriate action from their point of view (Mileti et al. 1992).

Risks are often ignored when they fall outside of human experience. For example, a society may ignore the risk of a volcanic eruption if one has not occurred in that area for several centuries. At the same time, a society may take strong measures to address a risk that has the same scientific probability of occurring as a volcanic eruption but that has occurred in recent history. The adoption and implementation of actions to mitigate risk in a dichotomous fashion—take action versus take no action—is largely the result of the perceptions and interpretations people have about risk. A variety of factors contribute to the formation of risk perception. These include: the ability of a society to estimate risk, perceived causes of natural disasters, experience, and the general propensity of people to deny risk. In general, as risk perceptions increase, the odds of a society taking actions to mitigate that risk also increase (Tweeddale 1996).

Aspects of perceived risk that have been examined are diverse. For example, it is known that people are poor probabilistic thinkers, overestimate small frequencies and underestimate high frequencies of major disasters, and rarely take scientific estimates into account when estimating risk (Tweeddale 1996). Societies are less likely to act to mitigate disaster losses if the perceived cause of disaster is God or nature. Societies are also less likely to take further action to mitigate hazard losses if that society values technology and has already adopted a technological

'fix,' for example, a flood control system to mitigate the hazard of flooding (Mileti 1999).

Interesting parallels about the dichotomization of natural hazards risk can be drawn in the area of the preservation of cultural property. Most property is not preserved—in much the same way that many people ignore natural hazards—while decisions are made to preserve some cultural property just as societies decide to address some natural hazards. A fundamental risk question that could be sharpened and addressed in both fields surrounds this risk dichotomization. For example, in the hazards arena, large amounts of time, effort, and money are put into mitigating earthquake risk, and yet the heat hazard is largely not addressed, even though more people die from heat exposure than earthquakes in nations like the United States. Risk assessment is not involved in influencing decision-making about which hazards get addressed and which do not. Similarly, in the arena of cultural property, risk assessment and analysis is used to inform decision-making about how to preserve what is being preserved, but is not included in assisting making decisions about what small percent of property we seek to preserve versus what is lost for future generations. Decisions about what to save and what to lose may not be the wrong decisions. The point is, a holistic risk assessment to document the wisdom of this decision-making process is absent. We know from the area of natural hazards that the hazards we ignore are becoming more perilous. Is this the case in the preservation of cultural property? If the same process is going on in the area of cultural property as with hazards, this might mean that the things most important to the culture and heritage of future generations are the very things that we are not preserving.

Societies Redistribute Risk, Costs, and Losses

Some societal actions intended to head off damages from natural disasters through mitigation measures actually only shift risk, costs, and losses from this generation onto others or from one segment of the population in today's society onto another segment. The reason is that actions taken to reduce future losses are often conceived of from narrow points of view that do not consider linkage to other parts of the system being addressed or linkages to other systems.

For example, constructing a more earthquake-resistant building for a major corporation may reduce future quake losses for that corporation, but it can also create greater risk for the poor who relocate in more dense numbers and in low-quality housing because of the service jobs that the corporation creates. It is now recognized in the natural hazards arena that actions which reduce losses in one system level may actually increase them in another.

SHIFTING LOSSES ONTO THIS GENERATION'S LESS POWERFUL

Research has shown that the individuals who live in most contemporary societies are typically unaware of all the risks and choices they face. They plan only for the immediate future, overestimate their ability to cope when disaster strikes, and rely heavily on emergency relief (Mileti 1999). It is also now recognized that social and demographic differences among members of a society play a large role in determining the risks people encounter, whether and how they prepare for disasters, and how they cope and recover when disasters do occur. For example, nonminorities and households with higher socioeconomic status fare better in post-disaster phases, while low-income households are at a greater risk primarily because they live in lower-quality housing and because disasters exacerbate poverty. As a result, the risk of natural disasters is unevenly distributed in a society as a product of social, political, and economic factors because of the way that these factors structure the lives of different groups of people (Blaikie et al. 1994).

Certain societal actions intended to mitigate risk reduce losses in the short-term for select segments of a population while increasing losses and shifting risk onto other segments. For example, society's most vulnerable groups are often the poor, women, racial and ethnic minorities, and other people who are members of other disenfranchised groups. Vulnerabilities to disaster are undoubtedly unequally distributed.

Unsustainable global patterns of settlement, resource management, social organization, and political economy increasingly put some population groups more at risk from disaster than others (see Enarson and Morrow 1998).

Women represent the population most at risk when hazardous conditions unfold as disastrous events (Schroeder 1987). Women are particularly subject to environmental risk through urban displacement and migration, environmental degradation, migration, poverty, and other social limitations and barriers to choice (Anderson 1994; Cutter 1995). As one might expect, the less economic and cultural power women possess before a disastrous event, the greater the suffering in the aftermath.

The poor are at greater risk from disastrous events worldwide mainly because they live in lower-quality housing, which is more likely to be damaged and is often located closer to technologically hazardous sites (Mileti 1999). Poor families around the world suffer the greatest losses and have access to the fewest public and private recovery assets, both in developing societies and wealthy industrialized nations like the United States (Bates 1982; Bolin 1982).

Existing research on race, ethnicity, and disasters suggests that minority group members of a society experience different and more devastating consequences as a result of disastrous events than nonminority citizens (Fothergill et al. 1999). In developed and highly stratified societies, minority group members are often disenfranchised from power and influence based on membership in that group, which most often results in a long and slow recovery phase after natural disaster strikes.

In sum, some actions intended to mitigate losses from natural disasters lead a society and its communities to believe that it is totally safe from the extremes of nature, which in turn allows for the increased concentration of people—typically the poor and less powerful—and property in hazardous areas. When a natural disaster does occur, the mitigation action often has contributed to a denser concentration of disenfranchised groups who are unable to benefit from the mitigation measures and are at greater risk from disastrous events.

SHIFTING LOSSES ONTO FUTURE GENERATIONS

Certain other current societal efforts intended to avoid damages and losses from natural hazards actually only postpone them. For example, communities located below dams or behind levees may avoid losses from floods those structures were designed to prevent. However, such communities often have more property to lose when those structures fail because additional development occurred, which relied on the constructed protection. Also, many dams, levees, bridges, roads, and other structures are approaching the end of their designed life, revealing how little consideration and forethought their backers and builders gave to events fifty years hence. Similarly, by providing advance warnings of severe storms such as hurricanes, societies may well have encouraged more people to build in fragile coastal areas. Such development, in turn, makes the areas more vulnerable by destroying dunes and other protective natural features. In the long term, risk, costs, and losses are not avoided but are in fact just deferred onto future generations. This is one of the root causes why the size and impact of catastrophic natural disasters are increasing exponentially worldwide.

SHIFTING COSTS ONTO NONVICTIMS

Part of the natural disaster problem is that many individuals who live in hazard-prone areas view natural disasters as low-probability, high-consequence events (Kunreuther 1998). Thus, societies, particularly more affluent societies, use financial mechanisms to shift losses from disasters away from victims who actually experienced the event onto the shoulders of nonvictims, or onto potential future victims before disaster strikes. Such mechanisms involve addressing the question: Who should pay for disaster losses? A society which believes that every citizen should share in the losses of disaster victims may find that taxation is the best way to provide the revenue to cover these costs. If, on the other hand, a society believes that individuals are responsible for bearing their own burdens, some form of insurance with risk-based rates may be appropriate. According to Petak (1998), insurance has traditionally served the purpose of reducing the economic impact of individual losses by arranging for the transfer of all or part of the loss to others who share the same risk.

This brings up the issue of whether certain individuals or groups should receive special treatment at the expense of others. If so, the treatment should be such that situations will not be created which have long-term negative consequences. For example, if uninsured disaster victims are guaranteed grants and low interest loans that enable them to continue to locate their properties in hazard-prone areas and more people continue to move into the hazardous areas, taxpayers will be subject to increasingly larger expenditures for bailing out more victims in the future. What may be viewed as equitable immediately after a disaster, may be viewed as inefficient from a long-term perspective.

If certain victims' disaster costs are to be subsidized by others, private risk-based insurance cannot be relied upon to cover damages from these events over an extended period, although it can be counted on for a limited time. In the long run, such socially motivated subsidies can only be successfully achieved and maintained by some form of government insurance. Historically, attempts to require private businesses to overcharge some groups in order to subsidize others have broken down in a competitive marketplace, despite more and more elaborate enforcement procedures. There is an important difference in the underlying principles of private insurance, where premiums are based on risk and a system in which taxpayers are expected to absorb disaster costs for that segment of the population deemed to require special consideration.

NO SOCIETAL INTERVENTION

Some societies either choose not to or do not have the resources to make decisions and devise interventions about risk, losses, and vulnerability. As a result, the risk of natural disasters is not owned at the societal level and is, thereby, shifted onto the shoulders of the individuals who live in that society (Platt 1999). While this is the case, particularly for societies with limited resources, it is also important to note that the international community will often absorb at least a portion of the individual burden. For example, in

August of 1999, when Turkey was devastated by one of the 20th century's most powerful earthquakes, 87 countries from around the world provided emergency disaster relief assistance (Office of U.S. Foreign Disaster Assistance 1999).

Implications for the Preservation of Cultural Property

What is known in the natural hazards arena about these varied impacts of decisions to redistribute future risk, costs, and losses raises a significant question regarding decision-making for the preservation of cultural property. What are the implications of a preservation decision made at one level of one system for other levels of the same system, and what are the implications of that decision in other systems? As is the case with natural hazards, a more holistic approach may be needed for cultural property decision-making that considers the implications of any decision across system levels and across time. Such an approach might yield different preservation decisions—both in terms of what is preserved and what is not preserved as well as what actions are taken to preserve—if a broader range of cultures and time perspectives are considered. Take, for example, world culture versus the home culture of the object being preserved: if different segments of today's societies are considered (the poor as well as the powerful, women as well as men, minorities as well as the dominant ethnic group) and if different time periods are considered, one generation might, for example, choose to eliminate the Berlin Wall whereas future generations may wish to have a significant portion of it preserved.

How societies dichotomize and/or redistribute the risks, costs, and losses from natural hazards is influenced by that society's fundamental cultural values. Every human community has its own cultural values—beliefs, ideals, and customs. Culture is shared by most members of a society but can differ between societies (Mileti and Passerini 1996). A society's general cultural values often direct and determine the approaches and types of hazards mitigation choices which are favored in that society. As a result, these choices direct risks, costs, losses, and vulnerability to natural disasters. In general, societies use solutions that are valued while ignoring approaches and solutions that would contradict societal values.

For example, most developed contemporary societies value technology. The result of how this cultural value plays out regarding societal choices for managing the risk of natural hazards is that choices are made based on the notion that technology can and eventually will make humans safe from all of the forces of nature. This value yields societal responses to disasters such as believing and/or acting as if losses are caused by surprise extreme events, rather than by choices about how and where buildings are located and other development takes place. Societies that value technology favor technological 'fixes' for natural hazards. More often than not, when technology is used in an attempt to control nature, citizens end up believing that they are totally safe. In the United States, for example, dams and levees are often constructed to manage floods; development then occurs and people move onto the flood plains under the assumption that the dams and levees will not fail. Societies that highly value technology put less emphasis on alternate mitigations to natural hazards, since alternative approaches such as land-use restrictions contradict other basic values like individualism and the sanctity of private property.

Values not only influence the mitigation actions selected by a society but can also direct the approaches a society uses to make choices from the range of actions available (White 1974). For example, capitalistic societies emphasize profit and often use rational economic decision-making tools to help them select among alternative actions to mitigate hazards.

Such nations tend to favor economic efficiency in determining a choice from among a range of actions, for example, economic cost-benefit analysis. Mitigation actions that are selected make cost-benefit sense and actions that do not are ignored even when the ignored alternatives would accomplish more in the long term.

As with natural hazards decision-making, values also play a critical role in the preservation of cultural property. A current emphasis is on making the right decision about how to use what is known about cultural preservation, and how to deal with competing value systems.

Many value questions are used to guide this decision-making process. What is preserved? Are today's preservation decisions consistent with the values of future generations? What gets preserved: the physical object or the information that it contains? Why is something being preserved: to keep the object or to provide accessibility of the object to the general public?

These questions illustrate the extremely contextual nature of value-based decision-making in cultural property preservation. This is similar to the field of natural hazards where values determine our approach, and our approach and values determine what is and is not lost in the future disasters. Currently, the field of natural hazards has shifted to being responsible for future losses by deciding what might be reasonable losses in the future and making today's decisions consistent with that vision. Thus, perhaps a significant issue regarding values in cultural preservation is not any of those previously stated. Perhaps it is a question to those who preserve for the future. What is preserved today will impact what and who people in the future will know us to be. Consequently, preservationists create values, and this is analogous to the natural hazards field. What might come next for preservationists is to adopt the manifest role of deciding what values to create in the minds of people in the future about who we were, and then making today's preservation decisions consistent with that intention.

A Shift in Approach to Sustainable Development

It has recently been recognized in the natural hazards arena that societies need to shift their strategy for hazards and disasters to a sustainable development approach that includes the following:

- a global systems perspective that recognizes that disasters arise from the interactions among the earth's physical systems, its human systems, and its built infrastructure;
- people and societies accept responsibility for hazards and disasters by viewing human actions—not nature—as the cause of disaster losses, which stem from choices about where and how human development will proceed;
- the notion that a final solution to natural hazards has been abandoned, since technology cannot make the world safe from all the forces of nature;
- ambiguity and change are now anticipated, and the view that hazards are relatively static, which led to the false conclusion that any mitigation effort is desirable and will—in some vague way—reduce the grand total of future losses, has been discarded;
- short-term thinking and planning horizons are being replaced with a long-term view;
- societal factors, such as how people view both hazards and mitigation efforts or how the free market operates, that have long been ignored are now recognized as playing a critical role in determining future losses; and
- sustainable development principles have been embraced since disasters are more likely where unsustainable development occurs; the converse is also true.

Sustainability regarding hazards means that a locality can one day tolerate—and overcome—damage, diminished productivity, and reduced quality of life from an extreme event without significant outside assistance. To achieve sustainability, communities must move toward taking responsibility for choosing where and how development proceeds. Toward that end, each locality evaluates its environmental resources and hazards, chooses future losses that it is willing to bear, and ensures that development and other community actions and policies adhere to those goals. Six objectives must simultaneously be reached to mitigate hazards in a sustainable way and stop the trend toward increasing catastrophic losses from natural disasters (see Table 1).

Events in the past quarter-century have shown that natural disasters and the technological hazards that accompany them cannot be solved in isolation. Rather, they are symptoms of broader and more basic problems. Losses from hazards—and the fact that the world has not successfully reduced them—result from shortsighted and narrow conceptions of the human relationship to the natural environment. To redress these shortcomings, a call has been made for a shift to sustainable hazard mitigation. This long-term, holistic, and comprehensive plan for averting disaster losses and encouraging sustainability offers a society the opportunity to coordinate its goals and policies. A society can best forge such a plan by tapping businesses and residents as well as experts and government officials. While actual planning and follow-through must occur at the local level, a great deal of impetus must come from society's leaders.

The proposed alternative natural hazards model is based on the sustainable development paradigm and values long-term holistic approaches to enhance environmental quality, economic vitality, quality of life, societal resiliency to natural disasters, as well as inter- and intragenerational equity. Nothing short of strong and innovative leadership will ensure that planning for sustainable hazard mitigation and development occurs.

Several interesting parallels from natural hazards were drawn to the preservation of cultural property. Foremost, the field of natural hazards has recently opted for a more holistic approach linked to sustainable development. Aspects of this new and emerging approach with comparisons for preservation include the following observations.

In much the same way that most people ignore the risk of natural hazards, most cultural property is not preserved, while decisions are made to preserve some small segment of what could be retained for future generations. Risk assessment and analysis is used to inform decision-making about how to preserve what is being preserved but is not applied to the risk of preservation decision-making in the first place.

What is known, regarding natural hazards, about the impacts of decisions that redistribute future risks, costs, and losses suggests another parallel for the preservation of cultural property.

TABLE 1.

Sustainable development objectives for the management of natural hazards risk

1. *Maintain and Enhance Environmental Quality:* Human activities to mitigate hazards should not reduce the carrying capacity of the ecosystem, for doing so increases losses from hazards in the longer term. Hazard mitigation activities should be linked to efforts to control and ultimately reverse environmental degradation by coupling hazard reduction to natural resource management and environmental preservation.

2. *Maintain and Enhance People's Quality of Life:* A population's quality of life includes, among other factors, access to income, education, health care, housing, and employment as well as protection from disaster. To become sustainable, local communities must consciously define the quality of life they want and select only those mitigation strategies that do not detract from any aspect of that vision.

3. *Foster Local Resiliency and Responsibility:* Resiliency to disasters means a locale can withstand an extreme natural event with a tolerable level of losses. It takes mitigation actions consistent with achieving that level of protection.

4. *Recognize That Vibrant Local Economies Are Essential:* Communities should take mitigation actions that foster a strong local economy rather than detract from one. A diversified local economy, not overly dependent on a single productive force, would not only be more sustainable over the long term, it would also be less easily disrupted by disasters.

5. *Ensure Inter- and Intragenerational Equity:* A sustainable community selects mitigation activities that reduce hazards across all ethnic, racial, and income groups, and between genders equally, now and in the future. The costs of today's advances are not shifted onto later generations or less powerful groups.

6. *Adopt Local Consensus Building:* A sustainable community selects mitigation strategies that evolve from full participation among all public and private stakeholders. The participatory process itself may be as important as the outcome.

The implications of a preservation decision made at one level of one system embrace other levels of the same system and influence decisions in other systems (e.g., world culture versus home culture).

We have compared the role of values in natural hazards decision-making to the role of values in cultural preservation decision-making. As is now accepted among those who work with hazards, we suggested that preservationists create values through the decisions made today, to determine how future generations will perceive us. As is currently the case with natural hazards professionals, we suggest that preservationists consider adopting the role of deciding what values to create in the minds of people in the future about who we are today, and then making today's preservation decisions consistent with that intention.

REFERENCES

Anderson, M.B. 1994. Understanding the disaster-development continuum. *Focus on Gender* 2 (1): 7–10.

Bates, F.L., ed. 1982. *Recovery, Change, and Development: A Longitudinal Study of the 1976 Guatemalan Earthquake.* Athens, GA: Univ. of Georgia.

Blaikie, P., T. Cannon, 1. Davis, and B. Wisner. 1994. *At Risk: Natural Hazards, People's Vulnerability, and Disasters.* New York: Routledge.

Bolin, R.C. 1982. *Long-term Family Recovery from Disaster.* Boulder, CO: Institute of Behavioral Science, Univ. of Colorado.

Cutter, S. 1995. The forgotten casualties: Women, children, and environmental change. *Global Environmental Change: Human Policy Dimensions* 5 (3): 181–194.

Enarson, E., and B.H. Morrow. 1998. Why gender? Why women? An introduction to women and disaster. In: *The Gendered Terrain of Disaster: Through Women's Eyes,* ed. E. Enarson and B. Hearn Morrow, pp. 1–10. Westport, CT: Praeger.

Fothergill, A., E. Maestas, and J.D. Darlington. 1999. Race, ethnicity and disasters in the United States: A review of the literature. *Disasters* 23: 156–173.

Kunreuther, H. 1998. Introduction. In: *Paying the Price: The Status and Role of Natural Disasters in the United States,* ed. H. Kunreuther and R.J. Roth, Sr., pp. 1–15. Washington, D.C.: Joseph Henry Press.

Mileti, D.S. 1999. *Disasters by Design: A Reassessment of Natural Hazards in the United States.* Washington, D.C.: Joseph Henry Press.

Mileti, D.S., C. Fitzpatrick, and B.C. Farhar. 1992. Fostering public preparations for natural hazards: Lessons from the Parkfield earthquake prediction. *Environment* 34 (3): 16–39.

Mileti, D.S., and E. Passerini. 1996. A social explanation of urhan relocation after earthquakes. *Intl. Journal of Mass Emergencies and Disasters* 14: 97–110.

Office of U.S. Foreign Disaster Assistance. 1999. Annual Report FY 1999. Washington, D.C.: U.S. Agency for Intl. Development.

Petak, W. 1998. Mitigation and insurance. In: *Paying the Price: The Status and Role of Natural Disasters in the United States,* ed. H. Kunreuther and R.J. Roth, Sr., pp. 155–170. Washington, D.C.: Joseph Henry Press.

Platt, R.H. 1999. *Disasters and Democracy: The Politics of Extreme Natural Events.* Washington, D.C.: Island Press.

Schroeder, R.A. 1987. *Gender Vulnerability and Drought: A Case Study of the Hausa Social Environment.* Boulder, CO: Institute of Behavioral Science, Univ. of Colorado.

Tweeddale, M. 1996. The nature and handling of risk. *Australian Journal of Emergency Management* 11: 2–4.

White, G.F. 1974. Natural hazards research: Concepts, methods, and policy implications. In: *Natural Hazards: Local, National, Global,* ed. G.F. White, pp. 3–16. New York: Oxford Univ. Press.

PETER WATERS

Excerpts from revised text of "Procedures for Salvage of Water-Damaged Materials"

July 1993 (web document: www.archives.gov/preservation/conservation/library-materials-01.html).

Introduction

Since the first publication in 1975 of 'Procedures for Salvage of Water-Damaged Materials' there has been no decrease in the frequency of accidents or unexpected disasters which have resulted in extensive water damage to library materials but there are many signs that we have begun to learn the immense value of disaster preparedness planning. Being familiar with the necessity of having to make a series of interrelated decisions promptly, understanding the effects of any particular course of action on subsequent ones—this is the best kind of preparation needed in the event of major water-damage problems. A well-organized plan can greatly reduce the costs of salvage and restoration as well as the proportion of outright losses. This preparedness can also go a long way to lessen the emotional and stressful impact upon human beings.

The various courses of action discussed in this revised edition are designed to save the maximum amount of material with minimum amounts of restoration on the one hand or replacement on the other. However, it cannot be emphasized too much that no general instructions can take the place of an assessment of a given situation on site by a qualified, experienced library or archive specialist, who has proven experience in the reclamation of fire and water-damaged collections. It is strongly recommended that such assistance and advice be sought at the earliest moment after a disastrous event has occurred. [...]

Library and archive staffs are now generally better informed about the mechanisms of drying cellulosic materials as well some of the technologies developed for this purpose. The use of vacuum chambers for drying large quantities of books and paper records has become an acceptable, almost common approach, but not without some confusion as to the differences and relative merits of vacuum drying and vacuum freeze-drying. Both methods effectively remove water but by quite different mechanisms and often with quite different results. An understanding of how these technologies function is essential in planning for a recovery operation, in order to make the best possible match between the nature, condition and needs of the materials and the capabilities of a particular drying system.

The use of fungicides to control the spread of mold growth has become an increasingly controversial subject because they may cause severe danger to workers and in some cases to the materials treated. Sterilizing by means of ethylene oxide and related chemicals has come under close scrutiny by the Environmental Protection Agency (EPA), to the extent that we cannot recommend its use except by a commercial business firm which is fully insured and licensed to perform this service. Treatments involving the use of ethylene oxide (ETO) are best carried out under controlled conditions, as in vacuum chambers at the end of a drying cycle, and they must be guaranteed to leave no residual toxicity in the material. ETO remains the most effective treatment for severe mold attack resulting from major disasters, especially those exposed to river water.

The critical decisions that have to be made following water damage require knowledge of available dry-

---

Editor's note: *In 1993, at the request of Dianne L. Van der Reyden, then at the Smithsonian Institution, later the Director of the Preservation Directorate at the Library of Congress, Peter Waters (1930-2003) updated his manual for inclusion in the document below, which was a joint effort of the four major cultural federal agencies that Van der Reyden coordinated (e-mail to Dianne Van der Reyden, December 4, 2011).*

ing technologies and their effects on a variety of composite materials. Ideally, materials removed from site, should be prepared and packed in a manner most suitable for the drying method to be used. Unfortunately, what tends to happen, particularly when no emergency plan exists, is that wet material is packed and shipped off to freezing facilities without knowledge of how the material will be dried. This may result in the material having to be re-packed before drying which adds considerably to the cost of drying and the potential for further damage.

The complete restoration of water-soaked documents, particularly bound items, can be a costly process even under the most favorable conditions. In the majority of cases, the high costs involved do not justify the salvage and restoration of books which are in print and can be replaced. However, decisions relating to these factors are virtually impossible to make during a salvage operation and even when a disaster plan exists. On the other hand it might be unwise not to attempt to salvage everything, if an insurance assessment is required and a claim is to be made.

Freezing, followed by vacuum freeze drying has been shown to be one of the most effective methods for removing water from large numbers of books and other paper records, but drying is not the final step in the reclamation process. In some cases, volumes which are only damp or which have suffered minor physical damage before freezing may come from a drying chamber in such good condition that they can be returned to the shelves. It is preferable that, where possible, the packing on site should be carried out in such a manner as to segregate very wet material from that which is partially wet and those that are damp from exposure to high humidity conditions This will not only result in cost savings during the drying operation but will help to avoid over drying of the least wet material. In the majority of instances, drying must be followed by restoration and rebinding, and therefore the technique and success of the drying method chosen will directly affect the final cost of restoration. This can be very expensive.

Thus, librarians and others faced with decisions which follow serious flooding and water damage from the aftermath of fire, and related water-damaged

exposure, need to be reminded that replacement is nearly always much less costly than salvage and restoration. The necessity for making sound, on-the-spot, cost-effective judgments is the best reason for being prepared in advance by developing a pre-disaster preparedness plan. There are a number of such plans that have been drawn up, which can be found in the literature, to serve as models.

We encourage all of our colleagues who care about the integrity of library collections, including those who are difficult to persuade that a disaster could ever occur, to formulate disaster preparedness plans without delay so that it may never be necessary to refer to this document in times of distress!

[…]

Part 9
Evaluation of Loss

When a flood or fire-damaged collection is covered by insurance, full settlement of a claim cannot be realized until the lost and damaged materials have been listed and their values established. The extent and success of possible restoration must also be determined. In the event that a claim is anticipated as a result of such damage, every item should be salvaged, frozen, and dried. After drying, the affected materials should be shelved in a specially equipped environmental storage area, isolated from the main stacks, and there inspected and monitored over a period of time. Such a policy is the best guarantee of sound judgments by custodians, consultants, and adjusters when they must calculate the degree of loss as a basis for compensation.

SUMMARY OF EMERGENCY PROCEDURES

Seek the advice and help of book and paper conservators with experience in salvaging water-damaged materials as soon as possible.

Turn off heat and create free circulation of air.

Keep fans and air-conditioning on day and night and use dehumidifiers and insure a constant flow of air is necessary to reduce the threat of mold.

Brief each worker carefully before salvage operations begin, giving full information on the dangers of proceeding except as directed. Emphasize the seriousness of timing and the priorities and aims of the whole operation. Instruct workers on means of recognizing manuscripts, materials with water-soluble components, leather and vellum bindings, materials printed on coated paper stock, and photographic materials.

Do not allow workers to attempt restoration of any items on site. This was a common error in the first 10 days after the Florence flood, when rare and valuable leather and vellum-bound volumes were subjected to scrubbing and processing to remove mud. This resulted in driving mud into the interstices of leather, vellum, cloth, and paper, caused extensive damage to the volumes, and made the later work of restoration more difficult, time consuming, and extremely costly.

Carry out all cleaning operations, whether outside the building or in controlled environment rooms, by washing gently with fresh, cold running water and soft cellulose sponges to aid in the release of mud and filth. Use sponges in a dabbing motion; do not rub. These instructions do not apply to materials with water-soluble components. Such materials should be frozen as quickly as possible.

Do not attempt to open a wet book. (Wet paper is very weak and will tear at a touch. One tear costs at least one dollar to mend!) Hold a book firmly closed when cleaned, especially when washing or sponging. A closed book is highly resistant to impregnation and damage.

Do not attempt to remove mud by sponging. Mud is best removed from clothes when dry; this is also true of library materials.

Do not remove covers from books, as they will help to support the books during drying.

When partially dry, books may be hung over nylon lines to finish drying. Do not hang books from lines while they are very wet because the weight will cause damage to the inside folds of the sections.

Do not press books and documents when they are water soaked. This can force mud into the paper and subject the materials to stresses which will damage their structures.

Use soft pencils for making notes on slips of paper but do not attempt to write on wet paper or other artifacts.

Clean, white blotter paper, white paper towels, strong toilet paper, and unprinted newsprint may be used for interleaving in the drying process. When nothing better is available, all but the color sections of printed newspapers may be used. Care must be taken to avoid rubbing the inked surface of the newspaper over the material being dried; otherwise some offsetting of the ink may occur.

Under no circumstances should newly dried materials be packed in boxes and left without attention for more than a few days.

Do not use bleaches, detergents, water-soluble fungicides, wire staples, paper or bulldog clips, adhesive tape, or adhesives of any kind. Never use felt-tipped fiber or ballpoint pens or any marking device on wet paper.

Never use colored blotting paper or colored paper of any kind to dry books and other documents.

Used and damp interleaving sheets should not be reused.

Frequent changing of interleaving material is much more effective than allowing large numbers of sheets to remain in place for extended periods.

Newsprint should not be left in books after drying is complete.

A good grade of paper toweling is more effective than newsprint, but the cost is much greater.

Editor's note: *For a recent analysis of the key components of emergency response plans, see Jordan Ferraro and Jane Henderson, "Identifying Features of Effective Emergency Response Plans,"* Journal of the American Institute for Conservation *50.1 (Spring/Summer 2011): 35–48.*

chapter 6

CONSERVATION

THE PHYSICAL CARE AND TREATMENT OF INDIVID-
ual items and collections is referred to as *conservation*. When carried out according to standard practices, it complements other
preservation strategies such as proper storage, environmental
monitoring, staff and patron training, reformatting, and security.
As **Caroline K. Keck**—one of the authors in this chapter—puts it,
conservation is similar to medicine in that it has amassed "a body of
knowledge founded on experience, experiments and observations."
With its focus on the object, conservation is at the heart of preservation strategies.
Before preservation was an established field, conservators were in charge of the aggregate care of institutional collections (and in some institutions, they still are).

Restoration is another word that is used to describe treatment. It has several meanings, some of which are derogatory. The word *restore* means to bring something back
that has been lost or to repair something that has been damaged. With film, where
there may be numerous edited versions of a work, restoration may refer to reintegrat-
ing lost footage. In a painting, restoration may refer to retouching pigments or toning
with varnish. In bookbinding, it might be a re-backing that is done so expertly that
the repair work might be indiscernible. The aim in such cases is to make the treatments as invisible as possible. (Though see Christopher Clarkson, "Conservation and
Restoration Defined," below, for a much more detailed distinction between book conservation and restoration.) When the intent of the restoration is deceit, the term has

a negative connotation. Unethical antique dealers, for example, may hope to increase the monetary value of their holdings by making objects look "better" or newer before selling them.

Of course there are degrees of practice. The work carried out on an object for the marketplace may be different from what is practiced in a museum, library, or archive. However, even among these types of institutions conservation treatments may have different aims. In a library, most items are not displayed, so "simply" making the text in a book legible may be the appropriate approach. Bleaching may not need to be an option because the pages don't need to look aesthetically pleasing. If an object is on exhibition or permanent display, stains on a print, missing paint on an oil, and so on, may be distracting to the viewer. In conservation, there are distinct standards of practice. Conservators would not add missing limbs to an ancient statue, for example. There are many nuances in conservation decision-making across fields and institutions.

Further complicating the term *restoration* is that, for a long time making objects look newer, better, or fresher, was perfectly acceptable practice. Caroline Keck describes it this way: "The restorer was the person employed to make an old item last longer. He concealed damages in tune with the tastes of his time without regard to original style, and often without regard to original composition. Until the late nineteenth century, few people disapproved of such an approach so long as the work complied with current interpretations." Today, however, most scholars, curators, architects, archivists, and librarians take a more minimalist approach to treatment. Less treatment— or even no treatment at all—is preferable.

In art conservation and historic preservation there is an ongoing debate as to how much focus there should be on the aesthetic qualities of a work, object, or building versus its historical and authorial authenticity. In historic preservation, there is an additional consideration: people live in historic structures. Thus it might not be practical—or desirable—to maintain an old building exactly as it was built.

Another term of art is *restauro di conservazione*, which translates as conservation-restoration. It refers to practice that falls somewhere between conservation and restoration. As Marie Berducou points out, "This definition has no universal support; in reality, the meaning given to the words *conservation* and *restoration* varies considerably according to author and country."[1] In this book, *conservation* is used, except when *restoration* has a particular meaning that must be respected.

Works about the treatment of items have been published for centuries. It is the nature of things to deteriorate, and techniques have long been developed to assure that objects, or the built environment, will last for as long as possible. Oral traditions have been preserved as well, initially solely through oral transmission and now also through sound recordings and/or transcriptions. Chapter 1, "Early Sources on Preservation," gives ample examples of early views on preservation and conservation.

More recently, many new issues are addressed in the conservation literature. These include the values of conservation, social and political contexts, outreach to expanding audiences, the environment and sustainability, new technologies of objects, new technologies for treatment, and so on. Some of these themes overlap with preservation and are covered throughout this book. The primary focus in this chapter is on treatment.

The decisions that conservators make are based on conservation research, ethics, standards, and best practices, as well on such pragmatic considerations as how an object will be used, stored, and exhibited. All of these issues are covered by the authors in this chapter, many of whom worked or studied with one another.

Paul N. Banks's "The Laws of Conservation" opens the chapter. The *Laws* have never been published, but have been disseminated for decades by Banks's former students. They are also known as *The Ten Laws of Conservation*.[2] These principles are an appropriate frame for the rest of the chapter. His first law, "No one can have access to a document that no longer exists," speaks to the essential reason for conservation. We preserve things so that they can be studied, used, viewed, experienced, and otherwise incorporated into our lives as well as into the lives of future generations.

Banks drew upon the work of many bookbinders, art conservators, and bibliographers; the works of several of them appear here. One influence was **Douglas Cockerell** (1870–1945), whose manual *Bookbinding and the Care of Books* appeared in many editions.[3] His sound practices and emphasis on quality materials established a foundation upon which the field of book conservation could be built. He was also pragmatic:

> Books for binding can be roughly divided into three classes: 1st. Books of value, or of special interest to their owners, that require to be bound as well as the binder can do them. 2nd. Books of permanent interest, but of no special value, that require to be well and strongly bound, but for which the best and most careful work would be too expensive. 3rd. Books of temporary interest that need to be held together and kept neat and tidy for occasional reference.
>
> In other words, some books must be bound as well as possible regardless of expense, some as cheaply as they can be bound well, and others as well as they can be bound cheaply.[4]

This chapter includes Cockerell's *A Note on Binding*.

Cockerell studied with T. J. Cobden-Sanderson (1840–1922), who was associated with the Arts and Crafts Movement. Cockerell taught Roger Powell (1896–1990) who later became his partner. Powell taught three of the authors included here: Peter Waters (who later became Powell's business partner), Christopher Clarkson, and Nicholas Pickwood. Banks became acquainted with Waters and Clarkson during the recovery efforts following the Florence flood in November 1966.

Back in the United States, Banks worked with Caroline and Sheldon Keck; all three played leadership roles in the American Institute for Conservation of Historic and Artistic Works (AIC). Banks was president from 1978–80 and there is an AIC award for excellence in teaching that recognizes the work of the Kecks. In 1960 at New York University, the Kecks founded the first American training program in conservation. A decade later, they started the Cooperstown Graduate Program in the Conservation

of Historic and Artistic Works at the State University of New York at Oneonta, New York (now at the State College at Buffalo). Banks started the Library Conservation Education Programs in the School of Library Service at Columbia University, which admitted its first class in 1981.

Paul Banks taught conservation and preservation to hundreds of students, mostly at Columbia University and The University of Texas; Jan Paris was one of them. Some of the authors whose works appear in this chapter are linked through their writings or by working with one another, but almost all of them had a connection to Paul Banks.

Nicholas Pickwood and **Christopher Clarkson** expand on the work of binders Cockerell and Powell and bibliographer Graham Pollard, whose article "Changes in the Style of Bookbinding, 1550-1830" was an early and important contribution to the description of bindings.[5] Clarkson's piece, "Minimum Intervention in Treatment of Books," written in 1999, addresses many critical points about book conservation. First, he considers what he calls "the original integrity of bindings and their contents," that is, the features, marks, and other pieces of evidence that help the conservator determine a book's history.

Of particular historical interest for this chapter, Clarkson describes developing the phrase "book conservation" in Florence, Italy in 1967. He, along with Peter Waters and several others who had gone to Florence after the November 1966 flood to help with recovery efforts, stayed on to establish a comprehensive program for treating the hundreds of thousands of items at the Biblioteca Nazionale Centrale that had been damaged. As Clarkson describes it "when I coined the phrase 'book conservation'…I was trying to express a clear break with European hand binding practices based on the past three centuries and to build a foundation of training based on the earlier periods of constructional creativity and diversity, using various materials in a wide range of qualities."

Interpretation of the artifact depends on a variety of specialists: the art historian, curator, bibliographer, conservator, and chemist or materials scientist. Clarkson explains through several examples how the lack of a thorough knowledge of bookbinding practices has led to poor treatment decisions.

Nicholas Pickwoad has systematically studied the individual components of book structures, such as sewing or rounding and backing, and uses his knowledge to date bindings. His techniques are detailed in "Distinguishing Between the Good and Bad Repair of Books." This work carries forward earlier work by conservators and bibliographers, some of whom have already been identified here. Recently, Pickwoad has focused his research on bookbinding documentation and creating a bilingual glossary with digital tools and resources to aid in the cataloging of bindings in St. Catherine's Library in Sinai, Egypt.[6]

In "Conservation and the Politics of Use and Value in Research Libraries," **Jan Paris** lays out the many challenges that conservators face in running institutional programs. Conservators are responsible for the care and treatment of a variety of materials such as rare books, manuscripts, posters, maps, photography, and ephemera. They must work collaboratively with curators and other librarians, and weigh competing priorities for their time. They must also prioritize items for treatment, prepare items for exhibitions, participate in short- and long-range planning for conservation and digitization, and facilitate the appropriate storage and use of materials.[7]

The conservation of archival materials has been far less written about than book or art conservation has been. Christine Ward describes the role of preservation—and by extension, conservation—in archives succinctly:

An archives is a place in which records of long-term, or enduring, value are systematically preserved and made available for use. Preservation ensures the continued availability and usability of the information contained in those records. *In a traditional sense, preservation is the archives' raison d'être.* But preservation of information is a means to achieve a desired end. A modern archives' primary goal is to provide access to its holdings. (Italics added.)[8]

There are challenges specific to archives conservation. For example, most materials in an archive are unique, so the replacement of a damaged item is not an option. Archival materials tend to be unbound, so permanent/durable folders housed in archival boxes are needed for these. Additionally, archival materials exist in an array of sizes, shapes, and media. Architectual plans and maps require treatment and storage strategies that differ from small pieces. The major text on archives preservation and conservation is by **Mary Lynn Ritzenthaler**. She lays out in detail a number of strategies for conservation of archives and manuscripts. One example is mass conservation procedures. Mass treatments include deacidification, fumigation, and paper strengthening. A short excerpt of this recently revised work is printed here.

Although Peter Waters wrote "Phased Conservation" with books in mind, he brought a systems approach to conservation that could be used for any type of collection. His ability to come up with solutions for addressing the needs of large collections was honed during the years that he spent after the 1966 Florence flood working at the Biblioteca Nazionale Centrale. While Christopher Clarkson's writings have focused on the treatment of individual items, Waters recognized that it was neither possible nor desirable to treat every item in need of attention and this is reflected in his publications. He found that providing simple protective enclosures for books alleviated the need for immediate treatment since the enclosure would protect the item for at least the short term. He fine-tuned this approach at the Library of Congress where the term *phased conservation* was coined. If a book needed repair, such treatments could be *phased*, since the enclosures would provide immediate protection and attention could be devoted to books that had the greater needs. Unfortunately, we were not able to reproduce the work here. Those interested in reading more should consult the webpages of the Library of Congress. Some of these ideas come through in his seminal work on disaster recovery, excerpts of which are in chapter 5.

There are many reasons not to treat an item. One is that conservation is time-consuming and expensive and thus may need to be justified; unless an object is in immediate danger of further deterioration, why treat it? A second reason is that treatment alters the original characteristics of an item. But perhaps the most compelling reason is covered by Paul Banks's

10th Law: "No treatment is reversible." **Andrew Oddy**, formerly of the British Museum Department of Conservation, explores this concept in his essay "Reversibility: Does it Exist?" which is one of the essays in a volume of the same title, based on a British Museum preservation conference. The volume follows an earlier British Museum meeting, and subsequent publication, *Restoration: Is it Acceptable?*[9]

Finally, **Sheldon Keck** reminds us how important a history of conservation is, for it allows us to gain insights into the philosophical approaches of the past. By understanding early treatments, conservators can understand how an object should be approached today. Part of the history of an object is embedded in the treatments it has had.

Banks's 9th law, "Conservation treatment is interpretation," is an appropriate note on which to close this introduction. All of the authors have thought deeply about the role of conservation in the life of an object as well as in cultural heritage.

NOTES

1. Marie Berducou, "Introduction to Archaeological Conservation," in *Historical and Philosophical Issues in the Conservation of Cultural Heritage*, ed. by Nicholas Stanley Price, et al. (Los Angeles, CA: The Getty Conservation Institute, 1996), p. 253.

2. I took a preservation course with Banks at Columbia University in summer 1976. My own notes include an eleventh law, "There will never be any more copies of a particular edition of a book than there are now." Thanks to Judy Walsh for providing me with her copies of the ten laws, and for Ellen Cunningham-Kruppa and Roberta Pilette for helping me to untangle the permissions.

3. Douglas Cockerell, *Bookbinding and the Care of Books*, first published in London in 1901; there were several subsequent editions.

4. Douglas Cockerell, *A Note on Bookbinding, with Extracts from the Special Report of the Society of Arts on Leather for Bookbinding*. (London: W.H. Smith, 1904), pp. 5–6.

5. Graham Pollard, "Changes in the Style of Bookbinding, 1550–1830," *The Library* 5th series, 11 (June 1956): 71–94.

6. See the profile of Nicholas Pickwoad at the website of Camberwell College, U.K., and a description of the Ligatus Bookbinding Glossary at http://www.ligatus.org.uk/glossary.

7. Some of these issues are also considered in the long-running Curators and Conservators Group (CACG) of the Rare Books and Manuscripts Section, Association of College and Research Libraries, a group that has been meeting since the 1980s. The purpose of this group is "[t]o add to the body of information on curator/conservator relations and to encourage the education of curators and conservators about their respective professions; to provide a forum for discussion about topics of mutual interest; to identify, recommend, and facilitate creation of continuing education seminars through the Seminars Committee; to publicize issues concerning curators and conservators by encouraging the publication of relevant articles in appropriate journals." (See www.rbms.info/rbms_manual/discussion_groups.shtml#curators_and_conservators).

8. Christine Ward, "Preservation Program Planning for Archives and Historical Records Repositories," in *Preservation Issues and Planning*, eds. Paul N. Banks and Roberta Pilette, 43 (Chicago: American Library Association, 2000).

9. Andrew Oddy and Sara Caroll, eds., *Reversibility— Does it Exist?* Occasional Paper, no. 135 (London: British Museum, 1999), and Andrew Oddy, ed., *Restoration: Is It Acceptable?* Occasional Paper, no. 99 (London: British Museum, Department of Conservation, 1994).

PAUL N. BANKS

"The Laws of Conservation"

N.p.: n.p., n.d.

1. No one can have access to a document that no longer exists.
2. Multiplication and dispersal increase chances for survival of information.
3. The physical medium of a book or document contains information.
4. No reproduction can contain all the information contained in the original.
5. Conservation treatment is interpretation and repair.
6. Authenticity cannot be restored.
7. No treatment is reversible.
8. Use causes wear.
9. Books and documents deteriorate all the time.
10. Deterioration is irreversible.

CHRISTOPHER CLARKSON

"Minimum Intervention in Treatment of Books"

Preprint from the 9th International Congress of IADA, August 15–21, 1999. Copenhagen: Royal Library of Denmark, 1999, pp. 89–96.

Interpretation has to be based on authentic qualities of the object. And if we want to pass down the objects to posterity as true documents, we have to care very much for the original substance. The extent to which this is spared during particular operations in conservation will depend on interpretation, mostly that by the conservator.[1]

Introduction

Thirty years ago 'conservation' was a word only used in the physical treatment of paintings and museum objects. When I coined the phrase 'book conservation' in Florence in 1967, I was trying to express a clear break with European hand binding practices based on the past three centuries and to build a foundation of training based on the earlier periods of constructional creativity and diversity, using various materials in a wide range of qualities.[2,3] I was concerned about the care and preservation of books and manuscripts; about the information conveyed not only by the text but by all aspects of the physical object as well—in fact the 'archaeology of the book.'[4] The 'objects', 'foreign marks', and 'foreign matter' found in and on a book can provide important evidence of the book's history and use, as well as the social history in which the book participated.

Another concern has been that as natural materials become more generalized and scarce in our synthetic age, books and libraries become a major resource for the wide variety of qualities displayed in everyday historic materials. The codex book has proved to be a very fine 'time capsule'; in the sense that if the materials used in its construction and decoration are of good quality, then the book may well have preserved them in their 'original state'. Hence we can find leaves in a medieval text-block looking as though they were made and printed yesterday, or an 18th-century book with water-colours quite fresh and bright. (If exhibited for a few days the 'fresh-state' can be lost forever). The codex was used deliberately as a repository and is also an accidental 'catch-all'. Therefore gutters of books are wonderful places where we can find early pins, needles, threads, and a wide variety of botanical specimens.[5] Very rarely have such marks or items caused any kind of damage; so please do not allow gutters of books to be brush-cleaned or page surfaces to be routinely dry-cleaned. Tidy-mindedness in such cases is misapplied. A general rule is that 'institutional dirt' if judged destabilizing may be removed, but not 'evidential dirt'. The devaluing of this type of information contained in our collections under the name of 'conservation' is now very great indeed. In such circumstances 'minimum intervention' is the only way forward.

I am fearful that the training of young conservators is not going in this direction, however, because it generally reflects only the past two to three hundred years of hand binding practice. During this time surface presentation was predominant, qualities of material deteriorated, and techniques continued to be abbreviated and generalized. There has been a further 'dumbing-down' over the last two decades, in the tendency to refer to 'conservation binding' as though it were a group of styles or binding types. This is quite wrong, for there are only conservation principles, which can be applied in different degrees and variation in order to stabilize or repair various binding types. This attitude, like misapplied mass-treatments (mass-treatments may, with great caution, have a place in our work; but 'mass-thinking' does not), can destroy our unique library and archive heritage, making our bookshelves neat and tidy, but altogether soulless.

Surprisingly, one is sometimes grateful for the crude patching of bindings of past custodians when comparing them with the thoughtless and ever increasing rebinding and restoration practices which

replace and fake original material far too much. In the former case, non-professional patching and mending (which may, with care, be recoverable), while impairing the surface of a binding, has occasionally preserved bibliographical integrity. In the latter case the historical and bibliographical integrity of a book is more than likely to be lost forever.

If we wish to preserve books and historic collections we must develop sensitive conservation practices relating and linking closely to preservation polices[6] within our institutions. Minimum intervention, refurbishing, rejuvenating materials (where possible), and stabilizing, although quite time consuming and labour intensive, have to be promoted as major priorities. Only then will rebinding be considered thoughtfully and sensitively; and become a far smaller part of conservation programmes than it is today.

Conservation and Restoration Defined

My definition of 'conservation' allows for minor interference with the object to stabilize it mechanically or chemically. This usually means the addition of a small amount of foreign or new material. Whether such material is visible is not my chief concern.

My use of the term 'restoration' implies a greater incursion into a particular area, for example 'tail spine-cap', 'first three quires resewn', etc. Where the encroachment of new material is greater I simply say 'restored'; the difference in how this is done determines whether I would judge it a sympathetic restoration or not. The difference between a sympathetic repair and 'facsimile' (the word facsimile embodies the idea that past cultures, materials and crafts can be recreated) can be extremely subtle and depends largely on the mind and intention of the restorer.

Minimum Intervention Defined

'Minimum intervention' means minimum interference. Paradoxically, however, a book conservator needs to acquire considerable knowledge and experience before attempting to practise 'minimum intervention'. Since the late 1960s I have been conscious that in order to be able to create simple and adaptable working methods one needs to have a deep historical awareness of books and manuscripts, considerable practical experience, a command over tools, a knowledge of a large variety of materials, and a broad repertoire of techniques. Many of my tools, materials, and techniques have evolved with each project.[7,8,9] It must be emphasised that these essential attributes and skills are quite different from those required to rebind books and will take time to acquire.

For minimum intervention to be practised correctly a damaged item must be very carefully analysed, understood, and assessed before any action is taken.

ANALYSIS

Part of the purpose of an analysis is to be able to describe a condition clearly. This involves using a well-defined terminology. The difficulties of describing in words the qualities or substance of a material are enormous but very important to document. To help in this I use many samples to touch, feel and compare but all the time one is making a personal judgement which is difficult to communicate in words, photographs or diagrams. Skin materials are a good example of what I mean because other than surface texture or general phrases such as 'soft handle', 'hard handle' etc., a useful description is very difficult to obtain. Even when new there are many variations within the manufacturing process of leather, parchment, or tawed skin—variations which may resolve or exacerbate a repair.[10]

Analysis also helps to better understand the cause of the condition. Moreover, a better understanding of the cause of the condition facilitates the process of finding a solution, for example:

- Has the damage been caused by abrasion or chafing?
- Has the damage been caused by a burst tear or by tensile force?
- Did the break/s occur due to strains in the original binding structure, strains caused by later restoration, awkward handling or exhibition display?

A thorough analysis of the problem may well lead to the conclusion that non-repair is an option, because a repair can throw up new stresses and endanger other areas of the binding structure. Some common examples that might be encountered:

- Replacing fore-edge clasps, stressing an original or aged sewing system or joints. A book-box which supplies gentle, even pressure overall would be a better option.
- A repair which dries, becoming less flexible than the surrounding period material endangers that material and/or neighbouring materials.
- A stiff-board vellum binding in which the upper joint has broken because the covering at the spine is too inflexible, a common problem of late 16th- and 17th-century vellum bindings with hollows (for stresses caused see comments below under 'Hollows').

In this paper I wish to give six examples which illustrate my various approaches and methods for repairing book structures and list other types of repair problems.

Example I

'Board leverage' is a term I use to refer to the readjustment of the text-block as its book-boards swing open. Good board-leverage depends on the weight, quality and condition of the layers of material (usually four: covering, bands, endleaf reinforcement and board-sheet) across the spine and at the joints. An important factor affecting the character of the leverage is how the bands enter the boards. For example, heavy alum-tawed bands entering the spine-edge of the boards produce an effect different to that of the North European Gothic attachment technique, where the wooden boards were so shaped at the spine-edge, and attached to the text-block in such a way, that when the boards were closed a convex spine and joint-shoulders were naturally, rather than artificially, formed.

DAMAGE

Damage can occur when text fragments that have been used as endleaf reinforcements are lifted; board leverage is then lost, allowing the boards to swing, hinging and dragging like doors. In this state the joints soon break down. Many collections are being seriously damaged in this way.

REPAIR

One must quickly restore the inner tension to the joint. This is not an easy task without causing major disruption, such as unsewing the first or last quires and re-introducing parchment or linen reinforcement pieces. A slightly less intrusive approach would be to insert comb-liners through the joints, pasting the 'tines' across the book's spine (under the covering material), and the liner overlay to the inner face of the board (under the board-sheet). Obviously there would be many instances where this should not or cannot be done, but assessing the problem and quick intervention is crucial in saving the binding.[11]

If one can obtain good board-leverage with a flatter action, there is less tendency for the joint edges of the cover material to form compression wrinkles each time a joint is flexed, compared to conventional tight-back or tight-jointed repairs where there is the need or desire to trim back considerably the original covering material from the joints.

Example II

In sharp contrast to the previous example are the late 19th-century European stiff-board, tight-back bindings in which 'third-of-a-circle' rounding and sharp, square backing shoulders force the covering and joint material to flex very acutely indeed. Characteristically in this binding type, the boards hinge independently and freely from a solid, compressed text-block; and covering leather is pared very thinly at the joints and board edges.

DAMAGE

Either the upper board or both boards have parted from their text-block and require reattaching. A major problem is the slick gold tooled and polished leather surfaces.

REPAIR

I started to work on a solution to this problem at the Library of Congress in the mid 1970s and came up with board-slotting, further developed at the Bodleian Library, where a slot is cut in the board to accept a tongue of cloth attached to text-block.[12,13] Attaching the tongue can be a problem when the leather is firmly adhered to the consolidated spine with a thin glue layer. A similar period binding with a tube hollow would be no problem.

Example III

A bookbinding with a hollow-back is one where the covering material at the spine is left free of the text-block's spine and so can flex independently when the book is opened. There are two types:

1. The type which I term 'natural hollow'—limp and semi-limp paper and vellum bindings, certain Germanic 17th–18th century stiff-board bindings and publishers' case bindings ('casing hollow') of the 19th and 20th centuries are all examples of this type. It has a slight gusset action at the joints.
2. 'Tube' or 'formed' hollows. In the 19th century a method of forming a hollow on the rounded shape of a spine was devised for certain leather work. It consisted of a paper tube exactly fitting the curved spine between the crown of the shoulders. One side of the tube supplies extra spine liner/s, and the other a spine stiffener for the cover, which often includes fake raised bands. By the time the third-of-a-circle spine shape came along, such hollows were the rule rather than the exception. Because it has tight joints with a tube-hollow, the joint materials hinge acutely at the crowns of the backing shoulders.
3. Another type should be listed: a tight-back where a hollow has developed through the strains of the books use, or where the adhesive

has deteriorated, so that the spine area now acts like a hollow-back.

Later in the century, and certainly up to the present day, the hollow-back has been considered the only solution for obtaining improved opening of many text-blocks without recourse to some fundamental changes in the conventional European hand-binding technique. On opening a book with a hollow the text-block's spine arch becomes concave while the portion of cover at the spine becomes more convex. Anything which impedes these movements will cause strain thus:

DAMAGE

There are several scenarios:

1. If the spine-stiffener is not flexible enough, or has become inflexible over the years, then the book's opening will be restricted.[14] If forced open, strains are thrown directly onto the edges of the tube hollow, or in the case of 'natural hollows' onto the joint area causing joints to break, or zigzag-type stress to appear at endleaf joint areas.

2. If the stiffener is in a brittle or weaker condition than the joints, instead of increasing in convexity the stiffener will peak and crack.

3. However, if the cover portion of the hollow is stronger or less flexible, opening the book will stress the sewing structure and joints. When the book is opened the text-block spine tries to arch and decrease in width. The joint will break if it is the weakest point and the opening is forced.

4. If joint areas are stronger, then on opening the book, the arch at the spine of the text-block will become pointed, causing liners to crack between the quires. When this happens, the bands will flex acutely at a place near the centre of the text-block. When the bands finally break, one is confronted with a major handling problem. An urgent repair is required because the text-block is in two halves, and the area of sewing thread retaining the neigh-

bouring quires can start slipping off the bands.

Do not make the mistake of imagining that maximum flexibility at the spine area is always what is required in a binding, for it depends much on the text-block dimensions, weight, material flexibility and other qualities, plus the book's intended use.

REPAIR

When analysing the problems of repair there are some general points to remember about books with hollow-backs:

A balance of flexibility between the text-block's spine and the 'cover spine piece' must be achieved. (I am not generally in favour of the technique of limiting a 'peaking' text-block by decreasing the flexibility of the 'spine-cover-piece' because this approach dramatically increases the strain on the joints.) To gain such a balance, attention to the substance and flexing properties of the text-block's spine liners and bands is required. Not much can usually be done to make the sewing supports more flexible, so they usually become the controlling factor in how much of the previous spine lining is removed and the type and quantity of new material that is applied. Unless one can satisfactorily solve such problems or permanently restrict the opening angle, then a sensible option is to stabilize the sewing system, leaving the cover to move separately and connected only at one joint (more acceptable to Special Collection personnel when an upper rather than a lower joint is concerned). This suggestion may appear to be an unacceptable compromise but repairing the joint could recreate the strains which caused the original damage. A warning, i.e. in the box lid, should always be given as to such a handling problem.

Another factor is that for spine liners especially, I never rely upon adhesive, because in time it will break down, particularly at the crown of the backing shoulders or at an area across the spine where the text-block's spine was 'peaking'. This is usually due to a break down of a band/s, or a break in a layer of hide glue or the lining material. At these points I will stitch the lining material with fine thread via the centres of appropriate quires/sections and always at the crown of the backing shoulders. If the headbands need to be rebuilt I will try to achieve this in such a way as to improve the consolidation and flexing across the spine. The introduction of 'end-of-spine-bands'—a wide band of cloth, parchment or alum-tawed skin, filling the area between the kettle and end of spine and held in place by paste and then firmly by the headband tie-downs—can often help to achieve a similar end.

To improve the flexibility, where required, of a 'spine-covering-piece' with false raised bands of glue-saturated cord or pieces of card, I may replace them with lightly pasted cords or strips of leather. The layers of paper from the previous tube hollow must nearly always be removed and the covering material treated. Both of these operations are more difficult if only one joint of the book is broken. Apart from making the spine parts more flexible, the aim is to retain the book's original dimensions; so the idea is to take away an equivalent amount of lining and hollow material to compensate for the thickness of the replacement plus the paste layer.

I hope enough has been said above to stress the kind of mechanical considerations and preparation required of the text-block's spine and the spine-covering-piece.

The next problem is the choice of joint repair. The gusset-like joints of the natural or case hollow allow a little more space and tolerance for the insertion of repair materials, compared with the tube hollow. This will often supply the opportunity to build-in the desired strength (on smaller format books especially I miss the very thin and fine handkerchief linens made famous by Roger Powell's effective use of them when rebinding Celtic manuscripts). When repairing natural hollows try to keep, or recreate, the original width or contour of the groove of the joint in such a way that the new material, when dry, does not shrink back, (all cloths should have been pre-shrunk).

The tight-jointed tube hollow should be thought of quite differently, because little space or tolerance exists for the repair materials at joints which hinge sharply from the backing shoulders. The folds of a hollow must exactly line-up with the crowns of the backing shoulders. One useful technique I designed while working and teaching at the Library of Congress which, with variations, has served me well over the years, is to build a hollow by taking two linen cloths, the length of the book's spine but wider than its thickness and stitch them together with two rows of stitches, their distance apart being exactly the width of the book's spine (measured from the crown of the backing shoulders). Cut the cloth on the bias for strength and after sewing one seam curve the two layers of cloth to reproduce the convexity of the spine before stitching the other seam. I place a thin barrier paper in the hollow before pasting it to the spine (removed after the repair is finished). When it is dry I stitch it with fine thread, via the centres of the outer quires or sections to the crown of the backing shoulders. This method supplies strong and precise hinging points, as opposed to the bulk of folds of a conventional hollow, resulting in two cloth overlays on either side of the text-block aiding the reattachment of the boards. If the opportunity arises I will paste one of the overlays to the board under the covering material and the other under the board-sheet, I may form them into a tongue to be inserted into a slot made in a board. Often only one fold of a hollow is broken in which case the two layers of cloth would be narrower and only require one seam. Where only one or two spine panels have broken away I will often use a similar technique, cutting the newly made hollow to panel size. Always test whether all parts of such a hollow open and move together and are in a straight line along backing shoulder/s, before continuing. For the small format publisher's case with a broken joint I may replace linen with a strong fibred Japanese paper.

Example IV

A bookbinding lying horizontally on a shelf is truly at 'rest'. However, when standing vertically, on the tail edge, a binding is under constant strain. Many structural, or once-structural, elements in a bookbinding had become conventions within a trade system by the time the bookshelf arrived in the late 16th century.

This is important to remember, as storing books vertically for long periods was a new idea, and it would have been immediately evident to earlier craftsmen that quite new stresses were being exerted. Since 1600 the bookbinder has never adequately solved the structural problems set by the vertically standing book. In a way, the last 400 years have been an attempt by the bookbinder to try to live, by various means, with this fundamental problem. Gradually, text-blocks were so consolidated, over-rounded, square jointed, and over-lined with such a reliance upon adhesive that they acted like solid blocks—further restricting the book's opening and ease of handling.

DAMAGE

Glancing along a shelf of books one can readily see the characteristics of 'text-block drag'—concavity at the head of the spine, and excessive convexity at the tail—which finally damages bands and/or covering material and endleaves at joint areas. Text-block drag within the boards is particularly acute with:

- large format books
- thick books
- heavy text-blocks
- books which are left standing on their own without restriction or support.

Text-block drag can be limited when a book is held tightly closed and has a text-block support filling the tail-square.

The distortion and expansion in the width of spine at the head, and the tendency for joints to break first at the head and spread downwards as the boards move away from the text-block, is exacerbated where the boards are of paste-board which also has a tendency to curl. This is a very common condition and, if caught early, many period bindings can be saved from further damage. It is a problem which has concerned me since the early 1970s.[15] For future preservation the minimal intervention methods suggested below are often combined with a housing which has an in-built text-block support. This would preferably be a book-box, but it could be a bookshoe[16] if the book is shelved

within an architectural feature such as a book-wall or glazed book-cabinet.

REPAIR

To operate correctly joints must be straight (see Example V), so the boards must be brought back in line with the backing-shoulder. Also the original spine and text-block shape need to be rescued as far as possible. After this how far the repairs can extend, depends upon the particular binding. One can introduce material to pull the boards back into line and at the same time fix spine shape with firm endbands. Since my rediscovery in 1968 of the two Italian primary sewn endbands—the 'figure-of-eight' and the 'back tie-down', I have used and taught their use and significance in much of my binding and repair work.[17] Future stresses will often be such that the endband cores must be laced into the boards, because one cannot rely upon the strength of modern covering leather for this purpose. In later periods of binding where headbands are used I disguise this lacing-in of the cores as far as is possible.

After the reforming of the text-block and its spine I must secure it in this position not by relying on adhesive (which will break down in time) but in a physical way. This is best done via quality endbands. If the end panels of the spine's cover can be lifted I will also paste aero-linen patch-liners between outer bands (or if not possible, between the kettle) and ends of spine. At present I prefer using the 'back tiedown', because it anchors the liner just as firmly as the 'figure-of-eight', and I feel it holds the spine shape better. I then prefer to paste the liner overlays between the board and the covering material, after which the endband cores are firmly laced-in and covering material replaced.

Example V

As mentioned above, bookboards need to be straight, at least along the joint edges. In a new binding one takes great care to balance the boards; this is usually achieved through building laminated boards. In the paste-board age they seemed to rely purely on the fact of the shrinkage of the board sheet correcting the boards after covering. It is not until later that occasionally one finds a correcting sheet underneath the board-sheet.

DAMAGE

Common reasons for board distortion:

- Curving outwards; where the board sheets have never been pasted down. Common with bindings of the paste-board period.
- Excessive inward curvature; repairer has replaced board sheets too damp.
- Curving outwards; repairer has placed the previous cover too damp.
- Excessive inward curvature; binder has recovered the book and saved the previous covers by adhering them to the inner face of the boards. However they have been pasted down too damp, resulting in this board distortion.
- Curve outwards; storage atmosphere too dry, a common problem with stiff-board vellum bindings. The natural average environment in which period books were made, bound, and stored is estimated to have been 60%–65% RH.[18]
- Curve outwards; cover material too damp when binding was first made.

REPAIR

The first on the list is a difficult problem, as I feel it is now part of the particular binding; also there are often interesting marks and notes on the inner face of such boards. If the binding were new one could stretch new board-sheets over the inner face. But with period items this is usually only a choice to consider if board-sheets have had to be lifted for reasons of major repair. Unfortunately a lifted board-sheet always looks disturbed.

Distorted stiff-board vellum bindings. First consider whether it is purely an environmental problem and if this can be corrected. If so, insert barrier sheets between text-block and boards and humidify at 65%

RH (if the item is to be placed in a humidity chamber then wrap the text-block in 'cling wrap'). When boards have corrected themselves, make repairs and consider housing in a pressure box. If the problem needs more treatment then the board sheets will have to be lifted. At this stage also you may make necessary repairs. Do this before humidifying the covers, unless boards have to be straight before some repairs. When covers have corrected themselves, and if necessary, stretch parchment or paper under board-sheets and dry them before the exterior sides. Leave in the correct storage environment 55%–60% RH for at least a week. If boards remain straight then paste down board-sheets, if not then correct further.

Example VI

The conventional method of repairing wooden boards is by cutting away weak or broken areas and splicing or scarfing in new wood, making sure there is good wood along the spine-edge where the lacing paths are, so that the joins can withstand the squeezing/leverage pressure exerted when the fore-edge is grasped.

REPAIR

Last year at West Dean College we had a 15th-century binding which had only fragments of its covering material remaining, exposing extremely split and worm-damaged boards and a spine corner missing. My colleague David Dorning and I decided that replacing damaged areas of the wood would destroy the historical integrity of the object, so we looked for a method of stabilising and strengthening the binding which would be as discreet as possible. This was finally achieved by impregnating with Paraloid B72 acrylic resin.[19] The breaks in the boards, bisecting lacing paths, were joined and strengthened by drilling and inserting silver steel rods which were glued using Araldite 20/20 epoxy adhesive. Missing areas of wood were rebuilt using a mixture of Paraloid B72 acrylic resin and inert glass micro-balloons.[20-24] The mixture was cast into the missing areas, supported on the rods, thus forming a very light filling which was then shaped and tinted to a sympathetic colour with acrylic paints. Some aspects of the treatment, such as the insertion of steel rods into the boards, constitute major intervention, but result in an aesthetically minimal effect.

Other Types of Damage & Possible Repair Techniques

(A) BROKEN OR YAWNING HEAD- AND TAIL-CAPS

When possible I insert thread or fine braid into the cap and paste or lace the ends to the board, making sure the repair moves with the flow of the book's spine. I often carry out this technique during the repair of a joint or reattachment of a board.

(B) APPLICATION OF NEW LEATHER PATCH REPAIRS

I do not use split or thinned grain layers, as the flexing and tear strength is in the corium. Instead, I edge-pare the new leather, fit and mould it into place, and while still damp I press and mark the silhouette of the period leather onto the new leather. When dry I grind away the new leather from the grain side using a flexi-drill with various shapes of diamond dust bits until the old leather fits into the ground recess.

(C) BROKEN ENDBANDS

Broken endband cores can often be repaired by piercing through their centres with fine threads (60/3) attached to a flexible beading needle (a blunted and polished tip will often follow the curve more easily than a sharp tip). The threads can be pasted to the board under the covering material. Finer threads can be used to reattach the endband more firmly to its text-block.

(D) LIFTING AN AREA OF A FRAGILE AND TENACIOUS PERIOD LEATHER SPINE

This can be extremely difficult, especially if its grain layer is flaking or friable. A facing of lens tissue adhered with a solution of Paraloid B72 in acetone (20%), or other facing methods,[25] is often a way to keep it together while one attempts to lift the spine

with a one-sided bevelled knife or shaped dental tool, dry or by applying minimal amounts of solvent.

ON COMPLETION

Please note that although a repair may appear successful directly after it is completed, no judgement should be made until all is bone dry. The book should then be handled so that one is sure that the repair moves with the flow of the leaves, spine, joints, etc.

It is worth adding that documentation must include not only descriptions and diagrams of the techniques employed but also samples of all materials used, so that future generations can compare the materials used for repair with the control samples.

Conclusion

Admittedly, some of the above examples may appear more major than my title suggests. However, the main purpose of this paper is to convey my approach to trying to save the original integrity of bindings and their contents. I hope I have emphasised and demonstrated that it is essential to have a good understanding of the book as a three-dimensional, mobile object and an appreciation of how a repair to one part of the functioning structure can effect others, before one can effectively simplify, adapt, and minimise treatments.

NOTES AND REFERENCES

1. Hanna Jedrzejewska, 'Ethics in Conservation', (Stockholm, 1976).

2. Christopher Clarkson, *Limp Vellum Binding and Its Potential as a Conservation Type Structure for the Rebinding of Early Printed Books* (Hitchen, 1982).

3. Christopher Clarkson, 'An Historical Study Collection: A Fundamental Tool for the Training of the Book-Conservator' (Florence, 1994).

4. Christopher Clarkson, 'The Conservation of Early Books in Codex Form: A Personal Approach: Part 1'. *The Paper Conservator*, 3 (1978), 34–38.

5. Jirí Vnoucek, 'Can we manage to restore medieval books without any loss of information', *IADA 7th International Conference,*' (Uppsala, 1991).

6. 'Preservation' meaning 'preventive measures' of all kinds; environmental, protective, supportive, handling training for staff and readers, display requirements etc.

7. For repair work one requires materials of the widest possible variety, highest qualities, weights, substances, etc. My attitude is that I must never stop collecting all forms of textiles, such as linen cloths, threads, braids, cords, etc.; papers, such as Japanese and European handmade paper, including fibre mixes and pulps; and skin materials, such as alum-tawed skins, tanned leathers, and parchments. I sometimes alter these basic materials in various ways, trying to make them more sympathetic to the item I am working upon—not simply in terms of colour or tone but in substance. An example of this would be creating semi-tans or -taws from parchment (a raw hide) to repair joint areas of a vellum binding. I do not reuse any period materials, such as old end leaves, or metal pins or rivets from old covers. Such confusion of the evidence (at best) and faking (at worst) does not belong in the world of conservation. With a fragmentary item I much prefer a straightforward and undisguised repair. The question of a guaranteed life expectancy of new materials used should be considered very seriously. There is a serious ethical obligation to contribute in every way possible to the improvement of the materials we use. I use a variety of binder's, model-maker's, artist's and dental tools, plus specific tools such as: syringes, flexible drill used with diamond dust burrs, stretch bandages, violin-maker's cramps, spade drills made from needles, knives tailored to shape made from high-speed steel; and essential equipment such as a non-traditional sewing frame, an ultrasonic humidifier, steam gun, and a humidification chamber.

8. Christopher Clarkson, 'A Conditioning Chamber for Parchment and Other Materials', *The Paper Conservator,* 19 (1995), 27–30.

9. Christopher Clarkson, 'Thoughts on Sewing Frame Design for the Book Conservator', *The Paper Conservator,* 19 (1995), 41–54.

10. Christopher Clarkson, 'Rediscovering Parchment: The Nature of the Beast', *The Paper Conservator,* 16 (1992), 5–26.

11. Christopher Clarkson, 'The Safe Handling and Display of Medieval Manuscripts and Early Printed Books,' *Ljubljana Book and Paper Conservation Conference Postprints* (Slovenia, 1996), 141–188.

12. Christopher Clarkson, 'Board Slotting: A New Technique for Re-attaching Bookboards', *IPC-Manchester Conference Postprints,* (Leigh, 1992), 158–164.

13. Edward Simpson, 'Setting up a Board-Slotting Programme', *The Paper Conservator,* 18 (1994), 77–89.

14. See reference 10.

15. It is a problem which I first began to address at the Library of Congress in 1972. Further developments were made in The Bodleian Library, most recently and publicly in Duke Humfrey's Library, because here Thomas Bodley introduced the bookshelf into England, and in Arts End he created probably the first architecturally conceived book-wall.

16. Christopher Clarkson, 'The Book Shoe: description & uses'. *Libraries Bulletin (Oxford University),* No. 42 (Trinity Term) 1984, pp. 4–7. For a good explanation of the book shoe in use see Pascale Regnault 'Putting shoes on Duke Humfrey. A Passive Conservation Measure in the Bodleian Library, Oxford. *8th. IADA Congress Pre-prints, Tübingen, September 1995, 21–28.*

17. See reference 2.

18. In a room of thick stone or brick walls with no ingress of water, this environment can be stable throughout the year. In England, it was as late as the 1960s that institutions started to dramatically alter their environments by installing central heating systems.

19. Obviously, direct application of a pure epoxy resin to a wooden object results in a dramatic and irreversible change in the characteristics of the wood. However, inert fillers can be added to these resins so that the resistance to compression of the resultant material is below that of the surrounding wood and its surface adhesion to a substrate very slight.

20. D.W Grattan & R. L. Barclay, 'A Study of Gap Fillers for Wooden Objects', *Studies in Conservation*, 33 (1988), 71–86.

21. P. Hatchfield, 'A Note on a Filler Material for Water Sensitive Objects', *Journal of the American Institute for Conservation*, 25 (1986), 93–96.

22. W.W. Phillips & J. Selwyn, 'Epoxies in Wood Repairs for Historic Buildings', *U.S. Department of the Interior, Heritage Conservation and Recreation Service Publication*, 1, (Washington, 1978).

23. D.W Grattan & R. L. Barclay, 'A Silicone Rubber/ Microballoon Mixture for Gap Filling in Wooden Objects', *ICOM Committee for Conservation- Proceedings of 6th Triennial Conference*, (Sydney, 1987).

24. R.L. Barclay & C. Mathias, 'An Epoxy/ Microballoon Mixture for Gap Filling in Wooden Objects', *Journal of the American Institute for Conservation*, 28, (1989), 31–42.

25. Anthony Cains, 'A Facing Method for Leather, Paper & Membrane', *IPC–Manchester Conference Postprints*, (Leigh, 1992), 153–157.

ACKNOWLEDGMENTS

I wish to thank Edward Adcock, Dana Josephson, and my wife Oonagh for reading through this text and making valuable contributions.

Selection 6.3

DOUGLAS COCKERELL

Excerpts from *A Note on Bookbinding*, with Extracts from *the Special Report of the Society of Arts on Leather for Bookbinding*

London: W.H. Smith & Son, 1904, pp. 5–11.

ALL OWNERS OF libraries have to get books bound from time to time, but comparatively few are able to give clear instructions to their binders. It doubtless saves some trouble if a previously bound volume is sent with a binding order, and the new work simply ordered "to pattern"; but this habit of sticking to old patterns tends to prevent the binder from improving his work. During the last few years great pains have been taken to improve bookbinding, and it is safe to say that most patterns now in use could be improved upon without increasing their cost.

The work of the Special Committee of the Society of Art on "Leather for Bookbinding" has done much to set standards for good work and good materials, and the report, with its detailed specifications, should prove of great assistance to those who have to give orders for binding books.

Books for binding can be roughly divided into three classes:

1st. Books of value, or of special interest to their owners, that require to be bound as well as the binder can do them.

2nd. Books of permanent interest, but of no special value, that require to be well and strongly bound, but for which the best and most careful work would be too expensive.

3rd. Books of temporary interest that need to be held together and kept neat and tidy for occasional reference.

In other words, some books must be bound as well as possible regardless of expense, some as cheaply as they can be bound well, and others as well as they can be bound cheaply. Rebinding a valuable old book is, at the best, a regrettable necessity, and if its value is to be preserved, the binder must take infinite pains with every detail. Such work should be done entirely by hand, and the binding built up step by step on the book—"made to measure" as it were to suit the needs of the particular volume. Work on which a binder is expected to exercise thought and care on every point must take a long time to do, and therefore must be costly. Cheap binding must be done quickly, and to be done quickly it must be treated "in bulk" without much regard to the requirements of any one book. Up to a point there is no reason why work done quickly should not be done well and strongly, and such work will suit ninety per cent of books. It is the exceptional book that takes time to bind. The thought that has to be expended on a single binding in the one case, in the other case is given to the first model only; leaving the actual workmen free to work more or less mechanically on repetitions of a model with binding, every detail of which they are familiar.

To bind a crown 8vo book (7½" x 5") in full sealskin or morocco of the best quality, carrying out the "Society of Arts" specification, and doing the work entirely by hand, and as well as it can be done, would cost from 21/- to 25/-, with little or no decoration. If the leaves needed special mending or any sizing or washing, or if the cover were decorated with gold tooling, the cost would be a good deal heavier.

As this is too expensive for the binding of any books but those of value or of special interest to their owners, the binder has to consider what features he can best modify or leave out in order to lessen the cost.

Obviously, the first thing to cut off will be the decoration; next, by making a "half," instead of a "whole," binding about three-quarters of the cost of the leather can be saved. A little more can be saved by mending the backs of the sections a little less neatly, and generally by lowering the standard of finish. By saving in every way, but still working to the specification, perhaps the cost can be halved without taking from the strength of the binding. This gives about 10/6 for the cost of a half-morocco or half-seal binding of a crown 8vo book, sewn flexibly round the bands, and forwarded and lettered by hand. The cost of the best material on such a binding would be about 1/8, and perhaps half of this could be saved by using inferior leather, millboards, etc., but for the sake of 10d. on a half-guinea binding this would be poor economy.

To reduce the cost of binding to this specification much below 10/6 a volume would necessitate a serious and unwarrantable lowering of the standard of work.

Recognising this, the Society of Arts Committee published a second specification for "Library binding."
To quote from their report:

This form of binding (Specification I.) must be expensive, as it takes a long time to do. For most books a cheaper form is needed, and after examining and comparing many bindings that had been subjected to considerable use, we have come to the conclusion that the bindings of books sewn on tapes, with 'French' joints, generally fulfil the conditions best.

The points of advantage claimed for a binding carried out under specification II. are:—

1.—It need not be expensive.
2.—The construction is sound throughout.
3.—A book so bound should open well.
4.—The 'French' joint enables comparatively thick leather to be used.
5.—In the absence of raised bands there is no reason for the undue stretching of the leather in covering.
6.—The backs of the sections are not injured by saw cuts.

By sewing on tapes instead of cords a smooth back is got, which saves time in the working, as it enables the backing to be done in the backing machine. Further time is saved by cutting the edges with the guillotine instead of with the plough; in fact, there is a saving of time at every point.

By substituting machine work for hand work in backing and cutting, and system for thought, the cost of a thoroughly strong half-seal binding for a crown 8vo book can be reduced to about 3/6. This allows of the use of the strongest leather and other sound materials. Further reductions in the price can only be the result of saving a penny here and a penny there, and unless the work is very roughly done, or the materials are inferior, 3/- or 3/6 is as cheap as any odd volume can be bound to this specification. Whole binding in the same style would cost about 8/- for a crown 8vo book. In all classes of binding where there are large numbers of volumes of the same size to be bound, the work goes through much more quickly, and therefore more cheaply.

For a cheaper class of work it would be impossible to keep strictly to the specification. To save time the backs of torn sections must be overcast instead of mended, and plates pasted in instead of being guarded.

For the cheapest work, cases are made apart from the books, and cloth is substituted for leather. The weak point in case work is the poorness of the connection between book and binding, but this can be overcome at a very slightly increased cost by sewing on tapes, and using split boards like those used for the "Library Binding." Strong buckram bindings can be made in this way for about 1/6 for a crown 8vo, and if what is known as art-vellum or other cloth is used the cost would be about 3d. less.

When bound books fail to open freely the binder is nearly always blamed for this serious defect, but quite often the fault lies with the choice of paper, which is habitually too thick and stiff for the size of the book.

All the binder can do is to get the bend of the leaves as far to the back as possible, and to manage that as few leaves as may be are bent at each opening. If a book is mended at the back instead of overcast, it should open right back to the sewing. If the back is overcast, or "sawn in," a portion of the backs of the leaves is taken up, and so the book cannot open flat.

When possible, and it would be possible in very many cases, it is better to bind "from the sheets." Binders can get unbound copies of books from the publishers, and such books will always be sounder than copies from which the publisher's cases have been removed.

Many modern books are printed on very poor paper. The heavily loaded "Art" paper used for printing half-tone blocks and music upon is perhaps the worst from the binder's point of view. This paper has a surface that readily flakes off, so that anything pasted to it is apt to come away, bringing the surface with it, and as folding breaks the paper at the fold, it cannot be held securely by the sewing thread. This is especially troublesome in the case of music, which must open flat and has to stand more than an ordinary amount of rough usage. Something can be done by strengthening the folds with guards, but this is an option that adds to the cost of binding.

CAROLINE K. KECK

"The Role of the Conservator"

In Preservation and Conservation: Principles and Practices. Proceedings of the North American International Regional Conference on Preservation and Conservation, Williamsburg and Philadelphia, September 10–16 1972. *Washington, DC; Preservation Press, 1976, pp. 25–34.*

ALL OF US joined in this conference share a commendable objective, the preservation of cultural heritage. This is an uneasy world. For any society to look backward with a sense of pride gives comfort that it may likewise look forward with hope. Evidences of man's creative genius serve to separate him from the insensitive destroyers whom we discredit as barbarians. In all periods, contemporary artists have found encouragement to refine their personal efforts by studying earlier masterpieces. As ordinary people, we are subconsciously moved by the expectation that if we show respect for the accomplishments of those now dead, the future might accord our era the same flattery. Weigh as we may these and other motives for our urge to prolong what we value in the present and the past, let us accept for our activities the burden of responsibility they entail. For however we may strive to avoid hypocrisy and shun exploitation in our preservation zeal, we who are gathered here are partners in the manufacture of illusions.

This is unavoidable. Anything we do or do not do in our preservation efforts expresses a decision on our part made in the light of our time. The dilemma that confronts us is that fabrications of man have a dual nature. They are constructed of matter and, as such, deteriorate according to the laws that govern all matter.

They are also imbued with an immaterial content, the fusion of an artist with his environment. The impact of any created form, a quality variously described as aesthetic, emotional, intellectual or spiritual, cannot be divorced from the form's physical components. No matter which specialist among us is expert in the identification of the form's original structure and the analysis of the subsequent changes it may have experienced, each generation and each separate individual will interpret the work of the past in subjective terms. While we may find that determining how to restrain or reverse the changes inflicted by deterioration is far from cut and dried, there is greater unanimity regarding these procedures than there will be in specifying the correct quality of an original impact. It would be senseless to deny that the forms that result from our activities will not color the face of history.

Reverence for the past has seldom been based on an inviolate image. Our ancestors considered the casual altering of an earlier form both practical and permissible. Like a remodeled building, the palimpsest, the recut ivory, the regilded statue and the repainted picture merely continued what was functional or beloved or wondrous. Instances of almost total transformation were not uncommon. Sometimes these were due to hostility toward the immediate past, but more often were due to a preference for modernization. Authenticity as a serious aim was neither philosophically evaluated nor lucrative. The restorer was the person employed to make an old item last longer. He concealed damages in tune with the tastes of his time without regard to original style, and often without regard to original composition. Until the late 19th century, few people disapproved of such an approach so long as the work complied with current interpretations.

The primary demand in restorations was a return to completeness. Except in periods of romanticism, which, after all, had their own methods for transformation, this held true throughout the centuries. No other fabrications appear to have suffered more from this prejudice for completeness than architecture and paintings. It is the special nature of a painting to be exposed to view. Exposure made paintings, like buildings, vulnerable to ravages from the environment and from the hands of man. Whereas sculpture is a three-dimensional actuality that retains its actuality even when a part is lost, buildings and paintings are two-dimensional compositions of three-dimensional structure that lose their impact as entities when voids occur. Why this is can be argued, but not dismissed. The Venus de Milo is acceptable without arms; the Mona Lisa with a great hole would not be tenable nor would the Lincoln Memorial. In certain forms of creative art, disruptions are too disturbing to viewers. If we combine this characteristic of human response with the long-term complacency toward surface alterations as the legitimate method for concealing damage, we can understand why restoration was deemed the art of disguise.

Semantics add to our difficulties. For many of us, the word *restoration* is synonymous with alteration and is a term that has acquired a derogatory flavor. It is foolhardy to take offense to a word that we happily claim for our personal state after the benefits of a fine vacation. Discredit associated with the title of restorer stems from our 20th-century concept that what is preserved should serve as a historical witness. It is as unfair for us to refute the labors of our predecessors in restorations as it will be for our descendants to damn ours for prolonging images that they may interpret offensively. As Sir Kenneth Clark points out in his television series on civilization, historical judgments are tricky. The truth is still circumscribed. We may not presume to establish absolutes.

The painter Eugène Delacroix is credited with saying that each pretended restoration is a hundred times more regrettable than the ravages of time because it gives us not a restored original, but *another* painting. Unless it be placed in a permanently static atmosphere, no painting—nor for that matter any other created form—whether recent or ancient, escapes constant change from the moment it leaves the hands of its creator. What we may claim today are facilities that enable us to approximate more closely the birth images compatible with the thinking of our time. We can scientifically record degradation and remains; we can photographically document for the future what we inherited and how we presume to alter it for survival. Call us *conservators* if the word suggests the improvement in our capabilities, as well as the broad-

ening of our field's scope, to confront the weighty problems of maintenance. Hazards of survival for all matter now assume mountainous proportions. Our world has added to the forces of uncivilized nature mechanical vibrations on, above and below the earth's surface, artificial light and heat and deadly pollutants. To restore anything is no mean task.

We think of ourselves as the medical end of the art world. The analogy is valid. When medicine emerged from its cloaks of secrecy and myth to become a profession, it commenced to amass a body of shared knowledge founded on experience, experiments and observations. With persistent research came innovations that honed the application of skills. The rise of universities devoted to the training of doctors assured that the hoard of information became part of a requisite background for succeeding generations of practitioners. This has provided society with a reliable standard for optimum medical performance. To a far lesser degree, both in length of time and in quantity of personnel, conservators have paralleled and are paralleling this development.

Most restorers in past centuries were artists who were otherwise incompetent to earn a living. Here and there, a few great masters would touch up their own and the works of others with the inevitable embellishments that creative genius is never able to suppress. As a rule, though, it remained for those not gifted enough to execute acceptable work to be paid pittances for abusing and embalming the productions of their betters. Case histories of famous art, extant and lost within memory, are replete with horror stories of the criminally destructive treatments inflicted on them in the name of preservation. Many a great work that we have inherited is sadly no more than a corpse decked by the ghostly mockery of its assassin's hand. We may take pride in our revulsion to these blatant malpractices. They were condoned partly because they did not offend majority opinion and partly because they were the only performances possible from the indifferent efforts of an untutored and unhonored category of worker.

The idea of training is to profit from the lessons learned by others. The idea that training is necessary to perform restoration is not unique to our time, but general consensus that it should be required for competent practice is a recent innovation. Only a little more than a decade ago, there was no formal academic schooling available in the United States where a student could acquire an education in the conservation of historic and artistic works. Today there are only three such institutions: New York University's Conservation Center, a five-year course accepting four to five students annually, the program of the Intermuseum Conservation Association at Oberlin, Ohio, which accepts three students a year for its three-year courses and the conservation training school of the Cooperstown Graduate Programs, where ten students are admitted yearly to a three-year course. All these are postgraduate curriculums with prerequisites in science, art history and manual dexterity. From their instructions, we may anticipate a limited number of professionally competent conservators, a hard-won, valuable change in attitude toward the status of the restorer.

Before we unduly inflate our egos for the wisdom of our time, let us note that almost 200 years ago a group of specially trained practitioners existed who for 20 years performed comprehensive restorations on the pictorial treasures of Venice until the end of that republic. In the forthcoming publication of the Edwards manuscripts,[1] four points of consideration are outlined for the establishment of a public school of restoration (in this case, within the Academy of Fine Arts in Venice) which could constitute a sound basis for any of our current funding appeals. These are (1) the need for such a school, (2) the theoretical and practical instructions to be offered, (3) the formal structure of the new institution and (4) the cost of this institution.

Freely transcribed from the almost illegible Italian script are precise statements that we could employ verbatim. Edwards held that a painting restorer need not possess the genius of a great artist nor his creative imagination, but before a youth passed into the workshop, he must have mastered the study of fabrication techniques and acquired skill in these techniques. Once admitted, the trainee should, with the instruction, supervision and example of an experienced professor of this art, begin to practice various restoration tasks, know the variety of solvents and their required degrees of concentration and learn that

great diligence is essential for the decisive success of a restoration! Edwards' attitude of mind, his concern for optimum execution stands forth as dedicated as our own. He made preliminary examinations, studied deterioration, identified materials and kept voluminous records. One of his most endearing comments on the subject of paintings was to the effect that their natural substances consist of complex heterogenous elements artificially held together contrary to their natural affinities, a deduction on the behavior of artistic works in almost any field continually frustrating to his contemporary colleagues. Although Edwards could hardly foresee the nightmares we face in problems of maintenance, it was his emphasis on the excessive deterioration suffered by paintings within the atmosphere of Venice, so humid and filled with salts, that impelled the old Venetian Senate to issue its Decree of September 3, 1778, ordering their great public undertaking in preservation.

We could use more like him today.

No, we cannot pride ourselves on unique superiority. We may boast the wealth of advantages supplied us by the Industrial Revolution and the progress of science. We may be justified in feeling there is a wider persuasion, spotty but spreading to the corners of our planet, that the preservation of cultural heritage is vital to social welfare. We had best think of ourselves as Edwards thought of himself, as temporary custodians of what is consigned to our care for its survival. If there are more of us on his side after 200 years, we have greater need of each other to cope with our increased problems.

Few classifications of historic and artistic works present the same contexts, purposes, preservation requirements or have identical responses to the environments in which we expect them to last. Not everyone may feel convinced that prolonging the existence of an image is requisite for his special use of it. Archaeologists are not always concerned with what happens to the materials they extricate, once they have rung from the bones every scrap of relevant information. Neither the resultant rubble at some digs nor the preservation of the uncovered finds are necessarily important to archaeological research. Historians and collectors would be better served if every archaeological expedition included in its membership at least one well-trained conservator. The change from an enveloping subsurface to an atmospheric exposure can be violent and its effects on vulnerable materials disastrous. Repeatedly, the uncontrolled methods employed to permit immediate viewing of encrusted finishes and designs have inflicted tragic loss; impatient haste has destroyed many retrieved objects. Admittedly, postponing detailed examination until such can be arranged within an often-distant laboratory to provide minimum degrading reaction for delicate treasures would cost time and money. However, such a procedure would permit initial observations to be enjoyed by other scholars and would take into account the fact that the impact of actual remains is not separable from physical components. If the archaeologist could curtail his personal drive for instant knowledge, this generosity would allow his colleagues in other professions to study his discoveries at optimum state. We do need each other.

Artifacts housed in collections are seldom destined for use. The rare porcelains, furniture, even rugs and costumes in museums are not intended to function as they once may have any more than the altarpieces that are displayed in dank surroundings lighted by smoking tapers. Discussions continue as to whether any museum rarities should even be touched by the public. The concept of preservation consistently applied to museum materials, which are kept in varying ranges of miniclimates, is to do nothing in your efforts to preserve that may not easily be undone or redone. The dictum of reversibility for treatments is viable and justified under the given circumstances. Nothing lasts forever, not even repairs; they wear out, too. The philosophy in this approach guarantees the ease with which future conservators may repeat or alter our preservation work with minimal hazard to the remains of the original. It also bows to the art historian to whom the museum conservator remains subservient. Scientific facilities may dictate what can be adjudged as superfluous and may advisedly be removed from an original artifact, but scholarly opinion will determine the eventual appearance to be exhibited. Scholars have been known to change their views. The conservator may produce and interpret evidence of physical alterations, but the final decision

on the desired impact of an image in a museum collection rests with the art historian.

The museum conservator can often diminish the speed of material deterioration by planning the control of destructive agents within a building environment. Light, relative humidity, air pollution and vandalism have feasible, if expensive, systems for their regulation. With the assistance of engineers, administrators and lawyers, these may be effectively applied. However, this is not so with outdoor displays, whether totem poles or obelisks, industrial equipment or vehicles, log cabins or the residences of Presidents. Here, the cherished principle of reversibility plays second fiddle to the need to defend against attacks from a belligerent environment and population. Methods for preservation of this category of artifact are forced to compromise with even our concept of proper impact. The integrity of the created image, so righteously governing the museum practitioner, cannot be accorded the same importance in the face of uncontrollable conditions for exhibition. Adjustments are necessary.

Nothing we attempt to preserve is hampered by more stringent regulations than old buildings. A building, ancient or contemporary, selected for long-term survival must either house some appropriate activity of a local group or function as a museum itself. However alien to its original impact within our crowded quarters, traffic and encompassing pressures, the form this prolongation will assume will be determined by the legal restrictions for human security. Originally, a building may have been surrounded by lawns and trees; warmed by fireplaces; illuminated with candles; its timbers, walls and roof fashioned in combustible wood; and accommodated with no more than an adjacent outhouse. Unavoidable for our society are the established standards of building codes, zoning, fire prevention, sanitation and provisions for bodily comfort. Area laws can be neither ignored nor bypassed. The consolidation of structure; the installation of plumbing, heating and artificial illumination; and provisions for occupancy will impose alterations inevitably influencing the appearance, inside and out, of any preserved edifice. Compromise between the original image and the preserved form it is forced to assume is an obvious necessity.

The ways in which we elect to preserve our separate specialties of interest are peculiar to their unique differences. If we can admit the diversity of demands we face and agree to disagree on applications of theory and practice, we can profit from sharing many portions of our expertise. Limited as we are, museum conservators can offer four main services: We are competent to determine the physical condition of collected items and what is involved for their remedial care and upkeep; we are knowledgeable to advise on whether an artifact is what it purports to be; we are useful consultants on the security for interior displays; the answers we supply on estimates of damage, cost and feasibility of repair for the items in our field are apt to be accurate. Our interpretation of the behavior of materials tends to be limited to the climatic confines in which we operate and inappropriate for those in which we have little experience. There are unknown factors everywhere. The exchange of information, however seemingly slight in its importance, might save colleagues in preservation the expense and time of exploring byways already mapped. To fail to invite help from one another is too costly for our common aim.

Giorgio Cavaglieri holds that "old buildings need a lot of new love."[2] So do all old forms, whether animate or inanimate. Our concern for what has lasted and for what we hope to have last longer is the same as that expressed by Edwards toward the paintings in 18th-century Venice and as that expressed today by the Rome Centre's vast embrace of universally valued inheritance. Only the adjective *new* differentiates the efforts of our generations. For us, *new* comprises our increased proficiencies to battle with our added difficulties. Accepting the good with the bad, if we can cooperate each with the other, we may be able to execute the best preservation possible within the confines of our human potential and the concepts of our period in time.

NOTES

1. Bettina Raphael, "Edwards Manuscripts," unpublished research done on Smithsonian-Rome Centre grant, Cooperstown Graduate Programs, Cooperstown, N. Y., 1971.

2. Giorgio Cavaglieri, president of the New York Chapter of ALA, in an address to technical personnel of the Port of New York Authority and the South Street Seaport Planning Conference, July 1970.

SHELDON KECK

"Further Materials for a History of Conservation"

In Preprints of Papers Presented at the Fourth Annual Meeting, American Institute for Conservation of Historic and Artistic Works, Dearborn, MI, 1976 *(Washington, DC: AIC, 1976), 11–19.*

A HISTORY OF conservation is valuable to us as conservators, not just to establish the antiquity of our vocation, but to give us insight into what we may encounter on examination and treatment of the same works today, as well as to give us an understanding of past philosophical approaches to the subject of restoration.

Although we know that methods of preservation, particularly in the funerary arts, were of profound importance to the ancient Egyptians, so far as artifacts are concerned, we know only that the Egyptians attempted to provide a favorable environment for the contents of their tombs as well as protection against damage or theft. The governing motive was religious. The incidental result was the preservation for millennia of arts and crafts sealed, hopefully for eternity, not only from the grasp of humanity but also from its site. Objects, repaired before burial, have been reported evacuated from Egyptian tombs. Inscriptions, reliefs and sculptures on earlier monuments were often obliterated to make way for new ones celebrating a succeeding royal personage. This circumstance permitted some monuments to survive. One could hardly call this conservation or restoration. Historical integrity was a matter of minimal concern.

In Greece, and later in Rome, individual artists were revered for their unique skills and creativity. Works of painting, sculpture and architecture were celebrated long after their creators had died. The desire existed to preserve works of art for their aesthetic significance as well as their monetary worth. Large collections were assembled first in Greece and in Rome, in temples, public buildings and in the dwellings of the affluent. Because of the great renown in which the works of art were held, we have in Greece relevant mentions as well as implications of restorations from Classical writers. Both Pliny and Vitruvius indicate that, during their time at least, the ancients were well aware of deterioration, damage and disfigurement caused by dampness, smoke, fire and ignorance.

In the second century A.D. the Greek traveler Pausanias[1] wrote that in the temple of Hera at Olympia there remained one ancient column of oak while all other columns were of stone. Archaeological excavations of the temple revealed that the stone columns were of different styles belonging to different periods.[2] As each original wooden column in the temple deteriorated it was replaced by a new column of stone according to the prevailing style over a span of some eight centuries. In this earliest of recorded architectural restorations the religious form of the temple remained inviolate, but the substance of its architectural members was transformed without regard to their original material or style. Rosi points out that the Greeks preserved in situ the last remaining vestige of the temple's original construction suggesting an interest in preserving contact with the cultural past.[3]

For his sources on the history of painting and sculpture the Roman encyclopedist Pliny the Elder drew extensively on now long lost writings of Greek historians and essayists. Paintings which he describes by renowned fourth-century B.C. Greek artists like Apelles, Protogenes, Pausias, and Polygnotos [sic] and were on exhibition at Rome, and were seen by him in the first century A.D. Restorations when required were performed by artists, a tradition already established in Greece. This tradition prevailed for centuries since the artist knew from long apprenticeship and experience, certainly better than anyone else, the nature of the materials and construction of the works of art he was called upon to restore.

Pliny records the Greek legend that Pausias of Sikyon learned the new encaustic technique from Pamphilos, and became the first well known master in this medium.[4] On being called upon to restore certain wall paintings by Polygnotos at Thespiae, Pliny explains that the restoration by Pausias suffered by comparison because, in order to conform to the style of Polygnotos, he had to work in an aqueous technique of which he was by no means a master.

Also of interest is the record by Pliny that Apelles' friend, Protogenes of Kaunos, on the island of Rhodes, painted a picture of "Ialysos bearing a Palm" with four coats of color to preserve it from injury and age, so that if the last upper coat peeled off, the lower one would take its place.[5] This painting hung in the Temple of Peace at Rome in the first century A.D. The story of the painting by Protogenes recalls the letter which Albrecht Dürer wrote to Herr Jacob-Heller, dated 26 August 1509, for whom he had just completed a painting. The letter describes a procedure very similar to that of Protogenes: "I have painted it with great care, as you will see, using none but the best colors I could get. It is painted with good ultramarine under, and over, and over that again, some five or six times; and then after it was finished I painted it again twice over so that it may last a long time. If it is kept clean I know it will remain bright and fresh 500 years, for it is not done as men are wont to paint. So have it kept clean and don't let it be touched or sprinkled with holy water."[6] Other paintings of Greek origin apparently were not so thoroughly painted and suffered as a result. For instance a picture by another contemporary of Apelles, Aristides of Thebes, representing a "Tragic Actor and Boy," which hung in the Temple of Apollo at Rome "was ruined through the ignorance of the painter to whom Marcus Junius as praetor (c. 25 B.C.) entrusted it to be cleaned before the games of Apollo."[7]

A masterpiece by Apelles portraying "Aphrodite Rising from the Sea" had been brought to Rome and was dedicated by the Emperor Augustus in the temple of his father, Caesar. "When the lower portion was damaged no artist could be found with the ability to restore it and thus the very injury redounded to the glory of the artist whose skills were inimitable. In the course of time the panel of the picture fell into decay and the Emperor Nero substituted for it another picture by the hand of Dorotheos." According to Sellers,

the commentator on Jex-Blake's translation of Pliny, the term "substituted" may be an exaggeration and probably the painting was only restored by Dorotheos, since the picture by Apelles seems to have continued in existence under Vespasian when Suetonius speaks of it being again restored.[8]

Three of the paintings mentioned above were easel paintings on wooden panels as were innumerable other works transported to Rome as spoils of war. Vitruvius confirms that wall paintings were transported there as well. "In Sparta paintings have been taken out of certain walls by cutting through the bricks, then have been placed in wooden frames, and so brought to the Comitium to adorn the aedileship of Varro and Murena."[9]

Boasting of the antiquity as well as the durability of wall paintings in Italy, Pliny further states that "To this day there are extant in the temples of Ardea paintings older than the city of Rome, which I admire beyond any others for though unprotected by a roof they remain fresh after all these years. At Lanuvium again there are two nude figured by the same artist, of Atalanta and Helen, painted side by side. Both are of great beauty, and the one is painted as a virgin; they have sustained no injury though the temple is in ruins. The Emperor Caligula from lustful motives attempted to remove them but the consistency of the plaster would not allow this to be done."[10]

Vitruvius warns against painting walls or ceilings of winter dining rooms with grand subjects or delicate decorations because they will be spoiled by the smoke from the fire and the constant soot from the lamps. Further he gives precautions on avoiding continuous dampness which will cause injury to plaster and stuccowork.[11]

… The artist craftsman directed and exploited by the early Christian Church furnished a utilitarian product. Its edifices required sacred images for worship and pictorial decorations to educate and impress the masses. I have seen only one example from this early period which was probably restored within a century or two of its time of origin. At the Istituto Central del Restauro in Rome in 1958 I was shown a large encaustic painting of the Madonna, on panel, dating from the sixth or seventh century from one of the Roman basilica churches. It showed extensive early repainting as well as some that was obviously much later. All during the Middle Ages it appears to have been customary to repaint completely panels, icons and polychrome sculpture when they became worn, darkened or damaged. The consecrated object retained its sacred nature in spite of repeated repaintings, whereas replacement with a new rendition could have meant sacrifice of miraculous spiritual properties inherent in the original object. Wall paintings, the primary purpose of which was public education, were also renewed by overpaint or frequently covered with fresh plaster upon which new subjects were painted.

An example of medieval restoration was elegantly brought to light some years ago in Florence, Italy, by the skilled hand of Leonetto Tintori.[12] His preliminary examination, including X-ray photography of an obviously repainted Tuscan crucifix, revealed that under the paint seen on the surface, consisting largely of restoration dating from the fifteenth to nineteenth centuries, were indeed two earlier layers each in reasonably good state of preservation. Tintori first removed the top layer of crude provincial restorations to uncover the upper of the two early layers. The surface revealed could be dated stylistically about the last decade of the thirteenth century. Still covered by this restoration was the original painting of about 1250. Between the tempera paint of 1250 and the tempera overpaint of the 1290s was a continuous and fairly thick layer of oil resin varnish. By attaching a protective facing to the entire upper layer of paint and employing a solvent which dissolved only the oil resin varnish, Tintori succeeded in separating both paint films. He removed as a complete and continuous unit the restoration of the 1290s and revealed the original painted panel of 1250. The two paintings, the artist's concept and the work of the first restorer mounted on a new support may now be viewed side by side. While this method of separating and preserving two contiguous paint films is extremely rare, not at all unusual is the example it provides of medieval restoration procedures. Numerous other specimens of that era which were completely overpainted have been uncovered in recent times. In fact, the medieval

concept of restoration by complete overpainting has continued in provincial churches even up to the middle of the nineteenth century.

———

By the time of the Renaissance in Italy, paintings were venerated as works of art and their conservation became a matter of serious concern. Nevertheless, much art and architecture was destroyed to make way for contemporary interpretations of the classical past. Vasari describes efforts both to preserve paintings faced with destruction and to restore those that had deteriorated. Giotto's frescoes which decorated the Old St. Peter's in Rome with scenes from the old and new testaments, were restored by artists of Vasari's day. During the building of the new walls of St. Peter's, some paintings on the old walls were carried away and set under the organ, others were destroyed. Among those saved "was a representation of Our Lady on a wall. In order that it might not be destroyed with the rest it was cut out, supported by beams and iron and so taken away. On account of its great beauty, it was afterwards built into a place selected by the devotion of M. Niccolo Acciaiuoli, a Florentine doctor enthusiastic over the excellent things of art, who adorned this work of art with stucco."[13]

Vasari himself restored Pietro Lorenzetti's frescoes in the Pieve at Arezzo together with the altarpiece in tempera of which he says: "I have entirely restored this altar at my own expense and with my own hands."[14]

———

Interesting, too, are the diagnoses of causes of deterioration recognized during the Renaissance. Of the frescoes by Pietro Cavallini in the vaulting of the church of Araceli sul Campidoglio in Rome, Vasari states that "the figures in this work as has been said elsewhere are much better preserved than the others because the vaulting suffers less from dust than the walls."[15]

The destructive effects of humidity are mentioned often by Vasari. He describes for example the last work of Giovanni Tossicani in the chapel of the Vescovado of Arezzo, "a fine Annunciation with St. James and St. Philip. As this work was on the north wall, it was all but destroyed by the damp, when Master Agnolo di Lorenzo of Arezzo restored the Annunciation, and soon after Giorgio Vasari, then quite a youth, restored Sts. James and Phillip to his great advantage as he learnt a great deal."[16]

––––––––

Restorations in Vasari's time were not always considered successful as we may observe from his account of what happened to the four battle scenes on panel painted by Uccello which were at Gualfonda on a terrace in the garden once belonging to the Bartolini. "These pictures being damaged, and having suffered a good deal, were restored in our day by Giuliano Bugiardini who has done them more harm than good."[17]

––––––––

A Pietà by Giovanni Bellini dating from about 1460, which hangs in the Ducal Palace in Venice, bears on its face the inscription "MDLXXI Renovatum" at which time it was enlarged and restored.[18] One wonders if the canvas on which it was painted was not also lined at the time.

Only one example is cited from the Renaissance in Northern Europe, a portrait by Holbein of Sir William Butts, the Younger. Painted in 1533–37, it depicts Butts as a young man in the style typical of Holbein. The portrait, hanging now in the Museum of Fine Arts, Boston, was said to have been restored for Butts years later on the occasion of a visit to his estate by Queen Elizabeth 1st. The restoration, by an unrecorded hand, brought the sitter's likeness up to date showing him as an elderly man, but bearing no relation to Holbein's style. Although the altered portrait was probably a reasonable likeness of Butts in his later years, as a recorded Holbein it was a complete falsification. The overpainting was removed in the twentieth century bringing to light the "lost" work by Holbein.

In 1603, letters by Peter Paul Rubens, written while he was an envoy in Spain, related his restoration of a collection of paintings extensively damaged by damp and mold during their transportation from Italy.[19] In 1618, an artist, J. Fisher, was employed to restore Dürer's "Paumgartner Altarpiece." His restorations transformed the wings of the altar painting by Dürer in 1498 into flamboyant specimens of the baroque style.

A conversation in the Volpato manuscript between painting apprentices gives insight into the cleaning of pictures in the seventeenth century. The elder apprentice warns of the dangers involved and the damage which may result. A solution of potash in pure water is advised, gently applied by sponge and washed off quickly with pure water. Rinsing is done a second time followed by drying with a linen cloth. The painting is then varnished with white of egg. Oiling is not recommended because it is not good for pictures except when applied to the back of a canvas from which the paint is "scaling." And as proof of this, remarks the apprentice, "see the St. Peter Martyr, at Venice, who having been oiled so many times by sacrilegious blockheads who have copied him, is so spoiled and blackened that there is no telling what sort of face he has, and yet I recollect when he was beautiful."[20]

We have no certainty when, in order to reconsolidate a torn or embrittled painting on canvas, a new fabric was first applied to cover completely the reverse of the original one. It is probable that the process was an outgrowth of the simpler expedient of locally patching a torn area with a piece of cloth or paper and an adhesive. As the size of the rupture increased, the thought eventually must have occurred to someone that a fabric which covered the entire reverse would not only disguise the fact that the painting had been torn, but would strengthen a canvas which had become fragile around its edges. Painting on canvas first became popular in Venice in the sixteenth century and spread quickly from there. It seems likely that the technique of "lining" an original canvas with a second fabric using water soluble adhesive of paste or glue was an established process well before the end of the seventeenth century.[21]

NOTES

1. Pausanias, *Description of Greece*, vol. 2, trans. W.H.S. Jones and H.A. Omerod (Cambridge: Harvard University Press, 1926), 471.

2. G. Rosi, "Safeguarding Our Artistic Heritage," *Unesco Chronicle* (May, 1959): 160.

3. Ibid., 159.

4. K. Jex-Blake, *The Elder Pliny's Chapters on the History of Art* (Chicago: Argonaut Inc. Publishers, 1968), 151.

5. Ibid., 127–29.

6. M. Conway, *Dürer's Literary Remains* (England: Cambridge University Press, 1889), 69.

7. Jex-Blake, *The Elder Pliny's Chapters*, 135.

8. Ibid., 127–129.

9. Vitruvius, *The Ten Books on Architecture*, trans. M.H. Morgan (New York: Dover Publications Inc., 1960), 53.

10. Jex-Blake, *The Elder Pliny's Chapters*, 87; and Pliny, *Natural History*, trans. H. Rackham, vol. 9 (Cambridge, Mass,: Harvard University Press, 1961), 27.

11. Vitruvius, *The Ten Books on Architecture*, 208–9.

12. U. Procacci, "Distacco di tempere ducentesche sovrapposte," *Bolletino d'Arte* I (1953): 31–37.

13. G. Vasari, *The Lives of the Painters, Sculptors, and Architects*, vol. I (New York: E.P. Dutton and Company, 1927), 70-71. See also 71, n. 1.

14. Ibid., 100.

15. Ibid., 126.

16. Ibid., 155.

17. Ibid., 237–38.

18. R. Longhi, "The Giovanni Bellini Exhibition," *Burlington Magazine* 91 (1949): 274–80.

19. R.S. Magurn, *The Letters of Peter Paul Rubens* (Cambridge, Mass.: Harvard University Press, 1955), 32ff.

20. M.P. Merrifield, *Original Treatises on the Arts of Painting*, vol. 2 (New York: Dover Publications, Inc., 1967), 750–52.

21. R.H. Marijnissen, *Dégradation, conservation, et restauration de l'oeuvre d'art*, vol. 1 (Brussels: Editions Arcade, 1967), 33–34, places the first mention of "relining" in 1660 followed by other references in 1680 and 1698.

ANDREW ODDY

"Does Reversibility Exist in Conservation?"[1]

In Reversibility—Does it Exist? *Ed. by Andrew Oddy and Sara Carroll. British Museum Occasional Paper no. 135 (London: British Museum Press, 1999), pp. 1–4.*

THE FIRST FORMAL training courses for teaching the conservation of museum objects were established at London University in the 1950s; at the Institute of Archaeology for archaeology and at the Courtauld Institute of Art for fine art. At least as far as the training in archaeological conservation was concerned, one of the basic tenets of the course was that any material applied to an artefact or work of art should be reversible.[2] The same was presumably true for the course on the conservation of fine art, but this paper is based mainly upon [my] more than 30 years' experience in the conservation of archaeological material and applied art and will only occasionally refer to the field of fine art.

When I entered the conservation profession in the 1960s, the emphasis was on the use of easily soluble adhesives and consolidants, and epoxy and polyester resins were seen as materials of last resort, although they could at least be softened with selected solvents, so that reversibility was, in theory, possible. This was the only meaning of the term reversibility at that time; could any material which was added to an object be removed?[3] In the generation which has passed since then, conservators have realised that the concept of reversibility can, *and must,* be applied to all stages of the conservation process.[4] The conservation of an artefact has four stages:

1. cleaning
2. stabilization
3. repair
4. restoration

although not all stages are necessary in many cases. The 1960s' view of reversibility was largely confined to stages 3 and 4, and nobody ever thought of cleaning archaeological objects as an irreversible process, *but it obviously is*.[5] The same is often true of stabilisation, and it is certainly true of restoration in many cases where reshaping of a 'distorted' object is carried out.

Cleaning

What is cleaning meant to achieve? The answer, of course, is clarification of surface detail, whether it be topography, texture or colour. Hence, dirty textiles and many dirty works of art on paper have been (almost) automatically washed in the past. Only recently, however, have conservators and conservation scientists begun to consider two aspects of washing—first, where and when did the dirt arise, and second, is washing harmful to the textile or paper?[6] (The possible effect of washing on pigments or dyes has, of course, long been an important factor in deciding whether to wash.)

The answers to both these questions have been to cast doubt on the wisdom of widespread washing. To take the second point first; fugitive dyes and pigments are easy to test before washing is begun, but what about the non-visible, but potentially soluble, components of paper and textile, such as sizes in paper and starch or other 'dressing' in textiles? These will be washed away, but *could* be replaced with equivalent materials after the washing process is complete. But is it ethical to resize a washed piece of paper, particularly if the nature of the original sizing material was not ascertained before the treatment? In the 1960s, and later, washing, bleaching and resizing of prints and drawings was commonplace, even in museums, and led to criticisms of conservators having 'laundered' many items of graphic art.

The result in the 1980s and 1990s, has been for curators of prints and drawings in the British Museum to require less and less interventive conservation. So far has this process advanced that even standard treatments for the removal of brown 'foxing' marks or for the reversal of the 'blackening' of white lead pigment are rarely requested.

In some ways, stopping the treatment of blackened lead white is understandable: as it is, by any standards, a process which is ethically questionable. After all, the original white lead pigment consists of basic lead carbonate. This 'blackens' by reaction with hydrogen sulphide in the atmosphere to form black lead sulphide. If this is treated with a solution of hydrogen peroxide in methyl ether, the black lead sulphide is oxidised to white lead sulphate. When the treatment is successful, as it usually is, the original *appearance* of the pigment is achieved (Daniels and Thickett 1992). However, the new white colour is due to lead sulphate, not to basic lead carbonate, and, hence, the original intentions of the artist have been thwarted by the conservator, however well-meaning he or she may be. No wonder that many curators are resisting this as a treatment, and it is certainly *not* reversible.

The refusal to have foxing removed is less understandable, except from the point of view of the absolute purist who resists all physical interventions with works of art. Needless to say, the bleaching of foxing is also irreversible but, unlike the treatment of blackened white lead, its elimination returns the image nearer to its original state from the point of view of the viewer. What, however, has happened to the physical and chemical properties of the paper is another question!

The discussion of cleaning has, so far, failed to face up to one fundamental question. *Before* anything is removed from the surface, the conservator must question its origin. Objects become covered in several different types of deposit, all of which can obscure the topography, the texture, and the colour(s) of the surface. These are:

1. dirt which has accumulated 'in the museum' (ie, since the object was first 'collected');
2. dirt which accumulated when the object was in use (ie, between manufacture and collection);
3. deposits applied intentionally during use;
4. soil deposits on archaeological objects;
5. alteration products arising from chemical changes to the object.

The first of these types of 'dirt' may be removed with impunity, as there can never be any doubt about the removal of 'museum dirt'. But is the same true for dirt which accumulated during use? Consider, for example, a collection of old agricultural tools. When collected, they will probably be covered with soil and the metal parts will be corroded. Should the soil be removed, or should it be preserved as evidence for use? There is no doubt that most museums will want the soil removed before the tools are displayed. However, museums could consider saving the soil (or a sample of it) in case some researcher in the future is interested in it.

Sometimes, however, dirt on an object actually tells a story. To take a slightly absurd example, some cricket players polish the ball on their trousers before bowling. The resulting red stain on one side of the trousers is evidence of this practice and if a pair of stained trousers were in a costume collection, the stain should not be removed. A similar example would be bloodstains on military uniforms, or, indeed, any deposit indicating the occupation of the wearer.

Of course, stains on clothing and textiles, especially food stains, make the textile even more vulnerable to insect attack, but that is a conservation problem which can be dealt with *without* removing the stains. Nevertheless, many curators would still react negatively to costumes with extensive deposits relating to the work of the original owner, and some might argue for washing in order to facilitate study by visiting scholars when, in reality, they (the curators) prefer a 'sanitised' collection.[7]

Deposits applied *intentionally* during use are often known as 'ethnographic dirt', although these deposits can also occur on archaeological objects. Food remains in cooking vessels are a classic example, but stains and deposits, such as blood on weapons and wax or oil in lamps and candlesticks, must also be preserved. The presence of food and wax/oil may well be obvious, but traces of blood on weapons may be almost invisible. Hence, conservators should take great care before washing any object to ensure that evidence of its use is not being removed. With modern methods of micro-analysis, even stains which are almost invisible may be induced to give up their secrets in a scientific laboratory.

Surface decoration, especially paint, and traces of religious offerings, have often gone unnoticed in the past, but conservators who have received a modern academic training are likely to look out for any such deposits, especially on the type of object where the presence of decoration or libations is to be expected. Unfortunately, paint has often been almost completely lost during burial, and it is only careful examination of finds from modern excavations, especially in waterlogged ground, that is revealing the extent of its use hitherto, especially on metalwork. It is a fact of modern museum life that few objects from antiquity now look like they did when originally made. In those days life was polychromatic and many surfaces were coloured, especially sculpture. But few pieces of classical stone sculpture now have traces of the original pigmentation; the few that do are witness to the rest having certainly been painted as well.

In the context of 'reversibility', ill-informed cleaning is not only irreversible, it is also unprofessional, as the job of the conservator is not only to preserve objects for the future, but also to preserve any evidence about their methods of manufacture or the way that they were used.

Soil deposits on archaeological objects can usually be removed with impunity, although it is essential to make sure that associated evidence is not lost; loose seeds inside a pottery vessel would, for example, be easy to lose. Sometimes, however, the analysis of soil deposits has played an important part in trying to establish a provenance for objects on the art market. If antiquities have been illegally exported from their country of origin, it will be in the interests of the vendor to have all traces of soil removed. With objects with a documented history, the removal of soil is not normally a problem—indeed, it is the 'bread and butter' of life for many conservators.

The main problem with the removal of soil comes when the interface between the soil and the object is reached, especially when the surface of the object consists of alteration products. Is it acceptable to remove corrosion products from metals and glass? In doing so, the conservator is removing part of the object, even if not an 'original' part, but in leaving them *in situ*, the conservator fails to reveal the contours of the original surface.[8] Few curators or conservators would doubt the wisdom of careful removal of corrosion products, but most conservators now do this process by hand, or using hand-held machinery, rather than by using chemical stripping agents. Nevertheless, removal of corrosion products is certainly irreversible, and it certainly compromises the integrity of the object.[9]

Stablisation

Stabilisation is the process of stopping active deterioration. It may consist merely of achieving stable environmental parameters, or of storing certain objects in the dark, or it may consist of an actual intervention.

Wood and ivory, which expand and contract with cycles of humidity, can only be stabilised by controlling the RH. However, ceramics and porous stones which are flaking because of the presence of soluble salts, can be stabilised either by controlling the RH or by removing the soluble salts. If the latter course of action is chosen, and if the stone or ceramic is able to withstand washing or poulticing, the desalination normally goes ahead. But should it? Where did the salts originate? If they have been absorbed from the soil, as is usually the case with ceramics, removal is not a problem, but if they have always been there, as may be the case with limestone, removal is an irreversible alteration to the nature of the object. It is, nevertheless, often carried out in the interest of preserving the stone as a work of art, even in the composition of the stone is slightly changed by the loss of the salts.

A similar 'stabilisation' process is the firing of cuneiform tablets before they are washed to remove salts. The firing process adds nothing and takes nothing away, but it does irreversibly change the nature of the tablet (Oddy 1999). Natural clay is turned into a ceramic, but unless this is done, salts cannot be removed, and unless the salts are removed, the tablets will often disintegrate (Organ 1960–61).

Fragile stone may need not only desalination, but also consolidation to strengthen it. Many different consolidants are available, and great play is made by conservators of the continuing solubility of many of them so that removal is possible and the treatment may be described as reversible. But is that true? In fact, deep consolidants can never be completely removed however soluble they are (Horie 1983), and if they could, the weakened object might well collapse before a replacement can be found and applied. So is there really a difference between using a completely soluble resin and a thermo-setting resin? The answer is more likely to lie with other properties of aging, such as colour change, rather than with continuing solubility.

There is a danger that these remarks might he interpreted as a licence to impregnate any object with any material. Far from it, *all* interventive treatments should be thought out and justified, but the message so far is that most interventive treatments, be they cleaning or stabilisation, are *not* reversible.

Repair

Repair means the reassembly of fragments and this very often is totally reversible. Whether paper is being stuck with starch paste, textiles by stitching, or ceramics with cellulose nitrate adhesive, the work can easily be reversed. Problems may arise if a very strong adhesive is necessary, but even epoxies and polyesters may be softened and removed provided the join line is not too deep.

When components to be joined are very heavy, it may be necessary to dowel the join, and this process is obviously irreversible in one sense because even if the dowel can be removed, the holes will remain in the two (or more) fragments.

One type of repair is not reversible, but fortunately it is little used (in museums at least): soldering and welding of metal. The development of modern adhesives has meant that many joins between fragments

of metal objects no longer require soldering, but it is sometimes the only way to effect a repair and, in such cases, the treatment must be thoroughly documented.

Another practice which was irreversible, but which has been rendered obsolete by modern adhesives, was the filing of edges of fragments to make them fit together. This was done for two reasons: first, when the fit between adjacent fragments was a bad one due to crumbling of the edges of the pieces, and second, when the thickness of the glue lines in a pot meant that the last few shards were too big for the space available. In this case, filing of edges used to be common.[10] Fortunately, modern adhesives have meant that only an infinitesimally thin layer of adhesive is needed in most joins, and where the joint is bad due to crumbling of edges, the adhesive can often be made more thixotropic by the addition of, for example, glass micro-balloons.

Restoration

The final stage of a conservation process may be what is known as restoration, be it gap-filling in the body of a ceramic vessel, or replacing the extremities of 'sculpture' (noses, cars, fingers, handles, spouts, etc). Gap filling and restoring missing parts are usually considered to be more or less reversible processes, and, in recent years, new techniques have been developed to simplify the removal of the restorations if this becomes necessary.[11] These new techniques usually involve the use of an easily soluble separator layer between the 'original' and the 'fill'.

There is, however, another meaning to the word restoration in a museum context—that of reshaping a distorted object. Reshaping is a process which has often been used on metal objects and on those made of organic materials, in particular, leatherwork and basketry. Where the original material is not 'elastic', reshaping is not normally a problem. Hence, the 'recreation' of an ancient suit of crocodile skin armour by humidification of the desiccated and crumpled 'leather' can hardly be disputed (Sully 1992). And if it is, further reshaping is possible. The same is true of baskets, or of other objects made of vegetable fibres, and of objects made of gut, such as Inuit parkas (Hill 1986; Morrison 1986). These processes of reshaping are reversible, but depend for their success on records of what the object looked like originally.

However, metals are in a different category as the very process of reshaping, if carried out without sufficient skill, may stretch the metal and produce a slightly different shape from that of the original object. When the metal is soft enough to be reshaped cold using gentle pressure from non-metallic tools, stretching is unlikely, if not impossible. In some cases, however, greater force may be needed unless the metal can be softened by annealing before the reshaping starts.

Nevertheless, reshaping of metals can be done without compromising the integrity of the object in many cases, but the process is always irreversible, both in terms of the physical shape and, when annealing has been necessary, in terms of the structure of the metal. This raises the question of under what circumstances can reshaping be considered.

1. Should damage which occurred during the 'lifetime' of the object be restored?
2. Should damage which occurred after the object lost its original function but before it was 'collected' he restored?
3. Should damage which occurred at the time of discovery (or more recently) be restored?

The answer to the first question is almost invariably negative. If a knife was thrown away because the blade had broken, no museum would want to restore the blade. However, if an object was damaged in a fire, which effectively ended its 'life', should it be restored? Or is the evidence of the burning part of the history of the object?

The second question refers to objects placed in tombs where they may be damaged by the collapse of a burial chamber. Some people would argue for restoration and others against, but it could be said that the collapse of a burial chamber is part of the history of the object and so such damage should not be repaired. Similar examples are the numerous weapons which were ritually bent before being thrown into

a river as an offering to the gods. This was common practice in the European Iron Age. At the moment when a sword was deliberately bent, it ceased to be a sword, but it did become a religious offering and, as such, took on a new identity. Thus, this kind of deliberate damage should not be restored.

Most types of objects, except high-fired ceramics and some kinds of stone, are adversely affected by burial. This type of damage can be restored *if restoration is seen as essential.*[12] However, more and more curators are opting for a reduction in the amount of restoration. If a metal bowl has a hole in it due to corrosion in the ground, does the hole really need filling before it can be exhibited? A few years ago, the answer was invariably 'yes', now it is often 'no'.

The aim of this paper has been to discuss aspects of reversibility and to consider the question posed by the title of the paper. A generation ago, reversibility was taken to mean that any material added to an object should be easily removable. Now it includes all conservation processes applied to antiquities, and conservators must consider not only the shape of the object, but also potential changes to its chemical composition and to its micro-structure. The result is to realise that very few processes are, in fact, truly reversible, so the decision on whether and how to conserve becomes not only a practical one, but also an ethical one. As Smith has pointed out, 'the time has come for professional judgement to be substituted for the principle of reversibility' (Smith 1988) and Appelbaum has stated that 'the notion of retreatability is one that is often more helpful … than the idea of reversibility itself (Appelbaum 1987).

NOTES

1. This paper is reprinted with minor changes from G. Kamalakar and V. Pandit Rao (eds), *Conservation, Preservation and Restoration: Traditions, Trends and Techniques*, Birla Archaeological and Cultural Research Institute, Hyderabad, 299–306.

2. Appelbaum has pointed out that a 'material' cannot be 'reversible'. Conservators have, however, come to mean 'soluble' when they say 'reversible' (Appelbaum 1987, p. 65). Smith has also pointed out that

'the principle of reversibility is visually flawed' as it asserts that conservators can reverse time (Smith 1988, p. 200).

3. R.D. Smith defined 'reversibility' in paper conservation as 'the ability of the conservator to remove any residue introduced into the paper by a preservation treatment' (Smith 1966).

4. Richard Smith updated his definition in 1988 to 'reversibility is the ability of a conservator to reverse, that is remove, any residue or effect introduced to, in, or on an object by a conservation treatment. A conservator needs to be able to return objects to the appearance and chemical and physical condition existing just prior to treatment' (Smith 1988). Even here the emphasis is on materials used in conservation. Only by implication is the definition extended to what may be removed and to the question of restoration.

5. As Barbara Appelbaum has pointed out (Appelbaum 1987, p. 66).

6. Smith (1988) points out on p. 203 that washing may improve the appearance of paper, but it will irreversibly change its physical properties.

7. In addition to the 'curator's desire for the immaculate', a 'demonstration of the conservator's skills' has also been cited as a spurious justification for restoration (Child 1988).

8. Child (1988) has drawn attention to the fact that discoloured original varnish is removed from easel paintings, but preserved on furniture.

9. The UKIC Guidance for Conservation Practice (1990) allows the removal of corrosion products by stating that 'nothing should be removed from an object without sufficient evidence that it is not part of the original condition of the object.'

10. An example in the British Museum of a well-known object where pieces were filed by early 'restorers' is the Portland Vase (see Smith 1992).

11. For example, the manufacturing of 'false' shards for restoring pottery (see Koob 1987).

12. Child defines restoration as a 'somewhat subjective process of altering the appearance of an object in order to 'improve' some factor, such as the object's safety, appearance or interpretation' (Child 1988).

REFERENCES

Appelbaum, B. 1987. Criteria for treatment: reversibility, *JAIC*, 26, 65–73.

Child, R.E. 1988. Ethics in the conservation of social history objects, *Preprint for the UKIC 30th Anniversary Conference*, (V. Todd, ed.), UKIC, London, 8–9.

Daniels, V., and Thickett, D. 1992. The reversion of blackened lead white on paper, in *Conference Papers: Manchester 1992* (S. Fairbrass, ed.), Institute of Paper Conservation, 109–115.

Hill, L.K. 1986. The conservation of Eskimo seal-gut kagools, *Bulletin of the Scottish Society for Conservation and Restoration*, 7, 17–20.

Horie, C.V. 1983. Reversibility of polymer treatments, in *The Proceedings of the Symposium 'Resins in Conservation' held at the University of Edinburgj ... 1982* (J.O. Tate, N.H. Tennant and J.H. Townsend, eds), SSCR, 3–1 to 3–6, especially 3–4.

Koob, S. 1987. Detachable plaster restorations for archaeological ceramics, in *Recent Advances in the Conservation and Analysis of Artifacts*, (J. Black, ed.), Summer Schools Press, London, 63–65.

Morrison, L. 1986. The conservation of seal gut parkas, *The Conservator*, 10, 17–24.

Oddy, A. 1999. Keep taking the tablets: a conservator's guide to the conservation of cuneiform documents, paper read to the Annual Meeting of AIC, St. Louis, Missouri, June 1999.

Organ, R.M. 1960-61. The conservation of cuneiform tablets, *British Museum Quarterly*, 23 (2), 52–7.

Smith, R.D. 1966. Paper deacidification: a preliminary report, *Library Quarterly*, 36 (4), 273–92.

Smith, S. 1992. The Portland Vase, in *The Art of the Conservator*, (A. Oddy, ed.), British Museum Press, London, 42–58, especially 56.

Sully, D.M. 1992. Humidification: the reshaping of leather, skin, and gut objects for display, in *Conservation of Leathercraft and Related Objects Interim Symposium* (P. Hallebeek, M. Kite and C. Calnan, eds.), Victoria and Albert Museum, London, 50–54.

UKIC. 1990. Guidance for Conservation Practice, *Members Handbook*, UKIC, 8–9.

JAN PARIS

"Conservation and the Politics of Use and Value in Research Libraries"

In The Book and Paper Group Annual, *vol. 19 (Washington, DC: AIC, 2001), pp. 61–65.*

BEHIND THE EVERYDAY activities in a library conservation lab there exists a web of assumptions derived from both conservation and library cultures. These assumptions underlie a range of philosophical questions about how we prioritize special collections[1] materials for conservation treatment, how this selection process may affect the historical record, and what we as conservators have to do with how this all works. It seems self-evident that curators and conservators are in the business of preserving the historical record, but what isn't so clearly seen is the way that we also play an invisible role in its shaping, as decisions we make ultimately affect what is saved and what is not. I'd like to direct a spotlight at the intersection of use and value as materials are selected for treatment. Using my experience with a recent exhibit, I'll describe the evolution of my thinking about the work we do and some of the issues that I believe lie at its core.

As library conservators, we think especially about the concept of current use, which may include an exhibit, a class assignment, an item requested frequently, or an item so fragile that it can't be handled safely even once. In a library, current use may demand intervention simply to allow the pages of a book to be turned or a manuscript with acidic ink to be handled without losing text. But it is also our responsibility to think about future use. These questions, of course, are not unique to conservation in libraries and archives. At the recent Getty Conservation Institute's conference called "Mortality Immortality?," then-director Miguel Angel Corzo put it simply in relation to twentieth-century art when he asked, "…how do we choose what will be saved? [and] Who will make the choices?"[2] Decisions for prioritizing conservation work are the result of a complex equation based on many factors, primary among them use and value.

But the question remains, "How is value defined and who defines it?"

Over time, I have watched my definition of value shift. After working in the field of conservation for about fifteen years, I became aware of a significant change in my thinking about the work I was doing. An elusive sensation, it would periodically emerge as a general feeling of discontent and a sense of alienation from the profession. As I tried to become more conscious of this experience, I recognized that it was particularly present when I was working on certain materials and less so when I was working on others. I began to notice a pattern.

Working on more ephemeral materials—the collection underdogs, the "other" in traditional library collections of highspots—I felt far more engaged than when I worked on the "high art" of the canon. At first, I thought it was simply a matter of personal preference, but then I began to see that my subjective experience was running parallel to cognitive changes in my relationship to the two distinct professional contexts within which I work—the field of conservation and the library world in which materials are selected for conservation.

Looking back, I began to see that I brought assumptions from my conservation training, which had taught me to view an object—in my case, a book—primarily in terms of its physical structure and chemical makeup. This materials-based perspective allowed room for aesthetics (and history to a limited extent), but chiefly in the realm of evaluating tangible attributes—determining what is original and what is not, what is damage and what is not, in short, what "belongs" and what does not. And it was implied, though not directly stated, that subject content is not considered part of our domain as conservators.

Parallel to my self-questioning about this perspective, the conservation field as a whole was addressing the issue of how to broaden its intellectual framework, which had grown out of a Western art historical model, to better address the needs of a wide range of objects that require a different type of approach. This was particularly true for materials that have been used in the course of daily life, be they Native American shoes, nineteenth-century scrapbooks, or a plantation owner's account book. In the special collections of libraries and archives, an object's meaning often lies in its history, not its appearance or an ideal version of its condition at the time it was produced.

Across the conservation specialties, we are now broadening our approach and adopting perspectives that privilege the cultural context of an object's production and use over the values of Western art history. Library and archives conservators have also begun to look at these issues, but my experience and a review of current literature indicate that the discussion remains generally focused within the context of making treatment decisions for individual items. Troubled by this narrow focus, I've begun questioning why our intellectual understanding of the collections in our care is not allowed to influence the way we look at *whole* collections as we address the issues of selecting and prioritizing materials.

My own interest in conservation admittedly began from an object-oriented base as well—I like old books. But after working for some time, I began to experience a shift from considering primarily aesthetic or even material qualities to considering research value to scholars. Now, the *first* questions I ask myself are "what can this tell us?" and "how will it be used in research?" Only after that do I ask "what is this material?" and "how was it made?"

My understanding of research value has taken time to develop because my conservation training had so often identified the researcher as an adversary—a destroyer of books! I realize now how completely this attitude shuts down the potential for dialogue and separates us from the people for whom we do this work and the intellectual community in which we can and—dare I say—should participate. It isolates us within a paradigm of the detached specialist—which ultimately casts us in a technical and thus more limited role. The shift in my awareness of how an artifact may be "read" not only expands my sensitivity to the objects in my care, it also increases my ability to assess materials for research potential.

At the same time that I was thinking about cultural bias in the field of conservation, I came to realize that the manner in which librarians and archivists selected materials for treatment also had a cultural bias. This was dramatically brought home to me in 1997 when I co-curated an exhibit called "The Invisible Process: Ingenuity and Cooperation in Finding Women's Lives"[3] and looked more closely at the relationship between conservation and research on women.

It was then that I first became conscious of biases in the ways conservation resources are allocated—biases that can be virtually invisible to us, because many of us in conservation are so thoroughly participants in the dominant culture. Because the exhibit was about women, I came face to face with issues of gender bias, though it is clear that a race or class analysis of how materials are privileged for conservation would reveal similar assumptions at work.

Of the 200,000 rare books and sixteen million manuscripts in our collection, a quick review of those assigned high priority and sent for treatment in the conservation lab revealed that these choices had been driven by unspoken assumptions in which value is historically equated with men (and men of European descent especially).

At the time of the exhibit, 364 items from three different special collections had been prioritized for treatment over the previous several years. Of these, only thirty-five were by or for women specifically, and fourteen of those were selected only because of the exhibit—by me! Where were the women writers, their pamphlets, their magazines? Why wasn't I treating these? Remembering that each time an item receives treatment, another remains on the path to disintegration, it's clear that these choices will ultimately have an irreversible effect on the historical record. Virginia Woolf put it well in *A Room of One's Own*, "Speaking crudely, football and sport are 'important'; the workings of fashion and the buying of clothes 'trivial'! And these values are inevitably transferred from life to fiction." And, apparently to the selection for conservation as well.

The issue of women's (and other overlooked groups') representation has been considered from the point of view of collection-building strategies in libraries, archives, and in many museums for some time. It takes only a small leap from there to see that it's time for a similar effort to assure a conscious consideration of representation in the materials being prioritized for conservation. What is the point of collecting materials that we then allow to disappear?

As I continued to think further about where women's lives were documented, I realized that not only were many of the sources that could illuminate their lives historically undervalued, but that often these materials were the most vulnerable to loss. Many popular culture materials, such as advertisements, posters, and magazines, were ephemeral and never intended to survive. The quality of the materials used in their production (and often, even in books published for women) is usually insubstantial and susceptible to rapid deterioration. Without a conscious understanding of their often unique value as documentation of ordinary women's lives—and a concerted effort to preserve them—they will not survive.

As contemporary scholars across disciplines rely more frequently on artifacts of material culture and artifacts of cultures outside the mainstream, library conservators have been confronted by the need to understand the cultural context in which these materials were produced and, just as importantly, how they will be used by researchers. Scholars looking, for example, at a young woman's diary may see it not only as text, but may also value the physical object as a carrier of information about the social setting in which the diarist lived. A first glance at Martha Ryan's Cipher Book (fig. 1a) tells us that the original binding is highly damaged; a second glance (fig. 1b) reveals that it is handmade of sacking cloth, lined with fragments of penmanship practice with such moral admonitions as, "Avoid all appearance... , Honour Father and Mother... , A good girl

will mind... ." Clearly, if this volume were rebound and the original cover discarded—still a common practice in more libraries than I care to think about— we would lose vital evidence about the social milieu and historical period in which this book was created.

Likewise, as materials are prioritized for conservation at the collection level, we must allow both research value and physical vulnerability to play important roles in our decisions. A good example is the manuscript of a sermon delivered in 1890 by Primus Priss Alston, on the twenty-fifth anniversary of the Emancipation Proclamation (fig. 2). Alston was an ex-slave who studied for the ministry and went on to serve almost thirty years as an ordained priest in Charlotte, North Carolina. There is no question

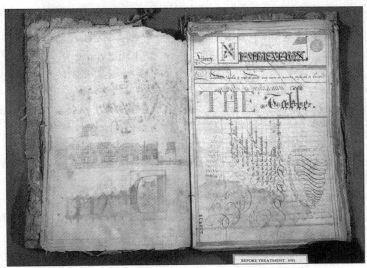

Figure 1a.

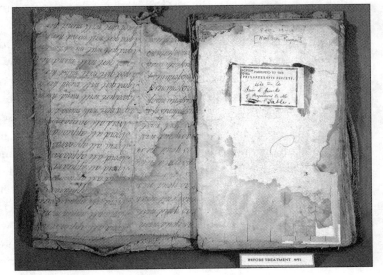

Figure 1b.

that this highly deteriorated document doesn't *look* like it's very valuable when placed next to an illuminated manuscript or an early printed book. But in fact, its research value is enormous, and it's clear that this material is vulnerable to loss if not treated.

When viewed at a collection-wide level, the impact of perceived value can multiply exponentially if we look at a situation like my own in the context of a major research collection where I am the only conservator for hundreds of thousands of rare books and millions of manuscripts. Let's make a hypothetical comparison. How do we weigh the time needed to treat a fifteenth-century printing of a classic text—even if the pages are badly stained and the twentieth-century binding is partially detached and historically inappropriate—against the use of the same amount of time to treat the memoir of an American woman traveler in Europe after the Napoleonic Wars, three country music posters, a diary of a nineteenth-century merchant's voyage to Africa, and a small collection of anti-lynching broadsides. Can we say that the fifteenth-century volume, an incunabulum (something "everyone" agrees is "valuable"), actually needs treatment when these other items, some of them in far more compromised condition, might receive more intense research use and document more diverse experiences?

Without digging too deeply, it's fairly obvious that at the University of North Carolina at Chapel Hill far more primary research is carried out on nineteenth- and twentieth-century issues of race, class, and gender in American society than textual analysis of fifteenth-century works.[4] So even though the older item may have cost more to acquire or have more value on the open market, based on its limited research potential within this institution and its basically usable condition, I'd assert that it is not a conservation priority. If suggested for treatment, it becomes part of my job not only to recognize, but to *point out* that the privileging of this one volume comes at the expense of other items that have been historically overlooked as conservation candidates.

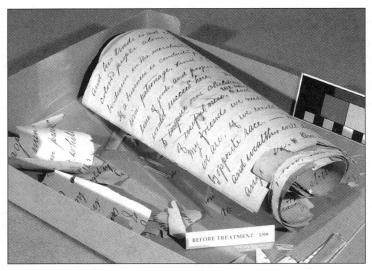

Figure 2.

I know that some people think that it's not the conservator's job to be involved in those decisions. I've come to believe that it is. In a research library, our charge is the care of the *collection* in the service of the library's mission, however that may be defined. Our responsibility goes beyond the individual object that's brought to us for treatment and even beyond our decisions to prioritize one volume over another, for example, because it has pressure-sensitive tape all over it. If large areas of the collection with high research value and a high level of vulnerability to deterioration are systematically ignored, I believe it is the conservator's job to be an advocate for those materials. This knowledge must be brought to bear no matter who brings it to the table or how their role has been traditionally defined.

As a result of my thinking about these issues, my traditional interactions with curators, where we juggle my time as a primary factor for prioritizing treatment choices, now include a look at subject matter in the context of my knowledge of each collection, its research strengths, and physical condition. In an effort to open the dialogue even further about possible candidates that have not been traditionally privileged, I also consider library- and even university-wide efforts and concerns to propose conservation projects. For example, several years ago, I initiated work with the Rare Book Collection to prioritize and treat items among our nineteenth-century African-American materials. I began with first-person narratives, since these were the most heavily used and are often extremely rare. Eventually, as some of these materials became important to our *Documenting the American South*[5] digitization project and required conservation before they could be safely handled for scanning, their priority as conservation candidates became more widely acknowledged.

As a profession, we've discussed, dissected, and debated the shift of the conservator from the bench to administration. And as a profession, I believe that we're gradually coming to see that our movement up into the administrative levels of our libraries and museums ultimately protects the collections we care for as our voices become more powerful in decision-making contexts. The questions I'm raising about selection and the knowledge that we as conservators are "allowed" to bring to bear are related to some of the same conflicting views about our roles.

I would like to suggest that we step farther out of our technical role and assert the knowledge that many of us have gained, either through scholarly training or direct experience with our collections and users. Today, gaps in the historical record are widely acknowledged, but a conscious change in patterns of selection for all functions—acquiring, retaining, *and* conserving—is needed to begin to redress the situation and prevent its perpetuation in the future. And especially within the group of materials that are already classed as rare or unique and identified as part of special collections, we must overcome the tendency to think about value in chiefly monetary terms and history as defined by the powerful. I'd like to see us become advocates for the historical importance of less privileged materials. Even in situations where curatorial prerogative is firmly entrenched, conservators can begin to ask questions that challenge the status quo.

I am comfortable asserting my role as conservator and intellectual advocate for "other-ness," and I am also fortunate to work in an institution open to my changing role. The task of prioritizing for conservation is always daunting. Working with such massive collections, we recognize that there is not a single answer for every institution or conservation program. But for me, it's critically important that we acknowledge our role as cultural workers who are players—either consciously or not—in the creation of the his-

torical record and public memory. If we continue to invest all of our resources in materials that have been traditionally valued, will those that have not been so privileged be available for use by the researcher of the future? The issue of what survives is obviously closely tied to both library and conservation work at many levels. Is it so different to censor or discard materials than to systematically ignore those in categories that are often the most vulnerable to loss? It may be different in intent, but the results are similar.

As conservators, we can, and in some cases should, make it our responsibility to go beyond the individual object and look at the whole collection in radically new ways. We must *all* be conscious of *whose* history/culture/art we are preserving. As I see it, part of my job as a conservator is to challenge the invisible assumptions about value in the world of library conservation.

Acknowledgments

Many thanks go to Lynn Holdzkom, without whom I would never have undertaken curating the exhibit that sparked my thinking about these issues. Both she and Lyn Koehnline willingly submitted to *many* discussions over the past several years and provided invaluable assistance with the writing of this paper. For their careful reading, editorial comments, and general all-around support, I would also like to thank Jill Snider, Claudia Koonz, Libby Chenault, and S. A. Bachman.

NOTES

1. "Special collections" refers to a range of primary source materials, including rare books, manuscripts, photographs, maps, art works, audio-visual materials, and other artifacts that are maintained in their original format.

2. Miguel Angel Corzo, ed., *Mortality immortality?: The legacy of 20th-century art* (Los Angeles: Getty Conservation Institute, 1999), xv.

3. "The Invisible Process: Ingenuity and Cooperation in Finding Women's Lives," Wilson Library, University of North Carolina at Chapel Hill, 3 July–30 September 1997. Exhibit catalog (66p.), including all

text and selected images, is available upon request from the author.

4. For example: *Like a Family: The Making of a Southern Cotton Mill World* (1987), Jacquelyn Dowd Hall, James Leloudis, Robert Korstad, Mary Murphy, Lu Ann Jones, and Christopher B. Daly; *Within the Plantation Household: Black and White Women of the Old South* (1988), Elizabeth Fox-Genovese; *Gender and Jim Crow: Women and the Politics of White Supremacy in North*

Carolina (1996), Glenda Gilmore; *Mothers of Invention: Women of the Slaveholding South in the American Civil War* (1996), Drew Faust; *Constructing Townscapes: Space and Society in Antebellum Tennessee* (1999), Lisa C. Tolbert.

5. *Documenting the American South* is a collection of digitized sources on Southern history, literature, and culture from the colonial period through the first decades of the twentieth century. See http://www.ibiblio.org/docsouth.

NICHOLAS PICKWOAD

"Distinguishing Between the Good and Bad Repair of Books"

In Conservation and Preservation in Small Libraries, *eds. Nicholas Hadgraft and Katherine Swift (Cambridge, UK: Parker Library Publications, 1994), 141–49.*

I AM OFTEN asked by owners and curators to look at repaired books and comment on the work done on them. Often the work looks neatly done, but betrays inadequacies of one sort or another. It may be that materials of clearly inferior quality have been used, or that detached boards show no sign of proper reattachment, or, quite often, that, as a result of the repairs done to it, the book simply will not open. Such things, to a trained binder, are not too hard to comment on, and I will return to some of the more detailed points later, but without seeing the book before it was repaired, it is always hard to do complete justice to the work done, and to know whether in fact the type of repair chosen was the most suitable and whether as much as possible has been saved from an original binding. In addressing the question of what may and may not constitute good and bad repair, we have to look at the process by which repairs are first undertaken, and look at some of the steps by which we can hope to arrive at good repairs and avoid the bad. Implicit in the acknowledgement that there are such things as bad repairs is the fact that not all binders, whether they call themselves conservators or not, are either trained in or capable of the work that they are often asked to do. Of all the decisions made when sending books out to be repaired, that of to whom to

send them is often the one which effectively seals the fate of the book, for good or ill.

The subject is immensely complex, and there are many ways in which most basic types of repair can be executed. In addition, decisions can be made which may seem to the uninitiated to be contradictory. It is quite possible that similar damage to copies of the same book from different collections, even within one library, may require to be treated in entirely different ways. But whilst there will always be to a greater or lesser extent a subjective element in selecting the type of repair, according to circumstances and to the particular interests of the people involved in the decision, I do believe that there are some basic ground rules which should be common to all such decisions, and my aim in this paper is to try to establish a checklist of the things to be considered when a book is brought forward for repair. I do not wish to come up with a list of rules, because the very variety of book types will make inflexible rules inevitably damaging in some cases. Rather, I hope to compile a set of questions which will prompt a rational consideration of the treatment options available.

Often there will be quite legitimate and apparently irreconcilable differences of opinion over what should be done to individual books, when the interests of curator, scholar and conservator cannot be made to agree. Most commonly this will arise over the need to gain access to the text, but where the binding, or the nature of some form of damage, will not allow this, discussion then comes down to one of the perceived relative importance of different components of the book. Money, or the lack of it, will also create difficulties, where the work that the conservator feels a book needs will cost far more than is either available, or is felt by the curator to be justifiable for a particular book. In such circumstances, the decision eventually arrived at, even if it is to decide to defer a decision—often the best solution for the book anyway—will run counter to the wishes of one or other of the parties involved. There is no way to avoid this, but what can be avoided is making decisions without properly exploring the issues involved.

It will be thought by many involved in the repair of books that the issues just mentioned are essentially curatorial and do not concern whether or not repairs are good, but the real quality of any repair will and must start with the decisions which initiate the whole process of repair. A skilful conservator can execute a brilliant repair which will still be seen as mistaken if the need for such a repair or the consequences of that repair are subsequently questioned.

At the very start, two questions immediately present themselves: **What is any repair trying to achieve?** and, **What are the treatment options available for achieving those ends?**

Like most fundamental questions, they sound simple, but can encompass immensely complex issues. The answers to both questions may involve not only a considerable knowledge of bibliography and conservation, but broader cultural and institutional concerns as well, and it is quite likely that no individual will have sufficient knowledge and experience to answer both of them—nor indeed to give a full answer to either.

Therefore, whilst I will divide the process into the two broad categories suggested by the questions—bibliography (in which I include other curatorial responsibilities) and conservation—it must not be thought that they are mutually exclusive, or that a properly considered repair can result from answering only one of them. The expertise of both the bibliogra-

pher and the conservator should be used in combination to arrive at the necessary answers.

It is also undoubtedly true that this process, the specification of repairs, should never be regarded as being suitable work for people who do not have a considerable knowledge of the type of book being considered for repair. Whilst some basic processes of identifying material which may be in need of repair can be carried out effectively by inexperienced personnel, decisions concerning treatment need to be made by people who will be able to identify the significance both of the books and of the actions decided on. Because in many cases this process will, when carried out by knowledgeable people, actually take very little time and will appear quite straightforward, delegation of the task may appear very tempting, especially where books of a rather mundane nature are being processed. The appearance, for instance, of a gilt title blocked directly onto the cloth spine of the second volume of the 1832 octavo edition of the works of Byron[1] (Figure 1) may not attract the notice of anyone unfamiliar with the history of nineteenth-century trade binding. Yet its consequent loss in rebacking will remove yet another example of what is probably the first commercial use of a significant technical advance.[2] If the people involved in making such decisions cannot recognise possibly unexpected and significant details of provenance, binding, marginalia etc., damaging mistakes will inevitably be made. Selection and specification are areas which need a high level of knowledge and, above all, an open mind.

Figure 1.

The specification may well only result from consultation with a conservator, but not necessarily the person who will do the work. It will help to have advice from an experienced conservator when drawing up specifications, as he/she should be aware of the treatment options available, when the binder who might otherwise have been asked to do the work might not. By these means, it may well be possible to make fuller use of locally available skills than would otherwise be the case, whilst avoiding some of the worst pitfalls. Unfortunately for the peace of mind of the curator, there is now available to the conservator a whole host of structural techniques in particular which do not form part of more conventional (i.e. old fashioned) bookbinding training. Anyone who is not aware of these techniques is not really in a position to draw up a specification.

The specification must also deal with the materials to be used, and here again professional expertise is needed. One cannot, unfortunately, rely on all binders to know as much as they might about materials—I don't suppose any of us do that and to some extent we are all working in the dark, in the absence of even basic research in some areas. But the materials should be agreed beforehand. So far as is possible, you must ensure that only materials which are of proven durability are used in the repairs, and not simply the materials that look good or are used in conventional commercial practice. The techniques used in the repair should be adapted to the right materials, and not the other way round. Where durable materials are available, but rather awkward to handle, it is incumbent on the binder to adapt otherwise conventional techniques to suit the material rather than reject them because they do not behave like more familiar, but less durable materials. The expense of the right materials (where they are available) may be alarming, but if used correctly, they will prove more cost effective in the long term.

It does, of course, go without saying that you must go to a binder who will understand what is required and has the technical range to cope with the work. It may not be easy to find such a binder, and if you cannot, it may be wiser to have only those repairs carried out which are within the range of the binders you can find. In most collections there is usually

work at all levels of sophistication to be done, and a large scale first-aid repair programme, using only the simplest techniques, will always be of greater benefit than ill-advised repair concentrating on the most valuable books.

The answers to the two basic questions asked above can be arrived at by asking two further parallel series of questions, which refer to the bibliographical and conservation implications of any proposed repairs, and which will allow a decent specification to be drawn up. The answers to these questions will be to a large extent interdependent. To put it simply, there is no future in demanding work which cannot be done, nor is it sensible to allow the successful outcome of the work to be threatened by the ability (or more properly, the inability) of a binder who is perhaps not qualified to take on the work. Furthermore, a specification should not be confused with listing simple repair requirements, which are often no more precise than 're-attach boards', as that information can be gathered by simple survey work. The specification should aim to establish as exactly as possible how the work is to be done, and, in particular, what must not be done in the process. Where work is not properly specified, the curator has no redress against well executed work which turns out not to be what was expected.

The 'bibliographical' questions will concern themselves very largely in establishing wherein the value or values of the book lie. I assume that a curatorial decision has already been made which establishes that the book is worth repairing; what the conservator needs to know from the curator is why it is worth repairing. All too often the conservator is simply asked to repair damaged books without any further briefing, and this is a recipe for accident and loss. The questions will include the following, though individual books may well prompt further specific lines of inquiry.

What exactly is it that is thought to need attention? I am often shown books for repair which simply do not need repair and have many years life in them without repair. Then again, in some badly damaged books, it may be only one area or type of damage which needs to be repaired. This needs to be stated clearly at the outset, so that unnecessary and unwanted repairs are avoided.

Are there any features within the textblock which require special attention? Too few binders have any training in bibliography, and may not therefore be able to recognise the significance of such things as cancels, stubs and so on. Such features will need to be pointed out. Are there any indications of provenance (including old shelf marks) which must be preserved at all costs? The possession of an otherwise unremarkable book by a famous historical or literary figure will give that book an importance far beyond normal, and it may be that any form of rebinding or radical repair would be thought damaging, by reducing the strength of the association between the owner and the book. A classic instance of this is to be found in a book which once belonged to Dr. Johnson, and has in it a note to the effect that it was that volume which the good Doctor threw at the head of Robert Norris M.D.[3] Not surprisingly it is somewhat damaged, and the very damage is an integral part of its history; it should not be repaired if it is at all possible not to (Figure 2). As a general rule, all indications of provenance should be preserved, whether attractive or not, and some of them may be very inconspicuous and quite possibly meaningless to most people likely to look at the book. John Donne's habit of marking passages in his books with pencil lines in the margins is one such, and all too easily erased by the tidy-minded.[4]

What is the significance of the binding (structure and decoration)? Most people can recognise a fine binding, but few are prepared to look for the significance of structural details. In some cases these can be of considerable interest, even though on books otherwise of little interest and value. An example of this comes in a curious English binding of the period 1670–1690 on a copy of the works of Sextus Empiricus printed in Cologne in 1621 (Figure 3). It is in pieces, and thus a candidate for repair, but it is in fact one of only five recorded glued bindings (that is, without any sewing). To sew it—or put it back together in any way—would destroy this tantalising insight into the way in which binders (or booksellers?) at a much earlier date than one might have guessed were trying to defraud their clients by making their books look as if they were properly bound (some even have false raised bands) when they were not. Where bindings of such historical interest are found on books of little intellectual or financial value, they are often most at risk, because if any repairs are considered ('to tidy them up a little'), they are likely to be of the cheapest, and thus the most damaging sort.

Is there additional importance offered by the book in some other form, such as the evidential value of the damage itself? Inserted material may be understood only in the context of the book in which it is found, and types of damage, especially soiling, may well give important information about the history of the book. The grime marks left by the inner edge of the back board on the present outer margin of the second cathedral waterworks plan in the Canterbury psalter indicate not only that it has been reversed at some point in its history, but also that it was at some stage immediately adjacent to the board, and not separated from it by flyleaves! Damage left

Figure 2.

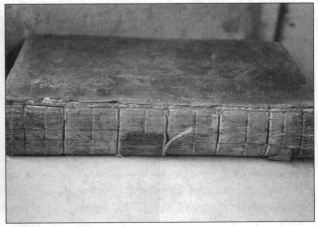

Figure 3.

by fires can not only help to date repairs and material added to damaged books (one looks to see whether it too has been damaged), but also may be useful in dating the fire—a matter of some interest when dealing with long established collections.

What is the future use of the book likely to be? It is impossible to work out how best to repair a book without some idea of the type of use to which it will be put. Books which are unlikely to get any sort of regular use may not actually need to be repaired at all, but a book known to receive regular use will have to be repaired in ways which will give it a chance of survival.

Where and how will the book be stored? If a large book can be stored horizontally, then much less in the way of repair may be needed than if it is to be kept vertically. If the storage conditions are inadequate, repairs are unlikely to be the answer to damage caused by them, and are best put off until adequate conditions can be established.

If you can establish, by these and other similar questions, what the repairs are attempting to do, you must then make sure that the qualities you have identified are in no way damaged by the repairs which may then be carried out. This may involve on the part of the binder a considerable degree of ingenuity and apparently unconventional binding technique, by which I mean that the repairs should refer directly to the structural and historical requirements of the damaged book and not be imposed on it by the limited range of techniques currently accepted as conventional bookbinding. Rebinding is by no means always the best course of action, and will always involve sometimes considerable amounts of historical (and physical) damage. But there are many ways in which even quite badly damaged structures can be reinforced without undue interference, particularly if the future use of the book can be properly controlled. Essentially, the techniques should be made to fit the book and what is required of it, and not the other way around.

The conservation questions will in the first place depend on an assessment of the damage and its effect on the book and of the necessity of repair. It must then be considered how any proposed repair will be affected by the answers given to the curatorial questions given above. Damage itself, whilst it provides the opportunity for repair, should not inevitably be seen as necessitating repair, and one basic question should be borne in mind when considering all possible repairs.

How much (or little?) repair is absolutely necessary to do what is required? Most libraries have so much work to do that they cannot afford to do more than is absolutely necessary, and the survival of the historical interest of many books is often dependent on how little work is done to them. All too often, though, the desire to carry out work which is little more than cosmetic (though this is not always a minor consideration) leads to the quite unnecessary destruction of physical evidence in books. To answer this question, however, further questions will have to be answered:

Does the damage threaten the survival of the book even without use?

Does the damage make the book unsafe to handle (given the likely future demand on the book)?

If the damage is stable and does not greatly interfere with the handling of the book, can it be repaired without gross interference with the rest of the book? If the answer to any of these questions is yes, then a further series of questions will be needed, prompted always by the need to approach the question of repair by asking how little is needed to achieve the desired ends, rather than how much. If the answer to all the questions is no, then the book should, perhaps, be returned to its shelf, possibly in some form of protective box or wrapper. Where any of the answers is yes, further questions are:

Is it possible to repair or support the existing structure without taking the book apart? As elsewhere, the answer to this question is going to depend very much on the skill and experience of the conservator. Many books are now repaired without being pulled, but some of the techniques needed are used by only a small number of binders. If the answer is no, then it may be thought better to leave the book alone, as either the disruption or the expense (or both) may be thought too great.

How much of the existing binding can be saved? The answer to this question will again be directly related to the skill and experience of the conservator, and may be subject to revision in the course of work as materials behave as expected or not. Generally, much more can be saved than is often recognised.

Is it possible to preserve all the original materials in place and allow the book to be read safely? If the answer to this question is no, it must be decided whether to abandon the proposed repairs, preserve the displaced materials off the book or modify the existing structure to allow an effective compromise.

If the existing structure is too badly damaged to keep together, is there a better way of putting it back together? It must be remembered that a facsimile of a binding structure taken down in order, perhaps, to carry out extensive and unavoidable repairs to text leaves, will never have the authenticity of the original, and that an opportunity is therefore afforded of modifying or altogether changing a structure better to suit the characteristics of the text leaves. For instance, a medieval vellum-leaved book in a later, tight-back binding could be given an unglued spine or a zig-zag guard when repaired, though both would be, strictly speaking, anachronistic. The replication of unsuitable binding structures in the interests of a notional authenticity does not necessarily make sense.

Each of these questions posits still more questions of an increasingly technical kind which may well need to be referred to curatorial decision, even during the course of repair. For example, while repairing the two volumes of the works of Etienne Dolet (Lyons, 1536 and 1538)[5] in contemporary English bindings, I discussed with the curator the treatment of the leaves of a commentary on the Decretals of Gregory IX (*Lectura super V libri decretalium*, Basel, 1477) used to make up the boards. Given the large number of copies of the text available elsewhere, it was decided to re-use the now de-laminated leaves as the boards of the book. Further work, however, revealed two leaves of a much rarer and more interesting text (the French translation by Simon de Hesdin and Nicolas de Gonesse of Valerius Maximus, *Facta et Dicta memorablia*, printed in the Southern Netherlands by the anonymous printer known as the Printer of Flavius Josephus, about 1475–7),[6] which it was then decided to extract and mount in the back of the relevant volume. In this case, the use of the leaves in an English binding provided the earliest (if not the only)

evidence of the existence of a copy of this book in England.

However, I have not yet tackled the central difficulty faced by most people with a curatorial responsibility but who do not have training in practical conservation work, which is **How do you make sure that you obtain work of the quality required and how do you recognise it when you see it?**

The issue is unfortunately complicated by the straightline and right-angle philosophy of binding and the deeply rooted belief that all books should look neat and tidy. There is a distressing amount of work done more with a view to eradicating untidiness from library shelves than to putting right more fundamental types of damage, and much of it is either done to books which have little need of repair in the first place, or done in such a way that it has little chance of surviving long enough to justify its expense. If more people could only accept that it is entirely natural for books which may be several hundred years old to look a little knocked about, then perhaps a lot less work would be done, and less damage with it. If a further conceptual leap could be made into accepting that even a repaired book might not necessarily end up with a gleaming new spine, but might, without unnecessary interference into its binding and structure, have been made safe to handle, then once again a lot of unnecessary damage through rebinding might be avoided.

This requires that the person examining the repaired book does not restrict his examination to checking the regularity of the squares and the tooling, which I have often seen done, and can understand that exact precision of finish does not necessarily contribute to either longevity or usability, and that such qualities should not be seen as reliable indications of quality in terms of conservation. This should be apparent to any perceptive observer of books bound before the eighteenth century, where a lack of attention to the finer points of finish has in no way contributed to their premature decay. In fact, the opposite is more likely to be the case, because more substantial (that is, to a binder working in the nineteenth-century tradition, 'clumsy') materials have often lasted better than their more heavily worked later replacements. Besides, the neatness of finish that has come to be expected as a result of an increasingly mechanistic approach to binding is not only inappropriate for some early books, but can also be expensive. If curators were better able to accept less intrusive repairs—the simple reattachment of boards rather than complete rebacking, for instance[7]—the work might prove not only cheaper in the long term (through increased durability), but also cheaper in the short term (through less work). Given contemporary problems with obtaining suitable materials, especially covering materials, for conservation binding, such a course of action may, in fact, be the only sensible option open in some cases.

But, to return to the question of distinguishing between good and bad repairs. I have in fact already discussed one of the more important prerequisites—the existence of an accurate specification against which to compare the repaired book. All too often it is easy to forget exactly the condition of a book before it went off to be repaired, and therefore it is hard to know exactly what to expect when it is returned. A specification will help clear up such confusion. So too will a report from the conservator when the work is finished.

Let us imagine, then, that the specification has been drawn up, the conservator has repaired the book and the book has been returned to its library. What procedure should then be followed?

Read the conservation report. All repaired books should be accompanied by a coherent written account of what has been done, listing the new materials and adhesives used (and where they have been used) and any alterations made to the format and original structure and materials of the book. This need not be very long, especially when repairs are simple, and need not explain at length what is clear to the eye, but must give sufficient information to allow future conservators and bibliographers to know what they need to know. Comments therefore such as 'boards reattached' or 'corners repaired' do not help much—anyone looking at the book can see that this work has been done— but comments such as 'linen cord whipped to existing sewing supports with linen thread and slips frayed out and pasted to the outside of the boards, leaving the original slips undisturbed' and 'corners repaired with Japanese tissue stuck with wheat starch paste' will help, and this will tell you whether work has been properly

done even when it may no longer be visible in the repaired book. Similarly, the remark 'book re-sewn' will be obvious to most people and therefore give little useful information, but 'book re-sewn all along on three recessed linen cords in place of two-on on the original two tawed thongs, which left central recess empty' does give information no longer evident on the repaired book. The quality of information given in such reports can actually serve as an indication of the binder's awareness of the implications of the work that he/she is doing. Binders who are reluctant to supply reasonably detailed reports may have reasons for doing so which do not reflect well on their techniques.

Check against the specification. A simple administrative task which will tell you whether the agreed work has been done.

Do the repairs work? This is the critical question. The repairs, if they are to be worth doing, must work, and all too often they do not. If the aim was to produce a book which is safe to read, it must be precisely that. If it is impossible to do so, then the repairs should not be carried out in the first place. It should open adequately (within the limits imposed by the textblock and old binding, if there is one) and place no undue strain on the original materials of the book preserved in the repair, and it should continue to do this for a considerable length of time. Where it is not possible to repair a book so that it will open easily, careful control of its future handling must be used to preserve it intact. The use of a book must be adapted to what the book can cope with. It is perhaps worth saying that the rightness and wrongness of a technique will depend almost entirely on whether or not it works and will continue to work. It is very apparent from some modern bookbinding manuals that in many cases techniques tend to be seen as inviolable, and are executed in certain ways and used in certain circumstances without room for variation. When this attitude confronts books which themselves do not conform to such techniques (as is usually the case with most books bound before the late eighteenth century), the results are usually lamentable.

So far as possible, the coherence of a book structure should not rely on adhesive alone, and should always be underpinned by a sound sewing structure, whether new or repaired. The moving parts should flex easily but must not be loose. This may sound contradictory, but flexibility which is gained by a loose connection between component parts will result in wear, abrasion and comparatively rapid collapse. Flexibility with strength is obtained by the firm and secure attachment of each component to the next within a structure built up from compatible materials which are in themselves of a suitable weight and flexibility. This means that when the book is opened, the component parts do not move independently of each other as they will if loosely connected, but within a firmly secured structure. The current revival of interest in non-adhesive structures makes this point all the more important, and it must be remembered that there are many books whose text-leaf material makes them unsuitable for non-adhesive structures of any sort. Basically, a book which opens too easily may be just as much at risk as one that hardly opens at all.

What to look for. It is impossible to give examples of everything here, but I will try to give examples of some of the things which can be done and the ways in which they ought to be done if they are used.

Paper repair. A great deal of paper repair done to the text-leaves of books is far too heavy and clumsy and will sooner or later cause further damage. The so-called Bodleian repair, using a handmade paper of the same weight as the leaf to be repaired, almost inevitably creates stress areas where the two papers overlap, usually weakening the old paper along the edge of the new. The carefully judged use of Japanese tissues, stuck either with paste or with reversible heat-set adhesives, will give strong, flexible and unobtrusive repairs. It is essential that the repaired leaves will flex and flow with the opening of the book without obstruction. Any awkwardness will inevitably result in damage. The same is true of vellum repairs: the repair vellum must be of the same weight and thickness, the same spine direction and with minimal overlap to prevent localised stiffness of the repaired leaf. On paper leaves, overall heatset lamination (as opposed to local repair) should be avoided wherever possible, and stiffly laminated leaves should not be combined in a textblock with unlaminated leaves. There may be cases in which overall lamination is the only sensible option, but it is all too often used as a cheap repair and not as a considered repair.

Lamination also destroys type-impression and the characteristic shape given to paper by early printing techniques. At the same time, the paper must be left sufficiently strong to take the sewing.

Endleaves. Old paper salvaged from other books should never be used, nor should the old end leaves be discarded or the old pastedowns covered up. Do not be fooled into thinking that pastedowns are of importance only when they have names or writing on them. Quite apart from the structure of the end leaves themselves, the very absence of an owner's name may be significant within the context of an historic collection. The endpapers, when either replaced or renewed, should also be sewn to the structure of the book. They should not be tipped to the first and last leaves of the textblock, where they will drag and eventually detach the leaves they are tipped to. They can, if required, be tipped to loose guards around the first and last gatherings. Where possible, linen joints should be incorporated, both to reinforce the sewing and, if the joint is pasted or glued to the board, to reinforce the joint—two different functions. It is quite possible not to paste down across the joint, and leave it open, a technique which was very common in the seventeenth century, and which can make for much easier repairs.

Sewing. Unless there are compelling reasons for doing otherwise, all books bound in boards should be sewn on, or the existing structures repaired with high-quality linen cords, tapes or braids with linen thread—all of which are available. Limp vellum bindings should be sewn on alum-tawed goatskin, which must be plump and soft and not glued to the vellum cover. Thin, hard skins will not function properly in the structures of limp vellum bindings and require adhesive to reinforce the link between sewing structure and cover—something which will often cause problems. Overcasting single or damaged leaves and then sewing them to the supports results in an essentially flawed structure, which will always depend for its stability on the strength of the spine linings. Where the linings are too strong, the book will not open, where they are too weak, it will break down into its component sections. Where such a structure is used on books with stiff leaves and/or narrow inner margins, the early breakdown of the structure is inevitable. It is always better, where practicable, to guard such leaves into pairs and sew through the guards—and explain what has been done in the conservation report, so that the book is not subsequently collated by reference to the sewing threads.

Spine linings. These, and the adhesives used to attach them, must always be listed in the conservation report. Such linings, in current conventional binding practice, are often used to reinforce inadequate sewing structures and give support to a spine that would otherwise collapse in vertical storage or open too sharply in use. All too often they either prevent reasonable access to the text, especially when used with heavy applications of glue, or they delaminate or crease and cause the premature collapse of the structure—the cause of the loud crack which can be heard in so many reading rooms. A properly designed sewing structure, using one of the many different structures and variations available, can be used to do what such heavy linings are supposed to do, but still leave the spine sufficiently flexible to allow a satisfactory opening. Where linings are used and need to be flexible, good quality linen should be used and not mull and jaconet, materials which have little initial strength and little long-term durability. A barrier layer of tissue and paste or paste alone should be used to protect the outer folds of the gatherings from the glue used to attach these linings. Hollow backs on books bound in boards should be avoided if possible, but if not, can be made of strong handmade paper, perhaps reinforced with linen, to give the strength normally lacking. Hollow backs can also be used very effectively in repairing books with fragile original spine leather which would either be crushed on a tight back or give such a stiff spine that the book will not open, and can be used even on books with raised bands. There are thousands of books where such tight-back rebacks have left the spines completely rigid—a question not of being sewn too tightly (the phrase all too often used), but of being lined and glued too heavily.

Boards. When new or replacement boards are required, they should both suit the weight and character of the book. Dense, hard millboard will not match the boards on, say, early seventeenth-century books, and a lighter-weight millboard or even museum mounting board (and acid-free or at least neutral pH as well) may prove better. It is also worth remembering that the heavier the board, the

Figure 4.

greater the strain on the joint and sewing structure of the book. Old boards—or indeed old material of any sort—should never be used to repair books to which they do not belong, despite the ease with which boards from books of the same size can be exchanged. When well done, the results can be indistinguishable from an entirely original, but repaired, book, which is, of course, historically indefensible. Where wooden boards are required, quarter-sawn timber should be used for maximum stability.

Board attachment. On all but the smallest books, the boards must be firmly attached to the sewing structure by the cords, tapes, braids, etc., used to sew the book or to reinforce the structure (Figure 4). This will mean that the woven textile attachment does not rely on the durability of any new covering material, which may indeed be dispensed with if this will mean leaving alone a fragile tooled spine which cannot safely be disturbed. For smaller and lightweight books, casing-in, or variations on it, can be used quite successfully, provided as always that the basic structure of the book is quite secure. If, however, the textblock is too heavy, then cased-in joints are likely to break down. It is always possible to support weak board attachment by the use of boxes or book-shoes with textblock supports or by storing the book horizontally. This is very useful if particular books cannot be successfully repaired perhaps because they have elaborately tooled spines which are too fragile to lift. Boards must never be re-attached by gluing strips of paper or cloth down the inside of the joint. This only attaches the heavy board to a single sheet of paper, often the title page or frontispiece, which will soon be removed or torn (Figure 5).

Endbands. The endbands (the generic term often now used to describe both head and tailbands) are, or

Figure 5.

rather should, be structural features of the book, supporting the spine at head and tail and possibly providing extra board attachment as well. They should be tied down regularly, in every gathering if possible, through a linen lining and can be used to re-attach the boards of a book, even whilst preserving in place the original end bands, which may never have been anything more than decorative. Where the spine of the book is flexible, they should be able to flex with it, and frequent tie-downs are essential here. Once again, linen thread should be used for strength and durability, and silk, if required, can be used as a secondary sewing over a primary sewing in linen, so that it will not matter when it rots. The absence (rather than loss) of end bands is also a feature of a binding which should be preserved, as it appears that the presence or otherwise of end bands on retail bindings is an indication of the economic status of the binding. Adding endbands to such bindings can lead people to think that the new endbands are replacements rather than additions—though a good conservation report should make this clear. Stuck-on bands, which have a long history, do not have the same function, and act

more like extensions of a spine lining. Though they were used in Germanic countries to reinforce board attachment from at least the early sixteenth century, they often do not serve well in regular use, though if still present they should be preserved (Figure 6). Their early use is not properly recorded, and we need the evidence of their introduction. Worked endbands are likely to be stronger, but need to be sewn in such a way that they are very firmly attached to the textblock. The conventional method of working them leaves them able to move independently of the textblock and thus likely to break away and cause damage.

Covering materials. Given the paucity of decent materials to use for covering books and the prominent position such materials have on the book, their selection and use is extremely problematical. We know that alum-tawed skins are extremely durable, and it is now possible to obtain high quality tawed calf as well as goat. Although the material is not always easy to stain evenly, particularly over large areas, it can be done and the material can be used with confidence that it will prove durable. Semi-chrome and semi-alum skins have also offered superior durability compared to skins prepared with synthetic tanning agents, but high quality sumac tanned goatskins are still available, as well as oakbark tanned calf, both traditional materials with a proven history of long-term stability behind them. If there is doubt about the quality of a skin that may have to be used for over-riding aesthetic reasons or needs to be pared so thin as to lose the greater part of its strength, then covering leather must not be called on to perform any vital structural function. That is, it should be accepted that the leather has only a cosmetic function, and that the real strength of the book is supplied by the

Figure 6.

underlying structure. Alternatively, it is quite possible to carry out the structural work and not put on a new spine at all. This prevents unnecessary work, and does not prevent or complicate the future use of a durable leather should the need arise, whilst leaving the book in a safe state to use.

Box design. It may appear that the design of a box is a very simple matter, and often it is. But there are several basic points of design to remember. The box must fit the book. If it is loose, then the book will be damaged as it slops around inside the box during transit, and will not receive proper support from the box when it is on the shelf. If the fit is too tight, the book will be damaged when it is moved in and out of the box. The normal drop-back box concentrates the handling of the book on the spine, and this may be a weak and vulnerable area. If this is so, then alternative designs are required. Textblock supports can be fitted if vertical storage is unavoidable, and so stop the textblock sagging and relieve strain on the joints. Pressure boxes can be used to keep vellum-leaved or vellum-covered books flat. Much simpler 'phase' boxes made out of acid-free card can be used to give immediate low cost—but also fitted—protection. Special cases can be made for the permanent protection of pamphlets, and all manner of special requirements can be catered for by inventive box design (Figure 7). In all these, acid-free and durable materials must be used, or the sometimes high cost of a customised box will be wasted. Some types of protective enclosure are very risky, in particular the slip case, and can cause more damage than no box at all.

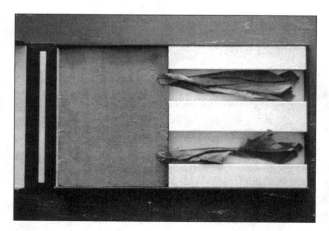

Figure 7.

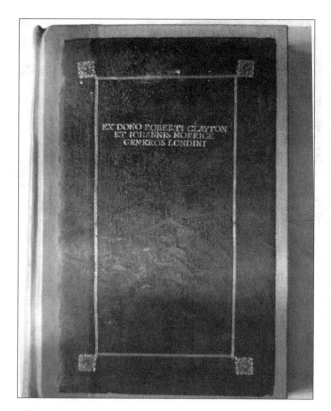

Figure 8.

Finally, a warning. We talk about reversible repairs, but what is meant by that is that the repairs, and the repairs alone, can be removed—and this is an extremely important aim of all proper conservation work. But what cannot be reversed is the fact that books have been repaired. The moment the structure of a book is interfered with it becomes impossible to put it back exactly as it was. Really crude repairs, like gluing a coarse thick piece of leather all around a book with detached boards, though sometimes laughable and certainly not to be recommended, often do much less damage than more 'professional' work. Even a book 'repaired' by having a piece of rexine glued all over it with Bostik (I have visited a library full of these) is probably salvageable, in that all the original components of the book are still there under the new cover, and can be retrieved. What we cannot undo is the sort of work where material has been discarded, the structure interfered with (if not entirely replaced) and only a sad ghost remains of the original binding (Figure 8). To avoid this sort of thing, we need to work out in advance what should be done, to make only informed and properly reasoned decisions and then make sure that what is decided on is done as well as it can be. Where this cannot be done, it is usually best to leave well alone.

REFERENCES

1. *The Works of Lord Byron*, 17 vols. (London: John Murray, 1832–3).

2. Bernard Middleton, *A History of English Craft Bookbinding Technique* (London: The Holland Press, 1978), p.172 and 172n. Further to complicate the history of the publication of this edition, I recently became aware of the fact that there were two slightly different versions of the block used on the spine. There is also a later issue in which the title on the first volume is also blocked directly onto the cloth.

3. Gruteras, Lampas, sive fax artium liberalium, hoc est Thesaurus Criticus, Frankfurt, 1602, in a seventeenth-century stiffboard parchment laced-case binding. It bears on the front flyleaf the manuscript note: "Mr Verdier's Servant is ready to attest, upon oath that the Volume which wounded the head of Robert Norris M.D., was Gruterus Lampas Critica, and that which broke Mr Lintot's Shin was Scaliger's Poetices. It was bought at the sale of Dr. Johnson's books by William Wyndham of Felbrigg Hall, Norfolk, where it has remained ever since." Now in the possession of the National Trust.

4. See Geoffrey Keynes, *A Bibliography of Dr. John Donne, Dean of St. Paul's,* 4th ed. (Oxford: Clarendon Press, 1973), and Mary Hobbs, *Bibliographical Notes and Queries*: Note 419 (Winter 1978). More books from the library of John Donne, *The Book Collector*, 29, No.4, (Winter 1980), p. 590.

5. See Nicholas Pickwood, "Codicology" in *The Eadwine Psalter. Text, Image, and Monastic Culture in Twelfth-Century Canterbury*, ed. Margaret Gibson, T.A. Heslop and Richard W. Pfaff (MHRA,1992), pp. 5–6.

6. Etienne Dolet, *Commentariorum Linguae Latinae*, (Lyon: 1536 and 1538), Southwell Minster Library.

7. I am grateful to Dr. Lotte Hellinga of the British Library for the identification of these leaves.

8. See in particular: Christopher Clarkson, "Board Slotting—a New Technique for Re-attaching Book- boards," in The Institute of Conservation, *Conference Papers Manchester 1992*, ed. Sheila Fairbrass (Leigh: The Institute of Paper Conservation, 1992), pp. 158–164.

Postscript

This paper was first written some 20 years ago, and in that time things have changed. I have become more and more strongly aware of the archæological value of bindings and of their importance as a means of throwing light on the history and culture of the book. Therefore, while I would not want to alter the main thrust of my argument, I would certainly be even more cautious about any interference into the structures of bindings, knowing as I do now how much significance can attach even to small and apparently unimportant details of those structures. I would also want, in the light of research done into German laced-case parchment bindings of the sixteenth century in more recent years, to amend my recommendation on the type of alum-tawed skin best used for the sewing supports on laced-case parchment bindings. The German examples typically used the thin, hard skins that I recommended should not be used (for valid structural reasons), but I had not seen enough of them when I wrote this paper—which goes to show how wary we must be of making pronouncements based on incomplete knowledge.

The more important development in those 20 years has been the increasing availability of full-colour, high-resolution digitised copies of books. This is having the somewhat unexpected effect, given the many reports we have seen of the death of the codex-form book in the face of the electronic revolution, of making real books, especially those in 'original condition', more not less special, and allowing the object-oriented values attached to books to assume greater importance in relation to the traditional text-oriented values. Could it be that on-line access to text is allowing our rare book collections slowly to transform themselves into museums? If so, it will certainly affect the argument put forward in this paper, if the requirement to prepare books for traditional use is being gradually eroded.

—*Nicholas Pickwoad, April 2012*

MARY LYNN RITZENTHALER

Excerpts from "Conservation Treatment"[1]

In ch. 10, Preserving Archives and Manuscripts, *2nd ed. (Chicago: Society of American Archivists, 2010), pp. 331–71.*

Treatment Approaches

Mass conservation procedures have been seen by some as the most viable hope for the long-term preservation of large archival and manuscript collections. In theory, mass procedures allow high-volume treatment of materials evidencing the same problem; individual handling is thus minimized and the cost of treatment per item greatly reduced. The potential for mass treatment seems most feasible in the areas of deacidification, fumigation, and some paper-strengthening techniques.[1] Most progress has been made with mass or batch deacidification of printed library materials, but, even here, the projected cost per item may place such advances out of the financial reach of most institutions. Archival materials are less likely candidates for most mass treatments than are library materials, given the eclectic nature of archival collections and the great diversity of materials and formats that can be encountered in even a single archives box. With a potentially large universe of papers, inks, photographs, and other media intermingled in a collection, it is impossible to know in advance the possible effect of a mass treatment on the majority of materials in any given container. The necessity of pre-screening holdings to segregate materials that could not be subjected to a particular treatment would eliminate one of the most appealing aspects of the concept and would also add time and cost to the project.

Because mass conservation treatments are unlikely to be available in the near future or appropriate for archival records, an archivist must consider provision of a temperature- and relative humidity-controlled environment as a mass preservation tool that is more realistically within the capability of most repositories. Such controls will effectively slow the rate of deterioration of most materials and should be a top priority. The concept of holdings mainte-

nance is also relevant in this context. This phased approach to preservation emphasizes measures that will benefit all holdings by housing them in protective and non-damaging enclosures and also provides a responsible foundation for implementing treatment programs as necessary.

Controlling the environment and providing proper housing fall within the realm of preventive preservation. Conservation treatment is a step beyond this. In an archival context, treatment is intended to return damaged materials to a usable condition with the goal of physical and chemical stability, not render cosmetic improvement. A condition survey undertaken by a conservator is one means of gathering data on the condition of the holdings and specific treatment needs. Treatment priorities can then be established based on an assessment of the data, the value of the records, and their expected use. From cost and time perspectives, condition surveys would likely focus on selected groups or subsets of records identified during collection-wide preservation risk assessment activities (see "Preservation Needs Assessment Collection Level," Chapter 2). This would appropriately narrow the focus to records that potentially warrant conservation treatment.

The concepts of *batch* and *single-item* treatments as they are evolving in archives conservation deserve brief mention. While conservators intend to carry out all treatments on archival records to the same high standard and precede each with necessary examination and testing, the nature of *many* records and their intended uses is such that it is possible to group them together as a batch treatment unit. Records composed of the same materials and exhibiting the same treatment requirements often can be subjected to the same sequence of treatment steps. A batch might consist of twenty-five, fifty, or one hundred or more documents, while batch treatments might include humidification, deacidification, mending, or a similar procedure that permits simultaneous or sequential treatment of materials in small groups. Batch treatment approaches are often appropriate for archival materials of low to moderate value or those that require routine treatments. Similarly, large groups of records being stabilized for digitizing are often efficiently treated in small groups to carry out mending or adhesive removal. Single-item treatment, on the other hand, is required for materials of high value as well as for treatments that are complex and require extensive testing and documentation. There is a need for both approaches in archives conservation.

Conservation Philosophy

RULE OF REVERSIBILITY

To the degree possible, a conservator should not undertake any procedure or treatment that he or she cannot later, if necessary, undo without harm to the document. Unfortunately, not all treatments or materials used in the past have withstood the test of time. If, a number of years after a treatment was carried out on a document, it becomes apparent that a particular procedure or material is causing damage-such as staining, yellowing, or a document to break along a mend line, or the document exhibits an accelerated rate of deterioration, it should be possible to reverse the procedure (i.e., return the document as nearly as possible to its pretreatment state). It is thus important to know the physical and chemical nature of all materials involved—both the collection items and the materials used in treatment—and how they may react together under various conditions over time. For example, will a given adhesive interact (cross link) with the material to which it is applied so that future removal is difficult or impossible? It is important to know the method of removing or reversing a material used in treatment. If the reversal process involves the use of water or other solvents, will these have any adverse effect on the paper, inks, or other media that may be present? It is also necessary to know the aging properties of treatment materials to select stable materials that will not yellow, discolor, or break down

over time. Treatment documentation (see Figure 1) should thoroughly describe treatments carried out and all materials used, including trade names. This can be invaluable information in later evaluating how a treatment has aged as well as in removing mends or linings, should that prove necessary.

With ongoing research and the passage of time, which allows for critical observation, techniques that once were considered acceptable may fall out of favor. One example is silking, an early method of reinforcement that provided support to paper documents by lining them with crepeline silk. Once it was determined that the silk could break down much sooner than the paper it was meant to support, this practice was discontinued. Another problem with silking was the adhesive used, which sometimes contained alum. This additive is now known to damage paper. Fortunately, most silking is reversible because the adhesives used are water soluble, and the inks on silked documents are of an age and type that tend to be stable in water.

Conservators are aware that reversibility is a difficult concept and one that is technically impossible. For example, if a conservator decides to bathe a paper document to reduce staining or discoloration, he or she could never return that document to an unbathed state (nor would one wish to do so). In a similar vein, if a conservator mended a paper manuscript with Japanese paper and starch paste, it is theoretically possible to remove the mend. In fact, however, it is probably impossible to remove every last vestige of paste from the paper, and a minute paste residue would be harmless at any rate. Thus, in actual application, the rule of reversibility is applied in a reasonable manner and with the understanding that materials and procedures used during the course of treatment must be stable and incapable of interacting with the item being treated in ways that alter its physical, chemical, aesthetic, or historical integrity. This is an area in which archival and conservation concerns are thoroughly congruent. The conservator's concerns in carrying out treatment are mirrored in the archivist's, who, as custodian of the records, must ensure that no actions undertaken on records—whether in the name of conservation, preservation, or archival processing—alter the nature of the records or their informational, evidential, or legal values.

APPLYING THE RIGHT TREATMENT SOLUTION

It is important to match the treatment solution to the problem to be remedied. The particular condition problem must be weighed against a range of possible solutions. The chosen solution should be most compatible in terms of like strength and material. In mending a torn document, for example, the tissue used to repair the tear must be of the appropriate weight, texture, flexibility, and color to approximate the strength and character of the item to be repaired. A mending tissue that is thinner and weaker than the document will not effect a strong, lasting repair. Conversely, a mending tissue that is much stronger and heavier than the paper to which it is applied will essentially overpower the problem and cause the weakened area to break down or deteriorate further.

The principle of compatibility also may be applied to treatment systems or technologies. There is sometimes the tendency to apply a given technology just because the ability to do so exists, whether or not it constitutes an appropriate solution in a particular situation. The factors of existing equipment, staff expertise in a given technique, or the weight of tradition should not influence or mandate the choice—or continuance—of inappropriate treatments. For example, in the past cellulose acetate lamination was an acceptable treatment solution in some instances (such as preparing newspapers for reformatting), but now it serves as an example of a procedure that was misapplied when individual decisions were not made regarding its appropriate application. It may be necessary to reject all potential treatment solutions at a given time if they are not right for the records in question. Treatment procedures that are routinely applied to everything require special scrutiny to ensure that proper decisions are made and that no single procedure becomes a rote activity.

It is important to accept the fact that, in some instances, it may be best to do nothing at all. There may be no currently acceptable treatment solutions for the problem, or the possibilities may be out of

reach due to technical or financial limitations. In such cases, it is better to provide optimum storage and to create a reproduction, if possible, to reduce handling of the material rather than to impose the wrong solution, which could cause even more serious problems over time. A document will experience much less damage by waiting until suitable treatment can be undertaken than by applying potential, harmful half-steps or having technically demanding work done by well-meaning but unqualified personnel.

Ethical approaches to conservation require the use of stable materials and treatment procedures that are sympathetic to the character of the original document or artifact. It is important to consider the age and composition of a given document as well as its physical and chemical stability in evaluating the suitability of potential treatments. The materials used in any treatment must be safe, must not hasten the deterioration of the original document, and must not appear in jarring contrast to its historic period.

RESTORATION

Although the term *conservation* has largely replaced *restoration,* both in common usage and in the approaches each term evokes, it is important to consider the differences because there are still many restoration workshops and practitioners of the art. The primary ethical consideration in treatment that might be described as restoration relates to how far reconstruction or replication of components of a historical document should be taken. There are a number of highly sophisticated techniques available that can be used to replace lost textual or image areas as well as to replicate antique paper and such characteristics as watermarks. A highly skilled craftsperson can easily "fool the eye," making new additions appear aged and timeworn. Archival—and ethical—considerations must be weighed to assure that the historical, legal, and evidential values of a document are not lost or obscured as a result of treatment.

The primary aim in most archives conservation is to ensure that the document is physically intact and as chemically stable as possible to assure long-term availability and use. While neat and careful work using appropriate materials is always important, cosmetic improvements for most archival records are less a concern than is physical and chemical stability. When the importance of an archival document warrants conservation treatment, it must be done with great care to ensure that its essential qualities, integrity, and authenticity are not cast into doubt. The goal is not to make the document appear pristine and new. Evidence of conservation treatment that involves paper fills or similar additions should be discernable to the practiced eye but not stark and glaring. Repairs should be subtle so that the eye does not travel immediately to them rather than focusing on the content of the document. Re-creation of missing text or image is normally considered unacceptable in archival contexts.

DOCUMENTATION

Adherence to conservation ethics requires that all treatments be documented. From a conservation standpoint, it is important to record all procedures and materials used, ensuring the possibility of future removal should it become necessary. Also, treatment records permit the assessment over time of the stability of treatment approaches and materials and the ways in which they react with various types of paper, other support materials, and media. From an archival perspective, documentation is also important because of the need to maintain a complete and accurate record of any changes to the records. For legal purposes, it may be necessary to detail any alteration of a document to assure its authenticity and continued validity.

Documentation may be a narrative description, a checklist, or a combination of the two (see Figure 1). Photographic documentation before, during, and after treatment can supplement written reports and is critical for documents of high value and/or for complex treatments. Typically, batch treatments are documented via a form or checklist, while single-item treatments are documented with more extensive narrative condition reports, treatment proposals, and treatment reports. Whatever the format, the treatment description should be specific in indicating precise procedures and materials used, including any trade names, if appropriate.

Other data to be recorded include a clear citation of the item(s) treated and its location in the holdings, description of original condition, date and place of treatment, name of conservator or firm, and any other information that is relevant to the document. All treatment should be fully documented, whether done in-house or on a contractual basis by an outside conservator or laboratory. Treatment documentation should be considered a permanent institutional record and should become part of the permanent file kept on each collection, along with such other vital records as the deed of gift, accession entry, and inventory or finding aid. All such reports should be generated on permanent-quality paper or, if maintained electronically, stored in a managed environment that will assure persistence of the information.

NOTE

1. Ideally, fumigation can be avoided if staff follows integrated pest management procedures that include environmental control and good housekeeping practices. When fumigation is necessary, however, it is advisable to consult a conservator or conservation scientist to discuss proposed fumigants and their potential affect on record materials. For a discussion of issues and options, see "Fumigation" in Chapter 8.

Figure 1.

Conservation Treatment Checklist

Collection/Record Group _____ Lab Transaction # _____

Accession Number/Series _____ Title _____

Description of Materials (media, support, format) _____

Number of Items, Volumes, Boxes _____ Value _____

Archivist Requesting Treatment _____ Date _____

Accepted in Lab by _____ Date _____

Assigned to _____ Date _____

Condition _____ Previous Treatment _____

Examination/Testing _____ Photography _____

Treatment Performed   **Materials Used**

Surface cleaned

Previous mends removed

Adhesive removed/reduced

Humidified/flattened

Washed

Deacidified

    Aqueous solution

    Non-aqueous solution

Mended

Encapsulated

Disbound/disassembled

Removed from frame

Matted/mounted for exhibit

Custom housed

Stabilized for duplication

Treatment Notes

Number of Items Treated _____ Date _____

Received from Lab by _____ Date _____

chapter 7

FRAMEWORKS FOR DIGITAL PRESERVATION

RECORDS THAT ARE BORN DIGITAL OR CONVERTED to digital form need to be continuously sustained to assure long-term access to them. That deceptively simple statement belies the complexity of such an endeavor. The components of preservation are many: technical, organizational, public policy, educational, legal, fiscal, social, and so on. One problem is that best practices are difficult to define and standards are still evolving as technology evolves. Content creation, integrity, and maintenance must conform to standards and best practices. Added to all of the above, there must be sustainable economic models on which digital preservation actions can rest. This chapter includes readings relating to most of these themes, though two, legal issues and metadata, are not represented here with their own readings. However, these subjects are addressed throughout the readings in this book.[1]

Over a thousand publications, in print and online, are devoted to preserving digital content;[2] this chapter contains just eight, along with some definitions. While it is not possible to synthesize such a complex field in just one chapter, it is possible to present seminal thinking about these matters. The goal, then, is not to present the reader with the most up-to-date developments in the field. Rather it is to frame the key issues by presenting the reader with some "classic" pieces published between the mid-1990s and 2010. References in this introduction will be made to some recent works, and readers are encouraged to peruse the web, where many new writings now solely reside.

Definitions

What does preservation mean in the digital environment? That question is posed by Ross Harvey in his *Preserving Digital Materials*.[3] The focus is shifting from a concentration on preserving the physical object to a broader need to determine which information must be preserved, regardless of its medium, its creator, or where it is held. This shift is concomitant with the changing nature of the collections themselves.

New terms are coming into use that signal not only the growing complexity of preserving our digital heritage, but the broadening of responsibilities and activities. For example, librarians are called upon to help e-science researchers gain access to large data sets, develop data sustainability plans, or develop user-focused and repository-based services to manage scholarly content. Museum curators need to be "stewards of an artist's intentions"[4] when there is no physical work to be preserved. Universities need professionals who can provide strategic direction for preserving institutionally produced content. Thus, in addition to "digital preservation," we also see "digital stewardship," "digital curatorship," and "data curation" in job descriptions to describe the responsibilities of those who work in heritage institutions.

Digital preservation is the term that has been used the longest, and the Association for Library Collections & Technical Services, a division of the American Library Association, developed short, medium, and long definitions for it in 2007:

Short Definition

Digital preservation combines policies, strategies and actions that ensure access to digital content over time.

Medium Definition

Digital preservation combines policies, strategies and actions to ensure access to reformatted and born digital content regardless of the challenges of media failure and technological change. The goal of digital preservation is the accurate rendering of authenticated content over time.

Long Definition

Digital preservation combines policies, strategies and actions to ensure the accurate rendering of authenticated content over time, regardless of the challenges of media failure and technological change. Digital preservation applies to both born digital and reformatted content.

Digital preservation policies document an organization's commitment to preserve digital content for future use; specify file formats to be preserved and the level of preservation to be provided; and ensure compliance with standards and best practices for responsible stewardship of digital information.

Digital preservation strategies and actions address content creation, integrity and maintenance.

Content creation includes:
- Clear and complete technical specifications
- Production of reliable master files
- Sufficient descriptive, administrative and structural metadata to ensure future access
- Detailed quality control of processes

Content integrity includes:
- Documentation of all policies, strategies and procedures
- Use of persistent identifiers
- Recorded provenance and change history for all objects
- Verification mechanisms
- Attention to security requirements
- Routine audits

Content maintenance includes:
- A robust computing and networking infrastructure
- Storage and synchronization of files at multiple sites
- Continuous monitoring and management of files
- Programs for refreshing, migration and emulation
- Creation and testing of disaster prevention and recovery plans
- Periodic review and updating of policies and procedures

Traditional preservation was a set of linear operations: information was created and/or published, and it was acquired, organized, and cared for by libraries, museums, and archives. Sometimes items had to be repaired and conserved when acquired; usually treatment came later in the life of the item, unless damage occurred due to an accident or a disaster. Proper environmental care, handling, and storage assured long-term preservation of, and access to, items.

The digital preservation life cycle is dynamic, not linear, and it requires constant and multiple actions. For example, as soon as a digital item is created, metadata is needed to support and document preservation. Provisions for copying and backup must be made, legal issues such as copyright must be attended to, and user expectations must be met. Finally, digital content needs to be stored in a trusted digital repository which provides storage, migration capabilities, and access.

Butch Lazorchak, a regular blogger on the Library of Congress's site *The Signal: Digital Preservation*, compares digital preservation to digital curation and digital stewardship:

> [The] idea of "preserving" has long been part of the Library of Congress' mission, so it was with little surprise that our program to address the challenges of digital materials was named the "National Digital Information Infrastructure and **Preservation** Program"; the founding NDIIPP report was called "**Preserving** our Digital Heritage"; and that our website is called "**digitalpreservation.gov.**" Working to figure out how to "not lose" existing digital information was a significant early driver of NDIIPP.
>
> In contrast, "digital curation" concepts started to appear after "digital preservation" had already put a stake in the ground. "Curation" takes a "whole life" approach to digital materials to address the selection, maintenance, collection and archiving of digital assets in addition to their preservation.
>
> Digital curation concepts largely arose from the scientific data and e-science communities, who have traditionally been driven more by immediate data re-use concerns than by "preserving" as an abstract concept... .

"Curation" is a useful concept for describing the evolving whole-life view of digital preservation, but [it] concentrates on underpinning activities of building and managing collections of digital assets and so does not fully describe a more broad approach to digital materials management... .

Enter "stewardship." "Stewardship" concepts evolved out of the environmental community, but that community's idea of holding resources in trust for future generations has long resonated in the digital preservation community.

"Digital Stewardship" satisfyingly brings preservation and curation together ... pulling in the life-cycle approach of curation along with research in digital libraries and electronic records archiving, broadening the emphasis from the e-science community on scientific data to address all digital materials, while continuing to emphasize digital preservation as a core component of action.[5]

Terminology is never static, and other terms may emerge by the time the ink in this volume has dried.

———

The earliest readings in this chapter date to the 1990s, a decade in which a number of professionals identified the preservation problems inherent in preserving digital content, such as the fugitive nature of digital media, the lack of administrative and technical infrastructures to support initiatives, and the lack of standards in the field. And many of these pieces were written before the World Wide Web and all of its attendant preservation opportunities and challenges.

In *Preservation in the Digital World,* **Paul Conway** addresses these issues while also observing that traditional preservation concepts and ethics can be a starting point for thinking about digital content. He proposes that

> the real challenge is creating appropriate organizational contexts for action. Cooperative strategies adopted from ongoing preservation practice are not all that is needed to address the complexities or the costs of digital technologies. Libraries and archives must do more than simply divide the

preservation pie. The national digital libraries that are now under construction should be built under an umbrella of guiding preservation concepts. Additionally, new approaches to creating and maintaining digital files cooperatively must be developed. The acceptance of shared responsibility and shared funding commitments will preserve access to what are, in essence, unique electronic collections.

Margaret Hedstrom's 1991 article, "Understanding Electronic Incunabula," calls for a framework for research on electronic records issues. She views electronic records as an evolving form of documentation that can be better understood by studying the history of technology as well as the historical, social, and cultural uses of records. She uses the term *incunabula*—which refers to the first fifty years of printing in the West, roughly 1455 to 1500—to refer to early electronic records, since the term is often used to refer to origins of things. The most obvious difference between early electronic records and incunabula documents and books is that many of the latter still survive, over 500 years later. Metaphors aside, this is an important article because Hedstrom provides a blueprint for research. She herself would become an important researcher in digital preservation—a term not yet used in 1991.

Jeff Rothenberg was another early researcher to address the challenges of preserving electronic records. Although he has long published in professional journals, his 1995 article in *Scientific American* brought the issues of digital preservation to a wide audience in a succinct and engaging way. Advocacy continues to be a key component of preservation. We need the support of the public to solve the challenges of digital preservation.

In *Why Digitize?* **Abby Rumsey** presents an analysis of what digitization is and is not. She addressed concerns about digitization at a time (1999) in which many publications were merely finding fault with it. A good example is the section "Digitization is not Preservation—at Least not Yet" in which she considers issues of durability and authenticity. Although these were—and still are—serious concerns, digital files can be refreshed and stored properly, and do not decay with use, unlike other media. "Analog is a dif-ferent way of knowing than digital, and each has its intrinsic virtues and limitations." More broadly, she concludes that digital technology holds much promise to reshape scholarly communication. Fifteen years later, this thoughtful piece still has much to offer.

Brian Lavoie and **Lorcan Dempsey** focus on the role of preservation in supporting research and learning in digital-information environments in "Thirteen Ways of Looking at…Digital Preservation" (2004). The focus, they believed, had been primarily on the technical preservation issues and not enough on *digital stewardship*. They say, "digital preservation is not an isolated process, but instead, one component of a broad aggregation of interconnected services, policies, and stakeholders which together constitute a digital information environment." The authors present thirteen ways of viewing digital preservation, some of which have been covered elsewhere in the literature, such as their first description of "preservation as an … ongoing activity." Other ways of viewing are more provocative, such as XI, "digital preservation as…an arm's length transaction." The authors posit that digital preservation is not just about stewardship, and that most institutions do not have the resources to play the role of stewards. Rather, preservation must focus equally on third-party services, sustainable pricing models, and so on.

Number V, "Digital preservation as…an economically sustainable activity," is an area in which Brian Lavoie has continued to work. He has co-chaired the Task Force on Sustainable Digital Preservation and Access; an excerpt from the report *Sustainable Economics for a Digital Planet* closes this chapter.

Clifford Lynch addresses the concept of stewardship in a novel way in his "Repatriation, Reconstruction, and Cultural Diplomacy in the Digital World," through the digitization of collections and photographs of items in collections. Repatriation of cultural heritage implies global stewardship; "cultural heritage belongs to everybody, and everybody shares some obligation to exercise responsible stewardship over it." However, there are some challenges to the stewardship of digital representations of museum objects. At the same time, "in an age of repatriation, cultural memory organizations can…still make available high-quality surrogates not only of their holdings but also of materials that they no longer hold—or, for that matter, of materials that they never held." Responsible stewardship should make these images widely available as a safeguard against disasters that may damage or destroy collections. Further, good photo-documentation is an aid in recovering stolen goods. While digital images can never replace damaged or lost originals, they do at least preserve some of the information inherent in those originals.

The final two pieces provide some measure of how digital preservation initiatives have progressed over the past fifteen-plus years. The first is an excerpt from *Preserving Digital Information,* a report of the Task Force on Archiving of Digital Information that was published by the Council of Library and Information Resources (CLIR) in 1996. The Task Force was created in 1994 and included representatives from libraries, archives, museums, publishing, industry, government, and other constituencies. Their task was to frame the key issues that would need to be resolved to assure continuing access to digital records.

The Task Force made a number of recommendations that seem obvious today, but were forward-looking back then. Indeed, many of the recommendations were subsequently acted upon, such as "Engage actively in national policy efforts to design and develop the national information infrastructure to ensure that longevity of information is an explicit goal." The National Digital Information Infrastructure Preservation Program (NDIIPP), was established by the Library of Congress in 2000; its work is being extended by the National Digital Stewardship Alliance, which began in 2010. National initiatives and collaborations now exist throughout the world.

Another recommendation was that standards, criteria, and mechanisms be established for certifying "repositories of digital information as archives." Today such repositories abound, including DSpace, created by MIT Libraries and Hewlett Packard in 2002, and now in partnership with Fedora as DuraSpace. However, work still needs to be done to assure the support and maintenance of the many home-grown repositories. In 2008, JISC founded the Repositories Support Project in the UK. Resources will continue to grow.

The CLIR report also addressed the need for funding digital preservation. Work in this area has been slow to evolve because of the enormous complexities inherent in ensuring ongoing access to digital content. A 2010 report tackles these multi-faceted issues: *Sustainable Economics for a Digital Planet: Ensuring Long-Term Access to Digital Information* (**Blue Ribbon Task Force** [written and edited by Abby Smith Rumsey]). As the title suggests, it is about more than the cost itself; rather, it addresses a host of sustainability issues.

The Task Force focused on four "content domains with diverse preservation profiles":

Scholarly discourse: the published output of scholarly inquiry;
Research data: the primary inputs into research, as well as the first-order results of the research;
Commercially owned cultural content: culturally significant digital content that is owned by a private entity and is under copyright protection; and
Collaboratively produced Web content: Web content that is created interactively, the result of collaboration and contributions by consumers ("Executive Summary").

The report also addresses the concept of digital preservation as an economic good by examining the four core attributes that are common to all preserved digital assets: "The demand for digital preservation is a *derived demand*, digital materials are *depreciable durable assets*, digital assets are *nonrival in consumption* and create a free-rider potential, and the digital preservation process is *temporally dynamic and path-dependent*."

These last two publications are bookends to the many issues that we have considered in this chapter. However, there is recent research in the field that focuses on creators and users of digital content. It is worth mentioning this scholarship even though it was not possible to include examples here.

In the late 1990s, Margaret Hedstrom and her doctoral students at the University of Michigan began to undertake research related to digital preservation from the user's perspective. In their CAMiLEON Project they studied the significant properties that users consider worth preserving in old computer games such as Chuckie Egg. One of the articles in which they report on their several studies is "'The Old Version Flickers More': Digital Preservation from the User's Perspective."[6]

Megan Winget, also studying games, in 2011 published a useful literature review on videogame preservation and massively multiplayer online role-playing games.[7] Jerome P. McDonough studied the preservation of games using data models such as the Functional Requirements for Bibliographic Records (FRBR) and the Open Archival Information System (OAIS).[8]

Scholars are also now studying how users archive and preserve their digital possessions. Catherine C. Marshall has found that consumers are not well aware of the impermanence of their digital possessions, and if aware, feel powerless to do anything about it.[9] Andrea J. Copeland studied the personal preservation decision-making of public library users, a group not generally included in preservation research. She examined their social, cognitive, and affective influences.[10]

The focus on preservation from the perspective of the user adds an important dimension to research. As people become ever more engaged in the creation and management of new forms of digital content (e.g., through social networking) they will have an enhanced role in its preservation.

NOTES

1. A recently published article relates to issues addressed in this chapter. See Tomas A. Lipinski and Andrea Copeland, "Look Before You License: The Use of Public-Sharing Websites in Building Co-Created Community Repositories," *Preservation, Digital Technology & Culture* 42.4 (2013): 174–98.

2. *See* Charles W. Bailey, Jr., *Digital Curation Bibliography: Preservation and Stewardship of Scholarly Works* (Houston, TX: Digital Scholarship, 2012). This is a selective bibliography of over 650 English-language publications, mostly from 2000–

2011. There were hundreds of publications by 1999, when I was gathering resources for a publication. Much has been published in Chinese, and a host of other languages as well, so the total of publications in this area probably approaches 2,000.

3. Ross Harvey, *Preserving Digital Materials,* 2nd ed. (Berlin and Boston: Walter de Gruyter, 2012), p. 7.

4. Maxwell Anderson, "Ownership Isn't Everything—The Future Will Be Shared," *The Art Newspaper* 216 (September 2010), accessed August 29, 2012, www.theartnewspaper.com/articles/Ownership-isn-t-everything-The-future-will-be-shared/21425.

5. Butch Lazorchak, "Digital Preservation, Digital Curation, Digital Stewardship: What's in (Some) Names?" In *The Signal: Digital Preservation* (August 23, 2011), accessed August 29, 2012, http://blogs.loc.gov/digitalpreservation/2011/08/digital-preservation-digital-curation-digital-stewardship-what%E2%80%99s-in-some-names.

6. Margaret L. Hedstrom, et al. "'The Old Version Flickers More': Digital Preservation from the User's Perspective," *American Archivist* 69 (Spring/Summer 2006): 159–87.

7. Megan A. Winget, "Videogame Preservation and Massively Multiplayer Online Role-Playing Games: A Review of the Literature." *Journal of the American Society for Information Science and Technology* 62.10 (2011): 1869–83.

8. Jerome P. McDonough, "Packaging Videogames for Long-Term Preservation: Integrating FRBR and the OAIS Reference Model," *Journal of the American Society for Information Science and Technology* 62.1 (2011): 171–84.

9. Catherine C. Marshall, "Rethinking Personal Digital Archiving, Part 1: Four Challenges from the Field," *D-Lib Magazine* 14.3–4 (March/April 2008), accessed August 29, 2012, www.dlib.org/dlib/march08/marshall/03marshall-pt1.html.

10. Andrea J. Copeland, "Analysis of Public Library Users' Digital Preservation Practices," *Journal of the American Society for Information Science and Technology* 62.7 (2011): 1288–1300.

TASK FORCE ON ARCHIVING OF DIGITAL INFORMATION

Excerpts from *Preserving Digital Information: Report of the Task Force on Archiving of Digital Information*

By Donald Waters and John Garrett. Commissioned by the Commission on Preservation and Access and the Research Libraries Group. Washington, DC: CPA and RLG, May 1, 1996.

Pages III–IV. Executive Summary

In December 1994, the Commission on Preservation and Access and the Research Libraries Group created the Task Force on Digital Archiving. The purpose of the Task Force was to investigate the means of ensuring "continued access indefinitely into the future of records stored in digital electronic form." Composed of individuals drawn from industry, museums, archives and libraries, publishers, scholarly societies and government, the Task Force was charged specifically to:

> "Frame the key problems (organizational, technological, legal, economic etc.) that need to be resolved for technology refreshing to be considered an acceptable approach to ensuring continuing access to electronic digital records indefinitely into the future.
>
> "Define the critical issues that inhibit resolution of each identified problem.
>
> "For each issue, recommend actions to remove the issue from the list.
>
> "Consider alternatives to technology refreshing.
>
> "Make other generic recommendations as appropriate" (see Appendix A for the full charge).

The document before you is the final report of the Task Force. Following its initial deliberations, the Task Force issued a draft report in August, 1995. An extended comment period followed, during which a wide variety of interested parties located both here in the United States and abroad contributed numerous helpful and thoughtful suggestions for improving the draft report. The Task Force benefited greatly from the comments it received and incorporated many of them in this final report.

In taking up its charge, the Task Force on Archiving of Digital Information focused on materials already in digital form and recognized the need to protect against both media deterioration and technological obsolescence. It started from the premise that migration is a broader and richer concept than "refreshing" for identifying the range of options for digital preservation. Migration is a set of organized tasks designed to achieve the periodic transfer of digital materials from one hardware/software configuration to another, or from one generation of computer technology to a subsequent generation. The purpose of migration is to preserve the integrity of digital objects and to retain the ability for clients to retrieve, display, and otherwise use them in the face of constantly changing technology. The Task Force regards migration as an essential function of digital archives.

The Task Force envisions the development of a national system of digital archives, which it defines as repositories of digital information that are collectively responsible for the long-term accessibility of the nation's social, economic, cultural and intellectual heritage instantiated in digital form. Digital archives are distinct from digital libraries in the sense that digital libraries are repositories that collect and provide access to digital information, but may or may not provide for the long-term storage and access of that information. The Task Force has deliberately taken a functional approach in these critical definitions and in its general treatment of digital preservation so as to prejudge neither the question of institutional structure nor the specific content that actual digital archives will select to preserve.

The Task Force sees repositories of digital information as held together in a national archival system primarily through the operation of two essential mechanisms. First, repositories claiming to serve an archival function must be able to prove that they are who they say they are by meeting or exceeding the standards and criteria of an independently-administered program for archival certification. Second, certified digital archives will have available to them a critical fail-safe mechanism. Such a mechanism, supported by organizational will, economic means and legal right, would enable a certified archival repository to exercise an aggressive rescue function to save culturally significant digital information. Without the operation of a formal certification program and a fail-safe mechanism, preservation of the nation's cultural heritage in digital form will likely be overly dependent on marketplace forces, which may value information for too short a period and without applying broader, public interest criteria.

In order to lay out the framework for digital preservation that it has envisioned, the Task Force provides an analysis of the digital landscape, focusing on features, including stakeholder interests, that affect the integrity of digital information objects and which determine the ability of digital archives to preserve such objects over the long term. The Task Force then introduces the principle that responsibility for archiving rests initially with the creator or owner of the information and that digital archives may invoke a fail-safe mechanism to protect culturally valuable information. The report explores in detail the roles and responsibilities associated with the critical functions of managing the operating environment of digital archives, strategies for migration of digital information, and costs and financial matters.

The report concludes with a set of recommendations on which the Commission on Preservation and Access and the Research Libraries Group need to act, either separately or together and in concert with other individuals or organizations as appropriate. The Commission and the Research Libraries Group should:

1. Solicit proposals from existing and potential digital archives around the country and provide coordinating services for selected participants in a cooperative project designed to place information objects from the early digital age into trust for use by future generations.

2. Secure funding and sponsor an open competition for proposals to advance digital archives, particularly with respect to removing legal and economic barriers to preservation.

3. Foster practical experiments or demonstration projects in the archival application of technologies and services, such as hardware and software emulation algorithms, transaction systems for property rights and authentication mechanisms, which promise to facilitate the preservation of the cultural record in digital form.

4. Engage actively in national policy efforts to design and develop the national information infrastructure to ensure that longevity of information is an explicit goal.

5. Sponsor the preparation of a white paper on the legal and institutional foundations needed for the development of effective fail-safe mechanisms to support the aggressive rescue of endangered digital information.

6. Organize representatives of professional societies from a variety of disciplines in a series of forums designed to elicit creative thinking about the means of creating and financing digital archives of specific bodies of information.

7. Institute a dialogue among the appropriate organizations and individuals on the standards, criteria and mechanisms needed to certify repositories of digital information as archives.

8. Identify an administrative point of contact for coordinating digital preservation initiatives in the United States with similar efforts abroad.

9. Commission follow-on case studies of digital archiving to identify current best practices and to benchmark costs in the following areas: (a) design of systems that facilitate archiving at the creation stage; (b) storage of massive

quantities of culturally valuable digital information; (c) requirements and standards for describing and managing digital information; and (d) migration paths for digital preservation of culturally valuable digital information.

Given the analysis in this report and its findings, we expect the Commission and the Research Libraries Group to pursue these recommendations on a national and, where appropriate, an international front, and to generate dialogue, interaction and products that will advance the development of trusted systems for digital preservation. There are numerous challenges before us, but also enormous opportunities to contribute to the development of a national infrastructure that positively supports the long-term preservation of culturally significant digital information.

John Garrett (co-chair)
CyberVillages Corporation

Donald Waters (co-chair)
Yale University

Pages 1–4. Introduction

Today we can only imagine the content of and audience reaction to the lost plays of Aeschylus. We do not know how Mozart sounded when performing his own music. We can have no direct experience of David Garrick on stage. Nor can we fully appreciate the power of Patrick Henry's oratory. Will future generations be able to encounter a Mikhail Baryshnikov ballet, a Barbara Jordan speech, a Walter Cronkite newscast, or an Ella Fitzgerald scat on an Ellington tune?

We may think that libraries and archives have stemmed the tide of cultural memory loss. We rely on them to track our genealogies, to understand what science has discovered, to appreciate the stories people told a hundred years ago, and to know how we educated our children during the Depression. Even seemingly trivial, ephemeral, or innocuous information that libraries maintain has unanticipated uses. For example, early in this century railways provided the primary means of transporting oil. The competition for this lucrative business led to rebates, kickbacks and other dubious business practices. The United States countered such practices by enacting severe antitrust laws. Germany, however, prohibited secret rates by requiring all oil carriage firms to publish their tariffs in the railway trade press. During World War II, nobody in Germany thought to repeal the law. Every week, an American agent went to a Swiss library, read the relevant newspaper, and worked out how much oil the Nazis were transporting and where.

Society, of course, has a vital interest in preserving materials that document issues, concerns, ideas, discourse and events. We may never know with certitude how many children Thomas Jefferson fathered or exactly how Hitler died. However, to understand the evils of slavery and counter assertions that the Holocaust never happened, we need to ensure that documents and other raw materials, as well as accumulated works about our history, survive so that future generations can reflect on and learn from them. The Soviet Union stands as an example of a society in which history was routinely rewritten and pages of encyclopedias were cut out and replaced according to current political whim. The ability of a culture to survive into the future depends on the richness and acuity of its members' sense of history.

THE FRAGILITY OF CULTURAL MEMORY IN A DIGITAL AGE

But our ability and commitment as a society to preserve our cultural memory are far from secure. Custodians of the cultural record have always had to manage the inherent conflict between letting people use manuscripts, books, recordings or videos, and being sure that they are preserved for future use. For works printed on acidic wood pulp paper, as most books have been since 1850, we measure the remaining lifetime of those materials in decades, not centuries.

And what of the information we are now creating and storing using digital technology? In 1993, forty-five percent of U.S. workers were using a computer (United States Census Bureau 1993); the number is surely larger now. Virtually all printing and a rapidly increasing amount of writing is accomplished with computers. Professional sound recording is digital, and digital video is on the verge of moving from experimental to practical applications.

As a means of recording and providing access to our cultural memory, digital technology has numerous advantages and may help relieve the traditional conflict between preservation and access. For materials stored digitally, users operate on exact images of the original works stored in their local computers. Separating usage from the original in this way, digital technology affords multiple, simultaneous uses from a single original in ways that are simply not possible for materials stored in any other form. Digital technology also yields additional, effective means of access. In full text documents, a reader can retrieve needed information by searching for words, combinations of words, phrases or ideas. Readers can also manipulate the display of digital materials by choosing whether to view digital materials on a screen, store them on their computer or external media, or to print them.

THE LIMITS OF DIGITAL TECHNOLOGY

Digital technology, however, poses new threats and problems as well as new opportunities. Its functionality comes with complexity. Anyone with a compass (or a clear night to view the position of the stars in relation to true north) could theoretically set up or repair a sundial. A digital watch is more useful and accurate for telling time than a sundial, but few people can repair it or even understand how it works. Reading and understanding information in digital form requires equipment and software, which is changing constantly and may not be available within a decade of its introduction. Who today has a punched card reader, a Dectape drive, or a working copy of FORTRAN II? Even newer technology such as 9-track tape is rapidly becoming obsolete. We cannot save the machines if there are no spare parts available, and we cannot save the software if no one is left who knows how to use it.

Rapid changes in the means of recording information, in the formats for storage, and in the technologies for use threaten to render the life of information in the digital age as, to borrow a phrase from Hobbes,

"nasty, brutish and short." Some information no doubt deserves such a fate, but numerous examples illustrate the danger of losing valuable cultural memories that may appear in digital form. Consider, for example, the now famous, but often misrepresented, case of the 1960 Census.

As it compiled the decennial census in the early sixties, the Census Bureau retained records for its own use in what it regarded as "permanent" storage. In 1976, the National Archives identified seven series of aggregated data from the 1960 Census files as having long-term historical value. A large portion of the selected records, however, resided on tapes that the Bureau could read only with a UNIVAC type II-A tape drive. By the mid-seventies, that particular tape drive was long obsolete, and the Census Bureau faced a significant engineering challenge in preserving the data from the UNIVAC type II-A tapes. By 1979, the Bureau had successfully copied onto industry-standard tapes nearly all the data judged then to have long-term value.

Though largely successful in the end, the data rescue effort was a signal event that helped move the Committee on the Records of Government six years later to proclaim that "the United States is in danger of losing its memory." The Committee did not bother to describe the actual details of the migration of the 1960 census records. Nor did it analyze the effects on the integrity of the constitutionally-mandated census of the nearly 10,000 (of approximately 1.5 million) records of aggregated data that the rescue effort did not successfully recover. Instead, it chose to register its warning on the dangers of machine obsolescence in apocryphal terms. With more than a little hyperbole, it wrote that "when the computer tapes containing the raw data from the 1960 federal census came to the attention of NARS [the National Archives and Records Service], there were only two machines in the world capable of reading those tapes: one in Japan and the other already deposited in the Smithsonian as a relic" (1985:9, 86–87).[1]

Other examples lack the memorable but false details accompanying the 1960 Census story, but they do equally illustrate how readily we can lose our heritage in electronic form when the custodian makes no plans for long-term retention in a changing technical environment. In 1964, the first electronic mail message was sent from either the Massachusetts Institute of Technology, the Carnegie Institute of Technology or Cambridge University. The message does not survive, however, and so there is no documentary record to determine which group sent the pathbreaking message. Satellite observations of Brazil in the 1970s, critical for establishing a time-line of changes in the Amazon basin, are also lost on the now obsolete tapes to which they were written (cf. National Research Council 1995a: 31; Eisenbeis 1995: 136, 173–74).

Similarly, in the late 1960s, the New York State Department of Commerce and Cornell University undertook the Land Use and Natural Resources Inventory Project (LUNR). The LUNR project produced a computerized map of New York State depicting patterns of land usage and identifying natural resources. It created a primitive geographic information system by superimposing a matrix over aerial photographs of the entire state and coding each cell according to its predominant features. The data were used for several comprehensive studies of land use patterns that informed urban planning, economic development, and environmental policy. In the mid-1980s, the New York State Archives obtained copies of the tapes containing the data from the LUNR inventory along with the original aerial photographs and several thousand mylar transparencies. Staff at the State Archives attempted to preserve the LUNR tapes, but the problems proved insurmountable. The LUNR project had depended on customized software programs to represent and analyze the data, and these programs were not saved with the data. Even if the software had been retained, the hardware and operating system needed to run the software were no longer available. As a consequence, researchers wishing to study changes in land use patterns now have to re-digitize the data from the hard-copy base maps and transparencies at the State Archives or rekey data from printouts at Cornell's Department of Manuscripts & University Archives.[2]

Today, information technologies that are increasingly powerful and easy to use, especially like those that support the World Wide Web, have unleashed the production and distribution of digital information. Such information is penetrating and transforming nearly every aspect of our culture. If we are effectively to preserve for future generations the portion of this rapidly expanding corpus of information in digital form that represents our cultural record, we need to understand the costs of doing so and we need to commit ourselves technically, legally, economically and organizationally to the full dimensions of the task. Failure to look for trusted means and methods of digital preservation will certainly exact a stiff, long-term cultural penalty. The Task Force on Archiving of Digital Information here reports on its search for some of those means and methods.

NOTES

1. The Task Force on the Archiving of Digital Information is indebted to Margaret Adams and Thomas Brown of the Center for Electronic Records at the National Archives and Records Administration for essential information in this brief account of the preservation of the 1960 Census data and its aftermath. Responding to a query from the Task Force, they reviewed the correspondence, memoranda and records schedules of the Center for Electronic Records and prepared a useful historical narrative about the actual treatment of the 1960 census data. See Adams and Brown (1996).

   In a separate correspondence addressed to the Task Force, Adams emphasizes that the story about there being only two machines in 1985 that could read the 1960 census data is "apocryphal" and observes that custodians did not, because of machine obsolescence, lose any census data that they intended to save. However, she notes that custodians did form their intentions based on the best knowledge that they had at the time (Adams 1995). The Report of the Committee on the Records of Government (1985: 88 n. 40) makes a similar point. It argues that "in the early years of data processing, archivists and historians failed to recognize the potential use of many machine-readable data files" and so routinely destroyed some of those files pertaining to earlier censuses.

   In the early days of data processing, custodians of data records simply had no basis to anticipate potential uses that seem obvious today to us in hindsight. There is a potent research topic here. As the Task Force goes on to argue in the next sections of this report, archiving is, in the end, a matter of human organization and the exercise of best judgment. The power and danger of technological obsolescence is that it sometimes requires judgments from actors and organizations on a schedule that may not match their willingness and competence to make them.

2. Margaret Hedstrom, the former Chief of the State Records Advisory Service in the New York State Archives and Records Administration, brought this example to the attention of the Task Force.

Pages 21–39.
Archival Roles and Responsibilities

As the networked environment for digital information expands and matures, intense interactions among the parties with stakes in digital information are providing the opportunity and stimulus for new stakeholders to emerge and add value, and for the relationships and division of labor among existing stakeholders to assume new forms. For example, naming authorities for digital information objects are being organized, creators are assuming the role of publishers, publishers are contemplating the construction of digital archives, and collector/disseminators are facing the need to resolve the names and locations of digital objects. Moreover, all of the stakeholders, including the new ones who are emerging, are exercising their various functions simultaneously in relation to particular digital information objects. That is, for example, the creator of an object may retain a financial or other stake in its dissemination and use for an extended period, just as a publisher/disseminator of the object exercises the same or similar interest. Similarly, stakeholders acting as collectors/disseminators may retain an interest in the continuing use of the object, at the same time as they or other stakeholders acting as digital archives take steps to preserve it for future use (Wiederhold 1995).

In a time of such sustained flux and change, during which these various divisions of labor are taking shape, the most effective and affordable strategy for developing a system of digital archives is to assume a distributed, rather than centralized, structure for collecting digital information objects, protecting their integrity over the long term, and retaining them for future use. A distributed structure, built on a foundation of electronic networks, places archival responsibility with those who presumably care most about and have the greatest understanding of the value of particular digital information objects. Moreover, such a structure locates the economic and cultural incentives where they are most likely to prompt those preserving digital information to respond with the greatest agility to the changing digital landscape and to the shifting tides of technology.[12]

Effective structures for digital archives in a distributed network will surely take various forms and will include corporations, federations and consortia, each of which may specialize in the archiving of digital information and range over regional and national boundaries. Both informal collaborations (associations and alliances) and formal partnerships among contractors and subcontractors, will also surely arise, in which responsibilities for archiving are allocated among various other interests in digital information. Moreover, shared interests in, for example, intellectual discipline, in type of information, in function, such as storage or cataloging, and even interests in the output of information within national boundaries will all form a varied and rich basis for the kinds of formal and informal interactions that lead to the design of particular archival organizations. In the end, existing archival organizations may successfully adapt their current roles and responsibilities to changing needs, existing archival roles and responsibilities may be redistributed among other kinds of organizations with stakes in digital information, and focused attention on the division of labor in the digital information economy will lead to the emergence and growth of new kinds of archival structures.

GENERAL PRINCIPLES

Whatever the particular structural outcomes may be as stakeholders, new and old, interact and give shape to the distributed network of digital information, distributed responsibility for preserving that information requires commitment at least to the following set of organizing principles:

1. Information creators/providers/owners have initial responsibility for archiving their digital information objects and thereby ensuring the long-term preservation of those objects.

   i. The creator/provider/owner may engage other parties, such as certified digital archives, to take over some or all of the archival responsibility.

   ii. Libraries and archival organizations may interact with creators/providers as subcontractors for maintaining digital archives during and after the active life of their information objects.

2. Certified digital archives have the right and duty to exercise an aggressive rescue function as a fail-safe mechanism to preserve information objects that become endangered because the creator/provider/owner does not accept responsibility for the preservation function and does not take steps formally to convey responsibility, or because there is no natural institutional home for the objects.

The conditions of creating digital information and giving it a useful life are essentially the same as those required for the information to persist over time. That is, it must be stored and maintained in an accessible form. It is not unreasonable, therefore, to assert, as the first principle does, that initial responsibility for preservation begins with creation of the information and rests with the creator, owner or provider of it. Individuals and public and private agencies already regard such a responsibility as a natural one for their critical internal records. Creators of knowledge in other spheres depend on past knowledge and regularly acknowledge their responsibility to add to the enduring record when they publish their own ideas and findings. As the properties and usefulness of other kinds of information objects become more widely known, the ability in the digital environment to reuse and repackage these objects may generate revenue or other benefits. Creators, owners or providers of these objects, including some publishers, who may not have otherwise counted long-term pres-

ervation among their key responsibilities, may thus be more inclined to do so and may either assume the responsibility themselves or find a qualified partner to do so. Among potential partners, they will likely find libraries, archives or similar agencies, which have specific collection agendas and will seek to take or share responsibility for preserving organized collections of digital materials.[13]

The second organizing principle calls, in effect, for a fail-safe mechanism. A variety of factors—budgetary constraints, reorganization of priorities or focus, change of business, the need to go out of existence, or expiration of copyright—might prompt custodians to neglect, abandon or destroy their collections of digital information. No distributed system of digital archives will afford effective protection of electronic information unless it provides for a powerful rescue function allowing one agency, acting in the long-term public interest of protecting the cultural record, to override another's neglect of or active interest in abandoning or destroying parts of that record.[14]

Digital archives operating normally and those operating in fail-safe mode differ mainly in the rights and obligations they have with respect to rescuing materials that have fallen in jeopardy because a custodian no longer accepts preservation responsibility. Section 108 of the 1976 Copyright Act of the United States defines the rights and obligations for libraries and archives operating normally to preserve copies of printed materials. The proposed revision of the copyright law reserves to libraries and archives similar rights and duties for digital materials. However, neither in its present form nor in its proposed revision does the Copyright Act provide a legal foundation defining the rights and duties that must come into play to facilitate and encourage an aggressive rescue function.

The Copyright Act, in fact, may not provide the best legal and institutional framework for establishing fail-safe mechanisms for digital archives. However, such a framework is urgently needed because we know that one of the greatest dangers to the long life of digital information is the ease with which it can be abandoned and then deliberately or inadvertently destroyed. One appropriate foundation for an archival fail-safe mechanism against this danger might rest in articulating for the various domains of intellectual property—on analogy from the domain of real estate—a definition of the concept of abandonment and of the rights and duties that follow for digital archives operating in fail-safe mode when they can show that present custodians have abandoned, or are in the process of abandoning, culturally valuable objects. Other means of providing a fail-safe mechanism for digital archives also exist, however. For example, a depository system might well serve the purpose. Under such a system, publishers could be legally bound to place with a certified digital archives a copy of their published digital works in a standard archival format (cf. European Commission 1996 and Consortium of University Research Libraries 1996).[15]

Given the principles articulated here, it follows that a commitment to preservation—collecting digital information objects, protecting their integrity over the long term, and retaining them in an accessible form for future use—is a defining feature of a digital archives, whether it is operating in normal or fail-safe mode. This commitment is fulfilled in practice in any digital archives by the exercise of three crucial functions: managing the operating environment of the archives, the migration of the archivs as the operating environment changes, and the costs and finances of the operating environment and of periodic migrations.

THE OPERATING ENVIRONMENT OF DIGITAL ARCHIVES

For assuring the longevity of information, perhaps the most important role in the operation of a digital archives is managing the identity, integrity and quality of the archives itself as a trusted source of the cultural record. Users of archived information in electronic form and of archival services relating to that information need to have assurance that a digital archives is what it says that it is and that the information stored there is safe for the long term. In the view of the Task Force, a formal process of certification, in which digital archives meet or exceed the standards and criteria of an independent certifying agency, would serve to establish an overall climate of value and trust about the prospects of preserving digital information.[16]

Appropriate organizations and individuals need to begin now developing such standards and criteria, including standard methods for a repository to declare its existence as a digital archives and therefore its intentions to preserve the contents over which it has custody, and for describing what the archives contains and what services it provides. The certification process must also address the standards and best practices for other dimensions of archival operation, including selection and accessioning of material, its storage and access and the engineering of the systems environment.

Appraisal and Selection

Archives cannot save all information objects; they must appraise and select for retention the most valuable items. Selection processes for archives of all kinds—paper and digital—are matters of intellectual judgment about what to include and save and what to exclude. Criteria for such judgments are largely tied to the intrinsic qualities of the material and many of the criteria that have proven useful in the paper world will no doubt translate to and prove equally effective in the digital environment. In general, selection criteria include an appraisal of the content of the object—its subject and discipline—in relation to the collection goals of the digital archives, the quality and uniqueness of the object, its accessibility in terms of available hardware and software, its present value and its likely future value (see National Research Council 1995a: 33–41, Owen and van de Walle 1995: 13; see also Atkinson 1986).

Selection is also dependent on a number of extrinsic factors. For example, it is acutely dependent on search and retrieval mechanisms to help place and evaluate candidate objects in a larger universe of related materials. Search and retrieval in large universes of diverse digital materials is the subject of very active computer science research, but search and retrieval today against a rapidly expanding universe of materials in all forms—digital, paper, microform—remains difficult, and the relatively primitive systems currently in operation may, in the short term at least, inhibit the effective selection of materials for digital archives.

Redundancy of information is also important for effective selection. Selectors need to know before accepting an object where a copy of record is stored and if and where additional copies are distributed either as backup or for more efficient retrieval. In addition, selectors ultimately need to have a rich understanding of the software and hardware dependencies of candidate digital information objects so that they can factor the carrying costs for an object into their overall assessment of its value. Such understandings remain in relatively short supply in some measure because the educational processes for wedding selection and technical skills still need to be devised and perfected. In larger measure, however, technical understandings are deficient because the digital environment is so immature that the dependencies of information objects on underlying hardware and software are still in many respects unknown.

Finally, selection for digital archives must be a continuing process. Given the need to migrate digital information regularly from its hardware and software environment, the stimulus and occasion will recur to reappraise the value of the material being migrated. Materials may lose value over time and may need to be withdrawn and discarded (deaccessioned). Hard decisions may also be necessary about how and whether digital objects migrate if changes in a technical environment force alters what is preserved so that it differs in fundamental ways from what existed in the original object. Digital archives thus need to formulate and implement policies and practices for ongoing appraisal (Conway 1996a).

Accession

Once an information object is identified for inclusion in a digital archives, it needs to be accessioned, that is, prepared for the archives. The accession process involves both describing and cataloging selected objects, including their provenance and context, and securing them for storage and access. Standards for description are well developed for certain kinds of materials that are likely to appear in digital archives, such as monographs and serials. Because of the high degree of standardization, one might reasonably expect such descriptions eventually to accompany the digital object, thus simplifying the accessioning process. For other kinds of materials, such as WWW pages, motion video and multimedia, relevant attributes are less well understood. Standards of description are less well practiced and one cannot reasonably expect satisfactory descriptive material to accompany the digital object. In all cases, special attention is needed in the accession process to creating, describing and tracking the versions of the object in the digital archives to satisfy the various requirements for display and other forms of access and for long-term storage. If material is to be deaccessioned then public declarations need to be made to that effect, particularly if it is the last known copy, so that rescue efforts by others can proceed if appropriate.

In the accession process, selected digital objects also need to be made secure for indefinite future use. A digital archives may need to establish access controls for its information objects and the means for authenticating them to future users. Establishing access controls involves setting terms and conditions for authorized use by specific users or classes of users. For certain extreme cases, such as rescued objects still under intellectual property protection, there may be no authorized uses for certain periods of time except for internal use within the digital archives to ensure that the object will be accessible in the future. Authentication, which may make use of cryptography, provides verification that a digital object is what it purports to be and contains the contents that the author/creator or publisher originally intended. One of the characteristics of materials in digital archives may need to be that they contain a digital digest or signature that users can independently verify to assure themselves that the object is unchanged from its archival state.[17]

Storage

The storage operation in digital archives attends primarily to the media level formatting of information objects. Primary considerations include levels of hierarchy and redundancy. In any digital archives, there may be multiple levels of storage graded to levels of expected use and needed performance in retrieval. Little used material may be stored most efficiently off-line, usually in tape format. For objects in high demand, where retrieval time is at a premium, on-line storage in magnetic media may serve best. In a distributed network, they may need to be stored on-line in multiple locations. An intermediate solution is near-line storage, where information objects may be stored on optical or tape media and loaded in a jukebox. Retrieval time in near-line storage systems suffers by comparison to on-line storage, but is considerably more responsive to user demand than off-line storage. Digital archives may use any or all of these methods. The most sophisticated systems combine the resources so that objects in use or recent use are stored on-line and, as they age from the time of most recent use, they move to near-line storage and then eventually off-line.

Another important storage consideration is redundancy. In a system that is completely dependent on the interaction of various kinds and levels of hardware and software, failure in any one of the subsystems could mean the loss or corruption of the information object. Effective storage management thus means providing for redundant copies of the archived objects as an insurance against loss. Depending on the copyright status of the objects, digital archives may choose to make backup copies on their own or to make arrangements for other sites, which hold the same object, in the network of digital archives to serve as backup, or they may choose to do both.

Access

Providing access to digital information in a distributed network environment means above all that digital archives are connected to networks using appropriate protocols and with bandwidth suitable for delivering the information in their control. Digital archives have an obligation to maintain the information in a form so that users over the network can find it with appropriate retrieval engines and view, print, listen to or otherwise use it with appropriate output devices. In the descriptions of the resources they hold, responsible digital archives must provide to their users what they know about the provenance and context of their digital objects so that users can make informed decisions about the reliability and quality of the evidence before them. With respect to access, digital archives also have the responsibility to manage intellectual property rights by facilitating transactions between rights-holders in the information and

users and by taking every reasonable precaution to prevent unauthorized use of the material.

SYSTEMS ENGINEERING

Because so many of the operational responsibilities of the digital archives—selection, accessioning, storage and access—are functionally identical to those of more traditional permanent repositories, they may successfully extend their scope to include digital materials. Many traditional archives have already embraced digital materials, and libraries and museums are not far behind. Wherever digital archives may reside organizationally, their operation is highly distinctive in one crucial respect. That is, they need, at least now and for the foreseeable future, a high level of systems engineering skill to manage the interlocking requirements of media, data formats, and hardware and software on which the operation of the digital archives essentially depends.

As the digital environment matures, the role of systems engineer will serve to integrate new technical developments that promise to streamline and strengthen the operation of digital archives. Commercially available systems for user authorization, and document authentication, systems for using resource descriptions to automate the maintenance and delivery of archived information objects, and networked-based services that help manage the conventions for naming digital resources and provide means for conducting intellectual property transactions all will need the attention of systems engineers to ensure that they are effectively incorporated into the normal operation of digital archives. In addition, the systems engineering function will serve an essential role in helping to determine when objects in digital archives should migrate to new hardware and software.

MIGRATION STRATEGIES

As the operating environments of digital archives change, it becomes necessary to migrate their contents. There are a variety of migration strategies for transferring digital information from obsolete systems to current hardware and software systems so that the information remains accessible and usable. No single strategy applies to all formats of digital information and none of the current preservation methods is entirely satisfactory. Migration strategies and their associated costs vary in different application environments, for different formats of digital materials, and for preserving different degrees of computation, display, and retrieval capabilities.

Methods for migrating digital information in relatively simple files of data are quite well established, but the preservation community is only beginning to address migration of more complex digital objects. Additional research on migration is needed to test the technical feasibility of various approaches to migration, determine the costs associated with these approaches, and establish benchmarks and best practices. Although migration should become more effective as the digital preservation community gains practical experience and learns how to select appropriate and effective methods, migration remains largely experimental and provides fertile ground for research and development efforts.

Stewards of digital material have a range of options when faced with the need to preserve digital information. One might preserve an exact replica of a digital object with complete display, retrieval, and computational functionality, or a representation of it with only partial computation capabilities, or a surrogate such as an abstract, summary, or aggregation. Detail or background noise might be dropped out intentionally through successive generations of migration, and custodians might change the form, format or media of the information. Enhancements are technologically possible through clean-up, mark-up, and linkage, or by adding indexing and other features. These technological possibilities in turn impose serious new responsibilities for presenting digital materials to users in a way that allows them to determine the authenticity of the information and its relationship to the original object.

Change Media

One migration strategy is to transfer digital materials from less stable to more stable media. The most prevalent version of this strategy involves printing digital information on paper or recording it on microfilm. Paper and microfilm are more stable than most digital media, and no special hardware or software are needed to retrieve information from them. Retaining the information in digital form by copying it onto new digital storage media may be appropriate when the information exists in a "software-independent" format as ASCII text files or as flat files with simple, uniform structures. Several data archives hold large collections of numerical data that were captured on punch cards in the 1950s or 1960s, migrated to two or three different magnetic tape formats, and now reside on optical media. As new media and storage formats were introduced, the data were migrated without any significant change in their logical structure.

Copying from one medium to another has the distinct advantage of being universally available and easy to implement. It is a cost-effective strategy for preserving digital information in those cases where retaining the content is paramount, but display, indexing, and computational characteristics are not critical. As long as the preservation community lacks more robust and cost-effective migration strategies, printing to paper or film and preserving flat files will remain the preferred method of storage for many institutions and for certain formats of digital information.

Yet the simplicity and universality of copying as a migration strategy may come at the expense of great losses in the form or structure of digital information. When the access method for some non-standard data changes, one must, in order to migrate them, often eliminate, or "flatten," the structure of documents, the data relationships embedded in databases, and the means of authentication which are managed and interpreted through software. Computation capabilities, graphic display, indexing, and other features may also be lost, leaving behind the skeletal remnant of the original object. This strategy is not feasible, however, for preserving complex data objects from complex systems. It is not possible, for example, to microfilm the equations embedded in a spreadsheet, to print out an interactive full motion video, or to preserve a multimedia document as a flat file.

Change Format

Another migration strategy for digital archives with large, complex, and diverse collections of digital materials is to migrate digital objects from the great multiplicity of formats used to create digital materials to a smaller, more manageable number of standard formats that can still encode the complexity of structure and form of the original. A digital archives might accept textual documents in several commonly available commercial word processing formats or require that documents conform to standards like SGML (ISO 8879). Databases might be stored in one of several common relational database management systems, while images would conform to a tagged image file format and standard compression algorithms (e.g., JFIF/JPEG).

Changing format as a migration strategy has the advantage of preserving more of the display, dissemination, and computational characteristics of the original object, while reducing the large variety of customized transformations that would otherwise be necessary to migrate material to future generations of technology. This strategy rests on the assumption that software products, which are either compliant with widely adopted standards or are widely dispersed in the marketplace, are less volatile than the software market as a whole. Also, most common commercial products provide utilities for upward migration and for swapping documents, databases, and more complex objects between software systems. Nevertheless, software and standards continue to evolve so this strategy simplifies but does not eliminate the need for periodic migration or the need for analysis of the potential effects of such migration on the integrity of the digital object.

Incorporate Standards

Digital archives will benefit from the widespread adoption of data and communication standards that facilitate reference to digital information objects and enable their interchange among systems. Business needs in many institutions are driving the development and adoption of data standards. Organizations that create, use and maintain Geographic Information Systems (GIS), for example, are trying to reduce data conversion and maintenance costs by creating data that conform to widely accepted standards so that they can be exchanged, reused, or sold. Rapid implementation of electronic commerce depends on widespread development and adoption of standards for EDI (electronic data interchange) transaction sets under auspices of the ANSI X.12 committee. Standards initiatives that address business needs for the secure and reliable exchange of digital information among the current generation of systems will impose standardization and normalization of data that ultimately will facilitate migrations to new generations of technology. Digital archives must keep abreast of standards developments and make sure that their own technological infrastructure conforms to widely adopted standards.

Build Migration Paths

Planning for long-term preservation is a critical element of digital preservation. To the extent that creators/providers/owners of digital information accept initial responsibility for archiving their objects, they may begin to see the wisdom of incorporating migration paths or other provisions for preservation as an integral part of the process or system that generates digital information. To assist in this educational process, digital archives might work one-on-one with potential donors to develop agreements early in their careers and establish arrangements for regular, on-line deposit of digital materials in a format acceptable to the repository. In government, institutional, and corporate settings, archivists and librarians can issue guidelines and advice for digital preservation and encourage their parent institutions to adopt common usage rules, comply with data standards, and select applications software that supports migration. The preservation community as a whole needs to work with industry to create information systems and standards that build in archival considerations, such as backward compatibility from the point of initial design. Backward compatibility or migration paths would enable new generations of software to "read" data from older systems without substantial reformatting. Although backward compatibility is increasingly common within software product lines, migration paths are not commonly provided between competing software products or for products that fail in the marketplace.[18]

Use Processing Centers

Although standards and migration paths may become commonplace at some future date, a large body of digital material exists today in non-standard formats, and organizations and individuals continue to produce digital materials in formats that will require migration. Developing "processing centers" that specialize in migration and reformatting of obsolete materials may provide a cost-effective method of digital preservation. Processing centers might provide reformatting services for particular types of materials, such as text, certain database structures, geographic information systems (GIS), or multimedia products. Such centers might maintain older versions of hardware and software to support migration. They might provide a platform for reading and viewing digital information with the same "look and feel" as the original version by developing "software emulators" as suggested by Rothenberg (1995). Processing centers would take advantage of economies of scale and maximize the use of uncommon technical expertise. Migration/preservation services centers might resemble commercial firms that reformat old home movies and obsolete video formats or consortia of libraries and archives with distributed preservation programs. A national laboratory for digital preservation, modeled after the National Media Laboratory, is another alternative. Feasibility studies and cost/benefit analyses would be necessary to determine the technological, economic, and commercial viability of such processing centers.

MANAGING COSTS AND FINANCES

In addition to managing their operating environment and the migration of information through hardware and software platforms, a third function by which digital archives fulfill their commitment to preserve electronic information is in managing the costs of these activities. The principal cost factors of the operating environment are those associated with selection, accession, storage, use, migration, property rights transactions, and the systems engineering needed to manage migration and to maintain the digital archives within a distributed network infrastructure. Some costs, like those for hardware and software as well as those for intellectual property if rights are purchased rather than leased, will appear as capital costs and will need to be amortized.

Operating costs will vary by the form of the information, by usage and over time. Digital information in full text form will be relatively cheap to store and use compared to other forms, such as image, sound, video and multimedia information. Full-text takes up less space in storage and less bandwidth in transmission than other forms. The modes of usage for full-text are relatively well, though by no means completely, understood, and so the delivery and access software is relatively more stable and less subject to costly turnover than that for information in other forms.

Usage will also substantially affect operating costs. Healthy demand for particular information objects will push the digital archives that provide them to shift delivery to more costly on-line storage or to sophisticated and expensive systems of hierarchical storage. The costs of software and intellectual property may also be pegged to demand. Another usage factor affecting costs is the high variability in the kinds of user access devices. For many types of information objects, modes of access are still closely tied to the type of workstation available to the user. The tradeoff for the digital archives is either to limit access only to "approved" devices or to support multiple platforms and incur the added associated costs in hardware, software, intellectual property and systems engineering.

Operating costs will also vary over time. Storage costs will likely continue to decline both absolutely and relative to other cost factors. The costs of access and of managing property rights transactions are relatively high today because the supporting systems are virtually non-existent; these systems are developing very rapidly and their relative costs will likely also fall. The costs of the property rights transactions themselves, however, cannot be reasonably predicted at this stage and the danger is that costs will rise to the point that they become a barrier to access. In the long run, the cost factor that will most likely determine the success or failure of digital archives is the investment in the systems engineering and infrastructure needed to support highly distributed network-based functions.

Migration costs will vary depending on the complexity of the original data objects, the frequency of migration, the extent to which the functionality for computation, display, indexing, and authentication must be maintained, and the need to compensate for acquisition of intellectual property rights. Migration costs are much greater for complex objects, such as geographic information systems, where it is necessary to retain multiple formats of data, color display, and complex relations between the "layers" of a geographic information system than for flat files of data or ASCII characters. Computer models that drive artificial intelligence systems are of little long-term value if their computation capabilities are not retained; but migrating the models from one generation of software to the next involves complex and expensive transformations. Some types of digital information may require frequent migration—as often as every three to five years—if they are stored in formats that are subject to frequent change. Digital archives may have to compensate for intellectual property rights and may be required to purchase software or site licenses in order to migrate digital information stored in proprietary formats.

Planning for migration is difficult because there is limited experience with the types of migrations needed to maintain access to complex digital objects. When a custodian assumes responsibility for preserving a digital object it may be difficult to predict when migration will be necessary, how much reformatting is needed, and how much migration will cost. There are no reliable or comprehensive data on costs associated with migrations, either for specific technologies and formats or for particular collections.

Cost Modeling

Answering questions about the costs and affordability of digital information and of preserving it in a system of digital archives is essential but exceedingly complex. There is a large array of cost factors to understand for a panoply of differing kinds of digital information objects in which numerous parties have a variety of different kinds of interests. A multidimen-

sional matrix—with present and future stakeholders mapped along one axis, kinds of digital information along a second, and cost factors against a third—might serve well as a framework for systematically assessing the value of digital information and the affordability of preserving it.

There is much we need to know before we can fully elaborate an economic framework of this kind, and much to be learned from detailed studies of a wide variety of public and private institutional experiences with preserving digital materials. A number of organizations, including the National Aeronautics and Space Administration (NASA), the National Oceanic and Atmospheric Administration (NOAA), and the Inter-university Consortium for Political and Social Research (ICPSR), have relatively long and rich experiences in maintaining huge archives of certain kinds of digital information, and they are increasingly doing so in a distributed environment over electronic networks. Yet, despite these various experiences, little systematic understanding has yet emerged of the actual costs of digital archiving. As a result, there is almost no sense of the detailed interplay of cost factors that might promote the kinds of specialization, division of labor and competition needed, in turn, to drive digital archives not just to manage costs against a standard of information quality and integrity, but to strive vigorously to lower those costs while maintaining and improving the standard of quality.[19]

To advance our overall understanding of the long-term implications of digital preservation, and to help define a context for developing the economy of archival management, we need formal, detailed models of the actual costs now being encountered in digital archives. One such model, which projects the costs needed to preserve the digital products of Yale's Project Open Book, is presented below. Within the larger framework of archival activity, this model represents just one small, restricted domain—namely, the preservation of images of textual documents produced by a research university library in a networked context. The analysis embedded in the Yale model illustrates how we can begin systematically to enrich our understandings of the value and usefulness of specific digital preservation efforts. It also suggests where we need to focus our energies as we undertake the fundamental work needed to advance the economy of digital archiving.

The Yale Cost Model

Assumptions about the value of digital information frequently turn on assertions that cheap storage and easy access are uniquely available in the digital environment. At the same time, many publishers, librarians and others contemplating the digital future express considerable fear that the digital world of information will not prove less expensive than the traditional paper environment, but in fact more expensive. Given a body of digital works, what resources are needed to store and provide access to them indefinitely into the future?

Through Project Open Book, the Yale University Library has accumulated an archives of over 2,000 digital texts. The texts are collections of black and white TIFF images at 600 dots per inch resolution under CCITT Group IV compression. Based on experience it has gained to date in handling these texts, the Yale Library has begun constructing a model that projects the costs of storage and access for a much larger digital archives, and has provided some of the details for presentation here (see also Waters 1994).

The fundamental assumption of the projection in the Yale model is that the digital archives is built primarily for the Yale community and is composed not of converted volumes, but of newly published digital texts distributed in bit-mapped form.[20] According to the model, the archives purchases or leases these new texts and they accumulate at an annual rate of 200,000 volumes per year. Only a fraction of the newly acquired material is used each year. The usage rate is based on actual circulation rates at the Yale Library of about 15% of volumes. Such a rate is not unusual for large research libraries and seems appropriate as a basis for modeling a digital archives intended to collect material for future use as well as present use. The usage rate in the digital archives, however, is assumed to be 20%, slightly more than 15% in the traditional library on the theory that access is easier and therefore demand is more for materials in digital form.

Costs of Digital Archives. Table 1 below contains a summary of the estimated digital archives storage and access costs per volume for Year 1 (See Appendix 2 for details). Components of storage costs in the digital archives include storage device costs—a jukebox, in this model—storage media costs, and the costs of operating and maintaining the storage equipment, and of periodically refreshing the media and migrating the data. The costs of providing access to the digital archives include providing a document server and software for the server that will support client machines on users' desks, maintaining the server and access software and of operating the server, and printing on demand a selected portion of volumes used and of delivering those printed copies to the user. Systems engineering and management overhead costs

TABLE 1.

Costs of the Digital Archives

COST FACTORS	COSTS PER VOLUME IN YEAR 1
Storage	
Device Costs	$0.97
Device Maintenance	0.40
Operations Costs	0.40
Media Costs	0.25
Media Refreshment and Data Migration	0.49
Storage Systems Engineering	0.04
Storage Management Overhead	0.03
Total Storage Costs per Volume	**$2.58**
Access	
Document Server	$2.13
Server Maintenance	0.88
Server Operations	0.88
Access Software	1.22
Software Maintenance	0.50
Access Systems Engineering	0.04
Access Management Overhead	0.03
Printing	0.96
Delivery	0.09
Total Access Costs per Volume	**$6.72**

are also included for both the storage and access services. Note, however, that many costs—for example, those for acquisitions, cataloging and reference services—are factored out of the model for purposes of this discussion.

In this model, all equipment and software are capitalized over a life of five years, whereupon it is assumed to be obsolete. The media are assumed to be refreshed and the data migrated as the technology changes on the same five year cycle. Hardware and software maintenance costs as well as equipment operations costs are estimated as a proportion of the original purchase price. The model assumes the cost of hardware and software, as well as migration and operational services all to be declining at a relatively rapid rate of 50% every 5 years. On the other hand, the management and systems engineering services costs are calculated as a proportion of the salary of a full-time, benefited employee whose salary rises each year at a 4% rate of inflation.

One can reasonably assume that local printers are available to network users of the digital archives, and that many users would not avail themselves of the printing and delivery services posited here. This model is built on the assumption that only 10% of the use of the archives would result in use of the archives' own printing and delivery services. The unit costs represented here are thus 10% of the actual unit costs for on-demand printing and delivery. Moreover, the printing costs include an estimated charge for copyright clearance and are assumed to be stable into the future. Delivery charges are assumed to be labor intensive and to inflate by 4% per year over time.

Are the storage and access costs for this first year high or low? How would the costs compare of over time? What is an appropriate standard of comparison?

Depository Library Costs. To generate a comparison benchmark, Yale imagined that the same 200,000 volumes that it assumed it would acquire each year for the digital archives could just as readily be acquired in paper form. Note that this kind of benchmark is only possible for document-like objects and is simply not an option for many of the materials that originate in digital form and cannot exist in any other form.

Yale further imagined, because its libraries are full or nearly so, that all new volumes would be stored, not in a new and expensive full-service library in the center of campus but in a low-cost depository facility from which a highly responsive service would deliver needed items directly to faculty offices and student rooms. Leaving all competitive rivalries aside, Yale granted for purposes of the model that it could not build and run a depository facility at unit costs lower than the published unit prices at the Harvard Depository Library. Yale thus projected its depository costs based on the depository prices charged by Harvard. For purposes of this presentation, other relevant costs—for example, those for acquisitions, cataloging, and reference services—are factored out and assumed to be equal to similar costs factored out of the digital archives model.

Table 2 contains a summary of the storage and access costs per volume in a depository library for Year 1. Given an average size of document and an average number of documents per linear foot, the projected library storage costs for paper documents are easily calculated from the published price list of the Harvard Depository Library, and presumably include in their base a means of recovering the costs of building construction and other capital costs as well as maintenance costs and management overhead. The costs of providing access to the paper-based depository library consist of four components: retrieval from the depository shelf, transfer to the campus service point, circulation of the volume and delivery to the

TABLE 2.

Depository Library Costs

COST FACTORS	COSTS PER VOLUME IN YEAR 1
Total Storage Costs per Volume	**$0.21**
Access	
Retrieval	$2.63
Courier	0.27
Circulation	0.60
Delivery	0.90
Total Access Costs per Volume	**$4.40**

user. Estimates of retrieval and courier service costs are also based on the published price list of the Harvard Depository Library.[21] The estimate of circulation cost is derived from actual circulation costs at Yale. And a cost is assigned for delivery service to the faculty office or student room as a substitute for reader use of a browsable stack in a full service library. All these costs are assumed to rise with inflation at an annual rate of 4%.

Today, in Year 1, the differences between the unit costs of the depository library compared to those of the digital archives are striking. The storage costs in this model are more than 12 times higher for a digital archives composed of texts in image form, and the access costs are 50% higher. Skepticism about the purported cost advantages of digital libraries over traditional libraries thus seems well-founded in this model, at least in Year 1. What would happen over the longer term?

A Ten-Year Scenario. Proponents of digital libraries rest their case, at least in part, on arguments about the rapidly declining rates of technology costs. This highly simplified model highlights that argument and sets up a stark contrast between the digital archives, the costs of which (except for management overheard, systems engineering, demand printing and delivery) decline at a steady rate, while the costs of the depository library rise by an inflationary rate each year.[22] If these assumptions are set in play over a ten year period, the changes in unit costs are remarkable (see Table 3).

The calculation for this table ignores the annual carrying costs a digital archives would incur to maintain the material it acquires each year. Instead, the table presents the costs as if each year was the first year of an archives' operations. By centering on the operational costs in this way, the table clearly reveals that real unit costs of storage for the digital archives fall by about 70% over the period. However, in Year 10 they still remain more than double the unit costs of storage in the depository library. By contrast, unit costs of access in the digital archives fall to less than half of the unit access costs in the depository library over the period, overtaking them in about Year 5.

So formulated, the model seems to confirm a widespread sense of the value of the digital world in providing easy access to digital information. However, if over the next decade storage in the digital archives is managed the same as storage in conventional paper-based libraries—that is, if the number of volumes stored is the same as the number of volumes acquired—then the overall cost advantage would still favor the depository library. In Year 10, the cost to store 200,000 new volumes in the digital archives is $164,000; the costs of access to 20%, or 40,000, of the volumes is $112,000; together these yield a total cost of $276,000. By contrast, the cost to store 200,000 new volumes in the depository library in Year 10 is $61,000; the costs of access to 15%, or 30,000, volumes would be $188,000; together these total $249,000.

Obstacles and Prospects for Digital Archives

With its stark assumptions that seem to favor the digital archives and its surprising results that favor the paper-based library, the cost analysis presented here

TABLE 3.

Projected Costs per Volume Over 10 Years

	Year 1	Year 4	Year 7	Year 10
Depository Library				
Depository Storage Costs Per Volume	$0.21	$0.24	$0.27	$0.30
Depository Access Costs Per Volume Used	$4.40	$4.95	$5.57	$6.27
Digital Archives				
Digital Storage Costs Per Volume	$2.58	$1.73	$1.18	$0.82
Digital Access Costs Per Volume Used	$6.72	$4.84	$3.60	$2.79

raises a critical question. If the costs of providing storage and access to texts in digital image form are truly greater than the costs of providing storage and access to the same texts in paper form, are the highly touted advantages of the digital environment merely a chimera?

There are at least two answers to this question. One is to challenge the high costs of the digital archives over time by asserting, for example, that the assumed rate of decline in technology-based costs should be steeper. This kind of challenge to the model and its results is risky for two reasons. First, although there may be evidence today that some technology costs are declining at a steeper rate than the overall rate posited in the model, it is difficult to argue from the evidence that the overall rate should be lowered or that such a lowered rate could be sustained over the period. It is difficult because, second, any expectation of declining costs has to be balanced against the equally persistent expectation of rising functionality, which tends to drive technology-based costs up—or, at least, to slow their decline.

Another, and perhaps more fruitful, answer is to think of the organization of digital information stor-

age and access in fundamentally different terms from those which govern the conventional paper library. As we have seen, one of the significant qualities of digital information is that it lives in a networked environment. Given sufficient capacity or bandwidth, adequate security and reliability and wide extension of the network, one can alter a fundamental assumption of the model, namely, that the digital archives, like the paper-based library, best serves its client community by taking physical possession of *all* the materials it acquires. Instead, one can imagine a distributed storage environment, supported by various kinds of consortia, partnership and other kinds of contractual arrangements with suppliers. Under these arrangements, a digital archives or other user agent could purchase or license the full 200,000 volumes, but then secure the right, either for a period of time or in perpetuity, to move a digital work from another archives on the network into local storage only when it is needed. And exercising a fail-safe prerogative might comprise one highly specialized definition of need.

With the prospect of a viable system of distributed networked-based digital archives, one can thus cast

TABLE 4.

Costs for All Volumes Stored and Used

	Year 1	Year 4	Year 7	Year 10
New Volumes	*200,000*	*200,000*	*200,000*	*200,000*
Depository Library (volumes stored = new volumes)				
Estimated Annual Use (15% of volumes)	*30,000*	*30,000*	*30,000*	*30,000*
Depository Storage Costs for New Volumes	$42,769	$48,110	$54,117	$60,874
Depository Access Costs for Volumes Used	$132,090	$148,583	$167,136	$188,005
Total Depository Storage and Access Costs	**$174,859**	**$196,693**	**$221,253**	**$248,879**
Digital Archives (volumes stored = volumes used)				
Estimated annual use (20% of volumes)	*40,000*	*40,000*	*40,000*	*40,000*
Digital Storage Costs for Volumes Used	$103,208	$69,371	$47,207	$32,763
Digital Access Costs for Volumes Used	$268,870	$193,400	$143,977	$111,785
Total Digital Storage and Access Costs	**$372,078**	**$262,771**	**$191,184**	**$144,549**
Difference: Depository - Digital	**($197,219)**	**($66,078)**	**$30,069**	**$104,331**

the model of a digital archives in the following way: assume that it begins storing permanently the volumes it has acquired only as they are needed. Observe in Table 4, the effects of this changed assumption. Note that in Year 10, because the digital archives is now storing only the volumes used, its storage costs have dropped from $160,000 (as calculated above) to $32,763. Still, the depository library continues to hold an overall cost advantage until Year 7. Access costs shift to the benefit of the digital archives in Year 6 and storage costs follow suit in the next year. Beginning in Year 7 and continuing on through the rest of the period, the digital archives, conceived in a digital networked environment, begins to demonstrate its affordability compared to conventional paper-based modes of information storage and access.

A different construction of the organization of digital storage and access compared to paper-based storage and access thus leads to a compellingly different construction of the relative economies. Even under highly restrictive assumptions—the very specialized case of bit-mapped images of text and the arguably conservative expectations about the rate of decline in technology-based costs—the digital archives embedded in a highly distributed network of information resources begins to look economically attractive in a relatively short time.[23]

Now, if one begins to relax these restrictive assumptions, then the model of distributed digital archives starts bearing even more economic fruit. Incorporate in the model a faster rate of decline in technology-based costs. Or, rather than bit-mapped, inject into the model a different format, such as compressed TeX, which is much less storage intensive than bit-mapped images. In all these cases, one can expect the costs to fall relative to both the digital and paper-based scenarios initially presented here.

Richer and more detailed cost models than the simple analytic model advanced here—ones that include costs of acquisition, cataloging, reference services and so on—are needed to accurately assess the value and affordability of the digital environment. The Yale model, however, has the distinct advantage of helping to reveal that the key that unlocks the path to the economies of the digital environment is not technological, but organizational. Developing suitable and effective modes of distribution in a networked environment that lead to cost effective digital archives for preserving digital information is an organizational task requiring much ingenuity and numerous creative partnerships and alliances of various kinds among stakeholders.[24] We can look forward to this organizational effort as the digital environment matures, but a key question still remains: who will pay?

Financing

A key question in the management of archival costs for operations and migration, of course, is how to balance them with income, either from a sponsoring organization or philanthropy that absorbs the costs or from direct or indirect charges for use. Uncertainty about the answer to this question, as much as any other factor, creates a significant barrier to the coherent, systematic preservation of digital information. Some general actions might help relieve the uncertainty about archival costs. For example, tax incentives and accounting rules that favor the preservation of digital information in archives as investment in long-term capital stock might spur the growth of digital archives. Otherwise, solutions to cost questions are likely to be found in relation to specific bodies of digital materials and the communities that are interested in them.

For some kinds of digital information direct charging for use will be entirely acceptable to the relevant user communities. One can imagine making an actuarial calculation of the lifetime cost of preserving a digital information object, finding creators/providers/owners with an economic interest in paying to preserve their information, and constructing an archival service that functions much like a safety deposit system for digital information objects. As facilities are developed and refined to exact charges, conduct transactions for intellectual property and maintain confidentiality, and as experience with such mechanisms grows, some communities of interest that presently resist the notion of charging for information services, such as archiving, may grow less resistant. In any case, more imaginative solutions need to be found by asking hard questions about who benefits from the archived information, when do they benefit and do the answers suggest how the costs of preservation might be afforded. Some instructive examples are beginning to emerge from communities in which the members have asked and tried to answer these hard questions.

Consider physics, for example. The direct beneficiaries of archived physics information are physicists and related professionals, who have, as their professional organization, the American Physical Society (APS). The APS already publishes the central corpus of physics information. It keeps a copy of most of what it has published and owns the copyrights to its publications. It has stability and longevity (it was founded earlier than the New York Public Library and considerably earlier than most extant commercial organizations), and a membership keenly aware of the value of its publications and thereby able to help select the most valuable among them. The Society has the technical skill and organizational wherewithal to manage its archives in digital form. It has mechanisms which could finance the digital archives, including member dues and access charges, and it has recently adopted a digital form of publication for its key journals. Moreover, after careful study, the Society has recently decided to embark on a systematic program that would lead it to build complete digital archives of its publications, past and present, and to maintain them into the future.

Like the APS, other professional associations are actively reconsidering how economically to preserve their key information assets in digital form. The Association for Computing Machinery (ACM), for example, has also embarked on a ambitious program designed to place the entire ACM literature in an on-line digital library and is explicitly questioning how to afford it: "Should there be an archiving fee replacing the current practice of page charges? Should uncited items be deleted from the archive after a minimum holding time? Should highly cited items be guaranteed a permanent place in the archive?" (Denning and Rous 1995: 103). Other associations are more concerned with preserving critical data than with the published literature. The American Geological Institute, a federation of geoscientific and professional associations, is in the process of forming a National Geoscience Data Repository System to capture and preserve geoscientific data (see American Geological Institute 1994). As these various efforts mature, and others emerge, what kind of imaginative solutions to the problems of managing the costs of digital preservation will they produce or, with incentives and stimuli from partners and competitors, could they be provoked to produce?

NOTES

12. See the National Research Council (1995a: 50), which argues that "the only effective and affordable archiving strategy is based on distributed archives managed by those most knowledgeable about the data." Against this view, the background paper on digital preservation prepared for the European Commission takes the position that "decentralised models in which the archiving of electronic publications is delegated to publishers or network resource providers are therefore not recommended. Preservation of electronic materials is better guaranteed by local storage under the control of the deposit library" (Owen and van de Walle 1995: 11). The apparent opposition between centralized and distributed (or decentralized) models is misleading, however. Viewed globally, a national depository model for archiving is merely a special case of a decentralized model, where the criteria for distributed collection depend on national boundaries, rather than discipline interests or functional divisions.

13. Several readers of the first draft of the Task Force report expressed skepticism that creators will accept responsibility for archiving digital information (Graham 1995b, Owen and van de Walle 1995: 11, and Parrott 1995). The "Draft Statement of Principles for the Preservation of and Long Term Access to Australian Digital Objects," however, follows the Task Force formulation when it asserts that "creators of original digital objects hold an initial, and in many cases a continuing responsibility for their preservation; creators have the power to facilitate or deny the continuing existence of digital information" (Lyall 1996).

14. Some readers of the first draft of the Task Force report objected that the notion of a fail-safe mechanism unreasonably assumes that archives will have knowledge of the existence and impending demise of digital information (Parrott 1995).

Moreover, they questioned the apparent negative connotations of the phrase "fail-safe mechanism": it implies efforts to "prevent" the demise of an object rather than causing it to endure (Graham 1995) and it is "essentially punitive" because it assumes that those who have accepted preservation responsibilities cannot be trusted (Parrott 1995). To overcome these negative connotations, the commentators suggested strengthening existing structures of cooperation and coordination (Parrott 1995) and abandoning the idea of a "fail-safe mechanism" in favor of establishing a "trigger" mechanism (Graham 1995).

Having considered these concerns, the Task Force remains convinced of the need for a "fail-safe mechanism" for digital archiving. In the world of paper, there are numerous ways of knowing of the existence of information objects and of their potential demise; it is no less reasonable in the digital world to assume that similar, and perhaps better, ways of knowing will develop. Moreover, the Task Force does not view a fail-safe mechanism as a negative force or as punitive to an a custodian of information. Rather, it regards the mechanism as an enabling tool for a rescuing agent and, therefore, as contributing to the general social good. If a custodian were to regard a fail-safe mechanism as a threat, then perhaps such a perception would serve the greater good of stimulating responsible archiving behavior. In any case, the Task Force intends the fail-safe mechanism only as a last resort. Such a protection of last resort would be necessary even if there were appropriate "trigger mechanisms" causing archiving behavior proactively to occur and if cooperative and collaborative structures were running smoothly. It would be necessary because custodians can ignore "triggers" to right behavior and because cooperation can break down.

15. The Task Force is grateful to Scott Bennett (1995) for drawing attention to the need for legal principles that could be called into play when digital works in copyright are in danger of being abandoned or destroyed. Bennett particularly cites the work of Patterson and Lindberg (1991: 204–207) on the concept of abandonment. Patterson and Lindberg, however, do not develop the concept and merely refer to it in the context of their discussion of the fair use of copyrighted materials. The sense of the Task Force is that an interpretation of fair use, however articulate it may be, is too slender a thread on which to base a fail-safe mechanism for the protection of our cultural heritage. Alternatively, the legal deposit system currently in place in the United States is not designed organizationally as a fail-safe mechanism for the preservation of culturally significant works. In the judgment of the Task Force, the time is right for a comprehensive examination of possible fail-safe mechanisms and a thorough understanding of both their legal and organizational foundations.

16. There are at least two models of certification. On the one hand, there is the audit model used, for example, to certify official depositories of government documents. The depositories are subject to periodic and rigorous inspection to ensure that they are fulfilling their mission. On the other hand, there is a standards model which operates, for example, in the preservation community. Participants claim to adhere to standards that an appropriate agency has certified as valid and appropriate; consumers then certify by their use whether the products and services actually adhere to the standards. In its call for certified digital archives, the Task Force has not judged the relatives merits of applying either of these particular kinds of models of certification.

17. Inattention to even minor details can sometimes compromise all other efforts to preserve the integrity of a digital information object and can hamper efforts to authenticate the objects to future users. For example, consider the Task Force's experience with the first draft of its report. Each page of the draft contained a date. The date changed with each date of printing. During the composition phase, before the Task Force publicly released the draft, the changing date helped distinguish earlier versions of the report from oe another. When it formally released the first draft, however, the Task Force did not fix the date on each page so that it would not change with each printing. Every time a reader retrieved and printed a copy of the report from its on-line location, the date printed on the report thus changed, generating much confusion about whether the Task Force had changed the substance of the draft report or not. Diane Hopkins (1995) of the World Bank kindly called the Task Force's attention to this subtle but very serious

problem for preserving digital documents from a word processing environment.

18. There has recently emerged the Standard for the Exchange of Product Model Data (STEP). It is a data representation standard intended to provide a complete unambiguous representation of data throughout its life cycle, including an archival phase. The application of STEP would facilitate the storage of data and a data model or representation, and would enable the data to be retrieved even if the software that created it is defunct or not able to run on the current computer hardware or operating system. Early implementations of the STEP standard are currently under development in industry for specific kinds of product documentation. The standard may have wider application, but these developments serve as an example of a comprehensive effort to design information systems to a standard that considers archival issues for information objects from the point of their creation. See, for example, Herbst and Malle (1995).

19. The National Research Council, in its study on *Preserving Scientific Data on Our Physical Universe,* is conscious of the costs of archiving but mainly points to what it regards as the chronic underfunding of archival efforts. See, for example, the working papers for the report in National Research Council (1995b: 79). There are, however, throughout the working papers and the final report a number of references that together suggest that the problem of cost is more than a simple matter of underfunding. For example, the final report (1996a: 29, 31) notes that "NOAA's budget for its National Data Centers in FY 1980 was $24.6 million, and their total data volume was approximately one terabyte. In FY 1994, the budget was on $22.0 million (not adjusted for inflation), while the volume of their combined data holdings was about 220 terabytes!" The report cites this comparison as evidence of the low priority given to data archiving in budgets. Such an assessment may in fact be accurate, but surely the change in funding also reflects the effects of dramatic increases in the cost efficiencies of digital storage technologies over the period.

So what level of funding priority is appropriate? The working papers that accompany the final National Research Council report tentatively probe several alternatives. The Department of Energy, for example, is cited with approval because one of its programs provides "about 15 percent of the total program budget for data management and archiving." Elsewhere, the working papers refer to the budget of the Jet Propulsion Laboratory, which manages the archives of a joint U.S. and French satellite data system, and observes that the cost of maintaining the resulting data sets for any 10-year period "appears to average less than 1 percent of the cost of collecting the data set" (National Resource Council 1995b: 79, 91). Without a closer benchmarking and deeper analysis of the cost factors at work in these various archival programs, it is, of course, impossible to judge the relative merits of these two different measures of appropriate funding, and the final report of the National Research Council does not attempt to make such a judgment. However, the National Research Council work does suggest that the archives of the nation's scientific data offer fertile ground for systematic studies that would yield very useful benchmarks and models of archival costs.

20. One commentator on the first draft of this report read the use of the Yale cost model here to mean that the Task Force "envisages a total replacement of one format with another" (Parrott 1995). The Task Force envisions no such thing. Although the cost projections in this model are based in part on the costs of maintaining digital objects that the Yale Library converted from its paper and microfilm collections, the plainly stated assumption is that the digital archive being modeled here is composed not of converted material but of newly published material in digital form.

21. The Task Force is indebted to Curtis Kendrick, the Assistant Director for the Depository in the Harvard University Library, for carefully reading this section in the first draft of the report and for providing an updated price list for the relevant Depository services cited in the Yale cost model. See Kendrick (1995). The presentation here incorporates the corrected prices. Kendrick also notes that the Harvard Depository is currently averaging about a 3% circulation rate and only operates for 250 days per year and observes that the Yale model extrapolates the Harvard unit prices to an hypothetical environment operating 360 days per year

at a 15% circulation rate. Kendrick worries that the Harvard fee structure could not sustain the heightened level of activity posited in the Yale model. Although it is possible that a higher level of activity would result in higher unit prices, it is more likely that economies of scale would obtain and that unit costs would in fact be lower. In simply extrapolating the current costs, and assuming no economies (or diseconomies) of scale, the Yale model takes a relatively conservative position.

22. In his comments on the first draft of the Task Force report, Scott Bennett of the Yale Library (1995) urges caution upon the Task Force in its use of the Yale cost model, which assumes a steady decline in hardware, software and certain operational costs over its ten-year horizon. "No trend line in technology or economics," he writes, "can reasonably be expected to continue indefinitely." The Task Force agrees that any projections beyond the 10 year horizon set in the Yale cost model would be highly suspect, and believes that the assumptions posited in the model about declining unit costs for hardware and software within the ten-year period are reasonable and plausible.

23. Fully distributed storage models, like the one envisioned here for digital materials, do exist for paper and microfilm materials. The Center for Research Libraries serves its members in allowing them to distribute among themselves the costs of storing paper or film materials. The preservation program for brittle books also operates on a distributed storage model in that it assumes no duplication in the creation and storage of masters that will serve the needs of the entire community. One commentator on the first draft of the Task Force report suggested that these kinds of distributed storage models for paper and microfilm would, for the purpose of cost comparison, provide a true parallel environment to the distributed model posited for digital materials (Bennett 1995). The fully distributed models for storing paper and film, however, work only for materials that are highly specialized and for which there is little demand. The models are not otherwise widely applied because the means of distributing paper and film among the nodes in the distributed network are so costly and cumbersome. The proposed comparison, while interesting theoretically, would contribute little to the argument of the Task Force.

24. The JSTOR project, sponsored by the Andrew W. Mellon Foundation, is one such creative venture that is seeking to demonstrate the organizational economies of scale unique to the digital environment. See Bowen (1995).

PAUL CONWAY

Excerpts from *Preservation in the Digital World*

Washington, D.C.: Council on Library and Information Resources, March 1996.
[Editor's Note: Not all of the original images were reproducible.]

Author's Preface

Digital images are everywhere in libraries and archives. In many cases, the quality of digital image products from demonstration projects is spectacular, while others are less satisfactory. Nevertheless, there is widespread belief that the ability to produce high-quality images will improve as the technology matures. Even though a major investment is required for digital image conversion, libraries are rearranging budgets, raising funds, and anticipating income streams to make it happen. Can any institution—library, archives, historical society, or museum—afford to squander this investment in moving from pilot project to a fully operational system? The risk of loss extends beyond the financial, however, without a serious effort to ensure long-term access to digital image files. Understanding how to adapt preservation concepts to manage risk in the midst of rapid technological ferment is what preservation in the digital world is all about.

In the public at large, preservation is a concern chiefly in the world of paper. Digital information gives us worry-free preservation, it is asserted, because an exact copy of a file can be made with the click of a button. However, those who have been involved in digital imaging projects, including university and library administrators, technology system specialists, product vendors, and research scholars, have learned quickly that digital imaging technology, in and of itself, provides no easy answers for preservation. Indeed, simply defining what preservation means in the digital imaging environment is a challenge. This report suggests a framework for applying fundamental preservation concepts, derived from the best present practices of paper and film, to the world of digital image documents so that the highest level of responsible preservation planning, management, and action can continue.

Introduction

In *Motel of the Mysteries* (1979), illustrator David Macaulay speculates about how people 2,000 years from now might interpret the cultural significance of a low-budget roadside motel buried intact under junk mail and pollution. Beyond being a wry satire on the science of archaeology, the book is a clever reminder of the danger of interpreting the past without documentary evidence. A "Do Not Disturb" sign becomes a sacred seal "placed upon the handle of the great outer door by the necropolis officials following the closing of the tomb." A television represents "the essence of religious communication."

Anthropologists and historians know that the impulses to record and to keep are a part of human nature. Truth is embedded in the symbols and artifacts that we create and then keep by choice or by accident. And yet, as we approach the end of the twentieth century, we find ourselves confronting a dilemma such as the one faced by Howard Carson, Macaulay's amateur digger: a vast void of knowledge

> ### The Digital World
> This era and what we are building go by many names, including Cyberspace, Global Information Infrastructure, Infobahn, Information Age, Information (Super) Highway, Interspace, and Paperless Society. They are all supported by networking (e.g., the Internet). However, their essence is information. Information is what flows over the networks, what is presented to us by our consumer electronics devices, what is manipulated by our computers, and what is stored in our libraries.
> —*Edward A. Fox, "Digital Libraries: Introduction,"* Communications of the ACM *38, April 1995.*

filled by myth and speculation. Information in digital form—the evidence of the world we live in—is more fragile than the fragments of papyrus found buried with the Pharaohs.

We are living in a digital world. Computers now far outnumber office workers in many parts of the globe. We bank by phone, enjoy digitally mastered music, fax carry-out orders, and communicate with each other through keyboarded thoughts. One of the sure signs that the global village has a digital face is the high investment of money and competitive energy now being directed toward changing the Internet into the National Information Infrastructure. After only a few years of life, the World Wide Web is crowded with time-sensitive data, news summaries, chat, and multimedia entertainment. The electronic landscape changes so rapidly—and the lines between the old and the new seem drawn so sharply—that *Wired* magazine can refer to a four-year-old network service provider as a "dinosaur," and get this retort: "It's very funny that a petroleum-based product like a magazine can call an online service that has an integrated Web browser irrelevant" (Nollinger 1995, p. 204).

It has long been the responsibility of libraries and archives to assemble, organize, and protect documentation of human activity. The ethic of preservation as coordinated, conscious management, however, is a more recent phenomenon. Librarians and archivists—like the clerks and scribes who went before them—have increased the chances that evidence about how we live, how we think, and what we have accomplished will be preserved. Traditional preservation, as responsible custody, works only when this evidence has a physical form; when the value of the evidence exceeds the cost of keeping it; and when the roles of evidence creators, evidence keepers, and evidence users are mutually reinforcing.

Digital imaging technology is more than another reformatting option. Imaging involves transforming the very concept of format, rather than creating an accurate picture of a book, document, photograph, or map on a different medium. The power of digital enhancement, the possibilities for structured indexes, and the mathematics of compression and communication together alter the concept of preservation. The digital world transforms traditional preservation concepts from protecting the physical integrity of the object to specifying the creation and maintenance of the object whose intellectual integrity is its primary characteristic. This transformation, along with the new leadership possibilities it creates, will force librarians and archivists to transform their services and programs in turn. Just as the invention of the vacuum tube created an entirely new form of mass communication—radio—instead of simply making point to point messaging possible without wires, digital imaging technologies create an entirely new form of information. Yet, many of the core tenets of preservation developed in the analog world can be carried forward to the digital world to continue the necessary roles of stewardship and service.

A Central Dilemma

The earliest known evidence of writing—pictorial signs on sun-dried clay tablets—originated roughly 6,000 years ago. Tens of thousands of examples of Sumerian and Babylonian writing exist today in the world's major research centers. Archaeologists unearth hundreds more every year. From ancient times to the present, the entire technology of writing has undergone steady evolution. Today, we have the capacity to store detailed bit-mapped images of hundreds of books on an optical disk the size of a coaster. This capacity to record and store gives rise to one of the central dilemmas of recorded history: Our capacity to record information has increased exponentially over time while the longevity of the media used to store the information has decreased equivalently.

The graph below illustrates these changes in broad strokes. The "X" axis lays out ten "writing" surfaces in the chronological order of their widespread introduction. The "Y" axis is a logarithmic scale where each level increases in order of magnitude—a factor of ten. The dotted line is a plot of the approximate number of characters per square inch that can be conveniently recorded on any particular surface. There is relative stability in density—fewer than 150 characters per square inch—in the centuries before modern printing presses and electronic technologies caused storage densities to skyrocket. Today's typical 5-1/2 inch

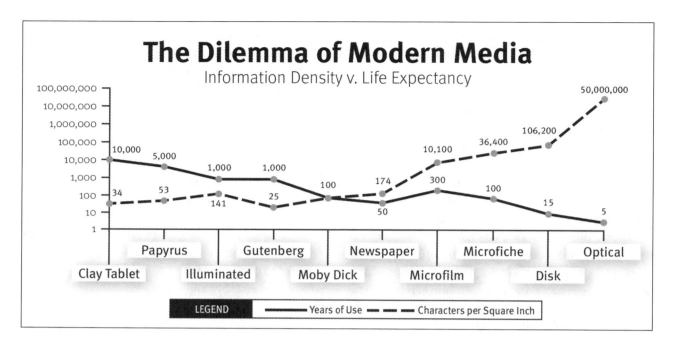

rewritable optical disk can hold 650 million characters on each of its two sides—yielding an equivalent density of 51 million characters per square inch of writable surface.

The solid line—representing the life expectancy in years of each recording medium—declines through the years. Papyrus fragments of Egyptian writing from 4,500 years ago, while quite fragile today, are still legible. Moving ahead in time, stunning examples of illuminated manuscripts and other documents from Medieval times are quite able to withstand centuries more study and admiration. A similar situation prevails with early modern book printing technologies. Herman Melville's *Moby Dick, or The Whale*, first published in 1851 on typically acidic paper, symbolizes the worldwide preservation challenges of all nineteenth- and twentieth-century publishing (Banks 1969). The introduction of wood pulp and acidic compounds to paper, required at the time by a manufacturing industry desperate to keep up with demand, started the "slow fires" of deterioration that preservation efforts are now attempting to squelch.

During the twentieth century, the permanence, durability, and stamina of newer recording media have continued to decline, with the exception of microfilm (Sebera 1990). Magnetic tape may be unreadable just thirty years after manufacture (Van

Bogart 1995, p. 11). The newest recording medium—optical disk—may indeed have a longer life than the digital recording surfaces that have gone before. It is likely, however, that today's optical storage media may long outlast the life of the computer system that created the information in the first place. This is the ultimate irony of recorded history. In order to achieve the kind of information density that is common today, we must depend on machines that rapidly reach obsolescence to create information and then make it readable and intelligible (Dollar 1992).

The mix of machinery and media of the digital world increases the need for responsible preservation activity in institutions. To help discover how to meet this increased need, this report first presents a framework of primary preservation concepts as they have evolved in past decades. It then redefines and transforms these concepts into a new framework for action in the digital world.

A Framework of Preservation Concepts

In the past two decades, a community of practitioners has reached consensus on a set of fundamental preservation concepts for managing available resources in a mature preservation program (Conway 1989). At one time, advocates for the protection of cultural artifacts, including books, primary source documents, and museum objects, used the terms "conservation" and "preservation" interchangeably. Today, preservation is an umbrella term for the many policies and options for action, including conservation treatments. Preservation is the acquisition, organization, and distribution of resources to prevent further deterioration or renew the usability of selected groups of materials.

The essence of preservation management is resource allocation. People, money, and materials must be acquired, organized, and put to work to ensure that information sources are given adequate protection. Preservation is concerned with evidence—what Michael Buckland (1991) calls "information as thing"—embedded in the intellectual content of objects and in the objects themselves. Nearly endless varieties of forms and formats are preserved so that people can use them for equally varied purposes, scholarly and otherwise. Those with the responsibility to do so find the small portions of the vast sea of information—structured as collections of documents, books, photographs and films, sound recordings, and other "things"—that have research value as evidence of thought and action well beyond the time and intentions of those who created or published them.

Cost-effective preservation action cannot take place without compromising ideal outcomes. Preservation management encompasses all the policies, procedures, and processes that together prevent further deterioration of physical objects, renew the information they contain, and increase their functional value. This distinction between the value of the content (usually text and illustration) and the value of the artifact is at the heart of a decision-making process that itself is central to effective management. Preservation management includes an ongoing, iterative process of planning and implementing prevention activities (e.g., maintaining a stable, safe, and secure environment, ensuring disaster preparedness, and building a basic collection-level maintenance program) and renewal activities (e.g., undertaking conservation treatments, replacing the content of library materials, or reformatting them on microfilm).

Figure 1. Clay tablet. 34 char./in² (per square inch)

In the world of paper and film, preservation and access are separate but related activities. It is possible to fulfill a preservation need of a manuscript collection, for example, without solving the collection's access problems. Similarly, access to scholarly materials can be guaranteed for a very long period of time with taking concrete preservation action. Modern preservation management strategies, however, posit that preservation action is taken on an item so that it may be used. In this view, creating a preservation copy of a deteriorated book on microfilm without making it possible to find the film (usually by cataloging it and then depositing the bibliographic record in a national database) is a waste of money. Preservation in the digital world puts to rest any lingering notion that preservation and access are separable activities.

Significant financial barriers slow the design and implementation of effective preservation strategies. Some leaders in the field have suggested, however, that inadequate funding may not be the only brake on preservation success. "The major obstacle to the development and administration of preservation programs is the shortage, not of money, as many suppose, but of knowledge," wrote Pamela Darling (1981, p. 185). "Financial constraints are serious and will become more so; but until the preservation field reaches the point at which most people know what ought to be done and how it should be done, the lack of money to do it on a scale appropriate to the need is not terribly significant." The basic consciousness-raising task for preservation may have been accomplished for the world of paper and film. It is just beginning for the digital world.

At this critical juncture in the evolution of preservation thinking, there is a large body of knowledge upon which to draw. The literature documents some fundamental concepts that have been described, tested, and codified (Swartzburg 1995). The following nine concepts, defined below in part by the words of some of the most articulate preservation advocates of past decades, form the framework for a comprehensive preservation perspective.

Figure 2. Papyrus. 53 char./in²

Context for Action

Four concepts describe what might be called the context for preservation action.

Custody: Fifty years ago, one of the foremost and persistent advocates for quality bookbinding put his finger on the centrality of preservation to the mission of modern research libraries and archives. Preservation, wrote Pelham Barr in his most frequently cited work, "as responsible custody, is the only library function which should be continuously at work twenty-four hours a day. It is the only function which should be concerned with every piece of material in the library from the moment the selector becomes aware of its existence to the day it is discarded" (1946, pp. 218-19). Barr's allusion to the life-cycle of information sources is highly relevant today. The concept is at the center of information management theory and practice, including specifications for the disposition of government archives, the management of book collections, and the maintenance of large-scale information technology systems (Atherton 1986).

Social value: Organizations that accept preservation as central to their mission also serve a larger societal need. The fundamental value of keeping intact the documentation of people and institutions has endured through years of changing practice.

Almost sixty years ago Robert C. Binkley, a pioneer of preservation microfilming, pinpointed the cultural value of preservation. "The objective of archival policy in a democratic country cannot be the mere saving of paper," he said to one of the first gatherings of professional archivists. "It must be nothing less than the enriching of the complete historical consciousness of the people as a whole" (1939, p. 168). More recently, educator Guy Petherbridge echoed the same sentiments. "The perpetuation of society as we are accustomed to conceive or idealize it is dependent to a very large extent on the preservation *en masse* of our accumulated group memories and consciousness stored in the form of the written, printed and otherwise recorded word or symbol" (1987, p. 1).

Efforts to explain and illustrate the overarching value of preservation have had a positive effect. Today, the widespread recognition of the value of an investment in preservation action—fueled, perhaps, by the persuasive message in the film "Slow Fires"—has resulted in national and regional planning efforts and new dollars for preservation programs. Even the word "archives," carrying the mandate to preserve and protect the secrets they contain, has entered the popular vocabulary (Cox 1993). Part of the service that libraries and archives provide to society is (or will be) their investment in converting, storing, and making available research resources in digital image form. Protecting this investment through prudent preservation action will continue to be the social role of hundreds of organizations that participate in digital library initiatives.

Structure: An organizational structure that enables preservation resource allocation is imperative. The mission of an institution and the relevance of that mission to a larger social purpose are necessary, though insufficient on their own, to mobilize preservation action. Robert Patterson suggested a mechanism for a library-wide preservation development process that was equal parts consciousness raising and strategic planning. His argument on the administrative difficulties of building an effective new program rings true today when it is read with the recognized challenges of digital image technologies in mind. "Historically, many librarians have felt that a conservation program was too technically complex a matter for them to undertake. ... Armed with some basic principles and facts, a program with realistic goals can be developed" (1979, p. 1116). The overwhelming trend in the development of mature preservation programs has been the coalescing of responsibility in a single department, which then sets about making itself, in the best Weberian tradition, essential to the organization.

Cooperation: Resource sharing and cooperation among institutions to select and preserve the best and most valuable cultural artifacts are core preservation values. The ups and downs of cooperative activities are well documented, as are the challenges of maintaining momentum when taking any action that does not immediately benefit the local institution (Gwinn 1985). The largest and most prestigious research libraries—spurred by the ready availability of external funding—may have led preservation program development in the last two decades, but advocates for peer-to-peer or regional cooperation have sounded a warning about the dangers of elitism. Vartan Gregorian reminded a large audience of preservation activists that "all of us are in the same boat. When the boat sinks, no one can claim the fact that

they had a first class ticket as solace" (Morrow 1991, p. 85).

The need to organize for local action often creates a direct tension with national cooperative initiatives. Rutherford Rogers, Yale University's librarian during the heyday of preservation program growth, called for an emphasis on local goals, informed but not controlled by national priorities. National planning, he declared, "cannot supplant local programs or relieve us of our responsibility to develop them. Instead, we must take advantage of the large support network of collective research and educational activities to develop local programs suited to local needs, a network that may serve as the basis of a true national program" (1985, p. 8). When properly managed, inter-institutional cooperative preservation programs supplement local priorities.

Priorities for Action

Five concepts together can be seen to help direct the priorities for preservation action.

Longevity: The central concern in traditional preservation practice has been the media upon which information is stored. The term "archival" used to

Figure 3. Illuminated manuscript. 141 char./in²

mean "permanent" and preservation focused on infinity. Jim O'Toole reviews the transformation of the definition of longevity: "The idea of permanence as it is understood by archivists has changed considerably over time, passing from an unattainable desire to an absolute value within the realm of achievement to an extremely relative notion of little clarity" (1989, p. 23). Today, archivists and librarians evaluate storage media in terms of their life expectancies. The top priority is extending the useability of papers, films, magnetic tapes, and other media by stabilizing their structures and limiting the ability of internal and external factors to cause deterioration. The focus on external factors led to specifications for proper environmental controls, care and handling guidelines, and disaster recovery procedures. Progress on efforts to control the internal factors of deterioration has resulted in alkaline paper standards, archival quality microfilm, and more rugged magnetic media (Calmes 1987).

Choice: Preservation adds value through selection. Choice involves defining value, recognizing it in something, and then deciding to address preservation needs in the way most appropriate to that value. Selection in archives and research libraries was once thought to be primarily a one-time decision about the potential for future use, made near the time of publication or when the documents ceased to serve the primary purposes for which they had been created originally (Atkinson 1986, p. 345). Over decades the act of preservation has evolved from saving material from oblivion and assembling it in secure buildings to encompass more sophisticated condition, value, and use assessments on the already-collected. Preservation selection in libraries has been dictated largely by the need to stretch limited resources in as wise a fashion as possible, resulting in the dictum that "no item shall be reformatted twice." The end result is a growing "virtual" special collection of items preserved using a variety of techniques, most notably by microfilming. Selection is perhaps the most difficult of undertakings precisely because it is static and conceived by practitioners as either completely divorced from present use or completely driven by demand (Demas 1994).

Quality: Maximizing the quality of all work performed is such an important maxim in the preservation field that few people state this fundamental

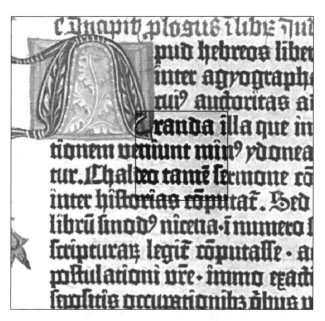

Figure 4. Gutenberg Bible. 25 char./in² (per square inch)

principle directly. Instead, the preservation literature dictates high quality outcomes by specifying standards for treatment options, reformatting processes, and preventive measures. The commitment to quality standards—do it once, do it right—permeates all preservation activity, including library binding standards, archival microfilming guidelines, conservation treatment procedures, the choice of supplies and materials, and a low tolerance for error. The evolution of microfilming as a central strategy for preserving brittle library materials has placed the quality of the medium and the quality of the image on an equal plane (Fox 1996). In the pursuit of quality microfilm, compromise on visual truth and archival stability is dictated more by the characteristics of the item chosen for preservation and less by cost or the present state of display technologies.

Integrity: The concept of integrity has two dimensions in the preservation context: physical and intellectual. Physical integrity largely concerns the item as artifact and plays out most directly in the conservation studio, where skilled bench staff use water-soluble glues, age-old hand-binding techniques, and high-quality materials to protect historical evidence of use, past conservation treatments, and intended or unintended changes to the structure of the item (Tanselle 1989). The ethics of conservation recognize that all physical treatments change the nature of the object and, therefore, are not really reversible by nature (Dureau 1986).

The preservation of intellectual integrity is based upon concern for evidence of a different sort. The authenticity, or truthfulness, of the information content of an item—maintained through careful and complete reformatting or sensitive treatment—is at the heart of intellectual integrity (Duranti 1995). Ideally, documentation supports the preservation of intellectual and physical integrity by creating a chain of evidence connecting multiple formats of the object and recording what has been or needs to be done to any one of these formats in the name of preservation. Preservation also protects and documents the relationships among items in a collection. The concepts of quality and integrity reinforce each other.

Access: For years, preservation simply meant collecting. The sheer act of pulling a collection of manuscripts from a barn, a basement, or a parking garage and placing it intact in a dry building with locks on the door fulfilled the fundamental preservation mandate of the institution. In this regard, preservation and access have been mutually exclusive activities often in constant tension. "While preservation is a primary goal or responsibility, an equally compelling mandate—access and use—sets up a classic conflict that must be arbitrated by the custodians and caretakers of archival records," states a fundamental textbook in the field (Ritzenthaler 1993, p. 1). Access mechanisms, such as bibliographic records and archival finding aids, simply provide a notice of availability and are not an integral part of the object.

After years of disciplined practice, most librarians, archivists, conservators, and scientists recognize these nine concepts of preservation action. The same learning curve that has led to the acceptance of current preservation practice must now take place for digital imaging technology in a time-frame of years instead of decades.

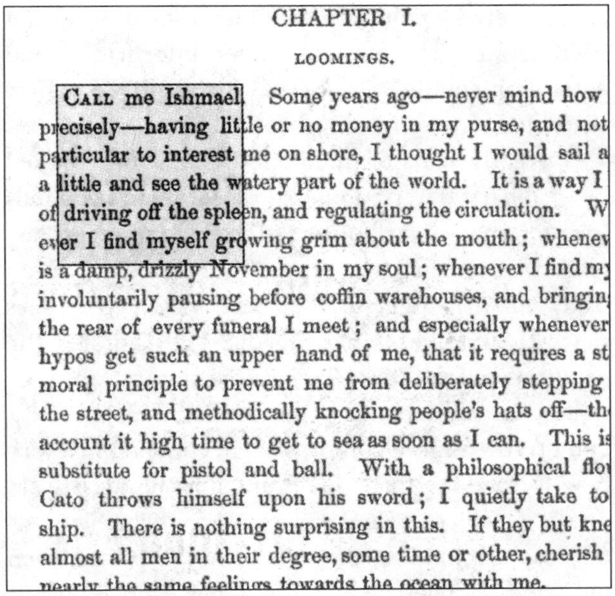
CHAPTER I.

LOOMINGS.

CALL me Ishmael. Some years ago—never mind how
precisely—having little or no money in my purse, and not
particular to interest me on shore, I thought I would sail a
a little and see the watery part of the world. It is a way I
of driving off the spleen, and regulating the circulation. W
ever I find myself growing grim about the mouth; whenev
is a damp, drizzly November in my soul; whenever I find my
involuntarily pausing before coffin warehouses, and bringin
the rear of every funeral I meet; and especially whenever
hypos get such an upper hand of me, that it requires a st
moral principle to prevent me from deliberately stepping
the street, and methodically knocking people's hats off—th
account it high time to get to sea as soon as I can. This is
substitute for pistol and ball. With a philosophical flo
Cato throws himself upon his sword; I quietly take to
ship. There is nothing surprising in this. If they but kne
almost all men in their degree, some time or other, cherish
nearly the same feelings towards the ocean with me.

Figure 5. Nineteenth-century novel. 101 char./in^2

Technology and Organizational Change

Technologies and organizations affect each other in different ways, depending in large part upon the characteristics of technologies and how organizations choose to use them. In this regard, it is important, first, to distinguish between acquiring digital imaging technology to solve a particular problem and adopting it as an information management strategy. Acquiring an imaging system to experiment with its capability to enhance access to library and archive materials is now almost as simple as purchasing tools in a hardware store. Simply buying a technology "solution" has no long-term implications for an organization. However, when pilot imaging projects are transformed and adopted as core systems for creating and delivering electronic documents with long-term value, preservation in the digital world becomes an important organizational issue.

Microfilm technology, as it has quickly proliferated in libraries and archives, has been largely a means for achieving ends already decided upon. Microfilm was, and remains, well-suited for reproducing bulky and fragile newspapers and for distributing research materials largely unknown or unusable in their native locations. Continuous wave radio, on the other hand, created a world of new possibilities for which new corporate goals had to be formulated. "In that sense it acquired a determinative force to which organizational decision-making had to adapt," writes Hugh Aitken. Unlike microphotography, radio broadcasting "encountered a cultural phenomenon that it has not itself created: a mass market for information and entertainment the existence of which had been barely suspected" (Aitken 1985, p. 562).

The early years of microphotography are marked by visionary descriptions of revolutionary possibilities for mass distribution of books on small glass plates rather than on paper (Luther 1959). Susan Cady (1990) suggests that any vision that sees new technologies replacing old ones ignores the centuries-old reality that new communication technology merely expands opportunities, adds diversity, and creates a more complex environment. For every new technology that today functions beside an old one (*e.g.*, television and radio), it is possible to identify a new technology that actually was replaced by an old one (*e.g.*, teletype by radio, typewriters by printers). People cherish convenience and will ignore any technology whose characteristics (*e.g.*, cumbersome equipment, poor image quality, weak indexing) limit that convenience.

Digital image technologies present a similar situation for libraries that radio presented more generally for the corporate world some sixty years ago. In the digital world, preservation becomes possible because preservation—as it is defined in this paper—is an intimate part of the new possibilities. In the digital world, preservation must be concerned with entire technology systems, not one or another component, such as a film or a storage disk. Like radio, television, and electric power networks, digital imaging is not one technology. It is an interlinked, open system of hardware, software, and service subsystems, each with their own components, that develops in cycles. Digital systems are characterized by multiple core subsystems (scanners and transmission devices). Data storage is but one of many peripheral subsystems, among them compression hardware and software, display technologies, and output devices.

Early students of the history of communication and technology wanted to know in what sense an individual, an organization, or a social class can be said to be in control of, or to be managing, a body of information (Innis 1950). They wrote in terms of monopolies of knowledge and the degree to which different media—clay tablets, papyrus, the printed book,

---

Preserving Visionary Technology

Enthusiasm for the potential of new information technologies is nothing new. A century ago, electrical engineers imagined a publishing revolution driven by mass storage on glass plate negative. One such engineer, Henry Morton, related a perhaps apocryphal tale of a microscopic version of the Lord's prayer, "written in characters so small that the entire 227 letters of that petition are engraved within an area measuring 1/294 by 1/441 of an inch." At that rate, he claimed, "a square inch of glass would accommodate the entire text of the Bible eight times over" (Norton, 1895, p. 432).

Reginald A. Fessenden, an engineer on the eve of his breakthrough invention of the modern radio transmitter, used Dr. Morton's story as a point of departure for describing his own use of microphotography to reproduce technical notes gathered in his investigations. He had a miniature camera built that was capable of recording a single page on a single glass plate negative measuring 1-1/2 by 1-1/4 inches. He developed batches of these negatives himself in his bathtub and stored them in small envelopes pasted to the reverse side of the blank library catalog cards that he used to index the contents.

Fessenden's success led him to speculate on how microphotography could revolutionize book publishing. "It is well within the bound of possibility that the scientific student of the future will do his book work with the aid of a small projection lantern and a library of small positives, purchased at a small fraction of the price now paid." Rapid access was an essential part of Fessenden's model. "It would be an extremely easy matter, for instance, to arrange the mechanism of a plate containing a German dictionary so that by the pressure of a couple of keys the page commencing with any given letters would be thrown on the screen" (Fessenden, 1896, p.224).

The glass strip containing the Lord's prayer in miniature has apparently vanished. The only evidence of Fassenden's extensive glass-plate microfiles is his scrapbook of photos and notes in the North Carolina Division of Archives and History. Yesterday's new technology is today's rare specimen. What is the prospect for digital technology?

LP vinyl disks—lent themselves to the formation of such monopolies. More recent scholarship suggests that understanding and influencing technological change encompasses not only managing a technology process but also managing the consequences of technology on people and organizations (Czitrom 1982). Expanding this argument further, Columbia University scholar Michael Tushman suggests that we cannot even begin to understand technological progress by examining technical characteristics alone. At critical junctures, he suggests, "organizational action (and inaction) dramatically affects the shape and direction of technological change" (1992, p. 312).

Libraries and archives are an interrelated part of this new and complex digital marketplace, but not necessarily a critical element. They need to recognize their role in the development of digital imaging technologies, as well as the new demands that these technologies will place on them as organizations.

Preservation Management in the Digital World

As librarians and archivists have experimented with the capabilities of digital imaging technologies, the concept of preservation has come to have at least three distinct meanings.

Make Use Possible: For a very small subset of valuable but deteriorated documents, digital imaging technology is a viable, and possibly the only, cost-effective mechanism for facilitating research use. A recent experiment involving digitizing oversize color maps (Gertz 1995) demonstrated that the only way to really use the maps, which have faded badly and are very brittle, is to view them on a large color monitor after they have been digitized and enhanced. Similarly, the managers of the Andrew Wyeth estate have found that reproductions of the artist's work are most faithfully represented in digital form (Mintzer and McFall 1991).

Protect Original Items: Digital image technology can be used to create a high quality copy of an original item. By limiting direct physical access to valuable documents, digital imaging becomes a "preserva-

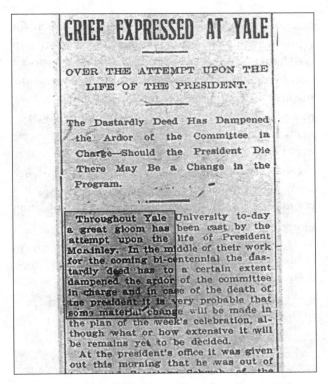

Figure 6. Newspaper. 174 char./in²

tion application" as distinct from an "access application." The original order of the collection, or book, is "frozen," much like microfilm sets images in a linear sequence. Sophisticated indexing schemes facilitate browsing and minimize the potential for damage or disruption to a collection caused by "fishing expeditions" through the published or unpublished record. Preservation via digital copying has been the most compelling force motivating archives and libraries to experiment with hardware and software capabilities.

Maintain Digital Objects: Once digital conversion of the original document has been completed, the challenge of protecting the digits from corruption or destruction becomes the preservation focus. This facet, now being called "digital preservation," typically centers on the choice of interim storage media, the life expectancy of a digital imaging system, and the concern for migrating the digital files to future systems as a way of ensuring future access (*Preserving Digital Information* 1995).

A workable framework for preservation in the digital world could encompass the initial choice of the technology, the use of digital imaging technology for reproducing research materials, and the protection of the digital information for as long as that information has value to the institution and the patrons the institution serves. The process of converting library materials to an electronic form—a process which in many aspects is similar to the one used to create preservation microfilm—is distinct from any particular medium upon which the images may be stored at a particular point in time. This distinction allows for a continuing commitment to creating and maintaining digitized information while entertaining the possibility that other, more advanced systems may render digital storage media obsolete. Preservation management of digital image files encompasses their creation, organization and indexing, storage, transmission, and continued intellectual integrity.

The following section proposes how the nine fundamental concepts of preservation described above can be transformed in response to the particular characteristics of digital information.

Context for Action

Custody: In the digital world, a library, archives, or museum cannot make a decision to adopt imaging technologies for long-term conversion and storage of research collections in digital form without a deep and continuing commitment to preservation by the parent institution. The preservation mission that was once largely the prerogative of the library must become the preservation mandate of the parent institution. The necessary financial and technological commitments to maintain image system life and migrate image system data to future generations must permeate the highest levels of the organization.

Social Value: The particular value to society of preservation in the digital world has less to do with historical consciousness and group memory—as advocates for traditional preservation have claimed—and much more to do with service to academic, scholarly, and public communities. Active use is the lifeline of the loosely connected clusters of unique (in digital form), highly valuable, and intensely consulted digital collections that form a digital library worth preserving.

Structure: Organizing for preservation in the digital world is not, first and foremost, a search for process efficiency, as has been the case with traditional preservation, but rather an ongoing process of risk management, where the cost of digital file migration is judged against the cost of failure to preserve the files in terms of the patrons who need the information. The stakeholders in this organization extend well beyond the bounds of a preservation department or the administration of a library or archives to encompass technology specialists, marketing experts, and commercial vendors.

Cooperation: As preservation in the digital world becomes less a centrally managed enterprise at the institutional level and more a mutually reinforcing shared responsibility, cooperation and institutional self-interest should reinforce each other. When approaching the challenges of preservation, institutions will contribute to the required cost and the technical expertise because there will simply be no other way to satisfy their patrons' information needs.

Priorities for Action

Longevity: Preservation in the digital world has little concern for the longevity of optical disks, magnetic tape, and other new, fragile storage media. The viability of digital image files is much more dependent on the life expectancy of the access system—a chain only as strong as its weakest component. Digital storage media must be handled with care, but they most likely will far outlast the capability of systems to retrieve and interpret the data stored on them. Since we can never know for certain when a system has become obsolete, libraries must be prepared to migrate valuable image data, indexes, and software to future generations of the technology. Migration is now and will remain a very challenging task, as the recent digital archiving task force has pointed out (*Preserving Digital Information* 1995).

Choice: Selection for preservation in digital form is not a one-time choice made near the end of an item's life cycle, but rather an ongoing process intimately connected to the active use of the digital files. The value judgments applied when making a decision to convert documents from paper or film to digital image are valid only within the context of the original system. With the need to migrate data to another storage and access system comes the mandate to revisit again and again the decision to continue preserving the information. It is a rare collection of digital files, indeed, that can justify the cost of a comprehensive migration strategy without factoring in the larger intellectual context of related digital files stored elsewhere and their combined uses for research and scholarship (Conway 1996).

Quality: Quality in the digital world—that is, the usefulness and useability of systems—is conditioned significantly by the limitations of capture and display technology. Digital conversion places less emphasis on obtaining a faithful reproduction of the original in favor of finding the best representation of the original in digital form. Mechanisms and techniques for judging quality of digital reproductions are different and more sophisticated than those for assessing microfilm or photocopy reproductions (Kenney and Chapman 1995). Additionally, the primary goal of preservation quality is to capture as much intellectual and visual content as is technically possible and then display that content to viewers in ways most appropriate to their needs.

Integrity: In the digital world, both physical and intellectual integrity have their place in preservation. A commitment to the physical integrity of a digital image file has far less to do with the media upon which the data are stored than with the loss of information that occurs when a file is created originally and then compressed mathematically for storage or transmission across a network. In the domain of intellectual integrity, index information is not independent of the content of the item but rather is an integral part of the digital file. Structural indexes and data descriptions traditionally published with an item as tables of contents or prepared as discrete finding aids or bibliographic records must be preserved—as metadata—along with the digital image files themselves (Weibel 1995). The preservation of intellectual integrity also involves authentication procedures, like audit trails, to make sure files are not altered intentionally or accidentally (Lynch 1994).

Access: In the digital world, the concept of access is transformed from a convenient byproduct of the preservation process to its central motif. The content, structure, and integrity of the information object assume center stage; the ability of a machine to transport and display this information object becomes an assumed end result of preservation action rather than its primary goal. Preservation in the digital world is not simply the act of preserving access but also includes a description of the "thing" to be preserved. In the context of this report, the object of preservation is a high-quality, high-value, well-protected, and fully integrated version of an original source document.

Administrators who have responsibility for selecting systems for converting materials with long-term value also bear responsibility for providing long-term access to the digital versions. This responsibility is a continuing one. Decisions about long-term storage and access cannot be deferred in the hope that technological solutions will emerge. An appraisal of the present value of a book, a manuscript collection, or a series of photographs in its original format is the necessary point of departure for making a judgment about preservation of the digital image version. The mere potential for increased access to a digitized collection does not add value to an underutilized collection. Similarly, the powerful capabilities of a relational index cannot compensate for a collection of documents whose structure, relationships, and intellectual content is poorly understood.

If libraries, archives, and museums expect to adopt digital imaging technology for purposes of transforming the way they serve their patrons and each other, then they must move beyond the experimental stage. Digital image conversion in an operational environment requires a deep and longstanding institutional commitment to preservation, the full integration of the technology into information management procedures and processes, and significant leadership in developing appropriate definitions and standards for digital preservation.

A New Framework for Effective Leadership

One view of leadership involves establishing control through the application of standards and procedural guidelines. Those who hope to exercise comprehensive control over digital imaging technology most probably will find that moral persuasion cannot often prevail in the absence of a significant market share. Others have argued that the rapid pace of technological change and the sheer complexity of information technologies render librarians and archivists helpless in influencing product developments. Yet, those who prefer to wait and see how digital imaging technology shakes out before making the administrative commitments necessary to ensure long-term preservation are shirking their responsibility to help define the terms of the debate.

Each of these perspectives ignores an imperative of leadership. "A leader is one who mobilizes others toward a goal shared by leader and followers," writes Garry Wills (1994, p. 70). Preservation in the digital world must encompass shared goals that leaders and followers elicit together. It is the responsibility of many people in many institutions fulfilling many roles of both leader and follower. Accepting the differentiation of roles is crucial if librarians and archivists are to identify which of the many facets of digital technology they can control, where their expertise is one of many important influences, and when they must accept the processes and products of the socio-economic system of which libraries and archives are but one part.

The following table summarizes key aspects of digital imaging technology that are important for creating and maintaining access to digital image files over a long period of time. It arrays these aspects on two dimensions: the priorities for action and the degree of power that librarians and archivists can have over accomplishing the goals implied by the priorities.

Longevity: Librarians can exercise a large measure of control over the life expectancy of digital image data through the careful selection, handling, and maintenance of rugged, well-tested recording and storage systems. They can influence the life expectancy of the information by making sure that local budgetary commitments are made consistently and at an appropriate level in support of long-term migration strategies. Ultimately, the library community may have little control over the evolution of the imaging marketplace, especially corporate research and development activities that have a tremendous impact on the life expectancy of the digital files being creating today.

Choice: Even while recognizing that selection decisions cannot be made autonomously or in a vacuum, librarians and archivists can choose which books, articles, photographs, films, and other materials are converted from paper or film into digital image form.

Leadership Options for Preservation Action

	Control	Influence	Accept
Longevity	Choice of Storage Media	Institutional Budgetary Commitments	Imaging Marketplace
Choice	Intellectual Content	Migration Strategy and Timing	Impact of Patron Problem Solving
Quality	Conversion Quality Standards	Image Compression and Display Standards	System Technical Capabilities
Integrity	Index Content and Structural Standards	Metadata Interchange Standards	Network Protocols and Speed
Access	Purchase of Non-proprietary Equipment	Backward Compatibility of Systems	System Life Expectancy

Influence over the continuing value of digital image files is largely vested in the right to decide when it is time to migrate image data to a future storage and access system and in knowing when a digital file has outlived its usefulness to the institution charged with preserving it. Librarians and archivists, while not directly responsible for the capabilities of their patrons, can nonetheless help determine how digital information will be provided and help educate users about use of new technologies to meet their needs.

Quality: The commercial imaging market has transformed the principle of maintaining the highest possible quality over time to one of finding the minimal level of quality acceptable to today's system users. Quality of the digital object, including the richness of both the image and the associated indexes, is the heart and soul of preservation in the digital world. This means maximizing the amount of data captured in the digital scanning process, documenting image enhancement techniques, and specifying file compression routines that do not result in the loss of data during telecommunication. Librarians and archivists can control standards of digital image quality, just as they have done for microfilm. They can only influence the development of standards for data compression, communication, and derivatives for display and output. Research laboratories and the imaging marketplace will have the greatest influence over improvements in the technical capabilities of digital conversion and storage systems.

Integrity: Librarians and archivists can help exercise control over the integrity of digital image files by authenticating access procedures and documenting successive modifications to a given digital file. They can also create and maintain structural indexes and bibliographic linkages within well-developed and well-understood database standards. Librarians and archivists are acknowledged experts in organizing information and so have a vital role to play in influencing the development of metadata interchange standards, including the tools and techniques that will allow structured, documented, and standardized information about data files and databases to be shared across platforms, systems, and international boundaries. However, librarians and archivists may find they are but bystanders in the rapid development of network protocols, bandwidth, or data security techniques.

Access: The digital imaging marketplace is highly competitive. Librarians and archivists can do the most to ensure continuing access to digital image files through prudent purchases of nonproprietary hardware and software components. In the present environment, true "plug and play" components are becoming more widely available; purchase decisions are the most powerful incentives for vendors to adopt open system architectures or at least provide better documentation on the inner workings of their systems. Additionally, librarians and archivists can influence vendors and manufacturers to develop new systems that are "backwardly compatible" with existing ones. This capability assists image file system migration in the same way that today's word processing software allows access to documents created with earlier versions. The life expectancy of a given digital image system and the requirement to migrate valuable digital image files to future generations of the technology are profoundly important matters over which librarians and archivists have little or no control. It seems that the commitment of a vendor to support and maintain an old system is inversely related to that vendor's ability to market a new system.

Conclusion

Preservation in the digital world challenges librarians and archivists, but not necessarily due to a lack of understanding of digital technologies, selection criteria, or appropriate preservation options. The technologies are becoming understood well enough. Informed choices about what to preserve in the digital world and the best ways to accomplish preservation goals both derive from this understanding.

The real challenge is creating appropriate organizational contexts for action. Cooperative strategies adopted from ongoing preservation practice are not all that is needed to address the complexities or the costs of digital technologies. Libraries and archives must do more than simply divide the preservation pie. The national digital libraries that are now under construction should be built under an umbrella of guiding preservation concepts. Additionally, new approaches to creating and maintaining digital files cooperatively must be developed. The acceptance of shared responsibility and shared funding commitments will preserve access to what are, in essence, unique electronic collections.

Will the totality of the national digital library—whether it is a single entity or many things to many people—be of such high quality and of such extraordinary value to a university, a state government, or other institution that each participant will make a long-term commitment to help support its preservation? Only if the answer to this question is yes will it be possible to build that library cooperatively. Establishing such commitments requires the kind of leadership that has set the context for traditional preservation action in the past two decades.

List of Figures

1. Clay tablet: *Akkadian Love Song*. Early 18th century BC. "Early Incantations and Rituals" #24, Museum # YBC4643, Yale Babylonian Collection, Sterling Library, Yale University. 133x173x33 mm.

2. Papyrus: *Unidentified Fragment*. P.Ct.YBR inv. 422(A)fol. Beinecke Photo File, Beinecke Library, Yale University. 215.9x228.6 mm.

3. Illuminated manuscript: *Rothschild Canticles*. 1300-1400, 182v.-183r. MS404, Beinecke Photo File, Beinecke Library, Yale University. 118x84 mm.

4. Gutenberg Bible: *Bible. Latin. Vulgate.* [Mainz, Printer of the 42-line Bible (Johann Gutenberg), ca. 1454-55.]. Zzi 561, 43 cm. Beinecke Photo File, Beinecke Library, Yale University.

5. Nineteenth-century novel: Melville, Herman. *Moby Dick, or, the Whale*. New York: Harper & Brothers, 1851, p. 1. Tinker 1545, Beinecke Library, Yale University. 1:1 Reproduction.

6. Newspaper: *Evening Leader*. New Haven, CT. September 7, 1901, p. 1. Sterling Library Stacks, Yale University. 1:1 Reproduction.

7. Microfilm: Melville, Herman. *Moby Dick, or, the Whale*. New York: Harper & Brothers, 1851. Film #B838, V2, reel M-17, no. 1701. Sterling Library, Yale University. Microtext RR. [Figure not included.]

8. Microfiche: *American City Directories, through 1860-New Haven*. Fiche B1272, #817. Sterling Library, Yale University. Microtext RR. [Figure not included.]

9. Floppy disk: 1.44 megabyte floppy disk. Preservation Department, Yale University Library. [Figure not included.]

10. Optical disk: 1.3 gigabyte magneto-optical disk. Project Open Book, Yale University Library. [Figure not included.]

Bibliography

PRESERVATION

Atherton, Jay. "From Life Cycle to Continuum: Some Thoughts on the Records Management-Archives Relationship." *Archivaria* 21 (Winter 1985–86): 43–51.

Atkinson, Ross. "Selection for Preservation: A Materialistic Approach." *Library Resources & Technical Services* 30 (October/December 1986): 341–53.

Banks, Paul N. "The Treatment of the First Edition of Melville's *The Whale*." *Guild of Bookworkers Journal* 7 (Spring 1969): 15–22.

Barr, Pelham. "Book Conservation and University Library Administration." *College & Research Libraries* 7 (July 1946): 214–19.

Bearman, David. *Archival Methods*. Pittsburgh: Archival and Museum Informatics, 1989.

Binkley, Robert C. "Strategic Objectives in Archival Policy." *American Archivist* 2 (July 1939): 162–68.

Calmes, Alan. "To Archive and Preserve: A Media Primer." *Inform* (May 1987): 14–17, 33.

Conway, Paul. "Archival Preservation: Definitions for Improving Education and Training." *Restaurator* 10 (1989): 47–60.

Cox, Richard J. "International Perspectives on the Image of Archivists and Archives: Coverage by *The New York Times*, 1992–1993." *International Information & Library Review* 25 (1993): 195–231.

Cummings, Anthony M., et al. *University Libraries and Scholarly Communication: A Study Prepared for the Andrew W. Mellon Foundation.* Washington, D.C.: Association of Research Libraries, 1992.

Darling, Pamela W. "Creativity v. Despair: The Challenge of Preservation Administration." *Library Trends* 30 (Fall 1981): 179–88.

Demas, Samuel. "Setting Preservation Priorities at Mann Library: A Disciplinary Approach." *Library Hi Tech* 12 (1994): 81–88.

Duranti, Luciana. "Reliability and Authenticity: The Concepts and Their Implications." *Archivaria* 39 (Spring 1995): 5–10.

Dureau, Jean Marie and D. W. G. Clements. *Principles for the Preservation and Conservation of Library Materials.* The Hague: IFLA, 1986.

Morrow, Carolyn Clark, ed. *National Conference on the Development of Statewide Preservation Programs.* Washington, D.C.: Commission on Preservation and Access, 1991.

O'Toole, James M. "On the Idea of Permanence." *American Archivist* 52 (Winter 1989): 10–25.

Ogden, Barclay. *On the Preservation of Books and Documents in Original Form.* Commission on Preservation and Access, October 1989.

Patterson, Robert H. "Organizing for Conservation: A Model Charge to a Conservation Committee," *Library Journal* 104 (May 15, 1979): 1116–19.

Petherbridge, Guy, ed. *Conservation of Library and Archive Materials and the Graphic Arts.* London: Butterworths, 1987.

Ritzenthaler, Mary Lynn. *Preserving Archives and Manuscripts.* Chicago: Society of American Archivists, 1993.

Rogers, Rutherford D. "Library Preservation: Its Scope, History, and Importance." In *The Library*

Preservation Program: Models, Priorities, Possibilities, pp. 7–20. Edited by Jan Merrill-Oldham and Merrily Smith. Chicago: American Library Association, 1985.

Sebera, Donald. "The Effects of Strengthening and Deacidification on Paper Permanence: Some Fundamental Considerations." *Book & Paper Group Annual*, vol. 9, pp. 65–117. Washington, D.C.: American Institute for Conservation, 1990.

Swartzburg, Susan G. *Preserving Library Materials: A Manual.* 2nd. ed. Metuchen, N.J.: Scarecrow, 1995.

Tanselle, G. Thomas. "Reproductions and Scholarship." *Studies in Bibliography* 42 (29 Sept. 1989): 25–54.

Walch, Victoria Irons, "Checklist of Standards Applicable to the Preservation of Archives and Manuscripts," *American Archivist* 53 (Spring 1990): 324–38.

Winger, Howard W. and Daniel Smith. *Deterioration and Preservation of Library Materials: The Thirty-fourth Annual Conference of the Graduate Library School.* Chicago: University of Chicago Press, 1970.

DIGITAL PRESERVATION

Ackerman, Mark S., and Roy T. Fielding. "Collection Maintenance in the Digital Library." *Proceedings of Digital Libraries* 95, Austin, TX, June 1995, pp. 39–48.

Battin, Patricia. "From Preservation to Access: Paradigm for the Nineties." *IFLA Journal* 19 (1993): 367–73.

Conway, Paul. "Digital Preservation: Paper and Microfilm Go Electronic." *Library Journal* 119 (February 1, 1994): 42–45.

Conway, Paul. "The Implications of Digital Imaging for Preservation." In *Preservation of Library and Archival Materials*, 2nd ed. Edited by Sherelyn Ogden. Andover, MA: Northeast Document Conservation Center, 1994.

Conway, Paul. "Selecting Microfilm for Digital Preservation: A Case Study from Project Open Book." *Library Resources & Technical Services* 40, (January 1996): 67–77.

Digital-Imaging and Optical Digital Data Disk Storage Systems: Long-Term Access Strategies for Federal Agencies. Technical Information Paper No. 12. Washington, D.C.: National Archives and Records Administration, 1994.

Dollar, Charles M. *Archival Theory and Information Technologies: The Impact of Information Technologies on Archival Principles and Methods.* Macerata: University of Macerata Press, 1992.

Fox, Edward A., et al. "Digital Libraries: Introduction," *Communications of the ACM* 38 (April 1995): 23–28.

Gertz, Janet, et al. *Oversize Color Images Project, 1994-1995: Final Report of Phase I.* Washington, D.C.: Commission on Preservation and Access, 1995.

Graham, Peter S. "Requirements for the Digital Research Library." *College & Research Libraries* 56 (July 1995): 331–39.

Kenney, Anne R. "Digital-to-Microfilm Conversion: An Interim Preservation Solution." *Library Resources & Technical Services* 37 (1993): 380–401.

Kenney, Anne R., and Stephen Chapman. *Digital Resolution Requirements for Replacing Text-Based Material: Methods for Benchmarking Image Quality.* Washington, D.C.: Commission on Preservation and Access, 1995.

Lesk, Michael. *Preservation of New Technology: A Report of the Technology Assessment Advisory Committee.* Washington, D.C.: Commission on Preservation and Access, 1992.

Lesk, Michael. *Electronic Libraries and Electronic Journals.* London: The British Library, 1994.

Levy, David M. and Catherine C. Marshall. "Going Digital: A Look at Assumptions Underlying Digital Libraries." *Communications of the ACM* 38 (April 1995): 77–84.

Lynch, Clifford. "The Integrity of Digital Information: Mechanics and Definitional Issues." *Journal of the American Society for Information Science* 45 (December 1994): 737–44.

Mintzer, Fred, and John D. McFall. "Organization of a System for Managing the Text and Images that Describe an Art Collection." *SPIE Image Handling and Reproduction Systems Integration* 1460 (1991): 38–49.

Mohlhenrich, Janice. *Preservation of Electronic Formats: Electronic Formats for Preservation.* Fort Atkinson, WI: Highsmith, 1993.

Preserving Digital Information: Draft Report of the Task Force on Archiving of Digital Information. Version 1.0 August 23, 1995. Research Libraries Group and Commission on Preservation and Access. URL: http://www.oclc.org:5046/~weibel/archtf.html.

Robinson, Peter. *The Digitization of Primary Textual Sources.* Office for Humanities Communication Publication, no. 4. Oxford: Oxford University Computing Services, 1993.

Rothenberg, Jeff. "Ensuring the Longevity of Digital Documents." *Scientific American* 272 (January 1995): 42–47.

Waters, Donald J. "Transforming Libraries Through Digital Preservation." In *Digital Imaging Technology for Preservation.* Proceedings from an RLG Symposium held March 17 & 18, 1994, pp.115–27. Edited by Nancy E. Elkington. Mountain View, CA: Research Libraries Group, 1994.

Van Bogart, John W. *Magnetic Tape Storage and Handling: A Guide for Libraries and Archives.* Washington, D.C.: Commission on Preservation and Access, 1995.

Weibel, Stuart. "Metadata: The Foundations of Resource Description." *D-Lib Magazine,* July 1995. URL: http://www.dlib.org.

MICROPHOTOGRAPHY

Bourke, Thomas A. "Scholarly Micropublishing, Preservation Microfilming, and the National Preservation Effort in the Last Two Decades of the Twentieth Century: History and Prognosis." *Microform Review* 19 (Winter 1990): 4–16.

Cady, Susan A. "The Electronic Revolution in Libraries: Microfilm Deja Vu?" *College & Research Libraries* 51 (July 1990): 374–86.

De Stefano, Paula. "Use-Based Selection for Preservation Microfilming." *College & Research Libraries* 56 (September 1995): 409–18.

Fessenden, Reginald A. "Use of Photography in Data Collections." *Electrical World* 28 (August 22, 1896): 222–24.

Fox, Lisa L., ed. *Preservation Microfiming: A Guide for Librarians and Archivists.* 2nd ed. Chicago: American Library Association, 1996.

Gabriel, Michael R. and Dorothy P. Ladd. *The Microform Revolution in Libraries.* Greenwich, CT: JAI Press, 1980.

Gwinn, Nancy E. "The Rise and Fall and Rise of Cooperative Projects." *Library Resources & Technical Services* 29 (January/March 1985): 80–86.

Luther, Frederic. *Microfilm: A History, 1839–1900.* Annapolis: The National Microfilm Association, 1959.

Morton, Henry. "Engineering Fallacies." *Cassier's Magazine* 8 (August 1895): 428–39.

Rider, Fremont. *The Scholar and the Future of the Research Library: A Problem and Its Solution.* New York: Hadham Press, 1944.

Veaner, Allen B. "Incredible Past, Incredible Future." *Library Resources & Technical Services* 26 (January-March 1982): 52–56.

TECHNOLOGY, CULTURE, AND LIBRARIES

Aitken, Hugh G. J. *The Continuous Wave: Technology and American Radio, 1900–1932.* Princeton, NJ: Princeton University Press, 1985.

Bolter, Jay David. "Text and Technology: Reading and Writing in the Electronic Age." *Library Resources & Technical Services* 31 (January/March 1987): 12–23.

Buckland, Michael K. "Information as Thing." *Journal of the American Society for Information Science* 42 (June 1991): 351–60.

Constant, Edward W. II. "The Social Locus of Technological Practice: Community, System, or Organization?" In *The Social Construction of Technological Systems: New Directions in the Sociology and History of Technology*, pp. 223–42. Edited by Wiebe E. Bijker, Thomas P. Hughes, and Trevor J. Pinch. Cambridge, MA: MIT Press, 1987.

Czitrom, Daniel J. *Media and the American Mind: From Marx to McLuhan.* Chapel Hill, NC: University of North Carolina Press, 1982.

Hughes, Thomas P. *Networks of Power: Electrification in Western Society, 1880–1930.* Baltimore, MD: Johns Hopkins University Press, 1983.

Innis, Harold A. *Empire and Communication.* Cambridge: Oxford University Press, 1950.

Lewis, Tom. *Empire of the Air: The Men Who Made Radio.* New York: HarperCollins, 1991.

Macaulay, David. *Motel of the Mysteries.* Boston: Houghton Mifflin, 1979.

Marsalis, Wynton. *Marsalis on Music.* New York: Norton, 1995.

Nollinger, Mark. "America, Online!" *Wired* 3.09 (September 1995): 158–61, 199–204.

Segal, Howard P. *Future Imperfect: The Mixed Blessings of Technology in America.* Amherst, MA: University of Massachusetts Press, 1994.

Tushman, Michael L. and Lori Rosenkopf. "Organizational Determinants of Technological Change: Toward a Sociology of Technological Evolution." *Research in Organizational Behavior* 14 (1992): 311–47.

Wills, Garry. "What Makes a Good Leader?" *The Atlantic Monthly* (April 1994): 63–80.

MARGARET HEDSTROM

"Understanding Electronic Incunabula: A Framework for Research on Electronic Records"

American Archivist 54.3 (Summer 1991): 334–54.

"ELECTRONIC INCUNABULA" IS a metaphor for the current nature of electronic records as an evolving form of documentation. Incunabula, translated literally, means "out of the cradle," but in common parlance incunabula refers to the origins, infancy, or beginning of anything. In the history of printing, incunabula are the earliest printed books—generally those printed before 1500. Electronic records, as today's incunabula, present archivists with their greatest challenge in decades.[1]

The term "electronic incunabula" captures several themes from the framework for research that follows. Electronic records are in their infancy, and society has only begun to witness their transformative effects on documentation and communications. The shift from print to electronic communications will change the ways that organizations create and use information, much as the introduction of printing altered social practices, cultural conventions, institutions, economics, laws, and the politics of information. Change will be evolutionary, as was the case with the introduction of printing, because profound shifts in the production and dissemination of information incorporate some traditional habits and approaches for handling information, and at the same time render obsolete some skills, professions, and institutions. Lacking any certain guideposts to predict the future, it is useful to look back at earlier shifts in paradigms.

This framework for research on electronic records uses historical evidence and concepts from the history of technology, but it is oriented toward future research. It shares common origins and inspiration with recent research agendas on the identification of records of enduring value, the management of archives, and the use and users of archives, but it differs from those research agendas in several respects.[2] First, electronic records are relatively new, and most archivists are unfamiliar with their nature and characteristics. Second, electronic records issues are complex and multi-faceted. Consultation and collaboration with experts in other fields will be essential elements of successful research. Third, research on electronic records issues spans all archival functions and may challenge basic archival theory and practice. Consequently, the research framework proposed here is interdisciplinary, more theoretical, and less specific than research agendas for functionally specific core areas of archival work.

Research Objectives

Research on electronic records issues should produce generalizable policies, practices, methods, and applications for the management, preservation, and use of electronic records. Government agencies and large corporations have used computers extensively for recording and manipulating information since the 1960s, but archivists have made little progress toward developing specialized programs for electronic records or integrating them into core functions. There are few established and accepted standards, practices, or conceptual approaches to the management and preservation of electronic records. Social science data libraries and some traditional archives developed effective techniques for simple machine-readable data files, but those methods are not applicable to more complex forms of electronic records found in databases, office automation systems, geographic information systems, and compound documents. As the capabilities of modern information systems diverge from simple automated systems and forge sharper distinctions between electronic records and conventional paper files, some archivists question whether basic archival theories and practices can be applied to electronic records.[3] The absence of approaches and techniques that address the wide variety of electronic records created with today's information technology is a major obstacle to development and growth of electronic records programs.

Research on electronic records issues will help the archival profession adopt a more strategic position in relation to information technology and its use by organizations. To date, archivists have responded to electronic records problems after hardware, software, and storage media have reached the market and become well established.[4] Archivists have had no impact on the design of information technology and little influence over its use in organizations. As a consequence, individuals and organizations have developed their own conventions for handling information in automated systems. Many current institutional practices undermine retention, preservation, and secondary use of electronic records; and most are inefficient, non-standard, and difficult to reverse. Even the word *archive* has lost much of its traditional meaning and associations. In the vernacular of data processing professionals, "to archive" means to store data off-line. A "permanent medium" is one that cannot be erased or altered even if it only lasts a few years. These new definitions do not incorporate any of the concepts that archivists normally associate with the term *archive:* to understand information in its context, to identify what is valuable, or to retain records and make them accessible as long as they have value. Archivists have literally lost control over the definition of *archive.*[5]

A framework for research with ambitious goals and challenging questions encourages archivists to "think big enough" about electronic record keeping to make a difference. Whether electronic records are recognized as records, treated as an essential element of society's documentary heritage, and regarded as treasures that can preserve history and memory, depends to a large extent on the ability of archivists to influence how individuals and institutions use information technology and value its products.

One way to influence the policies and practices that govern the use of information technology is to intervene when new technologies are introduced into organizations. Such a strategic approach requires more research on emerging technologies and more emphasis on designing systems and tools that support archival and information management objectives from the outset. By concentrating on emerging technologies, archivists have the potential to build records management and archival requirements into software, applications, policies, and procedures, rather than trying to satisfy them retrospectively. Research can help archivists anticipate technology trends and forecast their likely effects on organizations and their records. This in turn would allow archivists to raise concerns about access, retention, preservation, and future retrieval before these issues have been defined as too cumbersome, too expensive, or irrelevant.

Several historical precedents suggest that such actions can succeed. Standards for microfilm products and processes include important archival requirements, and archivists have a history of involvement with descriptive standards.[6] Currently, archivists and librarians are engaged in an effort to persuade the paper products industry to convert from acid to alkaline paper. Major archival repositories have made initial forays into several information technology standards, whose widespread adoption would facilitate retention and accessibility of electronic records.[7] Well-focused research can identify opportunities for archivists to influence standards and products, and help archivists better articulate their requirements when opportunities arise to comment on or contribute to standards development or product design. Research on electronic records issues will help archivists account for the social, economic, and political aspects of organizational life that mediate how information technologies are adopted and used by organizations. Electronic record keeping is both a technological and a sociological phenomenon, and solutions lie in both the technical and administrative realm. Yet archivists are most familiar with the physical and technical barriers to preservation of electronic records. Equally significant changes in the ways that organizations define and carry out their missions, organize work processes, and meet the demands for inter- and intra-organizational communications are a fundamental, but neglected aspect of the problem. The technologies available to create, retrieve, store, and disseminate information are a factor in changing patterns of organizational work, documentation, and communications, but the role of technology in the process of change is not clearly delineated.

Archivists also can contribute to research on information technology and systems that support a wide range of organizational needs for usable, reliable, authentic, comprehensible, and lasting documentation. Archivists are in a unique position to contribute to information system designs because of their singular perspective on the relationship between the mission and structure of an organization, its need for records, its information flows, and document structures. A few thoughtful information professionals acknowledge that many current information systems are hampered by the narrow perspective of computer scientists, which focuses on optimal processing times and machine utilization rather than on information systems that help people do their jobs well. David Levy, a researcher at the System Sciences Laboratory, Xerox Palo Alto Research Center, contends that an essential perspective on advanced document systems is lacking in spite of a great deal of research on hardware and software tools from a computer systems perspective. According to Levy, "what is missing … is the set of complementary studies, in which documents—the subject matter, in effect, of our document systems—are investigated in their own right, as richly structured, cultural, communicative artifacts."[8] The failure of new information technologies to mesh with organizational structures and information handling practices is not a recent phenomenon. In fact, the history of information processing is littered with information systems that failed because system designers concentrated on operating efficiencies and ignored organizational and cultural issues that are indispensable elements of information handling.[9]

In order for the archival profession to gain the maximum benefits possible from the time, effort, and other resources it invests in research, questions must be ambitious, think far ahead, and account for the social and cultural environment in which new information technology is applied. An effective program of research cannot focus only on present technologies or specific computer applications. Unless research projects recognize the broad implications of technological change and the essential changes that have taken place in organizations, the conduct of business, and record keeping, they are likely to overlook what is at stake and concentrate on issues that are time-bound and narrow in scope.

A research framework can support these objectives by promoting careful planning, sound research methodologies, and interdisciplinary approaches. Archivists have much to learn from colleagues in related fields who are concerned about related electronic records issues and much to gain from interdisciplinary research. Although there is no single discipline or organized body of "computing studies," archivists can find relevant research in the vast literature of information and library science, sociology of organizations, computer science, electrical engineering, and management science.[10]

The research needed to respond effectively to electronic records issues will be time-consuming, expensive, and complex, but posing broad questions about the significance of electronic records does not mean that archivists will conduct abstract research on global issues. Rather, a research framework can provide the structure for a series of smaller, practical projects that build on each other's results, contribute to an understanding of broader issues, and yield cumulative results from what might otherwise be disparate efforts.

Understanding the Context of Information Technology

Electronic records do not exist in a vacuum; rather, they emerge in response to particular conditions and needs. Research on electronic records will be influenced by the researcher's definition of information technology and assumptions about the role of technology in social and organizational change.[11] The research framework presented here defines information technology broadly as "the machines, processes and know-how used to create, store, manipulate, disseminate, and retrieve information." Students of technology point out that the term *technology* may be associated with physical objects, such as bicycles, washing machines, or computers; with processes or activities, such as oil refining or data processing; and with practical knowledge such as the "know-how" that goes into designing a bicycle or the knowledge required to sort a stack of cards into alphabetical order.[12] According to the definition used here, *information technology* may consist of physical objects that produce or process information, such as pens or computers; the processes that organize and manipulate information, such as routines to balance accounts or programs to alphabetize a list of names; and the know-how needed to organize and interpret information, such as double-entry bookkeeping or alphabetical filing rules. Machines, processes, and know-how are all essential subjects for electronic records research.

A broad definition of information technology corresponds roughly to hardware, software, and the formal and implicit decision rules that govern information handling in automated systems. In information handling, the boundaries between machine, process, and know-how are constantly shifting. With the development of expanded machine instruction sets and specialized computer chips, for example, processes that used to be part of the software become fully incorporated into hardware functionality. Likewise, the line shifts between manual processes and software as each new computer program absorbs elements of know-how into an automated process.[13] A broad definition of information technology acknowledges the shifting line between machine, process, and knowhow and helps maintain the essential connection between the manual processes of the past and their automated analogs.

Research on electronic records should avoid overly simplistic notions of the relationship between technology and social forces. One common interpretation of the role of technology in society is *technological determinism*—a perspective that attributes causality to machines or to technological process. Technologically determinist interpretations often contend that a specific machine or process was the cause of a larger social change. To argue, for example, that the printing press caused literacy because it provided a superior technology for the inexpensive dissemination of printed works is a technologically determinist argu-

ment. As Langdon Winner explains, according to this perspective, technology develops "as the sole result of an internal dynamic and then, unmediated by any other influence, molds society to fit its patterns."[14]

Some analysts have adopted an equally unsatisfactory perspective that views technology as the product of raw political and economic power. This perspective, referred to as *social determinism,* compensates for technological determinism because it assumes that technical artifacts do not matter at all. Technology merely reflects the decisions of those individuals, industries, interest groups, or whoever had the power to decide which path technology ought to take.[15] Finally, some interpretations view technology as a completely neutral force in society that is autonomous from a social or economic context. According to this notion, technology is simply a tool under human control. One can choose to use or not to use a specific piece of technology, and the consequences of its use depend entirely on how humans apply it.

Recent research in the sociology and history of technology provides a framework to move beyond technology as a "black box" and to analyze technology as a rich social process.[16] Sometimes referred to as the "social construction of technology," this new perspective considers technology to be the embodiment of human choices that influence how a machine is designed, what it is designed to accomplish, and how it is intended to accomplish its objectives. The design, development, marketing, acceptance or rejection, and interpretation of a technology are social processes shaped by rich interactions between cultural norms, economic and political power, social values, and the potential of a new machine or process.[17] According to this perspective, however, technologies ultimately reach "closure"—a point at which debate over the features of the technology ceases and the artifact or process stabilizes. Upon reaching closure, technical features alone may limit or eliminate possibilities, require adjustments in social and political systems, undermine deeply-held cultural values, and alter power relations.[18]

A perspective that considers technologies as "socially constructed" provides grounds for a cautiously optimistic view that archivists can influence key information technologies because it acknowledges that humans retain varying degrees of control over the design of technology. Many aspects of today's information technology have not reached closure. Archivists are not alone in questioning how information technology will shape their profession and the institutions they serve. Debates continue in many fields about the potential capabilities of information technology, what it should be designed to do, and how it will accommodate or transform information-handling practices.[19]

A perspective that views information technology as socially constructed also supports the premise that electronic records issues cannot be addressed exclusively through research on technical problems because important social and economic factors shape the decisions that individuals and organizations make about information technology. Computers are extraordinarily versatile machines, and their ability to process information once it has been reduced to a digital form places few technical constraints on potential applications. To learn much about the impact of information technology on capture, creation, and use of information, research must reach beyond the technology and examine its application and the context in which it is applied. Research on electronic records will benefit from a clear understanding of the origins and evolutionary nature of change in information-handling technology and processes. A substantial body of literature discusses the "information revolution," but it often describes computer technology uncritically, and ascribes to it the power to transform economies from industrial- to information-based, to change the work force from manual laborers to knowledge workers, and to increase the availability of goods, services, and leisure time for all. Much of this literature speculates about the likely impact of computers, but claims of a "revolution" are seldom substantiated with evidence that distinguishes the role of computer technology from other social and economic factors.[20]

Often, the term *revolution* is misappropriated because changes in information handling are more evolutionary in nature. Formal institutions, procedures, and the know-how needed to manage and interpret information develop over an extended period of time and persist in spite of technological change. Organizations rarely have the luxury to abandon completely their old information systems, whether manual or automated, because information systems consist not only of hardware and software, but also of all the rules, procedures, skills, and habits that people have developed to handle information. Elements of information-handling practices often are carried forward from manual to automated systems, and from one automated system to the next.

If the industrial nations are in the midst of an information revolution, it is unclear how far they have traveled. James Beniger contends that data processing is the culmination, not the dawn, of a "control revolution" that began in the 1830s. Through centralized organizations and new infrastructures for transportation and telecommunications, bureaucratic organizations gained control over markets and communications. The establishment of marketing, advertising, and mass distribution, which relied on and produced massive volumes of information, was as central to this change as development of a physical infrastructure of ports and railroads.[21]

Shoshana Zuboff places society at the beginning, rather than the end, of a transformation in information-handling practices. Zuboff makes a distinction between "automate" and "informate." She uses the term *automate* to refer to the replacement of human capabilities with the capacities of a machine, in contrast to the term *informate*, which refers to the capacity of information technology to change the ways organizations both process and use information.[22] According to Zuboff, most computer applications in factories and offices have simply automated older processes. This approach merely reproduces the logic of the assembly line and speeds up the processing of paper. When organizations "informate," they use the capabilities of computer technology to handle information in fundamentally different ways that transform work and power relations.

Ronald Weissman finds a similar shift in the world of the compound document and the personal workstation. Weissman claims that fundamental changes in software and computer architecture are transforming our notions of software and documents. New visions of computing tools result not only from massive leaps in the power of computers, but also from new ideas "about what computing can do and should be."[23] According to Weissman, a new computing culture has emerged, in contrast to the world of mainframe computers and MIS, which believes that "computing ought to have a playful character and be personally empowering, more fun and far more imaginative and enriching than simple text processing, budget consolidation, or mainframe payroll processing."[24]

While focusing on emerging technologies, research on electronic records issues should be sensitive to social, cultural, economic, and political factors that mediate how rapidly technology can change information handling practices. A fundamental transformation of white collar work will require massive investments in software and telecommunications, changes in legal and social practices, and an infusion of new skills for handling electronic documents. Whether this transformation will take several years or several decades is a matter for debate, but it will evolve as a series of compromises between the potential of technology and the real needs and requirements of organizational life.

Lessons from the introduction of printing in the fifteenth century can help archivists gain a perspective on a profound change in information technology that may be applicable to research on the electronic incunabula facing the profession today. Because printed books are such an integral part of the material culture of Western society, we rarely stop to think about their historical origins, how they assumed the form and structure that they possess, or what the introduction of printing meant for the generations who observed the printed book as a new phenomenon. An understanding of the history of printing can help archivists discern how societies create new conventions for formatting and organizing recorded information.

The printing press created a new textual form, the printed book that could be reproduced in multiple identical copies, but eventually the impact of the printing press stretched beyond print technology and its immediate products. After books were printed new institutions developed, such as the book trade and eventually the lending library. The notion of literacy changed from a mystical faculty of clerics and scholars to an essential skill for survival as printed works reached deeper into the population. Books changed from treasured objects to everyday items that were bought and sold, loaned, and even discarded.

The structure and uses of books also evolved gradually during the first century or so of printing. Elizabeth Eisenstein reminds us that many of the conventions which we take for granted as part and parcel of the definition of a book—pagination, tables of contents, interspersion of graphics and text, and running headers—were invented gradually as the printed book diverged from hand-copied manuscripts.[25] The introduction of printing not only spread literacy, knowledge, and texts, it also changed behavior and cultural practices. Printed books, for example, were first read aloud, but eventually the practice of silent reading developed.[26]

History also informs us that societies accumulate recording and communications technologies, rather than replace one with another. Humans did not stop speaking when they learned to write; they did not stop writing when they learned to print, nor will they stop using paper when electronic media are widely accessible. As David Levy explains, "our literate culture retains and reinvests in its technological heritage, since the cost of discontinuous change is so high."[27] The traditions that surround information handling also have remarkable staying power, but they are not impervious to change. Even with widespread automation, people will continue to use paper documents when they provide familiar or convenient means for circulating and reading information. What is at issue is not the replacement of one form of material or one recording medium with another, but the significance of new forms of material that individuals and organizations create, using new information technologies.

The examples above support the premise that automation will bring about profound changes in the materials archivists handle and the processes used to create them. Electronic records will continue to diverge from paper records in their appearance, structure, uses, and significance as computer technology provides the capability for people to manipulate information in novel ways. Although no one knows how this new potential will be realized, archivists can frame research questions that are sensitive to the magnitude and evolutionary nature of this change and its social and cultural dimensions.

Framing Questions: Areas for Research

The concepts and perspectives discussed above suggest five broad areas for research. This section proposes ways to frame research questions in each area, but it does not outline a detailed research agenda.[28] Electronic record keeping is fertile ground for research, and the five areas are not meant to cover all potential research issues. Moreover, the research areas are not mutually exclusive. Well-designed research projects might address questions raised in several of the research areas.

1. What is the relationship between activities, organizational structures, information technology, information flows, decision-making, and documentation?

Researchers should examine electronic records in the overall context of organizations and their documentation. A priority area for research is the relationship between functions, activities, organizational structures, and information systems. Similar research has already been proposed by archivists concerned with appraisal and descriptive practices.[29] Archival theory posits an explicit relationship between the functions and activities of organizations and the documentation they create. In an era of rapidly changing information technology, archivists need to reexamine how information systems support organizational functions and relate to organizational structure within specific organizations and in a broader documentary context. Such research will help archivists determine where current theory can be applied and where new approaches and methods are needed to manage electronic records.

Research must also address the specific relationships between automation and the documentary requirements of organizations. Archivists would benefit from research that examines changes in communications and records when organizations automate. How does information flow through an organization and how does automation change patterns of information flow? Why do organizations decide to automate certain functions (and not automate others)? What factors influence selection and use of information technology by organizations? Do organizational characteristics such as size, type of organization, composition of the work force, complexity of work, and the power structure affect the form and content of its records? Do individual decision-making styles and corporate culture influence an organization's use of automated systems?

Research on these relationships must also account for the complex interactions between information technology, the transformation of information-handling processes, and changes in organizational structures and functions. Although researchers from a variety of disciplines contend that organizations modify their structures, alter their communication patterns, and change decision-making styles as a consequence of automation, there are widely varying explanations for these relationships.[30] Moreover, academic researchers rarely consider the effects of these changes on the recorded documentation that organizations create.[31] Participation by archivists in interdisciplinary research projects could lend an especially valuable perspective to studies of automation and organizational change.

2. What new forms of material do users create with information technology?

Forms of material influence many aspects of archival practice. In the broadest sense, forms of material define archivists as professionals who concern themselves with records and distinguish archivists from librarians who handle bibliographic items and museum curators who work with artifacts. The archival profession uses special arrangement, description, and preservation practices for specific forms of materials, such as maps, drawings, and motion pictures, particularly when they also constitute "special format" records.[32]

It is common to regard electronic records as a new form of material because of the special physical characteristics of automated records and the need for new methods for their care and handling. In the 1960s and 1970s, when most electronic records were in the form of machine-readable data files that contained numeric data, electronic records could be treated as a distinct form of material. However, as computer technology provides the capability to store almost any type of information in digitized form—words, pictures, sounds, graphics, and images—the distinction between electronic records and other forms of material becomes less meaningful, while differences among forms of electronic records become significant.[33] In the area of cartographic data, for example, archivists are uncertain whether digitized data used to produce the pictorial representation of a geographic area constitutes a map or an electronic record. Are there any unique aspects of a digitized "map" that distinguish it from a map that is drawn or printed on paper?

Understanding the forms of material that arise with the automation of record keeping requires more than a new taxonomy of record types. Research on this issue should be especially sensitive to the interaction between the technical capability to create, store, or display information in new formats and the meaning and values that users ascribe to that information. Only certain electronic information is created and used to support documentary requirements, and only certain electronic communications have the characteristics of authenticity, reliability, and stability to qualify as records.[34]

Linkages between forms of material traditionally stored on paper, such as memoranda, and similar forms of electronic documents must be explored. Networks, for example, have the capacity to transmit memoranda that can be viewed on a computer screen, but users may not define that electronic message as a record until it is printed on paper or captured and stored in an electronic "filing" system.[35] At the same time, electronic mail systems may capture messages that previously were transmitted over the telephone, and hence, defined as outside the realm of recorded documentation (unless an individual chose to create a written summary of important calls).

The introduction of new forms of material and the simultaneous transformation of traditional forms into something new raises a series of questions about the relationship between forms of material and archi-

val practice.[36] When should new forms of material be managed differently from more traditional forms of documentation? Are there any archival principles that apply to all new electronic record types? What characteristics does an electronic memo share with a memo on paper? What does it have in common with other machine-readable records? What roles do tradition, habit, and past practice play in defining how individuals and organizations handle electronic records? For instance, do automated office systems mimic manual systems with the use of such conventions as "filing" and "paginating" documents because these practices form a bridge with paper document based practices and terminology? Or are these superior and effective ways of organizing and handling textual information regardless of its physical form?[37] Answers to these questions will help archivists better understand the nature of electronic records and the relevance of archival theory.

3. Can archivists intervene at critical points in the development and introduction of new technologies?

Research is needed in a third broad area to identify strategic opportunities for intervention by archivists into processes that affect the design and deployment of information technology and its use by organizations. The proposed research questions are based on the premise that many aspects of information technology have not yet reached closure, that outside interest groups at times can insert their views into the design process, and that archivists have something to offer to designers of information systems. Research should address the perceived need for archivists to become involved in the design of information systems while recognizing that archivists have not determined when to intervene or which tactics to use.[38]

Research on a series of focused questions could test these assumptions. At what critical points are decisions made about the development and introduction of new information technologies? Can archivists and records creators articulate design requirements that meet archival needs and explain them to hardware designers, software engineers, and applications developers? Which strategies and tactics successfully influence developers of information technology and designers of automated applications? How can archivists learn about significant technology trends and forecast their impact on organizations and their records? Can archivists influence the ways organizations value and use electronic records through involvement in information systems design? Can archivists help organizations form sound management practices for their electronic records before new systems become established?

Answers to these questions will help archivists craft strategies that use the profession's limited resources and influence most effectively. They may identify key technologies or decisive moments in the design cycle where intervention by archivists is most effective. Research on this issue would also help archivists learn more about the technical and social aspects of information systems design and implementation.

4. How will changes in the supply of, demand for, and costs of storing and disseminating information change archival practice?

Behind questions about culture, values in society, and organizational structure lie some hard questions about supply, demand, and costs. The automation of record keeping changes many of the economic dynamics that have molded the archival profession. Because paper is a very low-density storage medium and storage space has become increasingly expensive during the twentieth century, archivists take extraordinary measures to keep the volume of paper records at the minimum necessary to achieve "adequate" documentation. The appraisal function is dedicated to identifying that small percentage of records—often cited as 3 to 5 percent—that is absolutely necessary for historical purposes. Archivists at times weed superfluous materials from collections, undertake complex sampling projects, and microfilm records solely for the purpose of bulk reduction.

When information is stored in digitized form, the costs of storage per se decrease dramatically. Recent advances in storage technology make it possible to store millions of pages on a single disk at a trivial cost, and the trend toward lower storage costs is only accelerating. The costs of maintaining the information in a form that is accessible, however, quite possibly will absorb any potential savings from reduced

space. David Bearman has argued that it will be prohibitively expensive to preserve electronic records in the physical custody of archives in the wake of constantly changing storage and retrieval technologies, the requirements of software systems to retrieve electronic records, and the need to migrate data from one generation of technology to another. As a consequence, archivists should not consider taking physical custody of electronic records.[39]

This radical recommendation is thought provoking because it encourages archivists to reexamine their role during a period of rapidly changing information technology and to reconsider basic practices designed to preserve paper records. However, to make sound decisions about the custody of archival records, archivists need to know more about the existing and potential demand for their services, the costs of meeting that demand, and the impact of major changes in information technology on access and preservation costs. Although it is impossible to calculate ultimate storage costs for records that are to be retained "permanently," the profession lacks any model to estimate the relative costs of retaining records in the various available media or to evaluate the benefits of different media options. Archivists should conduct research on the costs, benefits, risks, and feasibility of various preservation options and strategies that can contribute directly to an informed reconsideration of the custodial role of archives.

Such an examination would quickly depart from supply and demand factors to more fundamental research on the users of archival records, their interests, behavior and motivation, and the nature of the services they demand. In his proposed research agenda for the use of archives, Lawrence Dowler encouraged all archivists to examine use and users closely and to build services around demand for records rather than supply.[40] Research on users will not be applicable to electronic records issues unless research projects examine potential users whose needs are not met by current archival holdings and services, including current users of electronic records who obtain access directly from the creating agencies, from social science data libraries, and from private vendors.

Archivists should study current and projected markets for electronic records to develop useful models for electronic records programs in an era of fundamental change in potential services, user expectations, and the costs of meeting them.[41] The experience of private-sector vendors who have captured government records in electronic form, added value to them, and redisseminated them at a profit may provide instructive lessons for the decades ahead. Archivists might study how private vendors identify and reach markets for electronic records, determine when and how to add value to them, and distribute data to those markets. How do purchasers of private data services evaluate the quality of the "product" they purchase? What types of value-added services are users willing to purchase? What are the implications for equity of access? These are the types of broad issues that archivists must confront because electronic records carry with them vastly reduced storage costs, coupled with new possibilities for manipulating, packaging, and adding value to records. Archivists need research that evaluates new options for delivering information to users while protecting the authenticity of electronic records.

5. *How should the requirements for management and preservation of electronic records change archives as institutions and the archival profession?*

Archivists who administer machine-readable records programs agree that the traditional methods used to appraise, process, describe, disseminate, and preserve paper records are inadequate to administer electronic records. In light of both advancing technologies and the limited success of machine-readable records programs, some archivists are beginning to question whether fundamental archival principles, such as provenance and original order, are applicable to the administration of electronic records. The concepts of original order and provenance derive from the basic archival principle of *respects des fonds*—the practice in archives of grouping together records from an administration, organization, person, or corporate body, and of segregating records of one origin from records of other origins. This principle is based on the assumption that much of the meaning and value of records derives from knowledge of the context in which the records were created. Knowledge of the context of creation in turn can be ascer-

tained by examining records in their original order and by studying the administrative history, organizational structure, and functions of organizations and the life history and accomplishments of individuals.[42]

Many archivists are aware that modern technologies undermine or complicate the application of the principles of provenance and original order. Except for the simplest data file structures, the physical ordering of data is controlled by software and is distinct from its logical order. Database management packages and the software that controls sophisticated applications, such as geographic information systems, provide users with the capability of a multitude of logical views of the data.[43] Networks provide users with capabilities for inter- and intra-institutional collaboration in the creation of documents and the formation of policy.

The debate over the relevance of established archival principles to electronic records has many dimensions. Some archivists question whether provenance can be used to control and describe electronic records that document multi-institutional communications, while others suggest that the principle can be applied if it accounts for fundamentally different patterns of communications and collaboration.[44] Archivists also disagree whether limitations on the principle of provenance relate exclusively to electronic records, or whether the principle has limited use for modern records, regardless of format.

Answering questions about the applicability of basic theory and practice will be the most difficult because the relevance of theories and the effectiveness of practices must be measured against the purpose of archives and the mandates for their programs. Archives could continue to serve as central repositories for the small percentage of records in any format that have enduring value, selected against the increasingly sophisticated appraisal criteria necessary to control costs. Archives could continue to distinguish themselves from libraries and other information services by defining specific types of recorded information that fall exclusively under their purview. Likewise, archivists might identify strengths and value in traditional archival theory and devise new methods that apply traditional theory to a new technological and organizational environment. For example, the need to maintain information about provenance in order to understand and interpret records might form the basis for the distinction between archival records and library materials. Archives would administer programs for access to records that are unintelligible without knowledge of the context in which they were created. The archivist's main responsibility would be to maintain linkages between context and content, with or without physical custody of records. Although research can never define for archivists what archives ought to be, research projects can help archivists evaluate the conceptual, technical, and economic obstacles to preservation of contextual information about electronic records.[45]

Research should also evaluate models for programs that help organizations create and maintain adequate documentation of their history and accomplishments, ensure that sufficient and authentic records are created to hold organizations accountable for their decisions and actions, and promote preservation of electronic records with long-term value. In an era of widespread electronic record keeping, there are few good models of theories, practices, or programs that support these requirements. Social science data archives are the most fully developed institutions for preservation and dissemination of information in machine-readable form. Their history and programs provide instructive lessons about the benefits and drawbacks of possible approaches to electronic records preservation.

University campuses and government-supported research institutions around the world established specialized repositories for machine-readable data files during the 1960s and 1970s in response to a recognized need for access to disaggregate social and economic data by a community of researchers.[46] Early proponents of social science data archives regarded the availability of machine-readable data, use and promotion of quantitative methods, and the need to train young scholars in new research techniques as closely intertwined problems. As quantitative methods gained acceptance in the social sciences, data archives became an important component of the infrastructure for research.

Social science data archives concentrate on one form of material: social science research data commonly found in censuses, research surveys, and polling data; they cater successfully to a well-defined, although expanding, clientele.[47] Staff are well versed in the subject areas and research methodologies that the data supports, often having acquired their training in the social sciences rather than in library or archival practices. Data archivists also are experts in data file formats and structures, survey research methods, technical processing, documentation and description, and storage issues. This constellation of expertise is valuable, because data archivists not only locate data sources, but help researchers use and interpret them.

These experiences suggest that there is a close relationship between sources, methods, uses, the value of information, and value-added services. Archivists should study the nature of this relationship, and compare the social sciences to the physical sciences, where repositories are larger and more specialized, and the arts and humanities where the few existing repositories are highly decentralized.

The experience of social science data archives raises several specific research questions. First, can archivists identify constituencies of potential users who are concerned about the availability and preservation of new forms of electronic records? How closely are researchers' concerns about the availability of data linked to the research methods they use? Could archivists mobilize potential users to urge that preservation of electronic records become part of the research infrastructure in the arts and humanities just as noted social scientists did thirty years ago? Finally, the example of social science data archives suggests the types of services that users will expect of data providers in the future, such as assistance with the interpretation of data, preparation of data packages for educational uses, and remote access to records.

Social science data archives do not offer solutions to the most challenging questions about preservation of electronic records because they preserve data primarily for its "informational" value. Data archives methods are increasingly limited for handling records from on-line databases, automated office records, compound documents, software and software-dependent data structures, graphics, and other new types of electronic records. They do not provide models for capture, selection, or preservation of records needed for their evidentiary value, nor do they suggest ways to preserve essential contextual information. If archives are going to continue to play their traditional societal role of capturing and preserving an institutional history and memory, then there is need for considerable research on the ways that organizations make and document decisions using modern technologies. In understanding the relationship between the functions, structures, and documentation of organizational life, archivists have both the most to learn and the most to offer.

A Note on Methodology

The final section of this research framework proposes ways to move from broad questions to specific research projects.[48] As other observers of archival research have noted, archivists lack the time, resources, and facilities to conduct basic research. Most archival research uses the "inductive" model, whereby a practicing archivist examines evidence and then draws conclusions from it, often in response to a specific, practical concern.

The inductive model can contribute answers to broader questions, if a series of more manageable research projects are designed with fundamental issues in mind. Small, practical research projects can build on each others' results if they are coordinated and carefully controlled to account for the setting in which the project occurs. Archivists need to design research projects carefully and use sound methodologies to make sure that urgent and practical research needs do not eclipse more profound issues. Careful attention to research methodology and constant concern with the broader implications of research projects will help archivists overcome a narrow, time-bound perspective.

The design of a research project should begin with the development of a hypothesis that can be tested.

Unfortunately, too many archival studies ask broad, open-ended questions, review current literature, and then experiment with an approach to a problem within the confines of a single institution or program. Without testable hypotheses and adequate controls over such studies, the validity of the research results and their applicability to other institutions are uncertain.

What would constitute a good hypothesis that applies the theoretical perspectives presented here? First, it must be possible to accept, reject, or modify the hypothesis and use it to answer specific questions. Taking just one example, a variety of approaches can be used to examine the issues surrounding office automation. One could construct a research project that asks "what happens to information flows, documents, and records in an office when a local area network is installed?"[49] This approach is problematic because the results are likely to be speculative, impossible to verify, and difficult to apply in varied institutions. A better approach would develop a hypothesis that postulates likely impacts on verbal communications and written documentation. Comparing expected and actual consequences would help archivists determine whether more or less information was recorded, how use and distribution patterns changed, and which documentation and information management problems an organization encountered during such a transition. A follow-up study might test further hypotheses about temporary dislocation and long-term changes that result from automation of record keeping. The development of clear hypotheses will help focus research projects. Researchers should use literature about automation from a variety of disciplines to develop, refine, and evaluate hypotheses. The extensive literature on office automation and communications, for example, would narrow a hypothesis about the impact of local area networks on written and verbal communications.[50]

Even practical projects must account for the array of social, cultural, historical, and technological factors that influence records and record keeping practices. Research projects must control for factors such as structure and functions of organizations that use automated tools for record keeping, the history of information systems in the organization, past practices for managing and controlling records and information, the nature of the "computing package" being used, and the corporate culture of the organization. Looking at all of these factors will help archivists sort out cause and effect, avoid technologically determinist arguments, and identify those aspects of organizational structure, technology, and behavior that should become the focus of intervention intended to promote management and preservation of archival records. Furthermore, careful attention to the environment in which the research occurs will help archivists determine which approaches and methods can be exported from one organization and applied effectively elsewhere.

To return to the example of local area networks, a researcher would need considerable data on such factors as the degree of centralization in the organization, the extent to which office activities rely on written and verbal communications, the extent to which individuals shared information before the system was installed, whether policies and corporate culture promoted or discouraged informal communications, and the effectiveness of previous record keeping and communications practices for supporting office functions. A researcher should also evaluate such technical factors as whether the network connected everyone who needed to communicate, how convenient the system was to use, and the extent to which electronic documents resembled more familiar paper documents. Without addressing all of these factors, it would be difficult to reach valid conclusions about the relationship between the communications capabilities of a local area network and patterns of documentation.

Research projects should be designed to control for the gradual nature of change that accompanies automation. Extensive research on the history of computing in organizations during the past thirty-five years shows that automation is an evolutionary force in organizations. The effects of automation are not always obvious a few months or even a few years after a new information system is installed because well-established customs for handling information and records change gradually. If one accepts the premise that automation is a gradual yet momentous

change, then research must use longer time frames than "before" and "after" studies generally permit.

Research projects should also be designed to avoid a priori assumptions about the impact of computing on organizations. Society is barraged with advertising, popular literature, images, and messages that shape perceptions of what computers are and what they can do. Too often, we accept uncritically such dictums as "computers allow organizations to process information efficiently," "computerization cuts costs," and "computers help deliver the right information to decision makers." While all of these factors may be correct in specific situations or perhaps even in the aggregate, there are enough cases where this is not true to demonstrate that such statements should be the conclusions of a research project and not part of the hypothesis. One recent study of computing literature determined that the initial assumptions of a study were the most accurate predictors of its conclusions.[51]

In developing research projects, archivists should also determine what types of expertise are needed. Considerable discussion has focused on the need for technical expertise to resolve electronic records keeping problems. There is little doubt that archivists need access to technical information, advice, and expertise to address many issues, but expertise in such areas as sociology of organizations, communications, economics, and marketing should not be overlooked. A realistic assessment of the need for outside expertise should encourage interdisciplinary projects. This research framework stops short of proposing a list of specific research projects that archivists should design and conduct during the next few years. It is my hope, however, that the theoretical perspective and the framework presented here can provide archivists with a model to develop specific projects. By keeping the broader issues in mind, well-designed research projects could answer not only issues of immediate concern to specific institutions, but also contribute answers to more challenging issues facing all archivists.

1. Participants in an advanced institute for government archivists, sponsored by the National Association of Government Archives and Records

Administrators (NAGARA), concluded that "the archival management of electronic records is probably the most important, and certainly the most complicated, issue currently before the archival profession." National Association of Government Archives and Records Administrators, *Archival Administration in the Electronic Age: An Advanced Institute for Government Archivists* (Pittsburgh: NAGARA, 1989), iii. Electronic records problems are also discussed in Committee on the Records of Government, *Report* (Washington, 1985); National Academy of Public Administration, *The Effects of Electronic Record Keeping on the Historical Record of the U.S. Government: A Report for the National Archives and Records Administration* (Washington: National Academy of Public Administration, 1989); National Historical Publications and Records Commission, *Electronic Records Issues: A Report to the Commission,* Commission Reports and Papers #4 (Washington: National Archives and Records Administration, March 1990); U.S. Congress, House of Representatives, Committee on Government Operations, *Taking a Byte Out of History: The Archival Preservation of Federal Computer Records,* House Report No. 101-987 (Washington: U.S. Government Printing Office, 1990).

2. Richard J. Cox and Helen W. Samuels, "The Archivist's First Responsibility: A Research Agenda to Improve the Identification and Retention of Records of Enduring Value," *American Archivist* 51 (Winter and Spring 1988): 28–46; Paul H. McCarthy, "The Management of Archives: A Research Agenda," *American Archivist* 51 (Winter and Spring 1988): 52–69; and Lawrence Dowler, "The Role of Use in Defining Archival Practice and Principles: A Research Agenda for the Availability and Use of Records," *American Archivist* 51 (Winter and Spring 1988): 74–86. Recommendations to develop a research agenda for electronic records are found in *Planning for the Archival Profession: A Report of the SAA Task Force on Goals and Priorities* (Chicago: Society of American Archivists, 1986), 9; and "An Action Agenda for the Archival Profession: Institutionalizing the Planning Process: A Report to SAA Council by the Committee on Goals and Priorities," 31 August 1988, 45–17.

3. David Bearman, *Archival Methods* (Pittsburgh: Archives & Museum Informatics, 1989), 26–27, 36–37, and 57–58; Katherine Gavrel, *Conceptual Problem Posed By Electronic Records: A RAMP Study* (Paris: UNESCO, April 1990); Charles Dollar, "The Impact of Information Technologies on Archival Principles and Methods," draft version 1.6, 18 September 1991, to be published by the University of Macerata (Italy) in 1992; Richard Kesner, "Automated Information Management: Is There A Role for the Archivist in the Office of the Future?" *Archivaria* 19 (Winter 1984–85): 162–72; and United Nations, Advisory Committee for the Co-ordination of Information Systems (ACCIS), *Management of electronic records: Issues and guidelines* (New York: United Nations, 1990).

4. Archivists often do not address technological problems until a technology is becoming or has become obsolete. For a discussion of one emerging technology, see Margaret Hedstrom, "Optical Disks: Are Archivists Repeating the Mistakes of the Past?" *Archival Informatics Newsletter* 2 (Fall 1988): 52–53.

5. The data processing definition of *archive* is "a procedure for transferring information from an on-line storage device or memory area to an off-line storage medium." Common archival definitions are: "the noncurrent records of an organization or institution preserved because of their continuing value," or "the agency responsible for selecting, preserving, and making available archival materials." See United Nations, ACCIS, *Management of electronic records,* 137–38. For commentary on this problem, see Lee Stout, "From the Chair," *Mid-Atlantic Archivist* 19 (Summer 1990): 3.

6. For an extended discussion of the development of standards for archival description, see "Special Section: Standards for Archival Description," *American Archivist* 52 (Fall 1989): 432–526; and "Standards for Archival Description: Background Papers," *American Archivist* 53 (Winter 1990): 24–108.

7. For examples, see U.S. National Archives and Records Administration, Archival Research and Evaluation Staff, *A National Archives Strategy for the Development of Standards for the Creation, Transfer, Access, and Long-Term Storage of Electronic Records of the Federal Government,* National Archives Technical Information Paper No. 8 (June 1990); Margaret H. Law and Bruce K. Rosen, *Framework and Policy Recommendations for the Exchange and Preservation of Electronic Records,*

[Report prepared by the National Computer Science Laboratory, National Institute of Standards and Technology for the National Archives and Records Administration] (March 1989); Canadian Bureau of Management Consulting, *Data and Document Interchange Standards and the National Archive* [Project No. 1-6465) (Ottawa, June 1987); Protocols Standards and Communications, Inc., *The Application of ODA/ODIF Standards* [prepared for the National Archives of Canada] (Ottawa, 1989); and Protocols Standards and Communications, Inc., *Application Portability* [prepared for the National Archives of Canada] (Ottawa, 28 December 1989).

8. David M. Levy, "Topics in Document Research," System Sciences Laboratory, Xerox Palo Alto Research Center, Palo Alto, CA, (D. Levy 1988. 8.31.1039), 1. For similar points from an archival perspective, see Luciana Duranti, "Diplomatics: New Uses for an Old Science: Part V," *Archivaria* 32 (Summer 1991): 6–24; and "Diplomatics: New Uses for an Old Science, Part VI," *Archivaria* (forthcoming).

9. Critiques of office automation abound from many perspectives. Sociologists and political theorists have commented on the "macro" effects of automation on workers' skills and job satisfaction. Others have examined how a narrow perspective on office work, based in the principles of Taylorism, fails to account for the skills and knowledge needed to process information. From many perspectives, automated systems fail to work as well as their designers intended. For varying interpretations of this issue, see Harry Braverman, *Labor and Monopoly Capital: The Degradation of Work in the Twentieth Century* (New York and London: Monthly Review Press, 1974); U.S. Office of Technology Assessment, *Automation of America's Offices* (Washington, D.C.: U.S. Government Printing Office, December 1985), 125–68; Shoshana Zuboff, *In the Age of the Smart Machine* (New York: Basic Books, 1988), Chapter 4; William Bowen, "The Puny Payoff from Office Computers," in *Computers in the Human Context,* ed. Tom Forester (Cambridge, MA: MIT Press, 1989), 267–71; and Michael Hammer, "Reengineering Work: Don't Automate, Obliterate," *Harvard Business Review* 68 (July-August 1990): 104–12. Disparities between codified information handling procedures and the way workers actually accomplish their tasks are not unique to automated information systems. For an example of this phenomenon in a manual system, see Lucy A. Suchman, "Office Procedure as Practical Action: Models of Work and System Design," *ACM Transactions on Office Information Systems* 1 (October 1983): 320–28.

10. One anthology with an extensive bibliography of multi-disciplinary literature is Forester, ed., *Computers in the Human Context.* Comprehensive literature reviews include Rob Kling, "Social Analyses of Computing: Theoretical Perspectives in Recent Empirical Research," *Computing Surveys* 12:1 (1979): 61–110; and Kalle Lyytinen, "Different Perspectives on Information Systems: Problems and Solutions," *ACM Computing Surveys* 19:1 (1987): 5–6.

11. For a recent summary of the various perspectives on computer technology, see "Editor's Introduction: Making Sense of IT," in Forester, ed., *Computers in the Human Context,* 1–15, and Parts One and Two.

12. D. MacKenzie and J. Wajcman, eds., *The Social Shaping of Technology* (Milton Keynes: Open University Press, 1985), cited in Wiebe E. Bijker, Thomas P. Hughes, and Trevor Pinch, eds., *The Social Construction of Technological Systems: New Directions in the Sociology and History of Technology* (Cambridge, MA: MIT Press, 1987), 4.

13. A redistribution of functionality also is moving software features closer to the machine. Ronald Weissman points out that features which used to be part of end-user applications are becoming features of operating systems. Ronald E. F. Weissman, "Virtual Documents on an Electronic Desktop: Hypermedia, Emerging Computing Environments and the Future of Information Management," in *Management of Recorded Information: Converging Disciplines,* comp. Cynthia Durance, Proceedings of the 1989 International Council on Archives, Symposium on Current Records (New York: K.G. Saur, 1990), 41.

14. Langdon Winner, "Do Artifacts Have Politics?" in *The Whale and the Reactor* (Chicago: University of Chicago Press, 1986), 21.

15. Ibid., 20–21.

16. For examples, see Bijker et al., *The Social Construction of Technological Systems*; Winner, *The Whale and the Reactor*; and Bruno Latour, *Science in Action* (Cambridge: Harvard University Press, 1987).

17. Trevor J. Pinch and Wiebe Bijker, "The Social Construction of Facts and Artifacts: Or How the Sociology of Science and the Sociology of Technology Might Benefit Each Other," in MacKenzie and Wajcman, eds., *Social Shaping of Technology*, 40.

18. Pinch and Bijker, "The Social Construction of Facts and Artifacts," 44–46; and Winner, "Do Artifacts Have Politics?" 20–39.

19. For examples from several fields, see Alison B. Bass, "Computers in the Classroom," in *Computers in the Human Context*, 237–47; Donald P. Ely and Tjeerd Plomp, "The Promises of Educational Technology: A Reassessment," in *Computers in the Human Context*, 248–61; E. P. Krauss, "Magnetic Media and the Law," *Legal Studies Forum* 13 (1989): 301–12; Jonathan Javitt, ed., *Computers in Medicine: Applications and Possibilities* (Philadelphia: Saunders, 1986); and Julie C. Rutkowska and Charles Crook, eds., *Computers, Cognition and Development: Issues for Psychology and Education* (Chichester, NY: Wiley, 1987).

20. Examples of this perspective include Edward Feigenbaum and Pamela McCorduck, *Fifth Generation: Artificial Intelligence and Japan's Computer Challenge to the World* (Reading, MA: Addison-Wesley, 1983); Alvin Toffler, *The Third Wave* (New York: Bantam Books, 1980); and John Scully, "The Relationship Between Business and Higher Education: A Perspective on the Twenty-first Century," *Communications of the ACM* 32 (September 1989): 1056–61. This approach, referred to as "technological utopianism," is critiqued in Rob Kling, "Reading 'All About' Computerization: Five Common Genres of Social Analysis," (August 1990), forthcoming in *Directions in Advanced Computer Systems*, ed. Doug Schuler (Norwood, NJ: Ablex Publishing Co.). Some critics question the direction and significance of the information "revolution" and the role of information technology in it. For critiques of the instrumentalist view of computing, see Stephen S. Cohen and

John Zysman, "Manufacturing Matters: The Myth of the Post-Industrial Economy," in Forester, ed., *Computers in the Human Context*, 97–103; and "Mythinformation," in Winner, *The Whale and the Reactor*, 98–117.

21. James R. Beniger, *The Control Revolution: Technological and Economic Origins of the Information Society* (Cambridge, MA: Harvard University Press, 1986). JoAnne Yates looks more closely at the role of records and communications systems in this process. See JoAnne Yates, *Control Through Communication: The Rise of System in American Management* (Baltimore: Johns Hopkins University Press, 1989).

22. Zuboff, *In the Age of the Smart Machine*, 9–12.

23. Weissman, "Virtual Documents on an Electronic Desktop," 38.

24. Ibid., 39.

25. Elizabeth Eisenstein, *The Printing Press as an Agent of Change* (Cambridge, Eng.: Cambridge University Press, 1979), Volume 1.

26. Roger Chartier, "General Introduction: Print Culture," in *The Culture of Print: Power and the Uses of Print in Early Modem Europe*, ed. Roger Chartier, trans. Lydia G. Cochrane (Princeton: Princeton University Press, 1987), 1–10. For similar observations about the slow transition from oral to written communications, see M. T. Clanchy, *From Memory to Written Word: England 1066–1307* (Cambridge, MA: Harvard University Press, 1979); and Hugh Taylor, "'My Very Act and Deed:' Some Reflections on the Role of Textual Records in the Conduct of Affairs," *American Archivist* 51 (Fall 1988): 456–69.

27. Levy, "Topics in Document Research," 4.

28. The Minnesota Historical Society, with financial support from the National Historical Publications and Records Commission, sponsored a working meeting in January 1991 on research issues in electronic records. The final report includes descriptions of ten research and development projects that constitute a research agenda. See *Research Issues In Electronic Records: Report of the Working Meeting* (St. Paul: Minnesota Historical Society, 1991), 7–22.

29. For discussion of the significance of this type of research for appraisal, see Cox and Samuels, "The

Archivist's First Responsibility," 40; Bruce H. Bruemmer and Sheldon Hochheiser, *The High-Technology Company: A Historical Research and Archival Guide* (Minneapolis: Charles Babbage Institute, 1989); Bearman, *Archival Methods,* 14–15; and Margaret Hedstrom, "New Appraisal Techniques: the Effect of Theory on Practice," *Provenance* 7 (Fall 1989): 1–21.

30. Reviews of this literature are found in Kling, "Social Analyses of Computing," 61–110; Rob Kling and Walt Scacchi, "Computing as Social Action: The Social Dynamics of Computing in Complex Organizations," in *Advances in Computers,* vol. 19 (New York: Academic Press, 1980), 249–327; and Lyytinen, "Different Perspectives on Information Systems," 5–46.

31. The National Academy of Public Administration attempted to address this problem in a study it conducted for the National Archives and Records Administration. Unfortunately, the methodology employed was insensitive to broader issues of information flow within and between organizations and the gradual, evolutionary change in information recording and use patterns. See National Academy of Public Administration, *The Effects of Electronic Record Keeping on the Historical Record of the U.S. Government,* Volume 2, Appendix C. The questionnaires used to determine the effects of automation on record keeping appear instead to have elicited *opinions* of users and non-users about these effects.

32. Helena Zinkham, Patricia D. Cloud, and Hope Mayo, "Providing Access by Form of Material, Genre, and Physical Characteristics: Benefits and Techniques," *American Archivist* 52 (Summer 1989): 300–19.

33. For an initial attempt at such definitions, see United Nations ACCIS, *Management of electronic records,* 103–07.

34. Physical characteristics alone do not establish the authenticity, reliability, and stability of electronic records. Even the definition of an electronic record has social and administrative dimensions.

35. National Academy of Public Administration, *The Effects of Electronic Record Keeping,* 38–43.

36. For a systematic analysis of this problem, see Duranti, "Diplomatics: New Uses for an Old Science: Part V."

37. Bruno Latour has identified the advanges of documents for presenting and transmitting knowledge. They are mobile, immutable when they move, created-on a flat surface, have a scale that can be modified without change in the internal proportions; they can be reproduced, shuffled and recombined; several images of different origins and scales can be superimposed; they can be inserted into written text; and they can be merged with geometry in such a way that three-dimensional perspectives and concepts can be represented on a two-dimensional plane. Latour does not discuss the trade-offs among these various features. For example, which document technology is superior: one that produces "inscriptions" that, though fragile, are very inexpensive to reproduce and easy to shuffle and recombine? or one that produces permanent, but cumbersome documents? See Bruno Latour, "Visualization and Cognition: Thinking with Eyes and Hands," in *Knowledge and Society: Studies in the Sociology of Culture Past and Present* (Greenwich, CT: JAI Press, 1986), 20–29.

38. I have argued elsewhere that archivists are missing an opportunity to influence the values and practices associated with optical disk technology. See Hedstrom, "Optical Disks: Are Archivists Repeating the Mistakes of the Past?" 52–53. For a recent example of an organization's attempt to develop a more interventionist approach to electronic records, see United Nations, ACCIS, *Management of electronic records.*

39. Bearman, *Archival Methods,* 43–47; David Bearman, "An Indefensible Bastion: Archives as Repositories in the Electronic Age," in *Archival Management of Electronic Records,* ed. David Bearman, Archives and Museum Informatics Technical Report #13 (Pittsburgh: Archives and Museum Informatics, 1991), 14–24; and Dollar, "The Impact of Information Technologies on Archival Principles and Methods," 62–66. For counter arguments, see Ken Thibodeau, "To Be or Not to Be: Archives for Electronic Records," in *Archival Management of Electronic Records,* 14–24; and Margaret Hedstrom,

"Archives as Repositories—A Commentary," in *Archival Management of Electronic Records,* 25–30.

40. Dowler, "The Role of Use," 74–86. See also Paul Conway, "Facts and Frameworks: An Approach to Studying the Users of Archives," *American Archivist* 49 (Fall 1986): 393–407; Bruce W. Dearstyne, "What is the Use of Archives? A Challenge to the Profession," *American Archivist* 50 (Winter 1987): 76–87; and Elsie T. Freeman, "In the Eye of the Beholder: Archives Administration from the User's Point of View," *American Archivist* 47 (Spring 1984): 111–23.

41. For a proposal on criteria to evaluate the quality of electronic records user services, see Thomas E. Brown, "Machine-Readable Views" *Archival Informatics Newsletter* 2 (Summer 1988): 33–35.

42. For discussions of archival principles and electronic records, see Gavrel, Conceptual Problems, 13–15; and Dollar, "Impact of Information Technologies on Archival Principles and Methods," 56–61.

43. Gavrel, Conceptual Problems, 17–29. The implications for archives of database management systems are discussed in Thibodeau, "To Be Or Not To Be," 5–10.

44. Hedstrom, "New Appraisal Techniques," 17–21. For an example of an archival analysis of a multi-jurisdictional database, see Alan Kowlcwitz, Archival Appraisal of Online Information Systems, Archival Informatics Technical Reports, Part 2, (Fall 1988).

45. The research agenda developed in conjunction with the Working Meeting on Research Issues in Electronic Records elaborated on the broad questions raised here in one of its priority areas for research. See Research Issues in Electronic Records, 10–11.

46. Kathleen M. Heim, "Social Scientific Information Needs for Numeric Data: The Evolution of the International Data Archive Infrastructure," Collection Management 9 (Spring 1987): 1–53.

47. Carolyn Geda, "Social Science Data Archives," *American Archivist* 42 (April 1979): 158–66; Kathleen Heim, ed., *Library Trends: Data Libraries for the Social Sciences* 30 (Winter 1982), special issue on social science data libraries; and *Reference Services Review* 16: 1 & 2 (1988): 7–55, special issue on numerical and statistical data files.

48. For an excellent summary of methodological concerns, see Tora Bikson, "Research on Electronic Information Environments: Prospects and Problems," unpublished paper presented at the Working Meeting on Research Issues in Electronic Records, Washington, D.C., 23 January 1991.

49. The National Archives of Canada and the Canadian Department of Communications participated in an inter-disciplinary project on office automation which attempted to address a series of more specific research problems. See Public Archives of Canada, Interim Report on the PAC/DOCS Project (Ottawa: 1985).

50. For overviews of some of this literature, see U.S. Office of Technology Assessment, *Automation of America's Offices,* 125–68; Kling, "Social Analyses of Computing," 61–110; and Charles Babbage Institute, "Selected Readings in the History of Computing," Appendix B to *Resources for the History of Computing: A Guide to U.S. and Canadian Records* (Minneapolis: Charles Babbage Institute, 1987), 158–64.

51. R. A. Hirschheim, "The Effect of A Priori Views on the Social Implications of Computing: The Case of Office Automation," *Computing Surveys* 18 (June 1986): 165–95.

BRIAN LAVOIE AND LORCAN DEMPSEY

"Thirteen Ways of Looking at...Digital Preservation"

D-Lib Magazine *10.7-8 (July/August 2004), www.dlib.org/dlib/july04/lavoie/07lavoie.html.*

Introduction

Research and learning are increasingly supported by digital information environments. The as yet unfulfilled promise is a rich fabric of scholarly resources, learning materials, and cultural artifacts, seamlessly integrated and readily accessible, organized in ways that facilitate traditional uses and encourage new uses as yet undefined.

Fulfilling this promise requires the cultivation of stakeholder communities that, through their working and learning experiences, meaningfully engage with digital information environments. Meaningful engagement is, in turn, contingent on the following prerequisites:[1]

- *Predictability and comprehensiveness*:
  A critical mass of digital resources must be developed. Where coverage is intermittent and/or unpredictable, usefulness is diminished and stakeholder interest will not grow.
- *Interoperability*: Digital content must be easily shared between services or users; usable without specialist tools; surfaced in a variety of environments; and supported by consistent methods for discovery and interaction. Digital content should also be managed using well-understood practices, and supported by services that can be recombined to meet new user needs.
- *Transactionability*: Mechanisms are needed to establish authoritatively the identity of content, services, and users interacting within the information environment, as well as to manage intellectual property rights and privacy, and to secure the integrity and authenticity of content and services.

- *Preservability*: The long-term future of digital resources must be assured, in order to protect investments in digital collections, and to ensure that the scholarly and cultural record is maintained in both its historical continuity and media diversity.

Of these four requirements, the last—preservation—has been the slowest to work its way into digital information environments. That is not to say the issue has been ignored. In fact, there has been much concern and speculation regarding the prospects for long-term stewardship of digital materials. This has motivated an ambitious research agenda, shared by cultural heritage institutions, government agencies, and even private enterprise, aimed at identifying and resolving the challenges posed by digital preservation.

Much of this work approaches digital preservation as a self-contained problem, focusing on the technical obstacles that must be overcome in order to secure the long-term persistence of digital materials. Success, in this context, rests on the ability to prove that technical solutions, in one form or another, exist.

Even as this important and necessary work proceeds, our understanding of the totality of the challenges associated with maintaining digital materials over the long-term is coming more sharply into focus. New questions are emerging, having less to do with digital preservation as a technical issue *per se*, and more to do with how preserving digital materials fits into the broader theme of *digital stewardship*. These questions surface from the view that digital preservation is not an isolated process, but instead, one component of a broad aggregation of interconnected services, policies, and stakeholders which together constitute a digital information environment.

Digital preservation issues worked their way into the consciousness of cultural heritage institutions in the form of a sense of imminent crisis. Expressions such as "digital dark age" were put forward, with the implication that whole portions of the scholarly and cultural record were on the brink of disappearing. But accumulating experience in managing digital materials has tempered this view. While it is true that digital materials are inherently more fragile than analog materials, the degree of risk varies widely across classes of resources: there is appreciable risk, for example, that a Web site available today may be gone tomorrow, but there is little indication that the corpus of commercially published electronic journal content is under the same threat.

In this sense, the focus of digital preservation has shifted away from the need to take immediate action to "rescue" threatened materials, and toward the realization that perpetuating digital materials over the long-term involves the observance of careful digital asset management practices diffused throughout the information lifecycle. This in turn requires us to look at digital preservation not just as a mechanism for ensuring bit sequences created today are renderable tomorrow, but as a process operating in concert with the full range of services supporting digital information environments, as well as the overarching economic, legal, and social contexts. In short, we must look at digital preservation in many different ways. With apologies to Wallace Stevens,[2] this article suggests thirteen ways of looking at digital preservation.[3]

I. Digital Preservation As . . . an Ongoing Activity

Preservation traditionally proceeds in fits and starts, with extended periods of inactivity punctuated by bursts of intensive effort—witness the Brittle Book campaigns of the 1980s, or recent efforts to save movies filmed on nitrate cellulose film stock. The pattern is one in which materials are left to approach a state of crisis, at which point the situation is remedied through large-scale intervention.

But digital materials generally do not afford the luxury of procrastination. The fragility of digital storage media, combined with a high degree of technology dependence, considerably shortens the "grace period" during which preservation decisions can be deferred. Issues of long-term persistence can arise as soon as the time digital materials are created: for example, in choosing between a widely-used, stable digital format, and one that is obscure or on the verge of obsolescence. This sense of urgency is driven largely by the fact that it is problematic to apply digital preservation technique *sex post*—i.e., after deterioration has set in. While a print book with a broken spine can be easily re-bound, a digital object that has become corrupted or obsolete is often impossible (or prohibitively expensive) to restore. Digital preservation techniques are most effective when they are pre-emptive.

This suggests that as more and more digital materials come under the stewardship of collecting institutions, preservation will become less like an *event* occurring at discrete intervals, and more like a *process*, proceeding relatively continuously over time. As a consequence, it will become more difficult to distinguish preservation activities from the routine, day-to-day management of digital materials.

It is important that the sudden ubiquity of preservation processes in digital collection management does not interfere unduly with other components of the digital information environment. Implementation of preservation measures should be as transparent as possible to users of digital materials, and should not represent obstacles to access and use. In the print world, preservation of rare book collections is achieved in part by restricting usage: materials are accessed under the supervision of a librarian and off-premises circulation is prohibited. While these measures undoubtedly prolong the life of these valuable materials, they do little to promote their use. In the case of digital materials, mechanisms to ensure long-term persistence should operate harmoniously with mechanisms supporting dissemination and use.

II. Digital Preservation As . . . a Set of Agreed Outcomes

It is one thing to recognize that actions must be taken to secure the long-term persistence of digital materials; it is another to articulate precisely what the outcome of preservation should be.

This issue is not confined to digital materials. Nicholson Baker (2001), for example, has decried reformatting efforts that result in the loss of the original item; to Baker, preservation of the original is the measure of successful preservation. To others, however, destructive microfilming meets their preservation needs, in that content is transferred to a medium with a life expectancy of half a millennium.

Similar questions are attached to the preservation of digital materials, but the issues involved are amplified. Digital content often embodies a degree of structural complexity not found in physical materials. It can subsume multiple formats, being at once text, images, animations, sound, and video; it can be interactive, providing tools for the user to create alternate views of the content, or link to new content; it is mutable, in that it can be updated or enhanced over time; it can be broken apart, with the pieces distributed and used individually; or re-combined to create new resources. In short, digital content can incorporate features with no equivalent in the analog world. How many of these features can or should be preserved?

Unfortunately, there is no single answer to this question. For some purposes, a preserved digital object must be a perfect surrogate for the original, replicating the full range of functionality, as well as the original "look and feel". But for other purposes, intensive preservation of this kind is unnecessary: perpetuating the object's intellectual content alone, or even a diminished approximation of the original object, is enough. The period of archival retention is also a point of debate. For some, nothing less than retention in perpetuity constitutes successful preservation; for others, a finite period is sufficient.

These considerations suggest that the choice of preservation strategy will need to reflect a consensus of all stakeholders associated with the archived digital materials. Achieving such a consensus is dif-

ficult, and in some circumstances, impossible. A second-best solution is for the digital repository to articulate clearly what outcomes can be expected from the preservation process. These outcomes should in turn be understood and validated by stakeholders. Communication between the repository and stakeholders, either to promote consensus on preservation outcomes, or for the repository to disclose and explain its preservation policies, mitigates the risk that the repository's commitments are misaligned with stakeholder expectations.

III. Digital Preservation As . . . an Understood Responsibility

The likelihood that digital preservation activities will proceed continuously throughout the information lifecycle suggests that preservation responsibilities will extend beyond traditional stewards of the scholarly and cultural record. If, for example, preservation considerations must be taken into account at the time of a digital object's creation, it is authors and publishers, rather than libraries and archives, who must take the first steps toward securing the long-term persistence of digital materials.

The need for entities beyond collecting institutions to play a role in preservation is not new: the publishing industry, in response to the brittle books crisis, recognized and acted on the necessity to produce printed materials on acid-free paper. In the digital realm, entities who do not regard preservation as part of their organizational mission will find the scope for their involvement in the preservation process greatly expanded. Consequently, the responsibility for undertaking preservation will become much more diffused.

The rapid take-up of networked digital resources, obtained through license or subscription, has led to portions of the scholarly and cultural record—e.g., electronic journals, ebooks, and Web sites—lying outside the custody of collecting institutions. This has prompted anxiety about the long-term stewardship of these materials, in particular when economic value has diminished while cultural importance has not. Since the value of certain digital materials can persist indefinitely, those who have custody of these materials during the various stages of the information lifecycle must recognize and act upon the need to manage them in ways compatible with long-term preservation.

The division of labor for preserving print materials is well-established. The division of labor in regard to *digital* preservation has yet to be determined—for example, clarification of legal deposit requirements for digital materials will be a key factor in determining how much of the digital preservation burden will be allocated to national libraries or archiving agencies. But the distribution of digital preservation responsibilities is almost certain to include decision-makers outside the cultural heritage community. It is important that these decision-makers understand the necessity of taking steps to secure the long-term persistence of the digital materials under their control.

IV. Digital Preservation As . . . a Selection Process

Preservation of print materials is both a benign by-product of production and distribution modes, and a process of active decision-making and intervention. Preservation of digital materials will reflect a similar mix, although the dividing line between benign by-product and active decision-making remains to be drawn. But as the volume of information in digital form continues to expand rapidly, an issue emerges that will surely require active decision-making and intervention: what should be preserved?

It is safe to assume that preserving everything is not an option. Digital preservation is expensive, and it is therefore impractical to make every bit of information in digital form the subject of active preservation measures throughout its entire lifecycle. Given this, two options remain. One is to collect as many digital materials as possible and deposit them into mass storage systems. The stored materials could then be sifted over time, with selections for more intensive preservation periodically made as need and/or interest arises.

The "save now, preserve later" strategy is feasible only through the unique characteristics of digital information, where the steady decline in storage cost makes it conceivable to save everything. The chief criticism of this approach is summarized by the adage "saving is not preserving"; there is considerable uncertainty concerning the extent to which preservation techniques can be applied retrospectively to digital materials that have resided untouched in storage for long periods of time.

The second strategy is selection: that is, determining from the outset which digital materials should be preserved and taking steps to curate them throughout their lifecycle. The choice of which materials to preserve is a difficult one, and will depend on a number of factors, including institutional mission, cultural preferences, economic practicality, and risk management policies. The question will also hinge on the digital medium's impact on the scholarly and cultural record. Is an e-mail discussion list, for example, part of the scholarly record, and if so, should it be preserved with as much care as the contents of a peer-reviewed journal?

Selection is not just a "preserve or not preserve" issue. It also involves the level of desirable intervention for a particular set of digital materials. Is it necessary to go to the trouble and expense of preserving a digital object in its original form? Or is preservation of the intellectual content enough? This issue presents difficult choices, but in a world of scarce preservation resources, these choices must be confronted.

V. Digital Preservation As . . . an Economically Sustainable Activity

Two key economic challenges plague efforts to preserve digital materials. First, allocation of funds to digital preservation has been insufficient; Neil Beagrie (2003) observes that in the context of funding decisions, the need to take immediate and frequent actions to preserve digital collections usually is overshadowed by the desire to create and disseminate new forms of digital content. Second, funds that are made available are usually provided on a temporary basis, often as grants to support one-off undertakings or special projects. Few institutions have allocated ongoing, budgeted resources for the long-term care of digital materials.

The impulse to fund digital preservation activities is dampened by the expectation that the costs will be formidable. It is difficult to forecast the precise magnitude of these costs, which will depend on factors such as system architecture, length of archival retention, scale, and preservation strategy. But regardless of their form, digital preservation activities will require a substantial resource commitment to sustain them over time.

Economic sustainability is the ability to marshal sufficient resources, on an ongoing basis, to meet preservation objectives. There are many avenues by which sustainability can be achieved. An institutional commitment to budget a continuous supply of funds to support digital preservation is one; these funds might be used to extend a pilot project originally funded through seed money from a grant-giving organization. Digital preservation activities might also be self-sustaining, generating revenues as a by-product of day-to-day operations. In these circumstances, economic sustainability might be defined in terms of cost recovery, or a minimum level of profitability.

Strategies for attaining economic sustainability must be built on a sound empirical footing; consequently, much more data on the costs of digital preservation is needed. Digital preservation is still in its infancy, and much of the available data is heavily skewed toward upfront costs: reformatting, setting up the digital repository, ingestion of materials, etc. As projects mature, empirical descriptions of digital preservation's complete cost trajectory will emerge. This data must be consolidated and synthesized to produce reasonable benchmark estimates of the cost requirements associated with various forms of digital preservation.

VI. Digital Preservation As . . . a Cooperative Effort

The fact that digital preservation is expensive, funding is scarce, and preservation responsibilities are diffused suggest that digital preservation activities would benefit from cooperation. Cooperation can enhance the productive capacity of a limited supply of digital preservation funds, by building shared resources, eliminating redundancies, and exploiting economies of scale.

In order to persuade institutions to invest in bringing digital collections online, and to make these collections a meaningful part of research and learning experiences, there must be assurance that the collections will persist. But long-term stewardship may be beyond the means of an individual institution. Aggregating collections into "union archives", maintained and funded as a shared community resource, would serve the dual function of promoting shared access and distributing the costs of long-term maintenance over a larger stakeholder community. The fact that both the benefits of access and the costs of long-term maintenance are shared by a large number of institutions would furnish a strong incentive to contribute materials to these shared digital collections.

Cooperation would also minimize redundancy. The characteristics of digital information are such that relatively few archived copies of a digital resource will likely be required to meet preservation objectives. The rationale for this assertion can be framed as follows. Sharing analog materials is generally more expensive than sharing digital materials: to access an archived copy of a print book, users must either travel to the book's location, or request that the book be shipped via interlibrary loan. To reduce access costs, it is desirable to preserve many copies of the same print book in geographically dispersed locations. In contrast, the ease with which digital information can be replicated and shared over networks suggests greater scope for preserving a particular digital resource in a single location, rather than preserving copies in multiple locations.[4] This can introduce significant cost savings by minimizing the incidence of redundant, fragmented efforts, multiple learning curves and reinvention of wheels.

Finally, cooperation opens possibilities for realizing greater efficiencies through economies of scale. Maintaining digital materials over the long-term will require an elaborate and costly technical infrastructure, as well as specialized human expertise. It is economically impractical for every collecting institution to develop local digital preservation capabilities. A coordinated approach promises to be more cost effective, by spreading fixed costs over a greater number of institutions. It also might make certain kinds of highly specialized, or "niche", digital preservation activities economically feasible, by expanding them to a sufficiently large scale to bring costs in line with benefits. These activities might be otherwise impractical if done piecemeal on a small scale.

VII. Digital Preservation As . . . an Innocuous Activity

In some circumstances, digital preservation is perceived as a threat to intellectual property rights. Much of this resistance can be attributed to the current ambiguity surrounding copyright law as it pertains to digital materials; the principles of fair use and legal deposit are in particular need of clarification.

Digital materials purchased through license or subscription, such as electronic journals or e-books, illustrate the collision between the need to intervene to preserve digital materials and the need to protect intellectual property rights. These materials are typically accessed over the Web through a central server controlled by the content provider, rather than through locally maintained copies. In these circumstances, the entities who perceive the need to preserve—i.e., collecting institutions—are often distinct from the entities that hold the right to preserve, as well as custody of the materials. Publishers are reluctant to distribute digital copies of their revenue-generating assets, even for preservation purposes, to individual licensees or subscribers; few institutions would have the resources to preserve the materials even if they did.

This presents two options: the content provider must be persuaded or enjoined to preserve the materials in their custody; or alternatively, the content provider must cede the right to preserve to another entity who is willing and able to assume responsibility for preservation. Currently, the latter approach seems to be in ascendance, evidenced by the emergence of "escrow repositories" or "archives of last resort". For example, the publisher Elsevier has agreed to transfer a copy of the content available through its Science-Direct service to the National Library of the Netherlands,[5] with the understanding that the Library will maintain this material in perpetuity and assume the responsibility for making it available should circumstances prevent Elsevier from doing so through its own systems.

Other issues remain to be resolved. In order to meet preservation objectives, the archiving agency may have to alter the archived content in some way—for example, by migrating it to another format in order to keep pace with changing technologies, or by disaggregating complex objects into more granular resources, such as breaking up an issue of a journal into its constituent articles. In these circumstances, appropriate permissions must be obtained from the rights holders in order to give the repository sufficient control over the archived materials to carry out its preservation responsibilities.

Striking a balance between the interests of content providers and collecting institutions may best be achieved through appropriately designed contracts. In the United States, copyright law is generally superseded by contract law; therefore, regardless of current interpretations of fair use or legal deposit, all stakeholders in a set of digital materials may address preservation requirements through provisions included in licensing or subscription agreements. An example of this is found in the UK's Model License governing digital materials licensed to UK higher education institutions. The Model License includes archiving clauses which identify the need for libraries to have continued access to purchased materials following the license's expiration, and commits the publisher to address this need as part of the licensing agreement.[6]

VIII. Digital Preservation As . . . an Aggregated Or Disaggregated Service?

For the most part, digital preservation systems have been designed "holistically", combining raw storage capacity, ingest functions, metadata collection and management, preservation strategies, and dissemination of archived content into a physically integrated, centrally administered system. But other organizational structures are also possible: for example, digital preservation activities might adopt a "disaggregated" approach, where the various components of the preservation process are broken apart into separate services distributed over multiple organizations, each specializing in a focused segment of the overall process.

A digital preservation system can be deconstructed into several functional layers. The bottom layer includes hardware, software, and network infrastructure supporting the storage and distribution of digital content. The next layer includes more specialized services to manage the archived content residing in the system, including metadata creation and management, and validation of materials' authenticity or integrity. Preservation measures are implemented in the next layer of services, including monitoring the repository's environment for changes that could impact the ability to access and use archived content, as well as initiating processes such as migration or emulation to counteract these changes. The topmost layer includes services that support browsing or searching, access requests, validating access permissions, and arranging for delivery.

This range of functions can be offered as separate yet interoperable services that can be combined in various ways to support different forms of repository activities. For example, some digital materials might require only "bit preservation"—i.e., an assurance that the bit streams constituting the digital objects remain intact and recoverable over the long-term. Other materials, however, may require more sophisticated preservation services: i.e., migration to new formats, or the creation of emulators to reproduce the content's original look, feel, and functionality. Some preservation efforts will require "active archives", characterized by a relatively continuous process of ingest and access; other efforts might submit materials for preservation at irregular and widely-spaced intervals, with little or no user access.

These preservation activities utilize various combinations of some or all of the services described above. A fully integrated system may find that one or more services end up under-utilized and therefore of insufficient scale to realize technical or cost efficiencies. On the other hand, entities that specialize in only a few of these services may be able to spread them over a larger collection of digital materials, and in doing so, attain the necessary scale to realize economies within the limited sphere of their chosen service layer. This reflects Adam Smith's classic argument for specialization in production, or a *division of labor*. Determining the extent to which digital preservation can benefit from a division of labor, in the sense of finding 1) a sensible deconstruction of the digital preservation process into a set of more granular services, and 2) the optimal degree of specialization across preserving institutions, is a key issue in the design of digital repository architectures.

IX. Digital Preservation As . . . a Complement to Other Library Services

Although much work remains to be done to resolve the challenges specific to preserving digital materials, it is not too early to begin thinking about how digital preservation mechanisms will be integrated with, and operate alongside of, the wide range of other services which, taken together, constitute a digital library.

The notion of "dark archives", supporting little or no access to archived materials, has met with scant enthusiasm in the library community. This suggests that digital repositories will function not just as guarantors of the long-term viability of materials in their custody, but also as access gateways. Fulfilling this dual mission requires that preservation processes operate seamlessly alongside access services. Preservation should not impede access or reduce the scope for sharing information. Careful records of the outcome of preservation processes must be kept: for example, in cases where material is migrated to new formats, users must understand which versions of a particular digital resource are available for access, and what alterations, if any, have been made to these versions as a consequence of preservation.

As preservation assumes a more prominent role in the day-to-day management of digital collections, preservation activities will co-exist, and at times, operate in concert with, other routine collection management functions, such as acquisition, description, and ILL fulfillment. When a new digital resource is acquired, it is simultaneously ingested by the digital repository's archival system. At the same time that the resource is being prepared for circulation, it must also be prepared for long-term retention. Not only must the resource be surfaced in the library's access environments (e.g., through a new record in the OPAC), it must also be surfaced in the library's "preservation system". Digital content management systems must find ways to integrate preservation tools and services into their environments.

It is essential that preservation actions be as transparent as possible to users of archived digital materials. It would be unfortunate if the preservation process were such that the scope for sharing digital materials across systems, institutions, and users was reduced. In the print world, preservation often exacts a heavy toll on users' ability to access material, by removing books from the shelves while they are re-bound, filmed, or scanned; by placing rigorous restrictions on circulation; or even removing the materials from circulation entirely. The characteristics of digital information are such that access and use of archived materials can be supported without compromising preservation objectives, but achieving this in practice requires explicit recognition of the impact of preservation on access (and *vice versa*) in the design and implementation of digital library systems.

X. Digital Preservation As . . . a Well-Understood Process

There is as yet little consensus on best practice for carrying out the long-term preservation of digital materials. Prospects for cultivating a shared view on this issue hinge on three factors: identification and development of standards to support digital preservation; suitable benchmarks and evaluative procedures for assessing the outcomes of digital preservation processes; and mechanisms for certifying adherence to a minimum set of practices on the part of digital repositories.

The emergence of standards would benefit many aspects of the preservation process. Some progress can already be reported. The Open Archival Information System reference model (2002), which details a conceptual framework for an archival repository, as well as the environment in which it operates and the information objects it manages, has been well-

received and extensively applied in the digital preservation community. But many other areas remain to be addressed, ranging from preservation-quality digital formats to optimal preservation strategies for various classes of digital materials.

Digital preservation would also benefit from the articulation of benchmarks or metrics for evaluating the efficacy of preservation processes as they unfold. Preservation activities necessarily require institutions to incur costs well in advance of realizing benefits. How can decision-makers be assured that investments to preserve digital collections are producing tangible results? It would be useful to devise a widely accepted set of evaluative procedures, similar to a quality assurance audit and based on measurable aspects of the preservation process, that would serve as a reliable indicator of how well preservation activities are progressing toward meeting preservation objectives.

Finally, well-understood processes for preserving digital materials must be paired with mechanisms for assessing whether a particular digital repository commands the expertise and resources to carry them out. Preservation requires institutions to transfer valuable (and often, rare and priceless) materials into the custody of the repository and its staff. These transfers must be accompanied by a high degree of confidence that the materials will be preserved according to well-known, established procedures. Such conditions exist in preservation microfilming, where fragile printed materials such as old newspapers and books are entrusted to service providers with the understanding that the materials will be returned unharmed. A similar element of trust must be cultivated in the digital preservation community. One way to contribute to this is through the establishment of certification procedures for digital repositories. Certification would indicate that a repository has met certain minimum requirements in its curatorial policies and procedures, including conformance to what is regarded as current best practice in digital preservation.

Development and take-up of standards and evaluative metrics, along with certification of digital repositories, will help dispel fears that scarce resources devoted to preservation will be wasted as digital materials are managed using non-standard or outmoded practices, and as a consequence, fail to release their value in use.

XI. Digital Preservation As . . . an Arm's Length Transaction

The responsibility for ensuring the permanence of the scholarly and cultural record is deeply rooted in the library, museum, and archival communities. But the characteristics of digital materials—their fragility, technology-dependence, and networked access—have unsettled preservation's traditional division of labor.

While it is certain that collecting institutions will continue to serve as the primary stewards of society's memory, it is unlikely that every collecting institution responsible for the curation of digital materials will have the resources and expertise to implement the entire digital preservation process locally. Part of the preservation responsibility may be taken up by third-party services specializing in the preservation of digital materials. In this event, digital preservation activities would be conducted as an arm's length transaction between separate parties. This raises several questions concerning how such a transaction would take place.

An obvious issue is pricing. The costs of digital preservation are subject to the vagaries of numerous factors, chief among which is the constantly evolving technological environment to which digital materials are so closely intertwined. The more rapid the pace of technological change, the costlier it will be to ensure that archived digital objects remain usable. Given the uncertainty over the pace and direction of technological change, it is difficult to estimate future preservation costs, and therefore, suitable pricing scales. Widespread use of relatively stable digital formats and technology would mitigate this problem, but not eliminate it.

Sustainable pricing models must also be developed. Several possibilities exist: the repository could charge a one-time, upfront, capitalized archiving fee; alternatively, it could distribute the fees over time, perhaps as an annual fee. Pricing models must strike a bal-ance between customers' preferences (e.g., inability to pay a large upfront fee, or desire to avoid budgeting ongoing funds) and those of the repository (e.g., difficulty in collapsing future preservation costs into a one-time fee, or need to invest large sums upfront to meet future preservation commitments).

A related question concerns what is supplied in exchange for payment. What preservation *guarantees* can the digital repository offer? To what compensation is the depositor entitled if promised outcomes are not achieved? Should the repository guarantee a specific *outcome* associated with its preservation process ("these digital objects will be renderable, using contemporary technology, in fifty years"), or should only the *process* itself be guaranteed ("these digital objects will be recorded on up-to-date digital storage media, refreshed at regular intervals, and maintained under environmentally controlled conditions")? Resolution of these issues must emerge from a convergence of customer expectations and repository commitments.

XII. Digital Preservation As . . . One of Many Options

An implicit assumption attached to most discussions of digital preservation is that materials currently in digital form must be preserved in digital form. For some materials—i.e., born-digital materials with no obvious print equivalent—there may be no choice but to preserve them as digital objects. But a large class of materials, including digital surrogates of analog items, as well as born-digital objects for which analog equivalents can be easily produced, present other options in addition to digital preservation. Indeed, analog manifestations of digital materials may already be the subject of preservation efforts, even as their digital equivalents are perceived to be at risk. Efforts to preserve digital materials must take into account potential overlap with analog preservation activities, as well as circumstances where preservation in analog form may be preferable to digital preservation.

A document in digital form comprised solely of text and static images can be easily reproduced as a paper document with little or no loss of information. In making this document part of the permanent scholarly or cultural record, which form should take precedence? For example, most researchers in the digital preservation community are familiar with the Council on Library and Information Resources (CLIR) reports in the maroon covers. These reports are available in print form, and may also be downloaded from the Web in digital form. Which copy should be the focus of preservation activity? In this case, the print and digital versions are, for all intents and purposes, perfect substitutes.

In cases where digital and analog versions differ, preservation issues become more complex. Even minor differences, such as pagination, may elicit questions as to which version should be considered the authoritative version for scholarly citation. For example, print magazine articles are easily cited, by volume, issue, and page. However, online versions of these same magazines often omit pagination, presenting each article as one HTML file of unbroken text. More significant differences between digital and analog versions, impacting appearance, functionality, or content, amplify the problem. If one institution collects the analog version, while another collects the digital version, which institution holds the official "copy of record"? Should both versions be preserved, or just one? Who decides?

Preservation decision-making in regard to materials existing simultaneously in digital and analog form often must be informed by a longer view. Are multiple versions of the same item expected to co-exist indefinitely, or is this merely a transitional state, with analog versions gradually supplanted by digital equivalents? In the latter case, preservation of only the digital version may be appropriate; in the former case, preservation of both versions might be necessary, or an authoritative version must be selected for preservation.

The decision to preserve in digital or analog form may turn on a simple cost comparison of the two approaches, but ideally, it should also take into account the preferences of users. Librarians discovered some time ago that users were resistant to replacing paper publications such as newspapers and magazines with microfilm copies, despite the advantages the latter format offered in terms of prolonging the longevity of the materials and reducing storage space requirements. In the same way, users may prefer that certain information resources be preserved as analog objects, and others as digital objects. User preferences, such as concerns about ease of access, may override purely economic factors.

XIII. Digital Preservation As . . . a Public Good

Few would disagree that preserving an information resource benefits its owner, whether a library, museum, archive, publisher, or private collector. But preserving a resource, and in so doing, making it part of the permanent scholarly or cultural record, also confers benefits on society at large, by securing the resource's continued availability for use by current and future generations of researchers and students. An institution that preserves the last copy of a resource has performed a service of potentially incalculable value to the public. In these circumstances, the benefits from preservation are widely distributed; unfortunately, the costs of preservation are not.

A preserving institution can generate societal benefits extending well beyond its immediate stakeholders. The costs of producing these extra benefits often remain uncompensated. In the analog world, inequities in the distribution of preservation costs have little impact on collecting institutions' incentives to preserve. This partly reflects the mission of these institutions, which includes the responsibility to act as stewards of society's memory. But other factors also play a role. Institutions directly own, and have physical custody of, one or more copies of the analog materials in their collections. The institution is therefore uniquely placed to undertake the preservation of these materials, and this enhances the incentives to preserve.

Another factor that strengthens preservation incentives for analog materials is that the distribution of the benefits from preservation is, in a sense, self-limiting. Analog items, such as print books, can be difficult and/or expensive to access by individuals outside the collecting institution's direct user community. For example, inter-library loan can cost as much as $30–$50 per item. Extremely rare or valuable materials may not be circulated at all, further reducing the scope for access by outside users.

The factors that enhance incentives to preserve analog materials—physical custody and limited opportunities for sharing—break down in the digital world. Rather than being purchased outright and transferred into the custody of each collecting institution, digital resources are often obtained through license or subscription, and then accessed by users from all institutions via a central Web server operated by the publisher. Institutions, while considering the licensed digital materials part of their collections, nevertheless do not have physical custody, and therefore little or no opportunity to undertake their preservation.

In addition to diminishing the notion of physical custody, digital materials are also more easily shared than analog materials. Resources can be made available online and accessed from all over the world, making an institution's user community potentially limitless. In these circumstances, there may be some resistance to underwriting expensive preservation activities that benefit a large pool of users, most of whom make no contribution to the preserving institution's resource pool (via tuition, taxes, etc.). Incentives to preserve are further reduced if the materials in question are not unique, but instead held by multiple institutions. Which institution should go to the trouble and expense of preservation, when the benefits, in terms of making the materials part of the permanent scholarly or cultural record, will accrue to all?

As Donald Waters (2002) points out, digital preservation exhibits characteristics of a *public good*, chief among which is the difficulty in excluding those who do not contribute toward the provision of the good from enjoying its benefits. Once a digital resource has been preserved by one institution, it has, in a sense, been preserved for all. In an era of rising costs and shrinking budgets, activities that confer uncompensated benefits outside the institution's immediate stakeholder community may diminish in priority. Also, as preservation responsibilities diffuse beyond collecting institutions, preservation incentives will become even less assured: in the absence of a formal preservation mandate, incentives to preserve digital materials without compensation for the benefit of society as a whole may be weak indeed.[7]

Conclusion

Preserving our digital heritage is more than just a technical process of perpetuating digital signals over long periods of time. It is also a social and cultural process, in the sense of selecting what materials should be preserved, and in what form; it is an economic process, in the sense of matching limited means with ambitious objectives; it is a legal process, in the sense of defining what rights and privileges are needed to support maintenance of a permanent scholarly and cultural record. It is a question of responsibilities and incentives, and of articulating and organizing new forms of curatorial practice. And perhaps most importantly, it is an ongoing, long-term commitment, often shared, and cooperatively met, by many stakeholders.

As experience in managing the long-term stewardship of digital materials accumulates, there will likely be even more ways we will need to look at digital preservation in the course of building digital information environments that endure over time. But this should come as no surprise: after all, Wallace Stevens found at least thirteen ways of looking at a blackbird.

REFERENCES

Nicholson Baker, 2001. *Double Fold: Libraries and the Assault on Paper*. New York, NY: Random House.

Neil Beagrie, 2003. *National Digital Preservation Initiatives: An Overview of Developments in Australia, France, the Netherlands, and the United Kingdom and of Related International Activity*. Washington, D.C.: Council on Library and Information Resources. Available at: http://www.clir.org/pubs/abstract/pub116abst.html.

Consultative Committee for Space Data Systems, 2002. *Reference Model for an Open Archival Information System (OAIS) (CCSDS 650.0-B-1 Blue Book)*. Washington, D.C.: CCSDS Secretariat. Available at: http://

ssdoo.gsfc.nasa.gov/nost/wwwclassic/documents/pdf/CCSDS-650.0-B-1.pdf.

Donald Waters, 2002. "Good Archives Make Good Scholars: Reflections on Recent Steps Toward the Archiving of Digital Information", in *The State of Digital Preservation: An International Perspective*. Washington, D.C.: Council on Library and Information Resources, pp. 78–95. Available at: http://www.clir.org/pubs/abstract/pub107abst.html.

NOTES

1. Remarks in this section are adapted from Lorcan Dempsey and Dan Greenstein, 1999. "The Fabric of Culture and Learning: A Draft Briefing Paper" (Unpublished).

2. "Thirteen Ways of Looking at a Blackbird". Available at: http://www.poets.org/poems/poems.cfm?45442B7C000C07020B77.

3. This is not to say that there are only thirteen ways of looking at digital preservation!

4. Of course, some redundancy may be desirable as a disaster-recovery measure.

5. See http://www.kb.nl/kb/pr/pers/pers2002/elsevier-en.html for a description of this agreement.

6. To learn more about the Model License, visit http://www.nesli2.ac.uk/.

7. For more detailed discussion of the incentives to preserve digital materials, see Brian Lavoie (2003) The Incentives to Preserve Digital Materials: Roles, Scenarios, and Economic Decision-Making. Available at: http://www.oclc.org/research/projects/digipres/incentives-dp.pdf.

Selection 7.5

CLIFFORD LYNCH

"Repatriation, Reconstruction, and Cultural Diplomacy in the Digital World"

Educause Review *43.1 (January/February 2008): 70–71.*

THE REPATRIATION OF cultural treasures has been very much in the news of late. Francesco Rutelli, the Italian minister of culture, has been engaged in intensive negotiations with leading museums in the United States concerning the return of cultural artifacts that he has characterized as having been "looted" from Italy. The Metropolitan Museum of Art in New York City, the Boston Museum of Fine Arts, and the J. Paul Getty Museum in Los Angeles, among others, have agreed to return a number of these artifacts as part of broader agreements for the loan of other artifacts and for collaborations on research.

In these and similar negotiations, the international community is struggling with the framing of what amounts to a statute of limitations and a set of dates before which artifacts can be regarded as having been taken "fair and square." Key demarcation dates involve the 1972 UNESCO convention on cultural heritage and a 2001 treaty between the United States and Italy (one of about a dozen treaties the United States has signed with other nations in this area over the last decade). Of course, international resentment is timeless. The activities of Napoleon Bonaparte, for example, remain controversial to this day among some nations. And despite the successes of the Italians (successes that ironically involve some Greek materials), Greece has not yet been successful in its call for the return of the Elgin Marbles (which the Greeks now pointedly call the Parthenon Marbles) from the British Museum.

Repatriation is a controversial issue not only between traditional nation-states. In the United States, for example, the Native American nations have long called for the return of their cultural patrimony, leading to the passage of the Native American Graves Protection and Repatriation Act (NAGPRA) in 1990. Repatriation is also an important theme in the discussions between the Native American nations and the Smithsonian Institution's National Museum of the American Indian. Fundamentally, the NAGPRA legislation called for the return to the tribes of an array of materials—such as cultural objects and human remains—from scientific and cultural heritage institutions in the United States. Importantly, this issue involved not just the ownership but also the treatment of these artifacts, which were often viewed as sacred —and thus subject to view only by specific audiences or in specific contexts; indeed, some are intended to decay naturally rather than be preserved permanently.

The legal and moral issues of repatriation and cultural heritage are complex and contentious, but they are not my focus here. My concern here is with stewardship and scholarship. At some point, cultural heritage belongs to everybody, and everybody shares some obligation to exercise responsible stewardship over it. In addition, although ownership of specific artifacts is real and sometimes contested, there is no copyright dimension: current possession of these ancient public-domain artifacts does not convey control over images that have been made of the artifacts (though the owner of an artifact can of course limit the making of new images, or exert contractual controls over the use of these images, by restricting physical access to the artifact, and some museums do this).[1] It is in this spirit of collective stewardship that I hope museums, before signing off on any repatriation agreements, will capture extensive and detailed digital documentation of the contested objects and release this documentation onto the Internet—along with documentation of the rest of their collections, of course.

Museums are primarily concerned with original, authentic objects. But digital surrogates can serve adequately for many scholarly and educational purposes. We have made great strides, not only technically but also economically, in our ability to digitally document cultural materials—both in two and now, increasingly, in three dimensions through the creation of surrogates.

Although artifacts have historically been documented mainly by photographs, digital surrogates include not only digital photographs but also high-resolution laser scans of sculptures and buildings, multi-spectral imagery, and other data sets. Indeed, these digital surrogates offer scholarly opportunities that would be effectively impossible with the original artifact, and they are becoming, in effect, complements to the actual artifact. As these collections of surrogates have grown and become broadly accessible through the Internet, they are changing the nature of museums by making much more of the museums' collections visible and available for study, even though there's no space to put the collections physically on public display.

In an age of repatriations, cultural memory organizations can (and, in my view, often should) still make available high-quality surrogates not only of their holdings but also of materials that they no longer hold—or, for that matter, of materials that they have never held. Indeed, there's an emerging argument that responsible stewardship calls for the creation and *distribution* of high-quality digital surrogates as a way of providing a social "insurance policy" against disasters that could damage or destroy irreplaceable treasures—whether held in museums, library special collections, or archives. Total catastrophe should no longer be acceptable. And leaving aside the imperatives of stewardship, there are independently compelling reasons to make such surrogates broadly available simply to advance the core institutional mission of supporting scholarship—but this is a separate argument that deserves to be elaborated in its own right.

And as we have been reminded yet again by the looting of the National Museum in Iraq, good documentation of a collection is an essential prerequisite to trying to recover stolen artifacts. In recent years, digital surrogates have been used to enable cultural reconstruction programs intended to replenish the looted or destroyed national cultural heritage of nations like Iraq or Afghanistan. The Afghanistan Digital Library, hosted at New York University, aims to collect digital versions of works published in Afghanistan from 1870 to 1930. In fact, we are also seeing preemptive collaborations being formed to replicate endangered rare materials, perhaps most notably the British Library's Endangered Archives Programme, which has been underwritten by the Lisbet Rausing Charitable Fund. Although all of these efforts are relatively modest in scale, they point toward a future in which cultural heritage, enhanced by digital surrogates, may perhaps be more robust, less concentrated, and less vulnerable than when it was represented only by physical collections of artifacts.

U.S. colleges and universities hold in trust enormous treasure-houses of cultural materials, not just in their libraries and archives but also in their museums—museums of anthropology and history as well as museums of fine arts—and in more specialized collections such as ethnographic studies that may be held at the individual faculty, departmental, or research center level. Much of this is rare, unique, irreplaceable; in at least a few cases, ownership of the materials has been contested by other nations or cultural groups. These cultural treasures are part of the immense body of scholarly evidence and cultural history that is slated, gradually but inevitably, to be digitized over the coming decades. The mandates for responsible stewardship, the pressures for repatriation, and the potential to contribute to the reconstruction of the available cultural record are all part of the difficult calculus of priorities for and demands upon very limited resources for digitization. Funding agencies, recognizing the diplomatic and cultural dimensions, are making funds available for tar-

geted digitization programs. Indeed, decisions made regarding choices about digitization priorities will be one of the ways in which colleges and universities will build up their capital, and the capital of the nation as a whole, for cultural diplomacy in a digital world.

1. For out-of-copyright objects (in the United States, typically including those created pre-1923), there can be a separate copyright in a photo or other reproduction of such works if there is sufficient creativity involved; in general, however, the case law seems to suggest that if the intent is simply to document, that additional layer of copyright is at best very thin. See, for example, the case *Bridgeman Art Library v. Corel Corp.* But the legal situation here is still murky, particularly internationally.

   In the case of images that document sacred cultural objects originating from living societies, such as the Native American nations, additional complexities arise. These societies may consider their objects—or images documenting them— suitable for viewing only by specific individuals or in specific contexts. Here there's a clear conflict between cultural traditions and scholarly interests, and as I understand it, the solutions negotiated for the images are based on mutual respect and goodwill rather than on any actual legal framework such as copyright, at least in the United States; NAGPRA was about artifacts.

JEFF ROTHENBERG

"Ensuring the Longevity of Digital Documents"

Scientific American 272.1 (January 1995): 42–47; rev. and expanded,
February 22, 1999. See www.clir.org/programs/otheractiv/ensuring.pdf.

THE YEAR IS 2045, and my grandchildren (as yet unborn) are exploring the attic of my house (as yet unbought). They find a letter dated 1995 and a CD-ROM (compact disk). The letter claims that the disk contains a document that provides the key to obtaining my fortune (as yet unearned). My grandchildren are understandably excited, but they have never seen a CD before—except in old movies—and even if they can somehow find a suitable disk drive, how will they run the software necessary to interpret the information on the disk? How can they read my obsolete digital document?

This scenario questions the future of our computer-based digital documents, which are rapidly replacing their paper counterparts. It is widely accepted that information technology is revolutionizing our concepts of documents and records in an upheaval at least as great as the introduction of printing, if not of writing itself. The current generation of digital records therefore has unique historical significance; yet our digital documents are far more fragile than paper. In fact, the record of the entire present period of history is in jeopardy. The content and historical value of many governmental, organizational, legal, financial, and technical records, scientific databases, and personal documents may be irretrievably lost to future generations if we do not take steps to preserve them.

What Have We Already Lost?

Although there are few well-documented, undisputed cases of important digital documents or data that have been irretrievably lost, anecdotal evidence abounds. One of the best publicized cases concerns U.S. Census information for 1960. This was originally stored on digital tapes that became obsolete faster than expected. Although some information on these tapes was apparently unreadable, most of it was successfully copied onto newer media, and it appears that nothing irreplaceable was lost (since the raw census returns were saved on microfilm). Nevertheless, this case represents a narrow escape and is cited prominently in the 1990 House of Representatives Report *Taking a byte out of history: the archival preservation of federal computer records* (Nov. 6, 1990, House Report 101-978). Additional cases of possible loss noted in that report include hundreds of reels of tape from the Department of Health and Human Services; files from the National Commission on Marijuana and Drug Abuse, the Public Land Law Review Commission, the President's Commission on School Finance, and the National Commission on Consumer Finance; the Combat Area Casualty file containing POW and MIA information for the Vietnam war; herbicide information needed to analyze the impact of Agent Orange; and many others. Other sources suggest that scientific data is in similar jeopardy, as old NASA tapes and irreplaceable records from numerous experiments age ungracefully in the absence of funding to copy them to newer media. These cases exemplify all of the modes of loss discussed in this paper: physical decay of media, loss of information about the format, encoding, or compression of files, obsolescence of hardware, and unavailability of software.

To date there appear to be few documented cases of unequivocal loss, but this may simply reflect the fact that documents or data that are recognized as important while they are still retrievable are the ones most likely to be preserved. The historical significance of many of our digital documents—which we may not consider important enough to warrant saving—may become apparent only long after they have become unreadable.

Old Bit Streams Never Die— They Just Become Unreadable

My grandchildren's dilemma reveals some fundamental problems concerning digital storage. First, without the explanatory letter, they would have no reason to think that the disk in my attic was worth deciphering. Despite the much-touted immortality of digital information (stemming from its ability to be copied perfectly), it is the *letter* that will be immediately intelligible fifty years from now, not the digital disk. The letter possesses the enviable quality of being readable with no machinery, tools, or special knowledge—other than that of English, which it seems safe to assume will remain understandable for hundreds of years [see Figure 1].

Ironically, although its reproducibility makes digital information theoretically invulnerable to the ravages of time, the physical media on which it is stored are far from eternal. If the optical CD in my attic were instead a magnetic disk, attempting to read it would probably be a waste of time. The contents of most digital media evaporate long before words written on high quality paper, and they often become unusably obsolete much sooner, as they are superseded by new media or incompatible formats [see Figure 2]. The past few decades have witnessed the demise of numerous forms of digital storage. This has prompted my observation that digital information lasts forever—or five years, whichever comes first.

Yet neither the physical fragility of digital media nor their lemming-like tendency toward obsolescence comprise the worst of my grandchildren's problems. They must not only extract the content of the disk—they must also interpret it correctly. To understand what this entails, we must examine the nature of digital storage. Digital information can be stored on any physical medium that can record digits (such as the 0s and 1s that we call "bits"). Different media may store a given sequence of bits differently, according to the physical properties of the media and various conventions. We will use the term "bit stream" to mean an intended, meaningful sequence of bits (which may not be the same as the sequence in which they appear on some storage medium). A bit stream

Figure 1.

Shakespeare's immortal Sonnet 18 and its digital equivalent

As Shakespeare so eloquently notes in the couplet of the famous 18th sonnet, the printed word has a kind of immortality that few other things can claim. The word "this" in the final line refers to the sonnet itself, thereby proving its own point.

> Shall I compare thee to a Summers day?
> Thou art more lovely and more temperate:
> Rough windes do shake the darling buds of Maie,
> And Sommers lease hath too short a date:
> Sometime too hot the eye of heaven shines,
> And often is his gold complexion dimm'd,
> And every faire from faire some-time declines,
> By chance, or natures changing course un-trim'd:
> But thy eternall Sommer shall not fade,
> Nor loose possession of that faire thou ow'st,
> Not shall death brag thou wandr'st in his shade,
> When in eternall lines to time thou grow'st,
>   So long as men can breath or eyes can see,
>   So long lives this, and gives life to thee.

A modern, digital version of the couplet would have to be something like the following:

> So long as the magnetic flux on this disk has not been disturbed,
> and so long as humans retain the appropriate size and speed disk drives,
> and so long as they have hardware controllers and software device drivers capable of reading the bits from this disk,
> and so long as they have access to this software that encoded the file structure
> and character codes employed in the bit stream of this document,
> and so long as they can still find or recreate the computing environment necessary
> to run that software,
> *and* so long as they can still breathe or see,
>   So long lives this, ...

Figure 2.

The medium is a short-lived message

There is considerable controversy over the physical lifetimes of media: for example, some claim that tape will last for 200 years, whereas others report that it often fails in a year or two. However, physical lifetime is rarely the limiting factor, since at any given point in time, a particular format of a given medium can be expected to become obsolete within no more than 5 years.

MEDIUM	practical physical lifetime	avg. time until obsolete
optical (CD)	5–59 years	5 years
digital tape	2–30 years	5 years
magnetic disk	5–10 years	5 years

is simply a stream of binary digits, strung together in sequence [see Figure 3].

A bit stream can be stored in many different ways on different media. Retrieving a bit stream from its physical representation on some medium requires a hardware device, such as a disk drive, on which to "mount" that medium, as well as special "controller" circuitry that can retrieve the information stored on the medium—whether magnetic, optical, or other. A special program (called a "device driver") is also required to make this device accessible by a

given computer system. Yet even assuming that my grandchildren still recognize digital information that is encoded in binary form and that the intended bit stream can be retrieved from the medium, it must still be interpreted. This is not straightforward, because a given bit stream can represent almost anything—from an integer to an array of dots in a pointillist-style image [see Figure 4]. How can future generations interpret our bit streams correctly?

Compounding this problem, a bit stream has implicit structure that cannot be represented explicitly in the bit stream itself. For example, if a bit stream

Figure 3.

What is a bit stream?

Imagine that all the numbers in a monthly checking account statement were strung together with no punctuation or spacing to distinguish between check numbers, dates, or the dollar amounts of checks, deposits, or balances. The result would be a decimal "digit stream" containing all the important information in the statement—albeit in a decidedly unreadable form. In order to understand this stream, you would need to know its format, e.g., that it is a sequence of entries, each consisting of a number of pieces, such a date, followed by a check number—with zero indication a deposit—followed by a transaction amount, followed by an intermediate balance. You would also need to know where each piece starts and ends, i.e., how many digits comprise a date, a check number, and an amount. A bit stream is simply a digit stream in which each digit is binary (i.e., 0 or 1). Note that changing the length of the stream or rearranging it in any way wreaks havoc with its meaning.

date	chk/dep	amount	balance
4/5/94	deposit	$500.00	$500.00
4/26/94	chk# 314	$100.00	$400.00
4/27/94	deposit	$50.00	$450.00
11/3/94	chk# 315	$100.00	$350.00

Removing all spaces and punctuation and translating dates into 6 digits (mmddyy); check number into 4 digits; deposits into 0000; and amounts into 11-digits, the above entries become:

040594000000000005000000000050000
042694031400000010000000000040000
042794000000000005000000000045000
110394031500000010000000000035000

Concatenating these entries produces the following decimal digit stream:

040594000000000005000000000050000042694031400000010000000000040000042794000000000005000000000045000011039403150000001000000000035000

A bit stream is simply a digit stream in which each digit is either 0 or 1.

represents a sequence of alphabetic characters, it may consist of fixed-length chunks of information (called "bytes"), each of which represents a code for a single character [see Figure 5]. In current schemes, bytes are typically 7 or 8 bits long. But a bit stream cannot include enough information to describe how it should

be interpreted. In order to extract fixed-length bytes from a bit stream (thereby "parsing" it into its constituent pieces) we must know the length of a byte. We could in principle encode a "key" integer at the beginning of the bit stream, representing the length of each byte [see Figure 6].

Figure 4.

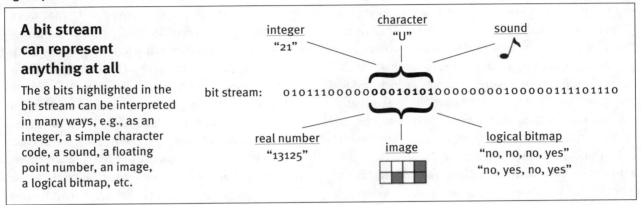

A bit stream can represent anything at all

The 8 bits highlighted in the bit stream can be interpreted in many ways, e.g., as an integer, a simple character code, a sound, a floating point number, an image, a logical bitmap, etc.

Figure 5.

Chunks (or bytes) can be of any length

Different length bytes allow different ranges of codes, which can in turn represent different numbers of characters. For example, 6-bit bytes provide barely enough codes to represent unadorned, uppercase text, whereas 8-bit bytes provide considerably more freedom.

byte-length	sample byte	code range	representable characters
6 bits	000101	0–63	{uppercase letters + digits + some punctuation}
8 bits	00000101	0–255	{upper + lowercase letters + digits + punctuation + "control" characters + graphical elements}

Figure 6.

Bit streams cannot be made self-explanatory

The 4 bits at the start of this bit stream are intended to be read as the "key" integer 7, meaning that the remaining bytes in the bit stream are each 7 bits long. However, there is no way to tell from the bit stream itself how long the key integer is: if we were to erroneously read the first 5 bits of the bit stream as the key (instead of the first 4), we would erroneously conclude that the remaining bytes were each 15 bits long.

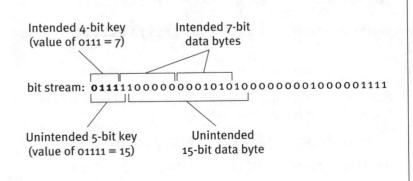

However, this key integer must itself be represented by a byte of some length. How can a reader interpret the key without knowing how long it is? We need another key to explain how to interpret the first key! Computer scientists describe such recursive problems as requiring a "bootstrap" (i.e., a way of doing something without help from any external source, as in pulling oneself up by one's own bootstraps). In order to provide such a bootstrap, we must annotate our digital storage medium with easily-readable information that explains how to read it. In our scenario, the letter accompanying the disk must fulfill this role.

In addition, compression schemes (which reduce the length of bit streams, to lower the cost of storing and transmitting them) and encryption schemes (which encode them for privacy) make bit streams quite difficult to parse [see Figure 7]. And even after a bit stream is correctly parsed, we face another problem: If the resulting stream of bytes represents a sequence of numbers or alphabetic characters, decoding it seems straightforward: we simply interpret each byte according to the appropriate code. Yet this leads to a problem similar to that of encoding a key to specify the length of each byte in a bit stream. To interpret each byte, we need to know what coding scheme it uses; but if we attempt to identify the coding scheme by encoding a "code-identifier" in the bit stream itself, we need another code-identifier to tell us how to read the first code-identifier! Again we must bootstrap this process by providing easily-readable annotations.

It's All in the Program

Yet the problem is deeper than this. Digital documents are typically saved as "files" of information: collections of bits corresponding to the bit streams representing specific documents. (Multiple documents are stored as separate files on a single digital medium; for simplicity we can assume a one-to-one correspondence between files and documents.) The bit stream in a document file may represent structures much more complex than sequences of fixed-length bytes. In particular, files often contain logically related but physically separate elements that are linked to each other by internal cross-references, consisting of pointers to other places within the bit stream or patterns to be matched. (Printed documents exhibit similar structure and cross-referencing, in which page numbers are used as pointers, while section names or other content references require the reader to search for specified text) [see Figure 8].

Figure 7.

Compressing a bit stream

As a simple example of compressing a bit stream without loss, "run-length encoding" replaces each sequence of 0s (000...0) by a count, indicating how many 0 bits were present in any given "run" (similarly for 1s). This can reduce the size of a bit stream without losing any information. For example, each run in the original bit stream can be represented by a 5-bit byte whose first bit specifies whether the run is of 0s or 1s and whose remaining 4 bits specify the length of a run (of up to 15 bits). This scheme is most appropriate for data that contains long sequences of 0s or 1s, such as digital imagery.

original bit stream: 00000011111111111111000000000000000111111111

        a run of 6 0-bits   a run of 14 1-bits

Representing each run in the original bit stream as a pair b:n (where b is 0 or 1 to indicate the contents of the run, and n is the length of the run) produces:

sequence of runs: 0:6,   1:14,   0:13,   1:9

resulting 5-bit bytes: 00110, 11110, 01101, 11001

compressed bit stream: 00110111100110111001 (20 bits)

In addition to having complex structure, many documents embed special information that is meaningful only to the software that created them. Word processing programs embed special format information in their documents to describe typography, layout, and structure (identifying titles, sections, chapter headings, etc.). Spreadsheet programs embed formulas specifying relationships among the cells in their documents. "Hypermedia" programs use embedded information to identify and link text, graphics, imagery, sound, and temporal information in arbitrarily complex ways. For convenience, we will refer to all embedded information of this kind—including all aspects of a bit stream's representation, such as its byte lengths, character codes, multi-media information, and structure—as "coding" (though this term is often used more narrowly).

As documents become more complex than simple streams of alphabetic characters, it becomes increasingly meaningless to think of them as existing at all except when they are interpreted by the software that created them. The bits in each document file are meaningful only to the program that created that file. In effect, document files are programs, consisting of instructions and data that can be interpreted only by the appropriate software. That is, a document file is not a document in its own right: it merely *describes* a document that comes into existence only when the file is "run" by the program that created it. Without this authoring program—or some equivalent viewing software—the document is held cryptic hostage to its own encoding.

As we discover the advantages of digital documents, we are coming to rely more and more heavily

Figure 8.

Document structure

Digital documents may encode structure as well as text. For example a document may consist of multiple subsections within sections:

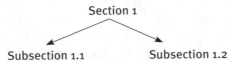

This can be represented by a bit stream that contains pointers (ptr1 and ptr2) that give the byte-count at which each subsection begins:

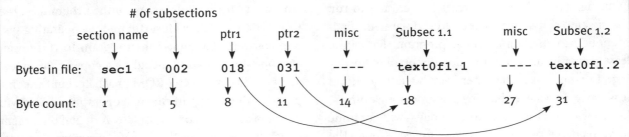

"Hypertext" documents may consist of elements that are linked together to form multiple alternative sequences, no one of which is any more "correct" than any other. In a document of this kind, a given element may appear as a subsection of several different sections (making the pointers in its bit stream even more essential for understanding its structure):

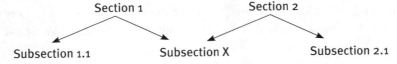

on those capabilities of the digital medium that transcend the limitations of the printed page. This may be partly a result of our infatuation with the novelty of information technology, but it nevertheless implies that nonlinear, multimedia documents will become increasingly prevalent, at least while our infatuation lasts. To the extent that we create digital documents of this kind, they will be impossible to access without appropriate software.

Suppose that my grandchildren manage to read the intended bit stream from the CD-ROM. Only then will they face their real problem: without further help from my accompanying letter, how can they interpret the coding of the document file on the disk? If the document is a simple sequence of fixed-length bytes representing alphabetic characters, then trial-and-error experimentation might decode the document as a stream of text. But if the document is more complex than this, a brute-force approach—trying to "decrypt" the structure and meaning of an arbitrary document file—is unlikely to succeed. The meaning of a file is not inherent in the file itself, any more than the meaning of this sentence is inherent in its characters or words. In order to understand a file, we must know what its content *signifies*, i.e., what meaning it has in the language of its intended reader. Unfortunately, the intended reader of a digital file is a computer program, not a human.

Digital documents therefore have the discouraging characteristic of being software-dependent. They cannot be "held up to the light" but must be viewed by using appropriate software. Is it necessary to run the specific software that created a document, or is it enough to run some similar program that can at least partially interpret the document file's encoding? In some cases the latter may be sufficient, but it is naive to believe that any document encoding—however natural it seems to us today—will continue to be readable by future software for very long. The information technology revolution continually creates new paradigms, which often abandon their predecessors instead of subsuming them. Collaborating authors and publishers are already confounded by a bewildering and ever-changing collection of incompatible document file formats that must be translated

back and forth, often with annoying losses of format, structure, and even content.

If "reading" a document means simply being able to extract its content—whether or not it is in its original form—then we may be able to avoid running the original software that created the document. But content can be subtle: translating from one word processing format to another, for example, often displaces headings or captions or eliminates them entirely. Is this merely a loss of structure, or does it impinge on content as well? If we transform a spreadsheet into a table, thereby deleting the formulas that relate the cells of the table to each other, have we retained its content?

As an extreme example, suppose that the document in my attic explains that my fortune can be found from a treasure map represented by visual patterns of inter-word and inter-line spacing in the digital version of this paper, stored on the CD. Since these patterns are artifacts of the formatting algorithm of my word-processing software, they do not appear in a printed or posted version of this paper: they will be visible only when the original digital version is viewed using the software that created it. Ultimately, if one needs to view a complex document as its author viewed it, one may have little choice but to run the software that created it.

In order to read the document file stored on the CD-ROM in my attic, my grandchildren must therefore know what program created the file; but what are their chances of finding that program fifty years from now? If I include a copy of the program on the CD-ROM itself, they must still find the operating system software that allows the program to run on an appropriate computer. Including a copy of this operating system on the CD-ROM may help, but the computer hardware required by that operating system will have long since become obsolete. A digital document depends not just on the specific program that created it but on the entire suite of hardware and software that allowed that program to run. How much of this can I store on the CD-ROM, to make it as self-sufficient as possible? What kind of digital Rosetta Stone can I leave to provide the key to understanding the contents of my disk? What can we do to ensure that the digital documents we are creating will not be lost to the future?

What's an Author to Do?

As a first step, we must preserve the bit streams of digital documents. This requires copying the bits onto fresh media to preserve their physical existence and copying them to new forms of media to ensure their accessibility. The need to refresh digital information by copying it onto new media (and possibly translating it into new formats, sometimes called "migration") has been recognized in the library sciences and archives literature, as well as in a number of scientific and commercial fields. This requires an ongoing effort: future access depends on an unbroken chain of migrations with a cycle time short enough to prevent media from becoming physically unreadable or obsolete before they are copied. A single break in this chain can render digital information inaccessible—short of heroic effort. Given the current lack of robustness and rate of evolution of media, migration cycles may need to be as frequent as every few years, requiring a significant commitment. Moreover, copying the bit streams of digital documents in this way is necessary but not sufficient. Like an illiterate monk dutifully copying text in a lost language, migration may save the bits but lose their meaning.

Preserving digital documents is analogous to preserving ancient written texts. Just as with digital documents, it is sometimes necessary to refresh an ancient text by transcribing it, since the medium on which it is recorded has a limited lifetime—though parchment or stone tablets last noticeably longer than magnetic disks. An ancient text can be preserved in one of two ways: either by copying it in its original language or by translating it into whatever language is current at the time of transcription.

Translation is attractive because it avoids the need to retain knowledge of the text's original language, yet few scholars would praise their ancestors for taking this approach. Not only does each translation lose information, but translation makes it impossible to *determine* whether information has been lost,

because the original is discarded. (In extreme cases, translation can completely destroy content, as when translating a dictionary. Imagine some misguided archaeologist having blindly translated all three copies of the text on the Rosetta Stone into English the moment it was discovered and discarding the original: an invaluable correspondence between languages would thereby have been translated into a trivial repetition of the same text.)

Copying text in its original language, on the other hand, guarantees that nothing will be lost— assuming that knowledge of the original language is retained along with the text. This amounts to saving the "bit stream" of the original text.

Similarly, there are two strategies for dealing with digital documents, both of which have received attention by archivists, library scientists, and others concerned with the preservation of records. The first attempts to translate documents into standard, system-independent forms, while the second attempts to extend the longevity of systems so that documents will remain readable using their original software. Unfortunately, neither approach promises a complete solution without considerable additional effort.

The Illusion that Standards Provide an Answer

On the surface, it may appear preferable to translate digital documents into standard forms that can be guaranteed to be readable in the future. This would circumvent the need to retain the ability to run the original software that created a document. Proponents of this approach cite the relational database model (developed by E.F. Codd in the 1970s) as a paradigmatic example. Since all relational database management systems (RDBMSs) implement this same underlying model, any relational database produced by any RDBMS can in principle be translated without loss into a form acceptable to any other RDBMS. A standard relational form could therefore be established, and all relational databases could be translated into this form. Files represented using this standard could be copied to new media as necessary, and the standard would provide readability for all time. This sounds tempting, but it is flawed in two fundamental ways.

First, although the formal mathematical definition of the relational database model leads all RDBMSs to provide equivalent baseline capabilities, most commercial RDBMSs distinguish themselves from each other precisely by offering features that extend the standard relational model in non-standard ways. Therefore relational databases are less amenable to standardization than they appear. If a Procrustean standard relational database form were imposed on existing relational databases, many of them would lose much of their richness.

Moreover, the relational model is rapidly giving way to an object-oriented database model (which represents entities as structured, composite objects), as the limitations of the relational approach become apparent. This evolution is neither accidental nor undesirable: it is the hallmark of information technology that it evolves at a rapid rate. Data saved in relational form may well become inaccessible as relational database systems give way to object-oriented systems.

Furthermore, the relational database model does not constitute a paradigmatic example, because it is practically unique. No other type of digital document comes close to having as formal a basis on which to erect a standard. Word processors, graphics programs, spreadsheets, and hypermedia programs each create documents with far greater variance in expressive capability and format than relational databases. The incompatibility of word processing file formats is a notorious example—nor is this simply an artifact of market differentiation or competition among proprietary products. Rather it is a direct outgrowth of the natural evolution of information technology as it adapts itself to the emerging needs of users. No common application other than relational database management is yet a suitable candidate for long-term standardization.

The False Promise of "Migration"

In the absence of long-term standards for each type of digital document, it might still be possible to trans-

late a document into successive standards, each having a relatively short life-span (on the order of one or two migration cycles). It is sometimes suggested that a variation of this approach occurs naturally, since documents that are in continuous use within organizations are translated into new formats as needed. However, this breaks down when a document ceases to be used in the ongoing business of the organization that owns it, since few organizations can justify the cost of translating documents that they no longer use.

The successive translation approach avoids the need for ultimate standards, but it compounds the problem of losing information, since each translation may introduce new losses. In theory, translating a document into a standard (or sequence of standards) retains a path back to the original. By keeping descriptions of each standard used in the sequence of translations (where these descriptions themselves would have to be translated into successive standards in order to remain readable), future scholars might reconstruct the original document. Unfortunately, this requires that each translation be reversible without loss, which is rarely the case. If all early versions of Homer had been discarded after translating them, there would be little hope of reconstructing them by translating backwards again.

Finally, the translation approach suffers from a fatal flaw. Unlike ancient Greek and English, which have roughly equivalent expressive power and semantics, digital documents are still evolving so rapidly that periodic paradigm shifts are inevitable. And new paradigms do not always subsume their predecessors: they represent revolutionary changes in what we mean by documents. By definition, paradigm shifts do not necessarily provide upward compatibility. Old documents cannot always be translated into new paradigms in meaningful ways, and translating backward is frequently impossible. The relational database model provides a case in point. Many earlier, "hierarchical" databases had to be completely redesigned to fit the relational model, just as relational databases are now being drastically restructured to make use of newer object-oriented models. Paradigm shifts of this kind can make it extremely difficult, if not meaningless, to translate old documents into new standard forms.

Although defining ultimate standards for digital documents may be an admirable goal, it is premature. Information technology is still on the steepest slope of its learning curve. The field is too new to have developed an accepted, formal understanding of the ways that humans manipulate information. It would be presumptuous to imagine that we are ready to enumerate the most important kinds of digital applications, let alone to propose that we are ready to circumscribe their capabilities by standardizing them. Any attempt to force users to settle for artificial limitations imposed by such standards would be futile, since the momentum of the information technology revolution derives directly from the attraction of new capabilities. It may become feasible to define long-term standards for digital documents sometime in the future, when information science rests on a more secure, formal foundation, but standards do not yet offer a solution to our problem.

Byting the Bullet

The alternative to translating a digital document is to view it by using the software that created it. In theory, this need not require that we actually *run* the software. Suppose we could describe its behavior in some system-independent way and save that description instead of the software itself. Future generations could interpret the saved description of the software to recreate its behavior, thereby reading the document. While this sounds promising, information science has not yet produced methods to describe the behavior of software in the depth required for this approach. High-level behavioral formalisms of this kind—that describe programs in terms of their interactions with humans in performing information processing tasks—may eventually emerge, but they are not yet on the horizon. In their absence, the only meaningful description of the detailed behavior of a program (in most cases) is the program itself. In order to recreate the behavior of an arbitrary program, there is currently little choice but to run it.

This requires saving digital document files and the programs that created them, as well as all system software required to run those programs. Though this is a daunting task, it is theoretically feasible. It is not uncommon to save and distribute digital documents along with appropriate viewing software—and sometimes even a copy of the appropriate version of the operating system needed to run that software. This is often the only way to ensure that a recipient will be able to read a document (assuming the required hardware is available). Furthermore, in many cases, it is necessary only to *refer* to the appropriate application and system software, since these programs are ubiquitous. Archives of free (public-domain) software are already proliferating on the Internet, and with luck, copyright and royalty restrictions for proprietary programs may expire when those programs become obsolete, making them available for future access to historical documents.

If digital documents and their programs are to be saved, their migration must be carried out with extreme care to ensure that their bit streams are not modified in any way that affects their interpretation, since programs and their data files can be corrupted by the slightest change. This is a reappearance of the translation problem discussed above. Copying bit streams must not inadvertently change byte size, introduce additional bits, reverse the order of bits, compress or encrypt data, or in any way modify the encoding of the bit stream. If such changes are unavoidable, it is not enough to record information sufficient to interpret the final encoding: one must also record sufficient detail about each such transformation to allow reconstructing the original encoding of the bit stream, on which its semantics may have relied. For example, if internal pointers in a document consist of bit counts, they would be invalidated by any transformation that changed the number of bits in the stream. (Finding all such pointers in a document and adjusting them to account for the changed bit count is analogous to—but much harder than—the "Year 2000" problem of finding all two-digit numbers in a program that represent years.) Although it is possible to design bit streams whose semantics are immune to any expected transformations of this sort, future migration cycles may introduce unexpected transformations, which the designer of the bit stream could not have foreseen.

Ideally, bit streams should be considered inviolable entities, sealed in virtual "envelopes" whose contents are preserved verbatim. If transformation is inescapable, it must be reversible without loss; easily-readable information associated with each envelope must describe its contents and its transformation history, if any. It will be a serious challenge to encapsulate bit streams in this way and ensure that they retain the necessary contextual information in a form that remains easily readable well into the future.

How Can We Run Obsolete Hardware?

We must still show how we can preserve the hardware needed to run the software to view a digital document. The migration process eliminates the need to preserve storage devices such as disk drives, but systems and application software still depend on hardware, both for computation and for input and output. One obvious approach is to try to maintain computers in working condition long after they become obsolete. Indeed a number of specialized museums and informal "retrocomputing" clubs are attempting to do this. However, despite a certain undeniable charm— attributable to its technological bravado— this strategy is futile in the long run: mechanical components fail, and even electronic circuits age as the "dopants" that make silicon into a useful semiconductor and the metal traces that connect components on each chip diffuse and "migrate" within their substrate. As components wear out, the cost of repairing or replacing them (and of retaining the expertise required to do so) will quickly outweigh the demand for maintaining any given computer. How long can we hope to keep current systems in operational condition? Twenty years? Fifty?

Moreover, since records cannot be expected to survive on their original media but will only be readable if they have migrated to new media, using old computers to read old records would require building special-purpose hardware interfaces between each old computer and each new generation of storage media, for example to allow a vintage-1960 computer to read data from a CD-ROM. The effort of designing,

building, and maintaining such interfaces would rapidly become prohibitive.

Fortunately, it is not necessary to preserve physical hardware to be able to run obsolete software. Emulators—programs that mimic the behavior of hardware—can be created to take the place of obsolete hardware as needed. Assuming that future computers will be orders of magnitude more powerful than ours, future users should be able to ask their computers to generate emulators for obsolete systems on demand. This may require accessing saved specifications for the desired hardware, but this hardware could not have existed in the first place if detailed specifications for its design and construction had not also existed. These specifications must be saved in a digital form that will be readable by future emulator generators (whether human or machine). Alternatively, specifications for emulators could be saved directly; since most new computers are emulated prior to being produced (as part of the design and evaluation process) machine-independent specifications for emulators could be derived from these existing machine-specific emulators. In the six years since I first suggested this approach, it has begun to occur spontaneously in an unlikely context. Special interest network groups are currently creating and sharing emulators for obsolete video game processors and early personal computers. Obsolete programs for these processors are being copied to current media by ingenious methods, such as digitizing audio signals generated by makeshift devices that read obsolete media, and these programs are then run under emulation on modern computers.

Putting It All Together

As we have seen, interpreting a bit stream depends on knowing how it has been encoded, and a bit stream cannot be fully self-describing, since any description that we encode in the bit stream must itself be interpreted. The only way to bootstrap this process is to include easily-readable annotation with every digital document, explaining how to interpret its bits. The letter accompanying the disk in my attic serves this purpose; but if the disk had been copied onto newer media, how would the information in the letter have been preserved? A unit of storage in the year 2045 may hold the bit streams of thousands of CDs. Even if each disk had an associated letter supplying the necessary context, how could this be carried along with the bit stream from each disk?

Clearly, any annotation must itself be stored digitally, along with its associated bit stream; but it must be encoded in a digital form that is more readable than the bit stream itself, in order to serve as a bootstrap. This is an ideal role for standards: a simple text-based standard should be able to encode sufficient explanatory information to allow interpreting an encapsulated bit stream. Whenever bit streams migrate to newer media, their annotations must be translated from their previous form to whatever standard is current at the time of the migration.

Reading current digital documents in the future will not be easy. Eventually, information science may develop models of human information processing and computation that will allow digital documents to be stored in system-independent form, but this cannot happen in time to save the current generation of these documents. Similarly, long-lived storage media may ultimately make migration less urgent (the cost of migration may motivate the acceptance of such media, overriding our appetite for improved performance), but there is no sign of this happening yet. In the meantime, we must act quickly and decisively if we are to help our descendants read our documents.

We must develop evolving standards for encoding explanatory annotations to bootstrap the interpretation of digital documents that are saved in nonstandard forms. We must develop techniques for saving the bit streams of software-dependent documents and their associated systems and application software. We must ensure that the hardware environments necessary to run this software are described in sufficient detail to allow their future emulation. We must save these specifications as digital documents, encoded using the bootstrap standards developed for saving annotations so that they can be read without special software (lest we be recursively forced to emulate one system in order to learn how to emulate another). We must associate contextual information

Figure 9.

> ## Using emulation to read an obsolete digital document
>
> HW description interpreter
>
> orig. HW description
>
> current HW'
>
> current OS'
>
> (migrated) media intact
>
> drives + logic for media
>
> orig. HW emulator
>
> OS' runs
>
> media physically accessible
>
> orig. OS
>
> orig. HW "runs" under emulation
>
> media drivers
>
> orig. SW
>
> orig. OS runs
>
> media logically accessible
>
> orig. SW runs
>
> document readable!

with our digital documents to provide provenance as well as explanatory annotations in a form that can be translated into successive standards so as to remain easily readable. Finally, we must ensure the systematic and continual migration of digital documents onto new media, preserving document and program bit streams verbatim, while translating their contextual information as necessary. If all of these factors come together, they should enable obsolete digital documents to be read as illustrated in Figure 9.

Conclusion

Beyond having obvious pragmatic value, the digital documents we are currently creating are the first generation of a radically new form of record-keeping. As such, they are likely to be viewed by our descendants as valuable artifacts from the dawn of the information age. Yet we are in imminent danger of losing them even as we create them. We must invest careful thought and significant effort if we are to preserve these documents for the future. If we are unwilling to make this investment, we risk substantial practical loss, as well as the condemnation of our progeny for thoughtlessly consigning to oblivion a unique historical legacy.

Where does this leave my grandchildren? By assumption, the information on their fifty-year-old CD has not migrated to newer media; but if they are fortunate, it may still be readable by some existing disk drive, or they may be resourceful enough to construct one, based on instructions in my accompanying letter. If I include all necessary system and application software on the disk, along with a complete and easily decoded specification of the hardware environment required to run it, they should be able to generate an emulator that will display my document by running its original software. I wish them luck.

SHORT BIBLIOGRAPHY

Archival Management of Electronic Records, Archives and Museum Informatics Technical Report no. 13, David Bearman, ed., Archives and Museum Informatics, Pittsburgh, 1991 (ISSN 1042-1459).

"Text and Technology: Reading and Writing in the Electronic Age," Jay David Bolter, *Library Resources and Technical Services*, 31 (January/March 1987), pp. 12–23.

"Understanding Electronic Incunabula: A Framework for Research on Electronic Records," Margaret Hedstrom, *The American Archivist*, 54:3 (Summer 1991), pp. 334–54.

"Scholarly Communication and Information Technology: Exploring the Impact of Changes in the Research Process on Archives," Avra Michelson and Jeff Rothenberg, *The American Archivist*, 55:2 (Spring 1992), pp. 236–315 (ISSN 0360-9081).

Research Issues in Electronic Records, published for the National Historical Publications and Records Commission, Washington, D.C., by the Minnesota Historical Society, St. Paul, Minn. 1991.

"Ensuring the Longevity of Digital Documents," Jeff Rothenberg, *Scientific American*, January 1995 (Vol. 272, Number 1), pp. 24–29.

"Metadata to Support Data Quality and Longevity," *The First IEEE Metadata Conference*, April 16-18, 1996, NOAA Auditorium, NOAA Complex, Silver Spring, MD, available only online at http://www.computer.org/conferen/meta96/rothenberg_paper/ieee.data-quality.html.

Taking a byte out of history: the archival preservation of federal computer records, Report of the U.S. House of Representatives Committee on Government Operations, Nov. 6. 1990 (House Report 101-978).

ABBY RUMSEY

Why Digitize?

Washington DC: Council on Library and Information Resources, 1999. [Editor's note: Published under Abby Smith.]

> *The dream of the virtual library comes forward now not because it promises an exciting future, but because it promises a future that will be just like the past, only better and faster.*
> —James J. O'Donnell, Avatars of the Word.

Introduction

In the digital world, all knowledge is divided into two parts. The binary strings of 0s and 1s that make up the genetic code of data allow information to be fruitful and multiply, and allow people to create, manipulate, and share data in ways that appear to be revolutionary. It is often said that digital information is transforming the way we learn, the way we communicate, even the way we think. It is also changing the way that libraries and archives not only work, but, more fundamentally, the very work that they do. It is easy to overstate—and underestimate—the transformative power of a new technology, especially when we do not yet understand the full implications of its many applications. Nonetheless, people have embraced this technology enthusiastically, often as an answer to questions that had not, in many cases, yet been posed. Librarians everywhere hear the voices of people speaking like evangelicals, urging the conversion of text and visual materials into digital form as if conversion per se were a self-evident good. But because we tend to imagine the future in terms of the present, as O'Donnell points out, such projections of the present onto the future may, at best, be misleading. If this new technology does, indeed, turn out to be revolutionary, then we cannot anticipate its impact in full, and we should be cautious about letting the radiance of the bright future blind us to its limitations.

While we may not yet fully understand the ways in which this technology will and will not change libraries, we can already discern some simple, yet profoundly important, patterns in digital applications that presage their effective and creative use in the traditional library functions of collecting, preserving, and making information accessible. A critical mass of experience is accumulating among libraries and archives active in digitizing parts of their collections, ranging in size from the Library of Congress, the National Archives, and major research libraries in the Digital Library Federation, to smaller institutions such as the Huntington and Denver Public libraries. Their experiences reveal patterns that can help us assess when the technology is able to meet expectations for improvement of traditional library services, when it cannot, and when it may do so, but not in a cost-effective manner. This paper will address the question of why a library should invest in the conversion of its traditional materials into digital form—in other words, what are the advantages and disadvantages of converting traditional analog materials into digital form.

What Is Digital Information?

Until very recently, all recorded information was analog—that is, a continuous stream of information of varying density and type. Analog information can range from the subtle tones and gradations of the chiaroscuro in a Berenice Abbott photograph of Manhattan in early morning light, to the changes in volume, tone, and pitch recorded on a tape that might, when played back on equipment, turn out to be the basement tapes of Bob Dylan or the Welsh accents of Dylan Thomas reading *Under Milk Wood*. But when such information is fed into a computer, broken up into 0s and 1s and put together in a binary code, its character is changed in quite precise ways.

Digitally encoded data do not represent the infinitely variable nature of information as faithfully as analog forms of recording. Digits are assigned numeric values which are fixed, so that great precision is gained in lieu of the infinitesimal gradations that carry meaning in analog forms. For example, when a photograph is digitized for viewing on a computer screen, the original continuous tone image is divided into dots with assigned values that are mapped against a grid. The pattern of the dots is remembered and reassembled by the computer upon command.

Those bits of data can be recombined for easy manipulation and compressed for storage. Voluminous encyclopedias that take up yards of shelf space in analog form can fit onto a minuscule space on a computer drive, and that same digital encyclopedia can be searched in many ways other than alphabetically, making possible information retrieval that would have been unimaginable if one had only the analog copy, on paper or microfilm.

Data that are not being used are not like books on a shelf or the family correspondence and photos stored in shoe boxes at the back of a closet. They are more like the stacks of LPs or the 8mm family home movies in storage in a basement. That is, digital information is not eye-legible: it is dependent on a machine to decode and re-present the bit streams in images on a computer screen. Without that machine, and without active human intervention, those data will not last.

One of the most important qualities of information in digital form is that by its very nature it is not fixed in the way that texts printed on a paper are. Digital texts are neither final nor finite, and are fixed neither in essence nor in form except when a hard copy is printed out, for they can be changed easily and without trace of erasures or emendations. Flexibility is one of the chief assets of digital information and is precisely what we like about text poured into a word processing program. It is easy to edit, to reformat, and to commit to print in a variety of iterations without the effort required to produce hard copy from a typewriter. That is why visual designers like computer-assisted design programs. It is easy to summon up quickly any number of variations of value, hue, shape, and placement to see, rather than to imagine, what different visual options look like. Furthermore, we

can create an endless number of identical copies from a digital file, because the file does not decay by virtue of copying.

From the creator's point of view this kind of plasticity may be ideal, but from the perspective of a library or archives that endeavors to collect a text that is final and in one sense or another definitive, it can complicate things considerably. Because the digital text is flexible and easily changed, the matter of preserving digital information becomes conceptually problematic. Which version of the file, or how many versions, should be archived? There are also formidable technical obstacles to ensuring the persistence of digital information.

Digitization Is Not Preservation— At Least Not Yet

All recorded information, from the paintings on the walls of caves and drawings in the sand, to clay tablets and videotaped speeches, has value, even if temporary, or it would not have been recorded to begin with. That which the creator or transcriber deems to be of enduring value is written on a more or less durable medium and entrusted to the care of responsible custodians. Other bits of recorded information, like laundry lists and tax returns, are created to serve a temporary purpose and are allowed to vanish. Libraries and archives were created to collect and make available that which has long-term value. And libraries and archives serve not only to safeguard that information, but also to provide evidence of one type or another of the work's provenance, which goes towards establishing the authenticity of that work.

Though digitization is sometimes loosely referred to as preservation, it is clear that, so far, digital resources are at their best when facilitating access to information and weakest when assigned the traditional library responsibility of preservation. Regrettably, because digitization is a type of reformatting, like microfilming, it is often confused with preservation microfilming and seen as a superior, if as yet more expensive, form of preservation reformatting. Digital imaging is not preservation, however. Much is gained by digitizing, but permanence and authenticity, at this juncture of technological development, are not among those gains.

The reasons for the weakness of digitization as a preservation treatment are complex. Microfilm, the preservation reformatting medium of choice, is projected to last several centuries when made on silver halide film and kept in a stable environment. It requires only a lens and a light to read, unlike computer files, which require hardware and software, both of which are developed in often proprietary forms that quickly become obsolete, rendering information on them inaccessible. At present, the retrieval of information encoded in an obsolete file format and stored on an obsolete medium (such as 8-inch floppy diskettes) is extremely expensive and labor-intensive, when at all possible. Often the medium on which digital information is recorded is itself inherently unstable. Magnetic tape is one example of a common digital medium that requires special care and handling and has been known to degrade within a decade, beyond the point where information can be recovered. Magnetic forms of analog recording, such as video and audio tape, are equally fragile and unreliable for long-term storage. In its inherent physical fragility, magnetic tape is not different in essence from the acid paper so widely produced in the last 150 years, but its life-span is often dramatically shorter than that of poor quality paper.

More important even than the durability of the medium is the need to keep the data fresh and encoded in readable file formats. Ongoing investigations into two possible ways of ensuring data persistence—the migration of data from one software and hardware configuration to a more current one, and the creation of software that emulates obsolete encoding formats—may develop solutions to this problem. As yet, we have no tested and reliable technique for ensuring continued access to digital data of enduring value, although information stored on non-proprietary formats such as ASCII has been migrated successfully (in the case, for example, of specific government records). Nevertheless, migration from one software to another does not produce a new file exactly identical to the old one. Though data loss may not necessarily mean loss of intellectual content, the file has been changed.

Another reason that preservation goals are in some fundamental way challenged by digital imaging is that it is quite difficult to ascertain the authenticity and integrity of an image, database, or text when it is in digital form. How can one tell if a digital file has been tampered with and the content changed or falsified? Looked at from the traditional perspective of published or manuscript materials, it is futile even to try: there is no original with which to compare a suspect file. Copies can be deceptively faithful: one cannot tell the difference between the original output of a scan of the Declaration of Independence, and one that is output four months later. In contravention of a core principle of archival authenticity, one can change the bit stream of a file and leave no record of its having been altered. There is much research and development being dedicated to solving the dilemma posed by the stunning fidelity of digital cloning, including methods for marking images and time-stamping them, but as yet there is no solution.

Authenticity may not be important for a digital image of a well-known document like the Declaration of Independence, in which access to either the analog original or a good photographic image is easy enough to obtain for comparison's sake. But anyone who has seen the digitally engineered commercial in which Fred Astaire can be seen dancing with a vacuum cleaner can readily understand the ease with which improbable digital occurrences can become real because we can be made to see them. After all, the evidence is before our eyes, and our eyes cannot detect a falsehood. It is our cognitive reasoning that detects that falsehood, not our eyes. That image of the suave, gliding across the floor with the functional, startles and amuses us because it confounds our expectations.

But what if we arrive at a library Web site, for example, looking for an image that we have never seen and about which we have few expectations. The only reason that we expect that image to be a truthful representative of the original is that we can rely on the integrity of the institution that has mounted the files and makes them available to us. We transfer the confidence we experience in the reading room of that library to our work station, wherever it may be. We go to the New York Public Library Web site with the full expectation that the library "guarantees" the integrity of the images they mount. But it would be very hard indeed for a researcher in Alaska looking at New York Public Library's Digital Schomburg site to verify independently that any given image is indeed a faithful representation of the original.

The problem of authenticity is far from unique to the digital realm. Forgers and impostors have a distinguished history of operating successfully and often long undetected in print and photographic media, although they have had to work harder and smarter than their digital counterparts. The traditional methods for authenticating documents that have served the library and archival professions well until now have relied largely on practices derived from markers carried on the physical medium itself. After a textual examination to look for obvious differences in content, researchers have often then examined the physical carrier itself—the book or manuscript leaf—to see if there are any signs of modification or falsification. From a simple examination of watermarks to a variety of sophisticated chemical, optical, and physical tests that can verify the age of paper, the composition of inks, and the physical traces of erasures and palimpsests, researchers have resorted to a number of strategies to verify the authenticity of a document. Granted, there are few who routinely insist on that level of authentication in doing research, but that is because the pitfalls of using books, manuscripts, and visual materials are familiar to us and we tend to discount them without much conscious thought. We should be wary of reposing the same quality of trust in digital resources that we do in print and photographic media until we are equally familiar with their evidentiary weaknesses.

As in other forms of reformatting, digital scanning has implications for the original item and its physical integrity. Depending on the policy of a library or archival institution, the original of a scanned item may or may not be retained after reformatting. To the extent that a reader can make do without handling the original, the digital preservation surrogate can serve to protect it from wear and tear. If there is concern that the scanning process could damage materials, one would choose to scan a film version of the original.

The advantages of scanning for access purposes may be combined with those of preservation microfilming by using the model of hybrid conversion, that is, creating preservation-standard microfilm and scanning it for digital access purposes, or, conversely, beginning with a high-quality scan of the original and creating computer-output microfilm (COM) for preservation purposes. Work is presently underway to articulate and refine best practices for implementing the hybrid approach to reformatting so that it can be adopted by libraries across the country. Of course COM, unlike microfilm created from the original, is only a recording of digital images on an analog medium. Though it has been fixed on a durable medium, some would argue that the image itself, having been generated digitally, has lost some essential information—or has at least lost its fundamental analog character—and cannot therefore claim to be as desirable for preservation as film made by photographing the original source.

Although this may seem a minor point to those more interested in easy access than in that level of authenticity, it is still important to understand that digital technology transforms analog information radically. There has to be some loss of information when an analog item is made digital, just as there is when one analog copy is made from another. On the other hand, there is virtually no loss of information from one generation of a digital copy to another. Images will not degrade when copied, in contrast to microfilm, which loses about 10 percent of its information with each copy. Once there is more than one copy of a digital file, it is impossible to pick out the original, and one will never speak of "vintage files" the way that one now speaks of vintage photographs. On the other hand, digital images are less likely to decay in storage if they are refreshed, the images will not degrade when copied, and the digital files will not decay in use, unlike paper, film, and magnetic tape.

Digitization Is Access—Lots of It

Digital files can provide extraordinary access to information. They can make the remote accessible and the hard to see visible. Digital surrogates can bring together research materials that are widely scattered about the globe, allowing viewers to conflate collections and compare items that can be examined side by side solely by virtue of digital representation. The easy access to reference surrogates—images that provide a great deal of the information contained in the original, even if at fairly low resolution—is a boon to researchers when developing efficient and effective research strategies. Through the use of thumbnail images, which do not require high resolution, one can at a minimum acquaint oneself with the source enough to know whether or not one needs to consult the original. Very often one can make do with the digital surrogate because it provides all the information required. An image of the 1612 map of Virginia by John Smith may provide a scholar enough information to determine how far inland Smith actually traveled. The black crosses he laid down on paper to mark the furthest points he reached on various treks are clearly legible even on a low-resolution image.

One must think about the nature of the source materials (color, black and white, or shades of gray) and the use of the images (who will be consulting them and for what) when making decisions about the parameters for image capture. The quality and utility of an image depend upon the technology of capture and display, and the usefulness of an image, even if only for reference, can be severely compromised by a low-resolution monitor on which the image will be displayed. While work is ongoing to address the quality control and variability of computer monitors, as yet the lack of control over display mechanisms constitutes one of the weakest links in the digital chain of transmission.

Image processing—the manipulation of images after initial digital capture—can greatly expand the capacity of the researcher to compare and contrast details that the human eye cannot see unaided. Images can be enhanced in size, sharpness of detail, and color contrast. Through image processing, a badly faded document can be read more easily, dirty images can be cleaned up, and faint pencil marks can be made legible. The plan of the District of Columbia prepared by Pierre-Charles L'Enfant for George Wash-ington in 1791 is so badly faded, discolored, and brittle that it resembles a potato chip. It cannot be used by researchers and yields little detailed information to the unaided eye. Digitized several years ago, the map now can be displayed to allow us to make out all the subtle contours of the architect's plan and to read the numerous annotations made by Thomas Jefferson. Like successful archaeologists, we have, with our digital picks and brushes, excavated important historical evidence that has changed the way we understand the planning of the nation's capital.

Digital technology can also make available powerful teaching materials for students who would not otherwise have access to them. Among the most valuable types of materials to digitize from a classroom perspective are those from the special collections of research institutions, including rare books, manuscripts, musical scores and performances, photographs and graphic materials, and moving images. Often these items are extremely rare, fragile, or, in fact, unique, and gaining access to them is very difficult. Digitizing these types of primary source materials offers teachers at all levels previously unheard-of opportunities to expose their students to the raw materials of history. The richness of special collections as research tools lies in part in the representation of an event or phenomenon in many different formats. The chance to study the presidential election of 1860 by looking at digital images of daguerreotypes of the candidates, political campaign posters (a recent innovation of the time), cartoons from contemporary newspapers, abolitionist broadsides and notices of slave auctions, and the manuscript of Lincoln's inaugural address in draft form reflecting several different stages of composition—such an opportunity would be possible with a well-developed plan of digital conversion of materials from different repositories normally beyond the reach of students.

While we know, for example, that the daily number of hits at the Library of Congress American Memory site is greater than the number of readers who visit the library's reading rooms each day, we have very little data now as to how much these types of online images are used and for what purposes. Some large libraries are attempting to compile and analyze use statistics, but this labor-intensive task presents quite a challenge. We need more user studies before we can assert confidently what may seem self-evident to us now: that adding digitized special collections to the mass of information available on the Internet is in the public interest and enhances education. We also need to ensure that libraries are working collaboratively in their efforts to digitize materials so that together they create a critical mass of research sources that are complementary and not duplicative, and that begin to fulfill the promise of coordinated digital collection building. However, at present there is no central source of information about what has been digitized, and with what care in the process, as there is for titles that have been microfilmed for preservation.

Some of the drawbacks of digital technology for access, as for preservation, stem from the technology's uncanny ability to represent the original in a seemingly authentic way. Working with digital surrogates can distort the research experience somewhat by taking research materials out of the context of the reading room. The nature of computer display makes only serial viewing possible, very different indeed, for example, from spreading photographs in their original sizes around a flat surface and looking at them simultaneously and in different groupings. Every object, every page, is mediated by the screen, which automatically flattens and decontextualizes the images. And a digital image, no matter how high the resolution and sensitive the display monitor, is always presented through the relatively low density of information of the computer screen, compromising the high-density nature of analog materials, which can be critical for assessing some visual evidence.

Digital "raw materials" on the Web are not as raw as they might appear to be. Many of the items that may be viewed now on the Web sites of such institutions as the National Archives, the Library of Congress, and the New York Public Library, come from special collections that are large, often cataloged only at the collection level, and often unedited, with few descriptions that aid a scholar. In order to digitize them, curators familiar with the materials sift through collections and make selections from them. The amount of physical preparation and intellectual control work that is needed for every digital project is very large

indeed. Scanning is a very expensive process, and most of the cost occurs before the item is laid on the scanner. Part of that cost is the physical preparation of, research into, and description of an item. A collection of daguerreotypes that may have been in reasonably good physical condition but not very well cataloged may undergo extensive conservation review and treatment before it is scanned, and labor-intensive searches into the identities of faces that have been anonymous for decades may precede the cataloging and description of the digitized images. While these searches may be viewed as extraneous, or at least discretionary, editorial expenses, in fact they are more commonly incurred than not. The collections that are on the Web are, in a real sense, publications, accompanied as they are by a great deal of descriptive information created in order to make the items understandable in the context of the Internet.

The users of library Web sites need this information. Because they are used to having a reference librarian available to help them in their searches when they are at a library, they often want a library site to provide comparable reference and searching functions. They expect higher levels of functionality of digital objects than they do of library materials, in part because there is no online equivalent to a reference specialist available.

Despite the high cost of digital conversion, many institutions are taking on ambitious projects in order to find out for themselves what the technology can do for them. They are investing large amounts of money in projects to make their collections more accessible and, too often, believing that they are also accomplishing preservation goals at the same time. The impact of digitizing projects on an institution, its way of operating, its traditional audience, and its core functions, is often hard to anticipate. The challenge of selecting the parts of a large collection that will be scanned is, for some, a novel task that calls into question basic principles of collection development and access policies. Many libraries and archives have collections that are intrinsically valuable by virtue of being comprehensive and containing much information that is essentially unpublished. But they also may contain sensitive materials, those that deal with historical events or previously popular attitudes that may be offensive to us now and that must be understood in the larger context, and this is precisely what a comprehensive collection provides—context.

How does one deal with sensitive materials in a networked environment? Making information available on the Internet removes the very barriers from use that we take for granted in physical collections. No one has to travel to a library, nor do they have to present proof of their serious research interest in order to gain access to complex, disturbing, and uninterpreted material. On the other hand, if one makes the difficult decision to edit out materials that are readily served in a reading room, but are too powerful to broadcast on the Internet, what does that do to the integrity of a research collection? There are ways to build in electronic barriers to access for all or portions of a site, using much the same technology that commercial entities use in granting fee-based access. However, constructing these barriers adds a layer of administrative complexity to managing the site that libraries and archives may not be prepared to take on, even if the technology does exist. Only when digitization is viewed specifically as a form of publishing, and not simply as another way to make resources available to researchers, are the thornier issues of selection for conversion put into an editorial context that provides a strong intellectual and ethical basis for imaginative selection of complex materials.

Many of the collections that may be of the highest research and teaching value will not be digitized for Web access because of the strictures of copyright that might apply. For this reason, library Web sites these days contain a disproportionate amount of public domain material, which distorts the nature of the source base for research restricted to the Web. The notion on the part of many young students that, if it is not on the Web or in an online catalog, then it must not exist, has the effect of orphaning the vast majority of information resources, especially those that are not in the public domain. This is not what the Framers had in mind when they wrote the copyright code into the Constitution, "to promote the Progress of Science and useful Arts." This skewed representation of created works on the Web will continue for quite some time into the future, and the complications that surround moving image and recorded sound rights means, ironically, that these will be the least accessible resources on the most dynamic information source around. And until Optical Character Recognition (OCR), the post-processing technology that makes scanned text searchable, works as well for scripts using non-Latin characters as for as for those using Latin ones, resources from around the world in vernacular languages will not take their proper place in the scanning queue.

What Is Gained and What Is Lost

In contemplating a digital conversion project, an institution must ask itself what can be gained from digitization, and whether the value added is worth the price. Many libraries have begun the difficult task of developing criteria for selecting for digitization and have published their criteria on the Internet. Columbia University, for example, was among the first to post guidelines for selection of materials for digital conversion, which include the criterion of added value (available from http://www.columbia.edu/cu/libraries/digital/criteria.htm). They define the added value of digital capture as

- enhanced intellectual control through creation of new finding aids, links to bibliographic records, and development of indices and other tools;
- increased and enriched use through the ability to search widely, manipulating images and text, and to study disparate images in new contexts;
- encouragement of new scholarly use through the provision of enhanced resources in the form of widespread dissemination of local or unique collections;
- enhanced use through improved quality of image, for example, improved legibility of faded or stained documents; and
- creation of a "virtual collection" through the flexible integration and synthesis of a variety of formats, or of related materials scattered among many locations.

At present, however, the cost of digitization and of creating and maintaining a migration path for preserving the files is very expensive. The benefits of making an underused collection more accessible should be viewed in conjunction with other factors such as compatibility with other digital resources and the collection's intrinsic intellectual value. As the Society of American Archivists has said, "The mere potential for increased access to a digitized collection does not add value to an underutilized collection. It is a rare collection of digital files indeed that can justify the cost of a comprehensive migration strategy without factoring in the larger intellectual context of related digital files stored everywhere and their combined uses for research and scholarship." (Available from http://www.archivists.org/governance/resolutions/digitize.html.)

As Donald Waters of the Digital Library Federation has expressed it, the *promise of digital technology is for libraries to extend the reach of research and education, improve the quality of learning, and reshape scholarly communication.* This is not an extravagant claim for the technology, but rather a declaration of an ambition shared by many who are developing and managing the technology. And the key to fulfilling that promise lies within the communities of higher education, science, and public policy responsible for applying digital technology to those ends. Digital conversion of library holdings has its stake in this ambition, particularly to the extent that it can broaden access to valuable but scarce resources. But the cost of conversion and the institutional commitment to keeping

those converted materials refreshed and accessible for the long-term is high—precisely how high, we do not know—and libraries must also ensure the longevity of information that is created in digital form and exists in no other form. We need more information about what imaging projects cost, and about who uses those converted materials and how they use them, in order to judge whether the investment is worth it. In the meantime, libraries must continue to be responsible custodians of their analog holdings, the print, image and sound recording collections that are their core assets and the legacy of many generations. This task requires continuing use of tried-and-true preservation techniques such as microfilming to ensure the longevity of imperiled information.

Analog is a different way of knowing than digital, and each has its intrinsic virtues and limitations. Digital will not and cannot replace analog. To convert everything to digital form would be wrong-headed, even if we could do it. The real challenge is how to make those analog materials more accessible using the powerful tool of digital technology, not only through conversion, but also through digital finding aids and linked databases of search tools. Digital technology can, indeed, prove to be a valuable instrument to enhance learning and extend the reach of information resources to those who seek them, wherever they are, but only if we develop it as an addition to an already well-stocked tool kit, rather than a replacement for all of those tools which generations before us have ingeniously crafted and passed on to us in trust.

BLUE RIBBON TASK FORCE ON SUSTAINABLE DIGITAL PRESERVATION AND ACCESS

Excerpts from *Sustainable Economics for a Digital Planet: Ensuring Long-Term Access to Digital Information. Final Report.*

La Jolla, CA: Blue Ribbon Task Force, February 2010.

Pages 1–5. Executive Summary

Digital information is a vital resource in our knowledge economy, valuable for research and education, science and the humanities, creative and cultural activities, and public policy. But digital information is inherently fragile and often at risk of loss. Access to valuable digital materials tomorrow depends upon preservation actions taken today; and, over time, access depends on ongoing and efficient allocation of resources to preservation.

Ensuring that valuable digital assets will be available for future use is not simply a matter of finding sufficient funds. It is about mobilizing resources—human, technical, and financial—across a spectrum of stakeholders diffuse over both space and time. But questions remain about what digital information we should preserve, who is responsible for preserving, and who will pay.

The Blue Ribbon Task Force on Sustainable Digital Preservation and Access investigated these questions from an economic perspective. In this report, we identify problems intrinsic to all preserved digital materials, and propose actions that stakeholders can take to meet these challenges to sustainability. We developed action agendas that are targeted to major stakeholder groups and to domain-specific preservation strategies.

The Task Force focused its inquiry on materials that are of long-term public interest, looking at four content domains with diverse preservation profiles:

Scholarly discourse: the published output of scholarly inquiry

Research data: the primary inputs into research, as well as the first-order results of that research

Commercially owned cultural content: culturally significant digital content that is owned by a private entity and is under copyright protection; and

Collectively produced Web content: Web content that is created interactively, the result of collaboration and contributions by consumers.

Economic analysis of digital preservation of these materials reveals structural challenges that affect all digital preservation strategies: (1) long time horizons, (2) diffused stakeholders, (3) misaligned or weak incentives, and (4) lack of clarity about roles and responsibilities among stakeholders. These risks, once identified, can be anticipated and provided for throughout the digital lifecycle. Major findings can be summarized as three imperatives for sustainable digital preservation.

Articulate a compelling value proposition.

When making the case for preservation, make the case for use. Without well-articulated demand for preserved information, there will be no future supply.

Stakeholders for digital materials are often diffuse across different communities. The interests of future users are poorly represented in selecting materials to preserve. Trusted public institutions—libraries, archives, museums, professional organizations and others—can play important roles as proxy organizations to represent the demand of their stakeholders over generations.

A decision to preserve now need not be thought of as a permanent or open-ended commitment of resources over time. In cases where future value is uncertain, choosing to preserve assets at low levels of curation can postpone ultimate decisions about long-term retention and quality of curation until such time as value and use become apparent.

Provide clear incentives to preserve in the public interest.

The lack of clear incentives to act will stymie timely preservation actions. Policy mechanisms can play an important role in strengthening weak motivations. Lowering barriers to efficient decentralized stewardship can be spurred by individual creators' use of nonexclusive licenses granting preservation rights to third parties.

Misalignment of incentives among stakeholders may occur between communities that benefit from preservation (and therefore have an incentive to preserve), and those that are in a position to preserve (because they own or control the resource) but lack incentives to do so. Policy mechanisms that can mitigate these problems include: financial incentives and other benefits to private owners who preserve digital materials for the benefit of the public; mandates to preserve when appropriate; and revision of copyright to enable preservation of privately owned materials by stewardship organizations acting in the long-term interest of the public.

Define roles and responsibilities among stakeholders to ensure an ongoing and efficient flow of resources to preservation throughout the digital lifecycle.

The strongest incentives to preserve will be ineffective without explicit agreement on the roles and responsibilities of all the actors—those who create the information, those who own it, those who preserve it, and those who make it available for use. Every organization that creates and uses data should implement policies and procedures for preservation, including: selection of materials with long-term value; preparation of data for archiving; and protocols to ensure a smooth and secure transfer of digital assets across organizational boundaries and between institutions.

There is a particular risk of "free riding" with digital materials because the cost of preservation may be borne by one organization but the benefits accrue too many. Effective governance mechanisms are needed to aggregate the collective interest into an effective preservation strategy that ensures that the effort and cost of preservation are appropriately apportioned.

Funding models should be tailored to the norms and expectations of anticipated users. They should leverage economies of scale and scope whenever possible. Digital assets do not need to be treated as a public good in all cases. Market channels are often the most efficient means of allocating resources for preserving many types of digital content.

Digital assets provided as market goods or otherwise privately held must have some provision for handoff to a trustworthy steward when the owner decides to stop preserving them, if those materials are of value to society. For materials that are not amenable to market provision and are at risk of loss—such as certain types of research data, Web-based materials, and digital orphans—public provision is necessary.

Finally, as the rate of digital information production continues to escalate, it is vitally important to reduce the cost of preservation for all types of digital assets. Reducing the cost of storing materials, developing sustainable sources of energy to power preservation systems, and engineering ways to lower the cost of preserving, curating, and providing access are all important.

There is a great diversity of preservation strategies among the content types that have long-term societal value. In the four domains evaluated, we were able to identify significant risks to sustainability and the near-term actions that stakeholders can take to remedy them.

Scholarly discourse: This is a fairly mature field, with well-developed preservation and funding strategies as a legacy of the print world. Disruptions are occurring to longstanding sustainability strategies as a result of digital preservation and distribution. There are particular needs to align preservation incentives among commercial and nonprofit providers; ensure handoffs between commercial publishers and stewardship organizations in the interest of long-term preservation of the scholarly record; and address the free-rider problem. Clarification of the long-term value of emerging genres of digital scholarship, such as academic blogs and grey literature, is a high priority. Research and education institutions, professional societies, publishers, libraries, and scholars all have leading roles to play in creating sustainable preservation strategies for the materials that are valuable to them.

Research data: There is a remarkable growth of data-intensive research in all knowledge domains. In most fields, there is high recognition of the benefits of preserving research data for various purposes and lengths of time. But there are few robust systems for making decisions about what to preserve; and there is often a lack of coordination of roles, responsibilities, and funding sources among those best positioned to preserve data (researchers) and the preservation infrastructure (curation and archiving services) that should support them. Research and education institutions, professional societies, archives, researchers, and the funding agencies that support data creation all have leading roles to play in creating sustainable preservation strategies.

Commercially owned cultural content: There are well-established preservation and access strategies undergoing fundamental changes as a result of new information technologies. This includes the creation, distribution, and consumption of cultural content, most evident in the emergence of interactive genres such as games and the creation of a long tail of use and reuse. As a result, there may be two forms of benefits—commercial and cultural, or private and public—that compete with one another. When that occurs, proxy organizations must step in to represent the public interest. Leading players in preserving this content include private creators, owners, and trade associations, stewardship organizations, regulatory authorities, and leading national and international institutions that can sponsor public-private partnerships to ensure the long-term access to our digital cultural heritage.

Collectively created Web content: The Web environment is marked by great dynamism, uncertainty about long-term value of digital content, and obscure ownership and rights issues for many collectively produced Web assets. The priority here is for stewardship organizations, content creators, hosting sites, platform providers, and users to model and test preservation strategies, and to provide clarification about long-term value and selection criteria. The Task Force identified important next steps for each of these content areas; they are summarized in Tables 1 and 2.

Sustainable preservation is a societal concern, however, and transcends the boundaries of any particular content domain. All parts of society—national and international agencies, funders and sponsors of data creation, stakeholder organizations, and individuals—have roles in achieving sustainability. Leadership is needed at all levels of society. Table 1 presents a summary of the action agendas for these major stakeholders.

Areas of priority for near-term action include the following:

Organizational Action

- developing public-private partnerships
- ensuring that organizations have access to skilled personnel, from domain experts to legal and business specialists
- creating and sustaining secure chains of stewardship between organizations over time
- achieving economies of scale and scope
- addressing the free-rider problem

Technical Action

- building capacity to support stewardship in all areas
- lowering the cost of preservation overall
- determining the optimal level of technical curation needed to operationalize an option strategy for all types of digital material

Public Policy Action

- modifying copyright laws to enable digital preservation
- creating incentives and requirements for private entities to preserve on behalf of the public (financial incentives, handoff requirements)
- sponsoring public-private partnerships
- clarifying rights issues associated with Web-based materials

- empowering stewardship organizations to protect digital orphans from unacceptable loss

Education and Public Outreach Action

- promoting education and training for 21st century digital preservation (domain-specific skills, curatorial best practices, core competencies in relevant science, technology, engineering, and mathematics knowledge)
- raising awareness of the urgency to take timely preservation actions

Sustainable preservation strategies are not built all at once, nor are they static. Sustainable preservation is a series of timely actions taken to anticipate the dynamic nature of digital information. Decision makers will always face uncertainties. Changes in technologies, policy environments, investment priorities, and societal concerns will unfold over the course of the digital lifecycle. But we can develop practices that resolve or anticipate uncertainties, that leverage resources among stakeholders, and above all, that leave options open for decision makers in the future. Sustainable preservation strategies will find ways to turn the uncertainties of time and resources into opportunities for flexibility, adjustments in response to changing priorities, and redirection of resources where they are most needed.

Above all, sustainable digital preservation requires a compelling value proposition, incentives to act, and well-defined roles and responsibilities. Digital preservation is a challenge for all of society because we all benefit from reliable, authentic information now and into the future. Done well, all of society will reap the benefits of digital stewardship.

Pages 80–85. Conclusions

Preservation decisions are always made under conditions of uncertainty: technologies, policy environments, investment priorities, and societal concerns will change over the course of the digital lifecycle. But we can develop practices that anticipate or resolve uncertainties, that leverage resources among stakeholders, and above all, that leave options open for decision makers in the future. Sustainable preservation strategies will find ways to turn the uncertainties of time and resources into opportunities for flexibility, adjustments in response to changing priorities, and redirection of resources where they are most needed.

Commitments made today are not commitments for all time. But actions must be taken today to ensure flexibility in the future. There is an urgent need in all sectors of digital creation—public and private, cultural and scientific—for support in the near-term to model and test robust preservation strategies. All stakeholder communities must provide leadership and accept responsibility for the development of a common digital preservation infrastructure that is sustainable for generations to come.

Like other societal challenges, such as climate change and sustainable energy, preservation is a balancing act, weighing the needs and desires of the present day with those of the future. Preservation depends on the cooperation of generations to steward our most precious asset over time—knowledge. Society has long valued, supported, and protected the cultural heritage deeded to us by previous generations. Isaac Newton acknowledged that "If I have seen further it is by standing on the shoulders of giants." By attending to the value of digital information, providing incentives to preserve these digital assets, and ensuring allocation of roles and responsibilities among stakeholders that share a common interest in valuable digital assets, we can continue to build high the shared body of knowledge that will enable all of us to see farther.

Tables 1 and 2 summarize the recommendations proposed by the Task Force for economic sustainability. Table 1 lists actions to be taken by leading actors and organizations; and Table 2 list actions by content domain.

TABLE 1

Action Agenda for Leading Actors and Organizations

National and International Agencies

Trusted international, national, and public institutions—libraries, archives, museums, research institutes, consortia, regulatory agencies

1. Create mechanisms for public-private partnerships to align or reconcile benefits that accrue to commercial and cultural entities. These agencies can play a critical role in convening stakeholders, sponsoring cooperation and collaboration, and ensuring representation of all stakeholders.

2. Convene expert communities to address the selection and preservation needs of materials of particular interest to the public for which there is no stewardship (Web materials, digital orphans).

3. Act expeditiously to reform national and international copyright legislation to address digital preservation needs.

4. Create financial incentives to encourage private entities to preserve digital materials on the public behalf.

Funders and Sponsors of Data Creation

Private and public agencies and foundations

1. Create preservation mandates when possible, ensuring that they adhere to community selection criteria, and specifying roles and responsibilities of individuals and organizations.

2. Invest in building capacity throughout the system. The Library of Congress, the National Archives and Records Administration, the National Science Foundation, and JISC have set important precedents for supporting capacity building within specific communities of practice. Seeding stewardship capacity and developing sustainable funding models should, however, be a high priority for all funders.

3. Provide leadership in training and education for 21st century preservation, including domain expertise and core competencies in STEM. Such organizations as the National\ Archives, Library of Congress, National Library of Medicine, National Agricultural Library, National Science Foundation, Smithsonian Institution, Institute of Museum and Library Services, National Endowment for the Arts, and National Endowment for the Humanities in the United States; and the British Library, National Archives, JISC, Digital Curation Centre, and Digital Preservation Coalition in the United Kingdom each have a remit for promoting digital preservation skills.

4. Fund the modeling and testing of domain-specific preservation strategies. This would entail developing domain-specific requirements for lifecycle management to create a timeline of predictable risks, strategies to meet them, and triggering mechanisms to address them.

Stakeholder Organizations

Universities, research institutions, private companies, third-party archives, professional societies, trade organizations

1. Secure preservation of high-value institutional materials by making explicit roles and responsibilities across organizational boundaries.

2. Develop preservation strategies that assign responsibilities for achieving outcomes. Service-level agreements and MOUs with third-party archives should include contingency plans for handoffs and clauses for putting internal monitoring systems in place.

3. Leverage resources; create economies of scope and economies of scale by partnering with related organizations and industry professional associations.

4. Work with domain and preservation experts to ensure that personnel are fully equipped with the technical skills needed for selecting, curating, and preserving materials.

5. Fund internal preservation and access activities as core infrastructure.

Individuals

Principal investigators, data creators, individual authors, creators, and scholars

1. Provide nonexclusive rights to preserve content they create and to distribute this content through publicly accessible venues.

2. Partner with preservation experts early in the lifecycle of one's own digital data, to ensure that data are ready to hand off to an archive in forms that will be useful over the long term.

3. Actively participate in professional societies and relevant organizations in developing stewardship best practices and selection priorities.

TABLE 2

Action taken by Content Domain

Action Agenda for Scholarly Discourse

1. Libraries, scholars, and professional societies should develop selection criteria for emerging genres in scholarly discourse, and prototype preservation and access strategies to support them.

2. Publishers reserving the right to preserve should partner with third-party archives or libraries to ensure long-term preservation.

3. Scholars should consider granting nonexclusive rights to publish and preserve, to enable decentralized and distributed preservation of emerging scholarly discourse.

4. Libraries should create a mechanism to organize and clarify their governance issues and responsibilities to preserve monographs and emerging scholarly discourse along lines similar to those for e-journals.

5. All open-access strategies that assume the persistence of information over time must consider provisions for the funding of preservation.

Action Agenda for Research Data

1. Each domain, through professional societies or other consensus-making bodies, should set priorities for data selection, level of curation, and length of retention.

2. Funders should impose preservation mandates, when appropriate. When mandates are imposed, funders should also specify selection criteria, funds to be used, and responsible organizations to provide archiving.

3. Funding agencies should explicitly recognize "data under stewardship" as a core indicator of scientific effort and include this information in standard reporting mechanisms.

4. Preservation services should reduce curation and archiving costs by leveraging economies of scale when possible.

5. Agreements with third-party archives should stipulate processes, outcomes, retention periods, and handoff triggers.

Action Agenda for Commercially Owned Cultural Content

1. Leading cultural organizations should convene expert communities to address the selection and preservation needs of commercially owned cultural content and digital orphans.

2. Regulatory authorities should bring current requirements for mandatory copyright deposit into harmony with the demands of digital preservation and access.

3. Regulatory authorities should provide financial and other incentives to preserve privately held cultural content in the public interest.

4. Leading stewardship organizations should model and test mechanisms to ensure flexible long-term public-private partnerships that foster cooperative preservation of privately held materials in the public interest.

Action Agenda for Collectively Produced Web Content

1. Leading stewardship organizations should convene stakeholders and experts to address the selection and preservation needs of collectively produced Web content.

2. Creators, contributors, and host sites could lower barriers to third-party archiving by using a default license to grant nonexclusive rights for archiving.

3. Regulatory authorities should create incentives, such as preservation subsidies, for host sites to preserve their own content or seek third-party archives as preservation partners.

4. Regulatory authorities should take expeditious action to reform legislation to grant authority to stewardship institutions to preserve at-risk Web content.

5. Leading stewardship organizations should develop partnerships with one or more major content providers to explore the technical, legal, and financial dimensions of long-term preservation.

chapter 8

PRESERVATION POLICY

P RESERVATION POLICY: TWO WORDS OFTEN USED together, each containing various meanings. The history and theory of preservation have been discussed in earlier chapters. Policy is worthy of its own consideration. Preservation intersects with policy in a variety of ways, yet *preservation policy* has a variety of implications—as illustrated in this chapter's readings.

First, we should consider the differences between policies and policy. Policies are procedures and actions that influence decision-making. In preservation, administration actions such as environmental monitoring, reformatting, conservation treatment, and disaster preparedness and recovery may be influenced or determined by institutional or professional policies. Institutional policies may govern an entire organization. For example, a library or museum in a university setting may have to adhere to university policies and procedures. One example of how institutional policies may impact preservation practices is in disaster-recovery planning. Most likely, the university has policies about procuring supplies, gaining access to petty cash, the hiring of extra staff, using volunteers, the chain of command for decision-making, the distribution of responsibilities across units, and so on. Those who draft disaster-preparedness and recovery procedures will need to account for institutional policies in their planning. The role of policies in preservation administration is frequently addressed in the professional literature.

Policies developed by professional organizations generally relate to standards and best practices; once determined, they are usually re-visited regularly. Organizations tend to post their policies and practices prominently, such as the home page of their websites. In some professional organizations there is a governing body, for example a board of directors, that approves of all policies. Readers of this book should refer to such websites as those of the American Library Association, the Society of American Archivists, and the American Association of Museums for their preservation policy statements.

National libraries, archives, and museums may also post their preservation policies. For example, the National Library of Australia (NLA) describes its preservation policy as follows:

> The purpose ... is to present high level policy statements for the National Library of Australia regarding the preservation of its collections, and regarding the Library's role in fostering preservation of documentary heritage. The policy is intended to define the Library's preservation responsibilities, and to provide guidance to Library staff engaged in making decisions and undertaking other activities that may have impact on collections. It is also a fundamental accountability document concerning one of the Library's core business functions, and is intended to serve as the basis for communication with a range of external stakeholders. This policy has been endorsed by the Library's Corporate Management Group for implementation throughout the Library.[1]

The NLA policy further states that the Library's preservation role is mandated by the National Library Act 1960. The Act requires the NLA to maintain and develop a national collection of materials, including a comprehensive collection of items relating to Australia and the Australian people. This statement links the Library's policy to national public policy.

The word *policy* is used to refer to intentional goals or actions. Policy can be a guide, an action, a norm of professional practice, and so on. *Public policy* has a more specific meaning: the procedures and actions that lead to laws, regulatory measures, courses of action, and funding priorities.

Individuals and groups often attempt to shape public policy through education, advocacy, or mobilization of interest groups. Shaping public policy is obviously different in Western-style democracies from what it is in other forms of government. But it is reasonable to assume that the process always involves efforts by competing interest groups to influence policy makers.

A major aspect of public policy is law. In a general sense, the law includes specific legislation and more broadly defined provisions of constitutional or international law.[2]

Cultural policy is a separate field of public policy which is an outgrowth of arts policy, according to J. Mark Schuster. Cultural policy may include arts policy, heritage policy (the historical physical environment), and humanities policy.[3]

Most articles about library, museum, and archival preservation include consideration of institutional policies and/or professional practices, *not* of public or cultural policy. However, there is a paucity of scholarly writing focused on policy issues, though this topic is regularly explored as part of larger studies. In contrast, the historic preservation literature regularly addresses policy issues. This is probably because public sector historic preservation activities are often undertaken in accordance with local, tribal, state, or federal laws, regulations, and standards. Thus, the practice of historic preservation relates to community economic development, adaptive reuse, tax-credit programs, and land use as well as to general cultural heritage concerns.

The National Trust for Historic Preservation advises that,

> As an advocate for historic preservation, you can take part in lobbying your public officials across a broad range of issues that will affect the quality of life in diverse neighborhoods and communities across the country. The National Trust for Historic Preservation wants preservation advocates to engage in those issues that directly impact their communities, as well as to build a social network

that reaches other preservationists experiencing similar problems and/or successes in their neighborhoods. Sharing of anecdotal information, best practices, current public policies or regulations, and success stories will help build the historic preservation movement while simultaneously shaping public policy to utilize all the benefits that historic preservation can provide to our urban and rural environments.[4]

The site suggests how to do this: offer testimony to legislative bodies with jurisdiction over preservation matters; take civil action such as writing to elected officials, signing a petition, attending a rally; networking with peers and preservation professionals; and initiating legal actions or the enforcement of legal protections.

The National Trust's Public Policy Department and Center for State and Local Policy offers numerous resources to help people make the case for historic preservation to policy makers. One resource is their *Blueprint for Lobbying*, which is summarized on their website.[5]

This chapter includes three articles that specifically address broad policy issues: **Ellen Cunningham-Kruppa**, on Humanities Texas; **John H. Hammer**, on the political aspects of book preservation in the United States; and **John Henry Merryman** on art and cultural-property law.

Cunningham-Kruppa studies funding for libraries and archives in "Exploring Cultural Policy at Humanities Texas." First she considers humanities agencies as loci for library and archives policies. Then she looks at the creation of Humanities Texas as a public policy act. When the National Endowment for the Humanities (NEH) was created in the 1960s, by Public Law 209, Congress encouraged the new agency to decentralize some of its funding. Thus each state (and several territories) created their own humanities councils which have subsequently received funding from NEH as well as from state and private sources. Using J. Mark Schuster's "state level cultural policy model as a framework for studying the role of Humanities Texas in the state's cultural environment," she examines its grant funding and programs for libraries and archives.

In the United States, cultural preservation issues are played out in the public policy arena in a variety of ways. One example was the push in the 1980s for federal dollars to be spent on addressing the "brittle books" problem of deteriorating paper. John H. Hammer's "On the Political Aspects of Book Preservation in the U.S." considers the "highly complex process by which Americans determine which problems are of national significance and how the nation will address them, [which] has evolved into a unique pattern that reflects our social, economic, and political organization."[6] His paper discusses actions which led to the dramatic increase in funding for the Office of Preservation in the National Endowment for the Humanities from $4.5 million to $12.33 million in the late 1980s, as well as other related preservation activities. The increased funding enabled libraries and archives to undertake large-scale preservation microfilming, and, later, digitization projects.

Legal scholar John Henry Merryman, in "Art Systems and Cultural Policy," gives an overview of the "social construct that includes art players, art supporters and a paradigm." The paradigm is "the underlying set of assumptions and attitudes that direct the ways players and supporters think and act" in the area of cultural property. In other words, Merryman demonstrates that the development of museums in the United States as private *and* public institutions influences donations, deaccessioning, preservation and access, and so on. Today, American institutions are also influenced by international conventions promulgated by UNESCO and other organizations relating to protected cultural property, and the import, export, and transfer of ownership. Merryman speculates that aspects of the international world art system may negatively impact American art policies in the arena of cultural property.

Another important area of public policy relates to intellectual property. Copyright laws dictate preservation and access practices in most cultural heritage institutions. Here the literature is voluminous, and fair use is a topic touched on throughout chapter 7, "Frameworks for Digital Preservation." Merryman explains that society has an interest in preserving works of art and making them accessible to the public. Preservation activities take place within broad national and international cultural policy frameworks. Some of these frameworks are not compatible with one another, and Merryman suggests that additional international dialogues are need.

Hammer's observation that cultural policy is a "highly complex process" is echoed by Bill Ivey, in his *Arts, Inc.*[7] Ivey, who was Chairman of the National Endowment for the Arts from 1998–2001, believes that the arts in the United States suffer from increasingly restrictive copyright laws and a strong for-profit arts industry marketplace. He places blame on the government, which he thinks does not consider culture as deserving of adequate public policy. Until the arts are viewed as worthy of serious cultural discourse, they will suffer. For proof, he considers the continuing vulnerability of the National Endowment for the Arts and the National Endowment for the Humanities in the face of conservative congressional agendas. He proposes a Cultural Bill of Rights as a means of creating conversations about culture and the public interest. The contents of Ivey's Bill of Rights appear at the head of this chapter. There may not be a more apt representation of cultural policy, and, by extension, preservation policy.

NOTES

1. National Library of Australia, *Preservation Policy*, accessed November 30, 2012, www.nla.gov.au/policy-and-planning/preservation-policy.

2. Dean G. Kilpatrick, "Definitions of Public Policy and the Law," accessed June 10, 2012, www.musc.edu/vawprevention/policy/definition.shtml.

3. J. Mark Schuster, *Informing Cultural Policy: The Research and Information Infrastructure* (New Brunswick, NJ: Rutgers, Center for Urban Policy Research, 2002): 4, 15. Ellen Cunningham-Kruppa discusses Schuster's work in detail in her article.

4. National Trust for Historic Preservation, *Lobbying 101,* accessed December 4, 2012, www.preservationnation.org/take-action/advocacy-center/lobbying-101/#.UL1mumd5GSp.

5. National Trust for Historic Preservation, *Lobbying Rules for Non-profits*, accessed December 4, 2012, www.preservationnation.org/take-action/advocacy-center/lobbying-101/lobbying-rules-for-non.html#.UL1nQGd5GSo.

6. John H. Hammer, "On the Political Aspects of Book Preservation in the U.S.," in *Advances in Preservation and Access* 1 (1992): 22–40; this passage is on p. 22.

7. Bill Ivey, *Arts, Inc.: How Greed and Neglect Have Destroyed Our Cultural Rights* (Berkeley: University of California Press, 2008).

ELLEN CUNNINGHAM-KRUPPA

"Exploring Cultural Policy at Humanities Texas"

Written for this volume.

AS KEEPERS OF the documentary records of human experience, creativity, and discovery, libraries and archives are central to the development of society. Research libraries and archives charge themselves with identifying, collecting, describing, preserving, disseminating, and mediating the cultural record. While they exist in a larger context of memory institutions, including museums, cultural heritage institutions, monuments and places, botanical gardens, zoological gardens, and all kinds of "collecting institutions,"[1] for the purposes of this paper I will focus on libraries and archives as primary holders of the documentary record.[2]

Libraries and archives have long understood their role as cultural institutions acting for the public good; for centuries they have committed themselves to evaluating and responding to issues of how to understand and protect the inherent value in research collections, grappling with the preservation and access issues associated with the sheer number of items and increasingly wide-ranging material formats comprising the human record. However, as clearly as libraries and archives articulate and advocate for their role in society as social–cultural–knowledge institutions, curiously they are frequently absent in academic and political discourse on topics of cultural policy.[3] Why is this, and what are the implications for the human record and for society?

The Lone Star State, with 144 academic and just under 600 public libraries, as well as more than 120 archival repositories, boasts library and archival riches that document an extensive range of subjects. From The University of Texas at Austin's Nettie Lee Benson Collection and Harry Ransom Humanities Research Center, to the Texas State Archives, whose holdings document the history of the state, Texas repositories large and small, serve a range of user needs and interests with world-renowned collections.

Acclaimed internationally for its research riches, Texas provides a locus for examining cultural policy vis-à-vis its libraries and archives. State cultural policies are complex and extend well beyond the boundaries of state art agencies, community development initiatives, parks and recreation commissions, and any number of other agencies and programs. The policy ecology at a state level comprises a mix of state agencies, offices, programs, private nonprofit organizations, and individuals, which, in aggregate, define the state's cultural policy.[4] As one of a number of possible loci for state-level policy connected to libraries and archives—the most obvious of which is the Texas State Library and Archives—Humanities Texas is Texas's affiliate of the National Endowment for the Humanities. My goal has been to apply a cultural policy framework to reveal Humanities Texas's explicit cultural policy, as expressed, for example, in a mission statement, and its implicit policy, which can be defined as inferred intentionality from actual programs, initiatives, audiences, and alliances. Research methodologies applied in this study include examination of Humanities Texas publications, including its website, and a face-to-face interview and e-mail follow-up with the Executive Director of Humanities Texas, Michael Gillette.[5]

But why choose a humanities body as a locus for library and archives policy rather than, for example, one delineated for education or the arts? In "Sub-National Cultural Policy—Where the Action Is? Mapping State Cultural Policy in the United States," Mark Schuster, former MIT professor of urban studies and planning, suggests a classification scheme for cultural policy which places state libraries, archives, and historical societies—as they are funded and practiced in public by and for the public—under the rubric of humanities policy. Explicit in Schuster's definition of cultural policy is the assertion that "a state's cultural policy can be usefully thought of as the sum of its activities with respect to the arts (including the for-profit cultural industries), the humanities, and the heritage."[6] Schuster positions libraries—and I will infer archives—as "the humanities equivalent of the museums, local historical societies, and historic sites" administered and advised under state cultural policy.[7] He further notes that humanities policy has been an area often neglected by researchers and practitioners, who have increasingly replaced the phrase "arts policy" with "cultural policy," but with no accompanying change in the boundary of attention.[8]

Given that they collect in wide-ranging subject areas and often serve multiple audiences, libraries and archives cannot be conveniently classified purely in humanistic, artistic, or scientific terms. Libraries tend to traverse any number of disciplinary and audience-based categorizations. As defined by the Society of American Archivists, archives are "the non-current records of individuals, groups, institutions, and governments that contain information of enduring value."[9] Located in federal, state, and local governments, schools, colleges and universities, religious institutions, businesses, hospitals, museums, labor unions, and historical societies, archival repositories are as diverse as the institutions and people they serve.

At the federal level, the United States Department of Labor Standard Industrial Classification (SIC) codes categorize libraries, Industry Group 823, as a sub-group of Major Group 82: Educational Services.[10] Perhaps, not surprisingly, given their generally misunderstood mission and work, archives are unaccounted for in SIC codes. Though libraries, in particular, received significant funding for collection building in the 1960s and 1970s from federal grants awarded by the Department of Education, recent federal support for libraries and archives has most prominently emanated from humanities bodies, such as the National Endowment for the Humanities, the Institute of Museum and Library Services, and the National Historical Publications and Records Commission. In the past three decades, significant support has been directed to projects and programs for archiving and preserving cultural records.

The groundbreaking 1964 *Report of the Commission on the Humanities* provides a clear conceptualization of libraries as humanities bodies. In 1963, the National Commission on the Humanities, a body sponsored by the American Council of Learned Societies, the Council of Graduate Schools in the United States, and the United Chapters of Phi Beta Kappa, commenced a series of meetings resulting in a report to its sponsors stressing two fundamental points:

1. expansion and improvement of activities in the humanities are in the national interest and consequently deserve financial support by the federal government; and
2. federal funds for this purpose should be administered by a new independent agency to be known as the National Humanities Foundation.[11]

The sponsors distributed the report to influential congressmen, and in 1965 Congress passed Public Law 209, establishing the National Foundation on the Arts and Humanities Act that created a National Endowment for the Arts (NEA) and a National Endowment for the Humanities (NEH).

Prepared by the Commission's Committee on Library Needs, composed of high-level administrators from the nation's top private and public university libraries, the 1964 *Report* includes a substantial appendix, "Libraries for the Humanities." The appended report focuses on public, school, and academic research libraries, suggesting that though libraries cover all subjects, the humanities demands the most of them. The introduction to the report clearly states the Committee's stance on the role of libraries in the humanities:

> Libraries preserve more of the recorded memory of mankind than any other institutions, and in every field the scholar depends upon them for information on what other scholars have discovered. This may often be the library's sole function for the scientist who pursues his own investigations in a laboratory, but the humanist, in addition, usually finds in libraries the raw materials with which he works.

The library resources at his disposal affect both the direction and the quality of his research. Clearly, therefore, libraries ought to have a particularly important place in any broad program for support of the humanities.

In summarizing the report, the Committee states in the final sentence that it is the humanities that have the most to gain from strong and responsive libraries.[12]

Based on 1) historical federal funding legislation; 2) the 1964 *Report,* which provided the foundational evidence in support of establishing the NEA and the NEH; 3) Schuster's classification of libraries and archives as humanities; and 4) the applicability of Schuster's model to Texas, I chose Humanities Texas as a possible locus for state-level policy in regard to libraries and archives. Given the limited classification scheme Schuster defines for practicality and audience comprehension, his categorization of libraries and archives as humanities (versus arts or heritage) is logical.

Schuster's state-level cultural policy classification scheme is as follows:

- Cultural policy is a separate field of public policy;
- Cultural policy, an outgrowth of arts policy, is usefully subcategorized as:
  - Arts policy;
  - Heritage policy (the historic physical environment—archaeological sites, historic buildings);
  - Humanities policy.[13]

Varying Definitions

A range of variables determined the validity of Schuster's state-level cultural policy research model as a potential framework for evaluating Humanities Texas's role in the state's cultural environment. Schuster, noted for his great strength in organizing and classifying concepts and imposing order on policy chaos, purposefully adopts a solid analytical, empirical approach to cultural policy research—one that is unabashedly non-theoretical. On any number of ideological bases, cultural policy scholars either accept, reject, or synthesize "practical" methodologies like Schuster's.

An understanding of what comprises the cultural policy domain is critical to evaluating the legitimacy of Schuster's conceptual model for cultural policy analysis. What I discovered, and what Scullion and Garcia attest to, is that "[c]ultural policy research exists in many contexts, asks many different kinds of questions and adopts a wide repertoire of research methodologies from a raft of academic discourses."[14] Studying primary texts in the field reveals a play of varying and sometimes competing theories, definitions, stakeholders, and social and economic implications play in the cultural policy domain. An evaluation of these wide-ranging issues and points of view is far too complex to approach in a short paper. However, a summary of the major questions and concerns helps to describe and coalesce the issues delineated by the emerging cultural policy discipline.

To complicate matters, apprehending the varying concepts and definitions of "culture" and "policy"—not to mention "humanities"—is attendant to fully understanding the cultural policy discipline and its internal debates. The range of ideas about each of these concepts elucidates the complexities, fluidity, and unsettled nature of cultural policy as an academic discipline and practice. Though this paper cannot begin to fully characterize the historical debates, the reader must be aware that the discourse ranges widely, is highly nuanced, and reveals a spectrum of political ideologies.[15]

Cultural Policy As Academic Discipline

Cultural policy is a young, interdisciplinary field in academia. In succinct terms, the field defines itself as a "shared commitment to investigating the conditions under which culture is produced, reproduced, and experienced."[16] Recent developments have established the thematic area of cultural policy as a discipline. Significantly, it has become increasingly instantiated in academic centers[17] associated with research universities and in a growing number of "cultural observatories" and government and private research entities. The field publishes research in a handful of key journals, the most prominent of which is the *International Journal of Cultural Policy*. As the title attests, the conversation and scholarship in cultural policy is notably international. The primary research conference for the field, the International Conference on Cultural Policy Research, began in 1999, and has convened every other year to date around the world (Norway, New Zealand, Canada, Austria, and Turkey). As a sign of the field's emerging maturity, three recently published high-profile monographic anthologies embody the consonance and dissonance in the field: Justin Lewis and Toby Miller's edited volume *Critical Cultural Policy Studies: A Reader* (2003); Toby Miller and George Yudice's co-authored *Cultural Policy* (2002); and J. Mark Schuster's *Informing Cultural Policy: The Research and Information Infrastructure* (2002). These are "readers," and the titles of these works explicitly name and implicitly scope the discipline of "cultural policy."[18]

According to Oliver Bennett, who in 1999 established the Centre for Cultural Policy Studies at the University of Warwick, the collection brought together by Lewis and Miller's, and by Schuster's books are "largely oblivious to the preoccupations of [each] other." In attempting to define two seemingly different worlds, themselves represented by not-altogether similar topics, these works "have become emblematic" of a field in search of definition.[19] As Bennett and Scullion, and Garcia, suggest, we might distill the purpose and scope embodied in the two volumes (and in Miller and Yudice's *Cultural Policy*) as critical (Lewis and Miller) versus applied (Schuster) discourse. But the discontinuities present themselves in more complicated ways, most particularly in the delineation of definitional boundaries for the concept of culture.

Broadly characteristic of scholars whose disciplinary and ideological roots reside in cultural studies and who research and write in the area of cultural policy, the authors of *Cultural Policy* and of *Critical Cultural Policy Studies*—one is a co-editor of one work and a co-author of the other—define cul-

ture along two axes. One pertains to an aesthetic notion of culture that focuses on artistic output and is judged by aesthetic criteria; the second pertains to an anthropological register that describes culture as a marker of how humans live their lives—"the senses of place and person that make us human—neither individual nor entirely universal, but grounded by language, religion, custom, time and space."[20] The topical categories in the contents of these two volumes reflect these two notions of culture. Both define culture as a set of signifying practices, e.g., cultural studies, transnational cultural policy, and symbolic (artistic) goods, e.g., museums, radio, television, and film. *Critical Cultural Policy Studies*, in particular, points to the broader anthropological notion of culture (a whole way of life) by including sport and urban planning. Bennett says that what is needed is a rigorous account of how culture as a whole way of life is constituted analytically. He asks:

> How, for example, can policy for culture 'as a whole way of life' avoid being expanded to the point of meaninglessness? The symbolic…in some sense always reflects the anthropological, but to conflate the two in cultural policy leads to a great deal of analytical confusion.[21]

Schuster, too, acknowledges the full conception of culture in *Informing Cultural Policy*, but purposefully takes a middle ground, looking for policy research that goes beyond the arts and the aesthetic to other forms of cultural policy, "stopping somewhat short of the fullest, most anthropological conception of culture."[22] With regard to *cultural* policy, Schuster states that its "conceptualization…as a separate field of public policy is a relatively recent phenomenon, particularly in the United States where there has traditionally been a fear of uttering this phrase with all of its *dirigiste* implications," echoing an ideology opposing that explicitly stated in *Cultural Policy* and *Critical Cultural Policy Studies*.[23]

Whereas Schuster practically locates policy in government, private, or quasi-governmental agencies, Lewis and Miller disdain the concept and reality of state-imposed policy. They state that their book "takes its lead from cultural studies," and that it is "inclined towards a radical-democratic leftism."[24] They also tell us that cultural policies have traditionally been deployed to "instill fealty in the public" and to "produce a compliant citizen, who learns self-governance in the interests of the cultural–capitalist polity."[25] Bennett quips that this "somewhat paranoid formulation…assumes that there is some alliance of agencies…consciously directing cultural policies, and that these policies do indeed have the capacity to produce the psychological effects described." He also posits that the relation of *Critical Cultural Policy Studies* to cultural studies gives the book a political orientation and an overriding concern with issues of power, and that Lewis and Miller attach themselves uncritically to a simplistic notion of the "progressive."[26]

Likewise, Bennett criticizes Schuster's volume for lacking a clear conceptual approach to cultural policy research, noting that Schuster's work constitutes cultural policy and cultural policy research as what governments and their ministries of culture, arts councils, and similar organizations determine them to be, and that it is highly context driven and one-dimensional "as the investigation of instrumental questions through empirical social science."[27] Scullion and Garcia suggest that Schuster's book is, in effect, a guidebook to the international research infrastructure for cultural policy research and that it wants to inform cultural policy *making* (an advocacy role) more than *research*.[28] Clearly, as an exhaustive embodiment of research resources, it also informs cultural policy research. Schuster's work is often accused of lacking an ideological context. I suggest, however, that his research does in fact extend from an ideological point of view that reflects a public policy (rather than cultural studies) disciplinary discourse.

In the end, because cultural policy research is interdisciplinary, it draws on a wide range of ideologies and employs as many methodologies. Cultural policy studies are part of a new and, as Scullion and Garcia assert, "distinctive" academic discipline. It is predicated on competing and sometimes contradictory audiences, purposes, and academic traditions. Cultural policy research undertakes policy-relevant, applied research as well as critical, reflective, theoreti-

cal research.[29] I concur with the proposal put forward by Bennett and by Scullion and Garcia that applied and critical discourses—at once interdisciplinary and addressing multiple audiences—can co-exist and, in fact, enrich each other, creating a challenging, exciting, and fluid academic discipline.

Humanities Texas

In this section, I examine Humanities Texas under its current leadership for policy—explicit and implicit—that links its mission with libraries and archives. First, to understand Humanities Texas as a state-level political, public, and cultural entity, we must examine its historical formation and actions, including its federal roots, mission, and leadership. Armed with this contextual overview, we then will look specifically at Humanities Texas's chief activities—grant funding and programs—for signs of explicit and/or implicit policy.

History

In enacting Public Law 209, Congress encouraged the NEA and the NEH to decentralize at least a portion of their funding. To provide for the humanities at the state level, the NEH determined that nonprofit citizen committees afforded the best opportunity for promoting the humanities in the individual states.[30] NEH affiliates exist in all fifty states and in the five US territories. Humanities Texas, founded in 1972, is a nonprofit, tax-exempt educational organization.[31]

Following the receipt of a $20,000 planning grant award from NEH in early 1973, in summer 1973, Humanities Texas requested funds from NEH to support administration, programs, board meetings, development, and grants to local projects. A $170,000, eighteen-month implementation grant was approved, effective October 1973. Humanities Texas's board hired an executive director, Sandra L. Myres, a member of the history faculty at The University of Texas at Arlington. The Committee awarded its first grant in January 1974 to KUT 90.5 FM, Austin, for a series of weekly two-hour radio programs focusing on the Texas Constitutional Revision Convention. The original home for Humanities Texas was The University of Texas at Arlington, which provided office space on its campus and some support services. Humanities Texas moved to Austin in June 1980 to be closer to other statewide organizations and to state government.[32]

MISSION AND POLICY

As stated in its bylaws, the mission of Humanities Texas "shall be to engage the people of Texas in critical reflection on their individual and collective lives by providing opportunities for lifelong learning in the humanities." To realize its mission, the bylaws define broadly Humanities Texas's programmatic scope:

> Humanities Texas shall engage in a grant program which will provide funds for approved projects which carry out its mission… Such projects shall be conducted by appropriate organizations and institutions within Texas. The council shall also sponsor projects and programs designed to achieve the council's mission. All programs shall be nonprofit and comply with the provisions of Public Law 89-209 and subsequent federal legislation and the directives of the National Endowment for the Humanities.[33]

LEADERSHIP AND GOVERNANCE

An executive director and a board of directors lead Humanities Texas. Federal law allows the Governor of Texas to appoint six people to the volunteer board for two-year terms.[34] The board elects its other members, representatives of the academic and public sectors, as vacancies occur. Non-gubernatorial members serve terms of three years, with the possibility of being re-elected to a second three-year term.[35]

Humanities Texas has had five executive directors from 1973 to 2008. The current Executive Director, Michael L. Gillette, took up the position in 2003. During one unstable five-year period in the late 1990s and early 2000s, Humanities Texas had two directors who were removed by the board. According to Gillette, the current board represents strong oversight,

with people who understand the Texas political climate and who are publicly visible and have access to the legislature.[36]

NAME AND ORGANIZATIONAL CHANGES

Over the past forty years, Humanities Texas's history of name and programmatic changes has reflected the historical priorities of its parent funding body, NEH. Initially named the Texas Committee for the Humanities in 1972, one year after its founding, the Committee became the Texas Committee for the Humanities and Public Policy, reflecting the NEH requirement that state humanities committees focus on the relationship between the humanities and public policy issues.[37]

To ensure that the programs reflected the needs and interests of their individual states, in its 1976 legislation reauthorizing the NEH, Congress encouraged committees to undertake traditional humanities projects as well as those relating to public policy. The council funded a wide range of projects in traditional humanities fields, including US and Texas history, literature, and culture. A clear sign of the policy influence of federal funding, the organization was renamed the Texas Committee for the Humanities in 1978. In 1996, it was renamed the Texas Council for the Humanities to reflect the increasing use of the word "council" rather than "committee" by the Congress and other state programs.[38] On January 1, 2004, after thirty years of operation, the council changed its name to Humanities Texas to be more "reflective of its inclusive, accessible approach to supporting public humanities programs around the state."[39]

In 1978, The University of Texas at Arlington Library established the Texas Humanities Resource Center (THRC) as one of its units. THRC relocated to Austin in 1986, merged physically with Humanities Texas, but operated as an independent nonprofit corporation until 1992. Functioning as a division of Humanities Texas, it organized and circulated exhibits, audiovisual programs, and print materials for use by cultural and educational communities in Texas and beyond. As an active, high-profile educational arm of Humanities Texas, in the first eighteen months of its founding THRC had distributed materials to support over 100 programs attended by 340,000 Texans and held in a range of institutions—including a number of public libraries.[40] By 2003, THRC had held just under 3,000 programs in 247 Texas communities, "collected and created more than seventy-five exhibits representing wide-ranging topics, and developed a rental library comprising over 400 films, videos, and slide programs."[41] In 2003, the materials developed by the Resource Center became legally and programmatically part of Humanities Texas.[42]

FUNDING

As the state affiliate of the NEH, Humanities Texas receives support through federal appropriations to the NEH as well as from foundations, corporations, and individuals. State humanities councils experienced modest increases in annual funding from the federal government during the 1970s and through the early 1980s. In 1986, however, Humanities Texas's revenues were cut almost in half when federal funding dropped significantly and private-sector support diminished as the Texas oil economy languished. Funds were gradually restored by the early 1990s and held stable through 1995. As a result of the 1994 US presidential elections, a number of federal programs came under attack by the new Congress, including the NEA and the NEH. By 1996, the annual budget for the NEH had dropped from $178 million to $110 million. State humanities councils, however, experienced more modest cuts; Humanities Texas lost approximately 6 percent of its federal funding.[43]

As an independent nonprofit corporation working in cooperation with the NEH, Humanities Texas can solicit funding from the private sector. In addition to donations from its "friends" organization, the council has received significant support for projects from foundations and corporations. The lack of state funding has limited Humanities Texas's programs. James Veninga, Executive Director of Humanities Texas from 1973 to 1997, noted that Humanities Texas's "inability to augment federal and private sector funding with state appropriations proved to be my biggest disappointment as…executive director."[44] Mike Gillette, current Executive Director of Humanities Texas, commented in an October 2008 interview that Humanities Texas had never received funding from the state legislature and that it is a current priority for Humanities

Texas to obtain a state appropriation.[45] Though state funding will provide the cachet of state sanction for Humanities Texas and its initiatives, state appropriations entail another level of policy authority and priorities that could affect Humanities Texas and its programs and initiatives in any number of ways, directly and indirectly, and positively and negatively.

EXECUTIVE DIRECTOR JAMES F. VENINGA: 1973–1997

During James Veninga's long tenure as Executive Director of Humanities Texas, his philosophies and actions created an agenda implicitly punctuated with policy favorable to the relationship of libraries and archives to advancing the public humanities. From funding public and private libraries to create humanities programs and exhibits for their constituencies, to providing small grants to libraries to bring in traveling exhibits held by the Texas Humanities Resource Center, to connecting with the Texas Library Association to publicize the work of Humanities Texas to the state's libraries, Veninga's tenure actively embraced libraries in the execution of Humanities Texas's mission.

In his published addresses and essays, *The Humanities and the Civic Imagination: Collected Addresses and Essays, 1978–1998*, Veninga speaks to an unambiguous role of libraries as primary actors in and spaces where Humanities Texas's programs have engaged large audiences throughout its existence. In particular, he highlights public libraries as partners with Humanities Texas in both documenting the humanities through exhibits and acting as sites where the public can view exhibits and films, attend readings and lectures, and participate in public discussions.[46] As a particularly high-profile example, between 1991 through 2002, Humanities Texas adopted Prime Time Family Reading Time (PTFRT). Created in 1991 by the Louisiana Endowment for the Humanities and designed specifically for underserved families with young children, PTFRT "reinforced the role of the family, encouraged parents and children to read and learn together, and taught families to become active library patrons." Humanities Texas held PTFRT programs in Arlington, Diboll, Canyon, Beaumont, Houston, Longview, and Humble, Texas.[47]

Beyond the role of libraries in Humanities Texas programs, Veninga's tenure evidenced clear implicit policy in respect to the knowledge and leadership librarians bring to Humanities Texas's mission. In 1982 and 1998, the library directors of The University of Texas at Austin Tarlton Law Library and the Houston Public Library chaired Humanities Texas's Board of Directors, an influential policy-making body.[48]

IN SEARCH OF POLICY: 2003–2008

Humanities Texas bylaws do not state explicit policy in regard to the role of libraries and archives in its programs and initiatives. The encompassing nature and broad definition of the humanities stated in the bylaws, however, does not exclude libraries and archives; in this case, the open language of the bylaws conveys Humanities Texas's interest in embracing the humanities wherever and however they are instantiated. On the other hand, strong implicit policy can be inferred in Humanities Texas's traveling exhibit program, grant-making activities, and Teacher Institutes, all of which signal significant commitments of resources and a forging of strong alliances with Texas libraries and archives and with the National Archives and Records Administration (NARA). We can infer that the strength of these commitments is in some part due to Veninga's philosophy, and, concomitantly, to the practices established during his tenure, as well as to the humanities philosophies and professional background the current Executive Director, Michael Gillette, brings to Humanities Texas.

Gillette, a lifelong Texan born on the Gulf Coast, holds a PhD from The University of Texas at Austin. He headed the Oral History Division of the Lyndon Baines Johnson Presidential Library before becoming director of the Center for Legislative Archives at NARA, a position he held from 1991 to 2003, when he retired. Signaling his commitment to a humanities vision that embraces the role of libraries and archives, in a 2007 interview for *In Focus*, NEH's online news source, Gillette stated that he sees part of Humanities Texas's role as "disseminating the talent and resources of museums, libraries, and universities throughout the state."[49] In a recent address he delivered at the May 2008 meeting of the Society of South-

west Archivists, Gillette unfolded the recent history of the NARA, discussing his assignment to assist in transitioning NARA by raising funds for a renovation of the National Archives building. He directly associates NARA with the concept of a cultural institution, noting that the "enterprise was one of continuous salesmanship. John Constance devised hundreds of opportunities to pitch the renovated Archives as a cultural institution." And when highlighting then Arizona Representative Jim Kolbe's role in shepherding a $200-million piece of legislation through Congress for NARA's renovation, Gillette says Kolbe "cared deeply about history and understood the Archives' potential as a cultural institution."[50] Clearly, Gillette's longtime career as an archivist, his personal and professional ties with archives, and his stated, affirmative disposition to the role of libraries and archives in Humanities Texas's programs have influenced Humanities Texas's exhibit program, grant-making activities, and Teacher Institutes.

As a highly visible humanities program for Texas, the traveling exhibit program makes a significant impact across the state; a number of them have been made available online. With the goal to provide high-quality, affordable resources to cultural and educational institutions throughout Texas and the nation, Humanities Texas's exhibitions program circulates more than fifty traveling exhibitions on a variety of topics ranging from the signers of the annexation of Texas and German immigration to Texas to the art of Miguel Covarrubias to rural Texas women at work. Humanities Texas also makes available a large collection of documentaries and other media resources to supplement humanities programming. The exhibits are designed to fit all sizes and kinds of institutions, with budgets big and small. Many of the exhibit requesters and sites are, naturally, Texas libraries and archives, reinforcing Humanities Texas's implicit cultural policy in regard to the role of libraries and archives in Texas's cultural environment.[51]

A practice established during Veninga's tenure, Humanities Texas has produced exhibits in coordination with libraries and archives, featuring the documentary treasures of Texas institutions, or, in the case of *Running for Office: Candidates, Campaigns, and the Cartoons of Clifford Berryman*, a national collection of one of Washington's best-known graphic political commentators in the first half of the twentieth century. Created by the National Archives with the support of the Foundation for the National Archives (which Gillette created), Humanities Texas partnered with the National Archives to organize the Texas travel schedule and venues for *Running for Office.*[52]

In 2008, Humanities Texas created two new exhibits in partnership with The University of Texas at Austin Center for American History, a library and archival repository whose collections strongly reflect Texas history. *Behold the People: R.C. Hickman's Photographs of Black Dallas, 1949–1961,* portrays images of nationally popular entertainers and Dallas nightclubs, schools and universities, funerals, and notable Dallas citizens. *Russell Lee Photographs* highlights the poignant Depression-era images photographer Russell Lee produced in 1935 and 1936, when he began his photography career as part of the photography unit of the Federal Farm Security Administration, as well as the vast body of important work that Lee produced from 1947 through 1977.[53]

In the area of grant-making, Humanities Texas's clear, explicit support of the state's libraries reveals an implicit cultural policy.[54] Humanities Texas-funded projects take many different forms: lectures, panel discussions, and conferences; teacher institutes and workshops; reading and film discussion groups; site interpretations; the development and fabrication of interpretive exhibits; and the production of films, television, and radio programs, and interactive media.[55] In 2005, of a total $360,340 (ninety-five grants), $40,900 (11 percent of the total) was awarded to Texas libraries and library systems, the majority of them public; a number of the grants went to post-Rita hurricane relief. In 2006, of a total $304,650 (144 grants), $26,300 (8 percent of the total) went to libraries and library systems, including one award to the Texas Center for the Book. Given the wide range of institutions receiving grants from Humanities Texas, at an average of just less than 10 percent of the total number of grants funded in 2005 and 2006, Texas libraries received a notable share of the funding.

Teacher Institutes, a primary, high-profile programmatic initiative, delineate clearly Humanities Texas's implicit cultural policy in regard to the role of libraries and archives in the interpretation and teaching of Texas history. Commencing in June 2004 and co-sponsored by a constellation of annually changing libraries, archives, museums, and academic bodies, Teacher Institutes exist to "enhance student learning by providing teachers the opportunity to work closely with humanities scholars and explore topics at the heart of the state's social studies and language arts curricula."[56] With funding support from co-sponsors, partners, and NEH *We the People* grants, Teacher Institutes define a central role for libraries and archives in the education of Texas's K–12 population. To address a week-long topic for the seventy or more Texas teachers who apply to and are chosen to attend, Teacher Institutes draw on faculty and staff in the state's universities, libraries, archives, and museums, as well as the staff of NARA. For example, Humanities Texas and the Bob Bullock Texas State History Museum sponsored 2005's four-day institute "Gateway on the Gulf: Galveston and American Immigration, 1845–1915," in partnership with the Harris and Eliza Kempner Fund, NARA, Galveston's Rosenberg Library, the Texas Seaport Museum, the Galveston Historical Foundation, The University of Texas Medical Branch, and the Institute of Texan Cultures. With the stated goals "to illuminate immigration patterns distinct to Texas and the Galveston point of entry, thereby broadening participants' understanding of Texas and US history; and to provide opportunities for participants to use historic sites, museums, and primary sources in teaching local, state, and national history," "Gateway on the Gulf" situates libraries and archives central in and to the cultural landscape that informs the teaching enterprise.[57]

Topical lectures by specialist faculty, field trips to local libraries, museums, and history-oriented institutions, and workshops that introduce strategies for the teaching of history, with particular emphasis on the use and interpretation of primary sources, compose the multi-day institutes. In addition to the participation of the Head of Special Collections of Galveston's Rosenberg Library, NARA sent two staff to Galveston to serve as institute faculty for "Gateway on the Gulf." NARA also provided each institute participant with CD-ROMs of images of immigration related documents.[58]

Conclusions

If we accept Schuster's definitional model for state cultural policy, which locates cultural policy for libraries and archives within those bodies that promulgate humanities policy—both formally and informally, explicitly and implicitly—it is clear that Humanities Texas embodies and enacts broad-based, implicit policy vis-à-vis Texas libraries and archives. It would have been much easier to apply Schuster's definitional model to the Texas State Libraries and Archives Commission (TSLAC), where explicit policy is clearly articulated, but TSLAC would not have been a good testbed for detecting the finer, sometimes tacit nuances that infer a relationship between libraries and archives as cultural institutions and humanities-defined state-level organizations. Based on twenty-five years of professional and academic experience in the field of libraries and archives, in selecting Humanities Texas for this study, I hypothesized that explicit policy would be, in fact, undetectable. I did not begin to imagine, however, the significant implicit policy that I would uncover. In doing so, I learned that implicit policy can be as influential as those stated explicitly, in Humanities Texas's case providing direct support to libraries and archives through funding initiatives and, via the trickle-down effect of public policy, conveying to the citizens of Texas who use the resources and visit the cultural exhibits the social, cultural import of libraries and archives. Often, introducing children for the first time to Texas's primary source records, the inclusion of libraries and archives in teaching Texas history in the state's K–12 schools speaks to Humanities Texas's commitment to including libraries and archives in historical documentation and, importantly, to their active role in creating lifelong learners who consult primary resources to discover and interpret the history of human experience, creativity, and discovery. However, a primary danger in not expressing explicit policy evinces in the potential for shaky administrative turnover in organizations and institutions. The nature of political appointments to Humanities Texas's board also presents potential issues. If the appointees, *de facto* representatives of the governor, do not envision libraries and archives as inherent in Humanities Texas's mission, their voice may override dissenting opinions. An explicit policy that articulates a role for libraries and archives in Humanities Texas's mission would oblige board members to comply with that mandate.

But the question remains: Why should we care about state cultural policy, and, more specifically, about the inclusion of libraries and archives in that policy discourse? First, as Schuster documents, state-level agencies, organizations, and institutions provide the most visible support for culture, and, as such, are indicators of "a state's cultural vitality and its commitment to developing the cultural life of its citizens."[59] Without public policy and the advocacy and oftentimes material legality inherent in the promulgation and enactment of policy in and for the public sphere, libraries and archives would have difficulty carrying out—philosophically and fiscally—their social missions. If Texas's citizens are to positively impact the social, intellectual, and literary history of the Lone Star State and the broader world they inhabit, they must have access to—to dig through, compare, contrast, and make sense of—the abundant riches comprising the state's documentary records and the supporting resources held in the state's libraries. A comprehensive cultural policy embracing the arts, heritage, and humanities sectors provides the necessary, primary foundation to support the social imperative of libraries and archives.

NOTES

1. Roland Hjerppe, "A Framework for the Description of Generalized Documents," *Advances in Knowledge Organization* 4 (1994): 175. Other kinds of social memory institutions may be considered, e.g., scientific journals (in particular "archival journals"), educational institutions and teaching practices; these communicate knowledge from one generation to another and are, therefore, more implicit kinds of memory institutions.

2. For the purposes of this paper, "record" and "document" are synonymous. UNESCO's Memory of the World Programme, which aims to preserve and

disseminate valuable archival holdings and library collections worldwide, defines documentary heritage as "a single document, a collection, a holding or archival fonds" [Ray Edmondson, *Memory of the World: General Guidelines to Safeguard Documentary Heritage* (Paris: UNESCO, 2002: 2.6.4)]. For the purposes of the Memory of the World Programme, a document has two components—the information it contains and the medium that supports it. Documents may contain different forms of information and may be supported on different storage media. For example, textual materials such as manuscripts, books, newspapers, posters, etc., may have text in ink, pencil, paint, etc.; the support may be paper, plastic, papyrus, parchment, palm leaves, bark, textile (silk), stone, or other media. For non-textual materials such as drawings, prints, maps, music, etc., the images may be ink, pencil, paints, etc.; the supports are similar to those for textual materials. Traditional moving and still photographic images are created by a variety of chemical processes and are "eye readable," although devices such as projectors are often required; supports are usually paper or plastic but may be metal or glass. Electronic data of all types, including audio, video, text, and still images in analog or digital form, are created in a variety of ways and must be "read" by a device before being comprehensible; the supports are usually some form of plastic, metals, or glass ("Memory of the World," UNESCO, accessed July 2, 2012, http://www.unesco.org/new/en/communication-and-information/flagship-project-activities/memory-of-the-world/homepage/).

3. The American Library Association is the primary advocate for libraries. (See "Advocacy & Issues," American Library Association, accessed July 2, 2012, http://www.ala.org/advocacy/.) The Society of American Archivists advocates for archives. (See "Position Statements and Resolutions," Society of American Archivists, accessed July 2, 2012, http://www2.archivists.org/statements.)

4. J. Mark Schuster, "Sub-National Cultural Policy—Where the Action Is? Mapping State Cultural Policy in the United States" (working paper presented at "Cultural Sites, Cultural Theory, Cultural Policy," the Second International Conference on Cultural Policy Research, Te Papa, Wellington, New Zealand, January 23–26, 2002).

5. To revise this paper for publication, in 2012 I also had phone conversations and exchanged e-mail with Eric Lupfer, Director of Grants and Education, Humanities Texas.

6. J. Mark Schuster, ed., *Mapping State Cultural Policy: The State of Washington* (Chicago: University of Chicago, Cultural Policy Center, 2003), 1.

7. Schuster, *Mapping State Cultural Policy*, 103.

8. Schuster, "Sub-National Cultural Policy."

9. Society of American Archivists, "So You Want to Be an Archivist: An Overview of the Archival Profession," accessed July 2, 2012, http://www2.archivists.org/profession.

10. "Major Group 82: Educational Services," U.S. Department of Labor, Occupational Safety and Health Administration, accessed July 2, 2012, http://www.osha.gov/pls/imis/sic_manual.display?id=69&tab=group. It is interesting to note that museums, art galleries, and botanical and zoological gardens are also grouped under "services" but not as "educational services."

11. Commission on the Humanities, *Report of the Commission on the Humanities* (New York: American Council of Learned Societies, 1964), accessed July 2, 2012, http://www.acls.org/uploadedFiles/Publications/NEH/1964_Commission_on_the_Humanities.pdf.

12. Commission on the Humanities, *Report*, 33, 45.

13. J. Mark Schuster, *Informing Cultural Policy: The Research and Information Infrastructure* (New Brunswick, NJ: Rutgers University, Center for Urban Policy Research, 2002), 4, 15.

14. Adrienne Scullion and Beatriz Garcia, "What Is Cultural Policy Research?" *International Journal of Cultural Policy* 11 (2005): 113.

15. The following sources are but a few examples of works that discuss and define "policy," "culture," and "humanities": Mark Considine, *Public Policy: A Critical Approach* (South Melbourne, Vic.: Macmillan, 1994); Philip Doty, "What is [Public] Policy?" (handout for INF 390N.1, Federal Information Policy, course taught by Doty in the School of Information, The University of Texas at Austin, Fall 2007); Thomas R. Dye, *Understanding Public Policy* (Englewood Cliffs, NJ: Prentice Hall, 1995); Egon C. Guba, "The Effects of Definitions of Policy

on the Nature and Outcomes of Policy Analysis," *Educational Leadership* 42 (1984); B.W. Hogwood and L.A. Gunn, *Policy Analysis for the Real World* (Oxford: Oxford University Press, 1984); Ann Majchrzak, *Methods for Policy Research* (Newbury Park, CA: Sage, 1984); George Steinmetz, *State/Culture: State Formation after the Cultural Turn* (Ithaca, NY: Cornell University Press, 1999); and Raymond Williams, *Keywords: A Vocabulary of Culture and Society* (London: Collins, 1976).

Policy Egon Guba states that "one can safely conclude that the term policy is not defined in any uniform way; indeed the term is rarely defined at all." He offers eight uses of the term, as:

1. an assertion of intents or goals;

2. the accumulated standing decisions of a governing body…within its sphere of authority;

3. a guide to discretionary action;

4. a strategy undertaken to solve or ameliorate a problem;

5. sanctioned behavior, formally…or informally through expectations and acceptance established over (sanctified by) time;

6. a norm of conduct characterized by consistency and regularity in some substantive action area;

7. the output of the policy-making system;

8. the effect of the policy-making and policy-implementing system as it is experienced by the client.

Hogwood and Gunn assert that policy is a label for a field of activity, an expression of general purpose or desired state of affairs, specific proposals, decisions of government, formal authorization, a program, output, outcome, a theory or a model, and process.

Majchrzak, by implication, states that policies are "pragmatic, action-oriented" solutions to fundamental social problems.

Public policy Dye asserts that finding a "proper" definition of public policy has "proved futile…Public policy is whatever governments choose to do or not to do, i.e., government action and inaction."

Considine supports the notion of public policy as "an action which employs governmental authority to commit resources in support of a preferred value."

Philip Doty provides an integrating concept of public policy as:

1. the commitment of public resources;

2. to certain courses of action;

3. to achieve certain goals;

4. in the context of differential power of all kinds.

Culture At all levels of discourse, what constitutes culture reflects a broad spectrum of ideas; dictionaries, scholars, cultural sector practitioners, politicians, and the public differ on the social meaning of culture. Thus a strict definition of culture is neither possible nor particularly desirable, but it is important to be clear that the concept of culture is adopted by various actors to represent a range of ideologies and meanings, oftentimes implying, defining, or asserting an intent and goal, much like the concept of "policy." An interesting place to begin is the "Introduction" in George Steinmetz's book.

Williams says that "the problems of meaning have preoccupied me and have led to the sharpest realizationof the difficulties of any kind of definition." See his definition of "culture."

Humanities U.S. Federal Public Law 209 defines the humanities as the study of language; literature; history; law; philosophy; ethics; archaeology; comparative religion; and art history, criticism, and theory. Others have suggested varying disciplinary combinations to comprise the humanities.

16. Oliver Bennett, "The Torn Halves of Cultural Policy Research," review essay of Justin Lewis and Toby Miller, eds, *Critical Cultural Policy Studies: A Reader* and J. Mark Schuster, *Informing Cultural Policy: The Research and Information Infrastructure, International Journal of Cultural Policy* 10 (2004): 246.

17. For example, cultural policy centers have been established at the University of Glasgow, the University of Chicago, and Ohio State University.

18. Scullion and Garcia, "What Is Cultural Policy Research?" 115.

19. Bennett, "The Torn Halves of Cultural Policy Research," 237.

20. Toby Miller and George Yudice, *Cultural Policy* (London: Sage, 2002).

21. Bennett, "The Torn Halves of Cultural Policy Research," 237–38.

22. Schuster, *Informing Cultural Policy*, 15.

23. Schuster, "Sub-National Cultural Policy," 1.

24. Justin Lewis and Toby Miller, eds., *Critical Cultural Policy Studies: A Reader* (Oxford: Blackwell, 2003), 4.

25. Lewis and Miller, *Critical Cultural Policy Studies*, 5.

26. Bennett, "The Torn Halves of Cultural Policy Research," 238, 242.

27. Bennett, "The Torn Halves of Cultural Policy Research," 242.

28. Scullion and Garcia, "What Is Cultural Policy Research?" 118.

29. Scullion and Garcia, "What Is Cultural Policy Research,?" 122, 124–25.

30. The NEA, on the other hand, was to encourage state arts agencies to become an arm of state government.

31. Humanities Texas underwent a number of name changes between 1973 and 2003. Throughout this paper I use the current name, Humanities Texas, to refer to the state council.

32. Humanities Texas, "Mission and History," accessed July 4, 2012, http://www.humanitiestexas.org/about/mission-history.

33. Humanities Texas, "Bylaws," accessed July 4, 2012, http://www.humanitiestexas.org/about/mission-history/bylaws.

34. Michael L. Gillette, interview by author, October 20, 2008. Interestingly, though the Governor may appoint members on a bipartisan basis, Governor Rick Perry has appointed only Republicans to Humanities Texas's board. This practice is not explicated in official Governor's Office policy, but the practice in and of itself may have an implicit effect on the governance of Humanities Texas.

35. Humanities Texas, "Bylaws."

36. Gillette, interview. Richard T. Hull served from 1997 to 1999, and Monte Youngs served from 1999 until 2002.

37. Humanities Texas, "Mission and History."

38. James F. Veninga, *The Humanities and the Civic Imagination: Collected Addresses and Essays, 1978-1998* (Denton, TX: University of North Texas Press, 1999), 3–6.

39. Humanities Texas, "Mission and History."

40. Veninga, *The Humanities and the Civic Imagination*, 31.

41. Humanities Texas, "Mission and History."

42. Humanities Texas, "Mission and History."

43. Humanities Texas, "Mission and History."

44. Veninga, *The Humanities and the Civic Imagination*, 10–11.

45. Gillette, interview. Eric Lupfer, in a phone conversation in August 2012, informed me that Humanities Texas received its first state funding in 2009 from the State Historical Commission. Humanities Texas also received significant state funding for 2010, 2011, 2012, and 2013 to expand the Teacher Institutes program.

46. Veninga, *The Humanities and the Civic Imagination*, 1–52.

47. Humanities Texas, "Past Programs. Primetime Family Reading Time," accessed August 18, 2012, http://www.humanitiestexas.org/programs/past/reading-time.

48. Veninga, *The Humanities and the Civic Imagination*, 5.

49. Rebecca Onion, "In Focus," *Humanities* 48, no. 6 (2007).

50. Michael L. Gillette, "'An Offer You Can't Refuse': The National Archives in Transition" (address

presented at the annual meeting of the Society of Southwest Archivists, Houston, TX, May 22, 2008).

51. Humanities Texas, "Exhibits and Resources," accessed July 5, 2012, http://www.humanitiestexas .org/exhibitions.

52. Humanities Texas, "Running for Office: Candidates, Cartoons, and the Cartoons of Clifford Berryman," accessed July 5, 2012, http://www .humanitiestexas.org/exhibitions/list/by-title/ running-office-candidates-campaigns-and -cartoons-clifford-berryman. An online version of the exhibition is available at http://www .archives.gov/exhibits/running-for-office.

53. Humanities Texas, "Russell Lee Photographs," accessed July 5, 2012, http://www.humanitiestexas .org/exhibitions/list/by-title/russell-lee-photographs.

54. Oddly, given the number of grants to libraries, I did not detect that grants went to Texas archival institutions in 2005 and 2006.

55. Humanities Texas, "Grants: How to Apply," accessed July 5, 2012, http://www.humanitiestexas .org/grants/apply.

56. Humanities Texas, "Teacher Institutes," accessed August 12, 2012, http://www.humanitiestexas.org/ education/teacher-institutes.

57. Humanities Texas, *Gateway on the Gulf: Galveston and American Immigration, 1845-1915: An Institute for Texas Teachers. Final Report* (Austin, TX: Humanities Texas, 2005), 2, accessed August 12, 2012, http://www.humanitiestexas.org/sites/ default/files/teacher-institute/HTxGatewayonthe Gulf2005.pdf.

58. Humanities Texas, *Gateway on the Gulf.*

59. Schuster, *Mapping State Cultural Policy,* v.

JOHN H. HAMMER

"On the Political Aspects of Book Preservation in the U.S."

Advances in Preservation and Access *1 (1992): 22–40.*

ON SEPTEMBER 27, 1988, President Reagan signed the "Interior and Related Agencies Appropriation for Fiscal Year 1989," which included $153 million for the National Endowment for the Humanities (NEH).[1] One ramification of this largely routine final step for agency budgets was that through it the President made available significant new funding for NEH's Office of Preservation—an increase from $4.5 to $12.33 million—and officially set in motion a massive nationwide program designed to address the problems posed by the deterioration of tens of millions of books and other materials printed since the 1850s. The funding of the NEH initiative to microfilm "brittle books" and older library materials printed on acidic paper represented the culmination of years of effort by a loosely linked network of librarians, scholars, and scientists. This network also includes officials from government, foundations, higher education, and other organizations concerned with the problems that began with mid-nineteenth century changes in paper manufacturing which left most of the printed material produced since unstable and disintegrating, pondering the potential loss of information and records of history and culture too vast to describe.

The highly-complex process by which Americans determine which problems are of national significance and how the nation will address them has evolved into a unique pattern that reflects our social, economic, and political organization. The development of a federal commitment to address the problem of deteriorating books residing in the collections of private institutions may be viewed as a veritable textbook illustration of that American policy process.

The Problem

Before the nineteenth century, paper was handmade using linen and cotton rags; thus paper production was limited by the supply of rags and the slowness of the process, and absolutely unable to respond to an escalating demand for paper. By the middle of the nineteenth century, the demands of ever-widening literacy had begun to fuel the growth of a paper industry aimed at large-scale production and centered on bleached tree pulp with alum-rosin sizing; this new process left most paper highly acidic. Acid reduces paper strength, and book pages made from acidic paper become yellow and brittle, eventually disintegrating and destroying the information they record.

Subsequent changes in paper making led to the extensive use of groundwood, which produces paper with short fibers that break easily, thus compounding the problems inherent in contemporary papers. Ironically, the technologies that made possible the vast increase in paper production also led to the rapid disintegration of the materials printed or otherwise preserved on the resulting acidic paper.

The problem with the new papers was actually understood and was the subject of some scientific debate early in the last century. Shahani and Wilson quote a letter from an English science writer John Murray, in a letter to *Gentleman's Magazine* in 1823 [Editor's note: the full letter is reproduced in chapter 1]:

> Allow me to call the attention of your readers to the present state of that wretched compound called Paper. Every printer will corroborate my testimony ... our beautiful Religion, our Literature, our Science are all threatened... I have in my possession a large copy of the Bible printed at Oxford, 1816 (never used) and issued by the British and Foreign Office, crumbling literally into dust... I have watched for some years the progress of the evil, and have no hesitation in saying, that if the same ratio of progression is maintained, a century more will not witness the volumes printed within the last twenty years.[2]

It should be noted that while acidic or short-fibered paper is the most obvious threat to books, a number of other factors such as heat, humidity, pests, and heavy use also contribute to the deterioration of printed materials. For reasons relating to climate as well as the historical development of their respective paper industries, the problem of books at risk is somewhat greater in North America than in Europe but, in fact, the difficulty is a worldwide one.

Toward Understanding

For many years individuals and agencies in the U.S. government have been interested in the problems associated with acidic paper. As early as the 1930s the National Bureau of Standards was both testing paper for stability (and confirming that highly acidic paper is unstable), and conducting research which developed a process of cellulose lamination that could render some embrittled materials useable. The National Archives and the Library of Congress (LC) have long been active in research and development aimed at saving their collections from deterioration. Interestingly, one of the most important persons to provide leadership in understanding the impact of acidic paper and identifying possible solutions was a state government employee, William Barrow of the Virginia State Library.

There has also been research into various aspects of the acidic paper problem in the private sector. For example, in 1900 Edwin Sutermeister of the S. D. Warren Company first proved that paper formulated for stability should contain alkaline filler. Alkaline-filled papers made in 1901 under Sutermeister's direction remain in good condition today, ninety years later.[3] Because of such research, as well as economic and certain other factors, the manufacturing of book papers has been moving slowly toward increased stability since World War II.

Without doubt, the single most important force for broadening both governmental and non-governmental policy makers' understanding of the preservation challenge and encouraging the examination of the issue is the Council on Library Resources (CLR). The

Council, a non-profit organization, was founded in 1956 by the Ford Foundation for the purpose of promoting library research both through directly-managed projects and grants and contracts with other organizations and individuals; it was concerned with preservation issues from its inception. Over its first three decades, through grant-making, committees, and collaborative activities with other organizations, CLR touched on virtually every aspect of the brittle books problem, illuminating conservation issues, making various aspects of preservation better understood, and often facilitating the development of technologies to resolve specific problems. A brief review of CLR grants and activities reveals an impressive grasp of the problems at each stage.[4] With respect to its impact on federal policies, the Council has displayed what can only be called an uncanny sense of the policy process and the kind of research and data needed by policy makers:

- Over a twenty-year period beginning in 1957, CLR provided grants totaling nearly $2 million to the Virginia State Library. This money supported William Barrow as he worked to determine the causes of paper deterioration, develop specifications for permanent/durable paper, promote the acceptance of alkaline (i.e., acid-free) paper, develop deacidification techniques, design testing equipment, and produce publications drawing attention to the problems of preservation.
- The Council also made grants to the American Library Association (ALA) for publishing a series on the conservation of library materials, testing supplies used by conservators, and developing performance standards for binding.
- A grant was made to the Association of Research Libraries (ARL) to study bibliographic control of microforms and to conduct research that would establish the magnitude of the preservation problem. In 1960, ARL found that there were 7,665,000 unique titles published after 1869 in U.S.

research libraries; these were thought to be deteriorating in large numbers.
- A 1965 CLR grant established the Library of Congress unit that produced the first volume of the National Register of Microform Masters.
- CLR supported Richard D. Smith who as a graduate student at the University of Chicago developed a new deacidification process.
- The Library of Congress' preservation laboratory, where preliminary deacidification experiments using diethyl zinc (DEZ) were carried out, was equipped with funds provided by the CLR.
- The Council funded the establishment of the Northeast Document Conservation Center (1972–74) and in 1984 developed a mid-Atlantic regional conservation center.
- In 1979, CLR formed the Committee on Production Guidelines for Book Longevity, to underscore the need for permanent and durable book papers and bindings and to develop practical, realistic methods of promoting the use of permanent paper. The final report of the Committee (*Book Longevity*, 1982) provided guidelines designed to ensure permanence and durability. A committee (Z-39) of the American National Standards Institute (now the National Information Standards Organization) used the Committee's report to draft a standard for permanent paper for printed library materials.
- Beginning in 1981, CLR in collaboration with key library, higher education, and scholarly groups formed several important task forces. By 1986 these groups had produced a national strategy to preserve the nation's intellectual heritage—essentially, the strategy subsequently accepted and funded by Congress. These culminating activities are discussed in detail below.

Of course, the Council on Library Resources did not work on preservation problems in isolation. In fact, the success of its effort was possible because of collaborations with key private organizations, notably ARL, ALA, RLG, the Association of American Universities (AAU), and the American Council of Learned Societies (ACLS). The Library of Congress and, later, the National Endowment for the Humanities regularly worked with CLR. After 1976, when the Ford Foundation was no longer willing fully to underwrite the cost of CLR (as it had, singlehandedly, with millions of dollars for the first twenty years), a dozen major foundations joined Ford in supporting the Council. Several became deeply involved in preservation issues, notably the Andrew W. Mellon and Exxon Education Foundations.

By the late 1970s there was agreement among the groups and individuals with whom CLR worked that there were three potential approaches to the brittle books problem: (1) When books were already embrittled, preserve their contents in another medium. Most agreed that microfilm was the single proven format; little was known about the longevity of optical disks and other electronic media, and these were considered risky for archival investment. (2) When books were printed on acidic paper but were not yet embrittled, deacidify their pages by means of gaseous or liquid process. (3) Persuade publishers to issue new books on alkaline papers. ("Alkaline" is the term now commonly used to describe papers produced without an acid residue; "acid-free" and "permanent" carry the same general meaning but have declined in use because they suggest more than the paper may deliver.)

Beginnings of Federal Support for Private Preservation

Because of the nature of scholarly research, a tradition that demands familiarity with past work before new interpretations can be offered, the preservation of scholarly resources emerged early on the agenda of the National Endowment for the Humanities, following its establishment in 1965. In 1973, NEH began its historic special assistance to The New York Public Library, at the same time making all research libraries a part of its mission.[5] As early as 1978, the Endowment began making grants through its Division of Research Programs that in some part addressed the issue of deteriorating scholarly materials. In 1981 NEH grants at Columbia University supported the training of professional conservation personnel for libraries and archives, and the preparation of a handbook on the practical application of new photographic preservation methods.

One of the final acts of William Bennett as he left the NEH chairmanship to become Secretary of Education in January 1985 was to establish an Office of Preservation at the Endowment. The step was taken to give preservation greater visibility—especially the magnitude of the brittle books problem—and to underscore the leadership that NEH had assumed in the area. Building on the work of the Council on Library Resources and others, NEH focused on building an infrastructure in libraries that could effectively respond to the vast challenge of trying to save the information contained in millions of deteriorating volumes. A 1985 NEH description of the priorities for the new office describes the agency's plan to "foster the preservation of those materials most needed for humanities research, to encourage cooperative projects among library and archival institutions in order to ensure effective use of federal and nonfederal funds, to stimulate private-sector funding of preservation activities, to support training in preservation, and to help humanities institutions develop a long-term capability to address their own institutional problems."[6] It was also in 1985 that NEH launched an ambitious U.S. Newspaper Program to locate, catalog, and film the more than 300,000 U.S. newspapers published since 1690.

Two projects were funded by NEH as possible models for other like endeavors, and both provided experience of considerable importance for future preservation policy-making:

1. A 1983 cooperative microfilming project undertaken by the Research Libraries Group to microfilm about 30,000 U.S. imprints and Americana printed between 1876 and 1900. This $675,000 project was to preserve materials that were fundamental to American studies but that survived in brittle, critical condition

in nine major research libraries. One unanticipated outcome of the RLG project was the evidence it provided that even large research libraries have difficulty in securing the time, staff, and funds needed for a major microfilming effort.

2. A 1984 grant to the American Philological Association to support cooperative preservation microfilming of selected embrittled serials and books in classical studies, published between 1850 and 1918. The key feature of this project was to study carefully and report the process of bringing scholars and librarians together in selecting materials to be saved; as a result, much was learned or inferred about how scholars and librarians deal with triage.

In 1979, about the time NEH was becoming quite active in supporting preservation activities (and at least implicitly offering alternative funding for some of the work CLR had so long supported), CLR turned to a committee-centered approach to preservation which had the effect of broadening significantly the number of leaders from libraries, higher education, scholarly associations, and government who were aware of the massive nature of the preservation challenge. The first of these groups was the 1979 Committee on Production Guidelines for Book Longevity.

In 1981 CLR and the Association of American Universities began a collaboration aimed at strengthening the nation's research libraries. Discussions among CLR, AAU, and research librarians, scholars, and university administrators resulted in the appointment of five task forces. A preservation task force was asked to consider how a national strategy for addressing the deterioration of library resources could be developed. The task force recommended development and implementation of a plan building on certain actions already underway that would also include the various local effort in research libraries and other institutions across the country. The final report of the preservation task force served as a basic source document for two meetings involving key leaders from libraries, scholarly organizations, and higher education, as well as figures from the printing and paper industries, and federal agencies like the Library of Congress, NEH,

and the National Historical Publications and Records Commission.

The major outcome of this activity in terms of the evolution of federal preservation policy was the recommendation that CLR undertake to describe a national plan for preservation that could be considered by both the library and scholarly communities. The Council, with the assistance of a small working group, drafted a paper delineating a national strategy that was subsequently reviewed and endorsed by the governing bodies of ARL, AAU, and ACLS. Shortly thereafter, the Exxon Education Foundation made a $1.5 million grant to CLR to establish a preservation filming facility to serve the mid-Atlantic region and, importantly, to support planning and build public support for a national preservation program. Thus with the approval and backing of the leading organizations and with grant funds in hand, a group comprised of selected university officers, scholars, preservation specialists, and library directors formed the Committee on Preservation and Access (CPA).

Building the Case

The new Committee was assigned the tasks of devising its management structure, outlining a funding plan, and determining the characteristics of and conditions for a national preservation program. It was always understood that one of the Committee's key objectives was to establish the American preservation problem as a federal concern, one to whose costs and resolution the U.S. government would contribute significantly. By adding "access" to the name of the new committee, CLR and its collaborators took an important step forward in devising an approach that would have appeal for policy makers; even though many types of materials, including photographs, motion pictures, and so forth, were deteriorating on the shelves of American libraries, brittle books were to be the centerpiece for the Committee and the national plan.

From the beginning, the Committee on Preservation and Access performed its tasks in a highly effective and timely fashion; it also began its work with many advantages:

- Almost thirty years of CLR-supported activities provided strong research and demonstration support for a national plan.
- A core of leaders from major universities, libraries, and foundations, well informed about the problem and eager to facilitate its resolution, already existed.
- The Library of Congress and other federal libraries had done much work to address the preservation problems of their own collections and provide research and guidance for others. (LC's leadership in the development of a large-scale deacidification process was seen as particularly promising.)
- The National Endowment for the Humanities stood ready to provide support and leadership for private preservation efforts.

Conversely, the Committee also had enormous challenges to overcome if it were to succeed, chief among these the sheer immensity of the task, in terms of expense and manpower; some feared that federal officials would conclude the problem was too vast to address. Other important issues to be confronted were the federal budgetary climate whose massive annual deficits were unfriendly to new initiatives; local problems of costs (and cost sharing), management, and coordination; and the very significant dilemma associated with deciding which materials would be preserved, and which left to disintegrate.

The Committee proved equal to the task. Under the chairmanship of Billy E. Frye, Provost and Academic Vice-President of the University of Michigan (later the holder of parallel posts at Emory University), the Committee's initial members were Harold Billings (University of Texas at Austin), Margaret S. Child (the Smithsonian Institution and a former NEH employee with key responsibilities for preservation activities), Carole F. Huxley (New York State Department of Education), Peter Likins (Lehigh University), Herbert Morton (ACLS's Office of Scholarly Communication and Technology), Robert O'Neil (University of Virginia), Rutherford Rogers (Hamden, Connecticut), Neil L. Rudenstine (Princeton University), Peter G. Sparks (LC), Sidney Verba (Harvard University), Robert Warner (University of Michigan), and Ber-

nice Wenzel (University of California at Los Angeles), with Harold Cannon (NEH) and John Vaughn (AAU) as observers.

The Committee met three times during 1984-85, and an interim report was circulated in July 1985. In October 1985, a CPA subcommittee met to discuss the scholar's role in the preservation of library materials. The November meeting (the last in 1985) was followed by publication of CPA's final report *Brittle Books* in April of 1986. The Council on Library Resources commissioned studies for CPA, including a grant to the University of California at Los Angeles to study the dimensions of the preservation problem in U.S. libraries.

In March 1986 at the Wye Center of the Aspen Institute, CPA members met with representatives from organizations that had expressed support for their brittle books plan. As a result of the recommendations from the Wye meeting, a Commission on Preservation and Access was established to develop and carry out the plans and procedures that would enable libraries and preservation specialists to extend and integrate existing preservation work—in practice, to implement the national brittle books plan. Conveniently, the new Commission could use the CPA acronym of its precursor, the Committee on Preservation and Access.

At the same time, a National Advisory Council on Preservation was established to promote participation in a national program and to provide advice to the Commission. Funding for CPA's first three years was promptly secured; in addition to support from CLR itself, the H.W. Wilson Company, and the Hewlett Foundation, several major research universities pledged substantial annual contributions to support the work of the new Commission.

The initial goal of the brittle books program was to create a national microfilm library. Four requirements necessary for success were identified:

1. Widespread understanding of the preservation problem, in order to generate adequate institutional support. (The publication of *Brittle Books* by the Council on Library Resources was considered an important step here.)

2. Use of the most effective technology available at any given time. (CPA reiterated the view that, while other technologies were promising, at the time only microfilm met archival standards.)
3. An efficient bibliographic system, including an accurate and timely tracking system.
4. Systematic and purposeful collaboration among libraries and allied organizations.

Although Billy E. Frye continued as its chair, the new Commission was somewhat smaller than its predecessor and had little additional overlap. Other Commission members included Millicent D. Abell (University Librarian of Yale), Herbert Bailey (Director Emeritus, Princeton University Press), James Govan (University Librarian, University of North Carolina at Chapel Hill), Vartan Gregorian (President of The New York Public Library), Kenneth R. R. Gros Louis (Vice President of Indiana University), Carole F. Huxley (Deputy Commissioner for Cultural Education, New York State Department of Education), Sidney Verba (Director, Harvard University Library), and William J. Welsh (Deputy Librarian of Congress).

With a small staff and advice from its National Advisory Council on Preservation, CPA set about its mission with vigor. Its accomplishments during the first two years included:

- Fleshing out and refining the central brittle books preservation plan.
- Establishing preservation guidelines for use by libraries, publishers, and others concerned with brittle books.
- Promoting preservation information among a widening group of scholarly societies, library groups, and other organizations.
- Promoting a public understanding of preservation, including assisting in developing *Slow Fires: On the Preservation of the Human Record*, a film produced with support from the Council on Library Resources, the National Endowment for the Humanities, and the Andrew W. Mellon Foundation.

- Encouraging research in areas related to brittle books.
- Developing a monitoring system to collect and analyze information about preservation, including supporting bibliographic systems.
- Pursuing strategies that would ensure access to preserved materials.

Building the Public Record

By the close of 1985, the pieces needed to begin building a public (i.e., Congressional) record demonstrating federal interest in preserving at-risk materials held in private libraries were in place; Congressional hearings, highly stylized, occasionally theatrical legislative vehicles generally intended to be didactic, are the cornerstones for building such public records. While surprises occasionally occur during public hearings, it is the careful preliminary design and shaping of hearings that is more significant, in terms of policy development. As the majority staff and chairman or designate set out to develop a hearing, their interactions with the ranking minority member, other committee members with special concerns or experience, affected executive agencies and departments, and, of course, the public groups concerned with the issues contribute in varying degrees to shaping the event, including the selection of sponsors for witnesses, and the nature and tone of questions directed at the witnesses themselves during the hearing.

As previously noted, the question of the federal government's interest in preserving its own books, records, and other materials has never been a major policy issue. Rather, LC, the National Archives, and other offices have long recognized the problems of disintegrating collections and actively sought solutions. In many instances, federal agencies have been the developers or patrons of new technologies to address problems in conservation and preservation of deteriorating paper. However, winning a federal commitment to fund a significant part of the microfilming in an ambitious brittle books program designed to save the information in millions of books in public and private libraries across the nation was by no means obvious.

Key legislators concerned with libraries and other cultural policies such as Representatives Pat Williams (D-MI), Sidney R. Yates (D-IL), E. Thomas Coleman (R-MO), Thomas J. Downey (D-NY), and Mary Rose Oakar (D-OH), and Senators Claiborne Pell (D-RI) and Mark O. Hatfield (R-OR) were aware in general terms of the progress toward developing a national preservation plan. After the Commission on Preservation and Access produced a credible brittle books program, the need for federal action became more pressing. Acting for chairman Pat Williams, the staff of the Select Education Subcommittee of the House Education and Labor Committee met with CPA staff to discuss its plan. Although the subcommittee had authorizing responsibility for the National Endowment for the Humanities, the staff was interested in exploring a number ofpossibilities for administering funds, in the event Congress decided to allocate money for the program. (While CPA seemed to find NEH the best choice to manage a federal program, a number of other possibilities were considered, including the 1979 National Enquiry into Scholarly Communication's proposal that a new national library agency be established with preservation in its portfolio.)[7] There were also questions of appropriate levels of federal funding, as well as whether hearings should be mounted and if so, the matter of choosing suitable witnesses. These discussions were clearly helpful to Commission members and staff, who came to understand the ways in which their concerns would be perceived by lawmakers and how best to frame issues so that these would be perceived and would succeed as issues "in the national interest." One outgrowth of these discussions was the decision to make the "democratization of access" (i.e., microfilming books in the Harvard University libraries that then become part of a national library, available to citizens in cities and towns across America) a central theme in presenting the program.

The Congressional Opener

An "Oversight Hearing on the Problem or 'Brittle Books' in Our Nation's Libraries" was held on March 3, 1987 before the Subcommittee on Postsecondary Education or the House Committee on Education and Labor; Pat Williams had brought the hearing with him from the Select Education Panel when he assumed responsibility for the higher-profile Postsecondary Education Subcommittee. With a background as a teacher and Congressional staffer with strong interests in education, the arts and humanities, and libraries, Williams skillfully directed the hearing planning, assisted by subcommittee staff director Gray Garwood and professional staff member Anne Hausmann. The witness list included:

PANEL 1

- Lynne Cheney (Chairman, National Endowment for the Humanities)
- Vartan Gregorian (President, New York Public Library)

PANEL 2

- Daniel Boorstin (Librarian of Congress), accompanied by Peter Sparks (National Preservation Program Office, Library of Congress)
- Carole F. Huxley (Deputy Commissioner for Cultural Education, New York State Department of Education)
- Warren J. Haas (president, Council on Library Resources), representing the Council, the Association of American Universities, and the American Council of Learned Societies.
- David C. Weber (Director, University Libraries, Stanford University), representing the American Library Association and the Association of Research Libraries

The leading role of the Commission on Preservation and Access is underscored by the fact that three of seven witnesses were current members of CPA.

Representative Williams opened the hearing by declaring that the nation's heritage was literally eroding away.

We know [that] the major cause of the problem of brittle books is the acid content of the paper upon which they are printed. The technology to prevent this problem from occurring in the future is now being developed. We also have the technical capability through microfilming these documents to resolve part of the present dilemma, thus, there is reason to hope that the knowledge contained in brittle books can be saved... We want to explore solutions and we want to determine the appropriate Federal, State, and private sector roles.[8]

Lynne Cheney saw a precise role for NEH "to help build the infrastructure that has to be in place for a large and coordinated effort to take place." Rather than a single initiative,

What we need... are national efforts along several fronts in different subject areas involving different groupings of institutions, with all of them committed to the idea that whatever preservation effort is undertaken needs to be registered in some central source so there won't be duplication.[9]

In response to Pat Williams' question, "Is there, in your judgment, a role for expanded public financial support for this effort?" Cheney responded,

We see NEH's role as providing the infrastructure and as establishing model programs. What growth we see in coming years should be very slow. When you are building infrastructure, a great infusion of money up front is not useful—various libraries have to designate the people in charge of these projects, they have to decide to have a slot for someone who will be their preservationist. So from my own particular perspective, the role of public funding should be one that expands slowly.[10]

Vartan Gregorian sounded a central theme of the Commission's plan:

What we are trying to do... [at the] New York Public Library... Library of Congress... Yale or Harvard libraries... University of California libraries, or any research or university libraries... is to nationalize in a sense by democratizing our holdings.[11]

Despite the fact that all witnesses indicated that the situation was very grave—an enormous percentage of current library holdings were already embrittled or threatened, and hundreds of millions of dollars would be required to microfilm even a portion of these materials—it was clear that they did not perceive the problem to be intractable; indeed, with a timely expansion of resources, it was one which could be substantially alleviated. Points made by various witnesses included:

- Through the Council on Library Resources and its Commission on Preservation and Access, a clear picture of the brittle books problem and its dimensions was now available. Estimates of the number of threatened volumes which had been further refined would be forthcoming later in 1987.
- Various individual libraries, groups, and associations had accomplished much in developing systems, personnel, and facilities to deal with the preservation problem.
- Through microfilming technology, it was possible that a significant portion of the information in materials at risk could be saved, if resources were mobilized rapidly (CPA estimated that one-third of the endangered books could be filmed; once on film, the preserved material could be made available to users in any number of other media).
- The results of experimental projects indicated that mechanisms for timely and effective decision-making on materials to be saved were feasible.
- Foundations, state governments, universities, libraries, and archives were already devoting substantial sums of money to dealing with preservation problems.
- NEH was an important source of leadership in promoting public awareness of complex issues and providing well-targeted funds to develop both models and the necessary infrastructure to manage preservation effectively.
- Work on deacidification, in which the Library of Congress was a leader, offered

good promise that in the near future preventive treatment of new and not yet embrittled materials would circumscribe the dimensions of the problem. It was noted that the majority of books published in the U.S. in 1986 were printed on acidic paper. (Witnesses also sought to dispel the notion that deacidification holds promise for already embrittled materials.)

The hearing was rather well attended by subcommittee members, and witnesses received a number of questions. Thomas Coleman, the ranking minority member of the subcommittee, while speaking very supportively of the effort, sounded the question that would be raised repeatedly in the discussion of federal support for preserving brittle books—who decides what is to be saved? Major R. Owens (D-NY), the only librarian serving in Congress, spoke of the lack of microfilm readers in many local libraries and in effect cautioned the sponsors of the national plan that access is the main federal interest in brittle books.

The hearing was considered to have placed the issue on the public record effectively. Pat Williams wrote to Representative Sidney R. Yates, reporting on the hearing and suggesting that the Interior and Related Agencies Subcommittee (chaired by Yates) of the Appropriations Committee allocate additional, new funds to NEH's Office of Preservation, to enable direct support for filming activities beginning in 1988. The question of Cheney's perceived resistance to additional funds was widely discussed.

While it seemed likely that, from the Reagan administration point of view, an initiative such as that proposed should be discouraged (i.e., Cheney could have been urged or perhaps directed by the Office of Management and Budget to resist something that would increase the budget), it also was possible that she philosophically opposed rapid escalation of federal spending—throwing dollars at problems. On the other hand, Cheney had clearly become deeply engaged in the challenge offered by endangered books and was proud of NEH's contribution to its resolution. Thus CPA members advised the legislators that Cheney was correct that much needed to be done to build infrastructure, but that some of

the major libraries with established preservation programs and significant collections could readily expand their filming activities, while other libraries were continuing to build their capacities.

Shortly after the hearing, the CLR-NEH-Mellon film *Slow Fires: On Preservation of the Human Record* premiered at the Library of Congress. The film, which was prepared in half-hour and one-hour versions (the shorter considerably crisper in tone) is most compelling in its treatment of the brittle book problem; it seems to have been useful in persuading Congressional staff and the legislators themselves of the seriousness and urgency of the problem. The film was broadcast nationally by PBS in December 1987.

In April 1987, at the request of Representative Yates' staff, the National Humanities Alliance (NHA) provided the Congressman with estimates of the number of books that could be preserved on microfilm, using expanded NEH Office of Preservation dollars. The figures developed showed that 20,500 books could be filmed for each million dollars added to NEH's budget. Yates then used the NHA estimates to request a capability statement from Cheney, which was provided on May 13, 1987. Cheney objected to restricting the augmented activities to brittle books, but also provided estimates for up to an additional $4 million, a doubling of Office of Preservation activity.

In June, when the House bill was marked up, the budget was so tight that Yates added only $500,000 for preservation, and even that amount was transferred from another line item (Humanities in Libraries) in the NEH budget, rather than added as new money. Owing in part to appeals from Senator Pell to Chairman Robert C. Byrd (D-WV) and James McClure (R-ID), the ranking minority member, the Senate supported the House's rather modest increase.

The Final Push

The final push to secure major federal participation in the brittle books program occurred in 1988. While other agencies were active in preservation, NEH rapidly emerged as the leading agency for libraries and archives across the country, and the unquestioned choice to administer new resources to address the problem of brittle books. Likewise, consensus was reached among major libraries, scholarly and higher-education organizations, the Library of Congress, and NEH on a core plan to save a minimum of three million at-risk volumes, and the institutional mechanisms to begin this massive project were put in place.

At the March 17, 1988 regular hearing of the Yates subcommittee on NEH's FY-89 budget request, Patricia Battin (President of the Commission on Preservation and Access since August 1987 and formerly a vice-president of Columbia University) appeared as a witness representing ARL and NHA. Battin testified on the brittle books plan developed by CPA that would save three million books over twenty years and coordinate with the Library of Congress plan to save an additional one million books over the same period. In April, in response to a request from Yates, NEH developed a capability statement assessing the immediate and long-range funding requirements for a full response to the CPA plan.

The NEH plan was remarkably flexible in that it made provision for the many preparatory and other indirect costs associated with filming and (presumably with Yates' agreement and to Cheney's delight) gave attention to other areas of interest to NEH, such as the U.S. Newspaper Program and conservation training. In terms of budget projections for NEH's Office of Preservation, the plan was unprecedented in its decade: beginning with a jump to $12.5 million in FY-90 (from $4.5 million in FY-88), funding levels were to increase yearly until a level of $20.3 million was reached in FY-93. The plan, presented in the form of a letter from Cheney to Yates, also asserted that

> the proper federal role in this area should continue to be a limited one. The major roles must be played by state and local governments, foundations, professional groups and organizations, and the libraries, archives, and other repositories that hold endangered materials.[12]

NEH's capability statement served as the central focus for a special hearing convened by Representative Yates on April 21, 1988, which, in sympo-

sium fashion, brought together an extraordinary group of knowledgeable individuals from libraries, foundations, federal agencies, and other institutions concerned with preservation issues. Lynne Cheney (accompanied by George F. Farr, Jr., the director of NEH's Office of Preservation), James H. Billington, Patricia Battin, Warren J. Haas, William G. Bowen, and many others discussed the brittle books problem from three vantage points: (1) The new NEH/CPA plan for large-scale filming of three million volumes over twenty years; (2) the Library of Congress' efforts to develop a feasible mass deacidification process; and (3) issues surrounding the publication of books of potential lasting value on "permanent" paper.

A major outcome of the hearing was the recognition that libraries, foundations, and other organizations were ready to move ahead on the filming plan, and that NEH was both in agreement with the general plan and prepared to handle effectively a rapid increase in federal funds for the effort. Other important points to emerge from the hearing included:

> Three million volumes should be a minimum goal; efforts should be made to save the full ten million volumes estimated to be at risk in American libraries.
>
> Similarly, if the three million volumes could be saved in ten or fifteen years (rather than twenty), this should be done. The impediments lay in the funding, not in actual capacity to preserve the materials.
>
> Commission on Preservation and Access estimates of costs were for filming only: Congress should be aware that universities and foundations would continue to provide substantial contributions to preservation, but that it is not realistic to expect those institutions to be able to find all the funds to support the filming at the new intensified levels.
>
> Technological and other improvements are likely to lower some of the cost estimates as the project proceeds.
>
> Materials saved on microfilm will be available for inexpensive reproduction in film and other

media. In this way, it will be possible, as Warren J. Haas put it, "to transform cultural assets acquired over many years by a relatively small number of institutions into a truly national asset that will be available to all in the nation who have need of them, regardless of their communities or affiliations."[13]

In the weeks after the hearing, a number of steps were taken to broaden further understanding of preservation and brittle books among the legislators and their staff, including screenings of *Slow Fires* on both channels of C-Span (Congressional television). Representative Yates and his colleagues on the House Appropriations Committee included the full first year funding, as outlined by NEH. The Senate concurred, and the expanded NEH Office of Preservation moved swiftly into action.

The momentum of the initiative has been maintained. By mid-1991, the Commission on Preservation and Access estimated that 342,000 volumes had already been filmed or were in the process of being filmed during that fiscal year, through the NEH project. The projected step increases for the Office of Preservation were met for each of the first three years. In 1991 with a budget of $22,581,000, the renamed NEH Division of Preservation and Access has grown to be the third largest grant-making unit of NEH. Other preservation initiatives have followed, including a major effort to stabilize collections of material culture in museums that is also administered by NEH. However, it was the brittle books initiative that awakened federal policy makers as well as many others to the stake the nation has in preserving its cultural and intellectual heritage.

NOTES

1. "An Act Making Appropriations for the Department of the Interior and Related Agencies for the Fiscal Year Ending September 30, 1989 and Other Purposes," H.R. 4867. September 27, 1988, in *United States Statutes at Large, Containing the Laws and Concurrent Resolution Enacted During the Sec-*

ond Session of the One-Hundredth Congress of the United States of America, 1988, and Proclamations, vol. 102, pl. 2 (Washington, D.C.: U.S. Government Printing Office, 1990).

2. Chandru J. Shahani and William K. Wilson, "Preservation of Libraries and Archives," in *Preserving Knowledge: The Case for Alkaline Paper* (Washington, D.C.: Association of Research Libraries, 1990), 241.

3. Shahani and Wilson, 242.

4. I am grateful to the Council on Library Resources and the Commission on Preservation and Access for making available files on legislation, the 1984–86 Committee on Preservation and Access, and other background materials. The presentation of CLR's development of the preservation issue in this article is based upon those mostly unpublished materials.

5. Ronald Berman, *Culture & Politics* (Lanham, Md.: University Press of America, 1984), 33–35.

6. National Endowment for the Humanities, *Twentieth Annual Report, 1985*, 95.

7. *Scholarly Communication; The Report of the National Enquiry* (Baltimore: Johns Hopkins University Press, 1979), 155–57.

8. U.S. Congress, House Committee on Education and Labor, *Oversight Hearing on the Problem of 'Brittle Books' in Our Nation's Libraries: Hearing before the Subcommittee on Postsecondary Education of the Committee on Education and Labor, U.S. House of Representatives*, 100th Cong., 1st sess., March 3, 1987, 1–2.

9. Ibid., 30.

10. Ibid., 38.

11. Ibid., 21–23.

12. U.S. Congress, House Committee on Appropriations, *Department of the Interior and Related Agencies Appropriations for 1989-Part II: Hearings before the Subcommittee on the Department of Interior and Related Agencies*, 100th Cong., 2d sess., March 7, 21, 22; April 20, 21, 1988, 441.

13. Ibid., 514–15.

JOHN HENRY MERRYMAN

"Art Systems and Cultural Policy"

Art, Antiquity and Law *15.2 (July 2010)*.

INDEED, IT WOULD be hard to overestimate the importance of the private collector in the life of the American art museum.[1]

American art museums are unique in the world. … [T]he private sector, not the operation of the state, brought these institutions into being… Generally speaking, in contrast to American museums, the European museum is in every sense a public institution.[2]

The first part of this article describes the unique American art system and contrasts it with art systems in other countries. The second part describes what I call the "New Cultural Policy" and its growing impact on the American art system. We begin with the notion of an art system.

An "art system" is a social construct that includes art players, art supporters and a paradigm.[3] In the visual arts, the players are people and institutions whose lives are centrally concerned with works of art: principally artists, collectors, dealers and auction houses, museums, art historians, ethnologists and archaeologists. Supporters (the interested public, patrons, foundations, corporations and the State) provide moral and material support to the players. The paradigm is the underlying set of assumptions and attitudes that direct the ways players and supporters think and act.

Two contrasting paradigms dominate the world's visual art systems: public and private. In the public paradigm, the visual arts are a governmental responsibility. The government trains and subsidizes artists. The government establishes and funds museums and controls their programs and operations. Collectors and the art trade live and operate in a state regulatory environment. If they are permitted to possess and deal in important works they are subject to government restrictions. Mistreatment of an important work of art is a criminal offense.[4] Owners must reg-

ister major works and inform government authorities when they are to be sold or moved. Their owners may not export them without government permission.[5] During the twentieth century, many public paradigm nations enacted nationalization laws declaring that works of art and other cultural objects are property of the State or the People.[6]

In the private paradigm, artists learn to make art and achieve recognition without governmental support or certification. Private dealers and auctioneers sell and collectors acquire, enjoy and dispose of works of art, including major works of great cultural importance, without governmental supervision or assent. Art museums are private institutions founded and sustained by collectors and supporters. They are self-governing, with self-perpetuating boards of trustees that are dominated by collectors. Their decisions and operations are largely free of government supervision or control.

One system paradigm builds down from the government; the other builds up from a base of individual collectors. In one, art decision-making power and responsibility are concentrated in the State; in the other the power and responsibility are widely dispersed among the players and supporters. One is hierarchical; the other is coordinate. One is nourished by state funds; the other is nourished by private wealth.

Every existing visual art system differs from every other in some important respects, and none of them strictly conforms to either paradigm.[7] Most art systems, however, favor one or the other and can fairly be characterized either as publicly oriented with private variations or fundamentally private with public variations. In most nations the visual art systems are in this sense "public,"[8] as they are in the United Nations, the European Union, the Council of Europe and other international organizations.[9] The American art system is different.

The American Art System

No other country has anything like our system of cultural patronage, which indiscriminately mixes private and public monies, direct and indirect subsidies, and funding by agencies at every level of government. The system is a fair reflection of the American wariness of—and inexperience with—official arts patronage.[10]

The United States is the most prominent, perhaps the only, true example of a basically private art system. The government does not provide professional training or financial support to visual artists.[11] Most American art museums, including most of the most important ones, are private institutions, mainly funded by private donations and self-generated income (from admission fees, museum stores and restaurants, the sale of exhibition catalogs and copyright permission fees).[12] Their collections consist principally of objects donated by collectors or purchased with monetary gifts and bequests from collectors and other private players and supporters.[13] Collectors typically build their collections through art market transactions and in this sense are dependent on the existence of dealers and auction houses.[14] Collectors and the art trade have until recently been unregulated,[15] and they still are free to trade in and export virtually all forms of art, including antiquities found on private land.

American art museums compare favorably with those in other First World nations in their number and variety, in the richness of their collections, in the quality of their exhibitions and publications, in the extent of their outreach to the public[16] and in the prodigality of their finances. Any attempt at comparative evaluation of the two kinds of art systems, however, would be hopelessly complicated by the ways in which each of them varies from its paradigm.[17]

We can, however, describe and evaluate the principal ways in which the American art system varies from the private paradigm. The most commonly mentioned American deviations from the private art system paradigm are the existence of important governmental museums, direct governmental support through the National Endowments for the Arts and the Humanities and other federal and state govern-

ment programs, and indirect subsidies to collectors and museums through the tax system.

Governmental Museums. Although most American art museums are private non-profit entities, important governmental museums also exist at the federal and local levels. Most of them, however, were originally established at the instigation of, and endowed with gifts of art and money by, private collectors. As examples, at the federal government level the Smithsonian Institution was established by a legacy from James Smithson (an Englishman), the National Gallery of Art was endowed by Andrew Mellon and the Hirshorn Museum by Joseph Hirshorn. At the local level, San Francisco maintains three privately endowed governmental art museums: the DeYoung Museum, established and endowed by M. H. de Young; the Legion of Honor Museum, of which Alma de Bretteville Spreckels was the principal benefactor; and the Asian Art Museum, established with major gifts from Avery Brundage.

Even though they are government owned and supported, these museums live in an art system that is dominated by private museums, with which they compete for acquisitions, for travelling shows, for professional staff, for trustees, for individual and corporate donations and government and foundation grants, and for public attention and attendance. This has led government museums to adopt attributes of the private art system paradigm. They have governing boards that include private collectors and supporters, as well as ex officio government official members.[18] They establish private support organizations to encourage gifts and to enlist volunteers who help perform a variety of other support functions.[19] The directors and professional staff of these museums identify with their private museum counterparts and participate with them in the Association of Art Museum Directors (AAMD), the Association of Art Museum Curators and the American Association of Museums (AAM), which themselves are private associations.

Direct Public Support for the Visual Arts. The United States Government has never had a ministry of culture, but it does have the National Endowment for the Arts (NEA) and the National Endowment for the Humanities (NEH),[20] which were established in 1965.[21] Reading its self-description, one might assume that the NEA, in particular, is a major player in the American visual art system:

> The National Endowment for the Arts is the largest annual funder of the arts in the United States. An independent federal agency, the National Endowment for the Arts is the official arts organization of the United States government. ... The Arts Endowment has made America a better place to live. Before the establishment of the National Endowment for the Arts in 1965, the arts were limited mostly to a few big cities. The Arts Endowment has helped create regional theater, opera, ballet, symphony orchestras, museums and other art organizations that Americans now enjoy. In its 40-year history, the National Endowment for the Arts has awarded more than 120,000 grants that have brought art to Americans in communities large and small.[22]

Actually, however, the NEA, with its annual budget of less than $150 million for all of the arts[23], is a minor force in the American visual arts system (although it may have had a more substantial impact on other arts, particularly dance, music and theatre).[24] Its influence is trivial by comparison with the activity of collectors and the art trade in the primary and secondary art markets[25] and the value of charitable gifts to museums.[26] The NEA's greatest impact may be symbolic: it represents to a world accustomed to ministries of culture that the United States, too, officially recognizes and supports the arts.[27]

When it created the NEA Congress instructed it to give each state $50,000 to study the feasibility of establishing an "arts council". From this modest beginning, with continuing funding under the NEA and other sources, arts councils have multiplied at the state and local levels.[28] The federal government also provides direct support to art museums through the Institute of Museum and Library Services (IMLS)[29] and the Art and Artifacts Indemnity Act.[30]

Tax Incentives. Since it was established in 1917 the charitable deduction has been a significant feature of the American federal and state income and death tax systems. It provides that the value of a gift to a qualifying nonprofit institution[31] may be deducted from the donor's taxable income (not from the tax) or, if the charitable gift is testamentary, from the donor's taxable estate. Income from museum income-producing activities, such as museum stores, is exempt from income taxation. Museum land and buildings are typically exempt from local property taxes.

Such favorable tax treatment, of which the indirect subsidy to collectors and museums from the charitable deduction is particularly significant, and is generally agreed to be a major factor in the considerable growth of American museum collections and facilities. The charitable deduction is criticized by some scholars but is energetically defended by its beneficiaries, and its life does not at this writing seem to be in danger.[32] Other major nations have flirted with the charitable deduction,[33] but "In the United States tax expenditures are a significant source of indirect aid to the arts, whereas in the other countries their impact is marginal."[34]

One very important effect of the charitable deduction is to give art collectors and other donors the power to affect how public funds, in the form of tax expenditures, will be spent to build, operate and acquire works of art for private museums:

> deductibility for tax purposes transfers decision-making power regarding the allocation of resources in matters of public concern from government to givers. ... the prevalent American view of subsidy in this form appears to be that it is the ultimate decentralization of choice regarding who and what is subsidized. Americans generally see this not as the rich deciding on who and what receives subsidy at government expense, but as the only practical way to shift the decision-making from bureaucracies and politicians to a vastly larger number of individuals.[35]

This "ultimate decentralization of choice" to individuals and away from "bureaucracies and politicians" is combined with an analogous "decentralization of choice" to private art museums, which are for most purposes autonomous institutions. Each such museum is a kind of art mini-state whose policies and practices are governed by its own independent board of trustees, which is typically dominated by collectors and is generally unburdened by government regulation.[36]

One possible way to describe this aspect of the American art system is to say it shows that the United States lacks a national art policy, to which one commentator responded that "to have no policy is to have a policy," adding: "we have made a decision…to leave to private and local institutions the determination of the decisions most overtly affecting the creation and conduct of cultural institutions."[37]

Thus the American art system might be summarily contrasted with public art systems along two principal dimensions. First, the American system strongly favors private choice over government choice.[38] By encouraging individual donations to museums through the charitable deduction the US government not only permits but actually, if indirectly, subsidizes choices (made by art collectors, the art market and art museums.) Second, the American art system exemplifies an extreme dispersal of choice over the selection, acquisition, possession, care and use of works of art, as contrasted with the centralization of choice in public art systems.[39]

Preservation, Truth and Access. There is general international acceptance in the art world of the notion that works of art are part, in the eloquent words of the 1954 Hague Convention,[40] of "the cultural heritage of all mankind". Elsewhere I have attempted to translate this grandiose notion into the social concerns of visual arts policy as "preservation, truth and access."[41] Briefly, society has an interest in preserving works of art[42], in learning from them and in making them accessible to scholars for study and to the public for education and enjoyment. How well does the American system's widespread dispersal of private choice serve such social concerns?

It might appear that the American system leaves works of art at risk by permitting dealers and auctioneers to sell and collectors to acquire, own and dispose of them without significant official oversight. Great works that are monuments of art history may be held in private hands without any legal requirement, other than the artist's moral right, of care in their treatment. Nor is there any legal obligation that privately held art works be made available for study by scholars or accessible for public enjoyment.

The anemic American version of the moral right[43] enables the artist, during her lifetime, to assert her interest in the integrity and paternity of the work of art after it leaves her hands.[44] The only other American legal restriction on the treatment of works of art in the hands of an owner other than the artist is California's Cultural and Artistic Creations Preservation Act[45], which states that "The Legislature hereby finds and declares that there is a public interest in preserving the integrity of cultural and artistic creations." The statute gives non-profit art organizations standing to "commence an action for injunctive relief to preserve or restore the integrity of a work of fine art" if it is "of recognized quality, and of substantial public interest." A search found no application of this statute in any decision by any court.

In *Playing Darts with a Rembrandt*[46] Professor Sax suggested that the presence of important works in the stocks of American dealers and auction houses and in private collections exposed them to excessive risks and unduly limited access by scholars and the public. He described a number of troubling events and practices[47] and concluded that "Conventional notions of ownership and dominion are unable to provide adequately for public access, openness, and preservation"[48] and that the fate of such objects "should not be at the mercy of purely private will."[49]

Sax provided no examples of American owners actually playing darts with their Rembrandts. He discussed Graham Sutherland's portrait of Winston Churchill, which Churchill and his wife detested and eventually burned; the unfinished Diego Rivera mural demolished by the Rockefellers, who had commissioned it; the French collector Groult who, a French dealer said a collector friend told him (double hearsay), had threatened to burn his collection, but didn't; a Toulouse-Lautrec painting that the same French dealer said another dealer told him that the previous French owner had shot with a gun (double hearsay again); and the Japanese collector Ryoei Saito, who said he wanted his Renoir and van Gogh to be cremated with him, but later said it was a joke.[50] There are of course many examples of the deliberate or negligent destruction of art works[51], but what most of them show is that works of art are in much greater danger from war, political and religious zeal, and vandalism than from collectors, dealers or museums.[52]

It is also true that, as Sax stated, American possessors of important works of art commonly make them available for exhibition and study. Such exposure provides prestige to the lender and adds value to works that are lent, shown and published. At any moment one will find a variety of important works from private American collections exhibited at major museums in the United States and abroad. Occasional museum exhibitions consist entirely of objects from single private collections.[53] Still, American collectors have no legal obligation to make the contents of their collections known or to make them available for scholars to study or the public to enjoy.

Deaccessioning. In public art systems, works in museum collections are commonly classified as "inalienable public property", with the rigorous prohibition on deaccessioning that such a classification implies. American museums, on the contrary, are relatively free to remove and sell or trade works from their collections. There are no legal restraints on deaccessioning, although both the American Association of Museums[54] and the Association of Art Museum Directors[55] have adopted influential policies limiting the practice. Neither policy, however, requires that a deaccessioned work go to another museum or that it remain within the United States. Typically the work will be publicly sold at auction free of such restrictions and may be acquired by a foreign private collection.

To establish an American regime of governmental authority over important works of art in private hands would raise a number of formidable issues, and it is difficult to imagine the creation of such a regime that would not significantly compromise the private character of the American art system. In Sax's words: "Any effort to find solutions…is complicated by the difficulty of finding a substitute for the precepts that govern ordinary ownership."[56] Rather than propose a legal response to his book's concern, Sax finally rested with his notion of "The Collector as Steward"—a sort of *noblesse oblige*:

> The model is the responsible collector who does not destroy and who does not conceal his treasures… .

Collectors have long embraced the idea that owners of cultural treasures are only temporary custodians. They exact great personal benefits from their holdings, and often profit economically as well in other ways. But they welcome experts and artists who want to study their holdings. They are commonly willing to lend their most important works to responsible institutions that serve the general public and through their philanthropy (often subsidized by the state) many, perhaps most, of the greatest objects eventually find their way into public institutions… . As one author put it, "some people feel that they are no more than the fortunate, if provisional, trustees of certain works of art, having no right to deprive others who appreciate beautiful objects as much as they do themselves."[57]

Sax is right in arguing that most collectors (and dealers and museum personnel) act responsibly toward the works of art they possess, but there are occasional outliers.[58] Perhaps it should be possible for responsibly interested parties to act to control them. California's Cultural and Artistic Creations Preservation Act[59] provides a model that, suitably tweaked, might provide a workable private system of protection for threatened works of art, but that must be the subject of another article.

When Public Art Systems Go Wrong. What happens when public art systems go wrong? The twentieth-century examples of art under the Nazis and in the Soviet empire are still fresh in human memory as this is written.[60] In Germany, works by Jewish artists were purged from the museums. The notorious Entartete Kunst (Degenerate Art) exhibition of 730 modern works by 112 artists, insultingly displayed with vulgar captions, opened in June 1937, and the related confiscations continued into October of that year, resulting in the seizure and removal of 5,000 paintings and 12,000 graphic works[61] from public and private collections. Artists in the Third Reich were expected to produce works that supported Nazi militarism while projecting an idealized version of German history and culture, a racially pure country, depicting Jews as inhuman and inferior. Non-conforming artists were forbidden to make art and were not allowed to possess art materials.[62]

In the USSR the State was at first less preoccupied with art. Russians had been prominent early collectors of the works of Matisse, Picasso and other foreign artists, and the works of contemporary Russian Suprematist artists were admired and sought after by foreign collectors. Lunacharsky, the first cultural commissar, left Soviet artists free to pursue their own artistic interests, and he cooperated in planning an exhibition of contemporary Russian art in Berlin in 1922. In the same year, however, an "Association of Artists of the Revolution" announced that it was their duty to "perpetuate the Revolution, the greatest event in history, in artistic documents." In subsequent years the evolution in policy increasingly supported state use of artists and art as propaganda tools in the pursuit of revolutionary goals. In 1932 all other artistic organizations were officially disbanded and a lavishly supported official union of artists controlled by Communist factions took their place. "Socialist realism" was the officially dictated style, while art of other kinds was fiercely repressed.[63]

This kind of recent history makes Americans skeptical about state control of the art system. Nazi Germany and the USSR are of course extreme examples, but they were state-run art systems before they became extreme. In America, most of the hundreds of independent private art museums and the thousands of wealthy and influential collectors and other active supporters who currently run the art system would certainly oppose any effort to appropriate it for political purposes or to impose official taste. Or so we would like to believe.[64] That belief has come to seem less realistic since the advent of what I call the New Cultural Policy.

The New Cultural Policy[65]

The American art system has historically flourished in an art market free of significant import and export impediments in a political climate favoring private choice. Since the end of the Second World War and the creation of UNESCO, however, a new kind of politics has taken shape in the cultural property world. National art systems are under growing pressure to conform to an evolving set of international expecta-

tions. These expectations are expressed in UNESCO's international legal instruments[66], in policies adopted by international organizations and professional societies[67], in the practices of major art system players, in positions taken by parties in international cultural property disputes, and in the growing body of cultural property scholarship.[68] I here refer to the sum of these expectations as the New Cultural Policy (NCP).

The energy that drives the NCP is supplied by three principal sources: the cultural heritage policies of source nations, the professional concerns of archaeologists and ethnologists, and UNESCO's own cultural program. These components are interrelated and mutually reinforcing: most UNESCO member nations limit or prohibit the export of antiquities, ethnographic objects and/or works of art.[69] Interested professional groups, most prominently archaeologists and ethnologists, actively support such controls.[70] Together, these nations and groups strongly influence the content and direction of UNESCO's cultural program.

The 1970 *UNESCO Convention*[71], a basic component of the NCP, encourages each State Party to decide what to designate as "protected" cultural property and what restraints to place on its "import, export and transfer of ownership."[72] Any action contrary to those restraints is, under the Convention, "illicit". Other States Parties to the Convention are obliged to recognize and enforce such restraints on the movement of cultural property so designated. This gives every source nation a "blank check"[73]: whatever restrictions it chooses to adopt create obligations for the other States Parties.

So encouraged, source nation governments have not merely limited the export of objects of major importance that might qualify as "national cultural treasures."[74] They have declared State ownership and prohibited the export of wholesale categories of artworks and antiquities, including many that could not by any objective measure be considered "cultural treasures."[75] Each year, for example, thousands of antiquities are newly discovered in Greece.[76] The great majority of them are surplus objects, meriting no space in already well-supplied Greek museums or study centers, and are consigned to storage. There, since Greek law prohibits the export of all antiquities, they remain unavailable to collectors, museums, scholars and viewers throughout the world. Greece is only an example; other source nations have adopted similarly retentive policies.[77]

In 2008 the Association of Art Museum Directors, bowing to NCP pressure, issued a policy statement[78] on acquisitions that crystallized a group of related NCP propositions and affirmed the centrality of the 1970 UNESCO Convention. The statement:

> Recognizes the 1970 UNESCO Convention as providing the most pertinent threshold date for the application of more rigorous standards to the acquisition of archeological material and ancient art. Widely accepted internationally, the 1970 UNESCO Convention helps create a unified set of expectations for museums, sellers, and donors.
>
> States that AAMD members normally should not acquire a work unless research substantiates that the work was outside its country of probable modern discovery before 1970 or was legally exported from its probable country of modern discovery after 1970.[79]
>
> Provides a specific framework for members to evaluate the circumstances under which a work that does not have a complete ownership history dating to 1970 may be considered for acquisition.

In its reference in this statement to "sellers and donors" the AAMD appropriately acknowledged the central importance of these players to the American art system. The NCP, however, looks less kindly on collectors, dealers and the art and antiquities market. The first candid expression of this antipathy appeared in UNESCO's 1976 *Recommendation Concerning the International Exchange of Cultural Property*,[80] which disapproved of international trade in cultural objects because:

> the international circulation of cultural property is still largely dependent on the activities of self-seeking parties and so tends to lead to speculation which causes the price of such property to rise, making it inaccessible to poorer countries and institutions while at the same time encouraging the spread of illicit trading.[81]

Many of the surplus cultural objects held by source nations would be welcomed to the licit international market by museums, collectors, the art trade and the interested public.[82] The *Recommendation*, however, does not go there. Instead, UNESCO has interpreted its constitutional mandate to support "international exchange" of cultural property[83] to exclude market transactions. In the NCP the licit international movement of cultural property is restricted to governments and "cultural institutions" that deal only with each other:

> "International exchange" shall be taken to mean any transfer of ownership, use or custody of cultural property between States or cultural institutions in different countries—whether it takes the form of the loan, deposit, sale or donation of such property—carried out under such conditions as may be agreed [upon] between the parties concerned.[84]

To an American reader, this interpretation of "international exchange" seems oddly divorced from reality. There is no place in it for collectors or an active art trade and no scope for a licit market in cultural property. There is no recognition of the roles of collectors and dealers in supporting artists and promoting their work, in building private collections that ultimately enrich museums, and in pioneering the collection of objects that eventually are recognized for their cultural importance.[85] Nor is there any recognition of the utility of the market as an efficient transactional arena[86] and a provider of price indicators of value.

The 2001 UNESCO *Convention on Protection of the Underwater Cultural Heritage*[87] takes UNESCO's anti-market bias to an extreme. Article 2 (7) of the Convention states in its entirety: "Underwater cultural heritage shall not be commercially exploited."

This startling provision is elucidated in Rule 2 of the rules annexed to the Convention:

> The commercial exploitation of underwater cultural heritage for trade or speculation or its irretrievable dispersal is fundamentally incompatible with the protection and proper management of underwater cultural heritage. Underwater cultural

heritage shall not be traded, sold, bought or bartered as commercial goods.

The statement that market transactions are "fundamentally incompatible" with the protection and proper management of underwater cultural heritage expresses an NCP position that appears to be "fundamentally incompatible" with the American art system.

> The NCP impinges on the American art system in a number of ways. It has entered popular culture in a form that resonates throughout the art system. The popular media and public opinion generally accept as self-evident the dubious premise that cultural objects belong in nations of origin. Major American museums have felt it necessary to accommodate foreign demands for the return of important objects in their collections, and the Association of Art Museum Directors has thought it prudent to adopt the restrictive policy statement shown above. The NCP's most significant American effect, however, is a new and growing U.S. federal government regulatory presence in the importation of cultural property.[88]

That history began in the late 1960s, amid growing hemispheric concern about the violation of archaeological sites in Mexico and Central America.[89] The United States participated centrally in drafting and promulgating the 1970 UNESCO Convention and in 1972 was the first major market nation to ratify it.[90] There then began a lengthy legislative process in Congress that eventually produced the 1983 *Convention on Cultural Property Implementation Act* (CPIA).[91] The CPIA established a procedure and an administrative apparatus within the United States Information Agency (later transferred to the Department of State) through which foreign States Parties to the Convention could apply for the application of import restrictions by the United States in order to "deter the pillage of archaeological or ethnological materials" in their territories.[92]

While that legislation was forming but before its enactment, the decisions in *U.S. v. Hollinshead*[93] and *U.S. v. McClain*[94] established an entirely different basis, totally independent of the 1970 UNESCO Convention and the CPIA, for American enforcement of foreign cultural property nationalization laws. Those cases held that federal courts would enforce those laws by treating the importation of cultural objects removed contrary to their provisions as violations of the U.S. National Stolen Property Act.[95] Then in 1977, with an 'Advisory Memorandum' on the subject of pre-Columbian art and relying on the McClain doctrine and prior legislation[96], on its authority over customs declarations[97] and on its strategic position at ports of entry, U.S. Customs officials began routinely seizing or detaining shipments of suspected cultural objects.[98] And in 2008, in an apparent effort to extend to archaeological sites abroad the reach of a statute enacted to protect archaeological resources on U.S. federal and Indian lands, federal authorities raided four California museums accused of violating the Archaeological Resources Protection Act (ARPA)[99] by importing stolen Ban Chiang culture objects from Thailand.[100]

In these ways the government of the United States, a major market nation and the home of the world's most private, collector-driven art system, with only minimal regulation of the domestic art trade, has become the world's most enthusiastic enforcer of other nations' broadly retentive anti-market legislation and its restrictive implications for American collectors and museums.[101] Ironically, some of the foreign legislation we so enforce, if enacted in the United States, would probably violate the Fifth Amendment's injunction against taking private property for public use without due process and just compensation.[102]

It is possible to view the source of this American enthusiasm for government regulation of the international art and antiquities trade in different ways.[103] Some may simply see it as an obvious way of doing the right thing by helping source nations preserve the human record. Others might see it as reflecting a State Department-based policy calculated to please source nations and build a reservoir of good will toward the United States at little cost. Others may see the McClain invocation of the National Stolen Property Act, the 2008 attempt to make an analogous use of the Archaeological Resources Protection Act, and Customs' expansive interpretation of its own authority as elements of a skillfully engineered end run around the limiting terms of the Cultural Property Implementation Act.[104] Still others might wonder what new directions the federal regulatory regime, now focused on international trade in art and antiquities, may eventually take.

Conclusion

The New Cultural Policy has of course significantly affected the American art system. The licit flow of antiquities and ethnographic objects from abroad has diminished to a trickle. Source nation nationalizations and export controls ensure that collectors and museums wishing to build or upgrade their collections, and the dealers who normally supply them, will have little new licit material to choose from. The licit supply of new collectible material is further reduced by the "guilty until proved innocent" presumption that makes orphans of unprovenanced objects like the Sevso treasure.[105] American museums consequently offer poorer collections for scholars to study and the public to enjoy.[106]

Equally important, under the NCP every acquisition of a foreign antiquity, ethnographic object or work of art has become a potential disaster for the dealer, collector or museum. Museums are particularly vulnerable:

> [A]cquisition today carries significant risks for museums, especially the risks of legal battles, either over civil claims for return or over criminal charges. Museums caught in unlawful possession of antiquities pay a hefty price in terms of reputation and public trust as well as loss of the acquisition funds. The chilling effect of litigation has increased the reliance on loans and has made museums more cautious about accepting antiquities from collectors.[107]

The chilling effect is compounded by the resulting increases in compliance costs and lawyers' fees, which consume museum resources that might otherwise be available for acquisitions, exhibitions and educational programs. The threat of civil or criminal liti-

gation also has a serious distorting effect on acquisitions decisions: "Connoisseurship has been displaced by other considerations,"[108] and the more desirable acquisition may be foregone out of an excess of caution.

Is America's embrace of the New Cultural Policy a good thing? Is it in our interest to support other nations' unbridled cultural nationalism? Are we wise to indulge the antipathy of UNESCO and establishment archaeologists toward collectors, dealers and the art market? What is in it for America?

At a different level, what kind of a world art system should we support? Should we encourage the current NCP sentiment for a world of culturally parochial, retentive nationalist art regimes in which all Greek art treasures remain in or return to Greece, Italian masterpieces and antiquities to Italy, Egyptian antiquities to Egypt, and so on and on? That road ultimately leads to extreme specialization.[109] While Greek museums would hold even more splendid collections of Greek works than they already do, they would contain little else (as is largely true of Greek museums today). Indonesian museums, filled with only indigenous Indonesian art, would be unable to sell excess pieces to support and enrich their collections and unable to diversify them by purchasing, for example, western art. There would be no licit international art market. Private collections, if they were permitted, would be similarly restricted: collectors could only acquire and hold national art and artifacts.

Or should we favor the more cosmopolitan world art system implied by the concept of a 'cultural heritage of all mankind'[110] and by the statement in the preamble of the 1970 UNESCO Convention that:

> the interchange of cultural property among nations for scientific, cultural and educational purposes increases the knowledge of the civilization of Man, enriches the cultural life of all peoples and inspires mutual respect and appreciation among nations.

This leads to art systems in which collectors and museums acquire and show works from a variety of the world's cultures, as do the Louvre, the British Museum and the Metropolitan Museum, among many other universal museums?[111] It also accommodates a reality nicely expressed by classicist Mary Beard: "We may try to regulate the movement of cultural property, but—licit or illicit—we cannot stop it."[112]

In the existing cultural property dialogue in the popular press, in the scholarly literature on cultural heritage, in the halls of UNESCO and in the lobbies of national legislatures and ministries of culture such questions and realities seldom receive serious attention. There is little evidence that ministers of culture in source nations or UNESCO officials in Paris understand the American art system or care about its welfare. They are comfortable with their own public art systems and the positions they hold within them. Nor do our archaeologists show much concern for the interests of American dealers, collectors and museums.

On the contrary, most of the current cultural property "dialogue" is actually a hermetic monologue in which source nation cultural nationalism, the single-minded pursuit of archaeologists' professional goals, and the hostility to collectors and the art market expressed in UNESCO's cultural program combine to support each other. In that monologue, at its worst, American collectors are vilified.[113] Their interests, and those of our museums and art trade, are denigrated or ignored. The major players in our art system are dismissed as "self-seeking parties"[114] whose activities are "fundamentally incompatible"[115] with the New Cultural Policy.

This will not do. The American art system is itself a cultural treasure, a great national resource, unique in the world. Its encounter with the New Cultural Policy raises important questions that require thoughtful consideration. It is time for a genuine cultural property dialogue to begin.[116]

1. Perry T. Rathbone, "Influences of Private Patrons: The Art Museum as an Example", in *The Arts and Public Policy in the United States* 51 (W. McNeil Lowry ed., 1984).

2. Id. at 39–41.

3. This "art system" notion is for many purposes similar to the more familiar 'art world' described by Howard S. Becker in *Art Worlds* (1982). Although they only incidentally use the term in their excellent comparative study, Joan Jeffri and Yu Ding, *Respect for Art: Visual Arts Administration and Management in China and the United States* (2007) cover much of the same ground. Joseph Alsop uses the term "art system" in his remarkable book *The Rare Art Traditions: The History of Art Collecting and Its Linked Phenomena Wherever These Have Appeared* (1982). Alsop's "art system" concept refers to his group of eight "by-products of art". See Alsop at 15–24, passim. Niklas Luhmann, *Art as a Social System* (2000), despite its promising title, turns out to be part of an attempt to "elaborate a theory of society" far removed from the empirical description and comparison of art systems. See Luhmann at 1.

4. See, e.g., Italian Penal Code Art. 733; Paola Poggi, 'La tutela penale dei beni culturali' in *I beni culturali: tra interessi pubblici e privati* 181 (Giovanni Cofrancesco ed., 1996).

5. See John Henry Merryman, 'The Retention of Cultural Property', 21 *U.C. Davis L. Rev.* 122, reprinted in Merryman, *Thinking About the Elgin Marbles: Critical Essays on Cultural Property, Art and Law* 170 (2nd ed. 2009) [hereinafter *Critical Essays*]. For an instructive illustration of governmental supervision of the private art sector in action see the case of *Beyeler v. Italy*, Application No. 33202/96, European Court of Human Rights, Judgment of 5 Jan. 2000, reprinted in John Henry Merryman, Albert E. Elsen & Stephen K. Urice, *Law, Ethics and the Visual Arts* 122 (5th ed. 2007) [hereinafter *LEVA5*].

6. The tendency for source nations to enact such ownership laws accelerated after the *Hollinshead* and *McClain* decisions, cited *infra* note 15, held that the unauthorized removal of cultural property from Guatemala and Mexico, which had such laws, constituted theft subject to the U.S. National Stolen Property Act.

7. "Most museums lie somewhere between the extremes of purely public and purely private museums." Bruno S. Frey & Stephan Meier, "The Economics of Museums" in *Handbook of the Economics of Art and Culture* 1029 (Victor A. Ginsburgh and David Throsby, eds., 2006) [hereinafter *Handbook*].

8. See Frederick Dorian, *Commitment to Culture: Art Patronage in Europe; Its Significance for America* (1964); *The Patron State: Government and the Arts in Europe, North America, and Japan* (Milton C. Cummings, Jr. and Richard S. Katz, eds., 1987); Nicholas M. Pearson, *The State and the Visual Arts: A Discussion of State Intervention in the Visual Arts in Britain, 1760–1981* (1982).

9. "Most industrialized nations and many of the so-called developing ones have cabinet-level ministries of culture. Poland, Denmark, Argentina, Haiti, and France are among the highly diverse examples … The European Economic Community has a Commissioner of Cultural Affairs; and the European ministers of culture meet regularly on a monthly or bi-monthly basis to discuss their differences and possible modes of comparison." Michael Kammen, "Culture and the State in America", 83 *J. of Am. History* 791, 807 (1996).

10. Karl E. Meyer, The Art Museum: Power, Money, Ethics—A Twentieth Century Fund Report 64 (1979).

11. Dick Netzer, 'Cultural Policy: An American View', in *Handbook,* supra note 7, at 1223, 1237. A major exception occurred in the 1930s, during the Great Depression and the New Deal, when the Federal Art Project, a division of the Works Progress Administration, provided employment to more than 5,000 artists. The FAP was terminated in 1939. For an account, see Laura Hapke, *Labor's Canvas: American Working Class History and the WPA Art of the 1930s* (2008). The Alaska Contemporary Art Bank is a more current exception, in that one of its purposes is to "provide support to professional artists in Alaska through purchase of their work." See Alaska State Council on the Arts, Art Bank, http://www.eed.state.ak.us/aksca/gallery_3.htm (last visited Feb. 16, 2010).

12. In J. Mark Davidson Schuster, *Supporting the Arts: An International Comparative Study* (1985), the author compiled statistics and related information from eight nations: Canada, France, Germany, Great Britain, Italy, Netherlands, Sweden and the United States. The author concluded that: "[T]he overall picture is clear. With the exception of the United States, where private support is an extremely important source of funding for the arts, and Canada and Great Britain, where some elements of private support are important, private support from individuals, corporations, or foundations is very small." Id. at 54. Two art museum charts on p. 66 are particularly interesting. One indicates the percentage of museum operating income from private donations and earned income. Italy and France showed none, Great Britain 10%, West Germany 17%, Canada 30%, Sweden 32% and the U.S. nearly 90%. The other chart shows the percentage of operating income from government support. Here that of the U.S. is least, with 13%, while the others range from Sweden's 70% to Italy's and France's 100%. For European Union museums, A Guide to European Museum Statistics by the European Group on Museum Statistics (EGMUS) offers an extremely useful source of data at http://www.ne-mo.org/ fileadmin/Dateien/public/ service/guidemuseumstatistics.pdf (last visited Feb. 16, 2010).

13. See Rachel Derkits, *Fine Art Museums in the United States: A Survey on Acquisitions* (May 2005) (unpublished paper, Stanford Law School) (on file with author). Another source states that "about 80 percent of new acquisitions at American museums now come through donations." Jeremy Kahn, 'Museums Fear Tax Law Changes on Some Donations', *N.Y. Times,* Jan. 13, 2006, available at http://www.nytimes.com/2006/09/13/arts/design/13gift .html (last visited Feb. 16, 2010).

14. In both systems the symbiotic relationship between collectors and dealers has established new fields of collecting that influence artists and are later taken up by art museums. African and Oceanic art, which strongly influenced Matisse, Picasso and the German Expressionists, are the most obvious examples. See Jack Flam, *Matisse: The Man and His Art* 173, 181 (1986); *Picasso and Africa* (Lawrence Madeline and Marilyn Martin eds, 2006). The artists' access to African and Oceanic art was by way of the Trocadero Museum in Paris, founded in 1878 by ethnographer Ernst Hamy and explorer Alphonse Pinart. The sequence seems to have been first the explorers/collectors, next the ethnographic museum, then the artists, and then the art museum. Although controversial, William Rubin, Kirk Varnedoe & Philippe Peltier, *"Primitivism" in 20th Century Art: Affinity of the Tribal*

and the Modern (1984), the exhibition catalog for a 1984 Museum of Modern Art show, is a major scholarly treatment of the crucial influence of the tribal arts on modern painters and sculptors.

15. The decisions in *United States v. Hollinshead*, 495 F. 2d 1154 (9th Cir. 1974) and *United States v. McClain*, 545 F.2d 988 (5th Cir. 1977) and 593 F.2d 658 (5th Cir. 1979); U.S. ratification of the 1970 UNESCO Convention; enactment of the 1983 Cultural Property Implementation Act; and significant expansion of U.S. Customs activities have combined to restrict American collectors, museums and art trade participation in the importing side of the international trade in art and antiquities. Purely internal art world activities in the United States are still relatively unregulated, as are art exports. See discussion of the New Cultural Policy, below.

16. Historically, American museums have been widely admired abroad for their emphasis on education. Thus, after a cross-country tour of American museums in the 1950s, an Austrian art historian and museum educator opined: "the real contribution which America has made in the field of museums lies.., in the creative educational aim of its museums." Ferdinand Eckhardt, "American Museums Seen Through the Eyes of a European", 12 *College Art J.* 131, 133 (1953). Today, however, the contrast is less pronounced, as museums large and small have active education departments and advertise a variety of outreach programs on their websites.

17. Netzer, *supra* note 11; Milton H. Cummings Jr., 'Government and the Arts: An Overview' in *Public Money and the Muse*, 31–79 (Stephen Benedict ed., 1991). One important study calls American museums "half private, half public"; Karl E. Meyer, *The Art Museum: Power, Money, Ethics—A Twentieth Century Fund Report* 43 (1979).

18. For example, at the date of writing the Board of Trustees of the National Gallery of Art includes four *ex officio* members: the Chief Justice of the United States; the Secretary of State; the Secretary of the Treasury; and the Secretary of the Smithsonian Institution, and five "private" members: at this writing, Victoria P. Sant, Sharon Percy Rockefeller, John Wilmerding, Mitchell P. Rales, and Frederick W. Beinecke. Ms. Sant is President of the

Museum and Mr. Wilmerding is Chairman of the Board of Trustees.

19. For example, the Asian Art Museum of San Francisco is supported by the Asian Art Museum Foundation, the Society for Asian Art, the Museum Society, the Museum Society Auxiliary and the Connoisseurs Council, in addition to devoted individuals. Compare the late 20th-century establishment of similar non-governmental support organizations in France (Sociéte des Amis du Louvre and Cercle Louvre Entreprises), Italy (Amici degli Uffizi) and Spain (Fundacion de los Amigos del Museo del Prado).

20. There is some overlap in the programs of the two agencies. In particular, the NEH has helped finance a number of major traveling exhibitions of antiquities and works of art. See National Endowment for the Humanities, Timeline, http://www.neh .gov/whoweare/timeline.html (last visited Feb. 16, 2010).

21. Creation of the NEA and the NEH was opposed by people who saw them as the entering wedge of a cultural ministry that they feared would lead to politicization and bureaucratization of the cultural sector. See e.g., Michael Macdonald Mooney, *The Ministry of Culture: Connections among Art, Money and Politics* (1980); Edward C. Banfield, *The Democratic Muse: Visual Arts and the Public Interest* (1984). "The painter John Sloan said that he would welcome a ministry of culture because then he would know where the enemy was." Michael Kammen, *supra* note 9, at 793. The debate was revived in 1989–90 by Senator Jesse Helms's exploitation of public reaction to offensive works displayed in exhibitions partially funded by the NEA. See id. at 794–813; "Culture and Democracy: Social and Ethical Issues," in *Public Support for the Arts and Humanities* (Andrew Buchwalter, ed., 1992). For an enlightening account of the NEA's trajectory, see Alice Goldfarb Marquis, *Art Lessons: Learning from the Rise and Fall of Public Arts Funding* (1995).

22. National Endowment for the Arts, http://www.nea .gov/about/Facts/AtAGlance.html, (last visited Sept. 30, 2007).

23. The NEA's annual appropriation reached its high of $175,954,680 in 1992, sharply declined to less than $100 million in 1996–2000 (for an explanation of

the decline, see *National Endowment for the Arts v. Finley*, 524 U.S. 569 (1998) and Sullivan, "Subsidies for Indecent Art", 20 *Legal Times* No. 44 (Mar. 30, 1998)) and then began to recover, reaching $124,561,84 in 2007. Americans for the Arts, www.AmericansForTheArts.org (last visited Feb. 16, 2010). The NEA is required by law to pass on 40% of its appropriation to state arts councils. It divides the remainder of its appropriation among fourteen of what it calls 'disciplines', including Arts Education; Dance; Design; Folk and Traditional Arts; Literature; Local Arts Agencies; Media; Museums; Music; Musical Theater; Opera; Presenting; Theatre; and Visual Arts.

24. The role and influence of the NEA are accurately summarised in Netzer, *supra* note 11, at 1229–33.

25. Data published by the U.S. Department of Commerce show that American art dealers had sales of well over $4 billion in 2002. U.S. Department of Commerce, "Other Miscellaneous Store Retainers: 2002", *2002 Economic Census, Retail Trade* (Oct. 2004). This figure does not include sales at art auctions or sales by private dealers, each of which would alone have far exceeded the total NEA appropriation for the visual arts for that year.

26. Private giving to the arts, culture and humanities category totaled $13.99 billion in 2004, according to a Congressional Research Service Report to Congress: Susan Boren, *Arts and Humanities: Background on Funding*, Order Code RS20287 (Feb. 16, 2006).

27. The NEA's most visible public art impact came from its "Art in Public Places" program (APP), a matching grant activity that resulted in some remarkable outdoor art, beginning with the Alexander Calder "La Grande Vitesse" sculpture in Grand Rapids, Michigan. National Endowment for the Arts, "Initial Public Arts Project Becomes a Landmark", http://www.nea.gov/about/40th/grandrapids.html (last visited Feb. 16, 2010). Many other APP projects, however, were less successful, and eventually the APP program was terminated. Its decline and fall are vividly described in Marquis, above, note 21, at 191 *ff*. Cf Ronald Lee Fleming, "Public Art for the Public", *Public Interest*, April 1, 2005, at 55.

28. Marquis, *supra* note 21, at 86*ff*. describes the creation and rapid growth of the 56 state and jurisdictional arts councils. Their representation organization is the National Assembly of State Arts Agencies, http://www.nasaa-arts.org (last visited Feb. 16, 2010). Nina Friedlander Gibbons, *The Community Arts Council Movement* (1982) describes the local arts agency movement.

29. The IMLS was established by the Museum and Library Services Act of 1996, which brought under one roof the former Institute of Museum Services and the former Library Programs Office. The IMLS's mission is "to create strong libraries and museums ... work[ing] at the national level and in coordination with state and local organizations to sustain heritage, culture, and knowledge; enhance learning and innovation; and support professional development." The IMLS is the primary source of federal funds for the nation's libraries and museums, although funds are not equally distributed between the two categories. In each of the last ten years, the IMLS' annual appropriations to museums have been only 13–15% of its appropriations to libraries. In fiscal year 2008, for example, libraries received $199,963,000, while the 17,500 museums shared only $30,445,000.

30. The 1975 Art and Artifacts Indemnity Act authorizes the Federal Council on the Arts and Humanities to reduce the costs of insurance for American museums borrowing objects from abroad as part of traveling exhibitions. As of 2008, the NEA, which administers the indemnity program, estimates that the indemnity agreements have aided 900 exhibitions and saved American museums nearly $250 million in insurance premiums since its inception. In December 2007 the Act was amended to establish a parallel domestic indemnity program. As a result, up to $5 billion of total coverage is now available for domestic exhibitions taking place at one time, with a maximum indemnity of $750 million for a single exhibition.

31. The federal charitable deduction provision is Internal Revenue Code [section]501(c)(3). The deduction applies to gifts to other cultural (music, dance, literary, etc.) and to religious, educational, health and social welfare non-profits as well as to the visual arts. Stanley Surrey, in *Pathways to Tax*

Reform (1973), established the practice of treating taxes foregone by the charitable deduction as a "tax expenditure". There is general agreement among economists that the tax expenditure for the arts in the U.S. is substantially greater than direct government support. Attempts to calculate the exact size of the tax expenditure, however, have provided widely varying results. Thus O'Hare and Feld, "Indirect Aid to the Arts", 471 *Annals of the Am. Academy of Political and Soc. Sci.* 132–43 (1984), estimated the tax expenditure for the arts in 1973 to have been $458 million. Economist Herbert Stein estimated the tax expenditure on the arts to be $1.25 billion a year in 1997. Herbert Stein, "Art & Tax Breaks," *N.Y. Times*, July 3, 1997, at A22. Economist Tyler Cowen estimated the tax expenditure to be $26–41 billion in Tyler Cowen, *Good & Plenty: The Creative Successes of American Arts Funding* 34 (2006). For an excellent discussion of the charitable deduction see J. Mark Schuster, "Tax Incentives in Cultural Policy" in *Handbook, supra* note 7, at 1254*ff*.

32. Alan L. Feld, Michael O'Hare and J. Mark Davidson Schuster, *Patrons Despite Themselves: Taxpayers and Arts Policy* (1983). For additional reading in the critical literature see Dick Netzer, *The Subsidized Muse: Public Support for the Arts in the United States* (1978); *Public Money and the Muse* (Stephen Benedict ed., 1991); *Public Policy and the Aesthetic Interest* (Ralph A. Smith and Ronald Berman eds, 1992); James Heilbrun and Charles M. Gray, *The Economics of Art and Culture* (2d ed. 2001).

33. A growing number of foreign State-funded museums exploit the American charitable deduction by establishing private U.S. non-profit organizations that solicit tax deductible gifts from U.S. taxpayers. See, e.g., American Friends of the British Museum, American Friends of the Israel Museum, American Friends of the Louvre, American Friends of the Tate, American Friends of the Uffizi.

34. Schuster, *supra* note 12, at 55; Vivian F. Wang, "Deductions and Donations: Tax Policy as a Manifestation of Attitudes About Art in the United States, United Kingdom and Canada" *Art Antiquity and Law* 79 (2009).

35. Dick Netzer, "Cultural Policy: An American View", in *Handbook, supra* note 7, at 1241.

36. The state attorney-general typically has jurisdiction to oversee museums and remedy their misdeeds, but that jurisdiction is seldom exercised, for reasons explained in Merryman, "Museum Ethics", l *Art and Museum Law J.* 93–103 (2006), reprinted in *Critical Essays, supra* note.5, at 568. An earlier catalog of uncorrected museum misdeeds appeared in "Are Museum Trustees and the Law Out of Step?" *ARTnews* (Nov. 1975), at 24–27, reprinted, with a "Note on Museum Trustees" and some related correspondence in *Critical Essays, supra* note 5 at 445. The American Association of Museums, a private organization of which most U.S. museums are members, has an accreditation program that has a mild regulatory effect, which amounts to museums accrediting museums.

37. Stanley N. Katz, "Influences on Public Policies in the United States" in *The Arts and Public Policy, supra* note 1, at 36.

38. See generally Charles Wolf, Jr., *Markets or Governments: Choosing Between Imperfect Alternatives* (2d ed. 1993).Cf Chapter Two of John E. Chubb and Terry M. Moe, *Politics, Markets and American Schools* (1990). As used in these and other similar studies, "markets" refers to the entire area of private, non-governmental choice.

39. "[T]he American art museum universe is more like the Milky Way than the solar system." Karl E. Meyer, *supra* note 10, at 58. One possible effect of the dispersal of choice is to establish multiple opportunities for experimentation of the same kind as, but vastly more widely distributed than those suggested in a famous passage in which Mr. Justice Brandeis, dissenting in *New State Ice Co. v. Liebmann*, 285 U.S. 262, 311 (1932), wrote of American federalism that: "It is one of the happy incidents of the federal system that a single courageous state may, if its citizens choose, serve as a laboratory; and try novel social and economic experiments without risk to the rest of the country."

40. *Hague Convention for the Protection of Cultural Property in the Event of Armed Conflict*, The Hague, May 14, 1954. The Convention and its first (1954) and second (1999) Protocols are set out in *LEVA5* at 65*ff*.

41. In "The Public Interest in Cultural Property", 77 *Calif. L. Rev.* 339 (1989), reprinted in *Critical Essays* 142, and "The Nation and the Object", 3 *Int'l J. Cult. Prop.* 61 (1994), reprinted in *Critical Essays* 206.

42. The text expresses a widely held assumption, which I share [see John Merryman, "The Refrigerator of Bernard Buffet", 27 *Hastings L. J.* 1023 (1976), reprinted in *Critical Essays* 405] that preservation of art is socially important. For an interesting challenge to that assumption see Amy Adler, "Against Moral Rights", 97 *Calif. L. Rev.* 263 (2009).

43. California enacted the first American moral right statute as the California Fine Art Preservation Act, Cal. Civ. Code § 987, in 1979, and similar legislation was subsequently adopted in other states. In 1990 Congress enacted a much more limited moral right as the Visual Artists Rights Act, 17 U.S.C. § 106A. The extent to which the state moral right statutes have been preempted by the federal legislation has not been fully resolved as this is written.

44. The American version is described and compared with the more virile and enduring moral right in other nations in *LEVA5* at 419–99.

45. Cal. Civ. Code § 989, enacted in 1982.

46. Joseph L. Sax, *Playing Darts with a Rembrandt* (1999).

47. Id. at 1–47.

48. Id. at 197.

49. Id. at 198. In a response to Sax's book, Lior Jacob Strahilevitz presents "a qualified defense of an owner's right to destroy valuable resources" including works of art. Strahilevitz, "The Right to Destroy", 114 *Yale L. J.* 781, 826–30 (2005). Cf Edward J. McCaffery, 'Must We Have the Right to Waste?', in *New Essays in the Legal and Political Theory of Property* 76 (Stephen R. Munzer ed., 2001). Compare with Adler, *supra* note 42.

50. Sax, *above*, note 46, at 7.

51. Thomas D. Bazley, *Crimes of the Art World* (2010); Dario Gamboni, *The Destruction of Art: Iconoclasm and Vandalism Since the French Revolution* (1997); Julius Held, "Alteration and Mutilation of Works of Art," 62 *S. Atlantic Q.*, Winter 1963, at 1; Avis Berman, "Art Destroyed, Sixteen Shocking Case

Histories," *Connoisseur*, July 1989, at 74; Patricia Failing, "The Case of the Dismembered Masterpieces," *ARTnews*, Sept. 1980, at 71.

52. "[T]he value that collectors and art markets create has been in most cases the only reasons that much of the world's art has survived. This has been a phenomenon since Roman times and has preserved at least something in the face of history during which gold, silver, and bronze objects were regularly melted down for state debts and cannons." E.V. Thaw, "The Art of Collecting," *The New Criterion*, Dec. 2002, at 16.

53. For a discussion of questions which arose about the propriety of this practice in connection with the 1999 "Sensation" exhibition at the Brooklyn Museum, see Judith H. Dobrzynski, "Private Collections Routine at Museums.", *N.Y. Times*, Oct. 1, 1999, at B6; David Barstow, "After 'Sensation' Furor, Museum Group Adopts Guidelines on Sponsors," *N.Y. Times*, Aug. 3, 2000, at E1.

54. The AAM *Code of Ethics* states that: "Disposal of collections through sale, trade, or research activities is solely for the advancement of the museum's mission. Proceeds from the sale of nonliving collections are to be used consistent with the established standards of the museum's discipline, but in no event shall they be used for anything other than acquisition or direct care of collections."

55. The November 2007 AAMD *Position Paper on Art Museums and Deaecessioning* provides: "There are two fundamental principles that are always observed whenever an AAMD member art museum deaccessions an object: The decision to deaccession is made solely to improve the quality, scope, and appropriateness of the collection, and to support the mission and long-term goals of the museum; Proceeds from a deaccessioned work are used only to acquire other works of art—the proceeds are never used as operating funds, to build a general endowment, or for any other expenses."

56. Sax, *supra* note 46, at 198.

57. Id. at 201. This passage expresses a theme later employed in Joseph Sax, "Imaginatively Public: The English Experience of Art as Heritage Property," 38 *Vand J. Transnat'l L.* 1097 (2005).

58. The *San Francisco Chronicle* of Jan. 11, 1983, carried an Associated Press story headlined "Wealthy

Christian Smashes 'Pagan' Treasures to Bits.'"
The dateline was Fort Worth, Texas: "Wealthy
businessman Cullen Davis, a born-again Christian,
destroyed more than $1 million worth of gold,
silver, jade, and ivory art objects because they
were associated with Eastern religions, evangelist
James Robison said yesterday. Robison told the
Fort Worth Star Telegram that he and Davis used
hammers to smash the carvings, which Davis had
donated last September to help Robison pay off
debts. The evangelist decided not to accept the gift
after recalling a verse in Deuteronomy: 'The graven
images of their gods shall we burn with fire: or it is
an abomination to the Lord thy God.' Robison said
he considered Davis' actions 'a good testimony for
his Christian faith.'"

59. Cal. Civ. Code § 989. The statute is briefly
described *supra* note 45.

60. On the Italian Fascist government and the arts, see
Giuseppe Palma, *L'Intervento dello stato nel settore
artistico* (1986); Maria Susan Stone, *The Patron
State: Culture & Politics in Fascist Italy* (1998).

61. The Degenerate Art exhibition was recreated at
the Los Angeles County Museum of Art in 1991 as
*Degenerate Art: The Fate of the Avant-Garde in Nazi
Germany*, curated by Stephanie Barron, who also
edited the remarkable exhibition catalog.

62. Emil Nolde is a famous example. He became widely
known and successful in the 1920s, and in 1931
he was appointed to the Prussian Academy of Art.
Although he was an early party member his art was
declared degenerate by the Nazis and included in
the Degenerate Art exhibition, and his works were
removed from German museums. In 1941 he was
forbidden to paint. The small watercolors called
"Unpainted Pictures" he made secretly during this
period became well-known after the Second World
War, when Nolde's significance was recognized in
a number of retrospective exhibitions. A novel by
Siegfried Lenz, *The German Lesson* (1986), is based
on Nolde's experience during the Nazi period.

63. Hellmut Lehmann-Haupt, *Art Under a Dictatorship*
219–30 (1954).

64. But cf. Sinclair Lewis, *It Can't Happen Here: A
Novel* (1935).

65. "New Cultural Policy" is a convenient title for a
complex phenomenon that others have described

but not so named. See especially Kate Fitz Gibbon,
"Dangerous Objects: Museums and Antiquities in
2008", Mar. 1, 2009, available at http://ssrn.com/
abstract=1479424.

66. UNESCO is the principal source of such instruments, which are available at http://portal.unesco
.org/en/ev.php- URL_ID=13649&URL_DO=DO
_TOPIC&URL_SECTION=-471.html.

67. A representative group of ethics codes is set out in
LEVA5 at 232ff.

68. The leading specialized journals are the *International Journal of Cultural Property*, which began
publication in 1992, and *Art Antiquity and Law*,
which first appeared in 1996.

69. See the invaluable International Foundation for
Art Research (IFAR) Art Law & Cultural Property Website: www.ifar.org, with two components:
International Cultural Property Ownership and
Export Legislation (ICPOEL), which contains
legislation governing the export and ownership of
cultural property from dozens of countries in the
original language and in translation; and Case Law
and Statutes (CLS), an extensive body of primarily
U.S. case law, including both litigated cases and,
notably, hard-to-find, out-of-court settlements,
with links to relevant U.S. statutes, foreign legislation and a glossary.

70. For representative expressions, see Colin Renfrew,
*Loot, Legitimacy and Ownership: The Ethical Crisis
in Archaeology* (2000); Neil Brodie, *Archaeology,
Cultural Heritage, and the Antiquities Trade* (2006);
Patty Gerstenblith, "Controlling the International
Market in Antiquities: Reducing the Harm,
Preserving the Past," 8 *Chi. J. Int'l L.* 169 (2007).
I more fully describe the archaeological estab-
lishment's position in "Thinking About the Sevso
Treasure," *Critical Essays*, at 348.

71. *Convention on the Means of Prohibiting and
Preventing the Illicit Import, Export or Transfer of
Ownership of Cultural Property*, available at http://
portal.unesco.org/en/ev.php-URL_ ID=13039
&URL_DO=DO_TOPIC&URL_SECTION=201
.html. The Convention is also set out in *LEVA5*
at 178.

72. Article one of the Convention states: "For the
purposes of this Convention, the term 'cultural
property' means property which, on religious

or secular grounds, is specifically designated by each state as being of importance for archaeology, prehistory, history, literature, art or science [what else is there?] and which belongs to the following categories [here follows a broadly inclusive list]."

73. Professor Paul Bator has criticized the "blank check" rule in his canonical article "An Essay on the International Trade in Art," 34 *Stanford L. Rev.* 275, 370 (1982), later published as a monograph, Paul M. Bator, *The International Trade in Art* 52–54 (1983). Subsequent citations to Bator herein are to the monograph.

74. The basic instruments that regulate international trade—the World Trade Organization and European Union treaties—prohibit national impediments to international trade in 'goods', including works of art. Both treaties, however, specifically exempt measures that "protect national cultural treasures". In *Commission of the European Communities v. The Italian Republic*, the European Court of Justice held that Italian legislation taxing export of works of art did not "protect" them and accordingly violated the treaty. Since that case there has been no further Commission or ITO action to control excessive national restrictions on trade in cultural property.

75. "Almost nobody has any idea what enormous, fantastic mountains of such "duplicates" exist in the state-owned museums around the Mediterranean. Italian archaeologists laugh hollowly when newspapers report the theft of some "unique, priceless" Etruscan vase. They know, but the public does not, how many thousands of these "unique, priceless" vases they already have in storage and quite literally don't know what to do with." Gordon Gaskill, 'They Smuggle History', *Illustrated London News*, June 14, 1969, at 21.

76. During expansion of the Athens subway for the 2004 Olympic Games, archaeologists reportedly turned up 30,000 finds. Hannah Hoag, "A New Olympic Battleground," *Discovery Magazine*, Dec. 3, 2003, available at http://discovermagazine .com/2003/dec/a-new-olympic-battleground/ ?searchterm=new%20olympic%20%20battleground (last visited Feb. 16, 2010).

77. For examples of such legislation see the IFAR database cited above, note 69. The problems created by

source nation hoarding of art and antiquities, often euphemized as 'protection' of the nation's cultural 'patrimony' or 'heritage', are explored in Merryman, 'The Retention of Cultural Property', above, note 5.

78. Available at http://www.aamd.org/newsroom/ documents/2008ReportAndRelease.pdf. The AAMD represents directors of major art museums in the United States, Canada and Mexico.

79. The application of this provision to undocumented antiquities to produce "orphans," i.e. antiquities that museums should not acquire or borrow or show, is described in "Thinking About the Sevso Treasure," *supra* note 70.

80. Available at http://portal.unesco.org/en/ev.php -URL_ID=13132&URL_DO=DO_TOPIC&URL _SECTION=201.html.

81. The force of this statement is weakened by its evident misunderstanding of basic economics. Constricting the licit supply of antiquities, not "speculation," is the main cause of rising prices and illicit trading. As Bator put it: "'Embargo itself perversely fuels the black market." Bator, *supra* note 73, at 43.

82. "[I]n most art-rich countries there are thousands and thousands of objects that were uncovered long ago. Most of these are not important or unique. There is simply no point in preventing the export of much of this material ... Indeed, export of such material should be encouraged because it would help satisfy the foreign market and reduce the incentive of buyers to deal on the black market." Id. at 49–50.

83. Article I.2.c. of its Constitution commits UNESCO to "Maintain, increase and diffuse knowledge ... By encouraging ... the international exchange of ... objects of artistic and scientific interest ... "

84. 1976 *Recommendation* Article I. 1.

85. "Culture is enriched and diversified if private as well as public tastes can be gratified. It would be a great mistake to put all decisions about what is beautiful and worth collecting into the hands of officials, committees, and boards of trustees. Private wealth, just because it is comparatively irresponsible, can be adventurous and iconoclastic." Bator, *supra* note 73, at 24.

86. The *Recommendation*'s image of an art world composed solely of "States" and "cultural institutions" that barter with and lend to each other necessarily assumes a radical reduction, rather than the "encouragement," of international traffic in cultural goods contemplated by UNESCO's Constitution. See *supra* note 83.

87. Available at http://portal.unesco/org/en/ev.php -URL-ID=13520&URL_DO=DO_TOPIC &URL _SECTION=201.html. Slovakia became the 24th party to the Convention on March 11, 2009.

88. For a fuller description of the growth of federal regulation of the antiquities trade and its effects on American museums, see Fitz Gibbon, *supra* note 65.

89. An article by Clemency Coggins, "Illicit Traffic of Pre-Columbian Antiquities," 29 *Art J.* 94 (1969) is generally credited as an initiating event in the development of what has become the NCP. It was closely followed by the *Treaty of Cooperation between the United States of America and the United Mexican States Providing for the Recovery and Return of Stolen Archaeological, Historical and Cultural Properties*, 22 U.S.T.S. 494, T.I.A.S. No. 7088 (1971) and the U.S. *Regulation of Importation of Pre-Columbian Monumental or Architectural Sculpture or Murals Act*, 19 U.S.C. §§ 1091*ff.* (1972).

90. Paul Bator was a member of the U.S. Delegation to the UNESCO Special Committee that negotiated and drafted the Convention. His analysis of the Convention and account of its legislative history appear as an appendix in his monograph, *supra* note 73.

91. 19 U.S.C. §§ 2601*ff.*

92. 19 U.S.C. § 2602. As this is written, the U.S. has imposed such import restrictions on cultural objects from fourteen nations, most recently China. See U.S. Department of State, Cultural Property Center, http://culturalheritage.state.gov/ chart.html (last visited Feb. 16, 2010).

93. 495 F.2d 1154 (9th Cir. 1974).

94. 545 F.2d 988 (5th Cir. 1977); 593 F.2d 658 (5th Cir. 1979).

95. 18 U.S.C. § 2314.

96. 18 U.S.C. § 545.

97. Cultural objects, like other imports, must be "declared" on entry into the United States. Improperly declared objects may be seized by Customs as contraband.

98. See James R. McAlee, "The McClain Case, Customs, and Congress," 15 *N.Y.U.J. Int'l L. & Pol.* 813 (1983); the *Boston Raphael* case in *LEVA5* at 163–69; *United States v. An Antique Platter of Gold*, 991 F. Supp. 222 (S.D.N.Y. 1997); 184 F.3d 131 (2d Cir. 1998).

99. Archaeological Resources Protection Act of 1979, 16 U.S.C. §§ 470aa-470mm.

100. According to a report prepared by the Stanford University Archaeological Center, "The investigation had been conducted since 2003 by the Internal Revenue Service and Immigration and Customs Enforcement, with the help of an undercover investigator recruited from the National Park Service." See Stanford Cultural Archaeology Center, Cultural Heritage Resource, http://www .stanford.edu/group/chr/drupal/chron/january february-2008 (last visited Feb. 16, 2010). The Internal Revenue Service was involved because of accusations that articles were donated to museum with inflated valuations.

101. For a balanced description of how and why the U.S. arrived at this position see Asif Efrat, "Protecting against Plunder: The United States and the International Efforts against Looting of Antiquities", *Cornell Law School Working Paper Series* No. 47 (2009), available at http://lsr.nellco.org/cornell/ clsops/papers/47. Cf. the Fitz Gibbon article, *supra* note 65.

102. The "taking" issues raised by cultural property nationalization legislation have been litigated in a few foreign courts. In 1983 the Costa Rican Supreme Court actually held such a law unconstitutional as violating its constitution's property taking clause. Costa Rica, *Boletin Judicial* No. 90 of May 12, 1983. The law was subsequently modified to conform to constitutional requirements. The constitutionality of Italy's cultural property legislation was considered in two Corte Costituzionale decisions: 202/1974 and 245/1976. The Corte found no unconstitutional "taking" in either

case. In France, on the basis of existing legislation, the owner of a van Gogh painting for which an export permit was denied recovered its resulting diminution in market value from the French Government. Timothy P. Ramier, *"Agent Judiciaire du Trésor v. Walter: Fair du Prince* and a King's Ransom,"* 6 *Int'l J. Cult. Prop.* 337 (1997). Cf. the case of *Beyeler v. Italy*, Application No. 33202/96, European Court of Human Rights Judgment of 5 Jan. 2000, set out in *LEVA5* at 122–134.

103. Asif Efrat, *supra* note 101, at 86, asks a similar question: "Why was the United States the only major market country willing to compromise its self interest for the sake of archaeological preservation?" In response he cites (1) public scandals that created a sense of shame and embarrassment and a feeling that something had to be done and (2) advocacy by "the archaeological community."

104. See James F. Fitzpatrick, 'A Wayward Course: The Lawless Customs Policy toward Cultural Properties', 15 *N.Y.U. J. Int'l L. & Pol.* 837 (1983).

105. See "Thinking About the Sevso Treasure." *supra* note 70.

106. "What has been the impact of antiquities regulation on the conduct of museums? In recent years, the acquisition of antiquities by museums has diminished overall. Extensive restrictions on export from source countries coupled with growing demand for objects with clean provenance have driven prices up and have taken antiquities acquisition out of the financial reach of many museums." Efrat, *supra* note 101 at 84–85.

107. Id. at 85.

108. "Museum curators are forced to acquire objects, not based on their artistic or historical value, but rather on the criminal advice of counsel… . By triggering the extremely powerful federal

prosecutorial machinery, the U.S. has unwittingly shut off debate about the proper place for art and antiquities, and alienated the art market itself." Derek Fincham, "Why U.S. Federal Criminal Penalties for Dealing in Illicit Cultural Property Are Ineffective, and a Pragmatic Alternative," 25 *Cardozo Arts & Ent. L. J.* 597, 598 (2007).

109. "[I]t would be a disaster if all art stayed at home," Bator, *supra* note 73, at 30. "The idea of a world in which art was destined to stay in the place in which it was made is a terrible nightmare." Mary Beard, 'Sale or Return', *Times Literary Supplement*, Oct. 2, 2009, at 4.

110. See Kwame Anthony Appiah, 'Whose Culture Is It?', *The N.Y. Rev. of Books,* Feb. 9, 2006; Kwame Anthony Appiah, *Cosmopolitanism: Ethics in a World of Strangers* (2006).

111. James Cuno, *Who Owns Antiquity? Museums and the Battle Over Our Ancient Heritage* (2008) strongly argues the case for such "universal" museums. See also the 2003 *Declaration on the Importance and Value of Universal Museums*, signed by the Directors of eighteen museums, ten of them in the U.S. The *Declaration* and a range of reactions to it—some of them quite hostile—are published in *ICOM News* no. 1, 2004, available at icom.museum/universal.html.

112. Mary Beard, *supra* note 109.

113. See e.g., Colin Renfrew, "Collectors are the Real Looters," *Archaeology,* May–June 1993, at 16.

114. See *supra* note 77 and accompanying text.

115. See *supra* note 81 and accompanying text.

116. I have repeatedly argued for such a dialogue (see *Critical Essays* at 62–63, 139–40, 291–92, 344–46, 364–65, 400–01) but with little discernible effect.

chapter 9

ETHICS AND VALUES

THIS INTRODUCTION TO THE PRESENT CHAPTER IS in two sections. Section 1 covers the ethics and values of preservation and a description of the last five readings of the chapter. Section 2 offers selected international conventions and declarations and a sampling of professional codes of ethics. These selections are but a brief overview of a complex and nuanced topic.

Section 1

Daniel N. Robinson divides philosophy and intellectual history into three main currents of thought: the problem of knowledge (epistemology and metaphysics), the problem of conduct (ethics and moral philosophy), and the problem of governance (political science and law).[1] While this is necessarily a reductionist approach, it is apt for examining the components of preservation in which knowledge, conduct, and governance play a role in its practice.

This chapter focuses on ethics and values—the problem of conduct. Ethics is the branch of philosophy that focuses on morality. It is a problem that has been considered and debated for over 2000 years, since the Hindu scripture *Upanishads* and, not much later, the writings of the ancient Greek philosophers. Ethics, virtue, values, morality: can they be taught? Does one have to be receptive to such lessons to learn them? When ought we to do something and when ought we not to do something? We are probably no closer to answering these questions today than were Socrates or Plato.

One piece in this chapter deals specifically with values: "Conservation and Its Values," by **Samuel Jones** and **John Holden**, from their *It's a Material World,* a report published by the British think tank Demos. The authors point out that value is socially determined: an object has value if people give it value. Conservation, they reason, contributes to a conversation about values.

Morality and *ethics* are often used interchangeably, and moral codes and standards are attempts to articulate, and even enforce, conduct. Professional organizations favor the term *ethics* over *morality* because *morals* is often used to refer to beliefs that relate to conduct in personal relationships. Ethics refers more generally to principles regarding conduct. In this chapter we use *ethics*, except when referring to a text that uses the terms interchangeably.

William K. Frankena and John T. Granrose note that "there are three kinds of inquiries about morality: (1) descriptive and explanatory studies such as are made by historians and social scientists; (2) normative inquiries about the principles, standards, or methods for determining what is morally right or wrong, good or bad; and (3) 'meta-ethical' questions about the meanings of terms like 'right,' 'good,' 'responsible,' etc., about the meaning of 'morality' itself, or about the justification of ethical judgments."[2] The second and third types of inquiry are within the purview of professional practice.

Further intertwining morals and ethics, Frankena and Granrose describe morality as having an action-guide (an AG) which includes moral codes, ideals, or standards. "We also," they write, "sometimes call an AG an 'ethics'; in fact, we often use 'ethics' as a synonym for 'morality' or 'moral code,' not just as a word for the branch of philosophy."[3]

John Dewey provides a bridge from personal morality to professional ethics.[4] He distinguishes between customary morality—"ancestral habit"—and reflective morality. The latter "appeals to conscience, reason, or to some principle which includes thought."[5] Professional practices, guidelines, and codes of ethics provide a framework around which a person applies reflective thought, personal insight, rational choice, responsibility, and duty to her decision-making. Yet, what happens when personal beliefs interfere with professional obligations? What code of conduct should then be followed?

Library, archive, and museum professionals face many situations in which personal beliefs may come into conflict with professional duties. Would you decline to purchase a book for a library because its subject is morally offensive to you? To process a particular archival collection that was assembled by an extremist political group? Or (two well-known cases that might pit professional ethics against personal morals), would you exhibit Andres Serrano's photograph "Piss Christ" or the Danish cartoons from 2005 that depicted Mohammed, because of the political fallout that might thus occur?[6] Or because of your own views?

These are examples of situations in which personal beliefs might conflict with professional practices. There are also situations in which one's adherence to a professional code of ethics may conflict with the wishes of others—who may also be professionals. As a conservator, would you rebind a book whose original binding is in perfect condition, and that is not doing damage to the text block, simply because the curator wants a new binding on it? Display a watercolor in a gallery whose owners will not dim the lights? Lend an item to an institution that does not monitor its temperature and humidity levels? And so on.

Ellen Pearlstein takes a detailed look at the ethical considerations that went into conserving a Native American feather blanket. It had been thought to be an 18th- or 19th-century California blanket; it turned out to be a much earlier Pueblo blanket from northern Arizona which was originally intended for child burial. The case "illustrates how a study of methods, materials, and construction methods may aid in determining whether an unprovenanced object may fall into cultural categories subject to repatriation under NAGPRA," the Native American Graves Protection Act of 1990. The conservators' findings suggested that the blanket should no longer be on public display and that repatriation was appropriate. Thus, conservation can be an aid to ethical decision-making.

There are other players whose actions affect cultural heritage institutions. Some people may steal from collections; others might willfully damage items by setting them on fire, spray-painting them, or bombing them. These actions may stem from a variety of motives, perhaps expressed as religious or moral beliefs, and the actors may feel an obligation to carry out such crimes. We have now moved from ethical issues to purely moral ones. While this chapter's readings focus on ethics, cultural heritage is vulnerable to the destructive impulses of individuals, political parties, or governments, anywhere, and at any time. (Rebecca Knuth has described cultural destruction in two books; an excerpt from one of them, "Understanding Modern Biblioclasm," is included in chapter 5.)[7] **Richard Cox** and **James O'Toole** address some of the same issues in two pieces that are included in this chapter, "The Impulse to Save" and "The Impulse to Destroy." The impulse to save may stem from the need to save, the practicality of saving, the saving of artifacts for sentimental reasons, and so on. The impulse to destroy may come from the creators of the records themselves. Others who seek to destroy may do so for political, social, or cultural reasons. Cox and O'Toole observe that "records, archival or otherwise, are powerful factors in society, so they are often the targets for destruction."

Armed conflict—within a country or between countries—almost always leads to the damage and destruction of cultural heritage. Some damage is accidental, some is intentional. There are rules of engagement that spell out appropriate conduct in armed conflicts, *Jus in Bello*, as well as for justice after war has been carried out, *Jus post Bellum*.[8] Yet there are many instances when, during war, or in the aftermath of it, military personnel may not adopt a moral attitude or ethical practices. (One example is the World War II soldiers who, during the liberation of Europe, "liberated" fine art.) Of course, the very act of war calls morality into question, a topic that, while it may have a profound impact on cultural heritage, is beyond the scope of this book.[9]

While we generally cannot control natural and political forces, preservation professionals seek to minimize damage through public outreach and education. We have made strides in disaster recovery and outreach, for example, and through international professional networks, much can be accomplished. For example, at its August 19, 2011 meeting, the Governing Board of the International Federation of Library Associations and Institutions

… set up an Advisory Group to draft Principles of Engagement to be used by IFLA and its members in library-related activities of disaster risk reduction and in times of conflict, crisis or natural disaster; with reference to IFLA's engagement in the Haiti reconstruction activities and international treaties and agreements to which IFLA is a party. The recent turmoil in Syria and Mali, the earthquake in Haiti or the earthquake followed by a tsunami in Japan, [demonstrate why] IFLA is deeply concerned by the great loss of cultural heritage in recent years due to armed conflicts, crises and natural disasters. The principles aim to encourage safeguarding and respect for cultural property especially by raising awareness and promoting disaster risk management and to strengthen cooperation and participation in cultural heritage activities through UNESCO, the libraries, archives, museums, heritage buildings and sites group and the International Committee of the Blue Shield initiatives and activities. …

In the event of disaster, the Principles of Engagement will guide activities in recovery situations and advise IFLA and its members if and how to engage in a particular recovery situation within IFLA's strategic directions. They establish criteria to guide decisions on whether IFLA and its members would become engaged in post-conflict/disaster recovery and the terms under which it would do so. The Principles outline the conditions of an intervention by IFLA, its guiding principles, the levels of involvement, and methods for the needs assessment and evaluation.[10]

While Cox and O'Toole address ethical issues surrounding why we preserve and destroy records, art historian **Ernst van de Wetering** considers ethics in modern and contemporary art in his "Conservation-Restoration Ethics and the Problem of Modern Art." For pre-twentieth-century art, there have been conservation treatment conventions: a work is documented, whenever possible, treatments, are reversible, and so on. However, for much contemporary art "it is the 'here and now-ness' that counts." He reasons that the conservator is necessarily caught between conserving the work as it is at present, and perceiving of it as a soon-to-be historic object. Yet the transitory nature of art is inevitable, and the conservator must not be resigned to the disappearance of even the most ephemeral of works.

Section 2

In this section are presented the chapter's first readings, conventions, declarations, and so on, which are the underpinnings for the rest of the chapter. They put the other readings into an international, social, and moral context, which gives the reader a grounding to understand the content and impact of the ethical choices discussed in the professional readings that follow.

ETHICS AND VALUES: SELECTED CONVENTIONS, CHARTERS, DECLARATIONS, AND PROFESSIONAL ASSOCIATION CODES OF ETHICS

International law is based by nature upon this principle: that the various nations ought to do, in peace, the most good to each other, and in war, the least harm possible, without detriment to their genuine interests
—*Montesquieu, L'Esprit des lois (1748), I, 3*[11]

THE UNITED NATIONS was created during World War II as

a "parliament of nations" which meets regularly and in special sessions to consider the world's most pressing problems. Each Member State has one vote. Decisions on such key issues as international peace and security, admitting new members and the UN budget are decided by two-thirds majority. Other matters are decided by simple majority. In recent years, a special effort has been made to reach decisions through consensus, rather than by taking a formal vote. The [General] Assembly cannot force action by any State, but its recommendations are an important indication of world opinion and represent the *moral authority* [italics added] of the community of nations (accessed December 5, 2012, http://www.un.org/Overview/uninbrief/ga.shtml).

The United Nations, and, by extension, other international bodies that try to promulgate ethical standards, do so with a sense of moral authority. Moral authority is a philosophical or sociological construct, not a rule of law. The idea is to call a person, or a nation, to the performance of ethical duties, and to discourage wrongdoing. Moral authority stems from theories of justice and universal equality.

The UN's formative "statement of purpose" was the *Universal Declaration of Human Rights* (*UDHR*), adopted in 1948. It sought to assure basic human rights to everyone, everywhere, whether members of the UN or not. The *UDHR* was framed in response to the devastation brought about by World War II. The United Nations was then a new organization, and the *UDHR* was a declaration not only of human rights, but of the international reach that the United Nations hoped to acquire and maintain. The Declaration contains thirty articles, two of which, numbers 22 and 27, mention cultural rights. Later the United Nations Educational, Scientific, and Cultural Organization (UNESCO) would establish programs to protect the world's cultural heritage.

An excerpt is included here because of the inclusion of social and cultural rights. In declarations and conventions created after 1948, strategies would be articulated for the preservation of cultural heritage.

UNITED NATIONS

Excerpts from the *Universal Declaration of Human Rights (UDHR)*

Article 22

Everyone, as a member of society, has the right to social security and is entitled to realization, through national effort and international co-operation and in accordance with the organization and resources of each State, of the economic, social and cultural rights indispensable for his dignity and the free development of his personality.

[...]

Article 27

(1) Everyone has the right freely to participate in the cultural life of the community, to enjoy the arts and to share in scientific advancement and its benefits.

(2) Everyone has the right to the protection of the moral and material interests resulting from any scientific, literary or artistic production of which he is the author.

UNESCO IS A specialized agency of the United Nations. As its name suggests,

> UNESCO works to create the conditions for dialogue among civilizations, cultures and peoples, based upon respect for commonly shared values. It is through this dialogue that the world can achieve global visions of sustainable development encompassing observance of human rights, mutual respect and the alleviation of poverty, all of which are at the heart of UNESCO's mission and activities... . Thus UNESCO's unique competencies in education, the sciences, culture and communication and information contribute towards the realization of those goals (accessed December 5, 2012, http://www .unesco.org/new/en/unesco/about-us/who-we-are/ introducing-unesco).

UNESCO's most direct tie to preservation is the *Memory of the World* Programme, which it established in 1992.

> Impetus came originally from a growing awareness of the parlous state of preservation of, and access to, documentary heritage in various parts of the world. War and social upheaval, as well as severe lack of resources, have worsened problems which have existed for centuries. Significant collections world-wide have suffered a variety of fates. Looting and dispersal, illegal trading, destruction, inadequate housing and funding have all played a part. Much [has] vanished forever; much is endangered. Happily, missing documentary heritage is sometimes rediscovered.
>
> Preparation of General Guidelines for the Programme was initiated through a contract with the International Federation of Library Associations and Institutions (IFLA) and the International Council on Archives (ICA). These organizations prepared lists of damaged library collections and archive holdings. UNESCO itself prepared a list of endangered library and archive holdings and a world list of national cinematic heritage. The *Memory of the World Register* was founded on the 1995 *General Guidelines* and has grown through accessions approved by successive International Advisory Committee meetings (http://www.unesco.org/ new/en/communication-and-information/flagship -project-activities/memory-of-the-world/about-the -programme).

An early activity of UNESCO was the *Hague Convention for the Protection of Cultural Property in the Event of Armed Conflict* (1954). The *Hague Convention* is the first treaty to focus exclusively on the protection of cultural heritage during armed conflict. The treaty has its roots in the two Hague Peace Conferences of 1899 and 1907. The result of the conferences was the creation of several conventions aimed at protecting cultural heritage sites during warfare. It wasn't until after World War II, and the creation of UNESCO, that the *Hague Convention* was fully realized. The 1954 *Convention* has been amended twice and is subscribed to by over 115 countries. The excerpt below spells out the scope and provides definitions.

Selection 9.2

UNESCO

Excerpt from *Convention for the Protection of Cultural Property in the Event of Armed Conflict*

The High Contracting Parties,

Recognizing that cultural property has suffered grave damage during recent armed conflicts and that, by reason of the developments in the technique of warfare, it is in increasing danger of destruction;

Being convinced that damage to cultural property belonging to any people whatsoever means damage to the cultural heritage of all mankind, since each people makes its contribution to the culture of the world;

Considering that the preservation of the cultural heritage is of great importance for all peoples of the world and that it is important that this heritage should receive international protection;

Guided by the principles concerning the protection of cultural property during armed conflict, as established in the Conventions of The Hague of 1899 and of 1907 and in the Washington Pact of 15 April, 1935;

Being of the opinion that such protection cannot be effective unless both national and international measures have been taken to organize it in time of peace;

Being determined to take all possible steps to protect cultural property; have agreed upon the following provisions:

Chapter I. General provisions regarding protection

ARTICLE 1. DEFINITION OF CULTURAL PROPERTY

For the purposes of the present Convention, the term 'cultural property' shall cover, irrespective of origin or ownership:

(a) movable or immovable property of great importance to the cultural heritage of every people, such as monuments of architecture, art or history, whether religious or secular; archaeological sites; groups of buildings which, as a whole, are of historical or artistic interest; works of art; manuscripts, books and other objects of artistic, historical or archaeological interest; as well as scientific collections and important collections of books or archives or of reproductions of the property defined above;

(b) buildings whose main and effective purpose is to preserve or exhibit the movable cultural property defined in sub-paragraph (a) such as museums, large libraries and depositories of archives, and refuges intended to shelter, in the event of armed conflict, the movable cultural property defined in sub-paragraph (a);

(c) centers containing a large amount of cultural property as defined in sub-paragraphs (a) and (b), to be known as 'centers containing monuments.'

ARTICLE 2. PROTECTION OF CULTURAL PROPERTY

For the purposes of the present Convention, the protection of cultural property shall comprise the safeguarding of and respect for such property.

ARTICLE 3. SAFEGUARDING OF CULTURAL PROPERTY

The High Contracting Parties undertake to prepare in time of peace for the safeguarding of cultural property situated within their own territory against the foreseeable effects of an armed conflict, by taking such measures as they consider appropriate.

ARTICLE 4. RESPECT FOR CULTURAL PROPERTY

1. The High Contracting Parties undertake to respect cultural property situated within their own territory as well as within the territory of other High Contracting Parties by refraining from any use of the property and its immediate surroundings or of the appliances in use for its protection for purposes which are likely to expose it to destruction or damage in the event of armed conflict; and by refraining from any act of hostility, directed against such property.

2. The obligations mentioned in paragraph 1 of the present Article may be waived only in cases where military necessity imperatively requires such a waiver.

3. The High Contracting Parties further undertake to prohibit, prevent and, if necessary, put a stop to any form of theft, pillage or misappropriation of, and any acts of vandalism directed against, cultural property. They shall refrain from requisitioning movable cultural property situated in the territory of another High Contracting Party.

4. They shall refrain from any act directed by way of reprisals against cultural property.

5. No High Contracting Party may evade the obligations incumbent upon it under the present Article, in respect of another High Contracting Party, by reason of the fact that the latter has not applied the measures of safeguard referred to in Article 3.

[...]

ARTICLE 6. DISTINCTIVE MARKING OF CULTURAL PROPERTY

In accordance with the provisions of Article 16, cultural property may bear a distinctive emblem so as to facilitate its recognition.

[...]

Chapter V. The distinctive emblem

ARTICLE 16. EMBLEM OF THE CONVENTION

1. The distinctive emblem of the Convention shall take the form of a shield, pointed below, persaltire blue and white (a shield consisting of a royal-blue square, one of the angles of which forms the point of the shield, and of a royal-blue triangle above the square, the space on either side being taken up by a white triangle).

2. The emblem shall be used alone, or repeated three times in a triangular formation (one shield below), under the conditions provided for in Article 17.

ARTICLE 17. USE OF THE EMBLEM

1. The distinctive emblem repeated three times may be used only as a means of identification of:
   (a) immovable cultural property under special protection;
   (b) the transport of cultural property under the conditions provided for in Articles 12 and 13;
   (c) improvised refuges, under the conditions provided for in the Regulations for the execution of the Convention.

2. The distinctive emblem may be used alone only as a means of identification of:
   (a) cultural property not under special protection;
   (b) the persons responsible for the duties of control in accordance with the Regulations for the execution of the Convention;
   (c) the personnel engaged in the protection of cultural property;
   (d) the identity cards mentioned in the Regulations for the execution of the Convention.

3. During an armed conflict, the use of the distinctive emblem in any other cases than those mentioned in the preceding paragraphs of the present Article, and the use for any purpose whatever of a sign resembling the distinctive emblem, shall be forbidden.

4. The distinctive emblem may not be placed on any immovable cultural property unless at the same time there is displayed an authorization duly dated and signed by the competent authority of the High Contracting Party.

[...]

UNESCO

Excerpt from the *Convention Concerning the Protection of the World Cultural and Natural Heritage*

The Convention Concerning the Protection of the World Cultural and Natural Heritage pairs cultural heritage with natural heritage. In other words, it seeks to define the scope of heritage. It grew out of the 1972 World Heritage Convention in which the International Council on Monuments and Sites (ICOMOS) and UNESCO were key players.[12] It represents a broadening of the notion of cultural heritage (then referred to as cultural property) as described in the Venice Charter 1964,[13] from historical monuments, to communities, to landscapes and the environment. Today heritage is also described as including the tangible and intangible.

THE GENERAL CONFERENCE of the United Nations Educational, Scientific and Cultural Organization, meeting in Paris from 17 October to 21 November 1972, at its seventeenth session,

Noting that the cultural heritage and the natural heritage are increasingly threatened with destruction not only by the traditional causes of decay, but also by changing social and economic conditions which aggravate the situation with even more formidable phenomena of damage or destruction,

Considering that deterioration or disappearance of any item of the cultural or natural heritage constitutes a harmful impoverishment of the heritage of all the nations of the world,

Considering that protection of this heritage at the national level often remains incomplete because of the scale of the resources which it requires and of the insufficient economic, scientific, and technological resources of the country where the property to be protected is situated,

Recalling that the Constitution of the Organization provides that it will maintain, increase, and diffuse knowledge, by assuring the conservation and protection of the world's heritage, and recommending to the nations concerned the necessary international conventions,

Considering that the existing international conventions, recommendations and resolutions concerning cultural and natural property demonstrate the importance, for all the peoples of the world, of safeguarding this unique and irreplaceable property, to whatever people it may belong,

Considering that parts of the cultural or natural heritage are of outstanding interest and therefore need to be preserved as part of the world heritage of mankind as a whole,

Considering that, in view of the magnitude and gravity of the new dangers threatening them, it is incumbent on the international community as a whole to participate in the protection of the cultural and natural heritage of outstanding universal value, by the granting of collective assistance which, although not taking the place of action by the State concerned, will serve as an efficient complement thereto,

Considering that it is essential for this purpose to adopt new provisions in the form of a convention establishing an effective system of collective protection of the cultural and natural heritage of outstanding universal value, organized on a permanent basis and in accordance with modern scientific methods,

Having decided, at its sixteenth session, that this question should be made the subject of an international convention,

Adopts this sixteenth day of November 1972 this Convention.

I. Definition of the Cultural and Natural Heritage

For the purposes of this Convention, the following shall be considered as "cultural heritage":

ARTICLE 1

> **monuments:** architectural works, works of monumental sculpture and painting, elements or structures of an archaeological nature, inscriptions, cave dwellings and combinations of features, which are of outstanding universal value from the point of view of history, art or science;
>
> **groups of buildings:** groups of separate or connected buildings which, because of their architecture, their homogeneity or their place in the landscape, are of outstanding universal value from the point of view of history, art or science;
>
> **sites:** works of man or the combined works of nature and man, and areas including archaeological sites which are of outstanding universal value from the historical, aesthetic, ethnological or anthropological point of view.

ARTICLE 2

For the purposes of this Convention, the following shall be considered as "natural heritage":

> **natural features** consisting of physical and biological formations or groups of such formations, which are of outstanding universal value from the aesthetic or scientific point of view;
>
> **geological and physiographical formations** and precisely delineated areas which constitute the habitat of threatened species of animals and plants of outstanding universal value from the point of view of science or conservation;
>
> **natural sites** or precisely delineated natural areas of outstanding universal value from the point of science, conservation or natural beauty.

Selection 9.4

UNITED NATIONS

Excerpts from the *Declaration on the Rights of Indigenous Peoples*

The United Nations Declaration on the Rights of Indigenous Peoples (2007) *sets out the individual and collective rights of indigenous peoples, as well as their rights to culture, identity, language, employment, health, education and other issues. It also emphasizes the rights of indigenous peoples to maintain "their own institutions, cultures and traditions, and to pursue their development in keeping with their own needs and aspirations." The declaration seeks to prohibit discrimination against indigenous peoples, and it "promotes their full and effective participation in all matters that concern them and their right to remain distinct and to pursue their own visions of economic and social development." Of particular relevance to this chapter, Article 31 emphasizes that indigenous peoples will be able to protect their cultural heritage and other aspects of their culture and tradition. This is a critical component of cultural heritage preservation.*

ARTICLE 1

Indigenous peoples have the right to the full enjoyment, as a collective or as individuals, of all human rights and fundamental freedoms as recognized in the Charter of the United Nations, the Universal Declaration of Human Rights, and international human rights law.

ARTICLE 2

Indigenous peoples and individuals are free and equal to all other peoples and individuals and have the right to be free from any kind of discrimination, in the exercise of their rights, in particular that based on their indigenous origin or identity.

ARTICLE 3

Indigenous peoples have the right to self-determination. By virtue of that right they freely determine their political status and freely pursue their economic, social and cultural development.

ARTICLE 4

Indigenous people, in exercising their right to self-determination, have the right to autonomy or self-government in matters relating to their internal and local affairs, as well as ways and means for financing their autonomous functions.

ARTICLE 5

Indigenous people have the right to maintain and strengthen their distinct political, legal, economic, social and cultural institutions, while retaining their right to participate fully, if they so choose, in the political, economic, social and cultural life of the State.

[...]

ARTICLE 29

1. Indigenous peoples have the right to the conservation and protection of the environment and the productive capacity of their lands or territories and resources. States shall establish and implement assistance programmes for indigenous peoples for such conservation and protection, without discrimination.

2. States shall take effective measures to ensure that no storage or disposal of hazardous materials shall take place in the lands or territories of indigenous peoples without their free, prior and informed consent.

3. States shall also take effective measures to ensure, as needed, that programmes for monitoring, maintaining and restoring the health of indigenous peoples, as developed and implemented by the peoples affected by such materials, are duly implemented.

[...]

ARTICLE 31

1. Indigenous peoples have the right to maintain, control, protect and develop their cultural heritage, traditional knowledge and traditional cultural expressions, as well as the manifestations of their sciences, technologies and cultures, including human and genetic resources, seeds, medicines, knowledge of the properties of fauna and flora, oral traditions, literatures, designs, sports and traditional games and visual and performing arts. They also have the right to maintain, control, protect and develop their intellectual property over such cultural heritage, traditional knowledge, and traditional cultural expressions.

2. In conjunction with indigenous peoples, States shall take effective measures to recognize and protect the exercise of these rights.

Selection 9.5

SALZBURG GLOBAL SEMINAR

Salzburg Declaration on the Conservation and Preservation of Cultural Heritage[14] **31 October 2009**

Accessed December 5, 2012, www.salzburgglobal.org/mediafiles/MEDIA51506.pdf.

ON THE OCCASION of the Salzburg Global Seminar session on *Connecting to the World's Collections: Making the Case for the Conservation and Preservation of our Cultural Heritage*, sixty cultural heritage leaders from the preservation sector representing thirty-two nations around the world shared experiences to address the sustainability of cultural heritage.

The Assembly:

Recognizes that our global cultural heritage strengthens identities, well-being, and respect for other cultures and societies,

Affirms that cultural heritage is a powerful tool to engage communities positively and, as such, is a driving force for human development and creativity,

Reaffirms that an appreciation of diverse cultural heritage and its continuity for future generations promote mutual understanding between people, communities, and nations,

Acknowledges that although we have made tremendous gains in the cultural heritage sector in education, facilities, new technologies, and partnerships, our global cultural heritage is threatened by continuing deterioration and loss resulting from a shortage of trained conservation practitioners, natural and man-made emergencies and environmental risks, including climate change, and limited investment, and

Recommends that governments, non-governmental organizations, the cultural heritage sector, communities, and other stakeholders work together to:

- Integrate conservation projects with other sectors to provide a lever for social

and economic development,

- Commit to increased community engagement and raise public awareness regarding at-risk cultural heritage,
- Strengthen the investment in research, networking, educational opportunities, and the exchange of knowledge and resources globally, and
- Promote responsible stewardship and advance sustainable national/regional conservation policies and strategies, including risk management.

The deliberations at the Salzburg Global Seminar for the *Conservation and Preservation of Cultural Heritage* have established a new collaborative platform to more effectively preserve the world's cultural heritage and address global challenges now and in the future.[15]

CODES OF ETHICS FOR CULTURAL HERITAGE PROFESSIONAL ASSOCIATIONS: A SAMPLING[16]

Selection 9.6

AMERICAN ALLIANCE OF MUSEUMS

Excerpt from *Code of Ethics for Museums*

MUSEUMS MAKE THEIR unique contribution to the public by collecting, *preserving* [italics added] and interpreting the things of this world. Historically, they have owned and used natural objects, living and non-living, and all manner of human artifacts to advance knowledge and nourish the human spirit. Today, the range of their special interests reflects the scope of human vision. Their missions include collecting and preserving, as well as exhibiting and educating with materials not only owned but also borrowed and fabricated for these ends. Their numbers include both governmental and private museums of anthropology, art history and natural history, aquariums, arboreta, art centers, botanical gardens, children's museums, historic sites, nature centers, planetariums, science and technology centers, and zoos. The museum universe in the United States includes both collecting

and non-collecting institutions. Although diverse in their missions, they have in common their nonprofit form of organization and a commitment of service to the public. Their collections and/or the objects they borrow or fabricate are the basis for research, exhibits, and programs that invite public participation.

Taken as a whole, museum collections and exhibition materials represent the world's natural and cultural common wealth. As stewards of that wealth, museums are compelled to advance an understanding of all natural forms and of the human experience. It is incumbent on museums to be resources for humankind and in all their activities to foster an informed appreciation of the rich and diverse world we have inherited. It is also incumbent upon them to preserve that inheritance for posterity.

[...]

For museums, public service is paramount. To affirm that ethic and to elaborate its application to their governance, collections and programs, the American Association [now, Alliance] of Museums promulgates this *Code of Ethics for Museums*. In subscribing to this code, museums assume responsibility for the actions of members of their governing authority, employees and volunteers in the performance of museum-related duties. Museums, thereby, affirm their chartered purpose, ensure the prudent application of their resources, enhance their effectiveness and maintain public confidence. This collective endeavor strengthens museum work and the contributions of museums to society—present and future.

AMERICAN ASSOCIATION FOR STATE AND LOCAL HISTORY

Excerpts from *Statement of Professional Standards and Ethics*

THE AMERICAN ASSOCIATION for State and Local History is a membership organization comprised of individuals, agencies and organizations acting in the public trust, engaged in the practice of history and representing a variety of disciplines and professions. The Association expects its members to abide by the ethical and performance standards adopted by all appropriate discipline-based and professional organizations. The following ethical statements and related professional standards are provided for the guidance of all members of the Association.

HISTORICAL RESOURCES

Historical resources, including collections, built environment, cultural landscapes, archaeological sites, and other evidence of the past, provide the tools through which we interact with the past and are the bedrock upon which the practice of history rests. In fulfillment of their public trust, historical organizations and those associated with them must be responsible stewards and advocates on behalf of the historical resource within their care and throughout their communities.

A. Association members shall give priority to the care and management of the historical resources within their care and always shall act to preserve their physical and intellectual integrity.

B. Institutions shall manage historical resources in accord with comprehensive policies officially adopted by their governing authorities.

C. Collections shall not be capitalized or treated as financial assets.

D. Collections shall not be deaccessioned or disposed of in order to provide financial support for institutional operations, facilities maintenance or any reason other than preservation or acquisition of collections, as defined by institutional policy.

E. Historical resources shall be acquired, cared for and interpreted with sensitivity to their cultural origins.

F. It is important to document the physical condition of historical resources, including past treatment of objects, and to take appropriate steps to mitigate potential hazards to people and property.

ACCESS

... Providing non-discriminatory access to historical resources through exhibitions, tours, educational programs, publications, electronic media and research is critical in fulfilling the public trust and mission of historical organizations. Access and limitations of access are governed by institutional policies and by applicable rights of privacy, ownership and intellectual freedom.

AMERICAN INSTITUTE FOR CONSERVATION OF HISTORIC AND ARTISTIC WORKS

Excerpts from *Code of Ethics and Guidelines for Practice*

PREAMBLE

The primary goal of conservation professionals, individuals with extensive training and special expertise, is the preservation of cultural property. Cultural property consists of individual objects, structures, or aggregate collections. It is material which has significance that may be artistic, historical, scientific, religious, or social, and it is an invaluable and irreplaceable legacy that must be preserved for future generations.

In striving to achieve this goal, conservation professionals assume certain obligations to the cultural property, to its owners and custodians, to the conservation profession, and to society as a whole. This document, the Code of Ethics and Guidelines for Practice of the American Institute for Conservation of Historic & Artistic Works (AIC), sets forth the principles that guide conservation professionals and others who are involved in the care of cultural property.

CODE OF ETHICS

I. The conservation professional shall strive to attain the highest possible standards in all aspects of conservation, including, but not limited to, preventive conservation, examination, documentation, treatment, research, and education.

II. All actions of the conservation professional must be governed by an informed respect for the cultural property, its unique character and significance, and the people or person who created it.

III. While recognizing the right of society to make appropriate and respectful use of cultural property, the conservation professional shall serve as an advocate for the preservation of cultural property.

IV. The conservation professional shall practice within the limits of personal competence and educa-

tion as well as within the limits of the available facilities.

V. While circumstances may limit the resources allocated to a particular situation, the quality of work that the conservation professional performs shall not be compromised.

VI. The conservation professional must strive to select methods and materials that, to the best of current knowledge, do not adversely affect cultural property or its future examination, scientific investigation, treatment, or function.

VII. The conservation professional shall document examination, scientific investigation, and treatment by creating permanent records and reports.

VIII. The conservation professional shall recognize a responsibility for preventive conservation by endeavoring to limit damage or deterioration to cultural property, providing guidelines for continuing use and care, recommending appropriate environmental conditions for storage and exhibition, and encouraging proper procedures for handling, packing, and transport.

[...]

XI. The conservation professional shall promote an awareness and understanding of conservation through open communication with allied professionals and the public.

XII. The conservation professional shall practice in a manner that minimizes personal risks and hazards to co-workers, the public, and the environment.

XIII. Each conservation professional has an obligation to promote understanding of and adherence to this Code of Ethics.

[...]

AMERICAN LIBRARY ASSOCIATION

Excerpt from *Code of Ethics*

AS MEMBERS OF the American Library Association, we recognize the importance of codifying and making known to the profession and to the general public the ethical principles that guide the work of librarians, other professionals providing information services, library trustees and library staffs.

Ethical dilemmas occur when values are in conflict. The American Library Association Code of Ethics states the values to which we are committed, and embodies the ethical responsibilities of the profession in this changing information environment.

We significantly influence or control the selection, organization, preservation, and dissemination of information. In a political system grounded in an informed citizenry, we are members of a profession explicitly committed to intellectual freedom and the freedom of access to information. We have a special obligation to ensure the free flow of information and ideas to present and future generations.

The principles of this Code are expressed in broad statements to guide ethical decision making. These statements provide a framework; they cannot and do not dictate conduct to cover particular situations.

I. We provide the highest level of service to all library users through appropriate and usefully organized resources; equitable service policies; equitable access; and accurate, unbiased, and courteous responses to all requests.

II. We uphold the principles of intellectual freedom and resist all efforts to censor library resources.

III. We protect each library user's right to privacy and confidentiality with respect to information sought or received and resources consulted, borrowed, acquired or transmitted.

IV. We respect intellectual property rights and advocate balance between the interests of information users and rights holders.

[...]

ASSOCIATION OF MOVING IMAGE ARCHIVISTS

Excerpt from *Code of Ethics*

THE ASSOCIATION OF Moving Image Archivists (AMIA), a collective of individuals, recognizes the diversity of its membership and encourages each individual who acts as a custodian of our moving image heritage to strive towards the following common goals:

1) To respect the value of moving images for their cultural, historical and/or artistic significance.

2) To provide the best possible conservation environment for artifacts in his/her care, regardless of the medium or format.

3) To encourage collection development and to adopt collection management policies that define collection scopes and articulate how collections should be maintained.

4) To restore and preserve artifacts without altering the original materials, whenever possible. To properly document any restoration/preservation decisions and to make decisions consistent with the intentions of the creators, whenever appropriate.

5) To balance the priority of protecting the physical integrity of objects/artifacts with facilitating safe and non-discriminatory access to them.

6) To provide access to content, as much as possible, without infringing on current copyright or intellectual property rights laws.

7) To agree that archivists who care for collections should refrain from exploiting artifacts from those collections for personal benefit.

SOCIETY OF AMERICAN ARCHIVISTS

Excerpts from *Code of Ethics for Archivists*

ARCHIVES ARE CREATED by a wide array of groups and provide evidence of the full range of human experience. Archivists endeavor to ensure that those materials, entrusted to their care, will be accessible over time as evidence of human activity and social organization. Archivists embrace principles that foster the transparency of their actions and that inspire confidence in the profession. A distinct body of ethical norms helps archivists navigate the complex situations and issues that can arise in the course of their work.

[...]

The Society endorses this Code of Ethics for Archivists as principles of the profession. This Code should be read in conjunction with SAA's "Core Values of Archivists." Together they provide guidance to archivists and increase awareness of ethical concerns among archivists, their colleagues, and the rest of society. As advocates for documentary collections and cultural objects under their care, archivists aspire to carry out their professional activities with the highest standard of professional conduct. The behaviors and characteristics outlined in this Code of Ethics should serve as aspirational principles for archivists to consider as they strive to create trusted archival institutions.

[...]

JUDGMENT

Archivists exercise professional judgment in appraising, acquiring, and processing materials to ensure the preservation, authenticity, diversity, and lasting cultural and historical value of their collections. Archivists should carefully document their collections-related decisions and activities to make their role in the selection, retention, or creation of the historical record transparent to their institutions, donors, and users. Archivists are encouraged to consult with colleagues, relevant professionals, and communities of interest to ensure that diverse perspectives inform their actions and decisions.

AUTHENTICITY

Archivists ensure the authenticity and continuing usability of records in their care. They document and protect the unique archival characteristics of records and strive to protect the records' intellectual and physical integrity from tampering or corruption. Archivists may not willfully alter, manipulate, or destroy data or records to conceal facts or distort evidence. They thoroughly document any actions that may cause changes to the records in their care or raise questions about the records' authenticity.

SECURITY AND PROTECTION

Archivists protect all documentary materials for which they are responsible. They take steps to minimize the natural physical deterioration of records and implement specific security policies to protect digital records. Archivists guard all records against accidental damage, vandalism, and theft and have well-formulated plans in place to respond to any disasters that may threaten records. Archivists cooperate actively with colleagues and law enforcement agencies to apprehend and prosecute vandals and thieves.

ACCESS AND USE

Recognizing that use is the fundamental reason for keeping archives, archivists actively promote open and equitable access to the records in their care within the context of their institutions' missions and their intended user groups. They minimize restrictions and maximize ease of access. They facilitate the continuing accessibility and intelligibility of archival materials in all formats. Archivists formulate and disseminate institutional access policies along with strategies that encourage responsible use. They work with donors and originating agencies to ensure that any restrictions are appropriate, well-documented, and equitably enforced. When repositories require restrictions to protect confidential and proprietary information, such restrictions should be implemented in an impartial manner. In all questions of access, archivists seek practical solutions that balance competing principles and interests.

PRIVACY

Archivists recognize that privacy is sanctioned by law. They establish procedures and policies to protect the interests of the donors, individuals, groups, and institutions whose public and private lives and activities are recorded in their holdings. As appropriate, archivists place access restrictions on collections to ensure that privacy and confidentiality are maintained, particularly for individuals and groups who have no voice or role in collections' creation, retention, or public use. Archivists promote the respectful use of culturally sensitive materials in their care by encouraging researchers to consult with communities of origin, recognizing that privacy has both legal and cultural dimensions. Archivists respect all users' rights to privacy by maintaining the confidentiality of their research and protecting any personal information collected about the users in accordance with their institutions' policies.

TRUST

Archivists should not take unfair advantage of their privileged access to and control of historical records and documentary materials. They execute their work knowing that they must ensure proper custody for the documents and records entrusted to them. Archivists should demonstrate professional integrity and avoid potential conflicts of interest. They strive to balance the sometimes-competing interests of all stakeholders.

NOTES

1. Daniel N. Robinson, *The Great Ideas of Philosophy*, 2nd ed. Part 1 (Chantilly, VA: The Teaching Company, 2004), 1. Moral epistemology is an area of study, and moral authority falls within governance, both of which demonstrate the pitfalls of categorization.

2. William K. Frankena and John T. Granrose, eds., *Introductory Readings in Ethics* (Englewood Cliffs, NJ: Prentice-Hall, 1974), 1.

3. Frankena & Granrose, *Introductory Readings*, 2.

4. John Dewey, "Reflective Morality and Ethical Theory," in Frankena & Granrose, 12–17.

5. Dewey, "Reflective Morality," 12–13.

6. These are two extreme examples of ethical dilemmas that a curator might face in exhibiting controversial images. The Serrano photograph was controversial from the beginning; it depicts a crucifix of Christ that was allegedly submerged in the artist's urine. Display of it has resulted in protests, and the work itself has been vandalized more than once by museum-goers. The Danish cartoons, which were published in the *Jyllands-Posten* on September 30, 2005, are also explosive because they depict images of Mohammed, which is prohibited by Islamic law. Even a book published by Yale University Press about the cartoons did not publish them; see http://creepingsharia.wordpress.com/videos/ (accessed July 9, 2012). The decision to display them might involve violent protests, vandalism, and so on. Thus the curator has to weigh freedom of speech against potential harm to the objects or to the protestors. A curator who holds strong religious beliefs might decline to exhibit these works.

7. "Understanding Modern Biblioclasm" is chapter 1 in Knuth's *Burning Books and Leveling Libraries: Extremist Violence and Cultural Destruction* (Westport, CT: Praeger, 2006), 1–16. See also her *Libricide: The Regime-Sponsored Destruction of Books and Libraries in the Twentieth Century* (Westport, CT: Praeger, 2003).

8. See chapter 1 for excerpts from Francis Lieber's *Instructions for the Government of Armies of the United States in the Field* (also known as the *Lieber Code*), for one example.

9. The scholarship on the topic of war and morality is voluminous, especially in recent years, in response to the numerous conflicts in the Middle East. A classic work that examines war in an international relations context is Raymond Aron's *Peace and War: A Theory of International Relations*, first published in 1966. See especially Chapter 19, "In Search of a Morality: I. Idealism and Realism," and part II, "Conviction and Responsibility," 611–635 (New Brunswick, NJ: Transaction Publishers, 2006), pp. 579–610).

10. See http://www.ifla.org/en/publications/ifla-principles-of-engagement-in-library-related

-activities-in-times-of-conflict-crisis (accessed July 9, 2012).

11. Cited by Raymond Aron immediately preceding the beginning of *Peace and War*; see note 9 above.

12. Yahaya Ahmad, "The Scope and Definitions of Heritage: From Tangible to Intangible," *International Journal of Heritage Studies* 12.3 (2006): 292–300.

13. *International Charter for the Conservation and Restoration of Monuments and Sites* (the Venice Charter), Second International Congress of Architects and Technicians of Historic Monuments, Venice, May 25–31, 1964, accessed December 5, 2012, http://www.icomos.org/venicecharter2004/index.html.

14. Prepared at a conference in Salzburg Austria, sponsored by the Salzburg Global Seminar (Salzburg, Austria) and the Institute of Museum and Library Services (Washington, DC), which initiated, organized, and hosted the conference. The co-chairs were Vinod Daniel (Australian Museum) and Debra Hess Norris (University of Delaware).

ETHICS AND VALUES: ARTICLES

Selection 9.12

RICHARD COX AND JAMES O'TOOLE

"The Impulse to Save"

In Understanding Archives & Manuscripts. *Chicago: Society of American Archivists, 2006, pp. 15–17.*

INFORMATION IS USUALLY recorded with some direct, intended usefulness in mind, and thus keeping the records (or copies of them) as soon as they are made has an obvious benefit. Most records are probably not needed for more than a few months, however, and the question of what records to keep longer has always challenged archivists. The public's perception of archives is that they save everything forever, and this often produces amazement or even protest when it is discovered that they are in fact selective.[25] Each motive for creating a record may have its parallel reason for keeping it temporarily. But what is the source of the impulse to save them for a longer, perhaps even indefinite, period after that original usefulness has ceased?

Though records may not always be created exclusively for practical reasons, the impulse to save them frequently has a resolutely practical basis. We save records because we think we will need them again in the future, even if that specific time or particular use cannot now be foreseen precisely. Archivists acknowledge that these future uses are difficult to assess and can impede the careful appraisal of records; it is easy to fall into the trap of saving everything "just in case." Still, the information recorded today may be needed again, its potency or effectiveness undiminished by the passage of time. Especially when the record is made for legal, economic, or instrumental purposes, there may be an ongoing need to recall that information, and saving it thus has a pragmatic value.

Just as the origins of writing suggest utilitarian purposes with lists of property, commercial transactions, and public decrees, so the most obvious reasons for saving records suggest very practical uses. Proving ownership of a piece of land may be necessary, for instance, for both the original owner and any successor. Perhaps more likely, determining exactly where one's property ends and another's begins may be critical. Records may also set the terms and conditions for the performance of specified duties (as in contracts), and saving them will therefore provide the basis for judging whether those obligations have been fulfilled. Such practical reasons for saving records always exist within the given legal and economic structures of different societies, and the usefulness of saved records will thus vary with place and time. Understanding those legal and economic requirements is critical for any saver of records long term. Moreover, it is important to document why records are saved, thereby allowing archivists and researchers alike to comprehend the full documentary universe from which they came.

Though certain uses of records may be foreseen at the time of their creation, in most cases it is the unpredictability of future use that reinforces the impulse to save them. When we record information, we cannot always anticipate the uses to which it might be put in the future. We are reasonably certain that the financial data recorded today will be needed at the end of the fiscal year to balance the books. It may also be needed next year, however, in an outside audit, and perhaps even required again five or six years hence in connection with a government tax investigation. It may be useful in charting long-term trends: are we making money or going broke? Perhaps none of these specific needs will arise, but they are all at least possible, and the record is kept against that possibility. The unpredictability of future uses of records demands the security that saving them provides.

At the same time, however, there are also nonpractical reasons for saving records, reasons that are personal, social, and even symbolic. Records are saved because they are a form of individual or collective memory. People will often hang onto even the most innocuous stuff—scraps of paper, old receipts, ticket stubs, canceled checks—because the document helps them remember something that is special to them. What did we do, why and how did we do it, and what were our thoughts and feelings as we did it? Letters, diaries, and photographs can provide that information, and so we save them in the interest of remembering what we once knew but have since forgotten, or of remembering it more vividly. We want to relive happy experiences of the past or, perhaps, recall the lessons of unpleasant experiences, and so we save the records that will help us do so. For individuals, preserved love letters call good times to mind; for whole societies, records such as those of the Salem witch trials or the Holocaust remind us of a past we might want to forget but know we should not. It may also

be that we save records even when it would be in our best interests not to. One of the enduring mysteries of the Watergate scandal of the 1970s is why President Nixon did not simply destroy the tape recordings that eventually helped destroy his political career.[26] Like various kinds of physical objects, records can be prized as relics, things in themselves with both physical and intellectual meaning, and we save them in the hope of calling back the presence of persons, events, or emotions with immediacy. We reread letters we wrote and received in college, for instance, or we look again at drawings made in childhood and proudly preserved by parents. These feelings too may be somewhat unpredictable, but the desire to recollect our individual and social past is common enough that we preserve the records that will make recollection possible. Such impulses may well be unexplainable in a coolly rational way; they may place us, together with book collectors, "among the gently mad."[27] But can everything be saved? Archivists and curators know that it cannot; otherwise, the shelves would be full tomorrow and all further collecting would have to stop. How archivists decide what to save is therefore critical, but before making those decisions they must understand the impulse to destroy no less than the impulse to save.

NOTES

25. This is most dramatically seen in Nicholson Baker, *Double Fold: Libraries and the Assault on Paper* (New York: Random House, 2001). Responses include Richard J. Cox, *Vandals in the Stacks? A Response to Nicholson Baker's Assault on Libraries* (Westport, Conn.: Greenwood Press, 2002) and Nicholas Basbanes, *A Splendor of Letters: The Permanence of Books in an Impermanent World* (New York: HarperCollins, 2003).

26. Kenneth E. Foote, "To Remember and Forget: Archives, Memory and Culture," *American Archivist* 53 (Summer 1990): 378–92; David Lowenthal, *The Past is a Foreign Country* (Cambridge: Cambridge University Press, 1985), especially chapter 5.

27. Nicholas Basbanes, *Among the Gently Mad: Perspectives and Strategies for the Book Hunter in the Twenty-First Century* (New York: Henry Holt and Co., 2001).

RICHARD COX AND JAMES O'TOOLE

"The Impulse to Destroy"

In Understanding Archives & Manuscripts, *Chicago, Society of American Archivists, 2006, pp. 17–21.*

THE MIRROR IMAGE of the impulse to save records is the impulse to destroy them. This is done most directly by the literal physical destruction of documents through such means as burning or shredding—or, in the case of electronic records, deleting—but there are other forms of destruction as well, both real and metaphorical. It may be done by neglecting them, deliberately or through more "benign" methods, so that the normal processes of deterioration can do their damage unimpeded. Finally, it may be done by falsifying or misrepresenting them, causing records to seem to say things that they do not actually say. The motives for destruction are manifold, and every literate society has examples of them, although such efforts have been especially prevalent in the twentieth century. Germany, France, Japan, South Africa, Yugoslavia, Bosnia, and the United States all have engaged in efforts to eliminate or seal documentation concerning genocide, social injustice, and mere political high jinks. "Truth commissions" in many countries have tried to undo this damage, and their work has led to the creation of archives and to greater access to records of past injustices.[28]

Records, archival or otherwise, are powerful factors in society, and, as a result, they are often the targets for destruction. Book burning has occurred everywhere there are books. and the destruction of libraries usually includes the elimination of archival documents as well. Some scholars argue that the legendary ancient library at Alexandria was destroyed by subsequent struggles between Christians and Muslims, each eager to purge texts that were either sacred or diabolical, depending on which side one was on. During the Reformation, each denomination enthusiastically burned the heretical books of the others. Crowds in the French Revolution sometimes directed their fury against repositories of documents that embodied aristocratic privilege, destroying records

of debt and service obligations while plundering the finery of manor houses and noble coats of arms.[29] Nor should we think of such actions as confined to a remote past, perpetrated by those who did not have the sensibility we moderns claim for ourselves. The smashing of Confucian texts during the Cultural Revolution in China in the 1960s and 1970s is a reminder that no society, however advanced or sophisticated, can entirely avoid the temptation to destroy records.

The impulse to destroy may come first from the creators of records themselves. Some leaders seek to destroy the records of their predecessors, eager in effect to begin the world and history over again with themselves. Hitler and his lieutenants destroyed the evidence of those peoples they tried to eradicate, all the while documenting their own activities to create a supposedly purer version of history.[30] More common is the desire to destroy records so as to remove evidence of wrongdoing, illegality, moral turpitude, or simple incompetence. Once again, the Watergate scandal offers a good example, in which possession of the tape recordings of White House conversations became critical. Archivists, historians, and public interest groups joined in a lawsuit to establish the principle that presidential materials were public records, not the personal property of the president, precisely because they feared that the incriminating recordings would be destroyed if President Nixon retained control over them.[31] In the corporate accounting scandals of the early twenty-first century, the destruction of damaging records by company officers was added to charges of insider trading and mismanagement of funds.[32] Any record creator with something to hide could readily see the advantages of destroying records to keep the secrets secret.

The impulse of others to destroy records after the fact is no less common, and the destruction is often justified in the name of larger ideological or cultural causes. In the early 1990s, libraries and archives in Bosnia were burned as part of a concerted effort by Serbian nationalists to eradicate evidence of Muslim and Croatian peoples. "Throughout Bosnia," one reporter noted, "libraries, archives, museums and cultural institutions have been targeted for destruction, in an attempt to eliminate the material evidence, books, documents and works of art that could remind future generations that people of different ethnic and religious traditions once shared a common heritage in Bosnia. ...While the destruction of a community's institutions and records is, in the first instance, part of a strategy of intimidation aimed at driving out members of the targeted group, it also serves a long-term goal. These records were proof that non-Serbs once resided and owned property in that place, that they had historical roots there. By burning the documents, by razing mosques and Catholic churches and bulldozing the graveyards, the nationalist forces who have now taken over these towns and villages are trying to insure themselves against any future claims by the people they have driven out and dispossessed."[33]

After-the-fact destruction of records may also derive from less sinister, more personal, and perhaps even understandable motives. The son of a World War II veteran tells a story which, though heartbreaking to historians and archivists, offers an enlightening window into the intense emotional meaning records may have and how that may lead to their destruction. The American serviceman in question, the son of immigrants, wrote regular letters home throughout his service in the European theater of the war, and the letters were lovingly passed around to members of the extended family as a way of assuring everyone that he was safe. On the day he returned home, discharged at the war's end, his father ordered one of the soldier's sisters to shred the letters into confetti. They now offered only painful reminders of the danger their loved one had experienced, the persistent anxiety the whole family had felt for his return, and these troubles were to have no part of the brighter future they all looked forward to.[34] Better to enforce forgetfulness of those dark days by destroying the records of them.

Falsifying or consciously misrepresenting records may also be seen as a form of destruction—if not of the records themselves, then at least of the trust we

normally place in them. Together with outright plagiarism, the fabrication of documentary evidence is rightly condemned, but examples of it persist nonetheless. Those writers who have made a sinister cottage industry of denying the historical reality of the Holocaust have refined this technique to a fine art, but the practice is not unknown even among more apparently reputable scholars.[35] Michael A. Bellesile's *Arming America: The Origins of a National Gun Culture* was published in 2000 to wide acclaim: it won Columbia University's Bancroft Prize for the best book in American history. The work quickly sank into a sea of controversy, however, as charges were first made and then proved that the author had misquoted, miscited, and miscalculated documentary evidence from public and private archives, all (it appeared) in a conscious effort to support his predetermined conclusions. There were even suggestions that he cited records that did not exist: when asked to produce the research notes for some of his more controversial assertions, he could not. Other historians tried without success to find records he claimed to have seen, while still others followed his documentary footsteps and found very different evidence. He was eventually placed on leave from his university, his career ruined, and the prestigious prize was taken away, to the embarrassment of him and of the original judges.[36] While this did not involve the actual physical destruction of records, the effect was the same: it undercut the reliability of records and skewed the documentary basis for understanding the past no less than flames or the shredder would have done.

NOTES

28. Priscilla B. Hayner, *Unspeakable Truths: Facing the Challenge of Truth Commissions* (New York: Routledge, 2002).

29. Just as often, of course, rulers try to control and shape the past to cover their misdeeds or to fabricate an image in history undeserving for their role in it. It is reported that when King Leopold of Belgium was forced to give up his colony in the Congo, he endeavored to destroy all the evidence of his activities, claiming a privilege that this was his personal business and no one else's. Adam Hochschild,

King Leopold's Ghost: A Story of Greed, Terror and Heroism in Colonial Africa (Boston: Houghton Mifflin Co., 1998).

30. More remarkably, the controversies in the 1990s about the looting of Holocaust victims' assets and the laundering of funds and other assets through Swiss banks brought a renewed attention to the fact that even a government committed to genocide is likely to document fully its atrocities. There are many accounts of the Holocaust victims' assets, but for a good introduction see Stuart E. Eizenstat, *Imperfect Justice: Looted Assets, Slave Labor and the Unfinished Business of World War II* (New York: Public Affairs, 2003).

31. For a full perspective on this, see John Prados, *The White House Tapes: Eavesdropping on the President* (New York: The New Press, 2003).

32. Barbara Ley Toffler, with Jennifer Reingold, *Final Accounting: Ambition, Greed, and the Fall of Arthur Andersen* (New York: Broadway Books, 2003).

33. Quoted from András Riedlmayer, "Erasing the Past: The Destruction of Libraries and Archives

in Bosnia-Herzegovina," *Middle Eastern Studies Association Bulletin,* July 1995, available at: http://fp.arizona.edu/mesassoc/Bulletin/bosnia.htm.

34. Stephen C. Puleo, *30,000 Miles from Home: The World War II Journey of Tony Puleo* (Boston: privately printed, 1997), i–ii.

35. One of the most dramatic examples of this is the trial, initiated by Holocaust-denier David Irving, of Deborah Lipstadt for her book about these deniers. The trial put on the stand the veracity of historical evidence, the appropriateness of historical methodologies, and the importance of archival records. See Deborah Lipstadt, *Denying the Holocaust: The Growing Assault on Truth and Memory* (New York: The Free Press, 1993) and Richard Evans, *Lying About Hitler: History, Holocaust, and the David Irving Trial* (New York: Basic Books, 2001).

36. "Columbia University Rescinds Bancroft Prize," *Organization of American Historians Newsletter,* February 2003, available at http://www.oah.org/pubs/nl/2003feb/belleisles.html.

SAMUEL JONES AND JOHN HOLDEN

Excerpt from "Conservation and Its Values"

In It's a Material World, *London: Demos, 2008, pp. 27–29.*

The Idea of Conservation

The *Oxford English Dictionary* defines conservation as 'to keep in safety, or from harm, decay, or loss; to preserve with care; now usually, to preserve in its existing state from destruction or change'.[9] But conservation is not just about practice; it is also an idea and an attitude, and is about choices. Decisions as to what to treat, how to treat it, and whom to involve are rooted in the relationship conservators perceive between the object and its social context. In a white paper, *Heritage Protection for the 21st Century*, DCMS and the Welsh Assembly recognised this:

Designation [the identification of those aspects of our past that are most important to us and explaining why they are important] is the first step in an effective heritage protection system. It is a means of identifying those aspects of our past that are most important to us, and explaining why they are important. Effective designation is also the basis for decisions about the way we manage change to the historic environment.[10]

Value is socially determined: an object, artefact or building can only have value insofar as people give it value. Conservation is therefore rooted in social action, and refers to the *management* of change in objects that have fluctuating value in the society in which they exist. It is in conservation's favour that it is *not* objective. Conservation is about refreshing and renewing culture and heritage in ways that reflect and contribute to society's values, thereby making a statement about value to others, and a statement about the present to the future. Objects matter because they are powerful visual metaphors that can bypass language. At heart, conservation is a political act – it is a contribution to a conversation between values[11] (see box 1).

Conservation is rooted in professional practice, but extends well beyond it. As a report produced by the Getty Conservation Institute in California, a leading centre for conservation research and practice, put it:

Traditional conservation remains the core of the field's activity and its raison d'être, but... the conservation process is best seen more inclusively, encompassing the creation of heritage, interpretation and education, the many efforts of individuals and social groups to be stewards of heritage, and shifting economics and political tides, as well as more traditional practices of conservators, preservationists, curators and other professionals.[12]

Conservation has a fundamental place within the cultural and heritage sector, and a special relationship with science. In presenting evidence to the House of Lords Science and Technology Committee, the British Museum positioned the conservation sector 'at the interface of the arts and sciences; scientific examination, analysis and research inform an understanding of material culture and the susceptibility of artefacts to change, while historical, archaeological and art historical research place these results in the context of place, period, practice and belief—a two-way knowledge transfer across this often problematic interface.'[14] In fact, conservation is one way in which people can make the connection between the arts and the sciences.

A professional's definition of conservation

A good definition of conservation, which takes conservation beyond the OED definition, is provided by Dean Sully, a lecturer in conservation at University College, London, who sees conservation involving interpretation as much as preservation. He says that conservation is:

a complex and continual process that involves determining what heritage is, how it is cared for, how it is used, by whom, and for whom. Conservation as a developing social practise is not only concerned with definitions of best practise, but in continually reassessing the applicability of new approaches to changed circumstances... Conservation is a process of understanding and managing change rather than merely an arresting process; it is a means of recreating material cultural heritage that seeks to retain, reveal and enhance what people value about the material past and sustain those values for future generations... objects are conserved because they are valued for the effect they have on people.[13]

NOTES

9. Quoted in House of Lords Science and Technology Committee, *Science and Heritage*.

10. DCMS and Welsh Assembly, *Heritage Protection for the 21st Century*.

11. For fuller discussion of the politics of 'things', see Appadurai, 'Introduction'.

12. Avrami, Mason and de la Torre, *Values and Heritage Conservation*.

13. Sully, *Decolonising Conservation*.

14. House of Lords Science and Technology Committee, *Science and Heritage*.

ELLEN PEARLSTEIN

"Restoring Provenance to a Native American Feather Blanket"

Museum Management and Curatorship *25.1 (2010): 87–105*. [*Editor's note: Not all of the original images were reproducible.*]

Introduction

A case study involving Native American feather blankets pinpoints rich contextual differences that may occur when objects with possible connected origins evolve and develop different cultural meanings. In the museum environment, physical examination is often used to aid in the understanding of an object and to offer guidance about its attribution, care, and preservation. However, the case of the feather blankets illustrates that the type of inquiry conducted by conservators can also aide in the identification of burial objects and may influence whether materials are subject to The Native American Graves Protection and Repatriation Act (NAGPRA) legislation, and are inappropriate for display.

The NAGPRA legislation was passed in the USA in 1990, obligating museums and collections receiving federal funding to report on and, in some cases, repatriate their Native American holdings to federally recognized tribes. According to the official website, 'NAGPRA provides a process for museums and Federal agencies to return certain Native American cultural items—human remains, funerary objects, sacred objects, and objects of cultural patrimony—to lineal descendants, culturally affiliated Indian tribes, and Native Hawaiian organizations' (National Park Service n/d). Before the passage of NAGPRA legislation and decidedly since, staff in American museums holding Native American collections have been consulting with tribal members about appropriate care, storage, treatment, and display of indigenous collections (Flynn and Hull-Walski 2001). This case study illustrates how a study of materials and construction methods may aid in determining whether an unprovenanced object might fall into the cultural categories subject to repatriation under NAGPRA.

In 2004, a feather blanket consisting of cordage wrapped with strips of feather was purchased from private collectors by the Agua Caliente Cultural Museum (ACCM) in Palm Springs, California (Figure 1). The blanket, which measures 66 cm x 46 cm, is in fragmentary condition and was accompanied by an associated bag of soil. The blanket had changed hands between private individuals within California before being acquired by the museum. Upon acquisition, the museum staff contacted a vertebrate biologist in California and reported in an undated memo that the feathers are 'breast and flank of songbirds, quail, duck, raptor, and possibly others.' Specialists in southern California material culture were consulted and in the same memo it is reported that the blanket was constructed of waterfowl feathers with a likely origin in California.

Only 14 California feather blankets are known through McLendon's (2001, 132) important work in

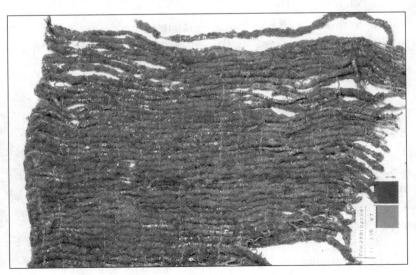

Figure 1.

which she traces the collecting history of each blanket to tribes in the north-central Sacramento River Valley. These California blankets are all in museum collections and their accompanying documentation indicates that the blankets were given by tribes as gifts to visitors as part of a display of wealth and status (McLendon 2001, 133) (Figure 2). In a context that implied regalia and rarity, the ACCM feather blanket was deemed a priority for conservation treatment and preparation for display.

The Agua Caliente Cultural Museum (ACCM) Artifact (2004.023.001)

DESCRIPTION AND CONSTRUCTION

The ACCM feather blanket is constructed of feather-wrapped plant fiber cordage. It has been made by

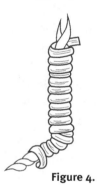

Figure 4.

first twisting slit feather quills, with barbs attached, continuously around two-ply plant fiber cord (Figures 3 [not shown] and 4). The plant fiber cords are S spun, and plied with a Z twist. No other mechanism for feather attachment aside from physical wrapping is visible. Another examiner noted a shiny material, suspected to be an adhesive, used to attach the feathers onto the fiber cordage; however, this is likely to be a natural plant gum left during the minimal processing of the leaf fiber (Rohn 1971, 6).

The feathered cord was initially prepared at considerable length and was then laid out and looped at either end, with each loop interlocked into the adjacent one. While it is likely that the feather cords were spliced to achieve the desired length, no evidence of splicing is apparent in X-radiographs taken of the blanket. Other researchers have found splicing difficult to discern in a comparably deteriorated blanket, despite finding feather-wrapped cordage measuring 42 m (137.5 feet) in total length (Rohn 1971, 16). Contemporary Hopi weaver, Ramona Sakiestewa, replicated a turkey feather blanket and twisted together the frayed yucca support fibers to increase length, producing cordage measuring 32 m or 105 feet (Southwest Productions 1983).

Figure 2.

These looped and feather-wrapped cords form the warp, which is held together and in parallel alignment with 17 rows of paired twining elements. Estimated from what is extant, 22 looped warps are visible at the more complete end, but it is estimated that there were loops at both ends, and the original object length is estimated at around 69 cm. In one corner is a knotted bundle of hair (Figure 5). At the opposite, more damaged end, the feathered cords retain a looped position but no loops are intact and the twining fibers have suffered greater losses. Despite the current condition which includes extensive insect damage and feather loss, it is apparent that the warp cordage was completely covered with feathers on all sides.

Materials in the Agua Caliente Cultural Museum (ACCM) Feather Blanket

FEATHERS

Specific materials analysis was conducted to help in assigning provenance to the feather blanket. The feathers on the blanket are all dull brown in color-

Figure 5.

ation and include downy and pennaceous (or smooth) feathers whose small size suggests sources on the bird body, and possibly trimmed feathers from the wings or tail. In spite of the varied appearance, the feathers appear to derive from a single type of bird. Carla Dove, Research Scientist in the Feather Identification Laboratory, Smithsonian Institution, was able to positively identify both the pennaceous and downy feathers as belonging to the turkey family. According to Dove's report, diagnostic traits include 'downy barbs with long barbules and ringed structures at the nodes' (Figure 6). The identification of turkey feathers contradicts the earlier designation that the blanket is made from waterfowl feathers.

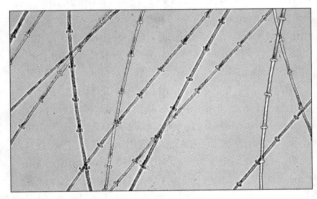

Figure 6.

CORDAGE FIBER

Two plant types were considered as comparative material for the fiber cordage used for both twining and around which the feathers are wrapped. The first is a species in the *Yucca* genus in the Agavaceae family and the second is *Apocynum cannabinum* L. in the Apocynaceae family. Undetermined yucca species have been identified as the source for cordage in feather blankets primarily from the Southwestern USA (Kidder and Guernsey 1919; Rohn 1971, 8-9; Webster 2003a). *A. cannabinum* L., known by the common names of Indian hemp, dogbane, and milkweed, is well established as a cordage fiber used by tribes throughout California, but is also cited as used in the Southwest (Anderson 2005, 229-31; USDA 2006) (Figure 7).

Examination of surface and cross-sections of the ACCM cordage fiber was conducted by preparing wet mounts and using polarized light micro-

scopy and transmitted light—methods which permit tiny samples to be viewed at up to 500 x magnification. The fibers used in the feather blanket are pale in color and coarse in texture, with a two-ply plant fiber cord that measures between 0.5 and 1.5 cm in diameter. Microscopic features indicate sclerenchyma (1) bundles and a structure derived from monocot (2) leaves. Mounted surface sections of both the feather wrapped and the twining fibers reveal bundles of flat, ribbon-shaped fibers, which have been processed to remove other plant tissue (Figure 8a and b [not shown]). Neither fiber sample has transverse dislocations (3) or a stem structure that might be associated with a bast (4) fiber, such as Indian hemp. The feather cord fiber bundle has a crescent shape in cross-section made up of tightly packed polygonal-shaped fibers with circular lumens, characteristic of Agave species (Mauersberger 1954; The Textile Institute 1965) (Figure 9 [not shown]). The twining fiber bundle has a semi-circular cross-section and the individual fibers are more circular. Traces of proto-xylem with spiral thickening are observed in the twining fiber surface section.

Examples of Indian hemp collected and processed in California were mounted as comparative material. The surface section revealed loosely connected fiber bundles with dislocations and striations parallel to the fiber length (Florian, Kronkright, and Norton 1990, 51). Indian hemp samples used for fiber by tribes all over California are described as either inner or outer bark fibers (Moerman 2006, 78-9). Morphological characteristics associated with Indian hemp were lacking in the ACCM blanket samples, which compared favorably with yucca leaf fiber. The ACCM blanket is markedly similar in characteristics to the feather wrapped yucca cordage found in Mug House, Mesa Verde, which is described as two-ply Z-twist cordage close to 0.5 cm in diameter (Rohn 1971, 8).

HAIR

The hair bundle at the more complete end of the blanket was identified by the author as human, based on morphological examination that included use of polarized light and environmental scanning electron microscopy. The hair is Z spun and is two ply in the

S direction, and it forms a figure-eight knot secured to the blanket. While the condition is extremely deteriorated, observable characteristics include a dark brown color and length up to about 13 cm. Polarized light microscopy with transmitted light indicated a very shallow scale pattern and a wide medulla (distinct inner region). Environmental scanning electron microscopy permitted clearer imaging of the hair, indicating a hair width of approximately 80 μm (micrometers) and scalloped-edged scales that are closely spaced at a count of about 20 scales per 100 μm—features consistent with human hair (McCrone and Delly 1973). The deteriorated condition of the hairs and the natural variability of features both contribute to an estimated identification as human, which was confirmed by a specialist at the US Fish and Wildlife Laboratories.

ASSOCIATED BOTANICALS

The associated botanicals were sifted from the soil accompanymg the feather blanket, and were submitted to a paleobotanist for identification. It is impossible to determine when the botanical materials became associated with the blanket, but their presence in the soil and the condition of the blanket suggest a burial association. The following items were reported: two *Juniperus* sp. leaf buds (Juniper); one *Portulaca* sp. seed (Purslane); one *Asteraceae akene* (sunflower family fruit); one *Poaceae culm* (grass family stem); and one unidentified seed or fruit (Wohlgemuth 2008). All of the plants identified are present in both the Southwest USA and north and central California. The California juniper (*J. californica*), however, grows in scattered localities in the inner southern and northern Coast Ranges and the Sierra Nevada foothills (Hickman 1993; Kuchler 1977), but it is not nearly as pervasive as juniper species in the Southwest.

Native North American Feather Blankets

The materials, technology, and cultural contexts of different feather blankets were investigated to provide comparative data for the ACCM blanket. Feather blankets under consideration are those in which cordage is made by wrapping vegetable fiber yarn with whole or split feathers, or with strips of bird skin, capturing tufts of feathers between twined cords, or rolling feather down into cordage without plant fiber support. Feather blankets from the Southwest Feather and fur blankets from the prehistoric Southwest are described by Kent and other investigators as made of cordage using different methods of twisting feather or fur tufts, or feathered or fur skins, together with or without plant fiber yarns (Haury 1950, Figure 93; Kent 1983, 24–6). Feather blankets excavated in the Southwest are commonly found in association with human burials. Feather blankets share construction methods with fur blankets which were excavated in levels associated with Basketmaker in Gypsum Cave in Nevada (Harrington 1933, 156–7). Of 11 fur blanket specimens from Gypsum Cave, seven are identified as twisted on yucca cordage measuring 0.32–0.48 cm (1/8" to 3/16") diameter, and three on Indian hemp, measuring 0.16–0.24 cm (1/16" to 3/32") (Harrington 1933, 157). A fur blanket with twining identical to that found in the ACCM feather blanket is documented from Basketmaker cave sites in northeastern Arizona, near Kayenta, and illustrated in Figure 11a in Guernsey and Kidder (1921, 65). The authors illustrate blankets and aprons from White Dog Cave and describe their materials as rabbit fur, both Indian hemp ('apocynum') and yucca, and human hair (Guernsey and Kidder 1921, 46; Plate 16). Harrington (1930, 116–7) published excavated examples from Paiute Cave in Southwestern Nevada of rabbit fur cordage dated by ceramic association to the Pueblo period. It is interesting that this fur blanket example is based on Z twist, two-ply skin strips lacking a vegetable fiber foundation cord, a feature which is observed on California feather blankets more than those of the Southwest (Harrington 1930, 116).

While fur blankets precede feather blankets chronologically in the Southwest, both fur and feather-wrapped cordage are found together in single burials. Archaeological feather-wrapped cords were found associated with a rabbit fur blanket in a cave burial dated to Pueblo I in north central Oregon (Cressman, Stewart, and Laughlin 1950, 375–6). The twining method reconstructed by Cressman for the rabbit skin blanket resembles the structure of the ACCM blanket (1950, 374). Kidder and Guernsey report on both fur and turkey feather cordage occurring at Basketmaker sites in northeastern Arizona (1919, 174). Early archaeologists working in the Southwest note a transition from fur to feather cordage. According to Guernsey's own excavation findings and examples found by others excavating in the Southwest, 'By Basketmaker III times, feather stripping was gradually taking the place of fur' (Roberts Jr. 1937, 8) and this material choice was used to separate Anasazi from Pueblo prehistory.

The earliest of the feather blanket remains are associated with Anasazi culture during Basketmaker II-III (100 BCE–AD 700) period, though this early date is assigned to an unexcavated blanket collected by early settlers in San Juan County, Utah, and now in the Museum of Peoples and Cultures at Brigham Young University (Brigham Young University 2007). Guernsey reports feather blanket remains from Cave 1 in Segi in northern Arizona in association with Pueblo I ceramics (ca. 750–950 AD), and illustrates a twining construction identical that used for the ACCM blanket (Guernsey 1931, 92–3 and Plate 54). Webster describes feather-wrapped yucca cordage found in association with Pueblo I finds in the Woods Canyon excavations northeast of Aztec, New Mexico (Webster 2003a). Webster's use of Nordenskiöld's drawing of a Pueblo feather blanket is effective for illustrating the construction found on the ACCM blanket (Figure 10). DNA and radiocarbon evidence have been used to place the manufacture of a macaw feather and squirrel pelt apron or blanket in the American Southwest at a Pueblo II/Pueblo III date (ca. 1050–1150 AD) (Borson et al. 1998).

Additional Southwest archaeological-find sites for feather blankets which date to the Pueblo periods include southern Arizona (Fewkes 1912, 148; Haury 1950, 428), New Mexico (Hough 1914, 71–3), Nevada (Gilmore 1953, 151), and Colorado (Burgh and Scoggin 1948, 66). Twelfth and thirteenth century finds from Mug House in Wetherhill Mesa in Mesa Verde, Colorado, include a well-documented turkey feather blanket and feather and fur cordage, although published reports do not indicate whether these finds are contemporary (Rohn 1971). Evidence for feather blankets in Nevada in the historic period comes from Gilmore (1953) who reports that 'early

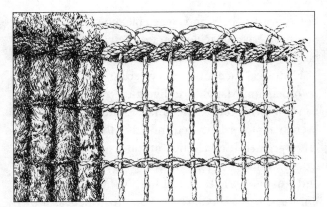

Figure 10.

native Paiutes in Nevada' used duck feathers to make beds and applied cut feather strips to make blankets, and that they further sold beds and pillows to early white settlers.

FEATHER BLANKETS FROM OUTSIDE THE SOUTHWESTERN USA

Compared to desert locations, prehistoric organic remains (i.e. perishables) from damp regions are not well preserved due to environmental conditions. Nonetheless, feather blankets have been documented from both archaeological and historic contexts in the southeast USA. Sibley, Jakes, and Swinker (1992) investigated feather blanket remains excavated from a habitation and mortuary Mississippian mound in Georgia, occupied between AD 900 and 1400. These authors identified plumaceous (or downy) waterfowl feathers used with and without fiber cordage. Where cordage is present it is based on a bast fiber wrapped with feathers (Sibley, Jakes, and Larson 1996, 76) and, where cordage is absent, down feathers were found matted together (Sibley, Jakes, and Swinker 1992). These authors (1992, 24) describe the fact that 88% of the bird bones found at Etowah, Mound C in Georgia derive from turkey, while waterfowl bones made up only 2% of the remains. The presence of waterfowl bones and feathers in the mound is associated with a high-status burial (1992, 24). In a review of feather cord construction used to produce fragments found in Southeast locations including Virginia, Louisiana, Arkansas, and Mississippi, methods include wrapping vegetable fiber cords with pennaceous feathers, beginning with the rachis or quill, and spinning feather down within hair and vegetable fibers (1992, 25). Southeastern archaeological feathered textile remains are always fragmentary and challenging to interpret.

Historical accounts of wearing blankets were recorded for Mauvilla indigenous populations surrounding Mobile, Alabama. Eighteenth century French explorer Levasseur noted of the Mauvilla that 'They are nearly all clothed in robes or turkey feather cloaks, which they plait or weave together' (Knight Jr. and Adams 1981, 182). Neither the material remains nor the site of Mauvilla have been identified, as it was believed to be burned by De Soto during a legendary massacre (Bond 1937).

Similarly, prehistoric organic remains from coastal California are generally not well preserved. Early reports about lost feather remains are aided by diaries of eighteenth and nineteenth century explorers throughout California and from ethnologist Harrington's papers describing interviews with the southern California Chumash (Forbes 1973; Hudson and Blackburn 1982–1987; Smith and Teggart 1909). In the eighteenth and nineteenth centuries in southern California, rabbit fur and eagle down were reported by a Gabrielino consultant as used interchangeably to form 'plush cordage' (Hudson and Blackburn 1982–1987, 162; Merriam 1955, 80). Forbes (1973) reports on fur and feathers being used interchangeably in northern California.

Other eighteenth and nineteenth century accounts from travels in California also refer to feather blankets. In Gaspar de Portolá's records of his travels to Monterey and San Diego in the mid-eighteenth century, he reports being given a 'present of fabric interwoven with beautiful feathers which in its arrangement looked like plush' (Smith and Teggart 1909, 47). Forbes compiled a history of California which he completed in 1839 and which was published posthumously by his brother. A trip to the Bay of San Francisco is described in which indigenous people are noted as wearing an outer garment in winter made from feathers which are 'twisted and tied together into a sort of ropes and then these are tied close together so as to have a feathery surface on both sides. They twist strips of otter skins in the same manner so as to have fur on both sides' (Forbes 1973, 183).

Comparison between Southwest and California Feather Blankets

TURKEY FEATHERS

The presence of turkey feathers and the state of preservation of the ACCM blanket are the most important diagnostics for placing the provenance in the American Southwest. Turkeys were wild and then domesticated by the Pueblo IV period (AD 1300–1540), and archaeological evidence indicates pre-European contact domestication of either an indigenous wild turkey, or a species traded from Mexico (Beacham and Durand 2007). The distribution of wild turkeys (Meleagris gallopavo) in America during the pre-Columbian period is restricted to the southern Southwestern states (Eaton 1992). Wild turkeys are not indigenous to California, and were first introduced there in 1908 by US Fish and Wildlife as a food source (Eaton 1992).

Feather selection and cordage

Known examples of eighteenth century California feather blankets are elaborate and decorative, and are made from select types of waterfowl with visual variety including banded, iridescent, and speckled feathers (McLendon 2001, 144) (Figure 11). McLendon notes five variations in style of California blankets, based on patterning occurring through the use of different feathers to create stripes. This variation found in California feather blankets is in contrast with feather blanket construction from the Southwest, where feather types used are limited and feather cordage is fairly uniform in color. However, the replica of a turkey feather blanket made by Ramona Sakiestewa is a plush and elaborate example, where long multicolored turkey body feathers were used to create a deep plush (Southwest Productions 1983).

Both California and Southwest blankets are made from warps which consist of lengths of feather-wrapped vegetable fiber cordage or tufts of feathers between twined cords, or cordage made by rolling feather down. Ineseño and Ventureño informants in southern California reported to Harrington that 'down cord' was made by rolling milkweed string on the thigh as they added feather down (Hudson

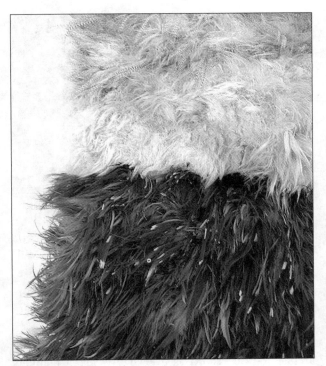

Figure 11.

constructed traditional Pueblo turkey feather blankets for workshops and display at Bandelier National Park; the Lovatos' methods include soaking the feathers in warm water to soften the quills and hand wrapping them around yucca cordage (Albuquerque Events Calendar 2008; Sakiestewa 2001).

DETAILS OF CONSTRUCTION

A significant feature of the California feather blankets is that the warps are horizontal and feather types are varied to create the stripes. Reporting about California blanket construction, Kroeber's Nisenan informant describes an upright pair of posts that was used to support horizontal warps (Kroeber 1929). McLendon (2001, 143) recognized the importance of the unpublished drawing of this support made by Kroeber's student, and published it in her work. McLendon further postulated that the red braided border which forms the neck tie at the top of each completed wearing blanket was secured first to the base of the posts and was used to anchor the initial warp and each of the wefts, suggesting that the construction occurs with the garment upside down (McLendon 2001, 143).

In discussing the construction of Pueblo feather blankets, Kent summarizes possible methods for securing the warps which include two tall posts for upright construction (perpendicular to the ground and identical to what is illustrated for California) and four short corner post supports for flat construction (parallel to the ground). In all instances, however, the warps are arranged vertically and the wefts are horizontal (Kent 1983, 116, Figure 56E). If the warp was vertical and secured to two upright supports, horizontal elements would be necessary at the top and bottom selvedge (an edge that prevents unraveling) in order to secure the warps. This element could be removable and need not become part of the blanket, and is not evident on the ACCM blanket, unless the human hair cord extant at one corner is part of this supporting cord.

As the loops in the ACCM feather blanket interlock, Kent's proposed supports in Figure 56E 3 or 4, which have each warp held separately by individual cords and posts, respectively, are not plausible (Kent

and Blackburn 1982-1987, 224). Examination of the American Museum of Natural History (New York) feather blanket, likely collected in California in 1830, indicated cordage made by rolling feather down with no vegetable fiber cordage present in the warp. In the Southwest, it is postulated that yucca leaf cords made to receive feathers were made by rolling fibers on the thigh (Rohn 1971, 13). Yucca leaves prepared for rolling and cordage have been found in northeastern Arizona, including 'sheaves of whole leaves, chewed or pounded leaves with the parenchyma partly removed, and lastly, hanks of the cleaned fiber ready for spinning' (Kidder and Guernsey 1919, 113).

While rolling feather down into cordage and capturing feathers between twisted cordage is visible on California blankets, feather application on Pueblo examples suggests wrapping. Southwest archaeological blankets are noted to have spiral wrapping of trimmed quills of turkey wing and tail feathers, and whole down feathers wrapped around yucca cordage (Kidder and Guernsey 1919, ll8). Contemporary Pueblo artists, Caroline and Darris Lovato (Santo Domingo) and Ramona Sakiestewa (Hopi), have

1983, 116). If the warp was horizontal, as in the case of the California blankets, then it could have been looped directly around two upright posts set apart at the desired blanket length or, in the case of flat construction, a horizontal warp could be secured to removable elements such as cords at each vertical selvedge. The preserved warp loops on the ACCM blanket have very little space available to accommodate a post diameter; however a cordage element may have been used during construction to secure the feathered warp to supports in either the vertical or horizontal orientation.

All of the 14 feather blankets from north-central Sacramento River Valley examined by McLendon (2001, 143) have a braided cord to secure the blanket around the shoulders as a cape. An important diagnostic trait noted by McLendon on the 14 feather blankets, and observed on two blankets examined by this author, is the presence of paired, tied off wefts. These wefts are secured with cow hitch knots around the braided red cord border on one long side, and they are tied off at the opposite long end (Figure 12). On Pueblo blankets, the weft fibers are either knotted at both selvages, or selected wefts are shifted at or near the selvage and then twined back toward the opposite selvage (Kent 1983, Figure 56). The selvage of Southwest blankets lack a braided border, but according to Kent and Webster the upper warp selvage is often twined with a very thick compound header cord and the lower warp selvage is interlaced by a pair of wefts worked in plain weave (Kent 1983; Webster 2007, pers. comm.). Further, the warps on California blankets examined by this author do not interlock, while interlocking is often found on warps of Southwest blankets.

Feather Blankets in Museums

Despite the remarkable similarity in material and construction methods for Native American feather blankets, significant contextual differences must be considered when conservation treatment and display are contemplated. Feather blankets recorded in California in the nineteenth century tend to be preserved in museum collections because they were given as gifts

Figure 12.

to visiting Europeans who treasured them as exotic and unusual (Hurtado 1983; McLendon 2001; Willoughby 1922). Such blankets are displayed in museums in America and Europe and, while many California blankets are in natural history museums, they are also found in art museums (Figure 2).

Pueblo turkey feather blankets are recorded in the archaeological record as everyday-wearing blankets and are most often found in the burial context. Most have been excavated as part of cave burials and were subsequently deposited with other finds in museums. Based on its size and construction, the ACCM feather blanket most closely parallels other examples found in child burials in caves in northern Arizona dating to the Pueblo period. In November 2004, the Colorado Historical Society reported in its NAGPRA summary a record of human remains collected prior to 1982 from Mesa Verde, and included an associated feather blanket along with ceramics and garments (Federal Register, 23 November 2004). A later accession included five Pueblo feather blankets identified as associated funerary objects. A total of four cases are presented when searching under 'feather blanket' on the National NAGPRA Online Database. In all cases, the associated cultural objects are considered diagnostic of ancestral Pueblo, which determined the list of tribes to which official notification was made by the collecting repositories (Federal Register Online, NAGPRA Notices of intent to repatriate, n.d). In February 2006, following the completion of a NAGPRA inventory by the University of Colorado, a notice to repatriate an anonymously donated set of human remains with a feather blanket was posted on the Federal Register (1 February 2006).

The significance of turkey feather blankets in the Southwest is indicated by their revival by contemporary Pueblo tribal members, and the display of contemporary examples is considered as an important representation of Pueblo history. The proud display of contemporary examples, along with strong interest in their preservation, (5) contrasts with the inappropriateness of display and request for repatriation of excavated examples.

Conclusions

The case study of the ACCM feather blanket is an excellent example of how professional conservation methods can be used in support of post-Colonial museum goals, where traditional owners become the beneficiaries of museological research (Simpson 2001, 253). The ability to correctly reattribute this blanket from historic California to a Pueblo child burial in northern Arizona changes not only conservation treatment and display, but also the disposition of this object in a museum's collection. The transmission of knowledge, which may be represented here by ancestral Pueblo feather blanket technologies reaching California, illustrates how dangerous it is to generalize about a shared context for these artifacts (Gunnerson 1962). The functions of objects can, and do, change over time, so that it is significant to consider each object and its cultural origins before planning conservation or display. Curation has to be understood in terms of the multiple values placed on objects with material and technological similarities.

Information obtained through this investigation, which supports an ancestral Pueblo burial context, makes the exhibition of this blanket inappropriate and, instead, supports repatriation. Among the outcomes of consultations between museums and Native Americans is an implicit ban on the display of grave goods. While the identification of materials and techniques can be decisive in understanding the cultural attribution of an object, the context is often more important than physical construction when considering museum stewardship. There are complex cultural differences between Pueblo and California

Native American feather blankets. California feather blankets, currently found in museum displays (Figure 2—Denver Art Museum), are best known from nineteenth century examples of elaborate wearing blankets which were given as gifts to Europeans and confer status (McLendon 2001, 133; Willoughby 1922). This contrasts sharply with prehistoric feather blankets from the Southwest which, while held in museums, are inaccessible in displays and websites. While Pueblo feather blankets were originally functional, they are found in mortuary contexts, and have been requested for repatriation as associated funerary objects through the NAGPRA. Despite the similarity in materials and construction, California feather blankets may be more appropriately considered for museum display, while Pueblo feather blankets may not.

Acknowledgments

The author wishes to thank Ginger Ridgway, Curator and Director of Programs, Agua Caliente Cultural Museum, for her invitation to conduct this study. Thanks also to Prof. Sally McLendon for sharing her thoughts about a draft of this paper, and to Prof. Frances Berdan for shared observations about the blanket, David Carson of the Getty Conservation Institute for analytical services, Smithsonian Scientist Carla Dove for feather analysis, UCLA Archaeology Ph.D. student John Marston for assisting with ethnobotanical materials, Laurie Webster for information about Southwest feather blankets, Far Western Anthropological Research Group Principal Investigator Eric Wohlgemuth for botanicals' identification, and US Fish and Wildlife specialist Bonnie Yates for confirming hair identification. Thanks are also extended to Gary Roybal at Bandelier National Park for providing access to the video on the Anasazi blanket recreation, and to Ramona Sakiestewa for sharing her insights. Judith Levinson and Vuka Roussakis at the American Museum of Natural History, NY and Deborah Hull-Walski and Greta Hansen at the National Museum of Natural History, Washington, DC are thanked for assisting with access to feather blankets in these collections.

NOTES

1. Sclerenchyma are non-living cells which impart strength to both monocot and dicot fibers.

2. Monocots refer to monocotyledonous plants which have one embryonic leaf in their seed, in contrast to dicotyledonous plants which have two embryonic leaves.

3. Dislocations are cross-markings which occur more frequently in hemp fibers and less in leaf fibers such as those in the Agavaceae family (Catling and Grayson 2004, 56).

4. Bast fibers are fibers prepared from woody stems of dicotyledonous plants.

5. In a conversation between the author and Ramona Sakiestewa in 2008, she expressed regret about the complete destruction, which was reported to be attacked by insects and rodents.

REFERENCES

Albuquerque Events Calendar. 2008. http://www .itsatrip.org/events (accessed May 31, 2008).

Anderson, M.K. 2005. *Tending the wild: Native American knowledge and the management of California's natural resources.* Berkeley/Los Angeles: University of California Press.

Beacham, E.B., and S.R. Durand. 2007. Eggshell and the archaeological record: New insights into turkey husbandry in the American Southwest. *Journal of Archaeological Science* 34: 1610–921.

Bond, J. 1937. *The Aboriginal Chickasaw Nation,* vol. 15, no. 4. http://digital.library.okstate.edu/ chronicles/v0l 5/v0I5p392.html (accessed August 1, 2007).

Borson, N., F. Berdan, E. Strak, J. States, and P.J. Wettstein. 1998. Origins of an Anasazi Macaw feather artifact. *American Antiquity* 63, no. I: 131–42.

Brigham Young University. 2007. Museum of peoples and cultures. http://mpc.byu.edu/Exhibitions, MPC 66.63.4.2 (accessed August 10, 2007).

Burgh, R.F., and C..R. Scoggin. 1948. *The Archaeology of Castle Park, Dinosaur National Monument, University of Colorado Studies, Series in Anthropology,* vol. 2. Boulder: University of Colorado Press.

Catling, D., and J. Grayson. 2004. *Identification of vegetable fibres.* London: Archetype.

Cressman, L.S., T.D. Stewart, and W Laughlin. 1950. Archaeological research in the John Day Region of North Central Oregon. *Proceedings of the American Philosophical Society* 94, no. 4: 369–90.

Eaton, S.W 1992. Wild Turkey (*Meleagris gallopavo*). In *The Birds of North America Online,* ed. A. Poole. Ithaca: Cornell Lab of Ornithology. http://bna.birds.comell.edu/bna/species/022doi: 10.2173/bna.22 (accessed August 7, 2008).

Federal Register, November 23, 2004. FR Doc 04-25918. Notices 69, no. 225: 68162–9.

Federal Register, February 1, 2006. FR Doc E6-1273. Notices 71, no. 21: 5369–73.

Federal Register Online, NAGPRA Notices of intent to repatriate, n.d. http://www.nps.gov/ history/nagpra/fed_notices/nagpradir/index2 .htm (accessed November 11, 2009).

Fewkes, J.W. 1912. *Antiquities of the Upper Verde River and Walnut Creek valleys, Arizona.* Twenty-eighth annual report 1906–07, Washington, DC.

Florian, M-L.E., D.P. Kronkright, and R.E. Norton. 1990. *The conservation of artifacts made from plant materials.* Marina del Rey: The Getty Conservation Institute.

Flynn, G., and D. Hull-Walski. 2001. Merging traditional indigenous curation methods with modern museum standards of care. *Museum Anthropology* 25, no. I: 31–9.

Forbes, A. 1973. *California: A history of upper and lower California from their first discovery to their present time.* Reprint of the 1839 edition of *The Far Western Frontier.* New York: Arno Press.

Gilmore, H.W 1953. Hunting habits of the early Nevada Paiutes. *American Anthropologist,* New Series 55, no. I: 148–53.

Guernsey, S.J. 1931. *Explorations in northeastern Arizona, report on the Archaeological Fieldwork of 1920-1923.* Papers of the Peabody Museum of American Archaeology and Ethnology, vol. XII, no. 1. Cambridge, MA: Harvard University.

Guernsey, S.J., and A.V Kidder. 1921. *Basket-maker caves of Northeastern Arizona.* Papers of the Peabody Museum of American Archaeology and Ethnology, vol. VIII, no. 2. Cambridge, MA: Harvard University.

Gunnerson, J.H. 1962. Plateau Shoshonean prehistory: A suggested reconstruction. *American Antiquity* 28, no. I: 41–5.

Harrington, M.R. 1930. Paiute Cave. *Southwest Museum Papers* 4: 106–26.

Harrington, M.R. 1933. Gypsum Cave, Nevada. *Southwest Museum Papers* 8: 1–197.

Haury, E.W. (with Byran, K. and others) 1950. *The stratigraphy and archaeology of Ventana Cave, Arizona.* Tucson: University of Arizona.

Hickman, J. 1993. *The Jepson manual: Higher plants of California.* Berkeley: University of California Press.

Hough, W. 1914. *Culture of the ancient Pueblos of the upper Gila River region,* New Mexico and Arizona. Smithsonian Institution. United States National Museum Bulletin 87. Washington, DC: Government Printing Office.

Hudson, T., and T.C. Blackburn. 1982–1987. *The material culture of the Chumash interaction sphere.* Los Altos, CA: Ballena Press and Santa Barbara: Santa Barbara Museum of Natural History.

Hurtado, A.L. 1983. Saved so much as possible for labour: Indian population and the New Helvetia work force. *American Indian Culture and Research Journal* 6, no. 4: 63–78.

Kent, K.P..1983. *Prehistoric textiles of the Southwest.* Santa Fe: School of American Research, Albuquerque, University of New Mexico.

Kidder, A.V., and S.J. Guernsey. 1919. *Archeological explorations in northeastern Arizona.* Smithsonian Institution. Bureau of American Ethnology. Bulletin 65.

Knight, Jr., V.J, and S.L. Adams. 1981. A voyage to the mobile and Tomeh in 1700, with notes of the interior of Alabama. *Ethnohistory* 28, no. 2: 179–94.

Kroeber, A.L. 1929. The Valley Nisenan. *American Archaeology and Ethnology* 24, no. 4: 253–90 (University of California Publications).

Kuchler, A.W. 1977. The map of the natural vegetation of California. Appendix of terrestrial vegetation of California. *California Native Plant Society Special Publication* Number 9. Sacramento.

Map of Western States Tribal locations. 1970. In *The National Atlas of the United States of America*, ed. A.C. Gerlach. Washington, DC: US Department of the Interior, Geological Survey, Courtesy of The University of Texas Libraries, The University of Texas at Austin. http://www.lib.utexas.edu/maps/united_states/early_indian_west.jpg (accessed January 10, 2009).

Mauersberger, H.R. 1954. *Matthews' textile fibers.* New York: John Wiley.

McCrone, W.C., and J.G. Delly. 1973. *The particle Atlas.* 2 ed. Vol. III of *The Electron Microscopy Atlas.* Ann Arbor, MI: Ann Arbor Science Publishers.

McLendon, S. 2001. California feather blankets; objects of wealth and status in two nineteenth-century worlds. In *Studies in American Indian Art: A memorial tribute to Norman Feder*, ed. C. Feest, 132-61. ERNAS Monograph 2. Vienna, Austria: European Review of Native American Studies.

Merriam, C.H. 1955. *Studies of the California Indians.* Berkeley: University of California Press.

Moerman, D.E. 2006. *Native American Ethnobotany.* Portland, OR: Timber Press.

National Park Service. n/d. US Department of the Interior. *National NAGPRA.* http://www.nps.gov/history/nagpra/ (accessed December 29, 2008).

Nordenskiöld, Gustaf. 1893. *The Cliff dwellers of the Mesa Verde, southwestern Colorado: their pottery and implements.* Trans. D. Lloyd Morgan. Stockholm; Chicago: P.A. Norstedt.

Roberts, Jr., F.H.H. 1937. Archaeology in the Southwest. *American Antiquity* 43, no. 1: 3–33.

Rohn, A 1971. *Mug House. Archeological Research Series,* No. 7-D, Chapter 7. Washington, DC: National Park Service. http://www.nps.gov/history/history/online_books/meve/7d/chap7.htm (accessed September 15, 2008).

Sakiestewa, R. 2001. Tapestry and beyond: Exploring the 'slender margins between real and unreal.' Courtesy of the Gloria F. Ross Center for Tapestry Studies. http://www.tapestryce nter.org/uploadl Transcript, %20Annual%20Lecture, %202001.pdf (accessed January 21, 2008).

Sibley, L.R., K.S. Jakes, and L.H. Larson. 1996. Inferring behavior and function from an Etowah Fabric

Incorporating Feathers. In *A most indispensable art; native fiber industries from Eastern North America*, ed. J.B. Petersen, 73–87. Knoxville, TN: The University of Texas Press.

Sibley, L.R., K.S. Jakes, and M.E. Swinker. 1992. Etowah feather remains from Burial 57: Identification and context. *Clothing and Textiles Research Journal* 10, no. 3: 21–8.

Simpson, M.G. 2001. *Making representations: Museums in the post-colonial era.* London/New York: Routledge.

Smith, D.E., and F.J. Teggart. 1909. *Diary of Gaspar de Portolá.* Berkeley: University of California.

Southwest Productions. 1983. *Recreating the Anasazi Turkey Feather Blanket.* Produced and written by Cindy Bellinger, VHS.

The Textile Institute. 1965. *Identification of textile materials.* 5th ed. Manchester.

USDA NRCS National Plant Data Center. May 2006. Indian Hemp; *Apocynum cannabinum* L. http://plants.usda.gov/javaiprofile?symbol=APCA (accessed May 10, 2008).

Webster, L. 2003a. Textiles and Basketry, Woods Canyon Project. http://www.woodscanyon.net/MAPL/basketry_report/lndex.html (accessed June 5, 2008).

Webster, L. 2003b. Textiles and Basketry, Woods Canyon Project. http://www.woodscanyon.net/MAPL/basketry_ reportiBasketry%20Images/Zoomed%20Images/Fig%20QQ-z.jpg (accessed January 10, 2009).

Willoughby, C.C.,1922. Feather mantles of California. *American Anthropologist*, New Series 24, no. 4: 432–7.

Wohlgemuth, E. 2008. *Plant materials identified from feather blanket.* Davis, CA: Far Western Anthropological Research Group.

ERNST VAN DE WETERING

"Conservation-Restoration Ethics and the Problem of Modern Art"

In Modern Art: Who Cares? *ed. by Ijsbrand Hummelen and Dionne Sillé. Amsterdam: Foundation for the Conservation of Modern Art/Netherlands Institute for Cultural Heritage, 1999, pp. 247–49.*

AT FIRST SIGHT conservation-restoration ethics seems to be a cultural, and thus temporal phenomenon. This may imply that it is only valid to a limited extent; that it is relative by nature. There is, however, a deeper significance in conservation-restoration ethics as enshrined in existing codes. This makes one wonder whether these codes do not in fact formulate truth instead of temporary conventions.

Conservation-restoration ethics is based on the a priori all too often confirmed by experience, that conservation-restoration is always an interpretation of the object concerned and therefore implies the risk of being a mistaken, anachronistic interpretation. Another a priori at the root of conservation-restoration ethics is that we have a responsibility for the future in allowing upcoming generations to have a past as we ourselves have had one, and that we do not have the right to interpret their past irreversibly on the basis of our own anachronistic interpretations.

Based on these a priories, Cesare Brandi came to the conclusion that besides relevant documentation it is primarily the original material of an object, or what is left of it, that can serve as a sound basis for future generations to build their own interpretations of the original appearance, function et cetera of the object. From this it follows that the conservation of the original material has the highest priority, in whatever condition it has survived.

This, however, does not mean that we are not allowed to reconstruct the object to a greater or lesser extent. Such reconstruction should—according to existing codes—be carried out as far as possible only in a reversible way, that is: without impairing or destroying the original material, nor the traces of its construction et cetera. This rule is in accordance with what was earlier stated.

Because of the aforegoing we are obliged to adequately document the object as we have found it. We are allowed to intervene in the object if this is inevitable or beneficial for a satisfactory 'reading' of the work, depending on the context in which it is seen or used; but then we should also document how we have intervened. Such documentation, as well as the treatment that may have been carried out, demand the greatest honesty.

It should be emphasised that although in this approach the object primarily has the function of a source about itself, this does not imply that we have to approach it as an historic 'ruin'. Nevertheless the original substance demands our highest respect, given our responsibility to the future.

This logical construction, which slowly developed in the nineteenth and twentieth century, is based on what could be called an anthropologically or even genetically determined human condition, constituted by humankind's need for a past on the one hand, and our need to care for future generations on the other. Basic to all this is humankind's need of a memory and a built-in urge regarding the transition of memories to later generations.

Torn between the Present and the Future

In theory, the only way to intervene in this natural continuum may be a cultural revolution: the destruction of the past in order to build a completely controlled future. We have seen in the last century that cultural revolutions fail in the end and that human nature, in the sense described above, cannot be bridled.

Nevertheless modern art, and to some extent art in general, tends to revolutionise culture by striving to influence the present and the future as well as

our perception of the past. One could say that much late nineteenth- and twentieth-century art by its very nature has, or tries to have, an existential impact on the way we experience the past as well as the future. It attempts to have the quality of a statement, a manifesto, which, as it were, determines the present with as much force as possible. It is the 'here and now-ness' that counts!

The conservator-restorer involved in putting the work of art as a statement across, by being involved in organising and shaping its presentation, can, according to the conservator Hiltrud Schinzel, be seen as an 'art-promoting person' while helping to present the work with maximum impact. In that situation, the conservator-restorer deals primarily with the visual impact of the work according to the artist's real or presumed wishes. He or she participates in a performance that is rather theatrical than museal in the traditional sense.

But: the theatre is the place where lies create truth—interventions are taken which in the view of conservation-restoration ethics are heavyhanded and highly unethical—radical repairs including complete reconstructions or, in the case of paintings, overpaintings. Such interventions may be carried out for the sake of the moment and may imply a serious loss of authenticity of the object as a source about itself and its maker.

Thus in the field of contemporary art the conservator-restorer is torn between two forces: the existential power of the work as a statement in the present and his or her awareness that the object at some point, probably very soon, will be absorbed into the stream of time, becoming an historical object as well and deserving the utmost care as a source about its original appearance, own meaning and function for future generations.

Different Speeds of Transformation

Apart from the anthropological and restoration ethics anchored in a conservator-restorer's role to preserve the past for the future, and the existential involvement of the artist to make a strong statement, there is thus a third aspect involved—the inevitability of the object's transformation over time. This transformation does not only involve the ageing and changing of the material but especially takes place in the minds of the beholders. As to this last type of transformation, Brandi noted in his *Teoria del Restauro* that the object is constantly reborn in the minds of those who see it and that it is undergoing a multitude of transformations in the process.

For the conservator-restorer it is important to be aware of this phenomenon. To someone, for instance, who has known the artist or was once an assistant in his/her studio or helped in the presentation of the object, the speed of transformation is much slower than for the young conservator-restorer of a later generation. The first category of conservators tends to prolong the present, in an effort to support the strength and actuality of the artist's statement. For the young conservator, the same artist and the same object may be already history, with all the consequences this may entail for the care of the object as a source about the past and the sense of responsibility for its transition to the future. In this situation, the autonomy of conservation-restoration ethics already takes over for younger conservator-restorers while for older ones the present and the 'theatrical' function of the object prevails.

The transformation of a work of art is tragic. Who would not like to prolong its 'here and now-ness'? No doubt, like other aspects of human life, the existential forces at first have priority over prudence and conservative forces. But, like in the existential situation of humankind, the transition of present into past is inevitable. And behind existential forces such as the lack of fear for risks, in a present situation there is also the natural inclination to care and the need to prolong life. It is then the classical ethics of conservation takes over even before the object's existential power as part of the (prolonged) present has faded.

Of course, given the transitoriness of many objects of contemporary art, the task to preserve is almost impossible. However, unless transitoriness is an integral and explicit part of the artist's statement, one should not be resigned to these objects decaying, believing that a proper documentation would suffice to maintain the memory of an object. Documentation is always biased. One should rather stick to the adage that conservation-restoration does not mean doing the possible, but that it should mean doing the impossible. The classical ethics of restoration may then be the force behind the development of technical innovation which, as so often happened in the past, would make seemingly impossible acts of preservation possible.

chapter 10

MULTICULTURAL PERSPECTIVES

THE AIM OF PRESERVATION IS TO SAFEGUARD CULTURAL heritage. But whose heritage? How is it to be preserved? And by whom, and for whom?

Two of the United Nations readings in chapter 9, the *Universal Declaration of Human Rights* (UDHR) and *Declaration on the Rights of Indigenous Peoples,* are a starting point for this chapter. The first of these, the *Universal Declaration,* written in 1948, set out to establish basic freedoms: the ability to work, go to school, live a healthy life, and have religious freedom, and the right to "participate in the cultural life of the community."[1] Although preservation is beyond the immediate scope of the UDHR, to assure cultural continuity there must be effective stewardship of it. UNESCO's mission is to promote collaboration among nations through its scientific, educational, and cultural programs. In keeping with this mission, over the past sixty years UNESCO has sponsored a number of activities aimed at preserving world heritage.

There are inherent limitations to the work of the United Nations and, by extension, UNESCO. Of the 196 countries in the world, 193 are UN members, referred to as Member States. Three countries do not belong to the United Nations: Kosovo, Taiwan, and Vatican City, which have important cultural heritages. The UN can take action on a wide range of issues and provide a forum for its 193 Member States to express their views, through the General Assembly and various councils and committees. However, Member States may opt *not* to sign declarations or other legal instruments that the UN may pass. While the UN can impose sanctions on countries that do not adhere to laws, these sanctions may not succeed. In other words, the power of the United Nations is limited.

At the same time, the work of the United Nations is truly global; no other organization has such reach. The UN works on a broad range of fundamental issues, including not only peacekeeping security, and better living conditions, but also the promotion of human, cultural heritage, and educational rights. The UN's recent *Declaration on the Rights of Indigenous People* addresses cultural rights. The *Declaration*, also known as the Daes Report, was spearheaded by Erica-Irene Daes, a Greek jurist, academic, diplomat, and United Nations expert. It grew out of the United Nations Working Group on Indigenous Populations (1984–2001) which promoted the cause of the world's indigenous peoples.

The Declaration asserts that indigenous people have the right to distinct cultural practices as provided for in the UDHR, but Article 5 adds that "Indigenous people have the right to maintain and strengthen their distinct political, legal, economic, social and cultural institutions while retaining their right to participate fully, if they so choose, in the political, economic, social and cultural life of the State."[2] Such rights allow, and may even force, preservation practices to shift.

Before we consider the Declaration's potential impact on conservation and preservation practices, it is worth considering cultural rights more broadly. Michael F. Brown calls the UN document which led to the Declaration "a canonical text that makes the case for Total Heritage Protection."[3] That is,

> The UN's key role in the area of universal human rights gives it moral standing useful for indigenous peoples even when their concerns are only awkwardly encompassed by a human-rights framework. But yoking the United Nations and aboriginal aspirations exacts a price. The rise of what has been called the "global cocktail circuit" promotes the emergence of a world-traveling indigenous elite and contributes to divisive internal struggles over resources and local accountability. On balance, however, the alliance has been useful to aboriginal peoples.[4]

As Brown implies, each country will need to work through these issues individually. Examples are the Native American Graves Protection and Repatriation Act (NAGPRA) of 1990 in the United States, and the Protection of Movable Cultural Heritage Act (PMCH) of 1986 in Australia. In fact, every country in which native peoples were colonized and subsequently deprived of access to their cultural birthright needs to facilitate the preservation of these cultures.

There are inherent challenges and contradictions implicit in the *Declaration of the Rights of Indigenous People*. Will it create boundaries among and between different indigenous groups? Will it discourage collaboration? What effect will it have on existing laws? What is the relationship between intellectual property protection and the safeguarding of cultural heritage? Between cultural heritage institutions that have collected indigenous objects and members of the communities whose heritage was collected? These open questions must be answered, lest, in the worst-case scenario, indigenous cultural heritage is completely removed from institutions and public consciousness.

This chapter includes passages and articles by four authors who have been addressing issues related to multicultural conservation and preservation for a long time. Some of them advocate directly for collaborative and community-based approaches; others have focused more specifically on conservation treatment issues. Each recognizes that cultural self-determination is a critical component of conservation today. All point the way towards new conservation and preservation strategies.

In "Cultural Heritage and Globalization," anthropologist **Lourdes Arizpe** discusses how our approaches to heritage are changing in the new global cultural commons "in which the web of meanings traditionally offered by different cultures is being rewoven." While access to cultural heritage was once limited to individual cultural communities or countries, today, objects and cultures are available to international audiences. This new world has led to "global creativity," a phrase that Arizpe attributes to Catherine Stimpson and Homi Bhabha. Arizpe's central question is, "How do we enhance the value of cultural heritage to safeguard it and to use it to build cultural understanding instead of cultural trenches?" To answer the question, she explores what she identifies as the two main views: the planetary (global) and the village (local) perspectives. Both can lead to valuing the past and focusing on living cultures, and in some cases bringing the two together.

Miriam Clavir, conservator emerita and research fellow at the Museum of Anthropology, the University of British Columbia, has focused on issues relating to the changes in museums and in conservation in response to indigenous peoples' concerns. She shows how museums can build relationships with First Nations communities on issues of preservation and conservation. This chapter includes an excerpt from her book *Preserving What Is Valued: Museums, Conservation, and First Nations*. Clavir illustrates how traditional museum perspectives contrast with the views of First Nations. For example, traditionally, museums have sought to *preserve objects* while tribes want to *preserve traditional cultural values*. For museums, the rationale for preservation is that it can prevent *loss of material culture and values; objects are witnesses to the past*. For First Nations, preservation may prevent *loss of parts of culture* and result in *positive identity,* [and] *control. Preservation is positive in the context of self-determination: renewal, living expression; objects are part of living cultures today* (italics represent quotes from Clavir's tables). In general, the traditional museum approach to conservation is object-based while the First Nations and Native American perspectives are people-based.

A new approach to conservation necessarily takes the conservator out of the museum and places her in the community.

In "'Accessories of Holiness': Defining Jewish Sacred Objects" (1992), **Virginia Greene** concludes that the definitions for Native American sacred objects—then recently articulated in the Native American Graves Protection and Repatriation Act—cannot necessarily be applied to other cultures. Guidelines must be established for each culture, religion, or tribal group. For example, in Jewish traditions there is a distinction between ritual objects that carry a quality of holiness and those that are essential to rituals but that are not necessarily sacred or holy. Once holy objects are no longer in ritual use, it is not appropriate to treat them,

whereas non-holy ritual objects can receive minor repairs. There are further considerations that the conservators must factor in, including storage and handling specifications, too detailed to summarize here. The critical takeaway is that conservators must never take objects at face value. Guidelines should be developed for each cultural group whose items are represented in museum, library, or archival collections.

The article points to the complexities in conserving sacred cultural objects and the limited use of the definitions in NAGPRA for such objects from other cultures. Greene advises that ethical standards for the treatment of sacred objects need to be developed for each culture, with the assistance, if possible, of a member of that group.

Sven Haakanson, Jr., director of the Alutiiq Museum in Kodiak, Alaska, answers the question, "Why Should American Indian Cultural Objects be Preserved?" in his essay of that title from Sherelyn Ogden's *Caring for Indian Objects*.[5] NAGPRA required over 5,000 museums to return to Native Americans tribal objects and human remains that they held in their collections. Not all Native American objects fall under NAGPRA. The remaining represent many aspects of Native American life and traditions. Many objects in museums may represent lost tribes or lost traditions in extant tribes. Haakanson sees opportunities for museums to build long-lasting relationships with Native American communities that would allow for exchanges, loans, exhibitions, and other educational programs.

Haakanson concludes with an observation also made by Clavir: that indigenous items in museums are not merely objects, they are part of living cultures. Haakanson observes that

> we can use these items to preserve our culture and to bring this knowledge into a living context that continues to be passed on from generation to generation, rather than tucked away in a book, archived, or hidden in a museum collection.

Some of the readings in this chapter address problems that are inherent when cultural institutions hold indigenous materials that were not originally intended to be housed there. NAGPRA and other laws throughout the world have assured that some categories of objects have been returned to indigenous communities. For other categories that remain in institutions, much work remains to be done. For example, Clavir points out that museums and indigenous communities may have conflicting viewpoints about preservation and "cultural retention." While museum professionals may adhere to particular practices and codes of ethics, tribes and other indigenous communities may not. Each may have its own perspective. Further complicating the conversations is that tribal members may themselves work in the very museums that hold their tribes' objects. In such instances, they may hold a variety of views.

Preserving the world's heritage can be a moral imperative, as fundamental as any other human right. Yet finding ways to accomplish this monumental task will depend on numerous global and local strategies. Existing laws have begun to change attitudes in museums, libraries, and archives towards managing diverse cultural materials. The readings in this chapter present us with some approaches for continuing to move forward. The conversations promise to remain rich and multi-textured.

NOTES

1. Article 27, UDHR, accessed December 1, 2012, http://www.un.org/en/documents/udhr/.

2. Article 5, DRIP, accessed December 1, 2012, social.un.org/index/IndigenousPeoples/DeclarationontheRightsofIndigenouspeoples.aspx.

3. Michael F. Brown, *Who Owns Native Culture?* (Cambridge, MA: Harvard University Press, 2003): 209-10. This work was published before the Declaration on the Rights of Indigenous People.

4. Brown, *Who Owns Native Culture?*, 210.

5. Sherelyn Ogden, *Caring for Indian Objects: A Practical and Cultural Guide* (St. Paul, MN: Minnesota Historical Society Press, 2004): 3–4.

Selection 10.1

LOURDES ARIZPE

"Cultural Heritage and Globalization"

In Values and Heritage Conservation: Research Report, *ed. by Erica Avrami, Randall Mason, and Marta de la Torre. Los Angeles: The Getty Conservation Institute, 2000, pp. 32–37.*

TODAY OUR PERCEPTION of cultural heritage is changing amid the rush of sights and images offered by an interactive world. Still anchored in history and ancestry, our perception must now be redefined in the new global cultural commons, in which the web of meanings traditionally offered by different cultures is being rewoven. To understand what is happening, many people are looking toward the site where culture and history intersect—that is, towards cultural heritage. They are finding, however, that the cultural heritage is also in process and flowing with the tide.

To think cultural heritage was to think of art objects, archeological sites, historic monuments. Yet the meanings that assign worth to such concrete things and places come from the values that people attach to them. Such values, until recently, were discussed within the circumscribed walls of cultural communities or nations; today, however, these concrete things and places are available to be appreciated by a much wider spectrum of international publics: by a young woman writer on the Internet in New Zealand; or by a Copt filmmaker in Egypt; or by a Xhosa youngster watching television in South Africa.

Among them a new global cultural commons is being created. It is multicultural by definition; it is patchy in its interactions; it is like the terra incognita of ancient maps. And people have stakes in it, and in the world cultural sites on which the new stakeholders of the commons may tie strings of recognition. This commons is also a place we must fill up, with "global creativity," a phrase used by Catherine Stimpson and Homi Bhaba, as they refer to the new historical phenomenon, which follows and incorporates older artistic and cultural work yet has an identity of its own.[1]

More and more, the concept of cultural heritage is opening up—to cultural landscapes, popular cultures, oral traditions. The weave of meanings that crystallize into recognition in a given time and place is becoming more and more visible. It is absolutely fascinating to find that, at exactly this time, quantum physics tells us that that world is not made up of objects but is instead made up of "states" that may change their functioning and appearance according to the way in which they are being observed. An anthropologist today also knows that ethnographic description is but a transitory, fleeting glance at a reality by an observer bound by his culture and his location in a certain time and a certain place.

If we take the above view, then, the value given to cultural heritage will depend on the meanings that are chosen among those constantly travelling along a web of cultural exchanges and recombinations. At present, as never before, trade globalization, migrations and tourism, as well as telecommunications and telematics, are rapidly adding more and more exchanges to that web.

More contact and more exchanges may lead to greater creativity, but they also lead to the shielding of cultures through the politics of difference. So the question which should concern us is: How do we enhance the value of cultural heritage to safeguard it and to use it to build cultural understanding instead of cultural trenches?

To answer this question, I will explore the two main perspectives from which value is assigned to cultural heritage: the planetary and the village perspectives. In the context of globalization I will analyze how cultural groups and nation-states are repositioning themselves today in the global cultural commons. I then propose several lines of analysis and reflection on cultural heritage so that different cultural groups may find new ways of preserving cultural heritage.

The Planetary Perspective

As the new century begins, we realize that the old maps based on the territorial juxtaposition of nation-states gave us a very different cosmovision from that of actual photographs of our blue planet taken from outer space. Among other things it makes visible the framework within which we must situate all human-made masterpieces: a single, spatially finite, spherical entity. Neither political borders nor cultural boundaries are visible from space.

The awareness of one world has also been reinforced by the various processes that make up globalization; in relation to culture, a central fact is that one can communicate instantly all over the world. In fact, as of May 18, 1998, a satellite system that circles the world was finally put in place, so that we may speak to anyone, anywhere, anytime around the globe. Telecommunications and audiovisuals have made it possible for people to become familiar with great cultural heritage from distant lands.

The globality, familiarity, and instantaneity that characterize this new planetary perspective are no doubt changing the perception and understanding of the cultural legacies of the past. How can such possibilities of communication be harnessed to help in the work of conservation and restoration of cultural heritage?

A Global Cultural Commons

Strategies to protect and conserve cultural heritage internationally have been successfully developed in the last decades through Unesco and a large number of nongovernmental organizations (NGOs) and foundations. Today, such strategies must be expanded and deepened, because global communications and audiovisuals, touching a majority of people in the world, are creating this new global cultural commons. In this new space, human-made cultural creations are beginning to be judged according to an emerging set of global standards. It is not only that, for example, an Akira Kurosawa, Ingmar Bergman, or Woody Allen film speaks to many cosmopolitan people across the world, or that a Hollywood blockbuster speaks to people of very different cultures. It is the way in which these films and images are creating a new language of meaning. They are, in fact, setting up a new metonymy in people's minds. Is this a new language that belongs to the global sphere, or is it a new dimension that will permeate all forms of communication internationally?

These are new themes to explore in terms of the local/global valuing of cultural heritage. Will this new language encourage people to give value to cultural heritage of other cultures? Do they assign relative value to cultural masterpieces according to the cultural distance between their own and other cultures? How important do they consider them for their emotional satisfaction or spiritual or cultural realization? Or, one may ask (as the World Bank has already done in a project on Fez in Morocco), in terms of the economics of cultural heritage, how much would you be willing to pay to conserve such heritage? Much more analytical work is needed on how collectivities of different kinds react towards cultural heritage in the context of a global cultural commons.

This knowledge is urgently needed to prevent a replication of the "tragedy of the commons" in relation to the protection of cultural heritage.[2] Some specialists are already concerned that this is the case for a number of sites inscribed in Unesco's World Heritage List. When a site is considered to have "world value," then safeguarding actions may be perceived as everybody's business—and, therefore, as no one's. Alternatively, it may be thought that saving such a site should be the main responsibility of only the rich and powerful, since poor people or nations are unable to give anything toward its safeguarding.

The Village View

If our planetary view (implying unity) comes from outer space, the village view (implying diversity) comes from everyday contact with people speaking other languages, exhibiting different symbols of identity, and wanting to choose all that is meaningful and exciting in today's cultural markets. This contact is leading to very rapid cultural change that is worrying people in many different regional settings, as the U.N. World Commission on Culture and Development discovered in the nine consultations it held in Europe, the Americas, Asia and Africa.[3] People everywhere are concerned that their traditions are no longer being followed, that young people especially may be choosing cultural symbols from other cultures. Artists are concerned about the difficulties they have found in continuing their local cultural production as foreign investments and cultural goods flow into national markets.

In times of such cultural fluidity, it is to be expected that people want to cling to the meanings that once held their immediate community together. Archaeological sites of historical importance, architectural or artistic masterpieces, the cultural texture of everyday life with dress codes and gastronomy, all become explicit consensual symbols of historical belonging. In many places, movements explicitly express such concerns: Afro-Americans and Chicanos, Celts and Catalans, Serbs and Albanokosovars, Chileans and the Mapuche people. Although all such movements have a cultural leitmotiv, they are extremely diverse in political aims, forms of action, and international strategies.

This situation has led to a current climate in which world cultural heritage must be dealt with globally, with unity of aims and strategies (the planetary view) at a time when there is a rising tide of the politics of difference (the village view). In my view, the way to advance in such a situation is to create new concepts to explain the new local/global structuring of the value of cultural heritage, while at the same time to support pilot projects with this aim in mind.

The Village Is Multicultural

Independent of the historical, cultural affiliation of a given site, monument, or art object, it is most probable that people living in a certain locality, or concerned with its heritage, will belong to multicultural communities. This is important vis-à-vis the valuing of cultural heritage. Thus, the way communities value that heritage will be influenced by the way they had previously defined their own cultural identity. And it is a matter of some urgency that the issue of multiculturalism with reference to cultural heritage be placed on the international agenda.

In recent years, several different situations have arisen as a result of the complexity of multicultural claims to cultural heritage. On the one hand, governments may be claiming, as "national" treasures, ancient masterpieces created many centuries ago by cultures totally different from theirs—or whose descendants may even be considered their cultural opponents. Such is the case of the Hindu government in India, which must protect the Muslim cultural heritage. If the country has a democratic system, appropriate political solutions may be arrived at, as they have been in India. Another kind of situation is that in which cultural minorities are given recognition and support for the management of their own cultural heritage and creativity. This has been the case, for example, in New Zealand with the Maori people.

This does not happen in cases in which cultural groups suffer ill treatment at the hands of the government. Such is the case of Guatemala, where the Maya heritage is considered a national asset, while the army continues to repress all political and cultural expressions of the Maya-Quiche and Cakchiquel Indians who are the direct descendants of the builders of the magnificent Maya heritage.

In the most negative situation, "cultural heritage cleansing" may be carried out by opponents in war, as has happened in the protracted war in the former Yugoslavia. In this case, along with "ethnic cleansing," there was a willful destruction of cultural heritage "to obliterate people's cultural roots," as Azzedine Beschaouch expressed it, when he described the case of the Old Bridge of Mostar, demolished with explosives by Croat extremists during the Bosnian war. To this example one would add the Serb destruction of the Library in Sarajevo, as well as the bombing of Dubrovnik.[4]

With the repositioning of actors in globalization, the more nation-states and cultural minorities need "distinction" to reposition themselves in the global cultural commons, the more they are apt to rely on the cultural heritage to build internal cohesion and an external image of their culture. Inevitably, then, questions about the historical origins and present control and management of culture heritage will be increasingly raised.[5]

Claims of the right to control cultural heritage will, in all probability, also proliferate for economic reasons. As multimedia and telecommunications open a market for the images of cultural heritage, and as the economic value of cultural heritage is increased through cultural tourism and other services, special interest groups will possibly increase their demands to share in the economic returns related to such heritage.

One example will illustrate the complexity of the issues involved: a Chol-speaking indigenous group in Chiapas, Mexico, is claiming that it should be getting a share of tourist fees for visits to Palenque, the Maya archaeological site. This opens up a Pandora's box of unanswerable questions: Was the site built by the Chol people? If so, are the Chol of today the real descendants of those historical Chol? If so, should only the Chol get this income to the exclusion of other Indian groups in the region, since there is not enough historical evidence to ascertain who built Palenque? And what about non-Chol Mexicans, for whom Palenque is part of their cultural heritage?

Counterbalancing such exclusionary claims will require a highly developed knowledge base for world cultural heritage. It will show (as the field of anthropology has recorded for many decades) that the creative process evolves by the slow, direct and indirect, accumulation of knowledge, skills and techniques, usually nurtured by exchanges with many other cultures. Along a different but related path, recent art theories now give greater emphasis to this creative process among artists and artistic communities than to the art objects themselves.

Highlighting the creative process in relation to world cultural heritage would, I believe, have several positive effects. First, it would bring in greater historical depth, thereby making visible the different layers of creativity and cultural exchanges that have crystallized in a particular cultural site, object, or landscape; this information would correctly situate cultural claims in a historical context.

Second, when the multicultural history of heritage is made visible, a wider range of today's communities could feel more directly related to a given cultural heritage.

Third, this multicultural history would strengthen the role of governments by eliminating the necessity for them to appear as defenders of a single cultural tradition, while providing them with greater legitimacy as the conveners of their countries' diverse cultural traditions of the past and the present. Of course, as conditions for this, a state must be democratic, open to expressions of different cultures, yet clear in its mandate to protect all the cultural heritage within its borders.

Finally, the multiculturality of the village also applies to the constituency that supports actions to safeguard world cultural heritage. Perhaps the phrase "global cultural stakeholders" could be used to signify people who share in giving value and, therefore, in creating the new meanings for world cultural heritage. Would it be possible to revive the project of creating a civil-society World Cultural Trust—a phrase used in the discussions that led to the Unesco World Heritage Convention? Such a project could contribute to strengthening civil-society initiatives to complement the work already being carried out by governments and international organizations. Their main role would be to act in the cultural commons by promoting awareness of the value of world cultural heritage.

Fostering Creativity about Cultural Heritage

In May 1995, a historic session of the Executive Board of Unesco was held in Fez, Morocco, during which many member states demanded a shift in the culture program of Unesco. They no longer wanted restored historic city centers that became ghost towns, where the bustle of people working, relating, and trading had been lost. Neither could their governments afford to open more and more museums that were not self-financing and that catered to elite publics. The concern was also expressed—and repeated in countless forums, including those of the World Commission on Culture and Development—that young people all over were increasingly uninterested in the cultural heritage of the past while they pursued totally new cultural activities.

Accordingly, Unesco's cultural program added to its successful conservation projects for cultural heritage a new focus on living cultures.[6] The premise for recasting the program was that cultural transformations previously took decades, even centuries; today such changes take only a few years and have unrivaled world coverage through the global cultural commons. Also, emphasis was placed on the enthusiasm of young people everywhere to create new meanings—their own cultural heritage, so to speak—so they can adapt to the unprecedented situations they are destined to live in. It seems to me that those youths who flock to Stonehenge for the summer solstice or to Teotihuacán for the spring equinox want a new freedom to recreate ancient rites so that these ancient stones and places may become new symbols around which to rally and recreate their own sense of place and purpose.

The language in which they are couching their search is that of a new spirituality and cosmology; most probably because they are offered no other language by traditional institutions, which are still caught up in political and social inertia and which mostly limit their activities to the conservation of what already exists.

New languages of expression must be offered to these young people. New, exciting experiences have been successful; for example, popular music concerts have been held in World Heritage sites, such as Nara, Japan, and El Tajin, Mexico. What is needed, in my view, is to instigate artists, writers, scientists, and other creators to renew the meetings that give life to the powerful symbolism of cultural masterpieces—a symbolism that is no longer imprisoned in the past but is instead shaping the future.

Fostering creativity around cultural heritage is valuable not only to mobilize people but also to keep "alive." The best way to save cultural heritage is to encourage new creative outlooks that will renew or add to its web of meanings. An image to illustrate this is that of the maypole, the origins of which are claimed by so many cultures. The larger the number of people taking the colored ribbons in their hands and the more they dance and intermingle around it, the tighter the mesh of ribbons will be and the more strongly they will be attached to the maypole.

The World Heritage List: Pride of All or Pride of the Few?

In 1972 the Convention Concerning the Protection of the World Cultural and Natural Heritage was adopted at the Unesco General Conference.[7] It built on the momentum created by the successful 1959 Unesco campaign to save the Philae and Abu Simbel temples in Egypt from flooding by the Aswan High Dam. After a 1965 White House conference that called for world action on cultural heritage, and after proposals from the Stockholm Conference on Human Environment for the Conservation of Nature (since the Convention also includes natural sites), the Convention was drawn up to protect the masterpieces of human creative genius by establishing the World Heritage List.

Other attempts, for example, to protect folk cultural productions have not been agreed upon internationally, nor have other conventions been ratified by as many countries.[8] In this light, the broad consensus and the widespread popularity of the Convention on World Heritage must be highlighted. This success has demonstrated that governments, spurred by public interest, have been able to agree on a world value on which to base a complex institutional charter and procedure to channel international cooperative actions.[9]

Knowing that it can be done is already a great step forward, but of course, the crucial issue is to what degree the Convention has been successful in actually helping conserve protected cultural monuments, sites, and landscapes. Most specialists agree that it has been successful, although some despair at the decline of many of the places on the list. In spite of such concerns, it is highly significant that—at a time when globalization is pushing people to retrench themselves in particularistic cultural identities—there is one value that people of all cultures seem to agree on.

Why is the Convention so highly respected and almost unanimously agreed upon? On one of my trips to Manila, in December 1995, as assistant director-general for culture at Unesco, I was told why. I had been taken to visit the Baroque churches of Manila on the World Heritage List. The guide showed me around with a special self-satisfaction and pride. So I asked, "And why does having a Unesco plaque of the World Heritage List help you in promoting these places?" He answered, "Because, madam, then we know that they are not only our pride but that of all of humanity, and this makes us even more proud."

It is people with local pride, then, who want to share their pride with others; and once others give this recognition, it adds to the value of the site. So the pride of the few becomes the pride of all. Thus, it is the interaction between local and global valorizing that gives strength and continuity to the World Heritage List.

Is The World Heritage List Representative?

A most interesting aspect of the World Heritage List is that while its main purpose is to ensure the safeguarding of world cultural heritage, it is also being interpreted as an inventory of cultural achievement. The fact, then, that the List is not balanced in terms of geographical and cultural regions has become problematic. In response to this and other similar concerns, a group of experts was commissioned in 1994 to assess how representative the World Heritage List was. This group concluded that there was an over-representation of European heritage; of historic cities and religious buildings, especially of the Christian religion; of "elite" architecture (in contrast to more "popular" architecture); and of historic sites (in comparison to prehistoric and twentieth-century sites).

One could already see a background metonymy emerging, which is being given fuller coverage with the new criteria for inclusion in the World Heritage List that have been negotiated. For example, a more flexible notion of "authenticity" now allows the inclusion of cultural heritage buildings that follow ancient designs yet have been rebuilt several times over the centuries, such as the wooden temples in Nara and Kyoto in Japan.

Similarly, the new category of "cultural landscape" was created, which, for example, has allowed for the inclusion of the Philippine rice terraces. Also, twentieth-century heritage is now taken into account; thus Brazil was able to inscribe Brasilia, its novel capital city, on the list.

For the purposes of this essay, however, I would also like to emphasize that the value of the List lies as much in its actual results as in the learning and negotiation process it has unleashed. Slowly, arduously, it is building agreements on the value of world cultural heritage and on the global standards for mechanisms and procedures to safeguard it. The program, however, now has to be recast in the terms of some of the points made in this essay, to give it relevance under the new conditions of globalization.

Summary

We know that the best way to safeguard world cultural heritage is for societies to care enough about it to mobilize to protect it and to support governments and specialized groups in working towards conservation. Today it should be possible to harness speeded-up cultural interactivity on a world scale for the protection of world cultural heritage.[10]

International programs and actions by governments, NGOs, and foundations have already been successful in broadening the base of the appreciation of heritage and of community participation in its protection. Fostering creativity in relation to cultural heritage would further broaden this base of support. Writers, filmmakers, and artists should be encouraged to breathe new life into the symbols and images of heritage through new cultural practices.

The World Heritage Convention could play an emblematic role in consolidating global, convergent actions for cultural heritage, in opposition to the narrow interests driven by competition in some aspects of globalization. New thinking is needed to open new imaginative avenues in caring for world cultural heritage. The global cultural commons must be explored, mapped, and furnished with global standards. It is crucial that cultural heritage be thought of as a historical process to which many individuals and cultures have always, and will always, contribute. And

the increasingly inescapable multicultural reality of the village—the consumers and publics for cultural heritage—must change perceptions, so that pride and cultural heritage may be shared by more and more people across cultural differences. Success in conserving the masterpieces of human creative genius will depend on our ability to interact, negotiate, and cultivate heritage as a creative process.

1. Catherine Stimpson and Homi Bhabha, Global creativity and the arts, *World Culture Report* 1 (June 1998):183–93.

2. Garret Hardin, The tragedy of the commons, *Science* 162(1968):1243–48.

3. The U.N. World Commission on Culture and Development, chaired by Javier Perez de Cuellar, published its report *Our Creative Diversity* in 1995. Lourdes Arizpe was a member of the Commission and was in charge of the secretariat of the Commission as assistant director-general for culture of Unesco.

4. Azzedine Beschaouch, The destruction of the Old Bridge of Mostar, *World Culture Report* 1 (June 1998):117.

5. This matter is raised without full consideration of the other complex aspects of the question—whether present governments legitimately represent the culture or cultures that created the heritage. This question is especially relevant in countries in which cultural minorities are persecuted while there heritage is claimed as part of the national heritage.

6. Unesco, *Draft Programme and Budget, 1998–1999*, 29 C/5 (1997). Unesco, *Approved Programme and Budget for 1998–1999*, 29 C/5 approved (1998).

7. In this section, for the purposes of discussion, I will refer exclusively to the cultural sites on the World Heritage List, although the list also includes natural sites.

8. Another convention with widespread support is the one for the Protection of Cultural Property in the Event of Armed Conflict, otherwise known as The Hague Convention of 1954, which was updated in 1997.

9. For an excellent analysis of how global standards for cultural heritage protection can counter some of the effects of globalization, see Lyndel Prott, International standards for cultural heritage, *World Culture Report* 1 (June 1998): 222–36.

10. One suggestion, for example, is to hyperlink Internet sites of popular artists, such as Cesaria Evora, to sites describing the cultural heritage of their places of origin. See Isabelle Vinson, Heritage and cyberculture: What cultural content for what cyberculture? *World Culture Report* 1 (June 1998): 237–49.

Selection 10.2

MIRIAM CLAVIR

"First Nations Perspectives on Preservation and Museums"

Chapter 3 in Preserving What Is Valued: Museums, Conservation, and First Nations. *Vancouver: University of British Columbia Press, 2002, pp. 69–97.*

THE CONSERVATION OF museum collections is not a frequent subject for First Nations writers, even within the small but growing Aboriginal-authored literature pertaining to museums and their collections. Repatriation and representation are the two most discussed areas in this literature. While both are beyond the specific focus of this book, they do reflect concerns about cultural authority and recognition, and these are also part of the museum/cultural preservation discourse. In addition, there is a growing Aboriginal-authored literature concerned with the protection of indigenous knowledge and creations. This literature extends through many fields, from pharmacy to archival studies.

Before proceeding with Part 2, it is important to consider whether separating museum perspectives and First Nations perspectives on preservation by relegating them to two separate chapters serves to create a structural paradigm of two distinct points of view, which could be misleading, generalizing, and falsely oppositional. Furthermore, does it serve to resurrect a professionally familiar but highly questionable "us" and "them" approach? Separate chapters can serve to lessen the acknowledgment of the fact that there is a reality of experiences and knowledge made up of both perspectives. For example, there are First Nations professionals in museums; there are First Nations cultural

centres that have professional museum components; and many contemporary Aboriginal people, both urban and nonurban, work closely with museums. Finally, categorizing museum and First Nations perspectives separately, with the former being presented first, risks creating a power/knowledge imbalance in which Western perspectives take precedence over non-Western perspectives.

I raise these points so that the reader does not unconsciously absorb the structure of this book in a way in which it was never intended. Because this book examines areas in which established museum conservation practice and First Nations have potentially conflicting viewpoints, it is necessary to consider each viewpoint separately to fully understand the meaning and context of preservation in differing value systems. Furthermore, considering "distinct viewpoints" is not merely a Western academic construct: contemporary First Nations are proud of their cultural traditions and place great significance on their "radically differing perceptions of reality and concepts of cultural retention" (Moses 1993, 2) *(Moses: Delaware/ Mohawk)*. For example, Atleo (1990, 3) compares Euro-based rational positivism with the "interconnected, holistic, and relational view which reflects a First Nations perspective of reality" *(Atleo: Nuh-Chh-Nulth)*. With regard to museums, this dichotomy will be seen, for example, in the comparison between the traditional museum and the National Museum of the American Indian (NMAI).

Bearing all of this in mind, I now turn to First Nations perspectives. Chapter 3 examines written and other publicly articulated First Nations perspectives on preservation. Chapter 4 provides background on the First Nations of British Columbia for readers unfamiliar with this area. Chapters 5 and 6 report on interviews and conversations about preservation with First Nations individuals, first in British Columbia and then in New Zealand. Chapter 7 serves as a conclusion to Part 2.

Before beginning, though, I would like to alert the reader to one further consideration. In both the literature and the interviews/conversations, most of the First Nations speakers clearly state that they are representing their own personal views and are not official spokespeople for their respective communities or nations. As Claxton (1994b, 1) states: "I cannot speak for other Nations, this is protocol, that we respect what belongs to others and not place our opinion on objects we know nothing about" *(Claxton: Coast Salish)*. With regard to the citations presented in these chapters, the reader is encouraged to recognize the limitations of quotations, which represent only a portion of what has been stated by the writers and speakers. In addition, it is worth remembering that the First Nations individuals cited represent people of different cultures as well as different ages, experiences, genders, and so on.

Mithlo (2001, 4), whom the reader met on the first page of this book, follows anthropologist Edward Spicer (Spicer and Thompson, 1972) in regarding historical experience as having precedence over language, kinship, and customs as the primary factor in constructing social identity. She adds that, in her country, the United States, Native Americans are treated federally as a common group, regardless of distinctive cultural classifications observed by the tribes and clans themselves. "This control of native identity results in shared experiences of natives in regards not only to the loss of land and language noted by Spicer, but also in relationship to contemporary social experiences

such as boarding school trauma, a high incidence of substance abuse, endemic poverty and continued racial discrimination ... Not only then is there internal justification for utilizing the concept of a Native American identity (following Spicer's argument of shared historical experience), there also exists a legal precedent for consideration of the many tribes composing a pan-Indian constituency" (4,5). In this book, however, peoples' statements should be regarded as individual opinions. Likewise, the information gathered throughout Part 2 in the form of tables should not be read as generalizations but, rather, as summaries of main points.

It is important to note that, while conservators also represent a diversity of social factors and opinions, their voluntary adherence to similar professional codes of ethics enables certain generalizations to be made about their values and beliefs. The same cannot be said of First Nations values and beliefs.

This chapter addresses First Nations viewpoints on the meaning of preservation, the role objects play in cultural preservation, and the role and nature of museums. I present published or publicly articulated perspectives from Aboriginal people in Canada, the United States, New Zealand, and, in a few cases, other countries. I present them together to illustrate that, despite great cultural differences, there exist shared perspectives regarding the fundamental importance of preserving indigenous cultural beliefs and lifeways. In addition, these perspectives often differ from those of museums.

The reader should note that, as I explained in the Introduction, in *Preserving What Is Valued*, First Nations names are written without their diacritical marks. Not all sources include diacritical marks in their orthography, and, rather than use them for some names but not all, I decided to use the spellings that are most often seen in English. For example, Sto:lo and Kwakwaka'wakw would read Stó:lo and Kwakwa̱ka'wakw in some First Nations sources; 'Namgis and Nisga'a would read 'Na̱lmgis and Nisga'a. I regret any inaccuracies the convention adopted for this book presents. I would also like the reader to note that a glossary of Maori words is included in Appendix C.

Meaning of Preservation

The following quotations illustrate the meaning of "preservation" for several indigenous organizations.

> The Keepers of the Treasures is a cultural council of American Indians, Alaska Natives and Native Hawaiians who preserve, affirm and celebrate their cultures through traditions and programs that maintain their native languages and lifeways. The Keepers protects and conserves places that are historic and sacred to indigenous peoples. (Keepers of the Treasures 1994, 9)
>
> [The seventeen Shuswap bands] declared their intentions to work *in unity* to *preserve, record, perpetuate and enhance the Shuswap language, history and culture.* It is with these principles in mind that the Shuswap people approach the work of the Task Force [Task Force on Museums and First Peoples cosponsored by the Assembly of First Nations and the Canadian Museums Association]. Any work or report which comes out of the meetings taking place between the museum and native communities must have at its heart the preservation, perpetuation and enhancement of native culture. These principles embody everything for which the Secwepemc [Cultural Education Society] strive[s]. (Secwepemc Cultural Education Society 1991,1)

Michael Pratt *(Osage),* sums up the meaning of preservation as follows: "We all possess one common goal. It is the retention and the preservation of the American Indian way of life" *(cited in Parker 1990, 3).*

The following quotations illustrate Aboriginal perspectives on the preservation of material culture:

> Ed Ladd *(Ladd: Zuni)* asked, "what is the significance to preservation" when there are only objects left? (Ladd, cited in Clavir 1992, 2)
>
> I called for a new approach to preservation that goes beyond the old concept of holding objects in the name of the public, and instead, sees the reconnection of objects to community as an essential step in cultural preservation. I said that museums are in a unique position to assist Indian commu-

nities in the revival and retention of their spiritual traditions ... The return of objects of cultural patrimony must take place while there are still tribal elders who remember their uses. If there is no one left who knows the stories, the songs, and the ways to properly handle the objects, how can their culture be preserved? (Hill 1993, 9) *(Hill: Mohawk)*

> The unique feature of a distinctively traditional First Nations approach to the preservation of a specific cultural property is that the very act of preservation typically marks the point of intersection between the performance of a ritual observance or the fulfillment of a religious obligation, and the physical maintenance of the object itself. (Moses 1993, 3) *(Moses: Delaware/ Mohawk)*
>
> Maori history is carried in material culture but also in spiritual and cultural mediums. They are all dependent on one another and important to sustaining Maori as a people. To conserve the material culture requires an understanding and participation in the culture itself to ensure the maintenance of all values and relationships significant to an object or structure. (Whiting 1995, 15) *(Whiting: Te Whanau-a-Apanui).*
>
> At the Woodland Cultural Centre, we have Policies for Sacred and Sensitive Items as part of Collections Management which guide us in caring for culturally significant items. The Woodland Museum was established as an integral element of the Woodland Cultural Centre, with a mandate to collect, preserve, research, exhibit and interpret a collection of archaeological material, historical material, arts, crafts, documents and archival photographs. (Harris 1993, 32) *(Harris: Iroquois/Six Nations)*
>
> The oldest of our material cultural treasures are those of the Maori ... [They have been] ... fashioned into a great variety of objects of great beauty, many of which have a spiritual and cultural significance which, along with the objects themselves, must not be lost to us. (McKenzie 1987/8, 35) *(McKenzie: Rangitane)*

According to the people quoted above preservation means cultural preservation: the active maintenance of continuity with indigenous values and beliefs that are part of a community's identity. As Parker (1990, i) says: "In meetings and correspondence with the National Park Service, Indian tribes made clear their unique perspectives on historic preservation. Tribes seek to preserve their cultural heritage as a living part of contemporary life: in other words, preserving not only historic properties but languages, traditions, and lifeways."

This holistic view can be seen not only in individual opinions, but also in the practices of Canadian First Nations cultural education centres such as the Woodland Cultural Centre and the Secwepemc Cultural Education Society, both of which have professional museum components with conventional museum mandates but also espouse the "wider objectives of community-based cultural conservation" (Galla 1994, 1) *(Galla: indigenous/India)*.

Within First Nations writing, it is important to observe how often words denoting activity and life are linked to words denoting preservation. Words and phrases such as "revival" and "performance of ritual" will be found in many subsequent quotations. Many of the following First Nations comments concern the experience of and reasons for losses and changes in cultural traditions as well as a positive feeling about being identified as Aboriginal peoples. Over the last several hundred years, traditional cultural memory has been broken up and elements have been lost. In words such as "retain," "renew," and "regain" the emphasis is on the active prefix "re."

Importance of Identity for First Nations

First Nations peoples have expressed a strong link between cultural preservation and a positive identity as First Nations. Cultural identity is particularly important for First Nations within today's changing socio-political situation. As has been discussed in the Introduction, within the last two decades First Nations in Canada and the United States are seeing the recognition of Aboriginal rights in legal, political, economic, territorial, and cultural spheres. In the 1990s this involved Aboriginal peoples regaining some measure of control over community and

territorial matters. It is not surprising to see the link between assuming control and building a strong cultural identity, especially after generations of government-supported policies that actively repressed Aboriginal socio-cultural expression. In addition, Aboriginal communities are striving to retain their languages and other cultural elements (e.g., through recording cultural information from the diminishing numbers of elders who grew up with a strong base in traditional cultural knowledge) and transmitting them to younger generations.

The cultural and societal changes experienced by First Nations have meant that their cultural losses differ qualitatively from those experienced by the dominant cultures. For example, in an article about Robert Davidson, a renowned Haida artist who works primarily with traditional styles, Laurence (1993, 7) writes:

> Although he heard his grandparents speaking Haida and saw his father and grandfather carving miniature poles in argillite, Davidson grew up speaking English only ... Achieving self-awareness in a community largely separated from its artistic, linguistic and ritual inheritance, he had no sense of being Haida. "I didn't hear my first Haida song until I was 16," Davidson says. "That's how far removed we were from the culture."

Although many museums preserve the surviving fragments of Western historical material culture, in the eyes of First Nations, anthropology museums preserve the history of colonialism and the rapid and extensive changes that it brought, "Firstly, we have suffered from a loss of our traditions and secondly, we lack the resources to stop this runaway process of cultural deterioration" (Crowshoe 1994, 1) *(Crowshoe: Peigan)*. Museum collections stand as a symbol of the power relationships that led to that "cultural deterioration."

> In the process of the making of Canada, there has been an attempt to subsume aboriginal cultures under Canadian political authority. This has led to the separation of contemporary Aboriginal communities from our own pasts. (Doxtator 1996, 62)

As will be seen in chapter 4 ("First Nations of British Columbia"), government policies suppressed Aboriginal cultural expression as well as many other aspects of Aboriginal societies. The museum-related literature written by the First Nations of various countries shows the importance of the link between the loss of indigenous cultural heritage (as well as the current efforts to restore it), positive identity, and community strength. This can be seen, for example, in the following comments regarding museum collections.

> The social, economic and political climate makes life extremely difficult for many Maori people. Museums, through the cultural treasures they possess, thus become more important as places where self-worth, identity and self-determination can be regained and act as catalysts for growth. (Hakiwai 1995, 289)
>
> Many First Nations now wish to access or regain control over their material and intellectual heritage stored and exhibited in non-Aboriginal museums. (Eastern Working Group 1991, 1)

Webster (1992a, 37) expresses the significance of regaining control over one's heritage as follows: "We are taking back, from many sources, information about our culture and our history, to help us rebuild our world which was almost shattered during the bad times" *(Webster: 'Namgis [Kwakwaka'wakw]).*

With regard to museums, First Nations want to regain control both in the area of collections and in the area of representation. McCormick was a spokesperson for the Native Council of Canada:

> We are talking about taking control over our own lives, our cultures, and most importantly, the interpretation of our cultures, past and present. (McCormick 1988, 1) *(McCormick: Cree)*
>
> Cultural autonomy signifies a right to cultural specificity, a right to one's origins and histories as told from within the culture and not as mediated from without. (Todd 1990, 24) *(Todd: Metis, Alberta)*

There is an emphasis on the importance of regaining both the tangible elements and the intangible elements of culture: "As bad as the losses were in terms of land, lives and culture, a greater loss was Indian pride. This essential source of strength, which kept them together as a people, was lost along with everything else. For people trying to contend with life and develop self-confidence it is essential that they have some control over their lives and their material culture. It is degrading to be forever at the whim of others" (Horse Capture 1991, 50) *(Horse Capture: Gros Ventre).*

The importance of regaining the past by bringing it—in the form of knowledge, materials, and representation—back into one's culture and under one's control is evident in how crucial this is to First Nations identity. Recovering from the experience of colonization, First Nations have a positive attitude towards their identity, especially those aspects of it that include intangible elements such as pride and strength. Having control over the tangible objects in museums plays a role in having control over the intangibles, as is seen in Hakiwai's comment. This also applies to the creation of contemporary Aboriginal art:

> It has been a life long dream of mine to help bring the art form of my ancestors to be recognized as great art, placed along side all the other great art of the world, to bring it beyond the curio attitude which it has suffered since contact...
>
> I have always felt alien to art galleries until my showing here. In showing my work you have opened the door to many other artists who are working to validate their work as true art. Our art has helped us as a people to reconnect with our cultural past, helped us in regaining our own identity, giving us strength to reclaim our place in the world. (Davidson 1993)

MUSEUM VALUES

Basic differences in emphasis between museum perspectives and First Nations perspectives can be represented schematically, as shown in Table 1.

I will now compare many of the museum values expressed in chapters 1 and 2 with First Nations values (as expressed in their literature and/or public statements). It is necessary to reiterate that any tendency towards generalization must be tempered with the knowledge that there are hundreds of distinct Aboriginal cultures in North America alone—all having various histories, cultural differences, and contemporary outlooks, and all containing individuals with various perspectives.

The National Museum of the American Indian (NMAI), which is part of the Smithsonian Institution, is a largely Native American-managed and -staffed museum that hopes, in the words of its director, "to re-analyze, redirect and, in many cases, reformulate entirely the concepts and presentations of the past concerning Indian culture" (West 1991, 24) *(West: Cheyenne-Arapaho)*. NMAI has conducted numerous consultations with Aboriginal people across North America on many aspects of museum development, collections, and programming. Table 2 briefly summarizes some of their conclusions with regard to museums and objects.

Other museum and First Nations values and beliefs that appear to be in conflict with one another can be summarized in Table 3. Note that this table highlights areas of apparent contradiction between museums and First Nations; later discussions will

expand on beliefs and values that appear less contradictory. Note also that this table represents conventional museum beliefs and that, as museums change, not all these statements will continue to hold true. The purpose of Table 3 is to set out and summarize key differences between the viewpoints of museums and those of First Nations. Beliefs pertaining specifically to conservation, such as object preservation versus use, and appropriate treatment of objects considered sacred or sensitive, are considered in more detail later in this chapter. I have included quotations in the table so that the reader can hear from individual First Nations members directly.

First Nations Perspectives on Museums

Museum and First Nations perspectives differ not only intellectually, but also emotionally. There is different emotional resonance implicit in many of the above statements. I now turn to some examples of differing perspectives and then to the positive and negative perceptions of museums held by First Nations people.

TABLE 1

"Preservation": Museum and First Nations Perspectives

Traditional Museum	First Nations
Preservation of objects	Preservation of traditional cultural practice, Aboriginal values
Rationale:	*Rationale:*
Loss of material culture, knowledge	Loss of parts of culture, positive identity, control
Preservation of the past as a positive value: objects are witnesses to the past	Preservation is positive in the context of self-determination: renewal, living expression; objects are part of living cultures today

TABLE 2

The Traditional Museum and the National Museum of the American Indian (NMAI)

Traditional Museum	NMAI
Preserves objects	Preserves culture
Conserves objects	Cares for objects
Displays objects	Uses objects
Object-based	People-based
Objects are out of their cultural context	Objects, people, and the environment are related to each other
Looks at the past	Integrates the past, the present, and the future
Objects are considered inert	Supports the Native American philosophy that objects are living and require air and natural light

Source: Swentzell 1991.

TABLE 3

Beliefs and Values, Museums and First Nations: Differences in Perspective [Excerpt]

Traditional Museum	First Nations
Importance of heritage objects	"The objects themselves are not important; what matters is what the objects represent. They represent the right to own that thing, and that right remains even if the object decays or is otherwise lost" (Webster 1986, 77). "The [Kwakiutl] elders spoke of the importance for young people to know and touch their past [the repatriated objects] if they are to have an identity in the future" (Morrison 1993, 6). "What will they remember if we don't show them anything?" (Alicie Araqutak, Avataq Cultural Institute, quoted in Haagen 1990, 77).
Prevention of deterioration, preservation of culturally designated objects	Some objects meant to deteriorate and complete their natural cycle. "The emphasis on preserving the [Athapascan] Native elders' material culture was often contrary to their holistic belief that these goods should return to nature to nurture future generations" (Wright 1994, 1). "One person stated that there is not a single item in his culture which is used for religious or ceremonial purposes which is meant to be preserved in perpetuity. All are gifts to the Gods which are meant to disintegrate back into the earth to do their work" (Clavir 1992, 8). "It is also patronizing to assume that indigenous people necessarily believe that all their works should complete a natural cycle and be allowed to degrade and eventually return to the soil. Like other people, Maori wish to keep records of their achievements and history" (Heikell, Whiting, et al. 1995, 15).
Objects contain encoded knowledge	Knowledge resides with the elders and is passed on generation to generation. "The attachment to material goods, however, did not ensure survival for these [Athapascan] people. It was the knowledge gained through oral narratives that provided necessary lessons in survival skills" (Wright 1994, 1).
Objects very important; provide tangible evidence	Songs, oral history and genealogy, rights and privileges, and other "intangibles" highly important as evidence. "The objects themselves confirm the stories that have been heard by native people over the years" (Hill 1993, 10).
Loss of authenticity/integrity in an object = loss of tangible link with past	Link with past is made tangible by participating in traditional lifeways.
Intangibles of culture are shown through animated museum environments (Macdonald 1992).	Intangibles are shown through rituals, community, and other culture events. "A museum is not necessarily the setting in which one can hope to experience or comprehend the significance of sacred objects, either from the viewpoint of those who created them, or from the viewpoint of those whose benefit they were created and originally maintained" (Moses 1995, 18).
Museums: a European tradition	Museums and similar institutions are not part of indigenous cultures. Culturally significant objects used and cared for by religious societies, within families, etc., and displayed in appropriate cultural contexts. Objects beyond usefulness often ritually retired (e.g., some burned or buried).

continued on next page

TABLE 3

Beliefs and Values, Museums and First Nations: Differences in Perspective *(continued)*

Traditional Museum	First Nations
Collecting and museums histori-cally represent European "superi-ority," European roots.	"To Canadian nationalists, the necessity of belief in the superiority of Anglo-Canadian society doomed aboriginal peoples to extinction and assimilation" (Doxator 1996, 61).
Ethnographic collections made to represent people who were believed to be disappearing.	"My culture has survived, but as a refugee in my own land" (McCormick 1988, 4). "We are not dead. We did not die out before the turn of the century and we're not a diluted form of the supposed 'real' and 'authentic' Maori" (Hakiwai 1995, 287). "All previous anthropological and social theorizations notwithstanding, and despite the best efforts of the combined European and western military, political and religious complexes the Native peoples of North American have not become extinct over the course of these past five centuries, and traditional indigenous systems of religion and spirituality remain vibrant features of daily life in many First Nations communities" (Moses 1993, 7). See also Tamarapa (1996, 42).
Public museums represent secular, scientific values.	Traditional spiritual values at the heart of cultural renewal. Preference for explain-ing world on basis of spiritual beliefs. "Some [museum people] place science as the ultimate human endeavor, above the law, above the religious rights or human rights of Indians" (Hill 1993, 9). See also Harris (1993). "The distinction between science and mythology has to be rejected because both are equally ideological" (Bedard 1993, 7–8).
Public service mandate	"Museums were not founded to serve the needs of the Maori people but rather to entomb us and our material culture. We were to become the prize exhibits of the nineteenth century, now safely 'domesticated' in museums" (Mead, as quoted in Tamarapa 1996, 162). "With the state presenting itself as the impartial coordinator and arbitrator among seemingly troublesome and demanding ethnic groups. It sees itself working 'for the benefit of all'" (Doxtador 1996, 61).
First Nations societies subject of scholarly studies; studies transmitted to public (e.g., via museums).	Desire not to be subjects of studies, especially if no benefit returns to them. (See, e.g., Nason 1981; Eastern Working Group 1991; Hill 1988.) Prefer co-equal partnerships in urban museum enterprise and control of community heritage.

continued on next page

TABLE 3

Beliefs and Values, Museums and First Nations: Differences in Perspective *(continued)*

Traditional Museum	First Nations
Importance of legal ownership by museum. In addition, frequent contemporary acknowledgement of "moral" rights of others.	Importance of First Nations Ownership of their cultural heritage. "The dominant society owns the concept of museology while the First Nations people own the heritage represented in the relevant collections" (Atleo 1990, 3). "Museums are to acknowledge that there is a living culture associated with these 'taonga,' and that Maori people are the spiritual and cultural custodians... Museums are the caretakers of the 'taonga,' not the owners' the 'mana' of the taonga resides with the 'iwi' from which it originates" (Tamarapa 1996, 163). "The somewhat illogical situation arises whereby the Crown of Canada, in existence for 127 years, assumes it has a greater right, a greater interest and connection, to aboriginal material of twenty-thousand years ago than do the aboriginal people who have always inhabited North America" (Doxtator 1996, 62). "Question: I was wondering whether the material that has been returned to your museum has its title of ownership actually transferred to your museum, or are the pieces on long-term loan? Answer: I guess it depends on who you are asking" (Webster 1986, 79).
Museum displays often represent static moments in linear time.	Cyclical and other concepts of time. "To most of Canadian society, the past is very separate from the present and future. The past is measured precisely in years and days... To Native societies, the past is not as distinctly separate from the present (p. 27). [In museums] to see change or European influence in the construction of an object was to see loss of culture (p. 26)... The physical expressions of traditions change... but the most basic principles that direct those traditions remain... and are not dependent upon chronological time" (Doxator 1988). "In our way of thinking, everything is a significant event, and the past is as real as us being here right now. We are all connected to the things that happened at the beginning of our existence. And those things live on as they are handed down to us" (Parris Butler, Fort Mohave, as quoted in Parker 1990, 5).
Democratic principles for public museums	1) Restrictions (viewing, handling, storage, use) may apply to certain objects (see Moses 1993, 5). 2) Access for average First Nations person to museum collections has been problematic. The "public" has been privileged to the detriment of particular stakeholders such as First Nations.

Positive Perceptions of Museums

Some First Nations people have expressed an appreciation of museums and their work. For example, according to Tamarapa (1996, 67): "Many Maori are aware of the benefits that museums have as places of professional care and responsibility."

Horse Capture (1991, 50-1), a museum curator and consultant from the Gras Ventre nation, tempers Tamarapa's positive view with the following observations:

> Native Americans, and perhaps other tribal peoples as well, have therefore a strange and special link with museums that has been described as a love/hate relationship. Many Indians appreciate the fact that for many reasons, the material that has survived is to be found in museums, where it is preserved and researched. The hate aspect comes from the fact that these museums are usually far away from Indian homes, and the materials are hence inaccessible to them. So the Indian people went to museums searching for ways to restore their culture. For the most part, they were viewed with suspicion or outright hostility.

The same mixed feelings have also been expressed in New Zealand: "For the Maori people there has been a great degree of ambivalence towards museums. They are important and respected places because of the cultural wealth they possess but concurrently many Maori people feel anger and resentment in the way that museums have acted as 'experts' and managers of cultural heritage and knowledge systems" (Hakiwai 1995, 287).

The importance of museum training and of First Nations museum and other specialist professionals has been acknowledged. The Museums Association of the Caribbean held a workshop in 1993 that made the following recommendation: "Museums should provide education in techniques for care and preservation of artifacts for cultural groups" (Branche 1996, 126). In Canada, in a more politicized context, McCormick (1988, 3) suggested: "It will be our elders and specialists, our historians and anthropologists, our scientists, who from now on will be the interpreters of our Culture. That is what self-determination means and we will have no less."

First Nations museum professionals uphold museum values as well as their own cultural values, and they have expressed that this sometimes causes conflict for them.

> To ask ourselves to relinquish our senior museum positions to the seer of a "tribe" or to allow leaders to bang drums or spread salt on votive bowls from a museum collection is like wrenching our museological souls from our very beings. (Branche 1996, 121)
>
> I never thought I would say this, but in a way it was fortunate that the collection was returned in such terrible shape, because we were able to convince people that the objects were much too fragile to be used. (Webster 1986, 78) (See also Harris 1993)

Moses (1993, 7), a conservator, writes about the contradiction between the purpose of museum preservation and the purpose of cultural preservation: "The specific issue at hand is whether such objects are to be artificially maintained within the sterile environment of the Euro-North American controlled museum, or whether they are to be returned to the heart of the living cultures from which they originate."

Negative Perceptions of Museums

Negative First Nations perceptions of museums have been given considerable voice. "As Gloria Cranmer-Webster stated at the concluding conference of the Task Force [Task Force, Museums and First Peoples, 1992]: 'We don't want museums.' The word 'museum' has a negative connotation signifying the place where dead things lie and where native people don't go" (Doxtator 1996, 64).

Moses (1995, 18) observes that museums "remain painful symbols and reminders of cultural loss and deprivation." Tamarapa (1996, 162) cites a Maori presenter at the national New Zealand museum conference in 1985: "The Museum represents a place of death, of bones, of plunder and relics and pillage." A Maori curator writes: "Museums are seen by many as a sad legacy of the past imbued with a continuing sense of paternalistic colonialism and monoculturalism" (Hakiwai 1995, 286).

Museums have housed the tangible symbols of fundamental aspects of the culture of many First Nations, and, in so doing, they have acquired a negative signification for many First Nations. Museums themselves have become the symbols of historic, repressive, and often racist dominance: "Museums remain to remind us of the horrors of our colonial past" (Atleo 1990, 13). Furthermore, the housing of these "signs" "placed the museum in the role of guardian of authentic symbols of 'Indianness'" (Doxtator 1988, 26). The museum developed a vested interest in presenting an image of First Nations as peoples of the past. Museums had been invested with the authority to speak about and display images of First Nations, while First Nations were excluded from any role in representing their own reality.

It is also offensive to many First Nations that museums often present a one-sided historical view of Aboriginal peoples. In 1994, for example, a resolution from the Commonwealth Association of Museums "support[ed]... re-defining ... the idea of 'museum' from houses of indigenous peoples from the past (not as dead) and considered that museums house cultures and cultural meanings that reflect for indigenous people living culture" (Commonwealth Association of Museums 1994, 1).

The following poem by a Native American captures the resentment that many Aboriginal people feel towards museums and the majority culture.

Evolution[1]

Buffalo Bill opens a pawn shop on the reservation
right across the border from the liquor store
and he stays open 24 hours a day, 7 days a week

and the Indians come running in with jewelry
television sets, a VCR, a full-length beaded
  buckskin outfit
it took Inez Muse 12 years to finish. Buffalo Bill

takes everything the Indians have to offer, keeps it
all catalogued and filed in a storage room. The Indians
pawn their hands, saving the thumbs for the last,
  they pawn

their skeletons, falling endlessly from the skin
and when the last Indian has pawned everything
but his heart, Buffalo Bill takes that for twenty bucks

closes up the pawn shop, paints a new sign over the
  old
calls his venture THE MUSEUM OF NATIVE AMERICAN
  CULTURES
charges the Indians five bucks a head to enter.

(Alexie 1992, 48) (Alexie: Spokane/Coeur d'Alene)

Negative Perceptions of Museum Practice

The museum process as well as the museum itself may carry a negative symbolic meaning for First Nations people. Moses (1993, 7) argues:

Conservation issues quite aside, many Native peoples, on principle, take exception to the imposition of any such requirements, (such as requiring repatriated materials to be provided with certain prescribed standards of physical care in terms of security, environmental control, and so on) and consider them to be essentially a means by which the Euro-North American museum community attempts to force from the First Nations a tacit acknowledgment that the dominant society has the right to control and regulate the access of First Nations peoples to their own cultural patrimony.

---

1. Reprinted from *The Business of Fancydancing*, © 1992 by Sherman Alexie, by permission of Hanging Loose Press.

A harsher view of museums and the museum process, which compares standard museum and conservation practice with prison practice, was manifested publicly in 1995 by two Shuswap (Interior Salish) men who went on a hunger strike outside the Royal British Columbia Museum (RBCM) in Victoria as a protest against the museum's refusal to return human remains. A newspaper reported that an unsigned statement, presumably from the protesters, described the human remains as "incarcerated ancestors—imprisoned in numbered cardboard boxes in a sterile cement room" (Crawley 1995, B1). (The RBCM said that it supports the return of human remains but that it requires First Nations community sanction of the request [e.g., having the request come from the band council].)

The word "collected," which usually has a positive value in Western society, has often been replaced in discussions by First Nations individuals with words such as "taken" and "stolen." Museums may also be particularly offensive to First Nations because they continue to house human remains.

A well-known First Nations artist writes negatively about museum practice and an exhibit shown at the UBC Museum of Anthropology:

> Desire. Is there desire in the museum? Oh no, desire would assume too many feelings: need, greed, jealousy, rapture. No, there is desire, but it is hidden. In the not so distant yesterday desire was hidden by the guise of objectivity. Today, this modern architecture with many windows, architecture with hints of traditional long houses or teepees, or buildings with columns and dark corridors all hide the desire ... But back in the museum the act of desiring has many foils: collecting, cataloguing, preserving, maintaining, educating. (Todd 1993-4, 57).

Moses (1993) points out that many First Nations have traditional practices that enable them to preserve significant objects and that museums, which present themselves as institutions specialized in the preservation of valued material culture, have in fact allowed many pieces to deteriorate.

The discourse with which this book is concerned is occurring within a highly politicized and emotionally charged atmosphere. In some countries, the values of conservation and museums are being challenged to work within a framework that supports both museum and First Nations perspectives. Rethinking their concept and purpose is what Branche (1996, 131), Director of Museums in the Department of Museums in Belize, had in mind for museums when she concluded: "All the words come together to describe this type of change—challenging, uncomfortable, fearful, emotional, and yes, even unscientific. It is in the best interests of all that we consciously come to grips with this issue and make deliberate moves in this great transformation."

First Nations Perspectives on Selected Conservation Beliefs

The following sections give First Nations perspectives on key concepts seen in museum conservation.

INTEGRITY

While preserving the integrity of the object is of primary concern to conservation, preserving the integrity of the indigenous culture and the cultural attributes of the objects within it is a primary concern of First Nations. This speaks to the holistic relationship of living people to their material culture and their desire that museums reflect this. "The most important fact that *Te Maori* taught the world is that Maoridom is a living culture and that our *taonga* express us as a people with a past, a present, and a future. As a result, museums were to admit they had not respected or acknowledged these intrinsic values" (Tamarapa 1996, 162).

Concerning heritage objects themselves, First Nations opinions reflect several ideas pertaining to the conservation model of "integrity." The first, as may be seen in the following quotations, is the view that First Nations cultural perspectives, not museological perspectives, should determine the parameters of the "integrity of the object."

> Culturally significant Maori works should be decided by Maori people. This seems to be a reasonable and logical view to take. However in our

colonial past acknowledged "experts" have often determined what is important about Maori people from historical (colonial) and aesthetic (colonial) considerations. (Heikell, Whiting et al. 1995, 15)

The artifact was initially made for a specific purpose, to perform a specific cultural function, and ... the natural deterioration of the artifact is therefore part of its actuality (Harris 1993, 32).

Preserving "conceptual integrity" (as conservators would think of it) is extremely important, and this is emphasized in many First Nations statements, as will be seen in the section on cultural significance and sacred/sensitive objects. Consider, however, an interesting comparative example related by Welsh in Clavir (1992). Welsh, at the time a senior curator at the Heard Museum in Phoenix, Arizona, said that Navaho consultants objected to a particular basket being displayed because it closely resembled sacred/sensitive material. The basket was a known reproduction and had never been used ritually. In addition, certain elements of it were evidently physically different from those of the "original" basket. Although the basket was not "sacred," it had sufficient conceptual authenticity for the consultants to believe that it should not be displayed, and it was withdrawn from the exhibit.

CULTURAL SIGNIFICANCE AND SACRED/SENSITIVE OBJECTS

Some First Nations people have stressed several issues pertaining to sacred/sensitive objects, the primary one being the overriding importance of respecting spiritual and ceremonial values. "Aboriginal people do believe in a grand narrative. We believe in the laws of the Creator. Laws are anathema to the postmodern. Some even call our Relationship to the Creator a covenant, a sacred agreement to protect the earth and the life it sustains" (Todd 1993-4, 60). This comment emphasizes the point that the cultural significance of certain objects, especially of sacred/sensitive objects, is far more important to the First Nations community than it is to the museum community. "There is a sense of balance that goes hand in hand with the restoration of the ritual associated with sacred objects ... The sacred duty has been performed. The people are

fulfilled in a way that can only be experienced, not fully explained" (Hill 1993, 10). The importance of the cultural significance of objects to their originating culture includes:

1. Recognition of their fundamental necessity to the First Nation:

In the traditional ceremony, the principal participants are the bundles/ceremonialists, the hosts [and others] ... Creator's authority is recognized in the bundles, thereby making the objects within them sacred ... At the signing of Treaty 7 in 1877, the Peigan Nitsitapi community was guided by 16 bundles/ceremonialists and 5 societies. (Crowshoe 1994, 6)

Most traditional materials are to some degree sacred in nature ... The most sacred items are communal and hence vitally important—meaning their repatriation could greatly benefit a living Indian community or group ... An essential part of these Indian beliefs is the material itself. This could include sacred material or material of cultural patrimony. Both give direction, hope, pride, strength, and all the other essentials to survival (Horse Capture 1991, 51).

2. The importance of the restoration/performance of ritual.

"The [repatriated] objects stimulate the restoration of the ceremony. The ceremony, in turn, revitalizes the community" (Hill 1993, 10).

3. The continuing role in Aboriginal communities for sacred/sensitive objects that have been/are being housed in museums:

When you get to the level of sacred objects, they shouldn't even be in collections with a curator. They should be back among the people who handle and care for them. They were given to us, each one of them was given to us by our Creator and they are for us. They are not for the general public (Pete Jemison, *Seneca*, in Parker 1990, 37).

We are asking for things back which have been with us for thousands of years (Tallbull, in Clavir 1992, 31).

Other concerns are:

Privacy: Many authors referred to respecting privacy protocols pertaining to certain sacred/sensitive objects. "The fact remains that uninitiated individuals, female or male, non-Native or Native, should not have access to sacred or secret materials" (Moses 1993, 8).

Power: This is considered an inherent quality of certain objects. An analogy might be found in the comparison between a sample of granite and a sample of uranium in a natural history collection: both have a physical integrity that can be described by standard procedures, but the uranium has a powerful, invisible, intrinsic attribute. Those who know how to use it can do so for good or for evil purposes. Those who ignore it can be damaged by it. Thus there are strict protocols for handling it and using it (Phillips 1982). "Traditionally [western Plains] bundles are not the only objects which can be imbued with medicine or power. Certain types of shields and shield covers, head-dresses, pipes, drums, and various articles of clothing and personal adornment, can also function as physical manifestations of this concept of medicine" (Moses 1993, 5).

Although objects in museums may have been separated from their originating community for a period of time, this rupture has not necessarily diminished their importance or their "power."

I know that respected elders from the Iroquois community in Oshwegan, called Six Nations, go there [Canadian Museum of Civilization] either annually or every two years to feed the false-face masks and that's needed (Barnes 1993, 2) *(Barnes: Mohawk)*.

She [Linda Poolaw, of Delaware and Kiowa ancestry] would not touch it [an eagle feather fan] because it was a ceremonial object, but she said museum staff could handle it for her (Kaminitz 1993, 6).

Spiritual items such as pipes, medicine bags or bundles can be documented for their educational or research value, and then returned to the people in the native community who are qualified to handle this material (Secwepemc Cultural Education Society 1991, 2).

This last quotation as well as the following also highlight the point made by First Nations that they too, not only museums, are able to look after heritage objects: "[After repatriation] many communities hold public meetings, rituals, and councils to teach each other about the care of the restored objects. People of all ages learn of the significance, intended use, stories and rituals associated with each object ... The entire community feels responsible for the welfare of the object" (Hill 1993, 10).

USE VERSUS PRESERVATION

There is a strong First Nations belief in the necessity to use heritage objects:

We know what conservators do or try to do; that is, preserve objects for as long as possible. But, diametrically opposed to this is the general Indian view as I know it, which is that objects are created to be used and when those objects are damaged or worn out, they are thrown away and new ones are made (Webster 1986, 77).

A lifetime of constant use is the artifact's only purpose. Since these objects were meant to deteriorate through functional use, they must remain crucial focal points of our traditional functions, available for use by the people to whom they belong (Harris 1993, 32).

For some people, the parameters of use for utilitarian objects are related to the condition of the object. (Other parameters will be seen in the personal conversations reported in subsequent chapters, and they include who has the right to use the object.) For example, the late Elizabeth Harry (Keekus), an elder and basket maker from the Sliammon Band in British Columbia, said that older baskets would traditionally be repaired in her culture, and, when they could no longer be used, they would be thrown out. They were useful objects, made to be used (Harry, personal communication, 1994).

On the other hand, Allison Nyce, from the Nisga'a and Tsimshian Nations, has commented that, when objects were sold to early anthropologists such as Boas, there were many more people who had "grown up with the culture," and therefore had the skills and the knowledge to continue to make the traditional objects in question. She noted that this is different from today's situation (Nyce, personal communication, 1995). Nyce might take further steps to preserve old baskets than would Keekus.

For ritual objects, however, use is continuous. A Salish spiritual leader, speaking at the Keepers of the Treasures Conference in 1992, talked about traditional cultural matters being put in the background rather than disappearing. He said that his culture had not gone away, it was just quiet, nobody was using it, and he was pleased to see that it was coming back strongly (from notes in Clavir 1992, 7). If objects in museum collections were to receive ritual caretaking, then this might well involve their being handled in non-museum ways. For example, Hill (personal communication, 1994) notes that ritual caretaking includes stroking, caressing (e.g., during ritual feeding, using sunflower oil) and the ritual burning of tobacco. "My granddad died in 1913 in Washington as part of a delegation petitioning the government. ... Three years ago his pipe came back. The family now has an annual sundance. The pipe is kept in a frame building without environmental controls—I don't call it a Museum—It's still alive" (Native Americans consultant, cited in Kaminitz 1993, 12). The living culture is continually emphasized in First Nations statements about heritage objects. They highlight the sense of continuity and the objects' importance in contemporary life, and they make the point that the cultural function of these objects does not and has not deteriorated. This stands in sharp contrast to the cultural function of many objects from Western material culture found in museum collections.

Again, for First Nations the emphasis is placed on cultural preservation. It includes the need to use and maintain objects ritually, and it often includes the need for them to be seen by community members and guests. It is also important that the histories of the objects be told and that the traditions associated with making them be passed on. In other words, the objects need to be part of the community's identity. The irony is that these objects left First Nations communities due, in part, to the activities of people (i.e.,

museum collectors) who, subscribing to the erroneous nineteenth-century belief that Aboriginal cultures would disappear, believed they were preserving cultural heritage.

At a Kwakiutl feast in 1900 anthropologist Franz Boas experienced the eerie irony of his own collecting work and remarked that although the speeches were still the same as he had heard in the past, "the bowls [were] no longer here. They are in the museums in New York and Berlin" (Doxtator 1996, 60, quoting Franz Boas as reported in Cole 1996, 276).

In contrast, Canadian museums have traditionally approached treasured material heritage by removing it from customary use and protecting, conserving and interpreting it in an institutional setting and in the name of the people of the country or region (Eastern Working Group 1991, 1).

First Nations wish to use objects from museum collections not only for the purposes of traditional ritual use, but also for the types of use normally found in museums: education and research. "Clearly the preservation of ethnographic collections is very important. But of equal importance in this country is the access to those collections by native people, particularly the carvers, for study purposes and, in special cases, for loans of material for ceremonial occasions" (Webster 1986, 78). In addition, one can note that the importance of cultural use to First Nations is often emphasized in the choice of certain words: for example, "to bring this generation back *in touch* with the power that used to be our birthright" (Hill 1993, 10). It is interesting to note how often words that museums associate with conservation are the same words that First Nations associate with cultural preservation: for example, "sacred knowledge is *fragile*" (9); "If it had taken any longer for the sacred objects to be *restored*, even those elders might not have survived" (10); "I had been wondering where negative stereotyping and imagery about the Native Indian was being *conserved*" (Watts 1988, 1); "The need to '*balance*' is what created the Peigan world view" (Crowshoe 1994, 3). (The last citation is analogous to the first principle of ethical behaviour for conservators in the Canadian code of ethics.) (All emphasis mine.)

Culturally Modified Practice in Museums

There are a growing number of examples of how Aboriginal cultural concerns are modifying museum practice. During a presentation in 1994, for example, Tamarapa (1996, 165) noted policy changes at the Museum of New Zealand *Te Papa Tongarewa,* where restrictions were placed on food being brought near any *taonga* (because food is believed to neutralize the life force of particularly sacred items), and where water bowls were placed near the door leading from *taonga* in storage so that people could spiritually cleanse themselves. Objects related to food and everyday functions were stored separately from sacred objects (166), and *nga toi moko* and *koiwi tangata,* which are "the most sacred objects of our collection," were kept in special sacred storage and referred to with Maori terms of respect (166). Tamarapa also stated that *karakia,* or prayers, were usually spoken when a new *taonga* either comes into the museum or is moved. She also noted that the museum had been restructured in 1991 and that this involved the creation of a Department of Maori Art and History that employed senior Maori staff knowledgeable in Maori protocol.

Another example of indigenous cultural concerns modifying museum practice was evident during the Te Maori exhibition. O'Biso (1987) has written that Maori ritual required that the welcoming museum have a ceremony at dawn, during which the doors of the museum were left unlocked and no guards or other museum personnel were permitted to be left inside; rather, they had to enter the museum in a ritually prescribed fashion. Regarding objects from the American Southwest, the ritual use of corn pollen and meal to feed masks was of concern to conservators at one museum because of the risk of insect infestation. A compromise was reached with the religious leaders whereby the food was ritually given to and left with the masks but was allowed to be frozen beforehand, thus eliminating the possibility that insect eggs would be brought into the museum (Welsh, Sease et al. 1992). Clavir (1994, 54) reported on changes being planned in 1992 for a storage room at the Museum of New Mexico (MNM) in order to address concerns from the pueblos:

The room for culturally sensitive objects at the Museum of New Mexico needs to be set apart from the rest of the collections. Features of this room include:

(1) A design similar to a traditional pueblo storage room in that

- the person who enters crosses a threshold into another area.
- the shelves are open.
- the room has access to a room with fresh air. The objects are considered living and have a need to breathe like all living things.

(2) The blinds pull down over the shelves or there are dust covers so people do not have to see all the objects at once, as the objects in the room may come from different cultures. This is the MNM's addition to try to avoid offending Pueblo people seeing other objects. It is a compromise in order to use a single room for all material.

(3) The objects are arranged by culture. Within this, the objects are arranged in a certain order, and sometimes piled, on the advice of the consultants. The consultants also advised interleaving piled objects with paper or cloth bags, like they do at home.

(4) The room is sealed off from the rest of the collections, so objects can be fed (cf. #1 re living objects) or smudged (exposed to smoke, [in many Native American cultures this is done using] smouldering sage, tobacco or sweetgrass), as required.

At the Six Nations Woodland Cultural Centre in Ontario, rituals are not performed in the museum; however, "the Woodland Museum has had the opportunity to 'loan' the Medicine Masks in our collection to the traditional community for ceremonial purposes. In these ceremonies, the Masks are 'renewed: meaning that they are cleaned and conserved according to customary procedures. These procedures are what preserves the Masks" (Harris 1993, 33). It is emphasized that ritual care is as necessary as scientific care. "Among the First Nations, traditions of proper care and handling and appropriate use, are well and long established, and have served to ensure the continued physical and spiritual well-being of a variety of ritual and sacred objects over the span of many generations" (Moses 1993, 6).

The experts who provide this kind of care are those who are considered appropriate by the First Nations community. Moses makes the point that these specialists should be regarded as part of the circle of professional advisors with whom a conservator normally consults. "Euro-North American museum workers should look upon Native elders and recognized spiritual leaders as a *professional* resource in their efforts to obtain a more complete understanding of the Native materials they come in contact with" (Moses 1993, 8).

First Nations Perspectives: A Summary

The overwhelming impression given by First Nations statements about the preservation of material culture is that preservation of objects is connected to regaining identity, respect, and cultural well-being through practising traditions and redressing historic power imbalances. Preservation of objects is defined as integral to maintaining the life of the community. In addition, objects housed in urban museums may remain in the museum or may be repatriated; however, in both cases the objects should be contextualized in such a way that First Nations are able to make decisions about them.

> If this place [NMAI] does nothing else but be a living entity that transmits human respect and sensitivity, then all the work we do and will do will be a success. (First Nations consultant, cited in Kaminitz 1993, 10)
>
> There needs to be an equal partnership which involves mutual respect and appreciation of the First Nations' culture and history. (Barnes 1993, 3)
>
> Ecotourism, equal partnership and empowerment seem to be the way of the future. (Branche 1996, 131)

Writers such as Moses (1995) have acknowledged that objects change their meaning as they progress through their life histories and that they are interpreted in different ways by different people. The original purpose for which an object was created is not necessarily the only purpose it will serve. Furthermore, Doxtator (1996) and Hakiwai (1995) comment that it is in fact museums that have not recognized the dynamism and changes in First Nations communities, tending to place Aboriginal peoples firmly in the past. Many Aboriginal authors do, however, confirm that the contemporary needs of First Nations communities are served by using sacred/sensitive objects from museum collections in accordance with their original purpose and that these needs take precedence over museological needs. It is also recognized that sacred/sensitive objects (depending on the point of view) may represent only a small proportion of existing museum collections.

Conclusion

The tables in this chapter show that there are often significant differences between First Nations and museum perspectives. Some of these differences, such as those pertaining to ownership, represent issues that have far-reaching implications and that are being influenced by decision-making processes situated within a broader socio-political and legal context. Other issues, such as the appropriate care of objects in museums, fall more within the individual museum's sphere of responsibility. In summary, while there may be significant differences in the points of view of some museums and First Nations, certain issues, depending on their scale, are potentially easier to resolve satisfactorily in discussions between the two groups.

The museum remains a charged negative symbol for many Aboriginal people; however, at the same time, they make use of its positive aspects. Seen as both positive and negative, museums occupy an ambiguous place, a place of decontextualization and of (often negative) recontextualization. Moreover, they both preserve against future loss, through conservation, and contribute to past loss: "A lot of cultural material has been lost, mostly to museums" (Webster 1986, 78).

In research on Aboriginal artists and their self-definitions (e.g., are they artists first or Aboriginal artists first), Mithlo (1994) states that, in times of change, when the boundaries people have set up for themselves are also changing, there exists a liminal zone, a state of ambiguity. In this zone people can be "both" as well as "either/or." "The maintenance of boundaries, or the manipulation of 'separateness' thus serves the interests of the disempowered" (Mithlo 1994, 1). Following Mithlo, in understanding why it is important for First Nations to maintain their "separateness," one can also understand why some individuals have defined themselves and their work as "both museums and First Nations" while others have posited First Nations concerns as being in opposition to those of museums.

This schema applies to the definition of preservation as well. For example, with regard to the use/preservation issue, in some cases use is regarded as the direct opposite of preservation (i.e., when the latter is defined as museum conservation), while in others use is seen as a form of preservation (i.e., when the latter is defined as the care of an object through ritual use).

First Nations believe strongly that they own their heritage, even if the museums own their objects. Within this atmosphere, how does one make decisions regarding the appropriate care of objects housed in urban museums? Do the contrasting viewpoints produce clear conflicts? Or is there a tendency to expand the conventional models of both conservation/museum practice and First Nations viewpoints so that the "and/both" model referred to by Mithlo can transform the either/or conflictual situation?

BIBLIOGRAPHY

Alexie, S. (1992). "Evolution." In *The Business of Fancydancing*, 48. Brooklyn, NY: Hanging Loose Press.

Atleo, R. (1990). "Policy Development for Museums: A First Nations Perspective." Policy research paper, Vancouver, UBC Museum of Anthropology.

Barnes, B. (1993). "The Co-operative Role of Native Cultural Centres and Museums." In *First Peoples Art and Artifacts: Heritage and Conservation Issues, Eighteenth Annual Conference, Art Conservation Training Programs,* ed. K. Spirydowicz, 1–4. Kingston, ON: Queen's University, Art Conservation Program.

Bedard, J. (1993). Comments at National Workshop on the History of Aboriginal Peoples in Canada, Canadian Museum of Civilization, 22–23 January 1993.

Branche, W. (1996). "Indigenes in Charge: Are Museums Ready?" In *Curatorship: Indigenous Perspectives in Post-Colonial Societies: Proceedings,* 119–31. Ottawa: Canadian Museum of Civilization with the Commonwealth Association of Museums and the University of Victoria.

Cernetig, M. (1989). "Letting the Totem Poles Topple." *Vancouver Sun,* 2 December D7.

Clavir, M. (1992). "IPAM: International Partnerships among Museums Report." *Report.* UBC Museum of Anthropology.

———. (1994). "Preserving Conceptual Integrity: Ethics and Theory in Preventive Conservation." In *Preventive Conservation Practice, Theory and Research: Preprints of the Contributions to the Ottawa Congress, 12–16 September 1994,* 15th IIC Congress, ed. R. Ashok and P. Smith, 53–7. London: International Institute for Conservation of Historic and Artistic Works.

Claxton, A. (1994b). "Deterioration in First Nation Artifacts." Class presentation and paper for course entitled "Curatorial Care of Artifacts," 30 November to 9 December 1994, University of Victoria.

Cole, D. (1996). *Captured Heritage: The Scramble for Northwest Coast Artifacts.* Vancouver, Douglas and McIntyre, 1985. Reprinted, Vancouver: UBC Press.

Commonwealth Association of Museums (1994). "Curatorship: Indigenous Perspectives in Post-Colonial Societies." *CAM Newsletter* December 1–4.

Crawley, M. (1995). "Hunger-strikers Battle BC Museum." *Vancouver Sun,* final edition, 21 July, B1.

Crowshoe, R. (1994). *Keep Our Circle Strong: Pagan Cultural Renewal.* Hand-out at conference entitled "Curatorship: Indigenous Perspectives in Post-Colonial Societies." University of Victoria, 16–19 May 1994.

Davidson, R. (1993). Letter to Directors and staff of the Vancouver Art Gallery, 19 October 1993.

Doxtator, D. (1988). "The Home of Indian Culture and Other Stories in the Museum." *MUSE* 6 (3): 26–31.

———. (1996). "The Implications of Canadian Nationalism for Aboriginal Cultural Autonomy." In *Curatorship: Indigenous Perspectives in Post-Colonial Societies: Proceedings*, 56–70. Ottawa: Canadian Museum of Civilization with the Commonwealth Association of Museums and the University of Victoria.

Eastern Working Group. (1991). "Towards a Partnership Between Aboriginal First Nations and Museums." Draft of submission to CMA/AFN Task Force.

Echo-Hawk, W. (1993). "Native American Burials: Legal and Legislative Aspects." In *Kunaltupii: Coming Together on Native Sacred Sites*, ed. B.O.K. Reeves and M.A. Kennedy, 38–45.

Galla, A. (1994). "Indigenous Peoples, Museums and Frameworks for Effective Change." Keynote address presented at the conference entitled *Curatorship: Indigenous Perspectives in Post-Colonial Societies*, University of Victoria, May (oral and written presentation).

Haagen, C.E.J. (1990). "Strategies for Cultural Maintenance: Aboriginal Cultural Education Programs and Centres in Canada." MA thesis, University of British Columbia.

Hakiwai, A.T. (1995). "The Search for Legitimacy: Museums in Aoreatoa, New Zealand." In *Proceedings of the International Conference on Anthropology and the Museum*, 21–23, December 1992, ed. T. Lin, 283–94, Taipei: Taiwan Museum.

Harris, J. (1993). "Cultural Function versus Conservation: Preserving the Sacred Artifact." *Ontario Museum Annual* 11 (October): 31–3.

Heikell, V., D. Whiting, M. Clavir, N. Odegaard, M. Kaminitz, and J. Moses. (1995). "The Conservator's Approach to Sacred Art." *Newsletter of the Western Association for Art Conservation* 17 (3): 15–8.

Hill, R. (1988). "Sacred Trust: Cultural Obligation of Museums to Native People." *MUSE* 6 (3): 32–7.

———. (1993). "Beyond Repatriation." *History News* 48 (2): 9–10.

Horse Capture, G.P. (1991). "Survival of Culture." *Museum News* 70 (1): 49–51.

Kaminitz, M. (1993). "The National Museum of the American Indian: Voices of the Museum Different." In *First Peoples Art and Artifacts: Heritage and Conservation Issues, Eighteenth Annual Conference, Art Conservation Training Programs*, ed. K. Spirydowicz, 1–5. Kingston, ON: Art Conservation Program, Queen's University.

Keepers of the Treasures (1994). "Keepers of the Treasures Mission Statement." *Keepers of the Treasures Newsletter* 2 (4): 9.

Laurence, R. (1993). "Art of the Healing Eagle." *Georgia Straight* (Vancouver) 27 (1332): 7–9.

MacDonald, G.F. (1992). "Change and Challenge: Museums in the Information Society." In *Museums and Communities: The Politics of Public Culture*, ed. I. Karp, C. Kreamer, and S. Lavine, 158–81. Washington: Smithsonian Institution Press.

McCormick, C. (1988). "Opening Remarks." Paper presented at "Preserving Our Heritage: A Working Conference for Museums and First Peoples," organized by the Assembly of First Nations and the Canadian Museums Association, Carleton University, Ottawa, November 1988.

McKenzie, M. (1987–8). "The Conservation of Cultural Property: The New Zealand Position." *AGMANZ* (Quarterly of the Art Galleries and Museums Association of New Zealand) 18 (3–4): 34–5.

Mithlo, N.M. (1994). "Cultural Property and Power." Grant application to Ford Foundation, 25 January 1994.

———. (2001). "'Red Man's Burden': The Politics of Inclusion in Museum Settings." Paper presented at Smith College, MA, 12 February.

Morrison, B. (1993). "Church Returns Native Artifacts." *Anglican Journal* 119 (9): 1 and 6.

Moses, J. (1993). "First Nations Traditions of Object Preservation." In *First Peoples Art and Artifacts: Heritage and Conservation Issues, Eighteenth Annual Conference, Art Conservation Training*

Programs, ed. K. Spirydowicz, 6–11. Kingston, ON: Art Conservation Program, Queen's University.

———. (1995). "The Conservator's Approach to Sacred Art." *Newsletter of the Western Association for Art Conservation* 17 (3): 18.

Nason, J. (1981). "A Question of Patrimony: Ethical Issues in the Collecting of Cultural Objects." *Museum Round-Up* 83: 13–20.

O'Biso, C. (1987). *First Light.* Auckland, NZ: Heinemann.

Parker, P. (1990). *Keepers of the Treasures: Protecting Historic Properties and Cultural Traditions on Indian Lands.* Washington, DC: National Park Service, US Department of the Interior.

Phillips, C. (1982). "Advocates for the Artifact: The Role of Conservation in State and Local History." *Museum Round-Up* 86 (Summer): 11–6.

Secwepemc Cultural Education Society. (1991). "Submission to the CMA/AFN Task Force on Museums and First Peoples." Secwepemc Cultural Education Society, 22 March.

Spicer, E.H., and R. Thompson, eds. (1972). *Plural Society in the Southwest.* New York: Interbook.

Tamarapa, A. (1996). "Museum Kaitiaki: Maori Perspectives on the Presentation and Management of Maori Treasures and Relationships with Museums." In *Curatorship: Indigenous Perspectives in Post-Colonial Societies: Proceedings*, 160–9. Ottawa: Canadian Museum of Civilization with the Commonwealth Association of Museums and the University of Victoria.

Todd, L. (1990). "Notes on Appropriation." *Parallelogramme* 16 (1): 24–33.

———. (1993–4). "Three Moments after 'Savage Graces.'" *Harbour* 3 (1): 57–62.

Webster, G.C. (1986). "Conservation and Cultural Centres: U'Mista Cultural Centre, Alert Bay, Canada." In *Symposium '86: The Care and Preservation of Ethnological Materials: Proceedings*, ed. R. Barclay, M. Gilberg, J.C. McCawley, and T. Stone, 77–9. Ottawa, ON: Canadian Conservation Institute.

———. (1988). "The 'R' Word." *MUSE* 6 (3): 43–4.

———. (1992a). "From Colonization to Repatriation." In *Indigena: Contemporary Native Perspectives*, ed. ed. G. McMaster and L-A. Martin, 25–37. Vancouver: Douglas and McIntyre.

Welsh, E., C. Sease, B. Rhodes, S. Brown, and M. Clavir. (1992). "Multicultural Participation in Conservation Decision-Making." *Newsletter of the Western Association for Art Conservation* 14 (1): 13–22.

West, W.R., Jr. (1991). "Press Statement of W. Richard West, Jr. on His Appointment as Director of the National Museum of the American Indian." *Museum Anthropology* 15 (2): 24.

Whiting, D. (1995). "The Conservator's Approach to Sacred Art." *Newsletter of the Western Association for Art Conservation* 17 (3): 15–6.

Wright, M. (1994). "Valuing Cultural Diversity and Treasuring Cultural Differences." *Newsletter of Western Museums Association* 1 (Winter): 1–2.

VIRGINIA GREENE

"'Accessories Of Holiness': Defining Jewish Sacred Objects"

Journal of the American Institute for Conservation *31:1 (1992): 31–39.*

1. Introduction

Recent congressional legislation on the repatriation of Native American material defines sacred objects as "specific ceremonial objects which are needed by traditional Native American religious leaders for the practice of traditional Native American religions by their present day adherents" (U.S. Congress 1990). This definition might be understood to imply that all objects needed for a ceremony are also sacred, thus requiring special consideration when treated by a conservator. This is not always the case even for Native American groups (Ladd 1991), and the definition certainly cannot be applied wholesale to other religions and cultures. The statement also implies the presence or participation of a religious leader when the objects are used, an implication that further restricts the applicability of the definition.

Traditional Judaism recognizes two categories of ritual objects: those that carry a quality of holiness and those that are essential to the performance of a particular ritual or commandment but have no intrinsic quality that can be defined as "sacred" or "holy."[1] This classification was specifically designed to answer two questions: Which objects used in a ritual context may also be used for secular purposes? What should be done with ritual objects when they are no longer fit for use? The first question is largely of academic interest, at least at the present time. The second, however, is a practical problem of considerable importance. The classification also provides a foundation for decisions about the conservation of these objects.

2. Holy Objects

The first category of ritual objects is called *tashmishey kedusha*, "accessories of holiness" or "objects which carry holiness." The classic example is a Torah scroll. This is so obvious that it is not even mentioned in the texts.

The category also includes:

(1) the mantle (often made of velvet embroidered with gold and silver thread) that is used to cover a Torah scroll in Ashkenazic communities, as well as the binder that keeps the scroll closed and silver and gold ornaments that are added after the mantle is in place (fig. 1); the special hinged wooden Torah case used by Sephardic and Oriental Jews[2]

Figure 1. Ark with torah scrolls. The velvet mantles are embroidered with silver and gold thread, and the ornaments (pointer, breastplates crowns, and finials) are silver. Contemporary mantles are often dedicated in honor of, or in memory of, a particular person or family.

(2) Torah ark curtains, decorated or plain

(3) the chair, or holder, on which the Torah is placed when it is removed from the ark (fig. 2)

(4) tefillin ("phylacteries," worn by men—and, in the Conservative movement, some women—during morning prayers on weekdays), including the leather cases, the biblical texts written on parchment that are inside, the leather straps used to fasten them to the head and arm during prayer, and any bag specifically made to hold them and used for that purpose on a regular basis (figs. 3–5)

(5) the mezuzza, which is fastened to the doorpost of a house (and, traditionally, to interior doorways as well), including both the case and the handwritten text (klaf) inside (figs. 6–7)

(6) cases for books, specifically a container for either a scroll or bound volume that contains one or more of the books of the Bible.

Figure 2. Torah resting on a holder. The pointer is used when reading the scroll to avoid abrading the letters and to keep dirt and oil from staining the parchment.

The three written texts, the Torah scroll, *tefillin*, and *klaf* for the *mezuzza*, form the core of this category. All are, or contain, biblical texts that must be handwritten on parchment, in a particular script, according to rigid rules, by men who are specially trained

Figure 3. Embroidered *tefillin* bag; *tefillin* with protective caps and with the straps wrapped around the cases.

Figure 4. *Tefillin,* showing the stitching on the cases. The lead seals are attached to the scribe to ensure the texts are not damaged before the *tefillin* are sold.

Figure 5. An unusual pair of tefillin with translucent backs. There are four texts on four pieces of parchment in the case worn on the head and the same texts on a single piece of parchment in the case worn on the arm.

as scribes (*sofrim*). Scribes also assemble the Torah scrolls, sewing the sheets of parchment together and mounting them on the rollers, and make the cases for *tefillin* (Cowan 1986; Ray 1986; Siegel, Strassfeld, and Strassfeld 1973).

The common feature of the objects in the group is that they contain words, specifically the name of God, but by extension any words divinely written or inspired, from which the quality of holiness is derived. The nontextual objects all come into intimate contact with the texts, and in so doing acquire some of the same quality of holiness. The transmission is not indefinite, however, extending a maximum of two layers. For example, curtains located outside of the ark curtain itself are not affected.

Over the years, this category has been expanded to include not only other handwritten biblical texts (such as the Scroll of Esther) but also printed Bibles, prayer books, volumes of the Talmud, law codes, and commentaries, not only in Hebrew but in other languages as well. In some communities, any document of any kind written in Hebrew letters was included;

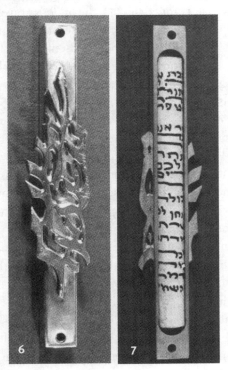

Figure 6. A silver *mezuzza* case, 3 in. long, for interior use.

Figure 7. The back of the *mezuzza* case, showing the parchment scroll.

the holy quality of the Hebrew language extending to other languages, such as Yiddish, written with the same alphabet.

According to the Shulchan Arukh (see note 1), *tashmishey kedusha*, when no longer fit for ritual use, must be "put away" (O.H. 154.3; Mishneh Torah, II 10.3). Traditionally, Ashkenazic Jews fulfill this requirement through burial, either in a specific part of a Jewish cemetery or, in some localities, next to or along with a man of exceptional piety and learning.

Many Sephardic/Oriental Jewish communities put *tashmishey kedusha* in a special room in the synagogue, called a *geniza* (from the root meaning "conceal," "hide," or "preserve"). Because of the extension of the category to include handwritten and printed books and documents along with the traditional items, these storerooms often contained a great deal of material. The most famous *geniza* is in the Ezra Synagogue in Cairo. Rediscovered at the end of the 19th century, it held more than 200,000 pages, some dating to the founding of the synagogue in 882 (Milgram 1971; *Encyclopedia Judaica* 1971), 7:404.

Once *tashmishey kedusha* have passed out of the traditional community and into the care of a museum, they can be further divided into two groups: (1) Torah scrolls, *tefillin* (both cases and texts), and the scroll (*klaf*) inside the *mezuzza*; and (2) all other material, including printed or handwritten documents, Torah mantles, ark curtains, *tefillin* bags, Torah ornaments, and *mezuzza* cases.

Objects in group (2) may be treated by any qualified conservator. In all cases it is preferable to treat Jewish ritual material as anthropological material rather than as art, keeping conservation treatment to a minimum and avoiding extensive restoration, but any ethical treatment is permitted. Conservators in private practice, who may not have the option of minimal treatment, may have to take on greater responsibility as a result. Original fabric or trimming removed from an ark curtain, for example, should be given to the owner for proper disposal. If the owner is unwilling to do this, it becomes the responsibility of the conservator to make the arrangements.[3]

Torah scrolls, *tefillin*, and *mezuzza* scrolls should be left as they are. Once they are no longer in use, there is no reason for them to be kosher—in proper condition to be used—and therefore no reason why missing or abraded letters should be restored or minor repairs made to the parchment. As the texts of these documents never vary and they are never illustrated, aesthetic considerations are not relevant.

If, for the safety of a Torah scroll, it is determined that repairs must be done to the rollers on which the scroll is mounted, these repairs should be done by a scribe, who will then remount the parchment onto the roller in the traditional manner. A Torah scroll that has a tear in the parchment can be kept rolled to another part of the scroll. If two pages are separated, the two parts of the scroll should be wrapped and stored separately. If it is considered both possible (considering the condition of the parchment) and essential to rejoin the separated leaves, this work should be done only by a scribe.

While they are in use, a pair of *tefillin* must be opened and examined periodically by a scribe to ensure that they are still ritually fit. Once they are no longer in ritual use, they should be left as they are. Undamaged *tefillin* should never be opened in a museum. The texts inside an already damaged pair of *tefillin* may be removed and examined, as the style of the writing may give clues to the time and place in which they were written. *Tefillin* may be exhibited in a damaged condition if there is some reason to do so, such as association with a famous person, or in an exhibit of Holocaust material. Alterations of any kind to an object that survived the Holocaust, unless absolutely necessary to ensure its physical survival, are inappropriate.

Repair of other books and documents, when done with the respect that should characterize any professional conservation treatment, is entirely appropriate. In Judaism, study of traditional texts is considered to be the equivalent of prayer. To restore any text, whether of aesthetic or historical value or not, to a state in which it can be studied is an act of merit whatever the religious or cultural affiliation of the person doing the work.

When Torah scrolls, Bibles, prayer books, or volumes of the Talmud are in the possession of a Jewish institution or a traditional Jew, photography (or making photocopies) of open scrolls or pages is normally permitted only for serious study or publication, as the copies are considered to be the equivalent of the

book or scroll itself and should be disposed of in the same way once they are no longer needed. Once the books and other documents are in a secular library or archive, the rules of the institution apply. These rules are usually based on condition and value, but restrictions on casual copying would be appropriate in all cases. The person obtaining the copies should be informed of the proper procedures for disposal, and the institution should offer to perform this service if the person returns the material.

3. Other Ritual Objects

The second category of ritual objects is termed *tashmishey mitzvah*, "accessories of religious observance," or, more clearly, "objects which make it possible to perform a commandment." This category includes most other ritual objects essential to Jewish life, including wine cups used on Sabbaths and holidays (fig. 8);[4] the Hanukkah menorah (*hanukiyah*, fig. 9); seder plates used on Passover (fig. 10); the *shofar* (ram's horn trumpet, fig. 11); the *tallit* (a prayer shawl with special knotted fringes, called *tzitzit*, (fig. 12); the *sukkah* (booth), a temporary dwelling built on the holiday of Sukkot as well as the *lulav* (a palm branch tied together with willow and myrtle) and *etrog* (citron) also used on Sukkot, *etrog* containers; Sabbath candlesticks; the spice box and candle holder used for the Havdalah service at the end of the Sabbath; challah and matzah covers; wedding canopies.

Most of these are permanent and often passed on for generations. Those associated with Sukkot (with the exception of the *etrog* container) are impermanent and must be built or acquired anew each year. At the conclusion of Sukkot, the *sukkah* is dismantled. Though some of the materials may be saved, the roof covering, which is made of fresh branches, is thrown away along with the palm branch and citron.

Other *tashmishey mitzvah* may be also discarded when they are no longer fit for ritual use. If a ceramic seder plate breaks or a silver wine cup is crushed, it will be repaired (for use or display) if not too badly damaged (as any secular item of value), or if not repairable, it will be discarded and replaced. A wine-stained challah or matzah cover will be saved if embroidered by one's grandmother, discarded and replaced if a modern commercial product. A *shofar*, however, may not be repaired. A small chip at the bottom of the horn can be trimmed down, but if there is major damage to the mouthpiece or body of the horn it must be replaced.

These objects may be discarded because they have no intrinsic quality of holiness. Great care and expense often go into their manufacture, so that they are objects of beauty (and hence of value in terms of Western aesthetics), but this is a consequence of the principle of *hiddur mitzvah*, "enhancing a commandment" (derived from Exodus 15.2). It is desirable, for example, to have the most beautiful *kiddush* cup that one can afford, but if one cannot afford silver, then glass will serve, and if a fine wine glass is unavailable, then one puts the wine in a plain glass—or a paper cup, if necessary. It is more important to have the wine and of primary importance to say the blessing over the wine and to say it in the proper frame of mind.

Over centuries, however, customary practice has become stricter than the original law, and several of the objects in this group are now treated as *tashmishey kedusha*. The best example is the *tallit*. It is clear that merely untying the knots or cutting the cords removes all special qualities from the *tzitzit* (Mishneh Torah, II 8.9), and the *tallit* itself was not special at all, as it was originally an ordinary garment. By the 16th century, the custom had already changed. The Shulchan Arukh states that *tzitzit* "should be treated with the consideration due to holy objects" (Klein 1979:5, O.H. 15.1, 21.1). Today most Conservative synagogues will set aside for burial any synagogue *tallit* that is no longer fit to be worn, and traditional Jews will do the same with their own, as well as with a damaged *shofar*.

Figure 8. Wine cups. The one on the far right is porcelain, the others silver.

Figure 9. The menorah on the right uses candles, the one on the left burns oil.

Figure 10. Ceramic seder plates, in many modern styles.

Figure 11. A *shofar*. notches on the lower edge or grooves along the side are the only decoration permitted.

Figure 12. A *tallit* with the fringes at each corner.

These objects may be treated by any qualified objects or textiles conservator, with the same preference for minimal treatment noted above. No attempt should be made, however, to retie or replace damaged fringes on a *tallit*.

4. Exhibition and Storage

There are few restrictions on the exhibit of Jewish ritual objects and generally none on the examination of this material for purposes of study by anyone of any religion or culture.

Torah scrolls, *tefillin*, and *mezuzza* scrolls are normally not exhibited unrolled, but this may be done if they are no longer fit for ritual use. In these cases, the advice of a rabbi should always be sought. These objects should be stored in a drawer or cabinet and covered. If a conservator judges it is unwise to leave an original mantle on a scroll, or a pair of *tefillin* in its bag, these can be separated.

Small Torah scrolls may be safely stored lying down in a drawer; large ones should be kept upright in a special rack. If a scroll has no mantle, or the original one must be removed, a plain cloth mantle should be made. Small scrolls in drawers may be covered by a clean white cloth or tissue paper. *Tefillin* should be kept in a special bag if one exists or placed in a plain cloth bag. *Mezuzzah* scrolls can be kept in their cases or wrapped in tissue. If properly cared for, there is no reason why these objects, if now in good condition, should ever require conservation treatment except in the event of a disaster.

If the parchment is in good condition, a Torah scroll should be completely rolled, front to back (or vice versa) and back to the center, once every year or two. This should be done only by people (it takes two) who are experienced in this procedure, with the advice of a conservator.

When taken out for study, *tashmishey kedusha* should be treated with the same respect one would show for a similar object still in ritual use. The table on which they are placed should be covered by a clean cloth, and the objects should be covered when not being examined or read. If left for a short period of time, a Torah scroll should be rolled up and the man-

tle or cloth placed on top. *Tefillin* or *mezuzzah* scrolls should be similarly covered.

5. Conclusion

Readers are cautioned that this is a discussion paper and that I have not provided a comprehensive set of rules for the treatment of all Jewish ritual objects, only guidelines that should enable a conservator to distinguish between pieces that may be treated as ordinary, "nonsacred" material, and those objects that should not normally be subject to conservation treatment. This paper also represents primarily a Conservative point of view, with a traditional bias. Orthodox practice may be even stricter in some cases; Reform practice may be more lenient or simply different. Specific questions should be directed to an experienced curator or conservator of Judaica and/or to a rabbi with specific expertise in this area.

The difficulties posed by broad definitions of sacred objects should be obvious. However valid the new congressional definition as a basis for a discussion of the repatriation of Native American material, it tells us nothing about the way in which such objects, or similar material from other cultures, should be handled in a museum. For conservators to observe appropriate ethical standards in the handling of sacred material, systems of classification together with guidelines for practical application will have to be developed for each cultural, religious, or tribal group, with the assistance (wherever possible) of a member of that group.

Acknowledgments

I would like to thank Dr. Saul Wachs, of Gratz College, and Cantor Mark Kushner, of Temple Beth Zion-Beth Israel, in Philadelphia, for information and advice; Rabbi Ira Stone, of Beth Zion-Beth Israel, for translating a passage from the Shulchan Arukh; the synagogue Sisterhood for permission to photograph objects from its gift shop; and Jerry Silverman, a *mensch* for all seasons, who lent me (at the very last minute, without a single question) some of the slides that I used at the AIC meeting in Albuquerque.

REFERENCES

Cowan, P. 1986. *A Torah is written*. Philadelphia: Jewish Publication Society.

Encyclopedia Judaica. 1971. Jerusalem: Keter Publishing House.

Klein, I. 1979. *A guide to Jewish religious practice*. New York: Jewish Theological Seminary.

Ladd, E. 1991. Personal communication.

Milgram, A. 1971. *Jewish worship*. Philadelphia: Jewish Publication Society.

Ray, E. 1986. *Sofer: The story of a Torah scroll*. Los Angeles: Torah Aura Publications.

Siegel, R., M. Strassfeld, and S. Strassfeld, eds. 1973. *The Jewish catalogue*. Philadelphia: Jewish Publication Society.

U. S. Congress. 1990. Native American Graves Protection and Repatriation Act, Public Law 101–601. United States Code Congressional and Administrative News, 101st Congress–Second Session. St. Paul, Minn.: West Publishing.

NOTES

1. Talmud, *Megillah* 26B; Maimonides, Mishneh Torah, II; Shulchan Arukh, O.H. 154.3. Moses Maimonides (1135–1204) was a physician, philosopher, and rabbinic scholar. The Mishneh Torah is a law code, i.e., a practical guide rather than a theoretical discussion of legal issues. The Shulchan Arukh is a medieval law code (first published 1565) still considered authoritative by traditional Jews.

2. Ashkenazic Jews trace their ancestry to communities in central and eastern Europe. Sephardic Jews are those who came originally from the Iberian Peninsula. After they were expelled in 1492, many settled in Greece, Turkey, and Palestine as well as in other parts of the world. Oriental Jews are those who trace their ancestry to the Arab world and Iran, as well as those whose families never left Palestine.

3. I am indebted to Paul Himmelstein for permission to transform his experiences with owners of Torah ark curtains into a general principle.

4. These cups are usually called *kiddush* cups, after the blessing over wine that is said at the beginning of every Sabbath and holiday. The word *kiddush* comes from the same root as *kedusha*, "holiness."

SVEN HAAKANSON, JR. (ALUTIIQ-SUGPIAQ)

"Why Should American Indian Cultural Objects Be Preserved?"

In Caring for Indian Objects: A Practical and Cultural Guide, *edited by Sherelyn Ogden.*
St. Paul, MN: Minnesota Historical Society Press, 2004, pp. 3–6.

American Indians have been viewed as a vanishing people. What if our cultural objects had not been preserved? Memories are sparked by them, and we learn through the oral history of our elders. Objects assist in having memories flourish. Elders see objects, and then stories flow from them, and younger Indians learn. Museums as well as other institutions have stored and preserved not only cultural objects but the remains of our ancestors. We have been seen as a thing of the past. While there is absolutely no justification for desecrating human remains, what if the cultural objects had not been preserved? We all have the responsibility now to restore the dignity that has been denied to us as a people and to breathe life into the cultural objects that have been preserved.*
—Kathryn "Jody" Beaulieu (Anishinabe/Ojibwe)

THE PRESERVATION OF American Indian cultural objects from the past, present, and future will always challenge their owners, collectors, and makers. Who legally owns the objects, their copyright, and the knowledge? This is a question that continues to plague museums and Native communities across our country. I do not know if we will ever solve this issue, but in my opinion it depends on what we, as individual people, agree to do. It has been my experience over the past fifteen years of working in museums that it takes human connections to make positive changes happen. No one wants to see their history forgotten or destroyed, while everyone wants to see their material culture and human remains given proper respect and treated in a way that follows their traditional path.

When the Native American Graves Protection and Repatriation Act (NAGPRA) was signed into law by President George Bush on November 17, 1990, over five thousand museums were obligated to reexamine, catalog, and inform Native Americans about the objects they held in their collections. Museums were required to offer to return certain types of objects to Indian people. At first, staff and administrators at museums were angered. Then they were confused and frustrated because they did not know what types of objects they held in their collections. They did not know whether their objects fit the definitions of NAGPRA—if, for example, they were associated or unassociated funerary objects, sacred objects, or cultural patrimony. Also, many scientists and curators felt it was a loss to science for human remains to be returned for reinterment and an even greater loss to repatriate sacred objects. Now, thirteen years later, museums that undertook this process have learned a tremendous amount about contemporary American Indian cultures and about how they can respectfully handle human remains and cultural objects. Because of NAGPRA, collaborative efforts between museums and American Indians began and discussions followed about future exchanges, exhibitions, and long-term projects that could educate the public and Natives themselves about their own histories.

But a major portion of objects held in museums does not fall under NAGPRA. During the past five hundred years, and especially in the past two hundred years, museums systematically built collections. Ritual objects, clothing, tools for hunting and transportation, and household utensils were collected to document as curiosity pieces what was assumed then to be the disappearing primitive societies of America. Little did the collectors or museums realize that their collections would hold far more value than just Native-made items of a disappearing people. Their

*Sidebar in the original essay

collections would embody American Indian history, heritage, and cultural knowledge.

These collections, if realized and understood, contain implicit information and knowledge about how each Native group made and used its material culture. Most American Indian groups have lost much of this knowledge and can learn about it only from collections of items that are usually found in American and European museums. This is why museums play a very important role in the preservation of American Indian history. They are caretakers of objects that have proven to be a way for us to learn and understand our past traditions. Without these collections Natives would have an even harder time demonstrating their links to their prehistory and the heritage of their people.

I was asked why some objects should be preserved and to demonstrate what we can do to build long-lasting relationships with museums that allow for exchanges, loans, and more. Currently, as a director of a Native-run museum, my mission is to promote our traditional heritage, history, language, and cultural knowledge. The Alutiiq Museum and Archaeological Repository in Kodiak, Alaska, was founded in 1995, and within the past seven years we have had several archaeological collections returned. We now house over one hundred thousand items, and manage four programs: *Alutiiq Word of the Week*, *Community Archaeology*, *Rural Schools Art Show*, and *Carving Traditions*. The first three received the Institute of Museum and Library Services 2000 National Award for Museum Service. We currently have a national traveling exhibition, *Looking Both Ways*, in partnership with the Arctic Studies Center of the Smithsonian Institution, and we are working with several European museums on Alutiiq collections from the 1800s. We have benefited in a positive way from NAGPRA. More importantly, the Alutiiq people now know more about their heritage than ever before and understand the importance of preserving traditional knowledge, culture, and objects held in museums.

Russians occupied our region from 1784 to 1867, and the Alutiiq people were nearly exterminated during the first twenty years of this occupation. From 1784 to 1804 our population dropped over 80 percent, and we lost much of our cultural and traditional knowledge at that time. Then in 1867 the United States purchased Alaska. It was during the 1800s that Russians, Europeans, and Americans made collections of Alutiiq objects. Many were private collections, but over the years the items made their way into museum collections. The collections that are housed in museums across Europe, Canada, and the United States have added a tremendous amount of information to the revitalization of our cultural knowledge and material culture. These objects are invaluable links to the understanding of our history.

For the past thirty years archaeological excavations have been conducted on Kodiak Island. These have allowed us to learn the depth of our history and have given us a broader understanding of what this type of research can do. One excavation in particular recovered over 35,000 objects, including wooden bowls, kayak parts, masks, baskets, human remains, bows, arrows, harpoons, and wooden shields. While extremely important, these collections of items are only fragments of what were hunting kits, tools, kayaks, household utensils, and buildings. We can only make educated guesses about the specific function and role that each object held within our culture and how it was constructed. Nevertheless, these fragments give us still more clues to our cultural past.

In the past ten years many Native groups across the United States have planned, developed, and built their own cultural centers and museums to care for and house the objects that fall under NAGPRA and to take pride in their own heritage. This has allowed Natives not only to promote and share their knowledge but to learn more about their history. For example, through a grant from the National Endowment for the Humanities, the Alutiiq Museum and the Arctic Studies Center of the Smithsonian Institution undertook a six-year collaborative project. They developed the traveling exhibit mentioned earlier titled *Looking Both Ways*, published a catalog, and produced education packets and a compact disc on Alutiiq heritage. This was not a typical exhibition where curators displayed ethnographic objects and told us with written display labels what they were. Instead, the voices of our elders narrated what the objects are and what they mean to them as Alutiiq people. This linked the items to our living culture and history, giving life to what would otherwise be a snapshot from the past. My father, Sven Sr., is quoted in the exhibit, saying "you've got to look back and find out the past, and then you look forward." This statement embodies what *Looking Both Ways* has done as an exhibition and for us. We have examined our past, through ethnographic objects, oral histories, and archaeological data, learned from these sources, and are building a deeper understanding of our history for our future.

Are Natives and museums to argue over the objects that do not fall under NAGPRA as they have previously over those that do? I pray not, because this will only further divide our abilities to work together in preserving and protecting our national, cultural, and local histories for our future generations. What is important is that we can continue to develop relationships that are win-win situations. We need museums to continue caring for and promoting our heritages, and they need us to inform them about objects they house, what they symbolize, and how they were made, used, and treated.

We have several challenges to meet and goals to achieve in the future. We need to convey that American Indian cultural items are more than objects of art or representations of primitive peoples. They are cultural links between the past, present, and future for specific groups of people. Additionally they may be the only history we have for these Native peoples. The items contain implicit information about how traditional materials were made into objects that were used everyday to fulfill both practical and ceremonial needs. What we can learn from these items is how our ancestors viewed their world, how they treated animals, and how they respected their ancestors. Most important, we can use these items to preserve our culture and to bring this knowledge into a living context that continues to be passed on from generation to generation, rather than tucked away in a book, archived, or hidden in a museum collection.

chapter 11

SUSTAINABILITY

A NTHOLOGIES PROVIDE READERS WITH AN appreciation and understanding of a given subject. In this chapter, the subject is relatively recent, and in the last few years, a profusion of writings has appeared, many of which are time sensitive, others of which are simply opinion pieces. I have included only three writings: Erica Avrami, et al., *Values and Heritage Conservation: Research Report*, David Lowenthal, "Stewarding the Future," and Rebecca Meyer, et al., "Sustainability: A Literature Review."

Erica Avrami, **Randall Mason**, **Marta de la Torre**, and eight other scholars examine a host of cultural challenges facing the field in *Values and Heritage Conservation*—the title of which might suggest that it should have been placed in chapter 9 of this volume, "Ethics and Values." However, it is included here because it provides a useful framework for any consideration of sustainability issues. As the authors stress in the opening pages, "Underpinning this research is an assumption that heritage is an integral part of civil society. ... Conservation shapes the society in which it is situated, and in turn, it is shaped by the needs and dynamics of that society." Conservation is a social and a technical activity, and it is "underpinned by the values of individuals, institutions, and communities." Consideration of sustainability must take full account of conservation activities.

Over the past twenty-five years, **David Lowenthal** has become the preeminent writer about cultural heritage in society. In "Stewarding the Future," he focuses on sustainability and its implied commitment to manage natural and cultural resources into the indefinite future. Lowenthal offers several reasons for his futurist stance: ethical, conscientious, familial, and pragmatic, all of which he considers in some detail. He suggests that perhaps a renewal of the "stewardly commitment" is needed to mitigate the many potential political, social, and environmental risks that we now face.

The final piece in this chapter is a nod to the voluminous recent publications about sustainability and preservation. **Rebecca Meyer**, **Shannon Struble**, and **Phyllis Catsikis** have written a review of the recent literature.

―――――――

Sustainability and preservation are closely related concepts, concerned with the protection of man-made and/or natural resources. At the heart of sustainability and preservation is *stewardship*, the belief that resources can be managed through successive generations. There are also notable distinctions between them.

Sustainability is used widely, almost ubiquitously today. It is usually defined in an environmental context:

> Sustainability is based on a simple principle: Everything that we need for our survival and well-being depends, either directly or indirectly, on our natural environment. Sustainability creates and maintains the conditions under which humans and nature can exist in productive harmony, that permit fulfilling the social, economic and other requirements of present and future generations.[1]

In 2010, the European Commission (EC) passed the Europe 2020 strategy to "generate smart, sustainable and inclusive growth in the EU [European Union]." Three interrelated priorities were established:

- Smart growth
- Sustainable growth
- Inclusive growth

The goal of sustainable growth is to promote "a more resource efficient, greener and more competitive economy."[2] There are five 2020 targets: Employment, R&D, Climate Change/energy, Education, and Poverty/social inclusion. "Climate change/energy" has three goals: reduce greenhouse gas emissions at least 20 percent from 1990 levels, derive 20 percent of energy from renewable sources, and realize a 20 percent increase in energy efficiency.[3] These targets will affect the operations of cultural heritage institutions.

Increasingly, sustainability is seen as having three components: economic, social, and environmental. This is referred to as the Triple Bottom Line (TBL), a concept that is borrowed from accounting and used frequently in articles about corporate responsibility. A perusal of the web shows that the three components are also described as "financial, social, and environmental," and "people, planet, and profits." There is a growing literature on the TBL.[4]

Preservation activities, on the other hand, usually focus on a particular collection, structure, or site. While preservationists may care about the natural environment, historically their foci have been more local than global. Nowhere is this more clearly illustrated than in cultural heritage institutions where the professionals who have preservation responsibilities have sustained the collections by controlling the environmental conditions in which objects are stored. For decades, institutions have tried to achieve the temperature and relative humidity standards set in the late 1960s and 1970s: 70 degrees F and 50 percent RH, with minimal fluctuation.[5] Since the 1990s, conservation scientists, such as Donald K. Sebera and James M. Reilly, have advocated for new environmental management approaches. Sebera developed the Isoperm method, which is a modeling technique for assessing the effects of particular temperature and humidity levels on paper-based collections,[6] while Reilly came up with new monitoring techniques.

Now Reilly also focuses on sustainable preservation practices, offering workshops and tools through the Image Permanence Institute at the Rochester Institute of Technology.[7] The impetus for this approach has come not only from conservation and preservation professionals, but from directors of cultural heritage institutions—who must necessarily think about environmental sustainability and financial stability. Steadily increasing energy costs, diminishing fossil fuels, and an increased awareness of climate change are causing leaders of cultural heritage institutions to reduce the carbon footprint of their institutions. Reducing our carbon footprint is no small task. In a recent article, Erica Avrami states that buildings account for up to 40 percent of energy consumption, and some 50 percent of all raw materials from nature are used in buildings.[8]

As Rebecca Meyer, Shannon Struble, and Phyllis Catsikis describe in "Sustainability: A Literature Review":

> In 2009, the National Museum Directors' Conference (NMDC), a UK-based organization, released *NMDC's Guiding Principles for Reducing Museums' Carbon Footprint*, which acknowledged that "seeking to achieve an internationally agreed narrow environmental standard for temperature and relative humidity has resulted in an unnecessarily high energy use." The recommendations encourage institutions to consider their local climate when deciding on appropriate targets for environmental control.[9]

Today, conservators and preservation administrators are changing their approach to environmental monitoring: "We want to attain the 'optimal preservation environment' that achieves the best possible preservation of collections, at the least possible consumption of energy, and is sustainable over time."[10]

But the environmental monitoring of collections is not the only area in which sustainability is at issue in institutions. Chemicals used in conservation treatments may pose risks to the environment. Materials used in building renovation projects, or in the construction of new buildings, may cause a host of environmental problems.

Environmental sustainability concerns the entire built environment. Two strategies for addressing these challenges are mitigation and adaptation. "Mitigation focuses on minimizing climate change. Adaptation addresses the effects of climate change."[11] Most conservation efforts focus on adaptation. Avrami views the future of built heritage conservation as a component of managing a sustainable built environment.

Disaster preparedness and response programs are now integrating weather patterns into planning. It is important for heritage professionals to understand how climate changes are leading to certain types of natural disasters.

Focusing on sustainability is an important way in which cultural heritage institutions can demonstrate their value to the communities in which they reside. How can we sustain the functions and services that our users and visitors most want? For starters, we can do so in an environmentally friendly way, such as using recycled paper, providing duplex printing services, recycling other materials, serving locally produced foods in our cafes, and so on.

It is possible that in a sustainable future, all of the issues considered in this chapter will be more closely linked. In the meantime, the topics under consideration here serve as a prelude.

NOTES

1. "Sustainability," United States Environmental Protection Agency, accessed December 5, 2012, http://www.epa.gov/sustainability/basicinfo.htm.

2. "Europe 2020 in a Nutshell," European Commission, accessed December 5, 2012, http://ec.europa.eu/europe2020/europe-2020-in-a-nutshell/index_en.htm.

3. "Europe 2020 in a Nutshell."

4. See for example, Timothy F. Slaper and Tanya J. Hall, "The Triple Bottom Line: What Is It and How Does It Work?" *Indiana Business Review*, Spring 2011, accessed December 5, 2012, http://www.ibrc.indiana.edu/ibr/2011/spring/article2.html.

5. See, for example, Garry Thomson, *The Museum Environment* (London: Butterworths, 1978); a second edition of this widely used book was published in 1986.

6. Donald K. Sebera, *Isoperms: An Environmental Management Tool* (Washington, D.C.: Commission on Preservation and Access, 1994).

7. For example, the workshop "Sustainable Preservation Practices for Managing Storage Environments," accessed December 5, 2012, https://www.imagepermanenceinstitute.org/about/what-we-do.

8. Erica Avrami, "Sustainability and the Built Environment: Forging a Role for Heritage Conservation," *Getty Conservation Institute Newsletter* 26.1 (2011): 4.

9. Rebecca Meyer, Shannon Struble, and Phyllis Catsikis, "Sustainabilty: A Literature Review." For the report go to http://www.nationalmuseums.org.uk/what-we-do/contributing-sector/environmental-conditions/.

10. Jeremy Linden, "Getting Greener and Creating the Optimal: The State of Sustainabilty Research and the Preservation Environment," *AIC News* 37.2 (2012): 1.

11. Erica Avrami, "Sustainability and the Built Environment," 5.

ERICA AVRAMI, RANDALL MASON, AND MARTA DE LA TORRE

"The Spheres and Challenges of Conservation" and "Conclusions," Excerpts from *Values and Heritage Conservation: Research Report*

Los Angeles: The Getty Conservation Institute (2000): 3–10, 68–70.

The Spheres and Challenges of Conservation

Underpinning this research is an assumption that heritage conservation is an integral part of civil society. Cultivating this role should, ideally, be one of the abiding concerns of our field. In some form, conservation of material heritage is a function observable in every modern society. Conservation shapes the society in which it is situated, and in turn, it is shaped by the needs and dynamics of that society.

Yet how conservation is approached and undertaken varies from culture to culture. The term *conservation* itself has varied meanings and connotations. In certain contexts, "conservation" has broad meaning, signifying the entire field or realm of cultural heritage preservation, from academic inquiry and historical research to policy making to planning to technical intervention (this meaning is akin to the American notion of "historic preservation"). At the same time,

"conservation" is used to indicate physical intervention or treatment specifically. This definition of conservation refers to the more technically oriented functions of the broader field. But the broader definition refers more widely to conservation as a complex, diverse, and even divergent social practice—and it is this definition that needs to be foregrounded.

It would seem that the latter, more narrow definition of conservation is an element of the former, more expansive definition. However, in practice, the work of intervention or treatment has become somewhat disconnected from this broader field and notion of conservation. Decisions about *what* to conserve and *why* are often taken independently from those dealing with *how* to conserve, and vice versa. This is due, in part, to the relative isolation of different groups or spheres of professionals that engage in the work of conservation (broadly defined).

Professionals working in the broader conservation field are drawn from the sciences, the arts, the social sciences, the humanities, and other areas—reflecting the fact that heritage conservation is truly a *multidisciplinary* endeavor. All the same, in practice *interdisciplinary* collaboration is not often achieved. If one were to map, simply and generally, the current shape of conservation policy and practice,[1] one would find a rather linear path with different groups of professionals engaged in distinct steps along the way.

As represented in Figure 1 (see [below]), at some initial stage, a product of material culture—be it an object or a place—is recognized as "cultural heritage." This is, in fact, the beginning of a process of heritage *creation* or *production*. Whether through academic discourse, archaeological excavation, a community movement, or political or religious trends, interest is generated about the object or place in question, and momentum builds. The next step entails protection of the "product" through, for example, designation as an historic site or acquisition by a museum. This step often involves individuals or groups, such as curators, heritage commissions, etc., who evaluate the significance of the product. Next, those who own or have responsibility for the product (collections managers, site managers, property owners, etc.) are charged with its overall management. This may (or may not) lead to a program of intervention or treatment to conserve the fabric of the object or place, involving conservators, architects, scientists, etc. And it may also include consultations made with communities and other stakeholders, or decisions made by politicians and investors.

As the diagram suggests, conservation policy and practice follow a sequence of steps that each involves a separate sphere of professionals and players, often with little interplay among the spheres. Intervention, in particular, has become its own, very distinct sphere, focusing mostly on the physical aspects of heritage and often losing sight of the interconnectedness of treatment to the preceding spheres.

In the current climate of globalization, technological advancement, population mobility, and the spread of participatory democracies and market economies, it has become quite clear to the broad conservation community that these and other societal trends are profoundly and rapidly changing cultures and communities. The future challenges of the conservation field will stem not only from heritage objects and sites themselves but from the *contexts* in which society embeds them. These contexts—the values people draw from them, the functions heritage objects serve for society, the uses to which heritage is put—are the real source of the meaning of heritage, and the raison d'être for conservation in all senses. As society changes, so does the role of conservation and the opportunities for conservation to shape and support civil society. These changed social conditions compel us to think expansively and realistically about the future standing of conservation in the social agenda.

Given these immediate challenges, many conservation professionals and organizations have recognized that greater cohesion, connection, and integration are needed in the conservation field. As suggested by

Figure 1.

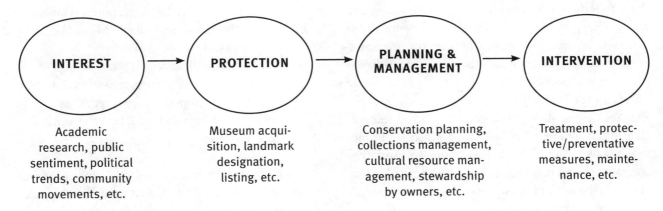

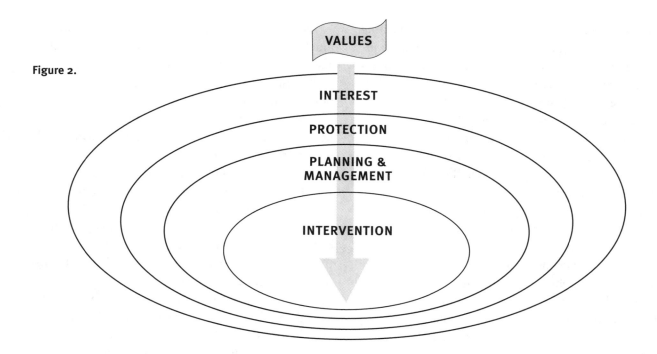

Figure 2.

Figure 2 (see above), rather than a disjointed sequence, the spheres of conservation ought to be integrated better and embedded within their relevant contexts, so as to ensure that conservation remains responsive to ever-changing cultural conditions.

In the last ten to fifteen years, the field (specifically those involved in the conservation of architecture and archaeological sites) has made significant advances in grappling with these challenges in a holistic way. Through comprehensive planning for conservation management,[2] integrated, interdisciplinary approaches to the preservation of the built environment have developed that address the changed conditions of contemporary society. Australia ICOMOS, the U.S. National Park Service, English Heritage, and many other government and nongovernmental agencies (NGOs) have established policies for integrated conservation management, employing value-driven planning methodologies that attempt to incorporate values more effectively in conservation decision making. Yet despite these advances, widespread integration of the spheres of conservation policy and practice has been slow. This is largely due to the rather fragmented and unbalanced body of knowledge that supports the work of conservation; also to the specialization of work in different disciplines. As a field, we

know a great deal about some aspects of conservation (science, documentation, listing); in other, important areas, we know very little (for instance, economics, or the use of heritage as a foil in identity or political struggles).

In the cultural heritage conservation field, we are consistently faced with challenges on three fronts:

- Physical condition: Behavior of materials and structural systems, deterioration causes and mechanisms, possible interventions, long-term efficacy of treatments, etc.
- Management context: Availability and use of resources, including funds, trained personnel, and technology; political and legislative mandates and conditions; land use issues, etc.
- Cultural significance and social values: Why an object or place is meaningful, to whom, for whom it is conserved, the impact of interventions on how it is understood or perceived, etc.

Traditionally, the research efforts of the conservation field have focused on the first front, physical condition. Great strides have been made to understand

and arrest material deterioration. As a result, in the area of material science and technical interventions, a considerable body of information, with specific applicability to conservation, has grown through the years.

In the realm of management issues, some conservation-specific discourse has emerged from the law and economics fields. Most of this research, though, has focused on issues of owners' rights and finance, rather than on the complexities of resource management within the field of conservation or on conservation as a "public good" within society.

Likewise, one finds extensive information about canons of art-historical value, personal values, responsibility to future generations, material culture and its societal functions, heritage as embodied in the natural environment, its stewardship, and so on. However, very little of this literature is applied to or developed in the context of conservation.

Although there is a great deal of information in related disciplines (anthropology, economics, psychology, philosophy, etc.) that can inform the work of conservation, relatively little research has addressed the specifics of cultural heritage conservation or has been undertaken in service of the conservation field. In fact, the greater part of *all* conservation research still focuses on the challenges of physical condition—namely, the deterioration of materials and possible interventions—concentrating on the objects as opposed to their contexts.

Every act of conservation is shaped by how an object or place is valued, its social contexts, available resources, local priorities, and so on. Decisions about treatments and interventions are not based solely on considerations of physical decay; yet the lack of a coherent body of knowledge that addresses and integrates all three fronts makes it very difficult to assess and incorporate these other, equally important factors in the work of conservation professionals. Likewise, this makes efforts to coalesce and connect the field at large and its multidisciplinary constituency formidable.

As a field, we have come to recognize that conservation cannot unify or advance with any real innovation or vision if we continue to concentrate the bulk of conservation discourse on issues of physical condition. Conservation risks losing ground within the social agenda unless the nontechnical complexities of cultural heritage preservation, the role it plays in modern society, and the social, economic, political, and cultural mechanisms through which conservation works are better understood and articulated.

Thus, the unmet need is for research that explains how conservation is situated in society—how it is shaped by economic, cultural, and social forces and how, in turn, it shapes society. With this type of research, the field can advance in a positive way by embedding the spheres of conservation within their relevant contexts, informing decision-making processes, fostering links with associated disciplines, and enabling conservation professionals and organizations to respond better in the future, through both practice and policy. Such research, coupled with strategic planning for how better to integrate conservation in the social agenda, will ensure that the next generation of conservation professionals will be educated and equipped to deal with conservation broadly and holistically.

CONSERVATION PERSPECTIVES

There is tremendous educational and practical potential to be realized by integrating and contextualizing the spheres and work of conservation, not only as a self-contained science or technological endeavor but as a social practice. Conservation is continually changing, mirroring the fact that cultures are constantly in flux from the local to the global scale. As social and cultural change intensifies, greater demands are made to conserve heritage as a brake against unwanted change and even as a means of effecting change. Heritage is one of the mainstays of culture, art, and creativity. In any case, the cultural context dictates that the pressure to conserve, and the stakes in doing so, rise dramatically. This is our current climate.

Insights gleaned from social theory, historical inquiry, and policy-related research about the nature of contemporary society suggest that the conservation field will only keep pace with recent trends if, collectively, we reexamine the core concepts of heritage and conservation. Echoing a great deal of social science and humanities research on culture in the postmodern era, heritage should be considered a very fluid phenomenon, a process as opposed to a static set of objects with fixed meaning. Building on this insight, heritage conservation should be recognized as a bundle of highly politicized social processes, intertwined with myriad other economic, political, and cultural processes.

Historically, cultural heritage—its very existence and its function within a society—has been taken for granted. That societies should save old things has been a matter of tradition, to be accepted and respected, and the reasons are not examined too closely. The norms dictating what things qualified as heritage were very stable—these were notions like "masterpieces," "intrinsic value," and "authenticity." However, in the last generation, cultural consensus and norms have been replaced by an atmosphere of openly contentious and fractious politics. Some of the best scholarship regarding conservation and society presents compelling evidence of precisely the opposite of what was previously held true: that heritage, at its core, is politicized and contested, and thus conservation must not hide behind its traditional philosophical matters of faith. (It should also be noted that the intense recent interest in professional ethics is another part of the development of critical perspectives on conservation.)

At the heart of contemporary, interdisciplinary, critical research on heritage is the notion that cultural heritage is a social construction; which is to say that it results from social processes specific to time and place. As noted, scholarship on culture in the past generation or so reinforces the notion that culture is a set of processes, not a collection of things. Artifacts are not static embodiments of culture but are, rather, a medium through which identity, power, and society are produced and reproduced. Objects, collections, buildings, and places become recognized as "heritage" through conscious decisions and unspoken values of particular people and institutions—and for reasons that are strongly shaped by social contexts and processes. Thus, the meaning of heritage can no longer be thought of as fixed, as the traditional notions of intrinsic value and authenticity suggest. Museology scholar Susan Pearce, for instance, suggests that cultural heritage is cognitively constructed and that "the notion of cultural heritage embraces any and every aspect of life that individuals, in their variously scaled social groups, consider explicitly or implicitly to be a part of their self-definition."[3]

All the same, a postmodernist tendency to reduce cultural heritage to simply a social construction runs up against the widely held understanding that heritage is in fact imbued with some universal, intrinsic qualities. Despite the tenor of identity politics and the pull toward cultural relativism, anthropologist Lourdes Arizpe argues the much-debated point that cultural heritage—in addressing the deepest, shared human longings for love and beauty and cooperation—has universal significance, or *etic* meaning, in addition to its more culturally bound *emic* meaning. Philosopher Uffe Jensen also suggests that the need for access to one's culture, one's heritage, crosses all cultures and contributes to human flourishing and happiness in the Aristotelian sense. As related to these values of human happiness and societal peace, there is a universal quality to the notion of cultural heritage that transcends relativistic interpretation but that is equally bound up in specificities of time and place. This is a major axis of debate, and each side suggests a very different approach to determining cultural significance as part of the conservation process.

All sides of the contingent-universal debate agree that heritage and its conservation (traditionally defined) play definite, even essential functions in most, if not all, societies. Yet the concept of conservation is itself paradoxical. As David Lowenthal notes in his essay below, "Heritage is never merely conserved or protected; it is modified—both enhanced and degraded—by each new generation." As with all other social activities, conservation is not objective; it is biased by the values and perspectives of various individuals and interest groups. Architectural historian Daniel Bluestone cautions that change must be understood as part of the richness of heritage and that, in the work of conservation, "understanding change is as important as understanding original intent." Conservation is a complex and continual process that involves determinations about what constitutes heritage, how it is used, cared for, interpreted, and so on, by whom and for whom. The decisions about what to conserve and how to conserve are largely defined by cultural contexts, societal trends, political and economic forces—which themselves continue to change.

Cultural heritage is thus a medium for the ever-evolving values of social groups (be they families, communities residing in certain places, ethnic groups, disciplines or professional groups, entire nations) as well as individuals. Social groups are embedded in certain places and times and, as a matter of routine, use things (including material heritage) to interpret their past and their future. In this sense, conservation is not merely an arresting process but a means of creating and recreating heritage.

Though this perspective on conservation challenges some widely held, traditional notions, we in the conservation field have come to recognize that we must integrate and contextualize our work. Conservation is a process that consistently recreates its product (cultural heritage), accumulating the marks of passing generations. As such, it must be situated in its larger social contexts—as part of the larger cultural sphere; as a basic phenomenon of public discourse; as a social activity constantly reshaped by forces such as globalization, technological developments, the widening influence of market ideology, cultural fusion, and myriad others. This process-centered model of conservation is at the heart of the future relevance of our field. It could serve as a basis for orienting practice, formulating and analyzing policy, understanding economic forces, and generally ensuring that conservation is "significant" for society at large.

VALUES, VALORIZATION, AND CULTURAL SIGNIFICANCE

Values and valuing processes are threaded through the various spheres of conservation and play an enormous role as we endeavor to integrate the field. Whether works of art, buildings, or ethnographic artifacts, the products of material culture have different meanings and uses for different individuals and communities. Values give some things significance over others and thereby transform some objects and places into "heritage." The ultimate aim of conservation is not to conserve material for its own sake but, rather, to maintain (and shape) the values embodied by the heritage—with physical intervention or treatment being one of many means toward that end. To achieve that end, such that the heritage is meaningful to those whom it is intended to benefit (i.e., future

generations), it is necessary to examine *why* and *how* heritage is valued, and by whom.

Cultural significance is the term that the conservation community has used to encapsulate the multiple values ascribed to objects, buildings, or landscapes. From the writings of [Alois] Riegl to the policies of the Burra Charter, these values have been ordered in categories, such as aesthetic, religious, political, economic, and so on.[4] Through the classification of values of different disciplines, fields of knowledge, or uses, the conservation community (defined broadly) attempts to grapple with the many emotions, meanings, and functions associated with the material goods in its care. This identification and ordering of values serves as a vehicle to inform decisions about how best to preserve these values in the physical conservation of the object or place. Though the typologies of different scholars and disciplines vary, they each represent a reductionist approach to examining the very complex issue of cultural significance.

However, this process of valuing is neither singular nor objective, and it begins even before the object becomes "heritage." With reference to Figure 1, one can see that some fraction of the material culture produced or inherited by society (artistic as well as utilitarian) becomes defined and recognized as heritage through designation. How does this happen? The creation of cultural heritage is largely derived from the way people remember, organize, think about, and wish to use the past and how material culture provides a medium through which to do this. The stories invested in objects, buildings, and landscapes, by individuals or groups, constitute a currency in which the valorizing of cultural heritage is transacted. The subtle distinction between *valuing* (appreciating existing value) and *valorizing* (giving added value) speaks to the interventionist and interpretative aspects of the simple act of identifying something as heritage. Simply labeling something as heritage is a value judgment that distinguishes that object or place from other objects and places for particular reasons, and as such, the labeling adds new meaning and value.

The process of valorizing begins when individuals, institutions, or communities decide that some object or place is worth preserving, that it represents something worth remembering, something about themselves and their past that should be transmitted to future generations. Through donation of an object to a museum or through the designation or listing of a building or site, these individuals or communities (be they political, academic, or so on) actively create heritage. But this is only the beginning of the process of creating and valorizing heritage.

Heritage is valued in a variety of ways, driven by different motivations (economic, political, cultural, spiritual, aesthetic, and others), each of which has correspondingly varied ideals, ethics, and epistemologies. These different ways of valuing in turn lead to different approaches to preserving heritage. For instance, conserving a historic house property according to historical-cultural values would lead one to maximize the capacity for the place to serve the educational function of telling the stories; the primary audiences in this case might be local schoolchildren and the local community, for whom association with this old place and its stories makes a significant contribution to their group identity. By contrast, conserving the same site to maximize economic value might lead to a conservation approach that favors revenue generation and tourist traffic over educational and other cultural values. Thus, parts of the property might be developed for parking, gift shops, and other visitor-support functions, instead of interpreting and conserving historic landscape or archaeological elements of the site; the overall conservation strategy might be driven by creating a popular (marketable) experience, as opposed to creating one that focuses on educational use by a target audience of schoolchildren. Neither option can be viewed as a priori better or more appropriate than the other, as the appropriateness is dependent upon the values prioritized by the community, or "stakeholders" involved (professionals, public, government, etc.), and the context in which the effort is undertaken.

Conservation (narrowly defined) has commonly been viewed as that which follows the act of heritage designation—that is, a technical response after a place or object has already been recognized as having value. The underlying belief has been that preservation treatment should not, and would not, change the meaning of the heritage object, yet the traditional practice of conserving—of preserving the physical fabric of a heritage object—does in fact actively interpret and valorize the object. Every conservation decision—how to clean an object, how to reinforce a structure, what materials to use, and so on—affects how that object or place will be perceived, understood and used, and thus transmitted to the future. Despite such postulated principles as minimum intervention, reversibility, and authenticity, a decision to undertake a certain conservation intervention gives priority to a certain meaning or set of values. For example, decisions in the management of an archaeological site may involve stabilizing one structure but excavating through another to expose an earlier structure below. Each decision affects how visitors experience the site and how they interpret and value the architectural forms and elements; these decisions likewise reflect how those responsible for care and protection interpret and value the forms and elements. In the realm of objects conservation, the issue of repatriation also captures such competing values. For instance, ethnographic objects associated with Native American groups are often collected in museums. There, the objects are conserved (and stored and/or displayed) to arrest decay, so that they may be viewed and studied by both scholars and the public. This course of action champions the value of the object as a means of providing information about and understanding of a certain Native American culture from outside the culture itself. Yet many Native American groups prefer that these objects be returned, so that they may be reburied in accordance with their spiritual beliefs. These options reflect different sets of values: one gives priority to the use of the object as a means of preserving cultural traditions, the other to its material form.

Values also inform policy decisions. Consider a hypothetical government agency with responsibility for managing the listing of official landmarks and investing public funds in preservation projects. A number of competing interests—competing values—typically viewed to be expressed through these decision-making processes. Different culture groups and political factions lobby to have their memories and messages sanctioned by government policy. To add complexity, economic values might trump these competing cultural values—projects are worth investing in, the logic goes, only if they are financially self-supporting.

These examples clearly illustrate that the values of individuals and communities—be they conservators, anthropologists, ethnic groups, politicians, or otherwise—shape all conservation. And in the conservation process, these values, as represented in the object or place, are not simply "preserved" but are, rather, modified. The meaning of the object or place is redefined, and new values are sometimes created.

What is the usefulness of such an insight? Analytically, one can understand what values are at work by analyzing what stories are being told. And analysis of meanings (which is to say, cultural significance) thus provides an important kind of knowledge to complement documentation and analysis of material conditions as the contexts for physical treatment. Yet the assessment of cultural significance is often *not* undertaken when conservation interventions are planned, or when it is, it is frequently limited to the one-time composition of a statement of significance by an archaeologist, historian, or other expert. Why is it that assessment of cultural significance is not more meaningfully integrated in conservation practice? As mentioned previously, with a body of information and a research agenda focused primarily on issues of physical condition, conservation education rarely involves training in how to assess complex meanings and values, whom to involve in such an assessment, and how to negotiate the decision making that follows.

Still largely regarded as a technical rather than a social endeavor, conservation has failed to attract significant input from the social sciences. As mentioned previously, despite emerging policies that promote value-driven planning for conservation management, there is a limited body of knowledge regarding how conservation functions in society—and specifically regarding how cultural significance might best be assessed and reassessed as part of a public and enduring conservation process. Cultural significance for the purposes of conservation decision making can no longer be a purely scholarly construction but, rather, an issue negotiated among the many professionals, academics, and community members who value the object or place—the "stakeholders."

Because of the complexity of contemporary society, it is important to recognize the diversity of potential stakeholders—they include, but are not limited to, the individual, the family, the local community, an academic discipline or professional community, an ethnic or religious group, a region, a nation-state, macrostates (such as the European Community or the North American Free Trade Area), the world. Relations among stakeholders at various levels are both intimate and tense; they sometimes build affiliation and community and other times sow discontent. Motivations for the valorization (or devalorization) of material heritage vary among these stakeholders. Broader cultural conditions and dynamics (for instance, marketization, technological evolution, cultural fusion) influence these interactions. Continuity and change, participation, power, and ownership are all bound up in the ways in which cultures are created and progress.

The effects of these phenomena of cultural change and evolution are manifested clearly in the heritage conservation arena. Rapid transformation in this technological age often has a dramatic effect on the dual forces of continuity and change, exacerbating political tensions among stakeholders. In conservation, this is manifested, for instance, in the prominent role of the "suburban sprawl" issue in American historic preservation, or the lures and pressures that come with worldwide development of tourism sites and industries. This dilemma can be made worse, since decision makers are having to take actions affecting heritage in shorter and shorter time frames, and the interests of local constituencies (as well as those of future generations) can easily vanish from consideration.

Lourdes Arizpe suggests that, for all conservation decision making, one must look at who is valorizing cultural heritage and why. "Governments value it in one way, elite national groups another, different from local populations, academics, or business people. To know what is the best strategy to preserve cultural heritage, we need to understand what each of these groups thinks and the relationship between these different groups." It is in our best interest, as conservation professionals, to facilitate some sort of agreement or understanding among these different stakeholders about the cultural significance of an object or place as part of common practice. An understanding of stakeholders' values—which define their goals and motivate their actions—provides critical insight for the long-term, strategic management of heritage resources by both the private and the public sectors.

To conserve in a way that is relevant to our own society in our own moment, we must understand how values are negotiated and determine how the process of analyzing and constructing cultural significance can be enhanced. There is also a parallel obligation, beyond preserving what is relevant to our own time— that is, preserving what we believe will be significant to future generations. The prospect of stewarding for future generations the material markers of the past, imbued with the cumulative stories and meanings of the past as well as of the present, is the essence of conservation. With wide acknowledgment that culture is a fluid, changeable, evolving set of processes and values and not a static set of things, the conservation of cultural heritage must embrace the inherent flux but not lose sight of this immutable cross-generational responsibility.

[…]

Conclusions

Over the past several decades, we have seen changes in society that have affected how we view and create cultural heritage. From a restricted, canonical perspective of masterpieces and historical monuments, the concept of heritage has expanded to include materials such as vernacular architecture, ensembles of buildings, natural and cultural landscapes, and other objects that are significant to specific groups of society. The meanings and functions of these artifacts and places are contested. The field of conservation itself is undergoing fundamental transformations—in some instances, as a direct result of these societal changes. Some of the changes in the field are generated by technical advances that concern the "first front" of conservation research (see "The Spheres and Challenges of Conservation" in the Report on Research, above), the physical condition of the heritage. Greater understanding of the deterioration processes of materials and the development of new techniques have increased the possibilities of treatments and interventions that extend the life of materials. Yet the understanding of when, where, and why to apply this new

technical knowledge has been less of a concern and has only recently been a subject for research.

As we in the conservation field acknowledge the importance of social and economic values along with the traditional notions of conservation (such as age, aesthetics, and historical significance), we find ourselves in a much larger arena of decision making. In earlier times, conservation was a relatively autonomous, closed field composed of specialists and experts. These experts, together with art historians and archaeologists, decided what was significant and thus needed special attention and care—and how to best render that attention and care. The right of these specialists to make decisions was tacitly recognized by those who funded the work (for the most part, government authorities), and there was a consensus among those with the power to act regarding the values to be conserved.

In the twentieth century, the conservation community and the heritage field have undergone an extraordinary expansion. There still are specialists— who are certainly needed—but new groups have become involved in the creation and care of heritage. These groups of citizens (some are professionals from such fields as tourism and economics, others are advocating the interests of their communities) arrive with their own criteria and opinions on how to establish significance, on what merits conservation, and on how it should happen. As such, heritage, and the right to make decisions about it, are sometimes the subject of confrontation and acrimonious debate between different groups in society.

All the same, democratization is a desirable development, and it has changed the heritage field: the old canons are questioned; the opinions of the specialists are not taken as articles of faith; and heritage decisions are recognized as complex negotiations to which diverse stakeholders bring their own values. Today heritage is seen as the source of important benefits to society, including stability, understanding, tolerance, recognition of and respect for cultural differences, and economic development.

This report has proposed a new definition of conservation: it should be understood as a social process, one that includes the work of many individuals and groups, not just conservation professionals. Traditional conservation remains the core of the field's activity and its raison d'être, but, as argued throughout this report, the conservation process is best seen more inclusively, encompassing the creation of heritage, interpretation and education, the many efforts of individuals and social groups to be stewards of heritage, and shifting economic and political tides, as well as the traditional practices of conservators, preservationists, curators, and other professionals. This report advocates acceptance of this broader definition—we see it as an imperative to the future success of the conservation field in responding to the demands of contemporary society.

This expanded notion of conservations reflects trends that have been developing throughout the world in the past several decades. In order to conserve heritage in ways most resonant with these realities, we must make larger sense of the forces behind heritage. But how to do so? The dynamics of this expanded notion of conservation—as well as the expanded purview of the conservation field—can be better understood through a conceptual framework for the heritage-creation process (as outlined above in "The Need for a Conceptual Framework"). Such a framework would not only foster understanding but also serve as a tool for informed decision making about the effective management of cultural heritage. As already mentioned, value-driven planning methodologies are being advocated more and more in the field of conservation; yet the mechanisms for applying these methodologies are inadequately documented and underdeveloped. In order for conservation planning processes to center on, and take into deeper consideration, the multitude of social values, we need to develop better tools and methods for the assessment of cultural significance, so that it can be effectively integrated into conservation practice. If the concept of heritage creation can be articulated and mapped as a social process through the development of a conceptual framework, we can create a common ground for the exchange of ideas among the many professionals, academics, and other citizens who can contribute to the increasingly public and interdisciplinary work of conservation.

Unless this critical link is forged, the conservation of cultural heritage risks being marginalized in the social agenda. Thus, in the development of this framework, we should aim to arrive at strategic options for how conservation might better function in society, rather than simply to document and theorize about how it currently operates.

To build on the development of such an explanatory framework, as well as to strengthen the work of conservation professionals in supporting the broader goals of society, research on the following topics is suggested.

STAKEHOLDERS IN THE NEGOTIATION PROCESS

As argued elsewhere in this report, our research suggests that understanding conservation in social contexts means looking at the entwined processes of valuing, valorizing, and decision making. Valuing and determinations of cultural significance have already been discussed. With regard to decision making, there are at least two kinds of conservation decisions: The first kind is *how* to conserve—this has been the traditional focus and strength of conservation professionals. The second kind of decision is *what* to conserve and, following on the heels of this, who plays what role and who pays. *What* to conserve has often been left to chance, or rather, the lead has been taken by public officials, legislators, and other policy makers.

Instead of focusing on the objects of conservation—the things and the methods of dealing with them—this research would center on subjects and would involve an investigation of the different actors and institutions and their motivations, habits, and other mediating factors.

THE NOTION OF UNIVERSALITY IN CULTURAL HERITAGE AND ITS CONSERVATION

Universality—the assumption that some heritage is meaningful to all of mankind—is one of the basic assumptions and matters of faith underlying conservation practice and one assumption that emphasizes the positive role of heritage in promoting unity and understanding.

The notion of universality remains one of the most important and pressing questions regarding conservation. Universality assumes that certain aspects of heritage are meaningful to all people, regardless of cultural, social, political, and economic differences—a notion that seems untenable if any of the assertions about postmodern culture are on target. Under the guise of the "intrinsic" value of art or of multinational conventions and declarations regarding the protection of heritage, universality has long been assumed to exist as a quality of heritage objects and to form the rationale for global diligence with regard to conservation. It is, for instance, the rationale behind Unesco's World Heritage List.

But universality warrants closer critical attention. There is a great deal of evidence to suggest that local, place- and community-bound values (i.e., those not, by definition, universally valued) are a more important impulse behind conservation. Cultural relativism (and, more generally, the postmodern questioning of canons in every corner of cultural and society) demands that the conservation field explore what universality is, why it is so influential, and what role it should play in conservation decisions—in particular, through determinations of cultural significance. Just such a critical dialogue already exists throughout the conservation community in informal ways, and formally addressing it through this topic could advance the dialogue significantly.

THE SIGNIFICANCE OF SCALE IN SHAPING THE VALUING AND CONSERVATION OF HERITAGE

Is geographical scale in itself a relevant factor vis-à-vis heritage conservation? Is it more or less effective to conserve heritage (or design conservation policy) at a local scale, versus a national or global scale? In reality, conservation is practiced at several scales—personal, family, community, city, region, nation, nation-state, continent, global. But what are the articulations among these scales of practice? Do they nest perfectly? Do they conflict?

CULTURAL HERITAGE CONSERVATION WITHIN THE CURRENT SOCIAL ADDRESS: "DIFFERENT, PLAUSIBLE FUTURES"

This topic calls for an investigation of the trends shaping the possible futures of cultural heritage conservation, given the forces affecting society today. The topic would deal explicitly with the externalities generated by larger social dynamics—which frame the conditions in which the conservation field works. Global trends certainly have an impact on the valuing and valorization of heritage (identity politics, democracy movements, privatization, market economics, and so on)—but how great an impact? Are these impacts different from those brought to bear by regional conflicts or local disputes? Where and how does conservation find a place in the constellation of public policy issues? Scenario building, a strategic-planning tool for envisioning several possible futures given today's complexity of driving forces, would be an excellent tool for addressing this question.

In the end, those concerned with the future of conservation are left with many questions, which undoubtedly will be the subject of continuing debates and research. Heritage is valued in myriad ways, for myriad reasons: to construct and negotiate identity; to build bonds within a social group, like a nation or a neighborhood; to turn an economic profit; to send a political message, and more. How do these complex dynamics concerning values and benefits affect the prospects, meaning, and reputation of the conservation field? As Lourdes Arizpe asks in her essay, will heritage conservation efforts in the future serve as bridges between cultures or as trenches separating them? Research and discussions will help us construct answers to such questions, by broadening our sense of purpose and by clarifying the challenges that lay before us.

NOTES

1. In this instance, as throughout the report, reference is made to the field of conservation as practiced in the Western world, namely Europe and the Americas.

2. Also known as heritage management, cultural resource management, site management, and so on.

3. This comment was made at the 1998 meeting that launched GCI's research on the values and benefits of cultural heritage conservation; it was quoted in an unpublished internal report of the meeting. Other uncited quotes in this section are from the same source.

4. Typologies for values related to cultural heritage have been put forth in publications by Ashworth, de la Torre, Hutter and Rizzo, Kellert, Lipe, and Riegl (for full citations, see the Appendix). These works represent a sampling and are by no means a definitive word on the diversity of values.

Selection 11.2

DAVID LOWENTHAL

"Stewarding the Future"

In CRM: The Journal of Heritage Stewardship *2.2 (Summer 2005): 1–17.*

"Think of your forefathers! Think of your posterity!"
— *John Quincy Adams, December 22, 1802*

SUSTAINABILITY IS AN iconic term in conservation stewardship. It implies a commitment to manage natural and cultural resources to ensure their continuance into an indefinite future. But how far ahead is that? No general agreement emerges. There is only a general assumption that it applies to a period beyond our own lifetime. For some, this means a concern merely for the next generation or two, while for others it involves many millennia, even an incalculably remote future.

Many reasons are advanced for a futurist stance. Some are ethical: it is only fair that future generations inherit a world that we have not shorn of health and wealth. Some are conscientious: we prefer to be blessed as good stewards rather than to be cursed as despoilers. Some are familial: we hope that our grandchildren will inhabit a world at least as fruitful as our own. Others are pragmatic: intergenerational equity is not merely just, it also helps to promote social stability and political well-being in the present. Moreover, active concern for a time beyond our own enhances not only our successors' lives but also our own.

Which if any of these futurist arguments are generally accepted and how far they are put into practice depend on culture and zeitgeist. So does the kind of time to which future concern applies. For example, the future as envisaged by science fiction in the West is almost always conceived in secular terms, forward from our own epoch, whereas outside the West, time is usually cyclical or recursive, wholly unlike mundane linear experience.[1] In the West many continue to regard eternity as a foreign country. Perturbed by daily auguries of global doom, I found it consoling to be assured, in a recent notice, that though old-style 20-pound notes would cease to be legal tender, they would nonetheless "remain payable at the Bank of England for all time." A cleric chided *The Times* of London for heading a letter "From here to eternity," for however protracted the longevity of the Bank of England, it was nonetheless temporal, "eternal investments [being] of a wholly different currency."[2]

Pious expressions of future concern are currently fashionable in commerce and politics alike. "You never actually own a Patek Philippe," says the watchmaker; "you merely look after it for the next generation." "We're developing the cures of the future," a pharmaceutical company touts its research program; "we'll care for your great-great grandchildren." Picturing a baby with a mobile phone, Nippon Telegraph & Telephone boasts that "we're already figuring out how his great-grandkids will communicate."[3] Yet in most societies and in most respects, future stewardship has lost ground over the past half century. What lies ahead matters less and less, and elicits ever less care.

The shift from future to present, from permanence to transience, was well under way a generation ago. Contrasting children's dolls once clutched lovingly until they disintegrated with disposable Barbie dolls turned in annually for new models, Alvin Toffler's *Future Shock* descried an accelerated love of evanescence, a propensity to think in terms of immediate returns and consequences.[4] Christopher Lasch's *Culture of Narcissism* blamed growing self-absorption: "We live these days for ourselves, not for predecessors or posterity"; narcissism was typical of "a society that has lost interest in the future."[5] Recent observers note "a growing incapacity or unwillingness…to identify with the future," as one psychologist put it, a tendency to be "less interested in offspring and willing to sacrifice for them." "Few cared about leaving the world in better shape for future generations."[6]

The consequences for natural resources are especially perilous. "We borrow environmental capital from future generations," the Bruntland Commission concluded, "with no intention or prospect of repaying." Our descendants "may damn us for our spendthrift ways, but they can never collect on our debt to them. We act as we do because we can get away with it: future generations do not vote; they have no political or financial power; they cannot challenge our decisions."[7] As is often said, the present is a ruthless dictator to the future.[8]

This seems paradoxical, for in recent times we have learned a great deal about how to preserve almost everything—endangered species, antiquities, art, archives, human life itself. Technology makes long-term conservation increasingly feasible. The means are there, but the ends are missing. The rationale for long-term stewardship is little discussed, let alone debated, still less realized as state or global policy. In the last few decades a plethora of international conventions have championed stewardship of resources for future generations, yet these principles are seldom if ever put into practice.

In this essay I attempt to explore why we have lost sight of the rationale for future stewardship that was well articulated from the late 18th century through the early 20th and have, by default, allowed the demands of the insistent present to dominate government and corporate action.

Sacred and Secular Concerns for the Future

Awareness of distant futures is a feature of most of the world's religions, which sanctify all time past and present.[9] Not that such awareness necessarily connotes much concern or responsibility; "the breathing in and out of the universe by Brahma every four hundred million years," Elise Boulding tartly notes, "is not an image of the future calculated to motivate record-keeping, planning, and action."[10] Yet distinctions between sacred and secular time are largely recent and are not even now embedded in popular thinking. In Judeo-Christian tradition, the length of the secular future varied with the felt imminence of the Second (or First) Coming. Were the end potentially far off, human responsibility to maintain a viable earth might stretch near to infinitude. But if the end were nigh, stewardship was pointless. Nor do doomsayers lament the breakdown of civil order consequent on neglect of the future; indeed, they often welcome signs of social disintegration as confirming the approach of the apocalypse.[11]

Fears of mounting collapse in the wake of the French Revolution engendered the first reasoned arguments for—as distinct from mere attachment to—long-term social stability. Many, to be sure, had always detested change and enjoined permanence as just and pious; but this preference was largely taken for granted. Only toward the end of the 18th century, when heirs of the Enlightenment foresaw an indefinite continuance of scientific and social advance, did they began to consider change historically, and to treat nations as persisting, though changing, social organisms.[12] In such societies, the organic community or commonwealth was treasured as the enduring, if not immortal, possession of all successive generations, not of the present alone. Concern for the future entailed respect for the past, and regard for both past and future were essential to a healthy and harmonious present.

The most eloquent avowal of this perspective was the Irish statesman and philosopher Edmund Burke's *Reflections on the Revolution in France* (1790). In Burke's view, French Jacobins were so inflamed against tradition that they rejected the whole of their past and were thus careless of the future. By contrast, the English, with due regard for what their forebears had bequeathed, took care to cherish what had come down to them and to pass it on to their descendants. And since the creation of such social institutions required [not] one but many lifetimes, a veneration of the past and a regard for the future were essential for their perfection and to their survival.

Bereft of the virtues of English organic traditionalism, in Burke's view, was the French revolutionary cult of newness. "People will not look forward to posterity, who never look backward to their ancestors.... Duration is no object to those who think little or nothing has been done before their time, place all their hopes in discovery, [and] think...that there needs no principle of attachment, except...present conveniency." As a consequence, "the temporary possessors and life-renters [in the French state], unmindful of what they have received from their ancestors, or of what is due to their posterity...act as if they were the entire masters [and] cut off the entail, or commit waste on the inheritance...hazarding to leave to those who come after them a ruin instead of a habitation—and teaching those successors as little respect for their contrivances, as they themselves respected the institutions of their forefathers." Hence "the whole chain and continuity of the commonwealth [are] broken. No one generation link[s] with the others" and life is meanly attenuated. "Men...become little better than the flies of a summer."[13]

Only "a contract...not to be dissolved by fancy" can avert such a calamitous rupture. To forge that contract takes far longer than any single lifetime. And "as the ends of such a partnership cannot be obtained in many generations, it becomes a partnership not only between those who are living, but between those who are living, those who are dead, and those who are to be born." Burke accepts the need for reform but rebukes those impatient for it. "Circumspection and caution are a part of wisdom" in restoring a building; no less so "when the subject of our demolition and construction is not brick and timber, but sentient beings.... A process of this kind is slow," and so it should be. "It is not fit for an assembly, which glories in performing in a few months the work of ages." He assails alike the presentism of Thomas Paine ("we owe nothing to the future") and of Thomas Jefferson ("the dead have no rights").[14]

More than a century after Burke, the French sociologist Emile Durkheim explained why humans generally rely on a construed sense of immortal continuity, an identity that transcends the duration of individual lifetimes. (Such construction comes naturally, for "our elders have talked their memories into our memories until we come to possess some sense of a continuity exceeding and traversing our own individual being.")[15] Social structure requires enduring communities, entities that outlast individual life spans and attach us to the heritage of our forebears and to the legacy we leave our descendants. Hence, as Burke had said, all communities are compacts between the living, the dead, and the yet unborn. Adherence to community implies reaching into a past and a future beyond what any one person can experience, a leap of imagination into two temporal unknowns. To thus extrapolate from personal experience is an essential act of faith without which life would be shorn of meaning. Only awareness of what we owe to those who preceded and concern for those who will follow enables us to care enough to plan ahead, both individually and in concert with our fellows.

Such faith begins, Durkheim stressed, with awareness of what we owe to the past. "We speak a language we did not create; we use instruments we did not invent; we claim rights we did not establish; each generation inherits a treasury of knowledge that it did not itself amass. We owe these varied benefits of civilization to society, and...we know...they are not of our own making." And we respect and revere them because they add mightily to our lives. They are, indeed, "the source of [man's] distinctive nature... help and protect him and guarantee him a privileged fate."[16]

Conserving Nature and Culture in the 19th and 20th Centuries

The virtues of regard for both past and future preached by Burke and explained by Durkheim were widely accepted and extolled during the century between them. Nineteenth-century circumstances were generally congenial to doctrines of stewardship, on behalf of individuals and nations alike. Religious piety enjoined concern for the long-term moral and social consequences not only of deeds but of thoughts. Divine judgment in the hereafter became a still more potent promise and threat, as science made every recorded act and impulse retrievable. "The air itself is one vast library, on whose pages are forever written all that man has ever said," famously warned the evangelical computer inventor Charles Babbage; "the atmosphere we breathe is the ever-living witness of the sentiments we have uttered," while earth and ocean "bear equally enduring testimony of the acts we have committed."[17] Victorian and Edwardian industrialists and city fathers built railroads, aqueducts, and sewer systems, libraries, parks, and gardens intended to endure for centuries to come, not only because they confidently expected to recoup their capital, but from a philanthropic regard for the future. "Society was working not for the small pleasures of today," explained the economist Keynes, "but for the future security and improvement of the race."[18] The immensely enlarged past unfolded by geologists and paleontologists seemed to many to herald a no less extended human future.

Conserving civilization's precious material and intangible legacies for posterity came to be considered crucial to national identity and pride, notably in the wake of Herder's path-breaking recognition of folklife, folklore, and folk structures as iconic to collective identity.[19] But the greatest stimulus to the doctrine of future stewardship was a dawning recognition of the extent of human impact on the natural environment, the threats thereby posed to sustainability, and the need for reform lest future generations inherit a ruined and lifeless earth.

The great pioneer of this insight was the 19th-century New England polymath George Perkins Marsh. Marsh's classic *Man and Nature* (1864) was the first text to cast doubt on, and then to overturn, the then-dominant view that lauded human agency, in obedience to divine command and to civilized advance, for transforming raw nature into an ever more fruitful and productive earth. Above all in Marsh's America, it had previously been a positive virtue, as well as the national destiny, to transform the unproductive wilderness into fields and pastures, towns and cities.

To the contrary, rejoined Marsh, many of mankind's so-called improvements—the felling of trees for timber, the ploughing of soils for intensive agriculture, the damming of rivers for power and industry—had subverted the balance of nature through deforestation and soil erosion, accentuating extremes of flooding and drought, and destroying the ecological stability of watersheds. Both the deliberate and the unintended consequences of reckless developmental greed, undertaken with thought only for the present, were fateful, even fatal. Marsh's apocalyptic warning resounded throughout both the New and the Old World

> [In] parts of Asia Minor, of Northern Africa, of Greece, and even of Alpine Europe…causes set in action by man have brought the face of the earth to a desolation almost as complete as that of the moon…. The earth is fast becoming an unfit home for its noblest inhabitant, and another era of equal human crime and human improvidence…would reduce it to such a condition of impoverished productiveness, of shattered surface, of climatic excess, as to threaten the depravation, barbarism, and perhaps even extinction of the species.[20]

The root cause, in Marsh's view, was lack of concern for the future. "Man has too long forgotten that the world was given to him for usufruct alone, not for consumption, still less for profligate waste." For the sake of our offspring we must mend our prodigal and thriftless ways. Above all, this required forest conservation. "The preservation of existing woods, and the far more costly extension of them where they have been unduly reduced, are among the most obvious of the duties which this age owes to those that are to come." Marsh felt such stewardship "especially incumbent upon Americans" who were deeply indebted to pioneer forebears' "toils and sacrifices," a debt repayable only "by a like self-forgetting care for the moral and material interests of our own posterity."

To heed the future, Americans had first to be more mindful of the past. A restless mobility severed them from home, from forebears, and from tradition. "It is rare that a middle-aged American dies in the house where he was born, or an old man even in that which he has built," noted Marsh. "This life of incessant flitting is unfavorable for the execution of permanent improvements."[21] Farmers shunned tree planting because trees grew slowly: "the longest life [of any individual owner] hardly embraces the seedtime and the harvest of a forest, the value of its timber will not return the capital expended and the interest accrued" for many generations. To plant trees "on a farm he expects to sell, or which he knows will pass out of the hands of his descendants," was poor economy. Hence "the planter of a wood must be actuated by higher motives than those of an investment"—namely, the future well-being of the wider community. And such altruism would serve the present too, Marsh argued; for setting "an approximately fixed ratio" between woodland, pasture, and arable land would reduce the "restlessness" and "instability" of American life. "The very fact of having begun a plantation would attach the proprietor more strongly to the soil for which he had made such a sacrifice."

Marsh initially trusted "enlightened self-interest [to] introduce the reforms, check the abuses, and preserve us from an increase of [the] evils" that he had listed. Unlike Old World serfs, American yeomen owned the land they tilled and could reap the benefits of their own improvements. But selfish individualism, the lure of instant profits, and growing corporate monopoly dimmed Marsh's hopes. Unless it were "his pecuniary interest to preserve them, every proprietor will fell his woods." Only public control could curb maltreatment of nature, protect national resources, and conserve the future commonweal. To be sure, government power spawned official abuse. "But the corruption thus engendered, foul as it is, does not strike so deep as the rottenness of private corporations."[22] Enlightened public management was required to prevent injustice today, desolation tomorrow.

Marsh's prescribed controls flew in the face of customary faith in individual liberty and free enterprise. But his warnings came as a thunderbolt to foresters, land and water engineers, and concerned statesmen in much of the world. In America, the much-heralded end of the frontier made the pace of environmental loss particularly noticeable—and especially alarming, as was the looming threat of a timber famine. Moreover, the industrial pillage and conspicuous waste of the post-Civil War era roused much disquiet. The last decades of the 19th century saw the enactment of unprecedented regulatory controls over environmental resources, notably forests and river regimes. And in a striking reversal of attitudes toward nature, these decades also saw the inception of park and forest reserves explicitly intended to preserve wild and untouched nature for aesthetic and spiritual refreshment forever. So canonical became the credo of future good that even the most avaricious get-rich-quick resource strippers deployed the rhetoric of stewardship for posterity.[23]

Future-oriented public policy-making peaked with President Theodore Roosevelt's official blessing to U.S. forestry chief Gifford Pinchot's national conservation program. Profoundly influenced by *Man and Nature* in his youth, Pinchot like Marsh aimed to husband and improve nature not only for today but for generations to come. And like Marsh, Pinchot sought government ownership to save public resources from private interest and corporate greed, for "the concentration of natural wealth…is one of the greatest of Conservation problems; monopoly of natural resources was only less dangerous to public welfare than their actual destruction." At the start of his forestry career in 1891 "not a single acre of Government, state, or private timberland was under systematic forest management," for "it had not dawned upon [Americans] that timber can be cut without forest destruction, or that the forest can be made to produce crop after crop."[24]

Above all, Pinchot was aghast at grab-and-get-out speculators and lumbermen who ignored the future because, as they and their congressional allies put it, the future had done nothing for them. Pinchot's devotion to the future, his visions of *perpetual* timber supply, *perpetual* forest cover, so alarmed the forestry industry that he had to parry the "misconception that conservation means nothing but the husbanding of resources for future generations." The present mattered as well, he assured them. But "the purpose of Forestry is to make the forest produce the largest possible amount of whatever crop or service will be the most useful, and keep on producing it for generation after generation of men and trees." He had timber in mind, but his dictum applied just as well to aesthetic and environmental benefits. Early Europeans in America could afford to ignore posterity; when soils were exhausted and forests gone, they and their heirs pulled out and went West.

But now the West was won and wholly engrossed; there was no more land; wasteful destruction must cease, bade Roosevelt and Pinchot in 1908. "The patriotic duty of insuring the safety and continuance of the Nation" meant stewarding natural resources against the no longer tenable "right of the individual to injure the future of the Republic for his own present profit."[25] Pinchot's stewardship ethos embodied W. J. McGee's classic goal: "the greatest good of the greatest number for the longest time"; it became, for a time, national policy. No generation had the right "wholly to consume, much less to waste, those sources of life without which the children or the children's children must starve or freeze."[26]

The American conservation movement exemplified, indeed inspired, the English economist A. C. Pigou's dictum that "it was the clear duty of government" to serve as "trustee for unborn generations as well as for its present citizens" against the "rash and reckless despoliation" of natural resources.[27] He noted that "the whole movement for conservation in the United States is based on this conviction." Writing in 1920, Pigou found "wide agreement that the State should protect the interests of the future" to offset, at least "in some degree…our preference for ourselves against our descendants." It was clear to him, as it had been to Marsh, that the time horizon of commerce was too short for enduring public interest; hence "the proper role of government in capitalistic societies," as Lester Thurow recently reiterated, "is to represent the interest of the future to the present."[28]

The Attenuated Postwar Future

Eighty years since Pigou, however, presentist bias is more than ever entrenched in popular attitudes and public policy. The idea of equity between generations remains the unrealized dream of a small minority.[29] This seems paradoxical, for scientists—ecologists, nuclear engineers, geneticists—have at the same time become more and more aware of how present actions pile up consequences for the unforeseeable future. For example, radiation damage has been shown to afflict the great-grandchildren of people exposed. In a risk authority's telling illustration, "the injured of Chernobyl, years after the catastrophe, are not even *all born* yet."[30]

The environmental well-being of our great-grandchildren can to some extent be planned for. But that of much remoter descendants is far more difficult, yet perhaps no less critical to secure. We are ever more aware that current actions have very long-term consequences, and that their impacts for good and for ill need to be factored into what we do. But deciding what precautions to take against nuclear byproducts that remain toxic for 15,000 human generations is exceedingly difficult. The United States has led the search for practical solutions to and realistic scenarios for this daunting problem.[31] But plans to bury nuclear waste in leakproof containers in strata guaranteed geologically stable for 10,000 years have proved hard to activate given anxieties over site selection, transport, and other uncertainties. And even assuming social stability and continuity thus far unprecedented, 10,000 years seems a lamentably brief time-span, since radioactive carbon-14 is lethal in air or groundwater for a million or more years.[32] Whatever the outcome, it is inspiring that a federal appeals court has expressed concern for American lives hundreds of thousands of years hence[33]—the farthest future publicly envisioned since Henry Clay in 1850 reminded fellow senators that "the Constitution of the United States was made not merely for the generation that then existed, but for posterity—unlimited, undefined, endless, perpetual posterity."[34]

For the most part, however, future concern dwindles in inverse proportion to the pressing demands of the voracious present.[35] Advocates of intergenerational equity are far outnumbered by economists who consider market forces and individual interests adequate guarantors of environmental and social heritage,[36] assume that "future generations are likely to be incomparably richer than people alive today,"[37] and rely on future technological miracles to deal, more cheaply and efficiently than can now be done, with our toxic legacies of nuclear waste, land and air and water pollution, lethal additives, corporate bankruptcies, and state indebtedness.[38]

Environmentalists, theologians, philosophers, and heritage managers implore us to have a care for the future, which should matter to us as both biological and cultural progenitors. "Who experiences their child's conception and birth," asks Benedict Anderson, "without dimly apprehending a combined connectedness, fortuity, and fatality in a language of 'continuity'?"[39] The visionary Stewart Brand promotes a long-term mind-set through enduring collective projects, echoing the multi-centuries' construction of medieval cathedrals and the 999-year property leases of Victorian and Edwardian England. One such embodiment of deep time is Daniel Hillis's 10,000-year clock, installed in London's Science Museum, that ticks just once a year, bongs once a century, and whose cuckoo comes out every millennium.[40]

To generate a culture of permanence is a herculean if not an insuperable task, however, for it runs counter to homo sapiens' built-in short-term thinking. The "human brain evidently evolved to commit itself emotionally only to…two or three generations into the future," writes the biologist Edward O. Wilson; to—

> think in this short-sighted way…is a hard-wired part of our Palaeolithic heritage. For hundreds of millennia those who worked for short-term gain… lived longer and left more offspring—even when their collective striving caused their chiefdoms and empires to crumble around them. The long view that might have saved their distant descendants required a vision and extended altruism instinctively difficult to marshal. The great dilemma for environmental reasoning stems from this conflict between short-term and long-term values.[41]

That care for the distant future may be essential to human survival is only now, thanks to bioterrorism and nuclear residues, transparently evident. Ecological counselors rightly lament human shortsightedness; echoing Marsh, they fear that unless we mend our ways the earth will be a wasteland within a few centuries or less.[42]

But who cares? Does the public share such concern? Who now echoes the angst of the New York planetarium visitor of the 1930s who asked a lecturer at the end of his talk on the sun, "Young man, did you say that life on earth would come to an end in three million years?" "No, I said three billion years." "Oh; what a relief!"[43] Who now would share James Jeans's 1928 expectation of two billion years' survival as "taking a very gloomy view of the future?"[44]

Environmental economists calculate one future discount rate for parents exclusively concerned with the welfare of their own immediate progeny, another for those whose concern extends to all humanity, altruists who "reap psychic satisfaction" from having assets transferred to the future, both by themselves and by others.[45] But unlike the Enlightenment philosopher Kant, who believed that humans "could not be indifferent even to the most remote epoch," most moderns sleep undisturbed by what may happen long after their death.[46] "Most human beings do not care in the least about the distant future," Charles Galton Darwin concluded half a century ago. "Most care about the conditions that will affect their children and grandchildren, but beyond that the situation seems too unreal…and uncertainties are too great."[47] After great-grandchildren "few men can project their concerns," held a philosopher in 1972. If some cared about their posthumous reputation, "most of us know that we will be anonymous to future generations and have no reputations to protect."[48]

Today the distant future seems even less real. "What [most] people really want to know," concludes one environmental economist, "is how things will be for their grandchildren."[49] Evidence even of such limited altruistic views is, however, at best scanty. Much of it is merely anecdotal. The economists cited above offer no evidence for selflessness, noting only that they "know numerous individuals who plan never to have children and yet profess great sympathy for the fate of posterity."[50] (It is, of course, one thing to profess sympathy for posterity, quite another to act on it.) My own experience over the last half-century suggests such sympathy has declined. In the early 1950s most of my college students said the future they cared about extended between 150 to 200 years ahead—as long as anyone they themselves might know and love would care about those younger than themselves. A substantial minority claimed they cared what might happen over the unlimited future. Many young people today disdain such long-term horizons. The "future" that concerns them is tomorrow, next weekend, perhaps next year. Few have any sense of themselves as future grandparents, even as parents.[51]

The whole 19th-century bourgeois ideal of life as a progressive career is now becoming obsolete, just as the notion of remaining in one job, or even with the same employer, is outmoded.[52] Attention spans become more and more abbreviated; speed is glorified, what would once have been chided as reckless irresponsibility is now lauded as swift, decisive action. The contemplated future gets ever more attenuated. "When I was a child," says Daniel Hillis, "people used to talk about what would happen by the year 2000. Now, thirty years later [in 1993], they still talk about what would happen by the year 2000. The future has been shrinking by one year per year for my entire life."[53] "When I pronounce the word future," a poet puts it, "the first syllable already belongs to the past."[54]

Spending Our Kids' Legacy

For today's generation the future is less predictable, and more bleak, than for any in at least two centuries. The great majority of North Americans and West Europeans polled in 2002 believed that their children would be worse off than they are;[55] two-thirds of children and young people themselves, in a 1996 Australian national opinion poll, expected their quality of life by 2010 to decline; two out of three British youths consider their prospects poorer than their grandparents', who had suffered World War II bombs, rationing, and unimaginable loss.[56] Since the future

is not only uncertain but apt to be more perilous and less attractive than the present, it is better not to dwell on it at all; we turn a deaf ear to our successors, lest we vilify, disown, abandon, or devour them.[57] Increasingly in the West, children are felt to be a burden; people who have them "are in worse economic shape than they've ever been in," judges a market analyst. "Having a child is now the best indicator" of imminent deep financial trouble.[58]

Any future that does compel attention is apt to be our own, not our children's, much less that of humankind, let alone of planet Earth in eons to come. Long gone are such iconic texts as Olaf Stapledon's *Last and First Men; a Story of the Near and Far Future* (1931) that explored continuity with extremely remote futures. Scholars conjuring up images of humanity's lot a thousand years hence speak to few beyond their own arcane subdiscipline.[59] The vogue for time capsules conveying artifacts and images of our own era to people millennia hence peaked between the 1930s and the 1950s and has since dwindled into obscurity.[60]

In the past, legacies like reputations were meant to be handed down intact; estates were not spent, they were stewarded. Except among environmentalists, stewardship is now out of fashion. Instead of conserving family heritage, we consume it. Inheriting and transmitting give way to self-indulgence, since many find any future too uncertain to be worth planning for. Nuclear fears led some young people in the 1950s to reject parenthood, to eschew mortgages and life insurance—even refusing, Alan Brien recalls, to "make any appointments of any kind more than a week ahead." So imminent seemed the end that it was pointless to plan for any future. Gloomy prognoses long prevailed; one American high school student in three, surveyed in the late 1980s, expected nuclear or biological annihilation within their lifetime.[61] Weakened family bonds and disposable wares curtail the handing on of household goods. "Virtually no one buys a home with the idea that it might become a 'family seat,'" writes Grant McCracken; few household items endure beyond two generations. Unlike our forebears, we rarely envisage descendants as replicas of ourselves.[62]

Decline of belief in a sentient hereafter also weakens posthumous concerns. Few conjure up images of heirs enjoying the legacies we have left them. Instead we muse like mummified Egyptians on what to take with us to the grave: a crowbar and a mobile phone, in case death proves premature; a fire extinguisher, in case divine justice miscarries; or, cannily, a proof of longevity, such as a 100th birthday telegram from Buckingham Palace. Treasures are stored up less for heirs than for our own futures. "We get them, bear them, breed, and nurse" them grumbled the American poet John Trumbull, echoing Joseph Addison's *Spectator*; "What has posterity done for us?"[63] As self-regard supplants intergenerational generosity, concern for the distant future "bespeaks a sort of mental corruption," in Garrett Hardin's phrase, a view he found held, by the mid-1970s, "by some of the most radical as well as some of the most reactionary people of our time."[64] Agonizing over the fate of the future, the historian Robert Heilbroner could think of "no argument based on reason [that] will lead me to care for posterity or to lift a finger in its behalf."[65]

The shift from stewardship to self-gratification is summed up in a cartoon that shows expectant heirs at a reading of the deceased's will: "Being of sound mind and body, I blew it all." The connoisseur who once aimed to leave his children a noble cellar no longer buys wine that will mature after his death; less and less wine is now grown to age. The tailor or shoemaker who once clinched a sale with "This will see you out" today has customers who prefer to outlast their wardrobes. "I don't want long-term bonds," an old woman tells her broker; "I'm so old I don't even buy green bananas any more." To survive long enough means having a future short enough to need no plans.

We increasingly take longevity as our inborn right. A service called "Cards from Beyond" will send your posthumous birthday greetings, with messages like "Take joy in the fact that those of us who have gone on before would give anything to be in your shoes." A few hopeful souls await being thawed from cold storage when a cure is found for what today would have killed them. Cryonic salesmen reckon most people would opt to be frozen if assured they could resume conscious life, however far in the future.[66] "The great problem with the future," in Brand's summary, "is that we die there. This is why it is so hard to take the future personally, especially the longer future, because that

world is suffused by our absence. Its very life emphasizes our helpless death."[67]

The Point of Posterity

What is needed is a modern restatement of Burke's principle.[68] Concern for future generations is not, or at least not mainly, a matter of altruistic self-sacrifice on behalf of people we will never know and who can do nothing for us. Nor is it simply a matter of calculating intergenerational equity, in John Rawls's terms, "balancing…how much [people] would be willing to save for their immediate descendants against what they feel entitled to claim of their immediate predecessors."[69] It is rather a matter of enriching our own lives with depth and purpose. "Human beings have a basic and pervasive need…to extend themselves," holds another philosopher, "to identify themselves as part of larger, ongoing and enduring processes, projects, institutions, and ideals." For "without the idea of posterity"—biological or intellectual—"our lives would be confined, empty, bleak, pointless and morally impoverished."[70] To say, as Rawls does, that "we can do something for posterity but it can do nothing for us," short-changes our imaginative capacity.[71] As beings uniquely capable of envisaging a future, humans have become dependent on doing just that.

Concern for the world to be inherited by generations to come was an Enlightenment obsession. Posterity replaced God as a judge and justifier of human behavior; personified, addressed as a deity, invoked in accents of prayer, posterity was the court of final appeal. It was invoked in the preamble to the United States Constitution and in the speeches of all the American founding fathers. The absence of posterity was unimaginably horrific. Were it known that humanity would become extinct (through a catastrophic comet collision, for example), Diderot predicted that "men would straightway rush into evil courses."[72]

Diderot's doom-laden prophecy is realized in P.D. James's The *Children of Men*, positing a world in which from 1995 on no children are born or conceived. Suicide is rife, lassitude and depression universal. Her protagonist "can understand how the aristocrats and great landowners with no hope of posterity leave their estates untended... . Our minds reach back through centuries for the reassurance of our ancestry, and without hope of posterity, for our race if not for ourselves, without the assurance that we being dead yet live, all pleasures of the mind and senses seem...no more than pathetic and crumbling defences shored up against our ruin.... Man is diminished if he lives without knowledge of his past; without hope of a future he becomes a beast."[73]

It was "the man within the beast" that led Adam Smith to elevate the rights of all humanity above immediate personal well-being, and enabled Heilbroner, glimpsing, like James, "the unbearable anguish" of a universe void of human life, to transcend narrow rationality.[74]

The pre-conditions for future concern are, however, highly demanding. In much of the world, poverty forces an insistence on immediate needs. To feed their children now, Mexican peasants have no choice but to forfeit resources whose loss their children may later bemoan. "We have to cut down trees to feed our families...so that our children can have enough to eat and go to school so they can have a future and more awareness," explained Eligio Corona. "The tragedy...is that, to feed his children today, he has to destroy that which would give them sustenance tomorrrow."[75]

"People take the long view when they feel a commitment to...posterity—their children and other people's children—and therefore see the need for actions to benefit the distant future." But they can afford to take that view, adds a management expert, only "when they believe the rules of the game are fair [and that] they will share equitably in the returns."[76]

Half a century ago the future was a bright and shining promise. Scientific progress, faith in social engineering, and impatience with tradition engendered countless cornucopian forecasts. The archetypal future, noted architectural historian Reyner Banham, was "a city of gleaming, tightly clustered towers, with helicopters fluttering about their heads and monorails snaking around their feet; all enclosed...under a vast transparent dome," where life would be "unmitigated bliss." Sometime around the late 1960s that modernist utopia disappeared. The future became a thing of the past. Visions of the white heat of technology gave way to hand-lettered tracts extolling pastoral scenes of "windmills and families holding hands."[77] Heritage, roots, and historic preservation made the past our favored abode to escape the fears and the perils of the present. The nostalgized past, I noted, was by the 1980s "the foreign country with the most profitable and rapidly growing tourist trade of them all."[78]

Could investment in the future now perhaps offer comparable rewards? That the future has become more open and less predictable, uncertain rather than foreordained, ought not to deter but to encourage engagement with it. We can still hearten venturers to chart ways beyond the present pall of gloom. Biologists suggest that biomedical research within the next quarter century may double our lifetimes; our grandchildren may coexist with five generations of their descendants. Physicists float prospects of being "truly at home in the universe" 50 years from now, when we'll probably know more about its history and properties "than we know now about...the surface of our planet."[79] Astronomer Martin Rees foresees a future shaped by human decisions that infuse the universe with "a teeming complexity of life beyond what we can even conceive."[80]

That the future, near and far alike, holds huge risks is undeniable. There is a small but finite possibility that we will "not survive the machinations of a technologically very knowledgeable, very depressed Luddite."[81] Rees himself fears that bioterror or bioerror will lead to a million casualties in a single event within the next 15 years.[82] Let us start coping with rather than shrinking from potential anthropogenic calamity, just as forward-looking science strives to deflect potential natural catastrophes like asteroid impacts and comet collisions. A century after Theodore Roosevelt bade us heed posterity's needs, another president's State of the Union message echoed his "responsibility to future generations...to build a better world for our children and grandchildren."[83] To carry out this pledge requires renewal of the stewardly commitment that inspired the first American conservation movement. We lend force to that inspiration when we see how we enrich our own lives, as well, through communion with the enduring collective humanity to which we owe our being and belonging.

ENDNOTES

1. Ivana Milojevic and Sohail Inayatullah, "Futures Dreaming: Challenges Outside and on the Margins of the Western World," *Futures* 35, no. 5 (June 2003): 493–507.

2. Bank of England notice, February 20, 2001; David Lowenthal, letter, "From Here to Eternity," February 27, 2001; Father Jonathan A. Hemmings, letter, "From Here to Eternity," (March 1, 2001), all in *The Times* (London).

3. Pfizer advertisement, *International Herald Tribune* (October 9, 2003); NTT DoCoMo ad, *International Herald Tribune* (October 11–12, 2003).

4. Alvin Toffler, *Future Shock* (London: Pan Books, 1971), 55.

5. Christopher Lasch, *The Culture of Narcissism* (New York: W.W. Norton, 1978), 211.

6. John Kotré, *Outliving the Self: Generativity and the Interpretation of Lives* (Baltimore, MD: Johns Hopkins University Press, 1984), 1.

7. The World Commission on Environment and Development, *Our Common Future* (Oxford, UK: Oxford University Press, 1987).

8. Daniel W. Bromley, *Environment and Economy: Property Rights and Public Policy* (Oxford, UK: Blackwell, 1999), 87.

9. Emmanuel Agius and Lionel Chircop, *Caring for Future Generations: Jewish, Christian and Islamic Perspectives* (Westport, CT: Praeger, 1998).

10. Elise Boulding, "The Dynamics of Imaging Futures," *World Future Society Bulletin* 12, no. 5 (September 1978): 6.

11. Eugen Weber, *Apocalypses: Prophesies, Cults, and Millennial Beliefs through the Ages* (Cambridge, MA: Harvard University Press, 1999); Paul Boyer, *When Time Shall Be No More: Prophecy Belief in Modern American Culture* (Cambridge, MA: Harvard University Press, 1992), 141.

12. I discuss this transition in *The Past Is a Foreign Country* (Cambridge, UK: Cambridge University Press, 1985) and in *The Heritage Crusade and the Spoils of History* (Cambridge, UK: Cambridge University Press, 1998), chapter 1.

13. Edmund Burke, *Reflections on the Revolution in France* [1790] (London: Dent, 1910), 31, 85, 92.

14. Ibid., 93. On Paine's and Jefferson's sovereignty of each generation, see Lowenthal, *The Past Is a Foreign Country*, 108.

15. Conor Cruise O'Brien, *Memoir: My Life and Themes* (London: Profile Books, 1999), 117.

16. Emile Durkheim, *The Elementary Forms of Religious Life* [1912], trans. Karen E. Fields (New York: Free Press, 1995), 213–214, 351–352, 372, 379.

17. Charles Babbage, *The Ninth Bridgewater Treatise: A Fragment*, 2d. ed. [1838] (London: Frank Cass, 1967), 112–115.

18. John Maynard Keynes, *The Economic Consequences of the Peace* [1919], in his *Collected Writings* (Cambridge, UK: Macmillan/Cambridge University Press, 1971), 2, 12, 41; "Futures—Confidence from Chaos," *Futures* 1, no. 1 (September 1968): 3.

19. Johann Gottfried von Herder, *Reflections on the Philosophy of the History of Mankind* (1784–91), ed. Frank E. Manuel (Chicago: University of Chicago Press, 1968).

20. George P. Marsh, *Man and Nature; or Physical Geography as Modified by Human Action* [1864] (Seattle: University of Washington Press, 2003), 42–43, 186–187.

21. George P. Marsh, Address Delivered before the Agricultural Society of Rutland County, September 30, 1847 (Rutland, VT, 1848), 17–19.

22. Ibid., 189, 277–280.

23. David Lowenthal, *George Perkins Marsh, Prophet of Conservation* (Seattle: University of Washington Press, 2003), chapters 13 and 14.

24. Gifford Pinchot, *Breaking New Ground* (New York: Harcourt, Brace, 1947), 27, 32.

25. Ibid., 32; "Theodore Roosevelt (1908)," in *American Environmentalism: Readings in Conservation History*, 3rd ed., ed. Roderick Frazier Nash (New York: Knopf, 1990), 52.

26. William John McGee, "Conserving Natural Resources" (1909–10), in Nash, *American Environment*, 45.

27. Arthur C. Pigou, *The Economics of Welfare* (1920), 4th ed. (London: Macmillan, 1952), 27ff.

28. Lester Thurow, *The Future of Capitalism* (New York: Penguin, 1997), 16.

29. Hazel Muir, "Suffer the Children," *New Scientist* (May 11, 2002): 5, citing Proceedings of the National Academy of Sciences 99, no. 21 (October 15, 2002): 68–77; Ulrich Beck, "Risk Society and the Provident State," in *Risk, Environment, and Modernity: Towards a New Ecology*, eds. Scott Lash, Bronislaw Szerszynski, and Brian Wynn (London: Sage, 1996), 27–43.

30. Kai Erikson, *A New Species of Trouble: Explorations in Disaster, Trauma, and Community* (New York: W.W. Norton, 1994), 203–225. See also "Chernobyl's Toll," *New Scientist* (May 21, 2004): 7.

31. Kathleen M. Trauth, Stephen C. Hora, and Robert Guzowski, *Expert Judgment on Markers to Deter Inadvertent Human Intrusion into the Waste Isolation Pilot Plant* (Albuquerque, NM: Sandia National Laboratories, 1993), cited in Julia Bryan-Wilson, "Building a Marker of Nuclear Warning," in *Monuments and Memory, Made and Unmade*, eds. Robert S. Nelson and Margaret Olin (Chicago, IL: University of Chicago Press, 2003), 183–204; Martin J. Pasqualetti, "Landscape Permanence and Nuclear Warnings," *Geographical Review* 87, no. 1 (January 1997): 73–91.

32. Thomas G. Hanks, Isaac J. Winograd, R. Ernest Anderson, Thomas E. Reilly, and Edwin P. Weeks, *Yucca Mountain as a Radioactive-Waste Repository*, U.S. Geological Survey Circular 1184 (Washington, DC: U.S. Government Printing Office, 1999), 15, 19. On the general issue, see Richard and Val Routley, "Nuclear Energy and Obligations to the Future" [1978], in *Responsibilities to Future Generations: Environmental Ethics*, ed. Ernest Partridge (Buffalo, NY: Prometheus Books, 1981), 277–301; Clive L. Spash, "Economics, Ethics, and Long-Term Environmental Damages," *Environmental Ethics* 15 (Summer 1993): 117–132.

33. Matthew. L. Wald, "Court Hears Arguments on Waste Site in Nevada," *New York Times* (January 15, 2004). A recent ruling reflects widespread doubts that the long-delayed Yucca Mountain nuclear waste repository would ever be licensed (Judge Susan G. Braden, Court of Federal Claims, cited in Matthew L. Wald, "Nuclear Waste Ruling," *International Herald Tribune* [April 28, 2005]).

34. Henry Clay, speech in the U.S. Senate, January 29, 1850.

35. Peter G. Brown, *Ethics, Economics and International Relations: Transparent Sovereignty in the Commonwealth of Life* (Edinburgh: Edinburgh University Press, 2000), 82.

36. James K. Glassman, September 22, 2003, cited in Carlo Stagnaro and Alberto Mingardi, "The 'Rights' of Future Generations," at http://www.techcentralstation.be; accessed April 27, 2005.

37. Wilfred Beckerman and Joanna Pasek, *Justice, Posterity, and the Environment* (Oxford, UK: Oxford University Press, 2001), 194–195.

38. See, for example, David Leonhardt, "U.S. Policy Fixated on Short Term," *International Herald Tribune* (May 26, 2003): 10. Christian Azar and Stephen H. Schneider, "Are the Economic Costs of Stabilising the Atmosphere Prohibitive?" *Ecological Economics* 42, no. 1 and 2 (2002): 73–80, charge that studies deploring carbon abatement policies as economically crippling vastly over-inflate actual costs.

39. Benedict Anderson, *Imagined Communities: Reflections on the Origin and Spread of Nationalism* (London: Verso, 1983), 18–19.

40. Stewart Brand, *The Clock of the Long Now: Time and Responsibility* (New York: Basic Books, 1999), 2–3. A precursor to Brand's Long Now Foundation was Gerald Feinberg's The *Prometheus Project: Mankind's Search for Long-Range Goals* (New York: Doubleday, 1968). An early prototype of Hillis's clock was Hisashige Tanaka's 1851 "Man-nen dokei," an ornate six-faced clock recently restored at Tokyo's Science Museum (John Boyd, "10,000-Year Japanese Clock Springs Back to Life," *New Scientist* [March 19, 2005]: 25).

41. Edward O. Wilson, *The Future of Life* (New York: Knopf, 2002), 40–41.

42. See, for example, Judith Miller, Stephen Engelberg, and William Broad, *Germs: Biological Weapons and America's Secret War* (New York: Simon & Schuster, 2001).

43. In the astronomer Martin Rees's version of this anecdote, the sun burns the earth to a crisp 6 billion rather than 6 million years hence (*Our Final*

Century: Will Civilisation Survive the 21st Century? [London: Heinemann, 2003], 182). A standard current estimate for the extinction of life on earth is 500 million years. See Peter D. Ward and Donald Brownlee, *The Life and Death of Planet Earth* (New York: Times Books, 2003).

44. James Jeans, *Eos or the Wider Aspect of Cosmogeny* (London: Kegan Paul, 1928), 12–13.

45. Richard B. Howarth and Richard B. Norgaard, "Intergenerational Transfers and the Social Discount Rate," *Environmental & Resource Economics* 3, no. 4 (1993): 337–358 at 345–352. See Stephen A. Marglin, "The Social Rate of Discount and the Optimal Rate of Investment," *Quarterly Journal of Economics* 77 (February 1963): 95–111.

46. John A. Passmore, *Man's Responsibility for Nature; Ecological Problems and Western Traditions* (London: Duckworth, 1974).

47. Charles Galton Darwin, *The Next Million Years* (New York: Doubleday, 1953), 207.

48. Thomas Sieger Derr, *Ecology and Human Need* [1972], reprinted in his "The Obligation to the Future," in *Responsibilities to Future Generations*, ed. Partridge, 37–44 at 39.

49. Richard B. Norgaard, "Optimists, Pessimists, and Science," *BioScience* 52, No. 3 (March 2002): 287–292 at 287.

50. Richard B. Howarth and Richard B. Norgaard, "Intergenerational Choices Under Global Environmental Change," in *Handbook of Environmental Economics*, ed. Daniel W. Bromley (Oxford, UK: Blackwell, 1995), 135, note 7.

51. Elaine Tyler May, *Barren in the Promised Land: Childless Americans and the Pursuit of Happiness* (Cambridge, MA: Harvard University Press, 1996); Madelyn Cain, *The Childless Revolution: What It Means to be Childless Today* (Cambridge, UK: Perseus, 2001).

52. Jonas Frykman and Orvar Löfgren, *Culture Builders: A Historical Anthropology of Middle-Class Life* (New Brunswick, NJ: Rutgers University Press, 1987), 29–30. I address this presentist trend in "The Forfeit of the Future," *Futures* 27, no. 4 (May 1995): 385–395, and "The Disenchanted Future," in *Progress: Geographical Essays*, ed. Robert E. Sack (Baltimore, MD: Johns Hopkins University Press, 2002), 61–77.

53. Daniel Hillis quoted in Brand, *Clock of the Long Now*, 2–3.

54. Wislawa Szymborska, "The three oddest words," *New York Times Magazine* (December 1, 1996): 49.

55. Pew global attitudes survey, *International Herald Tribune* (December 5, 2002): 8. Widespread pessimism about the future is confirmed in a June-August 2004 Gallup poll covering 60,000 people in 60 countries. See *International Herald Tribune* (November 19, 2004). See also Dennis Morgan, "Images of the Future: A Historical Perspective," *Futures* 34, no. 9 (November 2002): 889–893; Johan Galtung and Haakan Wiberg, eds., "Democracy Works: People, Experts and the Future," special issue of *Futures* 35, no. 2 (March 2003) assessing the accuracy of predictions made a generation back in Helmut Ornauer, Haakan Wiberg, Andrzej Sicinski, and Johan Galtung, eds., *Images of the World in the Year 2000: A Comparative Ten Nation Study* (The Hague, NL: Mouton, 1976).

56. Richard Eckersley, "Dreams and Expectations: Young People's Expected and Preferred Futures and Their Significance for Education," *Futures* 31, no. 1 (February 1999): 73–90; Populus poll cited in "Generation Ex," *The Times* (London) (October 30, 2003).

57. Kotré, *Outliving the Self*, 9, 18. These negative futures are explored by Erik H. Erikson in *Young Man Luther* (New York: Norton, 1958); and idem, *Gandhi's Truth* (New York: Norton, 1969).

58. James Surowiecki, "Leave No Parent Behind," *New Yorker* (August 18 and 25, 2003): 48, citing Elizabeth Warren and Amelia Warren Tyagi, *The Two-Income Trap* (New York: Basic Books, 2003).

59. For example, Seth Valamoor and Paige Heydon, ed., "Humanity 3000," special issue of *Futures* 32, no. 6 (August 2000): 509–612. The brief flurry of future interest triggered by the approach of the new millennium has left little trace. See Stephen Jay Gould, Umberto Eco, Jean-Claude Carrière, and Jean Delumeau, *Conversations about the End of Time*, ed. Catherine David, Frédéric Lenoir, and Jean-Philippe de Tonnac; trans. Ian Maclean and Roger Pearson (London: Penguin, 2000).

60. Jarvis, *Time Machines*, 138–174.

61. James W. Loewen, *Lies My Teacher Told Me: Everything Your American History Textbook Got Wrong* (New York: New Press, 1995), 263.

62. Grant McCracken, *Culture and Consumption: New Approaches to the Symbolic Character of Consumer Goods and Activities* (Bloomington: Indiana University Press, 1988), 42–43, 50; Carole Shammas, Marylynn Salmon, and Michael Dahlin, eds., *Inheritance in America from Colonial Times to the Present* (New Brunswick, NJ: Rutgers University Press, 1987), 211–212; Victor G. Kiernan, "Private Property in History," in *Family and Inheritance: Rural Society in Western Europe 1200–1800,* eds. Jack Goody, Joan Thirsk, and Edward P. Thompson (Cambridge, UK: Cambridge University Press, 1976), 397.

63. John Trumbull, "McFingal" [1782], canto II, lines 121ff; *The Spectator*, no. 583 (August 20, 1714).

64. Garrett Hardin, "Why Plant a Redwood Tree?" [1974], in his *Naked Emperors: Essays of a Taboo-Stalker* (Los Altos, CA: William Kaufman, 1982), 160–163.

65. Robert L. Heilbroner, "What Has Posterity Ever Done for Me?" *New York Times Magazine* (January 19, 1975), reprinted in *Partridge, Responsibilites to Future Generations*, 191–194.

66. Morton Schatzman, "Cold Comfort at Death's Door," *New Scientist* (September 26, 1992): 36–39; but see Phil Bagnall, "Cold Comfort for Christmas," *New Scientist* (December 23, 1995): 74.

67. Brand, *Clock of the Long Now,* 150.

68. Burke's significance was noted in a 1972 essay exhorting "reverence not just for the political, or even the social, order but for an inheritance so great that we have scarcely noticed it until recently"—that of nature. See "Notes and Comments: Concerning Conservation and Conservatism," *New Yorker* (May 13, 1972).

69. John Rawls, *A Theory of Justice* (Oxford, UK: Oxford University Press, 1980), 289.

70. Ernest Partridge, "Why Care about the Future?" in his *Responsibilities toward Future Generations*, 203–220 at 218–219.

71. Rawls, *Theory of Justice*, 291.

72. Carl L. Becker, *The Heavenly City of the Eighteenth-Century Philosophers* (New Haven: Yale University Press, 1932), 140–148.

73. Phyllis D. James, *The Children of Men* (London: Faber & Faber, 1992), 10–12, 114–115.

74. Heilbroner, "What Has Posterity Ever Done for Me?"

75. Lourdes Arizpe, "Perceiving Others as Guilty, Vulnerable, or Responsible," in *Culture and Global Change: Social Perception of Deforestation in the Lacandona Rain Forest in Mexico*, eds. Lourdes Arizpe, Fernanda Paz, and Margarita Velazquez (Ann Arbor: University of Michigan Press, 1996), 59–73 at 66–68.

76. Rosabeth Moss Kanter, *On the Frontiers of Management* (Cambridge, MA: Harvard University Press, 1999), 281–284.

77. Reyner Banham, "Come in 2001…," *New Society* (January 8, 1976): 62–63.

78. Lowenthal, *Past Is a Foreign Country*, 4.

79. Lee Smolin, "The Future of the Nature of the Universe," in *The Next Fifty Years: Science in the First Half of the Twenty-First Century*, ed. John Brockman (New York: Vintage, 2002), 9.

80. Martin Rees, "Our Changing Cosmic Perspecive and the Scope and Limits of Physical Laws," in *Meeting the Challenges of the Future*, Balzan Symposium 2002, ed. Walter Ruegg (Florence, Italy: Leo S. Olschki, 2003), 9.

81. Luigi Luca Cavalli-Sforza, "Are There Limits to Knowledge?" in Ruegg, *Meeting the Challenges of the Future*, 57.

82. Rees, *Our Final Century*, 74.

83. George W. Bush, "State of the Union Message to Congress and the Country," *New York Times* (February 3, 2005): A18.

REBECCA MEYER, SHANNON STRUBLE, AND PHYLLIS CATSIKIS

"Sustainability: A Review"

Written for this volume.

Introduction

Sustainability: the first connotation that is likely to come to mind today is *environmental* sustainability. This is a crucial type of sustainability, and resources on the subject abound. There are also, however, *economic* and *social* aspects of sustainability. Considering all three aspects of sustainability is critical to making the best sustainability decisions for cultural heritage institutions. We suggest that the universal recycling symbol (Figure 1), one of the best-known signs of the green movement, can be a visual metaphor for this relationship. All three aspects of sustainability inform and support one another in an integrated whole.

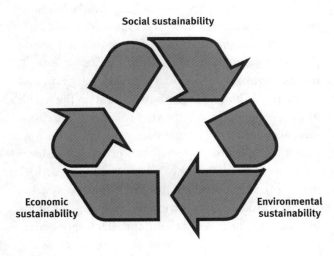

Social sustainability

Economic sustainability

Environmental sustainability

Figure 1.

Katy Lithgow, Head of Conservation at the National Trust, a UK organization dedicated to the preservation of buildings and natural history, refers to the three aspects of sustainability as "The Triple

Bottom Line." She identifies the first appearance of this concept in Freer Spreckley's 1981 book *Social Audit: A Management Tool for Co-operative Working*.[1] The three aspects of sustainability are often discussed separately in the literature, and often in relation to one type of cultural heritage institution. This is unfortunate, since there has been so much effort in recent years to break down institutional silos. Nevertheless, aspects of sustainability discussed in one specific type of cultural heritage institution are often applicable to other types.

Environmental Sustainability

As cultural heritage institutions recognize the imperative for environmental sustainability, libraries, archives, and museums must respond to the need for greener buildings. In the literature, sources address an increasing awareness of climate change and the need for strategies of mitigation and adaptation to reduce buildings' environmental impact and respond to future changes. As Avrami notes, "the climate change effects of greenhouse gas emissions, while debated, are well documented and widely acknowledged, as are the alarming contributions of the built environment to that carbon footprint."[2] Statistics indicate the immense impact buildings have on the environment.[3] Buildings use energy for heating, lighting, and electricity, and, therefore, emit carbon dioxide, generate waste and pollutants, consume natural resources, and contribute to the loss of natural habitat.

Many professional and technical guidelines now exist that encourage cultural heritage institutions to demonstrate accountability through responsible energy use. Webb stresses the need for museums to take greater responsibility for "the broader environmental impacts of environmental control."[4] Also addressing museums, Staniforth notes the need not only to "mitigate further climate change by reducing energy consumption and changing from fossil fuels to renewables," but also to adapt by making buildings "more resilient in the face of extreme weather events."[5] According to Brown in his "Future-Proof Design," sustainable library design means adaptability to meet the environmental and social realities of the future by engaging the community and featuring flexible facilities, reconfigurable spaces, multifunctional forms such as green or solar panel roofs, energy-positive capabilities, reusable building components, waste and water management, and disaster resistance.[6] Strategies for disaster resistance incorporate risk assessment; site selection; site planning; power supply, management, and storage; and passive design elements such as natural daylighting and natural ventilation.[7] Adopting sustainable design practices demonstrates a commitment to the strategies of mitigation and adaptation.

More general government recommendations and requirements regarding responsible energy use also exist. The US Green Building Council's Leadership in Energy and Environmental Design (LEED) rating system provides institutions with guidelines for effective resource and energy management. Library and museum sources document the development of standards and the importance of measuring a building's environmental performance as a way of showing commitment to sustainable design. Following its establishment in 2000, LEED rapidly gained "momentum as the standard for green design," as evidenced by Brown who noted the increasing number of LEED projects for green library design in 2003.[8] Numerous articles, including Antonelli's overview of green library actions from 1979–2008 and Stoss's 2010 study of green library resources, address library green building initiatives that have sought LEED certification.[9] According to Brophy and Wylie, museums are also among a growing number of buildings in a "green building movement" worldwide.[10] Litt and Brener both describe how museums are becoming more environmentally responsible through changes

in museum design and attention to LEED standards.[11] Recent literature continues to document the growing number of LEED-certified buildings, and many studies attest to the advances made by cultural heritage institutions.[12]

Sustainable buildings should maximize energy efficiency in a regional climate setting and minimize their impact on the built and natural environment locally and globally. Sources that provide overviews of sustainable building design and practice for libraries and museums identify recurrent central concerns, principles, and strategies of sustainable building.[13] Creating a sustainable building requires an understanding of institutional mission and promotion of an integrated design team approach.[14] Sustainable siting and orientation of green buildings should consider all aspects of their impact upon the local and global environment, and accommodate such things as recycling, waste management, alternative transportation, light pollution, landscaping, green roofs, water conservation, sensitivity to the surrounding microclimate and ecosystem, and local building traditions. Materials used should include certified wood (from ethically responsible forest management) and those that are readily renewable, locally available, nontoxic, low-emitting, and with recycled content.

Green building conditions that reduce impact on the surrounding natural environment also create an indoor environment conducive to the preservation of the materials housed in the building and to the health of the people using it. Attention to "specific environmental parameters" for maintaining the physical condition of collection materials is a primary consideration, as is balancing the "occasionally conflicting" needs of collections and people.[15] Energy systems should include energy-saving technologies for lighting, heating, and ventilation, and electricity generation from renewable sources of energy such as the sun and the wind. A healthy indoor environment is one that is monitored for air quality and energy use, in which green fittings and furnishings and cleaning products are used.

Research into the relationship between people and the built environment reveals that buildings exert a powerful effect upon their occupants. Writers in the library literature have drawn attention to the benefits of green buildings to the physical and mental well-being of their users. Twenty-five years ago, Veatch studied the relationship between the human experience and the built environment, psychologically, in terms of perception and human spatial behavior, and ergonomically, in terms of performance.[16] A few years later, James and Suzanne LaRue addressed concern over "Sick Building Syndrome," a toxic indoor environment caused by air pollution from contaminated ventilation systems that trap toxins from materials, cleaning supplies, and carpeting.[17] Windows are crucial in providing library users and staff with ventilation and sunlight. Waters maintains that planting and growing trees around library buildings has a positive impact on librarians and library users in addition to the environmental benefits of net cooling effect, carbon dioxide absorption, and improvement of water quality. According to Waters, "research has shown that visual exposure to settings with trees" results in considerable stress reduction.[18] It is important to note that Waters' position is at odds with long-established preservation practice which advises against having plants in and immediately around buildings that house collections. More in tune with this traditional advice are integrated pest management (IPM) recommendations for limiting or removing plants inside and in close proximity to repository buildings.[19] IPM is intended to prevent infestations, thus avoiding the use of pesticides and fumigants and preventing irreversible damage. Effective IPM is environmentally friendly in the sense that it eliminates or reduces the need for the use of harmful chemicals, so institutions need to consider the balance between the benefits and risks of greenery in and around their buildings. This issue provides one example of the tensions in environmental sustainability that are often evident between collection preservation needs, the needs of the building's inhabitants, and the needs of the natural environment.

Lighting strategies for green buildings must also balance the needs of people and of the environment to provide effective levels of indoor light for user activities, energy efficiency, and lighting that is sensitive to surrounding ecologies. Library sources address new lighting technology, day lighting, and exterior night lighting. According to McCabe, advances in "energy-

efficient and labor-saving applications" are aiding the adjustability of light levels while power-producing technologies are allowing libraries to adapt to on-site power-generating systems including solar power.[20] New designs for atria and skylights admit natural light and incorporate the necessary sun control devices.[21] According to Dean, library lighting should provide the reader with the proper illumination level while minimizing solar heat gain. He suggests that the use of natural light in a well-designed library can be more energy-efficient in the long term as well as more pleasant for the library staff and users.[22] As with plants and pest management in cultural heritage institutions, however, preservation needs should be considered when choosing lighting, as it is well established that sunlight damages many materials making the admission of natural light inappropriate in many circumstances.[23] Furthermore, LED lights, which are often recommended as a more environmentally-friendly lighting option, should be used with caution for illuminating objects susceptible to light damage because of their relative newness and lack of established data and standards.[24] Finally, Gallina and Mandyck advocate "dark sky lighting" as "safe, energy efficient, and environmentally sound."[25] The goal of exterior night lighting for libraries should be the reduction of light pollution (including light trespass, glare, and sky glow) and "a more conscious lighting design" that uses less energy and minimizes impact on the surrounding natural environment.

Sustainable buildings support a design that is "collaborative with nature" and takes inspiration from nature's design to minimize impact on the earth's resources.[26] Regional design approaches that adapt buildings to local environmental conditions are an important concern to cultural heritage institutions. Lachel discusses the benefits of creating sustainable museums using an approach known as "biophiliac design." Creating museums that mimic natural settings can elicit the same deep response people have for nature. Featuring local, natural materials and physical and visual contact with nature, biophiliac museums aim to combine energy efficiency with the positive effects of daylight and natural ventilation.[27] Consistent with biophiliac approaches to design, the Taiwanese government's construction of a new Taipei

Public Library branch is based on an eco-architectural concept situating the building harmoniously within the park that surrounds it. Tseng reports that specially designed desks and chairs "make patrons feel as if they are sitting in the woods," while the building's wood and steel construction "has the appearance of an oversized tree house."[28] Plants on the library's green roof "meld with the outdoor landscape" providing a green habitat.[29] Archives also use nature as a guide for designing sustainable buildings. Lebel considers the adaptation of archival building construction to tropical conditions on the French Caribbean island of Saint Martin.[30] Rowoldt and Hioki explore the use of local building traditions as a model for adapting archives buildings to local climate conditions in South Africa and Japan.[31]

Archives, museums, and libraries have much in common when it comes to meeting the needs of collections and of people in sustainable building design. Kim reviews the benefits to archives and risks of green construction, noting that green construction methods should be applied on a case-by-case basis depending on "the unique figure of archival facilities."[32] For museums, management of collections can also be compatible with green building practices, so a sustainable design approach must consider users as well as collections and attempt to balance the needs of both. Sue Wilkinson and her colleagues explain that collection "growth" is not just about increasing holdings or building bigger, newer buildings, but about connecting people with collections.[33] Just as collection growth in museums can be interpreted in various ways that reflect awareness of environmental sustainability, collection limits in libraries can also be a form of growth and greenness. Loder discusses how academic libraries' green building strategies, the shift to new technology (such as increased use of electronic resources and scanning of analog materials), and attention to collection size are benefiting users and reflecting the library's changing mission as an "intellectual gathering place."[34]

ENVIRONMENTAL CONTROL FOR PRESERVATION AND CONSERVATION

Adopting environmentally friendly strategies is fairly straightforward for a home or an office building. Cul-

tural heritage institutions, however, have a responsibility to take care of their collections, and this presents specific challenges when it comes to environmental sustainability.

It is not new knowledge that pollution is one of the biggest threats to cultural heritage objects. Writing in 1965, Thomson began with the assertion that "Most of the evil effects of the dirt and acid gases in town air on art and architecture have been recognized in a general way for more than a century."[35] Kucera and Fitz make a similar assertion: "The detrimental effects of air pollutants on materials exposed to the atmosphere have been known for a very long time and the adverse effects of smoke from coal burning was acknowledged several centuries ago."[36] These authors do not cite sources for their assertions, but they recall John Ruskin's "golden stain of time" in *The Seven Lamps of Architecture*, which Staniforth cites as an early expression of prevention- and maintenance-centered (rather than restoration-centered) preservation philosophy.[37] In addition, Grzywacz cites a passage from Homer concerning soot damage as evidence of early awareness of the effects of pollution on objects. Grzywacz also cites Thomson's article as a landmark in this understanding of the role of pollution, and describes Thomson's 1994 book *The Museum Environment* as including significant information on the topic.[38]

Environmental issues such as rising sea levels and air pollution are of great and immediate concern to organizations dedicated to the protection of buildings and monuments. UNESCO has demonstrated awareness and concern about the impact of climate change in recent years.[39] The UNESCO *Policy Document on the Impacts of Climate Change on World Heritage Properties* states that "Small Island Developing States (SIDS) are most vulnerable" to climate change effects, such as "sea level rise and severity of extreme weather conditions," but affirms "that the impacts of climate change are affecting many and are likely to affect many more World Heritage properties, both natural and cultural, in the years to come."[40] Reasons for this are given in the UNESCO documents on climate change and summarized by Cassar in her *Climate Change and the Historic Environment*:

Old buildings, archaeological sites, and historic parks and gardens are put at risk by the same dangers to the wider environment—flooding, coastal erosion, subsidence and possibly increased storminess—which have already been identified by other climate change studies. However, they present in addition a number of complexities that suggest they may be especially imperiled.

Changes in rainfall patterns and temperatures, even where these may not be perceived as a major threat to modern buildings, are likely to have dramatic effects on buried or exposed archaeological sites.... For old buildings and their preserved contents the problems are also likely to prove acute; it has long been understood that fluctuations in the local microclimate present the main danger to continued survival. Historic building materials are extremely permeable to the environment of air and soil; changes in moisture content can occur rapidly, and these can activate damaging cycles of salt crystallisation. Old rainwater goods may be unable to cope with changed patterns of rainfall, and acute events such as flooding have much worse and longer-term effects on historic than on modern buildings.[41]

Thus far in preservation practice, an effective and widely adopted method for protecting collections from damaging environmental conditions and pollutants has been environmental monitoring and control. This method does, however, have limits; it is possible to store a collection of objects in sealed, stable environmental conditions, but not to keep entire historic buildings thus. Protecting historic buildings from harmful environmental conditions requires addressing the planet's environmental conditions. This too has implications for collections, as many historic buildings house collections; the vulnerability of buildings renders the collections they house vulnerable also.

Another issue with environmental monitoring and control is that it tends to be energy-intensive, which is problematic in terms of environmental sustainability, as well for the economic or financial sustainability of cultural heritage institutions. The traditional, widely accepted parameters for environmental control are a stable temperature below 70 degrees F and a relative humidity of 30–50% maintained constantly.[42] Artigas cites an email from Dr. Shin Makaewa of The Getty Conservation Institute stating that maintaining these conditions typically costs $3 per square foot per year.[43] Brophy and Wiley claim that cultural heritage institutions that maintain environmental control conditions can use nearly twice as much energy as conventional office buildings.[44] They do not cite a source for this figure; it is likely an estimate based on the assumption that, because cultural heritage buildings maintain favorable environmental conditions at all times, they maintain these conditions for approximately twice as long as do office buildings that maintain the environment for human comfort only during business hours. Although no sources are cited for this assertion, which is troubling, it is generally accepted that reducing a building's temperature overnight reduces energy costs.[45]

Use of environmentally friendly fuels in maintaining environmental control could certainly reduce the environmental footprint, but this is not necessarily feasible for many institutions. Furthermore, as May Cassar, director of the Centre for Sustainable Heritage at the University College of London, asserts: "Replacing fossil fuels with other forms of energy while still consuming the same amount is not a sustainable strategy—we need to learn to do more with less."[46] A possible solution for reducing the environmental impact of environmental control that has emerged in recent years is to reconsider the stringency of control guidelines.

In 2009, the National Museum Directors' Conference (NMDC), a UK-based organization, released its *Guiding Principles for Reducing Museums' Carbon Footprint*, which acknowledged that "[s]eeking to achieve an internationally agreed narrow environmental standard for temperature and relative humidity has resulted in an unnecessarily high energy use."[47] The recommendations encourage institutions to consider their local climate when deciding on appropriate targets for environmental control. In the Spring of 2010, the Museum of Fine Arts, Boston and the Getty Conservation Institute held a conference titled "Rethinking the Museum Climate." One of the major issues discussed was the continued relevance of the environmental control standards established in Thomson's 1978 book *The Museum Environment*: 50+/-5% RH (relative humidity) and 70 +/-2 or 3°F. The conference attendees agreed that a relative humidity with an annual range of 40–60% could be an acceptable standard. This figure is potentially problematic, for it has been documented that "Temperatures above about 70°F and RH above about 55–60% encourage mold and insects."[48]

Despite these concerns, there is preliminary evidence that acceptance of a wider range of environmental control standards in institutions can result in lower energy costs. Artigas presents data showing "an exponential relationship between energy costs and consumption and the variance of the indoor temperature and relative humidity…as the variance increased the energy cost and consumption decreased exponentially."[49] Artigas collected data from five institutions, which he notes "is not statistically robust enough to allow one to conclude with any certainty the mathematical relationships between energy costs and consumption and the level of environmental control" but "does give an indication of that relationship."[50] The five institutions were all located in the mid-Atlantic or northeastern regions of the United States "to minimize the influence of variations in climatic conditions."[51] These regions have temperate climates with cooling, heating, and mixed or transitional seasons.

Considering the influence of local climate on environmental conditions within a building is a principal tenet of Staniforth's concept of "slow conservation," which she defines as "a holistic approach to conservation that looks not only at the collection in a museum or historic house but also at the building and the environment that surrounds the building."[52] The term "slow conservation" echoes the Slow Food movement, an organization and a philosophy dedicated to local and regional food traditions in response to the globalization of fast food. In the context of slow conservation, this translates to a consideration of local climate that echoes the NMDC's observation, cited above, that "[s]eeking to achieve an internationally agreed narrow environmental standard for

temperature and relative humidity has resulted in an unnecessarily high energy use."[53] Staniforth draws on her experience as Historic Properties Director at the National Trust to provide examples of how much variance is possible in maintaining protective environmental conditions when factors such as the building design and the local environmental conditions are taken into account. She highlights the example of the use of the *kura*, the traditional Japanese storehouse design, by the Archives of the Imperial Household Agency in Tokyo, which has preserved items for over 1000 years without a heating, ventilation, or air conditioning system. Use of the *kura* design also contributes to social sustainability, in the sense of preserving local culture identified by Avrami.[54] Other examples of buildings that are naturally suited to environmental control due to their design and their specificity to their regional location are described by Rowoldt, who identifies such buildings in locations as geographically diverse as Germany, the Netherlands, Israel, and South Africa, indicating that slow conservation is applicable in a variety of conditions.[55]

MATERIALS FOR PRESERVATION AND CONSERVATION

Despite the problems inherent in environmental control, it is crucial to understand what Staniforth describes as "modern prevention conservation philosophy":

> The aim is to avoid the need for major interventions using conservation materials with high embodied energy, often from non-renewable resources such as petrochemicals, and to replace it with a holistic approach to the care of collections that manages the environment surrounding the collection, creating conditions that reduce the rate at which damaging change occurs, whilst recognizing that some change in inevitable.[56]

When it is impossible to avoid "using conservation materials with high embodied energy," evaluating the environmental impact of conservation materials becomes complex and nuanced. The very characteristics of materials that threaten our environment, such as the extremely slow, or nonexistant degradition of plastics, are often the characteristics that make materials desirable for conservation and preservation.[57] For instance, a chemically inert plastic that does not degrade is exactly what is needed to encapsulate documents. Coming up with less toxic alternatives requires time-consuming research to determine suitability for use with valuable, irreplaceable objects.[58] Limited funding for conservation and the intensely laborious nature of conservation work only add to the difficulty.

Because of these challenges, efforts to reduce the environmental impact of conservation tend towards recycling and efficient use of materials. In 2008, the American Institute for Conservation of Artistic and Historic Works (AIC) formed a Green Task Force, which conducted a survey of the organization's members concerning sustainable practice. While "[o]ver 87% of respondents participate in workplace recycling, including active redistribution of equipment and supplies within and outside their institutions," only 14% reported being able to find "products that are 'greener' than those typically used in conservation activities."[59] The practices involving the more conservation-specific practices (rather than more general office-type practices such as reducing electricity use) consisted mostly of reusing materials of all types and adopting greener tools such as glass containers and washable cloths, rather than using greener conservation products. To put this low number in context, over 60% of respondents indicated that they feel conservation work is "especially wasteful or potentially damaging to the environment," and over 50% of respondents described themselves as being "very committed to adopting greener practices."[60] In spite of these encouraging numbers, several survey participants indicated that they did not feel it was appropriate for AIC to be concerned with green conservation practices.[61] Silence's report does not give their reasons, but it would be reasonable to surmise that this reluctance arises from conservators' preference for using materials and practices that have been well-established and well-documented.

Paper is a prime example of a material necessary for conservation for which more environmentally friendly options are available, but for which research is lacking. Recycled paper, while a common greener option, presents issues for those concerned about its longevity. Standards for paper permanence focus on the lignin content. ISO 11108 states that archival paper (as opposed to permanent paper, which is ISO 9706) can only be made from cotton, hemp, ramie or flax, in addition to meeting the requirements of permanent paper.[62] ISO 9706 expressed the limit for lignin not by percentage but by Kappa number, which measures sensitivity to oxidation. ANSI/NISO Z39.48, the American standard for permanent paper, allows a maximum of 1% lignin by weight. In 1991, McCrady expressed concern about the appropriateness of recycled postconsumer fiber for permanent and archival papers, due to the difficulty of removing fibers with higher lignin content.[63] There is also concern over the shorter fibers that result from the recycling progress, since longer fibers contribute to the strength of paper.[64]

If the suitability of recycled wood paper pulp is questionable, perhaps other materials should be considered. As mentioned, ISO 11108 states that archival paper can only be made from cotton, hemp, ramie, or flax. Two studies of the lignin content of hemp measured it at 2%[65] and 4.6%.[66] This is somewhat high in comparison to the 1% lignin by weight specified in Z39.48, but perhaps this should be reevaluated. McCrady's article "The Nature of Lignin" states that a draft of the ANSI Z39.48 standard allowed up to 7.5% lignin, based on the theory that including calcium carbonate would mitigate the effects of lignin. Hemp for permanent paper should be of interest not only because of the fiber's naturally low lignin content, but because of its environmental sustainability. It is a durable crop that requires few pesticides, if any, and it requires less water than cotton,[67] another one of the fibers specified in ISO 11108. Given the prevalence of paper in preservation—it is used for storage microenvironments in addition to being the material upon which documents and many works of art exist—investigating the suitability of alternative paper materials could be quite fruitful in reducing environmental impact.

Fidler, Wheeler, and Fuhlhage give another perspective that clarifies and complicates the issue of environmentally friendly materials in conservation.[68] It may also provide insight into the reasons behind some AIC survey participants' view that it is not appropriate for preservationists and conservationists to be concerned with green matters. The authors discuss three materials that have a history of being used in historic preservation—lead paint, ethyl silicate stone consolidant, and pentachlorophenol (PCP)—that have been recently classified as harmful to the environment. These materials, the authors assert, may be harmful, but they are the most suitable materials available for their preservation applications. The authors see these types of materials as being environmentally friendly in a different way. Of lead paint they write: "Original lead paint applications have saved carbon loads by continuing to function, and by reducing the need for additional carbon to be expended on new paint manufacture and frequent repainting."[69] They acknowledge, however, that this justification is not perfect:

> The hazardous loads on the environment are relatively small compared to other emission sources, and the long-lasting treatments can save carbon loads by limiting the need to repair and replace materials in the short to medium term. The cost-benefit analysis weighs in their favor, but is an uncomfortable truth.[70]

Careful consideration is necessary in making choices that balance the needs of collections with environmental impact.

Economic Sustainability: Ensuring the Future of Cultural Heritage Institutions

While Fidler, Wheeler, and Fuhlhage consider cost-benefit analysis in terms of the costs and benefits to the environment, the economic costs and benefits of sustainability must also be weighed. The ultimate goal when thinking about the economic aspects of sustainability is advocated by green economists. The theory of green economics changes the traditional model of sustainability from the three circles model, i.e., society, economy, and environment linked together but interdependent, to one in which the "economy operates within social relationships and the whole of society is embedded within the natural world."[71] In other words, instead of the recycling sign, the symbol is a circle within a circle within a circle, the idea being that nothing is more important than the environment because without it, society and the economy would not exist (Figure 2). Green economics favors a steady-state economy, or one that is balanced, with a "constant population and stock of capital and a lower rate of throughput (compared with today) that [does] not exceed the planet's ability to regenerate itself" over the relentless growth so important in traditional economic theories.[72] Green economists look at the big picture and a future that is globally sustainable.

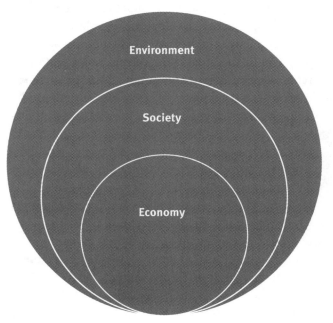

Figure 2.

It would be unrealistic for cultural heritage institutions to wait for steady-state economies to develop. If they were to do so, their survival would be at stake. In this time of economic uncertainty, repositories cannot afford to ignore economic realities in favor of environmental trends. However, they can make strategic physical, practical, and policy changes that balance the three functions of the system—society, environment, and economics—to create a sustainable institution. Of the three aspects of sustainability, economics is perhaps the most routine and practical, but it also has the most direct and obvious impact on the survival of an institution. A repository must be economically sustainable or it will not exist for long. Any programs it starts must also be economically sustainable if they are to continue into an uncertain future. Therefore, any changes implemented in an institution for the benefit of the environment and society must be balanced with the mission of the repository and the financial costs and benefits to the institution.

As discussed in the section "Environmental Control for Preservation and Conservation," maintaining environmental conditions conducive to preservation is expensive. Because of high energy costs and increasingly tighter budgets, the cost savings that come from reducing resource consumption were an early motivator for repositories to go green. The AIC's Green Task Force survey found that of the 475 respondents who completed the survey, 87% responded that their workplace participated in some form of recycling, which some respondents noted was "somewhat cost driven, as waste reduction and saving money go hand in hand."[73] Respondents also said that besides recycling, energy reduction was the second most prevalent green activity, of which the Task Force commented: "Rising fuel costs inspired much of this activity and continuing economic pressures give many facilities more than one good reason to reduce energy consumption."[74]

In addition to reducing energy usage, cultural institutions can reduce their consumption of other resources, from water to food to paper, and source those resources more sustainably, which not only contributes to a sustainable environment, but also saves money. It is encouraging to consider that in a field and industry that is constantly changing and innovating, such as the green sector, what is impractical and expensive today may be the next CFL light bulb, which is both practical and relatively inexpensive to change but low on energy use, and heat emission, and is long-lasting. Additionally, more and more industries and vendors are seeing the light when it comes to sustainability, partly as a result of "natural capitalism," or making "resources more productive in terms of money, time, materials and processes," but also because more consumers are demanding just that.[75]

Cultural institutions, including archives, libraries, and museums, are a commanding market presence, and if we use the power of that presence to push for better and cheaper green options, we can make changes.

One of the biggest components that contributes to the success or failure of sustainability efforts is the building. As previously mentioned, buildings are a heavy drain on energy, so the more sustainable the building design, the better the repository is able to reduce resource consumption and save money. A study by McGraw-Hill Construction and the University of San Diego released in 2010 reported that "[t]he value of green is undeniable—and delivering during a recession…Owners of green buildings consistently report financial benefits, such as 5% building value increase and 4% ROI."[76] The Environmental Protection Agency devotes a section of their website, "Why Build Green?," to encouraging green building practices. It states:

> By adopting green building strategies, we can maximize both economic and environmental performance. Green construction methods can be integrated into buildings at any stage, from design and construction, to renovation and deconstruction. However, the most significant benefits can be obtained if the design and construction team takes an integrated approach from the earliest stages of a building project.[77]

Economic benefits of green building construction can include reduced operating costs, the creation, expansion, and shaping of markets for green product and services, improvement of occupant productivity, and optimization of life-cycle economic performance (i.e., things will last longer).

As the EPA website notes, one option is to build a new building integrating sustainable design and technology from the beginning of the project. In 2007, the real estate consultancy firm Davis Langdon published a report that looked at the costs of sustainable building design versus the costs for conventional buildings during the construction phase.[78] The report specifically analyzed building costs of libraries and determined that there is no appreciable difference in costs to build a sustainable building versus a conventional one. Any extra costs that resulted from implementing sustainable design were offset and overtaken by savings in energy and resource use during the life of the building.

On the other hand, the National Trust for Historic Preservation's study found that reusing and retrofitting existing buildings was more environmentally friendly than tearing down existing buildings to construct new ones.[79] They concluded that "it can take between 10 and 80 years for a new, energy-efficient building to overcome, through more efficient operations, the negative climate change impacts that were created during the construction process."[80] However, they stated that "care must be taken in the selection of construction materials in order to minimize environmental impacts; the benefits of reuse can be reduced or negated based on the type and quantity of materials selected for a reuse project."[81] Presenters at *Library Journal*'s fifth Design Institute in 2009 also cautioned that buildings should be assessed on an individual basis "since, in many cases, the cost of reconstruction and bringing an old building up to code can often be higher than the cost of constructing anew."[82] Nevertheless, adapting an old building can be an appealing form of preserving the built environment.

A building does not necessarily require potentially expensive retrofitting to increase its energy efficiency. Sometimes low-tech or no-tech is both economically and environmentally sound. Techniques such as changing lights to activation by motion sensors, reducing or eliminating vampire electronics that use energy even when not in use, and changing landscaping, among others, make a difference. Working with the existing environment, using local building techniques, and knowing your collections can also facilitate practices that are both green and cost-effective, while still maintaining the integrity of the collections.

When thinking about the economic aspects of sustainability in cultural institutions, one might consider ways not only of reducing expenses, but also of raising funds. Green practices can open up entirely new avenues for fundraising and attract the attention of donors who otherwise might not have thought of

supporting cultural institutions. In some parts of the U.S., government programs offer grants, loans, or tax credits to support sustainable initiatives. For instance, in 2006, the Massachusetts Technology Collaborative, a state-run endowment, awarded the Massachusetts Museum of Contemporary Art $700,000 to install a solar array and energy-efficiency equipment.[83] Also in Massachusetts, the Massachusetts Board of Library Commissioners offers green incentive grants for the planning, design, and construction phases of library buildings.[84] The National Endowment for the Humanities and the Institute for Museum and Library Services are other grant-making organizations that have given awards to cultural institutions.[85] Private organizations, such as The Kresge Foundation and the David and Lucille Packard Foundation, have awarded grants to institutions to facilitate their transition to sustainable practices.[86] These endowments are more focused on the creation of processes than on the end result.[87] Other funding options include friends' groups and corporate sponsorships, which may help a repository move toward sustainability, even if they do so only in small or specific ways.

A crucial aspect of economic sustainability that has the potential to be overlooked is the promotion of an institution's sustainable practices. There are many reasons for advertising these practices, not the least of which is to educate and advocate for sustainability. By making the public aware of its efforts to be green, a repository may also attract donations, monetary and physical, and encourage its use. Public awareness of the efforts an institution is making to reduce its environmental impact and to ensure the environment visitors inhabit is clean and healthy can send a strong positive message to its community. A public library that is LEED certified, or has made other efforts to reduce its environmental impact, sets a visible example of a public building that follows sustainable practices that reduce the city's expenditure of taxpayers' money and thus benefits society and the environment. This can encourage taxpayers and library patrons to see the library as a valuable community investment, a viewpoint that contributes not only to the economic sustainability of such an institution, but to its social sustainability.

Social Sustainability: Fostering Awareness and Setting A Good Example

Cultural heritage institutions can use their unique positions of trust and prominence within their communities to serve as leaders in environmental stewardship. Libraries, archives, and museums play a crucial role in raising environmental awareness and fostering a connection with the natural world, providing information and education, and demonstrating sustainable building design and practices.

Libraries have a long history as community resource centers. Advocates of green libraries often note that the library, with its mission of sharing resources, is an inherently green concept.[88] Libraries not only provide users with environmental information, but also, according to Miller, author of the American Library Association's *Public Libraries Going Green*, have a role in educating the public in "environmental literacy." Miller defines this as "the ability to recognize that one's choices impact the environment; to identify the most sustainable solution for the situation; and to be able to act in the most environmentally friendly way on that solution."[89] Librarians can use their role as guides to information sources to raise awareness about environmental issues and sustainability practices inside and outside libraries.[90] Library programming can also help children and adults develop a personal appreciation of the natural world. Richard Louv suggests that libraries can get more involved by expanding information on outdoor activities, offering outdoor gear for checkout, expanding collections to include sections on regional natural history, and partnering with natural history museums and botanic gardens.[91] Demonstrating their commitment to creating socially sustainable communities, some public libraries are serving as local seed depositories and tool-lending libraries, and are creating community gardens "to educate patrons about gardening practices and local food issues."[92] According to Bryan, educating the public and connecting people with nature can begin with the planning stages of green library building design. Preparations for a green building can include establishing and enhancing the library's green space with multigenerational garden projects and partnering with other agencies such as community gardens and parks to create programs that "engage people in outdoor activities."[93]

Public libraries are particularly well situated to be community examples of sustainable design and the library building can serve as an example of local environmental responsibility. As Boyden and Weiner note, a green library "provides a highly visible and effective venue for communicating the benefits of environmentally responsible construction and building to the community."[94] Adopting green practice not only sets an example for a community but also involves the community in decision-making. According to Ames and Heid, the public play an important role in the decision to implement green design techniques in library construction and to pursue LEED certification,[95] and in this role the *sociable* aspect of social sustainability becomes clear. Green awareness not only encourages communication within a community, but also can provide opportunities for demonstrating a community's interconnectedness in decision-making.

Museums are also using green architecture as an example of environmental and social responsibility that connects projects to users. At the Museum of Contemporary Art Denver, Director Cydney Payton "wanted to connect the moral and social messages of the artworks inside the museum with the architecture of the building itself."[96] As the building's architect, David Adjaye, explains, green design is not just about technology but also about changing people's behavior. The exhibiting function of cultural heritage institutions can be used to this end as well. Even if an institution's collections do not focus on environmental issues, the institution can raise awareness by publicizing information about the steps that it takes to reduce the environmental impact of its activities. Lending materials for exhibition elsewhere can have a very high impact on the environment, as noted by Lambert and Henderson,[97] who suggest steps to reduce the impact and to reduce costs. Among these are the reusing packaging and using sea and train transportation in preference to air travel and couriers whenever possible.

Conclusion: Where do we go from here?

The literature discussed in this paper indicates that all aspects of sustainability—environmental, economic, and social—should play into sustainability decisions. When the discussion in the literature is focused on cultural heritage institutions, the social aspect often refers to the community-driven values of a repository and its ability to foster environmental awareness through education and the environmentally aware practices of the institution itself. Here the social, economic, and environmental aspects of the institution are deeply connected. Adopting green building and maintenance practices can demonstrate the institution's commitment to the well-being of the community it serves. This helps to establish it as a relevant and important part of the community, in addition to the educational and community services that the institution provides, thus supporting its financial sustainability. Green building and maintenance practices can also reduce costs, an important aspect of economic sustainability.

The focus on the environmental aspects of sustainability stemming from the Green Movement has widened to encompass economic and social aspects as well. The literature exploring these aspects of sustainability is also expanding, especially with respect to cultural heritage institutions, and being recognized by professional organizations concerning cultural heritage institutions. The American Institute for Conservation of Historic and Artistic Works has a Green Task Force, and the International Federation of Library Associations and Institutions (IFLA) has an Environmental Sustainability and Libraries Special Interest Group, sponsored by the Preservation and Conservation Section.[98] These groups are focused more on the preservation of collections, but the American Library Association has issued publications on the subject of green libraries, which expand on the social aspect of sustainability.[99]

The authors hope that as sustainability becomes more mainstream and recognized as an important element in the overall vision and management of an institution, there will be more sources on sustainable practices in cultural heritage institutions, especially sources that comment on all three aspects of sustain-ability. As Avrami observes, "while it is important for conservation to contribute to environmental and economic sustainability, its social contributions are the linchpin."[100] Recognition of this interconnectivity will ensure that the most comprehensively considered decisions will be made.

NOTES

1. Katy Lithgow, "Sustainable Decision Making: Change in National Trust Collections Conservation," *Journal of the Institute of Conservation* 34 (2011): 129–30. See also Erica Avrami, "Sustainability and the Built Environment: Forging a Role for Heritage Conservation," *Conservation Perspectives* 26.1 (2011): 4–9, and David Selden, "The Triple Bottom Line and Why We Care about Sustainability," *AALL Spectrum* 15.1 (2010): 14.

2. Avrami, "Sustainability and the Built Environment," 4.

3. "Why Build Green?" last modified December 2, 2010, http://www.epa.gov/greenbuilding/pubs/whybuild.htm.

4. Flemmich Webb, "Global Warning," *Museums Journal* 103.12 (2003): 25.

5. Sarah Staniforth, "Sustainability and Collections," *Conservation Perspectives* 26.1 (2011): 14.

6. William M. Brown, "Future-Proof Design," *Library Journal* 133.15 (September 15, 2008): 1, 8–10.

7. Brown, "Future-Proof Design," 10.

8. Bill Brown, "The New Green Standard," *Library Journal* 128.20 (December 2003): 61.

9. Monika Antonelli, "The Green Library Movement: An Overview and Beyond," *Electronic Green Journal* 27 (2008): 1–11; Frederick Stoss, "Libraries Taking the 'LEED': Green Libraries Leading in Energy and Environmental Design," *Online* 34.2 (2010): 20–27.

10. Sarah Brophy and Elizabeth Wylie, "It's Easy Being Green: Museums and the Green Movement," *Museum News* 85.5 (2006): 38–45.

11. Steven Litt, "The Greening of Museum Architecture," *ARTnews* 106.9 (2007): 190–3; Julie Brener, "Green Scenes," *Art + Auction* 31.5 (2008): 74–75.

12. For example, Greg Landgraf, "New Colorado Facility Becomes First Carbon-Positive Library," *American Libraries* 41.1/2 (2010): 26, 28; Suzanne Arist, "Going Green in Illinois: Diverse Libraries, Diverse Initiatives," *Illinois Library Association Reporter* 28.4 (2010): 4–7; Ted Strand, "All-Digital Information Commons Reduces Energy Consumption," *American Libraries* 41.8 (2010): 19–20; Jennifer T. Ries-Taggart, "Cleveland Public Library Completes First Freestanding LEED Certified Library in Ohio," *Public Libraries* 49.6 (2010): 10–11; Scott M. Bushnell, "Library's Green Annex Brings Acclaim, Growth," *Library Journal: Library by Design* (Spring 2009): 32; Peter Gisolfi, "A Sustainable Library, Inside and Out," *Library Journal: Library by Design* (Spring 2009): 6; Wanda Urbanska, "A Greener Library, A Greener You," *American Libraries* 40.4 (2009): 52–55; Stephanie Cash, "Green Acres" [Interview], *Art in America* 97.9 (2009): 112–117; Dorothy Waterfill Trotter, "Going for the Green," *American Libraries* 39.4 (2008): 40–43; Francine Fialkoff, "Green Libraries Are Local," *Library Journal* 133.11 (2008): 8; Rebecca Miller, "San Francisco's Green Branches," *Library Journal: Library by Design* (Fall 2008): 18–19.

13. For example, Johanna Sands, "Sustainable Library Design," Libris Design Project, 2001, http://www.librisdesign.org/docs/SustainableLibDesign.pdf; James Weiner and Lynn Boyden, "Creating Sustainable Libraries," *Library Journal: Buyers' Guide* (December 2001): 8–10; Alexander P. Lamis, "Greening the Library: An Overview of Sustainable Design," in *Planning the Modern Public Library Building*, ed. Gerald B. McCabe and James R. Kennedy (Westport, CN: Libraries Unlimited, 2003), 31–45; Kathryn Miller, *Public Libraries are Going Green* (Chicago: ALA, 2010); Sarah Brophy and Elizabeth Wylie, *The Green Museum: A Primer on Environmental Practice* (Lanham, MD: AltaMira Press, 2008); Sam McBane Mulford and Ned A. Himmel, *How Green is My Library?* (Santa Barbara, CA: ABC-CLIO, 2010). Studies of sustainable design decisions at specific institutions include: Brian Edwards, "The East Wing," *Architects' Journal* 233.5 (2011): 28–33; Vernon Mays, "Water + Life Campus," *Architect* 96.12 (2007): 41–46; and Sarah Bennett, "Horniman Museum, London," *Green Places* 16 (2005): 32–35.

14. Weiner and Boyden, "Creating Sustainable Libraries," 8; Sands, "Sustainable Library Design," 17–18.

15. Sands, "Sustainable Library Design," 13; Weiner and Boyden, "Creating Sustainable Libraries," 8.

16. Lamar Veatch, "Toward the Environmental Design of Library Buildings," *Library Trends* 36 (1987): 361–76.

17. James and Suzanne LaRue, "The Green Librarian," *Wilson Library Bulletin* 65 (1991): 27–33.

18. Richard L. Waters, "Why Your Library Should Plant Trees," *Public Library Quarterly* 22.1 (2003): 42.

19. Beth Lindblom Patkus, "Integrated Pest Management," Northeast Document Conservation Center, 2007, http://www.nedcc.org/resources/leaflets/3Emergency_Management/10PestManagement.php.

20. Gerald B. McCabe, "New Concepts for Technology in Library Design," in *Planning the Modern Public Library Building*, ed. Gerald B. McCabe and James R. Kennedy (Westport, CN: Libraries Unlimited, 2003), 205, 210. See also L. Blumenstein, "San José's Green Art," *Library Journal: Library by Design* (Spring 2009): 24–25.

21. McCabe, "New Concepts for Technology in Library Design," 206.

22. Edward Dean, "Natural Light in the Library," *Architecture Week* (December 2004): E1.1-E1.2, accessed September 19, 2012, http://www.architectureweek.com/2004/1201/environment_1-1.html.

23. Sherelyn Ogden, "Temperature, Relative Humidity, Light, and Air Quality: Basic Guidelines for Preservation," Northeast Document Conservation Center, 2007, http://www.nedcc.org/resources/leaflets/2The_Environment/01BasicGuidelines.php; Beth Lindblom Patkus, "Protection from Light Damage," Northeast Document Conservation Center, 2007, http://www.nedcc.org/resources/leaflets/2The_Environment/04ProtectionFromLight.php.

24. Steven Weintraub, Art Preservation Services, Inc., "Comments regarding LEDs and risks to light-sensitive materials," report to the Green Task Force of the American Institute of Conservation, April 28, 2010, accessed November 11, 2012, http://www.conservation-us.org/_data/n_0001/resources/live/Response%20from%20Steve%20Weintraub.pdf.

25. Carla Gallina and Jeffrey Mandyck, "Light Done Right," *Library Journal* (September 15, 2009), accessed September 19. 2012, http://www.library journal.com/article/CA6696205.html.

26. Sands, "Sustainable Library Design," 2.

27. Christian Lachel, "Nature Lovers," *Museums Journal* 104.11 (2004): 24.

28. Shu-Hsien Tseng, "An Eco-Building, A Healthy Life, and Good Service: A New Century in Public Library Architecture," *Public Libraries* 46.4 (2007): 53.

29. Tseng, "An Eco-Building, A Healthy Life, and Good Service," 54.

30. Anne Lebel, "Construction of an Archive Building in a Tropical Climate: The Saint Martin Media Library and Territorial Archives," *International Preservation News* 55 (2011): 27–30.

31. Sandra Rowoldt, "Going Archivally Green: Implications of Doing it Naturally in Southern African Archives and Libraries," *South African Journal of Library and Information Science* 66.4 (1998): 141–48; Kazuko Hioki, "From Japanese Tradition: Is Kura a Model for a Sustainable Preservation Environment?" *Studies in Conservation* 53.2 (2008): 131–35.

32. Sarah Kim, "Green Archives: Applications of Green Construction to Archival Facilities," *The Primary Source* 28.1 (2008).

33. Sue Wilkinson, Rachel Madan, Stephen Foulger, and Paul Goodman, "Can Museums Continue to Grow at a Time When They Need to be Reducing Their Carbon Footprint?" *Museums Journal* 108.10 (2008): 21.

34. Michael Wescott Loder, "Libraries with a Future: How Are Academic Library Usage and Green Demands Changing Building Designs?" *College & Research Libraries* 71.4 (2010): 348–60.

35. Garry Thomson, "Air Pollution: A Review for Conservation Chemists," *Studies in Conservation* 10 (1965): 147.

36. V. Kucera and S. Fitz, "Direct and Indirect Air Pollution Effects on Materials Including Cultural Monuments," *Water, Air, and Soil Pollution* 85 (1995): 153.

37. Sarah Staniforth, "Slow Conservation," *Studies in Conservation* 55.2 (2010): 75.

38. Cecily M. Gryzwacz, *Monitoring for Gaseous Pollutants in Museum Environments.* (Los Angeles: Getty Conservation Institute, 2006), vii.

39. See UNESCO, *Case Studies on Climate Change and World Heritage,* 2007, http://whc.unesco.org/uploads/activities/documents/activity-473-1.pdf; UNESCO, *Climate Change and World Heritage* (World Heritage Reports 22), 2007, http://whc.unesco.org/uploads/activities/documents/activity-474-1.pdf; UNESCO, *Policy Document on the Impacts of Climate Change on World Heritage Properties,* 2008, http://whc.unesco.org/uploads/activities/documents/activity-397-2.pdf.

40. UNESCO, *Policy Document on the Impacts of Climate Change,* 2–3.

41. May Cassar, *Climate Change and The Historic Environment* (London: UCL Centre for Sustainable Heritage, 2005), 6.

42. Odgen, "Temperature, Relative Humidity, Light, and Air Quality," 2007.

43. David John Artigas, "A Comparison of the Efficacy and Costs of Different Approaches to Climate Management in Historic Buildings and Museums" (Masters thesis, University of Pennsylvania, 2007): 2.

44. Brophy and Wylie, "It's Easy Being Green."

45. André Plourde, *Programmable Thermostats as Means of Generating Energy Savings: Some Pros and Cons* (Edmonton, Alberta: Canadian Building Energy End-Use Data and Analysis Centre, 2003).

46. May Cassar, "Energy Reduction and the Conservation of Cultural Heritage: A Review of Past, Present and Forthcoming Initiatives," *International Preservation News* 55 (2011): 7.

47. National Museum Directors' Conference, *NMDC Guiding Principles for Reducing Museums' Carbon Footprint,* 2009, http://www.nationalmuseums.org.uk/media/documents/what_we_do_documents/guiding_principles_reducing_carbon_footprint.pdf.

48. Beth Lindblom Patkus, "Monitoring Temperature and Relative Humidity," Northeast Document Conservation Center, 2007, http://www.nedcc.org/resources/leaflets/2The_Environment/02TemperatureAndHumidity.php.

49. Artigas, "A Comparison of the Efficacy and Costs of Different Approaches to Climate Management," 124.

50. Artigas, "A Comparison of the Efficacy and Costs of Different Approaches to Climate Management," 124.

51. Artigas, "A Comparison of the Efficacy and Costs of Different Approaches to Climate Management," 125.

52. Staniforth, "Slow Conservation," 75.

53. National Museum Directors' Conference, *NMDC Guiding Principles.*

54. Avrami, "Sustainability and the Built Environment," 8.

55. Rowoldt, "Going Archivally Green," 141.

56. Staniforth, "Slow Conservation," 75.

57. Mary Elizabeth Haude, Robin O'Hern, and Sarah Nunberg, "Plastics Are Forever: Wraps, Tools, Films, and Containers Used in Conservation Practice," AIC Committee for Sustainable Conservation Practices, 2008, http://www.conservation-wiki .com/w/index.php?title=Plastics_are_Forever: _Wraps,_Tools,_Films_and_Containers_used_in _Conservation_Practice.

58. Elizabeth Pye and Dean Sully, "Evolving Challenges, Developing Skills," *The Conservator* 30.1 (2007): 30.

59. Patricia Silence, "How Are US Conservators Going Green? Results of Polling AIC Members," *Studies in Conservation* 55.3 (2010): 160.

60. Silence, "How Are Us Conservators Going Green?" 160.

61. Silence, "How Are Us Conservators Going Green?" 161.

62. Ivar A.L. Hoel, "Standards for Permanent Paper," 64th IFLA General Conference, August 16–21, 1998, accessed December 5, 2012, http://ifla .queenslibrary.org/IV/ifla64/115-114e.htm; and Ellen McCrady, "The ANSI/NISO Z739.48 Standard and Other Standards," *North American Permanent Papers*, (Austin, TX: Abbey Publications, 1998), accessed December 5, 2012, http://cool .conservation-us.org/byorg/abbey/napp/std.html.

63. Ellen McCrady, "The Nature of Lignin," *Alkaline Paper Advocate* 4.4 (1991), http://cool.conservation -us.org/byorg/abbey/ap/ap04/ap04-4/ap04-402 .html.

64. Queensland State Archives, "Guide to Paper Selection for Permanent and Temporary Retention Public Records," accessed December 5, 2012, http://www .archives.qld.gov.au/Recordkeeping/Preserve Downloads/Documents/psa_1.pdf.

65. David Crônier, Bernard Monties, & Brigitte Chabbert, "Structure and Chemical Composition of Bast Fibers Isolated from Developing Hemp Stem," *Journal of Agricultural and Food Chemistry* 53.21 (2005): 8279–8289.

66. Ana Gutiérrez, Isabel M. Rodríguez, and José C. del Rio, "Chemical Characterizations of Lignin and Lipid Fractions in Industrial Hemp Bast Fibers Used for Manufacturing High-Quality Paper Pulps," *Journal of Agricultural and Food Chemistry* 54.6 (2006), 2138–144.

67. Tun, Lin and Catherine Chan-Halbrendt, "Sustainable Development: Building a Case for Hemp," *Journal of Textile and Apparel, Technology and Management* 4.3 (2005), 1–2.

68. John Fidler, George Wheeler, and Dwayne Fuhlhage, "Uncomfortable Truths," *Conservation Perspectives: The GCI Newsletter* 26.1 (2011): 15–17.

69. Fidler, Wheeler, and Fuhlhage, "Uncomfortable Truths," 15.

70. Fidler, Wheeler, and Fuhlhage, "Uncomfortable Truths," 15.

71. Molly Scott Cato, *Green Economics: An Introduction to Theory, Policy and Practice* (London: Earthscan, 2009), 37.

72. Cato, *Green Economics*, 40.

73. "Green Task Force Survey Summary Report," American Institute for Conservation of Historic and Artistic Works, accessed September 19, 2012, http://www.conservation-us.org/index.cfm?fuse action=page.viewpage&pageid=995.

74. "Green Task Force Survey Summary Report."

75. Brophy and Wylie, "It's Easy Being Green," 40.

76. "Building Performance and Occupant Satisfaction Tied to Green Investment" in *New Report: Findings from Multi-year Study* by CB Richard Ellis, McGraw-Hill Construction and the University of San Diego unveiled at Greenbuild Press Release, McGraw-Hill Construction, accessed September 19, 2012, http://srsweb.ei3.com/wp-content/uploads/

Building_Performance_Occupant_Satisfaction _Tied_to_Green_Investment_Nov10.pdf.

77. "Why Build Green?" U.S. Environmental Protection Agency.

78. Davis Langdon, "Cost of Green Revisited: Re-examining the Feasibility and Cost Impact of Sustainable Design in the Light of Increased Market Adoption," accessed September 19, 2012, http://www.davislangdon.com/upload/images/publications/USA/The%20Cost%20of%20Green%20Revisited.pdf.

79. "The Greenest Building: Quantifying the Value of Building Rescue," National Trust for Historic Preservation Preservation Green Lab, accessed September 19, 2012, http://www.preservationnation.org/information-center/sustainable-communities/sustainability/green-lab/lca/The_Greenest_Building_Exec_Summary.pdf.

80. "The Greenest Building."

81. "The Greenest Building."

82. Michael Rogers and Raya Kuzyk, "Green in Lean Times: Sustainability and Savings, Key Themes at LJ's Fifth Design Institute, in Arlington, VA," *Library Journal* (September 15, 2009).

83. Brophy and Wylie, "It's Easy Being Green," 41–42.

84. "The Massachusetts Public Library Construction Program Fact Sheet," Massachusetts Board of Library Commissioners, accessed September 19, 2012, http://mblc.state.ma.us/grants/construction/program/construction.php.

85. Richard L. Kerschner, "Providing Safe and Practical Environments for Cultural Property in Historic Buildings...and Beyond," in *From Gray Areas to Green Areas: Developing Sustainable Practices in Preservation Environments Symposium Proceedings* (Austin, TX: Kilgarlin Center for the Preservation of the Cultural Record, 2008), accessed September 19, 2012, http://www.ischool.utexas.edu/kilgarlin/gaga/proceedings2008/GAGA07-kerschner.pdf.

86. Brophy and Wylie, *The Green Museum*, 141.

87. Brophy and Wylie, "It's Easy Being Green," 42.

88. Mulford and Himmel, *How Green is My Library*, xv; Steven E. Smith, "The Library as an Environmental Alternative (Among Other Things)," *Wilson Library Bulletin* 65 (1991): 85. The opportunity also exists for archives to provide information for users in the growing field of environmental research and secure the patronage of researchers by promoting repository holdings and implementing customer services and marketing techniques (see Todd Welch, "'Green' Archivism: The Archival Response to Environmental Research," *American Archivist* 62.1 (1999): 74–94.

89. Kathryn Miller, "Environmental Literacy: An Opportunity for Illinois Libraries," *Illinois Library Association Reporter* 28.4 (2010): 30.

90. James and Suzanne LaRue, "The Green Librarian," 27–33. See also Urbanska, "A Greener Library, A Greener You" and Louise Schaper, "Our Zero-Carbon Campaign," *Library Journal* 136.2 (February 1, 2011): 33.

91. Richard Louv, "Libraries and the Nature Principle," *Booklist* 107.13 (March 1, 2011): 23. See also Louv, *Last Child in the Woods: Saving Our Children from Nature-Deficit Disorder* (Chapel Hill, NC: Algonquin Books, 2005) and *The Nature Principle* (Chapel Hill, N.C: Algonquin Books, 2011). See also Sarah Feldstein, "Expanding the Capacity of the Public Library: Partnerships with Community Based Environmental Groups," *Electronic Green Journal* 1.6 (1996): 1–7.

92. Antonelli, "The Green Library Movement," 7.

93. Cheryl Bryan, "Beginning Your Green Building," *Library Journal: Library by Design* (September 15, 2009): 31.

94. Lynn Boyden and James Weiner, "For the Public Good: Sustainability Demonstration in Public Library Building Projects," *Public Libraries* 40.1 (2001): 44. See also Lynn Boyden and James Weiner, "Sustainable Libraries: Teaching Environmental Responsibility to Communities," *The Bottom Line* 13.2 (2000): 74–83, and Peter Gisolfi, "This Old Library," *American Libraries* 42.3/4 (2011): 38–40.

95. Kathryn Ames and Greg Heid, "Leadership, Libraries, LEED for the Future," *Georgia Library Quarterly* 47.1 (Winter 2010): 13–17. See also Francine Fialkoff, "Educating a Community," *Library Journal: Library by Design* (Spring 2008): 14; and Louise

Schaper, "Public Input Yields Greener Library Design," *Library Journal* 128.20 (2003): 62–63.

96. Litt, "The Greening of Museum Architecture," 193.

97. Simon Lambert and Jane Henderson, "The Carbon Footprint of Museum Loans: A Pilot Study at Amgueddfa Cymru, National Museum Wales," *Museum Management and Curatorship* 26.3 (2011): 209–35.

98. International Federation of Library Associations and Institutions, "Environmental Sustainability and Libraries Special Interest Group," accessed Nov 23, 2012, http://www.ifla.org/environmental -sustainability-and-libraries.

99. See Miller's *Public Libraries Going Green.*

100. Avrami, "Sustainability and the Built Environment," 8.

BIBLIOGRAPHY

American Institute for Conservation of Historic and Artistic Works. "Green Task Force Survey Summary Report." Accessed September 19, 2012. http://www.conservation-us.org/index .cfm?fuseaction=page.viewpage&pageid=995.

Ames, Kathryn, and Greg Heid. "Leadership, Libraries, LEED for the Future." *Georgia Library Quarterly* 47.1 (2010): 13–17.

Antonelli, Monika. "The Green Library Movement: An Overview and Beyond." *Electronic Green Journal* 27 (2008): 1–11.

Arist, Suzanne. "Going Green in Illinois: Diverse Libraries, Diverse Initiatives." *Illinois Library Association Reporter* 28.4 (2010): 4–7.

Artigas, David John. "A Comparison of the Efficacy and Costs of Different Approaches to Climate Management in Historic Buildings and Museums." Masters thesis, University of Pennsylvania, 2007.

Avrami, Erica. "Sustainability and the Built Environment: Forging a Role for Heritage Conservation." *Conservation Perspectives: The GCI Newsletter* 26.1 (2011): 4–9.

Bennett, Sarah. "Horniman Museum, London." *Green Places* 16 (2005): 32–35.

Blumenstein, Lynn. "San José's Green Art." *Library Journal: Library by Design* (Spring 2009): 24–25.

Boyden, Lynn, and James Weiner. "For the Public Good: Sustainability Demonstration in Public Library Building Projects." *Public Libraries* 40.1 (2001): 44.

———. "Sustainable Libraries: Teaching Environmental Responsibility to Communities." *The Bottom Line* 13.2 (2000): 74–83.

Brener, Julie. "Green Scenes," *Art + Auction* 31.5 (2008): 74–75.

Brophy, Sarah, and Elizabeth Wylie. "It's Easy Being Green: Museums and the Green Movement." *Museum News* 85.5 (2006): 38–45.

———. *The Green Museum: A Primer on Environmental Practice.* Lanham, MD: AltaMira Press, 2008.

Brown, Bill. "The New Green Standard." *Library Journal* 128.20 (December 2003): 61–66.

Brown, William M. "Future-Proof Design." *Library Journal* 133.15 (September 15, 2008): 1, 8–10.

Bryan, Cheryl. "Beginning Your Green Building," *Library Journal: Library by Design* (September 15, 2009): 31.

"Building Performance and Occupant Satisfaction Tied to Green Investment in New Report: Findings from multi-year study by CB Richard Ellis, McGraw-Hill Construction and the University of San Diego unveiled at Greenbuild Press Release." McGraw-Hill Construction. Accessed September 19, 2012. http://srsweb.ei3.com/wp-content/ uploads/Building_Performance_Occupant _Satisfaction_Tied_to_Green_Investment _Nov10.pdf.

Bushnell, Scott M. "Library's Green Annex Brings Acclaim, Growth." *Library Journal: Library by Design* (Spring 2009): 32.

Cash, Stephanie. "Green Acres" [Interview]. *Art in America* 97.9 (2009): 112–17.

Cassar, May. *Climate Change and The Historic Environment.* London: UCL Centre for Sustainable Heritage, 2005.

———. "Energy Reduction and the Conservation of Cultural Heritage: A Review of Past, Present and

Forthcoming Initiatives." *International Preservation News* 55 (2011): 6–9.

Cato, Molly Scott. *Green Economics: An Introduction to Theory, Policy and Practice.* London: Earthscan, 2009.

Davis, Langdon. "Cost of Green Revisited: Reexamining the Feasibility and Cost Impact of Sustainable Design in the Light of Increased Market Adoption." Accessed September 19, 2012. http://www .davislangdon.com/upload/images/publications/ USA/The%20Cost%20of%20Green%20Revisited .pdf.

Dean, Edward. "Natural Light in the Library." *Architecture Week* (December 2004): pp. E1.1–E1.2. Accessed September 19, 2012. http://www .architectureweek.com/2004/1201/environment _1-1.html.

Edwards, Brian. "The East Wing." *Architects' Journal* 233.5 (2011): 28–33.

Feldstein, Sarah. "Expanding the Capacity of the Public Library: Partnerships with Community Based Environmental Groups." *Electronic Green Journal* 1.6 (1996): 1–7.

Fialkoff, Francine. "Educating a Community." *Library Journal: Library by Design* (Spring 2008): 14.

———. "Green Libraries Are Local." *Library Journal* 133.11 (2008): 8.

Fidler, John, George Wheeler, and Dwayne Fuhlhage. "Uncomfortable Truths." *Conservation Perspectives: The GCI Newsletter* 26.1 (2011): 15–17.

Gallina, Carla, and Jeffrey Mandyck. "Light Done Right." *Library Journal* (September 15, 2009). Accessed September 19, 2012. http://www.library journal.com/article/CA6696205.html.

Gisolfi, Peter. "A Sustainable Library, Inside and Out." *Library Journal: Library by Design* (Spring 2009): 6.

———. "This Old Library." *American Libraries* 42.3/4 (2011): 38–40.

Gryzwacz, Cecily M. *Monitoring for Gaseous Pollutants in Museum Environments.* Los Angeles, CA: Getty Conservation Institute, 2006.

Haude, Mary Elizabeth, Robin O'Hern, and Sarah Nunberg. "Plastics Are Forever: Wraps, Tools, Films, and Containers Used in Conservation Practice." AIC Committee for Sustainable Conservation Practices, 2008. http://www .conservation-wiki.com/w/index.php?title= Plastics_are_Forever:_Wraps,_Tools,_Films_and _Containers_used_in_Conservation_Practice.

Hioki, Kazuko. "From Japanese Tradition: Is Kura a Model for a Sustainable Preservation Environment?" *Studies in Conservation* 53.2 (2008): 131–35.

Kerschner, Richard L. "Providing Safe and Practical Environments for Cultural Property in Historic Buildings...and Beyond." In *From Gray Areas to Green Areas: Developing Sustainable Practices in Preservation Environments Symposium Proceedings.* Austin, TX: Kilgarlin Center for the Preservation of the Cultural Record, 2008. Accessed September 19, 2012. http://www.ischool.utexas .edu/kilgarlin/gaga/proceedings2008/GAGA07 -kerschner.pdf.

Kim, Sarah. "Green Archives: Applications of Green Construction to Archival Facilities." *The Primary Source* 28.1 (2008).

Kucera, V. and S. Fitz. "Direct and Indirect Air Pollution Effects on Materials Including Cultural Monuments." *Water, Air, and Soil Pollution* 85 (1995): 153–65.

Lachel, Christian. "Nature Lovers." *Museums Journal* 104.11 (2004): 24.

Lambert, Simon, and Jane Henderson. "The Carbon Footprint of Museum Loans: A Pilot Study at Amgueddfa Cymru, National Museum Wales." *Museum Management and Curatorship* 26.3 (2011): 209–35.

Lamis, Alexander P. "Greening the Library: An Overview of Sustainable Design." In *Planning the Modern Public Library Building*, ed. Gerald B. McCabe and James R. Kennedy, 31–45. Westport, CN: Libraries Unlimited, 2003.

Landgraf, Greg. "New Colorado Facility Becomes First Carbon-Positive Library." *American Libraries* 41.1/2 (2010): 26, 28.

LaRue, James, and Suzanne LaRue. "The Green Librarian." *Wilson Library Bulletin* 65 (1991): 27–33.

Lebel, Anne. "Construction of an Archive Building in a Tropical Climate: The Saint Martin Media

Library and Territorial Archives." *International Preservation News* 55 (2011): 27–30.

Lithgow, Katy. "Sustainable Decision Making: Change in National Trust Collections Conservation." *Journal of the Institute of Conservation* 34 (2011): 129–42.

Litt, Steven. "The Greening of Museum Architecture." *ARTnews* 106.9 (2007): 190–93.

Loder, Michael Wescott. "Libraries with a Future: How Are Academic Library Usage and Green Demands Changing Building Designs?" *College & Research Libraries* 71.4 (2010): 348–60.

Louv, Richard. *Last Child in the Woods: Saving Our Children from Nature-Deficit Disorder*. Chapel Hill, NC: Algonquin Books, 2005.

———. "Libraries and the Nature Principle." *Booklist* 107.13 (March 1, 2011): 23.

———. *The Nature Principle*. Chapel Hill, N.C: Algonquin Books, 2011.

Massachusetts Board of Library Commissioners. "The Massachusetts Public Library Construction Program Fact Sheet." Accessed September 19, 2012. http://mblc.state.ma.us/grants/construction/program/construction.php.

Mays, Vernon. "Water + Life Campus." *Architect* 96.12 (2007): 41–46.

McCabe, Gerald B. "New Concepts for Technology in Library Design." In *Planning the Modern Public Library Building*, ed. Gerald B. McCabe and James R. Kennedy, 205–214. Westport, CN: Libraries Unlimited, 2003.

Miller, Kathryn. "Environmental Literacy: An Opportunity for Illinois Libraries." *Illinois Library Association Reporter* 28.4 (2010): 30.

———. *Public Libraries Are Going Green*. Chicago: ALA, 2010.

Miller, Rebecca. "San Francisco's Green Branches." *Library Journal: Library by Design* (Fall 2008): 18–19.

Mulford, Sam McBane, and Ned A. Himmel. *How Green Is My Library?* Santa Barbara, CA: ABC-CLIO, 2010.

National Museum Directors' Conference, *NMDC Guiding Principles for Reducing Museums' Carbon Footprint*, 2009, http://www.nationalmuseums.org.uk/media/documents/what_we_do_documents/guiding_principles_reducing_carbon_footprint.pdf.

National Trust for Historic Preservation, Preservation Green Lab. "The Greenest Building: Quantifying the Value of Building Rescue." Accessed September 19, 2012. http://www.preservationnation.org/information-center/sustainable-communities/sustainability/green-lab/lca/The_Greenest_Building_Exec_Summary.pdf.

Ogden, Sherelyn. "Temperature, Relative Humidity, Light, and Air Quality: Basic Guidelines for Preservation." Northeast Document Conservation Center, 2007. http://www.nedcc.org/resources/leaflets/2The_Environment/01BasicGuidelines.php.

Patkus, Beth Lindblom. "Integrated Pest Management." Northeast Document Conservation Center, 2007. http://www.nedcc.org/resources/leaflets/3Emergency_Management/10Pest Management.php.

———. "Monitoring Temperature and Relative Humidity." Northeast Document Conservation Center, 2007. http://www.nedcc.org/resources/leaflets/2The_Environment/02TemperatureAnd Humidity.php.

———. "Protection from Light Damage." Northeast Document Conservation Center, 2007. http://www.nedcc.org/resources/leaflets/2The_Environment/04ProtectionFromLight.php.

Plourde, André. *Programmable Thermostats as Means of Generating Energy Savings: Some Pros and Cons*. Edmonton, Alberta: Canadian Building Energy End-Use Data and Analysis Centre, 2003.

Pye, Elizabeth, and Dean Sully. "Evolving Challenges, Developing Skills." *The Conservator* 30.1 (2007): 19–37.

Ries-Taggart, Jennifer T. "Cleveland Public Library Completes First Freestanding LEED Certified Library in Ohio." *Public Libraries* 49.6 (2010): 10–11.

Rogers, Michael, and Raya Kuzyk. "Green in Lean Times: Sustainability and Savings, Key Themes at LJ's Fifth Design Institute, in Arlington, VA." *Library Journal* (September 15, 2009).

Rowoldt, Sandra. "Going Archivally Green: Implications of Doing it Naturally in Southern African Archives and Libraries." *South African Journal of Library and Information Science* 66.4 (1998): 141–48.

Sands, Johanna. "Sustainable Library Design." Libris Design Project, 2001. http://www.librisdesign.org/docs/SustainableLibDesign.pdf.

Schaper, Louise. "Our Zero-Carbon Campaign." *Library Journal* 136.2 (2011): 33.

———. "Public Input Yields Greener Library Design." *Library Journal* 128.20 (2003): 62–63.

Selden, David. "The Triple Bottom Line and Why We Care about Sustainability." *AALL Spectrum* 15.1 (2010): 14.

Silence, Patricia. "How Are US Conservators Going Green? Results of Polling AIC Members." *Studies in Conservation* 55.3 (2010): 159–163.

Smith, Steven E. "The Library as an Environmental Alternative (Among Other Things)." *Wilson Library Bulletin* 65 (1991): 85, 156.

Staniforth, Sarah. "Slow Conservation." *Studies in Conservation* 55.2 (2010): 74–80.

———. "Sustainability and Collections." *Conservation Perspectives: The GCI Newsletter* 26.1 (2011): 12–14.

Stoss, Frederick. "Libraries Taking the 'LEED': Green Libraries Leading in Energy and Environmental Design." *Online* 34.2 (2010): 20–27.

Strand, Ted. "All-Digital Information Commons Reduces Energy Consumption." *American Libraries* 41.8 (2010): 19–20.

Thomson, Garry. "Air Pollution: A Review for Conservation Chemists." *Studies in Conservation* 10 (1965): 147–67.

Trotter, Dorothy Waterfill. "Going for the Green." *American Libraries* 39.4 (2008): 40–43.

Tseng, Shu-Hsien. "An Eco-Building, A Healthy Life, and Good Service: A New Century in Public Library Architecture." *Public Libraries* 46.4 (2007): 53.

UNESCO. *Case Studies on Climate Change and World Heritage.* 2007. http://whc.unesco.org/uploads/activities/documents/activity-473-1.pdf.

———. *Climate Change and World Heritage* (World Heritage Reports 22). 2007. http://whc.unesco.org/uploads/activities/documents/activity-474-1.pdf.

———. *Policy Document on the Impacts of Climate Change on World Heritage Properties.* 2008. http://whc.unesco.org/uploads/activities/documents/activity-397-2.pdf.

Urbanska, Wanda. "A Greener Library, A Greener You." *American Libraries* 40.4 (2009): 52–55.

U.S. Environmental Protection Agency. "Why Build Green?" Last modified December 2, 2010. http://www.epa.gov/greenbuilding/pubs/whybuild.htm.

Veatch, Lamar. "Toward the Environmental Design of Library Buildings." *Library Trends* 36 (1987): 361–76.

Waters, Richard L. "Why Your Library Should Plant Trees." *Public Library Quarterly* 22.1 (2003): 42.

Webb, Flemmich. "Global Warning." *Museums Journal* 103.12 (2003): 24–27.

Weiner, James, and Lynn Boyden. "Creating Sustainable Libraries." *Library Journal: Buyers' Guide* (December 2001): 8–10.

Weintraub, Steven. Art Preservation Services, Inc. "Comments Regarding LEDs and Risks to Light-Sensitive Materials." Report to the Green Task Force of the American Insitute of Conservation, April 28, 2012. Accessed November 11, 2012, http://www.conservation-us.org/_data/n_0001/resources/live/Response%20from%20Steve%20Weintraub.pdf.

Welch, Todd. "'Green' Archivism: The Archival Response to Environmental Research." *American Archivist* 62.1 (1999): 74–94.

Wilkinson, Sue, Rachel Madan, Stephen Foulger, and Paul Goodman. "Can Museums Continue to Grow at a Time When They Need to Be Reducing Their Carbon Footprint?" *Museums Journal* 108.10 (2008).

EPILOGUE

THIS ANTHOLOGY HAS PRESENTED PRESERVA-
tion writings, spanning nearly 3,000 years, on a variety of subjects. Authors have addressed long-debated issues, developed
theories, or offered historical or policy perspectives. For the
most part, the readings have focused on the preservation of cultural heritage, that is, the man-made environment. Inevitably,
fields grow and evolve. As keepers of cultural memory, we must
be concerned not only with the collections in our care, but with
global issues that affect us all, such as the environment and global warming. While
some of these broader issues were touched on in chapter 5, "Risks to Cultural
Heritage: Time, Nature, and People," and in chapter 11, "Sustainability," in the
near future there will be increasing opportunities for interdisciplinary research—
indeed, there is already a need for it. No single discipline can address all of the
challenges of saving our heritage. Preservation will continue to be shaped by
social, political, technological, and economic forces.

This epilogue identifies several new and potential research foci, some of which
may suggest the content of future anthologies. My aim is to encourage readers to
track these areas in the media, in journals and books, and on social networking sites.

Digital Media: How We Create and Use It
Will Affect How We Preserve It

Changes brought about by new technologies will continue to influence how we
learn, communicate, and create information. In a recent talk, Ken Thibodeau
described digital information as "polymorphous";[1] that is, occuring in different

forms and types. It can be repurposed, or presented in a number of text, image, and audio formats. We live in a "mashed-up" world in which texts and images will continue to be commingled, sometimes quite imaginatively. Users will access information in a variety of ways, using an array of technical devices. Stored data can be rendered in different ways, too, but it must be processed to be used. How we process, retrieve, and repurpose information will determine how it is preserved. Preservation itself is adapting to this great variety of technologies and the various uses and types of information. That is, preservation is already "shape shifting" and is flexible enough to adapt to the great variety it encounters in the materials and technologies it preserves.

Chapter 7, "Frameworks for Digital Preservation," identified authors who are studying the personal preservation decision-making processes of creators and users. This research spans many fields: library, archival, and information science, computer science, anthropology, art history, the sciences, and the digital humanities. Much more of this research is on the horizon, bringing many new possibilities for interdisciplinary collaboration.

Science

Two areas of science are parallel with the preservation and conservation of cultural heritage: transboundary conservation and taphonomy.

Scientists are concerned about humanity's natural and cultural legacies. One expression of collective action is transboundary conservation, a strategy for protecting the planet's biodiversity that creates a network of protected areas. A successful example of this approach was saving the southern white rhino from extinction. This "was only made possible by the strategic creation of protected areas from anthropogenic disturbances and in particular habitat loss—the number one threat to global biodiversity."[2] Such an approach requires that favorable financial and trade agreements are in place. But despite those and political obstacles as well, some 200 transboundary parks exist today in 820 protected natural areas in 112 countries.[3]

The concept of transboundary conservation has currency for the preservation of man-made artifacts as well; political, social, and religious boundaries are constantly changing. When changes occur, cultural heritage is sometimes destroyed for religious, cultural, political, and/or economic reasons. History is strewn with countless examples—the destruction of the Alexandrian Library—and, in modern times, the Nazi book burnings prior to and during World War II, and the destruction of the National and University Library of Bosnia and Herzegovina in 1992. Such destruction has continued with regularity in the twenty-first century: the destruction of the Bamiyan Buddhas in Afghanistan, on March 11, 2001; the burning and looting of the Iraqi National Library and Archive in spring 2004; and in 2008, the burning of Georgian books in the Gali district villages by Russians. Such examples are constant. A recent and ongoing example revolves around the intent of Northwestern University to tear down an architectural gem in Chicago: The Prentice Women's Hospital, which was designed by Bertrand Goldberg. While not a transborder dispute, the international architectural community has voiced its opposition to the proposed destruction of the building.

Much as conservationists have banded together, international organizations such as UNESCO have coordinated preservation initiatives such as the Blue Shield. These efforts were described in chapter 5, "Risks to Cultural Heritage: Time, Nature, and People," and in chapter 9, "Ethics and Values." The acceptance of universally shared heritage is urgent if we are to protect our natural and man-made heritage.

Another area of science concerned with preservation is taphonomy, the study of decaying organisms over time. Taphonomers examine organisms after they die and before they are discovered as fossils or remains. Taphonomy includes decomposition, and the chemical, biologic, or physical activity that affects the remains of the organism.

Taphonomy shares with preservation the concept of the *life cycle*, "a progression through a series of differing stages of development."[4] When used to refer to digital life cycle models, the term refers to the curation and preservation of data from their initial conceptualization through the iterative curation cycles. One might need to use preservation strategies at any stage in the life cycle. Comparing strategies across taphonomy and the conservation of objects might yield synergies.

Technology and Ecosystems

Life cycle is not the only term that has been lifted from science; *ecosystem* is used in a number of disciplines to examine how something functions within itself and within its greater environment. For example, computer scientists David G. Messerschmitt and Clemens Szyperski have used the ecosystem metaphor in their work *Software Ecosystem*.[5] The book examines technology; the development, dissemination, and use of software; the buyers and sellers of it; and legal and economic frameworks. By examining the *context* of software, one can draw conclusions about how software may continue to evolve.

Some scholars are already addressing the "ecosystem" of digital heritage; more such research is sure to follow.

Information Creators and Users

One of the most pressing issues in digital preservation is how to preserve content that is created through social media. A related subfield is *what* to preserve. It is impossible to save it *all*. It is challenging to preserve content when notions of authorship and text are themselves evolving. In particular, scholarly attention is beginning to turn to artistic projects that are created by large, sometimes diffuse, groups of creators. In such creations, the work of individuals plays a subsidiary role to the work of a community of creators. Also inherent in such creations are rights issues. It is likely to be many years before copyright law is in sync with innovations in communication technologies.

Another area of interest is how scholars will use new media. The issue is being studied by scholars in the digital arts and humanities, and a new vocabulary is growing around virtual heritage studies in particular.[6] For example:

Data artefact: data recorded and attributed to a data object as a product of human conception or agency.

Machinima: a film genre which involves making films and other works using in-game engines and some post-processing software.

Paradata: information about human processes of understanding and interpretation of data objects. Paradata is thus constantly being created, irrespective of whether they are systematically recorded or disseminated. Examples of paradata include a note recording method in a laboratory report, descriptions stored within a structured database of how evidence was used to interpret an artefact, or a comment on methodological premises within a research publication. Paradata differ in emphasis from 'contextual metadata': whereas the latter tends to focus upon how an object has been interpreted, the central focus of paradata tends to be the processes of interpretation through which understanding of objects or communicated [sic] is sought.[7]

How will the creation and use of new digital media influence its preservation? Scholarship in the field of Information Behavior and Searching continues to expand, particularly in the areas of "Everyday Life" and "Communities of Practice," which should help to shed light on best practices for preserving socially mediated work. The *Journal of the American Society for Information Science and Technology* is an excellent source for this research.

Citizen Science, Citizen Journalism, and Citizen Archivists

Archivists have for a long time recognized the importance of the inherent information of documents with respect to the documents' survival. That is, document creators are being schooled in helping archives to preserve the texts that they create.[8] The role of citizen-generated content in the preservation of our heritage needs to be studied further. Over the past decade, a literature on personal information management, or PIM, has emerged. In the case of unintentional digital archives, if they are not curated, they will not be preserved. Preservation begins at home.

Interdisciplinary Research

An academic discipline is variously viewed as a branch of learning, a distinct scholarly culture, an academic structure composed of faculty, pedagogy, and research, and—perhaps somewhat cynically—an administrative convenience. Disciplines are separate and distinct cultures. A discipline depends on a body of knowledge and a degree of consensus about problems, theories, and methods.

Is cultural heritage its own discipline or a combination of disciplines with a shared focused? A number of disciplines address aspects of the preservation of cultural heritage: library and information science, art history, geography, anthropology, archaeology, paleontology, urban studies, architecture, literature, and others. Two additional fields that include preservation are museum studies and historic preservation. Yet these fields are themselves embedded in a variety of disciplines. For example, historic preservation studies can be found in history departments and architecture schools. Museum studies departments may be found in anthropology, public history, art, and art history departments.

Preservation addresses a number of core areas: memory, meaning, value(s), ethics, international law, public access, use, treatment, documentation, reproduction, dissemination, and sustainability of material and digital objects. But preservation has not yet evolved into a distinct academic field, and the scattering of preservation and cultural heritage studies is not likely to be regularized soon. Thus there is a benefit to promoting new interdisciplinary collaboration to advance conservation and preservation research. Given the spread of preservation and conservation across many fields, new knowledge is likely to emerge. While interdisciplinary research is not new, the range of disciplinary collaborations in preservation could be expanded.

In all of the above areas, basic questions remain:

- What are we trying to preserve?
- Why are we trying to preserve it?
- Who will preserve it?
- How will we preserve it, and how will it be funded?
- Where will we preserve it?
- For whom will we preserve it? How will we make the preserved materials available? To whom?
- What is the scope of the preservation effort?

These questions will continue to be debated for as long as preservation exists. This anthology has presented some of the best efforts to address these questions to date. The contents of future anthologies remain to be conceptualized.

NOTES

1. Ken Thibodeau, "Wrestling with Shape-Shifters: Perspectives on Preserving Memory in the Digital Age," "The Memory of the World in the Digital Age: Digitization and Preservation, An International Conference on Permanent Access to Digital Documentary Heritage," September 26–28, 2012, Vancouver, British Columbia.

2. J. M. Baillie et al., eds. *IUCN Red List of Threatened Species: A Global Species Assessment* (Gland, Switzerland, and Cambridge, UK: IUCN, 2004), quoted in Russell A. Mittermeier et al., *Transboundary Conservation: A New Vision for Protected Areas* (Mexico City: CEMEX-Agrupación Sierra-Madre-Conservation International, 2005), 28.

3. Mittermeier et al., *Transboundary Conservation,* 11.

4. *American Heritage Dictionary of the English Language,* 4th ed. (Boston: Houghton, Mifflin, 2000), 1011.

5. David G. Messerschmitt and Clemens Szyperski, *Software Ecosystem: Understanding an Indispensible Technology and Industry* (Cambridge, MA: MIT Press, 2003).

6. See, for example, Anna Bentkowska-Kafel et al., eds., *Paradata and Transparency in Virtual Heritage* (Farnham, UK, and Burlington, VT: Ashgate Publishing, 2012).

7. Bentkowska-Kafel, *Paradata and Transparency,* 262.

8. Though it must also be recognized that some people and groups may not want their archives to wind up in institutions.

CONTRIBUTORS

EDWARD PORTER ALEXANDER (1907–2003) was an American historian and museum administrator. He was vice president of interpretation at Colonial Williamsburg and founded the Museum Studies program at the University of Delaware.

MARY ALEXANDER, daughter of the late Edward Porter Alexander, is a museum educator and grant administrator at the Maryland Historical Trust. She is author of the first edition of *Museums in Motion.*

LOURDES ARIZPE is a professor and researcher at Centro Regional de Investigaciones Multidisciplinarias, National University of Mexico. She is a writer and consultant whose interests include culture and intangible cultural heritage in rural Mexican communities, migration, and globalization.

JAN ASSMANN is a German Egyptologist, archaeologist, and writer and a member of the Heidelberg Academy, the German Institute for Archaeology, and other academic organizations.

ROSS W. ATKINSON (1945–2006) was a library leader and writer. At the time of his death, he was the Associate University Librarian for Collections at Cornell University.

ERICA AVRAMI is Director of Research and Education at the World Monuments Fund and Adjunct Assistant Professor at the Graduate School of Architecture, Planning, and Preservation at Columbia University.

PAUL N. BANKS (1934–2000) was a conservator, educator, and writer. At Columbia University, Banks founded the first graduate programs in conservation and preservation administration.

DAVID BEARMAN is an archivist, educator, and writer. He is founding partner of Archives and Museum Informatics in Toronto, Canada.

HOWARD BESSER is Professor of Cinema Studies and Director of the Moving Image Archiving and Preservation Program at New York University, and Senior Scientist for Digital Library Initiatives at NYU's Library.

PIERRE BOURDIEU (1930–2002) was a French sociologist, anthropologist, philosopher, and political activist.

LAURENCE BOUVARD is an editor, translator, and localization specialist. She holds a degree in linguistics from Harvard University, a Diploma of Specialised and Technical Translation from the University of Westminster, London, and an MSc from the University of London.

CESARE BRANDI (1906–1988), an art historian and conservation-restoration theorist, was the founder and director of the Istituto Centrale del Restauro (ICR) in Rome from 1939 through 1960.

PETER (P.A.T.I.) BURMAN is an architectural historian and cultural heritage scholar who lives and works in Scotland and Germany.

DAVID W. CARR, a retired faculty member at the University of North Carolina, Chapel Hill, is a consultant and author of *Open Conversations: Public Learning in Libraries and Museums* (2011).

PHYLLIS CATSIKIS is an independent researcher and scholar.

STANLEY CHODOROW is a historian. He is Emeritus Professor at the University of California, San Diego, where he was an administrator; he is also a former administrator at the University of Pennsylvania.

CHRISTOPHER CLARKSON is a book conservator, educator, and writer. In 2004, he was awarded the Plowden Gold Medal of the Royal Warrant Holders Association in recognition of his conservation work.

MIRIAM CLAVIR is Conservator Emerita and a research fellow at the University of British Columbia Museum of Anthropology, Vancouver, Canada.

MICHÈLE V. CLOONAN is Dean Emerita and Professor, Simmons College. A preservation educator, she was awarded the Paul Banks and Carolyn Harris Preservation Award from the American Library Association, 2010.

DOUGLAS COCKERELL (1870–1945) was an English bookbinder and author of the classic *Bookbinding and the Care of Books.* He apprenticed at the Doves Bindery in Hammersmith and launched his own bindery in 1897.

COLEMAN CONNOLLY received an A.B. in Classics from Princeton University. He is currently a doctoral candidate in Classical Philology at Harvard University.

PAUL CONWAY is Associate Professor of Information at the University of Michigan's School of Information and a Fellow of the Society of American Archivists. He received the American Library Association's Paul Banks and Carolyn Harris Preservation Award in 2005.

RICHARD J. COX is a Professor and lead educator at the Archives, Preservation, and Records Management Specialization at the University of Pittsburgh School of Information Sciences, and a Fellow of the Society of American Archivists.

ELLEN CUNNINGHAM-KRUPPA is a doctoral candidate in American Studies at The University of Texas at Austin, an adjunct assistant professor at the University of Delaware's Department of Art Conservation, and an adjunct faculty member at the Graduate School of Library and Information Science of Simmons College.

JAMES B. CUNO is President and CEO of the J. Paul Getty Trust; former President and Director of the Art Institute of Chicago; and Director of the Harvard University Art Museums, where he was also a professor of the history of art and architecture.

JOHN COTTON DANA (1856–1929) was a librarian, museum director, and writer who was the founder and first president of the Special Libraries Association.

PAMELA W. DARLING is a preservation advocate and writer. She is a former Head of the Preservation Department at Columbia University Libraries, and a Preservation Specialist at the Association of Research Libraries.

MARTA DE LA TORRE, formerly of The Getty Conservation Institute, is a cultural heritage consultant.

LORCAN DEMPSEY is Vice-President and Chief Strategist of OCLC and an Honorary Research Fellow at University of Wales, Aberystwyth.

PAULA DE STEFANO is a librarian and archivist. She is Associate Curator and Library Unit Head of Collections, Research Services, and Preservation at New York University.

HAKIM ABUL-QASIM FERDOWSI TUSI (940–1020) was a Persian poet and author of the epic poem the *Shahnameh.*

JAMES MARSTON FITCH (1909–2000), an American architect and preservationist, was one of the founders of Columbia University's Graduate School of Architecture, Planning, and Preservation.

KENNETH FOOTE is Professor of Geography at the University of Colorado at Boulder. His research focuses on cultural and historical geography as well as geographic information science.

ANNE J. GILLILAND [formerly Anne Gilliland-Swetland] is a Professor of Information Studies and Moving Image Archive Studies at the University of California, Los Angeles. She is a scholar in archival informatics and record-keeping and Fellow of the Society of American Archivists.

G. BROWN GOODE (1851–1896) was an American ichthyologist who also worked as a museum administrator and science historian. He was United States Commissioner for Fish and Fisheries from 1887 through 1888.

KAREN F. GRACY is Associate Professor at Kent State University's School of Library and Information Science, where she specializes in moving image archiving and digital preservation and curation.

VIRGINIA GREENE, an American museum conservator, is the former Head of Conservation at the University of Pennsylvania Museum of Archaeology and Anthropology.

SVEN HAAKANSON, JR. is an American anthropologist and artist. He is Executive Director of the Alutiiq Museum and serves on the Alaska Native Science Commission.

F. GERALD HAM is formerly the state archivist at the State Historical Society of Wisconsin. He is a Fellow and a former President of the Society of American Archivists.

JOHN H. HAMMER, Executive Director Emeritus at the National Humanities Alliance, writes about preservation policy and political issues. He is senior advisor, Humanities Initiatives, at the American Academy of Arts & Sciences.

ROSS HARVEY is Adjunct Professor at RMIT University, Melbourne, Australia and a former faculty member at Simmons College in Boston, MA. He has written extensively on preservation.

DAN HAZEN is Harvard College's Associate Librarian for Collection Development and a former librarian for Latin America, Spain, and Portugal in Widener Library Collection Development.

MARGARET HEDSTROM, Fellow of the Society of American Archivists, is Professor of Information and Associate Dean at the University of Michigan's School of Information. She led the CAMiLEON project in digital preservation and other international projects.

JOHN HOLDEN is Visiting Professor at the City University, London. He writes about policy in the cultural sector.

JEFFREY HORRELL, Dean of Libraries and Librarian of Dartmouth College, is the former Associate Librarian for Collections at Harvard College and Librarian of the Fine Arts Library at Harvard University.

THOMAS JEFFERSON (1743–1826) was a writer, inventor, architect, scholar, and President of the United States.

JUKKA JOKILEHTO is a Finnish architect and city planner. He is Extraordinary Professor at the University of Nova Gorica, where he teaches history and theory of conservation and management of the built environment.

SAMUEL JONES is a British scholar of international culture, arts, and conservation. He is an associate at the Demos think tank in London.

CAROLINE K. KECK (1908–2007) co-founded the Conservation Center of the Institute of Fine Arts at New York University and the Cooperstown Conservation training program with Sheldon Keck. She was the personal conservator to Georgia O'Keefe, and was the conservator of the collection of Nelson A. Rockefeller from 1973 through 1974.

SHELDON KECK (1910–1993) was an American art conservator. He co-founded the Conservation Center of the Institute of Fine Arts at New York University and the Cooperstown Conservation training program with his wife Caroline Keck.

REBECCA KNUTH is Professor, Library and Information Science, University of Hawaii at Manoa. She writes about intellectual freedom, the history of books and libraries, and international librarianship.

PIP LAURENSON is Head of Collection Care Research at the Tate in London, where she was formerly head of time-based media conservation there.

BRIAN LAVOIE is a research scientist at OCLC who focuses on economic issues associated with information and information services, system-wide organization of library resources, and digital preservation.

FRANCIS LIEBER (1798 or 1800–1872) was a German-American jurist, political philosopher, and author.

DAVID LOWENTHAL is Professor Emeritus of Geography at University College, London. He has written extensively on cultural heritage for over twenty-five years.

GREGORY LUKOW is Chief of the Motion Picture, Broadcasting, and Recorded Sound Division at the Library of Congress.

CLIFFORD LYNCH is Director of the Coalition for Networked Information and adjunct professor at the University of California, Berkeley. He is a former Director, Library Automation at the University of California.

MARCUS VALERIUS MARTIALIS (MARTIAL) (40 to ca. 102–104) was a Roman poet and satirist from Hispania.

RANDALL F. MASON is Chair of the Graduate Program in Historic Preservation and Associate Professor in the Department of City and Regional Planning at the University of Pennsylvania.

JAN MERRILL-OLDHAM (1947–2011) was a leader in the preservation field and the Malloy-Rabinowitz Preservation Librarian at Harvard University. She served on committees of the Amercan Library Association, Association of Research Libraries, the Council on Library and Information Resources, the National Information Standards Organizations, and others.

JOHN HENRY MERRYMAN is Nelson Bowman Sweitzer and Marie B. Sweitzer Professor of Law, Emeritus, and Emeritus Affiliated Professor in the Department of Art at Stanford University. He is an expert in art and cultural property law.

REBECCA L. MEYER is Curation and Preservation Assistant for MIT Libraries.

DENNIS S. MILETI is Professer Emeritus of Sociology at the University of Colorado at Boulder. His research interests include environmental sociology, research methods, and collective behavior.

WILLIAM MORRIS (1834–1896), English artist, writer, designer, and utopian socialist, was a central figure in the Arts and Crafts Movement.

JOHN MURRAY (1786–1851) was a Scottish science writer and lecturer.

GABRIEL NAUDÉ (1600–1653) was a physician, scholar, and librarian. He was the personal librarian to Henri de Mesme, and Cardinals Francesco Barberini, and Jules Mazarin, as well as to Queen Christina of Sweden.

ANDREW ODDY is a British conservator and former conservation scientist at the British Museum.

SHERELYN OGDEN is Head of Conservation at the Minnesota Historical Society. She writes extensively on preservation.

JAMES O'TOOLE is Professor and Clough Millennium Chair in History at Boston College and Fellow of the Society of American Archivists. He writes about the history of American religion and the history of information.

JAN PARIS is Conservator for Special Collections, Wilson Library, University of North Carolina at Chapel Hill.

SUSAN M. PEARCE is Professor Emerita of Museum Studies and Pro-Vice-Chancellor at the University of Leicester. She writes widely on material culture, collecting, and museum studies.

ELLEN PEARLSTEIN is Associate Professor in the Department of Information Studies and the Cotsen Institute of Archaeology at UCLA, and teaches about and researches American Indian tribal museums and cultural preservation in museums.

LORI PEEK is Associate Professor of Sociology at Colorado State University. She is Co-Director of the Center for Disaster and Risk Analysis and Associate Chair of the Social Science Research Council Task Force on Hurricane Katrina and Rebuilding the Gulf Coast.

PAUL PHILIPPOT is a lawyer, art historian, and archaeologist. He was Director-General of ICCROM (1971–1977).

NICHOLAS PICKWOAD is a faculty member at Camberwell College of Arts, Project Leader of the St. Catherine's Monastery Library Project (based at the University of the Arts London), and a Fellow of the IIC and of the Society of Antiquaries. He was awarded the 2009 Plowden Medal for Conservation.

MARY LYNN RITZENTHALER is an expert on archival preservation. She is Chief of the Document Conservation Laboratory at the National Archives and Records Administration.

MARK ROOSA is Dean of Libraries at Pepperdine University, Former Director for Preservation at the Library of Congress, and Chief Conservation Officer at the Huntington Library.

JEFF ROTHENBERG is a computer scientist formerly affiliated with the RAND Corporation who has written and spoken extensively on digital preservation in archives, libraries, and museums.

ABBY RUMSEY (SMITH) is a historian, writer, analyst, and consultant in cultural heritage.

DIETRICH SCHÜLLER is an ethnomusicologist and former Director of the Phonogrammarchiv at the Austrian Academy of Sciences.

WILLIAM SHAKESPEARE (1564–1616) was an English poet, playwright, and actor.

PERCY BYSSHE SHELLEY (1792–1822) was an English Romantic poet.

LAURAJANE SMITH is ARC Future Fellow at Australian National University. Her focus is heritage studies.

SHANNON STRUBLE, a graduate of the Simmons College dual-degree History/Archives Management graduate program, is a designer and Webmistress at Bromer Booksellers in Boston.

ERNST VAN DE WETERING is Chairman of the Rembrandt Research Project. He writes about art history as well as theory and ethics in conservation and restoration.

MARCUS VITRUVIUS POLLIO (ca. 80–70 BC; died after 15 BC) was a Roman writer, architect, and engineer.

PETER WATERS (1930–2003) was a book conservator and a leader of the preservation effort at the Biblioteca Nazionale Centrale Firenze after the 1966 flood of the Arno River. He was formerly a Conservation Officer at the Library of Congress.

JOHN WEEVER (1576–1632) was an English poet and antiquary known for his religious works and interest in funeral monuments.

CREDITS

CHAPTER 2

Jan Assmann, "Collective Memory and Cultural Identity," *New German Critique* 65 (Spring-Summer 1995): 125–33. Copyright, 1995, New German Critique, Inc. All rights reserved. Reprinted by permission of the publisher, Duke University Press. www.dukeupress.edu.

P.A.T.I. [Peter] Burman, "What Is Cultural Heritage?" in *Rational Decision-making in the Preservation of Cultural Property,* ed. Norbert S. Baer and Folke Snickars (Berlin: Dahlem University Press, 2001), 11–22. Reprinted from the *Dahlem Workshop Report 86: Rational Decision-Making in the Preservation of Cultural Property.* Courtesy of Dahlem Konferenzen of Freie Universität Berlin.

Australia International Council on Monuments and Sites (ICOMOS Inc.), *The Burra Charter: The Australia ICOMOS Charter for Places of Cultural Significance 1999 with Associated Guidelines and Code on the Ethics of Coexistence* (Victoria, Australia: ICOMOS, 1999). Australia ICOMOS' mission is to raise standards, encouraging debate and generating innovative ideas in cultural heritage conservation. ICOMOS (the International Council on Monuments and Sites) is a non-government organization that promotes expertise in the conservation of cultural heritage. Formed in 1965, it is primarily concerned with the philosophy, terminology, methodology and techniques of conservation. ICOMOS has national committees in over 100 countries and is linked to UNESCO. Australia ICOMOS, formed in 1976, links public authorities, institutions and individuals involved in the study and conservation of all places of cultural significance. Australia ICOMOS' goals are: 1) International: Participate in international activities, both within and beyond the ICOMOS International family. 2) Conservation Philosophy and Policy: Ensure that Australia ICOMOS leads conservation philosophy and practice for culturally significant places. 3) Education and Communication: Promote understanding of the cultural significance of places, raising conservation standards through education and communication programs. 4) Advocacy: Inform key decision-makers of Australia ICOMOS' aims and influence their adoption of best conservation philosophy and practice. 5) Membership: Develop, maintain and support a broad-based membership.

Susan M. Pearce, "The Making of Cultural Heritage," in *Values and Heritage Conservation: Research Report,* eds. Erica Avrami, Randall Mason, and Marta de la Torre (Los Angeles: The Getty Conservation Institute, 2000), 59–64. www.getty .edu/conservation/publications_resources/pdf _publications/values.pdf. Courtesy of the author and the Getty Conservation Institute.

Laurajane Smith, *Uses of Heritage* (London and New York: Routledge, 2006), chapter 2, 312–41. Copyright ©2006 Routledge. Reproduced by permission of Taylor & Francis Books UK.

CHAPTER 3

Paul N. Banks, "A Library Is Not a Museum," in *Training in Conservation: A Symposium on the Occasion of the Dedication of the Stephen Chan House,* October 1, 1983, Institute of Fine Arts, New York University, edited by Norbert S. Baer (New York: Institute of Fine Arts, 1989), 57–65. Reprinted courtesy of the Conservation Center of the Institute of Fine Arts, New York University.

David W. Carr, "In the Contexts of the Possible: Libraries and Museums as Incendiary Cultural Institutions," *RBM: A Journal of Rare Books, Manuscripts, and Cultural Heritage* 1.2 (September 2000): 117–34. Courtesy of the author.

Stanley Chodorow, "To Represent Us Truly: The Job and Context of Preserving the Cultural Record," *Libraries & the Cultural Record* 41.3 (Summer 2006): 372–80. Copyright ©2006 by the University of Texas Press, P.O. Box 7819, Austin, TX 78713-7819. All rights reserved.

Michèle Valerie Cloonan, "The Preservation of Knowledge," *Library Trends* 41.4 (Spring 1993): 594–605. Copyright © 1993 The Board of Trustees of the University of Illinois. This article first appeared in *Library Trends*, 41.4 (Spring 1993): 594–605.

F. Gerald Ham, "The Archival Edge," *American Archivist* 38.1 (January 1975): 5–13. Reprinted with the permission of the publisher, the Society of American Archivists. Used with permission of F. Gerald Ham.

Pamela W. Darling and Sherelyn Ogden, excerpt from "From Problems Perceived to Programs in Practice: The Preservation of Library Resources in the U.S.A., 1956–1980," *Library Resources & Technical Services* 25.1 (January/March 1981): 9–29. Reprinted with permission by the Association for Library Collections & Technical Services.

Ross Harvey, "Developing a Library Preservation Program," chapter 10 in his *Preservation in Australian and New Zealand Libraries,* 2nd ed. Riverina, Australia: Centre for Information Studies, 1993, 259–80. (Minor editorial emendations have been made by the author.) Republished with permission of the publisher, Chandos Publishing. www.woodheadpublisher .com/en/ChandosHome.aspx.

Jan Merrill-Oldham, "Taking Care: An Informed Approach to Library Preservation," in *To Preserve and Protect: The Strategic Stewardship of Cultural Resources. Essays from the symposium held at the Library of Congress, October 30–31, 2000* (Washington, DC: Library of Congress, 2002), 90–105.

David Bearman, "Retention and Preservation," chapter 2 in his *Archival Methods. Archives and Museum Informatics Technical Reports,* no. 9. N.p.: Archives & Museum Informatics, 1989. Used with permission of the author.

Richard J. Cox, "Digital Curation and the Citizen Archivist," paper given at Digital Curation: Practice, Promises & Prospects, April 1–3, 2009 (Chapel Hill, NC: School of Information and Library Science), 102–09. Used with permission of the author.

Kenneth E. Foote, "To Remember and Forget: Archives, Memory, and Culture," *American Archivist* 53.3 (Summer 1990): 378–92. Reprinted with the permission of the Society of American Archivists.

Anne J. Gilliland, *Enduring Paradigm, New Opportunities: The Value of the Archival Perspective in the Digital Environment*. An extended version of this paper was published in February 2000 by the Council on Library and Information Resources, Washington, DC, as report no. 89. The author excerpted and updated her report in August 2011 for this volume. Copyright ©2000 Council on Library and Information Resources. Reprinted with permission.

James M. O'Toole. "On the Idea of Permanence," *American Archivist* 52.1 (Winter 1989): 10–25. Reprinted with the permission of the Society of American Archivists.

Edward Porter Alexander and Mary Alexander, "To Conserve," chapter 9 in *Museums in Motion: An Introduction to the History and Functions of Museums*. 2nd ed. (Lanham, MD: Rowman AltaMira, 2008), 217–34. Reprinted with the permission of AltaMira Press.

James Cuno, excerpt from "The Object of Art Museums," in *Whose Muse? Art Museums and the Public Trust*, ed. by James Cuno (Princeton: Princeton University Press and Harvard University Art Museum, 2003), 52–53. ©2003 by Princeton University Press and Harvard University Art Museum. Reprinted by permission of Princeton University Press.

James Marston Fitch, "The Philosophy of Restoration: Williamsburg to the Present," chapter 14 in his *Selected Writings in Architecture, Preser-vation, and the Built Environment* (New York: W.W. Norton, 2006), 172–81.

Jukka Jokilehto, "Preservation Theory Unfolding," *Future Anterior* 3.1 (Summer 2006): 1–9. Copyright 2006 Graduate School of Architecture, Planning, and Preservation, Columbia University. Graduate School of Architecture, Planning, and Preservation Program. Reproduced with permission of University of Minnesota Press.

Paul Philippot, excerpts from "Historic Preservation: Philosophy, Criteria, Guidelines," in *Preservation and Conservation: Principles and Practices. Proceedings of the North American International Regional Conference. Williamsburg, VA and Philadelphia, PA, September 10–16, 1972*, edited by Sharon Timmons (Washington, DC: National Trust for Historic Preservation, 1976). Used with permission of the author.

CHAPTER 4

Ross W. Atkinson, "Selection for Preservation: A Materialistic Approach," *Library Resources & Technical Services* 30.4 (October/December 1986): 341–53. Reprinted with permission by the Association for Library Collections & Technical Services.

Paula De Stefano, "Selection for Digital Conversion in Academic Libraries," *College & Research Libraries* 62.1 (January 2001): 58–69. Reprinted by permission of the author.

Dan Hazen, Jeffrey Horrell, and Jan Merrill-Oldham, *Selecting Research Collections for Digitization*, Washington, DC: Council on Library and Information Resources, August 1998; Report 74; excerpts. Copyright ©1998 Council on Library and Information Resources. Reprinted with permission.

Karen F. Gracy, "Preservation in a Time of Transition: Redefining Stewardship of Time-Based Media in the Digital Age," written for this volume.

Howard Besser, "Digital Preservation of Moving Image Material?" *The Moving Image* 1.2 (Fall 2001): 39–55. Copyright 2001 Association of Moving Image Archivists.

Gregory Lukow, "The Politics of Orphanage: The Rise and Impact of the 'Orphan Film' Metaphor on Contemporary Preservation Practice," a paper delivered at the conference, Orphans of the Storm I, University of South Carolina, September 23, 1999 (www.sc.edu/film symposium/archive/orphans2001/lukow.html); (accessed February 14, 2014) by Gregory Lukow, Chief, Motion Picture, Broadcasting & Recorded Sound Division, the Library of Congress. Opening Keynote Address delivered at the Inaugural Orphan Films Symposium (corrected transcript), University of South Carolina, September 23, 1999.

Mark S. Roosa, "Sound and Audio Archives," *Encyclopedia of Library and Information Sciences,* 3rd ed. (New York: Taylor & Francis, 2010), 4913–20. Copyright 2009. Reproduced with permission of Taylor & Francis Group LLC.

Dietrich Schüller, "Socio-technical and Socio-cultural Challenges of Audio and Video Preservation," *International Preservation News* 46 (December 2008): 5–8. www.ifla.org/en/publications/international-preservation-news.

CHAPTER 5

Rebecca Knuth, "Understanding Modern Biblioclasm," chapter 1 in her *Burning Books and Leveling Libraries: Extremist Violence and Cultural Destruction* (Westport, CT: Praeger, 2006), 1–16. Copyright © 2006 by Rebecca Knuth. Reproduced with permission of ABC-CLIO, LLC.

Pip Laurenson, "Inside Installations. Preservation and Presentation of Installation Art. Part 1: Risk Assessment," May 2007. [Web document: www.inside-installation.org/OCMT/mydocs/Risk Assessment.pdf]. This essay was originally published in the *Inside Installations Booklet 2007* edited by Tatja Scholte and Paulien t'Hoen. Published by ICN and SBMK and alson online at http://www.inside-installations.org/OCMT/mydocs/Risk%20assessment.pdf. The essay was produced as part of the project *Inside Installations: Preservation and Presentation of Installation Art* supported by the European Commission's programme Culture 2000. Participants in this working group were: Bart Ankersmit (ICN), Reinhard Bek (Museum Jean Tinguely), Bryony Bery (Tate), Agnes Brokerhof (ICN), Anne de Buck (S.M.A.K.), Paulien 't Hoen (SBMK), Frederika Huys (S.M.A.K.), Kate Jennings (Tate), Pip Laurenson (Tate), Vivian Van Saaze (ICN), Tatja Scholte (ICN), Sanneke Stigter (Kröller-Müller Museum), Arianne Vanrell (MNCARS), and Tina Weidner (Tate). The author would like to thank Agnes Brokerhof and Bark Ankersmith of the Netherlands Cultural Heritage Agency (formally ICN) for their expert guidance.

Dennis S. Mileti and L.A. Peek-Gottschlich, "How Do Societies Manage Risk?" in *Rational Decision-making in the Preservation of Cultural Property,* eds. Norbert S. Baer and Folke Snickars. (Berlin: Dahlem University Press, 2001), 35–45. Reprinted from the Dahlem Workshop Report 86: Rational Decision-Making in the Preservation of Cultural Property. Courtesy of Dahlem Konferenzen of Freie Universität Berlin.

Peter Waters, excerpts from revised text of "Procedures for Salvage of Water-Damaged Materials," July 1993. [www.archives.gov/preservation/conservation/library-materials-01.html]. Reprinted with the permission of the American Institute of Conservation for Art & Historic Works, 1156 15th Street, NW, Suite 320, Washington, DC 20005, info@conservation-us.org, www.conservation-us.org.

CHAPTER 6

Paul N. Banks, "The Laws of Conservation." Reprinted with permission of the University of Texas Board of Regents.

Christopher Clarkson, "Minimum Intervention in Treatment of Books," Preprint from the 9th International Congress of IADA, August 15–21, 1999. (Copenhagen: Royal Library of Denmark, 1999), 89–96.

Caroline K. Keck, "The Role of the Conservator," in *Preservation and Conservation: Principles and Practices. Proceedings of the North American International Regional Conference on Preservation and Conservation, Williamsburg and Philadelphia, September 10–16, 1972.* Washington, DC; Preservation Press, 1976, pp. 25–34.

Sheldon Keck, "Further Materials for a History of Conservation," in *Preprints of Papers Presented at the Fourth Annual Meeting*, American Institute for Conservation of Historic and Artistic Works, Dearborn, MI, 1976 (Washington, DC: AIC, 1976), 11–19. Reprinted with the permission of the American Institute of Conservation for Art & Historic Works, 1156 15th Street, NW, Suite 320, Washington, DC 20005, info@conservation-us.org, www.conservation-us.org.

Andrew Oddy, "Does Reversibility Exist in Conservation?" in *Reversibility – Does it Exist?* ed. by Andrew Oddy and Sara Carroll. British Museum Occasional Paper no. 135 (London: British Museum Press, 1999), 1–4. Reprinted with permission of the British Museum Company.

Jan Paris, "Conservation and the Politics of Use and Value in Research Libraries," in *The Book and Paper Group Annual*, vol. 19 (Washington, DC: AIC, 2001), 61–65. Used by permission of the author.

Nicholas Pickwoad, "Distinguishing Between the Good and Bad Repair of Books," *Conservation and Preservation in Small Libraries*, edited by Nicholas Hadgraft and Katherine Swift, (Cambridge, UK: Parker Library Publications, 1994), 141–49. Reprinted with permission of the Masters and Fellows of Corpus Christi College, Cambridge. Copyright Parker Library, Corpus Christi College Cambridge.

Mary Lynn Ritzenthaler, excerpts from "Conservation Treatment," in chapter 10, *Preserving Archives and Manuscripts*, 2nd ed. (Chicago: Society of American Archivists, 2010), 331–71. Reprinted by permission of the Society of American Archivists, www.archivists.org.

CHAPTER 7

Task Force on Archiving of Digital Information, excerpts from *Preserving Digital Information: Report of the Task Force on Archiving of Digital Information*, by Donald Waters and John Garrett. Commissioned by the Commission on Preservation and Access and the Research Libraries Group. Washington, DC: CPA and RLG, May 1, 1996. Copyright © 1996 Council on Library and Information Resources. Reprinted with permission.

Paul Conway, Excerpts from *Preservation in the Digital World*. Pub. 62 (Washington, DC: Council on Library and Information Resources, March 1996). Copyright © Council on Library and Information Resources. Reprinted with permission.

Margaret Hedstrom, "Understanding Electronic Incunabula: A Framework for Research on Electronic Records," *American Archivist* 54.3 (Summer 1991): 334–54. Reprinted by permission of the Society of American Archivists, www.archivists.org.

Brian Lavoie and Lorcan Dempsey, "Thirteen Ways of Looking at…Digital Preservation," *D-Lib Magazine* 10.7–8 (July/August 2004), www.dlib.org/dlib/july04/lavoie/07lavoie.html. This article originally was published in *D-Lib Magazine*,

10.7–8 (July/August) 2004. © OCLC Online Computer Library Center, Inc.

Clifford Lynch, "Repatriation, Reconstruction, and Cultural Diplomacy in the Digital World," *Educause Review* 43.1 (January/February 2008): 70–71. Used with permission of the author.

Jeff Rothenberg, "Ensuring the Longevity of Digital Documents," *Scientific American* 272.1 (January 1995): 42–47; rev. and expanded, February 22, 1999. Used with permission of the author.

Abby Smith [Rumsey]. *Why Digitize?* Washington DC: Council on Library and Information Resources, 1999. Copyright © 1999 Council on Library and Information Resources. Reprinted with permission.

Blue Ribbon Task Force on Sustainable Digital Preservation and Access, excerpts from *Sustainable Economics for a Digital Planet: Ensuring Long-Term Access to Digital Information. Final Report.* La Jolla, CA: Blue Ribbon Task Force, February 2010. Excerpt from the Final Report of the Blue Ribbon Task Force for Sustainable Digital Preservation and Access. The full report is at brtf .sdsc.edu.

CHAPTER 8

Ellen-Cunningham-Kruppa, "Exploring Cultural Policy at Humanities Texas." Used with permission of the author.

John H. Hammer, "On the Political Aspects of Book Preservation in the U.S.," *Advances in Preservation and Access* 1 (1992): 22–40.

John Henry Merryman, "Art Systems and Cultural Policy," *Art, Antiquity and Law* 15.2 (July 2010). Used with permission of the author.

CHAPTER 9

United Nations, excerpts from Universal Declaration of Human Rights, 1948, and Declaration on the Rights of Indigenous Peoples, 2007. Courtesy United Nations.

UNESCO, excerpt from Convention for the Protection of Cultural Property in the Event of Armed Conflict, 1954, and excerpt from Convention Concerning the Protection of World Cultural and Natural Heritage, 1972. Courtesy UNESCO.

Salzburg Declaration on the Conservation and Preservation of Cultural Heritage, 2009.

American Alliance of Museums, excerpt from Code of Ethics for Museums, 1991, emended 2000. Courtesy American Alliance of Museums.

American Association for State and Local History, excerpts from Statement of Professional Standards and Ethics, June 2012. www.aalhs.org.

American Institute for Conservation of Historic and Artistic Works, excerpts from Code of Ethics and Guidelines for Practice, 1994. Reprinted with the permission of the American Institute of Conservation for Art & Historic Works, 1156 15th Street, NW, Suite 320, Washington, DC 20005, info@conservation-us.org, www.conservation-us.org.

American Library Association, excerpt from Code of Ethics, 1939, amended 1981, 1995, 2008.

Association of Moving Image Archivists, excerpt from Code of Ethics, 2009. Reprinted with permission from the Association of Moving Image Archivists. © 2010.

Society of American Archivists, excerpts from Code of Ethics for Archivists, 2005, revised 2012. Reprinted by permission of the Society of American Archivists.

Richard Cox and James O'Toole, "The Impulse to Save," in *Understanding Archives & Manuscripts* (Chicago: Society of American Archivists, 2006),

15–17. Reprinted with permission of the Society of American Archivists, www.archivists.org.

Richard Cox and James O'Toole, "The Impulse to Destroy," in *Understanding Archives & Manuscripts,* Chicago, Society of American Archivists, 2006, pp. 17–21. Reprinted with permission of the Society of American Archivists, www.archivists.org.

Samuel Jones and John Holden, excerpt from "Conservation and Its Values," in *It's a Material World,* London: Demos, 2008, pp. 27–29. http://demos.co.uk/files/Material%20World%20-%20web.pdf.

Ellen Pearlstein, "Restoring Provenance to a Native American Feather Blanket," *Museum Management and Curatorship* 25.1 (2010): 87–105. Reprinted by permission of the publisher (Taylor & Francis Ltd., www.tandfonline.com).

Ernst Van De Wetering, "Conservation-Restoration Ethics and the Problem of Modern Art," in *Modern Art: Who Cares?* ed. by Ijsbrand Hummelen and Dionne Sillé. Amsterdam: Foundation for the Conservation of Modern Art/Netherlands Institute for Cultural Heritage, 1999, pp. 247–49.

CHAPTER 10

Lourdes Arizpe, "Cultural Heritage and Globalization," in *Values and Heritage Conservation: Research Report,* ed. by Erica Avrami, Randall Mason, and Marta de la Torre. Los Angeles: The Getty Conservation Institute, 2000, pp. 32–37. www.getty.edu/conservation/publications_resources/pdf_publications/values.pdf. Courtesy of the author and the Getty Conservation Institute.

Miriam Clavir, "First Nations Perspectives on Preservation and Museums," chapter 3 in her *Preserving What Is Valued: Museums, Conservation, and First Nations.* Vancouver: University of British Columbia Press, 2002, pp. 69–97. Reprinted with permission of the publisher from *Preserving What Is Valued* by Miriam Clavir © University of British Columbia Press 2002. All rights reserved by the publisher.

Virginia Greene, "'Accessories of Holiness': Defining Jewish Sacred Objects," *Journal of the American Institute for Conservation* 31.1 (January 1992): 31–39. Reprinted with the permission of the American Institute of Conservation for Art & Historic Works, 1156 15th Street, NW, Suite 320, Washington, DC 20005, info@conservation-us.org, www.conservation-us.org.

Sven Haakanson, Jr. (Alutiiq-Sugpiaq), "Why Should American Indian Cultural Objects Be Preserved?" in *Caring for American Indian Objects: A Practical and Cultural Guide*, edited by Sherelyn Ogden (St. Paul, MN: Minnesota Historical Society Press, 2004), 3–6. Reprinted with permission of Minnesota Historical Society Press.

CHAPTER 11

Erica Avrami, Randall Mason, and Marta de la Torre, "The Spheres and Challenges of Conservation," 3–10, and "Conclusions," 68–70, from *Values and Heritage Conservation: Research Report,* edited by Avrami, Mason, and de la Torre. Los Angeles: The Getty Conservation Institute, 2000. www.getty.edu/conservation/publications_resources/pdf_publications/values.pdf. Courtesy of the authors and The Getty Conservation Institute.

David Lowenthal, "Stewarding the Future," in *CRM: The Journal of Heritage Stewardship* 2.2 (Summer 2005): 1–17. Used with permission of the author.

Rebecca Meyer, Shannon Struble, and Phyllis Catsikis. "Sustainability: A Review," 2012. Used with permission of the authors.

AUTHOR AND TITLE INDEX

SUBJECT INDEX